26th ANNUAL EDITION

2013 Poet's Market

Robert Lee Brewer, Editor

WRITER'S DIGEST
BOOKS
WritersDigest.*com*
Cincinnati, Ohio

Publisher: Phil Sexton

Writer's Market website: www.writersmarket.com
Writer's Digest website: www.writersdigest.com
Writer's Digest Bookstore: www.writersdigestshop.com

Distributed in Canada by Fraser Direct
100 Armstrong Avenue
Georgetown, Ontario, Canada L7G 5S4
Tel: (905) 877-4411

Distributed in the U.K and Europe by F&W Media International
Brunel House, Newton Abbot, Devon, TQ12 4PU, England
Tel: (+44) 1626-323200, Fax: (+44) 1626-323319
E-mail: postmaster@davidandcharles.co.uk

Distributed in Australia by Capricorn Link
P.O. Box 704, Windsor, NSW 2756 Australia
Tel: (02) 4577-3555

ISSN: 0883-5470
ISBN-13: 978-1-59963-598-9
ISBN-10: 1-59963-598-4

Attention Booksellers: This is an annual directory of F+W Media, Inc. Return deadline for this edition is December 31, 2013.

Edited by: Robert Lee Brewer
Cover designed by: Jessica Boonstra
Interior designed by: Claudean Wheeler
Page layout by: Ronson Slagle
Production coordinated by: Greg Nock
Cover illustration by: Joshua Roflow

CONTENTS

MARKETS

RESOURCES

INDEXES

FROM THE EDITOR

Every poet has his or her own unique story for beginning their poeming. For instance, my poetry writing ways began when I was trying to impress a girl. In the short term, the poem helped me get the girl, but in the long term, the relationship eventually fizzled. However, my love of poetry had only begun.

As with many poets, I wrote and wrote and wrote without a care for what was right or wrong. Mainly, I was writing for myself. But it didn't take long before I wanted to share with my friends to see what they thought. I remember filling up notebooks with poems and sending them off with my friends to "star" or "check" the poems they liked the best. Without realizing it, I was asking my target audience for feedback.

In college, I burned myself out and fell away from poetry when I realized just how amazing other contemporary poets wrote their poems. That's why my creative writing certificate is in fiction instead of poetry. I just thought getting poetry published was not for me.

Then, I had a life event that made me reconsider everything, including taking another chance on poetry. I began submitting my writing with the assistance of *Poet's Market*. I received several rejections, but every so often a poem would find a home in a publication. Each acceptance (or encouraging rejection note) kept me going.

With that in mind, I hope the *2013 Poet's Market* will help you make that leap forward in your poeming career. I know it doesn't matter where you started or what unexpected turns your writing has taken, you can do this.

Until next time, keep poeming!

Robert Lee Brewer
Senior Content Editor, *Poet's Market*
http://www.writersdigest.com/editor-blogs/poetic-asides
http://twitter.com/robertleebrewer

PHOTO: Al Parrish

WHISPERING INTO A CLOSED CHANNEL

Why We Need Poet's Market

by Nate Pritts

Getting your poems published is one way of having a voice—a speaking part!—in the larger conversation our contemporary culture is having about what poetry is and how it means. This is certainly an exciting and crucial part of being a poet. But that's not all it takes.

A poet isn't just someone who writes a poem, or even a bunch of poems, and it's not only someone who publishes a single poem or even a book full of them. It's not merely a craft or a skill, and it's not a path to an all-caps CAREER—though poetry can be those things, or lead to those things, for some people. To me, however, being a poet is something richer than a single action, even if it's a repeated action, and requires deep love for poetry, which is all at once a method of communion, a habit of mind and a discipline for how to live. It's maybe the last purely human creative act we have that offers direct connection to the consciousness of someone else unfettered by online social categorizations or the trappings of commerce.

Though there's no infallible, one-size-fits-all roadmap to success in this patchwork vocation, there is *Poet's Market* ready to provide the kind of navigation that matters. And while it's true that the book can't do the work for you—neither the deeply attentive work of being a writer nor the logistic clerical work needed to submit your oeuvre for publication—it is a massively helpful tool. Everyone will get something different from a book like this. Here's what I put into it, and what I got out of it.

A HAPPY FIRST STEP

I submit this recollection of my path as only one of an infinite number of possible trajectories. It's personal enough, and is fraught with ridiculous errors, so that there's no danger of anyone really thinking that I'm suggesting these are the exact dance steps anyone else should follow. It's merely one model for movement, proof that we still live in a cause/effect universe.

My initial dream was to be a novelist, or maybe write comic books. As a reader, it was all I really knew, it was what I really loved, and my head was full of a vague but relentless desire to be part of that dynamic—to write the kind of stories I enjoyed reading! So I wrote and wrote and wrote, and I read too—constantly, consistently and critically. It was a happy first step.

Only later did I start to become aware of the fact that I was missing out on something, or that my map didn't have all the locations filled in. I don't think I quite had the words for it then, but I started to become aware that there was a kind of community that consisted of writers and readers and publishers all doing what they could to advance their love of the art of writing. Up to that point, when I was maybe 22 years old, I was blindly confident that if I wrote a novel, it would be published. The writing itself was a pretty significant commitment on its own, but something much more was needed to really get my place at the table. Suddenly it didn't seem so easy—or rather, the road was starting to become clear to me, and it wasn't as straight as I thought it was.

A POET'S STORY

Despite my initial drive to write fiction, my story is a poet's story, and it's punctuated and given shape by two fortuitous revelations that took the top of my head off and stuffed it full of a new kind of breath. First, there was an administrative oversight. Second, I found the *Poet's Market.*

In just the last semester of my undergrad studies, the Advanced Fiction workshop I'd been primed for wasn't offered and I was forced to take an Advanced Poetry workshop, cold, with no background, or put off graduation by another year. I petitioned to be allowed to enroll, and was shoved into the class.

Luckily, I was instantly energized and enlivened by the flexible and fluid form of poetry, was truly giddy at all the possibilities for communication that it offered me. I've never fully recovered from that initial and stunning love. Everything I can think to say can make its way out as a poem. The possibilities for my voice in the world increased, got different and more voluptuous.

At the end of my undergrad experience, a professor of mine suggested I start sending poems out to magazines and journals. I didn't have any sense of what he meant by this, but he gave me a stack of literary magazines plucked from the shelves around his office and sent me away to figure it out. I was certainly aware that there was such a thing as contemporary poetry. Sure, I read a lot of dead poets, but my school had a pretty good visiting writers program, and my professor was writing poems so, anyway, I knew it could be done. What I didn't know was how to become part of that world myself.

In the few years between finishing my Bachelor's degree and starting my Master of Fine Arts degree, I was floundering. I had always wanted to be a writer; I certainly wasn't facing any kind of big crisis in that regard. I had enthusiasm and discipline, I thought (or hoped) I had talent (which is in itself a vague term that I'll let stand here but which I could write a lot more about). What I lacked was direction.

At the time, I was working as a mall bookstore manager so I had access to any book I wanted. I could just order a copy in to the store for a fake customer, put it on the shelf and read it on break, sitting in the back room behind boxes so as not to be disturbed with my official duties, or in good weather I could visit a picnic table behind the mall, in a green island area smack in the middle of the back parking lot.

Not even my closest friends read my poems in those days, though they meant more to me than anything.

Though I was reading and writing a lot during that time, it was obvious to me that I was whispering into a closed channel. No one, not even my closest friends, read my poems in those days, though they meant more to me than anything else. They weren't terrific, by any standards, and I could see the flaws in my work more clearly than anyone else would have been able to. But still my poems were expressions of my perspective, my sensitivity, in words I had chosen and ordered. In short, they didn't exist and then, because of my diligence, creativity and skill, they did.

But still I was aching because I wanted them out in the world, available for other people. And not because I thought the content of my poems, or the efficacy of my line breaks, would change the world. I thought it was important to share my poems with people because the fact that the poems existed at all would then help other people realize that their potential poems needed to be converted into actual poems.

JOINING THE POETRY COMMUNITY

This is when the second revelation happened in my early career as a writer. I stumbled across an edition of the *Poet's Market* (1995, to be exact, though this was probably early 1996 when I latched onto it). We all know that *Poet's Market* is a storehouse of knowledge. For me, it was like a Rosetta stone that helped decode a language I'd been eager to crack.

In my early, misguided attempts to be part of the conversation, I dog-eared pages and made lists of journals I wanted to submit to based simply on their names. Later, a little savvier, I ordered sample copies and bought full-length collections by poets—either because they were in these journals and I liked their work, or sometimes just because their name was mentioned in the "poets we've published" section of the old *PM* entries on individual journals.

Slowly, my low-tech web grew. I discovered other journals and poets by following the contributor notes, or from the blurbs on the back of books, and by following the preferences of presses and editors. Somewhere along the way, my own poems started to get published. And, weirdly, I wasn't satisfied in the way I thought I would be.

It wasn't because I was hungry for the next publication, or bigger publications—or even a chapbook of full-length collection representing my work. I figured those things would be nice, that I'd welcome them. What really had overtaken me was a love of poetry itself, the whole community. My own poems still make up a vital part of my identity, but it is only a part of it. However, I think what *Poet's Market* really helped me to see was the overall field of poetry, a field I could understand and contribute to.

Years later, I started my own magazine, *H_NGM_N*, and a few years ago we started publishing full-length books of poetry, in addition to the chapbooks we publish and the magazine. I started giving public readings of my work, something I'm still lucky enough to be asked to do, and I started organizing public readings of other people's work. The list, really, goes on and will continue to develop and change. There's no shortage of possibilities for how any single person can contribute to the field of poetry—can be made to feel truly a part of it.

Don't give up hope that the poems you write will be vital and necessary to the world. But let's remember that seeing your own poems as the only way to be of use to poetry and other people is a dangerous limitation. Rather than spending your life talking to the wall, or breathlessly hoping to be invited in, use every tool at your disposal—your discipline and your creativity and your *Poet's Market*—to blast your voice out big and clear, to walk in, sit down and start talking.

NATE PRITTS is the author of five books of poetry, most recently *Sweet Nothing* which *Publishers Weekly* describes as "both baroque and irreverent, banal and romantic, his poems [...] arrive at a place of vulnerability and sincerity." *POETRY Magazine* called his third book, *The Wonderfull Yeare*, "rich, vivid, intimate, & somewhat troubled" while *The Rumpus* called *Big Bright Sun*, his fourth book, "a textual record of mistakes made and insights gleaned...[in] a voice that knows its part in self-destruction." His poetry & prose have been widely published, both online & in print, at places like *Southern Review, Columbia, Court Green, Gulf Coast, Boston Review* & *Rain Taxi* where he frequently contributes reviews. He is the founder & principal editor of *H_NGM_N*, an online journal & small press. Visit his site at www.natepritts.com.

HOW TO USE *POET'S MARKET*

Delving into the pages of *Poet's Market* indicates a commitment—you've decided to take that big step and begin submitting your poems for publication. How do you *really* begin, though? Here are eight quick tips to help make sense of the marketing/submission process:

1. BE AN AVID READER. The best way to hone your writing skills (besides writing) is to immerse yourself in poetry of all kinds. It's essential to study the masters; however, from a marketing standpoint, it's equally vital to read what your contemporaries are writing and publishing. Read journals and magazines, chapbooks and collections, anthologies for a variety of voices; scope out the many poetry sites on the Internet. Develop an eye for quality, and then use that eye to assess your own work. Don't rush to publish until you know you're writing the best poetry you're capable of producing.

2. KNOW WHAT YOU LIKE TO WRITE—AND WHAT YOU WRITE BEST. Ideally, you should be experimenting with all kinds of poetic forms, from free verse to villanelles. However, there's sure to be a certain style with which you feel most comfortable, that conveys your true "voice." Whether you favor more formal, traditional verse or avant-garde poetry that breaks all the rules, you should identify which markets publish work similar to yours. Those are the magazines and presses you should target to give your submissions the best chance of being read favorably—and accepted. (See the Subject Index to observe how some magazines and presses specify their needs.)

3. LEARN THE "BUSINESS" OF POETRY PUBLISHING. Poetry may not be a high-paying writing market, but there's still a right way to go about the "business" of submitting and publishing poems. Learn all you can by reading writing-related books and magazines. Read the articles and interviews in this book for plenty of helpful advice. Surf the Internet for a wealth of sites filled with writing advice, market news and informative links.

4. RESEARCH THE MARKETS. Study the listings in *Poet's Market* thoroughly; these present submission guidelines, editorial preferences and editors' comments as well as contact information (names, postal and e-mail addresses, website URLs). In addition, the indexes in the back of this book provide insights into what an editor or publisher may be looking for.

However, studying market listings alone won't cut it. The best way to gauge the kinds of poetry a market publishes is to read several issues of a magazine/journal or several of a press's books to get a feel for the style and content of each. If the market has a website, log on and take a look. Websites may include poetry samples, reviews, archives of past issues, exclusive content, and especially submission guidelines. (If the market is an online publication, the current issue will be available in its entirety.) If the market has no online presence, send for guidelines and sample copies (include a SASE—self-addressed stamped envelope—for guidelines; include appropriate cost for sample copy).

Submission guidelines are pure gold for the specific information they provide. However you acquire them—by SASE or e-mail, online, or in a magazine itself—make them an integral part of your market research.

- ⊕ market new to this edition
- ⊘ market does not accept unsolicited submissions
- Canadian market
- market located outside of the U.S. and Canada
- online opportunity
- $ market pays
- tips to break into a specific market
- ○ market welcomes submissions from beginning poets
- ◐ market prefers submissions from skilled, experienced poets; will consider work from beginning poets
- ● market prefers submissions from poets with a high degree of skill and experience
- ◎ market has a specialized focus

5. START SLOWLY. It may be tempting to send your work directly to *The New Yorker* or *Poetry*, but try to adopt a more modest approach if you're just starting out. Most listings in this book display symbols that reflect the level of writing a magazine or publisher prefers to receive. The ○ symbol indicates a market that welcomes submissions from beginning or unpublished poets. As you gain confidence and experience (and increased skill in your writing), you can move on to markets coded with the ◐ symbol. Although it may tax your patience, slow and steady progress is a proven route to success.

6. BE PROFESSIONAL. Professionalism is not something you should "work up to." Make it show in your first submission, from the way you prepare your manuscript to the attitude you project in your communications with editors.

Follow those guidelines. Submit a polished manuscript. (See "Frequently Asked Questions" for details on manuscript formatting and preparation.) Choose poems carefully with the editor's needs in mind. *Always* include a SASE with any submission or inquiry. Such practices show respect for the editor, the publication and the process; and they reflect *your* self-respect and the fact that you take your work seriously. Editors love that; and even if your work is rejected, you've made a good first impression that could help your chances with your next submission.

7. KEEP TRACK OF YOUR SUBMISSIONS. First, do *not* send out the only copies of your work. There are no guarantees your submission won't get lost in the mail, misplaced in a busy editorial office, or vanish into a black hole if the publication or press closes down. Create a special file folder for poems you're submitting. Even if you use a word processing program and store your manuscripts on disk, keep a hard copy file as well (and be sure to back up your electronic files).

Second, establish a tracking system so you always know which poems are where. This can be extremely simple: index cards, a chart created with word processing or database software, or even a simple notebook used as a log. (You can enlarge and photocopy the Submission Tracker or use it as a model to design your own version.) Note the titles of the poems submitted (or the title of the collection if you're submitting a book/chapbook manuscript); the name of the publication, press, or contest; date sent; estimated response time; and date returned *or* date accepted. Additional information you may want to log: the name of the editor/contact, date the accepted piece is published and/or issue number of the magazine, type/amount of pay received, rights acquired by the publication or press, and any pertinent comments.

Without a tracking system, you risk forgetting where and when manuscripts were submitted. This is even more problematic if you simultaneously send the same manuscripts to different magazines, presses or contests. And if you learn of an acceptance by one magazine or publisher, you *must* notify the others that the poem or collection you sent them is no longer available. You run a bigger chance of overlooking someone without an organized approach. This causes hard feelings among editors you may have inconvenienced, hurting your chances with these markets in the future.

8. DON'T FEAR REJECTION. LEARN FROM IT. No one enjoys rejection, but every writer faces it. The best way to turn a negative into a positive is to learn as much as you can from your rejections. Don't let them get you down. A rejection slip isn't a permission slip to doubt yourself, condemn your poetry or give up.

Look over the rejection. Did the editor provide any comments about your work or reasons why your poems were rejected? Probably he or she didn't. Editors are extremely busy and don't necessarily have time to comment on rejections. If that's the case, move on to the next magazine or publisher you've targeted and send your work out again.

SUBMISSION TRACKER

Poem Title	Publication Contest	Editor/Contact	Date Sent	Date Returned	Date Accepted	Date Published	Pay Recieved	Comments

If, however, the editor *has* commented on your work, pay attention. It counts for something that the editor took the time and trouble to say anything, however brief, good or bad. And consider any remark or suggestion with an open mind. You don't have to agree, but you shouldn't automatically disregard the feedback, either. Tell your ego to sit down and be quiet, then use the editor's comments to review your work from a new perspective. You might be surprised by how much you'll learn from a single scribbled word in the margin; or how encouraged you'll feel from a simple "Try again!" written on the rejection slip.

GUIDE TO LISTING FEATURES

Below is an example of a Magazines/Journal listing (Book/Chapbook Publishers listings follow a similar format). Note the callouts that identify various format features of the listing. A key to the symbols displayed at the beginning of each listing is located on the inside cover of this book.

EASY-TO-USE REFERENCE ICONS

E-MAIL ADDRESSES AND WEBSITES

SPECIFIC CONTACT NAMES

TYPES OF POETRY CONSIDERED

DETAILED SUBMISSION GUIDELINES

EDITOR'S COMMENTS

ALASKA QUARTERLY REVIEW

ESB 208, University of Alaska-Anchorage, 3211 Providence Dr., Anchorage AK 99508. (907)786-6916. E-mail: aqr@uaa.alaska.edu. Website: www.uaa.alaska.edu/aqr. **Contact:** Ronald Spatz. "*AQR* publishes fiction, poetry, literary nonfiction and short plays in traditional and experimental styles."

- *Alaska Quarterly* reports they are always looking for freelance material and new writers.

MAGAZINES NEEDS *Alaska Quarterly Review*, published in 2 double issues/year, is "devoted to contemporary literary art. We publish both traditional and experimental fiction, poetry, literary nonfiction, and short plays." Wants all styles and forms of poetry, "with the most emphasis perhaps on voice and content that displays 'risk,' or intriguing ideas or situations." Has published poetry by Maxine Kumin, Jane Hirshfield, David Lehman, Pattiann Rogers, Albert Goldbarth, David Wagoner, Robert Pinsky, Linda Pastan, Ted Kooser, Kay Ryan, W. S. Merwin, Sharon Olds and Billy Collins. *Alaska Quarterly Review* is 224-300 pages, digest-sized, professionally printed, perfect-bound, with card cover with color or b&w photo. Receives up to 6,000 submissions/year, accepts 40-90. Subscription: $18. Sample: $6. Pays $10-50 subject to availability of funds; pays in contributor's copies and subscriptions when funding is limited.

HOW TO CONTACT No fax or e-mail submissions. Reads submissions mid-August to mid-May; manuscripts are *not* read May 15-August 15. Responds in up to 5 months, "sometimes longer during peak periods in late winter."

ADDITIONAL INFORMATION Guest poetry editors have included Stuart Dybek, Jane Hirshfield, Stuart Dischell, Maxine Kumin, Pattiann Rogers, Dorianne Laux, Peggy Shumaker, Olena Kalytiak Davis, Nancy Eimers, Michael Ryan, and Billy Collins.

TIPS "All sections are open to freelancers. We rely almost exclusively on unsolicited manuscripts. *AQR* is a nonprofit literary magazine and does not always have funds to pay authors."

FREQUENTLY ASKED QUESTIONS

The following FAQ (Frequently Asked Questions) section provides the expert knowledge you need to submit your poetry in a professional manner. Answers to most basic questions, such as "How many poems should I send?," "How long should I wait for a reply?" and "Are simultaneous submissions okay?" can be found by simply reading the listings in the Magazines/Journals and Book/Chapbook Publishers sections. See the introduction to each section for an explanation of the information contained in the listings. Also, see the Glossary of Listing terms.

Is it okay to submit handwritten poems?

Usually, no. Now and then a publisher or editor makes an exception and accepts handwritten manuscripts. However, check the preferences stated in each listing. If no mention is made of handwritten submissions, assume your poetry should be typed or computer-generated.

How should I format my poems for submission to magazines and journals?

If you're submitting poems by regular mail (also referred to as *land mail*, *postal mail* or *snail mail*), follow this format:

Poems should be typed or computer-printed on white 8½×11 paper of at least 20 lb. weight. Left, right and bottom margins should be at least one inch. Starting ½ inch from the top of the page, type your name, address, telephone number, e-mail address (if you have one) and number of lines in the poem in the *upper right* corner, in individual lines, single-spaced. Space down about six lines and type the poem title, either centered or flush left. The title may appear in all caps or in upper and lower case. Space down another two lines (at least) and begin to type your poem. Poems are usually single-spaced,

MAILED SUBMISSION FORMAT

S.T. Coleridge
1796 Ancient Way
Mariner Heights OH 45007 ❷
(852) 555-5555
albatross@strophe.vv.cy
54 lines

KUBLA KHAN ❹

❺ In Xanadu did Kubla Khan
a stately pleasure dome decree:
where Alph, the sacred river, ran
through caverns measureless to man
down to a sunless sea.
So twice five miles of furtile ground
with walls and towers were girdled round:
and there were gardens bright with sinuous rills,
where blossomed many an incense-bearing tree;
and here were forests ancient as the hills,
enfolding sunny spots of greenery.

❻ But oh! that deep romantic chasm which slanted
down the green hill athwart a cedarn cover!
A savage place! as holy and enchanted
as e'er beneath a waning moon was haunted
by woman wailing for her demon lover!
And from this chasm, with ceaseless turmoil seething,
as if this earth in fast thick pants were breathing, ❼
a mighty fountain momentarily was forced:
amid whose swift half-intermitted burst
huge fragments vaulted like rebounding hail,
or chaffy grain beneath the thresher's flail;
And 'mid these dancing rocks at once and ever
it flung up momently the sacred river.

① DO leave ½" margin on top, at least 1" on sides and bottom. ② DO list contact information and number of lines in upper right corner. ③ DO space down about 6 lines. ④ DO type title in all caps or upper/lower case. Type flush with left margin. ⑤ DON'T type a byline but DO space down at least 2 lines. ⑥ DO double-space between spaces. ⑦ DO type poems single-space unless guidelines specify double spacing. ⑧ For multi-page poems, DO show your name, keyword(s) from title, page number, and "continue stanza" or "new stanza." ⑨ DO space down at least 3 lines before resuming poem.

S.T. Coleridge

KUBLA KAHN, Page 2, continued stanza. 8

Five miles meandering with a mazy motion
through wood and dale the sacred river ran,
then reached the caverns measureless to man,
and sank in tumult to a lifeless ocean:
and 'mid this tumult Kubla heard from afar
ancestral voices prophesying war!

The shadow of the dome of pleasure
floated midway on the waves;
where was heard the mingled measure
from the fountain and the caves.
It was a miracle of rare device,
a sunny pleasure dome with caves of ice!

A damsel with a dulcimer
in a vision once I saw:
It was an Abyssinian maid,

although some magazines may request double-spaced submissions. (Be alert to each market's preferences.) Double-space between stanzas. Type one poem to a page. For poems longer than one page, type your name in the *upper left* corner; on the next line type a key word from the title of your poem, the page number, and indicate whether the stanza begins or is continued on the new page (i.e., MOTHMAN, Page 2, continue stanza *or* begin new stanza).

If you're submitting poems by e-mail:

First, make sure the publication accepts e-mail submissions. This information, when available, is included in all *Poet's Market* listings. In most cases, editors will request that poems be pasted within the body of your e-mail, *not* sent as attachments. Many editors prefer this format because of the danger of viruses, the possibility of software incompatibility, and other concerns associated with e-mail attachments. Editors who consider e-mail attachments taboo may even delete the message without opening the attachment.

Of course, other editors do accept, and even prefer e-mail submissions as attachments. This information should be clearly stated in the market listing. If it's not, you're probably safer submitting your poems in the body of the e-mail. (All the more reason to pay close attention to details given in the listings.)

Note, too, the number of poems the editor recommends including in the e-mail submission. If no quantity is given specifically for e-mails, go with the number of poems an editor recommends submitting in general. Identify your submission with a notation in the subject line. While some editors simply want the words "Poetry Submission," others want poem titles. Check the market listing for preferences. **Note:** Because of spam, filters and other concerns, some editors are strict about what must be printed in the subject line and how. If you're uncertain about any aspect of e-mail submission formats, double-check the website (if available) for information or contact the publication for directions.

What is a chapbook? How is it different from a regular poetry book?

A chapbook is a booklet, averaging 24-50 pages in length (some are shorter), usually digest-sized (5½×8½, although chapbooks can come in all sizes, even published within the pages of a magazine). Typically, a chapbook is saddle-stapled with a soft cover (card or special paper); chapbooks can also be produced with a plain paper cover the same weight as the pages, especially if the booklet is photocopied.

A chapbook is a much smaller collection of poetry than a full-length book (which runs anywhere from 50 pages to well over 100 pages, longer for "best of" collections and retrospectives). There are probably more poetry chapbooks being published than full-length books, and that's an important point to consider. Don't think of the chapbook as a poor relation to the full-length collection. While it's true a chapbook won't attract big

E-MAIL SUBMISSION FORMAT

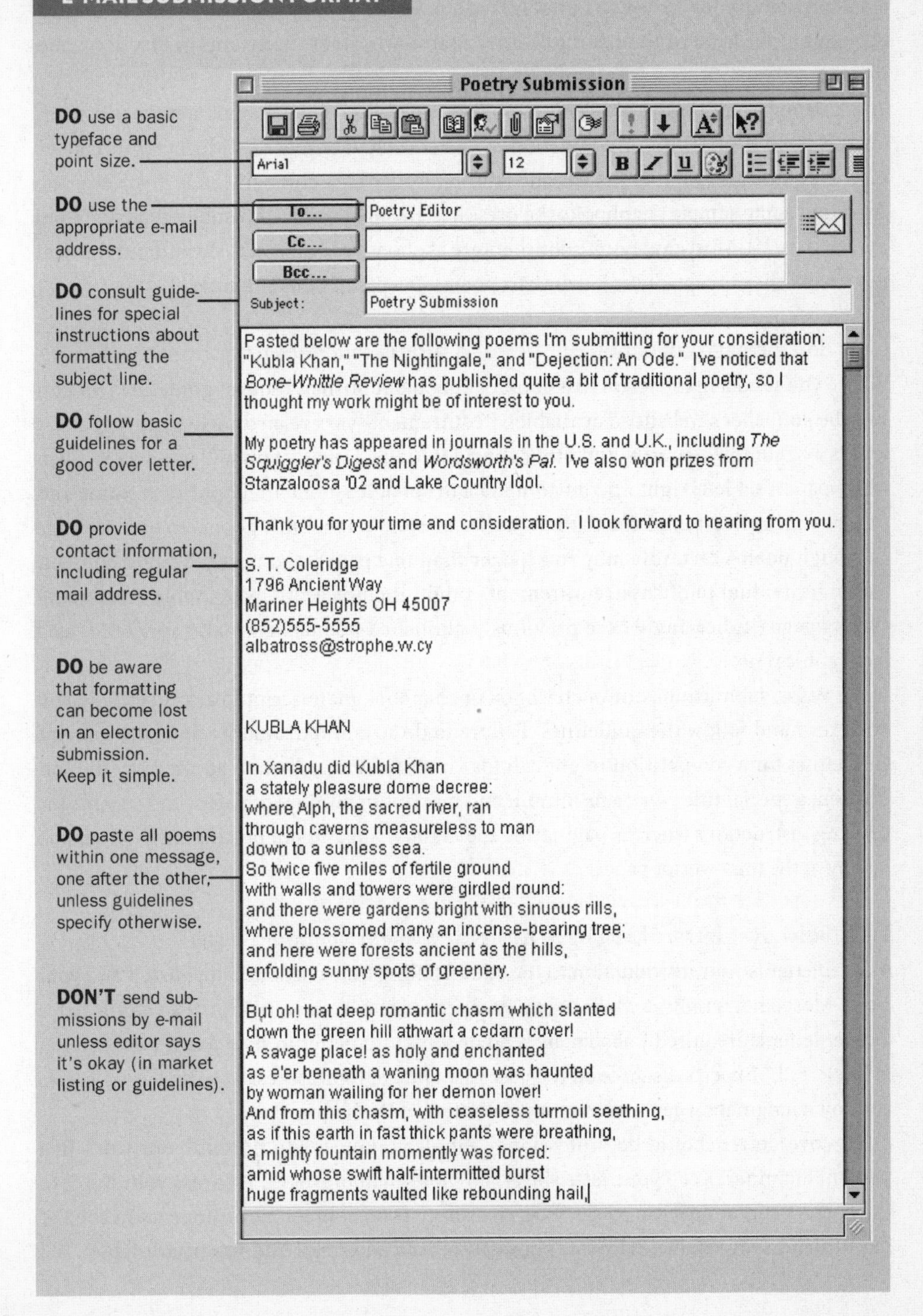

reviews, qualify for major prizes or find national distribution through chain bookstores, it's a terrific way for a poet to build an audience (and reputation) in increments, while developing the kind of publishing history that may attract the attention of a book publisher one day.

Although some presses consider chapbooks through a regular submission process, many choose manuscripts through competitions. Check each publisher's listing for requirements, send for guidelines or visit the website (absolutely vital if a competition is involved), and check out some sample chapbooks the press has already produced (usually available from the press itself). Most chapbook publishers are as choosy as book publishers about the quality of work they accept. Submit your best poems in a professional manner.

How do I format a collection of poems to submit to a book/chapbook publisher?

Before you send a manuscript to a book/chapbook publisher, request guidelines (or consult the publisher's website, if available). Requirements vary regarding formatting, query letters and samples, length, and other considerations. Usually you will use 8½×11, 20 lb. white paper; set left, right and bottom margins of at least one inch; put your name and title of your collection in the top left corner of every page; limit poems to one per page (although poems certainly may run longer than one page); and number pages consecutively. Individual publisher requirements might include a title page, table of contents, credits page (indicating where previously published poems originally appeared) and biographical note.

If you're submitting your poetry book or chapbook manuscript to a competition, you *must* read and follow the guidelines. Failure to do so could disqualify your manuscript. Guidelines for a competition might call for an official entry form to accompany the submission, a special title page, a minimum and maximum number of pages, and specific formatting instructions (such as paginating the manuscript and not putting the poet's name on any of the manuscript pages).

What is a cover letter? Do I have to send one? What should it say?

A cover letter is your introduction to the editor, telling him a little about yourself and your work. Most editors indicate their cover letter preferences in their listings. If an editor states a cover letter is "required," absolutely send one! It's also better to send one if a cover letter is "preferred." Experts disagree on the necessity and appropriateness of cover letters, so use your own judgment when preferences aren't clear in the listing.

A cover letter should be professional but also allow you to present your work in a personal manner. Keep your letter brief, no more than one page. Address your letter to the correct contact person. (Use "Poetry Editor" if no contact name appears in the listing.) Include your name, address, phone number and e-mail address (if available). If a

PREPARING YOUR COVER LETTER

Perry Lineskanner ❶
1954 Eastern Blvd.
Pentameter OH 45007
(852) 555-5555
soneteer@trochee.vv.cy

April 24, 2009

Spack Saddlestaple, Editor
The Squiggler's Digest ❷
Double-Toe Press
P.O. Box 54X
Submission Junction AZ 85009

Dear Mr. Saddlestaple:

❸ Enclosed are three poems for your consideration for The Squiggler's Digest: "The Diamond Queen," "The Boy Who Was Gromit," and "The Maker of Everything."

❹ Although this is my first submission to your journal, I'm a long-time reader of The Squiggler's Digest and enjoy the scope of narrative poetry you feature. I especially enjoyed Sydney Dogwood's poetry cycle in Issue 4.

My own poetry has appeared recently in The Bone-Whittle Review, Bumper-Car Reverie, and Stock Still.

Thank you for considering my manuscript. I look forward to hearing from you.

Sincerely,

Perry Lineskanner

❶ DO type on one side of 8½ × 11 20lb. paper. ❷ DO use a standard 12-point typeface (like Times New Roman). ❸ DO list the poems you're submitting for consideration. ❹ DO mention something about the magazine and about yourself.

biographical note is requested, include 2-3 lines about your background, interests, why you write poetry, etc. Avoid praising yourself or your poems in your letter (your submission should speak for itself). Include titles (or first lines) of the poems you're submitting. You may list a few of your most recent publishing credits, but no more than five; and keep in mind that some editors find publishing credits tiresome—they're more interested in the quality of the work you're submitting to *them*.

Use a business-style format for a professional appearance and proofread carefully; typos, misspellings and other errors make a poor first impression.

Show your familiarity with the magazine to which you're submitting: comment on a poem the magazine published, tell the editor why you chose to submit to her magazine, mention poets the magazine has published. Use a business-style format for a professional appearance and proofread carefully; typos, misspellings and other errors make a poor first impression. Remember that editors are people, too. Respect, professionalism and kindness go a long way in poet/editor relationships.

What is a SASE? An IRC (with SAE)?

A SASE is a self-addressed, stamped envelope—and you should never send a submission by regular mail without one. Also include a SASE if you send an inquiry to an editor. If your submission is too large for an envelope (for instance, a bulky book-length collection of poems), use a box and include a self-addressed mailing label with adequate return postage paper-clipped to it.

An IRC is an International Reply Coupon, enclosed with a self-addressed envelope for manuscripts submitted to foreign markets. Each coupon is equivalent in value to the minimum postage rate for an unregistered airmail letter. IRCs may be exchanged for postage stamps at post offices in all foreign countries that are members of the Universal Postal Union (UPU). When you provide the adequate number of IRCs and a self-addressed envelope (SAE), you give a foreign editor financial means to return your submission (U.S. postage stamps cannot be used to send mail *to* the United States from outside the country). Purchase price is $2 per coupon. Call your local post office to check for availability (sometimes only larger post offices sell them).

IMPORTANT NOTE ABOUT IRCS: Foreign editors sometimes find the IRCs have been stamped incorrectly by the U.S. post office when purchased. This voids the IRCs and makes it impossible for the foreign editor to exchange the coupons for return postage for your manuscript. When buying IRCs, make sure yours have been stamped correctly before you leave the counter. (The Postal Service clerk must place a postmark in the block with the heading *control stamp of the country of origin.*) More information about International Reply Coupons is available on the USPS website (www.usps.com).

To save time and money, poets sometimes send disposable manuscripts to foreign markets and inform the editor to discard the manuscript after it's been read. Some enclose an IRC and SAE for reply only; others establish a deadline after which they will withdraw the manuscript from consideration and market it elsewhere.

How much postage does my submission need?

As much as it takes—you do *not* want your manuscript to arrive postage due. Purchase a postage scale or take your manuscript to the post office for weighing. Remember, you'll need postage on two envelopes: the one containing your submission and SASE, and the return envelope itself. Submissions without SASEs usually will not be returned (and possibly may not even be read).

Note: New postage rates went into effect on January, 2012. There is now a new fee structure for First-Class Postage. For letters and cards (including business-size envelopes), the First-Class rate is 45 cents for the first ounce, and 20 cents per additional ounce up to and including 3.5 ounces. **Letter-sized mail that weighs more than 3.5 ounces is charged the "flats" rate** ("flats" include any envelope large enough to mail an 8½×11 manuscript page unfolded) of 90 cents for the first ounce, and 20 cents for each additional ounce up to and including 13 ounces. This means if you send a large envelope that weighs only one ounce, it costs 90 cents at the First-Class flats rate instead of the 45 cents charged for First-Class letters and cards. (See the charts on the next page for First-Class rates for letters and flats, or go to www.usps.com for complete information on all rates questions.)

The USPS also offers its Click-N-Ship® program, which allows a customer to print domestic and international shipping labels with postage, buy insurance and pay for postage by credit card. See the USPS website for a one-time software download, to check system requirements and to register for an account.

The website is also your source for ordering supplies (such as postage scale and labels), reviewing postal regulations, calculating postage and more. Canada Post information and services are available at www.canadapost.com.

POSTAGE INFORMATION

First Class Mail Rates: Letters & Cards

1 ounce	$0.45	3 ounces	$0.85
2 ounces	$0.65	3.5 ounces	$1.05
Postcard	$0.32		

First Class Mail Rates: Flats

Weight not over (ounces)	Rate	Weight not over (ounces)	Rate
1	$0.90	8	$2.30
2	$1.10	9	$2.50
3	$1.30	10	$2.70
4	$1.50	11	$2.90
5	$1.70	12	$3.10
6	$1.90	13	$3.30
7	$2.10		

Source: Website of the United States Postal Service (www.usps.com)

U.S. Postal Codes

AL	Alabama	KY	Kentucky	OK	Oklahoma
AK	Alaska	LA	Louisiana	OR	Oregon
AZ	Arizona	ME	Maine	PA	Pennsylvania
AR	Arkansas	MD	Maryland	PR	Puerto Rico
CA	California	MA	Massachusetts	RI	Rhode Island
CO	Colorado	MI	Michigan	SC	South Carolina
CT	Connecticut	MN	Minnesota	SD	South Dakota
DE	Delaware	MS	Mississippi	TN	Tennessee
DC	District of Columbia	MO	Missouri	TX	Texas
FL	Florida	NE	Montana	UT	Utah
GA	Georgia	NV	Nevada	VT	Vermont
GU	Guam	NH	New Hampshire	VI	Virgin Islands
HI	Hawaii	NJ	New Jersey	VA	Virginia
ID	Idaho	NM	New Mexico	WA	Washington
IL	Illinois	NY	New York	WV	West Virginia
IN	Indiana	NC	North Carolina	WI	Wisconsin
IA	Iowa	ND	North Dakota	WY	Wyoming
KS	Kansas	OH	Ohio		

Canadian Postal Codes

AB	Alberta	NS	Nova Scotia	QC	Quebec
BC	British Columbia	NT	Northwest Territories	SK	Saskatchewan
MB	Manitoba	NU	Nunavut	YT	Yukon
NB	New Brunswick	ON	Ontario		
NL	Newfoundland & Labrador	PE	Prince Edward Island		

What does it mean when an editor says "no previously published" poems? Does this include poems that have appeared in anthologies? What if one of my poems appeared online through a group or forum?

If your poem appears *anywhere* in print for a public audience, it's considered "previously" published. That includes magazines, anthologies, websites and online journals, and even printed programs (say for a church service, wedding, etc.). See the explanation for rights below, especially *second serial (reprint) rights* and *all rights* for additional concerns about previously published material.

One exception to the above guidelines is if your poem appears online in a *private* poetry forum, critique group, etc. As long as the site is private (i.e., a password is required to view and participate), your poem isn't considered "published." However, if your poem is printed on an online forum or bulletin board that's available for public viewing, even if you must use a password to post the poem or to comment, then your poem is considered "published" as far as rights are concerned.

What rights should I offer for my poems? What do these different rights mean?

Editors usually indicate in their listings what rights they acquire. Most journals and magazines license *first rights* (a.k.a. *first serial rights*), which means the poet offers the right to publish the poem for the first time in any periodical. All other rights to the material remain with the poet. (Note that some editors state that rights to poems "revert to poets upon publication" when first rights are acquired.) When poems are excerpted from a book prior to publication and printed in a magazine/journal, this is also called *first serial rights*. The addition of *North American* indicates the editor is the first to publish a poem in a U.S. or Canadian periodical. The poem may still be submitted to editors outside of North America or to those who acquire reprint rights.

When a magazine/journal licenses *one-time rights* to a poem (also known as *simultaneous rights*), the editor has *nonexclusive* rights to publish the poem once. The poet may submit that same poem to other publications at the same time (usually markets that don't have overlapping audiences).

Editors/publishers open to submission of work already published elsewhere seek *second serial (reprint) rights*. The poet is obliged to inform them where and when the poem previously appeared so they can give proper credit to the original publication. In essence, chapbook or book collections license reprint rights, listing the magazines in which poems previously appeared somewhere in the book (usually on the copyright page or separate credits page).

If a publisher or editor requires you to relinquish *all rights*, be aware that you're giving up ownership of that poem or group of poems. You cannot resubmit the work elsewhere, nor can you include it in a poetry collection without permission or by negotiating for reprint rights to be returned to you. Before you agree to this type of arrangement, ask the editor first if he or she is willing to acquire first rights instead of all rights. If you receive a refusal and you don't want to relinquish all rights, simply write a letter withdrawing your work from consideration. Some editors will reassign rights to a writer after a given amount of time, such as one year.

With the growth in Internet publishing opportunities, *electronic rights* have become very important. These cover a broad range of electronic media, including online magazines, CD recordings of poetry readings and CD-ROM editions of magazines. When submitting to an electronic market of any kind, find out what rights the market acquires upfront (many online magazines also stipulate the right to archive poetry they've published so it's continually available on their websites).

What is a copyright? Should I have my poems copyrighted before I submit them for publication?

Copyright is a proprietary right that gives you the power to control your work's reproduction, distribution and public display or performance, as well as its adaptation to other forms. In other words, you have the legal right to the exclusive publication, sale or distribution of your poetry. What's more, your "original works of authorship" are protected as soon as they are "fixed in a tangible form of expression," i.e., written down or recorded. Since March 1989, copyright notices are no longer required to secure protection, so it's not necessary to include them on your poetry manuscript. Also, in many editors' minds, copyright notices signal the work of amateurs who are distrustful and paranoid about having work stolen.

If you still want to indicate copyright, use the © symbol or the word *copyright*, your name and the year. If you wish, you can register your copyright with the Copyright Office for a $45 fee, using Form TX (directions and form available for download from www.copyright.gov). Since paying $45 per poem is costly and impractical, you may prefer to copyright a group of unpublished poems for that single fee. Further information is available from the U.S. Copyright Office, Library of Congress, 101 Independence Ave. S.E., Washington DC 20559-6000; by download from www.copyright.gov; or by calling (202)707-3000 between 8:30 a.m. and 5:00 p.m. (EST) weekdays.

SPECIAL NOTE REGARDING COPYRIGHT OFFICE MAIL DELIVERY: The "effective date of registration" for copyright applications is usually the day the Copyright Office actually receives all elements of an application (application form, fee and copies of work being registered). Because of security concerns, all USPS and private-carrier mail is screened off-site prior to arrival at the Copyright Office. This can add 3-5 days to delivery time and could, therefore, impact the effective date of registration. See the website for details about proper packaging, special handling and other related information.

OUT OF THE SLUSH AND INTO PRINT

by Kelly Davio

So you've written some poems. You've shared them with friends you trust for candid feedback, and they genuinely enjoy the poetry. Better still, your writing group, teachers or workshop compatriots think the work is strong enough to send to literary journals. You've done your homework by identifying venues that print poems like yours, and because you're a good literary citizen, you've subscribed to some of your favorite journals. Having identified the strongest three to five poems in your repertoire, you bundle your poems up, stamp the envelopes, rub said envelopes against your dog's head for luck, and say a little prayer as you pop them into the mail.

A few weeks or months pass, a rejection slip or two filtering in as you wait, but you don't worry that "your work does not meet our editorial needs at this time." You keep the faith. Then a few more slips find their way into your mailbox. When the very last journal rejects your work as well, you begin to wonder what's going wrong.

MY WRITING IS STRONG, SO WHY CAN'T I SEEM TO PUBLISH?

If you're asking this question, you're in good company with many other poets. Let's be clear: the odds of having work selected for publication are never in your favor. Consider the numbers of poems editors read: for each issue of *The Los Angeles Review*, for example, we consider more than 1,000 poems, eventually accepting about 40 or so. Many journals have room to showcase only half as many pieces. Not only are your poems pitted against many others, but in some cases, they also have to fight their way past early readers. At many journals, particularly those run by universities, undergraduate students of creative writing make initial calls on poems in the "slush pile" (the unsolicited manuscripts considered by journals) and determine whether an editor will even lay eyes on your work.

Depressed yet? Cheer up! There are a number of ways to increase the likelihood that your poetry will make it out of the slush, onto the editor's desk, and into print.

FIRST IMPRESSIONS

Think of your submission as a blind date with an editor. She doesn't know you, but she's hoping she finds that elusive spark with your work; you want to show her that your poetry is worth her time. When she opens your envelope or e-mail, the first thing she sees is your cover letter. Just as you would dress nicely to meet a possible romantic interest, your cover letter should show that you're competent, classy, and professional.

Start your date well by addressing the editor by name, not as "Sir or Madam," "To Whom it May Concern," or, worst of all, "Friend." Taking a few moments to find an editor's name on a journal's website, rather than dashing off a form letter, shows the editor you care about your submission.

Taking the time to follow simple instructions will get you places with an editor or reader.

Now that you're off to a good start, keep that cover letter strong by following all guidelines. It baffles editors that many—even most—writers who want to publish don't bother to read or follow guidelines. If an editor asks for three to five poems stapled to a cover letter, don't send six with a paperclip. If the editor asks for the titles of your submitted poems in the cover letter, don't omit them. Taking the time to follow simple instructions will get you places with an editor or reader; when I open that rare submission that is correctly formatted, is addressed to me, and—for the win—spells my name correctly, I automatically want to give more time and attention to that poet's work than to the poems of a writer who sent sloppy slush.

THE RIGHT KIND OF ATTENTION

Now that you've followed the journal's guidelines, the next step in presenting your work well includes telling a little about yourself. Your cover letter gives an editor a sense of you as a person and as a poet. By including information about where you went to school, what you do for a living, and how you heard about the publication in one, brief paragraph, you'll help the editor warm up to your work. It's also great to remind the editor that you met at a conference or reading, or that you are a loyal subscriber to the magazine (I shouldn't have to tell you it's a bad idea to make these claims if they're untrue). Showing that you're a friendly, engaged person puts an editor in a receptive frame of mind.

There is, however, such a thing as showing too much personality. Sure, using a quirky font, adding glitter to your envelope, or attaching photos of yourself in beachwear will get an editor's attention, but it's the wrong sort of attention. At literary journals, editors develop relationships with writers. If your submission suggests you might not be a person an editor would want to engage—let's say you include a sketch of yourself with your collection of medieval torture devices—she'll be understandably skittish about entering a working relationship with you. Making bold assertions about the importance or innovative nature of the enclosed poetry is a similarly bad idea; however much you may want to explain your work in detail, allow your poetry to speak for itself. As a rule, if you're in doubt as to whether any part of your submission is inappropriate or puts you in a bad light, take it out.

SECOND DATES

Every poet—fledgling or established—receives rejection. Sometimes rejection slips come as tiny scraps of paper that appear to have been cut by a toddler. Other times, a writer might be lucky enough to receive a whole sheet of paper on actual letterhead. And every now and then, an editor may put ink to paper or cursor to screen to give a writer some constructive feedback or request to see more work.

Let's be clear: being invited to resubmit is like being asked on a second date. There's no commitment at this stage, but there's genuine interest on the editor's part. She likes your poems, and now that you have her attention, you've got a chance to really impress her with the full range of your charms. You may be excited to have a second shot, but follow the rules of playing it cool: don't e-mail a group of poems five minutes after an editor has asked for them, and don't pop a new batch of work into the mail the same day as you receive a rejection. Just as calling your date moments after you've left the restaurant would smack of desperation, don't run the risk of turning your editor off with enthusiasm that resembles stalking. You needn't worry that the editor will forget you; if she's taken the time to ask for a resubmission, it's because she likes the work and finds it memorable. When you do resubmit, after having taken the time to consider what poems might be better suited to the journal's needs, you can jog the editor's memory by mentioning her offer to consider more work.

IT'S NOT PERSONAL UNLESS YOU MAKE IT PERSONAL

So let's say your second date doesn't go well, or that you never got to the second date at all. Maybe an editor flatly rejected your best poem, your magnum opus. You feel sure that the editor's taste is sorely lacking. While the editor may, in fact, be missing out, there are a number of reasons a journal might not be able to accept your work. The editor might be looking for variety, and your work may feel too similar to poems already accepted. Perhaps your poems do not fit the theme of the issue. Maybe the editor has already filled her allotted pages, and just can't squeeze another piece in the issue. A rejection of a poem isn't a rejection of a person.

However, some poets, in moments of frustration, have been known to dash off angry missives to editors, questioning levels of taste or qualification for the editorial position. When personal attacks are leveled, it discourages those editors who spend great swaths of their free time working to promote the craft and appreciation of poetry. In an industry that runs less on money than it does on good will, hostility will only breed a bad reputation. Spare yourself from becoming the pariah in the inbox by taking setbacks graciously.

PERSISTENCE PAYS ... IN CONTRIBUTOR'S COPIES

The longer you write and continue to send out work, the more you will find success in publishing. Given the vast number of publications in the Western world, there is undoubtedly a journal for every writer. And as you begin to see your poems come out in print, it will likely be a point of pride for you to see your collection of contributor's copies—copies given in payment for the use of the poet's work—grow to overfill your bookshelf.

But if you have visions of your bank account growing to such seam-bursting proportions, skim back up to the line about the literary world running on good vibes, not on hard cash. Placing poems in journals doesn't pay much, if anything. From time to time, a journal may be able to offer a poet a small honorarium, but publications can generally afford only to give complimentary or discounted copies.

So why put yourself through the rigmarole of writing, submitting, finding rejection and, somewhere down the line, getting some copies of magazines? Hopefully it's because you're genuinely in love with language and with poetry, and it brings you joy to share that love with others. As you go forward in your writing career, remember: be friendly, be courteous, be kind and, by all means, keep going.

KELLY DAVIO currently serves as the Managing Editor/Poetry Editor at the *Los Angeles Review*, and reads poetry for *Fifth Wednesday Journal*. Her work can be found in *Women's Review of Books*, *Cincinnati Review*, and *Best New Poets 2009*, among others. Her poetry collection, *Burn This House*, is forthcoming from Red Hen Press, and she is currently working on a novel in verse.

HOW TO INCREASE YOUR ODDS OF PUBLICATION

by Sage Cohen

Writing poetry is an art, and so is the process of submitting your poems for publication. If you'd like to increase your odds of getting noticed and getting published, this article can help you align your best work with the right opportunities—so you can give your poems the chance they deserve.

IDENTIFY THE RIGHT PUBLICATIONS FOR YOUR POETRY

You'll have the greatest odds of publication when you submit your poems to journals or contests that are most suited to your work—and therefore most likely to appreciate it. If you're not sure how to identify such possibilities, consider the following:

Read the work of poets you love

A good way to get a feel for publishing possibilities is by reviewing the acknowledgments pages of the poetry collections you admire. If you connect to a particular poet's work, chances are good that your poetry could also be well suited to the journals where s/he has been published.

Do your due diligence

Let's say you've collected a list of possible journals and contests based on the tip above. And let's say you've never sent out work for publication before. You can research here in *Poet's Market* to learn more about how your poetry and these opportunities might line up. For example, you'll want to submit only to journals that say they publish work by emerging as well as established poets. You'll want to confirm that contest submission fees and guidelines are in alignment with what you're willing to send and spend. And you may want to make sure your themes, poetic forms, and approach to language are compatible with the publication's description of what it is seeking. I also suggest learning what you can about the editors or contest judge(s)—and reading their poetry, if possible, so you get a feeling for their personal aesthetic.

Always experience a journal before submitting

Before submitting your work to a publication, purchase its latest issue or view content online to get a sense of the poets and poems it features. Also consider how the publication's front cover, inside art, website design, production, paper quality and font choice create a particular kind of experience. If you can imagine seeing your poetry in these pages, that's a good indication that the journal or site may be the right fit for you.

Track what you learn to grow your knowledge base

I suggest creating a simple system—a document, binder or folder—where you track what you've learned about each publication and record your thinking about how your poems align or do not align. This way, you'll have a growing knowledge base about the poetry market—and how various opportunities may be suited to your objectives—as you investigate, submit and publish over time.

CHOOSE THE RIGHT POEM/S

When you've chosen a publication or contest to which you'd like to submit, it's time to gather the poems for this opportunity. Consider running the poems you are considering through these filters of inquiry:

Does something significant or resonant happen?

Poems get editors' attention when they introduce a new possibility, provide a palpable experience or revelation, and say something in a way it has never been spoken (or written) before. Ask yourself:

- What happens in this poem? (Or, if the poem is non-narrative, do the language, sound and/or imagery create the kind of experience or journey I intended?)
- If this poem is about or addressed to someone I know, does it also reveal something meaningful or relevant to people outside of the dynamic?
- What is discovered or transformed or revealed?

Because it can be tricky to experience your own, highly subjective material objectively, you may want to share your poems with a reader or two you trust and ask these questions of them. If you're not sure you are creating an experience that has impact or resonance, your poem may not yet be ready for publication.

Have I found something fresh to say about a familiar theme?

If you're writing about a historical person or event or one that's been covered in the news in recent years, chances are good that most readers will have a good handle on the facts. To ensure that your poem makes an impact, ask yourself:

- What happens in this poem that is fresh, surprising, and different than the information already available on this topic?
- How is this poem departing from the work of "reporting" and moving into the territory of "illuminating"?
- How is this event or person serving as a leaping-off point for my own inquiry or discovery about myself, history, the natural world, or the human condition?

IS MY WORK AS POLISHED AS POSSIBLE?

These 10 revision tips may help you identify opportunities to nip, tuck, and shine. Ask yourself:

1. Could I trim exposition at the beginning or summary information at the end that is not serving the poem?
2. Could I use a different voice to influence the experience of this poem? (For example, consider changing a third-person voice into the first person and see if this shift in intimacy is of benefit.)
3. Could my similes and metaphors be more distilled or powerful? If I've used an extended metaphor, does it hold up throughout the poem?
4. Where can I bring more energy to the language I've used? Can I use more active language to communicate similar ideas? Can modifiers be cut?
5. What if I changed the past-tense verbs to the present tense (or vice versa)?
6. How might I shape the poem (line length, stanza breaks, white space) to more fully enact the emotion and rhythm of its content?
7. Are punctuation and capitalization and verb tense consistent? Would different choices (such as removing punctuation or capitalization) improve the experience?
8. Is there a music of repeating sounds throughout the poem? What words could I replace to create a more cohesive sound experience?

9. Are there opportunities to break lines in ways that give attention to important words or pace the momentum of the narrative more powerfully?
10. How might the title better encapsulate and add dimension to the experience of the poem? Could some of the exposition cut in step one be used to set the context of the poem in its title?

ARRANGE YOUR POEMS INTENTIONALLY

The order of the poems you've submitted can make a difference in an editor's experience and opinion of your work—even if you're just submitting three to five poems. Think about the arrangement as a single composition that provides a coherent reading journey. Where do you want the reader to start—and finish? How do you want them to enter the realm of your poetry, and how are you intending to send them off?

MAKE SUBMISSION GUIDELINES YOUR BIBLE

Every literary publication and contest will offer detailed guidelines about how and when they want to receive poems. Your job is to follow every single detail of those guidelines fanatically to ensure you don't rule yourself out with a simple oversight. Because it's easy to miss a detail when scanning instructions online, I recommend printing out the submission guidelines for any opportunity and then checking off each requirement as you meet it. Specifically:

- Follow simultaneous submission instructions. Some publications accept simultaneous submissions (meaning that you've sent the same poems to more than one publication for consideration at the same time) and others don't. Be careful to understand and honor each journal's parameters.
- Get your timing right. Publications have contest deadlines and specific reading windows. Make sure you are sending your work in advance of the specified deadline.
- Choose poems that fit. Ensure that you have chosen poems that match any specific requirements, such as: theme, form, length (number of lines or pages), number of poems allowed or required.
- Be deliberate about where you include your name. Some publications read and choose poems "blind," others don't. Be sure to understand whether the publication wants identifying information on the poems or not—and follow these guidelines carefully.
- Double-check the mailing address and editor names. No editor wants to see his or her name misspelled or receive mail addressed to his or her predecessor. It's also a

good idea to confirm the gender of the person you are addressing if you have any doubt.

- Follow binding requirements. Publications are often very specific about whether they want paper clips, staples or loose pages.
- Provide an SASE (self-addressed, stamped envelope) if this is required or requested by the publication. If they've made it clear that they intend to notify you some other way, follow whatever process is requested.
- Include a check if you are submitting to a contest that has a required reading fee. Make sure you make it out to the organization as requested in the amount required and specify the name of the contest to which you are submitting.

FORMAT, PROOF, AND POLISH

First impressions are often the last impression. Think of your submission package as a gift that an editor or selection committee will enjoy opening and experiencing—whether you're submitting online or by mail:

- Use a standard font that is easy to read—such as Times New Roman or Garamond or Calibri—using 12-point font, unless instructed otherwise. Your priority should be: legibility and ease for the person(s) who will be considering your poem.
- Unless you are doing so for a very specific reason, such as for dialogue or to distinguish a speaker's thoughts, think twice about bolding or italicizing fonts. Let your images, word choice and line breaks do the work of creating emphasis and momentum.
- Print your poems on white, unrumpled and unscented paper.
- Ensure that your toner is working or that your photocopies are clear and crisp.

WRITE A COVER LETTER THAT CONNECTS

Your cover letter should first and foremost provide whatever information is requested in the submission guidelines, if any. In the absence of specific instruction, write a concise note that covers the following:

- Explain that you are submitting poems for [name of contest, issue, or general consideration].
- Describe in a sentence or two what you admire about the publication and why you chose to submit your work—if you have something authentic to say. Or, if you've had a previous communication with an editor (such as, they sent an encouraging rejection with a note inviting you to submit again in the future) you can mention that here.

- Lists the names of the poems being submitted. If this is a simultaneous submission, it is good form to mention this and confirm that you intend to follow whatever process this publication has requested in its submission guidelines.
- Provide a brief biographical paragraph that describes key publishing or education highlights to reflect your literary experience and expertise. If you haven't published yet or don't have anything else relevant to report, no need to say anything here.
- Be polite and gracious.

Remember, this is a business communication. Some mistakes to avoid:

- Do not provide explanations about why you chose these poems for submission, why you wrote them, what they mean to you or your family, or how you have revised them.
- Do not advise editors about when you expect to hear back from them.
- Do not send a follow-up letter with a batch of poems that are edited versions of a previous submission.
- Do send a follow-up letter to withdraw any poems you have submitted as soon as they have been accepted elsewhere.

Over time, you'll get more efficient and adept with this process. Preparing your poems for submission will get faster, easier and more automatic as you know what steps to take and mistakes to avoid. Your commitment to consistently putting your best work forward—and willingness to learn from the feedback you get along the way—will give you the very best odds of publication.

SAGE COHEN is the author of *Writing the Life Poetic* and *The Productive Writer*, both from Writer's Digest Books, and the poetry collection Like the Heart, the World. She holds an MFA in creative writing from New York University and a BA from Brown University. Sage has won first place in the Ghost Road Press poetry contest, been nominated for a Pushcart Prize and published a number of articles in *Writer's Digest* magazine. In 2011, she judged the Writer's Digest contest for non-rhyming poetry. To learn more about Sage, visit pathofpossibility.com.

THE ORGANIZED POET

by Patricia Kennelly

If you're like many poets I've talked with, it's not uncommon to have your poems everywhere. My desktop held overflowing notebooks, file folders and piles of random pieces of paper, scribbled with favorite words, lines, and poem starts. My computer's desktop wasn't any better. Although I knew most of my work was saved, my lack of organization made finding a particular poem time-consuming.

This wasn't too much of a problem until I started submitting my body of work. I struggled with getting my work to the right market. I missed good opportunities and important deadlines and created unnecessary stress by entering my poems at the last minute. Finding contests, markets and journals was the easy part; tracking down a poem or trying to read my illegible note about a "must enter" contest became challenging.

Most organizational experts agree that organizing any part of your life will save you time, money and help to eliminate stress. So why do so many poets have resistance to organizing their work? Some poets think that organization is the opposite of creativity and that being too businesslike will stifle their voices. I found the opposite to be true. Working on organization fueled my desire to write poetry and get my poems published.

The result? More published pieces and a clearer picture of where I wanted to go with my poetry.

When I decided to take ownership of my body of work and organize, I naturally approached the submission process in a professional manner. Doing the hard work ahead of time meant I had more time to find and research markets. The result? More published pieces and a clearer picture of where I wanted to go with my poetry.

Whatever system you choose (pen and paper, computer based, online or a combination of all) make sure it's one that will work for you. And if it doesn't work, consider trying another. The best organizational systems only function if you're ready to get organized and if they fit your personality. If any of these tips seem too daunting, consider asking a fellow poet to work with you in exchange for doing the same for them.

10 WAYS TO GET ORGANIZED

If you don't already have an uncluttered writing space, create one. It's difficult to work on organization if your space causes additional stress or distraction. These tips might help you become a more organized poet:

1. Find all of your publishable poems as well as your incomplete poems. This may take some time. Don't rush this process; finding, reading and organizing your forgotten words may inspire new work. Consider typing up your poem starts into one document so you know where to begin when you're stuck for inspiration.

2. Print hard copies of all work and separate publishable poems and poems that need revision into separate accordion files or three-ring binders. You can choose to file by title, subject/theme or type/form. Other poets include length of poem and tone.

3. Generate a virtual folder on your desktop. I titled mine "All Poetry" and created subfolders entitled "Publishable Poems," "Needs Work," and "Published Poems." Choose subfolder titles that make sense to you, you can use poem title, subject matter, form, or theme. Your goal is to be able to find your poems easily.

4. Create or find a submission tracker. If your goal is publication, having a system that tracks your submissions and that is easy to use and update will help create a sense of order.

5. Write or type up a list of goal markets for the year. I do this by going through *Poet's Market* and my favorite poetry newsletters and websites to find markets that seem to be a good fit. This document will grow every month as you discover more markets, contests and literary journals. Some poets find including the hyperlinks to be helpful.

6. Make an appointment with yourself. At least once every week I set aside some time to follow up with upcoming deadlines and to write a to-do list. More productive writers than myself do a to-do list every day, but with a full time job I find that this weekly check-in is enough to keep me on task.

7. Subscribe to poetry newsletters and set Google alerts for specific contests you'd like to enter. Here is the challenging part–as soon as you receive the newsletter or alert, fill in your paper or virtual poetry calendar. And then delete the newsletter.
8. Keep office supplies including: envelopes, paper, file folders, printer ink and stamps stocked. While many magazines and journals are set up for e-mail submission, there are still some journals that require a hard copy submission.
9. Organize your books by genre. I keep chapbooks, craft books, journals, and poetry magazines on one shelf for reference and inspiration. While the Internet makes it easy to access information, having all of your reference materials within easy reach could prevent you from getting distracted online.
10. Do set a date for completion of your new organizational system by choosing a realistic goal date and sticking to it. As Barbara Sher writes in *Wishcraft: How to Get What You Really Want,* "...your true goal, or target, has to be a concrete action or event, not only so you'll know for sure when you get there, but so that you can make that date with success in advance!"

SETTING UP A POETRY CALENDAR

At the beginning of every year or starting today, consider purchasing a large spaced desk calendar specifically for poetry. Because I'm sitting at the desk every day it's easy to jot down poetry contests and submission deadlines I don't want to miss, especially the "no-entry fee" contests. If it's on my goal market list, I use different colored highlighters to show when the journal is open to submissions.

Writer Phyllis Kaelin also uses a similar paper-based calendar system but uses colorful sticky notes to chart her progress on a particular project. Her paper calendar system works hand in hand with her computer files. She says, "Within the project folder, I keep a running "notes document" where I put comments, plans, progress, word count etc. When I decide to submit I make a note there too."

If you don't already use an online calendar specifically for poetry set one up. If you're serious about poetry this can be used to track submissions, deadlines and markets but also helps keep you on track with readings, writing groups and poetry events. Popular online calendars include: Google Calendar (www.google.com/calendar), Convenient Calendar (www.convenientcalendar.com), and 30 Boxes (www.30boxes.com). I like using an online calendar that integrates with my smartphone so that I can send reminders to my phone, email and/or virtual desktop.

WHY USE A SUBMISSION TRACKER?

Even if you have a good memory, once you get in the habit of sending out your poems it's very easy to lose track of when and where your poems were sent. And there's nothing more frustrating than finding a good market for a particular poem and not remembering where or if it was sent out.

Poet's Market includes a basic submission tracker that you can enlarge and copy or if you're feeling creative design your own paper submission tracker using headlines that make sense to you. Another option many poets use is index cards or a simple journal log. Alternatively you can convert *Poet's Market*'s submission tracker to a computer spreadsheet program such as Excel. If you're not comfortable setting up your own tracking spreadsheet on your computer, there are several free submission trackers available online.

The most popular free submission trackers include: Duotrope (www.duotrope.com), Luminary Writer's Database (www.writersdb.com), Writers Market (www.writersmarket.com) *note*: your purchase of *Poet's Market* includes a 1-year online poetry subscription.

The benefits of using a submission tracker far outweigh the time it will take to set one up.

Rooze, an award-winning poet who is currently pursuing her MFA, says about Duotrope, "I like that they have a theme calendar and a deadline calendar. For each journal, they also list the average response time, percentage of submissions accepted, and the last time a response was received. This gives me a better context to know what to expect. Duotrope also specifies additional criteria, such as requirements around simultaneous submissions and previously printed poems."

The benefits of using a submission tracker far outweigh the time it will take to set one up. If you choose to include comments you can easily recognize when a poem needs a second look. If you use an online submission tracker your timely follow-up can also help other poets who use the database. Knowing that we're all in this submission process together, helping fellow poets just feels right.

If spreadsheets and submission trackers seem too left-brain, you might consider poet Jessy Randall's process. She says, "I write, with my hand and a pen, a poem. I mess around with, cross things out, rewrite lines, for a day or two. Then I set it aside for, if possible, at least a month, or even better, three months. Then I take a look at it again. If I think it's any good, I type it into a giant Word document that contains typed versions of all my poems, with the newest ones at the top. I fiddle around with it some more as I type it. I set it aside again for a while, maybe another month. If I still like it after all that, I submit it to a journal, bundling it together with other poems that somehow go with it. I keep track of where

I've sent it, and when, in a Word document (to tell the truth, it's the same giant document). I also try to keep track of the general response time so I know when I should send a query. So I'll have something like:

"Name of Journal: Poem Title 1, Poem Title 2, Poem Title 3, sent January 2012, should respond in 6 months."

For the submission process Randall adds that the "submission information is in the top of my Word document, along with a list of the poems that aren't sent out anywhere at the moment. Then come all the typed poems. At the bottom of this giant document is where I keep track of rejections, in alphabetical order by journal name. If I need to, I can do a word search in the document to see if a particular journal has already seen a particular poem."

YOU'RE PUBLISHED!

Unfortunately just being organized doesn't guarantee publication. But if you're committed to poetry and part of that commitment includes being organized and businesslike, with time and persistence, there's a very good chance that your work will be accepted.

If the poem was a simultaneous submission, be professional and notify the other publications that you are withdrawing your work.

When you do receive the letter or email that your work is being accepted make sure to follow through. Update your submission tracker as well as your computer and/or paper files. It's very rewarding to move the poem (physically or virtually) from the publishable folder to the published folder and/or to write where and when your poem will be published. If the poem was a simultaneous submission be professional and notify the other publications that you are withdrawing your work.

Blogger and poet Sonya Fehér of Mama True (www.mamatrue.com) includes a Published Worksheet as part of her organizational system.

"The Published Worksheet includes the following fields:

- **Market** – Name of market in which the poem was published
- **Details** – Volume # and other details from publication
- **Link** – If the poem was published online, this gives me the location."

For poet Jessy Randall, being organized makes poetry more gratifying: "This may sound weird, but I particularly enjoy the housekeeping side of poetry, the keeping-track-of-submissions part. When I open up the file that shows me what's where, what's been rejected, what's forthcoming, I feel a real sense of accomplishment even if I didn't write anything that day. Because look at all the stuff that's percolating along without me doing anything!"

That's the favorite part for me too; once I set my organizational system in place I had more fun with the submission process. I missed fewer deadlines and felt more in control of my poetic career. Whether your body of work consists of five or fifty poems there's no time like today to start organizing. Taking the time to organize your work goes beyond the practical; it's a way to honor your time, work, and commitment to craft. It could very well be the inspiration you need to get published.

PATRICIA KENNELLY is a published poet, business owner and editor in Colorado Springs, CO. Her poems have most recently appeared in *Haibun Today, Messages from the Hidden Lake* and *The Denver Post*. She gently nags about writing daily and creativity at http://www.writingnag.com.

WHY PUBLISHING A CHAPBOOK MAKES SENSE

by Jeannine Hall Gailey

Maybe you've published some poems in good literary journals, you've started giving readings around town, and you're ready for the next step. You have a lot of poems in your repertoire, but aren't sure exactly how to get your work into the hands of the public. Now is the time to consider putting together a chapbook. This article describes the benefits of publishing chapbooks and how to go about it, including advice from chapbook publishers and writers with successful chapbooks.

WHAT IS A POETRY CHAPBOOK?

Definitions abound (one is even included in the FAQ section at the beginning of *Poet's Market*), but today's chapbooks are primarily defined by length (usually fewer than 30 pages) and production (usually limited edition, sometimes handmade.) While some are beautiful book-arts products, perfect bound with high-quality covers, like those published by Washington State Chapbook Press, Floating Bridge or Tupelo Press, a chapbook can also be a stapled-together affair produced at the local copy shop.

As for the means of production, there are many chapbook presses out there (New Michigan Press, Concrete Wolf, Floating Bridge, Finishing Line Press, Pudding House Press…). But you can also self-publish a chapbook to sell at readings.

Chapbooks used to be mainly an emerging poet's way of getting their work out to the public, but these days, presses like Sarabande Press have created in-demand chapbooks for well-known authors such as Louise Glück and James Tate as well. Dorianne Laux, for instance, recently published a chapbook, "Superman," with Red Dragonfly Press.

WHY A POETRY CHAPBOOK?

The benefits are multiple. First, the task of putting together a chapbook collection of poems—thinking about organization, which poems to include or exclude, polishing up poems you meant to revise but never got around to—is great training for putting together a full-length book. Second, learning to market and sell your own work—getting over the embarrassment of asking bookstores to carry your chapbook, or telling friends about your chapbook publication—is essential for any poet, because the usual marketing machinery of publishing (talk shows, end-caps at Barnes & Noble, advertising campaigns) doesn't really exist in the poetry publishing world, which is run on slim margins by a very few overworked but dedicated people.

Kelli Russell Agodon, whose sold-out chapbook, "Geography," was one of Floating Bridge Press' bestsellers, talked about how the experience of having a chapbook had benefited her. "Having a chapbook has helped me by opening new doors. It has allowed me to have opportunities such as teaching or reading at poetry festivals and conferences that may not have been open to me if I didn't have a book. It also helped me understand the publishing process a little better before my full-length collection. Also, crafting the chapbook really allowed me to focus on one particular subject."

Chapbooks provide an opportunity for authors to produce tightly woven or themed collections.

Lana Ayers, editor and publisher at Concrete Wolf, a chapbook publisher, details further benefits: "Chapbooks provide an opportunity for authors to produce tightly woven or themed collections. And since most chapbooks, are less expensive than full-length collections, it is easier to convince a reader to take the plunge. Also, the shorter length of the collection can be less intimidating for readers new to poetry. So chapbooks are an all-around great opportunity for both poets and readers to get acquainted."

Kristy Bowen, editor and publisher at Dancing Girl Press, talks about why she started publishing chapbooks: "I also have a love for the chapbook itself as form, a small morsel of poetry that can be devoured in one sitting. Also, they are an affordable way to get new work into the hands of readers with very little fuss. I'm interested as well in how to expand the traditional notion of chapbooks further into the realm of book arts."

Writers have different motivations for publishing chapbooks—fascination with the form, building a relationship with an audience, or finding a home for a particular set of poems. Dorianne Laux described her decision to publish a chapbook after several highly successful full-length collections:

"I met Scott King, of Red Dragonfly Press, while I was at the Anderson Center for the Arts for a writing residency and he was producing letterpress broadsides. He later asked if I'd like to do a chapbook. At the time, I wasn't sure if I had enough poems on a theme to make a book, but said yes anyway, not wanting to miss a chance to work with Scott. It took me about a year to come up with the poems in 'Superman,' which are all loosely based around pop culture figures, icons and objects of the 20th century. I wasn't yet ready for a fifth book of poems and so a chapbook seemed a great way to have something in the interim. But more important was my desire to have a beautiful book, hand set on gorgeous paper and sewn together, something that would be a small, elegant gift I could give to friends. It was also a way to bring attention to this small press and its poet/editor, Scott King, who had taught me so much about the quality of labor that went into reproducing a page of words before the invention of carbon paper, mimeo and xerox machines, computers and desktop printers. It was exacting, dangerous and dirty work, performed amidst smoke, sparks and fire by some anonymous typesetter bent over in a greasy smock, delicately choosing the next stately letter with the deafening clatter of the molten lead foundry pounding against the drums in his ears. It's also wonderfully ironic to have a book about 20th-century characters like Cher and The Beatles produced using a 16th-century technology!"

So now you're intrigued. But how, exactly, do you put together a chapbook?

WHAT DOES PUTTING TOGETHER A CHAPBOOK ENTAIL?

The good news is that it's a lot like putting together a book, but a more compact, and perhaps, more tightly-themed collection. Usually, writers have obsessions, and those obsessions manifest themselves over time. You'll find 20 poems on superheroes, for instance, or on abandoned gas stations in the Midwest. Or you'll find 20 poems that tell their own story.

Kelli Russell Agodon's advice for someone putting together a chapbook for the first time? "My advice would be to focus your chapbook on one subject, theme, or story. The best chapbooks look deeply at a topic, but also make new discoveries in their poems throughout the book. I suggest choosing only your strongest poems for your chapbook, then determine if there are certain poems you need to write to make the chapbook stronger and more complete."

Kristy Bowen adds that "sometimes, especially poets at the beginning of their career see a chapbook as a stepping stone to the first book, which it usually is, but I suspect they sometimes see the chapbook merely as a shorter volume sort of tossed together without any real feel of cohesion in the chapbook itself. So what you get is an odd mismatch of the poems they consider best, but without any sort of thematic or formal binding." So what is Dancing Girl Press's editor looking for? "We particularly look for work that has a strong sense of image and music, cohesiveness as a manuscript, interesting and surprising, sometimes unusual, use of language. We love humor when done well, strangeness, wackiness. Hybridity, collage, intertextuality. Manuscripts that create their own worlds."

This brings us to the next subject—how to get your chapbook published.

HOW ARE CHAPBOOKS PUBLISHED?

You've got your manuscript of 15-30 pages of thematically engaged, tightly edited poetry together, so now what? Well, many chapbook publishers, just like poetry book publishers, decide what they are going to publish through a contest system. Presses like this include Tupelo Press, Concrete Wolf, Pudding House, and New Michigan Press. If you go this route, you should research the publisher by obtaining at least one of their previous publications, checking out the production and writing quality, and decide if it's a good fit for you. If it is, then you send off your manuscript with a cover letter, a check (usually $10-15), and a SASE, and hope for the best. Some presses publish runners-up and finalists as well as winners. Be sure to read the guidelines thoroughly, and follow them to the letter.

Some chapbook publishers, like Sarabande Press, only publish through solicitation—that is, they contact the person they want to publish directly—so unless you get a call, you won't be getting your chapbook published through them. Some chapbook publishers will read "open submissions," for a few months a year, like Dancing Girl Press, but these are few and far between.

Of course, there's always self-publishing, and this is an easier (and more affordable) feat if you're attempting a saddle-stitched chapbook than a perfect bound book. You could even put it all up—your poems, the cover art, your table of contents and acknowledgements—on your own computer, using basic publishing software, print it out on your own laser printer, and staple it at your kitchen table. If you Google "make your own saddle-stitched chapbook" you can find a couple of sets of instructions, or if you're lucky enough to have a book arts center near you, sign up for a class.

MARKETING A POETRY CHAPBOOK

A chapbook is, admittedly, more difficult to market than a poetry book. Many bookstores won't carry them because they are difficult to store and display. Your best bet is to talk an independent bookstore into carrying a copy or two on consignment. Most review outlets don't take chapbook reviews, and chapbooks are not usually eligible for major book awards.

Chapbooks are by nature ephemeral, and that can be an advantage. A limited run means an especially beautiful or well-written chapbook might later become a collector's item, and no writer keeps too many chapbooks on hand—though, unlike books, they don't take up too much space to store. Many people see chapbooks as a more intimate way to get to know a poet's work, and value the fact that the chapbooks may only be around for a short amount of time. Chapbooks are easy to sell at poetry readings, where the buyer is more likely to want a souvenir of that experience, and on poet's websites, where the buyers are already familiar with the poet and their work. If you have friends with blogs, send them a review copy of your chapbook and ask them to say a few words.

So, remember this—give readings. Be an interesting, enthusiastic reader who has actually organized their work and practiced it a few times. This will increase the odds that audience members might want to buy your chapbook! And, make sure you have a personal website or blog that your fans can come to and find out how to buy your chapbook—whether it's directly from you or from a link to your publisher or even Amazon. Don't make them hunt for it!

WHY SHOULD YOU CONSIDER PUBLISHING A CHAPBOOK?

A chapbook gives you a way to connect with your reader. It gives your reader a physical reminder of your work, and sometimes it's a beautiful artifact, sometimes a humble set of copies, folded over and stapled. Creating a chapbook helps you practice organizing your work into a coherent collection. Selling your chapbook orients you in the world of marketing poetry, and, if you do it yourself or watch it being produced, a way to understand the physical work of book publishing.

Creating a chapbook helps you practice organizing your work into a cohereent collection.

Because of these benefits, it's more than just a step towards a full-length poetry collection—it's a way for you to build an audience, to put your work out into the world in a considered, deliberate way. Take a look at the chapbook publishers listed in *Poet's Market*, and order some samples to get an idea of the diversity of the production and content of chapbooks available as well as figure out which publisher might be right for you. Before you know it, you'll have something in hand to share at readings and with friends and family.

JEANNINE HALL GAILEY is a San Diego writer whose first book of poetry, *Becoming the Villainess*, was published by Steel Toe Books. She was awarded a 2007 Dorothy Sargent Rosenberg Prize for Poetry and a 2007 Washington State Artist Trust GAP grant. Her poems have appeared in several publications, including *The Iowa Review, The Columbia Poetry Review*, and *Smartish Pace*. She currently teaches at the MFA program at National University.

10 CHAPBOOK DESIGN TIPS EVERY POET SHOULD KNOW

by Amy Miller

There's never been a better time to publish a chapbook. These days, desktop-publishing software is so easy to use that practically any poet who can turn on a computer can put together a chapbook—a small booklet of poems to sell at readings and book fairs. That's the good news. But the bad news is that it's easy to go mad with all that power and crank out a quick chapbook that doesn't do your poems justice. From cramped typography to scary author photos, there are lots of ways—some obvious, some subtle—to go wrong with a chapbook. But with a handful of tips and techniques, you can design a book that lures readers into its pages and presents your work in the best light.

And you don't have to be printing your own chapbook to take advantage of these tips. If you're just sending your work out to literary journals, some basic typography tweaks can help your poems look more polished on the page. And if you've been lucky enough to have your manuscript—chapbook-size or full-length—accepted by a publishing house, knowing a few tricks of the trade will help you communicate your wishes to your publisher in a language you both understand, perhaps making the difference between a book that just gets the job done and one that really pops.

FIGURE OUT THE BEST TYPE SIZE AND LEADING

This bit of typography-speak is one of the most important factors—some would say the most important—in making your poems look good on the page. Put simply, this is the relationship between the size of the letters (type size) and the vertical distance between the lines (leading). A common mistake is to make the leading too tight, resulting in lines that are too close together. It's a subtle business—this cramping won't make the type illegible, but even leading that's just a bit too tight will make it hard for the reader to discern one line from the next, making for an uncomfortable reading experience.

A good rule of thumb for poetry is to make your type size three points smaller than the leading: for instance, 11-point type on 14-point leading, or 12 on 15. But not all fonts are created equal; one font may look best at 11.5 on 15, while another may shine at 12 on 14.75. If you're trying to fit more lines onto the page (say, a poem is a line or two over), think twice before just decreasing the leading; you may be better off shrinking both the type size and the leading by a quarter or half point, resulting in smaller type but easy reading because the leading is still comfortable on the eye. And if you have to shrink the type on one page, do it for the whole book to keep your design consistent throughout.

CHOOSE A GOOD FONT

This may seem very basic, but picking out a font for poetry can be surprisingly difficult. There are many schools of thought on what makes a good poetry font—browse through a dozen chapbooks, and you'll probably see a dozen different text fonts. But if you look closely, you'll find that many fonts are too blocky, too narrow, or too rounded to make for smooth reading.

When in doubt, go with the old favorites—Garamond's a classic font for poetry, or something in the Times family may be a good choice. For a more modern look, try sans-serif fonts like Franklin Gothic or Helvetica. The most important thing is that the font should not be distracting—as your reader settles into her easy chair to enjoy your chapbook, you don't want her first thought to be, "What the heck font is that?"

The most important thing is that the font should not be distracting.

Bonus tip: When trying out a font, print out a poem or two in that font before deciding on it, and really scrutinize the printout—what looks good on your screen may look very different on the printed page, and your printer may render some fonts more crisply than others. Plan to use up some scrap paper while you experiment with printing out fonts.

FIND CENTER OF THE BOOK, AND PUT A GOOD POEM THERE

Most chapbooks are simply a stack of papers, folded in the middle and stapled along that fold. So when someone picks up your book to browse through it, it's likely to fall open to the center spot where the staples are. Because of this little chapbook phenomenon, that center spread is usually the third thing a reader will see, after the front cover and back cover, and the first poem he or she will read. So think of that center spot as prime real estate, and put a strong poem or two there that can be read without turning the page.

USE WHITE SPACE TO HELP YOUR READER

By its nature, poetry is a rich, dense reading experience. And as with a rich meal, it's wise to give your guest a little time to breathe between courses. Leaving some white space on the last page of a poem, or putting a blank left page before a new section (if you have sections) gives the reader a brief break to contemplate what he's just read and gear up for the next poem. One place where you should always have a blank page is on the left page before your first poem in the book.

That first poem should start on a right-hand page, and the blank page to its left serves as a little drumroll that lets the reader know the show's about to begin. And in the body of the book, it's fine to have the occasional poem spill over onto an extra page by five or six lines; again, the white space at the end of the poem gives the reader a mental resting spot.

PERFECT YOUR PUNCTUATION

Chapbooks, even ones from well-known publishers, seem to suffer more than their share of careless punctuation: double spaces, straight quote marks, two hyphens standing in for an em-dash, and other small glitches that a spell-check might not catch. Most typographers hate straight quotes (“, ‘) and prefer curly ones (”, ’), but there's nothing really wrong with straight quotes; just make sure you choose one or the other and don't mix them. As for em-dashes (—), you can get a true one on a PC by typing ctrl-alt-<minus sign on the number pad>; on a Mac, it's shift-option-hyphen. Set aside some time at the end of your design process to do some search-and-replaces and root out these inconsistences. This seemingly simple step will make a big difference to your reader.

EMBRACE ODD SIZES

Most chapbooks are 5-1/2 x 8-1/2 inches—not surprisingly, that's what you get when you take a stack of standard 8-1/2 x 11 sheets and fold them in half. That's all very convenient, but with a $30 guillotine-style paper trimmer (or the fancy one at the office), you can experiment with all sorts of other sizes—tall, small, horizontal, square—and come up with something unusual that will really pique your reader's interest. One popular size is a book that fits nicely in one hand—about 4 x 5 inches. And square books have an alluring power at the book table.

The challenge, of course, is getting your poems to fit into the format; poems with long lines will have a hard time squeezing into a narrow book, for instance. But sometimes fitting the trim size to the poems is part of the fun. A sweet size—and an easy cheat, requiring only one cut on the paper trimmer—is 4-1/4 x 5-1/2, which you can get by taking 8-1/2 x 11 sheets, cutting them in half, and then folding the resulting sheets in half.

BEWARE THE HASTY BACK COVER

Back covers are where a lot of otherwise good chapbooks go bad. It's not unusual to see strong poems and a good interior design marred by a back cover that was obviously thrown together in a hurry. Some poets opt out and just leave the back cover blank.

That's okay, but it's a missed opportunity; the back cover is a big chunk of free advertising space, a chance to give your prospective reader a taste of what's inside—a snippet of a poem, a short bio, and maybe an author photo. But don't try to jam too much on there; crowded typography is a common malady in back covers, often because of our old nemesis, type size vs. leading (see tip #1).

The back cover is a big chunk of free advertising space, a chance to give your prospective reader a taste of what's inside.

And if you do include an author photo, make it a good one. Whether it's serious or friendly, just make sure your photo isn't off-putting—a stiff grammar-school-type picture, or a badly lit mug shot that looks like it was ripped out of somebody's passport. If you can't find a good photo of yourself, leave it out; it is better to have no author photo than a bad one.

Bonus tip: Steal your back-cover design. A chapbook's back cover can look exactly like one on a full-length poetry collection, so grab a stack of poetry books from big publishers, study their back covers, and steal design elements that you like.

ENDPAPERS ADD ELEGANCE

Endpapers, also known as flyleaves, are the easiest way to add a hint of artistry to a chapbook. An endpaper is a single, blank sheet of paper just inside the cover of your book—a page that's there purely for decoration. These are fun to pick out, and the possibilities are almost limitless: a translucent vellum, textured stationery paper, a delicate sheet embedded with flower petals, or something bold and contrasting.

But there's some room for error—nothing says "cheap" like wrinkle-prone colored paper that you bought at the dollar store, and overly ornate endpapers may make your book look more like a tchotchke than a serious book of poetry.

BONUS TIP: When shopping for endpapers, take a sheet of your interior paper and cover stock (or, better yet, a printed cover) to the store with you to make sure the colors don't clash.

TRIM OFF THE OUTER EDGE

Any time you take a stack of papers and fold it in the middle, the outer edge—the right edge of your book, if you're looking at your front cover—will have a "peak" to it where the edges of the inner pages get pushed out beyond those of the outer pages. This isn't the worst thing in the world, but trimming off that outer edge so that it's flat, smooth, and flush with the edge of the cover will give the book a more finished, professional feel. A $40 rotary trimmer with a wheel-shaped blade, like the kind scrapbookers use, can do the trick with a little practice.

Or, if you have patience and a steady hand, you can trim off the edge with an X-Acto knife and a ruler. Another option is to take the books to a print shop and have them trim off the edges (for a few dollars) using one of their professional cutting machines.

BIND THE BOOK WITH STITCHING INSTEAD OF STAPLING

This one's an especially good trick because it looks hard to do, but it's actually very easy. All it takes to add this classic touch of elegance is a needle, an awl to make a few holes, some heavy thread in a color that complements or contrasts with your cover design, and a simple stitching diagram that you can find online (google "chapbook stitching").

This little upgrade will get an "ooh" out of almost everyone who picks up your book, making it that much more memorable—which is the whole point of having a chapbook in the first place.

AMY MILLER is the author of eight chapbooks of poetry and prose, and her writing has appeared in *Northwest Review, ZYZZYVA, Many Mountains Moving, Fine Gardening, The Writer's Journal*, and many other publications. During her 35-year career in publishing, she has worked as a layout artist, editor, and project manager for several magazines and book publishers. She blogs about writing, disaster movies, and life at writers-island.blogspot.com.

MISTAKES POETS MAKE

In putting together listings for *Poet's Market*, we ask editors for any words of advice they want to share with our readers. Often the editors' responses include comments about what poets should and shouldn't do when submitting work—the same comments, over and over. That means a lot of poets are repeating similar mistakes when they send out their poems for consideration.

The following list includes the most common of those mistakes—the ones poets should work hardest to avoid.

NOT READING A PUBLICATION BEFORE SUBMITTING WORK

Researching a publication is essential before submitting your poetry. Try to buy a sample copy of a magazine (by mail, if necessary) or at least see if an issue is available at the library. It may not be economically feasible for poets to purchase a copy of every magazine they target, especially if they send out a lot of poems. However, there are additional ways to familiarize yourself with a publication.

Read the market listing thoroughly. If guidelines are available, send for them by e-mail or regular mail, or check for them online. A publication's website often presents valuable information, including sample poems, magazine covers—and guidelines.

SUBMITTING INAPPROPRIATE WORK

Make good use of your research so you're sure you understand what a magazine publishes. Don't rationalize that a journal favoring free verse might jump at the chance to consider your long epic poem in heroic couplets. Don't convince yourself your experimental style will be a good fit for the traditional journal filled with rhyming poetry. Don't go into denial about whether a certain journal and your poetry are made for each other. It's counterproductive and ultimately wastes postage (not to mention time—yours and the editor's).

SUBMITTING AN UNREASONABLE NUMBER OF POEMS

If an editor recommends sending three to five poems (a typical range), don't send six. Don't send a dozen poems and tell the editor to pick the five she wants to consider. If the editor doesn't specify a number (or the listing says "no limit"), don't take that as an invitation to mail off 20 poems. The editors and staff of literary magazines are busy enough as it is, and they may decide they don't have time to cope with you. (When submitting book or chapbook manuscripts to publishers, make sure your page count falls within the range they state.)

Don't go to the other extreme and send only one poem, unless an editor says it's okay (which is rare). One poem doesn't give an editor much of a perspective on your work, and it doesn't give you very good odds on getting the piece accepted.

IGNORING THE EDITOR'S PREFERENCES REGARDING FORMATS

If an editor makes a point of describing a preferred manuscript format, follow it, even if that format seems to contradict the standard. (Standard format includes using 8½ × 11 white paper and conventional typeface and point size; avoid special graphics, colors or type flourishes; put your name and address on every page.) Don't devise your own format to make your submission stand out. Keep everything clean, crisp and easy to read (and professional).

Be alert to e-mail submission formats. Follow directions regarding what the editor wants printed in the subject line, how many poems to include in a single e-mail, whether to use attachments or paste work in the body of the message, and other elements. Editors have good reasons for outlining their preferences; ignoring them could mean having your e-mail deleted before your poems are even read.

OMITTING A SELF-ADDRESSED STAMPED ENVELOPE (SASE)

Why do editors continuously say "include an SASE with your submission?" Because so many poets don't do it. Here's a simple rule: Unless the editor gives alternate instructions, include a #10 SASE, whether submitting poems or sending an inquiry.

WRITING BAD COVER LETTERS (OR OMITTING THEM COMPLETELY)

Cover letters have become an established part of the submission process. There are editors who remain indifferent about the necessity of a cover letter, but many consider it rude to be sent a submission without any other communication from the poet.

Unless the editor says otherwise, send a cover letter. Keep it short and direct, a polite introduction of you and your work. (See "Frequently Asked Questions" for more tips on cover letters, and an example.)

Here are a few important don'ts:

- **DON'T** list all the magazines where your work has appeared; limit yourself to five magazine titles. The work you're submitting has to stand on its own.
- **DON'T** tell the editor what a good poet you are—or how good someone else thinks you are.
- **DON'T** tell the editor how to edit, lay out or print your poem. Some of those decisions are up to the editor, assuming she decides to accept your poem in the first place.
- **DON'T** point out the poem is copyrighted in your name or include the copyright symbol. All poems are automatically copyrighted in the poet's name as soon as they're "fixed" (i.e., written down), and editors know this.

NOT MAINTAINING GOOD EDITOR/POET RELATIONS

Most editors are hard-working poetry lovers dedicated to finding and promoting good work. They aspire to turn submissions around as quickly as possible and to treat all poets with respect. They don't want to steal your work. Often they aren't paid for their labor and may even have to dip into their own pockets just to keep their magazines going.

Poets should finesse their communications with editors regarding problems, especially in initial letters and e-mail. Editors (and their magazines and presses) aren't service-oriented businesses, like the phone company. Getting huffy with an editor as if arguing with your cable provider about an overcharge is inappropriate. Attitude isn't going to get you anywhere; in fact, it could create additional obstacles.

That's not to say poets shouldn't feel exasperated when they're inconvenienced or ill-treated. None of us likes to see our creations vanish, or to pay good money for something we're never going to receive (like a subscription or sample copy). However, exasperated is one thing; outraged is another. Too often poets go on the offensive with editors and make matters worse. Experts on how to complain effectively recommend you keep your cool and stay professional, no matter what kind of problem you're trying to work out.

For additional advice on editor/poet relations, see "Dealing With Problem Editors."

DEALING WITH PROBLEM EDITORS

There *are* problem editors out there, and we've all encountered them at one time or another. Some rip people off, prey on poets' desires to be published, or treat poets and their work with flagrant disregard. Fortunately, such editors are in the minority.

Now and then you may discover the disorganized editor or the overwhelmed editor; these two cause heartache (and heartburn) by closing up shop without returning manuscripts or failing to honor paid requests for subscriptions and sample copies. More often than not, their transgressions are rooted in chaos and irresponsibility, not malicious intent. Frustrating as such editors are, they're not out to get you.

There are many instances, too, where larger circumstances are beyond an editor's control. For example, a college-oriented journal may be student-staffed, with editors changing each academic year. Funds for the journal may be cut unexpectedly by administration belt-tightening, or a grant could be cancelled. The editorial office may be moved to another part of the university. An exam schedule could impact a publishing schedule. All of these things cause problems and delays.

Then again, a literary journal may be a one-person, home-based operation. The editor may get sick or have an illness in the family. Her regular job may suddenly demand lots of overtime. There may be divorce or death with which the editor has to cope. A computer could crash. Or the editor may need to scramble for money before the magazine can go to the printer. Emergencies happen, and they take their toll on deadlines. The last thing the editor wants is to inconvenience poets and readers, but sometimes life gets in the way.

Usually, difficulties with these kinds of "problem" editors can be resolved satisfactorily through communication and patience. There are always exceptions, though. Here are a few typical situations with problem editors and how to handle them.

AN EDITOR IS RUDE.

If it's a matter of bad attitude, take it with a grain of salt. Maybe he's having a rotten day. If there's abusive language and excessive profanity involved, let us know about it. (See the complaint procedure .)

COMPLAINT PROCEDURE

If you feel you have not been treated fairly by a market listed in *Poet's Market*, we advise you to take the following steps:

- First, try to contact the market. Sometimes one phone call, letter, or e-mail can quickly clear up the matter. Document all your communications with the market.
- When you contact us with a complaint, provide the details of your submission, the date of your first contact with the market and the nature of your subsequent communication.
- We will file a record of your complaint and further investigate the market.
- The number and severity of complaints will be considered when deciding whether or not to delete a market from the next edition of *Poet's Market*.

AN EDITOR HARSHLY CRITICIZES YOUR POEM.

If an editor takes time to comment on your poetry, even if the feedback seems overly critical, consider the suggestions with an open mind and try to find something valid and useful in them. If, after you've given the matter fair consideration, you think the editor was out of line, don't rush to defend your poetry or wave your bruised ego in the editor's face. Allow that the editor has a right to her opinion (which you're not obligated to take as the final word on the quality of your work), forget about it and move on.

AN EDITOR IS SLOW TO RESPOND TO A SUBMISSION.

As explained above, there may be many reasons why an editor's response takes longer than the time stated in the market listing or guidelines. Allow a few more weeks to pass beyond the deadline, then write a polite inquiry to the editor about the status of your manuscript. (Include an SASE if sending by regular mail.) Understand an editor may not be able to read your letter right away if deadlines are pressing or if he's embroiled in a personal crisis. Try to be patient. If you haven't received a reply to your inquiry after a month or so, however, it's time for further action.

AN EDITOR WON'T RETURN YOUR MANUSCRIPT.

Decide whether you want to invest any more time in this journal or publisher. If you conclude you've been patient long enough, write a firm but professional letter to the editor withdrawing your manuscript from consideration. Request that the manuscript be returned; but know, too, a truly indifferent editor probably won't bother to send it back or reply in any way. Keep a copy of your withdrawal letter for your files, make a new copy of your manuscript and look for a better market.

Also, contact *Poet's Market* by letter or e-mail with details of your experience. We always look into problems with editors, although we don't withdraw a listing on the basis of a single complaint unless we discover evidence of consistent misbehavior. We do, however, keep complaints on file and watch for patterns of unacceptable behavior from any specific market.

AN EDITOR TAKES YOUR MONEY.

If you sent a check for a subscription or sample copy and you haven't received anything, review your bank statement to see if the check has been cashed. If it has, send the editor a query. Politely point out the editor has cashed your check, but you haven't yet received the material you were expecting. Give the editor the benefit of the doubt: An upcoming issue of a magazine could be running late, your subscription could have been overlooked by mistake, or your copy could have been lost in transit or sent in error to the wrong address.

If your check has *not* been cashed, query the editor to see if your order was ever received. It may have been lost (in the mail or on the editor's desk), the editor may be holding several checks to cash at one time, or the editor may be waiting to cash checks until a tardy issue is finally published.

If you get an unsatisfactory response from the editor (or no response at all), wait a few weeks and try again. If the matter still isn't resolved, let us know about it. We're especially interested in publishers who take money from poets but don't deliver the goods. Be sure to send us all the details of the transaction, plus copies of any correspondence (yours and the editor's). We can't pursue your situation in any legal way or act as mediator, but we can ban an unscrupulous publisher from *Poet's Market* and keep the information as a resource in case we get later complaints.

Should you continue trying to get your money back from such editors? That's your decision. If your loss is under $10 (say, for a subscription or sample copy), it might cost you less in the long run to let the matter go. And the fee for a "stop payment" order on a check can be hefty—possibly more than the amount you sent the editor in the first place. Yes, it's infuriating to be cheated, but sometimes fighting on principle costs more than it's worth.

If your monetary loss is significant (for instance, you shelled out a couple hundred dollars in a subsidy publishing agreement), consider contacting your state attorney general's office for advice about small claims court, filing a complaint and other actions you can take.

HOW TO WRITE A SUCCESSFUL GRANT TO FUND YOUR WRITING

by Kris Bigalk

Whether it's applying for a $25,000 fellowship or applying for a $500 travel grant, writers have many opportunities to compete for money to fund their writing projects. The key to writing a successful grant lies in one general concept: writing the grant so that it meets the priorities and mission of the audience—in this case, the granting organization and/or the grant review committee.

Organizations offer grants for many reasons, but ultimately, their goals involve funding projects that line up with the organization's mission, values, and current initiatives. The first step in writing a successful grant is letting go of the focus on what the grant can do for you, and turning the focus around—what can you do with the grant that will reflect well on the granting organization? In other words, make the granting organization see how you will forward their mission, values, and initiatives.

FIND THE RIGHT GRANT

Writing a grant for a specific project is much more difficult than writing a grant with a general goal in mind. In other words, don't go into the search for a grant with a specific, inflexible schedule or plan. Never write or plan the grant before reading the guidelines. Most grants have limitations as to what they will and won't fund, and most also preference certain kinds of projects. Concentrate on moving your ideas toward the granting organization's preferences.

There are many lists and databases where writers can search for grant opportunities. A good place to begin is locally. Find the website of your city, county, regional, or state arts organizations and arts-oriented non-profits to search for grant opportunities. These grants are often a good bet, because the applicant pool is smaller and limited to a certain population. To search for national grant opportunities, check out the sidebar.

STUDY THE GUIDELINES

Once you've found a grant that interests you, print out the guidelines. These may be in one or two documents, so be sure to print everything related to the grant. The key to good grant writing is to be acutely aware of the audience—the people who will decide whether or not to fund your proposal.

In the guidelines you've printed out, locate the "Qualifications" or "Requirements" section. Highlight any prerequisites for application, such as a certain number of literary magazine publications, a published book, etc. If you don't meet the prerequisites, stop and find another grant. If you do meet the prerequisites, find the part of the application that outlines how you will prove that you have met those prerequisites (photocopies of magazines? links to online publications? a copy of the book?). Do you have the materials you need to prove you've met the prerequisite? If not, stop and find another grant. If so, gather them together.

Highlight any information on what the grant reviewers will be looking for, specifically.

Read through the grant guidelines again, with a highlighter. Highlight the main sections of the grant (usually bolded headings), and mark any instructions on how to write these sections. Also highlight any information on what the grant reviewers will be looking for, specifically. Often, the grant will include a list of desired characteristics of a proposal, for example, or even a list of characteristics that are more likely to be funded. Highlight keywords in those sections, as they will become keywords in your proposal.

IMAGINE YOUR "AUDIENCE"

Now that you have a general idea of what the organization is looking for in the grant, it's time to delve a little deeper into your audience's wants and needs. Go to the sponsoring organization's website, and collect any publications, podcasts, or other media generated by the organization. How does the organization present itself? What can you garner about the mission, values, and activities of the organization? Write a short paragraph that "profiles" the organization, again using any keywords you see repeated in the materials on the website.

Locate a list of past grants and projects the organization has funded. What do these projects have in common with one another? How do they connect with the mission and values of the organization? Write out the answers to these questions in another paragraph.

Sometimes sponsoring organizations will provide examples of past proposals that were funded. Another way to find these successful proposals is to ask your writer friends if they have examples. If you can locate an example of a successfully written grant for this specific opportunity, study it. Notice how it is formatted and what is emphasized by the grant writer. Highlight words or ideas you notice coming up more than once, especially if those words or ideas match what you've found in your highlighting and research.

GENERATE IDEAS/ROUGH DRAFTS

Now that you've done your research, write out the parameters of the grant on a separate sheet of paper, in your own words. What are the limitations of what the grant will fund/not fund? What projects will be preferenced? Refer to your paragraphs and analysis.

Make a list of ideas. What do you want to do that fits into these parameters? How could you do it so that it will be preferenced? Don't try to make a previous idea fit the parameters. Design a project that will definitely fit the parameters, even if it's different than the project you originally envisioned. Think about what your overall goals are, instead of a specific goal. So, for example, if a grant won't fund classes that count towards a degree, you could propose attending a series of writer's conferences or working with a writing mentor to achieve the goal of improving and honing your writing skills.

When an arts organization receives hundreds of grants and needs to cut them down to a manageable number, people need to be able to skim the proposals and find a reason to put yours in the "keeper" pile.

Before you begin drafting, keep in mind that it's very likely that your grant will not be read carefully, at least not in the first round. When an arts organization receives hundreds of grants and needs to cut them down to a manageable number, people need to be able to skim the proposals and find a reason to put yours in the "keeper" pile.

Additionally, many granting organizations serve people in all of the fine arts, and are not staffed by writers. The way to ensure your proposal will eventually make it to a final round and be read more carefully is to use headings, strategic bolds, underlines, and italics, and bulleted or numbered items, which tend to draw the eye to the criteria that will be important to the grant reviewers at all levels.

Begin writing out drafts of the sections of the grant. Use bolded headings that match the funding criteria; use exact keywords from the guidelines and the website to appeal to your audience. Make the proposal easy to read by using bulleted or numbered items and keeping the prose tight, succinct, and specific. Refer to the highlighted words that recurred in the guidelines, on the website, etc., and be sure to use these words and close synonyms to describe your project.

REVISE AND CHECK

Revise the sections of the grant application so that they flow well, make sense, and are proofread perfectly. While you can't assume that any of the reviewers are writers, you can't assume that they aren't writers, either. You're a writer, so reviewers will expect more from you than from other artists when it comes to writing. Poorly written or sloppy grants rarely get funded.

As you finish revising, check your work against the guidelines again to make sure you haven't strayed from them. Grants that veer off of guidelines do not get funded, because there are always plenty of others with merit that have stayed within the guidelines.

Finally, have a friend read your grant application and compare it to the guidelines, and give you feedback. Make any changes you deem necessary, and compile all of the materials together in a packet. Many grant guidelines include a checklist to help with this.

SUBMIT THE GRANT

Read over the instructions on how to submit the grant. Submit the grant exactly as detailed in the instructions, by the deadline listed. Grants that are incomplete, submitted in different formats, or submitted late are not funded. Take your time. Read things twice. Don't wait until the last day to submit the grant to start on this.

If you don't receive a confirmation that your application has been received, it's usually okay to call or e-mail and ask for that confirmation, unless this is expressly forbidden in the guidelines.

WAIT. PATIENTLY.

Most grants will list a ballpark date by which a decision will be made. Don't contact them before that date. Check the website and your junk mail folder, and then wait a week after that date to contact them if you still haven't heard anything.

If your grant is not funded, resist any urge to complain to the funding organization, judges, or anyone associated with the grant. Do not complain on Facebook, Twitter, or in any public forum. This is a great way to burn bridges and tends to make the writer look bitter and cantankerous; it rarely has the desired effect of making the granting organization look bad. Complain to your friends if you must, in private.

Do not complain on Facebook, Twitter, or in any public forum. This is a great way to burn bridges.

Like rejections for creative work, rejections for grants can sting, but it's often not a reflection on the writer or the project. Grant reviewers have a set of priorities for funding, and try to choose the projects that best meet those priorities. If a grant isn't funded, it may still have merit as a proposal, and a grant writer should not take such rejections personally.

If your grant is funded, feel free thank the funding organization, judges, or anyone associated with the grant. Celebrate as publicly as you wish, both online and in the real world. Tell others about your project and about the grant itself on your webpage and in other public forums.

It's a win-win situation for both the writer and the granting organization, and focuses on the mutual benefit to both. Organizations that make grants to writers serve a vital purpose in the writing community, and any time we can celebrate their contribution to the arts, we should do so.

KRIS BIGALK'S poetry collection, *Repeat the Flesh in Numbers,* will be released by NYQ Books in 2012. Her poetry has recently appeared in *Silk Road, Water~Stone Review, cream city review,* and *Mead,* and is forthcoming in *Rougarou.* Bigalk was awarded a 2010 Minnesota State Arts Board Individual Artist Grant in poetry, and attended Bread Loaf Writer's Conference as a contributor in 2010 and 2011. She is the Director of Creative Writing at Normandale Community College , where she founded and now directs a successful AFA in Creative Writing program.

BE CREATIVE IN YOUR CAREER: *Offer Private Writing Workshops*

by Chloe Yelena Miller

There is no single way to earn an income as a poet. I didn't realize that at first. After finishing an MFA program, I went the common route of teaching required composition writing classes at local colleges. On the side, I tutored Italian and English. I was at the whim of my many employers. I needed to take some of the creativity from my craft and put it into my career planning.

A few years later, I gave a workshop on just that—creativity—at a writing conference. An attendee asked me if I knew a private writing coach. I smiled and my eyebrows shot up. I realized I hadn't been using the right label to prompt me to lead private workshops. I answered a resounding, "Yes! I am one!" and my career shifted into gear.

Writing coaching was, in fact, exactly the work I had been doing all along in my day and moonlighting jobs. Are you in a similar situation?

WHY TEACH PRIVATELY?

Working as a private writing and workshop coach has been wonderful. I have the opportunity to set my own schedule and focus on topics I'm passionate about. I work with students who are motivated by interest instead of a university requirement. I make my own course and day-to-day schedule. The final reward is not only keeping 100% of the net profits, but also spending my days doing something I believe in. All of this ultimately nourishes my writing.

Writers teach because we love to discuss writing and encourage others as we've been encouraged. A private writing coach can continue talking about writing while organizing private workshops and earning enough to make it worthwhile. This is unlike the adjunct route that often leads to little money, running from campus to campus, and then committing to a program before discovering your class was cancelled.

That's not to say that you should abandon adjuncting. Teaching at a local university can help you gain authority in the eyes of potential private clients. Similarly, the experience of running successful private workshops might make you more attractive to a hiring committee for a better paying teaching position at a university. The two career paths can work in tandem.

STARTING YOUR OWN BUSINESS

Running your own business takes work to create, organize and maintain, not to mention to help it grow. Yes, writers can run businesses like the best entrepreneurs. If, like most writers, you freelance or juggle a number of part-time jobs, then you have already honed the right skills.

A private writing workshop can be as short as an hour or as long as an ongoing semester-length program. The workshop instructor must dedicate time not only to teaching and developing stimulating syllabi, but also to advertising, collecting and keeping track of fees paid, and finding new students while maintaining the current ones. It can be a balancing act, but one that pays off in the end on many levels.

To get started, think about your skills. Are you more knowledgeable in one topic or do you have particular fields of interest? For example, do you know a lot about both poetry and architecture? You could lead a subject-specific or themed creative writing workshop which will distinguish you from other courses.

Be sure to teach a topic that you not only know, but that interests you.

Start with a working title and course description of the first workshop. Be sure to teach a topic that you not only know, but that interests you. I run primarily free-verse poetry and creative nonfiction memoir workshops organized around food and memoir.

As you grow your business, you'll meet others who do similar work. As with any career, networking is necessary and you want to be a good colleague. If a potential student contacts you who might not be a good fit with your background, recommend a colleague. You will find that others will return the favor and recommend clients to you.

WHERE TO MEET?

The next step is to choose a venue. I've given readings and led talks in obvious venues, as well as train stations and lingerie stores (don't ask). When you consider a venue, think widely. Of course, some will work better than others.

The most successful creative writing workshops that I've led have been at an urban library, an upscale community center, a small town continuing education program and through school programs. The key to developing your business and class location is to think creatively.

Consider your connections in the community; walk around the town and think about spaces from a writing teacher's point of view. What organization's space might benefit from additional foot traffic? Which space has enough room, is accessible, has parking or access to mass transportation and enough light?

First, consider the obvious: a library, bookstore or community center. Then, think more widely: yoga studio, natural foods store, paper store, art gallery, bar, etc. You might also consider paying to rent out a space. Think about how long you'll need the space, how regularly, any costs involved, if the venue will help with advertising, if you'll be responsible for cleaning, any restrictions (food, moving furniture), if you'll need to bring chairs, lights or something to write on, surrounding noise level, etc.

You might also decide to teach solely online or combine online and in-person workshops. In these cases, you might be targeting different populations. When you choose dates, think about religious, local and state holidays, as well as the seasons. I currently run mainly online workshops around my in-person commitments.

LET POTENTIAL STUDENTS KNOW: ADVERTISE!

Now it is time to make an advertising plan. Think about the classes you've enjoyed taking, from a short workshop at a library to an MFA course. How did you hear about them? What about the title and course description drew you in? You, in the beginning of your career, were the market you are looking at now.

Think widely about your advertising plan. For example, I teach memoir writing and have blogged and written guest blogs and newspaper articles on related topics. This is a great way to connect with a related community who might be interested in creative writing. You definitely want to research similar businesses both in your area and elsewhere. Look at these businesses as models and see what you can do to make your services unique.

One great way to advertise is to offer donations. Perhaps there is an upcoming charity auction for an organization that you believe in. You could donate one hour, one workshop or a discount coupon. This is a win-win situation: potential clients will learn about you and the charity will benefit.

You might also consider contacting your alumni organizations and offering a workshop with one of those groups. Perhaps you could offer your services as a team-building exercise through a forwarding-thinking HR department of a nonprofit business?

You'll develop an e-mail mailing list by asking people who contact you if you may add them to the mailing list. Be sure to keep your communications brief and only when necessary to avoid the spam folder.

You don't want to be hard to find. Invite these folks to follow your blog and/or join a Facebook group. Be sure to regularly update your blog and Facebook page. As you read books, attend conferences, hear about submission opportunities, etc., share that information with your readers. Keep in touch every way that you promise.

LOOK THE PART

To run a business, you need to look like a business. This means a website and/or blog, business cards, social networking presence on sites like Facebook and perhaps even brochures. Use your blog or other social networking as a means to attract possible clients. You might want to guest blog on related blogs in order to gain readership. You can leave business cards and/or pamphlets in local coffee shops or bookstores.

You can set up most of your business for free. Your online presence takes time, but not money. As you get used to it, you'll work more quickly. You might, however, need to pay for space, computer equipment and business cards.

From the business side of things, you'll want to register your business. Check with the local town or city government and see what steps need to be taken. Unless you register and run your business as a not-for-profit, your services are for-profit.

MONEY DOESN'T HAVE TO BE A TABOO SUBJECT

Now for the potentially daunting question: What to charge? You don't have the overhead of a large school, but you want to make a profit. Consider the amount of time that you'll spend advertising, planning and actually running a class. Look around and see what local programs and individual writing coaches cost in your metro-area. Then, set a price that seems both fair and worth the time and effort that you'll put into your business.

Write a business plan and speak with an experienced professional for advice.

You might consider offering repeat students discounts and running the occasional special. To make your services available to a wider range of clients, offer a scholarship.

Regarding your income and net costs, you probably want to discuss possible deductions with a tax accountant. Write a business plan and speak with an experienced professional for advice.

Until your literary work is widely published, you'll be teaching mostly beginner to intermediate students. Therefore, you'll want to discuss poetry in an accessible and practical fashion. Learn more about the students before you start. See how much experience they've had in workshops and proceed accordingly. As your earlier teachers did, set ground rules in the workshop. Explain to the students who to best offer feedback in a workshop setting.

You should explain in your course descriptions how much experience the students are expected to have. Decide if there will be an application process to join the class. For example, will students be submitting work before being accepted to the class or will it be first come, first serve?

You should explain in your course descriptions how much experience the students are expected to have.

You might be asking why writers should pay you instead of working with you in a graduate-style workshop group free of charge? I've organized peer writing workshops and the difference is just that: we are peers and we all offer and receive feedback. In classes, I might share something I've written as a part of a lecture, but I don't expect the students to offer feedback.

If a potential client seems to be on the same level as you, perhaps you'll have less to offer that person. Chances are, however, that your students will mostly be beginning-level students. I find that most of my clients consider graduate school after our classes or are taking the class to see if they want to seriously pursue graduate school. If it seems that someone has moved beyond your skill set, she will appreciate your suggesting a higher-level coach or university class.

AVOID THE PITFALLS

There are possible reasons not to offer private writing workshops. All of the steps above can be time consuming, especially at the beginning of the learning curve. If it seems daunting, start small. Don't quit your day-job, but rather slowly build the necessary network. I have doubled my income each year that I've been doing this. I started off quite slowly as I was learning the ropes and meeting people.

Always check in regularly with the students. It is easy enough to tweak the curriculum to fit their needs. You might even send out a questionnaire before the class starts. This careful attention will help them to meet their goals and enjoy the class before sharing news about it with other people. Gather positive comments and ask the students if you can use these testimonials on your website.

Of course, there are always students who are less happy. Follow-up with them and ask questions. Sometimes it is a simple misunderstanding or perhaps the student had impossible expectations. Regardless of the reason, you can learn from this feedback. Your business will grow and change as you learn from your experiences.

I know that my students enjoy the workshops not only because they repeat classes, but because they keep in touch. If you teach in other settings, you know that teaching can be quite rewarding as you develop relationships and witness the long-term effects of your teaching.

Teaching writing keeps us honest as we continue to not only practice our craft, but examine it closely. Instead of working for someone else, work for yourself.

CHLOE YELENA MILLER is a poet, essayist and writing teacher in Washington, DC. She has work forthcoming or published in the *Cortland Review*, *Alimentum* and *Narrative*, among others. Her manuscript was a finalist for the Philip Levine Prize in Poetry. She teaches at George Mason University, Fairleigh Dickinson University and privately. Chloe blogs about writing at http://chloeyelenamiller.blogspot.com.

FROM A JUDGE'S PERSPECTIVE:

On Poetry Contests and Competitions

by Nancy Susanna Breen

Ever since I first helped judge a poetry contest 25 years ago, I've believed every poet could benefit from seeing the contest process from the other side. If you could read a stack of entries and weigh one poem against the other, you'd see competitions in a whole new light.

I used to enter poetry contests all the time, usually those sponsored by state poetry societies or literary magazines. Now I seem to participate more as a judge than an entrant. I've served as a screening, final, or sole judge for the National Federation of State Poetry Societies, small literary magazines, writers' groups, arts festivals, and *Writer's Digest*, among others.

I've learned a lot; and I'd like to share a few observations I hope will help you improve your next contest experience.

FOLLOW THE GUIDELINES

Guidelines are rules. Assume your work will be eliminated if you don't follow them. You wouldn't participate in a poker tournament or even a baking contest at the county fair without knowing the rules, would you? (Please say no.) Then do *not* enter a poetry contest without reading and following the guidelines to the letter.

LINE LIMITS. I toss out too many contest entries because they exceed the stated line limit. Sometimes the poet simply wasn't paying attention. Alarmingly, too many poets don't know how to break and count lines in a poem. In a few instances, the poet deliberately tries to fudge the line limit.

Example: Long prose poems often turn out to be rhymed; or line breaks have been removed so the poem appears to be several paragraphs of dense text. This is a sneaky way the poet can try to enter, say, a 64-line poem when the contest limit is 32 lines. My approach to such entries is to count the end rhymes within the paragraphs. If the poem, properly formatted, would have run over the line limit, out it goes.

FORMAT CORRECTLY. Depending on the contest, guidelines may state a variety of formatting requirements: standard 8½ × 11 white paper, certain margins, basic fonts (that means no italics or flowery typefaces), personal information in a specific area of the page or no personal information at all. The National Federation of State Poetry Societies (NFSPS) and its related groups have contest formatting rules that involve duplicate copies, how and where categories are listed on the page, and more. Contests that accept e-mail entries can be even stricter about formatting, such as requiring what must appear in the subject line of the e-mail. Know what's required before you prepare your entry.

NOTE THE DEADLINE. Pay attention to that date and whether it's a postmark or received-by deadline. Find out what happens to late entries. Your poems and fee may be returned or they might go right into the trash.

PROOFREAD

Review every line of your poetry carefully. I wouldn't eliminate an entry because of a typographical error, but that may not be true of other judges. What about a misspelled word? It would depend. Sometimes a word isn't misspelled; the poet used the wrong version of the word. I hate that (and yes, I've made that mistake). I also bristle if there's more than one error in a poem. That's just plain sloppy, and a judge questions how serious the poet is about his work.

Ignore punctuation if the poem is good, but I know from experience judges can be really unfair and sometimes old-fashioned about usage.

Punctuation is harder to pin down. Standards change according to the reference source and what the reader thinks is correct, plus there's that little matter of "poetic license." I ignore punctuation if the poem is good, but I know from experience judges can be really unfair and sometimes old-fashioned about usage. Don't get hung up on whether to use serial commas or dashes versus semicolons. Shoot for clarity. Really erratic punctuation or none at all may have an impact; you'll have to decide if that's a risk you want to take, but do what you feel is best for your poem.

HOW TO PICK A CONTEST

There are many reasons to enter a contest: prestige, publication, and even money. However, there are so many contests and most of them have entry fees. So it makes sense to figure out which contests are winners for your goals.

- **ENTER CONTESTS THAT OFFER PUBLICATION.** Most poets want validation, and there's no greater validation than publication.
- **ENTER CONTESTS THAT OFFER PAYMENT.** Did I say publication was the greatest validation? I meant money, because money and poetry usually mix about as well as running and scissors.
- **ENTER CONTESTS THAT ARE WELL-KNOWN.** Sure, it's nice to win contests, but it's even nicer if someone has heard of it before.
- **ENTER CONTESTS THAT PROVIDE A PREMIUM.** For instance, enter a contest that provides a subscription to the magazine or the winning collection as part of the entry fee. That way, you know you'll get something out of the experience.

—Robert Lee Brewer

CONTENT AND STYLE

AVOID THE "SAME OLD, SAME OLD." Often clichés and tired imagery turn up in poems because the poet is lazy. In other cases, the poet is overwriting. Seriously, say "she cried" instead of "the tears ran down her face." By the time a judge has seen the twentieth poem where tears are cascading like Niagara down someone's cheeks, she's ready to wet a few tissues herself. In fact, watch out for "tears" in general: rain falling like tears, wax dripping like tears...trust me, it's been done.

As an exercise, read some bad poetry. Come on, you know the Internet is full of it. Print some out and circle all the clichés and worn-out images. Make a list, if you like, and memorize it so you can avoid such lapses in your own work.

THINK TWICE ABOUT LOVE POEMS. One kind of love poem that doesn't win prizes resembles what a teenager might write to or about a new crush. Another kind emulates Elizabeth Barrett Browning ("How do I love thee…"), including the antiquated language. Many are heartfelt but simply don't distinguish themselves. They read as if they were written as private messages to the beloved, without any attempt at craft, and many have a taint of desperation. To a disinterested reader, they're usually pretty dull. Unless your love poetry has at least the snap and originality of boxed valentines for kids, don't enter it in contests.

THE NATURE OF NATURE IMAGES. Nature poems seem to be a breeding ground for stock images poets can't resist using over and over. Leaves, usually rust-colored or fiery, rain down in autumn. Snow always blankets the landscape in winter. Spring is all about bursting buds and renewal. In summer, the sun blazes and storm clouds gather on the horizon.

You're a poet! If you turn to such bland imagery, you're writing half-asleep. Okay, use these images as placeholders in the heat of composition; but when you revise your poem, stretch your imagination as you describe that snowy field, November forest, reawakening garden, or hot summer day.

GETTING RELIGIOUS. Religious contest poems tend to resemble the prayers or hymns of the poet's faith. Consequently, the poems all sound the same, without much of the poets' individual thoughts, fervor or perspectives. If you want to enter a religious poem in a general contest, make it yours, not a paraphrase of the "Our Father" or the lyrics of "A Mighty Fortress is Our God." Nobody said religious poems must sound a certain way. If you don't believe me, track down some good contemporary religious poetry and see how well-crafted and exciting it can be.

ABOUT RHYMING, METERED POEMS

Judging a contest of all-rhyming poetry usually makes my brain swell. Logic suggests the extra effort of writing in meter and rhyme would dissuade poets from even trying. Far from it! A well-publicized contest for rhyming poetry brings in a deluge of entries, many of them really bad. No one's reading poetry, yet everyone thinks he or she can write it if it rhymes.

Here are some tips to make your rhymed, metered poems stand out in competition:

- Keep *oo* and *ay* rhymes to a minimum. They're monotonous and contribute to your poem sounding the same as everyone else's.
- Avoid writing in rhymed couplets, especially iambic verse in lines shorter than five feet. Since it's the easiest, most familiar poetic style, the number of such entries overwhelms contests. Again, your poems fade into the crowd. Also, it's too easy to create that sing-song effect that destroys a poem.
- Shakespearean sonnets are very popular with entrants. Unfortunately, without finesse, these can come across as lightweight, especially if the closing couplet is too clever or on the nose. Go for individuality and try another sonnet form, or even another poetic form entirely.
- Always read your poem out loud. Better yet, have someone read it to you cold. You'll find out if you forced the meter in places, if the rhythm is rocky or awkward, or if you were so exacting your lines sound as if a metronome is ticking.
- If you think your poem would make a lovely greeting card, don't enter it.

- Understand that humorous or juvenile poems don't stand up well against serious entries. This is doubly true in a contest that welcomes all kinds of poetry. Save whimsy and cleverness for contests that call specifically for light verse or children's poetry.
- You live in the 21st century. Don't you dare use "thee," "thou," "whilst," or insert apostrophes for letters ("ne'er," "'tis," "enter'd").

FINAL THOUGHTS

Remember, judges are human and often poets themselves. They're supposed to remain objective, but their preferences regarding style and craft probably are going to influence their choices. I have my own ideas and prejudices—this article reflects some of them. I look for quality above all other considerations. In the end, though, I can't help the innate reasons I respond more favorably to one poem over another, especially when it comes to ranking the top poems.

That's why not winning is different from failure. Another judge may have chosen your work over that of the prizewinners, so move on to another contest.

Best of luck on your next poetry competition! I hope someday I get to choose *your* work for a prize.

NANCY SUSANNA BREEN is a published poet, contest judge, and former editor of *Poet's Market*. Her chapbooks include *Rites and Observances* (Finishing Line Press) and *How Time Got Away* (Pudding House Publications). She founded and maintains the writing website Nudged to Write (www.nudged2write.com).

IS IT A 'CON'?

Think Before You Trust

What is a "con?" Con is short for "confidence," an adjective defined by *Webster's* as "of, relating to, or adept at swindling by false promise," as in "confidence man" or "confidence game." While the publishing world is full of legitimate opportunities for poets to gain honor and exposure for their work, there are also plenty of "cons." How can you tell the difference? The following are some of the most common situations that cost poets disappointment, frustration—and cash. Learn to spot them before submitting your work, and don't let your vanity be your guide.

ANTHOLOGIES

Has this happened to you? You see an ad in a perfectly respectable publication announcing a poetry contest with big cash prizes. You enter, and later you receive a glowing letter congratulating you on your exceptional poem, which the contest sponsor wants to include in his deluxe hardbound anthology of the best poetry submitted to the contest. The anthology costs only, say, $65. You don't have to buy it—they'll still publish your poem—but wouldn't you be proud to own one? And wouldn't it be nice to buy additional copies to give to family and friends? And for an extra charge you can include a biographical note. And so on . . .

Of course, when the anthology arrives, the quality of the poetry may not be what you were expecting, with several poems crammed unattractively onto a page. Apparently everyone who entered the contest was invited to be published; you basically paid cash to see your poem appear in a phone-book-like volume with no literary merit whatsoever.

Were you conned? Depends on how you look at it. If you bought into the flattery and believed you were being published in an exclusive, high-quality publication, no doubt you feel duped. On the other hand, if all you were after was seeing your poem in print, even knowing you'd have to pay for the privilege, then you got what you wanted. (Unless you've deceived yourself into believing you've truly won an honor and now have a worthy publishing credit; you don't.)

HELPFUL WEBSITES

The following websites include specific information about questionable poetry publishers and awards. For more websites of value to poets, see Additional Resources.

- An Incomplete Guide to Print On Demand Publishers offers articles on POD publishing, comparisons of POD publishers (contracts, distribution, fees, etc.) and an online forum: http://booksandtales.com/pod/index.php
- Answers to frequently asked questions about poetry awards from the Academy of American Poets: www.poets.org/page.php/prmID/116
- Poets will find warnings and other valuable publishing information on the Preditors & Editors website: www.anotherealm.com/prededitors/
- Writer Beware tracks contests, publishers and literary agents: www.sfwa.org/beware
- Literary Contest Caution at http://windpub.com/literary.scams

If you don't want to add insult to injury, resist additional spiels, like having your poem printed on coffee mugs and T-shirts (you can do this yourself through print shops or online services like www.cafepress.com) or spending large sums on awards banquets and conferences. And, before you submit a single line of poetry, find out what rights the contest sponsor acquires. You may be relinquishing all rights to your poem simply by mailing it in or submitting it through a website. If the poem no longer belongs to you, the publisher can do whatever he wishes with it. Don't let your vanity propel you into a situation you'll always regret.

READING AND CONTEST FEES

Suppose you notice a promising market for your poetry, but the editor requires a set fee just to consider your work. Or you see a contest that interests you, but you have to pay the sponsor a fee just to enter. Are you being conned?

In the case of reading fees, keep these points in mind: Is the market so exceptional that you feel it's worth risking the cost of the reading fee to have your work considered? What makes it so much better than markets that do not charge fees? Has the market been around awhile, with an established publishing schedule? What are you paid if your work is accepted? Are reasonably priced samples available so you can judge the production values and quality of the writing?

Reading fees don't necessarily signal a suspicious market. In fact, they're increasingly popular as editors struggle with the costs of publishing books and magazines, including the man-hours required to read loads of (often bad) submissions. However, fees represent an additional financial burden on poets, who often don't receive any monetary reward for their poems to begin with. It's really up to individual poets to decide whether paying a fee is beneficial to their publishing efforts. Think long and hard about fee-charging markets that are new and untried, don't pay poets for their work (at the very least a print publication should offer a contributor's copy), charge high prices for sample copies or set fees that seem unreasonable.

Entry fees for contests often fund prizes, judges' fees, honorariums and expenses of running and promoting the contest (including publishing a "prize" collection or issue of a magazine). Other kinds of contests charge entry fees, from Irish dancing competitions to bake-offs at a county fair. Why not poetry contests?

> Watch out for contests that charge higher than average fees, especially if the fees are out of proportion to the amount of money being given.

That's not to say you shouldn't be cautious. Watch out for contests that charge higher-than-average fees, especially if the fees are out of proportion to the amount of prize money being given. (Look through the Contests & Awards section to get a sense of what most competitions charge.) Find out how long the contest has been around, and verify whether prizes have been awarded each year and to whom. In the case of book and chapbook contests, send for one of the winning publications to confirm that the publisher puts out a quality product. Regard with skepticism any contest that tells you you've won something, then demands payment for an anthology, trophy or other item. (It's okay if a group offers an anthology for a modest price without providing winners with free copies. Most state poetry societies have to do this; but they also present cash awards in each category of the contest, and their entry fees are low.)

SUBSIDY PUBLISHERS, PRINT-ON-DEMAND

Poetry books are a hard sell to the book-buying public. Few of the big publishers handle these books, and those that do feature the "name" poets (i.e., the major prize winners and contemporary masters with breathtaking reputations). Even the small presses publish only so many books per year—far less than the number of poets writing.

No wonder so many poets decide to pay to have their poetry collections published. While some may self-publish (i.e., take full control of their book, working directly with a printer), others turn to subsidy publishers (also called "vanity publishers") and print-on-demand (POD) publishers.

There are many differences between subsidy publishing and POD publishing, as well as similarities (having to pay to get published is a big one). Whether or not you get conned is entirely up to you. You have to take responsibility for asking questions, doing research on presses, and reading the fine print on the contract to make sure you know exactly what you're paying for. There are landmines in dealing with subsidy and POD publishers, and you have to investigate thoroughly and intelligently to avoid damage.

Some questions to keep in mind: Are fees inflated compared to the product and services you'll be receiving? Will you still own the rights to your book? Does the publisher put out a quality product that's attractive and cleanly printed? (Get a sample copy and find out.) How many copies of the book will you receive? How much will you have to pay for additional copies? How will your book be sold and distributed? (Don't count on seeing your volume in bookstores.)

Will you receive royalties? How much? Does the publisher offer any kind of promotional assistance or is it all up to you? Will those promotion efforts be realistic and results-oriented? (Sometimes "promotion" means sending out review copies, which is a waste—such volumes are rarely reviewed.) Don't wait until *after* you've signed a contract (and a check) to raise these issues. Do your homework first.

Obviously, poets who don't stay on their toes may find themselves preyed upon. And a questionable publishing opportunity doesn't have to be an out-and-out rip-off for you to feel cheated. In every situation, you have a choice *not* to participate. Exercise that choice, or at least develop a healthy sense of skepticism before you fling yourself and your poetry at the first smooth talker who compliments your work. Poets get burned because they're much too impatient to see their work in print. Calm your ego, slow down and devote that time, energy and money toward reading other poets and improving your own writing. You'll find that getting published will eventually take care of itself.

FINDING READERS:

How to Get Your Poetry Into Their Hands

by Diane Lockward

Poets who are fortunate enough to have a full-length collection from a large publishing house receive the services of a marketing department with a budget that covers advertising and a book tour. But if you, like most of us, get your book from a small press, you will find that your publisher has little or no budget for promotion. There are a number of benefits to working with a small press publisher, for example, more involvement in the design of the book and a personal relationship with your publisher. However, if you want your book to find its way into the hands of readers, you are going to have to work to make that happen.

SPREADING THE WORD

The work of promoting your book begins before the book is even out. Most small press publishers have found that ads are not cost effective, but they will design a press release and do a snail mailing for you. While you wait for your book to get published, compile an up-to-date snail mail list. Since mailings are expensive, include only your best prospects, not everyone you've ever met. Many publishers also do an e-mail blitz, so prepare a list of e-mail addresses. Your publisher will most likely send the press release and a review copy to journals that have published your work. Assemble a list of the names and addresses of those journals, but only the ones that run reviews.

After your book is published, supplement your publisher's mailings with your own. Many publishers provide postcards for this purpose, but if yours doesn't, you can design your own inexpensively at an online service such as vistaprint.com. Upload your cover image onto one side and add ordering information on the other, leaving space for the name and address of the recipient. In your e-mail notes include your cover image, but do not add an attachment as many people will not open it. It doesn't matter if people receive more than one notice about your book. Janet Holmes, publisher of Ahsahta Books, says, "Sometimes a reader needs to see the title of a book multiple times before it sinks in as something to acquire." Many recipients will appreciate—and act upon—the reminder.

Ask your publisher to provide you with the press release via attachment. Save it on your computer and include it with any additional review copies you mail out. Send the press release to your college alumni newsletter. Put one up on the bulletin board where you work. Fire off some to local libraries and bookstores. Send another with a fact sheet to your local newspaper. Request an article and offer to go in for an interview. My local paper interviewed me and ran an article for each of my books. That would not have happened if I hadn't asked.

LINING UP READINGS

Tom Hunley, director of Steel Toe Books, says, "Readings are far and away the #1 way for poets to sell books." Let your first reading be a book launch party. Invite your relatives, friends, and poet pals. Have food. This reading may well be your best sales event. If you have a friend with a book coming out around the same time, consider joining forces. Publisher Joan Cusack Handler celebrates each new CavanKerry Press book with a literary salon held in someone's home. Poet Claire Keyes (*The Question of Rapture*, Mayapple Press, 2008) had house readings held by friends. She and her hosts collaborated on the guest list and shared expenses.

After the initial round of readings, you need to get proactive. Poet Kate Greenstreet (*case sensitive*, Ahsahta Books, 2006) warns that "if you won't ask—and people aren't already inviting you—obviously, you won't be reading." To get readings, you need to compose a query letter. Keep it informative and succinct. I send most of mine by e-mail with links to my website and online sites where my work is available. Make a list of venues in your area. Try bookstores, libraries, art galleries, coffeehouses—all the usual places. Then get creative. I have friends who've read in chocolate stores, wine bars, and hip jewelry stores. Contact local book clubs and suggest that your book be a selection. Offer to present a reading and discussion for the group. Senior citizens' residences and nursing homes are often looking for social programs. Offer your services for a reading. If you have friends who teach, offer to do a reading, a Q & A, and a workshop. Apply to conferences, festivals, and book fairs.

Target audiences that might likely have an interest in your work and in poetry. For example, I'm a former high school English teacher. One of my most successful readings was for a district-wide English department meeting. I read 10 poems and offered 10 teaching tips. The supervisor purchased a copy of my book for each department member—all 40 of them. Plus, that presentation led to an offer to teach a six-hour workshop for a small group of teachers.

Also target groups that don't ordinarily attend readings but are somehow connected to your subject matter. Are your poems about flowers? Query nearby garden clubs and suggest a reading at one of their upcoming meetings. Do your poems deal with woman-related topics? Contact area women's clubs. Marion Haddad (*Somewhere Between Mexico and a River Called Home*, Pecan Grove Press, 2004) is the American-born daughter of Syrian immigrants and for 35 years lived a few minutes from the Mexican border, so she often seeks readings at Arab-American gatherings and border studies events. Richard Jeffrey Newman, whose *The Silence of Men* (CavanKerry, 2006) deals with gender, sexuality, and recovery from child sexual abuse, solicited and received an invitation to read at the 2008 Wellness and Writing Connections Conference. One of my favorite readings was at New York Life Investment Management, certainly an unlikely place for poetry, but the woman who heads Human Resources runs special programs for women employees. I proposed a reading entitled "Poetry and the Lives of Women." My host pre-ordered six of my books and had a drawing for them, a great alternative when reading at an event where selling books might not be appropriate.

Remember that the farther you cast your net, the fewer responses you're likely to get.

Eventually you will need to seek readings outside of your own area. Remember that the farther you cast your net, the fewer responses you're likely to get. Cast it anyhow because you will get some responses. To find out where readings are held, map out the distance you're willing to travel. Then do a Google search, for example, "poetry venues in New Jersey" or "poetry readings in Boston." That should bring up some listings. If there's contact information, send off your query letter. Check out reading schedules on other poets' websites. Visit online calendars, for example, those at The Academy of American Poets' and Poets & Writers' websites. Use these to suggest possible venues to query. When you get readings, publicize them as widely as possible. List them in online calendars and send out e-mail notices to people you know in the area of the reading. Do not rely solely on the venue host to drum up an audience for you.

Regardless of where you're reading, remember that you're promoting your book, so be prepared to read poems from the book. Greg Kosmicki, of The Backwaters Press, advises poets that while they may get tired of reading the same poems, the audience will be hearing them for the first time. Your listeners will be more inclined to buy your book if you hold it and read from it. Remember, too, that not everyone who attends your reading will buy your book. My own publisher, Charlie Hughes of Wind Publications, suggests that often the "value in a reading or personal appearance is not in the number of books sold at the event, but in getting the writer's name in the newspaper announcing the event—building name recognition." I usually bring along oversized postcards with my cover image on one side and a poem and ordering information on the other. I give these away and like to think that some of the recipients might make a later purchase. I also always carry some business cards with me, cover image on one side, contact information on the other.

USING THE INTERNET

The Internet is one of your best resources for promoting your book. If you don't already have a website, get one. Even if your publisher has a page for your book at the press website, you should have your own website. You can get a domain name very inexpensively. Since this is your website's address, use your own name so people can easily locate your website. If you design your own website, you will pay only for the hosting. If you use a free hosting site, be sure it's ad-free. A website with ads looks awful and unprofessional. If you use a web designer's services, you will, of course, pay more, but don't go wild. Your site should include a bio, an image of your book cover, purchase information, sample poems, links to other poems, links to online reviews and interviews, a calendar of your readings, and contact information. Be sure your website is attractive and up to date. A website that is not maintained does not make a good impression.

A blog takes some time, but it's a great place to establish contacts with other poets and another place to display your book cover and list readings.

Consider keeping a blog. There's a big community now of poet bloggers. A blog takes some time, but it's a great place to establish contacts with other poets and another place to display your book cover and list readings. You can add podcasts and videos, thus creating long-distance readings for potential fans who might not otherwise be able to get to a reading. Kate Greenstreet kept a blog for two years. She used it to do a series of more than 100 first-book interviews and undoubtedly earned many friends. As much as she gave to the poetry community, she got back in support when her own book came out.

Join an Internet social network such as Facebook, MySpace, or Red Room. These are hot gathering places for poets, and all are free. I'm on Facebook where I create event listings for my readings and send out invitations to "friends" who live in the area of an upcoming reading. Without this resource, I would not know these people's names or how to contact them. I've learned about venues and booked readings through Facebook contacts, gotten an online interview, and participated in a college student's poetry course project. Richard

Jeffrey Newman received an invitation from a Facebook contact to go to Chile as part of Chile Poesia, an international poetry festival. A poetry listserv will also put you among poets and offer opportunities for sales and readings.

A final suggestion for your Internet use, this one fast and easy. Use your e-mail signature to good advantage. Set your e-mail program to automatically add a link to your website at the bottom of each new message you write. If you like, you can add a link to your blog or anything special you have online such as a poem feature. Think of the signature area as free billboard space. You'll be amazed how many people will click on those links and go visiting.

KEEPING EXPECTATIONS REALISTIC

Promoting your book is the business of poetry, but don't expect to make money. As Kate Greenstreet says, "When we're talking about selling poetry books, we're talking about doing business, but it isn't conventional business even if you work really hard at it." Richard Jeffrey Newman reminds us that books of poetry "find their audience one reader at a time, slowly, over time." If you want your book to find those readers, you need to be industrious, adventurous, persistent and patient.

DIANE LOCKWARD'S second collection, *What Feeds Us* (Wind Publications), received the 2006 Quentin R. Howard Poetry Prize. Her poems appear in Garrison Keillor's *Good Poems for Hard Times* and in such journals as *Harvard Review, Spoon River Poetry Review,* and *Prairie Schooner.* (www.dianelockward.com)

10 TIPS FOR THE PERFECT READING

by Taylor Mali

The extent of the advice given to poets for how to present their work aloud at poetry readings usually boils down to reading slower, louder, and clearer. And while those are important improvements to almost anyone's style of recitation (albeit extremely difficult to make yourself do, especially at the same time), there are several other factors to keep in mind if you want your audience to appreciate your skills as a writer and perhaps even buy your book after the reading.

1. **TRY TO MAKE THE FIRST THING OUT OF YOUR MOUTH POETRY.** What else could be more important than immediately giving the audience an example of what they came to the reading to hear? Insipid chatter between poems is bad enough, but introductory insipid chatter is even worse and tends to go on and on. Sometimes it will be five minutes before a poet even gets to the first poem! Everything you think you need to say—thank yous, shout outs, announcements about journals in which your poetry will be forthcoming, or plugs for your books and next appearances—all of this can be mentioned after the first poem. Or maybe not at all (except for the thank yous).

2. **KNOW WHAT POEMS YOU WILL READ AND HAVE THEM CLOSE AT HAND.** Don't burden the audience with having to watch you flip through your own book or resort to looking at the table of contents while you make a self-deprecating joke only to realize finally that the poem you wanted to read is actually in your other book. Have your poems picked out in advance as well as the order in which you will read them. All of your fussing between poems counts toward the time you have been given to read.

3. **DON'T BE THE POET WHO READS FOREVER!** Time limits do not only apply to bad poets; they apply to brilliant poets like you as well. Unfortunately, it's usually the bad poets who have no concept of time. Before the reading, rehearse your set (with a stopwatch if possible) and do not go over the time you've been allotted. Losing track of how long you've been reading is no excuse for going over. Don't ask the organizer to give you a signal when you have five minutes left or periodically look up and ask, "How am I doing on time?" It's your responsibility to know how you are "doing on time." If anything, be a little under time and leave your audience wanting more.

4. **KEEP YOUR CHATTER BETWEEN POEMS TO A MINIMUM.** Most of what poets say between poems comes from nervousness and not any real need to explicate the poem.

5. **PERFORM ONE POEM BY SOMEONE ELSE.** Depending on how much time you have been given, it's a nice idea to celebrate the work of someone else beside yourself. Introduce your audience to one of your favorite poems by one of your favorite poets. Tell them where they can find this particular poem and two things you love about it. Then, at the end of your reading of the poem, say the author's name one last time.

6. **PERFORM AT LEAST ONE OF YOUR POEMS FROM MEMORY.** Once you experience the freedom of being able to make constant eye contact while having your hands completely free to gesture or hang naturally at your sides (which doesn't feel natural at all but looks perfectly normal), you will want to memorize more of your work. And you should! The roots of poetry are bardic, not literary, so it is entirely fitting to work on making the recitation of your poem a better performance. Work at memorizing more and more poetry every day. The mind is a muscle; the more you use it, the stronger it gets.

7. **LET THE AUDIENCE CLAP IF THEY WANT TO CLAP.** If one definition of a "performance" poem is that after it's over, the audience not only wants to applaud but knows that applause is appropriate, then you could say that one definition of an "academic" poem is that after it's over—assuming you know when that is—the audience doesn't even know if they are supposed to clap. Poets with limited performance skills will often request that audiences not applaud between poems because they are uncomfortable with the awkward silence that fills the room when they finish each poem. In fact, sometimes the only clue that such poets have finished a poem is when they say, "The next poem I'd like to read." Certainly don't telegraph the end of your poem by speeding up or trailing off or both. Rather build toward it, perhaps nodding your head ever so slightly at the end.

8. **MAKE EYE CONTACT.** Real eye contact. Look at different parts of the room as you glance up from your text every now and then. Poets who look at the exact same spot as they methodically lift their heads every seven seconds to pretend they are looking at the same person (whose chair is apparently attached to one of the lighting fixtures) aren't fooling anyone. It is better never to look up at all than to do so perfunctorily to mask your nervousness.

9. **IF THERE IS A MICROPHONE, USE IT.** Granted, when the microphone is attached to a podium, you won't have much choice but to use it. But faced with a solitary mic stand and the possibly awkward task of having to adjust it for your height while somehow also managing a bottle of water and the text from which you are about to read, you might decide you don't need a microphone at all. Not a good decision, even if you have a big, boomy voice. Without a microphone, you cannot get quiet when the poem invites it, or else no one will hear you when you do. Unless the system sounds like crap and has for the whole night, use the microphone, even if it takes a few extra seconds at the outset to adjust it.

10. **ENJOY YOURSELF.** This seems obvious, but audiences love to see people who love what they do, especially when they do it well. Smile a lot. Try reciting an entire poem while smiling. Let people suspect you are having the time of your life. And whatever you do, don't ever suggest that your reading is a kind of torture you are inflicting on the audience ("Don't worry. You only have to listen to three more!"). You are a genius, and your words are the proof. Knock 'em dead!

WHY POETS NEED PLATFORMS:

And How to Create One

by Sage Cohen

If you want your poetry to be read, people need to know who you are, what you write, and where to find it. A viable platform can take you there. The good news is that anyone who wants to establish a poetry platform can take the necessary steps to build one over time. No matter what your level of writing, publishing and social media savvy, you can have more fun end enjoy more success as you take small steps over time to cultivate your poetry platform. This article will tell you how.

WHAT A PLATFORM IS

Platform is the turf you name and claim as your area of writing expertise, and it's everything you do to make that expertise visible. Just as a thesis is the foundation of a term paper around which its argument is built, a platform is an organizing principle around which a poet's many expressions of work revolve. A platform says to both the poet and the world, "I am an expert in [fill in the blanks with your specialty]!"

Platform is both the destination and the path. Think of your platform as your portfolio of accomplishments (publications, leadership roles, Web presence, public appearances, classes) that demonstrate your authority on a given topic. You build it as you go. It keeps you moving forward, tells you where forward is, and is the measure against which you decide if you're getting there.

HOW A PLATFORM CAN HELP YOU

Every poet can benefit from having a platform—even you. Following are the primary advantages of platform consciousness:

- **POETIC PROWESS.** The more focused you are on taking your poetry forward, the more likely you will stay engaged in honing your craft, polishing drafts, completing poems and identifying organizing principles or themes in your growing collection of work.

- **PUBLISHING.** As you gain experience researching literary journals and sending out your work, your knowledge about the publications best suited (and most receptive) to your work will grow. Over time, you will develop relationships, insight and a publishing track record that may significantly increase your chances of publishing (both individual poems and collections of poems).

- **FUNDRAISING.** Platform gives success an opportunity to snowball. With each publication, award, recognition or other notch on your belt, you'll improve the odds of winning prizes and receiving grants and residencies if this is of interest to you.

- **AUTHORITY.** The more experience you have writing and publishing poetry (and potentially educating/exciting others about their own poetic process), the more you and others will trust in your authority.

- **OPPORTUNITY.** Once you have earned a reputable name among your poetic peers, requests for interviews, articles, speaking engagements, teaching, and more are likely to start rolling in. But more importantly, you will have paved the way to go after exactly what you want to create in your writing life, buoyed by the confidence that comes from proven expertise.

NAMING AND CLAIMING YOUR PLATFORM

Not sure what your platform is or what you want it to be? It may be as simple as "Poetry." Or you could name what you believe your poetry is serving or striving for—if this is relevant to your work. Several years ago I named my platform "Writing the Life Poetic," which quickly led to me authoring a nonfiction book by this name. One thing is certain: naming and claiming your area of expertise is going to give you a new sense of clarity and purpose. And you may be surprised at how quickly this clarity magnetizes new, relevant opportunities to you.

If you'd like to explore some of the possibilities for your poetic platform, the following exercise can help. I encourage you to map out your own Platform at a Glance using the example below as a starting place. It's OK if you don't have all the answers yet. Having a record of what you're aspiring to today can help you learn about where you're headed over time.

PLATFORM AT A GLANCE

PLATFORM BUILDING BLOCKS	INSIGHTS
Theme, topic, genre, or area of expertise	Poetry for the people: with a goal of encouraging writers of all levels to write, read, and enjoy poetry.
Audience(s) you serve	• People who feel afraid, unwelcome, or unsure of how to start writing poetry. • People already writing poetry who want to write more, improve their craft, and have more fun. • Writers of all stripes wanting to invigorate their relationship with language. • People who love poetry and read poems.
Needs, desires, and preferences of your audience(s)	• People who feel afraid: Want to be invited in to poetry and assured that they are welcome/can do it. • People already writing poetry: Seeking tools, techniques, and tips to help improve their craft. • Writers of all stripes: Seeking a poetic lens through which to better appreciate and apply language in anything and everything they write. • People who love reading poems: Want to find poems that connect, move them, reveal something new.
Value you bring to each different type of reader	• People who feel afraid: Friendly encouragement and useful information. • People already writing poetry: Vast selection of tips, tools, strategies, and examples. • Writers of all stripes: A way into—and an enjoyable exploration of—the life poetic. • People who love reading poems: Poems I've written that they can embrace and enjoy.

PLATFORM NAME	WRITING THE LIFE POETIC
Why you are the ideal person to develop this platform over time	I have more than 20 years of experience cultivating a poetic way of life. I have an advanced degree in creative writing, a great deal of teaching experience, and a well-established career of writing and publishing poetry.
Why you are passionate about doing so	Poetry matters—not just as a literary form, but as a way of life. I know from my own experience that a relationship with poetry can significantly expand a person's sense of possibility, delight, and camaraderie with one's self, universal human truths, and life itself. I want to make this gift available to anyone who's interested in receiving it—as a teacher, author and poet.

MULTIPLE PATHS TO PLATFORM DEVELOPMENT

Publishing is certainly a significant way to establish and build your platform. But it is one of many. The good news is that while you're waiting for your latest batch of poems to make a safe landing in just the right literary journal(s), there are many ways to grow your visibility as an expert in your field that are available to you right now. Let's consider a few:

- **GO PUBLIC.** Read your work publicly as much as possible—either as a featured reader through a reading series or special event or at an open mic reading. Open mics are far more widely accessible and encourage everyone to participate. They're a good way to establish a community of writers if you attend and share work regularly. Over time, people will start to recognize you and your work. This will help you learn who your audience is and what it is about your poems that appeals to them.

- **TEACH WHAT YOU KNOW.** If you are passionate about poetry and have been schooling yourself in the craft (either through formal education or self-study), chances are good that you have something to offer other poets. From tenured academic positions to workshops you've organized and publicized yourself, you can choose the forum that fits your experience and temperament—then bring people together to learn about what's possible in poetry.

- **GIVE SERVICE.** There are endless ways to give service to poets—both paid and volunteer. You could become active in an online community—or start your own—that writes or contemplates poetry. Depending on your level of expertise, you could offer coaching, consulting, or editing. If you enjoy working with people of certain ages or circumstances (such as students, prisoners, elders), you could find ways to share poetry in your community through religious, educational or civic organizations.

- **PUBLISH.** Most poets are likely to experience multiple types and stages of publishing throughout their career. Because publishing individual poems can be slow and full collections even slower, you may want to explore other ways of sharing your knowledge of poetry along the way by publishing how-to articles, interviews or essays about the life poetic. You can query print and online magazines, share free content with organizations or online communities that serve poets and writers and/or create Squidoo lenses on any number of craft or publishing issues. If self-publishing is of interest to you, you could write and sell instructional e-books or publish print-on-demand collections of your poems (only if you are not seeking "mainstream" publication for this work.)
- **GO SOCIAL.** Social media gives poets instantaneous access to a virtually limitless community that can help your poetry and your platform evolve over time. When you want to exchange ideas, inspiration, poems, encouragement, tips and resources, book reviews, links, or professional recommendations, you can do so using any number of social media outlets. Facebook, Twitter, GoodReads and LinkedIn are just a few of the most popular places to do so. Choose one or two online forums in which to start; spend some time investigating how others are using these; decide what kind of information exchange best reflects your platform; and then pace yourself as you become a relevant contributor to the online conversation.
- **BECOME YOUR OWN MEDIA CHANNEL.** With a wide range of simple and inexpensive interactive media available today, you have numerous options for getting your message out. First, consider your platform aspirations. Then, decide what kind of information you'd like to share—and whether your goal is to inspire, collaborate, teach, build community or some combination of these. Depending on your goals, you might consider employing interactive media such as: webinars, teleclasses, e-zines, podcasts, and specialized online communities such as Ning. Try one and commit to it for at least six months; then evaluate, refine and expand as you go.

COHERENCE AND YOUR POETIC SOUL

These days, readers expect to have a personal connection with the poets they enjoy through their websites, blogs, teaching and live appearances. Plus, with the widespread use of social media bridging the space between writer and reader, anyone who has admired your work can tap into your moment-by-moment publicized thinking through the social media communities you frequent.

Therefore, who you are (or more accurately, how you present yourself publicly) and what you write are often one continuous experience for readers. A writing life that grows out of and reflects who you authentically are is going to be the most grounded and sustainable path to success.

My friend Dan Raphael is an example of someone who has built a writing empire on the foundation of his wildly entertaining and unusual command of language and life. On the back of one of Dan's books is a quote that says:

She: Do you think he's ever taken acid?

He: Taken it? I think he wears a patch.

Dan delivers on this very engaging and entertaining promise. He is a transcendent force of nature and engaging linguistic acrobatics on stage when delivering his poems and behind the scenes, when sending e-mail to friends.

I have another friend who is a widely sought photographer who has recently been recognized in several national magazines. This photographer has a parallel platform as a poet; and a good number of her poems explore the socioeconomic dynamics of being a person providing a service for the elite and the wealthy. This presents a bit of a platform pretzel, as she has no desire to alienate valued clients with her poetry. The expert photographer/poet is very delicately navigating how to hold these two parts of her life with integrity and authenticity as she quickly becomes more visible and respected in both chosen fields.

How is your life in alignment or out of whack with your platform(s) today? Is there anything you need to reconcile to create a greater coherence between what you write and how you live?

HAVE PLATFORM, WILL PROSPER

With a clear platform as the organizing principle in your life poetic, you can take the steps that will make your poems and your life poetic more visible in the communities and publications that matter to you. As you become increasingly effective at creating the writing results you want, over time you will attract more readers, expand your sphere of influence and generate far more opportunities to share your love of poetry.

BLOGGING BASICS:

Get the Most Out of Your Blog

by Robert Lee Brewer

In these days of publishing and media change, writers have to build platforms and learn how to connect to audiences if they want to improve their chances of publication and overall success. There are many methods of audience connection available to writers, but one of the most important is through blogging.

Since I've spent several years successfully blogging—both personally and professionally—I figure I've got a few nuggets of wisdom to pass on to writers who are curious about blogging or who already are.

Here's my quick list of tips:

1. **START BLOGGING TODAY.** If you don't have a blog, use Blogger, WordPress, or some other blogging software to start your blog today. It's free, and you can start off with your very personal "Here I am, world" post.

2. **START SMALL.** Blogs are essentially very simple, but they can get very complicated (for people who like complications). However, I advise bloggers to start small and evolve over time.

3. **USE YOUR NAME IN YOUR URL.** This will make it easier for search engines to find you when your audience eventually starts seeking you out by name. For instance, my url is http://robertleebrewer.blogspot.com. If you try Googling "Robert Lee Brewer," you'll notice that My Name Is Not Bob is one of the top 5 search results (behind my other blog: Poetic Asides).

4. **UNLESS YOU HAVE A REASON, USE YOUR NAME AS THE TITLE OF YOUR BLOG.** Again, this helps with search engine results. My Poetic Asides blog includes my name in

the title, and it ranks higher than My Name Is Not Bob. However, I felt the play on my name was worth the trade off.

5. **FIGURE OUT YOUR BLOGGING GOALS.** You should return to this step every couple months, because it's natural for your blogging goals to evolve over time. Initially, your blogging goals may be to make a post a week about what you have written, submitted, etc. Over time, you may incorporate guests posts, contests, tips, etc.

6. **BE YOURSELF.** I'm a big supporter of the idea that your image should match your identity. It gets too confusing trying to maintain a million personas. Know who you are and be that on your blog, whether that means you're sincere, funny, sarcastic, etc.

7. **POST AT LEAST ONCE A WEEK.** This is for starters. Eventually, you may find it better to post once a day or multiple times per day. But remember: Start small and evolve over time.

8. **POST RELEVANT CONTENT.** This means that you post things that your readers might actually care to know.

Don't spend a week writing each post. Try to keep it to an hour or two tops and then post.

9. **USEFUL AND HELPFUL POSTS WILL ATTRACT MORE VISITORS.** Talking about yourself is all fine and great. I do it myself. But if you share truly helpful advice, your readers will share it with others, and visitors will find you on search engines.

10. **TITLE YOUR POSTS IN A WAY THAT GETS YOU FOUND IN SEARCH ENGINES.** The more specific you can get the better. For instance, the title "Blogging Tips" will most likely get lost in search results. However, the title "Blogging Tips for Writers" specifies which audience I'm targeting and increases the chances of being found on the first page of search results.

11. **LINK TO POSTS IN OTHER MEDIA.** If you have an e-mail newsletter, link to your blog posts in your newsletter. If you have social media accounts, link to your blog posts there. If you have a helpful post, link to it in relevant forums and on message boards.

12. **WRITE WELL, BUT BE CONCISE.** At the end of the day, you're writing blog posts, not literary manifestos. Don't spend a week writing each post. Try to keep it to an hour

or two tops and then post. Make sure your spelling and grammar are good, but don't stress yourself out too much.

13. **FIND LIKE-MINDED BLOGGERS.** Comment on their blogs regularly and link to them from yours. Eventually, they may do the same. Keep in mind that blogging is a form of social media, so the more you communicate with your peers the more you'll get out of the process.

14. **RESPOND TO COMMENTS ON YOUR BLOG.** Even if it's just a simple "Thanks," respond to your readers if they comment on your blog. After all, you want your readers to be engaged with your blog, and you want them to know that you care they took time to comment.

15. **EXPERIMENT.** Start small, but don't get complacent. Every so often, try something new. For instance, the biggest draw to my Poetic Asides blog are the poetry prompts and challenges I issue to poets. Initially, that was an experiment—one that worked very well. I've tried other experiments that haven't panned out, and that's fine. It's all part of a process.

SEO TIPS FOR WRITERS

Most writers may already know what SEO is. If not, SEO stands for *search engine optimization*. Basically, a site or blog that practices good SEO habits should improve its rankings in search engines, such as Google and Bing. Most huge corporations have realized the importance of SEO and spend enormous sums of time, energy and money on perfecting their SEO practices. However, writers can improve their SEO without going to those same extremes.

In this section, I will use the terms of *site pages* and *blog posts* interchangeably. In both cases, you should be practicing the same SEO strategies (when it makes sense).

Here are my top tips on ways to improve your SEO starting today:

1. **USE APPROPRIATE KEYWORDS.** Make sure that your page displays your main keyword(s) in the page title, content, URL, title tags, page header, image names and tags (if you're including images). All of this is easy to do, but if you feel overwhelmed, just remember to use your keyword(s) in your page title and content (especially in the first and last 50 words of your page).

2. **USE KEYWORDS NATURALLY.** Don't kill your content and make yourself look like a spammer to search engines by overloading your page with your keyword(s). You don't get SEO points for quantity but for quality. Plus, one of the main ways to improve your page rankings is when you...

3. **DELIVER QUALITY CONTENT.** The best way to improve your SEO is by providing content that readers want to share with others by linking to your pages. Some of the top results in search engines can be years old, because the content is so good that people keep coming back. So, incorporate your keywords in a smart way, but make sure it works organically with your content.
4. **UPDATE CONTENT REGULARLY.** If your site looks dead to visitors, then it'll appear that way to search engines too. So update your content regularly. This should be very easy for writers who have blogs. For writers who have sites, incorporate your blog into your site. This will make it easier for visitors to your blog to discover more about you on your site (through your site navigation tools).

If you interview someone on your blog, don't title your post with an interesting quotation. While that strategy may help get readers in the print world, it doesn't help with SEO at all.

5. **LINK BACK TO YOUR OWN CONTENT.** If I have a post on Blogging Tips for Writers, for instance, I'll link back to it if I have a Platform Building post, because the two complement each other. This also helps clicks on my blog, which helps SEO. The one caveat is that you don't go crazy with your linking and that you make sure your links are relevant. Otherwise, you'll kill your traffic, which is not good for your page rankings.
6. **LINK TO OTHERS YOU CONSIDER HELPFUL.** Back in 2000, I remember being ordered by my boss at the time (who didn't last too much longer afterward) to ignore any competitive or complementary websites—no matter how helpful their content—because they were our competitors. You can try basing your online strategy on these principles, but I'm nearly 100% confident you'll fail. It's helpful for other sites and your own to link to other great resources. I shine a light on others to help them out (if I find their content truly helpful) in the hopes that they'll do the same if ever they find my content truly helpful for their audience.
7. **GET SPECIFIC WITH YOUR HEADLINES.** If you interview someone on your blog, don't title your post with an interesting quotation. While that strategy may help get readers in the print world, it doesn't help with SEO at all. Instead, title your post as "Interview With (insert name here)." If you have a way to identify the person further, include that in the title too. For instance, when I interview poets on my Poetic Asides blog, I'll title those posts like this: Interview With Poet Erika Meitner. Erika's name is a keyword, but so are the terms *poet* and *interview*.

8. **USE IMAGES.** Many expert sources state that the use of images can improve SEO, because it shows search engines that the person creating the page is spending a little extra time and effort on the page than a common spammer. However, I'd caution anyone using images to make sure those images are somehow complementary to the content. Don't just throw up a lot of images that have no relevance to anything. At the same time...

9. **OPTIMIZE IMAGES THROUGH STRATEGIC LABELING.** Writers can do this by making sure the image file is labeled using your keyword(s) for the post. Using the Erika Meitner example above (which does include images), I would label the file "Erika Meitner headshot.jpg"—or whatever the image file type happens to be. Writers can also improve image SEO through the use of captions and ALT tagging. Of course, at the same time, writers should always ask themselves if it's worth going through all that trouble for each image or not. Each writer has to answer that question for him or herself.

10. **USE YOUR SOCIAL MEDIA PLATFORM TO SPREAD THE WORD.** Whenever you do something new on your site or blog, you should share that information on your other social media sites, such as Twitter, Facebook, LinkedIn, online forums, etc. This lets your social media connections know that something new is on your site/blog. If it's relevant and/or valuable, they'll let others know. And that's a great way to build your SEO.

Programmers and marketers could get even more involved in the dynamics of SEO optimization, but I think these tips will help most writers out immediately and effectively while still allowing plenty of time and energy for the actual work of writing.

BLOG DESIGN TIPS FOR WRITERS

Design is an important element to any blog's success. But how can you improve your blog's design if you're not a designer? I'm just an editor with an English Lit degree and no formal training in design. However, I've worked in media for more than a decade now and can share some very fundamental and easy tricks to improve the design of your blog.

Here are my seven blog design tips for writers:

1. **USE LISTS.** Whether they're numbered or bullet points, use lists when possible. Lists break up the text and make it easy for readers to follow what you're blogging.

2. **BOLD MAIN POINTS IN LISTS.** Again, this helps break up the text while also highlighting the important points of your post.

3. **USE HEADINGS.** If your posts are longer than 300 words and you don't use lists, then please break up the text by using basic headings.

4. **USE A READABLE FONT.** Avoid using fonts that are too large or too small. Avoid using cursive or weird fonts. Times New Roman or Arial works, but if you want to get "creative," use something similar to those.

5. **LEFT ALIGN.** English-speaking readers are trained to read left to right. If you want to make your blog easier to read, avoid centering or right aligning your text (unless you're purposefully calling out the text).

6. **USE SMALL PARAGRAPHS.** A good rule of thumb is to try and avoid paragraphs that drone on longer than five sentences. I usually try to keep paragraphs to around three sentences myself.

7. **ADD RELEVANT IMAGES.** Personally, I shy away from using too many images. My reason is that I only like to use them if they're relevant. However, images are very powerful on blogs, so please use them—just make sure they're relevant to your blog post.

If you're already doing everything on my list, keep it up! If you're not, then you might want to re-think your design strategy on your blog. Simply adding a header here and a list there can easily improve the design of a blog post.

GUEST POSTING TIPS FOR WRITERS

Recently, I've broken into guest posting as both a guest poster and as a host of guest posts (over at my Poetic Asides blog). So far, I'm pretty pleased with both sides of the guest posting process. As a writer, it gives me access to an engaged audience I may not usually reach. As a blogger, it provides me with fresh and valuable content I don't have to create. Guest blogging is a rare win-win scenario.

That said, writers could benefit from a few tips on the process of guest posting:

1. **PITCH GUEST POSTS LIKE ONE WOULD PITCH ARTICLES TO A MAGAZINE.** Include what your hook is for the post, what you plan to cover, and a little about who you are. Remember: Your post should somehow benefit the audience of the blog you'd like to guest post.

2. **OFFER PROMOTIONAL COPY OF BOOK (OR OTHER GIVEAWAYS) AS PART OF YOUR GUEST POST.** Having a random giveaway for people who comment on a blog post can help spur conversation and interest in your guest post, which is a great way to get the most mileage out of your guest appearance.

3. **CATER POSTS TO AUDIENCE.** As the editor of *Writer's Market* and *Poet's Market*, I have great range in the topics I can cover. However, if I'm writing a guest post for a fiction blog, I'll write about things of interest to a novelist—not a poet.

4. **MAKE IT PERSONAL, BUT PROVIDE NUGGET.** Guest posts are a great opportunity for you to really show your stuff to a new audience. You could write a very helpful and impersonal post, but that won't connect with readers the same way as if you write a very helpful and personal post that makes them want to learn more about you (and your blog, your book, your Twitter account, etc.). Speaking of which...

5. **SHARE LINKS TO YOUR WEBSITE, BLOG, AND SOCIAL NETWORKS.** After all, you need to make it easy for readers who enjoyed your guest post to learn more about you and your projects. Start the conversation in your guest post and keep it going on your own sites, and profiles. And related to that...

6. **PROMOTE YOUR GUEST POST THROUGH YOUR NORMAL CHANNELS ONCE THE POST GOES LIVE.** Your normal audience will want to know where you've been and what you've been doing. Plus, guest posts lend a little extra "street cred" to your projects. But don't stop there...

7. **CHECK FOR COMMENTS ON YOUR GUEST POST AND RESPOND IN A TIMELY MANNER.** Sometimes the comments are the most interesting part of a guest post (no offense). This is where readers can ask more in-depth or related questions, and it's also where you can show your expertise on the subject by being as helpful as possible. And guiding all seven of these tips is this one:

8. **PUT SOME EFFORT INTO YOUR GUEST POST.** Part of the benefit to guest posting is the opportunity to connect with a new audience. Make sure you bring your A-game, because you need to make a good impression if you want this exposure to actually help grow your audience. Don't stress yourself out, but put a little thought into what you submit.

ONE ADDITIONAL TIP: Have fun with it. Passion is what really drives the popularity of blogs. Share your passion and enthusiasm, and readers are sure to be impressed.

TWITTER CHEAT SHEET FOR WRITERS

by Robert Lee Brewer

With the publishing (and/or media) industry changing at the speed of light, so are the roles of writers (or content providers), editors (or content managers), agents (or content strategists), etc. One big change for writers (even in fiction, poetry, and other fields) is that they are expected to take an active role in building their own platforms via online and real world networking and exposure. One great tool for this online is Twitter.

It's easy (and free) enough to create a Twitter account, but how can writers take advantage of this social networking tool? What can they logically expect to gain from using it? What is a hashtag anyway? Well, hopefully, this cheat sheet will help.

First, let's look at some basic terminology:

- **TWEET** = Any message sent out to everyone on Twitter. Unless you direct message (DM) someone, everything on Twitter is a Tweet and viewable by anyone.
- **RT** = Retweet. Twitter created a RT-ing tool that makes for easy retweets, but the standard convention is to put an RT and cite the source before reposting something funny or useful that someone else has shared. For example, if I tweeted "Nouns are verbs waiting to happen," you could RT me this way: RT @robertleebrewer Nouns are verbs waiting to happen.
- **DM** = Direct message. These are private and only between people who DM each other.
- **# = HASHTAG.** These are used in front of a word (or set of letters) to allow people to easily communicate on a specific topic. For instance, I tweet poetry with other

poets on Twitter by using the hashtag #poettalk. Poets can click on the "poettalk" after the hashtag (no space) or they can search on the term "poettalk" in Twitter (right-hand toolbar).

- **#FF** = Follow Friday. This is a nice way to show support for other tweeters on Twitter. On Friday.

Second, here are 10 things you can do to optimize your use of Twitter:

1. **USE YOUR REAL NAME IF POSSIBLE.** Make it easy for people you know or meet to find you on Twitter.
2. **ADD A PROFILE PICTURE.** Preferably this will be a picture of you. People connect better with other people, not cartoons, book covers, and logos.
3. **LINK TO A WEBSITE.** Hopefully, you have a blog or website you can link to in your profile. If you don't have a website or blog, make one. Now. And then, link to it from your Twitter profile.
4. **WRITE YOUR BIO.** Make this memorable in some way. You don't have to be funny or cute, but more power to you if you can do this and still make it relevant to who you are.
5. **TWEET REGULARLY.** It doesn't matter if you have only 2 followers (and one is your mom); you still need to tweet daily (or nearly daily) for Twitter to be effective. And remember: If you don't have anything original to add, you can always RT something funny or useful from someone else.
6. **TWEET RELEVANT INFORMATION.** Don't be the person who tweets like this: "I am making a salad;" "I am eating a salad;" "That salad was good;" "I wonder what I'm going to eat next;" etc. These tweets are not interesting or relevant. However, if your salad eating experience rocked your world in a unique way, feel free to share: "Just ate the best salad ever. Now I'm ready to write a novel."
7. **LINK AND DON'T LINK.** It's good to link to other places and share things you're doing or that you've found elsewhere. At the same time, if all you do is link, people may think you're just trying to sell them stuff all the time.
8. **HAVE A PERSONALITY.** Be yourself. You don't have to be overly cute, funny, and smart. Just be yourself and remember that Twitter is all about connecting people. So be a person.
9. **FOLLOW THOSE WORTH FOLLOWING.** Just because you're being followed you don't have to return the follow. For instance, if some local restaurant starts following

me, I'm not going to follow them back, because they aren't relevant to me or to my audience.

10. **COMMUNICATE WITH OTHERS.** I once heard someone refer to Twitter as one big cocktail party, and it's true. Twitter is all about communication. If people talk to you or RT you, make sure you talk back and/or thank them. (*Here's a secret: People like to feel involved and acknowledged. I like it; you like it; and so does everyone else.*)

And, of course, if you're not already, please follow me on Twitter @robertleebrewer (http://twitter.com/robertleebrewer).

HERE ARE SOME EXTRA RESOURCES:

- **TwitterGrader.com** (http://twittergrader.com) This site allows you to enter your profile at any given time and find out how you're doing (according to them) in using Twitter effectively. Of course, the grade you receive is bound to not be perfect, but it is a good measuring stick.
- **What the Hashtag?** (http://wthashtag.com) This site allows you to search for hashtags, run reports on them, get transcripts between specific time periods, and more.
- **Hootsuite** (http://hootsuite.com) This is one of many tools that give the ability to Tweet and track your account without even going to Twitter. Many (maybe even most) people use these. There are others, such as TweetDeck, Seesmic, etc. Find one that you like and let it make your social networking life easier to manage.
- **bit.ly** (http://bit.ly) This is one of many URL shortening services out there, which is very helpful when tweeting URL links, since they can easily eat into your 140-character limit on Twitter. This particular one makes it easy for you to track clicks, though I'm sure that's fairly standard.

FACEBOOK VS. LINKEDIN:

Tips for Using Two Social Networking Sites

by Robert Lee Brewer

Many writers ask why start a LinkedIn account if they already have a Facebook, or conversely, why start a Facebook if they already have a LinkedIn? That's a fair question, but the answer is simple: These sites cater to different audiences, and both audiences are important to writers.

LinkedIn is the more professional site of the two. Many professionals use it to make meaningful connections with other like-minded professionals. HR departments use the site to find potential job candidates, and potential job candidates use their LinkedIn profiles as their resumes.

Facebook is a lot less professional, but smart writers treat this site as an important piece to their marketing puzzle. In fact, it's natural for writers to have more fun with their Facebook profiles, but they should still remember that editors, agents, writers, and other professionals may be interested in linking up on Facebook.

FACEBOOK TIPS FOR WRITERS

As of the writing of this article, Facebook is the most popular website on the Internet. Chances are good that you already have a profile on this social networking site. (If you don't have a Facebook profile, then you should create one now, since they're free.) However, you may or may not be optimizing your Facebook use.

Here are some tips for writers who are either new to Facebook or who aren't sure if they're using it the correct way:

1. **COMPLETE YOUR PROFILE.** You don't have to include EVERYTHING, but I'd suggest at least covering these bases: Current City, Birthday (you don't have to include the year), Bio, Education and Work, Contact Information.

2. **MAKE EVERYTHING PUBLIC.** As a writer, you should be using sites like Facebook and Twitter to connect with other writers, editors, agents, and your audience. So make it easy for them to find you and learn more about you by making everything available to the public. That said...

3. **THINK ABOUT YOUR AUDIENCE, FRIENDS, FAMILY, BOSS, FORMER TEACHERS, ETC., IN EVERYTHING YOU DO ON FACEBOOK.** Like it or not, you have to understand that if you are completely public on Facebook (and you should be if you want to connect with your audience) that you need to think about what you do on Facebook before you do it. Because Facebook isn't like Vegas: What happens on Facebook could easily go viral. But don't get paranoid; just use common sense.

Even though it's virtual, you want your profile to be as human as possible so that you can connect with others.

4. **INCLUDE A PROFILE PICTURE OF YOURSELF.** Don't use a picture of a cute animal, house pet, your children, an animated character, a famous celebrity, a model, etc. Just a nice pic of yourself. Even though it's virtual, you want your profile to be as human as possible so that you can connect with others.

5. **UPDATE YOUR STATUS REGULARLY.** You shouldn't update your status every hour, but once a day is a good pace. This just lets others on Facebook know that you are actively using the site.

6. **COMMUNICATE WITH FRIENDS ON FACEBOOK.** Don't stalk your friends; communicate with them. If you like a friend's status update, comment on it—or at the very least, click the Like button (to acknowledge that you liked their update). Speaking of friends...

7. **BE SELECTIVE ABOUT FRIENDS YOU ADD.** Don't blindly accept every friend request, because some may be bogus, and others may be from serial frienders (people who are trying to hit their friend limits). You want quality friends who share your interests or who you know from the "real world."

8. **BE SELECTIVE ABOUT ADDING APPS.** I'm not a huge fan of apps, because they are a distraction and time killer on Facebook. But there are some that could be useful. However, don't waste a month of your life playing Farmville or Mafia Wars; you'd be better off completing a crossword or sudoku puzzle.

9. **JOIN RELEVANT GROUPS.** For writers, there are an abundance of groups you could join, from professional organizations to those based around magazines, publishers and literary events. These are great places to connect with other writers. On that same note...

10. **FOLLOW RELEVANT FAN PAGES.** There are many who once had groups that migrated over to using fan pages, so there are fan pages for writing organizations, magazines, publishers, literary events, and more. (I even have a fan page on Facebook; just search for Robert Lee Brewer.)

BONUS TIP: If you have a blog, you can feed your Facebook profile automatically by using the Notes function. All you have to do is go to Notes, click the "Edit import settings" link, and enter your blog URL in the correct field. (Note: I had to enter my full URL, including the forward slash at the end, before the Notes function accepted my URL.)

OTHER SOCIAL NETWORKING SITES

This book contains articles on Twitter, Facebook, and LinkedIn, but there are many other powerful social networking sites on the Internet. Here's a list of some of them:

- **Bebo** (http://bebo.com)
- **Classmates** (http://classmates.com)
- **Digg** (http://digg.com)
- **Goodreads** (http://goodreads.com)
- **Google+** (http://plus.google.com)
- **Habbo** (http://habbo.com)
- **Hi5** (http://hi5.com)
- **MeetUp** (http://meetup.com)
- **MySpace** (http://myspace.com)
- **Orkut** (http://orkut.com)
- **Pinterest** (http://pinterest.com)
- **RedRoom** (http://redroom.com)
- **StumbleUpon** (http://stumbleupon.com)
- **Yelp** (http://yelp.com)
- **YouTube** (http://youtube.com)
- **Zorpia** (http://zorpia.com)

LINKEDIN TIPS FOR WRITERS

If Twitter and Facebook are the social networks where writers can just "hang out," then LinkedIn is the one where writers can "network" and make meaningful connections. Some writers may even be able to make connections with editors (like myself) and agents.

Many writers may not use LinkedIn anywhere near as much as they use Facebook or Twitter, but I believe in making yourself easy to find. Having a completed and optimized LinkedIn profile could lead to connections with editors, event coordinators, and other writers.

Here are a few tips I've picked up over time on how to use LinkedIn:

1. **USE YOUR OWN HEAD SHOT FOR YOUR AVATAR.** I recommend this on all social networks, because people want to make "real" connections on these sites. It's hard to take a picture of a family pet or cartoon character seriously.

2. **COMPLETE YOUR PROFILE.** There are many steps to completing your profile, including completing your resume and getting a few recommendations from connections, which leads to the next tip...

3. **GIVE THOUGHTFUL RECOMMENDATIONS TO RECEIVE THEM.** Give if you wish to receive. The recommendations you write will make you feel and look better, but the recommendations you receive in return will truly rock your solar system. Of course, to make and receive recommendations, you'll need to...

4. **SEARCH FOR CONNECTIONS YOU ALREADY HAVE.** These could be "real world" connections and/or connections from other social networks. The ones who are (or have been) most valuable to you are the best to make at first. Then...

5. **MAKE MEANINGFUL CONNECTIONS WITH OTHERS.** Search for other writers, editors, agents, or whoever you think might benefit your writing career. But don't ever spam. Look for meaningful connections and include a note about why you're contacting them through LinkedIn. Remember: Social networking is about *who* you know, not *how many*.

6. **ACCEPT INVITATIONS.** While I think it's a good rule of thumb to be selective about who you invite to connect with you, I also don't see any harm in accepting invitations with abandon—unless they are obviously not a good fit. My reasoning here is that you never know why someone is contacting you. Of course, you can always kill the connection later if it's not working.

7. **MAKE YOUR PROFILE EASY TO FIND.** If possible, put your name in your LinkedIn url. For instance, you can view my LinkedIn profile at http://www.linkedin.com/

in/robertleebrewer. Also, connect to your profile in blog posts and on other social networks.

8. **TAILOR YOUR PROFILE TO THE VISITOR.** It's easy to make me-centric profiles on social networks, because they're asking questions about you. However, remember that these descriptions are more beneficial to you if you're filling them out for the prospective connections you can make on social networking sites. Make it easy for them to figure out who you are, what you do, and how you might improve their lives. As such...

9. **UPDATE YOUR PROFILE REGULARLY WITH USEFUL CONTENT.** You can feed blog posts into your profile easily, and that will keep your profile active. You can also update your status by feeding in tweets or Facebook updates, but I refrain from doing that myself. My reasoning is that my updates are slightly different for each place. However, I can make meaningful tweets and LinkedIn status updates simultaneously by simply adding an #in hashtag to the tweet in question.

10. **JOIN (AND PARTICIPATE) IN GROUPS.** Heck, start your own group if you feel so inclined. Of course, participating in groups will require an extra level of engagement with the site, so this last tip is more of an extra credit assignment for those who want to unlock the full potential of LinkedIn.

THE INS AND OUTS OF PUBLISHING TRADITIONAL FORMS

by Shaindel Beers

It's no surprise to any seasoned writer that the majority of poetry published today is free verse, but what many don't realize is that most journals are open to publishing traditional forms. Too often, new poets send badly written form poems to journals and, upon rejection, assume that it is a bias against form that kept their work from being published. The truth is, if a poem is good enough, it will be published, whether it is free verse, a sonnet, villanelle, sestina, or traditional form of some other type. Writing in form takes the same persistence that writing in free verse does. One has to keep honing the poems, keep sending them out, and realize that rejection is part of the game because of the amount of competition in the marketplace.

In order to succeed at publishing form poems, one must take the same care in writing the poem as you would with any poem you intend to send out to publishers—make sure each word is the *right* word; get rid of any unnecessary words that are just taking up space. If you have an adjective plus a noun, maybe you're not using a specific enough noun. The same rule applies if you have an adverb plus a verb. Too many times writers get caught up in writing "the form" and forget that they must also be working to construct a great poem, not just a poem that fits the structure of the form they're going for.

The next major mistake new writers of form poetry make is that they automatically begin writing like they've been transported to a previous century when they write in form. There are rhymes that no one outside of the greeting card industry or the nineteenth century should attempt—love/above, true/you. Of course, there are exceptions to every rule; I'm sure someone under the right circumstances could make these rhymes work, but I've yet to see it. This tendency seems to occur because most of the form poems people have read are ones from their high school and college literature classes, usually nothing written within the last hundred years. To avoid this trap, read contemporary form poems. The anthology *Strong Measures: Contemporary American Poetry in Traditional Form*, edited by Philip Dacey and David Jauss is an excellent resource. Another valuable resource is Mark Jarman and David Mason's *Rebel Angels: 25 Poets of the New Formalism*. Any of the poets published in these anthologies are excellent examples of how to write form poetry that would be accepted for publication today.

One difference between contemporary form poems and form poems of the past is that modern poets use enjambment (the running over of a sentence from one line of poetry to the next) so that the rhyme scheme (or form in the case of non-rhyming forms) doesn't seem so obvious. Another is that modern form poems often rely on slant rhyme, which is rhyme in which there is a close but not exact correspondence of sounds. To see an example of both of these principles, here is an untitled sonnet by Marilyn Hacker from her volume, *Love, Death, and the Changing of the Seasons*:

> You did say, need me less and I'll want you more.
> I'm still shellshocked at needing anyone,
> used to being used to it on my own.
> It won't be me out on the tiles till four-
> thirty, while you're in bed, willing the door
> open with your need. You wanted her then,
> more. Because you need to, I woke alone
> in what's not yet our room, strewn, though, with your
> guitar, shoes, notebook, socks, trousers enjambed
> with mine. Half the world was sleeping it off
> in every other bed under my roof.
> I wish I had a roof over my bed
> to pull down on my head when I feel damned
> by wanting you so much it looks like need.

The rhyme scheme of this sonnet is *abbaabbacddccc*, making it more or less a Petrarchan sonnet. Hacker begins the poem with an end-stopped line, but from that point on, nearly all of the other lines rely upon enjambment. The fourth line is actually broken in the middle of a hyphenated word, "four-thirty." This keeps the poem, which does have some obvious rhymes—more, four, door, your—from sounding too sing-songy or simplistic. In the case of rhyming words that are in close proximity in the poem—the *bb* lines within the *abba* rhyme scheme, Hacker relies on slant rhyme—anyone/own, then/alone. While the reader can tell that these words don't quite rhyme, there is still a comfort found in the solidity of the *n* sounds at the ends of those words.

Hacker also plays with the rhyme scheme a bit by making this poem not an exact Petrarchan sonnet, in which the rhyme scheme of the sestet (the last six lines), would normally be: *cdcdcd* (a Sicilian sestet), *cddcdc*, *cdecde* (an Italian sestet), *cdeced*, or *cdcedc*. She might choose this unlikely rhyme scheme at the end of the poem as an act of rebellion against the beloved with whom the speaker seems to be having difficulty. Hacker also doesn't stick to a strict iambic pentameter in this sonnet, as there is an extra syllable in the first line. Too often, new writers of form poems sacrifice meaning for rhyme scheme or meter. An extra syllable or a missing syllable in a line here or there won't keep your form poem from being published; however, sacrificing meaning for rhyme or rhythm will.

Poets needn't be afraid to try their hand at formal poems. It's a rewarding practice, and venturing outside of one's comfort zone is always beneficial for a writer. By following the same principles you follow to write free verse poems—showing, not telling, and using concrete language—in addition to using flexibility of form to make your form poems seem new, you're sure to have some publication success with formal poems.

SHAINDEL BEERS' poetry, fiction, and creative nonfiction have appeared in numerous journals and anthologies. She is currently an instructor of English at Blue Mountain Community College in Pendleton, Oregon, in Eastern Oregon's high desert and serves as Poetry Editor of *Contrary*. *A Brief History of Time*, her first full-length poetry collection, was released by Salt Publishing, and Beers is currently working on her second poetry collection, *The Children's War*, for Salt Publishing.

AN APOLOGY FOR FREE VERSE:

or Let My Verse Go!

by Nate Pritts

I've never much liked the term "free verse" for three reasons—though I'll likely think of a few more, and maybe even a few reasons why I do like the term. But for starters:

1) It implies something *cheap* while the adjectiveless term VERSE sounds somehow stronger or purer (or costly?). Free verse thus seems particularly open to attacks disparaging anything labeled "free" as being "not worth it."
2) It is a label and labels are by their very nature static, an already existent condition, something that has stopped breathing and can be pinned down and labeled in a museum.
3) It sounds like a label cooked up by suits, by pie charts and textbooks. In short, it's not in any way descriptive nomenclature and is thus empty.

I'd like to invent a new term—like FREED VERSE, which imagines verse sprung loose and soaring on fire! Or, alternatively, I'd like to turn the term into an injunction, the kind you might find on a protestor's sign "FREE VERSE!" I'm imagining Poets everywhere picketing the Nonce Form factory where verse is being held captive without explanation!

Let my verse go!

Part of the problem stems from all the invectives aimed at free verse. We have prominent poets like Robert Frost famously declaring that "writing free verse is like playing tennis with the net down," and the respected, initialed, W.H. Auden equating the writing of free verse with an aversion to discipline, saying "But I can't understand—strictly from a hedonistic point of view—how one can enjoy writing with no form at all. If one plays a game, one needs rules, otherwise there is no fun. The wildest poem has to have a firm basis in common sense, and this, I think, is the advantage of formal verse."

This, I think, is the hole in the argument against free verse. The dangerous assumption underneath these attacks is that FORMAL verse is CONTROLLED while FREE verse is not only UNCONTROLED but also UNCONTROLLABLE. The truth is far more subtle, and far more empowering for the creative intellects that chose to write free verse. What Auden and Frost are assuming is that (to borrow their conceit) writing poetry is a game, and every game needs a set of objectives and parameters. But writers of free verse are not simply playing a game with no rules. We are—flagrantly! enthusiastically!—rejecting following *someone else's* rules! We are—unabashedly! belligerently!—playing by our own rules!

Many types of formal poetry are well-known and terrifying—the elegant and precise sonnet, the obsessive sestina, the smothery-sounding pantoum. They scare people off, partly, because in their awkward fusion of math and words, a writer might feel as if something outside of her own impulses may be guiding her utterance—sapping strength from her own volition and control as a writer. While this isn't entirely true, it foregrounds the fact that one of the qualities most prized by a writer is, in fact, control.

Formal poetry is constructed by a creative consciousness working in tandem with a scaffold of controlling mechanisms that are applied externally. Free verse is built as a record of a writer's attempts at control—their failures and successes at managing their own creative impulses.

Isn't it grand to have choices? Isn't it nice to have options?

I would assert that neither camp is right or wrong, neither is inherently more honorable or dishonorable. It's a matter of taste, preference, and (luckily) they are both always available to employ whenever! Isn't it grand to have choices? Isn't it nice to have options?

Also, I would submit that while end rhyme and syllable count and numerical repetition patterns make for interesting and generative parameters for a writer, isn't it also true that the writer of free verse is developing and deploying her own pressure-of-form in order to shape her utterance—to make a *different* urn, instead of shattering the well-wrought one?

Many writers end up creating their own forms and while these may not be as widely known or employed as the sonnet, they are still valid and interesting and wildly varied. Dancing to someone else's beat requires a rare precision and grace, and can force a dancer through contortions she might never have imagined on her own. But creating your own beat requires a scrappy and resilient sensibility, and the drive to see it through to its (hopefully) transcendent and transformative end.

Further, even when a writer doesn't create a form to follow there are myriad devices and strategies to be employed, sometimes intuitively and sometimes with patient consideration.

It's a long list of effects; grab any handy poetry textbook or toolbox and you'll find a hundred possibilities and then a hundred more.

So it might be helpful to end with a declaration, a consummation, a new manifesto (with caveats) of free verse:

1) Free verse joyfully and energetically relishes in the creative power of the writer to say whatever she wants to say, however she wants to say it! (so long as she remembers that without the pressure of craft and care and consideration, her words may be nothing more than an inarticulate cry...)
2) Free verse exists benignly alongside Formal verse, two siblings charged with facilitating expression. Write and let write! (though if either side attacks the other, or tries to assert that it is better than the other, an obfuscating cloud might descend making it impossible to write poems at all...)
3) Free verse exists for all of us—the yous and the mes, the grandly ambitious who seek to declaim their writings from the highest peak of immortality and those who seek to pass their writings quietly from row to row in class while the teacher's back is turned, and yes even the Audens and the Frosts!

Free verse is for all of us, for any of us—those with feelings, those with forms, those with formal feelings and those who are feeling formal. When we attempt to put our intellectual, emotional and physical experiences into words that take shape as lines and stanzas, we are engaging in a dizzying and humbling and human endeavor. We must not lose sight of the importance of writing verse, whether free or formal. And we must not let its importance intimidate us or keep us from doing it, often, however we please!

NATE PRITTS is the author of four full-length books of poems, most recently *Big Bright Sun* (BlazeVOX) and *The Wonderfull Yeare* (Cooper Dillon Books). His poetry and prose have been published widely, both online and in print, in journals such as *The Southern Review, Black Warrior Review, Columbia Poetry Review, DIAGRAM*, and *Gulf Coast* among many others. He is the founder and principal editor of *H_NGM_N* and H_NGM_N BKS. Learn more at www.natepritts.com.

WRITING EXPERIMENTAL POETRY

by Geof Huth

Poetry can be broken down into myriad categories, each of which might tell you something about the structure of the poem (the size and shape of a sonnet, for instance, is set exactly in place) but little about the actual content, the spark of life, the surprise of the poem itself. This gap between the definition of a kind of poem and an understanding of the poem is greatest, probably, when discussing experimental poetry, which covers such a huge area of writing that the term provides little guidance at all.

People write experimental poetry out of a desire to do something different, to avoid the mundane, and to eschew the overused practices of the past. That description doesn't quite demonstrate what an experimental poem might be, so here are a few concrete examples. A common type of poetry these days is visual poetry, which can be poetry whose visual presentation is essential to this meaning. Collage poetry that combines scraps of found text with visual images would be an example of this, because the poem just isn't the same thing if the words are extracted from the poem and presented in nice neat lines. Visual poetry also includes wordless textual designs made to give the reader a visual yet textual panorama to view and consider.

The poet Christian Bök has been working for years to write a poem that he can encode into the genome of a bacterium so that the body of that animal will manufacture a protein that will itself be another decodable poem. In this way, he hopes to preserve his poem in the only way that can outlast geological eras: within the genetic code of living things. The poet Vanessa Place, who is also a lawyer, has created poems that reuse legal briefs and depositions she creates as a part of her work as a lawyer. Sound poets create very musical poems, some with written scores, some created extemporaneously, made out of nothing but nonsense sounds. Still other experimental poems are experimental in milder ways, by combining dramatically different styles of writing in one poem or by writing poems in which each sentence of the poem seems unrelated to the other sentences in the piece. Because of these and many other examples, some people consider experimental poems not to be poems at all, questioning how poetic these literary forms are, just as experimental poets tend to question that value of a poem that does little more than tell a small piece of an individual poet's life.

Poetry, at its core, is a dramatic experiment with language. More than in any other form of writing, the poem is where the writer tries to create a transformative experience, one that changes the reader or the reader's perspective on the world, one that allows a little eureka to awaken within the person. Experimental poems do this sometimes very beautifully. The harshly fragmented writing of Leslie Scalapino's later years of life has a sweet aloofness to them, but they are made beautiful by their strange coldness and the way they are broken into bits of syntax that don't always cleave cleanly to one another. The late F.A. Nettebeck's great book *Bug Death* is filled with scraps of urban ugliness that don't cohere into a single narrative, but which hold together thematically. The result is a book that is deeply human and moving, and one that is also frightening and, finally, beautiful for all that it does. So an experimental poem is not necessarily anything ugly. It is still a little beast of words straining towards beauty. It is merely that the experimental poem allows for a broader definition of beauty.

And the reason for this is that the experimental poem is intent on the new. The experimental poem usually rejects the ways of the past (meter, rhyme, figurative language) and tries to find new paths towards poetic experience. Although the new is never perfectly possible, this striving for the new forces the experimental poet to question everything that might be written. The poet is required to find a new experience, find a new way to write a poem, a new form for the poem to take. So the poem might be a sequence of sounds spoken into the air or a found object encrusted with words. The experimental poem might require the reader to decrypt its message just to see what its actual words are. Digital poets even create poems where the experience of the poem changes with every viewing, based on what words the poem collects from the Internet and on how the reader interacts with the poem to make it move. Experimental poetry is about possibility and often combines separate kinds of experience (poetry and music, poetry and visual art) into one experience.

Experimental poets are an interesting band of poets, also, because they tend to be more connected to each other internationally than more traditional poets. One reason for this is that many of these poets have shared traditions of their own that bring them together—for instance, an interest in the Dadaists, the more experimental of the Modernists, or the concrete poets of the mid-twentieth century. This is why the vibrant band of visual poets in Turkey is well known across the world of visual poetry: this and the fact that they're talented visual poets. They have the same interests as the visual poets of the United States or Canada or Belgium.

It is difficult to define what an experimental poet is and what that poet does, because exactly what these might be changes with each experimental poet. These poets are scientists of sorts. They work hard to create forms of poetry that have not lived before, to breathe life into an idea that no one has ever had before, and to make a poetry of continuous surprise and enchantment. Sometimes, though, their ideas about enchantment are about disturbing our sometimes too-comfortable sense of what a poem is and should be.

The scope of **GEOF HUTH**'s poetic production includes handdrawn and computer-generated visual poems (some of them wordsless), one-word poems, and poems performed in a language that doesn't exist with melodies created on the spot. He writes almost daily on visual poetry and other poetry at his blog, dbqp: visualizing poetics. His latest book is *ntst: the collected pwoermds of geof huth*, a book of 775 one-word poems.

CRAFT OF POETRY

WHY PROSE POEMS?

by Nin Andrews

I always love it when other poets ask me, *Why prose poems?* It's the way they ask the question I particularly appreciate, as if prose poems are somehow defective. I am reminded of how Episcopalians spoke of Baptists when I was a girl. *He's not a Baptist?* my grandmother would ask of a boyfriend, her nose in the air. No wonder I used to shirk this definition of myself, pretend I wasn't *really* a prose poet. After all, I write verse poems and stories on occasion. But I'd have to admit to myself that I do have a deep love for the prose poem. I love both writing and reading them. So why shouldn't I accept the label? Who knows? Maybe it fits.

After years of being asked this question, I've decided I need to invent an answer. Never mind that I don't really have one, that I don't think there is a good definition of a prose poem out there, though Russell Edson's comparison of a prose poem to an airplane comes to mind. *A prose poem is a cast iron aeroplane that can actually fly, mainly because its pilot does not care if it does or not.* Like Edson I do believe that prose poems fly, at least as well as any other form of writing. The best prose poems give me a sensation of lifting off, defying gravity or the very weight of form, logic, and tradition. They move me beyond the familiar, the expected, and suggest the possibilities for bliss or insight, not easily defined. It's no wonder certain critics suspect and even despise prose poetry. After all, it's often the definition of the thing, rather than the thing itself, that inspires a critic.

But it's the very definition of things that makes me laugh, especially in this era. I sometimes feel as if I am living in a world that resembles a surreal prose poem, if not a science fiction novel. Language, as we use it, often seems stranger than Gertrude Stein's poetry. Instead of describing reality, it attempts to mask it. I am thinking of the names our government uses for military terminology. Names that are designed to hide death, bloodshed, accidents, and mass destruction associated with war. Names like special operations, smart bombs, friendly fire, collateral damage, peace-keeping missiles, and absolute duds. An absolute dud, for example, is a nuclear weapon that fails to explode. So one man's dud is another's absolute blessing. I am also thinking of how our culture treats death as if it were something we have a moral duty to put off forever. As a result, I have signed a piece of paper called a living will, which certifies I am willing to die. And it's hard not to think of all the millions of dollars made from products that promise eternal youth, extra-large penises, unblemished skin, infinite bliss and instant success. The printed words that are all around me in catalogs, newspapers, billboards and on the air provide an endless source of entertainment, wonder, and inspiration for prose poetry.

For me, the extreme pleasure of prose poetry is derived from the extent to which the form not only incorporates but also mocks and mimics other forms of writing. My favorite prose poems are like Houdinis or shape-shifters, slipping in and out of other forms. Amy Gerstler, for example, has written one prose poem that looks like a page of singles ads, another which looks like a page from a name-your-baby book, and another, which is a parody of a fan letter. Greg Boyd, Morton Marcus, and David Shumate have written prose poems which are parables, myths and fairy tales or perhaps anti-parables, anti-fairy tales and anti-myths, well-suited to our times.

> To me it makes no difference what someone calls a prose poem. ... I am simply happy they exist, in whatever shapes and forms and under whatever titles or labels they might occur.

In her new and stunning book, *Coronology*, Claire Bateman takes off on the form of a dictionary, and in her novel, *The Widening*, Carol Maldow writes what she calls a short novel in which each page, or chapter, is a prose poem. In my book, *The Book of Orgasms*, one poem is an interview with an orgasm, another an ad, and another a glossary of selected terms. In *Supernatural Overtones*, a book of prose poems by Ron Padgett and Clark Coolidge, it appears that Coolidge wrote language poems, and Padgett interpreted them as if they were old sci-fi movies. Then there are the darkly humorous and magical prose poems of Charles Simic, Russell Edson, Peter Johnson, and Maxine Chernoff. And I would be remiss if I left out the LANGUAGE poets who challenge the very nature and structure of meaning and language itself. Three of my favorite language poets are Gertrude Stein, Rosemary Waldrop, and Lyn Hejinian.

Some of the more traditional poets and writers who have written prose poems deny they have ever done so. They might call their prose poems something else—perhaps paragraphs or mini-stories with lyrical qualities. Other poets say they have simply found a prose poem, more or less, while looking at a billboard or reading the newspaper or listening to the radio or their neighbors. Others call prose poems flash fiction, and others ask, *What is the difference between flash fiction and prose poetry*? Still others spend their time trying to determine the exact line where prose poetry ends and flash fiction begins. To me it makes no difference what someone calls a prose poem. A poem in a paragraph, a paragraph in a poem. A story like a poem, a poem like a story. Nor does it matter where the poems come from, the gutter or the sky. I am simply happy they exist, in whatever shapes and forms, under whatever titles or labels they might occur.

NIN ANDREWS is the author of several poetry collections, including *The Book of Orgasms, Spontaneous Breasts, Why They Grow Wings, Midlife Crisis With Dick and Jane, Sleeping With Houdini,* and *Dear Professor, Do You Live in a Vacuum?* She also edited *Someone Wants to Steal My Name*, a book of translations of the French poet, Henri Michaux.

POETIC FORMS

by Robert Lee Brewer

Not every poet likes the idea of writing in poetic forms, but for many poets—including myself—poetic forms are a sort of fun challenge. Whether playing with a sestina or working haiku, I find that attempting poetic forms often forces me into corners that make me think differently than if I'm just writing in free verse.

If you don't have any—or much—experience with poetic forms, I encourage you to peruse the following list and try them. If you are very familiar with poetic forms, I hope the following list can act as a reference for when you're unsure of the rhyme scheme for a triolet versus a kyrielle—or shadorma.

Have fun poeming!

Abstract poetry

Apparently, *abstract* was a term used by Dame Edith Sitwell to describe poems in her book *Facade*. Abstract (or sound) poetry is more about how sounds, rhythms, and textures evoke emotions than about the actual meanings of words.

Acrostic poetry

Acrostic poetry is very easy and fun. The most basic form spells words out on the left-hand side of the page using the first letter of each line. For instance,

I like to write
Acrostic poems
Mostly because
Reading them
Out loud is
Bound to be fun.

If you notice, the first letter of every line makes the simple sentence, "I am Rob." It's very simple, and you can make it as difficult as you want—where the fun part begins.

The brave at heart can even try double acrostics—that is, spelling things out using the first and last letter of each line.

Alphabet poetry

There are many different ways to write an alphabet poem. You can write a poem in which the first letter of each word is a different letter of the alphabet. A tactic for writing this poem is to write out the alphabet ahead of time so that you can pay attention to which letters have been used and which letters are still up for grabs. Of course, you can also do this consecutively through the alphabet.

Another method for alphabet poems is to go through the alphabet using the first letter of the first word for each line.

Poets can always flip the alphabet, too. That is, instead of going A to Z, write alphabet poems from Z to A. It's all about having fun and stretching your mind. Kind of like school.

Anagrammatic Poetry

In Christian Bok's comments about his poem "Vowels" in *The Best American Poetry 2007*, he writes, "'Vowels' is an anagrammatic text, permuting the fixed array of letters found only in the title. 'Vowels' appears in my book *Eunoia*, a lipogrammatic suite of stories, in which each vowel appears by itself in its own chapter." So an anagrammatic poem uses only the letters used in the title.

For instance, if I titled a poem "Spread," it could use only words like red, dresses, drape, spare, pear, pressed, etc.

The real challenge with this kind of poem is first picking a word that has at least a couple vowels and a good mix of consonants. Then, brainstorm all the words you can think of using only those letters (as many times as you wish, of course).

The Blitz Poem

The blitz poem was created by Robert Keim and is a 50-line poem of short phrases and images. Here are the rules:

- Line 1 should be one short phrase or image (like "build a boat")
- Line 2 should be another short phrase or image using the same first word as the first word in Line 1 (something like "build a house")
- Lines 3 and 4 should be short phrases or images using the last word of Line 2 as their first words (so Line 3 might be "house for sale" and Line 4 might be "house for rent")

- Lines 5 and 6 should be short phrases or images using the last word of Line 4 as their first words, and so on until you've made it through 48 lines
- Line 49 should be the last word of Line 48
- Line 50 should be the last word of Line 47
- The title of the poem should be three words long and follow this format: (first word of Line 3) (preposition or conjunction) (first word of line 47)
- There should be no punctuation

There are a lot of rules, but it's a pretty simple and fun poem to write once you get the hang of it.

The Bop

The Bop is a poetic form that was developed by poet Afaa Michael Weaver at a Cave Canem summer retreat. Here are the basic rules:

- 3 stanzas
- Each stanza is followed by a refrain
- First stanza is 6 lines long and presents a problem
- Second stanza is 8 lines long and explores or expands the problem
- Third stanza is 6 lines long and either presents a solution or documents the failed attempt to resolve the problem

Cascade Poem

The cascade poem was a form invented by Udit Bhatia. For the cascade poem, a poet takes each line from the first stanza of a poem and makes those the final lines of each stanza afterward. Beyond that, there are no additional rules for rhyming, meter, etc.

So to help this make sense, here's what a cascade poem with a tercet would look like:

A
B
C

a
b
A

c
d
B

e
f
C

A quatrain cascade would look so:

A
B
C
D

a
b
c
A

d
e
f
B

g
h
i
C

j
k
l
D

And, of course, you can make this even more involved if you want.

Concrete poetry

Concrete poetry is one of the more experimental poetic forms available to poets. Concrete poems use space and sound to communicate the meanings of the words. Words can cover other words; and the poem has trouble standing without the structure. Concrete poetry is more visual than other poetic forms.

Of course, concrete poetry has plenty of detractors because of the weight structure has on the words, but as much thought goes into concrete poetry as any other form.

Elegy

An elegy is a song of sorrow or mourning—often for someone who has died. However, poets being an especially creative and contrary group have also written elegies for the ends of things, whether a life, a love affair, a great era, a football season, etc.

While there are such things as elegiac couplets and elegiac stanzas, form does not rule an elegy; content *is* king (or queen) when writing elegies.

Epitaphs

The epitaph is a note meant to appear on a tombstone. From the Greek, epitaph means "upon a tomb." Since it has to fit on a tombstone, this note is usually brief and often rhymes. Some epitaphs are funny; most are serious. Most try to get the reader thinking about the subject of the tombstone.

The Fib

Fibonacci poetry was founded by Gregory K. Pincus as a 6-line poem that follows the Fibonacci sequence for syllable count per line.

For the 6-line poem that means:

- 1 syllable for first line
- 1 syllable for second line
- 2 syllables for third
- 3 syllables for fourth
- 5 syllables for fifth
- 8 syllables for sixth

There are variations where the Fibonacci expands even further with each line, but to understand how to accomplish this, you need to understand the Fibonacci math sequence of starting with 0 and 1 and then adding the last two numbers together to add to infinity.

0+1=1
1+1=2
1+2=3
2+3=5
3+5=8
5+8=13
8+13=21
13+21=34
and so on and so forth...

Anyway, those lines can easily get more and more unwieldy the more you let them expand. So, there's another variation that has taken flight in making Fibonacci poems that ascend and descend in syllables. For poets who also like mathematics, this is definitely an interesting form to get your mind working.

Found Poems

Found poetry is all about taking words not originally meant to be a poem (as they originally appeared) and turning those words into a poem anyway. You can use newspaper articles, bits of conversation, instructions, recipes, letters, e-mails, direct mail and even spam e-mail.

With found poetry, you do not alter the original words, but you can make line breaks and cut out excess before and/or after the poem you've "found." The power of found poetry is how words not intended as poetry can take on new and profound meanings as found poems.

Ghazal

The ghazal (pronounced "guzzle") is a Persian poetic form. The original form was very simple: five to 15 couplets using the same rhyme with the poet's name in the final couplet. The main themes were usually love or drinking wine.

Contemporary ghazals have abandoned the rhymes and insertion of the poet's name in the final couplet. In fact, even the themes of love and drinking wine are no longer mandatory—as the poem now just needs the couplets which are complete thoughts on their own but also all work together to explore a common theme (whatever that might be).

If you wish to stay traditional though, here's the rhyme scheme you would follow:

a
a

b
a

c
a
and so on to the final stanza (depending upon how many you include).

Many traditional ghazals will also incorporate a refrain at the end of each couplet that could be one word or a phrase.

Haiku

Haiku is descended from the Japanese *renga* form, which was often a collaborative poem comprised of many short stanzas. The opening stanza of the renga was called *hokku.* Eventually, haiku evolved from the leftover and most interesting hokku that were not used in renga.

Most haiku deal with natural topics. They avoid metaphor and simile. While most poets agree that haiku have three short lines, there is some disagreement on how long those lines are. For instance, some traditional haiku poets insist on 17 syllables in lines of 5/7/5. Other contemporary haiku poets feel that the first and third lines can be any length as long as they're shorter than the middle line.

Haiku do not have to include complete sentences or thoughts. They do not have titles. The best haiku contain some shift in the final line.

Hay(na)ku

Hay(na)ku is a very simple poetic form created in 2003 by poet Eileen Tabios. Hay(na)ku is a 3-line poem with one word in the first line, two words in the second, and three in the third. There are no restrictions beyond this.

There are already some variations of this new poetic form. For instance, a reverse hay(na)ku has lines of three, two, and one word(s) for lines one, two, and three respectively. Also, multiple hay(na)ku can be chained together to form longer poems.

Insult poetry

There are no hard and fast rules to the insult poem, but it's usually done in a joking (all in good fun) fashion as opposed to seriously trying to annoy anyone. Many insult poems also have a repetitive form or recurring method of delivering the insults. The insult poem is a good way to show just how clever you are (or think you are). But beware writing them! Once you attack someone (even in jest), you are suddenly fair game to receive an insult poem in retaliation.

Kyrielle

The kyrielle is a French four-line stanza form—with 8 syllables per line—that has a refrain in the fourth line. Often, there is a rhyme scheme in the poem consisting of the following possibilities:

- aabb
- abab
- aaab
- abcb

The poem can be as long as you wish and as short as two stanzas (otherwise, the refrain is not really a refrain, is it?), and, as with many French forms, it is very nice for stretching your poetic muscles.

Limericks

The origin of the limerick is shrouded in some mystery, but most sources seem to point to the early 18th century—one theory being that soldiers returning from France to the Irish town of Limerick started the form, the other theory pointing to the 1719 publication of *Mother Goose Melodies for Children*. Either way, Edward Lear popularized the form in the mid-19th century.

Basically, the limerick is a five-line poem consisting of a tercet split by a couplet. That is, lines 1, 2, and 5 are a bit longer and rhyme, while the shorter lines of 3 and 4 rhyme. After studying many effective limericks, there is not a precise syllable count per line, but the norm is about 8-10 syllables in the longer lines and around 6 syllables in the shorter lines.

List Poems

A list poem (also known as a catalog poem) is a poem that lists things, whether names, places, actions, thoughts, images, etc. Even a grocery list could turn into a poem with this form.

Lune

The lune is also known as the American Haiku. It was first created by the poet Robert Kelly and was a result of Kelly's frustration with English haiku. After much experimentation, he settled on a 13-syllable, self-contained poem that has 5 syllables in the first line, 3 syllables in the second line and 5 syllables in the final line.

Unlike haiku, there are no other rules. No need for a cutting word. Rhymes are fine; subject matter is open. While there are fewer syllables to use, this form has a little more freedom.

There is also a variant lune created by the poet Jack Collom. His form is also a self-contained tercet, but it's word-based (not syllable-based) and has the structure of 3 words in the first line, 5 words in the second line and 3 words in the final line.

Monotetra

The monotetra is a poetic form developed by Michael Walker. Here are the basic rules:

- Comprised of quatrains (four-line stanzas) in tetrameter (four metrical feet) for a total of 8 syllables per line
- Each quatrain consists of mono-rhymed lines (so each line in the first stanza has the same type of rhyme, as does each line in the second stanza, etc.)
- The final line of each stanza repeats the same four syllables
- This poem can be as short as one quatrain and as long as a poet wishes

Personally, I like the rhyme scheme and the repetitive final line of each stanza. I also appreciate the flexibility of this form in terms of how long or short the poem can be.

Occasional Poems

There are no specific guidelines for occasional poems except that they mark a specific occasion. The poems can be long or short, serious or humorous, good or bad—just as long as they mark the occasion. Good occasions for poems include birthdays, weddings and holidays.

Odes

The ode is a poetic form formed for flattery. There are three types of odes: the Horation; the Pindaric; and the Irregular.

The Horation ode (named for the Latin poet, Horace) contains one stanza pattern that repeats throughout the poem—usually 2 or 4 lines in length.

The Pindaric ode (named for the Greek poet, Pindar) is made up of a pattern of three stanzas called triads. This type of ode can be composed of several triads, but the first (the strophe) and the second (antistrophe) should be identical metrically with the third (epode) wandering off on its own metrical path.

The irregular ode (named for no one in particular) does away with formalities and focuses on the praising aspect of the ode.

Palindrome poetry

The palindrome seems like a simple enough form—until you actually try to write a good one. The rules are simple enough:

1. You must use the same words in the first half of the poem as the second half, but
2. Reverse the order for the second half, and
3. Use a word in the middle as a bridge from the first half to the second half of the poem.

At first, the simplicity of the rules made me feel like this would be easy enough to do, but I ran into problems almost immediately. For instance, you can't start the poem with the word "the" unless you plan to end the poem on the word "the." And just because something makes sense in the first half doesn't guarantee it'll pass the same test on the way back.

Pantoum

The **pantoum** is a poetic form originating in Malay where poets write quatrains (4-line stanzas) with an *abab* rhyme scheme and repeat lines 2 and 4 in the previous stanza as lines 1 and 3 in the next stanza.

Poets differ on how to treat the final quatrain: Some poets repeat lines 1 and 3 of the original quatrain as lines 2 and 4 in the final quatrain; other poets invert lines 1 and 3 so that the beginning line of the poem is also the final line of the poem.

Also, the pantoum can be as long or as short as you wish it to be, though mathematically it does require at least 4 lines.

Paradelle

The paradelle is a poetic form that Billy Collins originally introduced as "one of the more demanding French forms," though eventually Collins fessed up that he created it as a joke.

However, Collins was not kidding about the demanding rules of the paradelle. Here they are:

- The paradelle is a 4-stanza poem.
- Each stanza consists of 6 lines.

- For the first 3 stanzas, the 1st and 2nd lines should be the same; the 3rd and 4th lines should also be the same; and the 5th and 6th lines should be composed of all the words from the 1st and 3rd lines and only the words from the 1st and 3rd lines.
- The final stanza should be composed of all the words in the 5th and 6th lines of the first three stanzas and only the words from the 5th and 6th lines of the first three stanzas.

Parody Poems

A parody poem is one that pokes fun at another poem or poet. For instance, I recently read a parody of "We Real Cool," by Gwendolyn Brooks, in an online version of *Coe Review* called "We Real White." The best parodies are those that are easily recognizable—and funny, of course.

Rondeau

The rondeau is a form that has a refrain and rhymes—two elements I love in many French poems. The traditional rondeau is a poem consisting of 3 stanzas, 13 original lines, and 2 refrains (of the first line of the poem) with 8 to 10 syllables per line and an A/B rhyme scheme.

The skeleton of the traditional rondeau looks like this:

A(R)
A
B
B
A

A
A
B
A(R)

A
A
B
B
A
A(R)

There are variations of the rondeau, including the rondeau redouble, rondel, rondel double, rondelet, roundel, and roundelay. Of course, poets tend to break the rules on each of these as well, which is what poets like to do.

Sestina

The sestina is one of my favorite forms. You pick 6 words, rotate them as the end words in 6 stanzas and then include 2 of the end words per line in your final stanza.

Let's pick 6 random words: bears, carving, dynamite, hunters, mothers, blessing. Here's how the end words would go:

Stanza 1

Line 1-bears (A)
Line 2-carving (B)
Line 3-dynamite (C)
Line 4-hunters (D)
Line 5-mothers (E)
Line 6-blessing (F)

Stanza 2

Line 7-blessing (F)
Line 8-bears (A)
Line 9-mothers (E)
Line 10-carving (B)
Line 11-hunters (D)
Line 12-dynamite (C)

Stanza 3

Line 13-dynamite (C)
Line 14-blessing (F)
Line 15-hunters (D)
Line 16-bears (A)
Line 17-carving (B)
Line 18-mothers (E)

Stanza 4

Line 19-mothers (E)
Line 20-dynamite (C)
Line 21-carving (B)
Line 22-blessing (F)
Line 23-bears (A)
Line 24-hunters (D)

Stanza 5

Line 25-hunters (D)

Line 26-mothers (E)
Line 27-bears (A)
Line 28-dynamite (C)
Line 29-blessing (F)
Line 30-carving (B)

Stanza 6

Line 31-carving (B)
Line 32-hunters (D)
Line 33-blessing (F)
Line 34-mothers (E)
Line 35-dynamite (C)
Line 36-bears (A)

Stanza 7

Line 37-bears (A), carving (B)
Line 38-dynamite (C), hunters (D)
Line 39-mothers (E), blessing (F)

While many poets try to write sestinas in iambic pentameter, that is not a requirement. Also, when choosing your six end words, it does help to choose words that can be altered if needed to help keep the flow of the poem going.

Sevenling

The sevenling was created by Roddy Lumsden. Here are the rules:

- The sevenling is a 7-line poem (clever, huh?) split into three stanzas.
- The first three lines should contain an element of three. It could be three connected or contrasting statements, a list of three details or names, or something else along these lines. The three things can take up all three lines or be contained anywhere within the stanza.
- The second three lines should also contain an element of three. Same deal as the first stanza, but the two stanzas do not need to relate to each other directly.
- The final line/stanza should act as either narrative summary, punchline, or unusual juxtaposition.
- Titles are not required. But when titles are present, they should be titled Sevenling followed by the first few words in parentheses.
- Tone should be mysterious, offbeat or disturbing.
- Poem should have ambience which invites guesswork from the reader.

Shadorma

Shadorma is a Spanish 6-line syllabic poem of 3/5/3/3/7/5 syllable lines respectively.

Skeltonic poetry

Skeltonic verse is named after the poet John Skelton (1460-1529), who wrote short rhyming lines that just sort of go on from one rhyme to the next for however long a poet wishes to take it. Most skeltonic poems average less than six words a line, but keeping the short rhymes moving down the page is the real key to this form.

Sonnet

The sonnet is a 14-line poem that usually rhymes and is often written in iambic pentameter, though not always. Over time, this Italian poem has been pushed to its limits and some contemporary sonnets abandon many of the general guidelines.

The two most famous forms of the sonnet are the *Shakespearean Sonnet* (named after William Shakespeare) and the *Petrarcan Sonnet* (named after Francesco Petrarca).

The rhyme scheme for a Shakespearean Sonnet is:

a
b
a
b

c
d
c
d

e
f
e
f

g
g

The rhyme scheme for the Petrarcan Sonnet is a little more complicated. The first eight lines (or octave) are always rhymed abbaabba. But the final six lines (or sestet) can be rhymed any number of ways: cdcdcd, cdedce, ccdccd, cdecde, or cddcee. Of course, this offers a little more flexibility near the end of the poem.

But sonnets don't necessarily need to be Shakespearean or Petrarcan to be considered sonnets. In fact, there are any number of other sonnet varieties.

A few extra notes about the sonnet:

- A crown of sonnets is made by seven sonnets. The last line of each sonnet must be used as the first line of the next until the seventh sonnet. The last line of that seventh sonnet must be the first line of the first sonnet.
- A sonnet redouble is a sequence of 15 sonnets. Each line from the first sonnet is used (in order) as the the last line of the following 14 sonnets.

Tanka

If a haiku is usually (mistakenly) thought of as a 3-line, 5-7-5 syllable poem, then the tanka would be a 5-line, 5-7-5-7-7 syllable poem. However, as with haiku, it's better to think of a tanka as a 5-line poem with 3 short lines (lines 2, 4, 5) and 2 very short lines (lines 1 and 3).

While imagery is still important in tanka, the form is a little more conversational than haiku at times. It also allows for the use of poetic devices such as metaphor and personification (2 big haiku no-no's).

Like haiku, tanka is a Japanese poetic form.

Triolet

The triolet (TREE-o-LAY) has 13th-century French roots linked to the rondeau or "round" poem. Like other French forms, the triolet is great for repetition, because the first line of the poem is used three times and the second line is used twice. If you do the math on this 8-line poem, you'll realize there are only three other lines to write: two of those lines rhyme with the first line, the other rhymes with the second line.

A diagram of the triolet would look like this:

A (first line)
B (second line)
a (rhymes with first line)
A (repeat first line)
a (rhymes with first line)
b (rhymes with second line)
A (repeat first line)
B (repeat second line)

Villanelle

The villanelle, like the other French forms, does have many of the same properties: plenty of rhyme and repetition. This French form was actually adapted from Italian folk songs (villanella) about rural life. One of the more famous contemporary villanelles is "Do Not Go Gentle Into That Good Night," by Dylan Thomas.

The villanelle consists of five tercets and a quatrain with line lengths of 8-10 syllables. The first and third lines of the first stanza become refrains that repeat throughout the poem. It looks like this:

A(1)
b
A(2)

a
b
A(1)

a
b
A(2)

a
b
A(1)

a
b
A(2)

a
b
A(1)
A(2)

CRAFT OF POETRY

FRESHEN YOUR POETRY BY REVISING STALE LANGUAGE

by Nancy Susanna Breen

During a recent stint of poetry judging, I decided to keep a running list of the words and phrases that turned up again and again in entries. What I discovered is that too many poets, especially new or developing poets, depend on clichés in their writing. Others simply don't stretch enough for originality when crafting their lines. Instead, they invoke wording and images that have become exhausted with use.

You can freshen your poetry and increase your individuality by targeting stale language during the revising process. Like mold on bread, instances of exhausted images and overused words act as alerts once you know what you're looking for.

CLICHÉS

A cliché is any trite phrase or expression; that is, a phrase or expression that has been run into the ground. Avoid clichés like the plague. (See how easy it is to work clichés into your writing? There are two in those two sentences.) Because of their familiarity, clichés are comfortable and seemingly add a conversational touch to a line of poetry. They seem to guarantee clarity as well, because readers know what the clichés mean.

However, when poets turn to the same tired phrases and overused words, their poems all sound alike. Cliché-ridden lines have a cookie cutter effect. They result in poems that seem prefabricated, assembled of standard parts.

Here's a brief list of clichés that turned up more than three times in the batch of poems I was judging:

lips are/were sealed
blood, sweat, and tears

into thin air
heart and soul
thick and thin
bitter end
on a silver platter
life is precious
time stands still
as far as the eye can see
tore like a knife
sands in an hourglass
sun, moon, and stars

If you need help recognizing clichés, the Internet offers some valuable sites. For example, ClicheList.net provides an alphabetized list of clichés, each example linked to an explanation of its meaning. Cliché Finder (www.westegg.com/cliche) allows you to search its 3,000-plus cliché bank by keyword; "cat" turned up over 50 examples, such as "cat has your tongue," "cat's meow," and "raining cats and dogs." There's also a cliché generator that provides 10 random clichés at a time. Make a practice of reading through those 10 random clichés daily for a month and you'll find it much easier to spot clichés in your poems.

OH, NO! NOT ANOTHER [BLANK] POEM

Clichés include dull, stereotypical ideas and situations. Consequently, entire poems can be clichés. Gather a large enough sample of poems, such as entries in a poetry contest or submissions to a magazine, and you'll probably see several examples of the same clichéd poem, sometimes with surprisingly little variation. Below are types of poems poets can't seem to resist writing. Exercise heightened originality if attempting these poems.

Butterflies

I have nothing against butterflies, and I appreciate how symbolic they are. However, they turn up constantly as poem subjects, accompanied by all the typical verbs: flit, flutter, and so on. Describing or referring to butterflies emerging from cocoons is also popular. Understand how commonplace butterflies are before writing an entire poem about them if you really want to set your work apart. For that matter, restrain yourself from using them as images or symbols without plenty of careful thought.

Sea and sand

Poets simply must write about the ocean. (I certainly have.) They stroll through the tide, meditate on the coming and going of the tide, study what the tide leaves behind, and compare life to the movements of the tide.

There's nothing wrong with writing about strolling on the beach, watching the waves, or examining the shells and driftwood at low tide. However, because they're so popular with poets, the ocean and beach are hard to write about in an original way, especially if the physical descriptions basically make up the poem.

Poets consistently choose the same words to describe the sea and shore, and the ring of familiarity isn't a virtue. Even a touching account of a dying person visiting the seaside for the last time or a broken-hearted lover examining a ruined relationship fades into sameness when the speakers' actions are similar and they seem to be viewing the scene through the same pair of eyes.

Seasonal

The most uninspired, and uninspiring, poetry I see usually focuses on one of the seasons or on all four at once. This is primarily because poets pull out all the standard images, as if putting up those colored cardboard cutouts in a classroom: colored leaves and pumpkins for fall, snowflakes for winter, buds and robins for spring, a big, smiling sun for summer. Such images are beloved and iconic; and because of this, you need to move past them when writing about a season. Read enough poems that cite "the golden leaves drift lazily to ground" and you'll wince at the mere thought of autumn.

I'm going to go a step farther and suggest that freshening the seasonal imagery you use isn't enough—you should avoid the seasons as the sole subjects of poems. Instead, use the season as a background. That way your poem develops into sometime more than a laundry list of the same old spring showers, hot July noons, and shimmering blankets of snow on a rolling landscape.

Love

It's a shame so many love poems come across as time-creased valentines. I've rarely read a clichéd love poem that made me doubt the sincerity of the writer's feelings. When such verse seems cribbed from the most mundane greeting card, though, especially when expressed in *oo-aa* rhymes, the poem appears mass-produced rather than the true expression of an individual. Poems about unrequited love or rejection are especially painful, not because of the sadness involved but because a kind of injured, righteous indignation overrides the poet's artistic common sense. And, of course, the same images are evoked and the same flowery language applied as though squeezed out of a tube of frosting.

When writing a poem that addresses a romantic partner or someone who has cast you aside, consider sending it only to the intended recipient or keeping it strictly to yourself. Otherwise, be sure you can treat the work as a piece of literary art, not a love letter. Even then, make it your own. Don't resort to gooey valentine verses or resentful poison notes.

A subset of the love poem is the "love is" poem. If you insist on defining love, have something new to say. "Love is" poems range from a list of clichéd comparisons, both positive and negative (a delicate rose, a knife to the heart, a blanket against the cold) to a series of unsurprising adjectives (kind, understanding, forgiving, harsh, demoralizing, etc.). Throw out the cookie cutter images and the threadbare language or don't bother at all, at least not if you're writing for a general readership. The same goes for "my love is like" poems.

OTHER CLICHÉ PITFALLS

Hearts

In poetry, hearts aren't mere organs that pump blood. Poets have them doing more tricks than a trained poodle in a one-ring circus: pounding, shrieking, weeping, dancing, swelling, bleeding, exploding, freezing, or stopping dead (without killing the poet). Poets assist their hearts in hyperactivity by opening them, shutting them, writing on them, exploring them, hiding things in them, and nursing them. Other people do things to poets' hearts as well: stomp on them, warm them, break them, steal them, stab them, fill them with joy or sadness, play with them, heal them, and reawaken them when they're dead (figuratively speaking).

"Heart" is one of those words you have to handle carefully, if at all. Despite its versatility, in most cases you can leave "heart" out of your poem. It's a cliché that can do more harm than good; and the more animated the heart is in your poem, the more danger of giving the reader a mental image that resembles a Wile E. Coyote cartoon.

Obviously, if you're writing about someone's cardiac event, *heart* is a necessary clinical term, not a cliché. Where emotions are concerned, though, don't go breaking, teasing, or exposing anyone's heart in your poems.

Despair

It's astonishing how many poets "plunge into the abyss" or "descend into oblivion" at some point in their poetry. Sometimes they hurtle their entire beings into the black pit of nothingness; in other instances, their minds or hearts take the dive of despair.

Sadly, it's hard for readers to take you seriously when you're melodramatic. Write with even more finesse when addressing such intense emotional conditions as grief and depression. Imagine an over-the-top actor in 19th-century theater wailing to the balcony, writhing on the stage, or whirling his cape around him like a shroud. This shouldn't be the effect you want your lines to convey.

Read the confessional poetry of Sylvia Plath, Robert Lowell, Anne Sexton, John Berryman, and others to learn how to calibrate your language so you express the most emotion with the least hyperbole.

Tears

Too many poets turn the human face into a Niagara Falls of tears. These tears run, cascade, course, drip, trickle, and flow. Or poets turn to clichés to describe weeping, such as "cried like a baby," "cried a river," or "cried her eyes out."

When you write skillfully, showing rather than telling, you can convey sorrow without using tears at all. Uncontrolled waterworks are just overkill; they don't make the scene more convincing. Think of a movie where an actor cries. It's usually an extreme situation when a character dissolves into heaving sobs; otherwise, the viewers don't buy it. Often a character struggling *not* to cry is more affecting than drenched cheeks. Remember that the next time you're inclined to flood someone's face with tears in your poem.

Colors

Although simply putting "green," "blue," or "red" into your descriptions is pretty mundane, it's almost worse to employ clichéd colors. If you notice "ruby red," "golden yellow," "baby pink," "sky blue," and similar color clichés in your poems, revise them to more specific colors or create original similes—in other words, don't just substitute "red as a ruby" or "blue as a summer sky." Come up with something vivid and new. If your color phrase turns up in the lyrics of pop songs or standards, it's too worn-out to use in your poetry. For inspiration, review some paint company Internet sites for the creative ways they name various colors, then work on original examples of your own.

While I'm discussing colors, I want to mention red, white, and blue. This combination is a favorite of poets writing about the military, patriotism, or the United States in general. Unfortunately, those colors used together have become cliché, detracting from verse that may otherwise make valid statements. There's plenty to say about a soldier's sacrifice, love of one's country, or the esteem for U.S. liberty and democracy without tying everything up in red, white, and blue bunting. Make your poem stirring enough and readers will see the stars and stripes without a specific reference.

A WORD ABOUT DEAD METAPHORS

When people repeat a metaphor so often its original imagery gives way to a new, literal meaning, the result is a *dead metaphor.* I once heard a talk at the Geraldine R. Dodge Poetry Festival by poet Donald Hall in which he cited the use of dead metaphors as one of the most common reasons he rejects poems. One of his examples was *sea of wheat*, which now means an expanse of wheat rather than an ocean-like view of the grain field.

Determining what constitutes a dead metaphor and when to delete it can be confusing. For instance, *eye of the needle* is considered a dead metaphor, yet it's also what we call that opening in the top of a needle. On the other hand, in the phrase *he plowed through the stacks of paper*, "plowed" at first glance seems a vigorous verb choice rather than a dead metaphor. However, consider how many times you hear this metaphor in televised news reports. "The robbery suspect plowed through the festival crowd." "The car plowed into the front porch of the home." *Plow* doesn't conjure up its original imagery of a blade digging through dirt; it's taken on a meaning of its own through heavy repetition as a popular term.

If you're unsure about dead metaphors, apply the yardstick of frequency: If the term in question gets repeated a lot, especially in the media, revise the term whether it's a dead metaphor or not.

BE ALERT, NOT OBSESSIVE

Don't inhibit your writing by being overly conscious about stale language as you're putting the words down. First or even second and third drafts aren't a time for self-editing. When you revise, watch carefully for overused words and tired imagery. They're tricky little devils to catch because we're so used to them. Reread this article and I'm sure you'll target some clichés or dead metaphors that slipped right by me. The point is to be aware of them as you hone your skills. Over time you'll become more astute about when you need to cast them aside to freshen up the lines of your poems.

NANCY SUSANNA BREEN is a poet, freelance writer, and editor. Her poetry is available in e-chapbook form at www.Smashwords.com as is an e-book of writing prompts, *Nudged by Quotes—20 Writing Prompts Inspired by The World's Great Poetry, Volume 10: Poetical Quotations*. She's the former editor of *Poet's Market* and judges poetry contests at the state and national levels.

THE IMPORTANCE OF READING POETRY

Even Poetry You Hate

by Nancy Susanna Breen

In his guide to poetry writing, *The Ode Less Travelled* (Gotham Books, 2005), British author Stephen Fry lists 10 habits of successful poets. Number four on his list is "Read poetry."

I agree. I firmly believe every poet should read poetry, even poets who simply write for a select circle in a critique group or in an online forum. Such poets often protest, "You don't *have* to read other poets to write poetry." Technically, they're right, but I admit I don't understand their reasoning or their aversion to reading a literary genre in which they're enthusiastic participants. I'm even more astonished by poets who say, "I'm intimidated by poetry" or "I don't like to read poetry because I usually don't understand it." I've even heard a few poets say, "I don't like to read other poets because I'm afraid they'll influence my style."

Those of you who write only for yourselves or for your coterie of fellow poets can get by with such an outlook. Your objective is self-expression, getting your feelings into words and nothing more. If you can share your poems with people you trust in a group or online forum, you're good with that. And you may be happier with your literary life than more ambitious poets. However, I can't fathom doing anything creative in a vacuum. Even knitters like to see what others are making, and cooks love to sample recipes, even if they wind up changing them. Plus you're missing out on so much great poetry that you may well understand if you just search it out. You might even learn to like it.

Those of you, though, who are concerned with craft and hope to gain a wide readership for your poems have no excuse. You *must* read others' poetry. After all, how can you justify ignoring the work of other poets while hoping others will read *your* poems? Poetry in modern society needs all the support, and all the readers, it can get. A golden rule for poets could be, "Read other poets as you would have them read you."

Beyond supporting your art form, there are many benefits to gain from reading poetry—even bad poetry or poetry you hate.

DEVELOPING AN EAR

Reading a variety of poems helps you develop an ear for the necessary music, rhythm, and flow of verse. This applies to free verse poems as well as rhymed, metered poetry. So much free verse falls flat because poets haven't learned how much sound variance and texture free verse actually can contain. This is why reading poems aloud can be even more effective than reading them silently to yourself. Read the same poem aloud more than once, tasting the shape of the vowels and consonants, playing with pauses and breathing according to punctuation, and exploring how lines flow into each other rather than ending where the lines break. You'll learn how naturally conversational a poem can be even when it plays with meter; eventually your own work will reflect such lessons.

Reading rhymed, metered poetry is also important, whether you write only formal poetry or stick strictly to free verse. However, those who write in rhyme and meter definitely need plenty of exposure to such poetry from all eras. Poets who never get past Shakespeare or the Romantic poets show it in their writing. Their metered lines sound like stiff imitations of the old masters, they think it's okay (or even required) to use "thee" and "'twere," and employ they such stale tricks as the order of their words inverting. Read modern formalist poets for contemporary approaches to this kind of verse to purge yourself of outmoded techniques.

Absolutely read poetry with meter and rhyme aloud. Study what the poet does to avoid a sing-song effect and how he or she chooses rhymes. Note the impact of repeated one-syllable end rhymes and the probably-unintended comic effect of multiple-syllable rhymes. In addition, reading (and listening) to structured verse will help you distance yourself from the "greeting card" taint that afflicts so many attempts at rhymed, metered poetry.

READING WHAT YOU DON'T LIKE

In *The Ode Less Travelled*, Fry notes, "Variety is important or you end up an imitative shadow of your favourites." Often poets stay in their comfort zones when reading poetry; that is, they gravitate toward poems they like and/or understand. The best way to stretch your writing muscles, though, is to read fine examples of work you do *not* enjoy. Yes, the experience isn't as satisfactory, but think of it as a kind of literary workout challenge. As you're reading, observe and even record all the things you don't like about the poem, including subject matter, style, voice, and sound. Bravely admit it when a line or even an entire poem leaves you clueless, but take a shot at deciding what you think it means. If you meet such a poem head-on and don't let it deflect you, you may find the struggle illuminating. The point is not to force yourself to like a certain style or poem but to encourage you to open your mind to poetry's many possibilities.

Adventurous reading may lead you to discover a poet, work, or style you never encountered before, one that may intrigue you into examining it further. Remember, you shouldn't write every poem with publication as your goal. Experimentation is vital to your artistic development, so try some of these alien forms and styles, doing it in secret, if necessary, to relieve your inhibitions. You may surprise yourself, and you'll certainly expand your abilities as a poet.

POETRY AS A HOW-TO REFERENCE

If you're unsure when to break the lines of your poems or you stumble over how to begin or end each work, reading the poetry of others can provide useful demonstrations of best practices. Don't assume only the renowned poets have something to teach you. An unknown, little-published poet may have a fresh arsenal of approaches for you to observe and imitate. Again, don't hesitate to experiment. It will help you understand what works for you and what doesn't; and even if you don't employ certain techniques in your own poems, you may begin to appreciate them in the work of others.

POETRY FROM VARIOUS CULTURES

Poets benefit not only from exposure to different forms of poetry but also to poetry from different cultures. If you know a second language, by all means read verse in a poet's native tongue. However, translations offer you access to the whole world of poetry going back to ancient times. Some poets and critics argue that too much is lost in translation to make the reading of translated poetry worthwhile. However, weigh the loss of never having read a given poem to the boon of being exposed to it in even a flawed translation. You may find yourself less hesitant about delving into translated poetry.

If a poem especially intrigues you, seek out alternate translations of the same piece to get a feel for the different ways translators interpret the words literally and stylistically. Go a step further and write your own version of the poem based on the translations you've reviewed. This is another of those don't-have-to-share exercises that can produce interesting results and beckon you down new paths in your own poetry writing.

Don't think solely in terms of language and foreign countries when seeking out poetry from other cultures. Your own background and experience determine what cultures may seem "foreign" to you. If you're straight, read gay, lesbian, bi-gender, and transgender (GLBT) poets. If you live in a small Midwestern town or a highly rural area, read poetry inspired by gritty urban life. If you were born and raised in the United States, read what immigrants have to say about venturing into American life and society. If you've never been a soldier or a member of a military family, read poems that capture the battlefield, the army base, experiences aboard ships or jets, or what it's like to watch a loved one leave for a tour of duty.

WHAT ABOUT BAD POETRY?

Naturally, you don't want to pick up poor writing habits. However, reading bad or simply mediocre poetry can be a strangely productive motivator.

Sometimes reading wonderful poetry makes me swoon; other times it makes me want to curl up in a ball of diminished self-confidence because I'm sure I'll never write anything that good. That's when I delve into some poetry I don't admire, whether in print or online. I'm not fishing for reasons to feel superior, but an inadequate poem can make my inner artist rear up and shout, "Hey, even *I* can write something better than that!"

It's also a great tonic for feeling flat and uninspired. I may prime the pump by rewriting someone else's poem in ways I think would improve it (an exercise only). Or that aforementioned inner artist squirms over the dull work I'm reading and whines, "I'm bored! Let's write something interesting."

I can't promise reading bad poetry will work for everyone. You may recoil from a terrible poem feeling more deflated than inspired. Sometimes a bad poem is simply a bad poem, and all I can do is wince and move on. Also, if you're suggestible or mimic work easily, reading lousy poetry may be exactly what you *don't* need.

There's another benefit of reading bad poetry, though, that you ought to consider. Read enough consistently poor work and you'll begin to pick up on the mistakes poets make again and again: overused words and phrases; wordy, flaccid poems that cry out for trimming and tension; trite scenes and perspectives that seemed so original when you thought only *you* were writing about them. Familiarity does breed contempt; and once you start spotting such flaws in your own work, you'll avoid the pitfalls of bad poetry writing and self-edit your own poems more diligently.

NURTURE THE HABIT

In *The Poetry Home Repair Manual* (University of Nebraska Press, 2005), former U.S. Poet Laureate Ted Kooser observes that imitation is how poets learn to write, "just as every painter learns to paint by looking at paintings" or composers learn from the work of other composers. The great thing about poetry is your art gallery or symphonic hall is as close as your bookshelf, e-reader, or computer screen.

If you're not a regular poetry reader, start out with a poem a day. Keep a volume of work by a single poet, a literary magazine, or an anthology where you're sure to pick it up and open it. Select daily readings randomly or move through the publication from cover to cover. Don't regard it as an assignment or a chore you have to complete. Stay relaxed and open as you read, and don't read too much at a time.

Another way to make regular poetry reading easier to achieve is to subscribe to daily poems by e-mail. Soon reading poems will become a basic part of checking your inbox; just make sure you do read them and don't let them build up over days and days.

Some of the most popular subscription sites include:

- Poem-a-Day at the Academy of American Poets (www.poets.org/poemADay.php)
- Poetry Daily (www.poems.com/about_newsletter.php)
- The Poetry Foundation, which offers RSS feeds for Poem of the Day and Audio Poem of the Day as well as a free mobile app for iPhone and Android (www.poetryfoundation.org/mobile/; links for the RSS feeds are at the bottom of the page)
- The Writer's Almanac with Garrison Keillor (http://mail.publicradio.org/content/506927/forms/twa_signup.htm)
- Poetry 180, with daily poems intended for American high school students, but the selections are excellent for poets of any age (http://www.loc.gov/poetry/180/)

In addition, Ted Kooser's "American Life in Poetry," a weekly newspaper feature, also offers a poem with accompanying comment by e-mail subscription (http://www.americanlifeinpoetry.org/email.html).

However you do it and whatever method you use, add reading poetry to your daily regimen. Once developed, it's a habit you won't want to break.

AS A BEGINNING

by Joannie Stangeland

Start with a tree, and always the one no.
Start with light and green spoken as sin,
elemental and forbidden, the apple's red skin
split open like a mouth, teeth marks
denting flesh, an invitation hissed bare,
truth a gate out, lives cast
into the sun, another kind of holy,
history recorded by men, but we weren't there.

~~~

We weren't there, with rib and words in our fists,
a belly fire. Sun on shoulders, hips.
Before words, raw—a mouthful of hunger,
no way to say bliss or feed me.
I'll take a bite, a nibble or lick, juice
dripping onto the calendar's sheets, millennia.
Grass turns to dirt, speaks to the feet.
After, a purple feeling. No light.

~~~

A purple feeling. No light on your skin.
How blind? Were eyes closed? Did they stumble
around exotic vines, tropical trees

like children in a game, ears tuned to sibilance.
Or is this metaphor? Vision a symbol
for knowing, knowledge for sin, code for sex.
Creation opens, flowers casting their seeds.
In a later generation, the lilies do not spin.

~~~

The lilies do not spin. They do not toil.
I come to my garden to bask in it, can't grow
an apple to save my life. Zucchini, the same story.
My beanstalks climb, but don't approach the sky,
no green path to the giant's palace,
not even a good meal of beans
and today, none of the clouds looks like a castle.
I live in the earthly, on this side of the gate.

~~~

The gate ajar and always the day leaving
its red stain across the sky's edge.
How was knowledge a sin? The seed was change,
a revelation, a new burden of the senses.
A day, and then another day, seasons.
Yes, winter. An apple, light banished,
and then vacations, always a garden, and sun
and truth clicks shut, the latch rattles.

GHOSTS

by Nin Andrews

You want to know the first time I saw one. Where I was, and if I was afraid. Did I believe my eyes? Because the other night when I saw you again, I knew it wasn't just the summer heat, the mist rising after a sudden rain. It's true what they say. Once you've seen a ghost, the seeing never stops. You develop an eye for it. And they keep coming back, connecting, maybe imagining you were the woman they met, once upon a time, way back when. Maybe they think you remember them the same way. Or that you're the ghost, not them. They want you to finish that sentence, the one you started when you were going to tell what you never told a soul. It's true. When they touch you, the words begin to form on your tongue.

OCCLUDED

by Shann Palmer

Some women have the capacity
to pick themselves up where they are
scattered, like chunks of glass
swept to the curb after a car crash,
the way a broken wall promises hope.
Messes must be cleared
so life can resume.

Men will talk like blustery winds
before a storm, changing
whole worlds in a handshake,
determined to make good fences,
build dynasties with a cursory kiss,
only to turn their backs in sleep,
murmuring someone else's name.

WIND CHIME, MINUS THE WIND

by Susan Laughter Meyers

They keep coming to a bowl of emptiness—hummingbirds. It's like mid-winter,
with cows grazing on air, sheep nuzzling their own good nature.

You came to us, nephew, swaddled in light and sky. Now the swift river
we navigate, alone and together, has broadened on its way to the sea.

Through the red nectar in the feeder I see a hummingbird hovering up and down,
over and over, like a tiny child jumping, arms flung wide.

When I reach my arms up and snap the sheet out over the bed, when it billows
and floats down, swelling then collapsing, I too ride the air.

The bright, hot day is a Panini with cheese running down its crust. One bite
and there's basil in the air, birds pecking seeds from tomatoes.

To stir the peanut butter is to see the oil mix with the paste, flaxseeds swirling,
lumps diminishing in a vortex of creaminess—is to dream.

This morning I am rain—soft, slow, melting into the crevices open to me.
To be rain is to be amenable to leafshine and ooze, puddle and weed.

To wear the wrong glasses is to be able to read the pages of the book that's not
here but not to be able to read the computer screen that is.

Up the road Bradford pears have been hacked back from the utility wires.
Here, the tea olive reaches up and out, on the verge of sprawling.

Intentions fly off in any direction. Paths intersect. Mostly, there's waiting.
So much to thwart and balance when a hummingbird is on guard.

A rubythroat sits on the loblolly limb, balancing and turning, never still:
tiny flower shifted by wind, lifting its brightness to the sun.

What was that quick move? No, that whisper. You can barely see it, barely
feel the stir, or not at all. Flutter. Wings, air, thoughts, heart.

Behind my eyelids, the storm's fireworks—strict, mercurial—kept waking me.
Drumming rain, a march I couldn't name. Now this glum morning.

Stillness isn't still for long, sunlight moving ever so slowly up the east side
of the tree trunks. And the quiver of the river birch leaves.

The new blossom and five buds atop the loblolly bay. A hummingbird perched
deep within the dense branches of the tea olive. Lucky me, here.

A wind chime, minus the wind. Green morning waiting for rain. Near the tea olive
a hummingbird feeder, tongue-ready. Always, the next bird.

THE WRECK OF BIRDS

by Rebecca Givens Rolland

If I had not thought to leave you? You left your luck at shooting birds.
Abstract, the red curtain flooded around you, a wreck of birds.

Younger then, I defined springtime by slag heaps, by balled ashes.
Can you think back to plant books, folded over, leaflets of birds?

Conch shells on ceramic plates, old man hanging a bittersweet head.
Startled, these images boomeranged in dreams, through flecks of birds.

One face lay inside another, nicked the forehead—I watched it.
Please, have you not attended to the lasso strikes, sparks of birds?

Tomorrow, a girl in the park slaps a hat on a melancholy woman.
Slain whites of plucked eyes will slip madly, trapping passels of birds.

Removing my face for you was simple—now the sculpture inside.
Younger than you or your brothers, but paler, no hint of birds.

Were you loved by an apple at one time, a stunningly nebulous cloud?
Doubtless, I cry to be burned, dragged off by thousands of birds.

Birth threatens constantly to run off—daily, I hinge farther from it.
Not a door you'd wrest open with me, not you, swift handler of birds.

Where's the dividing line of natural? Of carrying an entire new earth?
Hope had no intention for you, no castle, just migrations of birds.

Dead light on your face I cannot attribute to anger. I still refuse.
No joke: you'll go this morning, untouched, begging secrets of birds.

I'll defend you with a mirror in my pocket, snake in my fist: a first.
No woman has been seen around here? Three shadows of birds.

WHEN I RE-READ HIS LETTERS

by Patricia Fargnoli

Memories come
flying in like a flock of crows,
dark forms against the brightness
of sun on a cornfield, dozens of silhouettes,
beaks open, wing feathers outstretched
like spread fingers.
They bring their koww, koww, koww
and caw-ak-ak to the earth,
where the crops have already been carted off,
and forage there, scrabbling
among the rustling stalks.
Then as suddenly as they arrived,
they startle up into that clear sky
and fly off into another landscape.

DEAR FRITZ GUEST HOUSE,

by Sage Cohen

I sleep the sleep of seagulls.
Sucked-out shell and salt.

I fold my wings in and tuck
my head under like the idea

of a ship and slip along
the surface of time. It has taken

41 years to prepare this body
for living. Beside my bed

the blown-over trees seem
to be aching with every

arm they have for someone
across this ocean.

Last night soaking in sulfur
floating out over our world

I met a man. I didn't know it yet,
but he had a tiny, conch-like curl

of plastic whispering secrets
in his ear. I joined the chorus

as we soaked our skin in stars.
He was a gentle man, worn

smooth by pain. We asked
our questions and the ocean,

like all great teachers,
did not answer.

SEA GHOST, FIRE OF THE SEA

by Jeffrey H. MacLachlan

My brother's heart was born with a porthole like his hospital roommate's who didn't make it. The decrepit snow of late March withered atop dreamboat tulip bulbs. My parents attended the funeral and said she was sprinkled like fish flakes among minnows clear as first water gems. Her family called every weekend while we fried sweetbreads and I'd spirit my brother away to watch nature documentaries. *Noctiluca scintillans* is the floating bloom algae sometimes referred to as sea sparkle, sea ghost, fire of the sea. There, in estuaries, dark coastal water can rest for hours until a disturbance creates pulses of brightness that bubble green.

ECHOLOCATION

by Karen Rigby

Trench with profligate seaweed.   Ghost of a
sandbar traces of chain-link   the vessel
lowered entire.

Greening. Solitude.   Who survives salt against
wound /
against skin   coral filigreed   like blown
eggs
(cathedral of black / cathedral of blue)   down
  the laddering
    sea
      I cast my one lamp

across a city of drowned men   hair crowning.
We are nobody's fool.

Winter, the sea eclipsed sails.
Hooded my eyes.
White trunks
punctured the seabed.

In that deep-sea orangerie, a revolution
  with hatchets:
I was merman and huntress—

the sea a keyless ward, iron latch
  wet, then flaking—

FLINGING THE UNSAID INTO THE SURF

or Seeing You Again More Than 5 Years Later

by Heather M. Moore Niver

Our eyes meet
and I am suddenly aware
of our bare feet only inches apart
beneath the red kitchen table
we carefully keep between us.

We have never been alone
like this before.
I look down
—at your snoozing dog, my own toes, anything—
as the day's last rays waver,
glancing off the stones of my wedding ring.

When I meet your gaze
over the bowl of plums
again I say nothing,
just run one thumb
over the rim.

~~~

I carry the words
with me to the seaside
and drop syllables like stones
one by one by one,
making rings
in the roaring waves.
~~~

ARRIVAL: A LOVE VILLANELLE FOR HAITI

by Jen Karetnick

Nou led, Nou la. "We are ugly, but we are here,"
you say through the cracks of your lips, your hands
coated with the dust that masks any succor.

Your breasts may fall like bricks but still pucker
for the mouths of fashion-blind infants:
Nou led, Nou la. "We are ugly, but we are here."

For what use, really, are French manicures,
the Lancome creams on faces so life-beaten?
Coated with the dust that masks any succor,

now and throughout the centuries, since before
the men whose blood brought freedom, those little Toussaints:
Nou led, Nou la. "We are ugly, but we are here,"

spoken in greetings and leave-takings from mother
to daughter, cousin, friend, neighbor—women
coated with the dusk that masked any succor

until the buildings also denied their covers.
In Miami, we have been fooled by muted foundations,
coated with pearlized dust that masks any succor.
Sisters, *bonjou.* We have been ugly, but now we are here.

THE PAINTER'S PANTOUM

-after Melanie

by Jessie Carty

If I can borrow the phrase,
I will say bright burning
to describe the day she first
painted; her love of yellow.

I will say bright burning
also for her pedicured toenails
painted; her love of yellow;
her fingers unadorned.

Also for her pedicured toenails
she'd sometimes add designs.
Her fingers unadorned
because they *were* designers.

She'd sometimes add designs
to her scrabble-like signature.
Because they were designers—
each brush of each brush.

To her scrabble-like signature—
To describe the day she first...
Each brush of each brush:
If I can borrow the phrase.

HANDS TO

by Kelli Simpson

Hands to tend the cradle.
Cradle to the grave.
Grave dug with a ladle.
Ladle Grandma made.

Made it with a carving knife.
Knife between his ribs.
Ribs from man to woman.
Woman come to this.

AT THE BOWLING ALLEY

by Terri Kirby Erickson

Blind, the old man still beats you. He holds
the heavy ball as if it's made of Styrofoam, pitches
it down the alley and stands there, listening for
the strike. You marvel that this dreg of humanity
with his hawk-nosed face and unwashed body,
tattoos dripping down the slack skin of his arms
and between the lizard-like folds of his scrawny
neck, wins every game. The fact that he's blind,
too, is the final insult since you can spot a fly
circling a cup of greasy French fries from across
the dang building—the barrettes in Missy Cardwell's
curly blonde hair as she's walking to the restroom
at the far-end of the hall, her short skirt swinging
from side to side in that flirty way of hers that drives
you half-crazy. Maybe that's it—the old man has no
distractions. There's nothing but the feel of the ball
in his hands, the squeak of his beat-up bowling shoes
on the polished floor, and the sound of ten pins knocked
down in one fell swoop, hit so hard you wonder if
they'll ever get up. And even worse, he's your father,
the same sorry guy who took off when you were six.
You know he knows who you are, but he never
says a word—just whips the living fool out of you
and walks away, as if you're just another loser.

GREETINGS FROM MOTEL 6

by Linda Simoni-Wastila

I almost write wish you were here, but mama told me
never lie, so instead I say the remote feels good
in my hand, the highway noise screams a lullabye,
the donuts at the front desk set my teeth to ache,
the drunk trucker in the room next door reminds me
of home, and I don't wear make-up any more.

FROST AT MIDMORNING

by Nate Pritts

This is year one, right now, & there's
news of the world coming across the wire,
news on the march, or it's March
& it's really October & time ravages on
or it's Syracuse & I'm waking up lonely
with arms that can't do what they know to do,
palms shaped like empty rosebuds.
Someone wearing the stilly hush
of nature hands me an updated report
or I'm the report he gives me, I'm a gun
going off, I'm bang: frost weighs down
the leaves cluttering the ground, rainbow
patchwork puzzle that doesn't form
anything other than what it is. Frost
& red leaves, frost on the car, secret ministry
of frost on each of my lonely fingers
so they can't bend; they snap. The velocity
of this velocity careening through the thicket.
What about the gentle breathings of bodies
smashing into lakes? There's a line thin
as a lute string between romance & one hundred
possible deaths in each sunset we circle
as the big bright sun circles us, orbiting

all of this in a blind reverie haze determined
to gather the necessary information
to send back to base. Me a proud honorary
astronaut sent out as a lover of uncontained
& immortal beauty but, O, just a chump in love
with the ground, the feet of the real buried
in sand on a beach you can't reach except
in memory. Frost in autumn, frost at midnight,
Frost on a hotel bed, telescoping from mountains
to buzzsaws, each of your eyes a diamond
ripping through my wooden soul, a stunning
revelation no matter which of five mountain ranges
you're planted on & I am wildly annunciatory;
I am some pine tree utterance; I am a broken
sonnet shattered in the fall & fitted back together.
I'm a poem written on the back of a folded map
to your house. How simple the cavernous twists
& turns when we can see the ways we'll move in advance
of the broken life. I woke up from a dream of frost
covered leaves to a world of frost covered leaves.
I brooded all the following morn. I listened to my heart.

SACKCLOTH

by Pris Campbell

You come to me,
eyes like a bruised sky,
cherubs in your pocket,
beg my forgiveness.

Time is on my side,
the Stones sang.
I hum it off key.
Time has about-faced
and you want me again, but

how many nights
do I hit instant replay
before I see you're not
coming back, that groveling
never was your style, or
that my dreams are only
tempests sackcloth
is sewn from.

ON SOME OTHER PLANET WE'RE NEWLYWEDS

by Kelli Russell Agodon

You asked for sizzle, but it was late
and all I could give you was mumble.

You asked for sizzle and I gave you
myself as a fossil, dunes when you wanted waves.

In Jupiter years, we've been married
a couplet—two years. In a world

of purgatory that equals one grain of sand. If that.
If that and the oversized plates

we thought we needed, the Blue Danube pattern
of our shadows as we walked from the mall.

Now two calicos later, two calicos and a little less
sizzle, we chant our desires to ourselves

as we brush our teeth—*A little more,* you say.
A little more Jupiter. I rub your shoulders

trying to alienate the pain, our alien nation
of household, the pop and sizzle

not of bedroom, but of butter melting,
how in a different galaxy we might be young.

PHOTOGRAPHY LESSON, PT. REYES

by Iris Jamahl Dunkle

My father teaches me landscape
here, where the land itself cannot decide
to which age it raises its stiff thumb.

I have a decision to make—
a few names to throw in the ocean.

We walk up the bare beach—
We look through a machine—
He says *don't forget*
you are looking through a machine.

Your emotions will ruin it.

The hills beyond are almost bald—
a lone raven marks in an arc their curve
then lands in a still nest of waves.

Ravens, he says, *will never appear in pairs.*

I push the shutter down
let the machine realize
what I have learned,
as something scares the bird to flight.

Why must stories overlap? I ask
but my father is already walking,
the machine ticking faster
than waves can count.

FOLLOW THE LEADER

by Nancy Posey

A natural born leader with no sense of direction,
he always headed down the most unlikely path,

leading a string of smaller children, less sure,
more willing to turn over navigation to him

since he seemed so sure of himself, staff in hand,
his grandfather's compass hanging from his belt

and while they never ended up where they expected,
they were never disappointed, since what they sought,

adventure, could not be found on any map, but
could not be avoided with him at the head of the line.

They wove their way through cornfields, warned
to stay between the stalks, leaving no trace

of their presence. They learned to climb gingerly
over or between the strands of barbed-wire fence.

He taught them the difference between a toad
and a frog, the names of plants, which they learned

later he was probably making up as he went along,
much like the road they traveled in his wake.

POET BIOS

KELLI RUSSELL AGODON is the author of Letters From the Emily Dickinson Room, winner of the White Pine Press Poetry Prize, which is currently a finalist for the Foreword Book of the Year Award in Poetry. She is also the author of *Small Knots* and the chapbook, Geography. Her work has appeared in journals such as the Atlantic Monthly, Prairie Schooner, and Poetry Northwest. Kelli lives in Washington State with her family where she is an avid mountain biker as well as co-editor of Seattle's 28-year-old print journal, Crab Creek Review, and the co-founder of Two Sylvias Press. Find her blogging at Book of Kells, where she writes about living and writing creatively: www.ofkells.blogspot.com or visit her website at www.agodon.com.

NIN ANDREWS is the author of several poetry collections, including *Sleeping With Houdini* and *The Book of Orgasms.* Learn more at http://ninandrewswriter.blogspot.com.

The poetry of **PRIS CAMPBELL** has appeared in such journals as *Chiron Review, The Dead Mule, Boxcar Poetry Review, Underground Poetry Review, The Nervous Breakdown, Poets & Artists,* and *Wild Goose Poetry Review.* Her poems have been widely reviewed in journals and blogs, along with interviews about her writing. She has received three Pushcart Prize nominations and has published five collections of poetry. The most recent are *Sea Trails* by Lummox Press and *The Nature of Attraction,* with Scott Owens, by Main Street Rag Press. A former clinical psychologist, she was sidelined in 1990 with ME/CFS and now makes her home in the greater West Palm Beach, FL.

JESSIE CARTY is a North Carolina poet.

SAGE COHEN is the author of the poetry collection, *Like the Heart, the World,* and two nonfiction books from Writer's Digest Books: *Writing the Life Poetic* and *The Productive Writer.* Sage has won first place in the Ghost Road Poetry contest, been nominated for a Pushcart Prize and published numerous articles about the writing life in *Writer's Digest* magazine. She holds an MFA from New York University and a BA from Brown University. Visit Sage at pathofpossibility.com.

IRIS JAMAHL DUNKLE teaches at Clarion University. Her chapbook *Inheritance* was published by Finishing Line. Her poetry, creative nonfiction and scholarly articles have appeared in numerous publications, including *Fence, LinQ, Boxcar Poetry Review, Cleveland in Prose and Poetry, Eaden Water's Press Home Anthology* and *The Squaw Valley Writers Review.*

TERRI KIRBY ERICKSON is the award-winning author of three collections of poetry, including her latest book, *In the Palms of Angels* (Press 53), with an Introduction by Pulitzer Prize-winning journalist and author, Ron Powers. Her work has appeared in numerous literary journals, anthologies and other publications, and has been nominated for the Pushcart Prize and Best of the Net Award. For more information about her work, visit her website http://terrikirbyerickson.wordpress.com.

PATRICIA FARGNOLI'S newest book, *Then, Something* (Tupelo Press) won the ForeWord Poetry Book of the Year Award and the Shelia Mooton Book Award. She's published poems recently in *The Harvard Review, Green Mountains Review, Alaska Quarterly Review, Massachusetts Review, Poetry International,* etc.

JEN KARETNICK is the author/co-author of six books, including two collections of poetry: *Necessary Salt* (Pudding House) and *Bud Break at Mango House* (Portlandia Group), which won the Portlandia Press Chapbook Award. A Dorothy Sargent Rosenberg Award winner for a lyric poem, she recently won the Piccolo in Your Pocket poetry competition from the Alaska Flute Studies Center and was a finalist for the 2011 New Orleans Study Abroad and Knightsville/The New Guard poetry prizes. An award-winning restaurant critic for MIAMI Magazine as well as the Creative Writing Director for Miami Arts Charter School, she is currently writing *Romancing the Mango: Recipes for the Obsessed* for University Press of Florida. Jen was born in New Jersey and resides in Miami on the last acre of a historical plantation with her husband; two children; three dogs; four cats; and 14 mango trees.

JEFFREY H. MACLACHLAN also has recent or forthcoming work in *Blue Earth Review, Perceptions, Badlands,* and *The Rumpus.* He can be followed on Twitter @jeffmack.

SUSAN LAUGHTER MEYERS is the author of *Keep and Give Away* (University of South Carolina Press), which received the inaugural SC Poetry Book Prize. Her poetry has also appeared in numerous journals, as well as *Poetry Daily, Verse Daily,* and Ted Kooser's American Life in Poetry column. A long-time writing instructor with an MFA from Queens University of Charlotte, she lives with her husband in Givhans, SC.

HEATHER M. MOORE NIVER is a coffee-fueled freelance writer and editor in New York State. She has kept the ink flowing by participating in juried poetry workshops at the New York State Writer's Institute and The Edna St. Vincent Millay Society. Every winter, she leads an Adirondack arts retreat writing workshop. Her poetry has appeared in *Peer Glass, The Berkshire Review,* and *Pathways*; at swankwriting.com and YourDailyPoem.com; and at the 2008 National Poetry Month exhibit at the Sherry French Gallery. When she's not reveling in language and roasting coffee, she hikes, snowshoes, and dabbles in photography and music.

SHANN PALMER is a Texan living in Richmond, VA, where she hosts and participates in readings, workshops, and open mics to provide opportunities for other writers. Published in print and on the web, Shann has recent work *Short, Fast, and Deadly, Lingerpost,* and *Redheaded Stepchild.* Poems are forthcoming in *Poetry South, Qaartsiluni,* and *The Dead Mule School of Southern Literature.*

NANCY POSEY, an English instructor at Caldwell Community College, is the author of one chapbook, *Let the Lady Speak.* She enjoys involvement in the poetry community, both online and in her home state of North Carolina, home to a rich vein of poetry. An avid reader, she blogs about books at http://discriminatingreader.com. She also loves learning to play the mandolin.

NATE PRITTS is the author of five books of poetry, most recently *Sweet Nothing* from Lowbrow Press. He is also the founder and editor of *H_NGM_N*, an online journal and small press. His poetry and criticism have appeared in many journals, both online and in print, such as *Black Warrior Review, Gulf Coast, Forklift, Boston Review, Southern Review,* and *Rain Taxi* where he frequently contributes reviews. Find out more about him at www.natepritts.com.

KAREN RIGBY is the author of *Chinoiserie* (Sawtooth Poetry Prize, Ahsahta Press).

REBECCA GIVENS ROLLAND has recent or forthcoming work in *Stand, Zoland Poetry Annual,* and *Cincinnati Review*. Poems from this series are forthcoming in *American Letters & Commentary, Colorado Review,* and *Denver Quarterly*. Rolland is a doctoral student in education at Harvard; her website is www.rebeccarolland.com.

LINDA SIMONI-WASTILA crunches numbers by day and churns words at night. Her writing explores health, in particular the societal and personal facets of medication and medicating. Her poems and stories can be found in *The Sun, Thunderclap!, Monkeybicycle, Eclectic Flash, Tattoo Highway, Istanbul Literary Review,* and *Boston Literary Magazine*, among others. She lives and loves in Baltimore, a town where her Northern birthright and Southern breeding comfortably comingle. Find her online at http://linda-leftbrainwrite.blogspot.com.

KELLI SIMPSON is a freelance writer and daily blogger at The Zen of Motherhood. She lives in Oklahoma with her husband, Robert, her daughter, Ashli, and a rapidly growing collection of reptiles.

JOANNIE STANGELAND is the author of two poetry chapbooks—*A Steady Longing for Flight,* which won the Floating Bridge Press Chapbook Award, and *Weathered Steps.* Her new collection, *Into the Rumored Spring*, was released in 2011. Joannie's poems have also appeared in numerous journals and anthologies. Joannie has taught writing at Richard Hugo House and she also works as a technical writer.

MAGAZINES/ JOURNALS

Literary magazines and journals usually provide a poet's first publishing success. In fact, poets shouldn't think about book/chapbook publication until their poems appear in a variety of magazines, journals and zines (both print and online). This is the preferred way to develop an audience, build publishing credits and learn the ins and outs of the publishing process.

In this section you'll find hundreds of magazines and journals that publish poetry. They range from small black-and-white booklets produced on home computers to major periodicals with high production values and important reputations. To help you sort through these markets and direct your submissions most effectively, we've organized information in each listing according to a basic format.

HOW LISTINGS ARE FORMATTED

Content of each market listing was provided or verified by a representative of the publication (editor, poetry editor, managing editor, etc.). Here is how that content is arranged within the listing:

SYMBOLS. Icons at the beginning listings offer visual signposts to specific information about the publication. Refer to the Key to Icons & Abbreviations on the inside cover of the book.

CONTACT INFORMATION. Depending on what was provided, contact information includes: magazine/journal title; regular mail address; telephone number; fax number; e-mail address; website address; year the publication was established; the name of the person to contact (or an editorial title); and membership in small press/publishing organizations. (**Note:** If a magazine/journal publishes only online and/or wants submissions by e-mail exclusively, no street address may be given.)

MAGAZINE NEEDS. It's important to study this section as you research potential markets. Here you'll find such helpful information as the editor's overview of the publication, with individual poetry needs and preferences; a list of recently published poets; production information (number of pages, printing/binding details, type of cover); the number of poetry submissions the publication receives vs. the number accepted; and press run, distribution and price information.

HOW TO CONTACT. This section focuses on the specific details of submitting work: how many poems to send; minimum/maximum number of lines per poem; whether previously published poems or simultaneous submissions are considered; submission format preferences (including whether to submit by e-mail, and how); response times; payment; rights acquired and more.

ADDITIONAL INFORMATION. Editors may use this section to explain other publishing activities, elaborate on some aspect of the magazine/journal, suggest future plans—anything beyond the basic details that readers may find of interest.

CONTEST/AWARD OFFERINGS. This section discusses prizes and competitions associated with the publication, with either brief guidelines or a cross-reference to a separate listing in the Contests & Awards section.

ALSO OFFERS. Describes additional offerings associated with this publication (i.e., sponsored readings, website activities such as blogs and forums, related poetry groups, etc.).

TIPS. Provides direct quotes from editors about everything from pet peeves to tips on writing to perspectives on the state of poetry today.

GETTING STARTED, FINDING MARKETS

If you don't have a certain magazine or journal in mind, read randomly through the listings, making notes as you go. (Don't hesitate to write in the margins, underline, use highlighters; it also helps to flag markets that interest you with Post-It Notes). Browsing the listings is an effective way to familiarize yourself with the kind of information presented and the publishing opportunities that are available at various skill levels.

If you have a specific market in mind, however, begin with the General Index. Here all the book's listings are alphabetized along with additional references that may be buried within a listing (such as a press name or competition title).

REFINE YOUR SEARCH

To supplement the General Index, we provide the Subject Index to help you refine your marketing plan for submitting your poems to publications. Not every listing appears in this index, so use it only to reinforce your other research efforts.

2RIVER VIEW

7474 Drexel Dr., University City MO 63130. **E-mail:** long@2River.org. **E-mail:** submissions@2river.org. **Website:** www.2River.org. **Contact:** Richard Long. *2River View*, published quarterly online, restricts each issue to ten poets. "We prefer poems with these qualities: image, subtlety, and point of view; a surface of worldly exactitude, as well as a depth of semantic ambiguity; and a voice that negotiates with its body of predecessors." Robert Creeley, R. Virgil Davis, Tony Colella, David Appelbaum, Michelle Askin, Rebecca Givens. Accepts 1-5% of unsolicited submissions. Publishes ms 3 months after acceptance. Guidelines on website.

MAGAZINE NEEDS Submit up to 5 poems once per reading period. No previously published poems or simultaneous submissions. Accepts e-mail submissions pasted into the body of the e-mail; no fax or disk submissions. Reads submissions year round (see website for reading period for each issue).

5 AM

Box 205, Spring Church PA 15686. (715)284-0328. **Website:** www.5ampoetry.com. **Contact:** Ed Ochester and Judith Vollmer. "*5 AM*, published twice/year, is a poetry publication open in regard to form, length, subject matter, and style. Does not want religious poetry or "naive rhymers." Has published poetry by Virgil Suárez, Nin Andrews, Alicia Ostriker, Edward Field, Billy Collins, and Denise Duhamel. *5 AM* is 24-pages, tabloid size, offset-printed. Receives about 5,000 poems/year, accepts about 2%. Press run is 1,200. Subscription: $12 for 2 issues (one year), $20 for 4 issues (two years). Sample: $5." Responds in 4-6 weeks to mss.

TIPS "We read all year. Manuscripts cannot be returned without SASE with sufficient postage."

THE 13TH WARRIOR REVIEW

P.O. Box 5122, Seabrook NJ 08302-3511. **E-mail:** theeditor@asteriusonline.com. **Website:** www.asteriusonline.com/13thWR/. **Contact:** John C. Erianne, editor. *The 13th Warrior Review*, published 2-3 times annually online, seeks "excellent literary-quality poetry as well as fiction, essays, and reviews. All excellent poetry will be given serious consideration." Has published poetry by P.Q. Perron, Cindy Rosmus, B.Z Niditch, Genine Hanns, John Sweet, and Corey Ginsberg. Acquires first rights, first electronic rights, and non-exclusive anthology rights. Publishes ms 6 months after acceptance. Responds in 1 week to queries; 1-2 months to mss.

MAGAZINE NEEDS Submit no more than 5 poems at a time. Accepts e-mail submissions only, pasted as text into body of message. No attachments. "Use 'submission' as the subject header. Any submission that comes as a file attachment will be deleted without reply." Cover letter is preferred; "should be brief and to the point." Seldom comments on rejected poems. No previously published poems.

34TH PARALLEL

P.O. Box 4823, Irvine CA 92623. **E-mail:** tracesheridan@34thParallel.net. **Website:** www.34thparallel.net/submit.html. **Contact:** Trace Sheridan, Martin Chipperfield, editors. *34th Parallel*, published quarterly in print and online, seeks "to promote and publish the exceptional writing of new and emerging writers overlooked by large commercial publishing houses and mainstream presses. Wants work that experiments with and tests boundaries. Anything that communicates a sense of wonder, reality, tragedy, fantasy, and/or brilliance. Does not want historical romance, science fiction, erotica, Gothic horror, book reviews, or nonfiction." Single copy: $11; subscription: $36. Guidelines on website.

MAGAZINE NEEDS In the subject heading of your e-mail, type in 'story submissions' or 'poetry submission' or 'image submission'. Will discard as spam those submissions that do not contain one of these subject headings. Submit 1 poem only. Considers simultaneous submissions; no previously published poems. Accepts electronic submissions. Cover letter is required, containing a short bio about your life, your writing, and where we can see some of your other work online. Reads submissions year round. Often comments on rejected poems. Pays 1 contributor's copy in PDF format.

AASRA PUNJABI ENGLISH MAGAZINE

22619 97th Ave. S, Kent WA 98031. **E-mail:** aasra@q.com. **Contact:** Sarab Singh, editor. "Aasra Punjabi English Magazine, published bimonthly, features current events mainly Indian, but have featured others, too, of interest. Also features interviews, yoga, and other articles, and poetry." Has published poetry by Joan Robers, Elizabeth Tallmadge, Carmen Arhiveleta. Page count varies. Measures approximately 8.5x11, press printed, staple bound, includes ads. Single copy cost $3 (postage); subscription: $20/year. "The magazine is distributed free in the Seattle area and available through other libraries. We charge postage for a copy to be mailed. Please include $3 to allow us to send you the copy of the magazine. $2 per copy if more than 10 copies are purchased." Reads submissions year round. Sometimes comments on rejected poems. Sometimes published theme issues. Guidelines in magazine. Rights revert to poet upon publication. Best Poem of the Year is awarded one-year free subscription. Acquires one-time rights. Time between acceptance and publication is 2 months.

MAGAZINE NEEDS Submit 1-2 small poems at a time. Cover letter is required. Include SASE, name, address, telephone number, and e-mail address with age and sex on cover letter. Include a short bio. "If interested we can print 'About the Poet' also along with the poem."

CONTEST/AWARD OFFERINGS Best Poem of the Year is awarded one-year free subscription.

ABBEY

5360 Fallriver Row Court, Columbia MD 21044. **E-mail:** greisman@aol.com. **Contact:** David Greisman, editor. *Abbey* is "a more-or-less informal zine looking for poetry that does for the mind what the first sip of Molson Ale does for the palate." Does not want "pornography or politics." Has published poetry by Richard Peabody, Ruth Moon Kempher, Carol Hamilton, Harry Calhoun, Kyle Laws, Joel Poudrier, Wayne Hogan, and Edmund Conti. *Abbey* is usually 20-26 pages, magazine-sized, photocopied, and held together with 1 low-alloy metal staple in the top left corner. Receives about 1,000 poems/year, accepts about 150. Press run is 200. Subscription: $2. Sample: 50¢. Responds in 1 month "except during baseball season."

MAGAZINE NEEDS Pays 1-2 contributor's copies.

ADDITIONAL INFORMATION Abbey Cheapochapbooks come out once or twice every 5 years, averaging 10-15 pages. For chapbook consideration, query with 4-6 sample poems, bio, and list of publications. Responds in 2 months "including baseball season." Pays 25-50 author's copies.

ABLE MUSE

467 Saratoga Ave., #602, San Jose CA 95129-1326. **Website:** www.ablemuse.com. **Contact:** Alex Pepple, editor. "*Able Muse: a review of metrical poetry* published 3 times/year, predominantly publishes metrical poetry complemented by art and photography, fiction and non-fiction including essays, book reviews, and interviews with a focus on metrical and formal poetry. We are looking for well-crafted poems of any length or subject that employ skillful and imaginative use of meter and rhyme, executed in a contemporary idiom, that reads as naturally as your free verse poems." Acquires first rights. Time between acceptance and publication is 3 months. Sometimes comments on rejected poems. Responds in 4 months. Sometimes sends prepublication galleys.

Considers poetry by teens. "High levels of craft still required even for teen writers." Has published poetry by Mark Jarman, A.E. Stallings, Annie Finch, Rhina P. Espaillat, Rachel Hadas, and R.S. Gwynn. Receives about 1,500 poems/year, accepts about 5%. Subscription: $22 for 1 year.

MAGAZINE NEEDS Submit 1-5 poems and short bio. No previously published poems or simultaneous submissions. Electronic submissions only welcome through the online form at www.ablemuse.com/submit, or by e-mail to editor@ablemuse.com. "The e-mail submission method is being phased out. We strongly encourage using the online submission method." Will not accept postal submissions. Reviews books of poetry. Send materials for review consideration.

ABRAMELIN, THE JOURNAL OF POETRY AND MAGICK

E-mail: nessaralindaran@aol.com. **Website:** www.abramelin.net. **Contact:** Vanessa Kittle, editor. *Abramelin, the Journal of Poetry and Magick*, published biannually online and a yearly best of edition each December, offers "literary poetry and essays concerning the western esoteric traditions." Wants "poetry that shows rather than tells. Poems that make me jealous of the writer. Poems that are inspired with wonderful language and imagery. In short—literature. Poetry submissions needn't be about magick at all. I feel that real poetry is magick. In fact, poetry that is literally magickal in theme has to be twice as good." Does not want "rhyming poems. Very short fiction. But beware, I learned from the best." Has published poetry by Simon Perchik, Rich Kostelanetz, and Lyn Lifshin. *Abramelin* receives about 1,000 poems/year, accepts about 5%. Distributed free online. Number of unique visitors: 3,000/issue. Acquires one-time rights, with option to include in a yearly print anthology.

Rights revert to poets upon publication. Publishes 1-3 months after acceptance. Responds in 1 month. Guidelines available by e-mail or on website.

MAGAZINE NEEDS Submit 1-5 poems at a time. Considers previously published poems and simultaneous submissions (with notification). Accepts e-mail (pasted into body of message). Cover letter is preferred. Reads submissions year round. Often comments on rejected poems. Sometimes publishes theme issues. Upcoming themes available in magazine or on website. Lines/poem: no minimum/maximum. Pays 1 contributor's copy.

● ABRAXAS

P.O. Box 260113, Madison WI 53726-0113. **E-mail:** abraxaspress@hotmail.com. **Website:** www.abraxaspressinc.com/Welcome.html. **Contact:** Ingrid Swanberg, Editor/Publisher. *ABRAXAS*, published "irregularly; 9- to 12-month intervals or much longer," is interested in poetry that's "contemporary lyric, experimental, and poetry in translation. When submitting translations, please include poems in the original language. *ABRAXAS'* new format features longer selections of fewer contributors." Does not want "political posing; academic regurgitations." Has published poetry by Ivan Arguüelles, Denise Levertov, Ceésar Vallejo, d.a. levy, T.L. Kryss, and Andrea Moorhead. *ABRAXAS* is up to 80 pages, digest-sized, litho-offset-printed, flat-spined, with matte or glossy card cover with original art and photography. Press run is 700. Subscription: $16 (4 issues). Sample: $4 USD plus $1.90 s&h.

MAGAZINE NEEDS Submit 7-10 poems along with SASE. No electronic submissions. Payment is contributer's copy and 40% discount on additional copies.

ABZ

P.O. Box 2746, Huntington WV 25727. **E-mail:** editorial@abzpress.com. **Website:** www.abzpress.com.

MAGAZINE NEEDS *ABZ*, published annually, wants poetry using interesting and exciting language. Sample copies and subscriptions: $8. Submit 1 to 6 poems at a time. Reading period is September 1-December 1. Guidelines on website. "Contributors receive a small stipend and two copies of the magazine."

◐ ACM (ANOTHER CHICAGO MAGAZINE)

P.O. Box 408439, Chicago IL 60640. **Website:** www.anotherchicagomagazine.net. Jennifer Moore, poetry editor. **Contact:** Jacob S. Knabb, editor-in-chief. "*Another Chicago Magazine* is a literary magazine that publishes work by both new and established writers. We look for work that goes beyond the artistic and academic to include and address the larger world. The editors read submissions in Fiction, Poetry, Creative Nonfiction, and Et Al. year round. We often publish special theme issues and sections. We will post upcoming themes on our website. Fiction: Short stories and novel excerpts of 15-20 pages or less. Poetry: Usually no more than 4 pages. Creative Nonfiction: Usually no more than 20 pages. etc.: Work that doesn't quite fit into the other genres such as Word & Image Texts, Satire, and Interviews." Responds in 3 months to queries; 6 months to mss. Sample copy available for $8.

Work published in *ACM* has been included frequently in *The Best American Poetry* and *The Pushcart Prize.*

MAGAZINE NEEDS Submit 3-4 typed poems at a time, usually no more than 4 pages. Considers simultaneous submissions with notification; no previously published poems. Reads submissions year-round. Guidelines available on website; however, "The best way to know what we publish is to read what we publish. If you haven't read *ACM* before, order a sample copy to know if your work is appropriate." Responds in 3 months. Sends prepublication galleys. Pays monetary amount "if funds permit," and/or one contributor's copy and one-year subscription. Acquires first serial rights. Reviews books of poetry in 250-800 words. Send materials for review consideration. No more than 4 pages.

HOW TO CONTACT "Please include the following contact information in your cover letter and on your ms: Byline (name as you want it to appear if published), mailing address, phone number, and e-mail. Include a self-addressed stamped envelope (SASE). If a SASE is not enclosed, you will only hear from us if we are interested in your work. Include the genre (e.g., fiction, et al.) of your work in the address."

TIPS "Support literary publishing by subscribing to at least one literary journal—if not ours, another. Get used to rejection slips, and don't get discouraged. Keep introductory letters short. Make sure manuscript has name and address on every page, and that it is clean, neat and proofread. We are looking for stories with freshness and originality in subject angle and style, and work that encounters the world."

A COMPANION IN ZEOR

1622 Swallow Crest Dr., Apt. B, Edgewood MD 21040-1751. **Website:** www.simegen.com/sgfandom/rimonslibrary/cz/. **Contact:** Karen MacLeod, editor. *A Companion in Zeor*, published irregularly online, is a science fiction/fantasy fanzine. Acquires first rights. Guidelines available for SASE, by fax, email, or on website.

"Material used is now limited to creations based solely on works (universes) of Jacqueline Lichtenberg and Jean Lorrah. No other submission types considered. Prefer nothing obscene. Homosexuality not acceptable unless very relevant to the piece. Prefer a 'clean' publication image." Considers poetry written by young writers over 13; "copyright release form (on the web) available for all submissions."

MAGAZINE NEEDS Accepts fax, e-mail (pasted into body of message), and disk submissions. For regular mail submissions, "note whether to return or dispose of rejected mss." Cover letter is preferred. Sometimes sends prepublication galleys. "Always willing to work with authors or poets to help in improving their work." Reviews books of poetry. Poets may send material for review consideration.

ACUMEN MAGAZINE

Ember Press, 6 The Mount, Higher Furzeham, Brixham, South Devon TQ5 8QY, United Kingdom. **E-mail:** patriciaoxley6@gmail.com. **Website:** www.acumen-poetry.co.uk. **Contact:** Patricia Oxley, poetry editor. *Acumen*, published 3 times/year in January, May, and September, is "a general literary magazine with emphasis on good poetry." Wants "well-crafted, high-quality, imaginative poems showing a sense of form." Does not want "experimental verse of an obscene type." Has published poetry by Ruth Padel, William Oxley, Hugo Williams, Peter Porter, Danielle Hope, and Leah Fritz. *Acumen* is 120 pages, A5, perfect-bound. Receives about 12,000 poems, accepts about 120. Press run is 650.

MAGAZINE NEEDS Submit 5-6 poems at a time. All submissions should be accompanied by SASE. Include name and address on each separate sheet. Postal submissions only. Doesn't accept e-mail submissions, but will send rejections, acceptances, proofs and other communications via email overseas to dispense with IRCs and other international postage. Any poem that may have chance of publication is shortlisted and from list final poems are chosen. All other poems returned within 2 months. "If a reply is required, please send IRCs. One IRC for a decision, 3 IRCs if work is to be returned." Willing to reply by e-mail to save IRCs. Responds in 3 months. Staff reviews books of poetry in up to 300 words (single-book format) or 600 words (multi-book format). Send materials for review consideration to Glyn Pursglove, 25 St. Albans Rd., Brynmill, Swansea, West Glamorgan SA2 0BP Wales. Looking for poetry which is not trivial, not obvious, doesn't use outworn images or diction, and which works at many levels simultaneously. Receives around 10,00-15,000; publishes 150. Pays "by negotiation" and 1 contributor's copy.

TIPS "Read *Acumen* carefully to see what kind of poetry we publish. Also, read widely in many poetry magazines, and don't forget the poets of the past—they can still teach us a great deal."

THE ADIRONDACK REVIEW

Black Lawrence Press, 8405 Bay Parkway, Apt C8, Brooklyn NY 11214. **E-mail:** editors@theadirondackreview.com; angela@blacklawrencepress.com. **Website:** www.adirondackreview.homestead.com. **Contact:** Angela Leroux-Lindsey, Kara Christenson, Diane Goettel, editor. *The Adirondack Review*, published quarterly online, is a literary journal dedicated to quality free verse poetry and short fiction as well as book and film reviews, art, photography, and interviews. "We are open to both new and established writers. Our only requirement is excellence. We would like to publish more French and German poetry translations as well as original poems in these languages. We publish an eclectic mix of voices and styles, but all poems should show attention to craft. We are open to beginners who demonstrate talent, as well as established voices. The work should speak for itself." Acquires first rights. Responds to queries in 1-2 months. Responds to mss in 2-4 months.

HOW TO CONTACT Submit 2-7 poems at a time. Considers simultaneous submissions (with notification); no previously published poems. Accepts e-mail submissions only. "All submissions should be pasted into the body of an e-mail (no attached files, please). We no longer accept postal submissions. All postal submissions will be discarded unread." Cover letter is preferred. Reads submissions year round. Submit seasonal poems 3 months in advance. Time between acceptance and publication is 1-3 months. Seldom comments on rejected poems. Guidelines available on website. Rights revert to poet upon publication. "We reserve the right to reprint the work in the event of a print-based anthology at a later date." Reviews books of poetry. Send materials for review consideration.

ADVOCATE, PKA'S PUBLICATION

1881 Little Westkill Rd., Prattsville NY 12468. (518)299-3103. **E-mail:** advoad@localnet.com. **Website:** Advocatepka.weebly.com or www.facebook.com/pages/Advocate-PKAs-Publication/111826035499969. **Contact:** Patricia Keller, publisher. "Advocates for good writers and quality writings. We publish art, fiction, photos and poetry. *Advocate*'s submitters are talented people of all ages who do not earn their livings as writers. We wish to promote the arts and to give those we publish the opportunity to be published." Acquires first rights for mss, artwork, and photographs. Pays on publication with contributor's copies. Publishes ms 2-18 months after acceptance. Responds to queries in 6 weeks; mss in 2 months.

Gaited Horse Association newsletter is included in this publication. Horse-oriented stories, poetry, art and photos are currently needed.

MAGAZINE NEEDS *Advocate, PKA's Publication*, published bimonthly, is an advertiser-supported tabloid using "original, previously unpublished works, such as feature stories, essays, 'think' pieces, letters to the editor, profiles, humor, fiction, poetry, puzzles, cartoons, or line drawings." Wants "nearly any kind of poetry, any length." Circulation is 10,000; all distributed free. Subscription: $16.50 (6 issues). Sample: $5 (includes guidelines). Occasionally comments on rejected poems. Responds in 2 months. Guidelines available with sample copy ($5). Pays 2 contributor's copies. Acquires first rights only. No religious or pornographic poetry.

TIPS "Please, no simultaneous submissions, work that has appeared on the Internet, pornography, overt religiousity, anti-environmentalism or gratuitous violence. Artists and photographers should keep in mind that we are a b&w paper. Please do not send postcards. Use envelope with SASE."

AFRICAN VOICES

African Voices Communications, Inc., 270 W. 96th St., New York NY 10025. (212)865-2982. **Fax:** (212)316-3335. **E-mail:** africanvoices@aol.com. **Website:** www.africanvoices.com. *African Voices*, published quarterly, is an "art and literary magazine that highlights the work of people of color. We publish ethnic literature and poetry on any subject. We also consider all themes and styles: avant-garde, free verse, haiku, light verse, and traditional. We do not wish to limit the reader or author." Buys first North American serial rights. Pays on publication. Publishes ms an average of 3-6 months after acceptance. Responds in 3 months to queries. Editorial lead time 3 months. Sample copy for $5.

Considers poetry written by children. Has published poetry by Reg E. Gaines, Maya Angelou, Jessica Care Moore, Asha Bandele, Tony Medina, and Louis Reyes Rivera. *African Voices* is about 48 pages, magazine-sized, professionally printed, saddle-stapled, with paper cover. Receives about 100 submissions/year, accepts about 30%. Press run is 20,000. Single copy: $4; subscription: $12.

MAGAZINE NEEDS Submit no more than 2 poems at any 1 time. Accepts previously published poems and simultaneous submissions. Accepts submissions by e-mail (in text box), by fax, and by postal mail. Cover letter and SASE required. Seldom comments on rejected poems. Responds in 3 months. Pays 2 copies. Acquires first or one-time rights. Reviews books of poetry in 500-1,000 words. Send materials for review consideration to Layding Kaliba. Sponsors periodic poetry contests and readings. Send SASE for details. Length: 5-100 lines. Pays in contributor copies

TIPS "A ms stands out if it is neatly typed with a well-written and interesting story line or plot. Originality is encouraged. We are interested in more horror, erotic, and drama pieces. *AV* wants to highlight the diversity in our culture. Stories must touch the humanity in us all. We strongly encourage new writers/poets to send in their work. Accepted contributors are encouraged to subscribe."

AGNI

(617)353-7135. **Fax:** (617)353-7134. **E-mail:** agni@bu.edu. **Website:** www.agnimagazine.org. **Contact:** Sven Birkerts, editor. "Eclectic literary magazine publishing first-rate poems, essays, translations, and stories." Buys serial rights. Rights to reprint in *AGNI* anthology (with author's consent). Pays on publication. Publishes ms an average of 6 months after acceptance. Responds in 2 weeks to queries. Responds in 4 months to mss. Editorial lead time 1 year. Sample copy for $10 or online. Guidelines available online.

Reading period September 1-May 31 only. "Online magazine carries original content not found in print edition. All submissions are considered for both." Founding editor Askold Melnyczuk won the 2001 Nora Magid Award for Magazine Editing. Work from *AGNI* has been included and cited regularly in the *Pushcart Prize* and *Best American* anthologies.

MAGAZINE NEEDS *AGNI*, published semiannually, prints poetry, fiction, and essays "by both emerging and established writers. We publish quite a bit of poetry in forms as well as 'language'poetry, but we don't begin to try and place parameters on the 'kind of work' that *AGNI* selects." Wants readable, intelligent poetry—mostly lyric free verse (with some narrative and dramatic)—that somehow communicates tension or risk. Has published poetry by Patricia Goedicke, Stephen Dunn, Kim Addonizio, Kate Northrop, Matt Donovan, and Seamus Heaney. *AGNI* is typeset, offset-printed, perfect-bound. Circulation is 3,000 for subscriptions, mail orders, and bookstore sales. Subscription: $20. Sample: $10. Pays $20/page up to $150

HOW TO CONTACT Submit no more than 5 poems at a time. Considers simultaneous submissions; no previously published poems. No e-mail submissions. Cover letter is required ("brief, sincere"). "No fancy fonts, gimmicks. Include SASE or e-mail address; no preformatted reply cards." Reads submissions September 1-May 31. Pays $20/page ($150 maximum), a 1-year subscription, and for print publication: 2 contributor's copies and 4 gift copies. Acquires first serial rights.

TIPS "We're also looking for extraordinary translations from little-translated languages. It is important to read work published in *AGNI* before submitting, to see if your own might be compatible."

THE AGUILAR EXPRESSION

1329 Gilmore Ave., Donora PA 15033. (724)379-8019. **E-mail:** xyz0@access995.com. **Website:** www.wordrunner.com/xfaguilar. **Contact:** Xavier F. Aguilar, editor/publisher. *The Aguilar Expression*, published annually in October, encourages "poetics that deal with now, which our readers can relate to. Has published poetry by Martin Kich and Gail Ghai. *The Aguilar Expression* is 4-20 pages, 8×11, typeset, printed on 20 lb. paper. Receives about 10-15 poems/month, accepts about 10-15/year. Circulation is 150. Sample: $5. Make checks payable to Xavier Aguilar. Submit up to 5 poems at a time. Lines/poem: 30 maximum. No e-mail submissions. Cover letter is required (include writing background). SASE (for contact purposes) is required. Manuscripts should be submitted in clear, camera-ready copy. Submit copies, not originals; mss will not be returned. "We encourage all writers to send a SASE for writer's guidelines before submitting." Responds in 2 months.

"In publishing poetry, I try to exhibit the unique reality that we too often take for granted and acquaint as mediocre."

MAGAZINE NEEDS Submit up to 5 poems at a time. Lines/poem: 30 maximum. No e-mail submissions. Cover letter is required (include writing background). SASE (for contact purposes) is required. Mss should be submitted in clear, camera-ready copy. Submit copies, not originals; mss will not be returned. "We encourage all writers to send a SASE for writer's guidelines before submitting." Pays 2 contributor's copies.

ALASKA QUARTERLY REVIEW

ESB 208, University of Alaska-Anchorage, 3211 Providence Dr., Anchorage AK 99508. (907)786-6916. **E-mail:** aqr@uaa.alaska.edu. **Website:** www.uaa.alaska.edu/aqr. **Contact:** Ronald Spatz. "*AQR* publishes fiction, poetry, literary nonfiction and short plays in traditional and experimental styles." Buys first North American serial rights. Upon request, rights will be transferred back to author after publication. Honorariums on publication when funding permits. Publishes ms an average of 6 months after acceptance. Responds in 1 month to queries. Responds in 6 months to mss. Sample copy for $6. Guidelines available online.

Alaska Quarterly reports they are always looking for freelance material and new writers.

MAGAZINE NEEDS *Alaska Quarterly Review*, published in 2 double issues/year, is "devoted to contemporary literary art. We publish both traditional and experimental fiction, poetry, literary nonfiction, and short plays." Wants all styles and forms of poetry, "with the most emphasis perhaps on voice and content that displays 'risk,' or intriguing ideas or situations." Has published poetry by Maxine Kumin, Jane Hirshfield, David Lehman, Pattiann Rogers, Albert Goldbarth, David Wagoner, Robert Pinsky, Linda Pastan, Ted Kooser, Kay Ryan, W. S. Merwin, Sharon Olds and Billy Collins. *Alaska Quarterly Review* is 224-300 pages, digest-sized, professionally printed, perfect-bound, with card cover with color or b&w photo. Receives up to 6,000 submissions/year, accepts 40-90. Subscription: $18. Sample: $6. Pays $10-50 subject to availability of funds; pays in contributor's copies and subscriptions when funding is limited. No light verse.

HOW TO CONTACT No fax or e-mail submissions. Reads submissions mid-August to mid-May; manuscripts are *not* read May 15-August 15. Responds in up to 5 months, "sometimes longer during peak periods in late winter."

ADDITIONAL INFORMATION Guest poetry editors have included Stuart Dybek, Jane Hirshfield, Stuart Dischell, Maxine Kumin, Pattiann Rogers, Dorianne Laux, Peggy Shumaker, Olena Kalytiak Davis, Nancy Eimers, Michael Ryan, and Billy Collins.

TIPS "All sections are open to freelancers. We rely almost exclusively on unsolicited manuscripts. *AQR* is a nonprofit literary magazine and does not always have funds to pay authors."

◐ ALBATROSS

The Anabiosis Press, 2 South New St., Bradford MA 01835. (978)469-7085. **E-mail:** rsmyth@anabiosispress.org. **Website:** www.anabiosispress.org. **Contact:** Richard Smyth, editor. *Albatross*, published "as soon as we have accepted enough quality poems to publish an issue—about 1 per year," considers the albatross "to be a metaphor for the environment. The journal's title is drawn from Coleridge's *The Rime of the Ancient Mariner* and is intended to invoke the allegorical implications of that poem. This is not to say that we publish only environmental or nature poetry, but that we are biased toward such subject matter. We publish mostly free verse, and we prefer a narrative style." Wants "poetry written in a strong, mature voice that conveys a deeply felt experience or makes a powerful statement." Does not want "rhyming poetry, prose poetry, or haiku." Has published poetry Francis Blessington, Lyn Stefenhagens, Matthew J. Spireng, Lyn Lifshin, and Mitch LesCarbeau. *Albatross* is 28 pages, digest-sized, laser-typeset, with linen cover. Subscription: $8 for 2 issues. Sample: $5.

MAGAZINE NEEDS Submit 3-5 poems at a time. Lines/poem: 200 maximum. No simultaneous submissions. Accepts e-mail submissions if included in body of message (but is "often quicker at returning mailed submissions"). Name and address must accompany e-mail submissions. Cover letter is not required. "We do, however, need bio notes and SASE for return or response. Poems should be typed single-spaced, with name, address, and phone number in upper left corner." Time between acceptance and publication is up to 6 months to a year. Guidelines available for SASE or on website. Responds in 2-3 months. Pays 1 contributor's copy. Acquires all rights. Returns rights provided that "previous publication in *Albatross* is mentioned in all subsequent reprintings."

◐ ALIMENTUM, THE LITERATURE OF FOOD

P.O. Box 210028, Nashville TN 37221, Nashville TN 37221. **E-mail:** submissions@alimentumjournal.com. **Website:** www.alimentumjournal.com. **Contact:** Cortney Davis, Poetry Editor. "We're seeking fiction, creative nonfiction, and poetry all around the subject of food or drink. We do not read year-round. Check website for reading periods." Responds in 1-3 months to mss.

MAGAZINE NEEDS *Alimentum, The Literature of Food*, published semiannually in winter and summer, is "the only literary journal all about food." Wants "fiction, creative nonfiction, and poetry all around the subject of food." Has published poetry by Dick Allen, Stephen Gibson, Carly Sachs, Jen Karetnik, Virginia Chase Sutton. *Alimentum* is 128 pages, 6x7.5, perfect-bound, with matte coated cover with 4-color art, interior b&w illustration includes ads. Receives about 2,000 poems/year, accepts about 30-40. Press run is 2,000-3,000. Single copy: $10 ($18 Canada/foreign); subscription: $18 for 1 year ($30 Canada/foreign). Make checks payable to *Alimentum* (payment available online through credit card or PayPal).

HOW TO CONTACT Submit no more than 5 poems at a time. Lines/poem: no minimum or maximum. Considers simultaneous submissions; no previously published poems. No e-mail submissions; postal submissions only. Include SASE. Check website for reading periods which vary from year to year. Guidelines available on website. Responds 1-3 months. Pays contributor's copy. Acquires First North American Serial rights. Rights revert to poets upon publication.

ALSO OFFERS Publishes an annual broadside of "menupoems" for restaurants during National Poetry Month in April.

TIPS "No e-mail submissions, only snail mail. Mark outside envelope to the attention of Poetry, Fiction, or Nonfiction Editor."

ALIVE NOW

1908 Grand Ave., P.O. Box 340004, Nashville TN 37203-0004. **E-mail:** alivenow@upperroom.org. **Website:** www.alivenow.org; www.upperroom.org. **Contact:** Beth A. Richardson, editor. *Alive Now*, published bimonthly, is a devotional magazine that invites readers to enter an ever-deepening relationship with God. "*Alive Now* seeks to nourish people who are hungry for a sacred way of living. Submissions should invite readers to see God in the midst of daily life by exploring how contemporary issues impact their faith lives. Each word must be vivid and dynamic and contribute to the whole. We make selections based on a list of upcoming themes. Manuscripts which do not fit a theme will be returned." Considers avant-garde and free verse. *Alive Now* is 64 pages. Accepts 20 poems/year. Circulation is 70,000. Subscription: $17.95/year (6 issues); $26.95 for 2 years (12 issues). Additional subscription information, including foreign rates, available on website.

MAGAZINE NEEDS Submissions should invite readers to seek God in the midst of daily life by exploring how contemporary issues impact their faith lives. If ms does not fit a theme, it will not be considered. Themes can be found on website. Prefers electronic submissions, pasted into body of e-mail or attached as Word document. Postal submissions should include SASE. Include name, address, theme on each sheet. Payment will be made at the time of acceptance for publication. "We will notify contributors of manuscript status when we make final decisions for an issue, approximately two months before the issue date." Pays $35 or more on acceptance.

ALL GENRES LITERARY MAGAZINE

4625 Mormon Coulee Rd., #100, La Crosse WI 54601. **E-mail:** editor@allgenres24.com. **Website:** www.mikesharlowwritercom.fatcow.com/allgenres24. **Contact:** Michael Miller, managing editor; Elizabeth Miller. Buys first North American serial and electronic rights. Pays on publication. Publishes ms 3 months after acceptance. Responds to queries in 1 month; mss in 3 months. Editorial lead time 1 month. Sample copy and guidelines available online at website.

MAGAZINE NEEDS Length: no more than 1,000 words. Pays $25/poem.

AMAZE: THE CINQUAIN JOURNAL

10529 Olive St., Temple City CA 91780. **E-mail:** cinquains@hotmail.com. **Website:** www.amaze-cinquain.com. **Contact:** Deborah P. Kolodji, editor. *AMAZE: The Cinquain Journal*, published bianually online, is a literary webzine devoted to the cinquain poetry form. Wants American cinquains as invented by Adelaide Crapsey (5 lines with a 2-4-6-8-2 syllable pattern) and cinquain variations (mirror cinquains, crown cinquains, cinquain sequences, etc.). Has published poetry by an'ya, Ann K. Schwader, Michael McClintock, naia, and Denis Garrison. Receives about 1,500 poems/year, accepts about 100. Acquires 1-time rights. Rsponds in 6 weeks. Guidelines available for SASE or on website.

MAGAZINE NEEDS Submit 1-5 poems at a time. "E-mail submissions preferred, with poems in the body of the e-mail. Do not send attachments." Include SASE with postal mail submissions. "Poems are evaluated on quality, form, and content." Often comments on rejected poems.

AMBIT

17 Priory Gardens, Highgate, London N6 5QY, England. **E-mail:** info@ambitmagazine.co.uk. **Website:** www.ambitmagazine.co.uk. **Contact:** Edwin Brock, Carol Ann Duffy, and Henry Graham, Poetry Editors. *Ambit* magazine is a literary and artwork quarterly created in London, published in the UK, and read internationally. *Ambit* is put together entirely from unsolicited, previously unpublished poetry and short fiction submissions. Does not want "indiscriminately centre-justified poems; jazzy fonts; poems all in italics for the sake of it." Subscription: £28/1 year. (NOTE: online subcriptions renew automatically unless canceled.) Single Issue: £9. *Ambit*, published quarterly, is a 96-page quarterly of avant-garde, contemporary, and experimental work. *Ambit* is perfect-bound, with 2-color cover with artwork. Accepts about 3% of submissions received. Subscription: £28 UK, £30/€44 rest of Europe, £32/$64 everywhere else. Sample: £7 UK, £9/€15 rest of Europe, £10/$20 overseas.

MAGAZINE NEEDS Submit up to 6 poems at a time. No previously published poems or simultaneous submissions. No e-mail submissions. "SAE vital for reply;" include IRCs when submitting from outside of UK. Poems should be typed, double-spaced. Never comments on rejected poems. Guidelines available in magazine or on website. Responds in 3-4 months. Pays small token plus 2 contributor's copies. Staff reviews books of poetry. Send materials for review consideration to review editor.

TIPS "Read a copy of the magazine before submitting!"

◐ THE AMERICAN DISSIDENT: A JOURNAL OF LITERATURE, DEMOCRACY & DISSIDENCE

217 Commerce Rd., Barnstable MA 02630. **E-mail:** todslone@hotmail.com. **Website:** www.TheAmericanDissident.org. **Contact:** G. Tod Slone, editor. Journal, published 2 times/year, provides "a forum for, amongst other things, criticism of the academic/literary established order, which clearly discourages vigorous debate, cornerstone of democracy, to the evident detriment of American Literature. The Journal seeks rare poets daring to risk going against that established-order grain." Wants "poetry, reviews, artwork, and short (1,000 words) essays in English, French, or Spanish, written on the edge with a dash of personal risk and stemming from personal experience, conflict with power, and/or involvement." Submissions should be "iconoclastic and parrhesiastic in nature." 56-64 pages, digest-sized, offset-printed, perfect-bound, with card cover. Press run is 200. Single copy: $9; subscriptions: individuals, $18; institutions $20. Almost always comments on rejected poems. Pays 1 contributor's copy. Reviews books/chapbooks of poetry and other magazines in 250 words, single-book format. Send materials for review consideration. Acquires First North American serial rights. Up to 2 months between acceptance and publication. Responds in 1 month. Guidelines available for SASE.

MAGAZINE NEEDS Submit 3 poems at a time. Considers simultaneous submissions; no previously published poems. E-mail submissions from subscribers only. "Far too many poets submit without even reading the guidelines. Include SASE and cover letter containing not credits, but rather personal dissident information, as well as incidents that provoked you to 'go upright and vital, and speak the rude truth in all ways' (Emerson)." Time between acceptance and publication is up to 2 months. Almost always comments on rejected poems. Guidelines available for SASE. Responds in 1 month. Pays 1 contributor's copy. Acquires first North American serial rights. Reviews books/chapbooks of poetry and other magazines in 250 words, single-book format. Send materials for review consideration.

AMERICAN LETTERS AND COMMENTARY

E-mail: amerletters@satx.rr.com. **Website:** www.amletters.org. "Only previously unpublished work is considered. We publish creative nonfiction essays and critical essays with experimental slant/subject matter." Publishes ms an average of 1 year after acceptance. Guidelines available on website.

MAGAZINE NEEDS Length: 10 lines.

TIPS "Our reading period is October 1-March 1. A brief cover letter is always welcome. Read a recent issue before submitting—75% of submissions are rejected because they don't fit the journal's aesthetic or don't comply with our guidelines. No e-mailed submissions. We will make contact via e-mail by September 1 for forthcoming issue inclusions. Include an e-mail address in your contact info. All rights are returned to author upon publication."

◐ AMERICAN LITERARY REVIEW

University of North Texas, P.O. Box 311307, Denton TX 76203-1307. (940)565-2755. **E-mail:** americanliteraryreview@gmail.com; bond@unt.edu. **Website:** www.engl.unt.edu/alr. "The *American Literary Review* welcomes submissions of previously unpublished poems, short stories, and creative non-fiction. We also accept submissions for cover art. Please include an SASE and cover letter with your submission. Also include enough postage to return your work. Please mark envelopes and cover letters 'Fiction', 'Poetry', or 'Nonfiction'. Simultaneous submissions are acceptable if noted in your cover letter. For any questions not covered in this section, please refer to our 'Frequently Asked Questions' page. Our reading period extends from October 1 to May 1. Unsolicited manuscripts received outside this reading period will be returned unread. Currently, we do not accept submissions via email. Submissions should be directed to the appropriate editor (Fiction, Poetry, Nonfiction, or Art)."

MAGAZINE NEEDS *American Literary Review*, published semi-annually, considers all forms and modes of poetry, creative nonfiction, and fiction. "We are especially interested in originality, substance, imaginative power, and lyric intensity." Has published poetry by Kathleen Pierce, Mark Irwin, Stephen Dunn, William Olsen, David St. John, and Cate Marvin. *American Literary Review* is about 120 pages, digest-sized, attractively printed, perfect-bound, with color card cover with photo. Subscription: $14/year, $22 for 2 years. Sample: $8.

HOW TO CONTACT No fax or e-mail submissions. Cover letter is required. Include author's name, address, phone number, and poem titles. Reads mss October 1-May 1. Guidelines available on website. Responds in up to 3 months. Pays 2 contributor's copies. Considers simultaneous submissions.

CONTEST/AWARD OFFERINGS Check website for contest details.

TIPS "We encourage writers and artists to examine our journal. The *American Literary Review* publishes semi-annually. If you would like to subscribe to our journal, subscription rates run $14 for a 1-year subscription, $26 for a 2-year subscription, and $36 for a 3-year subscription. You may also obtain a sample copy of the *American Literary Review* for $7 plus $1 per issue for shipping and handling in the U.S. and Canada ($2 for postage elsewhere)."

THE AMERICAN POETRY JOURNAL

P. O. Box 2080, Aptos CA 95001-2080. **E-mail:** editor@americanpoetryjournal.com. **Website:** www.americanpoetryjournal.com. *The American Poetry Journal*, published annually (July), seeks "to publish work using poetic device, favoring image, metaphor, and good sound. We like alliteration, extended metaphors, image, movement, and poems that can pass the 'so what' test. *The American Poetry Journal* has in mind the reader who delights in discovering what a poem can do to the tongue and what the poem paints on the cave of the mind." Wants poems "that exhibit strong, fresh imagery, metaphor, and good sound." Does not want "narratives about family, simplistic verse, annoying word hodge-podges." Has published poetry by C.J. Sage, Natasha Sage, Lola Haskins, Dorianne Laux, and Sarah J. Sloat. *The American Poetry Journal* is 100 pages, 6×9, perfect-bound. Accepts about 1% of poems submitted. Single copy: $12; subscription: $12. Make checks payable to Dream Horse Press.

MAGAZINE NEEDS Submit 3-5 poems at a time. Considers simultaneous submissions; no previously published poems. E-mail submissions only. Cover letter is preferred. Considers unsolicited submissions February 1-May 31—All decisions made no later than June 30. (Poets may submit no more than twice during the reading period). "We consider submissions from subscribers year round." Time between acceptance and publication is between 2 and 6 months. "Poems are read first for clarity and technique, then read aloud for sound quality." Seldom comments on rejected poems. Guidelines available on website. Responds in 3 months. Pays one contributor's copy. Acquires first rights.

TIPS "Know the magazine you are submitting to, before you commit your work and yourself. It's not that difficult, but it helps your odds when the editor can tell that you get what the magazine is about. Reading an issue is the easiest way to do this."

THE AMERICAN POETRY REVIEW

1700 Sansom St., Suite 800, Philadelphia PA 19103. **E-mail:** sberg@aprweb.org. **Website:** www.aprweb.org. **Contact:** Stephen Berg, editor.

Accepts mss via postal mail only.

CONTEST/AWARD OFFERINGS "The Jerome J. Shestack Poetry Prizes of $1,000 are awarded annually to each of 2 poets whose work has appeared in APR during the preceding calendar year."

AMERICAN TANKA

E-mail: laura@lauramaffei.com. **Website:** www.americantanka.com. "*American Tanka* seeks to present the best and most well-crafted English-language tanka being written today, in a visually calm space that allows the reader's eye to focus on the single poem and linger in the moment it evokes." Acquires first North American serial rights. Responds in 3 months.

MAGAZINE NEEDS *American Tanka* is devoted to single English-language tanka. Wants "concise and vivid language, good crafting, and echo of the original Japanese form, but with unique and contemporary content." Does not want "anything that's not tanka. No sequences or titled groupings." Has published poetry by Sanford Goldstein, Marianne Bluger, Jeanne Emrich, Tom Hartman, Larry Kimmel, Pamela Miller Ness, and George Swede.

HOW TO CONTACT Submit up to 5 poems. No previously published poems or simultaneous submissions. Accepts submissions by online submission form found on website or by e-mail (pasted into body). Responds in 3 months. Acquires first North American serial rights. Welcomes submissions from anyone who has been writing tanka: experienced tanka poets, experienced poets in other forms, and novices. Seeks concise, well-crafted, 5-line tanka that evoke a specific moment in time.

ANCIENT PATHS

P.O. Box 7505, Fairfax Station VA 22039. **E-mail:** SSBurris@cox.com. **Website:** www.editorskylar.com. **Contact:** Skylar H. Burris, Editor. *Ancient Paths*, published biennially in odd-numbered years, provides "a forum for quality Christian poetry." Wants "traditional rhymed/metrical forms and free verse; subtle Christian themes. Seeks poetry that makes the reader both think and feel." Does not want 'preachy' poetry, inconsistent meter, or forced rhyme; no stream of conscious or avant-garde work; no esoteric academic poetry. Has published poetry by Nicholas Samaras, Paul David Adkins, Ida Fasel, and Donna Farley. *Ancient Paths* is 60+ pages, digital/e-book. Issue 17 will feature the work of multiple poets. Receives about 600 queries/year, accepts 10-20 poets. Press run to be determined. Acquires one-time or reprint rights. Pays $5 for the first poem and $2 for each additional poem published. Responds in 3-4 weeks "if rejected; longer if being seriously considered." Single copy: $5 for new e-book format; $10 for hard copy back issues. Make checks payable to Skylar Burris. Guidelines available for SASE or on website.

MAGAZINE NEEDS "Query with 3-6 of your best poems." Considers previously published poems and simultaneous submissions. Accepts e-mail submissions. "Submissions should be pasted directly into the message, single-spaced, 1 poem per message, using a small or normal font size, with name and address at the top of each submission. Use subject heading: ANCIENT PATHS SUBMISSION, followed by your title." For postal submissions, poems should be single-spaced; "always include name, address, and line count on first page of all submissions, and note if the poem is previously published and what rights (if any) were purchased." Check website for reading period and submission details for Issue 18. Time between acceptance and publication is up to 1 year. Sometimes comments on rejected poems. Guidelines available for SASE or on website. Lines/poem: 8 minimum; no maximum.

TIPS "Read the great religious poets: John Donne, George Herbert, T.S. Eliot, Lord Tennyson. Remember not to preach. This is a literary magazine, not a pulpit. This does not mean you do not communicate morals or celebrate God. It means you are not overbearing or simplistic when you do so."

THE ANTIGONISH REVIEW

(902)867-3962. **Fax:** (902)867-5563. **E-mail:** tar@stfx.ca. **Website:** www.antigonishreview.com. **Contact:** Bonnie McIsaac, office manager. *The Antigonish Review* is 144 pages, digest-sized, offset-printed, flat-spined, with glossy card cover with art. Receives 2,500 submissions/year, accepts about 10%. Press run is 1,000. Subscription: $24 CAD, $30 US, International $40. Sample: $7. TAR is open to poetry on any subject written from any point of view and in any form. However, writers should expect their work to be considered within the full context of old and new poetry in English and other languages. No more than 6-8 poems should be submitted at any one time. A preferable submission would be from 3-4 poems Literary magazine for educated and creative readers. Rights retained by author. Pays on publication. Publishes ms an average of 8 months after acceptance. Responds in 1 month to queries. Responds in 6 months to mss. Editorial lead time 4 months. Sample copy for $7 or online Writer's guidelines for #10 SASE or online

MAGAZINE NEEDS A preferable submission would be from 3-4 poems *The Antigonish Review*, published quarterly, tries "to produce the kind of literary and visual mosaic that the modern sensibility requires or would respond to. Has published poetry by Andy Wainwright, W.J. Keith, Michael Hulse, Jean McNeil, M. Travis Lane, and Douglas Lochhead. No previously published poems or simultaneous submissions. Submit 6-8 poems at a time. Lines/poem: not over 80, i.e., 2 pages. Pays $30/full page and 2 contributor's copies. Acquires first North American serial rights.

HOW TO CONTACT P.O. Box 5000, Antigonish NS-B2G 2W5, Canada. Accepts fax submissions; e-mail submissions accepted from overseas only. Include SASE (SAE and IRCs if outside Canada; "we cannot use U.S. postage") or we can respond by e-mail. Time between acceptance and publication is up to 8 months. Sometimes comments on rejected poems. Guidelines available for SASE, by e-mail, or on website. Responds in up to 6 months.

TIPS "Send for guidelines and/or sample copy. Send ms with cover letter and SASE with submission."

ANTIOCH REVIEW

P.O. Box 148, Yellow Springs OH 45387-0148. **E-mail:** mkeyes@antiochreview.org. **Website:** http://antioch-college.org/antioch_review/. Judith Hall, poetry editor. **Contact:** Muriel Keyes. Guidelines available on website. Responds in 8-10 weeks. Pays $15/published page plus 2 contributor's copies; additional copies available at 40% discount. Poetry submissions are not accepted between between May 1 and September 1. Literary and cultural review of contemporary issues, and literature for general readership. Pays on publication. Publishes ms an average of 10 months after acceptance. Responds in 3-6 months to mss. Sample copy for $7. Guidelines available online.

Work published in the *Antioch Review* has been included frequently in *The Best American Poetry, The Best New Poets* and *The Pushcart Prize.*

MAGAZINE NEEDS *The Antioch Review* "is an independent quarterly of critical and creative thought. For well over 50 years, creative authors, poets, and thinkers have found a friendly reception—regardless of formal reputation. We get far more poetry than we can possibly accept, and the competition is keen. Here, where form and content are so inseparable and reaction is so personal, it is difficult to state requirements or limitations. Studying recent issues of *The Antioch Review* should be helpful." Has published poetry by Peter Marcus, Jacqueline Osherow, Joanna Rawson, David Yezzi, and others. Receives about 3,000 submissions/year. Circulation is 3,000; 70% distributed through bookstores and newsstands. No light or inspirational verse. Pays $15/printed page.

HOW TO CONTACT Submit 3-6 poems at a time. No previously published poems or simultaneous submissions. Include SASE with all submissions.

AOIFE'S KISS

The Speculative Fiction Foundation, P.O. Box 782, Cedar Rapids IA 52406-0782. **E-mail:** aoifeskiss@yahoo.com. **Website:** www.samsdotpublishing.com. **Contact:** Tyree Campbell, Managing Editor. Member: The Speculative Literature Foundation (http://SpeculativeLiterature.org). "Aoife's Kiss is a print and online magazine of fantasy, science fiction, horror, sword & sorcery, and slipstream, published quarterly in March, June, September, and December. Aoife's Kiss publishes short stories, poems, illustrations, articles, and movie/book/chapbook reviews, and interviews with noted individuals in those genres." Responds in 2 weeks to queries. Editorial lead time is 2 months.

MAGAZINE NEEDS *Aoife's Kiss*, published quarterly, prints "fantasy, science fiction, sword and sorcery, alternate history, dark fantasy short stories, poems, illustrations, and movie and book reviews." Wants "fantasy, science fiction, spooky horror, and speculative poetry with minimal angst." Considers poetry by children and teens. Has published poetry by Bruce Boston, Karen A. Romanko, Mike Allen, Corrine De Winter, Julie Shiel, and Marge B. Simon. *Aoife's Kiss* (print version) is 54 pages, magazine-sized, offset-printed, saddle-stapled, perfect-bound, with color paper cover, includes ads. Receives about 300 poems/year, accepts about 50 (17%). Press run is 150; 5 distributed free to reviewers. Single copy: $7; subscription: $22/year, $40 for 2 years. Make checks payable to Sam's Dot Publishing.

HOW TO CONTACT Submit up to 5 poems at a time. Lines/poem: prefers less than 100. Considers previously published poems; no simultaneous submissions. Accepts e-mail submissions (pasted into body of message); no disk submissions. "Submission should include snail mail address and a short (1-2 lines) bio." Reads submissions year round. Submit seasonal poems 6 months in advance. Time between acceptance and publication is 2-5 months. Often comments on rejected poems. Guidelines available on website. Responds in 4-6 weeks. Pays $5/poem, $3/reprint, $1 for scifaiku and related forms, and 1 contributor's copy. Acquires first North American serial rights. Reviews books/chapbooks of poetry. Send materials for review consideration to Tyree Campbell.

APALACHEE REVIEW

Apalachee Press, P.O. Box 10469, Tallahassee FL 32302. (850)644-9114. **E-mail:** arsubmissions@hotmail.com (for queries outside of the U.S.). **Website:** http://apalacheereview.org/index.html. **Contact:** Michael Trammell, editor; Mary Jane Ryals, fiction editor.

MAGAZINE NEEDS *Apalachee Review*, published about twice/year, appears "as soon as we have enough good material." Has published poetry by Rita Mae Reese and Charles Harper Webb. *Apalachee Review* is 120 pages, digest-sized, professionally printed, perfect-bound, with card cover. Press run is 700. Subscription: $15 for 2 issues ($30 foreign). Sample: $5. Considers simulaneous submissions. Accepts submissions by postal mail only. "Submit clear copies, with name and address on each." SASE required. Reads submissions year round. Sometimes comments on rejected poems. Guidelines available for SASE or on website. Responds in 4 months, "but sometimes we get bogged down." Pays 2 contributor's copies. Poet retains rights. Staff reviews books of poetry. Send materials for review consideration. Member: CLMP, AAP.

APPARATUS MAGAZINE

E-mail: submissions@apparatusmagazine.com; editor@apparatusmagazine.com. **Website:** www.apparatusmagazine.com. **Contact:** Adam W. Hart, publisher/editor. "*Apparatus Magazine* strives to bring readers poetry and fiction from around the world that explores the mythos of 'man (or woman) vs. machine,' that conjures up words from the inner machine, and more. Each issue features work from around the world, bringing the reader literary updates from the *internal machine.*" Buys first North American serial rights, first and electronic rights, retains right to archive material on website. No payment offered, however, all published works will be considered for an annual *Apparatus Award* of $100 for each category (poetry, fiction) for work published in that publishing year (June to June). 1-3 months 1 week on queries; 2-3 months on mss. Guidelines also available on website.

Online monthly magazine which "strives to bring readers poetry and fiction from around the world that explores the mythos of "man (or woman) vs. machine," that conjures up words from the inner machine, and more. Each issue of apparatus magazine features work from around the world, bringing the reader literary updates from the internal machine. Fiction consists of short fiction/flash fiction (500 words or less), and each issue of the magazine has a specific theme.

MAGAZINE NEEDS Wants "shorter poetry, free verse. Attention given to poems with a strong, natural voice. apparatus magazine accepts poetry on general themes, but does feature monthly thematic issues." Does not want overtly inspirational poetry, poetry aimed at children, or confessional poetry. Avoid "work that is overtly racist, sexist, violent, homophobic, discriminatory, pornographic, or otherwise in questionable taste." Has published poetry by Rayne Arroyo, Anne Brooke, Lesley Dame, Gregg Shapiro, Inara Cedrins, and Chanming Yuan. Prefer shorter poetry, free verse. Attention given to poems with a strong, natural voice. No overtly inspirational poetry, poetry aimed at children, or confessional poetry.

HOW TO CONTACT Submit 3-5 poems at a time, 2 pages maximum/poem. Accepts submissions by e-mail pasted into body of e-mail message. Cover letter is required. "Please include list of submitted poems, as well as a (maximum) 3-line bio listing other publications/journals in which poet has published his/her work." Reads submissions year round. Submit seasonal poems 2-3 months in advance. Time between acceptance and publication is 1-3 months. Often comments on rejected poems. Regularly publishes theme issues. Upcoming themes available in magazine, by e-mail, and on website. Guidelines available in magazine, by e-mail, and on website. Acquires first North American serial rights, electronic rights, option with poet's permission to reprint accepted work in yearly anthology. Rights rever to poet upon publication.

CONTEST/AWARD OFFERINGS The Apparatus Award is offered annually for best poem published in *Apparatus Magazine* during the publication year (June to May). Award: $100. Guidelines available in magazine, on website, by e-mail.

TIPS "Be sure to read the guidelines as posted. Themes for each issue are typically posted 3 months (or more) in advance. Include cover letter and bio with emaill submissions. Submit more than just one poem, so I can get a feel for your work. Be sure to read back issues of the magazine. The journal tends to select work that focuses on specific themes, and usually tries to pick work that will compliment/contrast with other pieces selected for the issue. Send your best work and don't be afraid of trying again. I often suggest other publications/markets if a piece is not a good match for the journal."

APPLE VALLEY REVIEW: A JOURNAL OF CONTEMPORARY LITERATURE

88 South 3rd St., Suite 336, San Jose CA 95113. **E-mail:** editor@leahbrowning.net. **Website:** www.applevalleyreview.com. **Contact:** Leah Browning, editor. *Apple Valley Review: A Journal of Contemporary Literature*, published semiannually online, features "beautifully crafted poetry, short fiction, and essays." Wants "work that has both mainstream and literary appeal. All work must be original, previously unpublished, and in English. Translations are welcome if permission has been granted. Preference is given to short (under 2 pages), non-rhyming poetry." Does not want "erotica, work containing explicit language or violence, or work that is scholarly, critical, inspirational, or intended for children." Acquires first rights and first serial rights and retains the right to archive the work online for an indefinite period of time. "As appropriate, we may also choose to nominate published work for awards or recognition. Author retains all other rights." Time between acceptance and publication is 1-6 months. Sometimes comments on rejected poems and mss. Responds to mss in 1 week-2 months. Guidelines available by e-mail or on website.

Considers poetry by children and teens: "Our audience includes teens and adults of all ages."

Has published poetry by Vince Corvaia, Michael Lauchlan, Jin Cordaro, Gregory Lawless, Anna Evans, and Keetje Kuipers. Receives about 5,000+ poems/year, accepts less than 1%.

MAGAZINE NEEDS Submit 2-6 poems at a time. Lines/poem: "no limit, though we prefer short poems (under 2 pages)." No previously published poems. Accepts e-mail submissions (pasted into body of message, with "poetry" in subject line); no disk submissions. Reads submissions year round. Offers the annual *Apple Valley Review* Editor's Prize. Award varies. "From 2006-2011, the prize was $100 and a book of poetry or fiction." Submit 2-6 poems. **Entry fee:** none. **Deadline:** rolling; all submissions to the *Apple Valley Review*, and all work published during a given calendar year will be considered for the prize.

CONTEST/AWARD OFFERINGS Offers the annual *Apple Valley Review* Editor's Prize. Award varies. "From 2006-2011, the prize was $100 and a book of poetry or fiction." Submit 2-6 poems. **Entry fee:** none. **Deadline:** rolling; all submissions to the *Apple Valley Review*, and all work published during a given calendar year will be considered for the prize.

A PUBLIC SPACE

323 Dean St., Brooklyn NY 11217. (718)858-8067. **E-mail:** general@apublicspace.org. **Website:** www.apublicspace.org. **Contact:** Brigid Hughes, editor. 323 Dean St., Brooklyn, NY 11217. (718)858-8067. **E-mail:** general@apublicspace.org. **Website:** www.apublicspace.org. *A Public Space*, published quarterly, "is an independent magazine of literature and culture. In an era that has relegated literature to the margins, we plan to make fiction and poetry the stars of a new conversation. We believe that stories are how we make sense of our lives and how we learn about other lives. We believe that stories matter." Single copy: $15; subscription: $36/year or $60/2 years.

HOW TO CONTACT Submit up to 4 poems at a time. Considers simultaneous submissions; no previously published poems. Prefers submissions through online process; accepts mail. Include SASE. See website for submission dates and guidelines.

THE APUTAMKON REVIEW: VOICES FROM DOWNEAST MAINE AND THE CANADIAN MARITIMES (OR THEREABOUTS)

the WordShed, LLC, P.O. Box 190, Jonesboro ME 04648. **E-mail:** thewordshed@tds.net. **Website:** http://thewordshed.com. Send complete ms with cover letter. Accepts submissions in the body of an e-mail, on disk via USPS. Submission period is 12 months a year; reading January 1 through March 31. Responds only between Jan. 31 and April 31. Include age if under 18, and a bio will be requested upon acceptance of work. Responds to queries or submissions in 2-8 weeks. Send SASE (or IRC) for return of ms or a disposable copy of ms and #10 SASE for reply only. Considers simultaneous submissions, multiple submissions. Sample copy available for $12.85 US plus $2.75 US s/h. Guidelines available for SASE, via e-mail, via fax. Submissions receive $10-35 depending on medium, plus one copy. Pays on acceptance. Acquires first North American serial rights. Publication is copyrighted. All rights revert back to the contributors upon publication. "*The Aputamkon Review* will present a mismash of truths, half truths and outright lies, including but not limited to short fiction, tall tales, creative non-fiction, essays, (some) poetry, haiku, b&w visual arts, interviews, lyrics and music, quips, quirks, quotes that should be famous, witticisms, follies, comic strips, cartoons, jokes, riddles, recipes, puzzles, games. Stretch your imagination. Practically anything goes." Annual. Estab. 2006. Circ. 500. Member Maine Writers and Publishers Alliance. Pays on acceptance. Acquires first North American serial rights. Publication is copyrighted. All rights revert back to the contributors upon publication.

TIPS "Be colorful, heartfelt not mainstream. Write what you want and then submit."

ARC POETRY MAGAZINE

P.O. Box 81060, Ottawa ON K1P 1B1, Canada. **E-mail:** arc@arcpoetry.ca. **Website:** www.arcpoetry.ca. **Contact:** Pauline Conley, managing editor. "*Arc Poetry Magazine* has been publishing the best in contemporary Canadian and international poetry and criticism for over 30 years." Press run is 1,500. Subscriptions: 1 year—$35 CDN; 2 years—$60 CND (in Canada). US subscriptions: 1 year—$45 CAD; 2 years—$80 CAD. International subscriptions: 1 year—$55 CDN; 2 year—$90 CDN. Online ordering available for subscriptions and single copies (with occasional promotions). "*Arc Poetry Magazine* has been publishing the best in contemporary Canadian and international poetry and criticism for over 30 years." Acquires first Canadian serial rights. Pays $40 CAD/page plus contributor's copy. Responds in 4-6 months.

MAGAZINE NEEDS *Arc* is published 3 times a year, including an annual themed issue each fall. Canada's poetry magazine publishes poetry, poetry-related articles, interviews, and book reviews, and occasionally publishes on its website; *Arc* also runs a Poet-in-Residence program. Has published poetry by Don Coles, Karen Solie, Carmine Starnino, David O'Meara, Elizabeth Bachinsky, George Elliott Clarke, Daryl Hine, Michael Ondaatje, Stephanie Bolster, and Don Domanski. *Arc* is 130-160 pages, perfect-bound, printed on matte white stock "with a crisp, engaging design and a striking visual art portfolio in each issue." Receives over 2,500 submissions/year; accepts about 40-50 poems.

HOW TO CONTACT "*Arc* accepts unsolicited submissions of previously unpublished poems from September 1 to May 31; maximum of 5 poems, 1 submission per year per person. Please see arcpoetry.ca for full guidelines and to use our online submission manager. For reviews, interviews, and articles, please query first."

CONTEST/AWARD OFFERINGS Poem of the Year Contest—deadline: February 1; $5,000 grand prize; entry fee includes 1-year subscription. Confederation Poets Prize and Critic's Desk Award for best poem and reviews published in *Arc* in the preceding year. Other awards include the Archibald Lampman Award and the Diana Brebner Prize.

ARDENT!

Poetry in the Arts, Inc., 302 Cripple Creek, Cedar Park TX 78613. **E-mail:** rimer777@gmail.com. **Website:** www.poetryinarts.org/publishing/ardent.html. **Contact:** Dillon McKinsey, executive editor. *Ardent!*, published semiannually, is a journal of poetry and art. All forms and styles are considered. *Ardent!* is perfect-bound.

MAGAZINE NEEDS E-mail up to 3 poems (pasted in body of e-mail). "Include a statement giving Poetry in the Arts, Inc. your permission to use your work." Provide brief biography. Accepts attachments in e-mails. Strongly prefers e-mail submissions but will accept postal submissions. See website for guidelines.

◐ ARIES: A JOURNAL OF CREATIVE EXPRESSION

Dept. of Languages and Literature, 1201 Wesleyan St., Fort Worth TX 76105-1536. (817)531-4907. **E-mail:** sneeley@txwes.edu. **Website:** www.department.txwes.edu/aries/Aries.htm. **Contact:** Stacia Dunn Neeley, general editor. *Aries: A Journal of Creative Expression*, published annually in summer, prints quality poetry, b&w photography/art, fiction, creative nonfiction, essays, and short plays. Poetry 3 to 50 lines. Original poetry in languages other than English welcome if submitted with English translation as companion. Has published poetry by Virgil Suárez, Richard Robbins, Susan Smith Nash, Gerald Zipper, and Lynn Veach Sadler. *Aries* is 70-100 pages, digest-sized, offset-printed, perfect-bound, with slick cover. Receives about 800 poems/year, accepts about 10%. Press run is 300. Single copy: $7; back issues: $6.

HOW TO CONTACT Send 5 submissions maximum per year. Lines/poem: 3 minimum, 50 maximum. Considers simultaneous submissions with notification; no previously published poems. Cover letter required. Include titles of submissions and 100-word bio required; no names allowed on submissions themselves. Accepts submissions September 1-January 31 only. "At least 3 reviewers read every submission via blind review." Guidelines available in magazine, for SASE or by e-mail. Responds by May. Acquires first rights.

◐ ARKANSAS REVIEW

(870) 972-3043; (870)972-3674. **Fax:** (870)972-3045. **E-mail:** arkansasreview@astate.edu;. **E-mail:** jcollins@astate.edu; arkansasreview@astate.edu. **Website:** http://altweb.astate.edu/arkreview/. Tom Williams. **Contact:** Dr. Janelle Collins, general editor/associate professor of English. *Arkansas Review* is 92 pages, magazine-sized, photo offset-printed, saddle-stapled, with 4-color cover. Receives about 500 poems/year, accepts about 5%. Press run is 600; 50 distributed free to contributors. Subscription: $20. Sample: $7.50. Make checks payable to ASU Foundation. Submit any number of poems at a time. No previously published poems or simultaneous submissions. "All material, creative and scholarly, published in the *Arkansas Review*, must evoke or respond to the natural and/or cultural experience of the Mississippi River Delta region." Buys first North American serial rights. Responds in 2 weeks to queries. Responds in 4 months to mss. Editorial lead time 4 months. Sample copy for $7.50. Guidelines available online.

MAGAZINE NEEDS *Arkansas Review: A Journal of Delta Studies*, published 3 times/year, is "a regional studies journal devoted to the 7-state Mississippi River Delta. Interdisciplinary in scope, we publish academic articles, relevant creative material, interviews, and reviews. Material must respond to or evoke the experiences and landscapes of the 7-state Mississippi River Delta (St. Louis to New Orleans)." Has published poetry by Greg Fraser, Jo McDougall, and Catherine Savage Brosman. Length: 1-100 lines.

HOW TO CONTACT Accepts e-mail and disk submissions. Cover letter is preferred. Include SASE. Time between acceptance and publication is about 6 months. Occasionally publishes theme issues. Pays 3 contributor's copies. Acquires first rights. Staff reviews books/chapbooks of poetry "that are relevant to the Delta" in 500 words, single- and multi-book format. Send materials for review consideration to Janelle Collins ("inquire in advance").

TIPS Submit via mail. E-mails are more likely to be overlooked or lost. Submit a cover letter, but don't try to impress us with credentials or explanations of the submission. Immerse yourself in the literature of the Delta, but provide us with a fresh and original take on its land, its people, its culture. Surprise us. Amuse us. Recognize what makes this region particular as well as universal, and take risks. Help us shape a new Delta literature.

ARSENIC LOBSTER

E-mail: lobster@magere.com. **Website:** http://arseniclobster.magere.com. Guidelines available at http://arseniclobster.magere.com/1submission.html.

MAGAZINE NEEDS E-mail submissions to lobster@magere.com. "Poems should be timeless, rich in imagery and edgy; seeking elegant emotion, articulate experiment. Be compelled to write." "We do not want political rants or Hallmark poetry."

TIPS "All works must be previously unpublished. Include a lively, short biography. Poetry topics, reviews and criticism, and art/photographs (pdf or jpg attachment only) are also welcome."

ARTFUL DODGE

(330)263-2577. **E-mail:** artfuldodge@wooster.edu. **Website:** www.wooster.edu/artfuldodge. **Contact:** Daniel Bourne, editor-in-chief; Karin Lin-Greenberg, fiction editor; Marcy Campbell, associate fiction editor; Carolyne Wright, translation editor. There is no theme in this magazine, except literary power. We also have an ongoing interest in translations from Central/Eastern Europe and elsewhere. Buys first North American serial rights. Responds in 1-6 months to mss. Sample copy for $7. Guidelines for #10 SASE.

MAGAZINE NEEDS We are interested in poems that utilize stylistic persuasions both old and new to good effect. We are not afraid of poems which try to deal with large social, political, historical, and even philosophical questions—especially if the poem emerges from one's own life experience and is not the result of armchair pontificating. We don't want cute, rococo surrealism, someone's warmed-up, left-over notion of an avant-garde that existed 10-100 years ago, or any last bastions of rhymed verse in the civilized world. Pays $5/page honorarium and 2 contributor's copies.

TIPS Poets may send books for review consideration; however, there is no guarantee we can review them.

ART TIMES

A Literary Journal and Resource for All the Arts, P.O. Box 730, Mount Marion NY 12456-0730. (845)246-6944. **Fax:** (845)246-6944. **E-mail:** info@ArtTimesJournal.com. **Website:** www.arttimesjournal.com. **Contact:** Raymond J. Steiner. "*Art Times* covers the art fields and is distributed in locations most frequented by those enjoying the arts. Our copies are distributed throughout the lower part of the northeast as well as metropolitan New York area; locations include theaters, galleries, museums, schools, art clubs, cultural centers and the like. Our readers are mostly over 40, affluent, art-conscious and sophisticated. Subscribers are located across US and abroad (Italy, France, Germany, Greece, Russia, etc.)." Buys first North American serial rights, buys first rights. Pays on publication. Publishes ms an average of 3 years after acceptance. Responds in 6 months to queries. Responds in 6 months to mss. Sample copy for sae with 9×12 envelope and 6 first-class stamps. Writer's guidelines for #10 SASE or online.

MAGAZINE NEEDS *Art Times*, published monthly (combining Jan/Feb and July/Aug), is a tabloid newspaper devoted to the fine and performing arts. Focuses on cultural and creative articles and essays, but also publishes some poetry and fiction. Wants "poetry that strives to express genuine observation in unique language. All topics, all forms." *Art Times* is 20-26 pages, newsprint, includes ads. Receives 300-500 poems/month, accepts about 30-35/year. Circulation is 27,000; most distribution is free through galleries, performing arts centers, schools, museums, theatres, etc., in the Northeast Corridor of the U.S. Subscription: $15/year. Sample: $1 with 9×12 SAE and 3 first-class stamps. Submit 4-5 typed poems at a time. Lines/poem: up to 20. No e-mail submissions. Include SASE with all submissions. Has an 18-month backlog. Guidelines available for SASE. Responds in 6 months. Pays 6 contributor's copies plus one-year subscription. "We prefer well-crafted 'literary' poems. No excessively sentimental poetry." Publishes 2-3 poems each issue. 20 lines maximum. Offers contributor copies and 1 year's free subscription

TIPS "Competition is greater (more submissions received), but keep trying. We print new as well as published writers." "Be advised that we are presently on an approximate 3-year lead for short stories, 2-year lead for poetry. We are now receiving 300-400 poems and 40-50 short stories per month. Be familiar with *Art Times* and its special audience."

ASCENT ASPIRATIONS

1560 Arbutus Dr., Nanoose Bay BC C9P 9C8, Canada. **E-mail:** ascentaspirations@shaw.ca. **Website:** www.ascentaspirations.ca. **Contact:** David Fraser, Editor. *Ascent Aspirations Magazine*, publishes monthly on-line and publishes one anthology in print as a separate themed title in spring, specializes in poetry, short fiction, essays, and visual art. "A quality electronic and print publication, *Ascent* is dedicated to encouraging aspiring poets and fiction writers. We accept all forms of poetry on any theme. Poetry needs to be unique and touch the reader emotionally with relevant human, social, and philosophical imagery." Does not want poetry "that focuses on mainstream overtly religious verse." Considers poetry by children and teens. Has published poetry by Janet Buck and Taylor Graham. Work is considered for the print *The Yearly Anthology* through contests (see below). Receives about 1,500 poems/year, accepts about 15%. Submit 1-5 poems at a time. Considers previously published poems and simultaneous submissions. Prefers e-mail submissions (pasted into body of message or as attachment in Word); no disk submissions. "If you must submit by postal mail because it is your only avenue, provide a SASE with IRCs or Canadian stamps." Reads submissions on a regular basis year round. Time between acceptance and publication is 3 months or sooner. Editor makes decisions on all poems. Seldom comments on rejected poems. Occasionally publishes theme issues. Upcoming themes available on website. Responds in 3 months. Acquires one-time rights.To fund the printing of the annual anthology, *Ascent* offers a contest for poetry and fiction. 1st Prize: $100 CAD; 2nd Prize: $75 CAD; 3rd Prize: $50 CAD; 4th Prize: $25 CAD; 5 Honorable Mentions: $10 CAD each. All winners and honorable mentions receive 1-2 copies of anthology; all other entrants published in anthology receive 1 free copy. Guidelines available for SASE, by e-mail, or on website. **Entry fee:** $5 CAD/poem or $10 CAD/3 poems. **Deadlines:** "these vary for each contest." **NOTE: "Fee, awards, and the number of copies for winners of contests can change. Refer always to the website for the most up-to-date information."**

TIPS "Short fiction should, first of all tell, a good story, take the reader to new and interesting imaginary or real places. Short fiction should use language lyrically and effectively, be experimental in either form or content and take the reader into realms where they can analyze and think about the human condition. Write with passion for your material, be concise and economical and let the reader work to unravel your story. In terms of editing, always proofread to the point where what you submit is the best it possibly can be. Never be discouraged if your work is not accepted; it may just not be the right fit for a current publication."

ASHEVILLE POETRY REVIEW

P.O. Box 7086, Asheville NC 28802. (828)649-0217. **Website:** www.ashevillereview.com. **Contact:** Keith Flynn, founder/managing editor. *Asheville Poetry Review*, published annually, prints "the best regional, national, and international poems we can find. We publish translations, interviews, essays, historical perspectives, and book reviews as well." Wants "quality work with well-crafted ideas married to a dynamic style. Any subject matter is fit to be considered so long as the language is vivid with a clear sense of rhythm. We subscribe to the Borges dictum that great poetry is a combination of 'algebra and fire.'" Has published poetry by Sherman Alexie, Eavan Boland, Gary Snyder, Colette Inez, Robert Bly, and Fred Chappell. *Asheville Poetry Review* is 160-300 pages, digest-sized, perfect-bound, laminated, with full-color cover. Receives about 8,000 submissions/year, accepts about 5%. Press run is 3,000. Subscription: $22.50 for 2 years, $43.50 for 4 years. Sample: $13. **"We prefer poets purchase a sample copy prior to submitting."** Poems are circulated to an editorial board. Seldom comments on rejected poems. Occasionally publishes theme issues. Pays 1 contributor's copy. Rights revert back to author upon publication. Reviews books/chapbooks of poetry. Send materials for review consideration. Up to one year from acceptance to publishing time. Responds in up to 7 months. Guidelines available for SASE or on website.

MAGAZINE NEEDS Submit 3-5 poems at a time. No previously published poems or simultaneous submissions. No e-mail submissions. Cover letter is required. Include comprehensive bio, recent publishing credits, and SASE. Reads submissions January 15-July 15.

ASININE POETRY

E-mail: editor@asininepoetry.com. **Website:** www.asininepoetry.com. **Contact:** R. Narvaez, editor. *asinine poetry and prose*, published monthly online, "features 10-12 new works each month. We specialize in poetry that does not take itself too seriously." Wants "any form of poetry, but for us the poetry must be in a humorous, parodic, or satirical style. We prefer well-crafted poems that may contain serious elements or cover serious subjects—but which are also amusing, absurd, or hilarious." Does not want serious, straightforward poems. Has published poetry by Hal Sirowitz, William Trowbridge, Elizabeth Swados, Daniel Thomas Moran, and Colonel Drunky Bob. Receives about 1,000 poems/year, accepts about 10%.

MAGAZINE NEEDS Submit 3-4 poems at a time. Lines/poem: 50 maximum. Considers previously published poems and simultaneous submissions. Accepts e-mail (pasted into body of message).

CONTEST/AWARD OFFERINGS Sponsors 1 contest/year. Guidelines available on website.

ASSENT

Assent c/o Tracey Roberts, Room E701, Kedelston Rd., University of Derby, Derby DE22 1GB, England. **E-mail:** t.roberts@derby.ac.uk. **Website:** http://nottinghampoetrysociety.co.uk. **Contact:** Adrian Buckner, editor; Tracey Roberts, editorial assistant. Subscription Rates: £12.00 UK; £18.00 Sterling overseas (3 issues). Current issue: £4.00 + 80p p&p. Back issues: £1.50 inc p&p. Cheques payable to Derby University. Subscribers who wish to pay in $US: Please send cheque to 1036 Menlo Avenue, Apt. 301, Los Angeles, California 90006 USA. Subscription: $25 inc p&p. Current issue $7.00. Back issue $4.00. US Cheque payable to Karen Crosbie.

CONTEST/AWARD OFFERINGS The Nottingham Open Poetry Competition offers cash prizes, annual subscriptions, and publication in *Assent*. Open to all. Guidelines available on website.

ATLANTA REVIEW

P.O. Box 8248, Atlanta GA 31106. **E-mail:** atlrev@yahoo.com. **Website:** www.atlantareview.com. **Contact:** Dan Veach, Editor/Publisher. *Atlanta Review*, published semiannually, is devoted primarily to poetry, but occasionally features interviews and b&w artwork. Wants "quality poetry of genuine human appeal." Has published poetry by Seamus Heaney, Billy Collins, Derek Walcott, Maxine Kumin, Alicia Stallings, Gunter Grass, Eugenio Montale, and Thomas Lux. Atlanta Review is 128 pages, digest-sized, professionally printed on acid-free paper, flat-spined, with glossy color cover. Receives about 10,000 poems/year, accepts about 1%. Press run is 2,500. Single copy: $6; subscription: $10. Sample: $5.

Work published in *Atlanta Review* has been included in *The Best American Poetry* and *The Pushcart Prize*.

MAGAZINE NEEDS Submit no more than 5 poems at a time. No previously published poems. No e-mail submissions from within the U.S.; postal submissions only. Include SASE for reply. "Authors living outside the United States and Canada may submit work via e-mail." Cover letter is preferred. Include brief bio. Put name and address on each poem. Reads submissions according to the following deadlines: June 1 for Fall; December 1 for Spring. "While we do read year round, response time may be slower during summer and the winter holidays." Time between acceptance and publication is 6 months. Seldom comments on rejected poems. Guidelines available for SASE, by e-mail, or on website. Responds in 1 month. Pays 2 contributor's copies, author's discounts on additional copies. Acquires first North American serial rights.

THE ATLANTIC MONTHLY

The Watergate, 600 New Hampshire Ave., NW, Washington DC 20037. (202)266-6000. **Website:** www.theatlantic.com. **Contact:** James Bennet, editor; C. Michael Curtis, fiction editor; David Barber, poetry editor. "Interest is in the broadest possible range of work: traditional forms and free verse, the meditative lyric and the "light" or comic poem, the work of the famous and the work of the unknown. We have long been committed to the discovery of new poets. Our one limitation is length; we are unable to publish very long poems." General magazine for an educated readership with broad cultural and public-affairs interests. "The Atlantic considers unsolicited manuscripts, either fiction or nonfiction. A general familiarity with what we have published in the past is the best guide to our needs and preferences. Manuscripts must be typewritten and double-spaced. Receipt of manuscripts will be acknowledged if accompanied by a self-addressed stamped envelope. Manuscripts will not be returned. **At this time, the print magazine does not read submissions sent via fax or e-mail.** TheAtlantic.com no longer accepts unsolicited submissions." Buys first North American serial rights. Guidelines available onine.

MAGAZINE NEEDS Wants "the broadest possible range of work: traditional forms and free verse, the meditative lyric and the 'light' or comic poem, the work of the famous and the work of the unknown." *The Atlantic Monthly* publishes some of the most distinguished poetry in American literature. "We read with interest and attention every poem submitted to the magazine and, quite simply, we publish those that seem to us to be the best." Has published poetry by Maxine Kumin, Stanley Plumly, Linda Gregerson, Philip Levine, Ellen Bryant Voigt, and W.S. Merwin. Receives about 60,000 poems/year. Subscription: $24.50 for 10 issues. Sample: $7.50 (back issue).

HOW TO CONTACT Submit 2-6 poems at a time. No previously published poems or simultaneous submissions. No e-mail or disk submissions; postal submissions only. SASE required. Responds in 4-6 weeks. Pays upon acceptance. Always sends prepublication galleys. Acquires first North American serial rights only.

TIPS "Writers should be aware that this is not a market for beginner's work (nonfiction and fiction), nor is it truly for intermediate work. Study this magazine before sending only your best, most professional work. When making first contact, cover letters are sometimes helpful, particularly if they cite prior publications or involvement in writing programs. Common mistakes: melodrama, inconclusiveness, lack of development, unpersuasive characters and/or dialogue."

ATLANTIC PACIFIC PRESS

The Wale Inn Publishing House, P.O. Box 4394, Danbury CT 06813. (508)994-7869. **Fax:** (774) 263 2839. **E-mail:** lyric_songs@yahoo.com. **Website:** atlanticpacificpress.com. **Contact:** Christine Walen, editor. Quarterly. Has published poetry by D. Davis Phillips, Michael Foster, Lynn Veach Sadler, James Hoggard, Mediha F. Saliba, Sheryl L. Nelms, Marjorie Bixler, Sheila Golburgh Johnson, James Fowler, Claudia Barnett. APP is digest sized, 90+ pages, saddle stapled. Guidelines: send for with a SASE. Deadlines: Spg/Feb 20, Sum/May 20, Fall/Aug 20, Win/Nov 20. Single: $10 Subscription: $30/year. *Atlantic Pacific Press* is a quarterly journal of fiction, drama, poetry, prose poetry, flash fiction, lyrics, cartoons, sci-fi, fantasy, veterans/military, romance, mystery, horror, westerns, family life, children's stories, nonfiction, art, and photography. No porn. Acquires one time rights, first North American serial rights. First rights. Rights return to author upon publication.

ALSO OFFERS Offers annual drama contest. Deadline January 30. Send for guidelines with a SASE.

TIPS "Consider taking a writing class or workshop. Read your mss to someone before sending."

THE AVALON LITERARY REVIEW

CCI Publishing, P.O. Box 780696, Orlando FL 32878. (407)574-7355. **E-mail:** submissions@avalonliteraryreview.com. **Website:** www.avalonliteraryreview.com. **Contact:** Valerie Rubino, managing editor. Quarterly magazine. "*The Avalon Literary Review* welcomes work from both published and unpublished writers and poets. We accept submissions of poetry, short fiction, and personal essays. The author's voice and point of view should be unique and clear. We seek pieces which spring from the author's life and experiences. Submissions which explore both the sweet and bitter of life, with a touch of humor, are a good fit for our *Review*. While we appreciate the genres of fantasy, science fiction and horror, our magazine is not the forum for such work." Buys one-time rights. Pays on publication. Publishes ms an average of 3 months after acceptance. Editorial lead time is 3 months. Sample copy available for $10; by e-mail; available on website. Writer's guidelines available online at website or by e-mail.

MAGAZINE NEEDS No rhyming verse. Length: no more than 50 lines. Pays 5 contributor's copies.

TIPS "We seek work that is carefully structured. We like vivid descriptions, striking characters, and realistic dialogue. A humorous but not ridiculous point of view is a plus."

AVOCET, A JOURNAL OF NATURE POEMS

P.O. Box 1717, Southold NY 11971. **E-mail:** peter@avocetreview.com. **Website:** www.avocetreview.com. **Contact:** Peter C. Leverich, editor. *Avocet, A Journal of Nature Poems,* published quarterly, is "devoted to poets who find meaning in their lives from the natural world." Wants "imagist/transcendental poetry that explores the beauty and divinity in nature." Does not want "poems that have rhyme, cliché, or abstraction." Has published poetry by Louis Daniel Brodsky, Gary Every, Ruth Goring, Gayle Elen Harvey, Lyn Lifshin, Holly Rose Diane Shaw, and Kristin Camitta Zimet. *Avocet* is 60 pages, 4 1/4x5 1/2, professionally printed, saddle-stapled, with card cover. Single copy: $6; subscription: $24. Make checks payable to Peter C. Leverich.

MAGAZINE NEEDS Submit 3-5 poems at a time. Considers previously published poems, if acknowledged. Cover letter with e-mail address is helpful. Include SASE for reply only; mss will not be returned. Time between acceptance and publication is up to 3 months. Responds in up to 2 months.

THE AWAKENINGS REVIEW

P.O. Box 177, Wheaton IL 60187. **E-mail:** info@awakeningsproject.org. **Website:** www.awakeningsproject.org. **Contact:** Robert Lundin, editor. *The Awakenings Review,* published annually, prints works by people living with mental illness. Poet "must live with mental illness: consumer, survivor, family member, ex-patient." Wants "meaningful work, good use of the language. Need not be *about* mental illness." Has published poetry by Joan Rizzo, Wanda Washko, Ben Beyerlein, and Trish Evers. *The Awakenings Review* is 150 pages, digest-sized, perfect-bound, with glossy b&w cover. Receives about 800 poems/year, accepts about 10%. Press run is 1,000; 300 distributed free to contributors, friends. Single copy: $12 postpaid; subscription: $35. Make checks payable to *The Awakenings Review.* Acquires first rights. Publishes ms 8 months after acceptance. Responds in 1 month. Guidelines available in magazine, for SASE, by e-mail, or on website.

MAGAZINE NEEDS Submit 5 poems at a time. No previously published poems or simultaneous submissions. No e-mail submissions. Cover letter is preferred. Include SASE and short bio. Poems are read by a board of editors. Often comments on rejected poems. Occasionally publishes theme issue. Pays 1 contributor's copy, plus discount on additional copies.

BABEL: THE MULTILINGUAL, MULTICULTURAL ONLINE JOURNAL AND COMMUNITY OF ARTS AND IDEAS

E-mail: submissions@towerofbabel.com. **Website:** http://towerofbabel.com. **Contact:** Malcolm Lawrence, Editor-in-Chief. "Babel is an electronic zine recognized by the UN as one of the most important social and human sciences online periodicals. Writers whose work discriminates against the opposite sex, different cultures, or belief systems will not be considered." Time between acceptance and publication vis usually no more than 2 months." Seldom comments on rejected poems. Guidelines available on website. Responds in 2-4 weeks. Reviews books/chapbooks of poetry and other magazines, single- and multi-book format. Open to unsolicited reviews. Publishes regional reports from international stringers all over the planet, as well as features, round table discussions, fiction, columns, poetry, erotica, travelogues, and reviews of all the arts and editorials. We're interested in fiction, non-fiction and poetry from all over the world, including multicultural or multilingual work, as well as poetry that has been translated from or into another language, as long as it is also in English. We also appreciate gay/lesbian and bisexual poetry. Cover letter is required. Reviews books/chapbooks of poetry and other magazines, single- and multi-book format. Open to unsolicited reviews. Send materials for review consideration. 1-2 months Responds in 2-4 weeks. Guidelines available on website.

Babel is recognized by the UN as one of the most important social and human sciences online periodicals.

MAGAZINE NEEDS WordPress bloggers in the following languages: Arabic, Bulgarian, Bengali, Catalan, Czech, Welsh, Danish, German, English, Esperanto, Spanish, Persian, Finnish, Faroese, French, Hebrew, Croatian, Indonesian, Italian, Japanese, Korean, Latvian, Malay, Dutch, Polish, Portuguese, Russian, Albanian, Serbian, Swedish, Tamil, Thai, Ukrainian, Urdu, Uzbek, Vietnamese and Chinese.

HOW TO CONTACT Submit no more than 10 poems at a time. Considers previously published poems and simultaneous submissions. Accepts e-mail submissions only. Cover letter is required. "Please send submissions with a résumé or bio as a Microsoft Word or RTF document attached to e-mail."

ADDITIONAL INFORMATION Our bloggers include James Schwartz, the first out gay poet raised in the Old Order Amish community in Southwestern Michigan and author of the book *The Literary Party*; Susanna Zaraysky, author of the book *Language Is Music: Making People Multilingual*; James Rovira, Assistant Professor of English and Program Chair of Humanities at Tiffin University and author of the book *Blake & Kierkegaard: Creation and Anxiety*; and Paul B. Miller, Assistant Professor Department of French and Italian at Vanderbilt University.

TIPS "We would like to see more fiction with first-person male characters written by female authors, as well as more fiction first-person female characters written by male authors. We would also like to see that dynamic in action when it comes to other languages, cultures, races, classes, sexual orientations and ages. Know what you are writing about and write passionately about it."

BABEL FRUIT

E-mail: babelfruit@live.com. **Website:** http://web.mac.com/renkat/BABEL_FRUIT/BabelFruit.html. **Contact:** Ren Powell, founding editor; Cati Porter, associate editor. "Ezine that publishes literature of exile, expatriation, repatriation, integration and exploration. We want to read poetry 'under the influence of 'the other.' Travel, look around or reach within to wherever you see the other." Invites submissions from new and established poets. Send 4 poems max (or 5 pages, whichever comes first) with cover letter. Accepts simultaneous and previously published submissions; see guidelines online. Does not pay. Please read the guidelines online at website.

ADDITIONAL INFORMATION "Published biannually and nominates contributors for the Pushcart and other awards."

TIPS "If you use an attachment to submit, use: babelfruit.submission.doc and put your name in the subject line. We invite new and established writers."

BABYBUG

Carus Publishing, 70 East Lake St., Chicago IL 60601. **E-mail:** babybug@caruspub.com. **Website:** www.cricketmag.com. **Contact:** Marianne Carus, editor-in-chief; Suzanne Beck, managing art director. "A listening and looking magazine for infants and toddlers ages 6 to 24 months, *Babybug* is 6×7, 24 pages long, printed in large type on high-quality cardboard stock with rounded corners and no staples." Responds in 6 months to mss. Guidelines available online.

MAGAZINE NEEDS Submit no more than 5 poems at a time. Lines/poem: 8 lines maximum. Considers previously published poems. Include SASE. Guidelines available for SASE or on website. Responds in 6 months. Pays $25 minimum on publication. Acquires North American publication rights for previously published poems; rights vary for unpublished poems.

TIPS "Imagine having to read your story or poem—out loud—50 times or more! That's what parents will have to do. Babies and toddlers demand, 'Read it again!' Your material must hold up under repetition. And humor is much appreciated by all."

BABYSUE®

babysue ATTN: LMNOP aka dONW7, P.O. Box 15749, Chattanooga TN 373415. **E-mail:** LMNOP@babysue.com. **Website:** www.babysue.com; www.LMNOP.com. **Contact:** Don W. Seven, editor/publisher. *babysue* is an ongoing online magazine featuring continually updated cartoons, poems, literature, and reviews. It is also published twice/year and offers obtuse humor for the extremely open-minded. "We are open to all styles, but prefer short poems." No restrictions. Has published poetry by Edward Mycue, Susan Andrews, and Barry Bishop. "We print prose, poems, and cartoons. We usually accept about 5% of what we receive." Pays 1 contributor's copy. Responds "immediately, if we are interested." Seldom comments on rejected poems. Sample: $7; cash only (no checks or money orders).

TIPS "We do occasionally review other magazines."

THE BALTIMORE REVIEW

P.O. Box 36418, Towson MD 21286. **Website:** www.baltimorereview.org. **Contact:** Susan Muaddi Darraj, managing editor. *The Baltimore Review* is 144 pages, 6×9, offset-lithograph-printed, perfect-bound, with 10-pt. CS1 cover. Subscription: $15/year, $28 for 2 years. Sample: $10 (includes $2 p&h). Make checks payable to *The Baltimore Review*. Reads submissions year round. Time between acceptance and publication is up to 4-6 months. "Poems are circulated to at least two reviewers." Sometimes comments on rejected poems. Guidelines available on website. Responds in up to 4 months. Submit between 1-4 poems. No previously published work. Payment is in copies. "The Baltimore Review publishes poetry, fiction, and creative nonfiction from Baltimore and beyond." Buys first North American serial rights. Contributor paid in copies. Publishes ms an average of 6 months after acceptance. Responds in 6 weeks to queries. Responds in 4 months to mss. Sample copy for $10. Guidelines available online.

"We publish work of high literary quality from established and new writers. No specific preferences regarding theme or style, and all are considered."

MAGAZINE NEEDS *The Baltimore Review*, published twice/year (winter and summer), is "an eclectic collection of writing from Baltimore and beyond," showcasing creative nonfiction, short fiction, poetry, and book reviews. "We invite submissions from writers in the Baltimore region as well as nationally and internationally." Does not want "sentimental-mushy, loud, or very abstract poetry; corny humor; poorly crafted or preachy poetry." 4 pages Pays 2 contributor's copies, reduced rate for additional copies.

HOW TO CONTACT Submit 1-4 poems at a time. Considers simultaneous submissions, "but notify us immediately if your work is accepted elsewhere"; no previously published poems. Accepts submissions only via online submissions system at website (www.baltimorereview.org/submissions/). Cover letter is preferred.

CONTEST/AWARD OFFERINGS Sponsors an annual poetry contest. Offers 1st Prize: $300 plus publication in *The Baltimore Review*; 2nd Prize: $150; 3rd Prize: $50. Submit 1-4 poems (no more than 5 pages total). All forms and styles accepted, including prose poems. Guidelines available on website. **Entry fee:** $12 (includes copy of issue in which 1st-Prize winner is published) or $20 (includes one-year subscription).

TIPS "Please read what is being published in other literary journals, including our own. As in any other profession, writers must know what the trends and the major issues are in the field. We look for compelling stories and a masterful use of the English language. We want to feel that we have never heard this story, or this voice, before. Read the kinds of publications you want your work to appear in. Make your reader believe and care."

BARBARIC YAWP

BoneWorld Publishing, 3700 County Rt. 24, Russell NY 13684-3198. (315)347-2609. **Website:** www.boneworldpublishing.com. Acquires one-time rights. Responds in 2 weeks to queries; 4 months to mss. Sample copy for $4. Guidelines for #10 SASE.

TIPS "Don't give up. Read much, write much, submit much. Observe closely the world around you. Don't borrow ideas from TV or films. Revision is often necessary—grit your teeth and do it. Never fear rejection."

BARN OWL REVIEW

Olin Hall 342, The University of Akron, Akron OH 44325. **E-mail:** info@barnowlreview.com. **Website:** www.barnowlreview.com. **Contact:** Mary Biddinger and Jay Robinson, editors-in-chief. "We are a handsomely designed print journal looking for work that takes risks while still connecting with readers. We aim to publish the highest quality poetry from both emerging and established writers."

MAGAZINE NEEDS Barn Owl Review favors no particular poetic school or style; "however, we look for innovation and risk-taking in the poems that we publish." Submit 3-5 poems (in single attachment) via Submishmash between June 1-November 1. Contributors receive 2 copies of the issue.

BARROW STREET

P.O. Box 1831, New York NY 10156. **E-mail:** infobarrow@gmail.com. **Website:** www.barrowstreet.org. **Contact:** Lorna Blake, Patricia Carlin, Peter Covino, and Melissa Hotchkiss, editors. *Barrow Street*, published annually, "is dedicated to publishing new and established poets." Wants "poetry of the highest quality; open to all styles and forms." Has published poetry by Molly Peacock, Lyn Hejinian, Carl Phillips, Marie Ponsot, Charles Bernstein, and Stephen Burt. *Barrow Street* is 96-120 pages, digest-sized, professionally printed, perfect-bound, with glossy cardstock cover with color or b&w photography. Receives about 3,000 poems/year, accepts about 3%. Press run is 1,000. Subscription: $18 for 2 years, $25 for 3 years. Acquires first rights. Responds in 3-6 months. Sample copy for $10. Guidelines available on website.

Poetry published in *Barrow Street* is often selected for *The Best American Poetry*.

MAGAZINE NEEDS Submit up to 5 poems at a time. Online only-does not accept hard copy submissions. Considers simultaneous submissions (when notified); no previously published poems. Cover letter is preferred. Include brief bio. Must have name, address, e-mail, and phone on each page submitted or submission will not be considered. Reads submissions October 1-March 31. Poems circulated to an editorial board. Does not return or respond to submissions made outside the reading period. Always sends prepublication galleys. Pays 2 contributor's copies.

BATEAU

P.O. Box 1584, Northampton MA 01061. (413)586-2494. **E-mail:** info@bateaupress.org. **Website:** www.bateaupress.org. **Contact:** James Grinwis, editor. "*Bateau*, published semiannually, subscribes to no trend but serves to represent as wide a cross-section of contemporary writing as possible. For this reason, readers will most likely love and hate at least something in each issue. We consider this a good thing. To us, it means Bateau is eclectic, open-ended, and not mired in a particular strain." Has published poetry by Tomaz Salamun, John Olsen, Michael Burkhardt, Joshua Marie Wilkinson, Allison Titus, Allan Peterson, Dean Young. *Bateau* is around 80 pages, digest-sized, offset print, perfect-bound, with a 100% recycled letterpress cover. Receives about 5,000 poems/year, accepts about 60. Press run is 250. Single copy: $12; subscription $24. Make checks payable to Bateau Press. Acquires first North American serial rights, electronic rights. Publishes ms 3-8 months after acceptance. Responds in 3-6 months. Guidelines for SASE or on website.

MAGAZINE NEEDS Pays 2 contributor's copies.

HOW TO CONTACT Submit 5 poems at a time, up to 2 pages. Considers simultaneous submissions, no previously published poems or work concurrently available online. Work should only be submitted via our online submission upload system or the postal system. Reads submissions year round. Poems are circulated to an editorial board. Often comments on rejected poems. Sometimes publishes theme issues. Sometimes sends prepublication galleries. "We reserve the right to display work on internet for promotional, advertising, and to store, transmit, and distribute electronic copies of the work as required to facilitate the printing and distribution process of *Bateau*." Rights revert to poet upon publication.

BAYOU

English Dept. University of New Orleans, 2000 Lakeshore Dr., New Orleans LA 70148. (504)280-5423. **E-mail:** bayou@uno.edu. **Website:** http://137.30.242.125/cww/bayou/index.cfm. "A non-profit journal for the arts, each issue of *Bayou Magazine* contains beautiful fiction, nonfiction and poetry. From quirky shorts to more traditional stories, we are committed to publishing solid work. Regardless of style, at *Bayou* we are always interested first in a well-told tale. Our poetry and prose are filled with memorable characters observing their world, acknowledging both the mundane and the sublime, often at once, and always with an eye toward beauty. *Bayou* is packed with a range of material from established, award-winning authors as well as new voices on the rise. Recent contributors include Eric Trethewey, Virgil Suarez, Marilyn Hacker, Sean Beaudoin, Tom Whalen, Mark Doty, Philip Cioffari, Lyn Lifshin, Timothy Liu and Gaylord Brewer. And in one issue every year, *Bayou* features the winner of the annual Tennessee Williams/New Orleans Literary Festival One-Act Play Competition."

MAGAZINE NEEDS "Our poetry and prose are filled with memorable characters observing their world, acknowledging both the mundane and the sublime, often at once, and always with an eye toward beauty. Contains a range of material from established, award-winning authors as well as new voices on the rise." Has published poetry by Eric Trethewey, Virgil Súaréz, Marilyn Hacker, Sean Beaudoin, Tom Whalen, and Mark Doty. *Bayou* is 130 pages, digest-sized, professionally printed, perfect-bound, with matte cardstock cover (artwork varies). Receives "hundreds of submissions," accepts "very few." Press run is 500; distributed free to students and faculty of University of West Florida and University of New Orleans. Single copy: $8; subscription: $15. Make checks payable to the UNO Foundation. Considers simultaneous submissions; no previously published poems. Acquires first North American serial rights. Submit no more than 5 poems at a time. No e-mail or disk submissions. "A brief cover letter is necessary, but don't tell us your life story, explain your poems, or tell us how wonderful your poems are. Do give us your contact information." Reads submissions year round. Lines/poem: "We have no strict length restrictions, though obviously it is harder to fit in very long poems." Pays 2 contributor's copies.

TIPS "Do not submit in more than one genre at a time. Don't send a second submission until you receive a response to the first."

BEAR CREEK HAIKU

P.O. Box 3787, Boulder CO 80307. **Website:** www.coloradopoetscenter.org/links/bearCreek.html. **Contact:** Ayaz Daryl Nielsen, editor. Acquires first rights. Acceptance to publication time varies.

Reads submissions year round.

MAGAZINE NEEDS Lenth: 11 lines or less or haiku. Pays two contributor's copies.

THE BEAR DELUXE MAGAZINE

Orlo, 810 SE Belmont, Studio 5, Portland OR 97214. (503)242-1047. **E-mail:** bear@orlo.org. **Website:** www.orlo.org. **Contact:** Tom Webb, editor-in-chief; Kristin Rogers Brown, art director. Submit 3-5 poems at a time. Lines/poem: 50 maximum. Considers previously published poems and simultaneous submissions "so long as noted." Poems are reviewed by a committee of 3-5 people. Publishes 1 theme issue/year. Guidelines available for SASE. Responds in 6 months. Acquires first or one-time rights. "*The Bear Deluxe Magazine* is a national independent environmental arts magazine publishing significant works of reporting, creative nonfiction, literature, visual art and design. Based in the Pacific Northwest, it reaches across cultural and political divides to engage readers on vital issues effecting the environment. Published twice per year, *The Bear Deluxe* includes a wider array and a higher-percentage of visual art work and design than many other publications. Artwork is included both as editorial support and as stand alone or independent art. It has included nationally recognized artists as well as emerging artists. As with any publication, artists are encouraged to review a sample copy for a clearer understanding of the magazine's approach. Unsolicited submissions and samples are accepted and encouraged. *The Bear Deluxe* has been recognized for both its editorial and design excellence. Over the years, awards and positive reviews have been handed down from *Print* magazine, *Utne Reader, Literary Arts, Adbusters*, the Bumbershoot Arts Festival, *Orion, Fact Sheet 5*, the Regional Arts and Culture Council, *The Oregonian*, and the *Library Journal*, among others." Buys first rights, buys one-time rights. Pays on publication. Publishes ms an average of 6 months after acceptance. Responds in 3-6 months to mail queries. Only responds to e-mail queries if interested. Editorial lead time 6 months. Sample copy for $3. Guidelines for #10 SASE or on website.

"The magazine is moving away from using the term environmental writing. Quality writing which furthers the magazine's goal of engaging new and divergent readers will garner the most attention." The Orlo Office is open by appointment only.

MAGAZINE NEEDS 50 lines maximum. Pays $20, subscription, and copies.

HOW TO CONTACT Accepts e-mail submissions (pasted into body of message) but it is not as preferable as sending hard copy by mail. "We can't respond to e-mail submissions but do look at them."

TIPS "Offer to be a stringer for future ideas. Get a copy of the magazine and guidelines, and query us with specific nonfiction ideas and clips. We're looking for original, magazine-style stories, not fluff or PR. Fiction, essay, and poetry writers should know we have an open and blind review policy and should keep sending their best work even if rejected once. Be as specific as possible in queries."

THE BEATNIK COWBOY

Native Khymer Hotel, next to the new Nightmarket, Siem Reap , Cambodia. **E-mail:** randall_ro@yahoo.com; beatnik_cowboy@yahoo.com.au. **Contact:** David Soloman, assistant editor. *The Beatnik Cowboy*, published quarterly, wants "Beat-influenced poetry from all poets. We are a young and vibrant magazine, seeking to publish the best of the best poets of the world." Has published poetry by Steve Dalchinsky, David Pointer, Susan Maurer, Randall Rogers, and Joe Speer. *The Beatnik Cowboy*, published quarterly, wants "Beat-influenced poetry from all poets. We are a young and vibrant magazine, seeking to publish the best of the best poets of the world." Has published poetry by Steve Dalchinsky, David Pointer, Susan Maurer, Randall Rogers, and Joe Speer. Acquires one-time rights. Responds in 2 months. Guidelines available in the magazine, by SASE, or by e-mail request.

HOW TO CONTACT Submit 5 poems at a time. Shorter poems preferred. Considers previously published poems and simultaneous submissions. Accepts e-mail (as attachment) and disk submissions. Either post poems in the body of the text or as Word attachment. SAE with IRCs required for return of poems. Reads submissions year round. Submit seasonal poems 2 months in advance. Time between acceptance and publication is 3 months. "At times if we like your stuff we will encourage you to send in more." Sometimes comments on rejected poems. Guidelines available in the magazine, by SASE, or by e-mail request. Responds in 2 months. Acquires one-time rights.

BELLEVUE LITERARY REVIEW

NYU Langone Medical Center, Department of Medicine, 550 First Ave., OBV-A612, New York NY 10016.

(212)263-3973. **E-mail:** info@BLReview.org. **E-mail:** stacy.bodziak@nyumc.org. **Website:** www.blreview.org. **Contact:** Stacy Bodziak, managing editor.*Bellevue Literary Review*, published semiannually, prints "works of fiction, nonfiction, and poetry that touch upon relationships to the human body, illness, health, and healing." Has published poetry by Rafael Campo, Sharon Olds, James Tate, David Wagoner, John Stone, and Floyd Skloot.(Specialized: humanity, health, and healing) Member: CLMP.

Work published in *Bellevue Literary Review* has appeared in *The Pushcart Prize*.

MAGAZINE NEEDS *Bellevue Literary Review* is 160 pages, digest-sized, perfect-bound, includes ads. Receives about 1,800 poems/year, accepts about 3%. Press run is 5,000; distributed free to lit mag conferences, promotions, and other contacts. Single copy: $9; subscription: $15/year, $35 for 3 years (plus $5/year postage to Canada, $8/year postage foreign). Make checks payable to *Bellevue Literary Review*. *Bellevue Literary Review*, published semiannually, prints "works of fiction, nonfiction, and poetry that touch upon relationships to the human body, illness, health, and healing." Has published poetry by Rafael Campo, Sharon Olds, James Tate, David Wagoner, John Stone, and Floyd Skloot. Pays 2 contributor's copies and one-year subscription for author, plus one-year gift subscription for friend. Acquires first North American serial rights. Rights revert to poet upon publication.

HOW TO CONTACT Submit up to 3 poems at a time. Lines/poem: prefers poems of one page or less. Considers simultaneous submissions. No previously published poems; work published on personal blogs or Web sites will be considered on a case-by-case basis. No e-mail or disk submissions. "We accept poems via regular mail and through our website; when submitting via regular mail, please include SASE." Cover letter is preferred. Reads submissions year round. Time between acceptance and publication is about 6-7 months. "Poems are reviewed by two independent readers, then sent to an editor." Sometimes comments on rejected poems. Sometimes publishes theme issues. Upcoming themes available on website. Guidelines available for SASE or on website. Responds in 3-5 months. Always sends prepublication galleys.

BELLINGHAM REVIEW

Mail Stop 9053, Western Washington University, Bellingham WA 98225. (360)650-4863. **E-mail:** bhreview@wwu.edu. **Website:** wwww.bhreview.org. Brenda Miller, editor-in-chief. **Contact:** Marilyn Bruce, managing editor. Annual nonprofit magazine published once a year in the Spring. Seeks "Literature of palpable quality: poems stories and essays so beguiling they invite us to touch their essence. The *Bellingham Review* hungers for a kind of writing that nudges the limits of form, or executes traditional forms exquisitely." Buys first North American serial rights. Pays on publication when funding allows. Publishes ms an average of 6 months after acceptance. Responds in 1-6 months. Editorial lead time 6 months. Sample copy for $12. Guidelines available online.

The editors are actively seeking submissions of creative nonfiction, as well as stories that push the boundaries of the form. The Tobias Wolff Award in Fiction Contest runs December 1-March 15; see website for guidelines or send SASE.

MAGAZINE NEEDS *Bellingham Review*, published twice/year, has no specific preferences as to form. Wants "well-crafted poetry, but are open to all styles." Has published poetry by David Shields, Tess Gallagher, Gary Soto, Jane Hirshfield, Albert Goldbarth, and Rebecca McClanahan. Accepts submissions by postal mail and e-mail. Include SASE. Reads submissions September 15-December 1 only (submissions must be postmarked within this reading period). Responds in 2 months. Will not use light verse. Indicate approximate word count on prose pieces. Pays contributor's copies, a year's subscription, plus monetary payment (if funding allows).

TIPS "Open submission period is from Sept. 15-Dec. 1. Manuscripts arriving between December 2 and September 14 will be returned unread. The *Bellingham Review* holds 3 annual contests: the 49th Parallel Award for poetry, the Annie Dillard Award for Nonfiction, and the Tobias Wolff Award for Fiction. Submissions: December 1 - March 15. See the individual listings for these contests under Contests & Awards for full details."

BELL'S LETTERS POET

P.O. Box 14319 N. Swan Rd., Gulfport MS 39503. **E-mail:** jimbelpoet@aol.com. **Contact:** Jim Bell, editor/publisher. *Bell's Letters Poet*, published quarterly, **must be purchased by contributors before they can be published.** Wants "clean writing in good taste; no vulgarity, no artsy vulgarity." Guidelines available online or for SASE.

Has published poetry by Betty Wallace, C. David Hay, Mary L. Ports, and Tgrai Warden. *Bell's Letters Poet* is about 60 pages, digest-sized, photocopied on plain bond paper (including cover), saddle-stapled. Single copy: $7; subscription: $28. Sample: $5. "Send a poem (20 lines or under, in good taste) with your sample order, and we will publish it in our next issue."

MAGAZINE NEEDS Submit 4 poems at a time. Lines/poem: 4-20. Considers previously published poems "if cleared by author with prior publisher"; no simultaneous submissions. Accepts submissions by postal mail or e-mail. Submission deadline is 2 months prior to publication. Accepted poems by subscribers are published immediately in the next issue. Reviews chapbooks of poetry by subscribers. No payment for accepted poetry, but "many patrons send cash awards to the poets whose work they especially like."

TIPS "The Ratings" is a competition in each issue. Readers are asked to vote on their favorite poems, and the "Top 40" are announced in the next issue, along with awards sent to the poets by patrons. News releases are then sent to subscriber's hometown newspaper. *Bell's Letters Poet* also features a telephone and e-mail exchange among poets, a birth-date listing, and a profile of its poets."Tired of seeing no bylines this year? Subscription guarantees a byline in each issue."

BELOIT POETRY JOURNAL

Beloit Poetry Journal, P.O. Box 151, Farmington ME 04938. (207)778-0020. **E-mail:** bpj@bpj.org. **Website:** www.bpj.org. *Beloit Poetry Journal*, published quarterly, prints "the most outstanding poems we receive, without bias as to length, school, subject, or form. For more than 60 years of continuous publication, we have been distinguished for the extraordinary range of our poetry and our discovery of strong new poets." Wants "visions broader than the merely personal; language that makes us laugh and weep, recoil, resist—and pay attention. We're drawn to poetry that grabs hold of the whole body, not just the head." Responds in 1-16 weeks to queries. Sample copy for $5. Guidelines available on website.

Has published poetry by Sherman Alexie, Mark Doty, Albert Goldbarth, Sonia Sanchez, A.E. Stallings, Janice Harrington, Douglas Kearney, Susan Tichy, and Eduardo Corral.

MAGAZINE NEEDS Limit submissions to 5 pages or a single long poem. Pays 3 contributor's copies.

TIPS "We seek only unpublished poems or translations of poems not already available in English. Poems may be submitted electronically on our website Submission Manager, or by postal mail. Before submitting, please buy a sample issue or browse our website archive."

BEYOND CENTAURI

Website: www.samsdotpublishing.com. *Beyond Centauri*, published quarterly, contains "fantasy, science fiction, sword and sorcery, very mild horror short stories, poetry, and illustrations for readers ages 10 and up. " Wants "fantasy, science fiction, spooky horror, and speculative poetry for younger readers." Does not want "horror with excessive blood and gore." Considers poetry by children and teens. Has published poetry by Bruce Boston, Bobbi Sinha-Morey, Debbie Feo, Dorothy Imm, Cythera, and Terrie Leigh Relf. *Beyond Centauri* is 44 pages, magazine-sized, offset printed, perfect bound, with paper cover for color art, includes ads. Receives about 200 poems/year, accepts about 50 (25%). Press run is 100; 5 distributed free to reviewers. Single copy: $6; subscription: $20/year, $37 for 2 years. Make checks payable to Tyree Campbell/ Sam's Dot Publishing. Publishes ms 1-2 months after acceptance. Responds in 4-6 weeks.

MAGAZINE NEEDS Submit up to 5 poems at a time. Lines/poem: prefers less than 50. Considers previously published poems; no simultaneous submissions. Accepts e-mail submissions (pasted into body of message); no disk submissions. "Submission should include snail mail address and a short (1-2 lines) bio." Reads submissions year round. Often comments on rejected poems. Guidelines available on website. Acquires first North American serial rights. Reviews books/chapbooks of poetry. Send materials for review consideration to Tyree Campbell. Pays $2/original poem, plus 1 contributor's copy.

BIBLE ADVOCATE

Bible Advocate, Church of God (Seventh Day), P.O. Box 33677, Denver CO 80233. (303)452-7973. **E-mail:** bibleadvocate@cog7.org. **Website:** http://baonline.org/. **Contact:** Sherri Langton, associate editor. "Our purpose is to advocate the Bible and represent the Church of God (Seventh Day) to a Christian audience."

Buys first rights, buys second serial (reprint) rights, buys electronic rights. Pays on publication. Publishes ms an average of 9 months after acceptance. Responds in 2 months to queries. Editorial lead time 3 months. Sample copy for sae with 9×12 envelope and 3 first-class stamps. Guidelines available online.

MAGAZINE NEEDS Prefers e-mail submissions. Cover letter is preferred. "No handwritten submissions, please." Time between acceptance and publication is up to 1 year. "I read them first and reject those that won't work for us. I send good ones to editor for approval." Seldom comments on rejected poems. No avant-garde. Length: 5-20 lines. Pays $20 and 2 contributor's copies.

TIPS "Be fresh, not preachy! We're trying to reach a younger audience now, so think how you can cover contemporary and biblical topics with this audience in mind. Articles must be in keeping with the doctrinal understanding of the Church of God (Seventh Day). Therefore, the writer should become familiar with what the Church generally accepts as truth as set forth in its doctrinal beliefs. We reserve the right to edit manuscripts to fit our space requirements, doctrinal stands and church terminology. Significant changes are referred to writers for approval. No fax or handwritten submissions, please."

BIG PULP

E-mail: editors@bigpulp.com. **E-mail:** editors@bigpulp.com. **Website:** www.bigpulp.com. **Contact:** Bill Olver, editor. Quarterly literary magazine. Submissions accepted by e-mail only. Acquires one-time and electronic rights. Pays on publication. Publishes ms 1 year after acceptance. Responds in 2 months to mss. Sample copy available for $10; excerpts available online at no cost. Guidelines available online at website.

"We define "pulp fiction" very broadly—it's lively, challenging, thought-provoking, thrilling and fun, regardless of how many or how few genre elements are packed in. We don't subscribe to the theory that genre fiction is disposable; in our opinion, a great deal of literary fiction could easily fall under one of our general categories. We place a higher value on character and story than genre elements.

MAGAZINE NEEDS "All types of poetry are considered, but poems should have a genre connection." Length: 100 lines maximum. Pays $5/poem.

TIPS "We like to be surprised, and have few boundaries. Fantasy writers may focus on the mundane aspects of a fantastical creature's life, or the magic that can happen in everyday life. Romances do not have to requited, or have happy endings, and the object of one's obsession may not be a person. Mysteries need not focus on "whodunit?" We're always interested in science or speculative fiction focusing on societal issues, but writers should avoid being partisan or shrill. We also like fiction that crosses genre—for example, a science fiction romance, or fantasy crime story. We have an online archive or fiction and poetry and encourage writers to check it out. That said, Big Pulp has a strong editorial bias in favor of stories with monkeys. Especially talking monkeys."

BLACKBIRD

Virginia Commonwealth University Department of English, P.O. Box 843082, Richmond VA 23284. (804)827-4729. **E-mail:** blackbird@vcu.edu. **Website:** www.blackbird.vcu.edu. **Contact:** Mary Flinn, Gregory Donovan, senior editors.

HOW TO CONTACT Send complete ms online at www.blackbirdsubmissions.vcu.edu. Include cover letter, name, address, telephone number, brief biographical comment. Responds in 6 months to mss. Accepts simultaneous submissions. Sample copy online. Writer's guidelines online. Pays $200 for fiction, $40 for poetry. Pays on publication for first North American serial rights. Does not read from April 15-November 1. Publishes ms 3-6 months after acceptance. **Publishes 1-2 new writers/year.**

TIPS "We like a story that invites us into its world, that engages our senses, soul and mind."

BLACK WARRIOR REVIEW

P.O. Box 862936, Tuscaloosa AL 35486. (205)348-4518. **E-mail:** bwr@ua.edu; blackwarriorreview@gmail.com. **Website:** www.bwr.ua.edu. **Contact:** Jenny Gropp Hess, editor. "We publish contemporary fiction, poetry, reviews, essays, and art for a literary audience. We publish the freshest work we can find." Buys first rights. Pays on publication. Publishes ms 6 months after acceptance. Responds in 4 months to mss. Sample copy for $10. Guidelines available online.

Work that appeared in the *Black Warrior Review* has been included in the *Pushcart Prize* anthology, *Harper's Magazine, Best American Short Stories, Best American Poetry* and *New Stories from the South.*

MAGAZINE NEEDS *Black Warrior Review*, published semiannually in February and October, prints poetry, fiction, nonfiction, art and comics by up-and-coming as well as accomplished writers. Has published poetry by Joanna Klink, Claire Donato, Terrance Hayes, Sabrina Orah Mark, K.A. Hays, Andrew Zawacki, Catie Rosemurgy, Jaswinder Bolina, Oliver de la Paz, and Joshua Marie Wilkinson. *Black Warrior Review* is 180 pages, digest-sized. Press run is 2,000. Subscription: $16/year, $28 for 2 years, $40 for 3 years. Sample: $10. Make checks payable to the University of Alabama.

HOW TO CONTACT Submit up to 7 poems at a time. Considers simultaneous submissions if noted. No e-mail or disk submissions. Online submission system: http://bwrsubmissions.ua.edu. Responds in up to 5 months. Pays up to $75 and one-year subscription. Acquires first rights. Reviews books of poetry in single- or multi-book format. Send materials for review consideration.

TIPS "We look for attention to language, freshness, honesty, a convincing and sharp voice. Send us a clean, well-printed, proofread manuscript. Become familiar with the magazine prior to submission."

BLOOD LOTUS

E-mail: bloodlotusjournal@gmail.com; bloodlotuspoetry@gmail.com; bloodlotusfiction@gmail.com. **Website:** www.bloodlotusjournal.com. **Contact:** Stacia M. Fleegal, managing editor. *Blood Lotus*, published quarterly online, publishes "poetry, fiction, and anything in between!" Wants "fresh language, memorable characters, strong images, and vivid artwork." View submission guidelines online. Considers simultaneous submissions; no previously published work. Will not open attachments. Reads submissions year round. Guidelines on website. Acquires first North American rights, electronic archival rights.

MAGAZINE NEEDS "To us, excellent poems are well-crafted, image-heavy, and don't sound like something we've already read."

TIPS "Don't be boring."

BLOOD ORANGE REVIEW

E-mail: admin@bloodorangereview.com. **Website:** www.bloodorangereview.com. **Contact:** H.K. Hummel; Stephanie Lenox; Bryan Fry. *Blood Orange Review* publishes fiction, poetry, and nonfiction in an online quarterly. The *Review* is committed to cultivating an audience for exciting literary voices and promoting its writers. *Blood Orange Review*, published online quarterly, is "looking for more than an interesting story or a descriptive image. The pieces we publish are the ones that we remember days or even weeks afterward for their compelling characters, believable voices, or sharp revelations. We're not afraid of anything, but if we bristle or stop having fun, we figure there is a good chance our readers will too. In a word, write deftly. Leave us desiring more." Buys first North American serial rights. Publishes mss 3 months after acceptance. Responds in 8-10 weeks. Editorial lead time 2 months. Sample copy online. Guidelines on website.

MAGAZINE NEEDS Open to all forms and styles of poetry, but aims to publish the highest quality of work possible. Submit 3-5 poems through online submission manager in one document. Accepts simultaneous submissions; no previously published poems.

BLUE COLLAR REVIEW

Partisan Press, P.O. Box 11417, Norfolk VA 23517. **E-mail:** red-ink@earthlink.net. **Website:** www.partisanpress.org. **Contact:** A. Markowitz, editor; Mary Franke, co-editor. *Blue Collar Review (Journal of Progressive Working Class Literature)*, published quarterly, contains poetry, short stories, and illustrations "reflecting the working class experience—a broad range from the personal to the societal. Our purpose is to promote and expand working class literature and an awareness of the connections between workers of all occupations and the social context in which we live. Also to inspire the creativity and latent talent in 'common' working people."

Has published poetry by Simon Perchik, Jim Daniels, Mary McAnally, Marge Piercy, Alan Catlin, and Rob Whitbeck. *Blue Collar Review* is 60 pages, digest-sized, offset-printed, saddle-stapled, with colored card cover, includes ads. Receives hundreds of poems/year, accepts about 15%. Press run is 500. Subscription is $15/year; $25 for 2 years. Sample copy for $7. Make checks payable to Partisan Press.

MAGAZINE NEEDS Send no more than 5 poems. Include name and address on each page. Cover letter is helpful, though not required. Include SASE for response. Does not accept simultaneous submissions. Partisan Press looks for "poetry of power that reflects a working class consciousness and moves us forward as a society. Must be good writing reflecting social realism including but not limited to political issues." Publishes about 3 chapbooks/year; not presently open to unsolicited submissions. "Submissions are requested from among the poets published in the *Blue Collar Review*." Has published *A Possible Explanation* by Peggy Safire and *American Sounds* by Robert Edwards. Chapbooks are usually 20-60 pages, digest-sized, offset-printed, saddle-stapled or flat-spined, with card or glossy covers. Sample chapbooks are $7 and listed on website.

BLUELINE

120 Morey Hall, Dept. of English and Communication, Postdam NY 13676. (315)267-2043. **E-mail:** blueline@potsdam.edu. **Website:** www2.potsdam.edu/blueline. **Contact:** Donald McNutt, editor; Caroline Downing, art editor. *Blueline* is 200 pages, digest-sized. Press run is 600. "*Blueline* seeks poems, stories, and essays relating to the Adirondacks and regions similar in geography and spirit, or focusing on the shaping influence of nature. Payment in copies. Submission period is July through November. *Blueline* welcomes electronic submissions, either in the body of an e-mail message or in Word or html formatted files. Please avoid using compression software."

PROOFREAD ALL SUBMISSIONS. It is difficult for our editors to get excited about work containing typographical and syntactic errors.

MAGAZINE NEEDS *Blueline*, published annually in May, is "dedicated to prose and poetry about the Adirondacks and other regions similar in geography and spirit." Has published poetry by L.M. Rosenberg, John Unterecker, Lloyd Van Brunt, Laurence Josephs, Maurice Kenny, and Nancy L. Nielsen. Sample: $3 (back issue). Guidelines available for SASE or by e-mail. Responds in up to 3 months. "Decisions in early February." Pays 1 contributor's copy. Acquires first North American serial rights. Reviews books of poetry in 500-750 words, single- or multi-book format." We are interested in both beginning and established poets whose poems evoke universal themes in nature and show human interaction with the natural world. We look for thoughtful craftsmanship rather than stylistic trickery." Does not want "sentimental or extremely experimental poetry."

HOW TO CONTACT Submit 3 poems at a time. Lines/poem: 75 maximum; "occasionally we publish longer poems." No simultaneous submissions. Submit September 1-November 30 only. Include short bio. Poems are circulated to an editorial board. Sometimes comments on rejected poems.

ADDITIONAL INFORMATION "We are interested in both beginning and established poets whose poems evoke universal themes in nature and show human interaction with the natural world. We look for thoughtful craftsmanship rather than stylistic trickery."

TIPS "We look for concise, clear, concrete prose that tells a story and touches upon a universal theme or situation. We prefer realism to romanticism but will consider nostalgia if well done. Pay attention to grammar and syntax. Avoid murky language, sentimentality, cuteness or folkiness. We would like to see more good fiction related to the Adirondacks and more literary fiction and prose poems. If manuscript has potential, we work with author to improve and reconsider for publication. Our readers prefer fiction to poetry (in general) or reviews. Write from your own experience, be specific and factual (within the bounds of your story) and if you write about universal features such as love, death, change, etc., write about them in a fresh way. Triteness and mediocrity are the hallmarks of the majority of stories seen today."

BLUESTEM

Website: bluestem.submishmash.com. **Contact:** Olga Abella, editor.

"*Bluestem*, formerly known as *Karamu*, produces a quarterly online issue (December, March, June, September) and an annual print issue. Please submit no more than 5 poems at one time, or one short story, or one creative nonfiction essay, or 5 black & white drawings. Fiction / prose / essays should be no longer than 5,000 words. Query for writing longer than 5,000 words. Please include a brief (no more than 100 words) bio with your submission. All work is considered for both print and online publication. We will not read work for print only. All genres are welcome. We only accept submissions via our online submission manager, which can be accessed at bluestem.submishmash.com. No previously published work is accepted. Simultaneous submissions are fine. If your work is accepted elsewhere, please withdraw your work via the submission manager. Submissions are accepted year-round. Response times will be significantly longer during the summer. Expect a response in 6-8 weeks. The wait will be longer if we are seriously considering your work. Print contributors receive a complimentary copy of the issue containing their work, and may purchase extra copies at a discounted price. There is no compensation for online contributors but we will promote your work enthusiastically and widely. Sample back issues of *Bluestem (KARAMU)* are available for $4 for each issue you would like. The current issue is $8.00. Click here for subscription information. Watch for announcements of future themes or contests in Sept/Oct issue of *POETS & WRITERS*. Past issues have included themes such as: The Humor Issue, The Music Issue, The Millennium."

BOGG: A JOURNAL OF CONTEMPORARY WRITING

Bogg Publications, 422 N. Cleveland St., Arlington VA 22201-1424. **Contact:** John Elsberg, poetry editor. *Bogg: A Journal of Contemporary Writing*, combines "innovative American work with a range of writing from England and the Commonwealth. It features poetry (including haiku and tanka, prose poems, and experimental/visual poems), very short experimental or satirical/wry fiction, interviews, essays on the small press scene, reviews, review essays, and line art. We also publish occasional free-for-postage pamphlets." Uses a great deal of poetry in each issue (with featured poets). Wants "poetry in all styles, with a healthy leavening of shorts (under 10 lines). *Bogg* seeks original voices." Considers all subject matter. "Some have even found the magazine's sense of play offensive. Overt religious and political poems have to have strong poetical merits—statement alone is not sufficient." *Bogg* started in England and in 1975 began including a supplement of American work; it is now published in the U.S. and mixes U.S., Canadian, Australian, and UK work with reviews of small press publications from all of those areas. Has published poetry by Richard Peabody, Ann Menebroker, LeRoy Gorman, Marcia Arrieta, Kathy Ernst, and Steve Sneyd. *Bogg* is 56 pages, digest-sized, typeset, saddle-stapled, in a format "that leaves enough white space to let each poem stand and breathe alone." Receives more than 10,000 American poems/year, accepts about 100-150. Press run is 850. Single copy: $6; subscription: $15 for 3 issues. Sample: $4. Responds in 1 week. Guidelines available for SASE.

MAGAZINE NEEDS Submit 6 poems at a time. Considers previously published poems "occasionally, but with a credit line to the previous publisher"; no simultaneous submissions. Cover letter is preferred ("it can help us get a 'feel' for the writer's intentions/slant"). SASE required or material will be discarded ("no exceptions"). Prefers hard copy mss, with author's name and address on each sheet. Pays 2 contributor's copies.

TIPS "Become familiar with a magazine before submitting to it. Long lists of previous credits irritate us. Short notes about how the writer has heard about *Bogg* or what he or she finds interesting or annoying in the magazine are welcome."

BOMBAY GIN

Writing and Poetics Dept., Naropa University, 2130 Arapahoe Ave., Boulder CO 80302. (303)546-3540. **Fax:** (303)546-5297. **E-mail:** bgin@naropa.edu. **Website:** www.naropa.edu/bombaygin/index.cfm. **Contact:** Diana McLean. Bombay Gin, published annually in Fall and Spring, is the literary journal of the Jack Kerouac School of Disembodied Poetics at Naropa University."Produced and edited by MFA students, Bombay Gin publishes established writers alongside unpublished and emerging writers. It has a special interest in works that push conventional literary boundaries. Submissions of poetry, prose, visual art, translation, and works involving hybrid forms and cross-genre exploration are encouraged. Translations are also considered. Guidelines are the same as for original work. Translators are responsible for obtaining any necessary permissions." Has published poetry by Amiri Baraka, Joanne Kyger, Jerome Rothenberg, Lawrence Ferlinghetti, Edwin Torres, and Edward Sanders, among others. Bombay Gin is 150-200 pages, digest-sized, professionally printed, perfect-bound, with color card cover.

MAGAZINE NEEDS Please see website for current details on submission time frames and guidelines. Single copy: $12. One-year subscription: $20 + $6 for shipping. Pays 2 contributor's copies.

BOMB MAGAZINE

(718)636-9100. **Fax:** (718)636-9200. **E-mail:** firstproof@bombsite.com; generalinquiries@bombsite.com. **Website:** www.bombsite.com. **Contact:** Monica de la Torre. *BOMB Magazine* accepts unsolicited poetry and prose submissions for our literary pull-out *First Proof* by mail from January 1- August 31. Submissions sent outside these dates will be returned unread. "Written, edited and produced by industry professionals and funded by those interested in the arts. Publishes work which is unconventional and contains an edge, whether it be in style or subject matter." Buys first rights, buys one-time rights. Pays on publication. Publishes ms an average of 3-6 months after acceptance. Responds in 3-5 months to mss. Editorial lead time 3-4 months. Sample copy for $10. Guidelines by email.

MAGAZINE NEEDS "Pays $100, and contributor's copies. Pays on publication for Exclusive first-time serial rights and license in electronic, audio and print form in English language. Sends galleys to author

HOW TO CONTACT Send completed ms with SASE. Manuscripts should be typed, double-spaced (prose only), proofread, and should be final drafts, not exceeding 20 pages in length." Accepts simultaneous submissions. Include SASE.

TIPS "Mss should be typed, double-spaced, proofread and should be final drafts. Purchase a sample issue before submitting work."

BOSTON REVIEW

(617)324-1360. **Fax:** (617)452-3356. **E-mail:** review@bostonreview.net. **Website:** www.bostonreview.net. Timothy Donnelly. **Contact:** Dept. Editor. "The editors are committed to a society and culture that foster human diversity and a democracy in which we seek common grounds of principle amidst our many differences. In the hope of advancing these ideals, the *Review* acts as a forum that seeks to enrich the language of public debate." Buys first North American serial rights, buys first rights. Publishes ms an average of 4 months after acceptance. Responds in 4 months to queries. Sample copy for $5 or online. Guidelines available online.

Boston Review is a recipient of the Pushcart Prize in Poetry.

MAGAZINE NEEDS *Boston Review*, published bimonthly, is a tabloid-format magazine of arts, culture, and politics. "We are open to both traditional and experimental forms. What we value most is originality and a strong sense of voice." Has published poetry by Frank Bidart, Lucie Brock-Broido, Peter Gizzi, Jorie Graham, Allen Grossman, John Koethe, and Karen Volkman. Receives about 5,000 submissions/year, accepts about 30 poems/year. Circulation is 20,000 nationally. Single copy: $5; subscription: $25. Sample: $5. Responds in 2-4 months. Acquires first serial rights. Reviews books of poetry, solicited reviews only. Send materials for review consideration. Reads poetry between September 15 and May 15 each year. Payment varies.

HOW TO CONTACT Submit 5-6 poems at a time through online submissions system. Does not accept faxed or e-mailed submissions. Include brief bio. Time between acceptance and publication is 6 months to one year.

TIPS The best way to get a sense of the kind of material *Boston Review* is looking for is to read the magazine. (Sample copies are available for $6.95 plus shipping.) We do not consider previously published material. Simultaneous submissions are fine as long as we are notified of the fact. We accept submissions through our **online submissions system**. We strongly encourage online submission, however, if you must use postal mail, our address is *Boston Review*, P.O. Box 425786, Cambridge, MA 02142. We do not accept faxed or emailed submissions. Payment varies. Response time is generally 2-4 months. A SASE must accompany all postal submissions.

BOULEVARD

Opojaz, Inc., 6614 Clayton Rd., Box 325, Richmond Heights MO 63117. (314)862-2643. **Fax:** (314)862-2982. **E-mail:** kellyleavitt@boulevardmagazine.org; richardburgin@att.net; richardburgin@netzero.net. **Website:** www.boulevardmagazine.org. Kelly Leavitt, managing editor. **Contact:** Richard Burgin, editor. "*Boulevard* is a diverse literary magazine presenting original creative work by well-known authors, as well as by writers of exciting promise." Buys first North American serial rights. Rights revert to author upon publication. Pays on publication. Publishes ms an average of 9 months after acceptance. Responds in 2 weeks to queries. Responds in 3 months to mss. Sample copy for $10 Guidelines available online.

"*Boulevard* has been called 'one of the half-dozen best literary journals' by Poet Laureate Daniel Hoffman in *The Philadelphia Inquirer*. We strive to publish the finest in poetry, fiction and non-fiction."

MAGAZINE NEEDS *Boulevard*, published 3 times/year, strives "to publish only the finest in fiction, poetry, and nonfiction (essays and interviews). While we frequently publish writers with previous credits, we are very interested in publishing less experienced or unpublished writers with exceptional promise.

We've published everything from John Ashbery to Donald Hall to a wide variety of styles from new or lesser known poets. We're eclectic. We are interested in original, moving poetry written from the head as well as the heart. It can be about any topic." Has published poetry by Albert Goldbarth, Molly Peacock, Bob Hicok, Alice Friman, Dick Allen, and Tom Disch. *Boulevard* is 175-250 pages, digest-sized, professionally printed, flat-spined, with glossy card cover. Subscription: $15 for 3 issues, $22 for 6 issues, $25 for 9 issues. "Foreign subscribers, please add $6." Sample: $8 plus 5 first-class stamps and SASE. Make checks payable to Opojaz, Inc. Considers simultaneous submissions with notification; no previously published poems. Guidelines available for SASE, by e-mail, or on website. Responds in less than 2 months. Acquires first-time publication and anthology rights. Does not consider book reviews. "Do not send us light verse. Does not want "poetry that is uninspired, formulaic, self-conscious, unoriginal, insipid." Length: 200/max lines. $25-300 (sometimes higher) depending on length, plus one contributor's copy.

HOW TO CONTACT No e-mail submissions. All submissions must include SASE. Author's name and address must appear on each submission, with author's first and last name on each page. Cover letter is encouraged ("but not required"). Reads submissions October 1-April 30 only. Sometimes comments on rejected poems.

TIPS "Read the magazine first. The work *Boulevard* publishes is generally recognized as among the finest in the country. We continue to seek more good literary or cultural essays. Send only your best work."

THE BREAD OF LIFE MAGAZINE

P.O. Box 127, Burlington ON L7R 3X5, Canada. **E-mail:** info@thebreadoflife.ca. **Website:** www.thebreadoflife.ca. **Contact:** Fr. Peter Coughlin, editor. *The Bread of Life*, published semimonthly, is "a Catholic charismatic magazine designed to encourage spiritual growth in areas of renewal in the Catholic Church today." Includes feature articles, poetry, regular columns, quizzes and photography. "It's good if contributors are members of The Bread of Life Renewal Centre, a nonprofit, charitable organization. All of our contributors do so in humble service to our Lord on a volunteer basis." *The Bread of Life* is 48 pages, digest-sized, professionally printed, saddle-stapled, with glossy paper cover. Receives about 50-60 poems/year, accepts about 25%. Press run is 1,700. Membership: $35/year (includes magazine subscription). Cover letter is preferred. Publishes theme issues. Guidelines available for SAE with IRC.

THE BREAKTHROUGH INTERCESSOR

Breakthrough, Inc., P.O. Box 121, Lincoln VA 20160. **E-mail:** breakthrough@intercessors.org. **Website:** http://intercessors.org. Articles and Poetry *The Breakthrough Intercessor*, published quarterly, focuses on "encouraging people in prayer and faith; preparing and equipping those who pray." Accpets multiple articles per issue: 600-1,000 word true stories on prayer; **poetry very rarely due to space limitations.** Has published poetry by Norman Vincent Peale. *The Breakthrough Intercessor* is 36 pages, magazine-sized, professionally printed, saddle-stapled with self cover, includes art/graphics. Press run is 4,000. Subscription: $18. Make checks payable to Breakthrough, Inc.

MAGAZINE NEEDS Considers previously published articles and poems. Accepts fax, e-mail (pasted into body of message or attachment), and mailed hard copy. Time between acceptance and publication varies. Articles and poems are circulated to an editorial board.

THE BRIAR CLIFF REVIEW

3303 Rebecca St., Sioux City IA 51104-0100. (712)279-5477. **E-mail:** tricia.currans-sheehan@briarcliff.edu (editor); jeanne.emmons@briarcliff.edu (poetry). **Website:** www.briarcliff.edu/bcreview. **Contact:** Tricia Currans-Sheehan, Jeanne Emmons, Phil Hey, Paul Weber, editors. *The Briar Cliff Review*, published annually in April, is "an attractive, eclectic literary/art magazine." The *Briar Cliff Review* focuses on (but is not limited to) "Siouxland writers and subjects. We are happy to proclaim ourselves a regional publication. It doesn't diminish us; it enhances us." Acquires first serial rights. Sample copy available for $15 and 9×12 SAE. Guidelines available on website or for #10 SASE.

Magazine: 8×11; 125 pages; 70 lb. 100# Altima Satin Text; illustrations; photos; perfect-bound, with 4-color cover on dull stock. Member: CLMP; Humanities International Complete.

MAGAZINE NEEDS Wants "quality poetry with strong imagery and tight, well-wrought language; especially interested in, but not limited to, regional, Midwestern content." Receives about 1,000 poems/year; accepts about 30. Considers simultaneous submissions, but expects prompt notification of acceptance elsewhere. No e-mail submissions, unless from overseas. Cover letter is required. "Include short bio. Submissions should be typewritten or letter quality, with author's name and address on each page. No mss returned without SASE." Reads submissions August 1-November 1 only. Time between acceptance and publication is up to 6 months. Seldom comments on rejected poems. Responds in 6-8 months. Pays with 2 contributor's copies.

TIPS "So many stories are just telling. We want some action. It has to move. We prefer stories in which there is no gimmick, no mechanical turn of events, no moral except the one we would draw privately."

BRILLIANT CORNERS: A JOURNAL OF JAZZ & LITERATURE

P.O. Box 1206, Ann Arbor MI 48106. (888) 359-9188. **E-mail:** clare@bridgesjournal.org. **Website:** www.bridgesjournal.org. Established 1990. **Contact:** Clare Kinberg, managing editor.

MAGAZINE NEEDS *Brilliant Corners*, published semiannually, features jazz-related poetry, fiction, and nonfiction. "We are open as to length and form." Wants "work that is both passionate and well crafted—work worthy of our recent contributors." Does not want "sloppy hipster jargon or improvisatory nonsense." Has published poetry by Amiri Baraka, Jayne Cortez, Yusef Komunyakaa, Philip Levine, Sonia Sanchez, and Al Young. *Brilliant Corners* is 90 pages, digest-sized, commercially printed, perfect-bound, with color card cover with original artwork, includes ads. Accepts about 5% of work received. Press run is 350. Subscription: $12. Sample: $7.

HOW TO CONTACT Submit 3-5 poems at a time. No previously published poems or simultaneous submissions. No e-mail or fax submissions. Cover letter is preferred. Reads submissions September 1-May 15 only. Seldom comments on rejected poems. Responds in 2 months. Pays 2 contributor's copies.

ADDITIONAL INFORMATION Acquires first North American serial rights. Staff reviews books of poetry. Send materials for review consideration.

BRYANT LITERARY REVIEW

Faculty Suite F, Bryant University, 1150 Douglas Pike, Smithfield RI 02917. **E-mail:** blr@bryant.edu. **Website:** http://bryantliteraryreview.org. **Contact:** Tom Chandler, editor; Stasia Walmsley, managing editor; Lucie Koretsky, associate editor. *Bryant Literary Review* is an international magazine of poetry and fiction published annually in May. Features poetry, fiction, photography, and art. "Our only standard is quality." Has published poetry by Michael S. Harper, Mary Crow, Denise Duhamel, and Baron Wormser. Bryant Literary Review is 125 pages, digest-sized, offset-printed, perfect-bound, with 4-color cover with art or photo. Single copy: $8; subscription: $8. To submit work, please review the submission guidelines on our website. Acquires one-time rights. Publishes ms 5 months after acceptance. Responds in 3 months. Guidelines available online and in magazine.

MAGAZINE NEEDS Submit 3-5 poems at a time. Cover letter is required. "Include SASE; please submit only once each reading period." Reads submissions September 1-December 31. Pays 2 contributor's copies.

TIPS "We expect readers of the *Bryant Literary Review* to be sophisticated, educated, and familiar with the conventions of contemporary literature. We see our purpose to be the cultivation of an active and growing connection between our community and the larger literary culture. Our production values are of the highest caliber, and our roster of published authors includes major award and fellowship winners. The *BLR* provides a respected venue for creative writing of every kind from around the world. Our only standard is quality. No abstract expressionist poems, please. We prefer accessible work of depth and quality."

BURNSIDE REVIEW

P.O. Box 1782, Portland OR 97207. **Website:** www.burnsidereview.org. Burnside Review is 80 pages, 6x6, professionally printed, perfect-bound. Burnside Review, published every 9 months, prints "the best poetry and short fiction we can get our hands on." Each issue includes one featured poet with an interview and new poems. "We tend to publish writing that finds beauty in truly unexpected places; that combines urban and natural imagery; that breaks the heart." Acquires first rights. Publishes ms 9 months after acceptance. Responds in 2-4 months. Submit seasonal poems 3-6 months in advance. Single copy: $8; subscription: $13. Make checks payable to Burnside Review or order online.

MAGAZINE NEEDS Has published poetry by Linda Bierds, Dorianne Laux, Ed Skoog, Campbell McGrath, Paul Guest, and Larissa Szporluk. Reads submissions year-round. "Editors read all work submitted." Seldom comments on rejected work.

●$ BUTTON

E-mail: sally@moonsigns.net. **Website:** www.moonsigns.net. Has published poetry by Amanda Powell, Brendan Galvin, Jean Monahan, Mary Campbell, Kevin McGrath, and Ed Conti. *Button* is 30 pages, saddle-stapled, with cardstock offset cover with illustrations that incorporate 1 or more buttons. Press run is 1,200. Subscription: $5/4 issues. "We don't take email submissions, unless you're living overseas, in which case we respond electronically. But we *strongly* suggest you request writers' guidelines (send an SASE). Better still, look over our online issue or order a sample copy for $2.50, which includes postage." "*Button* is New England's tiniest magazine of poetry, fiction, and gracious living, published once a year. As 'gracious living' is on the cover, we like wit, brevity, cleverly-conceived essay/recipe, poetry that isn't sentimental or song lyrics. I started *Button* so that a century from now, when people read it in landfills or, preferably, libraries, they'll say, 'Gee, what a great time to have lived. I wish I lived back then.' Submit only between April 1 and September 30 please." Buys first North American serial rights. Pays on publication. Publishes ms an average of 3-9 months after acceptance. Responds in 1 month to queries. Responds in 2 months to mss. Editorial lead time 6 months. Sample copy for $2.50. Guidelines available online.

MAGAZINE NEEDS Quality poetry; "poetry that incises a perfect figure eight on the ice, but also cuts beneath that mirrored surface. Minimal use of vertical pronoun." Does not want "sentiment; no 'musing' on who or what done ya wrong." *Button*, published annually, is "New England's tiniest magazine of fiction, poetry, and gracious living." Pays $10-25 (honorarium) and at least 2 contributor's copies.

HOW TO CONTACT P.O. Box 77, Westminster, MA 01473. "Do not submit more than twice in one year." No previously published poems. Cover letter is required.

TIPS "*Button* writers have been widely published elsewhere, in virtually all the major national magazines. They include Ralph Lombreglia, Lawrence Millman, They Might Be Giants, Combustible Edison, Sven Birkerts, Stephen McCauley, Amanda Powell, Wayne Wilson, David Barber, Romayne Dawnay, Brendan Galvin, and Diana DerHovanessian. It's $2.50 for a sample, which seems reasonable. Follow the guidelines, make sure you read your work aloud, and don't inflate or deflate your publications and experience. We've published plenty of new folks, but on the merits of the work."

CAKETRAIN

P.O. Box 82588, Pittsburgh PA 15218. **E-mail:** caketrainjournal@hotmail.com. **Website:** www.caketrain.org. **Contact:** Amanda Raczkowski and Joseph Reed, editors. "Please submit up to seven poems, works of fiction or creative nonfiction (no book reviews), works of visual art, or any combination therein, to caketrainjournal@hotmail.com only; do not send work by mail. Submissions should include a cover letter with titles of pieces and a brief biographical statement. Caketrain does not accept previously published pieces. Simultaneous submissions are permitted; please notify immediately if a piece is chosen for publication elsewhere. Response time can take up to six months, but is often much shorter. Please do not submit additional work until a decision has been made regarding your current submission. Contributors receive one complimentary copy. All rights revert to authors upon publication." Price: $9.

◐ CALIFORNIA QUARTERLY

P.O. Box 7126, Orange CA 92863-7126. **E-mail:** pearlk@covad.net. Julian Palley, co-editor. The California State Poetry Society "is dedicated to the adventure of poetry and its dissemination. Although located in California, its members are from all over the U.S. and abroad." Levels of membership/dues: $30/year. Benefits include membership in the National Federation of State Poetry Societies (NFSPS); 4 issues of California Quarterly, *Newsbriefs*, and *The Poetry Letter*. Sponsors monthly and annual contests. Additional information available for SASE.

MAGAZINE NEEDS *California Quarterly*, the official publication of the California State Poetry Society (an affiliate of the National Federation of State Poetry Societies), is designed "to encourage the writing and dissemination of poetry." Submit up to 6 poems at a time. Lines/poem: 60 maximum. No previously published poems. Accepts submissions by postal mail only; no e-mail submissions. Put name and address on each sheet, include SASE. Acquires first rights. Rights revert to poet after publication. Pays 1 contributor's copy.

CALLALOO: A JOURNAL OF AFRICAN DIASPORA ARTS & LETTERS

Department of English, Texas A&M University, 4212 TAMU, College Station TX 77843-4227. (979)458-3108. **Fax:** (979)458-3275. **E-mail:** callaloo@tamu.edu. **Website:** http://callaloo.tamu.edu. *Callaloo: A Journal of African Diaspora Arts & Letters*, published quarterly, is devoted to poetry dealing with the African Diaspora, including North America, Europe, Africa, Latin and Central America, South America, and the Caribbean. Has published poetry by Aimeé Ceésaire, Lucille Clifton, Rita Dove, Yusef Komunyakaa, Natasha Tretheway, and Carl Phillips. Features about 15-20 poems (all forms and styles) in each issue along with short fiction, interviews, literary criticism, and concise critical book reviews. Circulation is 1,600 subscribers of which half are libraries. Subscription: $39, $107 for institutions.

MAGAZINE NEEDS Submit no more than 5 poems at a time; no more than 10 per calendar year. Submit using online ms tracking system only. Responds in 6 months.

TIPS "We look for freshness of both writing and plot, strength of characterization, plausibilty of plot. Read what's being written and published, especially in journals such as *Callaloo*."

CALYX

Calyx, Inc., P.O. Box B, Corvallis OR 97339. (541)753-9384. **Fax:** (541)753-0515. **E-mail:** editor@calyxpress.org. **Website:** www.calyxpress.org. **Contact:** Editor. *CALYX* is 6x8, handsomely printed on heavy paper, flat-spined, with glossy color cover. Single copy: $10 plus $4 shipping; subscription: $23/volume (3 issues), $41 for 2 volumes (6 issues). Sample: $14. See website for foreign and institutional rates. Guidelines available for SASE, by e-mail, or on website. Responds in 4-9 months. Send materials for review consideration. "*Calyx* exists to publish fine literature and art by women and is committed to publishing the work of all women, including women of color, older women, working class women and other voices that need to be heard. We are committed to discovering and nurturing developing writers." Publishes ms an average of 6-12 months after acceptance. Responds in 4-8 months to mss. Sample copy for $10 plus $4 postage and handling.

"Annual open submission period is October 1-December 31. Mss received when not open will be returned. Electronic submissions are accepted only from overseas. E-mail for guidelines only."

MAGAZINE NEEDS "Excellently crafted poetry that also has excellent content." *CALYX, A Journal of Art and Literature by Women*, published 3 times every 18 months, contains poetry, prose, art, book reviews, essays, and interviews by and about women. Has published poetry by Maurya Simon, Diane Averill, Carole Boston Weatherford, and Eleanor Wilner. Pays one contributor's copy/poem, plus subscription.

HOW TO CONTACT Send up to 6 poems at a time. Considers previously published poems "occasionally" and simultaneous submissions "if kept up-to-date on publication." No fax or e-mail submissions except from overseas. Include SASE and short bio. Prose and poetry should be submitted separately with separate SASEs for each submission category. "We accept copies in good condition and clearly readable. *CALYX* is edited by a collective editorial board." Reads submissions postmarked October 1-December 31 only. **Manuscripts received outside of reading period will be returned unread.**

ALSO OFFERS CALYX Books publishes one book of poetry/year. All work published is by women. Has published *Storytelling in Cambodia* by Willa Schneberg and *Black Candle: Poems about Women from India, Pakistan, and Bangladesh* by Chitra Banerjee Divakaruni. **Closed to submissions until further notice.**

TIPS "Most mss are rejected because the writers are not familiar with *Calyx*—writers should read *Calyx* and be familar with the publication. We look for good writing, imagination and important/interesting subject matter."

CANADIAN WRITER'S JOURNAL

Box 1178, New Liskeard ON P0J 1P0, Canada. (705)647-5424. **Fax:** (705)647-8366. **E-mail:** editor@cwj.ca. **Website:** www.cwj.ca. **Contact:** Deborah Ranchuk, editor. "Digest-size magazine for writers emphasizing short 'how-to' articles, which convey easily understood information useful to both apprentice and professional writers. General policy and postal subsidies require that the magazine must carry a substantial Canadian content. We try for about 90% Canadian content, but prefer good material over country of origin, or how well you're known. Writers may query, but unsolicited mss are welcome." Buys one-time rights. Pays on publication. Publishes ms an average of 2-9 months after acceptance. Responds in 2 months to queries. Sample copy for $8, including postage. Guidelines available online.

MAGAZINE NEEDS Poetry must be unpublished elsewhere; short poems or extracts used as part of articles on the writing of poetry. Submit up to 5 poems at a time. No previously published poems. Accepts e-mail submissions (pasted into body of message, with 'Submission' in the subject line). Include SASE with postal submissions. "U.S. postage accepted; do not affix to envelope. Poems should be titled." Responds in 3-6 months. Pays $2-5 per poem published (depending on length) and 1 contributor's copy. SASE required for response and payment.

TIPS "We prefer short, tightly written, informative how-to articles. US writers: note that US postage cannot be used to mail from Canada. Obtain Canadian stamps, use IRCs, or send small amounts in cash."

CANDELABRUM POETRY MAGAZINE

c/o 77 Homegrove House, Grove Rd. N., Southsea PO5 1HW, UK. **Website:** www.members.tripod.com/redcandlepress. *Candelabrum*, published twice/year in April and October, prints "good-quality metrical verse." Wants "rhymed verse especially. Elegantly cadenced free verse is acceptable. Accepts 5-7-5 haiku. Any subject, including eroticism (but not porn)—satire, love poems, nature lyrics, philosophical." Does not want "weak stuff (moons and Junes, loves and doves, etc.). No chopped-up prose pretending to be free verse. Nothing racist, ageist, or sexist." Has published poetry by Pam Russell, Ryan Underwood, David Britton, Alice Evans, Jack Harvey, and Nick Spargo. Receives about 2,000 submissions/year, accepts about 10% (usually holds poems for the next year). Press run is 900. Sample: $6 (in U.S. bills only; nonsterling checks not accepted).

MAGAZINE NEEDS Lines/poem: 40 maximum. No simultaneous submissions. No e-mail submissions. "Submit anytime. Enclose one IRC for reply only; 3 IRCs if you wish manuscript returned. If you'd prefer a reply by e-mail, without return of unwanted manuscript, please enclose one British first-class stamp, IRC, or U.S. dollar bill to pay for the call. Each poem on a separate sheet, please; neat typescripts or neat legible manuscripts. Please, no dark, oily photostats, no colored ink (only black or blue). Author's name and address on each sheet, please." Guidelines available on website. Responds in about 2 months. Pays one contributor's copy.Red Candle Press is "a formalist press, specially interested in metrical and rhymed poetry, though free verse is not excluded. We're more interested in poems than poets; that is, we're interested in what sort of poems an author produces, not in his or her personality."

TIPS "Formalist poetry is much more popular here in Britain, and we think also in the United States, now than it was in 1970, when we established *Candelabrum*. We always welcome new poets, especially formalists, and we like to hear from the U.S. as well as from here at home. General tip: Study the various outlets at the library, or buy a copy of *Candelabrum*, or borrow a copy from a subscriber, before you go to the expense of submitting your work. The Red Candle Press regrets that, because of bank charges, it is unable to accept dollar cheques. However, it is always happy to accept U.S. dollar bills."

THE CAPILANO REVIEW

2055 Purcell Way, North Vancouver BC V7J 3H5, Canada. (604)984-1712. **E-mail:** contact@thecapilanoreview.ca; tcr@capilanou.ca. **E-mail:** tcr@capilanou.ca. **Website:** www.thecapilanoreview.ca. **Contact:** Tamara Lee, managing editor. *The Capilano Review*, published 3 times/year, is a literary and visual arts review. *The Capilano Review* is 100-120 pages, digest-sized, finely printed, perfect-bound, with glossy full-color card cover. Circulation is 800. Sample: $15 CAD prepaid. Tri-annual visual and literary arts magazine that "publishes only what the editors consider to be the very best fiction, poetry, drama, or visual art being produced. *TCR* editors are interested in fresh, original work that stimulates and challenges readers. Over the years, the magazine has developed a reputation for pushing beyond the boundaries of traditional art and writing. We are interested in work that is new in concept and in execution." Buys first North American serial rights. Pays on publication. Publishes ms an average of within 1 year after acceptance. Responds in 4 months to mss. Sample copy for $10 (outside of Canada, USD). Guidelines with #10 SASE with IRC or Canadian stamps.

MAGAZINE NEEDS Length: No more than 4 pages. Pays $50-200.

HOW TO CONTACT No simultaneous submissions. No e-mail or disk submissions. Cover letter is required. Include SAE with IRCs; "submissions with U.S. postage will not be considered." Responds in up to 4 months.

THE CAROLINA QUARTERLY

CB #3520 Greenlaw Hall, University of North Carolina, Chapel Hill NC 27599-3520. (919)962-0244. **E-mail:** carolina.quarterly@gmail.com. **Website:** www.thecarolinaquarterly.com. *The Carolina Quarterly*, published 3 times/year, prints fiction, poetry, reviews, nonfiction, and graphic art. No specifications regarding form, length, subject matter, or style of poetry. Considers translations of work originally written in languages other than English. Has published poetry by Denise Levertov, Richard Wilbur, Robert Morgan, Ha Jin, and Charles Wright. *The Carolina Quarterly* is about 100 pages, digest-sized, professionally printed, perfect-bound, with glossy cover, includes ads. Receives about 6,000 poems/year, accepts about 1%. Press run is 900. Subscription: $24 for individuals, $30 for institutions. Sample: $9. Acquires first rights. Responds in 4-6 months.

MAGAZINE NEEDS Submit 1-6 poems at a time. No previously published poems or simultaneous submissions. No e-mail submissions. SASE required. Electronic submissions accepted, see website for majority consensus. "Manuscripts that make it to the meeting of the full poetry staff are discussed by all. Poems are accepted by majority consensus." Seldom comments on rejected poems. "Poets are welcome to write or e-mail regarding their submission's status, but please wait about four months before doing so." Reviews books of poetry. Send materials for review consideration (attn: Editor). Pays 2 contributor's copies.

CONTEST/AWARD OFFERINGS The Charles B. Wood Award for Distinguished Writing is given to the author of the best poem or short story published in each volume of *The Carolina Quarterly*. Only those writers without major publications are considered, and the winner receives a cash award.

CARUS PUBLISHING COMPANY

30 Grove Street, Suite C, Peterborough NH 03458. **Website:** www.cricketmag.com. "We do not accept e-mailed submissions. Manuscripts must be typed and accompanied by a self-addressed stamped envelope (SASE) so that we may respond to your submission. Manuscripts without an accompanying SASE will not be considered. UNFORTUNATELY, WE ARE UNABLE TO RETURN MANUSCRIPTS. Please do not send us your only copy. When submitting poetry, please send us no more than six poems at a time. Be sure to include phone and e-mail contact information. Please allow us up to 8 months for careful consideration of your submission. No phone calls, please."

CAVEAT LECTOR

400 Hyde St., Apt. 606, San Francisco CA 94109. (415)928-7431. **Fax:** (415)928-7431. **E-mail:** editors@caveat-lector.org. **Website:** www.caveat-lector.org. **Contact:** Christopher Bernard, co-editor. *Caveat Lector*, published 2 times/year, "is devoted to the arts and cultural and philosophical commentary. As well as literary work, we publish art, photography, music, streaming audio of selected literary pieces, and short films. Our website includes an art gallery and a multimedia section, including links to websites we think might be of interest to our readers." Acquires first rights.

MAGAZINE NEEDS Wants poems "on any subject, in any style, as long as the work is authentic in feeling and appropriately crafted. We are looking for accomplished poems, something that resonates in the mind long after the reader has laid the poem aside. We want work that has authenticity of emotion and high craft; poems that, whether raw or polished, ring true—and if humorous, are actually funny, or at least witty. Classical to experimental. Note: We sometimes request authors for audio of work we publish to post on our website." Has published poetry by Joanne Lowery, Simon Perchik, Les Murray, Alfred Robinson, and Ernest Hilbert. Submit poetry through postal mail only. Send brief bio and SASE with submission. Accepts submissions between February 1 and June 30. Pays contributor's copies.

CC&D, CHILDREN, CHURCHES & DADDIES MAGAZINE: THE UNRELIGIOUS, NONFAMILY-ORIENTED LITERARY AND ART MAGAZINE

Scars Publications and Design, 829 Brian Court, Gurnee IL 60031. (847)281-9070. **E-mail:** ccandd96@scars.tv. **Website:** http://scars.tv/ccd. **Contact:** Janet Kuypers. "Our biases are works that relate to issues such as politics, sexism, society, and the like, but are definitely not limited to such. We publish good work that makes you think, that makes you feel like you've lived through a scene instead of merely reading it. If it relates to how the world fits into a person's life (political story, a day in the life, coping with issues people face), it will probably win us over faster. We have received comments from readers and other editors saying that they thought some of our stories really happened. They didn't, but it was nice to know they were so concrete, so believable people thought they were nonfiction. Do that to our readers." Interested in many topics including adventure, ethnic/multicultural, experimental, feminist, gay, historical, lesbian, literary, mystery/suspense, new age, psychic/supernatural/occult, science fiction. Does not want religious or rhyming or family-oriented material. Manuscript published 1 yr after acceptance. Published Mel Waldman, Kenneth DiMaggio, Pat Dixon, Robert William Meyers, Troy Davis, G.A. Scheinoha, Ken Dean. Average length: 1,000 words. "Contact us if you are interested in submitting very long stories, or parts of a novel (if you are accepted, it would appear in parts in multiple issues)." Publishes short shorts, essays and stories. Also publishes poetry. Always comments on/critiques rejected mss if asked.

CELLAR DOOR POETRY JOURNAL

Dreamland Books, Inc., P.O. Box 1714, Minnetonka MN 55345. **E-mail:** dreamlandbooks@inbox.com. **Website:** www.cellardoorpoetry.com or www.dreamlandbooksinc.com. Digest-sized. "Cellar Door poetry celebrates the beauty of words, and revels in the dance between dark and light, truth, evil, goodness, and the glorious experience of being alive. We publish all forms and subjects of poetry." Reads submissions year round. Does not charge reading fees for the 5-piece poetry submission. We charge a $25 reading fee for chapbook manuscripts. Responds in up to 12 months to submissions. Poems are circulated to an editorial board; reviewed by a college writing professor and student interns of the journal. Sometimes comments on rejected poems (at N/C). Upcoming themes are on website; also guidelines. Acquires one-time rights. Rights revert to poet upon publication. Acquires one-time rights. Rights revert to poet upon publication. 12 months Guidelines available on website.

MAGAZINE NEEDS Does not want poetry promoting pornography, violence, racism, sexism, or any form of hate.

CONTEST/AWARD OFFERINGS Sponsors annual contest. See web page for guidelines. Prize: publication plus royalty.

ALSO OFFERS "Our authors and illustrators are available and equipped to do excellent workshops, speaking events, and/or fundraisers. As a small publishing house, we have much flexibility to do tremendous fundraisers for charitable organizations."

O CEREMONY, A JOURNAL OF POETRY AND OTHER ARTS

Dance of My Hands Publishing, 120 Vista Dr., Warminster PA 18974. **Website:** www.danceofmyhands.com. *Ceremony, a Journal of Poetry and Other Arts*, published biannually, encourages "all expression and articism. Beginning poets are especially encouraged." Wants poetry, short pieces of prose, photography and other printable arts. Considers poetry by teens. *Ceremony* is small, home-printed on 20 lb. recycled paper, and single staple-bound. Receives about 200 submissions/year, accepts 50%. Single copy: $3. Publishes ms 1-2 years after acceptance. Guidelines available on website under 'Contact.'

MAGAZINE NEEDS Submit up to 6 poems at a time. Poems of shorter length preferred. Considers previously published poems and simultaneous submissions. Accepts e-mail submissions only. Reads submissions year round. Sometimes comments on rejected poems. Sometimes publishes theme issues. Pays 1 contributor's copy.

◐ CERISE PRESS

P.O. Box 241187, Omaha NE 68124. **E-mail:** editors@cerisepress.com. **E-mail:** submissions@cerisepress.com. **Website:** www.cerisepress.com. **Contact:** Editors: Karen Rigby, Fiona Sze-Lorrain, Sally Molini. *Cerise Press*, published 3 times/year, is an "international, online journal of literature, arts, and culture (with a forthcoming print anthology) based in the US and France, offering poetry,nonfiction, translations, fiction, artwork, and photography." Has published Mahmoud Darwish, Auxeméry, Tess Gallagher, Yusef Komunyakaa, EleanorWilner, Pierre-Albert Jourdan, Abdelwahab Meddeb, Pura López-Colomé, Dorianne Laux, Ray Gonzalez, Victoria Chang.

MAGAZINE NEEDS Submit via e-mail. Considers simultaneous submissions. Cover letter is required. "Please let us know if work is accepted elsewhere. Do not query until 3 months from the date of submission." Reads submissions year round. Never comments on rejected poems. Guidelines on website. Responds in 2-3 months. Acquires one-time non-exclusive world rights and one-time non-exclusive reprint rights. Rights revert to poet upon publication. Reviews books and chapbooks of poetry, fiction, critical essays, biographies, photography, and more.

CHAFFIN JOURNAL

English Department, Eastern Kentucky University, C, Richmond KY 40475-3102. (859)622-3080. **E-mail:** robert.witt@eku.edu. **Website:** www.english.edu/chaffin_journal. **Contact:** Robert Witt, editor. *The Chaffin Journal* is 120 pages, digest-sized, offset-printed, perfect-bound, with plain cover with title only. Receives about 500 poems/year, accepts about 10%. Press run is 300; 40-50 distributed free to contributors. Single copy: $6; subscription: $6/year. Sample (back issue): $6. Make checks payable to *The Chaffin Journal*. Reads submissions June 1-October 1. Time between acceptance and publication is 6 months. Poems are reviewed by the general editor and 2 poetry editors. Never comments on rejected poems. Guidelines available in magazine or on website. Responds in 3 months. Acquires one-time rights. "We publish fiction on any subject; our only consideration is the quality." Annual. Ethnic/multicultural, historical, humor/satire, literary, mainstream, regional (Appalachia). "No erotica, fantasy." Receives 20 unsolicited mss/month. Accepts 6-8 mss/year. Does not read mss October 1 through May 31. **Publishes 2-3 new writers/year.** Recently published work by Meridith Sue Willis, Marie Manilla, Raymond Abbott, Marjorie Bixler, Chris Helvey. Length: 10,000 words per submission period; average length: 5,000 words. Send SASE for return of ms. Accepts simultaneous, multiple submissions. Pays 1 contributor's copy; additional copies $6. Pays on publication for one-time rights. Publishes 6 months after acceptance. Responds in 1 week to queries; responds in 3 months to mss. Sample copy for $6.

MAGAZINE NEEDS *The Chaffin Journal*, published annually in December, prints quality short fiction and poetry by new and established writers/poets. Wants any form, subject matter, or style. Does not want "poor quality." Has published poetry by Taylor Graham, Diane Glancy, Judith Montgomery, Simon Perchik, Philip St. Clair, and Virgil Suárez. *Pays 1 contributor's copy.*

HOW TO CONTACT Submit 5 poems per submission period. Considers simultaneous submissions (although not preferred); no previously published poems. No e-mail or disk submissions. Cover letter is preferred. "Submit typed pages with only one poem per page. Enclose SASE."

TIPS "All manuscripts submitted are considered."

CHALLENGER INTERNATIONAL

E-mail: lukivdan@hotmail.com. **Website:** http://challengerinternational.20m.com/index.html. *Challenger international*, published annually, contains "poetry and (on occasion) short fiction." Wants "any type of work, especially by teenagers (our mandate: to encourage young writers, and to publish their work alongside established writers), providing it is not pornographic, profane, or overly abstract." Has published poetry from Canada, the continental U.S., Hawaii, Switzerland, Russia, Malta, Italy, Slovenia, Ireland, England, Korea, Pakistan, Australia, Zimbabwe, Argentina, and Columbia. *Challenger international* is generally 20-50 pages, magazine-sized, laser-printed, side-stapled. Press run is 50. *Challenger international* is distributed free to McNaughton Centre Secondary Alternate School sudents.

MAGAZINE NEEDS Considers previously published poems and simultaneous submissions. Cover letter is required. Include list of credits, if any. Accepts e-mail submissions only; no postal submissions. "Sometimes we edit to save the poet rejection." Responds in 6 months. Payment is 1 e-copy (sent as an e-mail attachment) of the issue in which the author's work appears. Poet retains rights.

ADDITIONAL INFORMATION Island Scholastic Press publishes chapbooks by authors featured in *Challenger international*. Pays 3 author's copies. Copyright remains with author. Distribution of free copies through McNaughton Centre.

CHAMPAGNE SHIVERS

E-mail: ChampagneShivers@hotmail.com. **Website:** http://samsdotpublishing.com/vineyard/Champagne%20Shivers.htm. **Contact:** Cathy Buburuz, Editor. *Champagne Shivers* is "a classy horror magazine. This is not the place to submit offensive language. We prefer poetic, well-written horror." Wants "horror poetry only. We prefer poems that do not rhyme, but all verse will be considered. Poems 20-30 lines stand the best chance for acceptance, especially if they're scary and entertaining." Does not want "anything that isn't horror related, and always proof and edit before you send your submission. If your work does not have high entertainment or high impact, do not send it here." Has published poetry by Lee Clark Zumpe, Nancy Bennett, Steve Vernon, Kurt Newton, W.B. Vogel III, and Keith W. Sikora. *Champagne Shivers* is more than 60 pages, 8 1/2x11, professionally printed and perfect-bound, with full color cover art depicting a chilling, yet beautiful female. Receives about 1,000 poems/year, accepts 15 poems/issue. Press run and subscriber base vary; the only free copies go to reviewers and contributors. Single copy: $12 U.S. and Canada. Sample: $10 U.S. and Canada. ("Foreign countries, please inquire about costs.") Make checks payable to Tyree Campbell, Sam's Dot Publishing, P.O. Box 782, Cedar Rapids IA 52406-0782 (for subscriptions and sample copies only; DO NOT SEND SUBMISSIONS TO THIS ADDRESS).

"I want scary stuff, but I don't want anything that falls short of eloquent and poetic language.. To me, the word "Champagne" signifies quality and good taste, thus the title "Champagne Shivers."

MAGAZINE NEEDS Submit 1 poem at a time. Lines/poem: 20-30. No simultaneous submissions. Accepts e-mail submissions only (pasted into body of message; DO NOT SEND ATTACHMENTS) to ChampagneShivers@hotmail.com. Does not accept snail mail submissions. Cover letter is preferred. "Submit 1 poem with a bio written in the third person, your mailing address, and your e-mail address." Reads submissions year-round. Submit seasonal poems 4 months in advance. Time between acceptance and publication is less than 6 months. Always comments on rejected poems. Guidelines available by e-mail or on website. Pays 10¢/line for unpublished poems, plus 1 contributor's copy. Acquires first North American serial rights to unpublished poems. All rights revert back to the writer upon publication.

TIPS "Submit horror poems only. I love psychological horror poetry, horror poetry about the Old West, horror poems about asylums, or anything that's just plain scary. I do not want poems about werewolves, vampires, ghosts, or traditional monsters. I want to read poetry that's fresh and exciting. Most of all, send me something that's high in entertainment, that's never been done before. Send poems that will give me and my audience the shivers." Sam's Dot Publishing offers The James Award (Trophy) annually. The editor selects one poem per year from the pages of Champagne Shivers to nominate for the award. **Entry fee:** "None—it's free." **Deadline:** August. Guidelines available on website. "Never send snail mail submissions; always submit in the body of an e-mail after reading the information under How to Submit."

CHANTARELLE'S NOTEBOOK

E-mail: chantarellesnotebook@yahoo.com. **Website:** www.chantarellesnotebook.com. **Contact:** Kendall A. Bell and Christinia Bell, editors. *Chantarelle's Notebook*, published quarterly online, seeks "quality work from undiscovered poets. We enjoy poems that speak to us—poems with great sonics and visuals." Wants "all styles of poetry, as long as it's quality work." Does not want "infantile rants, juvenile confessionals, greeting card-styled verse, political posturing, or religious outpourings." Considers poetry by children and teens. "There are no age restrictions, but submissions from younger people will be held to the same guidelines and standards as those from adults." Has published poetry by Donna Vorreyer, Heather Cadenhead, Taylor Copeland, Taylor Graham, Stacey Balkun, and Bill Roberts. Receives about 500 poems/year, accepts about 20%. Sample: see website for latest issue. Submit 3-5 poems at a time. Lines/poem: "shorter poems have a better chance, but long poems are fine." Accepts e-mail submissions (pasted into body of message; "we will not open any attachments—they will be deleted"). Cover letter is required. "Please include a short bio of no more than 75 words, should we decide to accept your work." Reads submissions year round. Submit seasonal poems 2-3 months in advance. "The editors will review all submissions and make a decision within a week's time." Never comments on rejected poems. Guidelines available on website. "Please follow the guidelines—all the information is there!" "*Chantarelle's Notebook* is also accepting photo submissions. Please visit the website for guidelines on how to submit your photos to us. *Chantarelle's Notebook* will publish a 'best of' print journal that will cull poems from each of the previous 4 quarterly issues in the past year. The authors of the poems chosen will receive 1 contributor's copy and can buy additional copies at half price." Acquires one-time rights. Rights revert to poets upon publication. Responds in 6-8 weeks.

HOW TO CONTACT Submit 3-5 poems at a time. Lines/poem: "shorter poems have a better chance, but long poems are fine." Considers previously published poems; no simultaneous submissions. Accepts e-mail submissions (pasted into body of message; "we will not open any attachments—they will be deleted"). Cover letter is required. "Please include a short bio of no more than 75 words, should we decide to accept your work." Reads submissions year round. Submit seasonal poems 2-3 months in advance. "The editors will review all submissions and make a decision within a week's time." Never comments on rejected poems. Guidelines available on website. "Please follow the guidelines—all the information is there! *Chantarelle's Notebook* is also accepting photo submissions. Please visit the website for guidelines on how to submit your photos to us."

ADDITIONAL INFORMATION The deadline for Issue #23 submissions is April 10, 2011. Any submissions after that date will be considered for Issue #24 in July 2011.

ALSO OFFERS "*Chantarelle's Notebook* will publish a 'best of' print journal that will cull poems from each of the previous 4 quarterly issues in the past year. The authors of the poems chosen will receive 1 contributor's copy and can buy additional copies at half price."

CHARACTER I

443 W. Hight St., Suite D, Peoria IL 61606. **E-mail:** editor@characteri.com. **Website:** www.characteri.com. **Contact:** Edward Maximilian, editor. "character i is focused on publishing works that embody and explore the first-person narrative." Purchases worldwide print and electronic first rights. Responds in 1 week for queries and 2 weeks for mss. Editorial lead time 2 months. Writer's guidelines are available online at website.

MAGAZINE NEEDS Send complete ms.

TIPS "Please be sure to proofread your work prior to submission."

THE CHARITON REVIEW

Truman State University Press, The Chariton Review, Truman State University, 100 E Normal Ave., Kirksville MO 63501. (800)916-6802. **E-mail:** chariton@truman.edu; bsm@truman.edu. **Website:** tsup.truman.edu; http://tsup.truman.edu/aboutChariton.asp. **Contact:** Barbara Smith-Mandell, acquisitions editor. "Truman State University Press (TSUP) publishes peer-reviewed research in the humanities for the scholarly community and the broader public, and publishes creative literary works. TSUP is a resource to the Truman campus community, where students explore their publishing interests and scholars seek publishing advice." TSUP is now publishing The Chariton Review, an international literary journal. Guidelines available on website

MAGAZINE NEEDS Publishes two issues each year. This international literary journal was founded in 1975 by Andrew Grossbardt and edited by Jim Barnes from 1976 to 2010. James D'Agostino is editor effective July 2010. He is the author of *Nude with Anything*, and his work has appeared in numerous poetry magazines and journals. He teaches at Truman State University, which supported *The Chariton Review* for many years. Truman State University Press began managing production and distribution of the journal in 2008. See also The Chariton Review Short Fiction Prize. Send inquiries to our email. Please send a printout of the submission. *TSUP is currently not accepting unsolicited poetry manuscripts.* You may submit your manuscript to the ongoing T. S. Eliot Prize for Poetry by October 31 of any year. Please see the competition guidelines.

CONTEST/AWARD OFFERINGS T. S. Eliot Prize for Poetry.

THE CHATTAHOOCHEE REVIEW: EXPORTING THE SOUTH, IMPORTING THE WORLD

The Chattahoochee Review, 555 N. Indian Creek Dr., Clarkston GA 30021. **Website:** www.chattahoochee-review.org. **Contact:** Lydia Ship, managing editor. *The Chattahoochee Review*, published quarterly, prints poetry, short fiction, essays, reviews, and interviews. "We publish a number of Southern writers, but *The Chattahoochee Review* is not by design a regional magazine. All themes, forms, and styles are considered as long as they impact the whole person: heart, mind, intuition, and imagination." Has recently published work by George Garrett, Jim Daniels, Jack Pendarvis, Ignacio Padilla, and Kevin Canty. *The Chattahoochee Review* is 160 pages, digest-sized, professionally printed, flat-spined, with four-color silk-matte card cover. Press run is 1,250; 300 are complimentary copies sent to editors and "miscellaneous VIPs." Subscription: $20/year. Sample: $6. Publishes ms 6 months after acceptance. Responds in 1 week to 6 months. Guidelines for SASE or on website.

MAGAZINE NEEDS Submit 3-5 poems at a time. Submit one piece of fiction and/or nonfiction, up to 6,000 words, at a time. No previously published work. Simultaneous submissions okay only if we are told. No e-mail or disk submissions. Cover letter is "encouraged, but not required." Include bio material when sending cover letter. Poems and prose should be typed on one side of page with poet's name clearly visible. No reply without SASE. Publishes theme issues. Acquires first rights. Staff reviews books of poetry and short fiction in 1,500 words, single- or multi-book format. Send materials for review consideration. Pays $50/poem and 2 contributor's copies.

CHAUTAUQUA LITERARY JOURNAL CHAUTAUQUA

Department of Creative Writing, 601 S. College Rd., Wilmington NC 28403. **Website:** http://writers.ciweb.org. **Contact:** Jill Gerard, editor. *Chautauqua Literary Journal Chautauqua*, published annually in June, prints poetry, short fiction, and creative nonfiction. "The editors actively solicit writing that expresses the values of Chautauqua Institution broadly construed: A sense of inquiry into questions of personal, social, political, spiritual, and aesthetic importance, regardless of genre. We consider the work of any writer, whether or not affiliated with Chautauqua institution. The qualities we seek include a mastery of craft, attention to vivid and accurate language, a true lyric 'ear,' an original and compelling vision, and strong narrative instinct. Above all, we value work that is intensely personal, yet somehow implicitly comments on larger public concerns—work that answers every reader's most urgent question: Why are you telling me this?" Has published poetry by Robert Cording, Lucille Clifton, Carl Dennis, George Looney, Michael McFee, and many more. *Chautauqua* is approximately 230 pages, digest-sized, offset-printed, with notch adhesive binding and matte cover with original artwork. Receives about 4,000 poems/year, publishes about 30 poems per year. Press run is 1,500; 300 distributed free to contributors and others. Single copy: $14.95. Make checks payable to *Chautauqua Literary Journal*.

Poetry published in *Chautauqua Literary Journal Chautauqua* has been included in *The Pushcart Prize* anthology.

MAGAZINE NEEDS Submit 3 poems maximum at a time. Considers simultaneous submissions (if notified); no previously published poems. Prefers writers submit via Submishmash. Cover letter is preferred. "We prefer single-spaced manuscripts in 12 pt. font. Cover letters should be brief and mention recent publications (if any). SASE is mandatory." Reads submissions February 15-April 15 and August 15-November 15. Time between acceptance and publication is up to 1 year. "The editor is the sole arbiter, but we do have advisory editors who make recommendations." Sometimes comments on rejected poems. Guidelines available on website. Responds in 3 months or less. Always sends prepublication galleys. Pays 2 contributor's copies. Acquires first rights "plus one-time non-exclusive rights to reprint accepted work in an anniversary issue."

CHEST

3300 Dundee Rd, Northbrook IL 60062. 800-343-2222. **E-mail:** poetrychest@aol.com. **Website:** www.chestjournal.org. **Contact:** Michael Zack, M.D., poetry editor. *CHEST*, published monthly, "is the official medical journal of the American College of Chest Physicians, the world's largest medical journal for pulmonologists, sleep, and critical care specialists, with over 30,000 subscribers." Wants "poetry with themes of medical relevance." *CHEST* is approximately 300 pages, magazine-sized, perfect-bound, with a glossy cover, and includes ads. Press run is 22,000. Number of unique visitors: 400,000 to website. Subscription: $276. Make checks payable to American College Chest Physicians.

MAGAZINE NEEDS Submit up to 2 poems at a time, between 10 and 80 lines. Only accepts e-mail submissions (as attachment or in body of e-mail); no fax or disk submissions. Brief cover letter preferred. Reads submissions year round. Poems are circulated to an editorial board. Sometimes comments on rejected poems. Never publishes theme issues. Guidelines available in magazine and on website. Responds in 2 months; always sends prepublication galleys. Retains all rights.

CHIRON REVIEW

522 E. South Ave., St. John KS 67576. (620)786-4955. **E-mail:** editor@chironreview.com. **Website:** http://chironreview.com. **Contact:** Gerald and Zachary Locklin, poetry editors. *Chiron Review*, published quarterly, presents the widest possible range of contemporary creative writing — fiction and non-fiction, traditional and off-beat — in an attractive, professional tabloid format, including artwork and photographs of featured writers. No taboos. Has published poetry by Quentin Crisp, Felice Picano, Edward Field, Wanda Coleman, and Marge Piercy. Press run is about 1,000. Subscription: $20/year (4 issues). Single issue: $7.

MAGAZINE NEEDS Submit up to 5 poems or 1 long poem at a time. Only submit 4 times a year. Accepts e-mail and postal mail submissions. "Send all poems in ONE MS Word or translatable attachment. Complete postal address must accompany every single submission regardless of how many times you have submitted in the past. It helps if you put your name and genre of submission in subject line." Include SASE via postal mail. Does not accept simultaneous or previously published submissions. Guidelines available for SASE or on website. Responds in 2-6 weeks. Pays 1 contributor's copy. Acquires first-time rights. Reviews books of poetry in 500-700 words.

ADDITIONAL INFORMATION Will also publish occasional chapbooks; see website for details.

TIPS "Please visit website before submitting."

CHIZINE: TREATMENT OF LIGHT AND SHADE IN WORDS

"Subtle, sophisticated dark fiction with a literary bent." Quarterly. Experimental, fantasy, horror (dark fantasy, futuristic, psychological, supernatural), literary, mystery, science fiction (soft/sociological). Does not want "tropes of vampires, werewolves, mummies, monsters, or anything that's been done to death." Receives 100 mss/month. Accepts 3-4 mss/issue; 12-16 mss/year. Does not read June, July and August due to Chizine Short Story Contest. Length: 4,000 words (max). Publishes short shorts. Average length of short shorts: 500 words. Also publishes poetry. Send to savory@rogers.com to query. Always comments on/critiques rejected mss.

Received Bram Stoker Award for Other Media in 2000.

MAGAZINE NEEDS "Subtle, sophisticated dark fiction with a literary bent." Quarterly. Experimental, fantasy, horror (dark fantasy, futuristic, psychological, supernatural), literary, mystery, science fiction (soft/sociological). Does not want "tropes of vampires, werewolves, mummies, monsters, or anything that's been done to death." Receives 100 mss/month. Accepts 3-4 mss/issue; 12-16 mss/year. Does not read June, July and August due to Chizine Short Story Contest. Length: 4,000 words (max). Publishes short shorts. Average length of short shorts: 500 words. Also publishes poetry. Send to savory@rogers.com to query. Always comments on/critiques rejected mss. Received Bram Stoker Award for Other Media in 2000.

CHRISTIAN COMMUNICATOR

9118 W. Elmwood Dr., Suite 1G, Niles IL 60714-5820. (847)296-3964. **Fax:** (847)296-0754. **E-mail:** ljohnson@wordprocommunications.com. **Website:** acwriters.com. **Contact:** Lin Johnson, managing editor. Buys first rights, buys second serial (reprint) rights. Pays on publication. Publishes ms an average of 6-12 months after acceptance. Responds in 6-8 weeks to queries. Responds in 8-12 weeks to mss. Editorial lead time 3 months. Sample copy for SAE and 5 first-class stamps. Writer's guidelines for SASE, by e-mail, or online.

MAGAZINE NEEDS Length: 4-20 lines. Pays $5.

TIPS "We primarily use how-to articles and profiles of editors. However, we're willing to look at any other pieces geared to the writing life."

CHRISTIANITY AND LITERATURE

Humanities Division, Pepperdine University, 24255 Pacific Coast Highway, Malibu CA 90263. **E-mail:** christianityandliterature@pepperdine.edu. **Website:** www.pepperdine.edu/sponsored/ccl/journal. **Contact:** Julia S. Kasdorf, poetry editor (Pennsylvania State University, English Dept., 114 Burrows Bldg, University Park, PA 16802). "*Christianity & Literature* is devoted to the scholarly exploration of how literature engages Christian thought, experience, and practice. The journal presupposes no particular theological orientation but respects an orthodox understanding of Christianity as a historically defined faith. Contributions appropriate for submission should demonstrate a keen awareness of the author's own critical assumptions in addressing significant issues of literary history, interpretation, and theory." Subscription: $25/1 year; $45/2 years. Back issues: $10.

MAGAZINE NEEDS Submit 1-6 poems at a time. No previously published poems or simultaneous submissions. Accepts submissions by surface mail only. Cover letter is required. Submissions must be accompanied by SASE. Time between acceptance and publication is 6-12 months. "Poems are chosen by our poetry editor." Guidelines available on website. Responds within 4 months. Rights to republish revert to poets upon written request. Reviews collections of literary, Christian poetry occasionally in some issues (no chapbooks). Pays one contributor's copy and five offprints of poem.

TIPS "We look for poems that are clear and surprising. They should have a compelling sense of voice, formal sophistication (though not necessarily rhyme and meter), and the ability to reveal the spiritual through concrete images. We cannot return submissions that are not accompanied by SASE."

THE CHRISTIAN SCIENCE MONITOR

The Home Forum Page, 210 Massachussetts Ave., P02-30, Boston MA 02115. **E-mail:** homeforum@csmonitor.com. **Website:** www.csmonitor.com; http://www.csmonitor.com/About/Contributor-guidelines#homeforum. **Contact:** Susan Leach, Marjorie Kehe, editors. *The Christian Science Monitor*, an international daily newspaper, regularly features poetry in The Home Forum section. Wants "finely crafted poems that explore and celebrate daily life; that provide a respite from daily news and from the bleakness that appears in so much contemporary verse." Considers free verse and fixed forms. Has published poetry by Diana Der-Hovanessian, Marilyn Krysl, and Michael Glaser. Publishes 1-2 poems/week.

MAGAZINE NEEDS Submit up to 5 poems at a time. Lines/poem: Prefers short poems under 20 lines. No previously published poems or simultaneous submissions. Accepts e-mail submissions only (by attachment in MS Word, 1 poem/e-mail). Pays $20/haiku; $40/poem. Does not want "work that presents people in helpless or hopeless states; poetry about death, aging, or illness; or dark, violent, sensual poems. No poems that are overtly religious or falsely sweet."

CHRYSALIS READER

1745 Gravel Hill Rd., Dillwyn VA 23936. (434)983-3021. **E-mail:** editor@swedenborg.com; rlawson@sover.net. **E-mail:** chrysalis@hovac.com. **Website:** www.swedenborg.com/chrysalis. **Contact:** Robert F. Lawson, editor. *Chrysalis Reader* is 208 pages, 7×10, professionally printed on archival paper, perfect-bound, with coated coverstock. Receives about 1,000 submissions/year, accepts about 16 poems. Press run is 3,500. Sample: $10. (Sample poems available on website. Regularly publishes theme issues (the 2010 issue theme is "The Marketplace"). Themes and guidelines available with SASE or on website. Responds in 3 months. Always sends prepublication galleys. Pays $25 and 3 contributor's copies. Acquires first-time rights. "We expect to be credited for reprints after permission is given. "*The Chrysalis Reader* is a contemporary journal of spiritual discovery published in honor of Emanuel Swedenborg. Each issue focuses on a meaningful theme that inspires current writings and artwork that address today's questions on spirituality. Essays, fiction, poetry, and artwork give fresh and diverse perspectives from many traditions, personal experiences, and fields of study. As Swedenborg says, 'the essence of a thing cannot come into being unless it unites with a means that can express it." *The Chrysalis Reader* is published annually in the fall. Content of fiction, articles, poetry, etc. should be focused on that issue's theme and directed to the intellectual reader. Buys first North American serial rights. Pays on publication. Publishes ms an average of 15 months after acceptance. Responds in 4 weeks to queries. Responds in 6 months to mss. Sample copy for $10. Guidelines and themes by email and online at website.

"This journal explores contemporary questions of spirituality from a Swedenborgian multi-faith perspective."

MAGAZINE NEEDS *Chrysalis Reader*, published annually in September by the Swedenborg Foundation, is a "contribution to the search for spiritual wisdom, a book series that challenges inquiring minds through the use of literate and scholarly fiction, essays, and poetry." Wants "poetry that surprises, that pushes the language, gets our attention." Has published work by Robert Bly, Linda Pastan, Wesley McNair, Wyn Cooper, William Kloefkorn, and Virgil Suárez. "We are interested in all forms of poetry, but none of an overtly religious nature." (Specialized: spirituality; themes) Does not want anything "overly religious or sophomoric." Pays $75 for prose and $25 for poetry

HOW TO CONTACT Submit no more than 5-6 poems at a time. Considers simultaneous submissions "if notified immediately when work is accepted elsewhere"; no previously published poems. Include SASE. Reads submissions year round. Time between acceptance and publication is typically 18 months.

CICADA MAGAZINE

Cricket Magazine Group, 70 E. Lake St., Suite 300, Chicago IL 60601. (312)701-1720. **Fax:** (312)701-1728. **E-mail:** dvetter@caruspub.com. **Website:** www.cicadamag.com. **Contact:** Marianne Carus, editor-in-chief; Deborah Vetter, executive editor; John Sandford, art director. Bimonthly literary magazine for ages 14 and up. Publishes original short stories, poems, and first-person essays written for teens and young adults. *Cicada* publishes fiction and poetry with a genuine teen sensibility, aimed at the high school and college-age market. The editors are looking for stories and poems that are thought-provoking but entertaining. Pays on publication. Responds in 2 months to mss. Guidelines available online.

MAGAZINE NEEDS Reviews serious, humorous, free verse, rhyming (if done well) poetry. Limit submissions to 5 poems. Length: 25 lines maximum. Pays up to $3/line on publication.

TIPS "Quality writing, good literary style, genuine teen sensibility, depth, humor, good character development, avoidance of stereotypes. Read several issues to familarize yourself with our style."

CIDER PRESS REVIEW

P.O. Box 33384, San Diego CA 92163. **E-mail:** editor@ciderpressreview.com. **Website:** http://ciderpressreview.com. **Contact:** Caron Andregg, editor-in-chief; Ruth Foley, managing editor. "*Cider Press Review*, quarterly online, features 'the best new work from contemporary poets.' It was founded by Co-Publisher/Editors Caron Andregg and Robert Wynne. Since its inception, CPR has published thousands of poems by over 500 authors. Each year, Cider Press publishes an annual journal of poetry and the winning manuscript from the Cider Press Review Book Award. Our reading period is from Apr. 1 - Aug. 31 each year, and full mss. (in conjunction with the CPR Annual Book Award) between Sept. 1 - Nov. 30 each year." Submit up to 5 poems at a time. No previously published poems or simultaneous submissions. "International authors or special needs, please query via e-mail. Do not send unsolicited disk or e-mail submissions." Cover letter is preferred. Include short bio (25 words maximum). SASE or valid e-mail address required for reply. Reads submissions September 1-June 30 only. Poems are circulated to an editorial board. Always sends prepublication galleys. Pays 1 contributor's copy. *The Cider Press Review* also published two winning mss from their book awards: *The Cider Press Review* Book Award and The Editor's Prize. Our reading period for the online journal is from September 1 to May 31 each year. We accept submissions of full mss between April 1 and June 20, and September 1 through November 20. Mss entries must be accompanied by a require entry fee. Prize is $1,000 or $1,500 and publication for a full length book of poetry and 25 copies. Acquires first North American serial rights. Publishes ms 6-9 months after acceptance. Responds in 1-4 months. Guidelines available by SASE or on website.

MAGAZINE NEEDS *Cider Press Review*, published annually, features "the best new work from contemporary poets." Wants "thoughtful, well-crafted poems with vivid language and strong images. We prefer poems that have something to say. We would like to see more well-written humor. We also encourage translations." Does not want "didactic, inspirational, greeting card verse, empty word play, therapy, or religious doggerel." Also welcomes reviews in not more than 500 words of current full-length books of poetry. Has published poetry by Robert Arroyo, Jr., Virgil Suaárez, Linda Pastan, Kathleen Flenniken, Tim Seibles, Joanne Lowery, Thomas Lux, and Mark Cox. *Cider Press Review* is 128 pages, digest-sized, offset-printed, perfect-bound, with 4-color coated card cover. Receives about 2,500 poems/year, accepts about 3%. Press run is 500. Single copy: $13.95; subscription: $24 for 2 issues (1 journal, 1 book from the *Cider Press Review* Book Award). Sample: $12 (journal).

CIMARRON REVIEW

E-mail: cimarronreview@okstate.edu. **Website:** http://cimarronreview.okstate.edu. **Contact:** Toni Graham, fiction editor. *Cimarron Review* is 100-150 pages, digest-sized, perfect-bound, with color cover. Press run is 600. Single copy: $7; subscription: $24/year ($28 Canada), $42 for 2 years ($48 Canada), $65 for 3 years ($72 Canada). "We want strong literary writing. We are partial to fiction in the modern realist tradition and distinctive poetry—lyrical, narrative, etc." Buys first North American serial rights. Responds in 3-6 months to mss. Guidelines available.

MAGAZINE NEEDS *Cimarron Review*, published quarterly, is a literary journal "that takes pride in our eclecticism. We like evocative poetry (lyric or narrative) controlled by a strong voice. No restrictions as to subject matter." Wants "poems whose surfaces and structures risk uncertainty and which display energy, texture, intelligence, and intense investment." Has published poetry by William Stafford, John Ashbery, Grace Schulman, Barbara Hamby, Patricia Fargnoli, Phillip Dacey, Holly Prado, and Kim Addonizio. Submit 3-5 poems at a time. Pays 2 contributor's copies. Acquires first North American serial rights only.

HOW TO CONTACT English Dept., Oklahoma State Univ., 205 Morrill Hall, Stillwater, OK 74078. Considers simultaneous submissions. No e-mail submissions; accepts postal submissions only. "Writers outside North America may query by e-mail." No response without SASE. Guidelines available on website.

Responds in up to 6 months. Submit 3-6 poems at a time. Include cover letter.

ADDITIONAL INFORMATION Reviews books of poetry in 500-900 words, single-book format, occasionally multi-book.

TIPS "All work must come with SASE. A cover letter is encouraged. No email submissions from authors living in North America. Query first and follow guidelines." "In order to get a feel for the kind of work we publish, please read an issue or two before submitting."

CLARK STREET REVIEW

P.O. Box 1377, Berthoud CO 80513. **E-mail:** clarkreview@earthlink.net. **Contact:** Ray Foreman, editor. *Clark Street Review*, published 6 times/year, uses narrative poetry and short shorts. Tries "to give writers and poets cause to keep writing by publishing their best work." Wants "narrative poetry under 100 lines that reaches readers who are mostly published poets and writers. Subjects are open." Does not want "obscure or formalist work." Has published poetry by Charles Ries, Anselm Brocki, Ed Galling, Ellaraine Lockie, and J. Glenn Evans. *Clark Street Review* is 20 pages, digest-sized, photocopied, saddle-stapled, with paper cover. Receives about 1,000 poems/year, accepts about 10%. Press run is 200. Single copy: $2; subscription: $10 for 10 issues postpaid for writers only. Make checks payable to R. Foreman. Acquires one-time rights. Publishes ms 4 months after acceptance. Responds in 3 weeks. Guidelines for SASE or by e-mail.

"Editor reads everything with a critical eye of 30 years of experience in writing and publishing small press work."

MAGAZINE NEEDS Submit narrative poems only. Maximum 65 characters in width. Flush left. Considers previously published poems and simultaneous submissions. Send "disposable sharp hard copies. Include SASE for reply. No cover letter." No limit on submissions.

CLOUDBANK: JOURNAL OF CONTEMPORARY WRITING

P.O. Box 610, Corvallis OR 97339. **Website:** www.cloudbankbooks.com. **Contact:** Michael Malan, editor. Acquires one-time rights. Rights revert to poets upon publication. Publishes ms up to 6 months after acceptance. Responds in 4 months. Guidelines available in magazine, for SASE, by email or on website.

Has published poetry by Dennis Schmitz, Christopher Buckley, Paulann Peterson, Vern Rutsala, Penelope Schott.

MAGAZINE NEEDS Submit 5 poems or less at a time by mail with SASE. Cover letter is preferred. Does not accept fax, email, or disk submissions. Reads year round. Never sends prepublication galleys.

ADDITIONAL INFORMATION Considers poetry by teens.

CONTEST/AWARD OFFERINGS Cloudbank Biannual Contest for $200 prize and extra copy of issue in which the work appears. $15 entry fee.

TIPS "Please consider reading a copy of Cloudbank before submitting."

COAL CITY REVIEW

Coal City Press, University of Kansas, Lawrence KS 66045. **E-mail:** coalcity@sunflower.com. **E-mail:** briandal@ku.edu. **Website:** www.coalcityreview.com. Brian Daldorph, poetry editor. **Contact:** Mary Wharff, fiction editor. *Coal City Review* is 100 pages, digest-sized, professionally printed on recycled paper, perfect-bound, with colored card cover. Accepts about 5% of material received. Press run is 200. Subscription: $10. Sample: $6. Seldom comments on rejected poems. Guidelines available for SASE. Responds in up to 3 months.

MAGAZINE NEEDS *Coal City Review*, published annually in the fall, prints poetry, short stories, reviews, and interviews—"the best material I can find. As Pound said, 'Make it new.' Has published poetry by Gary Lechliter, Phil Miller, Cheela Chilala, Maggie Sawkins, and Denise Low. Does not want "experimental poetry, doggerel, five-finger exercises, or beginner's verse." Pays 1 contributor's copy.

HOW TO CONTACT Submit 6 poems at a time. Considers previously published poems "occasionally"; no simultaneous submissions. No e-mail submissions. "Please do not send list of prior publications." Include name and address on each page. Reviews books of poetry in 300-1,000 words, mostly single-book format. Send materials for review consideration.

ADDITIONAL INFORMATION *Coal City Review* also publishes occasional books and chapbooks as issues of the magazine, but **does not accept unsolicited book/chapbook submissions**. Most recent book is *Douglas County Jail Blues*, poetry from inmates at Douglas County Correctional Facility, Lawrence, Kansas (2001-2010).

TIPS "We are looking for artful stories—with great language and great heart. Please do not send work that has not been thoughtfully and carefully revised or edited."

COBBLESTONE

A Division of Carus Publishing, 30 Grove St., Suite C, Peterborough NH 03458. (800)821-0115. **Fax:** (603)924-7380. **E-mail:** customerservice@caruspub.com. **Website:** www.cobblestonepub.com. "We are interested in articles of historical accuracy and lively, original approaches to the subject at hand. Our magazine is aimed at youths from ages 9 to 14. Writers are encouraged to study recent COBBLESTONE back issues for content and style. (Sample issues are available for $6.95 plus $2.00 shipping and handling. Sample issues will not be sent without prepayment.) All material must relate to the theme of a specific upcoming issue in order to be considered. To be considered, a query must accompany each individual idea (however, you can mail them all together) and must include the following: a brief cover letter stating the subject and word length of the proposed article, a detailed one-page outline explaining the information to be presented in the article, an extensive bibliography of materials the author intends to use in preparing the article, a SASE. Authors are urged to use primary resources and up-to-date scholarly resources in their bibliography. Writers new to COBBLESTONE® should send a writing sample with the query. If you would like to know if your query has been received, please also include a stamped postcard that requests acknowledgment of receipt. In all correspondence, please include your complete address as well as a telephone number where you can be reached. A writer may send as many queries for one issue as he or she wishes, but each query must have a separate cover letter, outline, bibliography, and SASE. All queries must be typed. **Please do not send unsolicited manuscripts - queries only!** Prefers to work with published/established writers. Each issue presents a particular theme, making it exciting as well as informative. Half of all subscriptions are for schools. All material must relate to monthly theme." Buys all rights. Pays on publication. Guidelines available on website or with SASE; sample copy for $6.95, $2 shipping/handling, 10×13 SASE.

"*Cobblestone* stands apart from other children's magazines by offering a solid look at one subject and stressing strong editorial content, color photographs throughout, and original illustrations." *Cobblestone* themes and deadline are available on website or with SASE.

MAGAZINE NEEDS Serious and light verse considered. Must have clear, objective imagery. 100 lines maximum. Pays on an individual basis. Acquires all rights.

TIPS "Review theme lists and past issues to see what we're looking for."

COLD MOUNTAIN REVIEW

English Dept., Appalachian State University, ASU Box 32052, Boone NC 28608. **E-mail:** coldmountain@appstate.edu. **Website:** www.coldmountain.appstate.edu. **Contact:** Betty Miller Conway, managing editor. *Cold Mountain Review*, published twice/year (Spring and Fall), features poetry, interviews with poets, poetry book reviews, and b&w graphic art. Has published poetry by Sarah Kennedy, Robert Morgan, Susan Ludvigson, Aleida Rodriíguez, R.T. Smith, and Virgil Suárez. *Cold Mountain Review* is about 72 pages, digest-sized, neatly printed with one poem/page (or 2-page spread), perfect-bound, with light cardstock cover. Publishes only 10-12 poems/issue; "hence, we are extremely competitive: send only your best." Responds in 3 months. Guidelines for SASE.

MAGAZINE NEEDS Submit up to 5 poems at a time. No previously published poems or simultaneous submissions. No e-mail submissions; postal submissions only. Cover letter is required. Include short bio and SASE. "Please include name, address, phone number, and (if available) e-mail address on each poem. Poems should be single-spaced on one side of the page." Reads submissions August-May. Strongly suggest subscribing to magazing before submitting work. Pays 2 contributor's copies.

COLORADO REVIEW

Center for Literary Publishing, Colorado State University, 9105 Campus Delivery, Fort Collins CO 80523. (970)491-5449. **E-mail:** creview@colostate.edu. **Website:** http://coloradoreview.colostate.edu. **Contact:** Stephanie G'Schwind, editor-in-chief and nonfiction editor. Literary magazine published 3 times/year. Buys first North Americans erial rights. Rights revert to author upon publication. Pays on publication. Publishes ms an average of 6 months after acceptance. Responds in 2 months to mss. Editorial lead time 1 year. Sample copy for $10. Guidelines available online.

Work published in *Colorado Review* has been included in *Best American Poetry, Best New American Voices, Best Travel Writing, Best Food Writing*, and the *Pushcart Prize Anthology.*

MAGAZINE NEEDS Considers poetry of any style. Send no more than 5 poems atone time. Mss are read from August 1 to April 30. Mss received between May 1 and July 31 will be returned unread. Has published poetry by Sherman Alexie, Laynie Browne, John Gallaher, Kevin Prufer, Craig Morgan Teicher, Susan Tichy, Elizabeth Robinson, Elizabeth Willis, and Keith Waldrop. Pays minimum of $25 or $5/page.

COLUMBIA: A JOURNAL OF LITERATURE AND ART

Website: www.columbia.edu/cu/arts/journal. **Contact:** Emily Firetog, editor-in-chief; Megan Foley, managing editor; Sarah Perry, publisher. Columbia: A Journal of Literature and Art is an annual publication that features the very best in poetry, fiction, nonfiction, and art. We were founded in 1977 and continue to be one of the few national literary journals entirely edited, designed, and produced by students. You'll find that our minds are open, our interests diverse. We solicit manuscripts from writers we love and select the most exciting finds from our virtual submission box. Above all, our commitment is to our readers—to producing a collection that informs, surprises, challenges, and inspires.

MAGAZINE NEEDS Submit using online submissions manager.

CONTEST/AWARD OFFERINGS Sponsors annual contest with an award of $500. Submit no more than 5 poems/entry or 20 double-spaced pages for fiction and nonfiction submissions. **Entry fee:** $12. **Deadline:** see website or recent journal issue. All entrants receive a copy of the issue publishing the winners.

COMMON GROUND REVIEW

Western New England College, E-5309, Western New England College, 1215 Wilbraham Rd., Springfield MA 01119. **E-mail:** editors@cgreview.org. **Website:** http://cgreview.org. **Contact:** Janet Bowdan, editor. *Common Ground Review*, published semiannually (Spring/Summer, Fall/Winter), prints poetry and 1 short nonfiction piece in the Fall issue, 1 short fiction piece in Spring issue. Has published poetry by James Doyle, B.Z. Nidith, Ann Lauinger, Kathryn Howd Machan, and Sheryl L. Nelms. "We want poems with strong imagery, a love of language, a fresh message, that evoke a sense of wonder. This is the official literary journal of Western New England College." Publishes ms 4-6 months after acceptance. Responds in 2 months. Submit seasonal poems 6 months in advance. Guidelines available on website.

MAGAZINE NEEDS Poetry with strong imagery; well-written free or traditional forms. Submit up to 3 poems under 61 lines. No previously published poems. Simultaneous submissions are allowed; see website for details. Cover letter and biography are required. "Poems should be single-spaced indicating stanza breaks; include name, address, phone number, e-mail address, brief biography, and SASE (submissions without SASE will not be notified)." Reads submissions year round, but deadlines for non-contest submissions are August 31 and March 1. "Editor reads and culls submissions. Final decisions made by editorial board." Seldom comments on rejected poems. Does not want greeting card verse, overly sentimental or stridently political poetry. Length: 60 lines/max. Pays 1 contributor's copy. Acquires one-time rights.

CONTEST/AWARD OFFERINGS Sponsors an annual poetry contest. Offers 1st Prize: $500; 2nd Prize: $200; 3rd Prize: $100; Honorable Mentions. **Entry fee:** $15 for 1-3 unpublished poems. **Deadline:** March 1 for contest submissions only. All contest submissions are considered for publication in *Common Ground Review.*

TIPS "For poems, use a few good images to convey ideas. Poems should be condensed and concise, free from words that do not contribute. The subject matter should be worthy of the reader's time and appeal to a wide range of readers. Sometimes the editors may suggest possible revisions."

COMMON THREADS

3510 North High Street, Columbus OH 43214. (614)268-5094. **E-mail:** Team@ohiopoetryassn.org. **Website:** http://ohiopoetryassn.com. *Common Threads*, published semiannually in April and October, is the Ohio Poetry Association's member poetry magazine. **Only members of OPA may submit poems.** We use beginners' poetry, but like it to be good, tight, revised. In short, not first drafts. We like poems to make us think as well as feel something. Short poems 32 lines or under are treasured. We Do not want to see poetry that is highly sentimental, overly morbid, religiously coercive, or pornographic. Poetry by teens will be considered equally as members and prioritized if the teen poet is a high school contest winner. Poetry by Bill Reyer, Michael Bugeja, Timothy Russell, Yvonne Hardenbrook, Dalene Stull & other well published artists. Common Threads is 52 pages, digest-sized, computer-typeset, with matte card cover. Common Threads is a forum for OPA members, with reprints done so new members can see what is going well in more general magazines. Subscription: annual OPA dues, including 2 issues of Common Threads are $18; $15 for seniors (over age 65). Single copy: $2; $8 for students (through college).

MAGAZINE NEEDS Lines/poem: Nothing over 40 lines published (unless exceptional). Previously published poems are considered, if author notes when and where the work was previously published. Currently submissions are accepted by postal mail only. Submissions are accepted and read year round. Guidelines available for SASE. All rights revert to poet after publication.

COMMONWEAL

Commonweal Foundation, 475 Riverside Dr., Room 405, New York NY 10115. (212)662-4200. **Fax:** (212)662-4183. **E-mail:** editors@commonwealmagazine.org. **Website:** www.commonwealmagazine.org. **Contact:** Paul Baumann, editor; Tiina Aleman, production editor. (Specialized: Catholic) Subscription: $59. Buys all rights. Pays on publication. Responds in 2 months to queries. Sample copy free. Guidelines available online.

MAGAZINE NEEDS Serious, witty, well-written poems. Reviews books of poetry in 750-1,000 words, single- or multi-book format. *Commonweal*, published every 2 weeks, is a Catholic general interest magazine for college-educated readers. Does not publish inspirational poems. Length: 75 lines/poem max Pays 75¢/line plus 2 contributor's copies. Acquires all rights. Returns rights when requested by the author.

HOW TO CONTACT No simultaneous submissions. Only accepts hardcopy submissions with an SASE. Reads submissions September 1-June 30 only.

TIPS "Articles should be written for a general but well-educated audience. While religious articles are always topical, we are less interested in devotional and churchy pieces than in articles which examine the links between 'worldly' concerns and religious beliefs."

THE COMSTOCK REVIEW

4956 St. John Dr., Syracuse NY 13215. **E-mail:** poetry@comstockreview.org. **Website:** www.comstockreview.org. **Contact:** Georgia A. Popoff, managing editor. The magazine is 5 ¼" by 8 ¼", perfect bound. Page length maximum 38 lines (including spaces between the lines, not counting title and author's name). Exceptionally long titles or epigraphs are part of the line count. Our maximum character width is approximately 65 per line. Due to our size, and in an effort to feature as many fine poets as possible, we prefer poems that do not exceed the 38-line page length. Responds in 3 months.

"We accept submissions for the Open Reading Period postmarked from January 1 to March 15, yearly."

MAGAZINE NEEDS Submit 3-5 poems. Include SASE.

CONFRONTATION

English Department, C.W. Post Campus Long Island University, Brookville NY 11548. (516)299-2720. **Fax:** (516)299-2735. **E-mail:** confrontationmag@gmail.com. **Website:** confrontationmagazine.org. **Contact:** Jonna Semeiks, editor-in-chief. *Confrontation* is about 300 pages, digest-sized, professionally printed, flat-spined. Receives about 1,200 submissions/year, accepts about 150. Circulation is 2,000. Subscription: $15/year. Sample: $3. "We are eclectic in our taste. Excellence of style is our dominant concern. We bring new talent to light. We are open to all submissions, each issue contains original work by famous and lesser-known writers and also contains a thematic supplement that 'confront' a topic; the ensuing confrontation is an attempt to see the many sides of an issue rather than a formed conclusion." - Martin Tucker, director Confrontation Publications. Buys first North American serial rights, buys first rights, buys one-time rights, buys all rights. Pays on publication. Publishes ms an average of 1 year after acceptance. Responds in 3 weeks to queries. Responds in 2 months to mss. Sample copy for $3.

Confrontation has garnered a long list of awards and honors, including the Editor's Award for Distinguished Achievement from CCLP (to Martin Tucker) and NEA grants. Work from the magazine has appeared in numerous anthologies including the *Pushcart Prize, Best Short Stories* and *The O. Henry Prize*

Stories. Confrontation does not read mss during June, July, or August and will be returned unread unless commissioned or requested.

MAGAZINE NEEDS Prefers lyric poems. Considers poetry by children and teens. *Confrontation Magazine*, published semiannually, is interested "in all forms. Our only criterion is high literary merit. We think of our audience as an educated, lay group of intelligent readers. Has published poetry by David Ray, T. Alan Broughton, David Ignatow, Philip Appleman, Jane Mayhall, and Joseph Brodsky. Submit no more than 10 pages at a time (up to 6 poems). No sentimental verse. No previously published poems. Lines/poem: Length should generally be kept to 2 pages Pays $10-100. Pays $5-50 and 1 contributor's copy with discount available on additional copies.

HOW TO CONTACT "Prefer single submissions. Clear copy." No e-mail submissions; postal submissions only. Reads submissions September-May. "Do not submit mss June through August." Publishes theme issues. Upcoming themes available for SASE. Guidelines available on website. Responds in 2-3 months. Sometimes sends prepublication galleys.

ADDITIONAL INFORMATION Staff reviews books of poetry. Send materials for review consideration. Occasionally publishes "book" issues or "anthologies." Most recent book is *Plenty of Exits: New and Selected Poems* by Martin Tucker, a collection of narrative, lyrical, and humorous poems.

TIPS Most open to fiction and poetry. Prizes are offered for the Sarah Tucker Award for fiction and the John V. Gurry Drama Award. "We look for literary merit. Keep trying."

CONNECTICUT REVIEW

Connecticut Review, Connecticut State University System, 39 Woodland Street, Hartford, CT 06105-2337. (860)493-0095. **Fax:** (860)493-0120. **E-mail:** ctreview@southernct.edu. **Website:** www.ctstateu.edu/ctreview/index.html. JP Briggs, Jian-Zhong Lin, Mary Collins. **Contact:** Vivian Shipley, editor. Connecticut Review is published twice each year by the Connecticut State University System as a public service contribution to the national literary and intellectual discourse. Each issue of the journal is 200-212 pages in perfect bound 6 x 9 format and contains poetry, fiction, short essays, scholarly articles and fine artwork. The journal publishes the best in contemporary literature and essays. The selection process focuses on bringing to general readers cutting edge work that is both thought provoking and accessible. "*Connecticut Review* is a high-quality literary magazine. We take both traditional literary pieces and those on the cutting edge of their genres. We are looking for poetry, fiction, short-shorts, creative essays, and scholarly articles accessible to a general audience. Each issue features an 8-page color fine art section with statements from the painters or photographers featured." Buys first rights, buys first electronic rights. Publishes ms an average of 18 months after acceptance. Responds in 6 weeks to queries. Responds in 4 months to mss Sample copy for $12 and 3 first-class stamps Guidelines for #10 SASE

Poetry published in *Connecticut Review* has been included in *The Best American Poetry* and *The Pushcart Prize* anthologies; has received special recognition for Literary Excellence from Public Radio's series *The Poet and the Poem*; and has won the Phoenix Award for Significant Editorial Achievement from the Council of Editors of Learned Journals (CELJ).

MAGAZINE NEEDS Essays, poetry, articles, fiction, b&w photographs, and color artwork No doggerel poetry.

HOW TO CONTACT Submit 3-5 typed poems at a time. Accepts submissions by postal mail only. Name, address, and phone number in the upper left corner of each page. Include SASE for reply only. Guidelines available for SASE. Pays 2 contributor's copies. Acquires first or one-time rights.

TIPS "We read manuscripts blind—stripping off the cover letter—but the biographical information should be there. Be patient. Our editors are spread over 4 campuses and it takes a while to move the manuscripts around."

THE CONNECTICUT RIVER REVIEW

P.O. Box 516, Cheshire CT 06410. **E-mail:** patriciamottola@yahoo.com. **Website:** www.ct-poetry-society.org/publications.htm. **Contact:** Pat Mottola, editor. *Connecticut River Review*, published annually in July or August by the Connecticut Poetry Society, prints "original, honest, diverse, vital, well-crafted poetry." Wants "any form, any subject. Translations and long poems welcome." "Poet retains copyright." Responds in up to 8 weeks. Guidelines available for SASE or on website.

Has published poetry by Marilyn Nelson, Jack Bedell, Maria Mazziotti Gillan, and Vivian Shipley. *Connecticut River Review* is digest-sized, attractively printed, perfect-bound. Receives about 2,000 submissions/year, accepts about 100. Press run is about 300. Membership in the Connecticut Poetry Society is $30 per year and includes *Connecticut River Review* and *Long River Run*, a members-only magazine

MAGAZINE NEEDS Submit no more than 3-5 poems at a time. Considers simultaneous submissions if notified of acceptance elsewhere; no previously published poems. Cover letter is preferred. Include bio. "Complete contact information typed in upper right corner; SASE required." Reads submissions January 1-April 15. Pays 1 contributor's copy.

CONTEMPORARY HAIBUN

P.O. Box 2461, Winchester VA 22604-1661. (540)722-2156. **E-mail:** jim.kacian@comcast.net; ray@raysweb.net. **Website:** www.contemporaryhaibunonline.com; www.redmoonpress.com. **Contact:** Jim Kacian, editor/publisher. *contemporary haibun*, published annually in April, is the first Western journal dedicated to haibun. Considers poetry by children and teens. Has published poetry by Steven Carter, Penny Harter, Ce Rosenow, and Jeffrey Woodward. *contemporary haibun* is 128 pages, digest-sized, offset-printed on quality paper, with 4-color heavy-stock cover. Receives several hundred submissions/year, accepts about 5%. Print run is 1,000. Subscription: $17 plus $5 p&h. Sample available for SASE or by e-mail. *contemporary haibun*, published annually in April, is the first Western journal dedicated to haibun. Considers poetry by children and teens. Has published poetry by Steven Carter, Penny Harter, Ce Rosenow, and Jeffrey Woodward. *contemporary haibun* is 128 pages, digest-sized, offset-printed on quality paper, with 4-color heavy-stock cover. Receives several hundred submissions/year, accepts about 5%. Print run is 1,000. Subscription: $17 plus $5 p&h. Sample available for SASE or by e-mail.

MAGAZINE NEEDS Submit up to 3 haibun at a time. Considers previously published poems. Accepts e-mail submissions. Include SASE for postal submissions. Time between acceptance and publication varies according to time of submission. Poems are circulated to an editorial board. Acquires first North American serial rights.

HOW TO CONTACT Submit up to 3 haibun at a time. Considers previously published poems. Accepts e-mail submissions. Include SASE for postal submissions. Time between acceptance and publication varies according to time of submission. Poems are circulated to an editorial board. Acquires first North American serial rights.

CONTRARY

3133 S. Emerald Ave., Chicago IL 60616-3299. **E-mail:** chicago@contrarymagazine.com (no submissions). **Website:** www.contrarymagazine.com. **Contact:** Jeff McMahon, editor.

MAGAZINE NEEDS "Fiction, poetry, literary commentary, and prefers work that combines the virtues of all those categories" Member: CLMP. *Contrary* is published quarterly online. Founded at the University of Chicago, it now operates independently and not-for-profit on the South Side of Chicago. Reads submissions year round. See website for submission deadlines per issue. Often comments on rejected poems. Guidelines on website. " $20 per byline, $60 for featured work."Upon acceptance, *Contrary* acquires the following rights: 1) exclusive rights for the three-month period that the accepted work appears in the current issue of *Contrary* magazine, 2) the right to permanent inclusion of the work in *Contrary's*electronic archive, and 3) the right to reproduce the work in print and electronic collections of our content. After the current issue expires, the author is free to seek republication elsewhere, but *Contrary* must be credited upon republication."

HOW TO CONTACT No mail or e-mail submissions; submit work via the website. Considers simultaneous submissions; no previously published poems. Accepts submissions through online form only.

ADDITIONAL INFORMATION "We like work that is not only contrary in content, but contrary in its evasion of the expectations established by its genre. Our fiction defies traditional story form. For example, a story may bring us to closure without ever delivering an ending. And we value fiction as poetic as any poem. We look especially for plurality or meaning, for dual reverberation or beauty and concern. *Contrary's* poetry in particular often mimics the effects of fiction or commentary. We find ourselves enamored of prose poems because they are naturally ambiguous about form — they tug overtly on the forces of narrative —

but prose poems remain the minority of all the poetic forms we publish."

TIPS "Beautiful writing catches our eye first. If we realize we're in the presence of unanticipated meaning, that's what clinches the deal. Also, we're not fond of expository fiction. We prefer to be seduced by beauty, profundity and mystery than to be presented with the obvious. We look for fiction that entrances, that stays the reader's finger above the mouse button. That is, in part, why we favor microfiction, flash fiction and short-shorts. Also, we hope writers will remember that most editors are looking for very particular species of work. We try to describe our particular species in our mission statement and our submission guidelines, but those descriptions don't always convey nuance. That's why many editors urge writers to read the publication itself; in the hope that they will intuit an understanding of its particularities. If you happen to write that particular species of work we favor, your submission may find a happy home with us. If you don't, it does not necessarily reflect on your quality or your ability. It usually just means that your work has a happier home somewhere else."

CONVERGENCE: AN ONLINE JOURNAL OF POETRY AND ART

E-mail: clinville@csus.edu. **E-mail:** clinville@csus.edu. **Website:** www.convergence-journal.com. **Contact:** Cynthia Linville, managing editor. "We look for well-crafted work with fresh images and a strong voice. Work from a series or with a common theme has a greater chance of being accepted. Seasonally-themed work is appreciated (spring and summer for the January deadline, fall and winter for the June deadline). Please include a 75-word bio with your work (bios may be edited for length and clarity). A cover letter is not needed. Absolutely no simultaneous or previously published submissions."

Deadlines are January 5 and June 5.

MAGAZINE NEEDS New interpretations of the written word by pairing poems and flash fiction with complementary art. "We are open to many different styles, but we do not often publish formal verse. Read a couple of issues to get a sense of what we like; namely, well-crafted work with fresh images and a strong voice." *Convergence*, published quarterly online, Has published poetry by Oliver Rice, Simon Perchik, Mary Ocher. Receives about 800 poems/year, accepts about 10 per issue plus monthly selections for "Editor's Choice." Has about 200 online subscribers. Guidelines available on website. Does not often publish formal verse. Does not want "poetry with trite, unoriginal language or unfinished work." Length: 60 max. No payment.

HOW TO CONTACT No simultaneous or previously published submissions. Accepts e-mail submissions only. Reads submissions year round. Time between acceptance and publication is 1-2 months. Poems are circulated to an editorial board. Responds in 6 months. Acquires first rights.

TIPS "We look for freshness and originality and a mastery of the craft of flash fiction. Working with a common theme has a greater chance of being accepted."

COTTONWOOD

1301 Jayhawk Blvd. Room 400, Kansas Union, University of Kansas, Lawrence KS 66045. **E-mail:** tlorenz@ku.edu. **Website:** www.cottonwoodmagazine.org/read. **Contact:** Tom Lorenz, fiction editor.

MAGAZINE NEEDS *Cottonwood*, published semiannually, emphasizes the Midwest "but publishes the best poetry received regardless of region." Wants poems "on daily experience, perception; strong narrative or sensory impact, non-derivative." Does not want "'literary,' not 'academic.'" Has published poetry by Rita Dove, Virgil Suárez, Walt McDonald, Oliver Rice, and Luci Tapahonso. *Cottonwood* is 112 pages, digest-sized, printed from computer offset, flat-spined. Receives about 3,000 submissions/year, accepts about 20. Press run is 500-600. Single copy: $8.00. Sample: $5.

HOW TO CONTACT Submit up to 5 pages of poetry at a time with SASE. Lines/poem: 60 maximum. No simultaneous or e-mailed submissions. Sometimes comments on rejected poems. Responds in up to 5 months. Pays 1 contributor's copy.

ADDITIONAL INFORMATION Cottonwood Press "is auxiliary to *Cottonwood Magazine* and publishes material by authors in the region. **Material is usually solicited.**" Has published *Violence and Grace* by Michael L. Johnson and *Midwestern Buildings* by Victor Contoski.

TIPS "We're looking for depth and/or originality of subject matter, engaging voice and style, emotional honesty, command of the material and the structure. *Cottonwood* publishes high quality literary fiction, but we are very open to the work of talented new writers. Write something honest and that you care about and write it as well as you can. Don't hesitate to keep trying us. We sometimes take a piece from a writer we've rejected a number of times. We generally don't like clever, gimmicky writing. The style should be engaging but not claim all the the attention itself."

● THE COUNTRY DOG REVIEW

E-mail: countrydogreview@gmail.com. **Website:** www.countrydogreview.org. **Contact:** Danielle Sellers, editor. *The Country Dog Review*, published semiannually online, publishes "poetry, book reviews, and interviews with poets." Wants "poetry of the highest quality, not limited to style or region. Also accepts book reviews and interviews. Query first." Does not want "translations, fiction, nonfiction." Receives about 400 poems/year, accepts about 10%.

MAGAZINE NEEDS Submit 3-5 poems at a time. No previously published poems or simultaneous submissions. Only accepts e-mail submissions with attachment; no fax or disk submissions. Subject of e-mail should read: last name, date, poetry. Bio is required. Reads submissions year round. Submit seasonal poems 6 months in advance. "Please submit no more than twice a submission period." Time between acceptance and publication is 1-4 months. Never comments on rejected poems. Sometimes publishes theme issues. Upcoming themes and guidelines available by e-mail and on website. Responds in 1-2 months. Sometimes sends prepublication galleys. Acquires first North American serial rights. Reviews books of poetry in 500 words, single-book format.

CRAB CREEK REVIEW

7315 34th Ave. NW, Seattle WA 98117. **E-mail:** crabcreekreview@gmail.com. **Website:** www.crabcreekreview.org. Buys first North American rights. Responds in 3-5 months to mss. Guidelines available online.

"Nominates for the Pushcart Prize and offers annual Crab Creek Review Editors' Prize of $100 for the best poem, essay, or short story published in the previous year."

MAGAZINE NEEDS Has published poetry by Oliver de la Paz, Dorianne Laux, Greg Nicholl, and translations by Ilya Kaminsky and Matthew Zapruder. Fiction by karen Heuler and Daniel Homan. *Crab Creek Review* is an 80- to 120-page, perfect-bound paperback. Subscription: $15/year, $28/2 year. Sample: $6. Pays 1 copy.

CONTEST/AWARD OFFERINGS Offers annual poetry contest with deadline of May 31st. Entry fee: $10. Submit up to 5 poems. All entries will be considered for publication. See website for more information.

TIPS "We currently welcome submissions of poetry, short fiction, and creative nonfiction. Shorter pieces in all genres preferred. We are an international journal based in the Pacific Northwest that is looking for poems, stories, and essays that pay attention to craft while still surprising us in positive ways with detail and content. We publish well-known and emerging writers."

CRAB ORCHARD REVIEW

(618)453-6833. **Fax:** (618)453-8224. **Website:** www.craborchardreview.siuc.edu/. "We are a general interest literary journal published twice/year. We strive to be a journal that writers admire and readers enjoy. We publish fiction, poetry, creative nonfiction, fiction translations, interviews and reviews." Buys first North American serial rights. Publishes ms an average of 9-12 months after acceptance. Responds in 3 weeks to queries. Responds in 9 months to mss. Sample copy for $8. Guidelines for #10 SASE.

MAGAZINE NEEDS *Crab Orchard Review*, published semiannually in March and September, prints poetry, fiction, creative nonfiction, interviews, book reviews, and novel excerpts. Wants all styles and forms from traditional to experimental. Does not want greeting card verse; literary poetry only. Has published poetry by Luisa A. Igloria, Erinn Batykefer, Jim Daniels, Bryan Tso Jones. *Crab Orchard Review* is 256-280 pages, digest-sized, professionally printed, perfect-bound, with (usually) glossy card cover with color photos. Receives about 12,000 poems/year, accepts about 1%. Press run is 3,500; 100 exchanged with other journals; remainder in shelf sales. Subscription: $20. Sample: $12.

HOW TO CONTACT Submit up to 5 poems at a time. Considers simultaneous submissions with notification; no previously published poems. Postal submissions only. Cover letter is preferred. "Indicate stanza breaks on poems of more than 1 page." Reads submissions April-November for Summer/Fall special theme issue, February-April for regular, non-thematic Winter/Spring issue. Time between acceptance and publication is 6 months to a year. "Poems that are under serious consideration are discussed and decided on by the managing editor and poetry editor." Seldom comments on rejected poems. Publishes theme issues. Upcoming themes available in magazine, for SASE, or on website. Guidelines available for SASE or on website. Responds in up to 9 months. Pays $20/page ($50 minimum), 2 contributor's copies, and 1 year's subscription. Acquires first North American serial rights. Staff reviews books of poetry in 500-700 words, single-book format. Send materials for review consideration to Jon C. Tribble, managing editor.

TIPS "We publish 2 issues per volume—1 has a theme (we read from May to November for the theme issue); the other doesn't (we read from January through April for the non-thematic issue). Consult our website for information about our upcoming themes."

CRAZYHORSE

College of Charleston, Dept. of English, 66 George St., Charleston SC 29424. (843)953-7740. **E-mail:** crazyhorse@cofc.edu. **Website:** www.crazyhorsejournal.org. *Crazyhorse*, published semiannually, prints fine fiction, poetry, and essays. "Send your best words our way. We like to print a mix of writing regardless of its form, genre, school, or politics. We're especially on the lookout for writing that doesn't fit the categories. Before sending, ask 'What's reckoned with that's important for other people to read?'" Has published poetry by David Wojahn, Mary Ruefle, Nance Van Winkle, Dean Young, Marvin Bell, and A.V. Christie. See website for e-book and print subscriptions. We like to print a mix of writing regardless of its form, genre, school, or politics. We're especially on the lookout for original writing that doesn't fit the categories and that engages in the work of honest communication. Buys first North American serial rights. Publishes ms an average of 6-12 months after acceptance. Responds in 1 week to queries. Responds in 3-5 months to mss. Sample copy for $5. Writer's guidelines for SASE or by e-mail.

HOW TO CONTACT Submit 3-5 poems at a time. Considers simultaneous submissions; no previously published poems. No fax, e-mail, or disk submissions. Cover letter is preferred. Reads submissions year round. "We read slower in summer." Time between acceptance and publication is 6 months. Seldom comments on rejected poems. Guidelines available in magazine, for SASE, by e-mail, or on website. Responds in 3 months. Sometimes sends prepublication galleys. Pays $20-35/page, 2 contributor's copies, and one-year subscription (2 issues). Acquires first North American serial rights.

TIPS Write to explore subjects you care about. The subject should be one in which something is at stake. Before sending, ask, "What's reckoned with that's important for other people to read?"

◐ CRUCIBLE

Barton College, College Station, Wilson NC 27893. (252)399-6343. **E-mail:** crucible@barton.edu. **Website:** www.barton.edu/academics/english/crucible.htm. **Contact:** Terrence L. Grimes, editor. *Crucible*, published annually in November, uses "poetry that demonstrates originality and integrity of craftsmanship as well as thought. Traditional metrical and rhyming poems are difficult to bring off in modern poetry. The best poetry is written out of deeply felt experience which has been crafted into pleasing form." Wants "free verse with attention paid particularly to image, line, stanza, and voice." Does not want "very long narratives, poetry that is forced." Has published poetry by Robert Grey, R.T. Smith, and Anthony S. Abbott. *Crucible* is under 100 pages, digest-sized, professionally printed on high-quality paper, with matte card cover. Press run is 500. Sample: $8. Acquires first rights. Responds in 6 weeks to queries; 4 months to mss. Writer's guidelines free.

MAGAZINE NEEDS Submit no more than 5 poems at a time. No previously published poems or simultaneous submissions. "We require electronic submission of work and a short biography including a list of publications." Receives submissions between Christmas and mid-April only. Pays contributor's copies.

CONTEST/AWARD OFFERINGS The Sam Ragan Prize ($150), in honor of the former Poet Laureate of North Carolina, and other contests (prizes of $150 and $100). Guidelines available on website.

⊕ CURA: A LITERARY MAGAZINE OF ART AND ACTION

441 E. Fordham Rd., English Department, Dealy 541W, Bronx NY 10548. **E-mail:** curamag@fordham.edu. **Website:** www.curamag.com. **Contact:** Sarah Gambito, managing editor. "CURA: A Literary Magazine of Art and Action is a multi-media initiative based at Fordham University committed to integrating the arts and social justice. Featuring creative writing, visual art, new media and video in response to current news, we seek to enable an artistic process that is rigorously engaged with the world at the present moment. CURA is taken from the Ignatian educational principle of "cura personalis," care for the

whole person. On its own, the word "cura" is defined as guardianship, solicitude, and significantly, written work. Each year, CURA will feature a sustaining theme in dialogue with a non-profit organization that reflects the vision of "care for the whole person." Our aim is to provide support for and to raise awareness of the critical work these organizations are undertaking. For information on this year's theme, please check out our website at curamag.com. All publication proceeds will directly benefit the featured non-profit organization. We seek to foster a movement of creative response guided by concrete and meaningful action—to celebrate informed and active citizenship where a republic of writers, filmmakers, visual and digital artists converge. What Martín Espada has written about the social responsibility of the "Republic of Poetry" we believe applies to a Republic of all the Arts. It is "a place where creativity meets community, where the imagination serves humanity. It is a republic of justice because the practice of justice is the highest form of human expression." Content is published in print and in online and Kindle editions. CURA holds first serial rights on featured material." Acquires first rights. Publishes ms 5 months after acceptance. Editorial lead time is 5 months. Sample copy available online at website. Guidelines available online at website.

MAGAZINE NEEDS Pays 1 contributor's copy.

CURRENT ACCOUNTS

Current Accounts, Apt. 2D, Bradshaw Hall, Hardcastle Gardens, Bolton BL2 4NZ, UK. **E-mail:** bswscribe@gmail.com; fjameshartnell@aol.com. **Website:** http://bankstreetwriters.webs.com/currentaccounts.htm. **Contact:** FJ Hartnell. *Current Accounts*, published semiannually, prints poetry, fiction, and nonfiction by members of Bank Street Writers, and other contributors. Open to all types of poetry. "No requirements, although some space is reserved for members." Considers poetry by children and teens. Has published poetry by Pat Winslow, M.R. Peacocke, and Gerald England. *Current Accounts* is 52 pages, A5, photocopied, saddle-stapled, with card cover with b&w or color photo or artwork. Receives about 300 poems/year, accepts about 5%. Press run is 80; 8 distributed free to competition winners. Subscription: £6. Sample: £3. Make checks payable to Bank Street Writers (sterling checks only).

MAGAZINE NEEDS Submit up to 6 poems at a time. Lines/poem: 100 maximum. No previously published poems (unpublished poems preferred) or simultaneous submissions. Prefers e-mail submissions (pasted into body of message). Cover letter is required. SAE or IRC essential for postal submissions. Time between acceptance and publication is 6 months. Seldom comments on rejected poems. Guidelines available for SASE, by fax, e-mail, or on website. Responds in 3 months. Pays 1 contributor's copy. Acquires first rights. Published semiannually. Doesn't want rhyming poetry. "Travel or tourist poetry needs to be more than just exotic names and places. Titles need care. Poetry should be poetic in some form. Experimental work is welcome. As a writer you are expected to be able to spell." Welcomes submissions from any writers or any age. Subscription: $15/3 issues.

TIPS Bank Street Writers meets once/month and offers workshops, guest speakers, and other activities. Write for details."We like originality of ideas, images, and use of language. No inspirational or religious verse unless it's also good in poetic terms."

CUTBANK

English Dept., University of Montana, LA 133, Missoula MT 59812. **E-mail:** cutbank@umontana.edu. **Website:** www.cutbankonline.org. **Contact:** Josh Fomon, editor-in-chief.

MAGAZINE NEEDS Submit up to 5 poems at a time. Considers simultaneous submissions ("discouraged, but accepted with notification").

TIPS "Familiarity with the magazine is essential. *Cutbank* is very open to new voices—we have a legacy of publishing acclaimed writers early in their careers—but we will consider only your best work. Cutbank only accepts online submissions."

CUTTHROAT, A JOURNAL OF THE ARTS

P.O. Box 2414, Durango CO 81302. (970) 903-7914. **E-mail:** cutthroatmag@gmail.com. **Website:** www.cutthroatmag.com. **Contact:** William Luvaas, fiction editor.

MAGAZINE NEEDS Literary magazine/journal and "one separate online edition of poetry, translations, short fiction, and book reviews yearly. 6×9, 180+ pages, fine cream paper, slick cover. Includes photographs. "We publish only high quality fiction and poetry. We are looking for the cutting edge, the endangered word, fiction with wit, heart, soul and meaning." Annual. Estab. 2005. Member CCLMP.

HOW TO CONTACT Submit 3-5 poems attn: William Pitt Root, poetry editor. International submissions can be electronic. Reading periods for online editions are March 15-June 1; for print editions, July 15-October 10. Please include cover letter and SASE for response only; ms are recycled.

TIPS "Read our magazine and see what types of stories we've published. The piece must have heart and soul, excellence in craft. "

DALHOUSIE REVIEW

E-mail: dalhousie.review@dal.ca. **Website:** http://dalhousiereview.dal.ca. Anthony Stewart, editor. **Contact:** Poetry editor. *Dalhousie Review*, published 3 times/year, is a journal of criticism publishing poetry and fiction. Considers poetry from both new and established writers. *Dalhousie Review* is 144 pages, digest-sized. Accepts about 5% of poems received. Press run is 500. Single copy: $15 CAD; subscription: $22.50 CAD, $28 USD. Make checks payable to *Dalhousie Review*. Responds in 3-9 months.

MAGAZINE NEEDS Submit up to 5 poems, no more than 40 lines each. Does not accept simultaneous submissions or previously published submissions. Accepts postal submissions only, include e-mail address on submission. Reads year round. Pays 2 contributor's copies and 10 offprints.

DARKLING MAGAZINE

Darkling Publications, 28780 318th Avenue, Colome SD 57528. (605)455-2892. **E-mail:** darkling@mitchelltelecom.net. **Contact:** James C. Van Oort, editor-in-chief. *Darkling Magazine*, published annually in late summer, is "primarily interested in poetry. All submissions should be dark in nature and should help expose the darker side of man. Dark nature does not mean whiny or overly murderous, and being depressed does not make an artist's work dark. Pornography will not be considered and will merit no response. Profanity that is meritless or does not support the subject of any piece is unacceptable. Has published poems by Robert Cooperman, Kenneth DiMaggio, Arthur Gottlieb, Simon Perchik, Cathy Porter and Susanna Rich, among others. Subscription: $10 with s&h. Sample copies are $10.00. Make checks payable to Darkling Publications.

MAGAZINE NEEDS Submit up to 8 poems at a time. Lines/poem: any length is acceptable, but "Epic poems must be of exceptional quality. Considers simultaneous submissions but please no previously published poems. Will accept e-mail submissions; no disk submissions. Cover letter is required. Reads submissions June or July. Time between acceptance and publication is varies. Poems are circulated to an editorial board. Sometimes comments on rejected poems. Guidelines available in magazine. Announces rejections and acceptance in May or June. Pays 1 contributor's copy. All rights revert to author upon publication.

THE DEAD MULE SCHOOL OF SOUTHERN LITERATURE

E-mail: deadmule@gmail.com. **E-mail:** submit.mule@gmail.com. **Website:** www.deadmule.com. **Contact:** Valerie MacEwan, publisher and editor; Helen Losse, poetry editor. "No good southern fiction is complete without a dead mule." Celebrating over 15 years online means the dead mule is one of the oldest, if not "the" oldest continuously published online literary journals alive today. Publisher and editor Valerie MacEwan welcomes your submissions. "The Dead Mule School of Southern Literature wants flash fiction, poetry, visual poetry, essays, and creative nonfiction. We usually publish new work on the first and fifteenth of the month, depending on whims, obligations, and mule jumping contest dates. Helen Losse, poetry; Phoebe Kate Foster, fiction; Valerie MacEwan editor/publisher; Robert MacEwan, technical & design; and other volunteers who graciously donate their time and love to this fine journal.

MAGAZINE NEEDS "Submissions: see the instruction page located at: www.deadmule.com/submissions. Follow the guidelines. Query about photography. Contact publisher/editor through facebook.com/deadmule or www.deadmule.submishmash.com/submit or facebook.com/deadmuleschool. Publication on the dead mule grants us first electronic rights and indefinite archival rights. All other rights revert to author upon publication. We look forward to hearing from you."

TIPS "Read the site to get a feel for what we're looking to publish. Limit stories and essays to 1,000 words. All submissions must be accompanied by a "southern legitimacy statement," details of which can be seen within each page on the dead mule and within the submishmash entrypage. We've been around for over 15 years, send us something original. Chapbooks published by invitation, also short fiction compilations. Sporadic payment to writers whenever cafepress/

deadmule sales reach an agreeable amount and then we share!"

DENVER QUARTERLY

University of Denver, 2000 E. Asbury, Denver CO 80208. (303)871-2892. **Website:** www.denverquarterly.com. **Contact:** Bill Ramke. "We publish fiction, articles and poetry for a generally well-educated audience, primarily interested in literature and the literary experience. They read DQ to find something a little different from a stictly academic quarterly or a creative writing outlet." Quarterly. Reads between September 15 and May 15. Acquires first North American serial rights. Publishes ms 1 year after acceptance. Responds in 3 months.

Denver Quarterly received an Honorable Mention for Content from the American Literary Magazine Awards and selections have been anthologized in the *Pushcart Prize* anthologies. *Denver Quarterly.* received an Honorable Mention for Content from the American Literary Magazine Awards and selections have been anthologized in the *Pushcart Prize* anthologies.

MAGAZINE NEEDS Poetry submissions should be comprised of 3-5 poems. Submit ms by mail, include SASE. Accepts simultaneous submissions. Sample copy for $10. Pays $5/page for fiction and poetry and 2 contributor's copies.

TIPS "We look for serious, realistic and experimental fiction; stories which appeal to intelligent, demanding readers who are not themselves fiction writers. Nothing so quickly disqualifies a manuscript as sloppy proofreading and mechanics. Read the magazine before submitting to it. We try to remain eclectic, but the odds for beginners are bound to be small considering the fact that we receive nearly 10,000 mss per year and publish only about ten short stories."

THE DERONDA REVIEW

P.O. Box 55164, Madison WI 53705. **E-mail:** derondareview@att.net. **Website:** www.derondareview.org; www.pointandcircumference.com. Mindy Aber Barad, co-editor for Israel, P.O.B. 1299, Efrat 90435, Israel. Email: maber4kids@yahoo.com. **Contact:** Esther Cameron, editor-in-chief; Mindy Aber Barad (Israel only). *The Deronda Review*, published semiannually, seeks to "promote a literature of introspection, dialogue, and social concern." Wants "poetry of beauty and integrity with emotional and intellectual depth, commitment to subject matter as well as language, and the courage to ignore fashion. Welcome: well-crafted formal verse, social comment (including satire), love poems, philosophical/religious poems. The website will also publish essays and fiction. *The Deronda Review* has a standing interest in work that sees Judaism as a source of values and/or reflects on the current situation of Israel and of Western civilization. Open, in principle, to writers of all ages." *The Deronda Review* is now experimenting with a predominantly electronic format. Accepted poems will appear in a running journal on www.derondareview.org. Semiannually, the poems will be gathered into an issue, similar in format to former issues of the magazine, which will be posted online in PDF format. Printouts will be sent to contributors who do not have Internet connections, and bound printouts will be sent to libraries. Submit 3-5 poems at a time or, for the website, prose of any length. Longer works will be considered for installment publication. "The paper magazine rarely accepts reprints; the website invites submission of poems already published in paper format. All poems published for the first time on the website will be printed in the magazine." Cover letter is unnecessary. If submitting by surface mail, "do include SASE with sufficient postage to return all mss or with 'Reply Only" clearly indicated. First-time contributors in the U.S. are requested to submit by surface mail. Poets whose work is accepted will be asked for titles of books available, to be published in the magazine." Often comments on rejected poems. Does not offer guidelines because "the tradition is the only 'guideline.'" Encourages contributors to obtain a sample." Pays 2 contributor's copies for magazine publication. Acquires first rights. Publishes ms 1 year after acceptance. Responds in up to 4 months; "if longer, please query via the website."

TIPS *The Deronda Review* publishes the addresses of poets who would welcome correspondence. Longer selections of poets frequently published in the magazine are posted on www.pointandcircumference.com.

DESCANT

P.O. Box 314, Station P, Toronto ON M5S 2S8, Canada. (416)593-2557. **Fax:** (416)593-9362. **E-mail:** info@descant.ca. **Website:** descant.ca. Pays on publication. Publishes ms an average of 16 months after acceptance. Editorial lead time 1 year. Sample copy for $8.50 plus postage. Guidelines available online.

Pays $100 honorarium, plus 1-year's subscription for accepted submissions of any kind.

MAGAZINE NEEDS "*Descant* seeks high quality poems and stories in both traditional and innovative form." Annual. Circ. 500-750. Member CLMP. Literary. Pays $100. Pays on pubication.

CONTEST/AWARD OFFERINGS Sponsors the $500 Betsy Colquitt Award for the best poem in an issue; the $250 Baskerville Publishers Award for outstanding poem in an issue. Several stories first published by *descant* have appeared in *Best American Short Stories.*

TIPS "Familiarize yourself with our magazine before submitting."

DESCANT: FORT WORTH'S JOURNAL OF POETRY AND FICTION

English Department, Texas Christian University, Box 297270, Fort Worth TX 76129. **Fax:** (817)257-6239. **E-mail:** descant@tcu.edu. **Website:** www.descant.tcu.edu. **Contact:** Dave Kuhne, editor. *descant: Fort Worth's Journal of Poetry and Fiction*, published annually during the summer, seeks "well-crafted poems of interest. No restrictions as to subject matter or form."

"For 50 years, *descant*, the literary journal of Texas Christian University, has been publishing outstanding poetry and fiction, and, over the course of 5 decades, *descant* has become Fort Worth's journal of poetry and fiction. A forum for fiction and poetry, *descant* seeks high-quality work in either innovative or traditional forms." *descant* is 100+ pages, digest-sized, professionally printed and bound, with matte card cover. Receives about 3,000 poems/year. Press run is 500. Subscription: $12 ($18 outside US). Sample: $10.

MAGAZINE NEEDS Submit no more than 5 poems at a time. Lines/poem: 60 or fewer, "but sometimes longer." Accepts simultaneous submissions. Include SASE. No fax or e-mail submissions. Reads submissions September 1-April 1 only. Responds in 6 weeks. Pays 2 contributor's copies. Sponsors the annual Betsy Colquitt Award for Poetry, offering $500 to the best poem or series of poems by a single author in a volume. *descant* also offers a $250 award for an outstanding poem in an issue. No application process or reading fee; all published submissions are eligible for consideration.

CONTEST/AWARD OFFERINGS Sponsors the annual Betsy Colquitt Award for Poetry, offering $500 to the best poem or series of poems by a single author in a volume. *descant* also offers a $250 award for an outstanding poem in an issue. No application process or reading fee; all published submissions are eligible for consideration.

DEVIL BLOSSOMS

Asterius Press, P.O. Box 5122, Seabrook NJ 08302-3511. **Website:** www.asteriuspress.com. **Contact:** John C. Erianne, Editor. *Devil Blossoms*, published irregularly 1-2 times/year, seeks "poetry in which the words show the scars of real life. Sensual poetry that's occasionally ugly. I'd rather read a poem that makes me sick than a poem without meaning." Wants poetry that is "darkly comical, ironic, visceral, horrific; or any tidbit of human experience that moves me." Does not want "religious greetings, 'I'm-so-happy-to-be-alive' tree poetry." Has published poetry by Marie Kazalia, Stephanie Savage, Mitchell Metz, Normal, John Sweet, and Alison Daniel. *Devil Blossoms* is 32 pages, 712x10, saddle-stapled, with matte card cover with ink drawings. Receives about 10,000 poems/year, accepts about 1%. Press run is 750. Single copy: $5; subscription: $14. Make checks payable to John C. Erianne.

MAGAZINE NEEDS Submit 3-5 poems at a time. Considers simultaneous submissions "if so informed." Accepts e-mail submissions (pasted into body of message; no attachments). Must have "submission" in the subject header. Cover letter is preferred. Time between acceptance and publication is up to one year. "I promptly read submissions, divide them into a 'no' and a 'maybe' pile. Then I read the 'maybes' again." Seldom comments on rejected poems. Guidelines available on website. Responds in up to 2 months. Pays one contributor's copy. Acquires first rights.

TIPS "Write from love; don't expect love in return, don't take rejection personally, and don't let anyone stop you."

DEVOZINE

1908 Grand Ave., P.O. Box 340004, Nashville TN 37203-0004. **E-mail:** smiller@upperroom.org. **Website:** www.devozine.org. **Contact:** Sandi Miller, Editor. *devozine,* published bimonthly, is a 64-page devotional magazine for youth (ages 12-19) and adults who care about youth. Offers meditations, scripture, prayers, poems, stories, songs, and feature articles to "aid youth in their prayer life, introduce them to spiritual disciplines, help them shape their concept of God, and encourage them in the life of discipleship." Considers poetry by teens. Lines/poem: 10-20. No e-mail submissions; submit by regular mail with SASE or use online submmission form. Include name, age/birth date (if younger than 25), mailing address, e-mail address, phone number, and fax number (if available). Always publishes theme issues (focuses on nine themes/issue, one for each week). Indicate theme you are writing for. Guidelines available for SASE or on website. Pays $25.

DIAGRAM

Dept. of English, Univ. of Arizona, P.O. Box 210067, Tucson, AZ 85721-0067. **E-mail:** editor@thediagram.com. **Website:** www.thediagram.com. *DIAGRAM*, published semimonthly online, prints "poetry, prose, and schematic (found or created), plus nonfiction, art, and sound. We're especially interested in unusual forms and structures, and work that blurs genre boundaries." Does not want light verse. Has published poetry by Arielle Greenberg, Jason Bredle, Lia Purpura, GC Waldrep. Receives about 1,000 poems/year, accepts about 5%. Number of unique visitors:1,500/day. "*Diagram* is an electronic journal of text and art, found and created. We're interested in representations, naming, indicating, schematics, labelling and taxonomy of things; in poems that masquerade as stories; in stories that disguise themselves as indices or obituaries." Buys first North American serial rights. Responds in 1 month to mss

"We sponsor yearly contests for unpublished hybrid essays and innovative fiction. Guidelines on website."

HOW TO CONTACT Submit 3-6 poems at a time. Lines/poem: no limit. Considers simultaneous submissions; no previously published poems. Electronic submissions accepted through submissions manager; no e-mail, disk, or fax submissions. Electronic submissions MUCH preferred; print submissions must include SASE if response is expected." Cover letter is preferred. Reads submissions year round. Time between acceptance and publication is 1-10 months. Poems are circulated to an editorial board. Sometimes comments on rejected poems. Sometimes publishes theme issues. Guidelines available on website. Responds in 1-3 months. Always sends prepublication galleys. Acquires first rights and first North American serial rights. Rights revert to poet upon publication. Reviews books/chapbooks of poetry in 500-1,500 words, single- or multi-book format. Send materials for review consideration to Pablo Peschiera, reviews editor. Info on website

ADDITIONAL INFORMATION *DIAGRAM* also publishes periodic perfect-bound print anthologies.

TIPS "Submit interesting text, images, sound and new media. We value the insides of things, vivisection, urgency, risk, elegance, flamboyance, work that moves us, language that does something new, or does something old—well. We like iteration and reiteration. Ruins and ghosts. Mechanical, moving parts, balloons, and frenzy. We want art and writing that demonstrates/interaction; the processes of things; how functions are accomplished; how things become or expire, move or stand. We'll consider anything. We do not consider email submissions, but encourage electronic submissions via our submissions manager software. Look at the journal and submissions guidelines before submitting."

DIG MAGAZINE

Carus Publishing Co., 30 Grove St., Suite C, Peterborough NH 03458. (603)924-7209. **Fax:** (603)924-7380. **Website:** www.digonsite.com. **Contact:** Rosalie Baker, editor. Buys all rights. Pays on publication. Publishes ms an average of 1 year after acceptance. Responds in several months. Editorial lead time 1 year. Sample copy for $5.95 with 8×11 SASE or $10 without SASE. Guidelines available online.

MAGAZINE NEEDS *DIG Magazine*, published 9 times/year in partnership with *Archeology* magazine, features archeology and exploration for children ages 9-14. "All material must relate to the theme of a specific upcoming issue in order to be considered." Wants "clear, objective imagery. Serious and light verse considered. Must relate to theme." Subscription: $32.97/year (9 issues). Sample: $5.95 plus $2.00 s&h (include 10×13 SASE); sample pages available on website.

HOW TO CONTACT Query first. Lines/poem: up to 100. No e-mail submissions or queries. Include SASE. Reads submissions according to deadlines for queries (see website for schedule and details). Always publishes theme issue. Themes and guidelines available on website. Pays varied rates. Acquires all rights.

TIPS "Please remember that this is a children's magazine for kids ages 9-14 so the tone is as kid-friendly as possible given the scholarship involved in researching and describing a site or a find."

DIODE POETRY JOURNAL

Virginia Commonwealth University in Qatar, Doha Qatar, Qatar. +9744134812. **Fax:** +9744920332. **Website:** www.diodepoetry.com. **Contact:** Patty Paine, editor. "*Diode* is looking for 'electropositive' poetry. What is electropositive poetry? It's poetry that excites and energizes. It's poetry that uses language that crackles and sparks. We're looking for poetry from all points on the arc, from formal to experimental." Acquires one-time rights. Rights revert to poet upon publication. Responds in 3-5 weeks. Always sends prepublication galleys. Guidelines available on website, by e-mail, in magazine.

Does not want "light verse, erotic." Has published poetry by Bob Hicok, Beckian Fritz Golberg, G.C. Waldrep, Dorianne Laux, Ada Limon, Joshua Maries Wilkinson. Receives about 6,000 poems/year; accepts about 3%.

MAGAZINE NEEDS Submit 3-5 poems at a time. Considers simultaneous submissions, no previously published poetry. Accepts submissions by e-mail; attach document. Cover letter is required. Reads submissions year round. Time between acceptance and publication is 3-5 weeks. Sometimes comments on rejected poems. Considers reviews books and chapbooks of poetry of 1,500-4,000 words, single and multi-book format.

DISLOCATE

University of Minnesota English Department, the Edelstein-Keller Endowment, and Adam Lerner of the Lerner Publishing Group., Dept. of English, University of Minnesota, 1 Lind Hall, 207 Church St. SE, Minneapolis MN 55455. **Website:** http://dislocate.umn.edu. *dislocate* is a print and online literary journal dedicated to publishing the literature that pushes the traditional boundaries of form and genre. We like work that operates in the gray areas, that resists categorization, that ignores the limits; we like work that plays with the relationship between form and content. We publish fiction, nonfiction, and poetry, but we don't mind if we can't tell which one we're dealing with. In addition to our more "literary" content, dislocate also publishes articles and columns of interest to readers, writers, and other aesthetically curious individuals.

Reading period currently closed.

ADDITIONAL INFORMATION "We are now using Submishmash for all submissions. (Submissions will become available when the reading period begins.) We will not consider or respond to submissions or by post or e-mail."

CONTEST/AWARD OFFERINGS dislocate.umn.edu also runs a monthly Short Forms Contest; winners are published on the website and awarded prizes that vary from month to month. See contest submission guidelines and prize details.

TIPS "Looking for excellent writing that rearranges the world."

DMQ REVIEW

E-mail: editors@dmqreview.com. **Website:** www.dmqreview.com. **Contact:** Sally Ashton, editor-in-chief; Marjorie Manwaring, editor. We seek work that represents the diversity of contemporary poetry and demonstrates literary excellence, whether it be lyric, free verse, prose, or experimental form. Buys first North American serial rights. Publishes ms 1-3 months after acceptance. Responds in 3 months. Guidelines available online.

MAGAZINE NEEDS Has published poetry by David Lehman, Ellen Bass, Amy Gerstler, Bob Hicok, Ilya Kaminsky, and Jane Hirshfield. Receives about 3,000-5,000 poems/year, accepts about 1%. E-mail submissions only; NO attachments. Include a brief bio, 50 words/max. Type Poetry Submission followed by your name in the subject line.

ADDITIONAL INFORMATION Nominates for the Pushcart Prize. "We also consider submissions of visual art, which we publish with the poems in the magazine, with links to the artists' Web sites."

TIPS Check our current and past issues and read and follow submission guidelines closely. Important: Copy and include the permission statement with your submission (it's in our guidelines online). For Visual Art submissions: Type 'Art Submission' followed by your name in your email. Send a working URL where we may view samples of your work.

DOWN IN THE DIRT

829 Brian Court, Gurnee IL 60031-3155. (847)281-9070. **E-mail:** alexrand@scars.tv. **Website:** scars.tv. **Contact:** Alexandria Rand, editor.

MAGAZINE NEEDS *Down in the Dirt*, published monthly online, prints "good work that makes you think, that makes you feel like you've lived through a scene instead of merely read it." Also can consider poems. Does not want smut, rhyming poetry, or religious writing. Has published work by I.B. Rad, Pat

Dixon, Mel Waldman, and Ken Dean. *Down in the Dirt* is published "electronically as well as in print, either on the Web or in e-book form (PDF file)." Sample: available on website.

HOW TO CONTACT Lines/poem: any length is appreciated. Considers previously published poems and simultaneous submissions. Accepts e-mail submissions (vastly preferred to snail mail; pasted into body of message or as Microsoft Word .doc file attachment) and disk submissions (formatted for Macintosh). Guidelines available for SASE, by e-mail, or on website. No payment. "Currently, accepted writings get their own web page in the "writings" section at http://scars.tv, and samples of accepted writings are placed into an annual collection book Scars Publications produces."

ADDITIONAL INFORMATION Also able to publish electronic chapbooks. Write for more information.

CONTEST/AWARD OFFERINGS Scars Publications sponsors a contest "where accepted writing appears in a collection book. Write or e-mail (editor@scars.tv) for information."

◐ DROWN IN MY OWN FEARS

E-mail: drowninmyownfears@yahoo.com. **Website:** http://drowninmyownfears.angelfire.com. **Contact:** Chantal Hejduk, Alla Kozak and Kaia Braeburn, editors. Publishes ms 1-2 months after acceptance. Responds in 2-4 weeks.

MAGAZINE NEEDS *Drown In My Own Fears*, published quarterly online, "is a poetry journal about the human condition, therefore, we want poems reflecting that. Poems submitted should be about love, hate, pain, sorrow, etc. We don't want maudlin sentimentality, we want the depths of your very being. We want well-written, deeply conceived pieces of work. Anything that isn't about the human condition really isn\ rquote t for us." Wants "all styles of poetry, as long as it's your best work." Does not want "syrupy sweet, gooey nonsense, religious rants, political grandstandings." Considers poetry by teens. Has published poetry by Kendall A. Bell, April Michelle Bratten, Natalie Carpentieri, MK Chavez, James H. Duncan and Taylor Graham. Receives about 300 poems/year, accepts about 10%. Submit 3-5 poems at a time. "We prefer short poems, but long ones are ok." Considers previously published poems; no simultaneous submissions. Accepts e-mail submissions (pasted into body of e-mail message); no fax or disk submissions. Cover letter is rquired. Include a brief bio with your submission. Reads submissions year round. Never comments on rejected poems. Sometimes publishes theme issues. Upcoming themes and guidelines available on website. Acquires first rights. Rights revert to poets upon publication.

DRUNKEN BOAT

119 Main St., Chester CT 06412. **E-mail:** editor@drunkenboat.com. **Website:** www.drunkenboat.com. *Drunken Boat*, published twice yearly online, is a multimedia publication reaching an international audience with an extremely broad aesthetic. Considers poetry by teens. "We judge by quality, not age. However, most poetry we publish is written by published poets with training in creative writing. "Has published more than 500 poets, including Heather McHugh, Jane Hirshfield, Alfred Corn, Alice Fulton, Ron Silliman, and Roseanna Warren. Received about 3,000 poems/year, accepts about 5%. Responds in 3 months to mss. Guidelines available online.

MAGAZINE NEEDS "Submit no more than 3 poems, in a single document. Our aesthetic is very broad. We welcome work ranging from received form to the cutting edge avant-garde, from one line to the multi-page, from collaborations to hybridizations & cut-ups as well as works that use other media in their composition, originality & in translation (with the writer's permission), American, & from around the globe." Length: 1 lines.

TIPS "Submissions should be submitted in Word & rtf format only. (This does not apply to audio, visual & web work.) Accepts chapbooks. See our submissions manager system."

◐ DUCTS

P.O. Box 3203, Grand Central Station, New York NY 10163. **E-mail:** fiction@ducts.org; essays@ducts.org. **Website:** www.ducts.org/content. **Contact:** Jonathan Kravetz. *DUCTS* is a webzine of personal stories, fiction, essays, memoirs, poetry, humor, profiles, reviews and art. "*DUCTS* was founded in 1999 with the intent of giving emerging writers a venue to regularly publish their compelling, personal stories. The site has been expanded to include art and creative works of all genres. We believe that these genres must and do overlap. *DUCTS* publishes the best, most compelling stories and we hope to attract readers who are drawn to work that rises above." Semi-annual.

HOW TO CONTACT Reading period is January 1 through August 31. Send complete ms to poetry@ducts.org. Accepts submissions by e-mail to appropriate departments. Responds in 1-4 weeks to queries; 1-6 months to mss. Accepts simultaneous and reprints submissions. Writer's guidelines on ducts.org.
TIPS "We prefer writing that tells a compelling story with a strong narrative drive."

EARTHSHINE

P.O. Box 245, Hummelstown PA 17036. **E-mail:** poetry@ruminations.us. **Website:** www.ruminations.us. **Contact:** Sally Zaino and Julie Moffitt, poetry editors. *Earthshine*, published irregularly in print, and constantly online, features poetry and 1-2 pieces of cover art per volume. "When the online journal is full, a printed volume is produced and offered for sale. Subscriptions will be available as the publication becomes regular. The voice of *Earthshine* is one of illumination, compassion, humanity, and reason. Please see submission guidelines Web page for updated information. Poems are the ultimate rumination, and if the world is to be saved, the poets will be needed; they are who see the connections between all things, and the patterns shared. We seek poetry of high literary quality which will generate its own light for our readers." Has published poetry by Richard Schiffman, Anne Pierson Wiese, Steven Keletar, Mario Susko, Daniel J. Langton. Acquires first rights and requests ongoing electronic rights. Responds in 1-2 months. Guidelines available in magazine, for SASE, and online at website.
MAGAZINE NEEDS Considers previously published poems; no simultaneous submissions. Accepts e-mail submissions (pasted into body of message); no fax or disk submissions. Cover letter is preferred. "Please let us know where you heard about *Earthshine*. If submitting by mail, please include a SASE for reply only. Please do not send the only copy of your work." Reads submissions year round. Time between acceptance and publication is: "online publication is almost immediate, printed publication TBD." Sometimes comments on rejected poems. Never publishes theme issues. Pays 2 contributor's copies.
ALSO OFFERS "The parent of *Earthshine* is also at Ruminations.us, and offers full editing and review services for a fee."

ECLECTICA

E-mail: editors@eclectica.org. **E-mail:** submissions@eclectica.org. **Website:** www.eclectica.org. **E-mail:** editors@eclectica.org; submissions@eclectica.org. **Website:** www.eclectica.org. Online magazine. "Eclectica is a quarterly World Wide Web journal devoted to showcasing the best writing on the Web, regardless of genre or subject matter. 'Literary' and 'genre' work appear side-by-side in each issue, along with pieces that blur the distinctions between such categories. Pushcart Prize, National Poetry Series, and Pulitzer Prize winners, as well as Nebula Award nominees, have shared issues with previously unpublished authors." Magazine seeks outstanding poetry, fiction, nonfiction, opinion, and reviews. "A sterling quality literary magazine on the World Wide Web. Not bound by formula or genre, harnessing technology to further the reading experience and dynamic and interesting in content." Buys first North American serial rights, buys one-time, nonexclusive use of electronic rights rights. Guidelines available.
MAGAZINE NEEDS Magazine seeks outstanding poetry, fiction, nonfiction, opinion, and reviews.
HOW TO CONTACT Accepts submissions by e-mail. E-mail: submissions@eclectica.org. Must be plain text, no attachments. Poetry submissions should be limited to 5 works per author. "While we will consider simultaneous submissions, please be sure to let us know that they are simultaneous and keep us updated on their publication status." Guidelines available on website. Acquires first North American serial rights, electronic rights.
TIPS "Works which cross genres—or create new ones—are encouraged. This includes prose poems, 'heavy' opinion, works combining visual art and writing, electronic multimedia, hypertext/html, and types we have yet to imagine. No length restrictions. We will consider long stories and novel excerpts, and serialization of long pieces. Include short cover letter."

THE ECLECTIC MUSE

Suite 307, 6311 Gilbert Rd., Richmond BC V7C 3V7, Canada. (604)447-0979. **E-mail:** jrmbooks@hotmail.com. **Website:** mbooksofbc.com; thehypertexts.com. **Contact:** Joe M. Ruggier, publisher. *The Eclectic Muse*, published annually at Christmas, is devoted "to publishing all kinds of poetry (eclectic in style and taste) but specializing in rhyme- and neo-classicist revival." Does not want "bad work (stylistically bad or thematically offensive)." Has published poetry by Mary Keelan Meisel, John Laycock, Philip Higson, Roy Harrison, Michael Burch, and Ralph O. Cunningham. *The Eclectic Muse* is magazine-sized, digitally copied, saddle-stapled, with paper cover. The number of pages varies from year to year (32 minimum to 56 maximum). Receives about 300 poems/year, accepts about 15%. Press run is 200; distributed free to all contributing authors plus selected gift subscription recipients. Reads submissions year round. Sometimes comments on rejected poems. **"If authors wish to have a manuscript carefully assessed and edited, the fee is $250 USD; will respond within 8 weeks."** Responds in 2 months. Pays 2 contributor's copies. Reviews books/chapbooks of poetry and other magazines/journals at varying length. Send materials for review consideration to Joe M. Ruggier, managing editor. Time between acceptance and publication is 1 year. Single copy: $15 includes shipping and handling; subscription: $25. Make checks payable to Joe M. Ruggier. Guidelines available in magazine or on website.

MAGAZINE NEEDS Submit no more than 5 poems at a time. Lines/poem: 60 maximum; "please consult if longer." Accepts e-mail submissions (as ONE .doc or .rtf attachment containing all 5 poems) and disk submissions. "Send your submission by regular mail only if you have no access to a computer or you are computer illiterate. Typeset everything in Times New Roman 12 point. If your poetry features indents and special line spacing, please make sure you reproduce these features yourself in your data entry since it will not be possible for the editor to determine your intentions." Cover letter is preferred. "Include brief bio (100 words maximum) with your name, credentials (degrees, etc.), occupation and marital status, your most major publication credits only, and any hobbies or interests." Provide SASE plus clear e-mail and postal addresses for communication and for sending contributor's copy. "Look us up on www.thehypertexts.com, where myself and my services are listed (featured) permanently. The host of this splendid poetry website is my U.S. associate, Mr. Michael Burch. He features, on this site, most of the leading names in contemporary North America."

ECOTONE

(910)962-2547. **Fax:** (910)962-7461. **E-mail:** info@ecotonejournal.com. **Website:** www.ecotonejournal.com. "*Ecotone* is a literary journal of place that seeks to publish creative works about the environment and the natural world while avoiding the hushed tones and cliches of much of so-called nature writing. Reading period is Aug. 15 - Apr. 15." Responds in 3-6 months to mss.

◐ EKPHRASIS

Frith Press, P.O. Box 161236, Sacramento CA 95816-1236. **E-mail:** frithpress@aol.com. **Website:** ekphrasisjournal.com. **Contact:** Laverne Frith and Carol Frith, editors. Acquires first North American serial rights or one-time rights. Publishes ms 1 year after acceptance. Responds in 4 months. Guidelines available for SASE or on website.

Ekphrasis, published semiannually in March and September, is an "outlet for the growing body of poetry focusing on individual works from any artistic genre." Poetry should transcend mere description. Open to all forms." Does not want "poetry without ekphrastic focus. No poorly crafted work. No archaic language." Submit 3-5 poems at a time. Has published poetry by Jeffrey Levine, Peter Meinke, David Hamilton, Barbara Lefcowitz, Molly McQuade, and Annie Boutelle. *Ekphrasis* is 32-50 pages, digest-sized, photocopied, saddle-stapled. Subscription: $12/year. Sample: $6. Make checks payable, in U.S. funds, to Laverne Frith. Poems from *Ekphrasis* have been featured on *Poetry Daily*. Nominates for Pushcart Prize.

MAGAZINE NEEDS Considers previously published poems "infrequently, must be credited." Cover letter is required, including short bio with representative credits and phone number. Include SASE. Seldom comments on rejected poems. Pays 1 contributor's copy. Until further notice, Frith Press will publish **occasional chapbooks by invitation only.**

ELLERY QUEEN'S MYSTERY MAGAZINE

Dell Magazines Fiction Group, 267 Broadway, 4th Floor, New York NY 10017. (212)686-7188. **Fax:** (212)686-7414. **E-mail:** elleryqueenmm@dellmagazines.com. **Website:** www.themysteryplace.com/eqmm. "*Ellery Queen's Mystery Magazine* welcomes submissions from both new and established writers. We publish every kind of mystery short story: the psychological suspense tale, the deductive puzzle, the private eye case—the gamut of crime and detection from the realistic (including the policeman's lot and stories of police procedure) to the more imaginative (including 'locked rooms' and 'impossible crimes'). We look for strong writing, an original and exciting plot, and professional craftsmanship. We encourage writers whose work meets these general criteria to read an issue of *EQMM* before making a submission." Buys first North American serial rights. Pays on acceptance. Publishes ms an average of 6-12 months after acceptance. Responds in 3 months to mss. Sample copy for $5.50. Guidelines for SASE or online.

MAGAZINE NEEDS *Ellery Queen's Mystery Magazine*, published 10 times/year, uses primarily short stories of mystery, crime, or suspense—little poetry. *Ellery Queen's Mystery Magazine* is 112 pages (double-issue, published twice/year, is 192 pages), digest-sized, professionally printed on newsprint, flat-spined, with glossy paper cover. Single copy: $5.50 by check to publisher, available for $4.99 on newsstands; subscription: $55.90. Short mystery verses, limericks. Length: 1 page, double spaced maximum.

HOW TO CONTACT Considers simultaneous submissions; no previously published poems. Guidelines available on website. Responds in 3 months. Pays $15-65 and 3 contributor's copies. "EQMM uses an online submission system (http://eqmm.magazinesubmissions.com) that has been designed to streamline our process and improve communication with authors. We ask that all submissions be made electronically, using this system, rather than on paper. All stories should be in standard ms format and submitted in .DOC format. We cannot accept .DOCX, .RTF, or .TXT files at this time. For detailed submission instructions, see http://eqmm.magazinesubmissions.com or our writers guidelines page (http://www.themysteryplace.com/eqmm/guidelines)."

TIPS "We have a Department of First Stories to encourage writers whose fiction has never before been in print. We publish an average of 10 first stories every year. Mark subject line Attn: Dept. of First Stories."

ELLIPSIS MAGAZINE

(801)832-2321. **E-mail:** ellipsis@westminstercollege.edu. **Website:** www.westminstercollege.edu/ellipsis. Submit 3-5 poems at a time. Considers simultaneous submissions if notified of acceptance elsewhere; no previously published poems. Reads submissions August 1 - November 1. Responds in up to 8 months. Pays $10/poem, plus two contributor's copies. Buys first North American serial rights. Pays on publication. Publishes ms an average of 3 months after acceptance. Responds in 6 months to mss. Sample copy for $7.50. Guidelines available online.

Reads submissions August 1 to November 1.

MAGAZINE NEEDS Pays $10/poem, plus 1 copy.

HOW TO CONTACT No fax or e-mail submissions; postal submissions only. One poem per page, with name and contact information on every page. Include SASE and brief bio.

CONTEST/AWARD OFFERINGS All accepted poems are eligible for the *Ellipsis* Award which includes a $100 prize. Past judges have included Jorie Graham, Sandra Cisneros, and Stanley Plumly.

EPICENTER: A LITERARY MAGAZINE

P.O. Box 367, Riverside CA 92502. **E-mail:** submissions@epicentermagazine.org. **Website:** www.epicentermagazine.org. **Contact:** Jeff Green, Cali Linfor, Rowena Silver, editors. *Epicenter: A Literary Magazine* published semiannually, is open to all styles. "*Epicenter* is looking for poetry, essays, short stories, creative nonfiction, and artwork. We publish new and established writers." Considers translations. Does not want "angst-ridden, sentimental, or earthquake poetry. We are not adverse to graphic images as long as the work contains literary merit." Has published poetry by Virgil Suarez, Alba Cruz-Hacher, B.Z. Niditch, Egon Lass, and Zdravka Evtimova. *Epicenter* is 100 pages, perfect-bound. Receives about 2,000 submissions/year, accepts about 5%. Press run is 800. Single copy: $9. Make checks payable to *Epicenter: A Literary Magazine*. Acquires one-time and electronic rights. Guidelines in magazine, by e-mail or for SASE.

MAGAZINE NEEDS Submit up to 5 poems at a time. Send poetry with vivid imagery and fresh ideas. Accepts any style of poetry. Submit through postal mail or e-mail. "Due to the volume of e-mail submissions, we do not respond unless we wish to use a piece." Include SASE with postal mail. Pays 1 contributor's copy.

EPIPHANY

E-mail: contact@epiphmag.com. **E-mail:** submissions@epiphmag.com. **Website:** http://epiphmag.com. **Contact:** JW Smith, editor. Epiphany was started in 2010, solely to be an online venue in which writers and artists can display their works. "Epiphany's dynamic formatting sets our publication apart from other online magazines. We strive to bring poetry, prose, fiction, nonfiction, artwork, and photography together to form a visually and creatively stimulating experience for our readers." Six issues/year in February,

April, June, August, October, and December. Contributors retain their rights. Publishes ms an average of 3 months after acceptance. Responds in 1-4 weeks to queries; 1-4 months to mss. Sample copy available on website.

"Epiphany is a non-paying market at this time."

TIPS "We are open to a variety of writing styles and content subject matter. Our audience includes writers, artists, students, teachers, and all who enjoy reading short fiction, poetry, and creative nonfiction. We will not publish any works which we feel have a derogatory nature. Please visit our submission guidelines page at www.epiphmag.com/guide.html for more details."

EPOCH

(607)255-3385. **Fax:** (607)255-6661. "Well-written literary fiction, poetry, personal essays. Newcomers always welcome. Open to mainstream and avant-garde writing." Buys first North American serial rights. Pays on publication. Publishes ms an average of 6 months after acceptance. Responds in 2 weeks to queries. Responds in 6 weeks to mss. Editorial lead time 6 months. Sample copy for $5. Guidelines for #10 SASE.

MAGAZINE NEEDS *Epoch*, published 3 times/year, has a distinguished and long record of publishing exceptionally fine poetry and fiction. Has published poetry by Kevin Prufer, Peter Dale Scott, Martin Walls, Maxine Kumin, Heather McHugh, and D. James Smith. *Epoch* is 128 pages, digest-sized, professionally printed, perfect-bound, with glossy color cover. Accepts less than 1% of the many submissions received each year. Has 1,000 subscribers. Subscription: $11/year domestic, $15/year foreign. Sample: $5. Pays $5 up/printed page.

HOW TO CONTACT No simultaneous submissions. Manuscripts not accompanied by SASE will be discarded unread. Reads submissions September 15-April 15. Responds in up to 10 weeks. Occasionally provides criticism on mss. Pays 3 contributor's copies and at least $10/page. "We pay more when we have more!" Acquires first serial rights.

TIPS "Tell your story, speak your poem, straight from the heart. We are attracted to language and to good writing, but we are most interested in what the good writing leads us to, or where."

ESSAYS & FICTIONS

526 S. Albany St. Apt. 1N, Ithaca NY 14850. (914)572-7351. **E-mail:** essaysandfictions@gmail.com. **Website:** http://essaysandfictions.com. **Contact:** David Pollock and Danielle Winterton, co-founding editors. Essays & Fictions is an online journal of literature and criticism. Acquires first and electronic rights. Publication is copyrighted. Publishes ms 1-4 months after acceptance. Responds to mss in 1-3 months. Sample copy: $15. Guidelines available by e-mail or on website.

MAGAZINE NEEDS Contributors get one free copy and 15% off additional copies of the issue in which they are published.

TIPS "We look for confident work that uses form/structure and voice in interesting ways without sounding overly self-conscious or deliberate. We encourage rigorous excellence of complex craft in our submissions and discourage bland reproductions of reality. Read the journal. Be familiar with the *Essays & Fictions* aesthetic. We are particularly interested in writers who read theory and/or have multiple intellectual and artistic interests, and who set high intellectual standards for themselves and their work."

EUROPEAN JUDAISM

LBC, The Sternberg Centre, 80 East End Rd., London N3 2SY, England. **E-mail:** european.judaism@lbc.ac.uk. **Website:** www.berghahnbooks.com/journals/ej. *European Judaism*, published twice/year, is a "glossy, elegant magazine with emphasis on European Jewish theology/philosophy/literature/history, with some poetry in every issue. Poems should (preferably) be short and have some relevance to matters of Jewish interest." Has published poetry by Linda Pastan, Elaine Feinstein, Daniel Weissbort, and Dannie Abse. *European Judaism* is 110 pages, digest-sized, flat-spined. Press run is 950 (about 500 subscribers, over 100 libraries). Subscription: $45 individual, $20 student, $162 institution.

MAGAZINE NEEDS Submit 3-4 poems at a time. Lines/poem: short poems preferred. "I prefer unpublished poems, but poems from published books are acceptable." Cover letter is required. "No material is read or returned if not accompanied by SASE (or SAE with IRCs). We cannot use American stamps." Pays 1 contributor's copy.

EVANGEL

Free Methodist Publishing House, P.O. Box 535002, Indianapolis IN 46253-5002. (317)244-3660. **Contact:** Julie Innes, editor. *Evangel*, published quarterly, is an adult Sunday School paper. "Devotional in nature, it lifts up Christ as the source of salvation and hope. The mission of *Evangel* is to increase the reader's understanding of the nature and character of God and the nature of a life lived for Christ. Material that fits this mission and isn't longer than 1 page will be considered." Buys second serial (reprint) or one-time rights. Pays on publication. Sample copy and writer's guidelines for #10 SASE. "Write 'guidelines request' on your envelope so we can sort it from the submissions."

Evangel is 8 pages, 5.5 x 8.5, printed in 4-color, unbound, color and b&w photos. Does not want rhyming work. Accepts about 5% of poetry received. Fiction involves people coping with everday crises, making decisions that show spiritual growth. Weekly distribution. Recently published work by Kelli Wise and Hope Byler. Press run is about 10,000. Subscription: $2.59/quarter (13 weeks).

MAGAZINE NEEDS Submit no more than 5 poems at a time. Considers simultaneous submissions. Cover letter ispreferred. "Poetry must be typed on 8.5 x 11 white paper. In the upper left-hand corner of each page, include your name, address, phone number, and social security number. In the upper right-hand corner of cover page, specify what rights you are offering. One-eighth of the way down the page, give the title. All subsequent material must be double-spaced, with 1-inch margins." Responds in up to 2 months. Pays $10 plus 2 contributor's copies. Acquires one-time rights.

TIPS "Desire, concise, tight writing that supports a solid thesis and fits the mission expressed in the guidelines."

EVANSVILLE REVIEW

University of Evansville English Dept., 1800 Lincoln Ave., Evansville IN 47722. (812)488-1402. **E-mail:** evansvillereview@evansville.edu. **Website:** http://evansvillereview.evansville.edu. **Contact:** Editor. *The Evansville Review*, published annually in April, prints "prose, poems, and drama of literary merit." Wants "anything of quality." No excessively experimental work; no erotica. Has published poetry by Joseph Brodsky, J.L. Borges, John Updike, Willis Barnstone, Rita Dove, and Vivian Shipley. *The Evansville Review* is 140-200 pages, digest-sized, perfect-bound, with art on cover. Receives about 2,000 poems/year, accepts about 2%. Press run is 1,500. Sample: $5.

HOW TO CONTACT Submit 3-5 poems at a time. Considers previously published poems and simultaneous submissions. No fax or e-mail submissions; postal submissions only. Cover letter is required. Include brief bio. Manuscripts not returned without SASE. Reads submissions September 1-December 1 only. Time between acceptance and publication is 3 months. Poems are circulated to an editorial board. Seldom comments on rejected poems. Guidelines available for SASE or on website. Responds within 3 months of the deadline. Pays 2 contributor's copies. Rights remain with poet.

TIPS "Because editorial staff rolls over every 1-2 years, the journal always has a new flavor."

EXIT 13 MAGAZINE, "THE CROSSROADS OF POETRY SINCE 1988"

P.O. Box 423, Fanwood NJ 07023-1162. **E-mail:** exit13magazine@yahoo.com. **Contact:** Tom Plante, editor. *Exit 13*, published annually, uses poetry that is "short, to the point, with a sense of geography. It features poets of all ages, writing styles and degrees of experience, focusing on where and how we live and what's going on around us. The emphasis is on geography, travel, adventure, and the fertile ground of the imagination. It's a travelogue in poetry, a reflection of the world we see, and a chronicle of the people we meet along the way." Acquires one-time and possible anthology rights. Pays 1 contributor's copy. Responds in 4 months. Guidelines available in magazine or for SASE.

Has published poetry by Paul Brooke, Ruth Moon Kempher, Sandy McCord, Sander Zulauf, Paul Sohar, and Charles Rammelkamp. *Exit 13* is about 76 pages. Press run is 300. Sample: $8.

MAGAZINE NEEDS Submit through postal mail or e-mail. Paste in body of e-mail. Considers simultaneous submissions and previously published poems.

EYE ON LIFE ONLINE MAGAZINE

P.O. Box 534, Brookline MA 02445. **E-mail:** eyeonlife.ezine@gmail.com. **Website:** http://eyeonlifemag.com. **Contact:** Tom Rubenoff, senior poetry editor. Poets keep all rights. Responds in 4-6 weeks.

MAGAZINE NEEDS Publishes up to 5 poems/week. Submissions through online submission form only. Seeking poetry with vivid imagery that either works well within its form or transcends it in less than 400 wirds. Does not pay for poetry at this time.

CONTEST/AWARD OFFERINGS Eyes on Life Poetry Contest first prize $100, second prize $50. E-mail tomr@rubecome.us for details.

FACES MAGAZINE

Cobblestone Publishing, Editorial Dept., 30 Grove St., Suite C, Peterborough NH 03458. (603)924-7209. **E-mail:** facesmag@yahoo.com. **Website:** www.cricketmag.com. *FACES Magazine*, published 9 times/year, features cultures from around the globe for children ages 9-14. "Readers learn how other kids live around the world and about the important inventions and ideas that a particular culture has given to the world. All material must relate to the theme of a specific upcoming issue in order to be considered." Wants "clear, objective imagery. Serious and light verse considered. Must relate to theme." Subscription: $33.95/year (9 issues). Sample pages available on website. Acquires all rights.

MAGAZINE NEEDS Query first. Accepts e-mail queries. Include SASE for postal submissions and queries. Reads submissions according to deadlines for queries (see website for schedule and details). Always publishes theme issue. Themes and guidelines available on website. Length: up to 100 lines. Pay varies.

FAULTLINE

Dept. of English and Comparative Literature, University of California at Irvine, Irvine CA 92697-2650. **E-mail:** faultline@uci.edu. **Website:** www.humanities.uci.edu/faultline. Buys first North American serial rights. Pays on publication. Publishes ms an average of 5 months after acceptance. Responds in 4 weeks to queries. Responds in 4 months to mss. Editorial lead time 4 months. Sample copy for $5 or online. Writer's guidelines for #10 SASE or online.

Reading period is September 15-February 15. Submissions sent at any other time will not be read.

MAGAZINE NEEDS *Faultline*, published annually each spring, features new poetry, fiction, and translation. Has published poetry by C.K. Williams, Larissa Szporluk, Yusef Komunyakaa, Amy Gerstler, and Killarney Clary. *Faultline* is about 200 pages, digest-sized, professionally printed on 60 lb. paper, perfect-bound, with 80 lb. coverstock. Receives about 5,000 poems/year, accepts less than 1%. Press run is 1,000. Single copy: $10. Sample: $5. Pays in contributor copies.

HOW TO CONTACT Submit up to 5 poems at a time. Considers simultaneous submissions, "but please note in cover letter that the manuscript is being considered elsewhere." No fax or e-mail submissions. Cover letter is required. Include name, postal and e-mail addresses, and titles of work submitted; do not put name and address on ms pages themselves. SASE required. Reads submissions September 15-February 15 only. Poems are selected by a board of up to 6 readers. Seldom comments on rejected poems. Guidelines available for SASE or on website. Responds in 3 months. Pays 2 contributor's copies. Acquires first or one time serial rights.

TIPS "Our commitment is to publish the best work possible from well-known and emerging authors with vivid and varied voices."

FICKLE MUSES

E-mail: fiction2@ficklemuses.com. **Website:** www.ficklemuses.com. (Specialized: myth and legend). **E-mail:** editor@ficklemuses.com. **Website:** www.ficklemuses.com. Established 2006. **Contact:** Sari Krosinsky, editor.

MAGAZINE NEEDS *Fickle Muses*, published weekly online, is a journal of myth and legend printing poetry, fiction and art. Open to all styles and forms. Has published poetry by J.V. Foerster, Ray Hinman, Maureen Seaton, Kenneth P. Gurney, Doug Ramspeck. Accepts about 10% of poems received. Number of unique visitors: 160/week.

HOW TO CONTACT Submit up to 5 poems at a time. Lines/poem: no limits on length. Considers previously published poems and simultaneous submissions. Accepts e-mail submissions (pasted into body of message preferred, unless special formatting requires an attachment); no disk submissions. Cover letter is preferred. Reads submissions year round. Time between acceptance and publication is up to 3 months. Never comments on rejected poems. Guidelines available on website. Responds in up to 3 months. Acquires one-time and archival rights. Rights revert to poets upon publication. Reviews books/chapbooks of poetry and other magazines/journals in 500 words, single-book format. For review consideration, query by e-mail.

TIPS "Originality. An innovative look at an old story. I'm looking to be swept away. Get a feel for our website."

THE FIDDLEHEAD

University of New Brunswick, Campus House, 11 Garland Court, Box 4400, Fredericton NB E3B 5A3, Canada. (506)453-3501. **Fax:** (506) 453-5069. **E-mail:** fiddlehd@unb.ca; scl@unb.ca. **Website:** www.thefiddlehead.ca. Mark Anthony Jarman or Gerard Beirne, Fiction Editors. **Contact:** Kathryn Taglia, Managing Editor. Literary. Receives 100-150 unsolicited mss/month. Accepts 4-5 mss/issue; 20-40 mss/year. Publishes ms within 1 year after acceptance. Agented fiction: small percentage. **Publishes high percentage of new writers/year.** Send SASE and *Canadian* stamps or IRCs for return of mss. Responds in 6 months to mss. No email submissions. Simultaneous submissions only if stated on cover letter; must contact immediately if accepted elsewhere. Sample copy for $15 (US). Pays up to $40 (Canadian)/published page and 2 contributor's copies. Pays on publication for first or one-time serial rights. "Canada's longest living literary journal, *The Fiddlehead* is published four times a year at the University of New Brunswick, with the generous assistance of the University of New Brunswick, the Canada Council for the Arts, and the Province of New Brunswick. It is experienced; wise enough to recognize excellence; always looking for freshness and surprise. *The Fiddlehead* publishes short stories, poems, book reviews, and a small number of personal essays. Our full-colour covers have become collectors' items, and feature work by New Brunswick artists and from New Brunswick museums and art galleries. *The Fiddlehead* also sponsors an annual writing contest."

MAGAZINE NEEDS *The Fiddlehead* is open to good writing in English from all over the world, looking always for freshness and surprise. Our editors are always happy to see new unsolicited works in fiction and poetry. Work is read on an ongoing basis; the acceptance rate is around 1-2%. Response time is typically from 3 to 9 months. Apart from our annual contest, we have no deadlines for submissions.

CONTEST/AWARD OFFERINGS Sponsors poetry contest.

TIPS "If you are serious about submitting to *The Fiddlehead*, you should subscribe or read an issue or two to get a sense of the journal. Contact us if you would to order sample back issues ($10-$15 plus postage)."

FIELD: CONTEMPORARY POETRY & POETICS

Oberlin College Press, 50 N. Professor St., Oberlin OH 44074-1091. (440)775-8408. **Fax:** (440)775-8124. **E-mail:** oc.press@oberlin.edu. **Website:** www.oberlin.edu/ocpress. **Contact:** managing editor. *FIELD: Contemporary Poetry and Poetics*, published semiannually in April and October, is a literary journal with "emphasis on poetry, translations, and essays by poets." Has published poetry by Michelle Glazer, Tom Lux, Carl Phillips, Betsy Sholl, Charles Simic, Jean Valentine and translations by Marilyn Hacker and Stuart Friebert. *FIELD* is 100 pages, digest-sized, printed on rag stock, flat-spined, with glossy color card cover. Subscription: $16/year, $28 for 2 years. Sample: $8 postpaid. Buys first rights. Pays on publication. Responds in 6-8 weeks to mss. Editorial lead time 4 months. Sample copy for $8. Guidelines available online and for #10 SASE.

"See electronic submission guidelines."

MAGAZINE NEEDS Submissions are read August 1 through May 31. Submit 3-5 of your best poems. No previously published poems or simultaneous submissions. No e-mail submissions. Include cover letter and SASE. Reads submissions year round. Submit using our submission manager at http://www.oberlin.edu/ocpress/submissions.html. Pays $15/page and 2 contributor's copies.

TIPS "Keep trying!"

THE FIFTH DI...

Tyree Campbell, attn: Sam's Dot Publishing, P.O. Box 782, Cedar Rapids IO 52406-0782. **Website:** www.samsdotpublishing.com/fifth/fifth.htm. *The Fifth Di..*, published quarterly online, features fiction and poetry from the science fiction and fantasy genres. Open to most forms, but all poems must be science fiction or fantasy. Does not want horror, or anything that is not science fiction or fantasy. Considers poetry by children and teens. Has published poetry by Bruce Boston, Cathy Buburuz, Marge Simon, Aurelio Rico Lopez III, Terrie Relf, and John Bushore. Receives about 200 poems/year, accepts about 20.

MAGAZINE NEEDS Submit 1 poem at a time. Lines/poem: no limit. No previously published poems or simultaneous submissions. Accepts e-mail submissions only (as attachment); no disk submissions. Cover letter is preferred. Reads submissions year round. Time between acceptance and publication is 1 month.

Sometimes comments on rejected poems. Guidelines available on website. Responds in 1-3 months. Pays $5. Acquires first rights.

FILLING STATION

E-mail: mgmt@fillingstation.ca; poetry@fillingstation.ca; fiction@fillingstation.ca; nonfiction@fillingstation.ca. **Website:** www.fillingstation.ca. **Contact:** Caitlynn Cummings, managing editor. *filling Station*, published 3 times/year, prints contemporary poetry, fiction, visual art, interviews, reviews, and articles. "We are looking for all forms of contemporary writing. but especially that which is original and/or experimental." Has published poetry by Fred Wah, Larissa Lai, Margaret Christakos, Robert Kroetsch, Ron Silliman, Susan Holbrook, and many more. *filling Station* is 64 pages, 8×11, perfect-bound, with card cover, includes photos and artwork. Receives about 100 submissions for each issue, accepts approximately 10%. Press run is 700. Subscription: $20/3 issues; $36 for 6 issues. Sample: $8. Responds in 3-4 months. "After your work is reviewed by our Collective, you will receive an email from an editor to let you know if your work has been selected for publication. If selected, you will later receive a second email to let you know which issue your piece has been selected to appear in. Note that during the design phase, we sometimes discover the need to shuffle a piece to a future issue instead. In the event your piece is pushed back, we will inform you."

MAGAZINE NEEDS Up to 6 pages of poetry may be sent to poetry@fillingstation.ca. A submission lacking mailing address and/or bio will be considered incomplete.

TIPS "*filling Station* accepts singular or simultaneous submissions of previously unpublished poetry, fiction, creative nonfiction, nonfiction, or art. We are always on the hunt for great writing!"

FIRST CLASS

P.O. Box 86, Friendship IN 47021. **E-mail:** christopherm@four-sep.com. **Website:** www.four-sep.com. **Contact:** Christopher M, editor.

MAGAZINE NEEDS *First Class*, published in May and November, prints "excellent/odd writing for intelligent/creative readers." Does not want "traditional work." Has published poetry by Bennett, Locklin, Every, Ui-Neill, Catlin, and Huffstickler. *First Class* is 48-56 pages, 414x11, printed, saddle-stapled, with colored cover. Receives about 1,500 poems/year, accepts about 30. Press run is 300-400. Sample: $6 (includes guidelines). Make checks payable to Christopher M.

HOW TO CONTACT Submit 5 poems at a time. Considers previously published poems and simultaneous submissions. No fax or e-mail submissions. Cover letter is preferred. "Manuscripts will not be returned." Time between acceptance and publication is 2-4 months. Often comments on rejected poems. Guidelines available in magazine, or on website. Responds in 4-8 weeks. Pays 1 contributor's copy. Acquires one-time rights. Reviews books of poetry and fiction. Send materials for review consideration.

ADDITIONAL INFORMATION Chapbook production available.

TIPS "Don't bore me with puppy dogs and the morose/sappy feeling you have about death. Belt out a good, short, thought-provoking, graphic, uncommon piece."

FLINT HILLS REVIEW

Dept. of English, Box 4019, Emporia State University, Emporia KS 66801-5087. **Website:** www.emporia.edu/fhr/. *Flint Hills Review*, published annually in late summer, is "a regionally focused journal presenting writers of national distinction alongside new authors." Magazine: 9×6; 115 pages; 60 lb. paper; glossy cover; illustrations; photos. "FHR seeks work informed by a strong sense of place or region, especially Kansas and the Great Plains region. We seek to provide a publishing venue for writers of the Great Plains and Kansas while also publishing authors whose work evidences a strong sense of place, writing of literary quality, and accomplished use of language and depth of character development." Annual. Circ. 300. CLMP. Acquires one-time rights. Publishes ms 4-12 months after acceptance. Sample copy $5.50 Writer's guidelines for SASE, by e-mail, fax, or on website.

MAGAZINE NEEDS Wants all forms of poetry except rhyming. Does not want sentimental or gratuitous verse. Has published poetry by E. Ethelbert Miller, Elizabeth Dodd, Walt McDonald, and Gwendolyn Brooks. Submit 3-5 poems at a time. Considers simultaneous submissions; no previously published poems. Accepts submissions by fax or e-mail (pasted into body of message). Cover letter is required. Include SASE. Reads submissions January-March only.

CONTEST/AWARD OFFERINGS FHR hosts an annual nonfiction contest. **Entry Fee**: $10. **Deadline:** March 15.

TIPS "Strong imagery and voice, writing that is informed by place or region, writing of literary quality with depth of character development. Hone the language down to the most literary depiction that is possible in the shortest space that still provides depth of development without excess length."

FLOYD COUNTY MOONSHINE

720 Christiansburg Pike, Floyd VA 24091. (540)745-5150. **E-mail:** floydshine@gmail.com. **Contact:** Aaron Moore, editor-in-chief. *Floyd County Moonshine*, published biannually, is a "literary and arts magazine in Floyd, Virginia, and the New River Valley. We accept poetry, short stories, and essays addressing all manner of themes; however, preference is given to those works of a rural or Southern/Appalachian nature. We welcome cutting-edge and innovative fiction and poetry in particular."

Wants "rustic innovation." Has published poetry by Steve Kistulentz, Louis Gallo, Ernie Wormwood, R.T. Smith, Chelsea Adams, and Justin Askins. Single copy: $8; subscription: $20/1 year, $38/2 years.

MAGAZINE NEEDS Accepts e-mail submissions only. Submit a Word document as attachment. Accepts previously published poems and simultaneous submissions. Cover letter is unnecessary. Include brief bio. Reads submissions year round.

FLYWAY

Iowa State University, 206 Ross Hall, Ames IA 50011. **E-mail:** flyway@iastate.edu. **Website:** www.flyway.org. *Flyway* is 120 pages, digest-sized, professionally printed, perfect-bound, with matte card cover with color. Press run is 500. Subscription: $24. Sample: $8. Submit 4-6 poems at a time. Cover letter is preferred. "We do not read mss between the first of May and the end of August." Responds in 6 weeks (often sooner).10-12 poetry mss/issue. Reads mss September 1-May 1. Publishes ms 6-8 months after acceptance. Accepts 10/12 poetry mss/issue. **Publishes 7-10 new writers/year.** Pays 2 contributor's copies. Acquires first rights. *Flyway, A Journal of Writing and Environment*, published 3 times/year, "is one of the best literary magazines for the money. It's packed with some of the most readable poems being published today—all styles, forms, lengths, and subjects. We publish quality fiction, creative nonfiction, and poetry with a particular interest in place as a component of 'story,' or with an 'environmental' sensibility. Accepted works are accompanied by brief commentaries by their authors, the sort of thing a writer might say introducing a piece at a reading." Biannual. Acquires one-time rights.

CONTEST/AWARD OFFERINGS Sponsors an annual award for poetry, fiction, and nonfiction. Details available for SASE or on website.

TIPS "Quality, originality, voice, drama, tension. Make it as strong as you can."

FOGGED CLARITY

Fogged Clarity and Nicotine Heart Press, P.O. Box 1016, Muskegon MI 49443-1016. (231)670-7033. **E-mail:** editor@foggedclarity.com. **E-mail:** submissions@foggedclarity.com. **Website:** www.foggedclarity.com. Ryan Daly, managing editor. **Contact:** Ben Evans, executive editor/managing editor. "*Fogged Clarity* is an arts review that accepts submissions of poetry, fiction, non-fiction, music, visual art and reviews of work in all mediums. We seek art that is stabbingly eloquent. Our print edition will be released once every year, while new issues of our online journal will come out the beginning of every month. Artists maintain the copyrights to their work until they are monetarily compensated for said work. If your work is selected for our print edition and you consent to its publication, you will be compensated." All work selected for print is purchased. Averages 1-2 months from acceptance to publishing. Accepts queries by e-mail only. Sample copy available on website. Guidelines available at www.foggedclarity.com/submissions.

"By incorporating music and the visual arts and releasing a new issue monthly, *Fogged Clarity* aims to transcend the conventions of a typical literary journal. Our network is extensive and our scope is as broad as thought itself; we are, you are, unconstrained. With that spirit in mind *Fogged Clarity* examines the work of authors, artists, scholars, and musicians, providing a home for exceptional art and thought that warrants exposure."

MAGAZINE NEEDS Send no more than 6 poems, with short bio and complete contact information. Does not accept simultaneous submissions. Averages 1-2 months from acceptance to publishing. Does not accept previously published work. Responds in 2 weeks to queries; 1-2 months on mss. Editorial lead time is 2 months. Sample copy and guidelines available on website. Payment varies

TIPS "The editors appreciate artists communicating the intention of their submitted work and the influences behind it, in a brief cover letter. Any artists with proposals for features or special projects should feel free to contact our editors directly at editor@foggedclarity.com."

FOLIATE OAK LITERARY MAGAZINE

University of Arkansas-Monticello, Arts & Humanities, 562 University Dr., Monticello AR 71656. Phone: (870)460-1247. Email: foliateoak@uamont.edu. **Website:** www.foliateoak.uamont.edu. **Contact:** Diane Payne. Estab. 1973. "We are a general literary magazine for adults." Monthly magazine covering fiction, creative nonfiction, poetry, and art. Circ.: 500. "We are a general literary magazine for adults." Acquires one-time, nonexclusive rights. Publishes ms an average of 1 month after acceptance. Responds in 1 week to queries. Responds in 1 month to mss. Editorial lead time 1 month. Sample copy for #10 SASE. Guidelines available online.

"After you receive a rejection/acceptance notice, please wait one month before submitting new work. **Submission Period: August 1 -April 24.** We do not read submissions during summer break. If you need to contact us for anything other than submitting your work, please write to: foliateoak@uamont.edu."

MAGAZINE NEEDS No homophobic, religious rants, or pornographic, violent stories. Please avoid using offensive language.

HOW TO CONTACT Submit all material via online submission manager (5 poems/max, 2 prose). We love previously unpublished quirky writing that makes sense, preferably flash fiction (less than 1000 words). We enjoy poems that we understand, preferably not rhyming poems, unless you make the rhyme so fascinating we'll wonder why we ever said anything about avoiding rhymes. Give us something fresh, unexpected, and will make us say, Wow!

ADDITIONAL INFORMATION "At the end of the year, we'll use selected works from our website for the annual print anthology. **Snail mail submissions will not be returned.** Paste all your poems into one attachment. Always include a short (less than 50 words) third person bio. Please send no more than two prose selections and no more than 5 poems. Wait until your hear from us before you send more work. If your work is accepted by another publication, please notify us immediately."

TIPS "Please submit all material via our online submission manager." Read our guidelines before submitting. http://www.foliateoak.uamont.edu/submission-guidelines.

FOLIO, A LITERARY JOURNAL AT AMERICAN UNIVERSITY

Dept. of Literature, American University, Washington DC 20016. (202)885-2971. **Fax:** (202)885-2938. **E-mail:** folio.editors@gmail.com. **Website:** www.american.edu/cas/literature/folio/. Jenny Dunnington; Abdul Ali, poetry editors. *Folio*, published 2 times/year, Since 1984, we have published original creative work by both new and established authors. Past issues have included work by Michael Reid Busk, Billy Collins, William Stafford, and Bruce Weigl, and interviews with Michael Cunningham, Charles Baxter, Amy Bloom, Ann Beattie, and Walter Kirn. We look for well-crafted poetry and prose that is bold and memorable. *Folio* is 80 pages, digest-sized, with matte cover with graphic art. Receives about 1,000 poems/year, accepts about 25. Press run is 400; 50-60 distributed free to the American University community and contributors. Single copy: $6; subscription: $12/year. Make checks payable to "*Folio* at American University." Acquires first North American serial rights. Publishes ms 2 months after acceptance. Guidelines available online at website.

"Poems and prose are reviewed by editorial staff and senior editors."

MAGAZINE NEEDS Submit up to 5 poems or one prose piece at a time. Considers simultaneous submissions "with notice." No fax, e-mail, or disk submissions. Cover letter is preferred. Include name, address, e-mail address, brief brio and phone number. "SASE required for notification only; manuscripts are not returned." Reads submissions August 1-February 14. Pays 2 contributor's copies.

FOOTHILL: A JOURNAL OF POETRY

165 E. 10th St., Claremont CA 91711. (909)607-2583. **Fax:** (909)621-8029. **E-mail:** foothill@cgu.edu. **Website:** www.foothilljournal.com. **Contact:** Kevin Riel; editor-in-chief. Directed by students at Claremont Graduate University, *Foothill: a journal of poetry*, is the only literary journal devoted exclusively to poetry written by graduate students who are based in the United States. It is published online quarterly, with

one print edition each year. Digest-sized, 72 pages, digital press, perfect bound. Press run is 500. No ads. Never publishes theme issues. Sometimes comments on rejected poems. Single copy, $25; subscription, $25. Make checks payable to CGU. *Foothill* acquires electronic rights as well as right to print poem in year-end print journal. Rights revert to poets upon publication. Responds in 5 weeks. Guidelines available in magazine, by e-mail, and on website.

MAGAZINE NEEDS Will accept "any poetry by graduate students in the United States. Students do not need to be enrolled in an MFA or writing program. We welcome poetry submissions from those in other disciplines. Submit via fax or e-mail. Include document as attachment in e-mail. Cover letter preferred. Poems are circulated to an editorial board. Accepts submissions year round. Welcomes submissions from beginning poets. Does not consider poetry by children or teens. No limit for poem length.

● FORPOETRY.COM

E-mail: sub@ForPoetry.com. **Website:** www.forpoetry.com. **Contact:** Jackie Marcus, editor. *ForPoetry.Com*, published online with daily updates, wants "lyric poetry, vivid imagery, open form, natural landscape, philosophical themes—but not at the expense of honesty and passion." Does not want "city punk, corny sentimental fluff, or academic workshop imitations." Has published poetry by Sherod Santos, John Koethe, Robert Hass, Kim Addonizio, and Brenda Hillman.

MAGAZINE NEEDS Submit no more than 2 poems at a time. Considers simultaneous submissions; no previously published poems. Accepts e-mail submissions only (pasted into body of message; no attachments). Cover letter is preferred. Reads submissions September-May only. Guidelines available on website. Responds in 2 weeks. "If you do not hear back from us within two weeks, then your poems were not accepted. Rejection of poems may have more to do with a back-log; i.e., there are periods when we cannot read new submissions." Reviews books/chapbooks of poetry and other magazines in 800 words.

◐ FOURTEEN HILLS

Dept. of Creative Writing, San Francisco State Univ., 1600 Holloway Ave., San Francisco CA 94132-1722. **E-mail:** hills@sfsu.edu. **Website:** www.14hills.net. "Always send prepublication galleys. Pays 2 contributor copies. Submit 3-5 unpublished, unsolicited poems. 1 Prose ms, max of 25 pages; visual art, experimental and cross-genre literature also accepted; see website for guidelines. Writers may submit once per submission period. The submission periods are: Sept. 1 - Jan. 1 for inclusion in the spring issue (released in May) Feb. 1 - July 1 for inclusion in the winter issue (released in Dec.). Response times vary from 4-9 months, depending on where your submission falls in the reading period, but we will usually respond within 5 months. Mss and artwork should be mailed and addressed to the proper genre editor, and MUST be accompanied by a sase for notification, in addition to an e-mail and telephone contact. Due to the volume of submissions, mss CANNOT BE RETURNED so please, do not send any originals. We accept simultaneous submissions; however, please be sure to notify us immediately by email should you need to withdraw submissions due to publication elsewhere. Please note that we do not accept electronic submissions at this time in the form of an email or otherwise. However, check website for changes in submission policies." Acquires one time rights.

TIPS "Please read an issue of *Fourteen Hills* before submitting."

THE FOURTH RIVER

Chatham College, Woodland Rd., Pittsburgh PA 15232. **E-mail:** 4thriver@gmail.com. **Website:** http://fourthriver.chatham.edu. **Contact:** Sheryl St. Germain, executive editor; Peter Oresick, editor-in-chief. "*The Fourth River*, an annual publication of Chatham University's MFA in Creative Writing Programs, features "literature that engages and explores the relationship between humans and their environments." Wants "writings that are richly situated at the confluence of place, space, and identity, or that reflect upon or make use of landscape and place in new ways." *The Fourth River* is digest-sized, perfect-bound, with full-color cover by various artists. Accepts about 30-40 poems/year. Press run is 500. Single copy: $10; subscription: $16 for 2 years. Back issues: $5. Make checks payable to Chatham University." Buys first North American serial rights. Pays with contributor copies only. Responds in 3 months to mss. Sample copy for $10. Guidelines available online.

MAGAZINE NEEDS Submit 7 poems at a time. Lines/poem: submit 25 pages maximum. No previously published poems. Submit by post or through Submittable. Cover letter is preferred. "SASE is required for response." Reads submissions September

1-March 15. Time between acceptance and publication is 5-8 months. Poems are circulated to an editorial board. Sometimes comments on rejected poems. Sometimes publishes theme issues. Guidelines available on website. Responds in 3-5 months. Acquires first North American serial rights. Maximum 7 poems.

FREEFALL MAGAZINE

Freefall Literary Society of Calgary, 922 Ninth Ave. SE, Calgary AB T2G 0S4, Canada. **E-mail:** freefallmagazine@yahoo.com. **Website:** www.freefallmagazine.ca. **Contact:** Lynn S. Fraser, managing editor. Established 1990. Pays $25 per poem and one copy of the issue poems appeaer in. Wants prose of all types, up to 3,000 words; pays $10/page to a maximum of $100 per piece and one copy of issue piece appears in. "Magazine published biannually containing fiction, poetry, creative nonfiction, essays on writing, interviews, and reviews. Submit up to 5 poems at once. Pays $25 per poem and one copy of the issue poems appeaer in. Wants prose of all types, up to 3,000 words; pays $10/page to a maximum of $100 per piece and one copy of issue piece appears in. We are looking for exquisite writing with a strong narrative." Buys first North American serial rights (ownership reverts to author after one-time publication). Pays on publication. Writers' guidelines online.

MAGAZINE NEEDS "We are looking for exquisite writing with a strong narrative." Circ.: 1,000. Buys first North American serial rights (ownership reverts to author after one-time publication). Pays on publication. 100% freelance.

ADDITIONAL INFORMATION See website for information about the Freefall Literary Society of Calgary activities and services, and for additional information about *FreeFall Magazine*.

CONTEST/AWARD OFFERINGS Hosts an annual fiction and poetry contest. **Deadline:** December 31. Guidelines available by e-mail or on website.

TIPS "We look for thoughtful word usage, craftmanship, strong voice and unique expression coupled with clarity and narrative structure. Professional, clean presentation of work is essential. Carefully read *FreeFall* guidelines before submitting. Do not fold manuscript, and submit 9×11 envelope. Include SASE/IRC for reply and/or return of manuscript. You may contact us by e-mail after initial hardcopy submission. For accepted pieces a request is made for disk or e-mail copy. Strong Web presence attracts submissions from writers all over the world."

FREEXPRESSION

P.O. Box 4, West Hoxton NSW 2171, Australia. **E-mail:** peter@freexpression.net. **Website:** www.freexpression.com.au. **Contact:** Peter F. Pike, managing editor. *FreeXpresSion*, published monthly, contains "creative writing, how-to articles, short stories, and poetry including cinquain, haiku, etc., and bush verse." Open to all forms. "Christian themes OK. Humorous material welcome. No gratuitous sex; bad language OK. We don't want to see anything degrading." Has published poetry by Ron Stevens, Ellis Campbell, John Ryan, and Ken Dean. *FreeXpresSion* is 28 pages, magazine-sized, offset-printed, saddle-stapled, with paper cover. Receives about 2,500 poems/year, accepts about 30%. Subscription: $15 AUS/3 months, $25 AUS/6 months, $42 AUS/1 year.

FreeXpresSion also publishes books up to 200 pages **through subsidy arrangements with authors**. "Some poems published throughout the year are used in *Yearbooks* (annual anthologies)."

MAGAZINE NEEDS Submit 3-4 poems at a time. Lines/poem: "very long poems are not desired but would be considered." Considers previously published poems and simultaneous submissions. Accepts e-mail (pasted into body of message) and disk submissions. Cover letter is preferred. Time between acceptance and publication is 2 months. Guidelines available in magazine, for SAE and IRC, or by fax or e-mail. Responds in 2 months. Sometimes sends prepublication galleys. Acquires first Australian rights only. Reviews books of poetry in 500 words. Send materials for review consideration.

CONTEST/AWARD OFFERINGS Sponsors an annual contest with 3 categories for poetry: blank verse (up to 60 lines); traditional verse (up to 80 lines), and haiku. 1st Prize in blank verse: $200 AUS; 2nd Prize: $100 AUS; 1st Prize in traditional rhyming poetry: $250 AUS; 2nd Prize: $150 AUS; 3rd Prize: $100 AUS. Haiku, one prize $100 AUS. Guidelines and entry form available by e-mail.

THE FRIEND

The Friend Publications Ltd, 173 Euston Rd., London England NW1 2BJ, United Kingdom. (44)(207)663-1010. **Fax:** (44)(207)663-1182. **E-mail:** editorial@thefriend.org. **Website:** www.thefriend.org. Completely independent, *The Friend* brings readers news and views from a Quaker perspective, as well as from a wide range of authors whose writings are of interest to Quakers and non-Quakers alike. There are articles on issues such as peace, spirituality, Quaker belief, and ecumenism, as well as news of Friends from Britain and abroad. Guidelines available online.

Prefers queries, but sometimes accepts unsolicited mss.

MAGAZINE NEEDS There are no rules regarding poetry, but doesn't want particularly long poems.

THE FROGMORE PAPERS

Website: www.frogmorepress.co.uk. **Contact:** Jeremy Page, editor. *The Frogmore Papers*, published semiannually, is a literary magazine with emphasis on new poetry and short stories. "Quality is generally the only criterion, although pressure of space means very long work (over 100 lines) is unlikely to be published." Has published poetry by Marita Over, Brian Aldiss, Carole Satyamurti, John Mole, Linda France, and Tobias Hill. *The Frogmore Papers* is 46 pages, photocopied in photo-reduced typescript, saddle-stapled, with matte card cover. Accepts 2% of poetry received. Press run is 500. Subscription: £10/1 year (2 issues); £15/2 years (4 issues). Responds in 6 months.

MAGAZINE NEEDS Submit 4-6 poems at a time. Lines/poem: prefers 20-80 lines. Considers simultaneous submissions. Pays 1 contributor's copy.

CONTEST/AWARD OFFERINGS Sponsors the annual Frogmore Poetry Prize. Write for information.

FROGPOND: JOURNAL OF THE HAIKU SOCIETY OF AMERICA

Haiku Society of America, 985 S. Grandview Ave., Dubuque IA 52003. **E-mail:** fnbanwarth@yahoo.com. **Website:** www.hsa-haiku.org/frogpond. **Contact:** Francine Banwarth, editor. *Frogpond*, published triannually, is the international journal of the Haiku Society of America, an affiliate of the American Literature Association. "Its primary function is to publish the best in contemporary English-language haiku and senryu, linked forms including sequences, renku, rengay, and haibun, essays and articles on these forms, and book reviews." Subscription: $33/year. Single issue: $12. Responds at the end of each submission period (June 1-August 1; September 15-November 15; February 15-April 15). Guidelines available for SASE or on website. Detailed instructions on website.

MAGAZINE NEEDS Submissions to *Frogpond* by e-mail preferred. "Postal submissions should be accompanied by SASE with sufficient US postage to reach your location. Submit to fnbanwarth@yahoo.com or 985 S. Grandview, Dubuque, IA." No simultaneous submissions. Reviews books of poetry, usually in 1,000 words or less. Also accepts articles, 1,000-4,000 words, that are properly referenced according to 1 of the 3 style guides: MLA, APA, Chicago Manual.

CONTEST/AWARD OFFERINGS The "best of issue" prize is awarded to a poem from each issue of *Frogpond* through a gift from the Museum of Haiku Literature, located in Tokyo. The Haiku Society of America also sponsors a number of other contests, most of which have cash prizes: The Harold G. Henderson Haiku Award Contest, the Gerald Brady Senryu Award Contest, the Bernard Lionel Einbond Memorial Renku Contest, the Nicholas A. Virgilio Memorial Haiku Competition for High School Students, the Mildred Kanterman Merit Book Awards for outstanding books in the haiku field. Guidelines available on website.

FUGUE LITERARY MAGAZINE

200 Brink Hall, University of Idaho P.O. Box 44110, Moscow ID 83844-1102. **E-mail:** fugue@uidaho.edu. **Website:** http://www.uiweb.uidaho.edu/fugue/. **Contact:** Jennifer Yeatts, Managing Editor. Biannual literary magazine. See website for details. Submissions of poetry, essays, and short stories are accepted Sept. 1 through May 1 (online submissions only). All material received outside of this period will be unread. See website for submission instructions. at: www.uiweb.uidho.edu/fugure/submit.html. Sample copies available for $8.00. Guidelines available online.

Work published in *Fugue* has won the Pushcart Prize and has been cited in *Best American Essays*.

MAGAZINE NEEDS *Fugue*, published semiannually in summer and winter, is a literary magazine of the University of Idaho. "There are no restrictions on type of poetry; however, we are not interested in trite or quaint verse." Has published poetry by Sonia Sanchez, Simon Perchik, Denise Duhamel, Dean Young, and W.S. Merwin. *Fugue* is up to 200 pages, perfect-bound. Receives about 400 poems/semester, accepts only 15-20 poems/issue. Press run is 250. There is also an online version. Sample: $8. All contributors receive payment and 2 complimentary copies of the journal.

HOW TO CONTACT Submit 3-5 poems at a time (10 pages maximum). No previously published poems. Considers simultaneous submissions "with the explicit provision that the writer inform us immediately if the work is accepted for publication elsewhere." E-mail submissions only. Include brief cover letter in body of e-mail with name, address, e-mail, phone number, poem titles, and a brief bio citing any awards/publications. Paste poems in body of e-mail and include one attached file which includes all poems in .pdf, .rtf, or .doc format. Reads submissions September 1-May 1 only. Time between acceptance and publication is up to 1 year. "Submissions are reviewed by staff members and chosen with consensus by the editorial board. No major changes are made to a manuscript without authorial approval." Publishes theme issues. Guidelines available for SASE or on website. Responds in up to 5 months. Pays at least 1 contributor's copy plus an honorarium (up to $25 as funds allow). Acquires first North American serial rights.

CONTEST/AWARD OFFERINGS "For information regarding our annual spring poetry contest, please visit our website."

TIPS "The best way, of course, to determine what we're looking for is to read the journal. As the name *Fugue* indicates, our goal is to present a wide range of literary perspectives. We like stories that satisfy us both intellectually and emotionally, with fresh language and characters so captivating that they stick with us and invite a second reading. We are also seeking creative literary criticism which illuminates a piece of literature or a specific writer by examining that writer's personal experience."

FULLOSIA PRESS

P.O. Box 280, Ronkonkoma NY 11779. **E-mail:** deanofrpps@aol.com. **Website:** rpps_fullosia_press.tripod.com. **Contact:** J.D. Collins, editor; Geoff Jackson, associate editor.

MAGAZINE NEEDS *Fullosia Press*, published monthly online, presents news, information, satire, and right/conservative perspective. Wants any style of poetry. "If you have something to say, say it. We consider many different points of view." Does not want "anti-American, anti-Christian." Considers poetry by children with parental consent. Has published poetry by Awesome David Lawrence, John Grey, Peter Vetrano, Michael Levy, and Taylor Graham. Receives about 50 poems/year, accepts about 40%. Single copy: $15 and SASE (free online); subscription: $25/year (free online). Make checks payable to RPPS-Fullosia Press.

HOW TO CONTACT Accepts e-mail (pasted into body of message) and disk submissions. "E-mail preferred. Final submission by disk or e-mail only." Cover letter is required. Reads submissions when received. Submit seasonal poems 1 month in advance. Time between acceptance and publication varies. "I review all poems: 1) Do they say something?; 2) Is there some thought behind it?; 3) Is it more than words strung together?" Always comments on rejected poems. Publishes theme issues. Guidelines available for SASE, by e-mail, or on website. Responds in 1 month. Acquires one-time rights. Reviews books/chapbooks of poetry and other magazines/journals. Send materials for review consideration to RPPS-Fullosia Press.

TIPS "Make your point quickly. If you haven't done so, after five pages, everybody hates you and your characters."

THE FURNACE REVIEW

E-mail: editor@thefurnacereview.com. **E-mail:** submissions@thefurnacereview.com. **Website:** http://thefurnacereview.com. **Contact:** Ciara LaVelle, editor.

MAGAZINE NEEDS *The Furnace Review*, published quarterly online, is "dedicated to new writers and unique or groundbreaking work." Wants "all forms, from haiku to sonnets to free verse to totally experimental. Just make it interesting." Has published poetry by Carolynn Kingyens, Charles Geoghegan-Clements, Curtis Evans, and Richard Matthes. Receives about 1,500 pieces/year, accepts about 30.

HOW TO CONTACT Submit up to 5 poems at a time. Lines/poem: 75 maximum. Considers simultaneous submissions; no previously published poems. Accepts e-mail submissions; no disk submissions. Cover letter is preferred. "Include a short biography with all submissions." Reads submissions year round. Time between acceptance and publication is 3 months. Poems are circulated to an editorial board. Sometimes comments on rejected poems. Guidelines available on website. Responds in 6 months. Acquires first North American serial rights.

GARGOYLE

Paycock Press, 3819 N. 13th St., Arlington VA 22201. (703)525-9296. **E-mail:** hedgehog2@erols.com. **Website:** www.gargoylemagazine.com. **Contact:** Richard Peabody, co-editor, Lucinda Ebersole, co-editor. *Gargoyle Magazine*, published annually, has always been a scallywag magazine, a maverick magazine, a bit too academic for the underground and way too underground for the academics. We generally run short, one-page poems. We like wit, imagery, killer lines." Has published poetry by Nin Andrews, Kim Chinquee, Kate Braverman, Laura Chester, Thaisa Frank, Thylias Moss, Patricia Smith, Elizabeth Swados, and Paul West. *Gargoyle* is about 500 pages, digest-sized, offset-printed, perfectbound, with color cover, includes ads. Accepts about 10% of the poems received each year. Press run is 2,000. Subscription: $30 for 2 issues (individuals); $40 (institutions). Sample: $10. Reads submissions "all summer—June, July, and August." Time between acceptance and publication is 12 months. "The 2 editors make some concessions but generally concur." Often comments on rejected poems. Responds in 3 months. Always sends prepublication galleys. Pays 1 contributor's copy and offers 50% discount on additional copies. Acquires first North American serial, and first British rights. 12 months Responds in 1month to queries, proposals, and to mss. Sample copy for $12.95. Catalog available online at FAQ link "We don't have guidelines; we have never believed in them."

MAGAZINE NEEDS Not looking for poetry volumes for 2012.

HOW TO CONTACT Query by email. Submit 5 poems at a time. Considers simultaneous submissions. Submit electronically.

TIPS "We have to fall in love with a particular fiction."

O GEORGETOWN REVIEW

Box 227, 400 East College St., Georgetown KY 40324. (502)863-8308. **Fax:** (502)868-8888. **E-mail:** gtownreview@georgetowncollege.edu. **Website:** http://georgetownreview.georgetowncollege.edu. **Contact:** Steven Carter, editor. *Georgetown Review,* published annually in May, is a literary journal of poetry, fiction, and creative nonfiction. " Does not want "work that is merely sentimental, political, or inspirational." *Georgetown Review* is 192 pages, digest-sized, offset-printed, perfect-bound, with 60 lb. glossy 4-color cover with art/graphics, includes ads. Press run is 1,000. Single copy: $7. Make checks payable to *Georgetown Review.* Acquires first North American serial rights. Publication is copyrighted. Pays on publication. Publishes ms 1 year after acceptance. Responds to mss in 1-3 months. Sample copy $7.00 Guidelines available on website.

MAGAZINE NEEDS We have no specific guidelines concerning form or content of poetry, but are always eager to see poetry that is insightful, rooted in reality, and human." Has published poetry by Denise Duhamel, X.J. Kennedy, Fred Chappell, Frederick Smock, Mark Halperin, David Citino, William Greenway, James Harms, and Margarita Engle. Submit 1-10 poems at a time. Lines/poem: open. Considers simultaneous submissions; no previously published poems. No fax, e-mail, or disk submissions. Cover letter is preferred. "In cover letter, please include short bio and a list of publications. Also, must include SASE for reply." Reads submissions September 1-March 15. Pays 2 contributor's copies.

CONTEST/AWARD OFFERINGS Sponsors annual contest, offering $1,000 prize and publication; runners-up also receive publication. Guidelines available for SASE, by e-mail, or on website. **Entry fee:** $10/poem, $5 for each additional poem.

TIPS "We look for fiction that is well written and that has a story line that keeps our interest. Don't send a first draft, and even if we don't take your first, second, or third submission, keep trying."

THE GEORGIA REVIEW

The University of Georgia, Athens GA 30602. (706)542-3481. **Fax:** (706)542-0047. **E-mail:** garev@uga.edu. **Website:** www.uga.edu/garev. **Contact:** Stephen Corey, editor. Our readers are educated, inquisitive people who read a lot of work in the areas we feature, so they expect only the best in our pages. All work submitted should show evidence that the writer is at least as well-educated and well-read as our readers. Essays should be authoritative but accessible to a range of readers. Buys first North American serial rights. Pays on publication. Publishes ms an average of 6 months after acceptance. Responds in 2 weeks to queries. Responds in 2-3 months to mss. Sample copy for $10 Guidelines available online.

No simultaneous or electronic submissions.

MAGAZINE NEEDS We seek original, excellent poetry. Submit 3-5 poems at a time. We do not accept submissions via fax or e-mail. If a submission is known to be included in a book already accepted by a publisher, please notify us of this fact (and of the anticipated date of book publication) in a cover letter. Reads year-round, but submissions postmarked May 15-August 15 will be returned unread. Always sends prepublication galleys. Pays $4/line, one-year subscription, and 1 contributor's copy. Acquires first North American serial rights. Reviews books of poetry. "Our poetry reviews range from 500-word 'Book Briefs' on single volumes to 5,000-word essay reviews on multiple volumes." Pays $4/line.

TIPS "Unsolicited manuscripts will not be considered from May 15-August 15 (annually); all such submissions received during that period will be returned unread. Check website for submission guidelines."

GERTRUDE

P.O. Box 83948, Portland OR 97283. **E-mail:** poetry@gertrudepress.org. **Website:**www.gertrudepress.org. **Contact:** Steven Rydman, poetry editor.

MAGAZINE NEEDS *Gertrude*, published semiannually, is the literary publication of Gertrude Press (see separate listing in Books/Chapbooks), "a nonprofit 501(c)(3) organization showcasing and developing the creative talents of lesbian, gay, bisexual, trans, queer-identified, and allied individuals." Has published poetry by Judith Barrington, Deanna Kern Ludwin, Casey Charles, Michael Montlack, Megan Kruse, and Noah Tysick. *Gertrude* is 64-112 pages, digest-sized, offset-printed, perfect-bound, with glossy 4-color cardstock cover with art. Receives about 500 poems/year, accepts about 6-8%. Press run is 300; 50 distributed free. Single copy: $8.25; subscription: $15/year, $27 for 2 years. Sample: $6.25. Make checks payable to Gertrude Press.

HOW TO CONTACT Submit via online submission form on website. Submit 6 poems at a time. Lines/poem: open. Considers simultaneous submissions; no previously published poems. Accepts e-mail submissions via the website only; no disk submissions. Cover letter is preferred. Include short bio and SASE. Reads submissions year round. Time between acceptance and publication is 3-6 months. Poems are circulated to an editorial board. Sometimes comments on rejected poems. Guidelines available in magazine, by e-mail, or on website. Responds in 3 months. Sometimes sends prepublication galleys. Pays 1 contributor's copy plus discount on additional copies/subscriptions. Acquires one-time rights. Rights revert to poets upon publication.

TIPS "We look for strong characterization, imagery and new, unique ways of writing about universal experiences. Follow the construction of your work until the ending. Many stories start out with zest, then flipper and die. Show us, don't tell us."

THE GETTYSBURG REVIEW

(717)337-6770. **Fax:** (717)337-6775. **Website:** www.gettysburgreview.com. *The Gettysburg Review*, published quarterly, considers "well-written poems of all kinds." Has published poetry by Rita Dove, Alice Friman, Philip Schultz, Michelle, Boisseau, Bob Hicok, Linda Pastan, and G.C. Waldrep. Accepts 1-2% of submissions received. Press run is 4,500. Subscription: $28/year. Sample: $10. "Our concern is quality. Manuscripts submitted here should be extremely well written. Reading period September-May." Buys first North American serial rights. Pays on publication. Publishes ms an average of 6 months after acceptance. Responds in 1 month to queries. Responds in 3-6 months to mss. Editorial lead time 1 year. Sample copy for $11. Guidelines available online.

MAGAZINE NEEDS Pays $2.50/line.

HOW TO CONTACT Submit 3-5 poems at a time. Considers simultaneous submissions; no previously published poems. Cover letter is preferred. Include SASE. Reads submissions September-May only. Occasionally publishes theme issues. "Response time can be slow during heavy submission periods, especially in the late fall." Pays $2.50/line, one-year subscription, and 1 contributor's copy. Essay-reviews are featured in most issues. Send materials for review consideration.

GINOSKO

P.O. Box 246, Fairfax CA 94978. **E-mail:** ginoskoeditor@aol.com. **Website:** www.ginoskoliteraryjournal.com. **Contact:** Robert Paul Cesaretti, editor. "*Ginosko* (ghin-océ-koe): To perceive, understand, realize, come to know; knowledge that has an inception, a progress, an attainment. The recognition of truth by experience." Accepting short fiction and poetry, creative nonfiction, interviews, social justice concerns, and spiritual insights for www.GinoskoLiteraryJournal.com. Member CLMP. Copyright reverts to author. Editorial lead time 1-2 months. Receives postal submissions and e-mail—prefers e-mail submissions as attachments in .wps, .doc, or .rtf files.

Reads year round. Length of articles flexible; accepts excerpts. Publishing as semiannual ezine. Check downloadable issues on website for tone and style. Downloads free; accepts donations. Also looking for books, art, and music to post on website, and links to exchange.

GLASS: A JOURNAL OF POETRY

E-mail: glasspoetry@yahoo.com. **Website:** www.glass-poetry.com. **Contact:** Holly Burnside, editor. "We are not bound by any specific aesthetic; our mission is to present high quality writing. Easy rhyme and 'light' verse are less likely to inspire us. We want to see poetry that enacts the artistic and creative purity of glass." Buys first North American serial rights. Responds in 4 months to queries.

Submissions must follow our guidelines.

TIPS "Accepts submissions from Sept. - May. We like poems that show a careful understanding of language, sound, passion and creativity and poems that surprise us. Include brief cover letter and biography. Include your email address."

GRAIN

P.O. Box 67, Saskatoon SK S7K 3K1, Canada. (306)244-2828. **Fax:** (306)244-0255. **E-mail:** grainmag@sasktel.net. **Website:** www.grainmagazine.ca. **Contact:** Rilla Friesen, editor. "*Grain, The Journal Of Eclectic Writing*, is a literary quarterly that publishes engaging, diverse, and challenging writing and art by some of the best Canadian and international writers and artists. Every issue features superb new writing from both developing and established writers. Each issue also highlights the unique artwork of a different visual artist. *Grain* has garnered national and international recognition for its distinctive, cutting-edge content and design." Has published poetry by Lorna Crozier, Don Domanski, Cornelia Haeussler, Patrick Lane, Karen Solie, and Monty Reid. *Grain* is 112-128 pages, digest-sized, professionally printed. Press run is 1,100. Receives about 3,000 submissions/year. Subscription: $35 CAD/year, $55 CAD for 2 years. Sample: $13 CAD. (See website for U.S. and foreign postage fees.)

MAGAZINE NEEDS "High quality, imaginative, well-crafted poetry."

HOW TO CONTACT Submit up to 12 pages of poetry, typed in readable font on 1 side only. No previously published poems or simultaneous submissions. No fax or e-mail submissions; postal submissions only. Cover letter with all contact information, title(s), and genre of work is required. "No staples. Your name and address must be on every page. Pieces of more than 1 page must be numbered. Please only submit work in one genre at one time." Reads submissions September-May only. "Manuscripts postmarked between June 1 and August 31 will not be read." Guidelines available by SASE (or SAE and IRC), e-mail, or on website. Typically responds in 3-6 months. Pays $50-225 CAD (depending on number of pages) and 2 contributor's copies. Acquires first Canadian serial rights only. Copyright remains with the author.

TIPS "Submissions read September-May only. Mss postmarked between June 1 and August 31 will not be read. Only work of the highest literary quality is accepted. Read several back issues."

THE GREAT AMERICAN POETRY SHOW

The Muse Media, P.O. Box 69506, West Hollywood CA 90069. (323)424-4943. **E-mail:** info@tgaps.net. **Website:** www.tgaps.net. **Contact:** Larry Ziman, editor/publisher. *The Great American Poetry Show*, published about every 3-5 years, is an 8×11 hardcover serial poetry anthology. Wants poems on any subject, in any style, of any length. "For Volume 1, we read over 8,000 poems from about 1,400 poets and accepted only 113 poems from 83 poets. For Volume 2, we read over 15,000 poems and accepted 134 poems from 92 poets." Press run is 1,000. Single copy: $35 (print), $.99 (e-book, download only). Responds usually within 1-2 weeks ("depends on how busy we are").

The Great American Poetry Show is 150 pages, sheet-fed offset-printed, perfect-bound, with cloth cover with art/graphics. Has published poetry by Carol Carpenter, Philip Wexler, Fredrick Zydek, Patrick Polak, Steve de Frances, Lois Swann, Alan Catlin, and Julie M. Tate.

MAGAZINE NEEDS Submit any number of poems at a time. Considers previously published poems and simultaneous submissions. Accepts e-mail submissions in body of e-mail or as attachment. Cover letter is optional. Include SASE. "If we reject a submission of your work, please send us another group to go through." Pays 1 contributor's copy.

TIPS "Please visit our websjte where anyone can have us post poetry news, reviews, essays, articles, and recommended books, and where you can link to over 10,000 literary subjects such as articles, essays, interviews, reviews, magazines, publishers, and blogs."

GREEN HILLS LITERARY LANTERN

McClain Hall, Truman State University, Kirksville MO 63501. (660)785-4513. **E-mail:** jbeneven@truman.edu. **Website:** http://ll.truman.edu/ghllweb/. **Contact:** Joe Benevento, poetry editor. "The mission of GHLL is to provide a literary market for quality fiction writers, both established and beginners, and to provide quality literature for readers from diverse backgrounds. We also see ourselves as a cultural resource for North Missouri. Our publication works to publish the highest quality fiction—dense, layered, subtle—and, at the same time, fiction which grabs the ordinary reader. We tend to publish traditional short stories, but we are open to experimental forms." Annual. The GHLL is now an online, open-access journal. Acquires one-time rights. Publishes ms up to 1 year after acceptance. Responds in 4 months. Guidelines for SASE, by e-mail, or online.

MAGAZINE NEEDS Wants "the best poetry, in any style, preferably understandable. There are no restrictions on subject matter. Both free and formal verse forms are fine, though we publish more free verse overall." Has published poetry by Jim Thomas, David Lawrence, Mark Belair, Louis Philips, Francine Tolf, and Julie Lechevsky. Sample: $7 (back issue). Submit 3-7 poems at a time. Considers simultaneous submissions, "but not preferred"; no previously published poems. No e-mail submissions. Cover letter is preferred. Include list of publication credits. Type poems one/page. Often comments on rejected poems. Does not want "haiku, limericks, or anything over 2 pages. Pornography and gratuitous violence will not be accepted. Obscurity for its own sake is also frowned upon."

GREEN MOUNTAINS REVIEW

Johnson State College, 337 College Hill, Johnson VT 05656. (802)635.1350. **E-mail:** gmr@jsc.vsc.edu. **Website:** http://greenmountainsreview.com/. **Contact:** Elizabeth Powell, poetry editor. The editors are open to a wide rane of styles and subject matter. Acquires first North American serial rights. Rights revert to author upon request. Publishes ms 6-12 months after acceptance. Responds in 1 month to queries; 6 months to mss. Sample copy for $7. Guidelines available free.

"Manuscripts received between March 1 and September 1 will not be read and will be returned."

MAGAZINE NEEDS Has published poetry by Carol Frost, Sharon Olds, Carl Phillips, David St. John, and David Wojahn. Submit no more than 5 poems at a time.

TIPS We encourage you to order some of our back issues to acquaint yourself with what has been accepted in the past. Unsolicited mss. are read from Sept. 1 - Mar. 1.

THE GREENSBORO REVIEW

MFA Writing Program, 3302 HHRA Building, UNC Greensboro, Greensboro NC 27402-6170. (336)334-5459. **E-mail:** jlclark@uncg.edu. **Website:** www.greensbororeview.org. **Contact:** Jim Clark, editor. *The Greensboro Review*, published twice/year, showcases well-made verse in all styles and forms, though shorter poems (under 50 lines) are preferred. Has published poetry by Carl Dennis, Jack Gilbert, Linda Gregg, Tung-Hui Hu, A. Van Jordan, and Natasha Tretheway. *The Greensboro Review* is 144 pages, digest-sized, professionally printed, flat-spined, with colored matte cover. Subscription: $14/year, $24 for 2 years, and $30 for 3 years. Sample: $8.

Stories for *the Greensboro Review* have been included in *Best American Short Stories, The O. Henry Awards Prize Stories, New Stories from The South*and *Pushcart Prize.*

HOW TO CONTACT Submit no more than 5 poems at a time. Lines/poem: under 50 lines preferred. No previously published poems. Simultaneous submissions accepted. No fax or e-mail submissions. Cover letter is preferred. Include number of poems submitted. Provide SASE for reply; manuscripts arriving after those dates will be held for consideration for the next issue. Reads submissions according to the following deadlines: mss must arrive by September 15 to be considered for the Spring issue (acceptances in December), or February 15 to be considered for the Fall issue (acceptances in May). "Manuscripts arriving after those dates will be held for consideration for the next issue." Guidelines available in magazine, for SASE, or on website. Responds in 4 months. Always sends prepublication galleys. Pays 3 contributor's copies. Acquires first North American serial rights. Submit by regular mail or submission form on website.

TIPS "We want to see the best being written regardless of theme, subject or style."

GUERNICA

165 Bennett Ave., 4C, New York NY 10040. **E-mail:** editors@guernicamag.com; art@guernicamag.com; publisher@guernicamag.com. **Website:** www.guernicamag.com. **Contact:** Erica Wright, poetry; Dan Eckstein, art/photography. "*Guernica* contributors come from dozens of countries and write in nearly as many languages." Publishes mss 3-4 months from acceptance. Responds in 4 months. Guidelines available online.

Received Caine Prize for African Writing, Best of the Net, cited by *Esquire* as a "great literary magazine."

MAGAZINE NEEDS In subject line (please follow this format exactly): "poetry submission." Submit up to five poems, any length to poetry@guernicamag.com. Please send 3-5 poems to poetry@guernicamag.com. Attn: Erica Wright. Translations welcome (with rights to publish). Accepts 15-20 poems/year. Has published James Galvin, Barbara Hamby, Terrance Hayes, Richard Howard.

TIPS "Please read the magazine first before submitting. Most stories that are rejected simply do not fit our approach. Submission guidelines available online."

GULF COAST: A JOURNAL OF LITERATURE AND FINE ARTS

University of Houston, Dept. of English, University of Houston, Houston TX 77204-3013. (713)743-3223. **E-mail:** editors@gulfcoastmag.org. **Website:** www.gulfcoastmag.org. Christine Ha, Eric Howerton, Edward Porter, fiction editors. **Contact:** The Editors. Buys 5-10 ms/year. Receives 300 unsolicited mss/month. Accepts 4-8 mss/issue; 12-16 mss/year. Agented fiction 5%. **Publishes 2-8 new writers/year.** Recently published work by Matt Bell, Megan Mayhew Bergman, Sarah Shun-Lien Bynum, Jenine Capot Crucet, Benjamin Percy, John Weir. Publishes short shorts. Sometimes comments on rejected mss. Buys one-time rights. 6 months-1 year Responds in 4-6 months to mss. Writer's guidelines for #10 SASE or on website.

MAGAZINE NEEDS *Gulf Coast: A Journal of Literature and Fine Arts*, published twice/year in April and October, includes poetry, fiction, essays, interviews, and color reproductions of work by artists from across the nation. While the journal features work by a number of established poets, editors are also interested in "providing a forum for new and emerging writers who are producing well-crafted work that takes risks." Has published poetry by Anne Carson, Carl Dennis, Terrance Hayes, Bob Hicok, Alice Notley, Srikanth Reddy, Karen Volkman, and Dean Young. *Gulf Coast* is 270 pages, 7×9, offset-printed, perfect-bound. Single copy: $10; subscription: $16/year, $28 for 2 years. Sample: $8.

HOW TO CONTACT Submit up to 5 poems at a time. Considers simultaneous submissions with notification; no previously published poems. Cover letter is required. List previous publications and include a brief bio. Reads submissions September-April. Guidelines available for SASE or on website. Responds within 4-6 months. Pays $50/poem and 2 contributor's copies. Returns all rights (except electronic) upon publication.

CONTEST/AWARD OFFERINGS The 2011 Gulf Coast Contests, awarding publication and $1,000 each in Poetry, Fiction, and Nonfiction, are now open. Honorable mentions in each category will receive a $250 second prize. Ilya Kaminsky will judge the contest in poetry, Frederick Reiken will judge in fiction, and John D'Agata will judge in nonfiction. Postmark/Online Entry deadline: March 15, 2011. Winners and Honorable Mentions will be announced in May. **Entry fee:** $20 (includes one-year subscription). Make checks payable to *Gulf Coast*. Guidelines available on website.

TIPS "Submit only previously unpublished works. Include a cover letter. Online submissions are strongly preferred. Stories or essays should be typed, double-spaced, and paginated with your name, address, and phone number on the 1st page, title on subsequent pages. Poems should have your name, address, and phone number on the 1st page of each." The 2011 Gulf Coast Contests, awarding publication and $1,000 each in Poetry, Fiction, and Nonfiction, are now open. Honorable mentions in each category will receive a $250 second prize. Ilya Kaminsky will judge the contest in poetry, Frederick Reiken will judge in fiction, and John D'Agata will judge in nonfiction. Postmark/online entry deadline: March 15, 2011. Winners and Honorable Mentions will be announced in May. Entry fee: $20 (includes one-year subscription). Make checks payable to *Gulf Coast*. Guidelines available on website.

GULF STREAM MAGAZINE

Florida International Univ., English Dept., N. Miami FL 33181-3000. **E-mail:** gulfstreamfiu@yahoo.com. **Website:** www.gulfstreamlitmag.com.

"Submit online only. Please read guidelines on website in full. Submissions that do not conform to our guidelines will be discarded. We do not accept emailed or mailed submissions. We read from Sept 15- Dec 15; Jan 15 - Mar 15." Does not pay writers' expenses.

MAGAZINE NEEDS *Gulf Stream*, published semiannually, is associated with the Creative Writing program at Florida International University. Wants "poetry of any style and subject matter as long as it's of high literary quality." Has published poetry by Robert Wrigley, Jan Beatty, Jill Bialosky, and Catherine Bowman. *Gulf Stream* is 124 pages, digest-sized, flat-spined, printed on quality stock, with matte card cover. Accepts less than 10% of poetry received. Print back-issue sample: $5.

HOW TO CONTACT Submit no more than 5 poems at a time. Considers simultaneous submissions with notification. Accepts electronic online submissions only; no snail mail/hard copy or e-mail submissions. "See website for details." Cover letter is required. Reads submissions September 15-December 15; January 15-March 15 only. Publishes theme issue every other issue. Guidelines available in magazine or on website. Responds in 3 weeks to 3 months. Acquires first North American serial rights.

TIPS "Looks for fresh, original writing—well plotted stories with unforgettable characters, fresh poetry and experimental writing. Usually longer stories do not get accepted. There are exceptions, however."

◐ HAIGHT ASHBURY LITERARY JOURNAL

558 Joost Ave., San Francisco CA 94127. (415)584-8264. **E-mail:** haljeditor@gmail.com. **Website:** http://haightashburyliteraryjournal.wordpress.com/; www.facebook.com/pages/Haight-Ashbury-Literary-Journal/365542018331. **Contact:** Alice Rogoff, Taylor Landry. *Haight Ashbury Literary Journal*, publishes "well-written poetry and fiction. HALJ's voices are often of people who have been marginalized, oppressed, or abused. HALJ strives to bring literary arts to the general public, to the San Francisco community of writers, to the Haight Ashbury neighborhood, and to people of varying ages, genders, ethnicities, and sexual preferences. The Journal is produced as a tabloid to maintain an accessible price for low-income people." Has published poetry by Dan O'Connell, Diane Frank, Dancing Bear, Lee Herrick, Al Young, and Laura Beausoleil. *Haight Ashbury* is 16 pages, includes ads. Includes fiction under 20 pages, one story/issue, and b&w drawings. Press run is 1,500. Subscription: $10/ 2 issues, $20 for 4 issues; $50 for a lifetime subscription. Sample: $4.

MAGAZINE NEEDS Submit up to 6 poems at a time. Submit only once/6 months. No e-mail submissions (unless over seas); postal submissions only. "Please type 1 poem to a page, put name and address on every page, and include SASE. No bio." Sometimes publishes theme issues (each issue changes its theme and emphasis). Guidelines available for SASE. Responds in 4 months. Rights revert to author.

ADDITIONAL INFORMATION An anthology of past issues, *This Far Together*, is available for $12.

◐$ HANGING LOOSE

Hanging Loose Press, 231 Wyckoff St., Brooklyn NY 11217. **E-mail:** editor@hangingloosepress.com. **Website:** www.hangingloosepress.com. **Contact:** Robert Hershon, Dick Lourie, and Mark Pawlak, poetry editors. *Hanging Loose*, published in April and October, "concentrates on the work of new writers." Wants "excellent, energetic" poems. Considers poetry by teens ("one section contains poems by high-school-age poets"). Has published poetry by Sherman Alexie, Paul Violi, Donna Brook, Kimiko Hahn, Harvey Shapiro, and Ha Jin. *Hanging Loose* is 120 pages, offset-printed on heavy stock, flat-spined, with 4-color glossy card cover. Sample: $12.

MAGAZINE NEEDS Submit up to 6 poems at a time. No fax or e-mail submissions; postal submissions only. No simultaneous submissions. "Would-be contributors should read the magazine first." Responds in 3 months. Pays small fee and 2 contributor's copies.

ADDITIONAL INFORMATION Hanging Loose Press does not consider unsolicited book mss or artwork.

HARPUR PALATE

English Department, P.O. Box 6000, Binghamton University, Binghamton NY 13902-6000. **E-mail:** harpur.palate@gmail.com. **Website:** http://harpurpalate.blogspot.com. **Contact:** Barrett Bowlin, managing editor. *Harpur Palate*, published biannually, is "dedicated to publishing the best poetry and prose, regardless of style, form, or genre." Single copy: $10; subscription: $16/year (2 issues). Sample: $5. Make checks payable to *Harpur Palate*. "We have no restrictions on subject matter or form. Quite simply, send us your highest-quality fiction and poetry." Buys first North American serial rights, buys electronic rights. Publishes ms an average of 1-2 months after acceptance. Responds in 8 months to mss. Sample copy for $8. Guidelines available online.

MAGAZINE NEEDS Has published poetry by Sherman Alexie, Tess Gallagher, Alex Lemon, Marvin Bell, Ryan G. Van Cleave, Sascha Feinstein, Allison Joseph, Neil Shepard, and Ruth Stone. *Harpur Palate* is 180-

220 pages, digest-sized, offset-printed, perfect-bound, with matte or glossy cover. Receives about 1,000 poems/year, accepts about 50. Press run is 800. Single copy: $10; subscription: $16/year (2 issues). Sample: $5. Make checks payable to *Harpur Palate*. No more than 10 pages total. No response without SASE. Pays 2 contributor copies

HOW TO CONTACT Submit 3-5 poems at a time. Lines/poem: "No restrictions; entire submission must be 10 pages or fewer." Considers simultaneous submissions, "but we must be notified immediately if the piece is taken somewhere else"; no previously published poems. No e-mail submissions. Accepts postal submissions. Cover letter and SASE is required. Reads submissions year round. Time between acceptance and publication is 2 months. Poems are circulated to an editorial board. Seldom comments on rejected poems.

TIPS "*Harpur Palate* now accepts submissions all year; deadline for Winter issue is November 15, for Summer issue is April 15. We also sponsor a fiction contest for the Summer issue and a poetry contest for the Winter issue. We do not accept submissions via e-mail. We are interested in high quality writing of all genres, but especially literary poetry and fiction."

HAWAI'I PACIFIC REVIEW

1060 Bishop St., Honolulu HI 96813. (808)544-1108. **Fax:** (808)544-0862. **E-mail:** pwilson@hpu.edu. **E-mail:** hprsubmissions@hpu.edu. **Website:** www.hpu.edu/hpr. Establ. 1987. *Hawai'i Pacific Review*, published annually in September by Hawai'i Pacific University, prints "quality poetry, short fiction, and personal essays from writers worldwide. Our journal seeks to promote a world view that celebrates a variety of cultural themes, beliefs, values, and viewpoints. We wish to further the growth of artistic vision and talent by encouraging sophisticated and innovative poetic and narrative techniques." Has published poetry by Wendy Bishop, Rick Bursky, Virgil Suárez, Bob Hikok, Daniel Gutstein, and Linda Bierds. *Hawai'i Pacific Review* is 80-120 pages, digest-sized, professionally printed on quality paper, perfect-bound, with coated card cover. Receives 800-1,000 poems/year, accepts up to 30-40. Press run is about 500 (100 shelf sales). Single copy: $8.95. Sample: $5.

HOW TO CONTACT Submit up to 5 poems at a time. Lines/poem: 100 maximum. No previously published poems or simultaneous submissions. No fax or e-mail submissions. Cover letter is required. Include 5-line professional bio including prior publications. SASE required. "One submission per issue. No handwritten manuscripts. Include name on all pages." Reads submissions September 1-December 31 annually. Seldom comments on rejected poems. Guidelines available for SASE, by e-mail, or on website. Responds within 3 months. Pays 2 contributor's copies. Acquires first North American serial rights. Rights revert to poet upon publication. "Must acknowledge *Hawai'i Pacific Review* as first publisher."

TIPS "We look for the unusual or original plot; prose with the texture and nuance of poetry. Character development or portrayal must be unusual/original; humanity shown in an original insightful way (or characters); sense of humor where applicable. Be sure it's a draft that has gone through substantial changes, with supervision from a more experienced writer, if you're a beginner. Write about intense emotion and feeling, not just about someone's divorce or shaky relationship. No soap-opera-like fiction."

HAWAII REVIEW

University of Hawaii Board of Publications, 2445 Campus Rd., Hemenway Hall 107, Honolulu HI 96822. (808)956-3030. **Fax:** (808)956-3083. **E-mail:** hawaiireview@gmail.com. **Website:** www.kaleo.org/hawaii_review. Buys first North American serial rights, buys electronic rights. Publishes ms an average of 3 months after acceptance. Responds in 3 months to mss. Sample copy for $10. Guidelines available online.

TIPS "Make it new. Offers yearly award with $500 prizes in poetry and fiction."

HAYDEN'S FERRY REVIEW

c/o Virginia G. Piper Center for Creative Writing, Arizona State University, P.O. Box 875002, Tempe AZ 85287-5002. (480)965-1337. **E-mail:** HFR@asu.edu. **Website:** www.haydensferryreview.org. **Contact:** Beth Staples, managing editor. *Hayden's Ferry* is a handsome literary magazine appearing in November and April. Has published poetry by Dennis Schmitz, Raymond Carver, Maura Stanton, Ai, and David St. John. *Hayden's Ferry Review* is 120 pages, digest-sized, flat-spined, with glossy card cover. Press run is 1,300 (400 subscribers, 100 libraries, 400 shelf sales). Accepts about 1% of 12,000 submissions annually. Subscription: $22. Sample: $13. Word length open. "*Hayden's Ferry Review* publishes the best quality fiction, poetry, and creative nonfiction from new, emerging, and established writers." Buys first North American serial rights. Pays on publication. Publishes ms an average of 6 months after acceptance. Responds in 1 week or less to e-mail queries. Responds in 3-4 months to mss. Editorial lead time 5 months. Sample copy for $7.50. Guidelines available online.

Work from *Hayden's Ferry Review* has been selected for inclusion in *Pushcart Prize* anthologies and *Best Creative Nonfiction*.

MAGAZINE NEEDS Word length open. Pays $50.

HOW TO CONTACT "No specifications other than limit in number (6)." Now accepting submissions online. Submissions are circulated to two poetry editors. Editors comment on submissions "sometimes". See guidelines online. Sends contributor's page proofs. Pays $50 per contributor, one year subscription, and 2 contributor's copies.

THE HELIX

E-mail: helixmagazine@gmail.com. **Website:** helixmagazine.org. **Contact:** Collin Q. Glasow, editor-in-chief; Ashley Gravel, managing editor. **The Helix Magazine** is a Central Connecticut State University student run biannual publication. The magazine accepts submission from all over the globe, as it went national in 2007 and global in 2009. The magazine features CCSU student writing, writing from the Hartford County community and an array of submissions from all over the world. The magazine contains multiple genres of literature and art submissions including: poetry, short fiction, playwright, creative non-fiction paintings, photography, watercolor, collage, stencil and computer generated artwork. It is a student run and funded publication.

HIGHLIGHTS FOR CHILDREN

803 Church St., Honesdale PA 18431. (570)253-1080. **Fax:** (570)251-7847. **Website:** www.highlights.com. **Contact:** Christine French Clark, editor-in-chief; Cindy Faber Smith, art director. "This book of wholesome fun is dedicated to helping children grow in basic skills and knowledge, in creativeness, in ability to think and reason, in sensitivity to others, in high ideals, and worthy ways of living—for children are the world's most important people. We publish stories for beginning and advanced readers. Up to 500 words for beginners (ages 3-7), up to 800 words for advanced (ages 8-12)." Buys all rights. Pays on acceptance. Responds in 2 months to queries. Sample copy free. Guidelines on website in "About Us" area.

MAGAZINE NEEDS Lines/poem: 16 or less ("most poems are shorter"). Considers simultaneous submissions ("please indicate"); no previously published poetry. No e-mail submissions. "Submit typed manuscript with very brief cover letter." Occasionally comments on submissions "if manuscript has merit or author seems to have potential for our market." Guidelines available for SASE. Responds "generally within one month." Always sends prepublication galleys. Pays 2 contributor's copies; "money varies." Acquires all rights.

TIPS "Know the magazine's style before submitting. Send for guidelines and sample issue if necessary." Writers: "At *Highlights* we're paying closer attention to acquiring more nonfiction for young readers than we have in the past." Illustrators: "Fresh, imaginative work encouraged. Flexibility in working relationships a plus. Illustrators presenting their work need not confine themselves to just children's illustrations as long as work can translate to our needs. We also use animal illustrations, real and imaginary. We need crafts, puzzles and any activity that will stimulate children mentally and creatively. We are always looking for imaginative cover subjects. Know our publication's standards and content by reading sample issues, not just the guidelines. Avoid tired themes, or put a fresh twist on an old theme so that its style is fun and lively. We'd like to see stories with subtle messages, but the fun of the story should come first. Write what inspires you, not what you think the market needs. We are pleased that many authors of children's literature report that their first published work was in the pages of *Highlights*. It is not our policy to consider fiction on the strength of the reputation of the author. We judge each submission on its own merits. With factual material, however, we do prefer that writers be authorities in their field or people with first-hand experience. In this manner we can avoid the encyclopedic article that merely restates information readily available elsewhere. We don't make assignments. Query with simple letter to establish whether the nonfiction subject is likely to be of interest. A beginning writer should first become familiar with the type of material that *Highlights* publishes. Include special qualifications, if any, of author. Write for the child, not the editor. Write in a voice that children understand and relate to. Speak to today's kids, avoiding didactic, overt messages. Even though our general principles haven't changed over the years, we are contemporary in our approach to issues. Avoid worn themes."

HIRAM POETRY REVIEW

P.O. Box 162, Hiram OH 44234. (330)569-5331. **E-mail:** poetryreview@hiram.edu. **Website:** http://hirampoetryreview.wordpress.com/. **Contact:** Willard Greenwood, poetry editor. *Hiram Poetry Review*, published annually in spring, features "distinctive, beautiful, and heroic poetry." Wants "works of high and low art. We tend to favor poems that are pockets of resistance in the undeclared war against 'plain speech,' but we're interested in any work of high quality." Press run is 400 (300 subscribers, 150 libraries). Subscription: $9/year; $23/3 years. Acquires first North American serial rights. Rights return to poets upon publication. Responds in 6 months.

MAGAZINE NEEDS Send 3-5 poems at a time. Lines/poem: under 50 (3 single-spaced pages or less). Considers simultaneous submissions. No e-mail submissions unless international. Cover letter is required. Include brief bio. Reads submissions year round. Pays 2 contributor's copies.

HOLINESS TODAY

Nazarene Global Ministry Center, 17001 Prairie Star Pkwy., Lenexa KS 66220. **Website:** www.holinesstoday.org. **Contact:** Carmen Ringhiser, managing editor. *Holiness Today*, published bimonthly online and in print, is "the primary print voice of the Church of the Nazarene, with articles geared to enhance holiness living by connecting Nazarenes with our heritage, vision, and mission through real life stories of God at work in the world." Holiness Today (print) is 40 pages. Subscription: $12/year U.S.

THE HOLLINS CRITIC

P.O. Box 9538, Hollins University, Roanoke VA 24020-1538. **E-mail:** acockrell@hollins.edu. **Website:** www.hollins.edu/academics/critic. **Contact:** Cathryn Hankla. Buys first North American serial rights. Pays on publication. Publishes ms an average of 1 year after acceptance. Responds in 2 months to mss. Sample copy for $3. Guidelines for #10 SASE.

Uses a few short poems in each issue, interesting in form, content, or both. Has published poetry by Natasha Trethewey, Carol Moldaw, David Huddle, Margaret Gibson, and Julia Johnson. *The Hollins Critic* is 24 pages, magazine-sized. Press run is 500. Subscription: $10/year ($15 outside US). Sample: $3. No postal or e-mail submissions.

MAGAZINE NEEDS Submit up to 5 poems at a time using the online submission form at www.hollinscriticsubmissions.com, available from September 15-December 1. Submissions received at other times will be returned unread. Responds in 6 weeks. Pays $25/poem plus 5 contributor's copies. "We read poetry only from September 1-December 15."

TIPS "We accept unsolicited poetry submissions; all other content is by prearrangement."

HOME PLANET NEWS

P.O. Box 455, High Falls NY 12440. (845)687-4084. **E-mail:** homeplanetnews@yahoo.com. **Website:** www.homeplanetnews.org. **Contact:** Donald Lev, editor. *Home Planet News*, published 3 times/year, aims "to publish lively and eclectic poetry, from a wide range of sensibilities, and to provide news of the small press and poetry scenes, thereby fostering a sense of community among contributors and readers." Wants "honest, well-crafted poems, open or closed form, on any subject." Does not want "any work which seems to us to be racist, sexist, ageist, anti-Semitic, or imposes limitations on the human spirit." Considers poetry by children and teens. Has published poetry by Enid Dame, Antler, Lyn Lifshin, Gerald Locklin, Hal Sirowitz, and Janine Pommy Vega. *Home Planet News* is 24 pages, tabloid, Web offset-printed, includes ads. Receives about 1,000 poems/year, accepts up to 3%. Press run is 1,000 (300 subscribers). Single copy: $5; subscription: $12/3 issues, $18/6 issues.

HPN has received a small grant from the Puffin Foundation for its focus on AIDS issues.

HOW TO CONTACT Submit 3-6 poems at a time. Lines/poem: no limit on length, "but shorter poems (under 30 lines) stand a better chance." No previously published poems or simultaneous submissions. Cover letter is preferred. "SASE is a must." Time between acceptance and publication is 1 year. Seldom comments on rejected poems. Occasionally publishes theme issues. Upcoming themes available in magazine. Guidelines available for SASE or on website; "however, it is usually best to simply send work." Responds in 4 months. Pays one-year gift subscription plus 3 contributor's copies. Acquires first rights. Rights revert to poet upon publication. Reviews books/chapbooks of poetry and other magazines in 1,200 words, single- and multi-book format. Send materials for review consideration to Donald Lev. "Note: we do have guidelines for book reviewers; please write for them or check website. Magazines are reviewed by a staff member."

TIPS "We use very little fiction, and a story we accept just has to grab us. We need short pieces of some complexity, stories about complex people facing situations which resist simple resolutions."

HOMESTEAD REVIEW

Box A-5, 156 Homestead Ave., Hartnell College, Salinas CA 93901. (831)755-6943. **Website:** www.hartnell.edu/homestead_review. *Homestead Review*, published annually in April, seeks "avant-garde poetry as well as fixed form styles of remarkable quality and originality." Does not want "Hallmark-style writing or first drafts." Considers poetry written by children and teens. Has published poetry by Sally Van Doren, Kathryn Kirkpatrick, Laura Le Hew, Allison Joseph, and Hal Sirowitz. Receives about 1,000 poems/year, accepts about 15%. Press run is 500 (300 subscribers/libraries); 200 are distributed free to poets, writers, bookstores. Single copy: $10; subscription: $10/year. Make checks payable to *Homestead Review*. Acquires one-time rights. Publishes ms 6 months after acceptance. Responds in 5 months. Guidelines for SASE.

Manuscripts are read by the staff and discussed. Poems/fiction accepted by majority consensus."

MAGAZINE NEEDS Submit 3 poems at a time. No previously published poems or simultaneous submissions. Postal submissions preferred. Cover letter is required. "A brief bio should be included in the cover letter." Pays 1 contributor's copy.

CONTEST/AWARD OFFERINGS Contest with categories for poetry and fiction. Offers 1st Prize: $250 plus publication in *Homestead Review*. All entries will be considered for publication in *Homestead Review*. Guidelines available on website. **Entry fee:** $15 for 3 poems. **Deadline:** see website for current dates.

HOOT

A postcard review of {mini} poetry and prose, 1413 Academy Lane, Elkins Park PA 19027. **E-mail:** info@hootreview.com. **E-mail:** onlinesubmissions@hootreview.com. **Website:** www.hootreview.com. **Contact:** Amanda Vacharat and Dorian Geisler, editors. "*HOOT* publishes 1 piece of writing, designed with original art/photographs, on the front of a postcard every month. The postcards are intended for sharing, to be hung on the wall, etc. Therefore, we look for very brief, surprising-yet-gimmick-free writing that can stand on its own, that also follows 'The Refrigerator Rule'—something that you would hang on your refrigerator and would want to read and look at for a whole month. This 'rule' applies to our online content as well." Buys first North American serial rights and electronic rights. Pays on publication. Publishes ms 2 months after acceptance. Sample copy available for $2. Writer's guidelines available on website.

MAGAZINE NEEDS Length: 10 lines. Pays $10-100 for print publication.

TIPS "We look for writing with audacity and zest, from authors who are not afraid to take risks. We appreciate work that is able to go beyond mere description in its 150 words. We offer free online workshops every Wednesday for authors who would like feedback on their work from the *HOOT* editors. We also often give feedback with our rejections. We publish roughly 6-10 new writers each year."

HOSPITAL DRIVE

Hospital Drive, P.O. Box 800761, Charlottesville VA 22908-0761. **E-mail:** hospitaldrive@virginia.edu. **Website:** http://hospitaldrive.med.virginia.edu. **Contact:** Dr. Daniel Becker, editor. *Hospital Drive*, published irregularly, "encourages original creative work that examines themes of health, illness, and healing. Submissions will be accepted from anyone, but preference is given to those involved in providing, teaching, studying, or researching patient care. All work will be judged anonymously by reviewers and the editorial board. Poems, short fiction, personal essays, reviews, photography, and visual art (painting, drawing, sculpture, mixed media) will be considered. Issues will be released at least once a year, and include invited work. Please review our web site thoroughly and direct any additional questions to query@hospitaldrive.med.virginia.edu."

MAGAZINE NEEDS Submit up to 5 poems. Accepts e-mail submissions as attachment; no fax or disk submissions. Cover letter is unnecessary. All works must be submitted by e-mail, accompanied by basic contact information and the titles of each piece. Attach each poem as a separate document to 1 e-mail. Put "poetry submission" in the e-mail subject line. Time between acceptance and publication is 3-6 months. "All submissions will be reviewed anonymously by the editorial board, and only the highest quality work will be published." Never comments on rejected poems. Guidelines available on website.

HOTEL AMERIKA

Columbia College, English Dept., 600 S. Michigan Ave., Chicago IL 60605. **Website:** www.hotelamerika.net. **Contact:** David Lazar, editor; Adam McOmber, managing editor.

Work published in *Hotel Amerika* has been included in *The Pushcart Prize* and *The Best American Poetry* and featured on *Poetry Daily.*

HUBBUB

5344 SE 38th Ave., Portland OR 97202. **E-mail:** lisa.steinman@reed.edu. **Website:** http://www.reed.edu/hubbub/. J. Shugrue, co-editor. **Contact:** Lisa M. Steinman, co-editor. *Hubbub*, published once/year in the spring, is designed "to feature a multitude of voices from interesting contemporary American poets." Wants "poems that are well-crafted, with something to say. We have no single style, subject, or length requirement and, in particular, will consider long poems." Does not want light verse. Has published poetry by Madeline DeFrees, Cecil Giscombe, Carolyn Kizer, Primus St. John, Shara McCallum, and Alice Fulton. *Hubbub* is 50-70 pages, digest-sized, offset-printed, perfect-bound, with cover art. Receives about 1,200 submissions/year, accepts up to 2%. Press run is 350. Subscription: $7/year. Sample: $3.35 (back issues), $7 (current issue). Responds in 4 months.

MAGAZINE NEEDS Submit 3-6 typed poems at a time. No previously published poems or simultaneous submissions. Include SASE. Guidelines available for SASE. Acquires first North American serial rights. "We review 2-4 poetry books/year in short (3-page) reviews; all reviews are solicited. We do, however, list books received/recommended." Send materials for review consideration. Pays $20/poem.

TIPS Outside judges choose poems from each volume for 3 awards: Vi Gale Award ($500), Stout Award ($75), and Kenneth O. Hanson Award ($100). There are no special submission procedures or entry fees involved.

THE HUDSON REVIEW

The Hudson Review, Inc., 684 Park Ave., New York NY 10065. **Website:** www.hudsonreview.com. **Contact:** Paula Deitz. Pays on publication. Publishes ms an average of 6 months after acceptance. Responds in 6 months. Editorial lead time 3 months. Sample copy for $10. Guidelines for #10 SASE or online

Send with SASE. Mss sent outside accepted reading period will be returned unread if SASE contains sufficient postage.

MAGAZINE NEEDS Reads poems only between April 1 and June 30. Pays 50¢/line.

TIPS "We do not specialize in publishing any particular 'type' of writing; our sole criterion for accepting unsolicited work is literary quality. The best way for you to get an idea of the range of work we publish is to read a current issue. We do not consider simultaneous submissions. Unsolicited manuscripts submitted outside of specified reading times will be returned unread. Do not send submissions via e-mail."

HUNGER MOUNTAIN

Vermont College of Fine Arts, 36 College St., Montpelier VT 05602. (802)828-8517. **E-mail:** hungermtn@vermontcollege.edu. **Website:** www.hungermtn.org. Member: CLMP Accepts high quality work from unknown, emerging, or successful writers. No genre fiction, drama, or academic articles, please. Buys first worldwide serial rights. Pays on publication. Publishes ms an average of 1 year after acceptance. "Submit online or by mail. Please see www.hungermtn.org for complete guidelines before submitting." Responds in 4 months to mss. Sample copy for $10. Writer's guidelines online.

MAGAZINE NEEDS Has published poetry by Hayden Carruth, Matthew Dickman, Mark Doty, Maxine Kumin, Charles Simic, and Ruth Stone. *Hunger Mountain* is about 200 pages, 7×10, professionally printed, perfect-bound, with full-bleed color artwork on cover. Receives about 3,000 poems/year, accepts about 1%. Press run is 1,000; 10,000 visits online monthly. Single copy: $10; subscription: $12/year, $22 for 2 years. Make checks payable to Vermont College of Fine Arts. No light verse, humor/quirky/catchy verse, greeting card verse.

HOW TO CONTACT Reads submissions year round. Time between acceptance and publication is 2-12 months. Mss are circulated to an editorial board. Occasionally comments on rejected poems. Guidelines available on website. Responds in 4 months. Always sends prepublication galleys. Payment varies and includes 2 contributor's copies. Acquires first worldwide serial rights.

CONTEST/AWARD OFFERINGS Annual contests: Ruth Stone Poetry Prize; The Howard Frank Mosher Short Fiction Prize; the Katherine Paterson Prize for Young Adult and Children's Writing; The Hunger Mountain Creative Nonfiction Prize. Visit www.hungermtn.org for information about prizes.

TIPS "Mss must be typed, prose double-spaced. Poets submit at least 3 poems. No multiple genre submissions. Fresh viewpoints and human interest are very important, as is originality. We are committed to publishing an outstanding journal of the arts. Do not send entire novels, mss, or short story collections. Do not send previously published work."

HUNGUR MAGAZINE

P.O. Box 782, Cedar Rapids IA 52406-0782. **E-mail:** hungurmagazine@yahoo.com. **Website:** www.samsdotpublishing.com. **Contact:** Terrie Leigh Relf, editor. *Hungur Magazine*, published bi-annually, features "stories and poems about vampires, and especially about vampires on other worlds." Prefers a "decadent literary style." *Hungur Magazine* is 32 pages, magazine-sized, offset-printed, saddle-stapled, with paper cover with color art, includes ads. Press run is 100/issue. Subscription: $13/year. $23/2 years. Make checks payable to Tyree Campbell/Sam's Dot Publishing. Member: The Speculative Literature Foundation (http://SpeculativeLiterature.org). Publishes ms 4-6 months after acceptance. Responds in 2-3 weeks.

MAGAZINE NEEDS Submit up to 5 poems at a time. Lines/poem: prefers less than 100. No previously published poems or simultaneous submissions. Accepts e-mail submissions (pasted into body of message); no disk submissions. Reads submissions year round. Reviews books and chapbooks of poetry. Send materials for review consideration to Tyree Campbell. Pays $4/poem and 1 contributor's copy.

THE HYCO REVIEW

P.O. Box 1197, Roxboro NC 27573. **E-mail:** langled@piedmontcc.edu; reflect@piedmontcc.edu. **Website:** www2.piedmontcc.edu/hycoreview/index.html. **Contact:** Dawn Langley, editor. The Hyco Review, an online arts and literary magazine, published by Piedmont Community College, proudly announces the publication of its first online version. The magazine, originally titled Reflections and published in the traditional manner (paper), focuses on showcasing the works of artists and writers from Person and Caswell counties, North Carolina, as well as of alumni from the College. We publish annually and welcome quality submissions in any of the formats listed on our submission page. **Accepts submissions from NC authors only (residents or natives).** "If time and space permit, we'll consider submissions from southeastern U.S. authors and from authors we've previously published." Has published poetry by Robert Cooperman, Fredrick Zydek, Bruce Bennett, Fred Chappell, Shari O'Brien, and Daniel Green. Acquires first North American serial rights (if poem is unpublished) or one-time rights (if poem is previously published). Responds in up to 9 months (in March or April). Guidelines available in magazine, for SASE, or by e-mail.

MAGAZINE NEEDS Submit 5 poems maximum at a time. Lines/poem: no longer than 1 page (single-spaced). Considers previously published poems and simultaneous submissions (if notified). Accepts e-mail submissions (pasted into body of message or as attachment in MS Word). "Include a 25-word bio with submission. Include 2 copies of each poem—1 with name and address, 1 without. Affix adequate postage to SAE for return of manuscript if desired, or use First-Class stamps on SAE for notification. Poems are read by an 8- to 12-member editorial board who rank submissions through 'blind' readings. Board members refrain from ranking their own submissions." Pays 1 contributor's copy.

IBBETSON ST. PRESS

25 School St., Somerville MA 02143-1721. **E-mail:** doug_holder@post.harvard.edu. **Website:** http://ibbetsonpress.com. *Ibbetson St. Press*, published semi-annually in June and November, prints "'down to earth' poetry that is well-written; has clean, crisp images; with a sense of irony and humor." Wants "mostly free verse, but are open to rhyme." Does not want "maudlin, trite, overly political, vulgar for vulgar's sake work." Has published poetry by Miriam Goodman, Elizabeth Swados, Sarah Hannah, Gloria Mindock, Harris Gardner, Diana-der Hovanessian, Robert K. Johnson, Gary Metras, and others. *Ibbetson St. Press* is 50 pages, magazine-sized, desktop-published, with glossy white cover, includes ads. Receives about 1,000 poems/year, accepts up to 10%. Press run is 200. Also archived at Harvard, Brown, University of Wisconsin, Poets House-NYC, Endicott College and Buffalo University Libraries. Single copy: $8; subscription: $13. Make checks payable to *Ibbetson St. Press.* Publishes ms 6 months after acceptance. Responds in 2 months.

MAGAZINE NEEDS Submit 3-5 poems at a time. Considers previously published poems; no simultaneous submissions. No e-mail submissions; postal submissions only. Cover letter is required. "3 editors comment on submissions." Guidelines available for SASE. Acquires one-time rights. Reviews books/chapbooks of poetry and other magazines in 250-500 words. Send materials for review consideration. Pays 1 contributor's copy.

ADDITIONAL INFORMATION Does not accept unsolicited chapbook mss. Has published *King of the Jungle*, by Zvi Sesling; *Steerage*, by Bert Stern; *From the Paris of New England*, by Doug Holder; *Ti and Blood Soaked*; *East of the Moon*, by Ruth Kramer Baden; and *Lousia Solano: The Grolier Poetry Book Shop*, edited by Steve Glines and Doug Holder.

IDEALS MAGAZINE

2630 Elm Hill Pike, Suite 100, Nashville TN 37214. (615)333-0478. **Fax:** (888)815-2759. **Website:** www.idealsbooks.com. **Contact:** Melinda Rathjen Rumbaugh, editor.

TIPS "For submissions, target our needs as far as style is concerned, but show representative subject matter. Artists are strongly advised to be familiar with our magazine before submitting samples of work."

IDIOM 23

Central Queensland University, Idiom 23 Literary Magazine, Rockhampton QLD 4702, Australia. **E-mail:** idiom@cqu.edu.au; l.hawryluk@cqu.edu.au. **Website:** www.cqu.edu.au/faculties/faculty-of-arts,-business,-informatics-and-education/schools/humanities-and-communication/idiom-23-literary-magazine. **Contact:** Dr. Lynda Hawryluk, editorial board. Idiom 23, published annually, is "named for the Tropic of Capricorn and is dedicated to developing the literary arts throughout the Central Queensland region. Submissions of original short stories, poems, articles, and black-and-white drawings and photographs are welcomed by the editorial collective. Idiom 23 is not limited to a particular viewpoint but, on the contrary, hopes to encourage and publish a broad spectrum of writing. The collective seeks out creative work from community groups with as varied backgrounds as possible. The magazine hopes to reflect and contest idiomatic fictional representations of marginalized or non-privileged positions and values." Single copy: $20, available here: http://bookshop.cqu.edu.au.

MAGAZINE NEEDS Cover letter is required. [delete this information] Poems are circulated to an editorial board. Reviews books of poetry in single-book format. Send materials for review consideration to Dr. Lynda Hawryluk. Electronic submissions only. Considers poetry written by children and teens (16 years of age and older).

ILLOGICAL MUSE

115 Liberty St. Apt. 1, Buchanan MI 49107. **E-mail:** illogicalmuseonline@yahoo.com. **Website:** www.illogicalmuse.blogspot.com. *Illogical Muse*, an internet quarterly, welcomes "submissions of poetry, fiction, essays and artwork. Looks for well-crafted, intelligent verse in any form and on any subject." Does not want "anything overly graphic or explicit in content." Considers poetry written by children and teens. Has published poetry by Michael Lee Johnson, Sandra Hedin, B.Z. Niditch, Sara Crawford, and Marianne Lavalle-Vincent. Accepts 90% of the material received. Simultaneous submissions and previously published material are welcome as long as you keep me informed on the status of your submission. A brief bio and cover letter is perferred but not necessary, and a link to your personal website or blog is also acceptable. Response time can be 6 months or longer and you may have to wait one year before your accepted ms appears. Responds to postal submissions faster than email submissions.

MAGAZINE NEEDS Submit up to 6 poems at a time. Lines/poem: no more than 100. Considers previously published poems and simultaneous submissions. Absolutely no multiple submissions. Accepts e-mail submissions (pasted into body of message); no disk submissions. Cover letter is preferred. Include SASE, IRC's or valid e-mail for response. Work will be returned if proper postage is provided. Reads submissions year-round. Submit seasonal poems 6 months in advance. Time between acceptance and publication is up to 1 year. Sometimes comments on rejected poems. "Current theme is Nature but there are special requirements for this issue so check guidelines before submitting. Guidelines available for SASE or on website. Responds in 6 months. Reviews books/chapbooks of poetry and fiction and other magazine/journals. Send materials for review consideration. Acquires one-time rights and electronic/archival rights for website. All rights remain with poet.

TIPS "Quarterly writing contest. More information available on the blog. Link from the website."

ILLUMEN

Sam's Dot Publishing, P.O. Box 782, Cedar Rapids IA 52406-0782. **E-mail:** illumensdp@yahoo.com. **Website:** www.samsdotpublishing.com/aoife/cover.htm. **Contact:** Karen L. Newman, editor. "*Illumen* publishes speculative poetry and articles about speculative poetry, and reviews of poetry and collections." Buys first North American serial rights, buys one-time rights, buys second serial (reprint) rights. Responds in 2 weeks to queries. Responds in 3-4 months to mss. Editorial lead time 2 months. Sample copy for $8. Guidelines available online.

MAGAZINE NEEDS *Illumen*, published biannually, contains speculative poetry and articles about speculative poetry. "Speculative poetry includes, but is not limited to, fantasy, science fiction, sword and sorcery, alternate history, and horror." Wants "fantasy, science fiction, spooky horror, and speculative poetry with minimal angst." Does not want "horror with excessive blood and gore." Considers poetry by children and teens. Has published poetry by Ian Watson, Bruce Boston, Sonya Taaffe, Mike Allen, Marge B. Simon, and David C. Kopaska-Merkel. *Illumen* is 50 pages, digest-sized, offset-printed, perfect-bound, with color cover with color art, includes ads. Receives about 200 poems/year, accepts about 50 (25%). Press run is 100/issue (20 subscribers, 50 shelf sales); 5 distributed free to reviewers. Single copy: $9; subscription: $15/year. Make checks payable to Tyree Campbell/Sam's Dot Publishing. "Scifaiku is a difficult sell with us because we also publish a specialty magazine—*Scifaikuest*—for scifaiku and related forms." Length: 200 lines. Pays 1-2¢/word

HOW TO CONTACT Submit up to 5 poems at a time. Lines/poem: prefers less than 200. Considers previously published poems; no simultaneous submissions. Accepts e-mail submissions (pasted into body of message); no disk submissions. "Submission should include snail mail address and a short (1-2 lines) bio." Reads submissions year round. Submit seasonal poems 6 months in advance. Time between acceptance and publication is 1-2 months. Often comments on rejected poems. Guidelines available on website. Responds in 4-6 weeks. Pays 2 cents/word (minimum: $3) for original poems and 1 contributor's copy. Acquires first North American serial rights. Reviews books/chapbooks of poetry. Send materials for review consideration to Tyree Campbell.

TIPS "*Illumen* publishes beginning writers, as well as seasoned veterans. Be sure to read and follow the guidelines before submitting your work. The best advice for beginning writers is to send your best effort, not your first draft."

◐ ILLUMINATIONS

Dept. of English, College of Charleston, 66 George St., Charleston SC 29424-0001. (843)953-1920. **Fax:** (843)953-3180. **E-mail:** lewiss@cofc.edu. **Website:** www.cofc.edu/illuminations. **Contact:** Simon Lewis, editor. *Illuminations: An International Magazine of Contemporary Writing*, published annually, provides "a forum for new writers alongside already established ones." Open as to form and style, and to translations. Does not want to see anything "bland or formally clunky." Has published poetry by Brenda Marie Osbey, Geri Doran, Dennis Brutus, and Carole Satyamurti. *Illuminations* is 64-88 pages, digest-sized, offset-printed, perfect-bound, with 2-color card cover. Receives about 1,500 poems/year, accepts up to 5%. Press run is 400. Subscription: $15/2 issues. Sample: $10. Returns rights on request. Sample copy $10.

HOW TO CONTACT Submit up to 6 poems at a time. No previously published poems or simultaneous submissions. Accepts fax, e-mail (pasted into body of message, no attachments), and mail. Cover letter is preferred (brief). Time between acceptance and publication "depends on when received. Can be up to a year." Occasionally publishes theme issues. Guidelines available by e-mail or on website. Responds within 2 months. Pays 2 contributor's copies plus 1 subsequent issue. Acquires all rights. Returns rights on request.

●$ IMAGE: ART, FAITH, MYSTERY

3307 3rd Ave. W., Seattle WA 98119. **E-mail:** image@imagejournal.org. **Website:** www.imagejournal.org. *Image: Art, Faith, Mystery*, published quarterly, "explores and illustrates the relationship between faith and art through world-class fiction, poetry, essays, visual art, and other arts." Wants "poems that grapple with religious faith, usually Judeo-Christian." Has published work from Philip Levine, Scott Cairns, Annie Dillard, Mary Oliver, Mark Jarman, and Kathleen Norris. *Image* is 136 pages, 10x7, printed on acid-free paper, perfect-bound, with glossy 4-color cover, includes ads. Receives about 800 poems/year, accepts up to 3%. Has 5,000 subscribers (100 are libraries). Subscription: $39.95. Sample: $16 postpaid. Submit up to

4 poems at a time. No previously published poems. No e-mail submissions. Cover letter is preferred. Guidelines available on website. Always sends prepublication galleys. Pays 4 contributor's copies plus $2/line ($150 maximum). Reviews books of poetry in 2,000 words, single- or multi-book format. Send materials for review consideration. Acquires first North American serial rights. Publishes ms 1 year after acceptance. Responds in 3 months.

MAGAZINE NEEDS Submit up to 4 poems at a time. No previously published poems. No e-mail submissions. Cover letter is preferred. Always sends prepublication galleys. Reviews books of poetry in 2,000 words, single- or multi-book format. Send materials for review consideration. Pays 4 contributor's copies plus $2/line ($150 maximum).

INDIANA REVIEW

Ballantine Hall 465, 1020 E. Kirkwood, Indiana University, Bloomington IN 47405-7103. (812)855-3439. **E-mail:** inreview@indiana.edu. **Website:** www.indiana.edu/~inreview. "*Indiana Review*, a nonprofit organization run by IU graduate students, is a journal of previously unpublished poetry and fiction. Literary interviews and essays are also considered. We publish innovative fiction, nonfiction, and poetry. We're interested in energy, originality, and careful attention to craft. While we publish many well-known writers, we also welcome new and emerging poets and fiction writers." Buys first North American serial rights. Pays on publication. Publishes ms an average of 3-6 months after acceptance. Responds in 2 or more weeks to queries. Responds in 4 or more months to mss. Sample copy for $9. Guidelines available online.

Work published in *Indiana Review* received a Pushcart Prize (2001) and was included in *Best New American Voices* (2001). *IR* also received an Indiana Arts Council Grant and a NEA grant.

MAGAZINE NEEDS *Indiana Review*, published semiannually, includes prose, poetry, creative nonfiction, book reviews, and visual art. "We look for an intelligent sense of form and language, and admire poems of risk, ambition, and scope." Wants "all types of poems—free verse, traditional, experimental. Reading a sample issue is the best way to determine if *Indiana Review* is a potential home for your work. Any subject matter is acceptable if it is written well. Translations are welcome." Has published poetry by Denise Duhamel, Sherman Alexie, Marilyn Chin, Julianna Baggott, and Alberto Rios. *Indiana Review* is 160 pages, digest-sized, professionally printed, flatspined, with color matte cover. Receives more than 9,000 submissions/year, accepts up to 60. Has 2,000 subscribers. "We look for poems that are skillful and bold, exhibiting an inventiveness of language with attention to voice and sonics. Experimental, free verse, prose poem, traditional form, lyrical, narrative." 5 lines minimum Pays $5/page ($10 minimum), plus 2 contributor's copies.

HOW TO CONTACT Submit 4-6 poems at a time. Lines/poem: "do not send more than 10 pages of poetry per submission." Considers simultaneous submissions with notification; no previously published poems. Cover letter with brief bio is desired. SASE is mandatory for response. Guidelines available on website. "We try to respond to manuscripts in 3-4 months. Reading time is often slower during summer and holiday months." Pays $5/page ($10 minimum), 2 contributor's copies, and remainder of year's subscription. Acquires first North American serial rights only. Reviews books of poetry. Send materials for review consideration.

CONTEST/AWARD OFFERINGS Holds yearly poetry and prose-poem contests. Guidelines available for SASE or on website.

TIPS "We're always looking for nonfiction essays that go beyond merely autobiographical revelation and utilize sophisticated organization and slightly radical narrative strategies. We want essays that are both lyrical and analytical where confession does not mean nostalgia. Read us before you submit. Often reading is slower in summer and holiday months. Only submit work to journals you would proudly subscribe to, then subscribe to a few. Take care to read the latest 2 issues and specifically mention work you identify with and why. Submit work that `stacks up' with the work we've published. Offers annual poetry, fiction, short-short/prose-poem prizes. See website for full guidelines."

INKWELL

(914)323-7239. **Fax:** (914)323-3122. **E-mail:** inkwell@mville.edu. **Website:** www.inkwelljournal.org. *Inkwell*, published semiannually, features "emerging writers, high quality poems and short stories, creative nonfiction, artwork, literary essays, memoir and interviews on writing by established figures, and yearly compeitions in poetry and fiction." Wants "serious work—very well made verse, any form, any genre." Does not want "doggerel, light or humorous verse." Please review archives online or send for sample copy. *Inkwell* is 150 pages, digest-sized, press-printed, perfect-bound, with cover with illustration/photography. Receives about 2,500 poems/year, accepts about 30. Press run is 700. Single copy: $10; subscription: $18/year. Sample: $6 (back issue). Make checks payable to Manhattanville College—*Inkwell*. Buys first North American serial rights. Pays on publication. Publishes ms an average of 4 months after acceptance. Responds in 1 month to queries. Responds in 4-6 months to mss. Editorial lead time 4 months. Sample copy for $6. Guidelines free.

Inkwell is produced in affiliation with the Master of Arts in Writing program at Manhattanville College, and is staffed by faculty and graduate students of the program.

MAGAZINE NEEDS Does not want doggerel, funny poetry, etc. Pays $5-10/page.

HOW TO CONTACT Submit up to 5 poems at a time. Lines/poem: 70 maximum. Considers simultaneous submissions; no previously published poems. ("Previously published" work includes poetry posted on a public website/blog/forum, but not on a private, password-protected forum.) No fax, e-mail, or disk submissions. Cover letter is required. Include SASE. Reads submissions August 1-November 30. Time between acceptance and publication is 6 months. Poems are circulated to an editorial board. Never comments on rejected poems. Guidelines available for SASE or on website. Responds in 4 months. Pays $10/page and 2 contributor's copies. Acquires first North American serial rights. Rights revert to poets upon publication.

TIPS "We cannot accept electronic submissions."

INNISFREE POETRY JOURNAL

E-mail: editor@innisfreepoetry.org. **Website:** www.innisfreepoetry.org. **Contact:** Greg McBride. Buys first North American serial rights. Guidelines available on website.

MAGAZINE NEEDS Submit up to 5 poems by e-mail; single Word attachment. "Include your name, as you would like it to appear in *Innisfree*, in the subject line of your submission. Format all poems flush with the left margin—no indents other than any within the poem itself. Simultaneous submissions are welcome. If a poem is accepted elsewhere, however, please be sure to notify us immediately." Does not accept previously published poetry. Acquires first publication rights, including the right to publish it online and maintain it there as part of the issue in which it appears, to make it available in a printer-friendly format, to make the issue of *Innisfree* in which it appears downloadable as a PDF document and available as a printed volume. All other rights revert to the poet after online publication of the poem in *The Innisfree Poetry Journal*.

TIPS "Welcomes original previously unpublished poems year round. We accept poems only via e-mail from both established and new writers whose work is excellent. We publish well-crafted poems, poems grounded in the specific which speak in fresh language and telling images. And we admire musicality. We welcome those who, like the late Lorenzo Thomas, 'write poems because I can't sing.'"

IN OUR OWN WORDS

Burning Bush Publications, P.O. Box 4658, Santa Rosa CA 95402. **Website:** www.bbbooks.com. **Contact:** Amanda Majestie, editor. *In Our Own Words*, published annually online, seeks poetry and prose poems for its literary e-zine. Wants "thought-provoking, creative, alternative writing. We choose work that inspires compassion, peace, and respect for diversity in original and unexpected ways." Does not want "manuscripts of full-length books." Sample: past issues available on website.

MAGAZINE NEEDS Cover letter is required. "Send submissions to us by U.S. mail only. Include SASE. If you want us to reply your letter via e-mail, include your e-mail address! We will ask you for a digital file via e-mail, if we want to publish your submission." Reads submissions according to the following deadline: Annual Edition, June 1st. Guidelines available on website. Rights revert to poet upon publication.

INTERPRETER'S HOUSE

9 Glenhurst Rd., Mannamead, Plymouth PL3 5LT, England. **Website:** www.interpretershouse.org.uk. **Contact:** Simon Curtis, editor. *Interpreter's House*, published 3 times/year in February, June, and October, prints short stories and poetry. Wants "good poetry, not too long." Does not want "Christmas-card verse or incomprehensible poetry." Has published poetry by Dannie Abse, Tony Curtis, Pauline Stainer, Alan Brownjohn, Peter Redgrove, and R.S. Thomas. *Interpreter's House* is 74 pages, A5, with attractive cover design. Receives about 1,000 poems/year, accepts

up to 5%. Press run is 300 (200 subscribers). Single copy: £3 plus 55p. postage; subscription: £12 for 3 issues. Sample: £3.50.

Business correspondence (including subscriptions) should go to Matt Bright, Upper Flat, 251 Abingdon Rd., Oxford OX1 4TH England.

MAGAZINE NEEDS All work is dealt with swiftly. Usually no more than one poem is accepted, and writers who have already appeared in the magazine are asked to wait for at least a year before submitting again. Submit 5 poems at a time. No previously published poems or simultaneous submissions. Cover letter is preferred. Time between acceptance and publication is 2 weeks to 3 months. Often comments on rejected poems. Guidelines available for SASE (or SAE and IRC). Responds "fast." Pays 1 contributor's copy.

INVERTED-A HORN

Inverted-A, Inc., P.O. Box 267, Licking MO 65542. **Contact:** Nets Katz, and Aya Katz, editors. *Inverted-A Horn*, published irregularly, welcomes political topics, social issues, and science fiction. Wants traditional poetry with meter and rhyme. Does not want to see anything "modern, formless, existentialist." *Inverted-A Horn* is usually 9 pages, magazine-sized, offset-printed. Press run is 300. Sample: SASE with postage for 2 ounces (subject to availability). Inverted-A, Inc. is a very small press that evolved from publishing technical manuals for other products. "Our interests center on freedom, justice, and honor." Publishes 1 chapbook/year. Responds in 4 months.

MAGAZINE NEEDS Considers simultaneous submissions. Accepts e-mail submissions (as attachment, ASCII). Pays 1 contributor's copy; offers 40% discount on additional copies.

IODINE POETRY JOURNAL

P.O. Box 18548, Charlotte NC 28218. (704)595-9526. **E-mail:** iodineopencut@aol.com. **Website:** www.iodinepoetryjournal.com. **Contact:** Jonathan K. Rice, editor/publisher. *Iodine Poetry Journal*, published semiannually, provides "a venue for both emerging and established poets." Wants "good poetry of almost any style, including form (e.g., pantoum and sestina) and experimental." Does not want rhyme, religion, or pornography. Has published poetry by Fred Chappell, Colette Inez, Ron Koertge, Dorianne Laux, and R.T. Smith. *Iodine Poetry Journal* is 84 pages, digest-sized, perfect-bound, with full-color laminated cover, includes ads. Receives about 2,000 poems/year, accepts about 75 poems/issue. Press run is 350. Single copy: $8; subscription: $14/year (2 issues) $26 for 2 years (4 issues). Sample: "Back issues vary in price." Make checks payable to *Iodine Poetry Journal*. Publishes ms 1 year after acceptance. Responds in 2-3 months. Guidelines available in magazine, for SASE, or on website.

Poetry published in *Iodine Poetry Journal* has been selected for inclusion in *The Best American Poetry*.

MAGAZINE NEEDS Submit 3-5 poems at a time. Lines/poem: 40 or less preferred, "but not totally averse to longer poems." No previously published poems or simultaneous submissions. Accepts e-mail submissions from international poets only; no disk submissions. Cover letter is preferred. "Always include SASE, and specify if SASE is for return of manuscript or reply only. I like a brief introduction of yourself in the cover letter." Reads submissions year round. Submit seasonal poems 6 months in advance. Time between acceptance and publication is 6 months to 1 year. Poems are circulated to an editorial board. "I occasionally have other readers assist in the selection process, but editor makes the final decision." Sometimes comments on rejected poems. Sometimes sends prepublication galleys. Pays 1 contributor's copy and discounts extra copies of the issue in which work appears. Acquires first North American serial rights.

TIPS "We no longer publish our broadside, *Open Cut*."

IOTA

P.O. Box 7721, Matlock, Derbyshire DE4 9DD, England. (44)01629 582500. **E-mail:** info@iotamagazine.co.uk. **Website:** www.iotapoetry.co.uk. *iota*, published quarterly, considers "any style and subject; no specific limitations as to length." Has published poetry by Jane Kinninmont, John Robinson, Tony Petch, Chris Kinsey, Christopher James, and Michael Kriesel. *iota* is 56 pages, professionally printed, perfect-bound, with b&w photograph litho cover. Receives 6,000 poems/year, accepts about 300. Press run is 300. Single copy: £6.50 UK; subscription: £15 UK.

MAGAZINE NEEDS Submit up to 6 poems at a time. No previously published poems or simultaneous submissions. Cover letter is required. Prefers name and address on each poem, typed. "No SAE, no reply." Responds in 3 months (unless production of the next issue takes precedence). Pays 1 contributor's copy.

Reviews books of poetry. Send materials for review consideration.

ADDITIONAL INFORMATION The editors also run Ragged Raven Press (www.raggedraven.co.uk), which publishes poetry collections, nonfiction, and an annual anthology of poetry linked to an international competition.

CONTEST/AWARD OFFERINGS Sponsors an annual poetry competition, offering 1st Prize: £200; 2nd and 3rd Prize: £25; publication in *iota* and on website. Guidelines available on website. **Entry fee:** free for up to 2 poems for subscribers, £2 for each subsequent poem; £2/poem for non-subscribers. **Deadline:** April 15.

THE IOWA REVIEW

308 EPB, The University of Iowa, Iowa City IA 52242. (319)335-0462. **Website:** iowareview.org. **Contact:** Russell Scott Valentino, editor. *The Iowa Review*, published 3 times/year, prints fiction, poetry, essays, reviews, and, occasionally, interviews. *The Iowa Review* is 5×8, approximately 200 pages, professionally printed, flat-spined, first-grade offset paper, Carolina CS1 10-point cover stock. Receives about 5,000 submissions/year, accepts up to 100. Press run is 2,900; 1,500 distributed to stores. Subscription: $25. Stories, essays, and poems for a general readership interested in contemporary literature. Buys first North American serial rights, buys nonexclusive anthology, classroom, and online serial rights. Pays on publication. Publishes ms an average of 12-18 months after acceptance. Responds in 4 months to mss. Sample copy for $9.95 and online. Guidelines available online.

"This magazine uses the help of colleagues and graduate assistants. Its reading period for unsolicited work is September 1-December 1. From January through April, we read entries to our annual Iowa Awards competition. Check our website for further information."

MAGAZINE NEEDS Submit up to 8 poems at a time. Online submissions accepted, but no e-mail submissions. Cover letter (with title of work and genre) is encouraged. SASE required. Reads submissions "only during the fall semester, September through November, and then contest entries in the spring." Time between acceptance and publication is "around a year." Occasionally comments on rejected poems or offers suggestions on accepted poems. Pays $1.50/line of poetry, $40 minimum. "We simply look for poems that, at the time we read and choose, we find we admire. No specifications as to form, length, style, subject matter, or purpose. Though we print work from established writers, we're always delighted when we discover new talent."

TIPS "We publish essays, reviews, novel excerpts, stories, poems, and photography. We have no set guidelines as to content or length, but strongly recommend that writers read a sample issue before submitting. Buys 65-80 unsolicited ms/year. Submit complete ms with SASE."

ISLAND

P.O. Box 210, Sandy Bay Tasmania 7006, Australia. (61)(3)6226-2325. **E-mail:** island.magazine@utas.edu.au. **Website:** www.islandmag.com. "*Island* seeks quality fiction, poetry, essays, and articles. A literary magazine with an environmental heart." Buys one-time rights. Subscriptions and sample copies available for purchase online. Guidelines available online.

MAGAZINE NEEDS Pays $100.

ITALIAN AMERICANA

80 Washington St., Providence RI 02903-1803. **E-mail:** itamericana@yahoo.com. **Website:** www.italianamericana.com. **Contact:** C.B. Albright, editor-in-chief.

MAGAZINE NEEDS *Italian Americana*, published twice/year, uses 16-20 poems of "no more than 3 pages." Does not want "trite nostalgia about grandparents." Has published poetry by Mary Jo Salter and Jay Parini. *Italian Americana* is 150-200 pages, digest-sized, professionally printed, flat-spined, with glossy card cover. Press run is 1,000. Singly copy: $10; subscription: $20/year, $35 for 2 years. Sample: $7.

HOW TO CONTACT Contact Michael Palma, poetry editor. Submit no more than 3 poems at a time. "Single copies of poems for submissions are sufficient." No previously published poems or simultaneous submissions. Cover letter is not required "but helpful." Name on first page of ms only. Occasionally comments on rejected poems. Responds in 6 weeks. Acquires first rights. Reviews books of poetry in 600 words, multi-book format. Send materials for review consideration to Prof. John Paul Russo, senior editor, English Dept., University of Miami, Coral Gables, FL 33124.

CONTEST/AWARD OFFERINGS Along with the National Italian American Foundation, *Italian Americana* co-sponsors the annual $1,000 John Ciardi Award for Lifetime Contribution to Poetry. *Ital-*

ian Americana also presents $250 fiction or memoir award annually; and $1,500 in history prizes.

TIPS "Check out our new website supplement to the journal at www.italianamericana.com. Read *Wild Dreams: The Best of Italian Americana* (Fordham University Press), the best stories, poems and memoirs in the journal's 35-year history."

JACK AND JILL

Children's Better Health Institute, P.O. Box 567, Indianapolis IN 46206-0567. (317)636-8881. **E-mail:** j.goodman@cbhi.org. **Website:** www.jackandjillmag.org. "Write entertaining and imaginative stories for kids, not just about them. Writers should understand what is funny to kids, what's important to them, what excites them. Don't write from an adult 'kids are so cute' perspective. We're also looking for health and healthful lifestyle stories and articles, but don't be preachy." Buys all rights. Pays on publication. Publishes ms an average of 8 months after acceptance. Responds to mss in 3 months. Guidelines available online.

MAGAZINE NEEDS Wants light-hearted poetry appropriate for the age group. Reviews submissions for possible use in all Children's Better Health Institute publications. Mss must be typewritten with poet's contact information in upper right-hand corner of each poem's page. SASE required. Pays $35 minimum for poetry.

TIPS "We are constantly looking for new writers who can tell good stories with interesting slants—stories that are not full of out-dated and time-worn expressions. We like to see stories about kids who are smart and capable, but not sarcastic or smug. Problem-solving skills, personal responsibility, and integrity are good topics for us. Obtain current issues of the magazine and study them to determine our present needs and editorial style."

JEWISH CURRENTS

P.O. Box 111, Accord NY 12404. (845)626-2427. **E-mail:** info@jewishcurrents.org. **Website:** www.jewishcurrents.org. **Contact:** Lawrence Bush, editor. *Jewish Currents*, published 4 times/year, is a progressive Jewish bimonthly magazine that carries on the insurgent tradition of the Jewish left through independent journalism, political commentary, and a 'countercultural' approach to Jewish arts and literature. *Jewish Currents* is 48 pages, magazine-sized, offset-printed, saddle-stapled with a full-color arts section, "Jcultcha & Funny Pages." Press run is 700. Subscription: $25/year. Publishes ms 2 years after acceptance. Responds in 3 months.

MAGAZINE NEEDS Submit 4 poems at a time with a cover letter. No previously published poems or simultaneous submissions. Cover letter is required. "Include brief bio with author's publishing history." Poems should be typed, double-spaced; include SASE. Pays 3 contributor's copies.

JEWISH WOMEN'S LITERARY ANNUAL

NCJW Women New York Section, 820 Second Ave., New York NY 10017. (212)687-5030. **E-mail:** info@ncjwny.org. **Website:** www.ncjwny.org/services_annual.htm. *Jewish Women's Literary Annual*, published in April, prints poetry and fiction by Jewish women. Wants "poems by Jewish women on any topic, but of the highest literary quality." Has published poetry by Linda Zisquit, Merle Feld, Helen Papell, Enid Dame, Marge Piercy, and Lesleéa Newman. *Jewish Women's Literary Annual* is 230 pages, digest-sized, perfect-bound, with laminated card cover. Receives about 1,500 poems/year, accepts about 10%. Press run is 1,500. Subscription: $18 for 3 issues. Sample: $7.50.

MAGAZINE NEEDS Submit previously unpublished poetry and prose written by Jewish women. Accepts any topic. Submit through postal mail only.

TIPS "Send only your very best. We are looking for humor, as well as other things, but nothing cutesy or smart-aleck. We do no politics; prefer topics other than 'Holocaust'."

THE JOURNAL

Original Plus Press, 17 High St., Maryport Cumbria CA15 6BQ, UK. 01900 812194. **E-mail:** smithsssj@aol.com. **Website:** http://thesamsmith.webs.com. *The Journal*, published 3 times a year, features English poetry/translations, reviews, and articles. Wants "new poetry howsoever it comes; translations and original English-language poems." Does not want "staid, generalized, all form/no content." Buys all rights. Pays on publication. Publishes ms an average of 6 months after acceptance. Responds in 4 weeks to queries. Editorial lead time 6 months. Guidelines free.

MAGAZINE NEEDS Submit up to 6 poems at a time. Considers previously published poems and simultaneous submissions. Accepts e-mail submissions. Cover letter is preferred. "Please send 2 IRCs with hard-copy submissions." Time between acceptance and publication is up to 1 year. Often comments on rejected poems. Guidelines available for SASE (or SAE and IRC). Always sends prepublication galleys. Pays 1 contributor's copy. Since 1997, Original Plus Press has been publishing collections of poetry. Has recently published books by Chris Hardy, Brian Daldorph, Siobhan Logan, Alice Lenkiewics and Helen Bunkingham. But from now will be publishing only chapbooks. Send SASE (or SAE and IRC) or e-mail for details

TIPS "Send 6 poems; I'll soon let you know if it's not *Journal* material."

JOURNAL OF ASIAN MARTIAL ARTS

Via Media Publishing Co., 941 Calle Mejia, #822, Santa Fe NM 87501. (505)983-1919. **E-mail:** info@goviamedia.com. **Website:** www.goviamedia.com. Buys first rights, buys second serial (reprint) rights. Pays on publication. Publishes ms an average of 1 year after acceptance. Responds in 1 month to queries. Responds in 2 months to mss. Sample copy for $10. Guidelines with #10 SASE or online.

MAGAZINE NEEDS *Journal of Asian Martial Arts*, published quarterly, is a "comprehensive journal on Asian martial arts with high standards and academic approach." Wants poetry about Asian martial arts and its history/culture. "No restrictions, provided the poet has a feel for, and good understanding of, the subject." Does not want poetry showing a narrow view. "We look for a variety of styles from an interdisciplinary approach." *Journal of Asian Martial Arts* is 124 pages, magazine-sized, professionally printed on coated stock, perfect-bound, with soft cover, includes ads. Press run is 12,000 (1,500 subscribers, 50 libraries, the rest mainly shelf sales). Single copy: $9.75; subscription: $32/year, $55/2 years. Sample: $10. No poetry that does not focus on martial arts culture. Pays $10-100, or copies.

HOW TO CONTACT Considers previously published poems; no simultaneous submissions. Accepts e-mail submissions. Cover letter is required. Often comments on rejected poems. Guidelines available for SASE or by fax or e-mail. Responds in 2 months. Sometimes sends prepublication galleys. Pays $1-100 and/or 1-5 contributor's copies on publication. Buys first world and reprint rights. Reviews books of poetry "if they have some connection to Asian martial arts; length is open." Open to unsolicited reviews. Send materials for review consideration.

TIPS "Always query before sending a manuscript. We are open to varied types of articles; most however require a strong academic grasp of Asian culture. For those not having this background, we suggest trying a museum review, or interview, where authorities can be questioned, quoted, and provide supportive illustrations. We especially desire articles/reports from Asia, with photo illustrations, particularly of a martial art style, so readers can visually understand the unique attributes of that style, its applications, evolution, etc. Location and media reports are special areas that writers may consider, especially if they live in a location of martial art significance."

JOURNAL OF NEW JERSEY POETS

English Dept., County College of Morris, 214 Center Grove Rd., Randolph NJ 07869-2086. (973)328-5467. **Fax:** (973)328-5425. **E-mail:** mayres1@ccm.edu. **Contact:** Acquisitions: Matthew Ayers, editor; Debra Demattio, Emily Birx, Matthew Jones, Philip Chase, associate editors.

MAGAZINE NEEDS *Journal of New Jersey Poets*, published annually in April, is "not necessarily about New Jersey—but of, by, and for poets from New Jersey." Wants "serious work that conveys the essential, real, whole emotional moment of the poem to the reader without sentimentality." Has published poetry by Joe Weil, X.J. Kennedy, Marvin Silbersher, Tina Kelley, Gerald Stern, Kenneth Burke, and Catherine Doty. *Journal of New Jersey Poets* is about 90 pages, perfect-bound, offset-printed on recycled stock. Press run is 600. Single copy: $10; subscription: $16 for 2 issues ($16/issue for institutions). Sample: $5. Poets who live or work in New Jersey (or who formerly lived or worked here) are invited to submit up to 3 poems with their New Jersey bio data mentioned in the cover letter. Accepts fax and e-mail submissions, "but they will not be acknowledged nor returned. Include SASE with sufficient postage for return of manuscript, or provide instructions to recycle." Annual deadline for submissions: September 1. Time between acceptance and publication is within 1 year. Guidelines available for SASE or by e-mail. Responds in up to 1 year. Pays 2 contributor's copies and a one-year subscription. Acquires first North American serial rights. All reviews are solicited. Send 2 copies of books for review consideration. (Specialized: of, by, for NJ poets).

ADDITIONAL INFORMATION Awarded first New Jersey poets prize to Stephen Dobyns in 2010. For prize guidelines, e-mail editor Matthew Ayres.

JOURNAL OF THE AMERICAN MEDICAL ASSOCIATION (JAMA)

(312)464-4444. **E-mail:** jamams@jama-archives.org. **Website:** www.jama.com.

MAGAZINE NEEDS *Journal of the American Medical Association (JAMA)*, published weekly, includes a poetry and medicine column and publishes poetry "in some way related to a medical experience, whether from the point of view of a health care worker or patient, or simply an observer. No unskilled poetry." Has published poetry by Jack Coulehan, Floyd Skloot, and Walt McDonald. *JAMA* is magazine-sized, flat-spined, with glossy paper cover. Receives about 750 poems/year, accepts about 7%. Has 360,000 subscribers (369 libraries).

THE JOURNAL

(614)292-4076. **Fax:** (614)292-7816. **E-mail:** thejournal@osu.edu; thejournalmag@gmail.com. **Website:** english.osu.edu/research/journals/thejournal/. "We're open to all forms; we tend to favor work that gives evidence of a mature and sophisticated sense of the language." Buys first North American serial rights. Pays on publication. Publishes ms an average of 1 year after acceptance. Responds in 2 weeks to queries. Responds in 2 months to mss. Sample copy for $7 or online. Guidelines available online.

> "We are interested in quality fiction, poetry, nonfiction, and reviews of new books of poetry. We impose no restrictions on category, type, or length of submission for Fiction, Poetry, and Nonfiction. We are happy to consider long stories and self-contained excerpts of novels. Please double-space all prose submissions. Address correspondence to the Editors. We will only respond to submissions accompanied by a SASE."

MAGAZINE NEEDS Pays $20.

CONTEST/AWARD OFFERINGS "However else poets train or educate themselves, they must do what they can to know our language. Too much of the writing we see indicates poets do not, in many cases, develop a feel for the possibilities of language, and do not pay attention to craft. Poets should not be in a rush to publish—until they are ready."

TIPS "Manuscripts are rejected because of lack of understanding of the short story form, shallow plots, undeveloped characters. Cure: Read as much well-written fiction as possible. Our readers prefer 'psychological' fiction rather than stories with intricate plots. Take care to present a clean, well-typed submission."

KAIMANA: LITERARY ARTS HAWAI'I

Hawai'i Literary Arts Council, P.O. Box 11213, Honolulu HI 96828. **E-mail:** reimersa001@hawaii.rr.com. **Website:** www.hawaii.edu/hlac. **Contact:** Poetry Editor. *Kaimana: Literary Arts Hawai'i*, published annually, is the magazine of the Hawai'i Literary Arts Council. Wants poems with "some Pacific reference—Asia, Polynesia, Hawai'i—but not exclusively." Has published poetry by Kathryn Takara, Howard Nemerov, Anne Waldman, Reuel Denney, Haunani-Kay Trask, and Simon Perchik. *Kaimana* is 64-76 pages, 7×10, saddle-stapled, with high-quality printing. Press run is 1,000. Subscription: $15, includes membership in HLAC. Sample: $10.

MAGAZINE NEEDS Cover letter is preferred. Sometimes comments on rejected poems. Guidelines available in magazine or on website. Responds with "reasonable dispatch." Pays 2 contributor's copies. "Hawai'i gets a lot of 'travelling regionalists,' visiting writers with inevitably superficial observations. We also get superb visiting observers who are careful craftsmen anywhere. *Kaimana* is interested in the latter, to complement our own best Hawai'i writers."

TIPS "Poets published in Kaimana have received the Pushcart Prize, the Hawaii Award for Literature, the Stefan Baciu Award, the Cades Award, and the John Unterecker Award."

KALEIDOSCOPE

Kaleidoscope Press, 701 S. Main St., Akron OH 44311-1019. (330)762-9755. **Fax:** (330)762-0912. **E-mail:** mshiplett@udsakron.org. **Website:** www.udsakron.org/kaleidoscope.htm. **Contact:** Mildred Shiplett. "Subscribers include individuals, agencies, and organizations that assist people with disabilities and many university and public libraries. Appreciates work by established writers as well. Especially interested in work by writers with a disability, but features writers both with and without disabilities. Writers without a disability must limit themselves to our focus, while those with a disability may explore any topic (although we prefer original perspectives about experiences with disability)." Buys first rights. Rights return to author upon publication. Pays on publication. Responds in 3 weeks to queries. Responds in 6 months to mss. Sample copy for $6 prepaid. Double-space your work, number the pages, & include name. Guidelines available online.

Kaleidoscope has received awards from the American Heart Association, the Great Lakes Awards Competition and Ohio Public Images.

MAGAZINE NEEDS *Kaleidoscope: Exploring the Experience of Disability through Literature and the Fine Arts*, published twice/year in January and July, is based at United Disability Services, a not-for-profit agency. Distributed by University of Akron Press. Poetry should deal with the experience of disability, but is not limited to that experience when the writer has a disability. Wants high-quality poetry with vivid, believable images and evocative language. Does not want "stereotyping, patronizing, or offending language about disability." Has published poetry by Gerald Wheeler, Jeff Worley, Barbara Crooker, and Sheryl L. Nelms. *Kaleidoscope* is 64 pages, magazine-sized, professionally printed, saddle-stapled, with 4-color semigloss card cover. Press run is 1,500 (for libraries, social service agencies, health care professionals, universities, and individual subscribers). Single copy: $7.50; subscription: $12.50 individual, $25 agency. Contact University of Akron Press at uapress@uakron.edu. "Do not get caught up in rhyme scheme. High quality with strong imagery and evocative language. Reviews any style."

HOW TO CONTACT Submit up to 6 poems at a time. Considers previously published poems and simultaneous submissions "as long as we are notified in both instances." Accepts fax and e-mail submissions. Cover letter is required. Send photocopies with SASE for return of work. "All submissions must be accompanied by an autobiographical sketch and should be double-spaced, with pages numbered and author's name on each page." Reads submissions by March 1 and August 1 deadlines. Publishes theme issues. Upcoming themes available in magazine, for SASE, by fax, e-mail, or on website. Guidelines available for SASE, by fax, e-mail, and on website. Responds within 3 weeks; acceptance or rejection may take 6 months. Pays $10-25 plus 2 contributor's copies. Rights revert to author upon publication. Staff reviews books of poetry. Send materials for review consideration.

TIPS "Articles and personal experiences should be creative rather than journalistic and with some depth. Writers should use more than just the simple facts and chronology of an experience with disability. Inquire about future themes of upcoming issues. Sample copy very helpful. Works should not use stereotyping, patronizing, or offending language about disability. We seek fresh imagery and thought-provoking language. Please double-space work, number pages & include full name and address."

KELSEY REVIEW

P.O. Box B, Liberal Arts Division, Trenton NJ 08690. **E-mail:** kelsey.review@mccc.edu. **Website:** www.mccc.edu/community_kelsey-review.shtml. **Contact:** Holly-Katharine Matthews. *Kelsey Review*, published annually in September by Mercer County Community College, serves as "an outlet for literary talent of people living and working in Mercer County, New Jersey only." Has no specifications as to form, length, subject matter, or style. Fiction: 4,000 word limit. Poetry: Not more than 6 pages. Non-Fiction: 2,500 word limit. Black and White art. Does not want to see poetry "about kittens and puppies." Has published poetry by Vida Chu, Carolyn Foote Edelmann, and Mary Mallery. *Kelsey Review* is about 90 glossy pages, 7x11, with paper cover. Receives 100+ submissions/year, accepts 10. Press run is 2,000; all distributed free to contributors, area libraries, bookstores, and schools.

HOW TO CONTACT Submit up to 6 poems at a time. No previously published poems or simultaneous submissions. No fax or e-mail submissions. Manuscripts must be typed. Submit poems by May 15 deadline. Send SASE for returns. Guidelines available by e-mail. Responds in August of each year. Pays 3 contributor's copies. All rights revert to authors.

TIPS Look for "quality, intellect, grace and guts. Avoid sentimentality, overwriting and self-indulgence. Work on clarity, depth and originality."

THE KENYON REVIEW

Finn House, 102 W. Wiggin, Gambier OH 43022. (740)427-5208. **Fax:** (740)427-5417. **E-mail:** kenyonreview@kenyon.edu. **Website:** KenyonReview.org. **Contact:** Marlene Landefeld. "An international journal of literature, culture, and the arts, dedicated to an inclusive representation of the best in new writing (fiction, poetry, essays, interviews, criticism) from established and emerging writers." Buys first rights. Pays on publication. Publishes ms an average of 1 year after acceptance. Responds in 4 months to mss. Editorial lead time 1 year. Sample copy $10, includes postage and handling. Please call or e-mail to order. Guidelines available online.

MAGAZINE NEEDS *The Kenyon Review*, published quarterly, contains poetry, fiction, essays, criticism, reviews, and memoirs. Features all styles, forms, lengths, and subject matters. Considers translations. Has published poetry by Billy Collins, Diane Ackerman, John Kinsella, Carol Muske-Dukes, Diane di Prima, and Seamus Heaney. *The Kenyon Review* is 180 pages, digest-sized, flat-spined. Receives about 6,000 submissions/year. Press run is 6,000. Also now publishes *KR Online*, a separate and complementary literary magazine. Sample: $12 (includes postage).

HOW TO CONTACT Submit up to 6 poems at a time. No previously published poems or simultaneous submissions. Accepts submissions **through online registration only** at www.kenyon-review.org/submissions (group poems in a single document; do not submit poems individually). Reads submissions September 15-January 15. Guidelines available on website. Responds in up to 4 months. Payment for accepted work is made upon publication. Author retains rights and will receive a contract upon acceptance. Does not consider unsolicited reviews.

TIPS "We no longer accept mailed or e-mailed submissions. Work will only be read if it is submitted through our online program on our website. Reading period is September 15-January 15. We look for strong voice, unusual perspective, and power in the writing."

◐ THE KERF

College of the Redwoods, 883 W. Washington Blvd., Crescent City CA 95531. (707) 476-4370. **E-mail:** ken-letko@redwoods.edu. **Website:** http://www.redwoods.edu/Departments/english/poets&writers/clm.htm. **Contact:** Ken Letko, editor. *The Kerf*, published annually in fall, features "poetry that speaks to the environment and humanity." Wants "poetry that exhibits an environmental consciousness." Considers poetry by children and teens. Has published poetry by Ruth Daigon, Alice D'Alessio, James Grabill, George Keithley, and Paul Willis. *The Kerf* is 54 pages, digest-sized, printed via Docutech, saddle-stapled, with CS2 coverstock. Receives about 1,000 poems/year, accepts up to 3%. Press run is 400 (150 shelf sales); 100 distributed free to contributors and writing centers. Sample: $5. Make checks payable to College of the Redwoods.

MAGAZINE NEEDS Submit up to 5 poems (7 pages maximum) at a time. No previously published poems or simultaneous submissions. Reads submissions January 15-March 31 only.

O KOTAPRESS LOSS JOURNAL

(928)225-5416. **E-mail:** editor@kotapress.com. **Website:** www.kotapress.com; www.kotapress.blogspot.com. **Contact:** Kara L.C. Jones, editor. *KotaPress Loss Journal*, published quarterly online with blogs almost daily, provides support "of the grief and healing process after the death of a child. We publish *only* non-fictional poetry that somehow relates to grief and healing in relation to the death of a child. Please do not make up poems about this kind of loss and send them just to get in the magazine; it is insulting to many of our readers who are living this reality. As always, our interest is more in the content and story rather than one's ability to write in form; more in the ideas of poetry therapy rather than the academic, critique, competitive ideas normally fostered in universities." Has published poetry by John Fox, Poppy Hullings, Patricia Wellingham-Jones, Carol Jo Horn, and Sarah Bain. Responds in 2-6 months.

MAGAZINE NEEDS "Please read the *Loss Journal* site and blog before sending anything. Then send a letter explaining your interest in contributing. We are interested in knowing how your personal experiences with death, dying, grief, and healing are playing out in the specific poems you are submitting. Include a bio. Send your letter, poems, and bio as text all in one e-mail. Submissions without letter explaining your interest will be ignored. Make sure the subject line of your e-mail says 'Loss Journal Submission'"

◐$ LADYBUG

Carus Publishing Co., 700 E. Lake St., Suite 300, Chicago IL 60601. (312)701-1720. **Website:** www.cricketmag.com. **Contact:** Marianne Carus, editor-in-chief; Suzanne Beck, managing art director. "We look for quality literature and nonfiction." Subscription: $35.97/year (12 issues). sample: $5; sample pages available on website. Pays on publication. Responds in 6 months to mss. Guidelines available online.

MAGAZINE NEEDS *LADYBUG Magazine*, published monthly, is a reading and listening magazine for young children (ages 2-6). Wants poetry that is "rhythmic, rhyming; serious, humorous, active." 20 lines maximum. Pays $3/line ($25 minimum).

TIPS "Reread ms before sending. Keep within specified word limits. Study back issues before submitting to learn about the types of material we're looking for.

Writing style is paramount. We look for rich, evocative language and a sense of joy or wonder. Remember that you're writing for preschoolers—be age-appropriate, but not condescending or preachy. A story must hold enjoyment for both parent and child through repeated read-aloud sessions. Remember that people come in all colors, sizes, physical conditions, and have special needs. Be inclusive!"

LA FOVEA

E-mail: editors@lafovea.org. **Website:** www.lafovea.org. **Contact:** Frank Giampietro, creator and senior editor. Published 20 times/year online. "Each Nerve editor (found on the main page of www.lafovea.org) is in charge of a nerve. The nerves are made up of poets who are invited to submit to La Fovea. Click on the editors name to see all the poets and poems in his or her nerve. The nerve editor asks a poet to submit two poems. After that poet has had his or her poems on La Fovea, he or she will ask another poet to submit poems. If the last poet on the nerve does not find a poet to submit poems for whatever reason, the nerve is dead. It's okay to have a dead nerve. The most important thing is for the never editor to notice a nerve has died and begin a new nerve from their first page of poems."

MAGAZINE NEEDS Wants any poetry. "If a poet wants to submit to La Fovea but has not been invited, he or she may submit to La Fovea and choose the editor whom the poet believes most matches his or her family of aesthetic style. The editor of the never may choose to send these poems to the current nerve editor and ask if he or she wishes to publish the poet's work. If the poet does not wish to publish the work, than the work will be returned to the submitter." Has published poetry by Denise Duhamel, Campbell McGrath, Julianna Baggott. Submit 2 poems at a time and short bio. Considers simultaneous submissions, no previously published poetry. Reads submissions year round. Time between acceptance and publication is 1 month. Guidelines available on website. Responds in 1 month. Acquires one-time rights. Rights revert to poet upon publication.

LAKE EFFECT: A JOURNAL OF THE LITERARY ARTS

School of Humanities & Social Sciences, Penn State Erie, 4951 College Dr., Erie PA 16563-1501. (814)898-6281. **Fax:** (814)898-6032. **E-mail:** goll@psu.edu. **Website:** www.pserie.psu.edu/lakeeffect. **Contact:** George Looney, editor-in-chief.

MAGAZINE NEEDS *Lake Effect* is looking for poems that demonstrate an original voice and that use multilayered, evocative images presented in a language shaped by an awareness of how words sound and mean. Each line should help to carry the poem. There is no length limit per poem, but send no more than four poems at a time. Lake Effect seeks poems from both established poets and from new and emerging voices.

LANDFALL: NEW ZEALAND ARTS AND LETTERS

Otago University Press, P.O. Box 56, Dunedin , New Zealand. (64)(3)479-8807. **Fax:** (64)(3)479-8385. **E-mail:** landfall@otago.ac.nz. **Website:** www.otago.ac.nz/press/landfall. **Contact:** Richard Reeve, coordinator. *Landfall: New Zealand Arts and Letters*, published twice/year in May and November, focuses "primarily on New Zealand literature and arts. It publishes new fiction, poetry, commentary, and interviews with New Zealand artists and writers, and reviews of New Zealand books." Single issue: $29.95 NZD; subscription: $49.95 NZD (2 issues) for New Zealand subscribers, $45 AUD for Australian subscribers, $42 USD for other overseas subscribers. Guidelines for SASE.

MAGAZINE NEEDS Submit no more than 10 poems. Prefers e-mail submissions. Accepts postal mail submissions, but must include SASE. Include contact information and brief bio. Publishes theme issues. Reads year round.

LANGUAGEANDCULTURE.NET

4000 Pimlico Dr., Suite 114-192, Pleasanton CA 94588. **E-mail:** review@languageandculture.net. **Website:** www.languageandculture.net. **Contact:** Liz Fortini, editor.

MAGAZINE NEEDS *Languageandculture.net*, published twice/year online, prints contemporary poetry in English. Also accepts translations of Spanish, French, German, Italian, and Russian; "other languages under review." No restrictions on form. Considers poetry by teens. Publishes 20-40 poems/issue. Submit 3-5 poems at a time. Lines/poem: 70 maximum. Considers previously published poems and simultaneous submissions. Accepts e-mail submissions; no disk submissions. "Return e-mail address must be included." Cover letter is preferred. Include brief bio. Reads submissions "yearly." Time between acceptance and publication "varies; no longer than 6-8 months." Poems are circulated to an editorial board. Rarely comments on rejected poems. No payment. Acquires one-time electronic rights.

LA PETITE ZINE

E-mail: lapetitezine@gmail.com. **Website:** www.lapetitezine.org. **Contact:** Melissa Broder and D.W. Lichtenberg, editors. Member: CLMP. *La Petite Zine*, an online literary magazine founded in 1999, which currently publishes fierce poetry and petite prose pieces of 1000 words or less. LPZ is not affiliated with a particular literary school or movement; we like what we like. Above all else, LPZ seeks to be un-boring, a panacea for your emotional hangover. Has published work by Anne Boyer, Arielle Greenberg, Johannes Goransson, Joyelle McSweeney, Joshua Marie Wilkinson, and Jonah Winter. Receives about 3,000 poems/year, accepts about 150 (5%). Sample: free online; there is no subscription, but readers are invited to sign up for e-mail notification of new issues at the submission address. *La Petite Zine*'s home page "indexes all authors for each specific issue and offers links to past issues, as well as information about the journal, its interests and editors, and links to other sites. Art and graphics are supplied by Web del Sol. Additionally, we publish graphic poems, excerpts from graphic novels, and the like." Acquires one-time rights. Publishes ms 6 months after acceptance. Responds in 2 weeks to 6 months.

Work published in *La Petite Zine* has appeared in *The Best American Poetry*. "Any deviation from our guidelines will result in the disposal of your submission."

MAGAZINE NEEDS Submit up to 5 poems at a time ("please adhere to this guideline"). Considers simultaneous submissions, "but please notify us immediately if poems are accepted elsewhere"; no previously published poems. Only accepts submissions using submission manager on website. Cover letter is required. Include brief bio listing previous publications. Wait four months before submitting again. Reads year round.

LEADING EDGE

E-mail: editor@leadingedgemagazine.com. **Website:** www.leadingedgemagazine.com. Twice yearly magazine. "We strive to encourage developing and established talent and provide high quality speculative fiction to our readers." Does not accept mss with sex, excessive violence, or profanity. "*Leading Edge* is a magazine dedicated to new and upcoming talent in the field of science fiction and fantasy." Has published work by Orson Scott Card, Brandon Sanderson, and Dave Wolverton. Has published poetry by Michael Collings, Tracy Ray, Susan Spilecki, and Bob Cook. Buys first North American serial rights. Pays on publication. Publishes ms an average of 2-4 months after acceptance. Responds in 2-4 months to mss. Sample copy for $5.95. Guidelines available online at website.

Accepts unsolicited submissions.

MAGAZINE NEEDS Single copy: $5.95; subscription: $10 (2 issues), $20 (4 issues), $27.50 (6 issues). "Publishes 2-4 poems per issue. Poetry should reflect both literary value and popular appeal and should deal with science fiction- or fantasy-related themes." Submit 1 or more poems at a time. No e-mail submissions. Cover letter is preferred. Include name, address, phone number, length of poem, title, and type of poem at the top of each page. Please include SASE with every submission." Pays $10 for first 4 pages; $1.50/each subsequent page.

TIPS "Buy a sample issue to know what is currently selling in our magazine. Also, make sure to follow the writer's guidelines when submitting."

THE LEDGE MAGAZINE

40 Maple Ave., Bellport NY 11713-2011. (631)286-5252. **E-mail:** info@theledgemagazine.com. **Website:** www.theledgemagazine.com. **Contact:** Tim Monaghan, Editor-in-Chief. *The Ledge* is 300 pages, 6×9, typeset, perfect-bound, with glossy cover. Accepts 3% of poetry received. Press run is 1,000. Single copy: $10; subscription: $20 for 2 issues, $36 for 4 issues, $48 for 6 issues. "The Ledge Magazine publishes cutting-edge contemporary fiction by emerging and established writers." Annual. Receives 120 mss/month. Accepts 9 mss/issue. Manuscript published 6 months after acceptance. Published Pia Chatterjee, Xujun Eberlein, Clifford Garstang, Richard Jespers, William Luvaas, Michael Thompson. Also publishes poetry. Rarely comments on/critiques rejected mss. Send complete ms with cover letter. Include estimated word count, brief bio. Send SASE (or IRC) for return of ms. Sample copy available for $10. Subscription: $20 (2 issues), $36 (4 issues). Guidelines available for SASE. Writers receive 1 contributor's copy. Additional copies $6. Sends galleys to author. Publication is copyrighted.

Acquires first North American serial rights Pays on publication. Responds to queries in 6 weeks; responds to mss in 8 months

MAGAZINE NEEDS *The Ledge* seeks "passionate poems that utilize language and imagery in a fresh, original fashion. We favor visceral poems that speak to the human experience. We want inspired, imaginative, well-crafted verse and we are open to all styles and schools of writing, including formal poems. Each issue of *The Ledge* features a diverse and eclectic group of poets from all backgrounds and persuasions. Excellence is the ultimate criterion." Has published poetry by Philip Dacey, Moira Egan, Tony Gloeggler, Melody Lacina, Rick Lott, and Jennifer Perrine. Pays 1 contributor's copy; $6 each additional copy. Acquires one-time rights.

HOW TO CONTACT Submit 3-5 poems at a time. Considers simultaneous submissions; no previously published poems. Include SASE. Reads submissions October-March. Responds in 4-6 months.

TIPS "We seek compelling stories that employ innovative language and complex characterization. We especially enjoy poignant stories with a sense of purpose. We dislike careless or hackneyed writing."

◐ LEFT CURVE

P.O. Box 472, Oakland CA 94604-0472. (510)763-7193. **E-mail:** editor@leftcurve.org. **Website:** www.leftcurve.org. **Contact:** Csaba Polony, editor.

MAGAZINE NEEDS *Left Curve*, published "irregularly, about every 10 months," addresses the "problem(s) of cultural forms, emerging from the crisis of modernity, that strives to be independent from the control of dominant institutions, and free from the shackles of instrumental rationality." Wants poetry that is "critical culture, social, political, 'post-modern.' We will look at any form of poetry, from experimental to traditional." Does not want "purely formal, too self-centered, poetry that doesn't address in sufficient depth today's problems." Has published poetry by John Berger, Vincent Ferrini, Devorah Major, Jack Hirschman, and Lawrence Ferllinghetti. *Left Curve* is 144 pages, magazine-sized, offset-printed, perfect-bound, with 4-color Durosheen cover, includes ads. Press run is 2,000 (250 subscribers, 100 libraries, 1,600 shelf sales). Subscription: $35/3 issues (individuals) , $50/3 issues (institutions). Sample: $12.

HOW TO CONTACT Submit up to 5 poems at a time. Lines/poem: "most of our published poetry is 1 page in length, though we have published longer poems of up to 8 pages." Accepts e-mail or disk submissions. Cover letter is required. "Explain why you are submitting." Publishes theme issues. Guidelines available for SASE, by e-mail, or on website. Responds in up to 6 months. Pays 2-3 contributor's copies. Send materials for review consideration.

TIPS "We look for continuity, adequate descriptive passages, endings that are not simply abandoned (in both meanings). Dig deep; no superficial personalisms, no corny satire. Be honest, realistic and gouge out the truth you wish to say. Understand yourself and the world. Have writing be a means to achieve or realize what is real."

LILITH MAGAZINE: INDEPENDENT, JEWISH & FRANKLY FEMINIST

250 W. 57th St., Suite 2432, New York NY 10107. (212)757-0818. **Fax:** (212)757-5705. **E-mail:** info@lilith.org. **Website:** www.lilith.org. Susan Weidman Schneider, editor-in-chief. *Lilith Magazine: Independent, Jewish & Frankly Feminist*, published quarterly, is "an independent magazine with a Jewish feminist perspective" that uses poetry by Jewish women "about the Jewish woman's experience." Does not want poetry on other subjects. "Generally we use short rather than long poems." Has published poetry by Irena Klepfisz, Lyn Lifshin, Marcia Falk, Adrienne Rich, and Muriel Rukeyser. *Lilith Magazine* is 48 pages, magazine-sized, with glossy color cover. Publishes about 4 poems/year. Press run is about 10,000 (about 6,000 subscribers). Subscription: $26/year. Sample: $7.

MAGAZINE NEEDS Send up to 3 poems at a time. No simultaneous submissions or e-mail submissions. "Please put name and contact info on each sheet submitted. Copy should be neatly typed and proofread for typos and spelling errors. Short cover letters only." Sometimes comments on rejected poems. Guidelines available for SASE or on website. Responds in up to 6 months.

TIPS "Read a copy of the publication before you submit your work. Please be patient."

O LINEBREAK

333 Kimpel Hall, University of Arkansas, Fayetteville AR 72701. **E-mail:** editors@linebreak.org. **Website:** http://linebreak.org. **Contact:** Johnathon Williams, founding editor. "*Linebreak* is a weekly online magazine of original poetry. Each poem we publish is read and recorded by another working poet selected by the

editors." Has published Dorianne Laux, Bob Hicok, D.A. Powell, C. Dale Young, Richard Siken, Sandra Beasley. Publishes ms 4 months after acceptance. Responds in 6 weeks. Guidelines available on website.

Poems published on *Linebreak* have been selected for the Best New Poets anthology and nominated for the Pushcart Prize.

MAGAZINE NEEDS Submit up to 5 poems at a time through upload form on website. Considers simultaneous submissions. Reads submissions year round. Poems are circulated to an editorial board. Sometimes comments on rejected poems. Guidelines available on website. Sometimes sends prepublication galleys. Acquires electronic rights: "We require the rights to publish and archive the work indefinitely on our website, and the right to create an audio recording of each poem, which is also archived indefinitely. Copyright remains with the author."

LIPS

7002 Blvd. East, #2-26G, Guttenberg NJ 07093. (201)662-1303. **E-mail:** LBoss79270@aol.com. **Contact:** Laura Boss, poetry editor. *Lips*, published twice/year, takes pleasure "in publishing previously unpublished poets as well as the most established voices in contemporary poetry. We look for quality work: the strongest work of a poet; work that moves the reader; poems that take risks that work. We prefer clarity in the work rather than the abstract. Poems longer than 6 pages present a space problem." Has published poetry by Robert Bly, Allen Ginsberg, Michael Benedikt, Maria Gillan, Ruth Stone, Maria Mazziotti Gillan, Stanley Barkan, Lyn Lifshin, and Ishmael Reed. *Lips* is about 150 pages, digest-sized, flat-spined. Receives about 16,000 submissions/year, accepts about 1%. Submit 6 pages maximum at a time. Poems should be typed. Reads submissions September-March only. Responds in 1 month (but has gotten backlogged at times). Sometimes sends prepublication galleys. Pays 1 contributor's copy. Acquires first rights. Sample: $10 plus $2.50 for postage. Guidelines available for SASE.

THE LISTENING EYE

Kent State University Geauga Campus, 14111 Claridon-Troy Rd., Burton OH 44021. (440)286-3840. **E-mail:** grace_butcher@msn.com. **Website:** http://reocities.com/Athens/3716/eye.htm. **Contact:** Grace Butcher, editor.

HOW TO CONTACT Submit up to 4 poems at a time. Lines/poem: "prefer shorter poems (less than 2 pages), but will consider longer if space allows." Accepts previously published poems "occasionally"; no simultaneous submissions. No e-mail submissions "unless from overseas." Cover letter is required. Poems should be typed, single-spaced, 1 poem/page—name, address, phone number, and e-mail address in upper left-hand corner of each page—with SASE for return of work. Reads submissions January 1-April 15 only: max four poems/ four pages. Time between acceptance and publication is up to 6 months. Poems are circulated to the editor and 2 assistant editors who read and evaluate work separately, then meet for final decisions. Occasionally comments on rejected poems. Guidelines available in magazine or for SASE. Responds in 3 months. Pays 2 contributor's copies. Acquires first or one-time rights. Awards $30 to the best sports poem in each issue.

TIPS "We look for powerful, unusual imagery, content and plot in our short stories. In poetry, we look for tight lines that don't sound like prose; unexpected images or juxtapositions; the unusual use of language; noticeable relationships of sounds; a twist in viewpoint; an ordinary idea in extraordinary language; an amazing and complex idea simply stated; play on words and with words; an obvious love of language. Poets need to read the 'Big 3'—Cummings, Thomas, Hopkins—to see the limits to which language can be taken. Then read the 'Big 2'—Dickinson to see how simultaneously tight, terse, and universal a poem can be, and Whitman to see how sprawling, cosmic, and personal. Then read everything you can find that's being published in literary magazines today, and see how your work compares to all of the above."

LITERAL LATTE

200 E. 10th St., Suite 240, New York NY 10003. (212)260-5532. **E-mail:** litlatte@aol.com. **Website:** www.literal-latte.com. "We want any poem that captures the magic of the form." *Literal Latté*, published continually online, is a literary journal of "pure prose, poetry, and art. Open to all styles of poetry—quality is the determining factor." Has published poetry by Allen Ginsberg, Carol Muske, Amy Holman, and John Updike. Receives about 3,000 poems/year, accepts 1%. Bimonthly online publication with an annual print anthology featuring the best of the website. "We want great writing in all styles and subjects. A feast is made of a variety of flavors." Buys first rights and requests permission for use in anthology. Responds in 6

months to mss. Editorial lead time 3 months. Writer's guidelines online, via e-mail, or for #10 SASE

HOW TO CONTACT Considers simultaneous submissions; no previously published poems. No e-mail submissions; postal submissions only. Cover letter is required. Include bio and e-mail address for response only. Time between acceptance and publication is within 1 year. Often comments on rejected poems. Guidelines available by e-mail or on website. Responds in 5 months.

ADDITIONAL INFORMATION "We will publish an anthology in book form at the end of each year, featuring the best of our Web magazine."

TIPS "Keeping free thought free and challenging entertainment are not mutually exclusive. Words make a manuscript stand out, words beautifully woven together in striking and memorable patterns."

LITERARY MAMA

E-mail: lminfo@literarymama.com. **Website:** www.literarymama.com. **Contact:** Caroline M. Grant, editor-in-chief. Departments include columns, creative nonfiction, fiction, Literary Reflections, poetry, Profiles & Reviews. We are interested in reading pieces that are long, complex, ambiguous, deep, raw, irreverent, ironic, body conscious. Responds in 3 weeks to 3 months to mss. "We correspond via e-mail only." Guidelines available at www.literarymama.com/submissions.

TIPS "We seek top-notch creative writing. We also look for quality literary criticism about mother-centric literature and profiles of mother writers. We publish writing with fresh voices, superior craft, vivid imagery. Please send submission (copied into e-mail) to appropriate departmental editors. Include a brief cover letter. We tend to like stark revelation (pathos, humor, and joy), clarity, concrete details, strong narrative development; ambiguity, thoughtfulness, delicacy, irreverence, lyricism, sincerity; the elegant. We need the submissions 3 months before the following months: October (Desiring Motherhood); May (Mother's Day Month); and June (Father's Day Month)."

THE LITERARY REVIEW: AN INTERNATIONAL JOURNAL OF CONTEMPORARY WRITING

Fairleigh Dickinson University, 285 Madison Ave., Madison NJ 07940. (973)443-8564. **Fax:** (973)443-8364. **E-mail:** tlr@fdu.edu; info@theliteraryreview.org. **Website:** www.theliteraryreview.org. **Contact:** Minna Proctor, editor. *The Literary Review*, published quarterly, seeks "work by new and established poets that reflects a sensitivity to literary standards and the poetic form." No specifications as to form, length, style, subject matter, or purpose. Has published poetry by David Citino, Rick Mulkey, Virgil Suárez, Gary Fincke, and Dale M. Kushner. *The Literary Review* is about 200 pages, digest-sized, professionally printed, flat-spined, with glossy color cover. Receives about 1,200 submissions/year, accepts 100-150. Press run is 2,000 (800 subscribers, one-third are overseas). Sample: $8 domestic, $8 + $3.99 shipping outside U.S.; request a "general issue." Acquires first rights. Responds in 6-9 months.

MAGAZINE NEEDS Submit up to 5 typed poems at a time. Accepts only online submissions at www.theliteraryreview.org/submit.html. No mail, fax, or e-mail submissions. Considers simultaneous submissions. **Read-time September 1 through May 31.** Publishes theme issues. Reviews books of poetry in 500 words, single-book format. Send materials for review consideration. Pays 2 contributor's copies + 1 year free subscription.

ALSO OFFERS *TLR Online*, available on the website, features original work not published in the print edition. Has published poetry by Reneée Ashley and Catherine Kasper.

LITTLE PATUXENT REVIEW

6012 Jamina Downs, Columbia MD 21045. (443)255-5740. **E-mail:** editor@littlepatuxentreview.org. **Website:** www.littlepatuxentreview.org. **Contact:** Laura Shovan, editor. "*The Little Patuxent Review (LPR)* is a biannual print journal devoted to literature and the arts. We are acommunity-based publication with a focus on poets, writers and artists,primarily from the Mid-Atlantic region. We profile the work of a major poet orfiction writer in each issue. We celebrate the launch of each issue with a series of readings. Highlights are broadcast on *LPR*'s YouTube channel." *LPR* is about 120 pages, digest-sized, 100# Finch Cover/Artwork (varies depending on featured artist). "*The Little Patuxent Review (LPR)* is a biannual print journal devoted to literature and the arts. We are acommunity-based publication with a focus on poets, writers and artists,primarily from the Mid-Atlantic region. We profile the work of a major poet orfiction writer in each issue. We celebrate the launch of each issue with a series of readings. Highlights are broadcast on *LPR*'s YouTube channel." First rights. 1 contributor's copy. 2 months. Responds in 3-5 months. Sample copy $10 (additional $5 postage). Make checks payable to: Little Patuxent Review. Guidelines available in magazine and on website.

Has published poetry by Lucille Clifton, Martín Espada, Donald Hall, Joy Harjo, Clarinda Harriss, Alan King.

MAGAZINE NEEDS "All forms and styles of highest quality considered. Please see our website for the current theme." Poetry must exhibit the highest quality to be considered. Please read a sample issue before submitting, or visit the 'Concerning Craft' section of *Little Patuxent Review's* website." No more than 100 lines/poem

HOW TO CONTACT Submit up to 3 poems via e-mail. "Poetry and prose must be typed using a standard, legible font (i.e, the equivalent of 12-point Times New Roman) with flush-left margins and submitted as a .doc, .docx, .pdf, .rtf, or .txt electronic file. Please include a biographical note of 60-75 words in cover letter. Let us know if you now live or have lived in the Mid-Atlantic area. We prefer submissions through the Submittable website. A direct link and instructions are given at www.littlepatuxentreview.org." All unsolicited submissions cannot be previously published elsewhere. Does not accept multiple submissions. Submission period for the winter 2013 issue is August 1-November 1, 2012. Guidelines available on website. Reponds in 3-5 months.

CONTEST/AWARD OFFERINGS 2011 Pushcart Prize for "Patronized," Tara Hart.

ALSO OFFERS "*LPR* co-sponsors arts 'Salon'events in conjunction with the Columbia Art Center including literary readings, art presentations, and musical performances. Events are free and open to the public. Contributors are invited to participate in reading series and literary festivals. As part of our outreach effort, the *LPR* in the Classroom Program provides *LPR* issues to high schools and colleges at the discounted rate."

LIVING POETS MAGAZINE

Dragonheart Press, 11 Menin Rd., Allestree, Derby DE22 2NL, England. **Website:** www.dragonheart-press.com. *Living Poets Magazine*, published irregularly online, provides a showcase for poetry. Wants "crafted poetry with strong imagery." Does not want "constrained rhyming structures." Receives about 400 poems/year, accepts about 20%. Digital sample: $10 (printable from PDF). Make checks payable to S. Woodward or via PayPal.

MAGAZINE NEEDS Submit 3 poems at a time no longer than 40 lines. Considers previously published poems and simultaneous submissions. Prefers e-mail submissions. Cover letter is preferred. Include bio and publication credits. Time between acceptance and publication is 1-2 months. Often comments on rejected poems. Publishes theme issues. Guidelines available on website or for SASE, by e-mail, or on website. Responds in 3 months. Pays 1 contributor's copy. Reviews books/chapbooks of poetry or other magazines in single-book format. Send materials for review consideration to Review Editor, Dragonheart Press.

CONTEST/AWARD OFFERINGS Sponsors Dragonheart Press Annual Poetry Competition. **Deadline:** December 31. Guidelines available for SASE (or SAE and IRC) or by e-mail (competition@dragonheart-press.com).

LOS

150 N. Catalina St., No. 2, Los Angeles CA 90004. **E-mail:** lospoesy@earthlink.net. **Website:** http://home.earthlink.net/~lospoesy. *Los*, published 4 times/year, features poetry. Has published poetry by John P. Campbell, Mark Cunningham, Jean Esteve, George J. Farrah, Bill Knott, Paul Lowe, and Charles Wuest. *Los* is digest-sized and saddle-stapled. Press run is 100.

MAGAZINE NEEDS Accepts e-mail submissions (pasted into body of message or as attachment). Time between acceptance and publication is up to 1 month. Guidelines available on website. Responds in 3 months. Pays 1 contributor's copy.

LOUISIANA LITERATURE

SLU Box 10792, Southeastern Louisiana University, Hammond LA 70402. **E-mail:** lalit@selu.edu; ngerman@selu.edu. **Website:** www.louisianaliterature.org. **Contact:** Jack B. Bedell, editor. *Louisiana Literature*, published twice/year, considers "creative work from anyone, though we strive to showcase our state's talent. We appreciate poetry that shows firm control and craft; is sophisticated yet accessible to a broad readership. We don't use highly experimental work." Has published poetry by Claire Bateman, Elton Glaser, Gray Jacobik, Vivian Shipley, D.C. Berry, and Judy Longley. *Louisiana Literature* is 150 pages, 6×9, handsomely printed on heavy matte stock, flat-spined, with matte card cover. Single copy: $8 for individuals; subscription: $12 for individuals, $12.50 for institutions.

HOW TO CONTACT Submit 3-5 poems at a time. No simultaneous submissions. No fax or e-mail submissions. "Send cover letter, including bio to use in the event of acceptance. Enclose SASE and specify whether work is to be returned or discarded." Reads submissions year round, "although we work more slowly in summer." Publishes theme issues. Guidelines available for SASE or on website. Sometimes sends prepublication galleys. Pays 2 contributor's copies. Send materials for review consideration; include cover letter.

TIPS "Cut out everything that is not a functioning part of the story. Make sure your manuscript is professionally presented. Use relevant specific detail in every scene. We love detail, local color, voice and craft. Any professional manuscript stands out."

● THE LOUISIANA REVIEW

Division of Liberal Arts, Louisiana State University at Eunice, P.O. Box 1129, Eunice LA 70535. (337)550-1315. **E-mail:** bfonteno@lsue.edu. **Website:** web.lsue.edu/la-review. Dr. Michael Alleman, poetry editor. **Contact:** Dr. Billy Fontenot, editor. *The Louisiana Review*, published annually during the fall or spring semester, offers "Louisiana poets, writers, and artists a place to showcase their most beautiful pieces. Others may submit Louisiana- or Southern-related poetry, stories, and b&w art, as well as interviews with Louisiana writers. We want to publish the highest-quality poetry, fiction, and art." Wants "strong imagery, metaphor, and evidence of craft." Does not want "sing-song rhymes, abstract, religious, or overly sentimental work." Has published poetry by Gary Snyder, Antler, David Cope, and Catfish McDaris. *The Louisiana Review* is 100-200 pages, digest-sized, professionally printed, perfect-bound. Receives up to 2,000 poems/year, accepts 40-50. Press run is 300-600. Single copy: $5.

HOW TO CONTACT Submit up to 5 poems at a time. No previously published poems. No fax or e-mail submissions. "Include cover letter indicating your association with Louisiana, if any. Name and address should appear on each page." Reads submissions year round. Time between acceptance and publication is up to 2 years. Pays one contributor's copy. Poets retain all rights.

TIPS "We do like to have fiction play out visually as a film would rather than static and undramatized. Louisiana or Gulf Coast settings and themes preferred."

◐ THE LOUISVILLE REVIEW

Spalding University, 851 S. Fourth St., Louisville KY 40203. (502)585-9911, ext. 2777. **Fax:** (502)992-2409. **E-mail:** louisvillereview@spalding.edu. **Website:** www.louisvillereview.org. **Contact:** Kathleen Driskell, associate editor. *The Louisville Review*, published twice/year, prints all kinds of poetry. Has a section devoted to children's poetry (grades K-12) called The Children's Corner. Considers poetry by children and teens. Has published poetry by Wendy Bishop, Gary Fincke, Michael Burkard, and Sandra Kohler. *The Louisville Review* is 150 pages, digest-sized, flat-spined. Receives about 700 submissions/year, accepts about 10%. Single copy: $8; subscription: $14/year, $27/2 years, $40/3 years (foreign subscribers add $6/year for s&h). Sample: $5.

MAGAZINE NEEDS Considers simultaneous submissions; no previously published poems. Accepts submissions via online manager; please see website for more information. "Poetry by children must include permission of parent to publish if accepted. Address those submissions to The Children's Corner." Reads submissions year round. Time between acceptance and publication is up to 4 months. Submissions are read by 3 readers. Guidelines available on website. Responds in 4-6 months. Pays in contributor's copies.

LULLWATER REVIEW

Emory University, P.O. Box 122036, Atlanta GA 30322. **Fax:** (404)727-7367. **E-mail:** lullwater@lullwaterreview.com. **E-mail:** emorylullwaterreview@gmail.com. **Contact:** Rachel Wisotsky, co-editor-in-chief. "We're a small, student-run literary magazine published out of Emory University in Atlanta, GA with two issues yearly—once in the fall and once in the spring. You can find us in the *Index of American Periodical Verse*, the *American Humanities Index* and as a member of the Council of Literary Magazines and Presses. We welcome work that brings a fresh perspective, whether through language or the visual arts." Buys first North American serial rights. Pays on publication. Publishes ms an average of 1-2 months after acceptance. Responds in 1-3 months to queries; 3-6 months to mss. Sample copy for $5. Guidelines with #10 SASE.

MAGAZINE NEEDS *Lullwater Review*, published in May and December, prints poetry, short fiction, and artwork. Wants poetry of any genre with strong imagery, original voice, on any subject. Has published poetry by Amy Greenfield, Peter Serchuk, Katherine McCord, and Ha Jin. Submit 6 or fewer poems at a time. Considers simultaneous submissions; no previously published poems. Cover letter is preferred. Prefers poems single-spaced with name and contact info on each page. "Poems longer than 1 page should include page numbers. We must have a SASE with which to reply." Reads submissions September 1-May 15 only. Poems are circulated to an editorial board. Seldom comments on rejected poems. No profanity or pornographic material. Pays 3 contributor copies.

TIPS "We at the *Lullwater Review* look for clear cogent writing, strong character development and an engaging approach to the story in our fiction submissions. Stories with particularly strong voices and well-developed central themes are especially encouraged. Be sure that your manuscript is ready before mailing it off to us. Revise, revise, revise! Be original, honest, and of course, keep trying."

THE LUTHERAN DIGEST

The Lutheran Digest, Inc., 6160 Carmen Ave. E, Inver Grove Heights MN 55076. (952)933-2820. **Fax:** (952)933-5708. **E-mail:** editor@lutherandigest.com. **Website:** www.lutherandigest.com. David Tank, editor. **Contact:** Nicholas A. Skapyak, editor. "Articles frequently reflect a Lutheran Christian perspective, but are not intended to be sermonettes. Popular stories show how God has intervened in a person's life to help solve a problem." Buys first rights, buys second serial (reprint) rights. Pays on acceptance. Publishes ms an average of 6 months after acceptance. Responds in 1 month to queries. Responds in 4 months to mss. No response to e-mailed mss unless selected for publication. Editorial lead time 9 months. Sample copy for $3.50. Guidelines available online.

The Lutheran Digest is 64 pages, digest-sized, offset-printed, saddle-stapled, with 4-color paper cover, includes local ads. Receives about 200 poems/year, accepts 10-20%. Press run is 60,000-65,000; most distributed free to Lutheran churches. Subscription: $16/year, $22/2 years.

MAGAZINE NEEDS Submit 3 poems at a time. Lines/poem: 25 maximum. Considers previously published poems and simultaneous submissions. Accepts fax and e-mail (as attachment) submissions. Cover letter is preferred. "Include SASE if return is desired." Time between acceptance and publication is up to 9 months. "Poems are selected by editor and reviewed by publication panel." Guidelines available for SASE or on website. Responds in 3 months. Pays credit and 1 contributor's copy. Acquires one-time rights.

TIPS "Reading our writers' guidelines and sample articles online is encouraged and is the best way to get a 'feel' of the type of material we publish."

THE LYRIC

P.O. Box 110, Jericho Corners VT 05465. **E-mail:** themuse@thelyricmagazine.com. **Website:** www.thelyricmagazine.com. *The Lyric*, published quarterly, is "the oldest magazine in North America in continuous publication devoted to traditional poetry." Prints about 55 poems/issue. Wants "rhymed verse in traditional forms, for the most part, with an occasional piece of blank or free verse; no translations, please. Most of our poems are accessible on first or second reading. Frost wrote: 'Don't hide too far away.'" Sample for $5, available in Europe through the Rom office for 18 euros/year sent to Nancy Mellichamp-Savo, via Lola Montez, #14, Rome, Italy 00135; sample: 5 euros.

Has published poetry by Michael Burch, Gail White, Constance Rowell Mastores, Ruth Harrison, Barbara Loots, and Glenna Holloway. *The Lyric* is 32 pages, digest-sized, professionally printed with varied typography, with matte card cover. Receives about 3,000 submissions/year, accepts 5%. Subscription: $15/year, $28/2 years, $38/3 years (US), $17/year for Canada and other countries (in US funds only).

MAGAZINE NEEDS Submit up to 6 poems at a time by postal service; out of country poems may be submitted by e-mail. Lines/poem: 40 maximum. Considers simultaneous submissions (although "not preferred"); no previously published poems. Cover letter is "often helpful, but not required. Subscription will not affect publication of submitted poetry." Guidelines available for SASE or by e-mail. Responds in 3 months ("average; inquire after 6 months"). Pays 1 contributor's copy. "Our themes are varied, ranging from religious ecstasy to humor to raw grief, but we feel no compulsion to shock, embitter, or confound our readers. We also avoid poems about contemporary political or social problems—'grief but not grievances,' as Frost put it. Frost is helpful in other ways: If yours is more than a lover's quarrel with life, we are not your best market. And most of our poems are accessible on first or second reading."

TIPS All contributors are eligible for quarterly and annual prizes totaling $650. Also offers *The Lyric* College Contest, open to undergraduate students in the US. Awards prize of $500; 2nd Place: $100. **Deadline:** December 15. Send entries by e-mail: tanycim@aol.com, or to Tanya Cimonetti, 1393 Spear St., S, Burlington, VT 05403."Our *raison d'etre* has been the encouragement of form, music, rhyme, and accessibility in poetry. As we witness the growing tide of appreciation for traditional/lyric poetry, we are proud to have stayed the course for 91 years, helping keep the roots of poetry alive."

LYRICAL PASSION POETRY E-ZINE

P.O. Box 17331, Arlington TX 22216. **Website:** http://lyricalpassionpoetry.yolasite.com. **Contact:** Raquel D. Bailey, founding editor. Founded by award-winning poet Raquel D. Bailey, Lyrical Passion Poetry E-Zine is an attractive monthly online literary magazine specializing in Japanese short form poetry. Publishes quality artwork, well-crafted short fiction and poetry in English by emerging and established writers. Literature of lasting literary value will be considered. Welcomes the traditional to the experimental. Poetry works written in German will be considered if accompanied by translations. Offers annual short fiction and poetry contests. Acquire first-time rights, electronic rights: must be the first literary venue to publish online or in any electronic format. Rights revert to poets upon publication. Publishes ms 1 month after acceptance. Responds in 2 months. Guidelines and upcoming themes available on website.

MAGAZINE NEEDS Multiple submissions are permitted but no more than 3 submissions in a 6 month period. Submissions from minors should be accompanied by a cover letter from parent with written consent for their child's submission to be published on the website with their child's first initial & last name accompanied by their age at the time of submission. Does not want: dark, cliché, limerick, erotica, extremely explicit, violent or depressing literature. Free verse poetry length: between 1 and 40/lines.

THE MACGUFFIN

18600 Haggerty Rd., Livonia MI 48152-2696. (734)462-4400, ext 5327. **E-mail:** macguffin@schoolcraft.edu. **Website:** www.macguffin.org. **Contact:** Steven A. Dolgin, editor; Nicholle Cormier, managing editor; Elizabeth Kircos, fiction editor. "Our purpose is to encourage, support and enhance the literary arts in the Schoolcraft College community, the region, the state, and the nation. We also sponsor annual literary events and give voice to deserving new writers as well as established writers." First rights. Once published, rights revert back to author. Responds in 2-4 months to mss. Guidelines available.

MAGAZINE NEEDS *The MacGuffin*, published 3 times/year, prints "the best poetry, fiction, nonfiction, and artwork we receive. We have no thematic or stylistic biases. We look for well-crafted poetry." Does not want "pornography, triteness, and sloppy poetry. We do not publish haiku, concrete, or light verse." Has published poetry by Thomas Lynch, Gabriel Welsch, Linda Nemec Foster, Conrad Hilberry, and Laurence Lieberman. *The MacGuffin* is 160 pages, 6×9, perfect-bound, with color cover. Press run is 500. Subscription: $22/year. Sample: $6/copy. Poetry should be typed, single-spaced, only one poem per page. There are no subject biases.

HOW TO CONTACT Submit no more than 5 poems at a time. Lines/poem: 400 maximum. Considers simultaneous submissions if informed; no previously published poems. Accepts fax, e-mail (as Word attachment only), and hard copy submissions via mail (SASE for reply only). Cover letter is required. "List titles and brief bio in cover letter. Do not staple work." Poems should be typed, single-spaced, 1 per page. Poet's name, address, and e-mail should appear on each page. Include SASE. Guidelines available for SASE, by fax, e-mail, or on website. Responds in 2-6 months. Pays 2 contributor's copies plus discount on additional copies. Acquires first rights if published; rights revert to poets upon publication.

CONTEST/AWARD OFFERINGS "Also sponsors the National Poet Hunt Contest. See contest rules online. For mail submissions: do not staple work. Include name, email, address, and the page no. on each page. Include SASE for reply only. Submit each work (single story or five-poem submission) as a Word .doc attachment."

TIPS "We strive to give promising new writers the opportunity to publish alongside recognized writers.

Follow the submission guidelines, proofread your work, and be persistent. When we reject a story, we may accept the next one you send. When we make suggestions for a rewrite, we may accept the revision. Make your characters come to life. Even the most ordinary people become fascinating if they live for your readers."

THE MADISON REVIEW

University of Wisconsin, 600 N, Park St., 6193 Helen C. White Hall, Madison WI 53706. **E-mail:** madisonreview@gmail.com. **Website:** wwww.english.wisc.edu/madisonreview/madisonReviewHome.htm. **Contact:** Joe Malone and Anna Wehrwein, fiction editors; Joyce Edwards and Alex Konrad, poetry editors. *The Madison Review* is a student-run literary magazine that looks to publish the best available fiction and poetry. Buys one-time rights. Publishes ms an average of 9 months after acceptance. Responds in 4 weeks to queries. Responds in 6 months to mss. Editorial lead time 6 months. Sample copy for $3. Guidelines free.

"We do not publish unsolicited interviews or genre ficion."

MAGAZINE NEEDS Submit up to 5 poems at a time. No simultaneous submissions. No e-mail submissions. Cover letter is preferred. Include SASE. Submissions must be typed. Does not want "religious or patriotic dogma and light verse." Pays 2 contributor's copies.

TIPS "Our editors have very ecclectic tastes, so don't specifically try to cater to us. Above all, we look for original, high quality work."

THE MAGAZINE OF FANTASY & SCIENCE FICTION

P.O. Box 3447, Hoboken NJ 07030. (201) 876-2551. **E-mail:** fandsf@aol.com. **Website:** www.fandsf.com. **Contact:** Gordon Van Gelder, editor. *The Magazine of Fantasy & Science Fiction* is 240 pages, digest-sized, offset-printed, perfect-bound, with glossy cover, includes ads. Receives about 20-40 poems/year, accepts about 1%. Press run is 35,000 (20,000 subscribers). Single copy: $7; subscription: $34.97. Sample: $6. Make checks payable to *The Magazine of Fantasy & Science Fiction*. "*The Magazine of Fantasy and Science Fiction* publishes various types of science fiction and fantasy short stories and novellas, making up about 80% of each issue. The balance of each issue is devoted to articles about science fiction, a science column, book and film reviews, cartoons, and competitions." Bimonthly." Buys first North American serial rights, buys foreign serial rights. Pays on acceptance. Publishes ms an average of 9-12 months after acceptance. Responds in 2 months to queries. Sample copy for $6. Guidelines for SASE, by e-mail or website.

The *Magazine of Fantasy and Science Fiction* won a Nebula Award for Best Novelet for "The Merchant and the Alchemist's Gate" by Ted Chiang in in 2008. Also won the 2007 World Fantasy Award for Best Short Story for "Journey into the Kingdom" by M. Rickert. Editor Van Gelder won the Hugo Award for Best Editor (short form), 2007 and 2008.

MAGAZINE NEEDS *The Magazine of Fantasy & Science Fiction*, published bimonthy, is "one of the longest-running magazines devoted to the literature of the fantastic." Wants only poetry that deals with the fantastic or the science-fictional. Has published poetry by Rebecca Kavaler, Elizabeth Bear, Sophie M. White, and Robert Frazier. "I buy poems very infrequently—just when one hits me right." Seldom comments on rejected poems. Guidelines available for SASE or on website. Responds in up to 1 month. Always sends prepublication galleys. Pays $50/poem and 2 contributor's copies. Acquires first North American serial rights.

HOW TO CONTACT Submit 1-3 poems at a time. No previously published poems or simultaneous submissions. No e-mail or disk submissions. Time between acceptance and publication is up to 2 years, but usually about 9 months.

TIPS "Good storytelling makes a submission stand out. Regarding manuscripts, a well-prepared manuscript (i.e., one that follows the traditional format, like that describted here: http://www.sfwa.org/writing/vonda/vonda.htm) stands out more than any gimmicks. Read an issue of the magazine before submitting. New writers should keep their submissions under 15,000 words—we rarely publish novellas by new writers."

THE MAGAZINE OF SPECULATIVE POETRY

P.O. Box 564, Beloit WI 53512. **Website:** www.sff.net/people/roger-dutcher/#mspgdln. **Contact:** Roger Dutcher, editor. *The Magazine of Speculative Poetry*, published biannually, features "the best new speculative poetry. We are especially interested in narrative form, but open to any form, any length (within reason); interested in a variety of styles. We're looking for the best of the new poetry utilizing the ideas, imagery, and approaches developed by speculative fiction, and will welcome experimental techniques as well as the fresh employment of traditional forms." Has published poetry by Joanne Merriam, Jeannine Hall Gailey, Ann K. Schwader, and Kendall Evans. *The Magazine of Speculative Poetry* is 24-28 pages, digest-sized, offset-printed, saddle-stapled, with matte card cover. Receives about 500 poems/year, accepts less than 5%. Press run is 150-200. Subscription: $19 for 4 issues. Sample: $5.

MAGAZINE NEEDS Submit 3-5 poems at a time. Lines/poem: "Some poems run 2 or 3 pages, but rarely anything longer. We're a small magazine, we can't print epics." No previously published poems or simultaneous submissions. "We like cover letters, but they aren't necessary. We like to see where you heard of us; the names of the poems submitted; a statement if the poetry manuscript is disposable; a big enough SASE; and if you've been published, some recent places." Poems should be double-spaced. Comments on rejected poems "on occasion." Guidelines available for SASE. Responds in up to 2 months. Pays 3¢/word ($7 minimum, $25 maximum) and 1 contributor's copy. Acquires first North American serial rights. "All rights revert to author upon publication, except for permission to reprint in any 'Best of' or compilation volume. Payment will be made for such publication." Reviews books of speculative poetry. Query regarding unsolicited reviews, interviews, and articles. Send materials for review consideration.

MAGMA POETRY

23 Pine Walk, Carshalton Surrey SM5 4ES, United Kingdom. **E-mail:** contributions@magmapoetry.com. **Website:** www.magmapoetry.com. info@magmapoetry.com for general questions. *Magma* appears 3 times/year and contains "modern poetry, reviews and interviews with poets." Wants poetry that is "modern in idiom and shortish (2 pages maximum). Nothing sentimental or old fashioned." Has published poetry by Thomas Lynch, Thom Gunn, Michael Donaghy, John Burnside, Vicki Feaver, and Roddy Lumsden. *Magma* is 64 pages, 8×8, photocopied and stapled, includes b&w illustrations. Receives about 3,000 poems/year, accepts 4-5%. Press run is about 500. Single copy: £5.70 UK and Ireland, £6.15 rest of Europe, £7.50 airmail ROW. Subscription: £14.50 UK and Ireland, £18 rest of Europe, £20.50 airmail ROW. Make checks payable to *Magma*. For subscriptions, contact Helen Nicholson, distribution secretary, Flat 2, 86 St. James's Dr., London SW17 7RR England.

"Triannual website covering the best in contemporary poetry and writing about poetry. We look for poems which give a direct sense ofwhat it is to live today—honest about feelings, alert about the world, sometimes funny, always well crafted. We showcase a poet in each issue. A rotating editorship results in different emphasis. Many poems are from poets living abroad, including Ireland, USA, Canada, Australasia. Please submit in the body of an email rather than as an attachment or with our online form." Enter contest for the Troubadour International Poetry Prize. See website for details.

MAGAZINE NEEDS Submit up to 6 poems at a time. Accepts simultaneous submissions. Accepts submissions by post (with SAE and IRCs) and by e-mail (preferably pasted into body of message; if attachment, only 1 file). Cover letter is preferred. Deadlines for submissions: end of February, mid-July, end of October. "Poems are considered for one issue only." Time between acceptance and publication is maximum 3 months. "Each issue has an editor who submits his/her selections to a board for final approval. Editor's selection very rarely changed." Occasionally publishes theme issues. Responds "as soon as a decision is made." Always sends prepublication galleys. Pays 1 contributor's copy.

ALSO OFFERS "We hold a public reading in London three times/year, to coincide with each new issue, and poets in the issue are invited to read."

TIPS "See 'About Magma' and the contents of our website to gain an idea of the type of work we accept." Keep up with the latest news and comment from *Magma Poetry* by receiving free updates via email. Sign up online to receive the Magma Blog and/or the *Magma* newsletter.

THE MAGNOLIA QUARTERLY

P.O. Box 10294, Gulfport MS 39506. **E-mail:** writerpllevin@gmail.com. **Website:** www.gcwriters.org. **Contact:** Phil Levin, editor. *The Magnolia Quarterly* publishes poetry, fiction, nonfiction, and reviews. **Membership required to submit to magazine** (exception: each issue features a non-member poet chosen by the poetry editor). Will consider all styles of poetry. Does not want "pornography, racial or sexist bigotry, far-left or far-right political poems." Has published poetry by Leonard Cirino, Catharine Savage Brosman, Angela Ball, Jack Bedell, and Larry Johnson. *The Magnolia Quarterly* is 40 pages, pocket-sized, stapled, with glossy cover, includes ads. Single copy: $5; subscription: included in $30 GCWA annual dues. Make checks payable to Gulf Coast Writers Assocation. Editing service offered on all prose.

MAGAZINE NEEDS Submit 1-5 poems at a time. Lines/poem: open. Considers previously published poems and simultaneous submissions. Prefers e-mail submissions. Cover letter is preferred. Reads submissions year round. Time between acceptance and publication varies. Guidelines available in magazine, for SASE, by e-mail, or on website. No payment. Returns rights to poet upon publication.

CONTEST/AWARD OFFERINGS "Let's Write" contest, with cash prizes for poetry and prose. Additional information available on website.

ALSO OFFERS The Gulf Coast Writers Association, "a nationally recognized organization dedicated to encouraging all writers."

◐ THE MAIN STREET RAG

P.O. Box 690100, Charlotte NC 28227-7001. (704)573-2516. **E-mail:** editor@mainstreetrag.com. **Website:** www.MainStreetRag.com. **Contact:** M. Scott Douglass, editor/publisher. *Main Street Rag*, published quarterly, prints "poetry, short fiction, essays, interviews, reviews, photos, art. We like publishing good material from people who are interested in more than notching another publishing credit, people who support small independent publishers like ourselves." Will consider "almost anything," but prefers"writing with an edge—either gritty or bitingly humorous. Contributors are advised to visit our website prior to submission to confirm current needs." Has published poetry by Silvia Curbelo, Sean Thomas Dougherty, Denise Duhamel, Cathy Essinger, Ishle Yi Park, and Dennis Must. *Main Street Rag* is about 130 pages, digest-sized, perfect-bound, with 12-point laminated color cover. Receives about 5,000 submissions/year; publishes 50+ poems and 3-5 short stories per issue. Press run is about 500 (250 subscribers, 15 libraries). Single copy: $8; subscription: $24/year, $45 for 2 years.

HOW TO CONTACT Submit 6 pages of poetry at a time. No previously published poems or simultaneous submissions. Cover letter is preferred. "No bios or credits—let the work speak for itself." Time between acceptance and publication is up to 1 year. Guidelines available for SASE, by e-mail, or on website. Responds within 6 weeks. Pays 1 contributor's copy. Acquires first North American print rights.

✪◐ THE MALAHAT REVIEW

(250)721-8524. **E-mail:** malahat@uvic.ca (for queries only). **Website:** www.malahatreview.ca. **Contact:** John Barton, editor. "We try to achieve a balance of views and styles in each issue. We strive for a mix of the best writing by both established and new writers." Buys first world rights. Pays on acceptance. Publishes ms an average of 6 months after acceptance. Responds in 2 weeks to queries. Responds in 3-10 months to mss. Sample copy for $16.95 (US). Guidelines available online.

MAGAZINE NEEDS *The Malahat Review*, published quarterly, is "a high-quality, visually appealing literary journal that has earned the praise of notable literary figures throughout North America. Its purpose is to publish and promote poetry, and fiction, and creative nonfiction of a very high standard, both Canadian and international." Wants "various styles, lengths, and themes. The criterion is excellence." Has published poetry by Steven Heighton, George Elliot Clarke, Daryl Hine, and Jan Zwicky. Receives about 2,000 poems/year, accepts about 100. Subscription: $35 CAD for individuals, $40 USD for individuals in the US, or $20 CAD for online subscription, $64 CAD for institutions (or US equivalent). Sample: $16.95 USD. 5-10 pages Pays $20/magazine page

HOW TO CONTACT Submit 5-10 poems at a time. No previously published poems or simultaneous submissions. No e-mail submmissions; postal submissions only. Include SASE with Canadian stamps or IRC with each submission. Guidelines available for SASE (or SAE and IRC). Responds usually within 3-10 months. Pays $30 CAD per printed page, 2 contributor's copies, and 1 year's subscription. Acquires first world serial rights. Reviews Canadian books of poetry.

CONTEST/AWARD OFFERINGS Presents the P.K. Page Founders' Award for Poetry, a $1,000 prize to the author of the best poem or sequence of poems to be published in *The Malahat Review*'s quarterly issues during the previous calendar year. Also offers the Open Season Awards, biennial Long Poem Prize, and Far Horizons Award for Poetry.

TIPS "Please do not send more than 1 submission at a time: 4-8 poems, 1 piece of creative non-fiction, or 1 short story (do not mix poetry and prose in the same submission). See *The Malahat Review*'s Open Season Awards for poetry and short fiction, creative non-fiction, long poem, and novella contests in the Awards section of our website."

THE MANHATTAN REVIEW

440 Riverside Dr., #38, New York NY 10027. **Website:** http://themanhattanreview.com. *The Manhattan Review*, published annually "with ambitions to be semi-annual," prints "American writers and foreign writers with something valuable to offer the American scene. We like to think of poetry as a powerful discipline engaged with many other fields." Wants to see "ambitious work. Interested in both lyric and narrative. We select high-quality work from a number of different countries, including the U.S." Does not want "mawkish, sentimental poetry." Has published poetry by Zbigniew Herbert, D. Nurkse, Baron Wormser, Penelope Shuttle, Marilyn Hacker, and Peter Redgrove. *The Manhattan Review* is 208 pages, digest-sized, professionally printed, with glossy card cover. Receives about 400 submissions/year, accepts few ("but I do read everything submitted carefully and with an open mind"). Press run is 500 (400 subscribers, 250 libraries). Single copy: $7.50; subscription: $15. Sample: $9 and 7×10 envelope. Responds in 3 months, if possible.

MAGAZINE NEEDS Submit 3-5 pages of poetry at a time. Simultaneous submissions "discouraged; notification required." Cover letter is required. Include short bio and publication credits. Sometimes comments on poems, "but don't count on it." Staff reviews books of poetry. Send materials for review consideration. Pays contributor's copies.

MANOA

(808)956-3070. **Fax:** (808)956-3083. **E-mail:** mjournal-l@listserv.hawaii.edu. **Website:** manoajournal.hawaii.edu. **Contact:** Frank Stewart, Poetry Editor. "High quality literary fiction, poetry, essays, personal narrative. In general, each issue is devoted to new work from Pacific and Asian nations. Our audience is international. US writing need not be confined to Pacific settings or subjects. Please note that we seldom publish unsolicited work." Buys first North American serial rights, buys non-exclusive, one-time print rights. Pays on publication. Responds in 3 weeks to queries; 1 month to poetry mss; 6 months to fiction. Editorial lead time 9 months. Sample copy for $15 (US). Guidelines available online.

Manoa has received numerous awards, and work published in the magazine has been selected for prize anthologies. *Manoa* has received numerous awards, and work published in the magazine has been selected for prize anthologies. See website for recently published issues.

MAGAZINE NEEDS *Manoa*, published twice/year, is a general interest literary magazine that considers work "in many forms and styles, regardless of the author's publishing history. However, we are not for the beginning writer. It is best to look at a sample copy of the journal before submitting." Has published poetry by Arthur Sze, Ai, Linda Gregg, Jane Hirshfield, and Ha Jin. *Manoa* is 240 pages, 7×10, offset-printed, flat-spined. Receives about 1,000 poems/year, accepts 1%. Press run is more than 2,500 (several hundred subscribers, 130 libraries, 400 shelf sales). "In addition, *Manoa* is available through Project Muse to about 900 institutional subscribers throughout the world." Subscription: $22/year. Sample: $10. No light verse. Pays $25/poem

TIPS "Not accepting unsolicited manuscripts at this time because of commitments to special projects. See website for more information."

THE MARLBORO REVIEW

The Marlboro Review Inc., P.O. Box 243, Marlboro VT 05344-0243. (802)254-4938. **E-mail:** editor@marlbororeview.com. **Website:** www.marlbororeview.com. **Contact:** Ellen Dudley, editor. Open to short fiction and poetry submissions. Include SASE with proper postage, otherwise your work will be discarded unread. Submissions received during the summer break will be returned unread. "Our only criterion for publication is strength of work." Semiannual. Estab. 1996. Circ. 1,000. Length: No line limits known. Check with publisher. Recent contributors include Stephen Dobyns, Joan Aleshire, Jean Valentine, Robert Hill Long, Carol Frost. Pays on publication. 1 year Responds in 3 months to queries; 4 months to mss. Works published in *The Marlboro Review* have received Pushcart prizes. Guidelines available online.

TIPS "Check Guidelines for details and restrictions. Open to most themes. We are particularly interested in translation, as well as cultural, scientific, and philosophical issues approached from a writer's sensibility. If you are overseas and must submit electronically, consult with Ellen Dudley before sending any files."

THE MASSACHUSETTS REVIEW

South College, University of Massachusetts, Amherst MA 01003-9934. (413)545-2689. **Fax:** (413)577-0740. **E-mail:** massrev@external.umass.edu. **Website:** www.massreview.org. Buys first North American serial rights. Pays on publication. Publishes ms an average of 18 months after acceptance. Responds in 3 months to mss. Sample copy for $8. Guidelines available online.

Does not respond to mss without SASE.

MAGAZINE NEEDS *The Massachusetts Review*, published quarterly, prints "fiction, essays, artwork, and excellent poetry of all forms and styles." Has published poetry by Catherine Barnett, Billy Collins, and Dara Wier. *The Massachusetts Review* is digest-sized, offset-printed on bond paper, perfect-bound, with color card cover. Receives about 2,500 poems/year, accepts about 25. Press run is 1,600 (1,100-1,200 subscribers, 1,000 libraries, the rest for shelf sales). Subscription: $27/year U.S., $35 outside U.S., $37 for libraries. Sample: $9 U.S., $12 outside U.S. Pays 50¢/line to $25 maximum

HOW TO CONTACT No previously published poems or simultaneous submissions. Reads submissions October 1-May 31 only. "Guidelines are available online at our website, as is our new online submission manager." Responds in 2 months. Pays $25 plus 2 contributor's copies.

TIPS "No manuscripts are considered May-September. Electronic submission process on website. No fax or e-mail submissions. No simultaneous submissions. Shorter rather than longer stories preferred (up to 28-30 pages)." Looks for works that "stop us in our tracks." Manuscripts that stand out use "unexpected language, idiosyncrasy of outlook and are the opposite of ordinary."

MATURE YEARS

(615)749-6292. **Fax:** (615)749-6512. **E-mail:** matureyears@umpublishing.org. Buys first North American serial rights. Pays on acceptance. Publishes ms an average of 1 year after acceptance. Responds in 2 weeks to queries. Responds in 2 months to mss. Sample copy for $6 and 9×12 SAE. Writer's guidelines for #10 SASE or by e-mail.

MAGAZINE NEEDS *Mature Years*, published quarterly, aims to "help persons understand and use the resources of Christian faith in dealing with specific opportunities and problems related to aging. Poems may or may not be overtly religious. Poems should not poke fun at older adults, but may take a humorous look at them." Does not want "sentimentality and saccharine. If using rhymes and meter, make sure they are accurate." *Mature Years* is 112 pages, magazine-sized, perfect-bound, with full-color glossy paper cover. Press run is 55,000. Sample: $6. Length: 3-16 lines. Pays $5-20

HOW TO CONTACT Lines/poem: 16 lines of up to 50 characters maximum. Accepts fax and e-mail submissions (e-mail preferred). Submit seasonal and nature poems for spring from December through February; for summer, March through May; for fall, June through August; and for winter, September through November. Pays $1/line upon acceptance.

TIPS "Practice writing dialogue! Listen to people talk; take notes; master dialogue writing! Not easy, but well worth it! Most inquiry letters are far too long. If you can't sell me an idea in a brief paragraph, you're not going to sell the reader on reading your finished article or story."

MEASURE: A REVIEW OF FORMAL POETRY

Department of English, The University of Evansville, 1800 Lincoln Ave., Evansville IN 47722. (812)488-2963. **E-mail:** measure@evansville.edu. **Website:** http://measure.evansville.edu. *Measure: A Review of Formal Poetry* is "dedicated to publishing the best metrical, English-language verse from both the United States and abroad. In each issue we strive to bring you the best new poetry from both established and emerging writers, and we also reprint a small sampling of poems from the best books of metrical poetry published the previous year. Likewise, each issue includes interviews with some of our most important contemporary poets and offers short critical essays on the poetry that has helped to shape the craft." Wants "English-language metrical poetry with no particular stanza preference. See our website or a back issue for examples. *Measure* also reprints poems from books; send copy for consideration." Does not want "fixed forms written in free verse; syllabics; quantitative." Has published poetry by Timothy Steele, R.S. Gwynn, Philip Dacey, X.J. Kennedy, Rachel Hadas, and Charles Rafferty. *Measure* is 180 pages, digest-sized, perfect-bound, with glossy cover with color artwork. Receives about 1,500 poems/year, accepts about 10%. Press run is 1,000. Single copy: $10; subscription: $18 for one year, $34 for 2 years, $50 for 3 years. Make checks payable to *Measure*. Responds in 3 months.

MAGAZINE NEEDS Submit 3-5 poems at a time at submissions website: measurepress.com. Lines/poem: no minimum or maximum. No previously published poems or simultaneous submissions. No e-mail or disk submissions. Cover letter is preferred. "All submissions should be typed. Each poem should include the poet's name and phone number. A self-addressed stamped envelope must accompany the submission." Reads submissions year round. Time between acceptance and publication "depends." Never comments on rejected poems. Guidelines available in magazine, for SASE, or on website. Pays 2 contributor's copies.

THE MENNONITE

722 Main St., Newton KS 67114-1819. (866)866-2872 ext. 34398. **Fax:** (316)283-0454. **E-mail:** gordonh@themennonite.org. **Website:** www.themennonite.org. **Contact:** Gordon Houser, associate editor. *The Mennonite*, published monthly, seeks "Christian poetry—usually free verse, not too long, with multiple layers of meaning." Does not want "sing-song rhymes or poems that merely describe or try to teach a lesson." Has published poetry by Jean Janzen and Julia Kasdorf. *The Mennonite* is 56 pages, magazine-sized, with full-color cover, includes ads. Receives about 200 poems/year, accepts about 5%. Press run is 9,500 (9,000 subscribers). Single copy: $3; subscription: $46 US. Acquires first or one-time rights. Publishes ms up to 1 year after acceptance. Responds in 2 weeks. Guidelines for SASE.

MAGAZINE NEEDS Submit up to 4 poems at a time. Considers previously published poems and simultaneous submissions. Accepts e-mail submissions (preferred). Cover letter is preferred. Occasionally publishes theme issues. Pays 1 contibutor copy.

MERIDIAN

University of Virginia, P.O. Box 400145, Charlottesville VA 22904-4145. (434)982-5798. **Fax:** (434)924-1478. **E-mail:** MeridianUVA@gmail.com; meridianpoetry@gmail.com; meridianfiction@gmail.com. **Website:** www.readmeridian.org. *Meridian*, published semiannually, prints poetry, fiction, nonfiction, interviews, and reviews. Pays 2 contributor's copies (additional copies available at discount). Time between acceptance and publication is 1-2 months. Seldom comments on rejected poems and mss. Responds in 1-4 months. Always sends prepublication galleys and author contracts. Guidelines available on website.

Has published poetry by Joelle Biele, David Kirby, Larissa Szporluk, and Charles Wright. *Meridian* is 190 pages, digest-sized, offset-printed, perfect-bound, with color cover. Receives about 2,500 poems/year, accepts about 30 (less than 1%). Press run is 1,000 (750 subscribers, 15 libraries, 200 shelf sales); 150 distributed free to writing programs. Single copy: $7; subscription: $12/year. Make checks payable to *Meridian*. Work published in *Meridian* has appeared in *The Best American Poetry* and *The Pushcart Prize*.

MAGAZINE NEEDS Submit up to 4 poems at a time. Considers simultaneous submissions (with notification of acceptance elsewhere); no previously published poems. No e-mail or disk submissions; accepts postal and online submissions (**$2 upload fee for up to 4 poems**; no fee for postal submissions). Cover letter is preferred. Reads submissions September-May primarily (do not send submissions April 15-August 15; accepts online submissions year round). Reviews books of poetry.

CONTEST/AWARD OFFERINGS *Meridian* Editors' Prize Contest offers annual $1,000 award. Submit online only; see website for formatting details. **Entry fee:** $8, includes 1-year subscription to *Meridian* for all US entries or 1 copy of the prize issue for all international entries. **Deadline:** December or January; see website for current deadline.

MICHIGAN QUARTERLY REVIEW

0576 Rackham Bldg., 915 E. Washington, University of Michigan, Ann Arbor MI 48109-1070. (734)764-9265. **E-mail:** mqr@umich.edu. **Website:** www.umich.edu/~mqr. **Contact:** Jonathan Freedman, editor; Vicki Lawrence, managing editor. "MQR is an eclectic interdisciplinary journal of arts and culture that seeks to combine the best of poetry, fiction, and creative nonfiction with outstanding critical essays on literary, cultural, social, and political matters. The flagship journal of the University of Michigan, MQR draws on lively minds here and elsewhere, seeking to present accessible work of all varieties for sophisticated readers from within and without the academy." Buys first serial rights. Pays on publication. Publishes ms an average of 1 year after acceptance. Responds in 2 months to queries. Responds in 2 months to mss. Sample copy for $4. Guidelines available online.

"The Laurence Goldstein Award is a $1,000 annual award to the best poem published in the *Michigan Quarterly Review* during the previous year. The Lawrence Foundation Award is a $1,000 annual award to the best short story published in the *Michigan Quarterly Review* during the previous year."

MAGAZINE NEEDS *Michigan Quarterly Review* is "an interdisciplinary, general interest academic journal that publishes mainly essays and reviews on subjects of cultural and literary interest." Wants all kinds of poetry except light verse. No specifications as to form, length, style, subject matter, or purpose. Has published poetry by Susan Hahn, Campbell McGrath, Carl Phillips, and Cathy Song. *Michigan Quarterly Review* is 160 pages, digest-sized, professionally printed, flat-spined, with glossy card cover. Receives about 1,400 submissions/year, accepts about 30. Press run is 2,000 (1,200 subscribers, half are libraries). Single copy: $7; subscription: $25. Sample: $4. Pays $10/published page

HOW TO CONTACT No previously published poems or simultaneous submissions. No e-mail submissions. Cover letter is preferred. "It puts a human face on the manuscript. A few sentences of biography is all I want, nothing lengthy or defensive." Prefers typed mss. Publishes theme issues. Upcoming themes available in magazine and on website. Guidelines available for SASE or on website. Responds in 6 weeks. Always sends prepublication galleys. Pays $8-12/page. Acquires first rights only. Reviews books of poetry. "All reviews are commissioned."

CONTEST/AWARD OFFERINGS The Laurence Goldstein Poetry Award, an annual cash prize of $1,000, is given to the author of the best poem to appear in *Michigan Quarterly* during the calendar year. "Established in 2002, the prize is sponsored by the Office of the President of the University of Michigan."

TIPS "Read the journal and assess the range of contents and the level of writing. We have no guidelines to offer or set expectations; every manuscript is judged on its unique qualities. On essays—query with a very thorough description of the argument and a copy of the first page. Watch for announcements of special issues which are usually expanded issues and draw upon a lot of freelance writing. Be aware that this is a university quarterly that publishes a limited amount of fiction and poetry and that it is directed at an educated audience, one that has done a great deal of reading in all types of literature."

MID-AMERICAN REVIEW

Bowling Green State University, Department of English, Box W, Bowling Green OH 43403. (419)372-2725. **E-mail:** mikeczy@bgsu.edu. **Website:** www.bgsu.edu/midamericanreview. **Contact:** Michael Czyzniejewski. "We try to put the best possible work in front of the biggest possible audience. We publish serious fiction and poetry, as well as critical studies in contemporary literature, translations and book reviews." Buys first North American serial rights, buys one-time rights. Pays on publication when funding is available. Publishes ms an average of 6 months after acceptance. Responds in 5 months to mss. Sample copy for $7 (current issue); $5 (back issue); $10 (rare back issues). Guidelines available online.

MAGAZINE NEEDS "Poems should emanate from textured, evocative images, use language with an awareness of how words sound and mean, and have a definite sense of voice. Each line should help carry the poem, and an individual vision must be evident. We encourage new as well as established writers. There is no length limit on individual poems, but please send no more than six poems." Pays $10/page up to $50, pending funding.

HOW TO CONTACT Submit by mail with SASE or through online submissions form at website.

TIPS "We are seeking translations of contemporary authors from all languages into English; submissions must include the original and proof of permission to translate. We would also like to see more creative nonfiction."

THE MIDWEST QUARTERLY

(620)235-4369; (620)235-4317. **E-mail:** midwestq@pittstate.edu; smeats@pittstate.edu. **Website:** www.pittstate.edu/department/english/midwest-quarterly. **Contact:** James B. M. Schick. Wants "well-crafted poems, traditional or untraditional, that use intense, vivid, concrete, and/or surrealistic images to explore the mysterious and surprising interactions of the natural and inner human worlds." Does not want "'nature poems,' per se, but if a poem doesn't engage nature in a significant way, as an integral part of the experience it is offering, I am unlikely to be interested in publishing it." Has published poetry by Peter Cooley, Lyn Lifshin, Judith Skillman,

Naomi Shihab Nye, Jonathan Holden and William Kloefkorn. *The Midwest Quarterly* is 130 pages, digest-sized, professionally printed, flat-spined, with matte cover. Press run is 650 (600 subscribers, 500 are libraries). Receives about 3,500-4,000 poems/year, accepts about 50. Subscription: $15. Sample: $5. *The Midwest Quarterly* publishes "articles on any subject of contemporary interest, particularly literary criticism, political science, philosophy, education, biography, and sociology. Each issue contains a section of poetry usually 12 poems in length. We seek discussions of an analytical and speculative nature and well-crafted poems. Poems of interest to us use intense, vivid, concrete and/or surrealistic images to explore the mysterious and surprising interactions of the nature and inner human worlds." Contest winnings. Guidelines available online.

"For publication in MQ and eligibility for the annual Emmett Memorial Prize competition, the Editors invite submission of articles on any literary topic, but preferably on Victorian or Modern British Literature, Literary Criticism, or the Teaching of Literature. The winner receives an honorarium and invitation to deliver the annual Emmett Memorial Lecture. Contact Dr. Stephen Meats, English Department, Pittsburg State University, Pittsburg, KS 66762."

HOW TO CONTACT Submit no more than 5 poems at a time. Lines/poem: 60 maximum ("occasionally longer if exceptional"). Considers simultaneous submissions; no previously published poems. No fax or e-mail submissions. "Manuscripts should be typed with poet's name on each page Include e-mail address for notification of decision. SASE only for return of poem." Comments on rejected poems "if the poet or poem seems particularly promising." Occasionally publishes theme issues or issues devoted to the work of a single poet. Guidelines available on website. Responds in 2 months. Pays 2 contributor's copies. Acquires first serial rights.

MIDWIFERY TODAY

P.O Box 2672, Eugene OR 97402-0223. (541)344-7438. **Fax:** (541)344-1422. **E-mail:** editorial@midwiferytoday.com and jan@midwiferytoday.com (editorial only); layout@midwiferytoday.com (photography). **Website:** www.midwiferytoday.com. **Contact:** Jan Tritten, editor-in-chief and publisher. Publishes ms an average of 5 months after acceptance. Responds in 2 weeks to queries. Responds in 1 month to mss. Editorial lead time 3-9 months. Sample copy and guidelines available online.

"Through networking and education, *Midwifery Today*'s mission is to return midwifery to its rightful position in the family; to make midwifery care the norm throughout the world; and to redefine midwifery as a vital partnership with women."

MAGAZINE NEEDS Accepts e-mail submissions (pasted into body of message or as attachment). Cover letter is required. Does not want poetry unrelated to pregnancy or birth. Does not want poetry that is "off subject or puts down the subject." Maximum line length: 25. Pays 2 contributor's copies. Acquires first rights.

TIPS "Use Chicago Manual of Style formatting."

MILLER'S POND

E-mail: mail@handhpress.com (C.J. Houghtaling); mpwebeditor@yahoo.com (Julie Damerell). **Website:** www. millerspondpoetry.com. **Contact:** C.J. Houghtaling, publisher; Julie Damerell, editor. *miller's pond* is exclusively an e-zine and does not publish in hard copy format. "All submissions must be sent electronically from our website. Mail sent through the post office will be returned. No payment for accepted poems or reviews. Current guidelines, updates, and changes are always available on our website. Check there first before submitting anything." E-mail submissions to mpwebeditor@yahoo.com. Web version is published three times each year. No simultaneous submissions but will use previously published poetry with credit to the original publication. Submissions accepted year round but read in December, April, and August. Response time varies from same day to 3 months.

TIPS "Follow submission guidelines on the website. Submissions that do not fulfill the guidelines are deleted without comment. Read the website to see the kind of poetry we like."

MINAS TIRITH EVENING-STAR: JOURNAL OF THE AMERICAN TOLKIEN SOCIETY

American Tolkien Society, P.O. Box 97, Highland MI 48357-0097. **E-mail:** editor@americantolkiensociety.org. **Website:** www.americantolkiensociety.org. **Contact:** Amalie A. Helms, editor. *Minas Tirith Evening-Star: Journal of the American Tolkien Society*, published quarterly, uses poetry of fantasy about

Middle-Earth and Tolkien. Considers poetry by children and teens. Has published poetry by Thomas M. Egan, Anne Etkin, Nancy Pope, and Martha Benedict. *Minas Tirith Evening-Star* is digest-sized, offset-printed from typescript, with cartoon-like b&w graphics. Press run is 400. Single copy: $3.50; subscription: $12.50. Sample: $3. Make checks payable to American Tolkien Society. Responds in 2 weeks. Guidelines for SASE or by e-mail.

MAGAZINE NEEDS Considers previously published poems ("maybe"); no simultaneous submissions. Accepts e-mail and disk submissions. Cover letter is preferred. Sometimes comments on rejected poems. Occasionally publishes theme issues. Sometimes sends prepublication galleys. Reviews related books of poetry; length depends on the volume ("a sentence to several pages"). Send materials for review consideration. Pays 1 contributor's copy.

ADDITIONAL INFORMATION Under the imprint of W.W. Publications, publishes collections of poetry of fantasy about Middle-Earth and Tolkien. Books/chapbooks are 50-100 pages. Publishes 2 chapbooks/year. For book or chapbook consideration, submit sample poems.

ALSO OFFERS Membership in the American Tolkien Society is open to all, regardless of country of residence, and entitles one to receive the quarterly journal. Dues are $12.50/year to addresses in U.S., $12.50 in Canada, and $15 elsewhere. Sometimes sponsors contests.

THE MINNESOTA REVIEW

Virginia Tech, ASPECT, 202 Major Williams Hall (0192), Blacksburg VA 24061. **E-mail:** editors@theminnesotareview.org; submissions@theminnesotareview.org. **Website:** www.theminnesotareview.org. **Contact:** Janell Watson, editor. *The Minnesota Review*, published biannually, features quality poetry, short fiction, and critical essays. Each issue is about 200 pages, digest-sized, flat-spined, with glossy card cover. Press run is 1,000 (400 subscribers). Also available online. Subscription: $30/2 years for individuals, $60/year for institutions. Sample: $15.

MAGAZINE NEEDS Submit up to 5 poems every 3 months online. Reads poetry August 1-November 1 and January 1-April 1. Pays 2 contributor's copies.

M.I.P. COMPANY

P.O. Box 27484, Minneapolis MN 55427. (763)544-5915. **Website:** www.mipco.com. **Contact:** Michael Peltsman. "The publisher of controversial Russian literature (erotic poetry)." Responds in 1 month.

Seldom comments on rejected poems.

MAGAZINE NEEDS (Specialized: Russian erotica) Considers simultaneous submissions; no previously published poems. Responds to queries in one month. Seldom comments on rejected poems.

MISSISSIPPI REVIEW

Univ. of Southern Mississippi, 118 College Dr., #5144, Hattiesburg MS 39406-0001. (601)266-4321. **Fax:** (601)266-5757. **E-mail:** elizabeth@mississippireview.com. **Website:** www.mississippireview.com. Buys first North American serial rights. Sample copy for $10.

"We do not accept unsolicited manuscripts except under the rules and guidelines of the *Mississippi Review* Prize Competition. See website for guidelines."

HOW TO CONTACT "Literary publication for those interested in contemporary literature—writers, editors who read to be in touch with current modes. We do not accept unsolicited manuscripts except under the rules and guidelines of the *Mississippi Review* Prize Competition. See website for guidelines."

THE MISSOURI REVIEW

(573)882-4474. **Fax:** (573)884-4671. **E-mail:** tmr@missourireview.com. **Website:** www.missourireview.com. Offers signed contract. Responds in 2 weeks to queries. Responds in 10 weeks to mss. Editorial lead time 6 months. Sample copy for $8.95 or online Guidelines available online.

"We publish contemporary fiction, poetry, interviews, personal essays, cartoons, special features—such as History as Literature series and Found Text series—for the literary and the general reader interested in a wide range of subjects."

MAGAZINE NEEDS *The Missouri Review*, published 3 times/year, prints poetry "features" only—6-14 pages for each of 3-5 poets/issue. "By devoting more editorial space to each poet, *The Missouri Review* provides a fuller look at the work of some of the best writers composing today." Has published poetry by Ellen Bass, Anna Meek, Timothy Liu, Bob Hicok, George Bilgere, and Camille Dungy. Subscription: $24. Sample: $8.95. Publishes 3-5 poetry features of 6-12 pages per issue. Please familiarize yourself with the magazine before submitting poetry. Pays $30/printed page.

HOW TO CONTACT Submit 6-12 poems at a time. Considers simultaneous submissions with notification; no previously published poems. No e-mail submissions; accepts postal and online submissions ($3 to download up to 20 pages of poetry at one time). Cover letter is preferred. Include SASE. Reads submissions year round. Responds in 10-12 weeks. Sometimes sends prepublication galleys. Pays $30/printed page and 3 contributor's copies. Acquires all rights. Returns rights "after publication, without charge, at the request of the authors." Staff reviews books of poetry.
ADDITIONAL INFORMATION The Tom McAfee Discovery Feature is awarded at least once/year to showcase an outstanding young poet who has not yet published a book; poets are selected from regular submissions at the discretion of the editors.
TIPS "Send your best work."

MOBIUS: THE JOURNAL OF SOCIAL CHANGE

E-mail: fmschep@charter.net. **Website:** http://mobiusmagazine.com. **Contact:** Fred Schepartz, publisher and executive editor; F.J. Bergmann, poetry and art editor. *Mobius: The Journal of Social Change*, published quarterly, prints socially and politically relevant poetry and fiction and is distributed free in Madison, WI, and to libraries and subscribers. Wants any form of poetry on themes of social change. Does not want heavy-handed, transparent didacticism. Considers poetry by teens; however, the publication is not directed at children. Has published poetry by Rob Carney, Wade German, Michael Kriesel, Simon Perchik, Wendy Vardaman. *Mobius* is published quarterly online. Receives about 700 poems/year, accepts less than 30. Acquires one-time electronic rights; rights revert to poets upon publication. Publishes ms 6 months after acceptance. "Usually responds in 3 days; query if no response within one week." Guidelines on website.
MAGAZINE NEEDS Submit 5 poems at a time. Considers previously published poems and simultaneous submissions. Accepts e-mail submissions (pasted into body of message); no fax or disk submissions. Cover letter is unnecessary. Include short bio and mailing address; postal submissions must include e-mail address or SASE. Reads submissions year round. Sometimes comments on rejected poems. Never publishes theme issues. Pays 2 contributor's copies.

THE MOCCASIN

The League of Minnesota Poets, 427 N. Gorman St., Blue Earth MN 56013. (507)526-5321. **Website:** www.mnpoets.org. *The Moccasin*, published annually in October, is the literary magazine of The League of Minnesota Poets. **Membership is required to submit work.** Wants "all forms of poetry. Prefer strong short poems." Does not want "profanity or obscenity." Considers poetry by children and teens who are student members of The League of Minnesota Poets (write grade level on poems submitted). Has published poetry by Diane Glancy, Laurel Winter, Susan Stevens Chambers, Doris Stengel, Jeanette Hinds, and Charmaine Donovan. *The Moccasin* is 40 pages, digest-sized, offset-printed, stapled, with 80 lb. linen-finish text cover with drawing and poem. Receives about 190 poems/year, accepts about 170. Press run is 200. Single copy: $5.25; subscription: free with LOMP membership.
MAGAZINE NEEDS Submit 6 or more poems at a time. Lines/poem: 24 maximum (unless poem has won a prize from the National Federation of State Poetry Societies in its annual competition). Considers previously published poems; no simultaneous submissions. No disk submissions. Cover letter is preferred. "No poems will be returned and no questions answered without a SASE." Reads submissions year round (deadline for each year's issue is mid-July). Sometimes comments on rejected poems. Guidelines available in magazine. No payment; poet receives contributor's copy as part of LOMP membership subscription. **Annual membership dues of $20.00 (Student membership dues $10.00) are payable by January 1** each year to Stash Hempeck, Membership Chair, P.O. Box 57, Hendrum, MN 56550. Acquires one-time rights.
TIPS To become a member of The League of Minnesota Poets, send $20 ($10 if high school student or younger) to Angela Foster, LOMP Treasurer, 30036 St. Croix Rd, Pine City MN 55063. Make checks payable to LOMP. You do not have to live in Minnesota to become a member of LOMP. "Membership in LOMP automatically makes you a member of the National Federation of State Poetry Societies, which makes you eligible to enter its contests at a cheaper (members') rate."

MODERN HAIKU

P.O. Box 33077, Santa Fe NM 87594-3077. **E-mail:** modernhaiku@gmail.com. **Website:** http://modernhaiku.org. "*Modern Haiku* publishes high quality material only. Haiku and related genres, articles on haiku, haiku book reviews, and translations comprise its contents. It has an international circulation; subscribers include many university, school, and public libraries." Buys first North American serial rights. Pays on acceptance. Publishes ms an average of 6 months after acceptance. Responds in 1 week to queries. Responds in 6-8 weeks to mss. Editorial lead time 4 months. Sample copy for $13 in North America, $14 in Canada, $17 in Mexico, $30 overseas. Payment possible by PayPal on the *Modern Haiku* website. Guidelines available online.

MAGAZINE NEEDS *Modern Haiku*, published 3 times/year in February, June, and October, is "the foremost international journal of English-language haiku and criticism. We are devoted to publishing only the very best haiku. We also publish articles on haiku and have the most complete review section of haiku books." Wants "haiku in English (including translations into English) that incorporate the traditional aesthetics of the haiku genre, but which may be innovative as to subject matter, mode of approach or angle of perception, and form of expression. No tanka or renku. No special consideration given to work by children and teens." Has published haiku by Roberta Beary, Billy Collins, Lawrence Ferlinghetti, Carolyn Hall, Sharon Olds, Gary Snyder, John Stevenson, George Swede, and Cor van den Heuvel. *Modern Haiku* is 140 pages (average), digest-sized, printed on heavy quality stock, with full-color cover illustrations 4-page full-color art sections. Receives about 15,000 submissions/year, accepts about 1,000. Press run is 650. Subscription: $35 ppd by regular mail in the US; sample: $15 ppd in the US. Payment possible by PayPal on the *Modern Haiku* website. Does not want "general poetry, tanka, linked verse forms." Pays $1 per haiku by postal mail only (not for e-mail).

HOW TO CONTACT Submissions: Guidelines available for SASE or on website. No previously published haiku or simultaneous submissions. Responds in 4-6weeks. No contributor's copies. Acquires first international serial rights. Postal submissions: "Send 5-15 haiku on 1 or 2 letter-sized sheets. Put name and address at the top of each sheet. Include SASE." Pays $1 per haiku. E-mail submissions: "May be attachments (recommended) or pasted in body of message. Subject line must read: MH submission. Adhere to guidelines on the website. No payment for accepted haiku." Reviews of books of haiku by staff and freelancers by invitation in 350-1,000 words, usually single-book format. Send materials for review consideration with complete ordering information.

CONTEST/AWARD OFFERINGS Sponsors the annual Robert Spiess Memorial Haiku Competition. Guidelines available for SASE or on website.

TIPS "Study the history of haiku, read books about haiku, learn the aesthetics of haiku and methods of composition. Write about your sense perceptions of the suchness of entities; avoid ego-centered interpretations. Be sure the work you send us conforms to the definitions on our website."

⊕ MOONSHOT MAGAZINE

416 Broadway, Third Floor, Brooklyn NY 11211. **E-mail:** info@moonshotmagazine.org. **Website:** http://moonshotmagazine.org. **Contact:** JD Scott, editor. "Moonshot, a magazine of the literary and fine arts, was conceived in 2009 to provide an equal opportunity space for writers and artists based solely on the merits of their work. Moonshot's mission is to eliminate the social challenges of publishing— encouraging all types of writers and artists to submit their work in the pursuit of exposing their creations to a wider range of audiences. It is our goal to utilize traditional printing techniques as well as new technologies and media arts to feature voices from all over the globe. Moonshot celebrates storytelling of all forms, embraces the dissemination of media, and champions diverse creators to construct an innovative and original literary magazine." Buys First North American serial rights, electronic rights. Pays on publication, contributor's copy. Sample copy online at website, $10.

O MUDFISH

Box Turtle Press, 184 Franklin St., New York NY 10013. (212)219-9278. **E-mail:** mudfishmag@aol.com. **Website:** www.mudfish.org. **Contact:** Jill Hoffman, editor.

MAGAZINE NEEDS *Mudfish*, published annually by Box Turtle Press, is an annual journal of poetry and art. Wants "free verse with energy, intensity, and originality of voice, mastery of style, the presence of passion." Has published poetry by Charles Simic, Jennifer Belle, Stephanie Dickinson, Ronald Wardall, Doug Dorph, and John Ashbery. Press run is 1,200. Single copy: $12 plus $3.50 subscription: $24 for 2 years (price includes s&h).

HOW TO CONTACT Submit 4-6 poems at a time. No previously published poems or simultaneous submissions. No e-mail submissions; postal submissions only. Responds "immediately to 3 months." Pays 1 contributor's copy.

CONTEST/AWARD OFFERINGS Sponsors the Mudfish Poetry Prize Award of $1,000. **Entry fee:** $15 for up to 3 poems, $3 for each additional poem. **Deadline:** varies. Guidelines available for SASE.

ALSO OFFERS Also publishes Mudfish Individual Poet Series #6 marbles, by Mary Du Passage.

MUDLARK: AN ELECTRONIC JOURNAL OF POETRY & POETICS

Dept. of English, University of North Florida, Jacksonville FL 32224-2645. (904)620-2273. **Fax:** (904)620-3940. **E-mail:** mudlark@unf.edu. **Website:** www.unf.edu/mudlark. **Contact:** William Slaughter, editor and publisher. *Mudlark: An Electronic Journal of Poetry & Poetics*, published online "irregularly, but frequently," offers 3 formats: issues of *Mudlark* "are the electronic equivalent of print chapbooks; posters are the electronic equivalent of print broadsides; and flash poems are poems that have news in them, poems that feel like current events. The poem is the thing at *Mudlark*, and the essay about it. As our full name suggests, we will consider accomplished work that locates itself anywhere on the spectrum of contemporary practice. We want poems, of course, but we want essays, too, that make us read poems (and write them?) differently somehow. Although we are not innocent, we do imagine ourselves capable of surprise. The work of hobbyists is not for *Mudlark*." Has published poetry by Sherman Alexie, Denise Duhamel, T. R. Hummer, Kurt Brown, Susan Kelly-DeWitt, and Michael Hettich. *Mudlark* is archived and permanently on view at www.unf.edu/mudlark. Submit any number of poems at a time. "Prefers not to receive multiple submissions but will consider them if informed of the fact, up front, and if notified immediately when poems are accepted elsewhere. Considers previously published work only as part of a Mudlark issue, the electronic equivalent of a print chapbook, and only if the previous publication is acknowledged in a note that covers the submission. Only poems that have not been previously published will be considered for Mudlark posters, the electronic equivalent of print broadsides, or for Mudlark flashes." Accepts e-mail or USPS submissions with SASE; no fax submissions. Cover letter is optional. Seldom comments on rejected poems. Always sends prepublication galleys "in the form of inviting the author to proof the work on a private website that *Mudlark* maintains for that purpose." Acquires one-time rights. No payment; however, "one of the things we can do at *Mudlark* to 'pay' our authors for their work is point to it here and there. We can tell our readers how to find it, how to subscribe to it, and how to buy it—if it is for sale. Toward that end, we maintain A-Notes on the authors we publish. We call attention to their work." Publishes ms no more than 3 months after acceptance. Responds in "1 day to 1 month, depending.." Guidelines for SASE, by e-mail or on website.

MYTHIC DELIRIUM

3514 Signal Hill Ave. NW, Roanoke VA 24017-5148. **E-mail:** mythicdelirium@gmail.com. **Website:** www.mythicdelirium.com. **Contact:** Mike Allen, editor. *Mythic Delirium*, published biannually, is "a journal of speculative poetry for the new millennium. All forms considered. Must fit within the genres we consider, though we have published some mainstream verse." Does not want "forced rhyme, corny humor, jarringly gross sexual material, gratuitous obscenity, handwritten manuscripts." Has published poetry by Sonya Taaffe, Theodora Goss, Joe Haldeman, Ursula K. Le Guin, Ian Watson, and Jane Yolen. *Mythic Delirium* is 32 pages, digest-sized, saddle-stapled, with color cover art, includes house ads. Receives about 750 poems/year, accepts about 5%. Press run is 150. Subscription: $9/year, $16/2 years. Sample: $5. Make checks payable to Mike Allen. Member: Science Fiction Poetry Association, Science Fiction & Fantasy Writers of America. Publishes ms 2 months after acceptance. Responds in 5 weeks.

MAGAZINE NEEDS Submit up to 6 poems at a time. No previously published poems or simultaneous submissions. Prefers electronic submissions; no disk submissions. Cover letter is preferred. Often comments on rejected poems. Guidelines available for SASE, by e-mail, or on website. Acquires first North American serial rights. **"Reading periods: March 1-May 1 for the Summer/Fall issue and August 1-October 1 for the Winter/Spring issue. Closed to submissions all other times."** Pays $5/poem, plus 1 contributor's copy.

TIPS "*Mythic Delirium* isn't easy to get into, but we publish newcomers in every issue. Show us how ambitious you can be, and don't give up."

NASSAU REVIEW

Nassau Community College, State University of New York, English Dept. Y9, 1 Education Dr., Garden City NY 11530-6793. (516)572-7792. **E-mail:** christina.rau@ncc.edu. **Contact:** Christina Rau, editor. "The Nassau Review, published annually, welcomes submissions of many genres, preferring work that is innovative, captivating, well-crafted, and unique, work that crosses boundaries of genres and tradition. New and seasoned writers are both welcome. All work must be in English. Simultaneous submission accepted. No children's lit, fan fiction, or previously published work (online included). Full guidelines will be available at www.ncc.edu. Email submissions in the body of the email only with the subject line indicating genre and your full name. No attachments. No hard copies. Nassau Review is about 190 pages, digest-sized, flat-spined. Press run is 1,100. Sample: free. Submit 3-5 poems with 50 lines max each or 1 prose piece with 3,000 words max. Reading period: September 1—February 1. Responds in up to 4 months. Pays 2 contributor's copies. Sponsors an annual aitjprs awards contest with two $250 awards. Check the website for announcements."

TIPS "We look for narrative drive, perceptive characterization and professional competence. Write concretely. Does not want over-elaborate details, and avoid digressions."

THE NATION

33 Irving Place, 8th Floor, New York NY 10003. **Website:** www.thenation.com. Steven Brower, art director. **Contact:** Jordan Davis, poetry editor. 33 Irving Place, 8th Floor, New York, NY 10003. **Website:** www.thenation.com. **Contact:** Jordan Davis, poetry editor. *The Nation*, published weekly, is a journal of left/liberal opinion, with arts coverage that includes poetry. The only requirement for poetry is "excellence." Has published poetry by W.S. Merwin, Maxine Kumin, James Merrill, May Swenson, Edward Hirsch, and Charles Simic. Submit up to 3 poems at a time, no more than 8 poems within the calendar year. No simultaneous submissions. No fax, e-mail, or disk submissions; send by first-class mail only. No reply without SASE.

Poetry published by *The Nation* has been included in *The Best American Poetry*.

HOW TO CONTACT *The Nation* welcomes unsolicited poetry submissions. You may send up to three poems at a time, and no more than eight poems during a calendar year. Send poems by first-class mail, accompanied by a SASE. Does not reply to or return poems sent by fax or e-mail or submitted without an SASE. Submissions are not accepted from June 1 to September 15. Manuscripts may be mailed to: Jordan Davis, poetry editor.

THE NATIONAL POETRY REVIEW

E-mail: editor@nationalpoetryreview.com; nationalpoetryreview@yahoo.com. **Website:** www.nationalpoetryreview.com. **Contact:** C.J. Sage, editor. *The National Poetry Review* seeks "distinction, innovation, and *joie de vivre.* We agree with Frost about delight and wisdom. We believe in rich sound. We believe in the beautiful—even if that beauty is not in the situation of the poem but simply the sounds of the poem, the images, or (and, ideally) the way the poem stays in the reader's mind long after it's been read." *TNPR* considers both experimental and 'mainstream' work." Does not want "overly self-centered or confessional poetry." Acquires first rights. Pays 1 contributor's copy "and small honorarium if funds are available." Time between acceptance and publication is no more than 1 year. "The editor makes all publishing decisions." Sometimes comments on rejected poems. Usually responds in about 1-12 weeks. Guidelines available in magazine or on website.

Has published poetry by Bob Hicok, Jennifer Michael Hecht, Larissa Szplorluk, Margot Schilpp, Nance Van Winkel, and Ted Kooser. *The National Poetry Review* is 80 pages, perfect-bound, with full-color cover. Accepts less than 1% of submissions received. Single copy: $15; subscription: $15/year. Make checks payable to *TNPR* only. Poetry appearing in *The National Poetry Review* has also appeared in *The Pushcart Prize.*

MAGAZINE NEEDS Submit 3-5 poems at a time. Considers simultaneous submissions "with notification only. Submissions are accepted through e-mail only. Submit only between December 1 and February 28 unless you are a subscriber or benefactor. Put your name in the subject line of your e-mail and send to tnprsubmissions@yahoo.com." Bio is required. Subscribers and benefactors may submit any time during the year ("please write 'subscriber' or 'benefactor' in the subject line"). See website before submitting.

NATURAL BRIDGE

Dept. of English, University of Missouri-St. Louis, One University Blvd., St. Louis MO 63121. (314)516-7327. **E-mail:** natural@umsl.edu. **Website:** www.umsl.edu/~natural. *Natural Bridge*, published biannually, seeks "fresh, innovative poetry, both free and formal, on any subject. We want poems that work on first and subsequent readings—poems that entertain and resonate and challenge our readers. *Natural Bridge* also publishes fiction, essays, and translations." Has published poetry by Ross Gay, Beckian Fritz Goldberg, Joy Harjo, Bob Hicok, Sandra Kohler, and Timothy Liu. *Natural Bridge* is 150-200 pages, digest-sized, printed on 60 lb. opaque recycled, acid-free paper, true binding, with 12 pt. coated glossy or matte cover. Receives about 1,200 poems/year, accepts about 1%. Press run is 1,000 (200 subscribers, 50 libraries). Single copy: $10; subscription: $15/year, $25/2 years. Make checks payable to *Natural Bridge*. Member: CLMP.

MAGAZINE NEEDS Submit 4-6 poems at a time. Lines/poem: no limit. Considers simultaneous submissions; no previously published poems. No e-mail or disk submissions. "Submissions should be typewritten, with name and address on each page. Do not staple manuscripts. Send SASE." Reads submissions July 1-August 31 and November 1-December 31. Time between acceptance and publication is 9 months. "Work is read and selected by the guest-editor and editor, along with editorial assistants made up of graduate students in our MFA program. We publish work by both established and new writers." Sometimes comments on rejected poems. Sometimes publishes theme issues. Upcoming themes available on website. Guidelines available in magazine or on website. Responds in 6 months after the close of the submission period. Sometimes sends prepublication galleys. Pays 2 contributor's copies plus one-year subscription. Rights revert to author upon publication.

TIPS "We look for fresh stories, extremely well written, on any subject. We publish mainstream literary fiction. We want stories that work on first and subsequent readings—stories, in other words, that both entertain and resonate. Study the journal. Read all of the fiction in it, especially in fiction-heavy issues like numbers 4 and 11."

NAUGATUCK RIVER REVIEW

P.O. Box 368, Westfield MA 01085. **E-mail:** naugatuckriver@aol.com. **Website:** http://naugatuckriverreview.wordpress.com/. **Contact:** Lori Desrosiers, publisher. The *Naugatuck River Review*, published semiannually, "is a literary journal for great narrative poetry looking for narrative poetry of high caliber, where the narrative is compressed with a strong emotional core." Acquires first North American serial rights. Pays 1 contributor's copy. Time between acceptance and publication is 2-3 months. "We have 6 poetry editors on staff and submissions are blind-read." Never comments on rejected poems. Responds in 2-12 weeks. Always sends prepublication galleys. Guidelines available in magazine and on website.

Considers poetry by teens. Has published poetry by Leslea Newman, Patricia Smith, Lyn Lifshin, Jeff Friedman, Pam Uschuk, Patricia Fargnoli. *Naugatuck River Review* is approximately 100 pages, digest-sized, perfect-bound with paper and artwork cover. Receives about 2,000 poems/year; accepts about 170. Press run is print-on-demand. Single copy: $15; Subscription (starting with next issue): $20/year. Make checks payable to *Naugatuck River Review*.

MAGAZINE NEEDS Submit 3 poems at a time. Lines/poem: 50. Prefers unpublished poems but will consider simultaneous submissions. Accepts online submissions through submission manager only; no fax or disk. Include a brief bio and mailing information. Reads submissions January 1-March 1 and July 1-September 1 for contest.

NECROLOGY SHORTS: TALES OF MACABRE AND HORROR

Isis International, P.O. Box 510232, St. Louis MO 63151. **E-mail:** editor@necrologyshorts.com; submit@necrologyshorts.com. **Website:** www.necrologyshorts.com. **Contact:** John Ferguson, editor. Consumer publication published online daily and through Amazon Kindle. Also offers an annual collection. "*Necrology Shorts* is an online publication which publishes fiction, articles, cartoons, artwork, and poetry daily. Embracing the Internet, e-book readers, and new technology, we aim to go beyond the long time standard of a regular publication to bringing our readers a daily flow of entertainment. We will also be publishing an annual collection for each year in print, e-book reader, and Adobe PDF format. Our main genre is suspense horror similar to H.P. Lovecraft and/or Robert E. Howard. We also publish science fiction and fantasy. We would love to see work continuing the Cthulhu Mythos, but we accept all horror. We also hold contests, judged by our readers, to select the top stories and artwork. Winners of contests receive various prizes, including cash." Acquires one-time rights, anthology rights. Does not currently pay for submissions Acceptance to publication is 1 month. Responds in 1 month to ms. Editorial lead time is 1 month. Sample copy online. Guidelines found on website.

MAGAZINE NEEDS *Necrology Shorts*, published online daily and through Amazon Kindle, is seeking avante-garde, free verse, haiku, light-verse, and traditional poetry in the genres of horror, fantasy, and science fiction. "We will also be publishing an annual collection for each year in print, e-book reader, and Adobe PDF format. Our main genre is suspense horror similar to H.P. Lovecraft and/or Robert E. Howard. We also publish science fiction and fantasy. We would love to see work continuing the Cthulhu Mythos, but we accept all horror." Buys 500 poems/year.

HOW TO CONTACT Submit up to 5 poems at one time. Length: 4-100 lines.

TIPS "*Necrology Shorts* is looking to break out of the traditional publication types to use the Internet, e-book readers, and other technology. We not only publish works of authors and artists, we let them use their published works to brand themselves and further their profits of their hard work. We love to see traditional short fiction and artwork, but we also look forward to those that go beyond that to create multimedia works. The best way to get to us is to let your creative side run wild and not send us the typical fare. Don't forget that we publish horror, sci-fi, and fantasy. We expect deranged, warped, twisted, strange, sadistic, and things that question sanity and reality."

NERVE COWBOY

Liquid Paper Press, P.O. Box 4973, Austin TX 78765. **Website:** www.jwhagins.com/nervecowboy.html. **Contact:** Joseph Shields or Jerry Hagins. *Nerve Cowboy*, published biannually, features contemporary poetry, short fiction, and b&w drawings. Editors will also consider color artwork for the front cover of an issue. "Open to all forms, styles, and subject matter, preferring writing that speaks directly and minimizes literary devices." Wants "poetry of experience and passion which can find that raw nerve and ride it. We are always looking for that rare writer who inherently knows what word comes next." Has published poetry by Mather Schneider, Suzanne Allen, Micki Myers, Charles Harper Webb, Karl Koweski, and David J. Thompson. *Nerve Cowboy* is 64 pages, 7x8, attractively printed, saddle-stapled, with color artwork cover. Accepts about 5% of submissions received. Press run is 400. Subscription: $22 for 4 issues. Sample: $6. "*Nerve Cowboy* publishes adventurous, comical, disturbing, thought-provoking, accessible poetry and fiction. We like to see work sensitive enough to make the hardest hard-ass cry, funny enough to make the most hopeless brooder laugh and disturbing enough to make us all glad we're not the author of the piece." Buys one-time rights. Publishes ms an average of 6-12 months after acceptance. Responds in 3 weeks to queries. Responds in 3 months to mss. Sample copy for $6. Guidelines available online.

HOW TO CONTACT Submit 3-7 poems at a time. No e-mail submissions. Considers previously published poems with notification; no simultaneous submissions. Cover letter is preferred. Include bio and credits. Put name and mailing address on each page of ms. Seldom comments on rejected poems. Guidelines available for SASE or on website. Responds within 3 months. Pays 1 contributor's copy. Acquires first or one-time rights.

TIPS "We look for writing which is very direct and elicits a visceral reaction in the reader. Read magazines you submit to in order to get a feel for what the editors are looking for. Write simply and from the gut."

NEW ENGLAND REVIEW

Middlebury College, Middlebury VT 05753. (802)443-5075. **E-mail:** nereview@middlebury.edu. **Website:** go.middlebury.edu/nereview; www.nereview.com. Literary only. Reads September 1-May 31 (postmarked dates). Buys first North American serial rights, buys first rights, buys second serial (reprint) rights. Pays on publication. Publishes ms an average of 6 months after acceptance. Responds in 2 weeks to queries. Responds in 3 months to mss. Sample copy for $10 (add $5 for overseas). Guidelines available online.

No e-mail submissions.

MAGAZINE NEEDS *New England Review*, published quarterly, is a prestigious, nationally distributed literary journal. Has published poetry by Carl Phillips, Lucia Perillo, Linda Gregerson, and Natasha Trethewey. *New England Review* is 200+ pages, 7×10, printed on heavy stock, flat-spined, with glossy cover with art. Receives 3,000-4,000 poetry submissions/year, accepts about 70-80 poems/year. Subscription: $30. Sample: $10. Overseas shipping fees add $25 for subscription, $12 for Canada; international shipping $5 for single issues. Pays $10/page ($20 minimum), and 2 copies

HOW TO CONTACT Submit up to 6 poems at a time. No previously published poems or simultaneous submissions. Accepts submissions by postal mail only; accepts questions by e-mail. "Cover letters are useful." Address submissions to "Poetry Editor." Reads submissions postmarked September 1-May 31 only. Time between acceptance and publication is 3-6 months. Responds in up to 3 months. Always sends prepublication galleys. Pays $10/page ($20 minimum) plus 2 contributor's copies. Send materials for review consideration.

TIPS "We consider short fiction, including short-shorts, novellas, and self-contained extracts from novels in both traditional and experimental forms. In nonfiction, we consider a variety of general and literary, but not narrowly scholarly essays; we also publish long and short poems; screenplays; graphics; translations; critical reassessments; statements by artists working in various media; testimonies; and letters from abroad. We are committed to exploration of all forms of contemporary cultural expression in the US and abroad. With few exceptions, we print only work not published previously elsewhere."

THE NEW LAUREL REVIEW

828 Lesseps St., New Orleans LA 70117. **Fax:** (504)948-3834. **Website:** www.nathanielturner.com/newlaurelreview.htm. **Contact:** Lewis Schmidt, managing editor. *The New Laurel Review*, published annually, is "an independent nonprofit literary magazine dedicated to fine art. The magazine is meant to be eclectic, and we try to publish the best we receive, whether the submission is poem, translation, short story, essay, review, or interview. We have no domineering preferences regarding style, and we do consult with invited readers and writers for their opinions. We are seeking original work without hackneyed phrases, indulgent voices, or tired thinking. We love surprises and to see a writer or artist enliven our too often dull, editorial worlds." Has published poetry by Gerald Locklin, Roland John (British), Joyce Odam, Ryan G. Van Cleave, Robert Cooperman, and Jared Carter. *The New Laurel Review* is about 115-130 pages, 6×9, laser-printed, perfect-bound, with original art on laminated cover. Receives 400-600 submissions/year, accepts about 30-40 poems. Press run is about 500. Single copy: $12 for individuals, $14 for institutions. Sample (back issue): $5.

MAGAZINE NEEDS Submit 3-5 poems at a time. No simultaneous submissions. "Poems should be typed; no handwritten submissions will be read. Name and address should appear on each poem submitted. Include a brief biography of three or four typed lines, including previous publications. Do not send cover letters, which may or may not distract from the submission. Be sure to include SASE; manuscripts will not be returned otherwise. If you are submitting from outside the U.S., provide International Reply Coupons. Because we are totally independent from various funding agencies, we sometimes take an inordinate time to reply." Reads submissions September 1-May 30 only. Time between acceptance and publication "can be as long as a year from acceptance." Pays one contributor's copy. Acquires first rights, but will gladly grant permission for the writer to reprint.

TIPS "READ, READ, READ. And it is wise to obtain a copy of any magazine to which you plan to submit work. Also, you might remember that you cannot be cummings, Eliot, Faulkner, or Hemingway. One of the most disheartening aspects of editing is to receive a submission of poems with low caps, no punctuation, or words sprawled all over the page, under the pretense that the work is original and not pseudo-cummings or Yawping Whitman. Find your own voice and techniques."

NEW LETTERS

University of Missouri-Kansas City, 5101 Rockhill Rd., Kansas City MO 64110. (816)235-1168. **Fax:** (816)235-2611. **E-mail:** newletters@umkc.edu. **Website:** www.newletters.org. Buys first North American serial rights. Pays on publication. Publishes ms an average of 6 months after acceptance. Responds in 1 month to queries; 5 months to mss. Editorial lead time 6 months. Sample copy for $10 or sample articles on website. Guidelines available online.

Submissions are not read between May 1 and October 1.

MAGAZINE NEEDS No light verse. Open. Pays $10-25.

TIPS "We aren't interested in essays that are footnoted, or essays usually described as scholarly or critical. Our preference is for creative nonfiction or personal essays. We prefer shorter stories and essays to longer ones (an average length is 3,500-4,000 words). We have no rigid preferences as to subject, style, or genre, although commercial efforts tend to put us off. Even so, our only fixed requirement is on good writing."

NEW MEXICO POETRY REVIEW

44 Via Punto Nuevo, Santa Fe NM 87508. **E-mail:** nmpr@live.com. **Website:** http://newmexicopoetryreview.com. **Contact:** Kathleen Johnson, editor. *New Mexico Poetry Review*, published semiannually in April and October, is dedicated to publishing strong, imaginative, well-crafted poems by both new talents and established writers. Wants "poems, prose poems, poetry-related essays, and interviews." Does not want "dull or pretentious writing." *New Mexico Poetry Review* is 80-120 pages, digest-sized, professionally printed, perfect-bound, with a full-color glossy card with art, includes ads. Press run is 500. Single copy: $12; subscription: $22/year. Make checks payable to New Mexico Poetry Review. Submit up to 5 poems at a time of no more than 70 lines. Accepts e-mail submissions pasted into body of e-mail message; no fax or disk submissions. Cover letter is not required. Reads submissions year round. Sometimes comments on rejected poems. Sometimes publishes theme issues. Sometimes sends prepublication galleys. Pays 1 contributor's copy. Reviews books and chapbooks of poetry by New Mexico poets in 500-700 words, single and multi-book format. Publishes occasional books and chapbooks, but does not accept unsolicited book/chapbook submissions. Acquires first North American serial rights. Publishes ms 4-6 months after acceptance. Responds in 1-3 months. Guidelines available for SASE, by e-mail, or on website.

ADDITIONAL INFORMATION Publishes occasional books and chapbooks, but does not accept unsolicited book/chapbook submissions.

NEW MILLENNIUM WRITINGS

New Messenger Writing and Publishing, P.O. Box 2463, Knoxville TN 37901. (865)428-0389. **E-mail:** donwilliams7@charter.net. **Website:** http://newmillenniumwritings.com. **Contact:** Don Williams, editor. "While we only accept general submissions January-March, we hold 4 contests twice each year for all types of fiction, nonfiction, short-short fiction, and poetry." Publishes mss 6 months to 1 year after acceptance. Rarely comments on/critiques rejected mss.

Annual anthology. 6×9, 204 pages, 50 lb. white paper, glossy 4-color cover. Contains illustrations. Includes photographs. "Superior writing is the sole criterion." Received Golden Presscard Award from Sigma Delta Chi (1997).

MAGAZINE NEEDS Accepts mss through biannual *New Millennium Writing* Awards for Fiction, Poetry, and Nonfiction; also accepts general submissions January-March.

TIPS "Looks for originality, accessibility, musicality of language, psychological insight, mythic resonance. E-mail for list of writing tips or send SASE. No charge."

NEW OHIO REVIEW

English Department, 360 Ellis Hall, Ohio University, Athens OH 45701. (740)597-1360. **E-mail:** noreditors@ohio.edu. **Website:** www.ohiou.edu/nor. **Contact:** Jill Allyn Rosser, editor. *NOR*, published biannually in spring and fall, publishes fiction, nonfiction, and poetry. Wants "literary submissions in any genre. Translations are welcome if permission has been granted." Billy Collins, Stephen Dunn, Stuart Dybek, Eleanor Wilner, Yusef Komunyakaa, Kim Addonizio, William Olson. Single: $9; Subscription: $16. Member: CLMP. Guidelines available online.

MAGAZINE NEEDS Submit up to 6 poems at a time. "Do not submit more than once every six months. "Considers simultaneous submissions. "Notify immediately if work is accepted elsewhere. "Accepts mail only. Include SASE or IRC, or provide a valid e-mail address (international submissions only). Primary reading period is September through May, but will accept submissions from subscriber e-mail address (international submissions only).

NEW ORLEANS REVIEW

Box 195, Loyola University, New Orleans LA 70118. (504)865-2295. **E-mail:** noreview@loyno.edu. **Website:** http://neworleansreview.org. **Contact:** Christopher Chambers, editor; Amberly Fox, managing editor. Biannual magazine publishing poetry, fiction, translations, photographs, and nonfiction on literature, art and film. Readership: those interested in contemporary literature and culture. New Orleans Review is a journal of contemporary literature and culture, publishing new poetry, fiction, nonfiction, art, photography, film and book reviews. The journal was founded in 1968 and has since published an eclectic variety of work by established and emerging writers including Walker Percy, Pablo Neruda, Ellen Gilchrist, Nelson Algren, Hunter S. Thompson, John Kennedy Toole, Richard Brautigan, Barry Spacks, James Sallis, Jack Gilbert, Paul Hoover, Rodney Jones, Annie Dillard, Everette Maddox, Julio Cortazar, Gordon Lish, Robert Walser, Mark Halliday, Jack Butler, Robert Olen Butler, Michael Harper, Angela Ball, Joyce Carol Oates, Diane Wakoski, Dermot Bolger, Roddy Doyle, William Kotzwinkle, Alain Robbe-Grillet, Arnost Lustig, Raymond Queneau, Yusef Komunyakaa, Michael Martone, Tess Gallagher, Matthea Harvey, D. A. Powell, Rikki Ducornet, and Ed Skoog. Buys first North American serial rights. Pays on publication. Responds in 4 months to mss. Sample copy for $5.

TIPS "We're looking for dynamic writing that demonstrates attention to the language, and a sense of the medium, writing that engages, surprises, moves us. We're not looking for genre fiction, or academic articles. We subscribe to the belief that in order to truly write well, one must first master the rudiments: grammar and syntax, punctuation, the sentence, the paragraph, the line, the stanza. We receive about 3,000 manuscripts a year, and publish about 3% of them. Check out a recent issue, send us your best, proofread your work, be patient, be persistent."

THE NEW ORPHIC REVIEW

706 Mill St., Nelson BC V1L 4S5, Canada. (250)354-0494. **Fax:** (250)354-0494. **E-mail:** dreamhorsepress@yahoo.com. **Website:** www.dreamhorsepress.com; www3.telus.net/neworphicpublishers-hekkanen. "Unsolicited manuscripts ARE considered year round. Send a ten poem query first, with an SASE proper postage (keeping in mind postage rate changes), include a cover letter with biography, and a reading fee of $10 or for an additional 1 dollar save yourself the postage, paper and envelopes and submit online. Response times vary, but we will either respond with a request to review the manuscript in its entirety or with a simple rejection note. If you have submitted a full manuscript under the old system and haven't received a response, please be patient, they are still being considered."

Margrith Schraner's story, "Dream Dig" was included in *The Journey Prize Anthology*, 2001.

ADDITIONAL INFORMATION *New Orphic Review*, published in May and October, is run "by an opinionated visionary who is beholden to no one, least of all government agencies like the Canada Council or institutions of higher learning. He feels Canadian literature is stagnant, lacks daring, and is terribly incestuous." Publishes poetry, novel excerpts, mainstream and experimental short stories, and articles on a wide range of subjects. Each issue includes a Featured Poet section. "*New Orphic Review* publishes authors from around the world as long as the pieces are written in English and are accompanied by a SASE with proper Canadian postage and/or U.S. dollars to offset the cost of postage." Wants "tight, well-wrought poetry over leggy, prosaic poetry. No 'fuck you' poetry; no rambling pseudo Beat poetry." Has published poetry by Robert Cooperman, Step Elder, Louis E. Bourgeios, and Art Joyce. *New Orphic Review* is 120-140 pages, magazine-sized, laser-printed, perfect-bound, with color cover, includes ads. Receives about 400 poems/year, accepts about 10%. Press run is 500. Subscription: $30 CAD for individuals, $35 CAD for institutions. Sample: $20. Submit 6 poems at a time. Lines/poem: 5 minimum, 30 maximum. Considers simultaneous submissions; no previously published poems. Cover letter is preferred. "Make sure a SASE (or SAE and IRC) is included." Time between acceptance and publication is up to 8 months. "The managing editor and associate editor refer work to the editor-in-chief." Seldom comments on rejected poems. Occasionally publishes theme issues. Guidelines available for SASE (or SAE and IRC). Responds in 2 months. Pays 1 contributor's copy. Acquires first North American serial rights. New Orphic Publishers publishes 4 paperbacks/year. However, **all material is solicited**.

TIPS "I like fiction that deals with issues, accounts for every motive, has conflict, is well written and tackles something that is substantive. Don't be mundane; try for more, not less."

NEW SOUTH

Campus Box 1894, Georgia State Univ., MSC 8R0322 Unit 8, Atlanta GA 30303-3083. (404)651-4804. **Fax:** (404)651-1710. **E-mail:** new_south@langate.gsu.edu. **Website:** www.review.gsu.edu. *New South*, published semiannually, prints fiction, poetry, nonfiction, and visual art. Wants "original voices searching to rise above the ordinary. No subject or form biases." Seeks to publish high quality work, regardless of genre, form, or regional ties. *New South* is 160+ pages. Press run is 2,000; 500 distributed free to students. Single copy: $5; subscription: $8/year; $14 for 2 issues. Single issue: $5. Sample: $3 (back issue). After more than 30 years *GSU Review* has become *New South*. Our role as George State University's journal of art & literature has not changed; however, it was time for a revision, a chance for a clearer mission. Sample copy for $3. Guidelines available online.

HOW TO CONTACT Submit up to 3 poems at a time. Considers simultaneous submissions (with notification in cover letter); no previously published poems. No e-mail submissions. Name, address, and phone/e-mail must appear on each page of ms. Cover letter is required. Include "a 3-4 line bio, a list of the work(s) submitted in the order they appear, and your name, mailing address, phone number, and e-mail address." Include SASE for notification. New South is now accepting submissions through Tell It Slant, an online submission manager. For a small fee that's roughly the cost of printing and posting paper submissions, Tell it Slant will save time, reduce paper waste, and increase our efficiency. Time between acceptance and publication is 3-5 months. Seldom comments on rejected poems. Pays 2 copies. Rights revert to poets upon publication.

CONTEST/AWARD OFFERINGS The *New South* Annual Writing Contest offers $1,000 for the best poem; copy of issue to all who submit. Submissions must be unpublished. Submit up to 3 poems on any subject or in any form. "Specify 'poetry' on outside envelope." Guidelines available for SASE, by e-mail, or on website. **Deadline:** March 4. Competition receives 200 entries. Past judges include Sharon Olds, Jane Hirschfield, Anthony Hecht, Phillip Levine and Jake Adam York. Winner will be announced in the Spring issue.

THE NEW VERSE NEWS

Tangerang , Indonesia. **E-mail:** nvneditor@yahoo.com; nvneditor@gmail.com. **Website:** www.newversenews.com. **Contact:** James Penha, editor. *The New Verse News*, published online and updated "every day or 2," has "a clear liberal bias, but will consider various visions and views." Wants "poems, both serious and satirical, on current events and topical issues; will also consider prose poems and short-short stories and plays." Does not want "work unrelated to the news." Receives about 1,200 poems/year; accepts about 300. Acquires first rights. Rights revert to poet upon publication. Responds in 1-3 weeks. Sometimes comments on rejected poems. Guidelines available on website.

MAGAZINE NEEDS Submit 1-5 poems at a time. Lines/poem: no length restrictions. No previously published poems or simultaneous submissions. Accepts only e-mail submissions (pasted into body of message); use "Verse News Submission" as the subject line; no disk or postal submissions. Send brief bio. Reads submissions year-round. Submit seasonal poems 1 month in advance. "Normally, poems are published immediately upon acceptance." Poems are circulated to an editorial board. No payment.

NEW WELSH REVIEW

P.O. Box 170, Aberystwyth, Ceredigion Wa SY23 1 WZ, United Kingdom. 01970-626230. **E-mail:** editor@newwelshreview.com. **Website:** www.newwelshreview.com. **Contact:** Gwen Davies, editor. "NWR, a literary quarterly ranked in the top five of British literary magazines, publishes stories, poems and critical essays. The best of Welsh writing in English, past and present, is celebrated, discussed and debated. We seek poems, short stories, reviews, special features/articles and commentary." Quarterly.

THE NEW WRITER

(44)(158)021-2626. **E-mail:** editor@thenewwriter.com. **Website:** www.thenewwriter.com. **Contact:** Sarah Jackson, poetry editor. "Contemporary writing magazine which publishes the best in fact, fiction and poetry." Buys one-time rights. Pays on publication. Publishes ms an average of 1 year after acceptance. Responds in 2 months to queries. Responds in 4 months to mss. Sample copy for SASE and A4 SAE with IRCs only. Guidelines for SASE.

MAGAZINE NEEDS *The New Writer*, published 6 times/year, is "aimed at writers with a serious intent, who want to develop their writing to meet the high expectations of today's editors. The team at *The New Writer* is committed to working with its readers to increase the chances of publication through masses of useful information and plenty of feedback. More than that, we let you know about the current state of the market with the best in contemporary fiction and cutting-edge poetry, backed up by searching articles and in-depth features." Wants "short and long unpublished poems, provided they are original and undeniably brilliant. No problems with length/form, but anything over 2 pages (150 lines) needs to be brilliant. Cutting edge shouldn't mean inaccessible. The poetry editor prefers poems which provide a good use of language, offering challenging imagery." *The New Writer* is 56 pages, A4, professionally printed, saddle-stapled, with paper cover. Press run is 1,500 (1,350 subscribers); 50 distributed free to publishers, agents. Single copy: £6.25 in U.S. (5 IRCs required); subscription: £37.50 in U.S. "We have a secure server for subscriptions and entry into the annual Prose and Poetry Prizes on the website. Monthly e-mail newsletter included free of charge in the subscription package." 40 lines maximum. Pays £3/poem.

HOW TO CONTACT Submit up to 3 poems at a time. Lines/poem: 150 maximum. Does not consider previously published poems. Accepts e-mail submissions (pasted into body of message). Time between acceptance and publication is up to 6 months. Often comments on rejected poems. Guidelines available for SASE (or SAE with IRC) or on website. Pays £3 voucher plus 1 contributor's copy. Acquires first British serial rights.

CONTEST/AWARD OFFERINGS Sponsors *The New Writer* Prose & Poetry Prizes annually. "All poets writing in the English language are invited to submit an original, previously unpublished poem or a collection of 6-10 poems. Up to 25 prizes will be presented, as well as publication for the prize-winning poets in an anthology, plus the chance for a further 10 shortlisted poets to see their work published in *The New Writer* during the year." Guidelines available by e-mail or on website.

TIPS "Hone it—always be prepared to improve the story. It's a competitive market."

THE NEW YORKER

4 Times Square, New York NY 10036. (212) 286-5900. **E-mail:** beth_lusko@newyorker.com; toon@cartoonbank.com. **Website:** www.newyorker.com; www.cartoonbank.com. **Contact:** Bob Mankoff, cartoon; David Remnick, editor-in-chief. A quality weekly magazine of distinct news stories, articles, essays, and poems for a literate audience. Pays on acceptance. Responds in 3 months to mss.

The New Yorker receives approximately 4,000 submissions per month.

MAGAZINE NEEDS *The New Yorker*, published weekly, prints poetry of the highest quality (including translations). Subscription: $47/year (47 issues), $77 for 2 years (94 issues). Send poetry to Poetry Department.

HOW TO CONTACT Submit no more than 6 poems at a time. No previously published poems or simultaneous submissions. Use online e-mail source and upload as pdf attachment. Include poet's name in the subject line and as the title of attached document. "We prefer to receive no more than two submissions per writer per year." Pays top rates.

TIPS "Be lively, original, not overly literary. Write what you want to write, not what you think the editor would like. Send poetry to Poetry Department."

NEW YORK QUARTERLY

P.O. Box 2015, Old Chelsea Station, New York NY 10113. **E-mail:** info@nyquarterly.org. **Website:** www.nyquarterly.org. **Contact:** Raymond Hammond, editor. *New York Quarterly*, published 3 times/year, seeks to print "a most eclectic cross-section of contemporary American poetry." Has published poetry by Charles Bukowski, James Dickey, Lola Haskins, Lyn Lifshin, Elisavietta Ritchie, and W.D. Snodgrass. *New York Quarterly* is digest-sized, elegantly printed, flat-spined, with glossy color cover. Subscription: $35. Responds in 6 weeks.

MAGAZINE NEEDS Submit 3-5 poems at a time. No e-mail submissions, but accepts electronic submissions on website. Considers simultaneous submissions with notification. No previously published poems. Include your name and address on each page. "Include SASE; no international postage coupons." Guidelines available on website. Pays in contributor's copies.

NEXUS LITERARY JOURNAL

W104 Student Union, Wright State University, Dayton OH 45435. **E-mail:** bruce.15@wright.edu. **Website:** www.wsunexus.com. **Contact:** Logan Bruce, editor. *Nexus Literary Journal*, published 3 times/year in fall, winter, and spring, is a student-operated magazine of mainstream and street poetry. Wants "truthful, direct poetry. Open to poets anywhere. We look for contemporary, imaginative work." *Nexus* is 80-96 pages. Receives about 1,000 submissions/year, accepts about 50-70. Circulation is 3,000. Sample: free for 10x15 SAE with 5 first-class stamps. Acquires first rights. Responds in 5 months except during summer. Upcoming themes and guidelines available in magazine, for SASE, or by e-mail.

MAGAZINE NEEDS Submit up to 5 poems at a time. Considers simultaneous submissions ("due to short response time, we want to be told it's a simultaneous submission"). Reads submissions year round. E-mail your prose/poetry to bruce.15@wright.edu with a subject line of "Short Story/Poetry/Other Submission" respective to your piece(s) you are submitting. Pieces should be attached to the e-mail as .doc, .docx, or .rtf files. The body of your e-mail should consist of a simple cover letter with your name, title of your piece, word count, what type of work it is, and contact information. Pays 2 contributor's copies.

O NIBBLE

1714 Franklin St., Suite 100-231, Oakland CA 94612. **E-mail:** nibblepoems@gmail.com. **Website:** http://nibblepoems.wordpress.com. **Contact:** Jeff Fleming, editor. *nibble*, published bimonthly, is a journal of poetry "focusing on short poems (less than 20 lines)." Does not want "inaccessible, self-important poems." *nibble* is 32 pages, digest-sized, laser-printed, side-stapled, with a cardstock, imaged cover. Receives about 1,500 poems/year, accepts about 250. Press run is 250; 50 distributed free to schools. Single copy: $6; Subscription: $24/6 issues. Make checks payable to Jeff Fleming.

MAGAZINE NEEDS Prefers e-mail submissions. Submit 3-5 poems at a time. SASE required for mail submissions; cover letter is required. Reads submissions year round. Time between acceptance and publication is 2 months. Often comments on rejected poems. Sometimes publishes theme issues. Upcoming themes available by e-mail. Guidelines available for SASE and by e-mail. Responds in 2-4 weeks. Pays 1 contributor's copy. Acquires one-time rights. Reviews books and chapbooks of poetry.Occasionally will publish chapbooks.

◐ NIMROD: INTERNATIONAL JOURNAL OF POETRY AND PROSE

University of Tulsa, 800 S. Tucker Dr., Tulsa OK 74104-3189. (918)631-3080. **Fax:** (918)631-3033. **E-mail:** nimrod@utulsa.edu. **Website:** www.utulsa.edu/nimrod. **Contact:** Francine Ringold, editor-in-chief; Elis O'Neal, managing editor. Magazine: 6×9; 192 pages; 60 lb. white paper; illustrations; photos. "We publish 1 thematic issue and 1 awards issue each year. A recent theme was 'Growing Season,' a compilation of poetry and prose from all over the world. We seek vigorous, imaginative, quality writing. Our mission is to discover new writers and publish experimental writers who have not yet found a 'home' for their work." Responds in 3 months to mss. Sample: $11. Guidelines available for SASE, by e-mail, or on website.

Semiannual. Receives 120 unsolicited mss/month. **Publishes 5-10 new writers/year.** Recently published work by Terry Blackhawk, Kellie Wells, Judith Hutchinson Clark, Tomaz Salamun. SASE for return of ms. Accepts queries by e-mail. Does not accept submissions by e-mail unless the writer is living outside the US. Subscription: $18.50/year U.S., $20 foreign. Poetry published in *Nimrod* has been included in *The Best American Poetry*.

MAGAZINE NEEDS Submit 5-10 poems at a time. No fax or e-mail submissions. Open to general submissions from January 1-November 30. Sponsors the annual *Nimrod* Literary Awards, including The Pablo Neruda Prize for Poetry. "During the months that the *Nimrod* Literary Awards competition is being conducted, reporting time on non-contest mss will be longer." Also sponsors the *Nimrod* workshop for readers and writers, a 1-day workshop held annually in October. Cost is about $50. Send SASE for brochure and registration form. Pays 2 contributor's copies, plus reduced cost on additional copies.

◐$ NINTH LETTER

Dept. of English, University of Illinois, 608 S. Wright St., Urbana IL 61801. (217)244-3145. **E-mail:** poetry@ninthletter.com. **Website:** www.ninthletter.com. Member: CLMP; CELJ. *Ninth Letter*, published semiannually, is "dedicated to the examination of literature as it intersects with various aspects of contemporary culture and intellectual life." Open to all forms of poetry. Wants "exceptional literary quality." Has published poetry by Paula Bohince, L.S. Asekoff, D.A. Powell, Bob Hicok, G.C. Waldrep, and Angie Estes. *Ninth Letter* is 176 pages, 7×10, offset-printed, perfect-bound, with 4-color cover with graphics. Receives about 9,000 poems/year, accepts about 40. Press run is 2,500 (500 subscribers, 1,000 shelf sales); 500 distributed free, 500 to contributors, media, and fundraising efforts. Single copy: $14.95; subscription: $21.95/year. Sample: $8.95 (back issue). Make checks payable to *Ninth Letter*.

Ninth Letter won Best New Literary Journal 2005 from the Council of Editors of Learned Journals (CELJ) and has had poetry selected for *The Pushcart Prize*, *Best New Poets*, and *The Year's Best Fantasy and Horror*.

MAGAZINE NEEDS Submit no more than 6 poems or 10 pages at a time. No previously published poems. Electronic submissions accepted through website. No e-mail or disk submissions. Cover letter is preferred. "SASE must be included for reply." Reads submissions September 1- April 30 (inclusive postmark dates). Time between acceptance and publication is 5-6 months. Poems are circulated to an editorial board. Sometimes comments on rejected poems. Guidelines available for SASE, by e-mail, or on website. Responds in 2 months. Always sends prepublications galleys. Pays $25/page and 2 contributor's copies. Acquires first North American serial rights. Rights revert to poet upon publication.

NITE-WRITER'S INTERNATIONAL LITERARY ARTS JOURNAL

158 Spencer Ave., Suite 100, Pittsburgh PA 15227. (412)668-0691. **E-mail:** nitewritersliteraryarts@gmail.com. **Website:** http://nitewritersinternational.webs.com. **Contact:** John Thompson. *Nite-Writer's International Literary Arts Journal*, published quarterly, is open to beginners as well as professionals. "We are 'dedicated to the emotional intellectual' with a creative perception of life." Has published poetry by Lyn Lifshin, Rose Marie Hunold, Peter Vetrano, Carol Frances Brown, and Richard King Perkins II. 30-50 pages, magazine-sized, laser-printed, with stock cover with sleeve. Receives about 1,000 poems/year, accepts about 10-15%. Press run is about 100 (more than 60 subscribers, 10 libraries).

MAGAZINE NEEDS Strong imagery and accepts free verse, avant-garde poetry, haiku, and senryu. Does not want porn or violence. Open to length.

HOW TO CONTACT Considers previously published poems and simultaneous submissions. Cover letter is preferred. "Give brief bio, state where you heard of us, state if material has been previously published and where. Always enclose SASE if you seek reply and return of your material." Time between acceptance and publication is within one year. Always comments on rejected poems.

ADDITIONAL INFORMATION Single copy: $6; subscription: $20. Sample (when available): $4. Guidelines available for SASE. Responds in one month.

TIPS "Read a lot of what you write — study the market. Don't fear rejection, but use it as learning tool to strengthen your work before resubmitting."

THE NOCTURNAL LYRIC

P.O. Box 542, Astoria OR 97103. **E-mail:** thenocturnallyric@rocketmail.com. **Website:** www.angelfire.com/ca/nocturnallyric. **Contact:** Susan Moon, editor.

MAGAZINE NEEDS *The Nocturnal Lyric, Journal of the Bizarre*, published annually, features "bizarre fiction and poetry, primarily by new writers." Wants "poems dealing with the bizarre: fantasy, death, morbidity, horror, gore, etc. Any length" Does not want "boring poetry." Has published poetry by Eric Martin, Michael J. Frey, David L. Paxton, Herbert Jerry Baker, Debbie Berk, and Kenneth C. Wickson. *The Nocturnal Lyric* is 40 pages, digest-sized, photocopied, saddle-stapled, includes ads. Receives about 200 poems/year, accepts about 35%. Press run is 400 (40 subscribers). Single copy: $3 U.S., $5 foreign. Make checks payable to Susan Moon.

HOW TO CONTACT Submit up to 4 poems at a time. Considers previously published poems and simultaneous submissions. No e-mail submissions. Seldom comments on rejected poems. Guidelines available in magazine, for SASE, or on website. Responds in up to 6 months. Pays 50¢ "discount on subscription" coupons. Acquires one-time rights.

TIPS "A manuscript stands out when the story has a very original theme and the ending is not predictable. Don't be afraid to be adventurous with your story. Mainstream horror can be boring. Surreal, satirical horror is what true nightmares are all about."

NORTH AMERICAN REVIEW

University of Northern Iowa, 1222 W. 27th St., Cedar Falls IA 50614. (319)273-6455. **Fax:** (319)273-4326. **E-mail:** nar@uni.edu. **Website:** northamericanreview.org. **Contact:** Kim Groninga, nonfiction editor. "The *NAR* is the oldest literary magazine in America and one of the most respected; though we have no prejudices about the subject matter of material sent to us, our first concern is quality." Buys first North American serial rights, buys first rights. Pays on publication. Publishes ms an average of 1 year after acceptance. Responds in 4 months to mss. Sample copy for $7. Guidelines available online.

"This is the oldest literary magazine in the country and one of the most prestigious. Also one of the most entertaining—and a tough market for the young writer."

MAGAZINE NEEDS No restrictions; highest quality only. Pays $1/line; $20 minimum, $100 maximum

TIPS "We like stories that start quickly and have a strong narrative arc. Poems that are passionate about subject, language, and image are welcome, whether they are traditional or experimental, whether in formal or free verse (closed or open form). Nonfiction should combine art and fact with the finest writing. We do not accept simultaneous submissions; these will be returned unread. We read poetry, fiction, and nonfiction year-round."

NORTH CAROLINA LITERARY REVIEW

East Carolina University, ECU Mailstop 555 English, Greenville NC 27858-4353. (252)328-1537. **Fax:** (252)328-4889. **E-mail:** nclrsubmissions@ecu.edu; bauerm@ecu.edu; rodmand@ecu.edu. **Website:** http://www.nclr.ecu.edu/submissions/artists-and-photographers.html. **Contact:** Diane Rodman, art acquisitions editor. "Articles should have a North Carolina slant. First consideration is always for quality of work. Although we treat academic and scholarly subjects, we do not wish to see jargon-laden prose; our readers, we hope, are found as often in bookstores and libraries as in academia. We seek to combine the best elements of magazine for serious readers with best of scholarly journal." Buys first North American serial rights. Rights returned to writer on request. Pays on publication. Publishes ms an average of 1 year after acceptance. Responds in 1 month to queries. Responds in 6 months to mss. Editorial lead time 6 months. Sample copy for $10-25. Guidelines available online.

MAGAZINE NEEDS *North Carolina Literary Review*, published annually in the summer, contains "articles and other works about North Carolina topics or by North Carolina authors." Wants "poetry by writers currently living in North Carolina, those who have lived in North Carolina, or those using North Carolina for subject matter." Has published poetry by Betty Adcock, James Applewhite, and A.R. Ammons. *North Carolina Literary Review* is 200 pages, magazine-sized. Receives about 100 submissions/year, accepts about 10%. Press run is 1,000 (350 subscribers, 100 libraries, 100 shelf sales); 100 distributed free to contributors. Subscription: $20 for 2 years, $36 for 4 years. Sample: $15. *North Carolina poets only.* Length: 30-150 lines. $50-100 honorarium, extra copies, back issues or subscription (negotiable)

HOW TO CONTACT Submit 3-5 poems at a time through online submission manager. Cover letter is required. Submit poetry September through April. "Because we do not read during the summer, submissions received during the summer will be sent through the review process after August 25th." Simultaneous submissions are permitted "as long as you notify *NCLR* immediately if accepted elsewhere." Time between acceptance and publication is up to 1 year. Often comments on rejected poems. Guidelines available for SASE, by e-mail, or on website. Responds in 3 months within reading period. Sometimes sends prepublication galleys. Pays 2-year subscription plus 1-2 contributor's copies. Acquires first or one-time rights. Reviews books of poetry by North Carolina poets in up to 2,000 words, multi-book format. Poets from North Carolina may send books for review consideration. Rarely reviews chapbooks.

TIPS "By far the easiest way to break in is with special issue sections. We are especially interested in reports on conferences, readings, meetings that involve North Carolina writers, and personal essays or short narratives with a strong sense of place. See back issues for other departments. Interviews are probably the other easiest place to break in; no discussions of poetics/theory, etc., except in reader-friendly (accessible) language; interviews should be personal, more like conversations, that explore connections between a writer's life and his/her work."

NORTH CENTRAL REVIEW

North Central College, CM #235, 30 N. Brainard St., Naperville IL 60540. (630)637-5291. **E-mail:** nccreview@noctrl.edu. **Website:** http://orgs.noctrl.edu/review. *North Central Review*, published semiannually, considers "work in all literary genres, including occasional interviews, from undergraduate writers globally. The journal's goal is for college-level, emerging creative writers to share their work publicly and create a conversation with each other. ALL styles and forms are welcome as submissions. The readers tend to value attention to form (but not necessarily fixed form), voice, and detail. Very long poems or sequences (running more than 4 or 5 pages) may require particular excellence because of the journal's space and budget constraints." Does not want "overly sentimental language and hackneyed imagery. These are all-too-common weaknesses that readers see in submissions; we recommend revision and polishing before sending work." Considers poetry by teens (undergraduate writers only). *North Central Review* is 120 pages, digest-sized, perfect-bound, with cardstock cover with

4-color design. Press run is about 750, distributed free to contributors and publication reception attendees. Single copy: $5; subscription: $10. Make checks payable to North Central College. Acquires first rights. Publishes ms 1-4 months after acceptance. Responds in 1-4 months. Guidelines for SASE, by e-mail, online and in magazine.

MAGAZINE NEEDS Submit up to 5 poems at a time. Lines/poem: "no limit, but poems running more than 4-5 pages may undergo particular scrutiny." No previously published poems or simultaneous submissions. Accepts e-mail submissions (as Word attachments only); no fax submissions. Cover letter is preferred. Include name, postal address, phone number, and e-mail address (.edu address as proof of student status). If necessary (i.e., .edu address not available), include a photocopy of student ID with number marked out as proof of undergraduate status. Reads submissions September-March, with deadlines of February 15 and October 15. Poems are circulated to an editorial board. "All submissions are read by at least 3 staff members, including an editor." Rarely comments on rejected poems. Pays 2 contributor's copies.

TIPS "Don't send anything you just finished moments ago—rethink, revise, and polish. Avoid sentimentalitity and abstraction. That said, the *North Central Review* publishes beginners, so don't hesitate to submit and, if rejected, submit again."

NORTH DAKOTA QUARTERLY

(701)777-3322. **E-mail:** ndq@und.edu. **Website:** www.und.nodak.edu/org/ndq. Merrifeild Hall Room 110, 276 Centennial Drive Stop 7209, Grand Forks, ND 58202-7209. (701)777-3322. **E-mail:**ndq@und.edu. **Website:** www.und.nodak.edu/org/ndq. **Contact:** Robert Lewis, editor. *North Dakota Quarterly* is published by the University of North Dakota. Seeks material related to the arts and humanities—essays, fiction, interviews, poems, reviews, and visual art. Wants poetry "that reflects an understanding not only of the difficulties of the craft, but of the vitality and tact that each poem calls into play." Has published poetry by Maxine Kumin, Paul Muldoon, Robert Bagg, James Scully, Patricia Schneider, and Marianne Boruch. *North Dakota Quarterly* is about 200 pages, digest-sized, professionally designed and printed, perfect-bound, with full-color artwork on white card cover. Has 550 subscribers. Subscription: $25/year. Sample: $8.

Work published in *North Dakota Quarterly* was selected for inclusion in *The O. Henry Prize Stories, The Pushcart Prize Seriesand Best American Essays.*

HOW TO CONTACT Submit 5 poems at a time. No previously published poems or simultaneous submissions. No e-mail submissions; accepts only typed hard-copy submissions by postal mail. Time between acceptance and publication varies. Responds in up to 6 weeks. Always sends prepublication galleys. Pays 2 contributor's copies. Acquires first serial rights.

NORTHWEST REVIEW

5243 University of Oregon, Eugene OR 97403-5243. (541)346-3957. **Fax:** (541)346-0537. **E-mail:** nweditor@uoregon.edu. **Website:** http://nwr.uoregon.edu. **Contact:** Geri Doran, general editor. *Northwest Review*, published 2 times/year is "looking for smart, crisp writing about poetry and poetics. The only criterion for acceptance of material for publication is excellence." Has published poetry and essays by Ai, Yusef Komunyakaa, Charles Wright, Brenda Hillman, Eavan Boland, and Marilyn Chin. *Northwest Review* is digest-sized, flat-spined. Receives about 3,500 submissions/year, accepts about 4%. Press run is 1,300. Single copy: $8-10; subscription: $20/year (two issues). Sample: $8-10.

Poetry published by *Northwest Review* has been included in *The Best American Poetry, Poetry Daily*, and *Verse Daily.*

HOW TO CONTACT Send complete ms. Essays 4,000-8,000 words. No simultaneous submissions. No email submissions; postal submissions only. Include SASE. Send only clear, clean copies. Guidelines and reading periods available on website. Responds within 3 months. Acquires first North American serial rights. Pays 2 contributor's copies.

TIPS "Our advice is to persist."

NORTHWIND

Chain Bridge Press, LLC., 4201 Wilson Blvd., #110-321, Arlington VA 22203. **Website:** www.northwindmagazine.com. **Contact:** Tom Howard, managing editor. "Our focus is originality and provocative, compulsively readable prose and poetry, in any style or genre. We look for smart, lyrical writing that will appeal to an intelligent and culturally sophisticated audience." Buys first rights. Pays on publication. Publishes ms 2 months after acceptance. Responds in 2 months to mss. Sample copy available online at website. Guidelines available online at website.

MAGAZINE NEEDS "Give us something lyrical and genuine. Avoid sentimentality. Trust your ideas and your metaphors, and trust that we'll recognize them and be moved by them as well."

TIPS "For fiction and nonfiction, make the first paragraph the strongest one. Love your characters and make us love them (or hate them) too. Respect your reader; we love subtlety. Don't be afraid to be lighthearted or playful—not all great stories are tragic or depressing. Show us that you care about your craft by editing carefully before you send it in to us."

NOTES ON THE STATE OF NEW JERSEY

37 Chelsea Ct., Franklin Park NJ 08823. **E-mail:** editor@notesonnj.com. **Website:** www.notesonnj.com. **Contact:** Melissa Morris, editor. Notes on the State of New Jersey publishes material from a variety of perspectives and voices to give an authentic representation of what is happening in New Jersey. Buys simultaneous rights. Responds in 2-4 weeks on queries. Editorial lead time 1-2 months. Sample copy available on website. Guidelines available on website.

MAGAZINE NEEDS Poetry must be about New Jersey or be written by a New Jersey poet to be considered.

TIPS "If you love to write about New Jersey, then we would love to hear from you."

NOTRE DAME REVIEW

(574)631-6952. **Fax:** (574)631-4795. **E-mail:** english.ndreview.1@nd.edu. **Website:** www.nd.edu/~ndr/review.htm. The *Notre Dame Review* is an indepenent, noncommercial magazine of contemporary American and international fiction, poetry, criticism, and art. We are especially interested in work that takes on big issues by making the invisible seen, that gives voice to the voiceless. In addition to showcasing celebrated authors like Seamus Heaney and Czelaw Milosz, the *Notre Dame Review* introduces readers to authors they may have never encountered before, but who are doing innovative and important work. In conjunction with the *Notre Dame Review*, the online companion to the printed magazine, the *Notre Dame Re-view* engages readers as a community centered in literary rather than commercial concerns, a community we reach out to through critique and commentary as well as aesthetic experience. Buys first North American serial rights. Pays on publication. Publishes ms an average of 6 months after acceptance. Responds in 4 or more months to mss. Sample copy for $6. Guidelines available online.

MAGAZINE NEEDS *Notre Dame Review*, published semiannually, aims "to present a panoramic view of contemporary art and literature—no one style is advocated over another. We are especially interested in work that takes on big issues by making the invisible seen." Has published poetry by W.S. Merwin, R.T. Smith, Moira Egan, Michael Harper, Floyd Skloot, and Kevin Ducey. *Notre Dame Review* is 170 pages, magazine-sized, perfect-bound, with 4-color glossy cover, includes ads. Receives about 400 poems/year, accepts 10%. Press run is 2,000 (500 subscribers, 150 libraries, 1,000 shelf sales); 350 distributed free to contributors, assistants, etc. Single copy: $8; subscription: $15/year.

HOW TO CONTACT Submit 3-5 poems at a time. Considers simultaneous submissions; no previously published poems. Cover letter is required. Reads submissions September-November and January-March only. Time between acceptance and publication is 3 months. Seldom comments on rejected poems. Publishes theme issues. Guidelines available on website. Responds in 3 months. Always sends prepublication galleys. Pays small gratuity on publication, plus 2 contributor's copies. Acquires first rights. Staff reviews books of poetry in 500 words, single- and multi-book format. Send materials for review consideration.

ADDITIONAL INFORMATION *nd[[re]]view* is the online companion to *Notre Dame Review*, offering "interviews, critique, and commentary on authors and artists showcased within the pages of the print magazine." See website for more details.

TIPS "We're looking for high quality work that takes on big issues in a literary way. Please read our back issues before submitting."

NOW & THEN; THE APPALACHIAN MAGAZINE

East Tennessee State University, Box 70556, Johnson City TN 37614-1707. (423)439-5348. **Fax:** (423)439-6340. **E-mail:** nowandthen@etsu.edu. **Website:** www.etsu.edu/cass/nowandthen. **Contact:** Jane Woodside, editor. Literary magazine published twice/year. "*Now & Then* accepts a variety of writing genres: fiction, poetry, nonfiction, essays, interviews, memoirs, and book reviews. All submissions must relate to Appalachia and to the issue's specific theme. Our readership is educated and interested in the region." Buys first

North American serial rights. Rights revert back to author after publication. Sample copy available for $8 plus $3 shipping. Guidelines and upcoming themes available on website.

Magazine: 8×11; 44-48 pages; coated paper and cover stock; illustrations; photos. *Now & Then* tells the stories of Appalachia and presents a fresh, revealing picture of life in Appalachia, past and present, with engaging articles, personal essays, fiction, poetry, and photography.

MAGAZINE NEEDS Submit up to 5 poems, with SASE and cover letter including "a few lines about yourself for a contributor's note and whether the work has been published or accepted elsewhere." Will consider simultaneous submissions; occasionally accepts previously published poems. Put name, address and phone number on every poem. Deadlines: March 31 (spring/summer issue) and August 31 (fall/winter issues). Publishes theme issues. Responds within 6 months. Sends prepublication galleys. Pays $20/poem plus 2 contributor's copies.

TIPS "Keep in mind that *Now & Then* only publishes material related to the Appalachian region. Plus we only publish fiction that has some plausible connection to a specific issue's themes. Get the guidelines. We like to offer first-time publication to promising writers."

NTHPOSITION

E-mail: val@nthposition.com; rquintav@gmail.com. **Website:** www.nthposition.com. **Contact:** Rufo Quintavalle, poetry editor; Val Stevenson, managing editor. *nthposition*, published monthly online, is "an eclectic, London-based journal with politics and opinion, travel writing,fiction and poetry, art reviews and interviews, and some high weirdness." Guidelines available online.

Rufo Quintavalle, poetry editor, wants "all kinds of poetry, from post modern to mainstream." Receives about 2,000 poems/year; accepts about 10%. "We can only notify people whose work we accept." Val Stevenson, managing editor, wants clear, vivid prose. Receives about 1,500 articles/year,accepts about 10%.

MAGAZINE NEEDS Accepts e-mail submissions only (pasted into body of message; no attachments). Cover letter is required. "Please include a brief (2 sentences) biographical note." Reads submissions throughout the year. Time between acceptance and publication is 4 months. "Poems are read and selected by the poetry editor, who uses his own sense of what makes a poem work online to select." Never comments on rejected poems. Occasionally publishes theme issues. Guidelines available by e-mail or on website. Responds in 6 weeks. No payment. Does not request rights but expects proper acknowledgement if poems reprinted later. Publishes special theme e-books from time to time, such as 100 Poets Against the War. "No racism, nastiness, silkworm farming or diabetes articles."

ALSO OFFERS Publishes special theme e-books from time to time, such as *100 Poets Against the War.*

TIPS "Submit as text in the body of an e-mail, along with a brief bio note (2-3 sentences). If your work is accepted it will be archived into the British Library's permanent collection."

NUTHOUSE

Website: www.nuthousemagazine.com. *Nuthouse*, published every 3 months, uses humor of all kinds, including homespun and political. Wants "humorous verse; virtually all genres considered." Has published poetry by Holly Day, Daveed Garstenstein-Ross, and Don Webb. *Nuthouse* is 12 pages, digest-sized, photocopied from desktop-published originals. Receives about 500 poems/year, accepts about 100. Press run is 100. Subscription: $5 for 4 issues. Sample: $1.50. Make checks payable to Twin Rivers Press. Acquires one-time rights. Publishes ms 6 months-1 year after acceptance. Responds in 1 month.

MAGAZINE NEEDS Pays 1 contributor's copy per poem.

OFF THE COAST

Resolute Bear Press, P.O. Box 14, Robbinston ME 04671. (207)454-8026. **E-mail:** poetrylane2@gmail.com. **Website:** www.off-the-coast.com. **Contact:** Valerie Lawson, editor/publisher. Quarterly journal with deadlines of March, June, September and December 15. *Off the Coast* is accepting submissions of poetry (any subject or style, e-mail submissions preferred, postal submissions OK with SASE), photography, graphics, and books for review (books only, no chapbooks). Subscriptions are $35 for 1 year, $60 for 2 years. Single issue: $10. *Off the Coast* prints all styles and forms of poetry. Considers poetry by children and teens. Has published poetry by Wes McNair, Kate Barnes, Henry Braun, Baron Wormser, Betsy Sholl, David Wagoner, Diana DerHovanessian, Simon Perchik, and Rhina Espaillat. *Off the Coast* is 80-100+ pages, perfect-bound, with stock cover with original art. Receives about 2,500 poems/year, accepts about 200. Press run is 300; occasional complimentary copies offered. Make checks payable to *Off the Coast*. Editorial decisions are not made until after the deadline for each issue. Notifications go out the first two weeks of the month following the deadline date eg: early April for March 15 deadline. **For samples of poetry, art and reviews, visit our website**. "The mission of *Off the Coast* is to become recognized around the world as Maine's international poetry journal, a publication that prizes quality, diversity and honesty in its publications and in its dealings with poets. *Off the Coast*, a quarterly print journal, publishes poetry, artwork and reviews. Arranged much like an anthology, each issue bears a title drawn from a line or phrase from one of its poems." The rights to each individual poem and print are retained by each individual artist. 1-2 months. Responds in 1-2 months. Editorial decisions are not made until after the deadline for each issue. Notifications go out the first two weeks of the month following the deadline date eg: early April for March 15 deadline. For samples of poetry, art and reviews, visit our website: www.off-the coast.com. Contributors receive one free copy. Additional copies of the issue their work appears in available for $5, half the cover price. Sample issue for $10. Guidelines available in magazine.

HOW TO CONTACT "Send 1-3 previously unpublished poems, any subject or style, using our submission manager: www.offthecoast.sumishmash.com/submit. We accept postal submissions with SASE with sufficient postage for return. Please include contact information and brief bio with submission. We accept simultaneous submissions, but please inform us if your work is accepted elsewhere. Pays one contributor's copy. "The rights to each individual poem and print are retained by each individual artist." For reviews, send a single copy of a newly published poetry book. Please send bound books only, we do not review chapbooks."

THE OLD RED KIMONO

Georgia Highlands College, 3175 Cedartown Highway SE, Rome GA 30161. **E-mail:** napplega@highlands.edu. **Website:** www.highlands.edu/ork/neworkweb/WELCOME.html. **Contact:** Dr. Nancy Applegate, professor of English. *The Old Red Kimono*, published annually, prints original, high-quality poetry and fiction. Has published poetry by Walter McDonald, Peter Huggins, Ruth Moon Kempher, John Cantey Knight, Kirsten Fox, and Al Braselton. *The Old Red Kimono* is 72 pages, magazine-sized, professionally printed on heavy stock, with colored matte cover with art. Receives about 500 submissions/year, accepts about 60-70. Sample: $3. Acquires one-time rights. Responds in 3 months.

MAGAZINE NEEDS Submit 3-5 poems at a time. Accepts e-mail submissions. Reads submissions September 1-March 1 only. Guidelines available for SASE or on website for more submission information. Pays 2 contributor's copies.

ON SPEC

P.O. Box 4727, Station South, Edmonton AB T6E 5G6, Canada. (780)413-0215. **Fax:** (780)413-1538. **E-mail:** onspec@onspec.ca. **E-mail:** onspecmag@gmail.com. **Website:** www.onspec.ca. "We publish speculative fiction and poetry by new and established writers, with a strong preference for Canadian authored works." Buys first North American serial rights. Pays on acceptance. Publishes ms an average of 6-18 months after acceptance. Responds in 2 weeks to queries. 3 months after deadline to mss. Editorial lead time 6 months. Sample copy for $8. Guidelines for #10 SASE or on website.

Submission deadlines are February 28, May 31, August 31, and November 30.

MAGAZINE NEEDS No rhyming or religious material. Length: 4-100 lines. Pays $50 and 1 contributor's copy.

TIPS "We want to see stories with plausible characters, a well-constructed, consistent, and vividly described setting, a strong plot and believable emotions; characters must show us (not tell us) their emotional responses to each other and to the situation and/or challenge they face. Also: don't send us stories written for television. We don't like media tie-ins, so don't watch TV for inspiration! Read, instead! Absolutely no e-mailed or faxed submissions. Strong preference given to submissions by Canadians."

OPEN MINDS QUARTERLY

The Writer's Circle, 680 Kirkwood Dr., Building 1, Sudbury ON P3E 1X3, Canada. (705)675-9193, ext. 8286. **E-mail:** openminds@nisa.on.ca. **Website:** www.nisa.on.ca. **Contact:** Dinah Laprairie, editor. *Open Minds Quarterly* provides a "venue for individuals who have experienced mental illness to express themselves via poetry, short fiction, essays, first-person accounts of living with mental illness, book/movie reviews." Wants "unique, well-written, provocative poetry." Does not want overly graphic or sexual violence.

Considers poetry by children and teens. Has published poetry by Pamela MacBean, Sophie Soil, Alice Parris, and Kurt Sass. *Open Minds Quarterly* is 24 pages, magazine-sized, saddle-stapled, with 100 lb. stock cover with original artwork, includes ads. Receives about 300 poems/year, accepts about 30%. Press run is 750; 400 distributed free to potential subscribers, published writers, advertisers, and conferences and events. Single copy: $5.40 CAD, $5 USD; subscription: $35 CAD, $28.25 USD (special rates also available). Make checks payable to NISA/Northern Initiative for Social Action.

MAGAZINE NEEDS Submit 1-5 poems at a time. Considers previously published poems and simultaneous submissions. Accepts e-mail and disk submissions. Cover letter is required. "Info in cover letter: indication as to 'consumer/survivor' of the mental health system status." Reads submissions year round. Submit seasonal poems at least 8 months in advance. Time between acceptance and publication is 6-18 months. "Poems are first reviewed by poetry editor, then accepted/rejected by the editor. Sometimes, submissions are passed on to a third party for input or a third opinion." Seldom comments on rejected poems. Guidelines available for SASE, by fax, e-mail, or on website. Responds in up to 4 months. "Rarely" sends prepublication galleys. "All authors own their work—if another publisher seeks to reprint from our publication, we request they cite us as the source."

CONTEST/AWARD OFFERINGS "The Brainstorm Poetry Contest runs in first 2 months of each year. Contact the editor for information."

ALSO OFFERS "All material not accepted for our journal will be considered for The Writer's Circle Online, our Internet publication forum. Same guidelines apply. Same contact person."

OPEN SPACES

Open Spaces Publications, Inc., PMB 134, 6327-C SW Capitol Hwy., Portland OR 97239-1937. (503)313-4361. **Fax:** (503)227-3401. **E-mail:** info@open-spaces.com. **Website:** www.open-spaces.com. "*Open Spaces* is an online quarterly which gives voice to the Northwest on issues that are regional, national and international in scope. Our readership is thoughtful, intelligent, widely read and appreciative of ideas and writing of the highest quality. With that in mind, we seek thoughtful, well-researched articles and insightful fiction, essays and poetry on a variety of subjects from a number of different viewpoints." Rights purchased vary with author and material. Pays on publication. Publishes ms an average of 6 months after acceptance. Editorial lead time 9 months. Sample copy for $10. Guidelines available online.

"*Open Spaces* is a forum for informed writing and intelligent thought. Articles are written by experts in various fields. Audience is varied (CEOs and rock climbers, politicos and university presidents, etc.) but is highly educated and loves to read good writing." Will not accept e-mail submissions.

MAGAZINE NEEDS Again, quality is far more important than type. Submit 3 poems with SASE. "No epics, please."

TIPS "*Open Spaces* reviews all manuscripts submitted in hopes of finding writing of the highest quality. We present a Northwest perspective as well as a national and international one. Best advice is read the magazine."

OPEN WIDE MAGAZINE

40 Wingfield Road, Lakenheath, Brandon SK Ip27 9HR, UK. **E-mail:** contact@openwidemagazine.co.uk. **Website:** www.openwidemagazine.co.uk. **Contact:** Liz Roberts. Online literary magazine/journal: Quarterly. Open Wide Magazine has been publishing poetry, fiction, reviews and interviews. With our Feel Free Press imprint we published two print anthologies 'Poems Written Whilst Staring Death In The Face' and 'Destination Anywhere', 32 broadsides, a paperback poetry collection by K.M Dersley and chapbooks by Debbie Kirk, Luke Buckham, Shane Allison and Dan Provost. Also as Open Wide Books we published online chapbook collections from Ben Myers, Melissa Mann, Ben Barton, James D Quinton and Emily McPhillips. Receives 100 mss/month. Accepts 25 mss/issue. Publishes 30 new writers/year. Length: 500-4,000. Average length: 2,500. Publishes short shorts. Also publishes poetry, reviews (music, film, art) and interviews. Rarely comments on/critiques rejected mss. Include estimated word count, brief bio. Send either SASE (or IRC) for return of ms

or disposable copy of ms and #10 SASE for reply only. Acquires one time rights. Publication is copyrighted. Published 3 months after acceptance. The magazine costs just £1.00 for a PDF copy that is mailed to you at the e-mail address you provide us with via your Paypal account, unless you specify otherwise.

MAGAZINE NEEDS Short fiction and poetry journal enjoys adventure, ethnic/multicultural, experimental, feminist, humor/satire, mainstream, mystery/suspense, principle beat.

ORBIS: AN INTERNATIONAL QUARTERLY OF POETRY AND PROSE

17 Greenhow Ave., West Kirby, Wirral CH48 5EL, England. **E-mail:** baldock.carole@googlemail.com. **Website:** www.kudoswritingcompetitions.com. **Contact:** Carole Baldock, editor. *Orbis: An International Quarterly of Poetry and Prose* features "news, reviews, views, letters, prose, and quite a lot of poetry." Wants "more work from young people (this includes 20-somethings) and women writers." *Orbis* is 84 pages, digest-sized, professionally printed, flat-spined, with full-color glossy card cover. Receives "thousands" of submissions/year. Publishes 180. Single copy: £5 UK, £6 overseas (€10, $15 USD); subscription: £17 UK, £23 overseas (€30, $46 USD).

MAGAZINE NEEDS Submit up to 4 poems at a time. Accepts e-mail submissions "from outside UK only; Send press release in 1st instance to: Nessa O'Mahony, 5 Walnut View, Brookwood, Scholarstown Road, Rathfarnham, Dublin 16, Ireland. For postal submissions; enclose SASE (or SAE and 3 IRCs) with all correspondence." Response: 1-3 months. Reviews books and other magazines.

CONTEST/AWARD OFFERINGS Prizes in each issue: £50 for featured writer (3-4 poems); £50 Readers' Award for piece receiving the most votes; £50 split among 4 (or more) runners-up.

OSIRIS

P.O. Box 297, Deerfield MA 01342-0297. **E-mail:** amoorhead@deerfield.edu. **Contact:** Andrea Moorhead, poetry editor. *Osiris*, published semiannually, prints contemporary poetry in English, French, and Italian without translation, and in other languages with translation, including Polish, Danish, and German. Responds in 1 month. Sometimes sends prepublication galleys. Sample: $6.

Wants poetry that is "lyrical, non-narrative, multi-temporal, post-modern, well-crafted. Also looking for translations from non-IndoEuropean languages." Has published poetry by Abderrahmane Djelfaoui (Algeria), George Moore (USA), Flavio Ermini (Italy), Mylene Durand (Quebec), Anne Blonstein (Switzerland), Astrid Cabral (Brazil), and Rob Cook (USA). *Osiris* is 48-56 pages, digest-sized, perfect-bound. Press run is 500 (50 subscription copies sent to college and university libraries, including foreign libraries). Receives 200-300 submissions/year, accepts about 12. Single copy: $10; subscription: $18.

MAGAZINE NEEDS Submit 4-6 poems at a time. "Poems should be sent by postal mail. Include short bio and SASE with submission. Translators should include a letter of permission from the poet or publisher as well as copies of the original text." Pays 5 contributor's copies.

OVER THE TRANSOM

825 Bush St. #203, San Francisco CA 94108. (415)928-3965. **E-mail:** jsh619@earthlink.net. **Contact:** Jonathan Hayes, editor. *Over The Transom*, published 2 times/year, is a free publication of poetry and prose. Open to all styles of poetry. "We look for the highest quality writing that best fits the issue." Considers poetry by children and teens. Has published poetry by Garrett Caples, Richard Lopez, Glen Chesnut, Daniel J. Langton. *Over The Transom* is 32 pages, magazine-sized, saddle-stapled, with cardstock cover. Receives about 1,000 poems/year, accepts about 5%. Press run is 300 (100 subscribers); 150 distributed free to cafes, bookstores, universities, and bars. Single copy: free. Sample: $3. Make checks payable to Jonathan Hayes. Publishes ms 2-6 months after acceptance. Responds in 2 months.

MAGAZINE NEEDS Submit 5 poems at a time. Considers previously published poems and simultaneous submissions. Accepts e-mail submissions; no disk submissions. Must include a SASE with postal submissions. Reads submissions year round. Never comments on rejected poems. Occasionally publishes theme issues. Pays 1 contributor's copy.

OXFORD MAGAZINE

356 Bachelor Hall, Miami University, Oxford OH 45056. **E-mail:** oxmagpoetryeditor@muohio.edu. **Website:** www.oxfordmagazine.org. *Oxford Magazine*, published annually in May online, is open in terms of form, content, and subject matter. "We have

eclectic tastes, ranging from New Formalism to Language poetry to Nuyorican poetry." Has published poetry by Lisa Jarnot, Eve Shelnutt, Denise Duhamel, and Walter McDonald. Acquires one-time rights.

Work published in *Oxford Magazine* has been included in the Pushcart Prize anthology.

MAGAZINE NEEDS Submit 3-5 poems at a time. Considers simultaneous submissions; no previously published poems. Accepts e-mail (pasted into body of message or as MS Word attachment) and disk submissions. Cover letter is preferred. Reads submissions September 1-December 31. No payment.

OYEZ REVIEW

Roosevelt University, Dept. of Literature & Languages, 430 S. Michigan Ave., Chicago IL 60605-1394. (312)341-3500. **E-mail:** oyezreview@roosevelt.edu. **Website:** legacy.roosevelt.edu/roosevelt.edu/oyezreview. Buys first North American serial rights. Pays 2 contributor's copies. Publishes ms an average of 2 months after acceptance. Responds in 3 months. Sample copy available by request. Guidelines available online. SASE required. Does not accept email submissions unless from abroad.

Reading period is August 1-October 1. Responds by mid-December.

MAGAZINE NEEDS *Oyez Review*, published annually in January by Roosevelt University's MFA Program in Creative Writing, receives "submissions from across the nation and around the world. We're open to poetic sequences and longer poems provided they hold the reader's attention. We welcome skilled and polished work from newcomers as well as poems from established authors. The quality of the individual poem is key, not the poet's reputation." Has published poetry by Gary Fincke, Moira Egan, Gaylord Brewer, Barbara De Cesare, Prairie Markussen, Gary Held. *Oyez Review* is 90 pages, digest-sized. Accepts 5% of poems received. Press run is 800. Single copy: $5. 10 pages maximum.

HOW TO CONTACT Submit up to 5 poems, no more than 10 pages of poetry at a time. No simultaneous submissions. No fax, e-mail, or disk submissions. Cover letter is required. "Be sure to include a three- to five-sentence biography and complete contact information, including phone and e-mail." Reads submissions August 1-October 1 only. Time between acceptance and publication is 2 months. Guidelines available on website. Responds in 3 months. Pays 2 contributor's copies. Acquires first North American serial rights.

OYSTER BOY REVIEW

P.O. Box 1483, Pacifica CA 94044. **E-mail:** email_2010@oysterboyreview.com. **Website:** www.oysterboyreview.com. **Contact:** Damon Suave, editor/publisher. Electronic and print magazine. *Oyster Boy Review*, published 4 times a year, is interested in "the underrated, the ignored, the misunderstood, and the varietal. We'll make some mistakes. 'All styles are good except the boring kind'—Voltaire." Considers poetry by children and teens. Has published poetry by Jonathan Williams, Cid Corman, Lyn Lifshin, and Paul Dilsaver. *Oyster Boy Review* is 60 pages, 612x11, Docutech printed, stapled, with paper cover, includes ads. Receives about 1,500 poems/year, accepts 2%. Press run is 200; 30 distributed free to editors, authors. Subscription: $20.

HOW TO CONTACT Submit up to 5 poems at a time. No previously published poems or simultaneous submissions. Accepts e-mail submissions if poems are included in body of message. Cover letter preferred. Postal submissions require SASE. Do not submit mss in late December. "Upon acceptance, authors asked to provide electronic version of work and a biographical statement." Time between acceptance and publication is 6 months. Seldom comments on rejected poems. Guidelines available by e-mail or on website. Responds in 3 months. Pays 2 copies. Reviews books/chapbooks of poetry in 250-500 words (first books only), in single or multi-book format. Send materials for review consideration.

ADDITIONAL INFORMATION Off the Cuff Books is not open to submissions or solicitations. Off the Cuff Books publishes "longer works on special projects of authors published in *Oyster Boy Review*."

TIPS "Keep writing, keep submitting, keep revising."

PACKINGTOWN REVIEW

The University of Illinois at Chicago, English Department, UH 2027 MC 162, University of Illinois at Chicago, 601 S. Morgan, Chicago IL 60607. (908)745-1547. **E-mail:** editors@packingtownreview.com. **Website:** www.packingtownreview.com. **Contact:** Editor. *Packingtown Review*, published annually in March, prints creative writing and critical prose by emerging and established writers. "We welcome submissions of poetry, scholarly articles, drama, creative nonfiction, fiction, and literary translation, as well as genre-bending pieces." Wants "well-crafted poetry. We are open to most styles and forms. We are also looking for poetry that takes risks and does so successfully. We will consider articles about poetry." Does not want "uninspired or unrevised work." *Packingtown Review* is 250 pages, magazine-sized. Press run is 500. Single copy: see website for prices.

HOW TO CONTACT Submit 3-5 poems at a time. Considers simultaneous submissions (with notification); no previously published poems (considers poems posted on a public website/blog/forum previously published, but not those posted on a private, password-protected forum). No e-mail or disk submissions. Cover letter is required. "Please include a SASE. If you have simultaneously submitted these poems, please indicate in the cover letter and let us know ASAP if a poem is accepted elsewhere." Reads submissions year round. Poems are circulated to an editorial board. Sometimes comments on rejected poems. Sometimes publishes theme issues. Guidelines available on website. Responds in 3 months. Always sends prepublication galleys. Pays 2 contributor's copies. Acquires first North American serial rights. Rights revert to poets upon publication. Review books/chapbooks of poetry and other magazines/journals. Send materials for review consideration to Lucas Johnson.

TIPS "We are looking for well-crafted prose. We are open to most styles and forms. We are also looking for prose that takes risks and does so successfully. We will consider articles about prose."

◐$ PAINTED BRIDE QUARTERLY

Drexel University, Dept. of English and Philosophy, 3141 Chestnut St., Philadelphia PA 19104. **E-mail:** pbq@drexel.edu. **Website:** http://webdelsol.com/pbq. *Painted Bride Quarterly*, published online, "aims to be a leader among little magazines published by and for independent poets and writers nationally. We have no specifications or restrictions. We'll look at anything." Has published poetry by Robert Bly, Charles Bukowski, S.J. Marks, and James Hazen. *Painted Bride Quarterly* is printed as one hardcopy anthology annually. Single copy: $15. *Painted Bride Quarterly* seeks literary fiction, experimental and traditional. Buys first North American serial rights. Responds in 6 months to mss. Guidelines available online and by e-mail.

HOW TO CONTACT Submit up to 5 poems at a time. Lines/poem: any length. No previously published poems. No e-mail submissions. "Submissions must be original, typed, and should include a short bio." Time between acceptance and publication is 6-9 months. Seldom comments on rejected poems. Occasionally publishes theme issues. Guidelines available on website. Pays one-year subscription, one half-priced contributor's copy, and $5/accepted piece. Publishes reviews of poetry books.

CONTEST/AWARD OFFERINGS Sponsors an annual poetry contest and a chapbook competition. **Entry fee:** required for both. Guidelines available for SASE or on website.

TIPS "We look for freshness of idea incorporated with high-quality writing. We receive an awful lot of nicely written work with worn-out plots. We want quality in whatever—we hold experimental work to as strict standards as anything else. Many of our readers write fiction; most of them enjoy a good reading. We hope to be an outlet for quality. A good story gives, first, enjoyment to the reader. We've seen a good many of them lately, and we've published the best of them."

PALABRA

P.O. Box 86146, Los Angeles CA 90086-0146. **E-mail:** info@palabralitmag.com. **Website:** www.palabralitmag.com. "*PALABRA* is about exploration, risk, and ganas—the myriad intersections of thought, language, story and art—*el mas alla of letters*, symbols and spaces into meaning." Responds in 3-4 months to mss.

PARADOXISM

200 College Rd., Gallup NM 87301. **Fax:** (503)863-7532. **E-mail:** smarand@unm.edu. **Website:** www.gallup.unm.edu/~smarandache/a/paradoxism.htm. **Contact:** Dr. Florentin Smarandache.

MAGAZINE NEEDS *Paradoxism*, published annually, prints "avant-garde poetry, experiments, poems without verses, literature beyond the words, anti-language, non-literature and its literature, as well as the sense of the non-sense; revolutionary forms of poetry. Paradoxism, a 1980s movement of anti-totalitarian protest, is based on excessive use of antitheses, antinomies, contradictions, paradoxes in creation." Wants "avant-garde poetry, 1-2 pages, any subject, any style (lyrical experiments)." Does not want "classical, fixed forms." Has published poetry by Paul Georgelin, Mircea Monu, Ion Rotaru, Micheéle de LaPlante, and Claude LeRoy. *Paradoxism* is 52 pages, digest-sized, offset-printed, with soft cover. Press run is 500; distributed "to its collaborators, U.S. and Canadian university libraries, and the Library of Congress as well as European, Chinese, Indian, and Japanese libraries."

HOW TO CONTACT No previously published poems or simultaneous submissions. Do not submit during the summer. "We do not return published or unpublished poems or notify the author of date of publication." Responds in up to 3 weeks. Pays 1 contributor's copy.

ADDITIONAL INFORMATION Paradoxism Association also publishes 2 poetry paperbacks and 1-2 chapbooks/year, including translations. "The poems must be unpublished and must meet the requirements of the Paradoxism Association." Responds to queries in 2 months; to mss in up to 3 weeks. Pays 50 author's copies. Sample e-books available on website at www.gallup.unm.edu/~smarandache/eBooksLiterature.htm.

TIPS "We look for work that refers to the paradoxism or is written in the paradoxist style. The Basic Thesis of the paradoxism: everything has a meaning and a non-meaning in a harmony with each other. The Essence of the paradoxism: a) the sense has a non-sense, and reciprocally b) the non-sense has a sense. The Motto of the paradoxism: 'All is possible, the impossible too!' The Symbol of the paradoxism: a spiral—optic illusion, or vicious circle."

THE PARIS REVIEW

62 White St., New York NY 10013. (212)343-1333. **E-mail:** queries@theparisreview.org. **Website:** www.theparisreview.org. Nathaniel Rich, fiction editor. **Contact:** Lorin Stein, editor. "Fiction and poetry of superlative quality, whatever the genre, style or mode. Our contributors include prominent, as well as less well-known and previously unpublished writers. Writers at Work interview series includes important contemporary writers discussing their own work and the craft of writing." Buys all rights, buys first English-language rights. Pays on publication. Responds in 4 months to mss. Sample copy for $12 (includes postage). Guidelines available online.

Address submissions to proper department. Do not make submissions via e-mail.

MAGAZINE NEEDS Submit no more than six poems at a time. Poetry can be sent to the poetry editor (please include a self-addressed, stamped envelope), or submitted online at http://www.theparisreview.org/poetry/. Pays $35 minimum varies according to length. Awards $1,000 in Bernard F. Conners Poetry Prize contest.

CONTEST/AWARD OFFERINGS Awards $1,000 in Bernard F. Conners Poetry Prize contest.

PARNASSUS: POETRY IN REVIEW

Poetry in Review Foundation, 205 W. 89th St., #8F, New York NY 10024. (212)362-3492. **E-mail:** parnew@aol.com. **Website:** www.parnassusreview.com. **Contact:** Herbert Leibowitz, editor and publisher. Buys one-time rights. Pays on publication. Publishes ms an average of 12-14 months after acceptance. Responds in 2 months to mss. Sample copy for $15.

MAGAZINE NEEDS Accepts most types of poetry.

TIPS "Be certain you have read the magazine and are aware of the editor's taste. Blind submissions are a waste of everybody's time. We'd like to see more poems that display intellectual acumen and curiosity about history, science, music, etc., and fewer trivial lyrical poems about the self, or critical prose that's academic and dull. Prose should sing."

PASSAGES NORTH

English Department, Northern Michigan University, 1401 Presque Isle Ave., Marquette MI 49855. (906)227-1203. **E-mail:** passages@nmu.edu. **Website:** www.passagesnorth.com. *Passages North*, published annually in spring, prints poetry, short fiction, creative nonfiction, essays, and interviews. Sample: $3 (back issue). Guidelines available for SASE, by e-mail, or on website.

Magazine: 7×10; 200-300 pgs; 60 lb. paper. Publishes work by established and emerging writers. Has published poetry by Moira Egan, Frannie Lindsay, Ben Lerner, Bob Hicok, Gabe Gudding, John McNally, Steve Almond, Tracy Winn, and Midege Raymond. *Passages North* is 250 pages. Single copy: $13; subscription: $13/year, $23 for 2 years.

MAGAZINE NEEDS Submit up to 6 poems at a time. Considers simultaneous submissions. Time between acceptance and publication is 6 months. Reads submissions September-May only. Responds in 2 months. Pays 2 contributor's copies. Sponsors the Elinor Benedict Poetry Prize every other year; 1st Prize: $1,000, plus 2 Honorable Mentions. Entry fee: $15 for 1-3 poems (each entrant receives the contest issue of *Passages North*). Make checks payable to Northern Michigan University. Deadline: reads entries October15-February 15.

TIPS "We look for voice, energetic prose, writers who take risks. We look for an engaging story in which the author evokes an emotional response from the reader through carefully rendered scenes, complex characters, and a smart, narrative design. Revise, revise. Read what we publish."

PASSION

Crescent Moon Publishing, P.O. Box 393, Maidstone Kent ME14 5XU, United Kingdom. (44)(162)272-9593. **E-mail:** cresmopub@yahoo.co.uk. **Website:** www.crescentmoon.org.uk. Crescent Moon Publishing, P.O. Box 393, Maidstone, Kent ME14 5XU United Kingdom. (44)(162)272-9593. **E-mail:** cresmopub@yahoo.co.uk. **Website:** www.crescentmoon.org.uk. Established 1988. **Contact:** Jeremy Robinson, editor. *Passion*, published quarterly, features poetry, fiction, reviews, and essays on feminism, art, philosophy, and the media. Wants "thought-provoking, incisive, polemical, ironic, lyric, sensual, and hilarious work." Does not want "rubbish, trivia, party politics, sport, etc." Has published poetry by Jeremy Reed, Penelope Shuttle, Alan Bold, D.J. Enright, and Peter Redgrove. Single copy: £2.50 ($4 USD); subscription: £10 ($17 USD). Make checks payable to Crescent Moon Publishing.

HOW TO CONTACT Submit 5-10 poems at a time. Cover letter is required. Include brief bio and publishing credits ("and please print your address in capitals"). Pays one contributor's copy.

ADDITIONAL INFORMATION Crescent Moon publishes about 25 books and chapbooks/year on arrangements **subsidized by the poet**. Wants "poetry that is passionate and authentic. Any form or length." Does not want "the trivial, insincere or derivative. We are also publishing two anthologies of new American poetry each year entitled *Pagan America*." Has also published studies of Rimbaud, Rilke, Cavafy, Shakespeare, Beckett, German Romantic poetry, and D.H. Lawrence. Books are usually about 76 pages, flat-spined, digest-sized. *Pagan America* available for £4.99 each ($8.95 USD) or £10 ($17 USD) for 2 issues.

THE PATERSON LITERARY REVIEW

Passaic County Community College, Cultural Affairs Dept., One College Blvd., Paterson NJ 07505-1179. (973)684-6555. **Fax:** (973)523-6085. **E-mail:** mGillan@pccc.edu. **Website:** www.pccc.edu/poetry. **Contact:** Maria Mazziotti Gillan, editor/executive director. *Paterson Literary Review*, published annually, is produced by the The Poetry Center at Passaic County Community College. Wants poetry of "high quality; clear, direct, powerful work." Has published poetry by Diane di Prima, Ruth Stone, Marge Piercy, and Laura Boss. *Paterson Literary Review* is 300-400 pages, magazine-sized, professionally printed, saddle-stapled, with glossy 4-color card cover. Press run is 2,500. Sample: $13.

Work for *PLR* has been included in the *Pushcart Prize* anthology and *Best American Poetry.*

HOW TO CONTACT Submit up to 5 poems at a time. Lines/poem: 100 maximum. Considers simultaneous submissions. Reads submissions December 1-March 31 only. Responds within 1 year. Pays 1 contributor's copy. Acquires first rights.

ALSO OFFERS Publishes *The New Jersey Poetry Resource Book* ($5 plus $1.50 p&h) and *The New Jersey Poetry Calendar.* The Distinguished Poets Series offers readings by poets of international, national, and regional reputation. Poetryworks/USA is a series of programs produced for UA Columbia-Cablevision. See website for details about these additional resources.

TIPS Looks for "clear, moving and specific work."

PAVEMENT SAW

Pavement Saw Press, 321 Empire St., Montpelier OH 43543. **E-mail:** info@pavementsaw.org. **Website:** http://pavementsaw.org. **Contact:** David Baratier, editor. "Pavement Saw Press has been publishing steadily since the fall of 1993. Each year since 1999, we have published at least 4 full length paperback poetry collections, with some printed in library edition hard covers, 1 chapbook and a yearly literary journal anthology. We specialize in finding authors who have been widely published in literary journals but have not published a chapbook or full-length book." *Pavement Saw*, published annually in August, wants "letters, short fiction, and poetry on any subject, especially work." Does not want "poems that tell; no work by a deceased writer, and no translations." Dedicates 15-20 pages of each issue to a featured writer. *Pavement Saw* is 88 pages, digest-sized, perfect-bound. Receives about 9,000 poems/year, accepts less than 1%. Press run is 550. Single copy: $8; subscription: $14. Sample: $7. Make checks payable to Pavement Saw Press. Sometimes sends prepublication galleys. Pays at least 2 contributor's copies. Acquires first rights. Responds in 4 months. Guidelines available in magazine or for SASE.

MAGAZINE NEEDS Submit 5 poems at a time. Lines/poem: 1-2 pages. Considers simultaneous submissions, "as long as poet has not published a book with a press run of 1,000 or more"; no previously published poems. No e-mail submissions; postal submissions only. Cover letter is required. "No fancy typefaces." Seldom comments on rejected poems.

ADDITIONAL INFORMATION Pavement Saw Press also publishes books of poetry. "Most are by authors who have been published in the journal." Published "7 titles in 2005 and 7 titles in 2006; 5 were full-length books ranging from 80 to 240 pages."

PEACE & FREEDOM

Peace & Freedom Press, 17 Farrow Rd., Whaplode Drove, Spalding, Lincs PE12 0TS, England. **Website:** http://pandf.booksmusicfilmstv.com/index.htm. Published semiannually; emphasizes social, humanitarian, and environmental issues. **Considers submissions from subscribers only.** "Those new to poetry are welcome. The poetry we publish is pro-animal rights/welfare, anti-war, environmental; poems reflecting love; erotic, but not obscene; humorous; spiritual, humanitarian; with or without rhyme/meter." Considers poetry by children and teens. Has published poetry by Dorothy Bell-Hall, Freda Moffatt, Andrew Bruce, Bernard Shough, Mona Miller, and Andrew Savage. *Peace & Freedom* has a varied format. Subscription: $20 U.S., £10 UK for 6 issues. Sample: $5 U.S., £1.75 UK. "Sample copies can be purchased only from the above address. Advisable to buy a sample copy before submitting. Banks charge the equivalent of $5 to cash foreign checks in the UK, so please only send bills, preferably by registered post." Responds to submissions in less than a month usually., with SAE/IRC. Submissions from subscribers only.

MAGAZINE NEEDS No previously published poems or simultaneous submissions. Accepts e-mail submissions (pasted into body of message, no attachments; no more than 3 poems/e-mail); no fax submissions. Include bio. Reads submissions year round. Publishes theme issues. Upcoming themes available in magazine, for SAE with IRC, by e-mail, or on website. Responds to submissions in less than a month ("usually"), with SAE/IRC. "Work without correct postage will not be responded to or returned until proper postage is sent." Pays one contributor's copy. Reviews books of poetry. Lines/poem: 32 max.

CONTEST/AWARD OFFERINGS "*Peace & Freedom* holds regular poetry contests as does one of our other publications, *Eastern Rainbow*, which is a magazine concerning 20th-century popular culture using poetry up to 32 lines." Subscription: $20 U.S., £10 UK for 6 issues. Further details of competitions and publications available for SAE with IRC or on website.

TIPS "Too many writers have lost the personal touch that editors generally appreciate. It can make a difference when selecting work of equal merit."

PEARL

3030 E. Second St., Long Beach CA 90803. (562)434-4523. **E-mail:** pearlmag@aol.com. **Website:** www.pearlmag.com. **Contact:** Joan Jobe Smith, Marilyn Johnson, and Barbara Hauk, poetry editors. *Pearl*, published semiannually in May and November, is interested "in accessible, humanistic poetry that communicates and is related to real life. Humor and wit are welcome, along with the ironic and serious. No taboos, stylistically or subject-wise." Does not want "sentimental, obscure, predictable, abstract, or clicheé-ridden poetry. Our purpose is to provide a forum for lively, readable poetry that reflects a wide variety of contemporary voices, viewpoints, and experiences—that speaks to real people about real life in direct, living language, profane or sublime. Our Fall/Winter issue is devoted exclusively to poetry, with a 12- to 15-page section featuring the work of a single poet." Has published poetry by Christopher Buckley, Fred Voss, David Hernandez, Lisa Glatt, Jim Daniels, Nin Andrews, and Frank X. Gaspar. *Pearl* is 112-136 pages, digest-sized, offset-printed, perfect-bound, with glossy cover. Press run is 700. Subscription: $21/year (includes a copy of the Pearl Poetry Prize-winning book). "*Pearl* is an eclectic publication, a place for lively, readable poetry and prose that speaks to real people about real life in direct, living language, profane or sublime." Pays with contributor's copy. Publishes ms an average of 6-12 months after acceptance. Sample copy for $10. Guidelines available online.

Submissions are accepted from Jan. - June only. Mss. received between July and Dec. will be returned unread. No e-mail submissions, except from countries outside the U.S. See guidelines.

MAGAZINE NEEDS "Our poetry issue contains a 12-15 page section featuring the work of a single poet. Entry fee for the Pearl Poetry Prize is $20, which includes a copy of the winning book." No sentimental, obscure, predictable, abstract or cliché-ridden poetry. 40 lines max. Send with cover letter and SASE.

HOW TO CONTACT Submit 3-5 poems at a time with cover letter and SASE. Lines/poem: no longer than 40 lines preferred, each line no more than 10-12 words, to accommodate page size and format. Considers simultaneous submissions ("must be acknowledged as such"); no previously published poems. NO e-mail submissions; postal submissions only. "Handwritten submissions and unreadable printouts are not acceptable." Reads submissions January-June only. Time between acceptance and publication is up to 1 year. Responds in 2 months. Sometimes sends prepublication galleys. Pays 1 contributor's copy. Acquires first serial rights.

TIPS "We look for vivid, *dramatized* situations and characters, stories written in an original 'voice,' that make sense and follow a clear narrative line. What makes a manuscript stand out is more elusive, though—more to do with feeling and imagination than anything else."

PEBBLE LAKE REVIEW

15318 Pebble Lake Dr., Houston TX 77095. **E-mail:** submissions@pebblelakereview.com. **Website:** www.pebblelakereview.com. **Contact:** Amanda Aucter, editor. *Pebble Lake Review*, published twice a year in June and December, seeks "high-quality, image-rich poetry that demonstrates attention to language, form, and craft. Looking for more experimental work." Does not want "anything cliché, Hallmark-style, racist, or erotic." Has published poetry by Kim Addonizio, Oliver De ala Paz, Denise Duhamel, Bob Hicok, Ilya Kaminksy, David Kirby, Noelle Kocot, Timothy Liu, Charles Harper Webb, Franz Wright, and others. *Pebble Lake Review* is available online and includes an audio component. Receives about 5,000 poems/year, accepts less than 3%.

Poems published in *Pebble Lake Review* have appeared on Verse Daily (www.versedaily.org) and were included in *Pushcart Prize XXXI: Best of the Small Presses.*

MAGAZINE NEEDS Submit September 1- February 1 annually, 3-5 poems at a time. Considers simultaneous submissions with notification; no previously published poems. Accepts e-mail submissions (pasted into body of message; attachments accepted if Word or RTF documents); no disk submissions. Cover letter is required. Time between acceptance and publication is 1-4 months. "Poems are circulated between the editors, and the decision is finalized by the editor-in-chief." Seldom comments on rejected poems. Guidelines available on website. Acquires one-time electronic rights; rights are returned to author upon publication. Reviews books/chapbooks of poetry in 500-1,000 words, single-book format. Send materials for review consideration.

ALSO OFFERS Selects poets to read work as part of the *Pebble Lake Review* Audio Project. E-mail the online editor at webmaster@pebblelakereview for details.

THE PEDESTAL MAGAZINE

6815 Honors Court, Charlotte NC 28210. (704)643-0244. **E-mail:** pedmagazine@carolina.rr.com. **Website:** www.thepedestalmagazine.com. **Contact:** Nathan Leslie, fiction editor; John Amen, editor-in-chief. Member: CLMP. "We are committed to promoting diversity and celebrating the voice of the individual." Buys first rights. All rights reverse back to the author/artist at publication time. "We retain the right to publish the piece in any subsequent issue or anthology without additional payment." Responds in 4-6 weeks to mss. Guidelines available online.

Pedestal 56 is now online.

MAGAZINE NEEDS *The Pedestal Magazine*, published bimonthly online, prints "12-15 poems per issue, as well as fiction, interviews, and book reviews. We are open to a wide variety of poetry, ranging from the highly experimental to the traditionally formal." Receives about 5,000 poems/year, accepts about 1%. "We have a readership of approximately 15,000 per month." "We are open to a wide variety of poetry, ranging from the highly experimental to the traditionally formal. Submit all poems in 1 form. No need to query before submitting." No length restriction. Pays $40/poem.

HOW TO CONTACT Submit up to 6 poems at a time. Lines/poem: open. Considers simultaneous submissions; no previously published poems. No e-mail or disk submissions. "Submissions are accepted via a submission form provided in the 'Submit' section of the website. Our submissions schedule is posted in the guidelines section." Time between acceptance and publication is 2-4 weeks. Poems are circulated to an editorial board. Sometimes comments on rejected poems. Sometimes publishes theme issues. Guidelines available on website. Responds in 4-6 weeks. Always sends prepublication galleys (by e-mail). Pays $40/

poem. Acquires first rights. Reviews books/chapbooks of poetry in 850-1,000 words. "Please query via e-mail prior to sending books or related materials."
TIPS "If you send us your work, please wait for a response to your first submission before you submit again."

THE PEGASUS REVIEW

P.O. Box 88, Henderson MD 21640-0088. (410)482-6736. **Website:** www.sgc.edu. Dr. William Webster, faculty adviser. *The Pegasus Review*, now a quarterly, focuses on a specific theme for each issue and issued in calligraphic format. "Since themes might change it is advisable to contact editor about current themes. With us, brevity is the key. Themes may be submitted in the way of poetry, short-short fiction and essays." Has published work by Jane Stuart, Ed Galing, John Grey, and Burton R. Hoffman. Press run is 120 (100 subscribers, 2 libraries). Subscription: $12. Sample: $2.50, including shipping and handling. "We are currently accepting original poetry, prose, and artwork for consideration. Poetry and prose should be submitted electronically. Simply cut and paste it directly into an email sent to: pegasus@sgc.edu." Responds within 1 month, often with a personal response.
MAGAZINE NEEDS Submit 3-5 poems at a time. Lines/poem: 24 maximum. Considers previously published poems, "if there is no conflict or violation of rights agreement," and simultaneous submissions, "but author must notify proper parties once specific material is accepted." "Brief cover letter with specifics as they relate to one's writing background are welcome." Include name and address on each page. "The usual SASE would be appreciated, unless told to recycle material." Pays 2 contributor's copies and an occasional book award.
TIPS "Write and circulate your work. Constantly strive to improve your writing craft through local writers' groups and/or writing conferences. Remember: writers need readers, so offer to read your work before a group (schools, senior citizen centers, libraries).

PENNINE INK MAGAZINE

1 Neptune St., Burnley BB11 1SF, England. **E-mail:** sheridansdandl@yahoo.co.uk. **Website:** pennineink.weebly.co.uk. **Contact:** Laura Sheridan, Editor.
MAGAZINE NEEDS *Pennine Ink*, published annually in January, prints poems and short prose pieces. *Pennine Ink* is 48 pages, A5, with b&w illustrated cover. Receives about 400 poems/year, accepts about 40. Press run is 200. "Contributors wishing to purchase a copy of *Pennine Ink* should enclose £2 ($4 USD) per copy." Submit up to 6 poems at a time. Lines/poem: 40 maximum; prose: no longer than 1,000 words. Considers previously published poems and simultaneous submissions. Accepts e-mail submissions. Seldom comments on rejected poems. Responds in 3 months. Pays 1 contributor's copy.

PENNSYLVANIA ENGLISH

Penn State DuBois, College Place, DuBois PA 15801-3199. (814)375-4785. **Fax:** (814)375-4785. **E-mail:** ajv2@psu.edu. **Website:** www.english.iup.edu/pcea. **Contact:** Antonio Vallone, editor. *Pennsylvania English*, published annually, is "sponsored by the Pennsylvania College English Association." Wants poetry of "any length, any style." Has published poetry by Liz Rosenberg, Walt MacDonald, Amy Pence, Jennifer Richter, and Jeff Schiff. *Pennsylvania English* is up to 200 pages, digest-sized, perfect-bound, with full-color cover. Press run is 500. Subscription: $10/year.
HOW TO CONTACT Submit 3 or more poems at a time. Considers simultaneous submissions; no previously published poems. No e-mail submissions. Submissions must be typed. Include SASE. Guidelines available for SASE. Responds in 6 months. Pays 2 contributor's copies.
TIPS "Quality of the writing is our only measure. We're not impressed by long-winded cover letters detailing awards and publications we've never heard of. Beginners and professionals have the same chance with us. We receive stacks of competently written but boring fiction. For a story to rise out of the rejection pile, it takes more than the basic competence."

PENNY DREADFUL: TALES & POEMS OF FANTASTIC TERROR

E-mail: MMPENDRAGON@aol.com. **Website:** www.mpendragon.com. *Penny Dreadful: Tales & Poems of Fanastic Terror*, published irregularly (about one/year), features goth-romantic poetry and prose. Publishes poetry, short stories, essays, letters, listings, reviews, and b&w artwork "which celebrate the darker aspects of Man, the World, and their Creator." Wants "literary horror in the tradition of Poe, M.R. James, Shelley, M.P. Shiel, and LeFanu—dark, disquieting tales and verses designed to challenge the reader's perception of human nature, morality, and man's place within the Darkness. Stories and poems should be set prior to 1910 and/or possess a timeless quality. Rhymed, metered verse preferred." Does not want "references to 20th- and 21st-century personages/events, graphic sex, strong language, excessive gore and shock elements." Has published poetry by Nancy Bennett, Michael R. Burch, Lee Clark, Louise Webster, K.S. Hardy, and Kevin N. Roberts. *Penny Dreadful* is about 170 pages, digest-sized, desktop-published, perfect-bound. Press run is 200. Subscription: $25/3 issues. Sample: $10. Make checks payable to Michael Pendragon. Acquires one-time rights. Guidelines available on website.

"Works appearing in *Penny Dreadful* have been reprinted in *The Year's Best Fantasy and Horror*." *Penny Dreadful* nominates best tales and poems for Pushcart Prizes.

MAGAZINE NEEDS Submit up to 12 poems at a time. Lines/poem: poems should not exceed 3 pages. Considers previously published poems and simultaneous submissions. "Due to the amount of submissions received, the editor cannot always respond. He encourages all contributors to submit work as simultaneous submissions." Accepts e-mail submissions (preferred; "include in body of message with a copy attached"). Put name and address on opening page, and name/title/page number on all following pages. SASE required with postal submissions. Reads submissions year round. Time between acceptance and publication is "indefinite." Poems are reviewed and chosen by editor. Always sends prepublication galleys. Pays 1 contributor's copy.

ADDITIONAL INFORMATION *Penny Dreadful* "includes market listings for, and reviews of, kindred magazines." Pendragon Publications also publishes *Songs of Innocence & Experience*.

THE PENWOOD REVIEW

P.O. Box 862, Los Alamitos CA 90720. **E-mail:** lcameron65@verizon.net. **E-mail:** submissions@penwoodreview.com. **Website:** www.penwoodreview.com. **Contact:** Lori Cameron, editor. *The Penwood Review* has been established to embrace high quality poetry of all kinds, and to provide a forum for poets who want to write intriguing, energetic, and disciplined poetry as an expression of their faith in God. We encourage writing that elevates the sacred while exploring its mystery and meaning in our lives. Semiannual. Wants "disciplined, high-quality, well-crafted poetry on any subject. Rhyming poetry must be written in traditional forms (sonnets, tercets, villanelles, sestinas, etc.)." Has published poetry by Kathleen Spivack, Anne Babson, Hugh Fox, Anselm Brocki, Nina Tassi, and Gary Guinn. *The Penwood Review* is about 40 pages, magazine-sized, saddle-stapled, with heavy card cover. Press run is 50-100. Single copy: $8; subscription: $16. Pays with subscription discount of $10 and, with subscription, 1 additional contributor's copy. Acquires one-time and electronic rights. Publishes ms 1 year after acceptance. Responds in up to 4 months. Sample copy for $6.00.

MAGAZINE NEEDS Submit 3-5 poems at a time. Lines/poem: less than 2 pages preferred. No previously published poems or simultaneous submissions. Prefers e-mail submissions (pasted into body of message). Cover letter is optional. One poem to a page with the author's full name, address, and phone number in the upper right corner. "Submissions are circulated among an editorial staff for evaluations." Never comments on rejected poems. Does not want "light verse, doggerel, or greeting card-style poetry. Also, nothing racist, sexist, pornographic, or blasphemous.

PEREGRINE

Amherst Writers & Artists Press, P.O. Box 1076, Amherst MA 01004. (413)253-3307. **Fax:** (413)253-7764. **E-mail:** peregrine@amherstwriters.com. **Website:** www.amherstwriters.com. **Contact:** Nancy Rose, editor. *Peregrine*, published annually, features poetry and fiction. Open to all styles, forms, and subjects except greeting card verse. "*Peregrine* has provided a forum for national and international writers since 1983, and is committed to finding excellent work by emerging as well as established authors. We publish what we love, knowing that all editorial decisions are subjective." Has published poetry by Willie James King, Virgil Suaárez, Susan Terris, Myron Ernst, Pat Schneider, Edwina Trentham, Sacha Webley, Fred Yannantuono, and Ralph Hughes. *Peregrine* is 104 pages, digest-sized, professionally printed, perfect-bound, with glossy cover. Press run is 1,000. Single copy: $15. Sample: $12. Make checks payable to AWA Press.

HOW TO CONTACT Submit 3-5 poems at a time. Lines/poem: 60 maximum (including spaces). Considers simultaneous submissions; no previously published poems. No e-mail submissions. Include cover letter with bio, 40 words maximum; indicate line count for each poem. Enclose sufficiently stamped SASE for return of mss; if disposable copy, enclose

#10 SASE for response. Reads submissions January 2-March 31 (postmark) only. Each ms read by several readers; final decisions made by the editor. Guidelines available for #10 SASE or on website. Pays 2 contributor's copies. Acquires first rights.

TIPS "Check guidelines before submitting your work. Familiarize yourself with Peregrine. We look for heart and soul as well as technical expertise. Trust your own voice."

PERMAFROST: A LITERARY JOURNAL

c/o English Dept., Univ. of Alaska Fairbanks, P.O. Box 755720, Fairbanks AK 99775. **Website:** www.uaf.edu/english/permafrost. *Permafrost: A Literary Journal*, published in May/June, contains poems, short stories, creative nonfiction, b&w drawings, photographs, and prints. "We survive on both new and established writers, hoping and expecting to see the best work out there. We publish any style of poetry provided it is conceived, written, and revised with care. While we encourage submissions about Alaska and by Alaskans, we also welcome poems about anywhere, from anywhere. We have published work by E. Ethelbert Miller, W. Loran Smith, Peter Orlovsky, Jim Wayne Miller, Allen Ginsberg, and Andy Warhol." *Permafrost* is about 200 pages, digest-sized, professionally printed, flat-spined. Subscription: $9/year, $16/2 years, $22/3 years. Back-issues $5.

MAGAZINE NEEDS Submit up to 5 poems at a time. Considers simultaneous submissions. "Poems should be typed, with author's name, address, phone, and e-mail at the top of each page." Reads submissions September 1-March 15. Included SASE; "e-mail submissions will not be read." Sometimes comments on poems. Guidelines available on website. Responds in 2-3 months. Pays 1 contributor copy; reduced contributor rate on additional copies. Pays 1 contributor's copy. reduced contributor rate on additional copies.

PHILADELPHIA STORIES

Fiction/Art/Poetry of the Delaware Valley, 93 Old York Road, Suite 1/#1-753, Jenkintown PA 19046. (215) 551-5889. **Fax:** (215) 635-0195. **E-mail:** christine@philadelphiastories.org; info@philadelphiastories.org. **Website:** www.philadelphiastories.org. **Contact:** Christine Weiser, co-publisher/managing editor. *Philadelphia Stories*, published quarterly, publishes "literary fiction, poetry, and art from Pennsylvania, New Jersey, and Delaware—and provide it to the general public free of charge." Wants "polished, well crafted poems." Does not want "first drafts." Considers poetry by teens. Has published poetry by Daniel Abdal-Hayy Moore, Scott Edward Anderson, Sandy Crimmins, Liz Dolan, Alison Hicks, and Margaret A. Robinson. *Philadelphia Stories* is 24 pages, magazine-sized, saddle-stapled, with 4-color cover with original art, includes ads. Receives about 600 poems/year, accepts about 15%. Press run is 12,000 per quarter, distributed free. Subscription: "we offer $20 memberships that include home delivery." Make checks payable to *Philadelphia Stories*. Member: CLMP.

HOW TO CONTACT Submit 3 poems at a time. Lines/poem: 36. Considers simultaneous submissions; no previously published poems. Accepts submissions through online submission form at www.philadelphiastories.org/submissions; no disk submissions. Cover letter is preferred. Reads submissions year round. Time between acceptance and publication is 3 months. Poems are circulated to an editorial board. "Each poem is reviewed by a preliminary board that decides on a final list; the entire board discusses this list and chooses the mutual favorites for print and Web." Guidelines available on website. Responds in 3 months. "We send a layout proof to check for print poems." Acquires onetime rights. Rights revert to poets upon publication. Reviews books of poetry.

TIPS "All work is screened by 3 editorial board members, who rank the work. These scores are processed at the end of the quarterly submission period, and then the board meets to decide which pieces will be published in print and online. We look for exceptional, polished prose, a controlled voice, strong characters and place, and interesting subjects. Follow guidelines. We cannot stress this enough. Read every guideline carefully and thoroughly before sending anything out. Send out only polished material. We reject many quality pieces for various reasons; try not to take rejection personally. Just because your piece isn't right for one publication doesn't mean it's bad. Selection is an extremely subjective process."

PHOEBE: A JOURNAL OF LITERATURE AND ART

MSN 2C5, George Mason University, 4400 University Dr., Fairfax VA 22030-4444. (703)993-2915. **E-mail:** phoebe@gmu.edu (inquiries only). **Website:** www.phoebejournal.com . Established 1970. **Contact:** Poetry Editor. Phoebe Magazine: 9×6; 112-120 pages; 80

lb. paper; 0-5 illustrations; 0-10 photos. "We publish mainly fiction and poetry with some visual art." Biannual. "*Phoebe* prides itself on supporting up-and-coming writers, whose style, form, voice, and subject matter demostrate a vigorous appeal to the senses, intellect, and emotions of our readers. No romance, western, juvenile, or erotica." Receives 300 unsolicited mss/month. Accepts 3-7 mss/issue. Does not read mss in summer. Publishes ms 3-6 months after acceptance. **Publishes 8-10 new writers/year.**

MAGAZINE NEEDS *Phoebe: A Journal of Literature and Art*, published semiannually in September and February, is interested in the uncanny, the assured—solid poetry. Has published poetry by C.D. Wright, Russell Edson, Yusef Komunyakaa, Rosemarie Waldrop, Charles Bernstein, and The Pines. Press run is 3,000, with 35-40 pages of poetry in each issue. Receives 4,000 submissions/year. Single copy: $6; subscription: $12/year.

HOW TO CONTACT Submit up to 5 poems at a time. No simultaneous submissions. No e-mail submissions; postal submissions only. Include SASE and a short bio. Reads submissions September 1-April 15 (postmark); mss postmarked April 16-August 31 will not be read. Guidelines available for SASE or on website. Responds in up to 3 months. Pays 2 contributor's copies or one-year subscription.

ADDITIONAL INFORMATION Check http://phoebejournal.blogspot.com for additional information and commentary about *Phoebe*.

THE PINCH

Dept. of English, The University of Memphis, Memphis TN 38152. (901)678-4591. **E-mail:** editor@thepinchjournal.com. **Website:** www.thepinchjournal.com. Laura Snider. **Contact:** Kristen Iverson, editor-in-chief. "Semiannual literary magazine. We publish fiction, creative nonfiction, poetry, and art of literary quality by both established and emerging artists." Give 2 copies of journal in which work appears on publication. Copyrighted. Acquires first North American serial rights. Responds in 3 months on mss. Sample copy available for $12. Guidelines available on website.

MAGAZINE NEEDS *The Pinch* (previously *River City*), published semiannually (fall and spring), prints fiction, poetry, interviews, creative nonfiction, and visual art. Has published poetry by Albert Goldbarth, Maxine Kumin, Jane Hirshfield, Terrance Hayes, S. Beth Bishop, and Naomi Shahib Nye. *The Pinch* is 160 pages, 7×10, professionally printed, perfect-bound, with colorful glossy cover and color art and photography. Press run is 2,500. Sample: $12.

HOW TO CONTACT Submit no more than 5 poems at a time. No e-mail submissions. Include SASE. "We do not read in the summer months." Reads submissions according to these deadlines only: August 15-November 1 (Spring issue) and January 15-March 15 (Fall issue). Guidelines available for SASE, by e-mail, or on website. Responds in up to 3 months. Pays 2 contributor's copies.

CONTEST/AWARD OFFERINGS Offers an annual award in poetry. 1st Prize: $1,000 and publication; 2nd- and 3rd-Prize poems may also be published. Any previously unpublished poem of up to 2 pages is eligible. No simultaneous submissions. Poems should be typed and accompanied by a cover letter. Author's name should not appear anywhere on ms. Manuscripts will not be returned. Guidelines available for SASE, by e-mail, or on website. **Entry fee:** $15 for up to 3 poems (includes one-year subscription). **Deadline:** January 15-March 15 (inclusive postmark dates). Winners will be notified in July; published in subsequent issue.

TIPS "We have a new look and a new edge. We're soliciting work from writers with a national or international reputation as well as strong, interesting work from emerging writers. The Pinch Literary Award (previously River City Writing Award) in Fiction offers a $1,500 prize and publication. Check our website for details."

THE PINK CHAMELEON

E-mail: dpfreda@juno.com. **Website:** www.thepinkchameleon.com. **Contact:** Mrs. Dorothy Paula Freda, editor/publisher. Needs fiction and nonfiction.

MAGAZINE NEEDS *The Pink Chameleon Online* published annually online, contains "family-oriented, upbeat poetry, any genre in good taste that gives hope for the future." Wants "poems about nature, loved ones, rare moments in time." Does not want "pornography, cursing, swearing; nothing evoking despair." Also considers poetry by children and teens. Receives about 50 poems/year, accepts about 50%. Submit 1-4 poems at a time. Considers previously published poems; no simultaneous submissions. Accepts e-mail submissions only (pasted into body of message; "please, no attachments"). Use plain text and include a brief bio. Reads submissions January-April 30th and September-October 31st. Time between acceptance and publication is up to 1 year depending on date of acceptance. Often comments on rejected poems. Guidelines available by e-mail or on website. Responds in 1 month. No payment. Acquires one-time, one-year publication rights. All rights revert to poet in 6 months to a year, depending on date of acceptance. Line Length: 6 lines/min-24 lines/max

TIPS "Simple, honest, evocative emotion, upbeat fiction and nonfiction submissions that give hope for the future; well-paced plots; stories, poetry, articles, essays that speak from the heart. Read guidelines carefully. Use a good, but not ostentatious, opening hook. Stories should have a beginning, middle and end that make the reader feel the story was worth his or her time. This also applies to articles and essays. In the latter two, wrap your comments and conclusions in a neatly packaged final paragraph. Turnoffs include violence, bad language. Simple, genuine and sensitive work does not need to shock with vulgarity to be interesting and enjoyable."

PINYON

Mesa State College, Languages, Literature and Mass Communications, Mesa State College, 1100 North Ave., Grand Junction CO 81501-3122. **E-mail:** pinyonpoetry@hotmail.com. **Website:** www.mesastate.edu/english/publications.html. **Contact:** Managing editor. *Pinyon*, published annually in June, prints "the best available contemporary American poetry and fiction. No restrictions other than excellence. We appreciate a strong voice." Does not want "inspirational, light verse, or sing-song poetry." Has published poetry by Mark Cox, Barry Spacks, Wendy Bishop, and Anne Ohman Youngs. *Pinyon* is about 120 pages, magazine-sized, perfect-bound. Receives about 4,000 poems/year, accepts 2%. Press run is 300; 100 distributed free to contributors, friends, etc. Subscription: $8/year. Sample: $5. Make checks payable to Pinyon, MSC.

HOW TO CONTACT Submit 3-5 poems at a time. No previously published poems or simultaneous submissions. Cover letter is preferred. "Name, address, e-mail, and phone number on each page. SASE required." Reads submissions August 1-December 1. "3 groups of assistant editors, led by an associate editor, make recommendations to the editor." Seldom comments on rejected poems. Guidelines available for SASE. Responds in February. Pays 2 contributor's copies. Acquires one-time rights.

TIPS "Ask yourself if the work is something you would like to read in a publication."

PIRENE'S FOUNTAIN

E-mail: pirenesfountain@gmail.com. **Website:** pirenesfountain.com. **Contact:** Oliver Lodge, Tony Walbran, editors; Lark Vernon, senior editor; Ami Kaye, publisher and managing editor. *Pirene's Fountain* is published online 2 times per year in April and October. Has published work by Lisel Mueller, Linda Pastan, J.P. Dancing Bear, Alison Croggan, Dorianne Laux, Rebecca Seiferle, Joseph Millar, Kim Addonizio, Jane Hirshfeld, and Jim Moore, among others. Receives about 1,500 poems/year, accepts about 20%. 50-100 word bio note is required. Poets retain copyright to their own work, rights revert to poets upon publication. Publishes ms 1-3 months after acceptance. Responds in 1-4 months. Guidelines available online.

MAGAZINE NEEDS "Poets whose work has been selected for publication in our journal during the past calendar year (with the exception of staff /featured poets) are automatically entered for the annual award. Our editors will each choose one poem from all of the selections. The 5 nominated poems will be sent "blind" to an outside editor/publisher for the final decision. The winning poet will be awarded a certificate and a $100 Amazon gift card via email. Pushcart and Best of the Net nominations: Editors select the best work published by PF during the year. This is open to all submitting and featured poets. Only previously unpublished poems will be considered; please indicate that in your submission. Nominated poets are notified after selections have been sent in." Submit 3-8 poems at a time. Considers previously published poems and simultaneous submissions. Considers poetry posted on a public website/blog/forum and poetry posted on a private, password-protected forum as published. Poems are circulated to an editorial board. Never comments on rejected poems. Sometimes publishes theme issues. Does not want "blatantly religious/political themes, anything obscene, pornographic, or discriminatory in nature."

TIPS "Please read submission guidelines carefully and send in at least 3 poems. We offer a poetry discussion group on Facebook, entitled Pirene's Fountain Poetry."

PLAINSONGS

Department of Languages and Literature, Hastings NE 68901. (402)461-7343. **Fax:** (402)461-7756. **E-mail:** plainsongs@hastings.edu. **Contact:** Laura Marvel Wunderlich, editor. Plainsongs, published 3 times/year, considers poems on any subject, in any style, but free verse predominates. Plainsongs' title suggests not only its location on the great plains, but its preference for the living language, whether in free or formal verse. Subscription: $15 for 3 issues. Sample: $5. Acquires first rights. Responds 2 months after deadline.

MAGAZINE NEEDS Submit up to 6 poems at a time. No fax, email, or disk submissions. Postal submissions only. Reads submissions according to the following deadlines: August 15 for winter issue; November 15 for spring issue; March 15 for fall issue. Pays 2 contributor's copies and one-year subscription.

CONTEST/AWARD OFFERINGS 3 poems in each issue receive a $25 prize. "A short essay in appreciation accompanies each award poem."

PLAIN SPOKE

Amsterdam Press, 6199 Steubenville Road SE, Amsterdam OH 43903. (740) 543-4333. **E-mail:** plainspoke@gmail.com. **Website:** www.plainspoke.net. Shaun M. Barcalow, fiction editor. **Contact:** Cindy Kelly, editor. *Plain Spoke*, published quarterly, publishes "poetry heavy in sense images and with a clear, plain-spoken voice." Wants "Americana, nostalgia, narrative." Does not want "esoteric, universal, clicheé." Has published poetry by Claudia Burbank, Deborah Bogen, Doug Ramspeck, Amy Sargent. *Plain Spoke* is 36-60 digest-sized, laser-printed, saddle-stitched, with a color art on cardstock cover. Receives about 2,500 poems/year, accepts about 5%. Press run is 300. Single copy: $8; subscription: $25. Make checks payable to Amsterdam Press.

HOW TO CONTACT Submit up to 6 poems at a time, preferably under 40 lines. Considers simultaneous submissions, no previously published poems (considers poetry posted on a public website/blog/forum). Accepts e-mail submissions (following guidelines on website at www.plainspoke.net. Cover letter is required. Paper submissions require an SASE. Submissions received without an SASE are recycled. No postcards. Reads submissions year round. Submit seasonal poems 3 months in advance. Time between acceptance and publication is 1-4 months. Poems are circulated to an editorial board. Sometimes comments on rejected poems. Never publishes theme issues. Guidelines available for SASE, by e-mail, and on website. Responds in 1 week. Pays 1 contributor's copy. Acquires first North American serial rights. Rights revert to poets upon publication. Reviews books and chapbooks of poetry in single-book format. Send cover letter and materials for review consideration to Reviews Editor, *Plain Spoke*.

TIPS "Work that surprises us stands out. We don't like the predictable. We don't want to feel like we're reading a story, pull us in. Make every word count and don't rely on adverbs."

PLANET-THE WELSH INTERNATIONALIST

P.O. Box 44, Aberystwyth Ceredigion SY23 3ZZ, United Kingdom. **E-mail:** planet.enquiries@planetmagazine.org.uk. **Website:** www.planetmagazine.org.uk. **Contact:** Emily Trahair, acting editor. A literary/cultural/political journal centered on Welsh affairs but with a strong interest in minority cultures in Europe and elsewhere. *Planet: The Welsh Internationalist*, published quarterly, is a cultural magazine "centered on Wales, but with broader interests in arts, sociology, politics, history, and science." Wants "good poetry in a wide variety of styles. No limitations as to subject matter; length can be a problem." Has published poetry by Nigel Jenkins, Anne Stevenson, and Les Murray. *Planet* is 128 pages, A5, professionally printed, perfect-bound, with glossy color card cover. Receives about 500 submissions/year, accepts about 5%. Press run is 1,550 (1,500 subscribers, about 10% libraries, 200 shelf sales). Single copy: £6.75; subscription: £22 (£38 overseas). Sample available. Publishes ms 4-6 months after acceptance. Responds in 3 months. Sample copy for £4. Guidelines available online.

MAGAZINE NEEDS Please submit 4-6 poems at a time. No previously published poems or simultaneous submissions. Accepts e-mail (as attachment) and disk submissions. SASE or SAE with IRCs essential for reply. Pays £30 minimum

TIPS "We do not look for fiction which necessarily has a 'Welsh' connection, which some writers assume from our title. We try to publish a broad range of fiction and our main criterion is quality. Try to read copies of any magazine you submit to. Don't write out of the blue to a magazine which might be completely inappropriate for your work. Recognize that you are likely to have a high rejection rate, as magazines tend to favor writers from their own countries."

PLEIADES

Pleiades Press, Department of English, University of Central Missouri, Martin 336, Warrensburg MO 64093. (660)543-4425. **Fax:** (660)543-8544. **E-mail:** pleiades@ucmo.edu. **Website:** www.ucmo.edu/englphil/pleiades. **Contact:** G.B. Crump, Matthew Eck and Phong Nguyen, prose editors. "We publish contemporary fiction, poetry, interviews, literary essays, special-interest personal essays, reviews for a general and literary audience from authors from around the world." Buys first North American serial rights, buys second serial (reprint) rights. Occasionally requests rights for TV, radio reading, website. Pays on publication. Publishes ms an average of 9 months after acceptance. Responds in 2 months to queries. Responds in 1-4 months to mss. Editorial lead time 9 months. Sample copy for $5 (back issue); $6 (current issue) Guidelines available online.

"Also sponsors the Lena-Miles Wever Todd Poetry Series competition, a contest for the best book ms by an American poet. The winner receives $1,000, publication by Pleiades Press, and distribution by Louisiana State University Press. Deadline September 30. Send SASE for guidelines."

MAGAZINE NEEDS *Pleiades*, published semiannually in April and October, prints poetry, fiction, literary criticism, belles lettres (occasionally), and reviews. Open to all writers. Wants "avant-garde, free verse, and traditional poetry, and some quality light verse." Does not want anything "pretentious, didactic, or overly sentimental." Has published poetry by James Tate, Joyce Carol Oates, Brenda Hillman, Wislawa Szymborska, Carl Phillips, and Jean Valentine. *Pleiades* is 160 pages, digest-sized, perfect-bound, with heavy coated cover with color art. Receives about 9,000 poems/year, accepts fewer than 1%. Press run is 2,500-3,000; about 200 distributed free to educational institutions and libraries across the country. Single copy: $6; subscription: $12. Sample: $5. Make checks payable to Pleiades Press. "Nothing didactic, pretentious, or overly sentimental. Do not send poetry after May 31. We resume reading poetry on Sept. 1." Pays $3/poem, and contributor copies

HOW TO CONTACT Submit 3-5 poems at a time. Considers simultaneous submissions with notification; no previously published poems. Cover letter is preferred. Include brief bio. Time between acceptance and publication "can be up to 1 year. Each poem published must be accepted by 2 readers and approved by the poetry editor." Seldom comments on rejected poems. Guidelines available for SASE or on website. Responds in up to 3 months. Payment varies. Acquires first and second serial rights.

TIPS "Submit only 1 genre at a time to appropriate editors. Show care for your material and your readers—submit quality work in a professional format. Include cover letter with brief bio and list of publications. Include SASE. Cover art is solicited directly from artists. We accept queries for book reviews. For summer submissions, the poetry and nonfiction editors will no longer accept mss sent between June 1 & August 31. Any sent after May 31 will be held until the end of summer. Please do not send your only copy of anything."

PLOUGHSHARES

Emerson College, Ploughshares, 120 Boylston St., Boston MA 02116. **Website:** www.pshares.org. **Contact:** Ladette Randolph, editor. *Ploughshares*, published 3 times/year, is "a journal of new writing guest-edited by prominent poets and writers to reflect different and contrasting points of view. Translations are welcome if permission has been granted. Our mission is to present dynamic, contrasting views on what is valid and important in contemporary literature and to discover and advance significant literary talent. Each issue is guest-edited by a different writer. We no longer structure issues around preconceived themes." Editors have included Carolyn Forché, Gerald Stern, Rita Dove, Chase Twichell, and Marilyn Hacker. Has published poetryby Donald Hall, Li-Young Lee, Robert Pinsky, Brenda Hillman, and Thylias Moss. Ploughshares is 200 pages, digest-sized. Receives about 11,000 poetry, fiction, and essay submissions/year. Press run is 6,000. Subscription: $30 domestic, $30 plus shipping (see website) foreign. Sample: $14 current issue, $7 back issue, please inquire for shipping rates. Buys first North American serial rights. Pays on publication. Publishes ms an average of 6 months after acceptance. Responds in 5 months to mss. Guidelines available online.

A competitive and highly prestigious market. Rotating and guest editors make cracking the line-up even tougher, since it's difficult to know what is appropriate to send. Reads submissions June 1-January 15 (postmark); mss submitted January 16-May 31 will be returned unread. "We doaccept electronic submissions — there is a $3 fee per submission, which is waived if you are a subscriber."

MAGAZINE NEEDS Submit 1-3 poems at a time.

TIPS "We no longer structure issues around preconceived themes. If you believe your work is in keeping with our general standards of literary quality and-value, submit at any time during our reading period."

PMS

(205)934-8578. **E-mail:** kmadden@uab.edu. **Website:** www.pms-journal.org/submissions-guidelines. **Contact:** Kerry Madden, Editor-in-Chief. "This is an all women's literary journal. The subject field is wide open." "Each issue of *PMS* includes a memoir written by a woman who has experienced a historically significant event. *PMS 10* features Masha Hamilton and her authors from the Afghan Women's Writing Project. Writer Donna Thomas's memoir, Kiddie Land, recalls Birmingham's segregated past when Kiddie Land opened to children of all colors. Look for excerpts of *PMS 10* to be online soon." Sample copy for $7.

Work from PMS has been reprinted in a number of award anthologies: *New Stories from the South 2005, The Best Creative Nonfiction 200* and *2008, Best American Poetry 2003* and *2004*, and *Best American Essays 2005* and *2007.*

MAGAZINE NEEDS All submissions should be unpublished original work that we can recycle and be accompanied by a SASE with sufficient postage for either return of your manuscript or notification. Writers will receive two complimentary copies of the issue of *PMS* in which their work appears and a one-year subscription. Copyright returns to the author after publication in *PMS*.

HOW TO CONTACT We will not acknowledge or return submissions not accompanied by SASE. Submissions should include a cover letter and a brief biographical statement of the writer. All manuscripts should be typed on one side only of 8 x 11 white paper with the author's name, address, phone number, and email address on the front of each submission. Prose should be double-spaced; poetry may be single-spaced. Poems of multiple pages should indicate whether or not stanza breaks accompany page breaks.

TIPS "We seek unpublished original work that we can recycle." Reading period runs Jan. 1-Mar. 31. Submissions received at other times of the year will be returned unread. Best way to make contact is through e-mail.

POCKETS

Upper Room, P.O. Box 340004, 1908 Grand Ave., Nashville TN 37203-0004. (800)972-0433. **Fax:** (615)340-7275. **E-mail:** pockets@upperroom.org. **Website:** pockets.upperroom.org/. **Contact:** Lynn W. Gilliam, editor. Magazine published 11 times/year. "*Pockets* is a Christian devotional magazine for children ages 8-12. Stories should help children experience a Christian lifestyle that is not always a neatly wrapped moral package but is open to the continuing revelation of God's will." Buys first North American serial rights. Pays on acceptance. Publishes ms an average of 1 year after acceptance. Responds in 8 weeks to mss. Each issue reflects a specific theme. Sample copy available with a 9×12 SASE with 4 First-Class stamps attached to envelope. Guidelines on website.

Does not accept e-mail or fax submissions.

MAGAZINE NEEDS *Pockets*, published monthly (except February), is an interdenominational magazine for children ages 8-12. "Each issue is built around a specific theme, with material (including poetry) that can be used by children in a variety of ways. Submissions do not need to be overly religious; they should help children experience a Christian lifestyle that is not always a neatly wrapped moral package but is open to the continuing revelation of God's will." Considers poetry by children. Length: 4-20 lines. $25 minimum.

TIPS "Theme stories, role models, and retold scripture stories are most open to freelancers. Poetry is also open. It is very helpful if writers read our writers' guidelines and themes on our website."

POEM

Huntsville Literary Association, P.O. Box 2006, Huntsville AL 35804. **E-mail:** poem@hla-hsv.org. **Website:** www.hla-hsv.org. **Contact:** Rebecca Harbor, editor. *Poem*, published twice/year in May and November, consists entirely of poetry. "We publish both traditional forms and free verse." Wants poems "characterized by compression, rich vocabulary, significant content, and evidence of 'a tuned ear and practiced pen.' We want coherent work that moves through the particulars of the poem to make a point. We equally welcome submissions from established poets as well as from less-known and beginning poets." Does not want translations. Has published poetry by Kathryn Kirkpatrick, Peter Serchuk, and Kim Bridgford. *Poem* is 90 pages, digest-sized, flat-spined, printed on good stock paper, with a clean design and a matte cover. Prints more than 60 poems/issue, generally featured 1 to a page. Press run is 500. Single copy: $10; subscription: $20. Sample: $7 (back issue).

MAGAZINE NEEDS Send 3-5 poems at a time. No previously published poems or simultaneous submissions. Include SASE. Reads submissions year-round. Guidelines available for SASE or on website. Responds in 1-2 months. Pays 2 contributor's copies. Acquires first serial rights.

● POEMELEON: A JOURNAL OF POETRY

E-mail: editor@poemeleon.org. **Website:** www.poemeleon.org. **Contact:** Cati Porter, editor. Volume VI Issue 2, The Unreal Issue, launched December 2012. The Unreal Issue featured work that could be considered magical realist, fabulist, speculative, or otherwise incorporates the strange, the surreal, and the unreal, whether or not it could possibly really exist. If you think it seems unreal, maybe we will, too. Please send only your best work, any length, any style. Expect a response within 1 - 3 months after close of submissions. If you have not heard from us after 3 months please inquire. Please submit 1 to 5 poems, 1 craft essay, or 1 book review, using the formsonline. Please include a brief third-person bio in your cover letter. Acquires one-time, non-exclusive rights.

MAGAZINE NEEDS *Poemeleon: A Journal of Poetry*, published semiannually online, wants all forms and styles of poetry. "Does not want overly religious or sentimental, greeting card verse." Has published poetry by Sherman Alexie, David Kirby, Tony Barnstone, Catherine Daly, Ann Fisher-Wirth, Richard Garcia, Eloise Klein Healy, Bob Hicok. Poemeleon receives about 1,000 poems/year, accepts about 150-200. Number of unique visitors: 25,000/year. Submit 3-5 poems at a time. Considers previously published poems (as long as they have not appeared online) and simultaneous submissions as long as we are notified promptly if a poem is taken elsewhere). Considers poetry posted on a public website/blog/forum as published. All submissions must come through online submissions form located on the guidelines page of the website; no fax, paper, e-mail or disk submissions. Cover letter is preferred. Each issue is devoted to a particular type of poetry (past issues include poems of place, ekphrastic poems, poems in form, and the prose poem, The persona poem, humor, gender, and collaborative poetry). Please check the guidelines page for specifics before submitting. Reads submissions year round.

ADDITIONAL INFORMATION Previously published is fine, as long as it was in print, not online, and as long as you as the author retain all copyright.

CONTEST/AWARD OFFERINGS Mystery Box Contest offers a prize of the Mystery Box and publication on the website. Submit 1 poem. Guidelines available on website. **Entry fee:** none. Deadline: none.

◐ POEMS & PLAYS

English Department, Middle Tennessee State University, Murfreesboro TN 37132. **E-mail:** gbrewer@mtsu.edu. **Contact:** Gaylord Brewer, editor. *Poems & Plays*, published annually in the spring, is an "eclectic publication for poems and short plays." No restrictions on style or content of poetry. Has published poetry by Naomi Wallace, Kate Gale, James Doyle, and Ron Koertge. *Poems & Plays* is 88 pages, digest-sized, professionally printed, perfect-bound, with coated color card cover. Receives 1,500 poems per issue, publishes 30-35 "typically." Press run is 800. Subscription: $10 for 2 issues. Acquires first rights. Pays 1 contributor's copy. Responds in 2 months. Sample copy for $6.

TIPS Considers chapbook mss (poems or short plays) of 20-24 pages for The Tennessee Chapbook Prize. "Any combination of poems or plays, or a single play, is eligible. The winning chapbook is printed within *Poems & Plays*." Winning author receives 50 copies of the issue. SASE required. **Entry fee:** $15 (includes 1 copy of the issue). **Deadline:** Same as for the magazine (October-November). Past winners include Tammy Armstrong and Judith Sornberger. "The chapbook competition annually receives over 150 manuscripts from the US and around the world."

◐ POESY MAGAZINE

P.O. Box 7823, Santa Cruz CA 95061. (831)239-4419. **E-mail:** info@poesy.org; submissions@poesy.org. **Website:** www.poesy.org. **Contact:** Brian Morrisey, editor and publisher. *POESY Magazine*, published biannually, is "an anthology of American poetry. *POESY*'s main concentrations are Boston, Massachusetts and Santa Cruz, California, 2 thriving homesteads for poets, beats, and artists of nature. Our goal is to unite the 2 scenes, updating poets on what's happening across the country." Wants to see "original poems that express observational impacts with clear and concise imagery. Acceptence is based on creativity, composition, and relation to the format of *POESY*." Does not want "poetry with excessive profanity. We would like to endorse creativity beyond the likes of everyday babble." Has published poetry by Lawrence Ferlinghetti, Jack Hirschman, Edward Sanders, Todd Moore, Diane Di Prima, and Julia Vinograd. *POESY* is 16 pages, magazine-sized, newsprint, glued/folded, includes ads. Receives about 1,000 poems/year, accepts about 10%. Press run is 1,000; most distributed free to local venues. Single copy: $1; subscription: $12/year. Sample: $2. Make checks payable to Brian Morrisey.

MAGAZINE NEEDS Submit 3-5 poems at a time. Lines/poem: 32 maximum. No previously published poems or simultaneous submissions. Accepts e-mail (submissions@poesy.org) and disk submissions. "Snail mail submissions are preferred with a SASE." Cover letter is preferred. Reads submissions year round. Time between acceptance and publication is 1 month. "Poems are accepted by the Santa Cruz editor/publisher based on how well the poem stimulates our format." Guidelines available in magazine, for SASE, by e-mail, or on website. Responds in 1 month. Sometimes sends prepublication galleys. Pays 3 contributor's copies. Acquires one-time rights. Reviews books/chapbooks of poetry and other magazines/journals in 1,000 words, single-book format. Send materials for review consideration to *POESY*, c/o Brian Morrisey.

TIPS "Stay away from typical notions of love and romance. Become one with your surroundings and discover a true sense of natural perspective."

◐ POETALK

Bay Area Poets Coalition, 1791 Solano Ave. #A11, Berkeley CA 94707-2209. **E-mail:** poetalk@aol.com. **Website:** www.bayareapoetscoalition.org. **Contact:** John Rowe (editorial board), acquisitions. *POETALK*, currently published 1-2 issues/year, is the poetry journal of the Bay Area Poets Coalition (BAPC) and publishes 60-plus poets in each issue. "*POETALK* is open to all. No particular genre. Rhyme must be well done." All rights revert to author upon publication. Usually responds in up to 6 months. Guidelines available early summer for SASE, by e-mail, or see posting on website.

○ *POETALK* is 36 pages, digest-sized, photocopied, saddle-stapled, with heavy card cover. Press run is 400. Subscription: $5/2 issues. Sample copy: $2. **Deadline:** Submit September 1-November 15 (postmark).

MAGAZINE NEEDS In general, poets may submit 3-5 poems at a time, no more than twice/year. Lines/poem: under 35 preferred; longer poems of outstanding quality considered. Considers previously published poems and simultaneous submissions, but must be noted. Cover letter is preferred. Include SASE. "Mss should be clearly typed, single-spaced, and include author's name and mailing address on every page. Please also provide an e-mail address." Pays 1 contributor's copy.

CONTEST/AWARD OFFERINGS Sponsors yearly contest.

TIPS "If you don't want suggested revisions, you need to say so clearly in your cover letter or indicate on each poem submitted." Bay Area Poets Coalition holds monthly readings (in Berkeley, CA). BAPC has 150 members; membership is $15/year (includes subscription to *POETALK* and other privileges); extra outside US.

POETICA MAGAZINE, REFLECTIONS OF JEWISH THOUGHT

P.O. Box 11014, Norfolk VA 23517. **Website:** www.poeticamagazine.com. *Poetica Magazine, Reflections of Jewish Thought*, published 3 times/year, offers "an outlet for the many writers who draw from their Jewish backgrounds and experiences to create poetry/prose/short stories, giving both emerging and recognized writers the opportunity to share their work with the larger community." Does not want long pieces, haiku, rhyming poetry. Considers poetry by children and teens, grades 6-12. *Poetica* is 70 pages, perfect bound, full color cover, includes some ads. Receives about 500 poems/year, accepts about 60%. Press run is 350. Single copy: $10; subscription: $19.50. Poets retain all rights. Publishes ms 1 year after acceptance. Responds in 1 month.

MAGAZINE NEEDS Submit 3 poems at a time to submission@poeticamagazine.com. Lines/poem: 2 pages maximum. Considers simultaneous submissions. No e-mail or disk submissions. Cover letter is optional. Reads submissions year round. Pays 1 contributor's copy.

CONTEST/AWARD OFFERINGS Offers annual poetry contest with up to $50 awarded for First Prize; up to 5 Honorable Mentions. Selected poems will be published in future issues of *Poetica*. Accepts simultaneous submissions. No limit on number of entries (3 poems constitute an entry). Submit 2 copies of each poem, single-spaced, no more than 1 poem/page. Include poet's name on all pages. No e-mail submissions. Include SASE for results only; mss will not be returned. Guidelines available on website. **Entry fee:** $15 for up to 3 poems. **Deadline:** March 31 annually. Judge: Jane Ellen Glasser. Notifies winners by June. Other contests include the Poet of the Month Award, Annual Chapbook Award, and annual anthology centered on a theme.

POETIC MATRIX, A PERIODIC LETTER

P.O. Box 1223, Madera CA 93639. **E-mail:** poeticmatrix@yahoo.com. **Website:** www.poeticmatrix.com. **Contact:** John Peterson, editor. *Poetic Matrix, a periodic letteR*, published 2 times/year online, seeks poetry that "creates a 'place in which we can live' rather than telling us about the place; poetry that draws from the imaginal mind and is rich in the poetic experience—hence the poetic matrix." Does not want poetry that talks about the experience. Has published poetry by Lyn Lifshin, Tony White, Gail Entrekin, James Downs, Joan Michelson, and Brandon Cesmat.

MAGAZINE NEEDS Accepts e-mail submissions (pasted into body of message, no attachments). Guidelines available by e-mail or on website. Acquires one-time rights."*Poetic Matrix* has a call for manuscripts for the Slim Volume Series every 2 years. See website for when reading dates are set and for additional guidelines and awards. The Slim Volume Series is for manuscripts of 65-75 pages." **Charges reading fee of $17.**

TIPS "We seek writing of quality, with passion and intelligence."

POET LORE

The Writer's Center, 4508 Walsh St., Bethesda MD 20815. **E-mail:** post.master@writer.org. **Website:** http://poetlore.com; www.writer.org. E. Ethelbert Miller, editor. **Contact:** Jody Bolz, editor. *Poet Lore*, published semiannually, is "dedicated to the best in American and world poetry as well as timely reviews and commentary." Wants "fresh uses of traditional forms and devices, but any kind of excellence is welcome." Has published poetry by Ai, Denise Duhamel, Jefferey Harrison, Eve Jones, Carl Phillips, and Ronald Wallace. *Poet Lore* is 144 pages, digest-sized, professionally printed, perfect-bound, with glossy card cover. Receives about 4,200 poems/year, accepts 125. Press run is at least 800. Single copy: $8; subscription: $18/nonmember, $12/member. "Add $1/single copy for shipping; add $5 postage for subscriptions outside U.S."

MAGAZINE NEEDS Considers simultaneous submissions "with notification in cover letter." No e-mail or disk submissions. "Submit typed poems (up to 5), with author's name and address on each page; SASE is required." Guidelines available for SASE or on website. Responds in 3 months. Pays 2 contributor's copies and a one-year subscription. Reviews books of poetry. Send materials for review consideration.

POETRY

The Poetry Foundation, 61 W. Superior St., Chicago IL 60654. (312)787-7070. **Fax:** (312)787-6650. **E-mail:** editors@poetrymagazine.org. **Website:** www.poetrymagazine.org. Christian Wiman, Editor. **Contact:** Helen Klaviter. *Poetry*'s website offers featured poems, letters, reviews, interviews, essays, and web-exclusive features. *Poetry*, published monthly by The Poetry Foundation (see separate listing in Organizations), "has no special manuscript needs and no special requirements as to form or genre: We examine in turn all work received and accept that which seems best." Has published poetry by the major voices of our time as well as new talent. *Poetry* is elegantly printed, flat-spined. Receives 90,000 submissions/year, accepts about 300-350. Press run is 16,000. Single copy: $3.75; subscription: $35 ($38 for institutions). Sample: $5.50. Buys first serial rights. Pays on publication. Publishes ms an average of 9 months after acceptance. Sample copy for $3.75 or online at website. Guidelines available online.

MAGAZINE NEEDS Accepts all styles and subject matter. Submit no more than 4 poems at a time. No previously published poems or simultaneous submissions. Electronic submission preferred. When submitting by post put return address on outside of envelope; include SASE. Submissions must be typed, single-spaced, with poet's name and address on every page. Responds in 1-2 months. Pays $10/line (with a minimum payment of $300). Reviews books of poetry in multi-book formats of varying lengths. Does not accept unsolicited reviews. Pays $10/line ($150 minimum payment).

CONTEST/AWARD OFFERINGS 7 prizes (Bess Hokin Prize, Levinson Prize, Frederick Bock Prize, J. Howard and Barbara M.J. Wood Prize, John Frederick Nims Memorial Prize, Friends of Literature Prize, Union League Civic and Arts Poetry Prize) ranging from $300 to $5,000 are awarded annually to poets whose work has appeared in the magazine that year. Only verse already published in *Poetry* is eligible for consideration; no formal application is necessary.

POETRYBAY

P.O. Box 114, Northport NY 11768. (631)427-1950. **E-mail:** poetrybay@aol.com; info@poetrybay.com. **Website:** www.poetrybay.com. **Contact:** George Wallace, editor. *Poetrybay*, published semiannually online, seeks "to add to the body of great contemporary American poetry by presenting the work of established and emerging writers. Also, we consider essays and reviews." Has published poetry by Robert Bly, Yevgeny Yevtushenko, Marvin Bell, Diane Wakoski, Cornelius Eady, and William Heyen.

MAGAZINE NEEDS Submit 5 poems at a time. Considers simultaneous submissions; no previously published poems. Accepts e-mail submissions (pasted into body of message to info@poetrybay.com); no disk submissions. Time between acceptance and publication is 6-12 months. Seldom comments on rejected poems. Occasionally publishes theme issues. Guidelines available on website. Sometimes sends prepublication galleys. Acquires first-time electronic rights. Reviews books/chapbooks of poetry and other magazines/journals. Send materials for review consideration.

THE POETRY CHURCH MAGAZINE

Moorside Words and Music, Eldwick Crag Farm, High Eldwick, Bingley, W. Yorkshire BD16 3BB, England. **E-mail:** reavill@globalnet.co.uk. **Contact:** Tony Reavill, editor. *The Poetry Church Magazine*, published quarterly, contains Christian poetry, prayers, and hymns. Wants "Christian or good religious poetry." Does not want "unreadable blasphemy." **Publishes subscribers' work only.** Considers poetry by children over age 10.

Has published poetry by Laurie Bates, Joan Sheridan Smith, Idris Caffrey, Isabella Strachan, Walter Nash, and Susan Glyn. *The Poetry Church Magazine* is 40 pages, digest-sized, photocopied, saddle-stapled, with illustrated cover. Receives about 1,000 poems/year, accepts about 500. Press run is 1,000. Single copy: free; subscription: £12 for 4 issues ($20 USD). Make checks payable in sterling to Feather Books.

MAGAZINE NEEDS Submit 2 poems at a time. Lines/poem: usually around 20, "but will accept longer." Considers previously published poems and simultaneous submissions. Cover letter is preferred (with information about the poet). No e-mail submissions; postal submissions only. Include SASE, or SAE and IRC. Submissions must be typed. **Publishes "only subscribers' poems as they keep us solvent."** Time between acceptance and publication is 4 months. "The editor does a preliminary reading, then seeks the advice of colleagues about uncertain poems." Responds within 1 week. Poets retain copyright.

ADDITIONAL INFORMATION Feather Books publishes the Feather Books Poetry Series, collections of around 20 Christian poems and prayers. Has recently published the Glyn family, Walter Nash, David Grieve, and Rosie Morgan Barry. "We have now published 300 poetry collections by individual Christian poets." Books are usually photocopied, saddle-stapled, with illustrated covers. "We do not insist, but **most poets pay for their work. Enquire for current costs.** If they can't afford it, but are good poets, we stand the cost. We expect poets to read *The Poetry Church Magazine* to get some idea of our standards."

ALSO OFFERS Each winter and summer, selected poems appear in *The Poetry Church Collection*, the leading Christian poetry anthology used in churches and schools.

POETRY INTERNATIONAL

San Diego State University, 5500 Campanile Dr., San Diego CA 92182-6020. (619)594-1522. **Fax:** (619)594-4998. **E-mail:** poetryinternational@yahoo.com. **Website:** http://poetryinternational.sdsu.edu. **Contact:** Fred Moramarco, Founding Editor. *Poetry International*, published annually in November, is "an eclectic poetry magazine intended to reflect a wide range of poetry being written today." Wants "a wide range of styles and subject matter. We're particularly interested in translations." Does not want "cliché-ridden, derivative, or obscure poetry." Has published poetry by Adrienne Rich, Robert Bly, Hayden Carruth, Kim Addonizio, Maxine Kumin, and Gary Soto. *Poetry International* is 200 pages, perfect-bound, with coated cardstock cover. Press run is 1,500. Subscription: $15/1 year. "We intend to continue to publish poetry that makes a difference in people's lives, and startles us anew with the endless capacity of language to awaken our senses and expand our awareness." Responds in 6-8 months to mss.

Features the Poetry International Prize ($1,000) for best original poem. Submit up to 3 poems with a $10 entry fee.

MAGAZINE NEEDS Features the poetry of a different nation of the world as a special section in each issue.

HOW TO CONTACT Submit no more than 5 poems at a time. Considers simultaneous submissions, "but prefer not to"; no previously published poems. No fax or e-mail submissions. Reads submissions September 1 - Decemeber 1 only. Time between acceptance and publication is 8 months. Poems are circulated to an editorial board. Seldom comments on rejected poems. Responds in up to 4 months. Pays 1 contributor's copy. Acquires all rights. Returns rights "50/50," meaning they split with the author any payment for reprinting the poem elsewhere. "We review anthologies regularly."

TIPS "Seeks a wide range of styles and subject matter. We read unsolicited mss. only between Sept. 1st and Dec. 31st of each year. Mss. received any other time will be returned unread."

POETRY KANTO

Kanto Poetry Center, 3-22-1 Kamariya-Minami Kanazawa-ku, Yokohama 236-8502, Japan. **E-mail:** alan@kanto-gakuin.ac.jp. **Website:** http://home.kanto-gakuin.ac.jp/~kg061001/. **Contact:** Alan Botsford, editor. *Poetry Kanto*, published annually in November by the Kanto Gakuin University, is a journal bridging east and west, featuring "outstanding poetry that navigates the divide of ocean and language from around the world. We seek exciting, well-crafted contemporary poetry in English, and also encourage and publish high-quality English translations of modern and emerging Japanese poets. All translations must be accompanied by the original poems." See website for sample poems. Has published poetry by Jane Hirshfield, Ilya Kaminsky, Beth Ann Fennelly, Vijay Seshadri, Michael S. Collins, Mari L'Esperance, Michael Sowder, and Sarah Arvio. Pays 3-5 contributor's copies. The magazine is unpriced. For sample, send SAE with IRCs. Guidelines available on website.

Poetry Kanto is 120 pages, 6×9, professionally printed on coated stock, perfect-bound, with glossy cover. Press run is 1,000; many are distributed free worldwide to schools, poets, and presses.

MAGAZINE NEEDS Submit 5 poems at a time maximum. Queries welcome. No previously published poems or simultaneous submissions. Prefers e-mail submissions (as attachment in Word). Cover letter is required. Include brief bio. All postal submissions require SAE and IRCs. Reads submissions December-April.

POETRY NORTHWEST

Everett Community College, 2000 Tower St., Everett WA 98103. (425)388-9395. **E-mail:** editors@poetrynw.org. **Website:** www.poetrynw.org. **Contact:** Kevin Craft, editor. *Poetry Northwest* is published semiannually in April and October. "The mission of *Poetry Northwest* is to publish poetry with a vibrant sense of language at play in the world, and a strong presense of the physical world in language. We publish new, emerging, and established writers. In the words of founding editor Carolyn Kizer, we aim to 'encourage the young and the inexperienced, the neglected mature, and the rough major talents and the fragile minor ones.' All styles and aesthetics will find consideration." Acquires all rights. Returns rights to poets upon request. Pays 2 contributor's copies. Time between acceptance and publication is 3-12 months. Sometimes comments on rejected poems. Responds in 8-12 weeks. Single copy: $8. Sample: $9. Make checks payable to *Poetry Northwest*. Guidelines available on website.

Has published poetry by Theodore Roethke, Czeslaw Milosz, Anne Sexton, Harold Pinter, Thom Gunn, and Philip Larkin, Heather McHugh, Richard Kenney. *Poetry Northwest* is 40+ pages, magazine-sized, Web press-printed, saddle-stapled, with 4-color cover, includes ads. Receives about 10,000 poems/year; accepts about 1%. Press run is 2,000.

MAGAZINE NEEDS Submit 3-5 poems at a time once per submission period. No previously published poems; simultaneous submissions OK with notice. Regular mail or online submission form only. No e-mail or disk submissions. Cover letter is required. Sometimes publishes theme issues. Upcoming themes available in magazine or on website. Reading period is September-March. Mss sent outside reading period will be returned unread. Always sends prepublication galleys. Reviews books of poetry in single- and multi-book format.

POETRY NOW

1719 25th Street, Sacramento CA 95816. Richard Hansen, design/layout. **Contact:** Trina Drotar, Managing editor. *Poetry Now* is a literary review with additional online content, published bimonthly by the Sacramento Poetry Center. *Poetry Now* is available on SPC's website in a downloadable format and also at www.issuu.com. The publication includes a calendar of events, book reviews, interviews, and poetry from adults and from poets under 18 in a special column, Young Voices. Seeks submissions of all genres and forms of poetry. Has published poetry by Frank Andrick, James Benton, Martha Ann Blackman, Carol Claassen, Quinton Duval, Bill Gainer, Ann Menebroker, Joshua McKinney, Joyce Odam, and A.D. Winans. Receives over 300 poems/year, and accepts approximately 40%.

MAGAZINE NEEDS Submit 3-5 poems at a time, 1-page maximum length, and a 30-50 word bio. No cover letter. For Young Voices (poets under 18), submit 1-3 poems at a time, 1-page maximum length, and a 20-30 word bio. No previously published poems accepted. Simultaneous submissions accepted but please notify if work is accepted elsewhere. Reads submissions year round. Time of acceptance is 1-3 months. Pays two contributor's copies. Email submission to SPCPoetryEditor@gmail.com. Include in subject line either "Submissions" or "Young Voices."

TIPS "Study the works of poets you love."

POETRY SALZBURG REVIEW

University of Salzburg, Department of English and American Studies, Erzabt-Klotz-Strasse 1, Salzburg A-5020, Austria. (43)(662)8044-4422. **Fax:** (43)(662)8044-167. **E-mail:** editor@poetrysalzburg.com. **Website:** www.poetrysalzburg.com. **Contact:** Dr. Wolfgang Goertschacher, editor. *Poetry Salzburg Review*, published twice/year, contains "articles on poetry, mainly contemporary, and 60% poetry. Also includes essays on poetics, review-essays, interviews, artwork, and translations. We tend to publish selections by authors who have not been taken up by the big poetry publishers. Nothing of poor quality." Acquires first rights. Responds in 2 months.

Has published poetry by Brian W. Aldiss, Rae Armantrout, Paul Muldoon, Alice Notley, Samuel Menashe, Jerome Rothenberg, Michael Heller, Nathaniel Tarn. *Poetry Salzburg Review* is about 200 pages, A5, professionally printed, perfect-bound, with illustrated card cover. Receives about 10,000 poems/year; accepts 3%. Press run is 500. Single copy: $13; subscription: $25 (cash preferred; subscribers can also pay with PayPal). Make checks payable to Wolfgang Goertschacher. "No requirements, but it's a good idea to subscribe to *Poetry Salzburg Review*."

MAGAZINE NEEDS No previously published poems or simultaneous submissions. Accepts e-mail submissions (as attachment). Time between acceptance and publication is 6 months. Seldom comments on rejected poems. Occasionally publishes theme issues. No payment. Reviews books/chapbooks of poetry as well as books on poetics. Send materials for review consideration.

THE POET'S ART

171 Silverleaf Lane, Islandia NY 11749. (631)439-0427. **E-mail:** davidirafox@yahoo.com. **Contact:** David Fox, editor. *The Poet's Art*, published quarterly, is "a family-style journal, accepting work from the unpublished to the well known and all levels in between." Wants "family-friendly, positive poetry; any form considered. Topics include humor, nature, inspirational, children's poetry, or anything else that fits the family-friendly genre." Does not want "violent, vulgar, or overly depressing work. Work is read and accepted by the mentally-ill population, but they should keep in mind this is a family-friendly journal." Considers poetry by children and teens, "any age, as long as it's good quality; if under 18, get parents' permission." Has published poetry by Sheila B. Roark, William J. Middleton, John W. (Bill) Williams, Cory Meyer, and Arthur C. Ford Sr. *The Poet's Art* is 40 or more pages, magazine-sized, photocopied, paper-clipped or stapled, with computer cover, includes ads. Receives about 100 poems a year; accepts about 50%. Press run is 30+. "I have had to institute a $2.50 per issue charge—limit 2— to cover mailing expenses."

MAGAZINE NEEDS Submit "as many poems that will fit on 1 page" at a time. Lines/poem: rarely accepts anything over 1 page. Considers simultaneous submissions ("list any other small press journals (if any) poem titles"). No e-mail or disk submissions; postal submissions only. Cover letter is preferred—"It's only polite. And include a SASE—a must! (I have been lax in this rule about SASEs, but I will now throw any submissions without a SASE away!)." Reads submissions year round, "but poets should be aware we are currently backlogged into December 2012, as of this listing. I review all poems submitted and then decide what I wish to publish." Always comments on rejected poems. Reviews chapbooks of poetry and other magazines/journals, "but editors and authors must write reviews themselves. After all, who knows your magazine/journal or chapbook better than you? (Little-known/newer journals sent in by editors or contributors get first consideration for reviews)." Send to David Fox.

POETS' ESPRESSO REVIEW

1474 Pelem Court, Stockton CA 95203. **E-mail:** poetsexpressoreview@gmail.com. **Website:** www.poetsespresso.com. Donald R. Anderson, editor-in-chief. **Contact:** Patricia Mayorga, editor. *Poets' Espresso Review,* published quarterly online and in print, is "a small black and white publication of poetry, art, photography, recipes, and local events." Sponsored by the Writers' Guild, a club of San Joaquin Delta College. "We value variety, appropriateness for most age groups, and poetry that goes well with the season of the issue, visual and bilingual poetry (side by side with translation), and of length that will fit on our half-sheet pages." Does not want "profanity, racially prejudiced, otherwise offensive material, porn, submissions that are excessively long, illegible writing, nor your only copy of the poem." Considers poetry by all ages. "Please include contact info of parent if from a minor." Has published poetry by David Humphreys, Nikki Quismondo, Susan Richardson Harvey, Marie J. Ross, Christine Stoddard, Michael C. Ford, and Allen Field Weitzel. *Poets' Espresso Review* (print edition) is 24-28 pages, digest-sized, printed "on College's industrial printers," stapled, with color card stock cover with b&w photograph/artwork, might include ads. Accepts about 100 poems/year. Number of unique visitors (online): "small count with rapid growth." Single copy: $2; subscription: $12/year (6 issues). Sample: free in return for review or swap for a desired publication. Make checks payable to Patricia Mayorga.

HOW TO CONTACT Submit "as many poems as you wish" at a time. Lines/poem: "from quote-size up to 80." Considers previously published poems and simultaneous submissions with notification. Accepts e-mail (as attachment in MS Word [.doc], MS Works [.wps], rich text [.rtf], InDesign Interchange [.inx], or notepad [.txt] formats) and disk submissions; no fax submissions. "If postal submissions, submit copies, not originals of works, bio, optional photo. Pieces will not be returned, will respond if accepted with copy of publication. Text must be typed/printed without illegible markings. In any submission except ads, 2 to 4 line biography about the poet/artist is required, written in third person. Biography photo is optional. You may include info for readers to contact you, if you wish." Reads submissions year round. "Deadline for submissions are on or before the onset of the quarter (September, December, March, June). Time between acceptance and publication is 1 to 12 months. Include SASE with cover requesting response if want release from publishing consideration of works after submission. Otherwise may publish up to 12 months after submission. The editor bases acceptance upon space available, interest and meeting the guidelines." Sometimes comments on rejected poems. Regularly publishes (seasonal) theme issues. Guidelines available for SASE with cover letter request, by e-mail, or on website. Responds in up to 2 months. Sometimes sends prepublication galleys (upon request). Pays 1 contributor's copy (extra copies at $3 plus postage per copy). Acquires one-time rights for print edition; acquires electronic rights "to keep an archived issue available online indefinitely in the future. Rights remain with author to publish in any way; rights are given to *Poet's Espresso Review* for indefinite archive on website and 1 issue of the newsletter." Send materials for review consideration to Patricia Mayorga by e-mail (poetsespressoreview@gmail.com) or by postal mail with cover letter.

ADDITIONAL INFORMATION "We occasionally publish anthologies. For info on other works we have published, please visit the websites for the books *Sun Shadow Mountain* and *Moon Mist Valley* other projects linked on the project page at www.rainflowers.org."

THE POET'S HAVEN

P.O. Box 1501, Massillon OH 44648. (330)844-0177. **Website:** www.PoetsHaven.com. **Contact:** Vertigo Xavier, publisher. *The Poet's Haven* is a website "featuring poetry, artwork, stories, essays, and more."

Wants work that's "emotional, personal, and intimate with the author or subject. Topics can cover just about anything." Does not publish religious material. Has published poetry by Robert O. Adair, Christopher Franke, T.M. Göttl, Mary I. Huang, and Anne McMillen. Work published on *The Poet's Haven* is left on the site permanently. Receives about 1,000 poems/year, accepts about 70%.

MAGAZINE NEEDS Considers previously published poems and simultaneous submissions. Accepts submissions through online form only. Time between acceptance and publication is about 2 weeks. Never comments on rejected poems. Guidelines available on website. No payment for online publication. Acquires rights to publish on the website permanently and in any future print publications. Poet retains rights to have poems published elsewhere, "provided the other publishers do not require first-time or exclusive rights."

ADDITIONAL INFORMATION Publishes audio podcast as "Saturday Night With *The Poet's Haven*." Check website for submission information or to download sample episodes.

POET'S INK

E-mail: poet_Kelly@yahoo.com. **Website:** www.PoetsInk.com. **Contact:** Kelly Morris, editor. *Poet's Ink*, published monthly online, seeks "poetry of all kinds. Work by new poets is published alongside that of more experienced poets." Does not want "bad rhyme, clicheés, poetry riddled with abstractions." Considers poetry by teens. "Will be judged by the same standards as poetry by adults." Has published poetry by Alexandria Webb, David Waite, Colin Baker, Megan Arkenburg, and Robert Demaree. Receives about 500 poems/year, accepts about 10%. Acquires one-time rights. Publishes ms 2 months after acceptance. Responds in 1 month. Guidelines by e-mail or online at website.

MAGAZINE NEEDS Submit 3-5 poems at a time. Lines/poem: 2 minimum, 100 maximum ("longer poems better not be long-winded!"). Considers previously published poems and simultaneous submissions. Accepts e-mail submissions (as attachment); no disk submissions. Cover letter is preferred. "No funky formatting of poems!" Reads submissions year round.

THE POET'S PEN

The Society of American Poets (SOAP), 6500 Clito Road, Statesboro GA 30461. 912-587-4400. **Website:** http://ihspub.com. **Contact:** Dr. Charles E. Cravey, editor. *The Poet's Pen*, published quarterly by The Society of American Poets, is "open to all styles of poetry and prose—both religious and secular." Does not want "gross or 'X-rated' poetry without taste or character." Has published poetry by Najwa Salam Brax, Henry Goldman, Henry W. Gurley, William Heffner, Linda Metcalf, and Charles Russ, among others. *The Poet's Pen* uses poetry **primarily by members and subscribers**, but outside submissions are also welcome. Subscription: included in membership, $30/year ($25 for students). Sample: $10.

MAGAZINE NEEDS Submit 3 poems at a time/quarter. Considers simultaneous submissions and previously published poems, if permission from previous publisher is included. Include name and address on each page. "Submissions or inquiries will not be responded to without a #10 business-sized SASE. We do stress originality and have each new poet and/or subscriber sign a waiver form verifying originality." Publishes seasonal/theme issues. Guidelines available in magazine, for SASE, or by e-mail. Sometimes sends prepublication galleys. Always comments on rejected poems.

CONTEST/AWARD OFFERINGS Sponsors several contests each quarter, with prizes totaling $100-250. Also offers Editor's Choice Awards each quarter. The President's Award for Excellence is a prize of $50. **Deadline:** November 1. Also publishes a quarterly anthology from poetry competitions in several categories with prizes of $25-100. Guidelines available for SASE or by e-mail.

POETS' PODIUM

2-3265 Front Rd., E. Hawkesbury ON K6A 2R2, Canada. Ken Elliott, Catherine Heaney Barrowcliffe, Robert Piquette, or Ron Barrowcliffe, associate editors. **Contact:** Ken Elliot. *Poets' Podium*, published quarterly, is a newsletter that aims "to promote the reading and writing of the poetic form, especially among those being published for the first time." Poetry specifications are open. "**Priority is given to valued subscribers.** Nevertheless, when there is room in an issue, we will publish nonsubscribers." Does not want poetry that is "gothic, erotic/sexual, gory, bloody, or that depicts violence." Subscription: $15 USD. Sample: $3 USD.

MAGAZINE NEEDS Submit 3 poems at a time. Lines/poem: 4 minimum, 25 maximum. Considers previously published poems and simultaneous submissions. Cover letter is required. Include SASE (or SAE and IRC), name, address, and telephone number; e-mail address if applicable. Time between acceptance and publication varies. Guidelines available for SASE (or SAE and IRC), or by fax or by e-mail. Pays 3 contributor's copies. All rights remain with the author.

TIPS "Poetry is a wonderful literary form. Try your hand at it. Send us the fruit of your labours."

POINTED CIRCLE

Portland Community College—Cascade, 705 N. Killing, Portland OR 97217. **E-mail:** lutgarda.cowan@pcc.edu. **Contact:** Lutgarda Cowan, English instructor, faculty advisor. Magazine: 80 pages; b&w illustrations; photos. "Anything of interest to educationally/culturally mixed audience." Annual. Ethnic/multicultural, literary, regional, contemporary, prose poem. "We will read whatever is sent, but encourage writers to remember we are a quality literary/arts magazine intended to promote the arts in the community. Be mindful of deadlines and length limits." Acquires one-time rights.

MAGAZINE NEEDS No pornography, nothing trite. Pays 2 contributor copies

HOW TO CONTACT Accepts submissions only October 1-March 1, for July 1 issue. Accepts submissions by e-mail, mail. Prose up to 3,000 words; poetry up to 6 pages; artwork in high-resolution digital form. Submitted materials will not be returned; SASE for notification only. Accepts multiple submissions.

POLYPHONY H.S., AN INTERNATIONAL STUDENT-RUN LITERARY MAGAZINE FOR HIGH SCHOOL WRITERS AND EDITORS

Polyphony High School, 1514 Elmwood Ave., Suite 2, Evanston IL 60201. (847)910-3221. **E-mail:** polyphonyhs@gmail.com. **Website:** www.polyphonyhs.com. "Our mission is to create a high-quality literary magazine written, edited, and published by high school students. We strive to build respectful, mutually beneficial, writer-editor relationships that form a community devoted to improving students' literary skills in the areas of poetry, fiction, and creative nonfiction." Acquires first rights. Pays on publication. Responds in 6-8 weeks. Sample copy available for $7.50 + $2.50 shipping/handling. Detailed guidelines online.

MAGAZINE NEEDS Pays 2 contributor's copies.

CONTEST/AWARD OFFERINGS "We manage the Claudia Ann Seaman Awards for Young Writers; cash awards for the best poem, best story, best work of creative nonfiction. See website for details."

THE PORTLAND REVIEW

Portland State University, P.O. Box 347, Portland OR 97207-0347. (503)725-4533. **E-mail:** theportlandreview@gmail.com. **Website:** portlandreview.tumblr.com. **Contact:** Jacqueline Treiber, editor. *The Portland Review*, published 3 times/year by Portland State University, seeks "submissions exhibiting a unique, compelling voice and content of substance. Experimental poetry welcomed." Has published poetry by Gaylord Brewer, Richard Bentley, Charles Jensen, Mary Biddinger, and Jerzy Gizella. *The Portland Review* is about 130 pages. Receives about 1,000 poems/year, accepts about 30. Press run is 1,000 for subscribers, libraries, and bookstores nationwide. Single copy: $9; subscription: $27/year, $54/2 years. Sample: $8. Buys first North American serial rights. Publishes ms an average of 3-6 months after acceptance. Responds in 2-4 months to mss. Sample copy for $9. Guidelines available online. "Automatic rejection of mss not following guidelines."

HOW TO CONTACT Submit up to 5 poems at a time. No previously published poems. To submit, use submission manager on website. Include phone number, e-mail address, and other contact information. Reads submissions between September 1 and April 1. "Our website is a general introduction to our magazine, with samples of our poetry, fiction, and art. *The Portland Review* will only consider one submission per writer, per reading period. **If you would like to be considered for online publication, please specify this within your cover letter.** "Responds in up to 4 months. Pays 2 contributor's copies. Acquires first North American rights.

TIPS "View website for current samples and guidelines."

POST POEMS

Raw Dog Press, 151 S. West St., Doylestown PA 18901-4134. **Website:** http://rawdogpress.bravehost.com. Post Poems, published annually by Raw Dog Press, is a postcard series. Wants "short poetry (3-7 lines) on any subject. The positive poem or the poem of understated humor always has an inside track. No taboos, however. All styles considered. Anything with rhyme had better be immortal." Has published poetry by Don Ryan, John Grey, and the editor, R. Gerry Fabian. Send SASE for catalog to buy samples.

MAGAZINE NEEDS Submit 3-5 poems at a time. Lines/poem: 3-7. Cover letter is optional. SASE is required. Always comments on rejected poems. Guidelines available on website. Pays in contributor's copies. Acquires all rights. Returns rights on mention of first publication. Sometimes reviews books of poetry. Raw Dog Press welcomes new poets and detests second-rate poems from "name" poets. "We exist because we are dumb like a fox, but even a fox takes care of its own." Send SASE for catalog to buy samples.

THE POTOMAC

2020 Pennsylvania Ave., NW, Suite 443, Washington DC 20006. **E-mail:** Charles.Rammelkamp@ssa.gov. **Website:** http://thepotomacjournal.com. **Contact:** Charles Rammelkamp, editor. *The Potomac*, published semi-annually online, features political commentary, cutting-edge poetry, flash fiction, and reviews. Open to all forms of poetry by new and established writers. Sample copy free online.

Has published poetry and fiction by Robert Cooperman, Michael Salcman, Joanne Lowery, Roger Netzer, Pamela Painter, and L.D. Brodsky. Receives a "variable" number of poems/year, accepts about 50-60.

MAGAZINE NEEDS Submit any number of poems at a time. Considers simultaneous submissions; no previously published poems. Accepts e-mail submissions (as attachment) only; no postal or disk submissions. Cover letter is preferred. Reads submissions year round. Time between acceptance and publication is 3 months. Often comments on rejected poems. Guidelines available on website. Responds in 2 months. Sometimes sends prepublication galleys. No payment. Acquires one-time rights. Reviews books/chapbooks of poetry and other magazines/journals in up to 2,000 words, single- and multi-book format. Send materials for review consideration.

POTOMAC REVIEW: A JOURNAL OF ARTS & HUMANITIES

Montgomery College, 51 Mannakee St., MT/212, Rockville MD 20850. (240)567-4100. **E-mail:** zachary.benavidez@montgomerycollege.edu. **Website:** www.montgomerycollege.edu/potomacreview. **Contact:** Zachary Benavidez, editor-in-chief. *Potomac Review: A Journal of Arts & Humanities*, published semiannually in November and May, "welcomes poetry, from across the spectrum, both traditional and nontraditional poetry, free verse and in-form (translations accepted). Essays and creative nonfiction are also welcome." Has published work by David Wagoner, Elizabeth Spires, Ramola D, Amy Holman, and Luke Johnson. *Potomac Review* is 150 pages, digest-sized, 50 lb paper; 65 lb cover stock. Receives about 2,500 poems/year, accepts 3%. Subscription: $18/year (includes 2 issues). Sample: $10. Publishes ms 1 year after acceptance. Responds in 3 months. Guidelines available on website.

MAGAZINE NEEDS Submit up to 3 poems (5 pages maximum) at a time. Considers simultaneous submissions; no previously published poems. Cover letter is preferred. Include brief bio; enclose SASE. Poems are read "in house," then sent to poetry editor for comments and dialogue. Often comments on rejected poems. Does not publish theme issues. Pays 2 contributor's copies and offers 40% discount on additional copies.

CONTEST/AWARD OFFERINGS Sponsors an annual poetry contest and annual fiction contest. Guidelines available in magazine (fall/winter issue), for SASE.

THE PRAIRIE JOURNAL

P.O. Box 68073, 28 Crowfoot Terrace NW, Calgary AB Y3G 3N8, Canada. **E-mail:** editor@prairiejournal.org (queries only); prairiejournal@yahoo.com. **Website:** prairiejournal.org. **Contact:** A.E. Burke, literary editor. "The audience is literary, university, library, scholarly, and creative readers/writers." Buys first North American serial rights, buys electronic rights. In Canada author retains copyright with acknowledgement appreciated. Pays on publication. Publishes ms an average of 4-6 months after acceptance. Responds in 2 weeks to queries. Responds in 6 months to mss. Editorial lead time 4-6 months. Sample copy for $5. Guidelines available online.

"Use our mailing address for submissions and queries with samples sor clippings."

MAGAZINE NEEDS *The Prairie Journal*, published twice/year, seeks poetry "of any length; free verse, contemporary themes (feminist, nature, urban, non-political), aesthetic value, a poet's poetry." Does not want to see "most rhymed verse, sentimentality, egotistical ravings. No cowboys or sage brush." Has published poetry by Liliane Welch, Cornelia Hoogland, Sheila Hyland, Zoe Lendale, and Chad Norman. *The*

Prairie Journal is 40-60 pages, digest-sized, offset-printed, saddle-stapled, with card cover, includes ads. Receives about 1,000 poems/year, accepts 10%. Press run is 600; the rest are sold on newsstands. Subscription: $10 for individuals, $18 for libraries. Sample: $8 ("use postal money order"). No U.S. stamps. No heroic couplets or greeting card verse. Length: 3-50 lines. Pays $5-50

HOW TO CONTACT No previously published poems or simultaneous submissions. No e-mail submissions. "We will not be reading submissions until such time as an issue is in preparation (twice yearly), so be patient and we will acknowledge, accept for publication, or return work at that time." Guidelines available for postage ("no U.S. stamps, please"; get IRCs from USPS) or on website. Sometimes sends prepublication galleys. Pays $10-50 and 1 contributor's copy. Acquires first North American serial rights. Reviews books of poetry, "but must be assigned by editor. Query first."

ADDITIONAL INFORMATION For chapbook publication by Prairie Journal Press, Canadian poets only (preferably from the plains region). Has published Voices From Earth, selected poems by Ronald Kurt and Mark McCawley, and In the Presence of Grace by McCandless Callaghan. "We also publish anthologies on themes when material is available." Query first, with 5 sample poems and cover letter with brief bio and publication credits. Responds to queries in 2 months; to mss in 6 months. Payment in modest honoraria. Publishes "Poems of the Month" online. Submit up to 4 poems with $1 reading fee by postal mail."Read recent poets! Experiment with line length, images, metaphors. Innovate."

TIPS "We publish many, many new writers and are always open to unsolicited submissions because we are 100% freelance. Do not send US stamps, always use IRCs. We have poems and reviews online (query first)."

PRAIRIE SCHOONER

The University of Nebraska Press, Prairie Schooner, 123 Andrews Hall, University of Nebraska, Lincoln NE 68588-0334. (402)472-7211, 1-800-715-2387. **E-mail:** jengelhardt2@unlnotes.unl.edu. **Website:** http://prairieschooner.unl.edu. Poetry published in Prairie Schooner has been selected for inclusion in *The Best American Poetry* and *The Pushcart Prize*. *Prairie Schooner*, published quarterly, prints poetry, fiction, personal essays, interviews, and reviews. Wants "poems that fulfill the expectations they set up." No specifications as to form, length, style, subject matter, or purpose. Has published poetry by Alicia Ostriker, Marilyn Hacker, D.A. Powell, Stephen Dunn, and David Ignatow. *Prairie Schooner* is about 200 pages, digest-sized, flat-spined. Receives about 5,500 submissions/year, uses about 300 pages of poetry. Press run is 2,500. Single copy: $9; subscription: $28/1 year. Sample: $6. "We look for the best fiction, poetry, and nonfiction available to publish, and our readers expect to read stories, poems, and essays of extremely high quality. We try to publish a variety of styles, topics, themes, points of view, and writers with a variety of backgrounds in all stages of their careers. We like work that is compelling—intellectually or emotionally—either in form, language, or content." Buys all rights, which are returned to the author upon request after publication. Pays on publication. Publishes ms an average of 1 year after acceptance. Responds in 1 week to queries. Responds in 3-4 months to mss. Editorial lead time 6 months. Sample copy for $6. Guidelines for #10 SASE.

Submissions must be received between September 1 and May 1.

MAGAZINE NEEDS *Prairie Schooner*, published quarterly, prints poetry, fiction, personal essays, interviews, and reviews. Wants "poems that fulfill the expectations they set up." No specifications as to form, length, style, subject matter, or purpose. Has published poetry by Alicia Ostriker, Marilyn Hacker, D.A. Powell, Stephen Dunn, and David Ignatow.

HOW TO CONTACT Submit 5-7 poems at a time. No simultaneous submissions. No fax or e-mail submissions; postal submissions only. Reads submissions September 1-May 1 (mss must be received during that period). Guidelines available for SASE or on website. Responds in 3-4 months, "sooner if possible." Always sends prepublication galleys. Pays 3 contributor's copies. Acquires all rights. Returns rights upon request without fee. Reviews books of poetry. Send materials for review consideration.

CONTEST/AWARD OFFERINGS "All manuscripts published in *Prairie Schooner* automatically will be considered for our annual prizes." These include The Strousse Award for Poetry ($500), the Bernice Slote Prize for Beginning Writers ($500), the Hugh J. Luke Award ($250), the Edward Stanley Award for Poetry ($1,000), the Virginia Faulkner Award for Excellence in Writing ($1,000), the Glenna Luschei Prize for Excellence ($1,500), and the Jane Geske Award ($250). Also, each year 10 Glenna Luschei Awards ($250 each) are given for poetry, fiction, and nonfiction. All contests are open only to those writers whose work was published in the magazine the previous year. Editors serve as judges. Also sponsors The *Prairie Schooner* Book Prize.

ALSO OFFERS Editor-in-Chief Hilda Raz also promotes poets whose work has appeared in her pages by listing their continued accomplishments in a special section (even when their work does not concurrently appear in the magazine).

TIPS "Send us your best, most carefully crafted work and be persistent. Submit again and again. Constantly work on improving your writing. Read widely in literary fiction, nonfiction, and poetry. Read *Prairie Schooner* to know what we publish."

PRAYERWORKS

P.O. Box 301363, Portland OR 97294-9363. (503)761-2072. **E-mail:** jay4prayer@aol.com. **Contact:** V. Ann Mandeville, editor. *PrayerWorks*, published weekly, is a newsletter "encouraging elderly people to recognize their value to God as prayer warriors." Established as a ministry to people living in retirement centers, *PrayerWorks* features "prayers, ways to pray, stories of answered prayers, teaching on a Scripture portion, articles that build faith, and poems." *PrayerWorks* is 4 pages, digest-sized, desktop-published, photocopied, folded. Receives about 50 poems/year, accepts about 25%. Press run is 1,100. Subscription: free. PrayerWorks is a ministry of THE MASTER'S WORK.

MAGAZINE NEEDS Submit 5 poems at a time. Considers previously published poems and simultaneous submissions. Accepts e-mail submissions (WordPerfect or Microsoft Word attachments). Cover letter is preferred. 1 poem/page. Time between acceptance and publication is usually within 1 month. Seldom comments on rejected poems. Publishes theme issues relating to the holidays (submit holiday poetry 2 months in advance). Pays 5 or more contributor's copies.

PRISM INTERNATIONAL

Department of Creative Writing, Buch E462, 1866 Main Mall, University of British Columbia, Vancouver BC V6T 1Z1, Canada. (604)822-2514. **Fax:** (604)822-3616. **Website:** www.prismmagazine.ca. A quarterly international journal of contemporary writing—fiction, poetry, drama, creative nonfiction and translation. Readership: public and university libraries, individual subscriptions, bookstores—a worldwide audience concerned with the contemporary in literature. Buys first North American serial rights. Selected authors are paid an additional $10/page for digital rights. Pays on publication. Publishes ms an average of 4 months after acceptance. Responds in 4 months to queries. Responds in 3-6 months to mss. Sample copy for $11, more info online. Guidelines available online.

MAGAZINE NEEDS *PRISM international*, published quarterly, prints poetry, drama, short fiction, creative nonfiction, and translation into English in all genres. "We have no thematic or stylistic allegiances: Excellence is our main criterion for acceptance of manuscripts." Wants "fresh, distinctive poetry that shows an awareness of traditions old and new. We read everything." Considers poetry by children and teens. "Excellence is the only criterion." Has published poetry by Margaret Avison, Elizabeth Bachinsky, John Pass, Warren Heiti, Don McKay, Bill Bissett, and Stephanie Bolster. *PRISM international* is 80 pages, digest-sized, elegantly printed, flat-spined, with original color artwork on a glossy card cover. Receives 1,000 submissions/year, accepts about 80. Circulation is for 1,200 subscribers. Subscription: $28/year, $46 for 2 years. Sample: $11. "Subscribers outside of Canada, please pay in U.S. dollars." **Buys 10 poems/issue.** Pays $40/printed page, and 1-year subscription

HOW TO CONTACT Submit up to 6 poems at a time. No previously published poems or simultaneous submissions. No e-mail submissions. Cover letter is required. Include brief introduction and list of previous publications. Poems must be typed or computer-generated (font and point size open). Include SASE (or SAE with IRCs). "Note: American stamps are not valid postage in Canada. No SASEs with U.S. postage will be returned. Translations must be accompanied by a copy of the original." Guidelines available for SASE (or SAE with IRCs), by e-mail, or on website. Responds in up to 6 months. Editors sometimes comment on rejected poems. Acquires first North American serial rights.

ADDITIONAL INFORMATION Sponsors annual Earle Birney Prize for Poetry. Prize awarded by the outgoing poetry editor to an outstanding poetry contributor published in PRISM *international*. Enter by regular submission only: no fee required. $500 prize.

CONTEST/AWARD OFFERINGS Annual Poetry Contest. First prize: $1,000; second prize: $300; third prize: $200. Entry fee: $28 for 3 poems; $7 per additional poem. Entry fee includes one-year subscription. Deadline: January 29. This year's poetry judge is **Brad Cran**, Vancouver poet laureate and author of *The Good Life* (2002; Nightwood Editions). He is a contributing editor at *Geist* magazine, and you can read some of his work on their site. The editorial board also awards an annual $500 prize to an outstanding poetry contributor in each volume. See below.

TIPS "We are looking for new and exciting fiction. Excellence is still our No. 1 criterion. As well as poetry, imaginative nonfiction and fiction, we are especially open to translations of all kinds, very short fiction pieces and drama which work well on the page. Translations must come with a copy of the original language work. We pay an additional $10/printed page to selected authors whose work we place on our online version of *Prism*."

◐ PRISM QUARTERLY

3232 S. First St., Springfield IL 62703. (217)529-5933. **E-mail:** prism@daybreakpoetry.com. **Website:** http://www.pwlf.com/prism_quarterly.htm. **Contact:** Michelle Delheimer. *Prism Quarterly*, published by Daybreak Press, a division of Pitch-Black LLC, considers "all styles and forms of poetry." Does not want poems over 100 lines long. Considers poetry by children and teens. Has published poetry by Marge Piercy, Marcellus Leonard, Barb Robinette, and Siobhan. *Prism Quarterly* is 128 pages, digest-sized, laser-printed, perfect-bound, with cardstock cover with original artwork, includes ads. Receives about 800 poems/year, accepts about 200. Press run is 200; 25 distributed free to contributors and reviewers. Single copy: $7.95; subscription: $29.95. Make checks payable to Pitch-Black LLC. Publishes ms 2-3 months after acceptance. Responds in 1-3 months.

MAGAZINE NEEDS Submit no more than 3 poems at a time. Lines/poem: 100 maximum. No previously published poems or simultaneous submissions. Accepts e-mail submissions (pasted into body of message or as attachment in Rich Text Format); no disk submissions. Cover letter is required. "Please include SASE and e-mail address (if available) if response is desired for any submission." Reads submissions year-round. Submit seasonal poems 3 months in advance. Poems are circulated to an editorial board. Always comments on rejected poems. Guidelines available on website. Acquires first rights. Rights revert to poet upon publication. Pays 1 contributor's copy.

TIPS "Intermittent contests are announced at our website. Please see site for frequent updates.""*Prism Quarterly* is a superlative journal of eclectic literature. The publishers welcome poets and writers in all (publishable) stages of their careers and seek a variety of themes, forms, and styles."

PROVINCETOWN ARTS

Provincetown Arts, Inc., 650 Commercial St., P.O. Box 35, Provincetown MA 02657. (508)487-3167. **E-mail:** cbusa@comcast.net. **Website:** www.provincetownarts.org. "*Provincetown Arts* focuses broadly on the artists and writers who inhabit or visit the Lower Cape, and seeks to stimulate creative activity and enhance public awareness of the cultural life of the nation's oldest continuous art colony. Drawing upon a 75-year tradition rich in visual art, literature, and theater, *Provincetown Arts* offers a unique blend of interviews, fiction, visual features, reviews, reporting, and poetry. Has published poetry by Bruce Smith, Franz Wright, Sandra McPherson, and Cyrus Cassells. 170 pages, magazine-sized, perfect-bound, with full-color glossy cover. Press run is 10,000. Buys first rights, buys one-time rights, buys second serial (reprint) rights. Pays on publication. Publishes ms an average of 4 months after acceptance. Responds in 3 weeks to queries; 2 months to mss. Editorial lead time 6 months. Sample copy for $10. Guidelines for #10 sase.

MAGAZINE NEEDS Submit up to 3 poems at a time. No e-mail submissions; "all queries and submissions should be sent via postal mail." Submissions must be typed. Pays $25-100/poem plus 2 contributor's copies. Acquires first rights.

ADDITIONAL INFORMATION The Provincetown Arts Press has published 8 volumes of poetry. The Provincetown Poets Series includes *At the Gate* by Martha Rhodes, *Euphorbia* by Anne-Marie Levine (a finalist in the 1995 Paterson Poetry Prize), and *1990* by Michael Klein (co-winner of the 1993 Lambda Literary Award).

O THE PUCKERBRUSH REVIEW

English Dept., University of Maine, 413 Neville Hall, Orono ME 04469. **E-mail:** sanphip@aol.com. **Website:** http://puckerbrushreview.com. **Contact:** Sanford Phippen, Editor. *The Puckerbrush Review*, a print-only journal published twice/year, looks for "freshness and simplicity." Has published poetry by Wolly Swist and Muska Nagel. Submit 5 poems at a time. Guidelines available for SASE. Pays 2 contributor's copies.

"Please submit your poetry, short stories, literary essays and reviews through our website link. Hard-copy submissions will no longer be accepted."

MAGAZINE NEEDS Does not want to see "confessional, religious, sentimental, dull, feminist, incompetent, derivative" poetry.

TIPS "Just write the best and freshest poetry you can."

PUDDING MAGAZINE: THE INTERNATIONAL JOURNAL OF APPLIED POETRY

81 Shadymere Lane, Columbus OH 43213. (614)986-1881. **Website:** www.puddinghouse.com. *Pudding Magazine: The International Journal of Applied Poetry*, published "every several months," seeks "what hasn't been said before. Speak the unspeakable. Long poems okay as long as they aren't windy." *Pudding* also serves as "a forum for poems and articles by people who take poetry arts into the schools and the human services." Wants "poetry on popular culture, rich brief narratives, i.e. 'virtual journalism' (see website)." Does not want "preachments or sentimentality; obvious traditional forms without fresh approach." Has published poetry by Knute Skinner, David Chorlton, Mary Winters, and Robert Collins. *Pudding* is 70 pages, digest-sized, offset-composed on Microsoft Word PC. Press run is 1,500. Subscription: $29.95 for 4 issues. Sample: $8.95. Responds same day, unless traveling. Guidelines available on website.

MAGAZINE NEEDS Submit 3-10 poems at a time. Previously published submissions "respected, but include credits"; no simultaneous submissions. Cover letter is preferred ("cultivates great relationships with writers"). "Submissions without SASEs will be discarded. No postcards." Sometimes publishes theme issues. Returns rights "with *Pudding* permitted to reprint." Send anthologies and books for review consideration or listing as recommended. Pays 1 contributor's copy; $10 and 4 contributor's copies to featured poets.

TIPS "Our website is one of the greatest poetry websites in the country—calls, workshops, publication list/history, online essays, games, guest pages, calendars, poem of the month, poet of the week, much more." The website also links to the site for The Unitarian Universalist Poets Cooperative and American Poets Opposed to Executions, both national organizations.

PUERTO DEL SOL

New Mexico State University, English Department, P.O.Box 30001, MSC 3E, Las Cruces NM 88003. (505)646-3931. **E-mail:** contact@puertodelsol.org. **Website:** www.puertodelsol.org. **Contact:** Carmen Giménez Smith, editor-in-chief. Wants "top-quality poetry, any style, from anywhere; excellent poetry of any kind, any form." Has published poetry by Richard Blanco, Maria Ercilla, Pamela Gemin, John Repp, and Lee Ann Roripaugh. *Puerto del Sol* is 150 pages, digest-sized, professionally printed, flat-spined, with matte card cover with art. Receives about 900 poetry submissions/year, accepts about 50. Press run is 1,250 (300 subscribers, 25-30 libraries). Subscription: $10/2 issues. Sample: $8. Acquires First North American serial rights. Sample copy and guidelines available online.

MAGAZINE NEEDS*Puerto del Sol*, published twice/year, is "interested in poems, fiction, essays, photos, and translations, usually from the Spanish; also (generally solicited) reviews and interviews with writers."

HOW TO CONTACT Submit 3-6 poems at a time. Considers simultaneous submissions. No e-mail submissions. Brief cover letter is welcome. "Do not send publication vitae." One poem/page. Reads mss September 1-February 1 only. Offers editorial comments on most mss. Tries to respond within 6 months. Sometimes sends prepublication galleys. Pays 2 contributor's copies.

TIPS "We are especially pleased to publish emerging writers who work to push their art form or field of study in new directions."

PULSAR POETRY MAGAZINE

Ligden Publishers, 34 Lineacre, Grange Park, Swindon, Wiltshire SN5 6DA, England. **E-mail:** pulsar.ed@btopenworld.com. **Website:** www.pulsarpoetry.com. **Contact:** David Pike, Editor. Acquires first rights. "Originators retain copyright of their poems." Publishes ms 1 year after acceptance. Responds in 1 month. Guidelines available for SASE (or SAE and IRC) or on website.

Now is a web-zine only. "We will publish poems on the Pulsar web on a quarterly basis, i.e. March, June, September and December. The selection process for poems will not alter and we will continue to publish on a merit basis only, be warned the editor is very picky! See poem submission guidelines online. We encourage the writing of poetry from all walks of life. Wants 'hard-hitting, thought-provoking work; interesting and stimulating poetry.' Does not want 'racist material. Not keen on religious poetry.' Has published poetry by A.C. Evans, Chris Hardy, Kate Edwards, Elizabeth Birchall, and Michael Newman."

MAGAZINE NEEDS No previously published poems or simultaneous submissions. Accepts e-mail submissions (pasted into body of message). "Send no more than 2 poems via e-mail; file attachments will not be read." Cover letter is preferred. Include SAE with adequate IRCs for a reply only (mss not returned if non-UK). Mss should be typed. "Poems can be published in next edition if it is what we are looking for. The editor and assistant read all poems." Seldom comments on rejected poems. Pays 1 contributor's copy.

TIPS "Give explanatory notes if poems are open to interpretation. Be patient and enjoy what you are doing. Check grammar, spelling, etc. (should be obvious). Note: we are a nonprofit-making society."

PULSE ONLINE LITERARY JOURNAL

12 Center St., Rockland ME 04841. (760)243-8034. **E-mail:** mainepoet@mac.com. **Website:** www.heartsoundspressliterary.com. **Contact:** Carol Bachofner, poetry editor. *Pulse Online Literary Journal* is open to formal poetry as well as free verse. Wants "your best. Send only work revised and revised again! Translations welcome with submitted original language piece." Does not want "predictable, sentimental, greeting card verse. No gratuitous sexuality or violence. No religious verse or predictable rhyme." Has published poetry by Walt McDonald and Lyn Lifshin. Receives about 400 poems/year, accepts about 30-45%. Acquires first rights. Publishes ms 3-4 months after acceptance. Responds in 3-4 weeks. Guidelines online.

MAGAZINE NEEDS Submit 3-5 poems at a time. Lines/poem: up to 120. Considers previously published poems. Only accepts e-mail submissions (pasted into body of e-mail); no disk submissions. Cover letter is required. "Send bio of 50-100 words with submission." Reads submissions year round; publishes February, April, June, August, September, October, December. Sometimes comments on rejected poems. Sometimes publishes theme issues. Themes for 2009 were April-September: Urban Landscape; September-December: Movements. Reviews books/chapbooks of poetry.

CONTEST/AWARD OFFERINGS Larry Kramer Memorial Chapbook Award; William Dunbar Book-length poetry contest. Submission ofr the contest is by USPS. See website for guidelines and deadlines. Entry fee: varies with contest (multiple entries okay with additional fee for each). Deadline: April 1.

PURPLE PATCH

25 Griffiths Rd., West Bromwich B71 2EH, England. **E-mail:** ppatch66@hotmail.com. **Website:** www.purplepatchpoetry.co.uk. **Contact:** Geoff Stevens, editor. *Purple Patch*, published quarterly, is a poetry and short prose magazine with reviews, comments, and illustrations. "All good examples of poetry considered." Does not want "poor rhyming verse, non-contributory swear words or obscenities, hackneyed themes." Has published poetry by Raymond K. Avery, Bryn Fortey, Bob Mee, B.Z. Niditch, and Steve Sneyd. *Purple Patch* is 24 pages, digest-sized, photocopied, side-stapled, with cover on the same stock with b&w drawing. Receives about 2,500 poems/year, accepts about 8%. Circulation varies. Subscription: £7 UK/3 issues; £12 US/3 issues. Make checks (sterling only) payable to G. Stevens. Acquires first British serial rights. Publishes ms 4 months after acceptance. Responds in 1 month. Guidelines available in magazine or on website.

MAGAZINE NEEDS Submit 2 or more poems at a time. Lines/poem: 40 maximum. No e-mail submissions; postal submissions only. Cover letter is preferred. Include self-introduction. Submissions must be sent return postage-paid. Reads submissions year round. Occasionally publishes theme issues. Upcoming themes available for SASE (or SAE and IRCs). Staff reviews poetry chapbooks, short stories, and tapes in 30-300 words. Send materials for review consideration. Pays 1 contributor's copy "to European writers only; overseas contributors must purchase a copy to see their work in print."

PURPOSE

616 Walnut Ave., Scottdale PA 15683. (724)887-8500. **Fax:** (724)887-3111. **E-mail:** CarolD@MennoMedia.org; purposeeditor@mpn.net. **Website:** www.mpn.net. **Contact:** Carol Duerksen, editor. *Purpose*, published monthly by Faith & Life Resources, an imprint of the Mennonite Publishing Network (the official

publisher for the Mennonite Church in the US and Canada), is a "religious young adult/adult monthly." Focuses on "action-oriented, discipleship living." *Purpose* is digest-sized with 4-color printing throughout. Press run is 8,000. Receives about 2,000 poems/year, accepts 150. Sample: (with guidelines) $2 and 9×12 SAE. Buys one-time rights. Pays on acceptance. Publishes ms an average of 18 months after acceptance. Responds in 3 months to queries. Sample copy and writer's guidelines for 6×9 SAE and $2.

MAGAZINE NEEDS Length: 12 lines. Pays $7.50-20/poem depending on length and quality. Buys one-time rights only.

HOW TO CONTACT Considers simultaneous submissions. Prefers e-mail submissions. Postal submissions should be double-spaced, typed on one side of sheet only. Responds in 6 months. Guidelines available electronically or for SASE. Pays $7.50 to $20 per poem plus 2 contributor's copies.

TIPS "Many stories are situational, how to respond to dilemmas. Looking for first-person storylines. Write crisp, action moving, personal style, focused upon an individual, a group of people, or an organization. The story form is an excellent literary device to help readers explore discipleship issues. The first 2 paragraphs are crucial in establishing the mood/issue to be resolved in the story. Work hard on the development of these."

QUANTUM LEAP

Q.Q. Press, York House, 15 Argyle Terrace, Rothesay, Isle of Bute PA20 0BD, Scotland. **Website:** www.qq-press.co.uk. *Quantum Leap*, published quarterly, uses "all kinds of poetry—free verse, rhyming, whatever—as long as it's well written and preferably well punctuated, too. We rarely use haiku." Has published poetry by Pamela Constantine, Ray Stebbing, Leigh Eduardo, Sky Higgins, Norman Bissett, and Gordon Scapens. *Quantum Leap* is 40 pages, digest-sized, desktop-published, saddle-stapled, with card cover. Receives about 2,000 poems/year, accepts about 15%. Press run is 200. Single copy: $13; subscription: $40. Sample: $10. Make checks payable to Alan Carter. "All things being equal in terms of a poem's quality, **I will sometimes favor that of a subscriber (or someone who has at least bought an issue) over a nonsubscriber**, as it is they who keep us solvent."

MAGAZINE NEEDS Submit 6 poems at a time. Lines/poem: 36 ("normally"). Considers previously published poems (indicate magazine and date of first publication) and simultaneous submissions. Cover letter is required. "Within the UK, send a SASE; outside it, send IRCs to the return postage value of what has been submitted." Time between acceptance and publication is usually 3 months "but can be longer now, due to magazine's increasing popularity." Sometimes comments on rejected poems. Guidelines available for SASE (or SAE and 2 IRCs). Responds in 3 weeks. Pays £2 sterling. Acquires first or second British serial rights.

ADDITIONAL INFORMATION Under the imprint "Collections," Q.Q. Press offers **subsidy arrangements** "to provide a cheap alternative to the 'vanity presses'—poetry only." Charges **£150 sterling ($300 USD) plus postage** for 50 32-page (A4) books. Write for details. Order sample books by sending $12 (postage included). Make checks payable to Alan Carter.

CONTEST/AWARD OFFERINGS Sponsors open poetry competitions as well as competitions for subscribers only. Send SAE and IRC for details.

QUARTERLY WEST

University of Utah, 255 S. Central Campus Dr., Room 3500, Salt Lake City UT 84112. **E-mail:** quarterlywest@gmail.com. **Website:** www.utah.edu/quarterlywest. **Contact:** Matt Kirkpatrick & Cami Nelson, editors. "We publish fiction, poetry, and nonfiction in long and short formats, and will consider experimental as well as traditional works." Buys first North American serial rights, buys all rights. Pays on publication. Publishes ms an average of 6 months after acceptance. Responds in 6 months to mss. Sample copy for $7.50 or online Guidelines available online.

Quarterly West was awarded first place for Editorial Content from the American Literary Magazine Awards. Work published in the magazine has been selected for inclusion in the *Pushcart Prize* anthology and *The Best American Short Stories* anthology.

MAGAZINE NEEDS *Quarterly West*, published semiannually, seeks "original and accomplished literary verse—free or formal." Also considers translations (include originals with submissions). No greeting card or sentimental poetry. Has published poetry by Quan Barry, Medbh McGuckian, Alice Notley, Brenda Shaughnessy, Bob Hicok, David Kirby, and Linh Dinh. *Quarterly West* is 160 pages, digest-sized, offset-printed, with 4-color cover art. Receives 2,500 submissions/year, accepts less than 1%. Press run is 1,500 (500 subscribers, 300-400 libraries). Subscription: $14/year, $25 for 2 years. One issue: $8.50. Back issues: $6. Pays $15-100.

HOW TO CONTACT Submit 3-5 poems at a time. Only considers submissions through submission manager on website. Will not consider postal or e-mail submissions. Considers simultaneous submissions, with notification; no previously published poems. Reads submissions September 1-May 1. Seldom comments on rejected poems. Responds in up to 6 months. Pays 2 contributor's copies and money when possible. Acquires first North American serial rights. Returns rights with acknowledgment and right to reprint. Reviews books of poetry in 1,000-3,000 words.

TIPS We publish a special section of short shorts every issue, and we also sponsor a biennial novella contest. We are open to experimental work—potential contributors should read the magazine! Don't send more than 1 story/submission. Biennial novella competition guidelines available upon request with SASE. We prefer work with interesting language and detail—plot or narrative are less important. We don't do Western themes or religious work.

QUEEN'S QUARTERLY

144 Barrie St., Queen's University, Kingston ON K7L 3N6, Canada. (613)533-2667. **Fax:** (613)533-6822. **E-mail:** queens.quarterly@queensu.ca. **Website:** www.queensu.ca/quarterly. **Contact:** Joan Harcourt, editor. *Queen's Quarterly* is "a general interest intellectual review featuring articles on science, politics, humanities, arts and letters, extensive book reviews, some poetry and fiction. We are especially interested in poetry by Canadian writers. Shorter poems preferred." Has published poetry by Evelyn Lau, Sue Nevill, and Raymond Souster. Each issue contains about 12 pages of poetry, digest-sized, 224 pages. Press run is 3,500. Receives about 400 submissions of poetry/year, accepts 40. Subscription: $20 Canadian, $25 US for US and foreign subscribers. Sample: $6.50 US.Submit up to 6 poems at a time. No simultaneous submissions. Submissions can be sent on hard copy with a SASE (no replies/returns for foreign submissions unless accompanied by an IRC) or by e-mail and will be responded to by same. Responds in 1 month. Pays usually $50 (Canadian)/poem, "but it varies," plus 2 copies. "A general interest intellectual review, featuring articles, book reviews, poetry, and fiction." Requires first North American serial rights. Pays on publication. Publishes ms on average 6-12 months after acceptance. Responds in 2-3 months to queries. Free sample copy online. Writer's guidelines online.

QUIDDITY INTERNATIONAL LITERARY JOURNAL AND PUBLIC-RADIO PROGRAM

Benedictine University at Springfield, 1500 N. 5th St., Springfield IL 62702. **Website:** www1.ben.edu/springfield/quiddity. **Contact:** Joanna Beth Tweedy, Founding editor. "Each work selected is considered for public-radio program feature offered by NPR-member station (WUIS (PRI affiliate). *Quiddity*, published semi-annually, is "a print journal and public-radio program featuring poetry, prose, and artwork by new, emerging, and established contributors from around the globe. Please visit the website for guidelines." Has published work by J.O.J. Nwachukwu-Agbada, Kevin Stein, Karen An-Hwei Lee, and Haider Al-Kabi. *Quiddity* is 176 pages, 7×9, perfect-bound, with 60 lb. full color cover. Receives about 3,500 poems/year, accepts about 3%. Press run is 1,000. Single copy: $9; subscription: $15/year. Make checks payable to *Quiddity*." Publishes ms 6 months to 2 years after acceptance. Responds in 6 months.

"International submissions are encouraged."

MAGAZINE NEEDS Query first. Submit up to 5 poems at a time, no more than 10 pages. Considers simultaneous submissions; no previously published poems (previously published includes work posted on a public website/blog/forum and on private, password-protected forums). Cover letter is preferred. "Address to poetry editor, SASE required (except international). See website for reading dates. Pays 1 contributor's copy.

CONTEST/AWARD OFFERINGS Sponsors the annual Teresa A. White Creative Writing Award and the Linda Bromberg Literary Award. **Entry fee**: $12. "See website for guidelines, deadline, and prize information. All entries are considered for publication."

RADIX MAGAZINE

Radix Magazine, Inc., P.O. Box 4307, Berkeley CA 94704. (510)548-5329. **E-mail:** radixmag@aol.com. **Website:** www.radixmagazine.com. **Contact:** Sharon Gallagher, editor. *"Radix Magazine*, published quarterly, is named for the Latin word for "root" and "has its roots both in the 'real world' and in the truth of Christ's teachings." Wants poems "that reflect a

Christian world-view, but aren't preachy." Has published poetry by John Leax, Czeslaw Milosz, Madeleine L'Engle, and Luci Shaw. *Radix* is 32 pages, magazine-sized, offset-printed, saddle-stapled, with 60-lb. self cover. Receives about 120 poems/year, accepts about 10%. Press run varies. Subscription: $15. Sample: $5. Make checks payable to *Radix Magazine*." interested in first North American serial rights. Publishes ms 3 months to 3 years after acceptance. Responds in 2 months to queries and to mss. Editorial lead time 6 months. Sample copy for $5. Guidelines by e-mail.

MAGAZINE NEEDS "Needs poetry." Submit 1-4 poems at a time. Length: 4-20 lines. Pays 2 contributor copies.

TIPS "We accept very few unsolicited manuscripts. We do not accept fiction. All articles and poems should be based on a Christian world view. Freelancers should have some sense of the magazine's tone and purpose."

THE RAG

11901 SW 34th Ave., Portland OR 97219. **E-mail:** raglitmag@gmail.com. **Website:** http://raglitmag.com. Krissy Marheine, webmaster. **Contact:** Seth Porter, editor; Dan Reilly, editor. Send complete ms. "The Rag focuses on the grittier genres that tend to fall by the wayside at more traditional literary magazines. The Rag's ultimate goal is to put the literary magazine magazine back into the entertainment market while rekindling the social and cultural value short fiction once held in North American literature." Purchases first rights only. Pays on acceptance. Responds in 1 month or less for queries and in 1-2 months for mss. Editorial lead time 1-2 months.

MAGAZINE NEEDS "We accept all themes and styles." "5 poems or 2,000 words, whichever comes first." Pays $20-100+.

TIPS "We like gritty material; material that is psychologically believable and that has some humor in it, dark or otherwise. We like subtle themes, original characters, and sharp wit."

RAILROAD EVANGELIST

Railroad Evangelist Association, Inc., P.O. Box 5026, Vancouver WA 98668. (360)699-7208. **E-mail:** rrjoe@comcast.net. **Website:** www.railroadevangelist.com. "The *Railroad Evangelist*'s purpose and intent is to reach people everywhere with the life-changing gospel of Jesus Christ. The railroad industry is our primary target, along with model railroad and rail fans." Editorial lead time 6 weeks. Sample copy for SAE with 10x12 envelope and 3 first-class stamps. Guidelines for #10 SASE.

All content must be railroad related.

MAGAZINE NEEDS Length: 10-100 lines. Pays in contributor copies.

THE RAINTOWN REVIEW

Central Ave. Press, 5390 Fallriver Row Court, Columbia MD 21044. **E-mail:** theraintownreview@gmail.com. **Website:** www.theraintownreview.com. **Contact:** Anna Evans, editor. We prefer poems that have NOT been previously published. *The Raintown Review*, published 2 times/year in Winter and Summer, contains poetry, reviews, and belletristic critical prose. Wants well-crafted poems. "We are primarily a venue for formal poetry." Has published poetry by Julie Kane, Alexandra Oliver, Rick Mullin, Annie Finch, Kevin Higgins, David Mason, A.E. Stallings, Richard Wilbur, and many others. The Raintown Review is 120 pages, perfect-bound. Receives about 2,500 poems/year, accepts roughly 5%. Press run is approximately 500. Subscription: $24/year, $45 for 2 years, $65 for 3 years. Sample: $12. Make checks/money orders payable to Central Ave Press. One can also subscribe online via our website preferred method.

MAGAZINE NEEDS Submit 3-5 poems at a time. Lines/poem: no restrictions. Considers simultaneous submissions. Accepts e-mail submissions only (pasted into body of message); no postal submissions. Guidelines available on website. Usually responds in 2 months, if possible. Pays one contributor's copy. Acquires one-time rights.

RATTAPALLAX

(212)560-7459. **E-mail:** info@rattapallax.com. **Website:** www.rattapallax.com. **Contact:** Alan Cheuse, fiction editor. *Rattapallax* is a literary magazine that focuses on issues dealing with globalization. Buys first North American serial rights, buys South American rights. Pays on publication. Publishes ms an average of 6 months after acceptance. Editorial lead time 6 months. Guidelines available online.

MAGAZINE NEEDS *Rattapallax*, published semiannually, is named for "Wallace Steven's word for the sound of thunder. The magazine includes a DVD featuring poetry films and audio files. *Rattapallax* is looking for the extraordinary in modern poetry and prose that reflect the diversity of world cultures. Our goals are to create international dialogue using literature and focus on what is relevant to our society." Has published poetry by Anthony Hecht, Sharon Olds, Lou Reed, Marilyn Hacker, Billy Collins, and Glyn Maxwell. *Rattapallax* is 112 pages, magazine-sized, offset-printed, perfect-bound, with 12-pt. CS1 cover. Receives about 5,000 poems/year, accepts 2%. Press run is 2,000 (100 subscribers, 50 libraries, 1,200 shelf sales); 200 distributed free to contributors, reviews, and promos. Single copy: $7.95; no subscriptions. Make checks payable to *Rattapallax*. Length: 5-200 lines.

HOW TO CONTACT Submit 3-5 poems at a time. Considers simultaneous submissions; no previously published poems. Accepts e-mail submissions (sent as simple text) from outside the U.S. and Canada; all other submissions must be sent via postal mail (SASE required). Cover letter is preferred. Reads submissions year round; issue deadlines are June 1 and December 1. Time between acceptance and publication is 6 months. "The editor-in-chief, senior editor, and associate editor review all the submissions and then decide on which to accept every week. Near publication time, all accepted work is narrowed, and unused work is kept for the next issue." Often comments on rejected poems. Guidelines available by e-mail or on website. Responds in 2 months. Always sends prepublication galleys. Pays 2 contributor's copies. Acquires first rights.

RATTLING WALL

c/o PEN Center USA, 269 S. Beverly Dr. #1163, Beverly Hills CA 90212. **E-mail:** therattlingwall@gmail.com. **Website:** http://therattlingwall.com. **Contact:** Michelle Meyering, editor. Acquires first rights. Rights revert to poet upon publication. Pays 2 contributor's copies on publication. Publishes ms 2 months after acceptance. Responds in 2-4 months. Sample copy for $15. Guidelines available online.

MAGAZINE NEEDS Submit 3-5 poems at a time. Considers simultaneous submissions. Accepts submissions by mail only. Cover letter is required. Reads submissions year round. Does not want sentimental love poetry or religious verse. Does not consider poetry by children or teens.

RAVING DOVE

P.O. Box 28, West Linn OR 97068. **E-mail:** editor@ravingdove.org. **E-mail:** ravingdog@gmail.com. **Website:** www.ravingdove.org/. **Contact:** Jo-Ann Moss, editor. Online literary journal published 4 times/year. "Our mission is to share thought-provoking poetry and prose that champions human rights and social justice, and opposes physical and psychological violence in all its forms, including war, discrimination against sexual orientation, and every shade of bigotry." Receives one-time, nonexclusive electronic publishing rights. Responds in 1-3 months to mss. Editorial lead time 1-3 months. Guidelines available online and by e-mail.

MAGAZINE NEEDS *Raving Dove*, published quarterly, "is an online literary journal that publishes original poetry, nonfiction, fiction, photography, and art with universal anti-violence, anti-hate, human rights, and social justice themes. We share sentiments that oppose physical and psychological violence in all its forms, including war, discrimination against sexual orientation, and every shade of bigotry." Wants free verse only, any length. Has published poetry by Howard Camner, Marguerite Bouvard, John Kay, Harry Youtt. Receives about 750 poems/year, accepts about 30. Number of visitors is "2,000/month and growing."

HOW TO CONTACT Considers simultaneous submissions. Accepts e-mail submissions only; allows attachments. No fax, disk, or postal submissions. Cover letter is unnecessary. "Poetry Submission" must appear as the subject of the e-mail; all submissions must include full name, general geographic location, and a third-person bio of 100 words or less. Weblinks are permitted. Reads submissions year round. Time between acceptance and publication is no more than 3 months. Sometimes comments on rejected poems. Guidelines available on website. Always sends prepublication galleys ("the link to the poet's Web page at *Raving Dove* is sent prior to publication"). Responds in 3 months. Payment is based on funding. Acquires first North American and Internet serial rights, exclusive for the duration of the edition in which the poetry appears (see submission guidelines on website for further information). Rights revert to poets at the end of the issue.

ADDITIONAL INFORMATION Nonprofit status granted by U.S. government.

REDACTIONS: POETRY, POETICS, & PROSE

58 S. Main St., 3rd Floor, Brockport NY 14420. **E-mail:** redactionspoetry@yahoo.com (poetry); redationsprose@yahoo.com (prose). **Website:** www.redactions.com. All rights revert back to the author.

MAGAZINE NEEDS "Anything dealing with poetry."

TIPS "We only accept submissions by e-mail. We read submissions throughout the year. E-mail us and attach submission into one Word, Wordpad, Notepad, .rtf, or .txt document, or, place in the body of an e-mail. Include brief bio and your snail mail address. Query after 90 days if you haven't heard from us. See website for full guidelines for each genre, including artwork."

REDHEADED STEPCHILD

E-mail: redheadedstepchildmag@gmail.com. **Website:** www.redheadedmag.com/poetry. **Contact:** Malaika King Albrecht. "*The Redheaded Stepchild* only accepts poems that have been rejected by other magazines. We publish biannually, and we accept submissions in the months of August and February only. We do not accept previously published work. We do, however, accept simultaneous submissions, but please inform us immediately if your work is accepted somewhere else. We are open to a wide variety of poetry and hold no allegiance to any particular style or school. If your poem is currently displayed online on your blog or website or wherever, please do not send it to us before taking it down, at least temporarily." Acquires first rights. Rights revert to poets upon publication. Time between acceptance and publication is 3 months. Poems are circulated to an editorial board. Sometimes comments on rejected poems. Responds in 3 months. Guidelines on website.

Wants a wide variety of poetic styles. Does not want previously published poems. Has published poetry by Kathryn Stripling Byer, Alex Grant, Amy King, Diane Lockward, Susan Yount, and Howie Good.

MAGAZINE NEEDS "Submit 3-5 poems that have been rejected elsewhere with the names of the magazines that rejected the poems. We do not want multiple submissions, so please wait for a response to your first submission before you submit again. As is standard after publication, rights revert back to the author, but we request that you credit *Redheaded Stepchild* in subsequent republications. We do not accept e-mail attachments; therefore, in the body of your e-mail, please include the following: a brief bio; 3-5 poems; the publication(s) that rejected the poems."

REDIVIDER

Department of Writing, Literature, and Publishing, Emerson College, 120 Boylston St., Boston MA 02116. **E-mail:** fiction@redividerjournal.com; poetry@redividerjournal.com. **Website:** www.redividerjournal.org. *Redivider*, published semiannually, prints high-quality poetry, art, fiction, and creative nonfiction. Wants "all styles of poetry. Most of all, we look for language that seems fresh and alive on the page, that tries to do something new. Read a sample copy for a good idea." Does not want "greeting card verse or inspirational verse." Has published poetry by Bob Hicok, Billy Collins, Paul Muldoon, Tao Lin, Claudia Emerson, and Bobby Byrd. *Redivider* is 100+ pages, digest-sized, offset-printed, perfect-bound, with 4-color artwork on cover. Receives about 1,000 poems/year, accepts about 30%. Press run is 1,000. Single copy: $6; subscription: $10. Make checks payable to *Redivider* at Emerson College.

HOW TO CONTACT Submit 3-6 poems at a time through online submissions manager. Considers simultaneous submissions, but requires notification if your work is taken elsewhere; no previously published poems. Cover letter is required. Reads submissions year-round. Seldom comments on rejected poems. Guidelines available in magazine, for SASE, by e-mail, or on website. Responds in 5 months. Pays 2 contributor's copies. Acquires first North American serial rights. Reviews books of poetry in 500 words, single-book format. Send materials for review consideration, Attn: Review Copies. "Book reviews and interviews are internally generated." Our deadlines are July 1 for the Fall issue, and December 1 for the Spring issue.

TIPS "Our deadlines are July 1 for the Fall issue, and December 1 for the Spring issue."

RED LIGHTS

2740 Andrea Drive, Allentown PA 18103-4602. (212)875-9342. **E-mail:** mhazelton@rcn.com; marilynhazelton@rcn.com. **Contact:** Marilyn Hazelton, editor. *red lights*, published semiannually in January and June, is devoted to English-language tanka and tanka sequences. Wants "print-only tanka, mainly 'free-form' but also strictly syllabic 5-7-5-7-7; will consider tanka sequences and tan-renga." Considers poetry by children and teens. Has published poetry by Sanford Goldstein, Michael McClintock, Laura Maffei, Linda Jeannette Ward, Jane Reichhold, and Michael Dylan Welch. *red lights* is 36-40 pages, 812x334, offset-printed, saddle-stapled, with Japanese textured paper cover; copies are numbered. Single copy: $8; subscription: $16 U.S., $18 USD Canada, $20 USD foreign. Make checks payable to "red lights" in the U.S.

TIPS "Each issue features a '*red lights* featured tanka' on the theme of 'red lights.' Poet whose poem is selected receives 1 contributor's copy."

THE RED MOON ANTHOLOGY OF ENGLISH LANGUAGE HAIKU

P.O. Box 2461, Winchester VA 22604-1661. **E-mail:** jim.kacian@redmoonpress.com. **Website:** www.redmoonpress.com. **Contact:** Jim Kacian, editor/publisher. *The Red Moon Anthology of English Language Haiku*, published annually in February, is "a collection of the best haiku published in English around the world." Considers poetry by children and teens. Has published haiku and related forms by John Barlow, Cherie Hunter Day, Gary Hotham, and Billie Wilson. *The Red Moon Anthology of English Language Haiku* is 184 pages, digest-sized, offset-printed on quality paper, with 4-color heavy-stock cover. Receives several thousand submissions/year, accepts less than 2%. Print run is 1,000 for subscribers and commercial distribution. Subscription: $17 plus $5 p&h. Sample available for SASE or by e-mail.

MAGAZINE NEEDS "We do not accept direct submissions to the *Red Moon Anthology*. Rather, we employ an editorial board who are assigned journals and books from which they cull and nominate. Nominated poems are placed on a roster and judged anonymously by the entire editorial board twice a year." Guidelines available for SASE or by e-mail. Acquires North American serial rights.

ALSO OFFERS *contemporary haibun*, "an annual volume of the finest English-language haibun and haiga published anywhere in the world."

RED ROCK REVIEW

College of Southern Nevada, CSN Department of English, J2A, 3200 E. Cheyenne Ave., North Las Vegas NV 89030. (702)651-4094. **Fax:** (702)651-4639. **E-mail:** redrockreview@csn.edu. **Website:** sites.csn.edu/english/redrockreview/. **Contact:** Rich Logsdon, Senior Editor. *Red Rock Review*, a nonprofit biannual journal, prints "the best poetry available," as well as fiction, creative nonfiction, and book reviews. Has published poetry by Dorianne Laux, Kim Addonizio, Ellen Bass, Cynthia Hogue, and Dianne di Prima. *Red Rock Review* is about 130 pages, magazine-sized, professionally printed, perfect-bound, with 10-pt. CS1 cover. Accepts about 15% of poems received/year. Press run is 2350. Subscriptions: $9.50/year. Sample: $5.50. "We are dedicated to the publication of fine contemporary literature." Buys first North American serial rights. All other rights revert to the authors & artists upon publication. No longer accepting snail mail submissions. Send all submissions as MS. Word, RTF, or PDF file attachment to redrockreview@csn.edu. Guidelines available online. Occasionally comments on rejections.

MAGAZINE NEEDS Length: 80 lines.

HOW TO CONTACT Submit 2-3 poems at a time by e-mail. Attach Word, RTF, or PDF file to redrockreview@csn.edu. Lines/poem: 80 maximum. Considers simultaneous submissions. No hard copy submissions will be accepted. "The e-mail to which the files are attached should serve as your cover letter clearly stating your contact information and the contents of your attachments. **We do not accept general submissions in June, July, August, or December."** Time between acceptance and publication is 2-3 months. "Poems go to poetry editor, who then distributes them to 3 readers." Occasionally comments on rejected poems. Guidelines available on website. Responds in 2-3 months. Pays 2 contributor's copies. Acquires first North American serial rights. Reviews books/chapbooks of poetry in 500-1,000 words, multi-book format. Send materials for review consideration.

TIPS "Open to short fiction and poetry submissions from Sept. 1-May 31. Include SASE and include brief bio. No general submissions between June 1st and August 31st. See guidelines online."

RENDITIONS: A CHINESE-ENGLISH TRANSLATION MAGAZINE

Website: www.renditions.org. *Renditions: A Chinese-English Translation Magazine*, published twice/year in May and November, uses "exclusively translations from Chinese, ancient and modern." Poems are printed with Chinese and English texts side by side. Has published translations of the poetry of Yang Lian, Gu Cheng, Shu Ting, Mang Ke, and Bei Dao. *Renditions* is about 150 pages, magazine-sized, elegantly printed, perfect-bound, with glossy card cover. Single copy: $19.90; subscription: $29.90/year, $49.90/2 years, $69.90/3 years.

MAGAZINE NEEDS Submissions should be accompanied by Chinese originals. Accepts e-mail and fax submissions. "Submissions by postal mail should include two copies. Use British spelling." Sometimes comments on rejected translations. Publishes theme issues. Guidelines available on website. Responds in 2 months. Mss usually not returned.

ADDITIONAL INFORMATION Also publishes a hardback series (Renditions Books) and a paperback series (Renditions Paperbacks) of Chinese literature in English translation. "Will consider" book mss; query with sample translations.

RHINO

The Poetry Forum, Inc., P.O. Box 591, Evanston IL 60204. **E-mail:** editors@rhinopoetry.org. **Website:** www.rhinopoetry.org. **Contact:** Ralph Hamilton Sr., Editor; Helen Degen Cohen, Sr. Editor and Founder. *RHINO*, published annually in spring, prints poetry, short-shorts, and translations. Wants "work that reflects passion, originality, engagement with contemporary culture, and a love affair with language. We welcome free verse, formal poetry, innovation, and risk-taking." Has published poetry by Geoffrey Forsyth, Penelope Scambly Schott, F. Daniel Rzicznek, and Ricardo Pau-Llosa. *RHINO* is 150 pages, 7×10, printed on high-quality paper, with card cover with art. Receives 8,000-10,000 submissions/year, accepts 90-100, or 1%. Press run is 800. Single copy: $12. Sample: $5 (back issue). Submit 3-5 poems. Considers simultaneous submissions with notification; no previously published poems. Expects electronic copy upon acceptance. Reads submissions April 1-October 1. Guidelines available on website. Responds in up to 6 months. Pays 2 contributor's copies. Acquires first rights only. "This eclectic annual journal of more than 30 years accepts poetry, flash fiction (1,000 words or less), and poetry-in-translation from around the world that experiments, provokes, compels. More than 80 poets are showcased. The regular call for poetry is from April 1 to October 1st, and the Founder's Contest submission period has been changed to July 1 to October 1st." Buys first North American serial rights. Response time may exceed 6 weeks. Guidelines available online.

"Founders' Contest submission period is from July 1-October 1."

MAGAZINE NEEDS "Please label each poem with your name, address, telephone number, and email address for ease in contacting you."

HOW TO CONTACT Submit online and by mail. Include SASE for USPS mail only.

TIPS "Please visit our website for further examples that will indicate the quality of poetry we look for, plus additional submission information, including updates on the Rhino Founders' Contest."

THE RIALTO

P.O. Box 309, Alysham, Norwich NR11 6LN, England. **Website:** www.therialto.co.uk. **Contact:** Michael Mackmin, editor. *The Rialto*, published 3 times/year, seeks "to publish the best new poems by established and beginning poets. We seek excellence and originality." Has published poetry by Alice Fulton, Jenny Joseph, Les Murray, George Szirtes, Philip Gross, and Ruth Padel. *The Rialto* is 64 pages, A4, with full-color cover. Receives about 12,000 poems/year, accepts about 1%. Press run is 1,500. Single copy: £7.50; subscription: £23 (prices listed are for U.S. and Canada). Make checks payable to *The Rialto*. "Checks in sterling only, please. Online payment also available on website."

MAGAZINE NEEDS Submit up to 6 poems at a time. Considers simultaneous submissions; no previously published poems. Cover letter is preferred. "SASE or SAE with IRCs essential. U.S. readers please note that U.S. postage stamps are invalid in UK." No poetry submissions will be accepted by e-mail or online. Time between acceptance and publication is up to 4 months. Seldom comments on rejected poems. Responds in 5-6 months. Pays £20/poem. Poet retains rights.

TIPS "*The Rialto* has recently commenced publishing first collections by poets. Please do not send book-length manuscripts. Query first." Sponsors an annual young poets competition. Details available in magazine and on website. Before submitting, "you will probably have read many poems by many poets, both living and dead. You will probably have put aside each poem you write for at least 3 weeks before considering it afresh. You will have asked yourself, 'Does it work technically?'; checked the rhythm, the rhymes (if used), and checked that each word is fresh and meaningful in its context, not jaded and tired. You will hopefully have read *The Rialto*."

RIBBONS: TANKA SOCIETY OF AMERICA JOURNAL

David Bacharach, TSA Editor, 5921 Cayutaville Rd., Alpine NY 14805. **E-mail:** davidb@htva.net. **Website:** www.tankasocietyofamerica.com. **Contact:** David Bacharach, editor. Published quarterly, seeks and regularly prints "the best tanka poetry being written in

English, together with reviews, critical and historical essays, commentaries, and translations." Wants "poetry that exemplifies the very best in English-language tanka, which we regard as 'the queen of short form poetry,' having a significant contribution to make to the short poem in English. All schools and approaches are welcome." Tanka should "reflect contemporary life, issues, values, and experience, in descriptive, narrative, and lyrical modes." Does not want "work that merely imitates the Japanese masters." Considers poetry by children and teens. "We have no age restrictions." Has published poetry by Cherie Hunter Day, Marianne Bluger, Sanford Goldstein, Larry Kimmel, John Stevenson, and George Swede. *Ribbons* is 60-72 pages, 6×9 perfect-bound, with color cover and art. Receives about 2,000 poems/year, accepts about 20%. Press run is 275; 15 distributed free. Single copy: $10; subscription: $30. Make checks payable to Tanka Society of America and contact Carole MacRury, Secretary/Treasurer (e-mail: macrury@whidbey.com; 1636 Edwards Dr., Point Roberts, WA 98281). Publishes ms 2 months after acceptance. Respond in 1-2 months.

MAGAZINE NEEDS Submit 1-8 poems at a time. Lines/poem: 5 minimum; sequences of up to 50 total lines considered. No previously published poems or simultaneous submissions. Prefers e-mail submissions (pasted into body of message); no disk submissions. "Postal submissions must include SASE." Reads submissions year-round. "See the publication or contact the editor for specific deadlines for each issue."

TIPS "Work by beginning as well as established English-language tanka poets is welcome; first-time contributors are encouraged to study the tanka form and contemporary examples before submitting. No particular school or style of tanka is preferred over another; our publications seek to showcase the full range of English-language tanka expression and subject matter through the work of new and established poets in the genre from around the world."

O RIO GRANDE REVIEW

University of Texas at El Paso, PMB 671, 500 W. University Ave., El Paso TX 79968-0622. **E-mail:** editors@riograndereview.com. **Website:** www.utep.edu/rgr. *Rio Grande Review*, published in January and August, is a bilingual (English-Spanish) student publication from the University of Texas at El Paso. Contains poetry; flash, short, and nonfiction; short drama; photography and line art. *Rio Grande Review* is 168 pages, digest-sized, professionally printed, perfect-bound, with card cover with line art. Subscription: $8/year, $15/2 years. Guidelines available for SASE, by e-mail, or on website.

MAGAZINE NEEDS Poetry has a limit of 10 pages. No simultaneous submissions. Accepts e-mail submissions only (as attachment or pasted into body of message). Include short bio. Any submissions received after a reception deadline will automatically be considered for the following edition. "Permission to reprint material remains the decision of the author. However, *Rio Grande Review* does request it be given mention." Pays 2 contributor's copies.

◐ RIVER OAK REVIEW

Elmhurst College, 190 Prospect Ave., Elmhurst IL 60126-3296. (630) 617-3137. **Fax:** (630) 617-3609. **E-mail:** riveroak@elmhurst.edu. **Website:** www.riveroakreview.org. Ann Frank Wake, poetry editor, annfw@elmhurst.edu. **Contact:** Ron Wiginton, fiction editor, ronw@elmhurst.edu. *River Oak Review*, published annually, prints high-quality poetry, short fiction, and creative nonfiction. "We are a national journal striving to publish midwestern poets in each issue." Has published poetry by Wendy Bishop, Jim Elledge, James Doyle, Ken Meisel, Blair Beacom Deets, and Robin Becker. *River Oak Review* is at least 128 pages, digest-sized, neatly printed, perfect-bound, with glossy color cover with art. Publishes about 5% of poetry received. Press run is 500. Single copy: $10; subscription: $10/year, $20/2 years. Sample: $5. Make checks payable to *River Oak Review*.

HOW TO CONTACT Submit 4-6 poems at a time. No previously published poems. SASE required. Reads submissions year round. Sometimes comments on rejected poems. Guidelines available for SASE or on website. Tries to respond in 3 months. Pays 2 contributor's copies. Acquires first North American serial rights.

TIPS "The voice is what we notice first. Is the writer in command of the language? Secondly, does the story have anything to say? It's not that 'fluff' cannot be good, but we note our favorites stories tend to have meaning beyond the surface of the plot. Thirdly, the story must by populated by 'real' peoples who are also interesting, characters, in other words, who have lives underneath the storyline. Finally, look before you leap."

ROAD NOT TAKEN: THE JOURNAL OF FORMAL POETRY, THE

29302 Sandalwood Ct, San Juan Capistrano CA 92675. **E-mail:** jimatshs@yahoo.com. **Website:** www.journalformalpoetry.com. **Contact:** Dr. Jim Prothero, co-editor. *The Road Not Taken: the Journal of Formal Poetry*, published quarterly online, prints formal poetry "in the tradition of Frost, Wordsworth, Tennyson, Hopkins, etc." Wants "formal poetry only. Nature and spiritual poetry always of interest but not required. Also essays/blogs on the topic of formal poetry would be of interest." Does not want free verse. Accepts poetry by children and teens; no age limitations—"it just has to be excellent." Acquires one-time rights. Rights revert to poets upon publication. Time between acceptance and publication is 2 months. Sometimes comments on rejected poems. Responds in 2 months. Guidelines available by e-mail and on website.

MAGAZINE NEEDS Submit 5 poems at a time. Considers previously published poems; no simultaneous submissions. (Considers poetry posted on a public website/blog/forum as published.) Accepts e-mail submissions (pasted into body of message); no fax or disk submissions. Cover letter is unnecessary. Reads submissions year round. Poems are circulated to an editorial board. "There are 2 editors: Dr. Jim Prothero and Dr. Don Williams. Poems must meet both of our approval."

ROANOKE REVIEW

Roanoke College, 221 College Lane, Salem VA 24153-3794. **E-mail:** review@roanoke.edu. **Website:** http://roanokereview.wordpress.com. **Contact:** Paul Hanstedt, editor. "We're looking for fresh, thoughtful material that will appeal to a broader as well as literary audience. Humor encouraged." Annual. Estab. 1967. Circ. 500.

MAGAZINE NEEDS Submit original typed mss, no photocopies. Guidelines available on website. Responds in 3-6 months. Pays 2 contributor's copies "plus cash when budget allows."

TIPS "Pay attention to sentence-level writing—verbs, metaphors, concrete images. Don't forget, though, that plot and character keep us reading. We're looking for stuff that breaks the MFA story style." "Be real. Know rhythm. Concentrate on strong images."

ROCKY MOUNTAIN RIDER MAGAZINE

P.O. Box 995, Hamilton MT 59840. (406)363-4085. **E-mail:** info@rockymountainrider.com. **Website:** www.rockymountainrider.com. **Contact:** Natalie Riehl, publisher. Buys first serial rights, one-time rights, as well as some reprint rights, if material has not been published in a competing publication in Montana, Idaho, Wyoming, Washington, Oregon, Colorado, or Utah. Pays on publication. Publishes ms an average of 6 months after acceptance. Responds in 2 months to queries. Responds in 3 months to mss. Sample copy for $3. Guidelines on website.

MAGAZINE NEEDS Wants "cowboy poetry; western or horse-themed poetry." *Rocky Mountain Rider Magazine* is 68+ pages, magazine-sized, Web offset-printed on SuperCal, stapled. Publishes 0-2 poems/issue. Press run is 16,500; distributed free through 500+ locations in 11 states. "Cowboy poetry should be no more than 4-5 stanzas, 6-36 lines. Please submit articles typed and double-spaced on 8-1/2x11 paper." Submit 1-10 poems at a time. Considers previously published poems and simultaneous submissions. No e-mail submissions; postal submissions only. Cover letter is preferred. Include SASE. Seldom comments on rejected poems. Occasionally publishes theme issues. Reviews books of poetry. Send materials for review consideration. Include SASE for returns Pays $10/poem.

TIPS "We aren't looking for 'how-to' or training articles, and are not currently looking at any fiction. Our geographical regions of interest is the US West, especially the Rocky Mountain states."

ROOM

P.O. Box 46160, Station D, Vancouver BC V6J 5G5, Canada. **E-mail:** contactus@roommagazine.com. **Website:** www.roommagazine.com. **Contact:** Growing Room Collective. "*Room* is Canada's oldest literary journal by, for, and about women. Published quarterly by a group of volunteers based in Vancouver, *Room* showcases fiction, poetry, reviews, art work, interviews and profiles about the female experience. Many of our contributors are at the beginning of their writing careers, looking for an opportunity to get published for the first time. Some later go on to great acclaim. *Room* is a space where women can speak, connect, and showcase their creativity. Each quarter we publish original, thought-provoking works that reflect women's strength, sensuality, vulnerability, and wit." Buys first rights.

MAGAZINE NEEDS *Room* is a quarterly using "poetry by and about women, written from a feminist perspective. Nothing simplistic, clichéd. Short fiction also accepted." *Room of One's Own* is 96 pages, digest-sized. Press run is 1,000 (420 subscribers, 50-100 libraries); 350 shelf sales. Subscription: $22 ($32 US or foreign). Sample: $8 plus IRCs. "We prefer to receive 5-6 poems at a time, so we can select a pair or group." Include bio note. No simultaneous submissions. The mss are circulated to a collective, which "takes time." Publishes theme issues. Guidelines and upcoming themes available for SAE and 1 IRC. Responds in 6 months. Acquires first North American serial rights. "We solicit reviews." Pays honorarium plus 2 copies.

HOW TO CONTACT Send material for review consideration, attn. book review editor.

ROSE & THORN JOURNAL

Website: www.roseandthornjournal.com. **Contact:** Barbara Quinn. "Adjective stacking doesn't make a poem better, but we do like strong, vivid images. Please avoid trite imagery like: 'Our hearts beat as one; our lips joined in passion.' While we prefer shorter poems, consideration is given to longer works if they meet the above criteria. Also, forms are welcome if they do not contain obtrusive rhyming." "We created this publication for readers and writers alike. Since 1998, the *R&T* has showcased the best of the Web with a unique blend of art and words. Visit this award-winning spot and find out for yourself why we are consistently rated a top spot for writers." Writer retains all rights. Responds in 2 weeks to queries. Responds in 1 month to mss. Guidelines available online.

MAGAZINE NEEDS Online journal specializing in literary works of fiction, nonfiction, poetry, and essays. "*Rose & Thorn Journal* welcomes emerging and established poets whose verse exhibits technical skill, distinctive style, lyric intensity, and is thematically fresh and substantive." Quarterly. Circ. 120,000. extreme erotica, political or social rants, gratuitous violence.

HOW TO CONTACT Copy and paste submission including a brief, third person bio into the body of an e-mail. Send to poetry@roseandthornjournal.com.

TIPS "Clarity, control of the language, evocative stories that tug at the heart and make their mark on the reader long after it's been read. We look for uniqueness in voice, style and characterization. New twists on old themes are always welcome. Use all aspects of good writing in your stories, including dynamic characters, strong narrative voice and a riveting original plot. We have eclectic tastes, so go ahead and give us a shot. Read the publication and other quality literary journals so you'll see what we look for. Always check your spelling and grammar before submitting. Reread your submission with a critical eye and ask yourself, 'Does it evoke an emotional response? Have I completely captured my reader?' Check your submission for 'it' and 'was' and see if you can come up with a better way to express yourself. Be unique."

ROSEBUD

N3310 Asje Rd., Cambridge WI 53523. (608)423-9780. **E-mail:** jrodclark@smallbytes.net. **Website:** www.rsbd.net. **Contact:** Roderick Clark, editor. Responds in 3 months. Sample copy for $6.95.

MAGAZINE NEEDS *Rosebud*, published 3 times/year in April, August, and December, has presented "many of the most prominent voices in the nation and has been listed as among the very best markets for writers." Wants poetry that avoids "excessive or well-worn abstractions, not to mention clicheés. Present a unique and convincing world (you can do this in a few words!) by means of fresh and exact imagery, and by interesting use of syntax. Explore the deep reaches of metaphor. But don't forget to be playful and have fun with words." *Rosebud* is "elegantly" printed with full-color cover. Press run is 10,000. Single copy: $7.95 U.S. Subscription: $20 for 3 issues, $35 for 6 issues. E-mail up to 3 poetry submissions to poetry editor John Smelcer at: jesmelcer@aol.com.

CONTEST/AWARD OFFERINGS Sponsors The William Stafford Poetry Award and the X.J. Kennedy Award for Creative Nonfiction. Guidelines for both available on website.

TIPS "Each issue will have six or seven flexible departments (selected from a total of sixteen departments that will rotate). We are seeking stories; articles; profiles; and poems of: love, alienation, travel, humor, nostalgia and unexpected revelation. Something has to 'happen' in the pieces we choose, but what happens inside characters is much more interesting to us than plot manipulation. We like good storytelling, real emotion and authentic voice."

SACRED JOURNEY

Fellowship in Prayer, Inc., 291 Witherspoon St., Princeton NJ 08542. (609)924-6863. **Fax:** (609)924-6910. **E-mail:** submissions@sacredjourney.org. **Website:** www.fellowshipinprayer.org. *Sacred Journey: The Journal of Fellowship in Prayer* is a quarterly multi-faith journal published winter, spring, summer, and autumn. Retains one-time rights and then the copyright is returned to the author. "Submissions may be selected for publication or on our fellowship in prayer website under 'web exclusives.' Your agreement for publication grants Fellowship in Prayer non-exclusive publication rights including the right to use and edit the work for publication in the print or electronic version of the journal *Sacred Journal* display on the Web and to retain the work indefinitly in an online archive." Responds within 4 months of receipt. Submission is considered permission for publication. "We reserve the right to edit. We will make every effort to contact the author with content revisions. Please include or be prepared to provide a bio of 50-words or less and/or a headshot phot to accompany your work, should it be selected for the print journal." Editorial lead time 3 months. Free sample copy available online. Writer Guidelines are available online or by request.

"We publish articles, poems, and photographs which convey a spiritual orientation to life, promote prayer, meditation, and service to others and present topics that will foster a deeper spirit of unity among humankind. The spiritual insights, practices, and beliefs of women and men from a broad spectrum of religious traditions are welcomed."

MAGAZINE NEEDS "No poetry highly specific to a certain faith tradition. Nothing laden with specific faith terminology, nor a lot of Bibe quotes or other quotes." Limited to 35 lines (occasionally longer).

TIPS "We are always seeking original prayers to share the richness of the world's religious traditions."

SALT HILL JOURNAL

E-mail: salthilljournal@gmail.com. **Website:** www.salthilljournal.com. **Contact:** "Please contact appropriate genre editor.". *Salt Hill*, published semiannually, is "published by a group of writers affiliated with the Creative Writing Program at Syracuse University. Our eclectic taste ranges from traditional to experimental. All we ask is that it's good. Open to most themes. Accepting translations." Has published poetry by Denise Duhamel, Edie Fake, Mary Gaitskill, Terance Hayes, H.L. Hix, Etgar Keret, Phil LaMarche, Dorianne Laux, Patrick Lawler, Maurice Manning, Eugene Marten, Patricia Smith, Lynne Tillman, among others. *Salt Hill* is 144-180 pages, digest-sized, includes ads. Receives about 3,000 poems/year, accepts about 2%. Press run is 1,000. Subscription: $15/year. Sample: $10 domestic. Guidelines available online

MAGAZINE NEEDS "As of August 1st, Salt Hill will accept only online submissions via Submishmash. Please submit your work, along with a cover letter, including contact information, here: http://salthill.submishmash.com/Submit. We read submissions between August 1 and April 1 of each year. Please read an issue of Salt Hill to get a feel for what we like.We ask that you do not send more work until hearing back from us.Due to the volume of submissions, we can't respond individually to submission status queries." No known line limits.

TIPS "*Salt Hill* seeks to publish writing that is exciting and necessary, regardless of aesthetic. Rather than trying to fit any subscribed style, send your best work. We recommend reading recent issues or samples on our website prior to submitting. Open submissions from Aug. 1-Apr. 1. Enclose SASE for reply. We recycle mss, and encourage you to use a 'Forever' stamp on your SASE. Clearly mark envelope to the appropriate genre editor's attention."

THE SAME

P.O. Box 494, Mount Union PA 17066. **E-mail:** editors@thesamepress.com. **Website:** www.thesamepress.com. **Contact:** Nancy Eldredge, managing editor. *The Same*, published biannually, prints nonfiction (essays, reviews, literary criticism), poetry, and short fiction. We want eclectic poetry (formal to free verse, "mainstream" to experimental, all subject matter.) The Same is 50-100 pages, desktop-published and perfect bound. Single copy: $6; subscription: $12 for 2 issues, $20 for 4 issues. Publishes ms 11 months after acceptance. Responds within 2 months.

MAGAZINE NEEDS Submit 1-7 poems at a time. Lines/poem: 120 maximum. No previously published poems or simultaneous submissions without query. Prefers e-mail submissions (pasted into body of message). Cover letter is optional. Include SASE if you want a snail mail response. If you don't want your manuscript returned, you may omit the SASE if we can respond by e-mail. Please query before submitting fiction and non-fiction. Submissions are read year round.

ADDITIONAL INFORMATION Publishes 1-3 chapbooks/year. **Solicited mss only.** Chapbooks are 24-32 pages, desktop-published, saddle-stapled, with cardstock covers. Pays 25 author's copies (out of a press run of 100).

O SAMSARA: THE MAGAZINE OF SUFFERING

P.O. Box 467, Ashburn VA 20147. **E-mail:** rdfgoalie@gmail.com. **Website:** www.samsaramagazine.net. **Contact:** R. David Fulcher, editor. *Samsara, The Magazine of Suffering*, published biannually, prints poetry and fiction dealing with suffering and healing. "Both metered verse and free verse poetry are welcome if dealing with the theme of suffering/healing." Has published poetry by Michael Foster, Nicole Provencher, and Jeff Parsley. *Samsara* is 80 pages, magazine-sized, desktop-published, with color cardstock cover. Receives about 200 poems/year, accepts about 15%. Press run is 300 (200 subscribers). Single copy: $5.50; subscription: $10. Make checks payable to R. David Fulcher. Acquires first rights. Publishes ms 3 months after acceptance. Responds in 2 months. Sample copy for $5.50. Guidelines for SASE or on website.

MAGAZINE NEEDS Submit up to 5 poems at a time. Lines/poem: 3 minimum, 100 maximum. Considers simultaneous submissions "if noted as such"; no previously published poems. Cover letter is preferred. No e-mail submissions; accepts submissions by postal mail only. Pays 1 contributor's copy.

● SANDY RIVER REVIEW

University of Maine at Farmington, 238 Main St., Farmington ME 04938. **E-mail:** srreview@gmail.com. **Website:** studentorgs.umf.maine.edu/~srreview. **Contact:** Kelsey Moore, editor. "*The Sandy River Review* seeks prose, poetry and art submissions twice a year for our Spring and Fall issues. Prose submissions may be either Fiction or Creative Non-Fiction and should be 15 pages or fewer in length, 12 pt., Times Roman font, double-spaced. Most of our art is published in black & white, and must be submitted as 300 dpi quaity, CMYK color mode, and saved as a .TIF file. We publish a wide variety of work from students as well as professional, established writers. Your submission should be polished and imaginative with strongly drawn characters and an interesting, original narrative. The review is the face of the University of Maine at Farmington's venerable BFA Creative Writing program, and we strive for the highest quality prose and poetry standard." Rights for the work return to the writer once we publish it. Pays on publication. Pays 5 copies of the published issue. Publishes ms 2 months after acceptance. Guidelines available by e-mail request.

TIPS "We recommend that you take time with your piece. As with all submissions to a literary journal, submissions should be fully-completed, polished final drafts that require minimal to no revision once accepted. Double-check your prose pieces for basic grammatical errors before submitting."

◐ THE SARANAC REVIEW

CVH, Department of English, SUNY Plattsburgh, 101 Broad St., Plattsburgh NY 12901. (518)564-2414. **Fax:** (518)564-2140. **E-mail:** saranacreview@plattsburgh.edu. **Website:** http://research.plattsburgh.edu/saranacreview. **Contact:** Poetry Editor. Estab. 2004. *The Saranac Review*, published annually in the fall, wants poetry from both U.S. and Canadian writers. Does not want "amateurish or 'greeting card' poetry." Has published poetry by Donald Revell, Ricardo Pau-Llosa, Jim Daniels, Rustin Larson, Rane Arroyo, Ross Leckie, Diane Swan, T. Alan Broughton, Brian Bartlett, Barry Dempster. *The Saranac Review* is magazine-sized, with color photo or painting on cover, includes ads. Press run is 1,000. Single copy: $12/$14CA; subscription: $15/year, $20 for 2 years, $28 for 3 years, $45 for 5 years ($18/year for institutions—multi-year subscriptions receive 15% discount); all Canadian subscriptions add $3/year. Make checks payable to Subscriptions/*The Saranac Review*.

HOW TO CONTACT Submit no more than 3 poems at a time. Considers simultaneous submissions if notified; no previously published poems. No e-mail or disk submissions. Cover letter is appreciated. Include phone and e-mail contact information (if possible) in cover letter. Manuscripts will not be returned without SASE. Reads submissions September 1-February 15 (firm). Poems are circulated to an editorial board. Sometimes comments on rejected poems. Guidelines available on website. Responds in 3-6 months. Pays 2 contributor's copies. Acquires first rights.

TIPS "We publish serious, generous fiction."

O SCIENCE EDITOR

P.O. Box 4082, Alexandria VA 22303. (703)786-2272. **Fax:** (571)366-2089. **E-mail:** csescienceeditor@gmail.com. **Website:** www.CouncilScienceEditors.org. **Contact:** Rebecca S. Benner, editor. *Science Editor*, published quarterly, is "a forum for the exchange of information and ideas among professionals concerned with publishing in the sciences." Wants "up to 90 typeset lines of poetry on the intersection of science (including but not limited to biomedicine) and communication. Geared toward adult scholars, writers, and editors in communication and the sciences." Has published poetry by Mary Knatterud, Judy Meiksin, David Goldblatt, Mary Donnelly, Nancy Overcott, Jyothirmai Gubili, Neil H. Segal, Michele Arduengo. *Science Editor* is approx. 32 pages, magazine-sized, 4-color process, saddle-stitched, with an 80 pd Dull Cover; includes ads. Press run is 1,500. Single copy: $12 US; $15 Int'l. "Journal is a membership benefit; dues are $164 per year; nonmember subscriptions: $55 US; $68 Int'l/year." Make checks payable to Council of Science Editors (CSE). Acquires one-time rights, electronic rights. Publishes ms 3-6 months after acceptance. Responds in 3-6 weeks. Guidelines by e-mail.

MAGAZINE NEEDS Submit up to 3 poems at a time, maximum 90 lines. Does not consider previously published poems or simultaneous submissions. Accepts e-mail submissions (pasted into the body of message), no fax or disk. "Submit both cover letter and poetry by e-mail only in the body of the same e-mail message, with no attachments." Sometimes comments on rejected poems. "*Science Editor* is posted online. Issues at least one year old are openly displayed accessible. Issues less than one year old can be accessed only by Council of Science Editors members." Rights revert to poet upon publication. Pays 3 contributor's copies.

SCIFAIKUEST

P.O. Box 782, Cedar Rapids IA 52406. **E-mail:** gatrix65@yahoo.com. **Website:** www.samsdotpublishing.com. **Contact:** Tyree Campbell, managing editor; Teri Santitoro, editor. *Scifaikuest*, published quarterly both online and in print, features "science fiction/fantasy/horror minimalist poetry, especially scifaiku, and related forms. We also publish articles about various poetic forms and reviews of poetry collections. The online and print versions of *Scifaikuest* are different." Wants "artwork, scifaiku and speculative minimalist forms such as tanka, haibun, ghazals, senryu. No 'traditional' poetry." Has published poetry by Tom Brinck, Oino Sakai, Deborah P. Kolodji, Aurelio Rico Lopez III, Joanne Morcom, and John Dunphy. *Scifaikuest* (print edition) is 32 pages, digest-sized, offset-printed, perfect-bound, with color cardstock cover, includes ads. Receives about 500 poems/year, accepts about 160 (32%). Press run is 100/issue; 5 distributed free to reviewers. Single copy: $7; subscription: $20/year, $37 for 2 years. Make checks payable to Tyree Campbell/Sam's Dot Publishing. Member: The Speculative Literature Foundation. *Scifaikuest* was voted #1 poetry magazine in the 2004 Preditors & Editors poll.

MAGAZINE NEEDS Submit 5 poems at a time. Lines/poem: varies, depending on poem type. No previously published poems or simultaneous submissions. Accepts e-mail submissions (pasted into body of message). No disk submissions; artwork as e-mail attachment or inserted body of e-mail. "Submission should include snail mail address and a short (1-2 lines) bio." Reads submissions year round. Submit seasonal poems 6 months in advance. Time between acceptance and publication is 1-2 months. "Editor Teri Santitoro makes all decisions regarding acceptances." Often comments on rejected poems. Guidelines available on website. Responds in 6-8 weeks. Pays $1/poem, $4/review or article, and 1 contributor's copy. Acquires first North American serial rights.

SEAM

P.O. Box 1051, Sawston, Cambridge CB22 3WT, United Kingdom. **Website:** www.seampoetry.co.uk. *Seam*, published twice/year in spring and autumn, is "international in outlook and open to experimental work and authorized translations." Wants "good contemporary poetry and "high-quality poems that engage the reader." Has published poetry by Mike Barlow, Jane Holland, Sheenagh Pugh, Julian Stannard, George Szirtes, and Tamar Yoseloff. *Seam* is 72 pages, A5, perfect-bound, with b&w cover. Receives about 2,000 poems/year, accepts about 5%. Press run is 300. Subscription: £8/year (£12 or $18 overseas). Sample: £4.50 (£5.50 or $9 overseas). Payments accepted through PayPal.

MAGAZINE NEEDS Submit 5-6 poems at a time. No simultaneous submissions or previously published poems (if published in UK). No e-mail submissions. Type each poem on 1 sheet of paper (A4 size). Sometimes comments on rejected poems. Can reply by e-mail to save postage and time standing in line at post office for International Reply Coupons. Pays 1 contributor's copy.

THE SEATTLE REVIEW

Box 354330, University of Washington, Seattle, WA 98195. (206)543-2302. **E-mail:** seaview@u.washington.edu. **Website:** www.seattlereview.org. "We are looking for exceptional, risk-taking, intellectual and imaginative poems between ten and thirty pages in length." *The Seattle Review* will publish, and will only publish, long poems and novellas. The long poem can be: a single long poem in its entirety, a self-contained excerpt from a book-length poem, a unified sequence or series of poems. Subscriptions: $20/three issues, $32/five issues. Back issue: $4. Includes general fiction, poetry, craft essays on writing, and one interview per issue with a Northwest writer. Buys first North American serial rights. Pays on publication. Responds in 8 months to mss. Sample copy for $6. Guidelines available online.

Editors accept submissions only from October 1 through May 31.

HOW TO CONTACT Submit 3-5 poems via mail between October 1 and May 31, or use submission manager on website year round. Include SASE in mail. Submissions must be typed on white, 8 1/2x11 paper. The author's name and address should appear in the upper right hand corner. No simultaneous submissions.

TIPS "Know what we publish: no genre fiction; look at our magazine and decide if your work might be appreciated. Beginners do well in our magazine if they send clean, well-written manuscripts. We've published a lot of 'first stories' from all over the country and take pleasure in discovery."

THE SECRET PLACE

American Baptist Home Mission Societies, ABC/USA, P.O. Box 851, Valley Forge PA 19482-0851. (610)768-2434. **E-mail:** thesecretplace@abc-usa.org. Buys first rights. Pays on acceptance. Editorial lead time 1 year. For free sample and guidelines, send 6×9 SASE.

MAGAZINE NEEDS Length: 4-30 lines. Pays $20.

TIPS "Prefers submissions via e-mail."

SEEMS

P.O. Box 359, Lakeland College, Sheboygan WI 53082-0359. **E-mail:** elderk@lakeland.edu. **E-mail:** seems@lakeland.edu. **Website:** www.seems.lakeland.edu. Acquires first North American serial rights and permission to publish online. Returns rights upon publication. Responds in 3 months (slower in the summer).

MAGAZINE NEEDS Lines/poem: open. No simultaneous submissions. No fax or e-mail submissions. Cover letter is optional. Include biographical information, SASE. Reads submissions year round. There is a 1- to 2-year backlog. "People may call or fax with virtually any question, understanding that the editor may have no answer." Guidelines available on website. Pays 1 contributor's copy.

CONTEST/AWARD OFFERINGS Subsequent issues may include themes and will alternate with chapbooks from Word of Mouth Books (query for the no-fee, any-genre, chapbook contest: elderk@lakeland.edu). See the editor's website at www.karlelder.com. "Links to my work and an interview may provide insight for the potential contributor."

SENECA REVIEW

Hobart and William Smith Colleges, Geneva NY 14456. (315)781-3392. **E-mail:** senecareview@hws.edu. **Website:** www.hws.edu/academics/senecareview/index.aspx. "The editors have special interest in translations of contemporary poetry from around the world. Publisher of numerous laureates and award-winning poets, we also publish emerging writers and are always open to new, innovative work. Poems from *SR* are regularly honored by inclusion in *The Best American Poetry* and *Pushcart Prize* anthologies. Distributed internationally." Accepts queries by mail or online at http://senecareview.submishmash.com/submit. Responds in 3 months to mss. Guidelines available online. E-mail quetions to senecareview@hws.edu.

TIPS "One submission per reading period. Mss received May1-September 1 are returned."

THE SEWANEE REVIEW

(931)598-1000. **Website:** www.sewanee.edu/sewanee_review. 735 University Ave., Sewanee, TN 37383-1000. (931)598-1000. **Fax:** (931)598-1145. **Website:** www.sewanee.edu/sewanee_review. The *Sewanee Review* is America's oldest continuously published literary quarterly. Only erudite work representing depth of knowledge and skill of expression is published. Solicits brief, standard, and essay-reviews.Winners of the Allen Tate Prize and the Aiken Taylor Award for Modern American Poetry are determined by the editorial board and a prize committee; poets cannot apply for these awards. Subscriptions: $25/year. Samples: $8.50. "A literary quarterly, publishing original fiction, poetry, essays on literary and related subjects, and book reviews for well-educated readers who appreciate good American and English literature." Buys first North American serial rights, buys second serial (reprint) rights. Pays on publication. Responds in 6-8 weeks to mss. Sample copy for $8.50 ($9.50 outside US). Guidelines available online.

Does not read mss June 1-August 31.

MAGAZINE NEEDS Send complete ms. Length: 40 lines.

HOW TO CONTACT Submit up to 6 poems at a time. Lines/poem: 40 maximum. No simultaneous submissions. No e-mail submissions; postal submissions only. "Unsolicited works should not be submitted between June 1 and August 31. A response to any submission received during that period will be greatly delayed." Guidelines available in magazine or on website. Responds in 2 months. Pays per line, plus 2 contributor's copies (and reduced price for additional copies).

TIPS "Please keep in mind that for each poem published in *The Sewanee Review*, approximately 250 poems are considered."

SHEMOM

2486 Montgomery Ave., Cardiff CA 92007. **E-mail:** pdfrench@cox.net. **Contact:** Peggy French, editor. *Shemom*, published 3 times/year, is a zine that "showcases writers of all ages reflecting on life's varied experiences. We often feature haiku." Includes poetry, haiku, and essays. Open to any style, but prefers free verse. "We like to hear from anyone who has a story to tell and will read anything you care to send our way." *Shemom* is 20-30 pages. Receives about 200 poems/year, accepts 50%. Press run is 60 (30 subscribers). Single copy: $4; subscription: $12/3 issues. Make checks payable to Peggy French. Publishes ms 3 months after acceptance. Responds in 1 month. Guidelines for SASE.

MAGAZINE NEEDS Submit 3-10 poems at a time. Considers previously published poems and simultaneous submissions. Accepts e-mail submissions (as attachment or pasted into body of message). "Prefer e-mail submission, but not required; if material is to be returned, please include a SASE." Pays 1 contributor's copy. Acquires one-time rights.

SHENANDOAH

(540)458-8765. **Fax:** (540)458-8461. **E-mail:** shenandoah@wlu.edu. **Website:** shenandoah.wlu.edu/faq.html. **Contact:** R. T. Smith, editor. "Unsolicited manuscripts will not be read between January 1 and October 1, 2010. All manuscripts received during this period will be recycled unread." Buys first North American serial rights, buys one-time rights. Pays on publication. Publishes ms an average of 10 months after acceptance. Responds in 3 months to mss. Sample copy for $12. Guidelines available online.

MAGAZINE NEEDS Considers simultaneous submissions "only if we are immediately informed of acceptance elsewhere." No e-mail submissions. All submissions should be typed on 1 side of the paper only, with name and address clearly written on the upper right corner of the ms. Include SASE. Reads submissions September 1-May 15 only. Responds in 3 months. Pays $2.50/line, one-year subscription, and 1 contributor's copy. Acquires first publication rights. Staff reviews books of poetry in 7-10 pages, multi-book format. Send materials for review consideration. (Most reviews are solicited.) "No inspirational, confessional poetry." Pays $2.50/line ($200 max)

CONTEST/AWARD OFFERINGS Sponsors the annual James Boatwright III Prize for Poetry, a $1,000 prize awarded to the author of the best poem published in *Shenandoah* during a volume year. The Shenandoah/Glasgow Prize for Emerging Writers $2,000 awarded for poetry on alternate years.

THE SHEPHERD

1530 Seventh St., Rock Island IL 61201. (309)788-3980. **Contact:** Betty Mowery, poetry editor. *The Shepherd*, published quarterly, features inspirational poetry from all ages. Wants "something with a message but not preachy." Subscription: $12. Sample: $4. Make all checks payable to *The Oak*.

MAGAZINE NEEDS Submit up to 5 poems at a time. Lines/poem: 35 maximum. Considers previously published poems. Include SASE with all submissions. Responds in one week. "*The Shepherd* does not pay in dollars or copies, but you need not purchase to be published." Acquires first or second rights. All rights revert to poet upon publication.

TIPS Sponsors poetry contest. Guidelines available for SASE.

SHIP OF FOOLS

Ship of Fools Press, University of Rio Grande, Box 1028, Rio Grande OH 45674. (740)992-3333. **Website:** http://meadhall.homestead.com/Ship.html. **Contact:** Jack Hart, editor. *Ship of Fools*, published "more or less quarterly," seeks "coherent, well-written, traditional or modern, myth, archetype, love—most types." Does not want "concrete, incoherent, or greeting card poetry." Considers poetry by children and teens. Has published poetry by Rhina Espaillat and Gale White. *Ship of Fools* is digest-sized, saddle-stapled, includes cover art and graphics. Press run is 200. Subscription: $8 for 4 issues. Sample: $2.

MAGAZINE NEEDS No previously published poems or simultaneous submissions. Cover letter is preferred.

Often comments on rejected poems. Guidelines available for SASE. Responds in one month. "If longer than six weeks, write and ask why." Pays 1-2 contributor's copies. Reviews books of poetry.

ADDITIONAL INFORMATION Ship of Fools Press has "no plans to publish chapbooks in the next year due to time constraints."

SIERRA NEVADA REVIEW

999 Tahoe Blvd., Incline Village NV 89451. **E-mail:** sncreview@sierranevada.edu. **Website:** www.sierranevada.edu/800. *Sierra Nevada Review*, published annually in May, features poetry and short fiction by new writers. Wants "image-oriented poems with a distinct, genuine voice. Although we don't tend to publish 'light verse,' we do appreciate, and often publish, poems that make us laugh. No limit on length, style, etc." Does not want "sentimental, clicheéd, or obscure poetry." Has published poetry by Virgil Suaárez, Simon Perchik, Carol Frith, and Marisella Veiga. *Sierra Nevada Review* is about 75 pages, with art on cover. Receives about 1,000 poems/year, accepts about 50. Press run is 500. Subscription: $10/year. Sample: $5. Responds in 3 months. Guidelines available for SASE, by e-mail, or on website.

MAGAZINE NEEDS Submit up to 5 poems at a time. Considers simultaneous submissions; no previously published poems. Accepts e-mail submissions (pasted into body of message, no attachments). Reads submissions September 1-March 1 only. Sometimes comments on rejected poems. Pays 2 contributor's copies.

SKIPPING STONES: A MULTICULTURAL LITERARY MAGAZINE

P.O. Box 3939, Eugene OR 97403-0939. (541)342-4956. **E-mail:** editor@skippingstones.org. **Website:** www.skippingstones.org. **Contact:** Arun Toke, editor. "*Skipping Stones* is an award-winning multicultural, nonprofit magazine designed to promote cooperation, creativity and celebration of cultural and ecological richness. We encourage submissions by children of color, minorities and under-represented populations. We want material meant for children and young adults/teenagers with multicultural or ecological awareness themes. Think, live and write as if you were a child, tween or teen. Wants material that gives insight to cultural celebrations, lifestyle, customs and traditions, glimpse of daily life in other countries and cultures. Photos, songs, artwork are most welcome if they illustrate/highlight the points. Translations are invited if your submission is in a language other than English. Upcoming themes will include cultural celebrations, living abroad, challenging, hospitality customs of various cultures, cross-cultural understanding, African, Asian and Latin American cultures, humor, international understanding, turning points and magical moments in life, caring for the earth, spirituality, and multicutural awareness." Buys first North American serial rights, non-exclusive reprint, and electronic rights. Publishes ms an average of 4-8 months after acceptance. Responds only if interested, send nonreturnable samples. Editorial lead time 3-4 months. Writer's guidelines online or for business-sized envelope.

MAGAZINE NEEDS *Skipping Stones*, published bi-monthly during the school year (5 issues), "encourages cooperation, creativity, and celebration of cultural and ecological richness." Wants "poetry by young writers under age 18, on multicultural and social issues, family, freedom—uplifting. No adult poetry, please." *Skipping Stones* is magazine-sized, saddle-stapled, printed on recycled paper. Receives about 500-1,000 poems/year, accepts 10%. Press run is 2,500. Subscription: $25. Sample: $6. Only accepts poetry from youth under age 18. Length: 30 lines maximum.

HOW TO CONTACT Submit up to 5 poems at a time. Lines/poem: 30 maximum. Considers simultaneous submissions; no previously published poems. Accepts e-mail submissions. Cover letter is preferred. "Include your cultural background, experiences, and the inspiration behind your creation." Time between acceptance and publication is 6-9 months. "A piece is chosen for publication when most of the editorial staff feel good about it." Seldom comments on rejected poems. Publishes multi-theme issues. Guidelines available for SASE. Responds in up to 4 months. Pays 1 contributor's copy, offers 40% discount for morecopies and subscription, if desired. Acquires first serial rights and non-exclusive reprint rights.

CONTEST/AWARD OFFERINGS Sponsors annual youth honor awards for 7- to 17-year-olds. Theme is "multicultural, social, international, and nature awareness." Guidelines available for SASE or on website. Entry fee: $3 (entitles entrant to a free issue featuring the 10 winners). Deadline: June 25.

TIPS "Be original and innovative. Use multicultural, nature, or cross-cultural themes. Multilingual submissions are welcome."

SLANT: A JOURNAL OF POETRY

University of Central Arkansas, P.O. Box 5063, 201 Donaghey Ave., Conway AR 72035. (501)450-5107. **Website:** www.uca.edu/english/poetryjournal/. **Contact:** James Fowler, editor. *Slant: A Journal of Poetry*, published annually in May, aims "to publish a journal of fine poetry from all regions of the United States and beyond." Wants "traditional and 'modern' poetry, even experimental; moderate length, any subject on approval of Board of Readers." Doesn't want "haiku, translations." Has published poetry by Richard Broderick, Linda Casebeer, Marc Jampole, Sandra Kohler, Charles Harper Webb, and Ellen Roberts Young. *Slant* is 120 pages, professionally printed on quality stock, flat-spined, with matte card cover. Receives about 1,000 poems/year, accepts 70-75. Press run is 175 (70-100 subscribers). Sample: $10.

MAGAZINE NEEDS Submit up to 5 poems at a time. Lines/poem: poems should be of moderate length. No previously published poems or simultaneous submissions. Submissions should be typed; include SASE. "Put name, address (including e-mail if available), and phone number at the top of each page." Accepts submissions September 1-November 15. Comments on rejected poems "on occasion." Guidelines available in magazine, for SASE, or on website. Responds in 3-4 months from November 15 deadline. Pays 1 contributor's copy. Poet retains rights.

SLATE & STYLE

2861 S. 93 Plaza APT 8, Omaha NE 68124. (402)350-1735. **E-mail:** bpollpeter@hotmail.com. **Website:** www.nfb-writers-division.org. **Contact:** Bridgit Pollpeter, editor.

MAGAZINE NEEDS *Slate & Style*, published quarterly, is the magazine of the Writers' Division of the National Federation of the Blind. Published for blind writers, *Slate & Style* is available in large print, in Braille, and by e-mail at: bpollpeter@hotmail.com, and includes resources and articles of interest to blind writers. "We prefer contributors be blind writers, or at least writers by profession or inclination. New writers welcome. No obscenities. Will consider all forms of poetry including haiku. Interested in new talent." Considers poetry by children and teens, "but please specify age." Has published poetry by Harriet Barrett, W. Burns Taylor, Chelsea Cook, Jennifer Shields, and David Thomas. *Slate & Style* (print format) is 28-32 pages, magazine-sized, stapled. Press run is 200 (160 subscribers, 4-5 libraries). Subscription/membership: $10/year (regardless of format). Sample: $3. Please specify format when subscribing, and make all checks out to the NFB writers' division.

HOW TO CONTACT Submit 3 poems at a time once or twice/year. Lines/poem: 5-36. No previously published poems or simultaneous submissions. Accepts submissions by e-mail at: bpollpeter@hotmail.com (pasted into body of message). "On occasion we receive poems in Braille. I prefer print, since Braille slows me down. Typed is best." Cover letter is preferred. Reads submissions according to the following deadlines: February 16, May 15, August 15, November 15; "do not submit manuscripts in July." Comments on rejected poems "if requested." Guidelines available in magazine, for SASE, by e-mail, or on website. Responds in 2 weeks "if I like it." Pays 1 contributor's copy. Reviews books of poetry. Send materials for review consideration.

CONTEST/AWARD OFFERINGS Sponsors an annual poetry contest, awarding 1st Prize: $100; 2nd Prize: $50; 3rd Prize: $25. Honorable mentions may also be awarded, and winning poems will be published in magazine. **Entry fee:** $5 for up to 3 poems. Make check or money order payable to NFB Writers' Division. "Include cover letter with title and your identifying information." Opens January 1st; **Deadline: June 1.** We are now sponsoring a poetry contest for blind students, K-12. Guidelines available for SASE, by e-mail, or on website.

TIPS "The best advice I can give is to send your work out; manuscripts left in a drawer have no chance at all."

SLEEPINGFISH

Via Titta Scarpetta #28, RM Rome 00153, Italy. **E-mail:** white@sleepingfish.net. **Website:** www.sleepingfish.net. *SleepingFish*, published 1-2 times/year, is "a print or online magazine of innovative text and art. " Wants "art, visual poetry, prose poems, experimental texts, graffiti, collage, multi-cultural, cross-genre work—anything that defies categorization." Does not want "conventional 'lined' or rhyming poetry (anything that looks like a 'poem'), conventional stories, genre fiction or poetry, political, religious, New Age, anything with an agenda." Acquires first rights. Returns all rights "as long as *SleepingFish* is acknowledged as first place of publication." Responds in 1-3 months. Guidelines available on website.

Considers poetry by teens. Has published writings by Rick Moody, Diane Williams, Blake Butler, David Baptiste-Chirot, Miranada Mellis, Brian Evenson, Norman Lock, Peter Markus. *SleepingFish* print issues are 100-120 pages, magazine-sized, digitally printed, perfect-bound or with other binding, with 110 lb. cardstock cover in full color. Receives about 500 poems/year, accepts about 25 (5%). Press run is 400 (10 libraries, 300 shelf sales, 100 online sales); 50 distributed free to contributors. Single copy: $15.

MAGAZINE NEEDS Submit 1-5 prose or visual poems at a time. Lines/poem: 1-3 pages (prose less than 1,000 words). Considers simultaneous submissions; no previously published poems. Accepts e-mail submissions only (pasted into body of message or as small attachments (less than 2 MB) in DOC, RTF, JPG, GIF, or PDF format); no disk submissions. Cover letter is preferred. "Please send e-mail only. Reading period varies; see website for details." Time between acceptance and publication is 2-6 weeks. "Currently, an online operation based out of Rome. Tastes and whims vary and are subject to change. Sometimes there is a loose theme, and acceptance may also be dependent on whether the admission fits in with other work in the issue." Sometimes comments on rejected poems. "Poet should be familiar with *SleepingFish*. Online samples and work on site (www.sleepingfish.net) if you can't afford a copy." Sometimes sends prepublication galleys. Pays 1 contributor's copy, with additional contributor copies available at half price. "Payment depends on funds." Does not review books.

SLIPSTREAM

Dept. W-1, Box 2071, Niagara Falls NY 14301. **E-mail:** editors@slipstream.org. **Website:** www.slipstreampress.org/index.html. **Contact:** Dan Sicoli, co-editor. "We prefer contemporary urban themes—writing from the grit that is not afraid to bark or bite. We shy away from pastoral, religious, and rhyming verse." Chapbook Contest prize is $1,000 plus 50 professionally printed copies of your chapbook. Guidelines available online.

If you're unsure, the editors strongly recommend that you sample a current or back issue of *Slipstream*.

MAGAZINE NEEDS No pastoral, religious, and rhyming verse.

SNOW MONKEY

E-mail: snowmonkey.editor@comcast.net. **Website:** www.ravennapress.com/snowmonkey/. Seeks writing "that's like footprints of the Langur monkeys left at 11,000 feet on Poon Hill, Nepal. Open to most themes." Responds in 2 months to mss.

MAGAZINE NEEDS Submit via e-mail. Does not pay.

TIPS "Send submissions as text-only in the body of your email. Include your last name in the subject line. We do not currently use bios, but we love to read them."

SNOWY EGRET

The Fair Press, P.O. Box 9265, Terre Haute IN 47808. **Website:** www.snowyegret.net. The Fair Press, P.O. Box 9265, Terre Haute IN 47808. **Website:** www.snowyegret.net. **Contact:** Editors. Guidelines available on website. Responds in 1 month. Always sends prepublication galleys. Pays $4/poem or $4/page plus 2 contributor's copies. Acquires first North American and one-time reprint rights. *Snowy Egret*, published in spring and autumn, specializes in work that is "nature-oriented: poetry that celebrates the abundance and beauty of nature or explores the interconnections between nature and the human psyche." Has published poetry by Conrad Hilberry, Lyn Lifshin, Gayle Eleanor, James Armstrong, and Patricia Hooper. *Snowy Egret* is 60 pages, magazine-sized, offset-printed, saddle-stapled. Receives about 500 poems/year, accepts about 30. Press run is 400. Sample: $8; subscription: $15/year, $25 for 2 years.

MAGAZINE NEEDS Guidelines available on website. Responds in 1 month. Always sends prepublication galleys. Pays $4/poem or $4/page plus 2 contributor's copies. Acquires first North American and onetime reprint rights.

TIPS Looks for "honest, freshly detailed pieces with plenty of description and/or dialogue which will allow the reader to identify with the characters and step into the setting; fiction in which nature affects character development and the outcome of the story."

SOFA INK QUARTERLY

E-mail: publisher@sofaink.com. **E-mail:** acquisitions@sofaink.com. **Website:** www.sofaink.com; www.sofainkquarterly.com. **Contact:** David Cowsert. "Sofa Ink Quarterly offers wonderful original stories, poetry, and nonfiction that is entertaining yet wholesome. Sofa Ink Quarterly showcases original writing and art that avoids sensationalism. There is no swearing, profaning deity, excessive gore, gratuitous violence or gratuitous sex. You will find exceptional storytelling, delightful poetry, and beautiful art."

MAGAZINE NEEDS Submit 5 poems maximum at a time. Considers simultaneous submissions. Accepts e-mail submissions (as attachment in Word). Submit seasonal poems 4 months in advance. Time between acceptance and publication is about 3 months. Guidelines available for SASE or on website. Responds in 1-3 months. Pays $5 and 3 contributor's copies. Acquires first North American serial rights. Submit 5 poems maximum at a time. Considers simultaneous submissions. Accepts e-mail submissions (as attachment in Word). Submit seasonal poems 4 months in advance. Time between acceptance and publication is about 3 months. Guidelines available for SASE or on website. Responds in 1-3 months. Pays $5 and 3 contributor's copies. Acquires first North American serial rights.

TIPS Follow the content guidelines. Electronic submissions should be in a Word attachment rather than in the body of the message.

SONG OF THE SAN JOAQUIN

P.O. Box 1161, Modesto CA 95353-1161. **E-mail:** info@ChaparralPoets.org. **Website:** www.ChaparralPoets.org/SSJ.html. **Contact:** The Editor. *Song of the San Joaquin*, published quarterly, features "subjects about or pertinent to the San Joaquin Valley of Central California. This is defined geographically as the region from Fresno to Stockton, and from the foothills on the west to those on the east." Wants all forms and styles of poetry. "Keep subject in mind." Does not want "pornographic, demeaning, vague, or trite approaches." Considers poetry by children and teens. Acquires one-time rights. Pays 1 contributor's copy. Time between acceptance and publication is 3-6 months. "Poems are circulated to an editorial board of 7 who then decide on the final selections." Seldom comments on rejected poems. Responds in up to 3 months.

Has published poetry by Joyce Odam, Wilma Elizabeth McDaniel, Margarita Engle, Marnelle White, Frederick Zydek, and Nancy Haskett. *Song of the San Joaquin* is 60 pages, digest-sized, direct-copied, saddle-stapled, with cardstock cover with glossy color photo. Press run is 200 (25 copies to libraries); 40 distributed free to contributors.

MAGAZINE NEEDS Submit up to 3 poems at a time. Lines/poem: open ("however, poems under 40 lines have the best chance"). Considers previously published poems; no simultaneous submissions. E-mail submissions are preferred; no disk submissions. Cover letter is preferred. "SASE required. All submissions must be typed on 1 side of the page only. Proofread submissions carefully. Name, address, phone number, and e-mail address should appear on all pages. Cover letter should include any awards, honors, and previous publications for each poem, and a biographical sketch of 75 words or less." Reads submissions "periodically throughout the year."

ADDITIONAL INFORMATION "Poets of the San Joaquin, which sponsors this publication, is a chapter of California Federation of Chaparral Poets, Inc., and publishes an annual anthology of members' works. Information available for SASE or by e-mail."

CONTEST/AWARD OFFERINGS Poets of the San Joaquin holds an annual local young poets' contest as well as regular poetry contests. Guidelines available for SASE or by e-mail.

SO TO SPEAK

George Mason University, 4400 University Dr., MSN 2C5, Fairfax VA 22030-4444. **E-mail:** sts@gmu.edu (inquiries only). **Website:** http://sotospeakjournal.org. Established 1991. **Contact:** Eleanor Smith Tipton, poetry editor. *So to Speak*, published semiannually, prints "high-quality work relating to feminism, including poetry, fiction, nonfiction (including book reviews and interviews), photography, artwork, collaborations, lyrical essays, and other genre-questioning texts." Wants "work that addresses issues of significance to women's lives and movements for women's equality and are especially interested in pieces that explore issues of race, class, and sexuality in relation to gender." *So to Speak* is 100-128 pages, digest-sized, photo-offset-printed, perfect-bound, with glossy cover, includes ads. Receives about 800 poems/year, accepts 10%. Press run is 1,000 (75 subscribers, 100 shelf sales); 500 distributed free to students/contributors. Subscription: $12. Sample: $7.

HOW TO CONTACT Accepts submissions only via submissions manager on website. Submit 3-5 poems at a time. Considers simultaneous submissions; no previously published poems. No e-mail or paper submissions. "Please submit poems as you wish to see them in print. Be sure to include a cover letter with full contact info, publication credits, and awards received." Reads submissions August 15-October 15 and

December 31-March 15. Time between acceptance and publication is 6-8 months. Seldom comments on rejected poems. Responds in 3 months if submissions are received during reading period. Pays 2 contributor's copies. Acquires one-time rights.

CONTEST/AWARD OFFERINGS *So to Speak* holds an annual poetry contest that awards $500. Guidelines available for SASE, by e-mail, or on website.

TIPS "We do not read between March 15 and August 15. Every writer has something they do exceptionally well; do that and it will shine through in the work. We look for quality prose with a definite appeal to a feminist audience. We are trying to move away from strict genre lines. We want high quality fiction, nonfiction, poetry, art, innovative and risk-taking work."

SOUL FOUNTAIN

90-21 Springfield Blvd., Queens Village NY 11428. (718)479-2594. **Fax:** (718)479-2594. **E-mail:** davault@aol.com. **Website:** www.TheVault.org. **Contact:** Tone Bellizzi, editor. *Soul Fountain*, published 3 times/year, is produced by The Vault, a not-for-profit arts project of the Hope for the Children Foundation, "committed to empowering young and emerging artists of all disciplines at all levels to develop and share their talents through performance, collaboration, and networking." Prints poetry, art, photography, short fiction, and essays. Open to all. "We publish quality submitted work, and specialize in emerging voices. We favor visionary, challenging, and consciousness-expanding material." Does not want "poems about pets, nature, romantic love, or the occult. Sex and violence themes not welcome." Welcomes poetry by teens. *Soul Fountain* is 28 pages, magazine-sized, offset-printed, saddle-stapled. Subscription: $24. Sample: $7. Make checks payable to Hope for the Children Foundation. Publishes ms 1 year after acceptance. Guidelines for SASE.

MAGAZINE NEEDS Submit 2-3 poems at a time. Lines/poem: 1 page maximum. Considers previously published poems and simultaneous submissions. Accepts e-mail submissions (pasted into body of message). Poems should be camera-ready. "When e-mailing a submission, it is necessary to include your mailing address. Cover letter not needed. SASE with postal mail submissions is not necessary, but $2 in postage is appreciated." Pays 1 contributor's copy.

SOUTH CAROLINA REVIEW

Clemson University, Strode Tower Room 611, Box 340522, Clemson SC 29634-0522. (864) 656-5399. **Fax:** (864) 656-1345. **E-mail:** cwayne@clemson.edu. **Website:** www.clemson.edu/cedp/cudp/scr/scrintro.htm. **Contact:** Wayne Chapman, editor.

MAGAZINE NEEDS Submit 3-10 poems at a time. No previously published poems or simultaneous submissions. Cover letter is preferred. "Editor prefers a chatty, personal cover letter plus a list of publishing credits. Manuscript format should be according to new MLA Stylesheet." Submissions should be sent "in an 8x10 manila envelope so poems aren't creased." Do not submit during June, July, August, or December. Occasionally publishes theme issues. Responds in 2 months. Pays in 2 contributor's copies. Staff reviews books of poetry.

SOUTH DAKOTA REVIEW

University of South Dakota, 414 E. Clark St., Vermillion SD 57069. (605)677-5184. **Fax:** (605)677-5298. **E-mail:** sdreview@usd.edu. **Website:** www.usd.edu/sdreview. *South Dakota Review*, published quarterly, prints "poetry, fiction, criticism, and scholarly and personal essays. When material warrants, emphasis is on the American West; writers from the West; Western places or subjects. There are frequent issues with no geographical emphasis; periodic special issues on one theme, one place, or one writer." Wants "originality, sophistication, significance, craft—i.e., professional work." Has published poetry by Allan Safarik, Joanna Gardner, Nathaniel Hansen, and Jeanine Stevens. Press run is 500-600 (450 subscribers, half libraries). Single copy: $10; subscription: $30/year, $45/2 years. Sample: $8. Acquires first, second serial (reprint) rights. Publishes ms 1-6 months after acceptance. Responds in 10-12 weeks.

Pushcart and *Best American Essays* nominees.

MAGAZINE NEEDS Submit up to 5 poems at a time. Postal submission or online submission using submission manager found on website. Cover letter is required. Must include SASE. Reads submissions year round.

TIPS Rejects mss because of "careless writing; often careless typing; stories too personal ('I' confessional); aimlessness of plot; unclear or unresolved conflicts; subject matter that editor finds clicheéd, sensationalized, pretentious or trivial. We are trying to use more fiction and more variety."

THE SOUTHEAST REVIEW

Florida State University, Tallahassee FL 32306-1036. **Website:** southeastreview.org. **Contact:** Katie Cortese, editor. Established 1979. **Contact:** Rebecca Hazelton, poetry editor. Acquires first North America serial rights which then revert to the author. 2-6 months Responds in 2-4 months.

"The mission of *The Southeast Review* is to present emerging writers on the same stage as well-established ones. In each semi-annual issue, we publish literary fiction, creative nonfiction, poetry, interviews, book reviews and art. With nearly 60 members on our editorial staff who come from throughout the country and the world, we strive to publish work that is representative of our diverse interests and aesthetics, and we celebrate the eclectic mix this produces. We receive approximately 400 submissions per month and we accept less than 1-2% of them. We will comment briefly on rejected mss when time permits. Publishes ms 2-6 months after acceptance." **Publishes 4-6 new writers/year**. Recently published work by Elizabeth Hegwood, Anthony Varallo, B.J. Hollars, Tina Karelson, John Dufresne, and more.

MAGAZINE NEEDS *The Southeast Review*, published biannually, looks for "the very best poetry by new and established poets." *The Southeast Review* is 160 pages, digest-sized. Receives about 5,000 poems/year, accepts less than 4%. Press run is 1,000 (500 subscribers, 100 libraries, 200 shelf sales); 100 distributed free. Single copy: $8; subscription: $15/year. Sample: $6. Make checks payable to *The Southeast Review*.

HOW TO CONTACT Submit 3-5 poems at a time. Considers simultaneous submissions; no previously published poems. Accepts submissions by postal mail only; SASE required. Cover letter is preferred ("very brief"). Reads submissions year round. Time between acceptance and publication is up to 1 year. Seldom comments on rejected poems. Guidelines available for SASE, by e-mail, or on website. Responds in up to 3 months. Pays 2 contributor's copies. Acquires first North American serial rights. Reviews books and chapbooks of poetry. "Please query the Book Review Editor (serbookreview@gmail.com) concerning reviews."

CONTEST/AWARD OFFERINGS Sponsors an annual poetry contest. Winner receives $500 and publication; 9 finalists will also be published. **Entry fee:** $15 for 3 poems. **Deadline:** March. Guidelines available on website.

TIPS *The Southeast Review* accepts regular submissions for publication consideration year-round exclusively through the **online Submission Manager**. Any breaks, hiatuses, or interruptions to the reading period will be announced online, and are more likely to occur during the summer months. *SER* does not, under any circumstances, accept work via e-mail. **Except during contest season, paper submissions sent through regular postal mail will not be read or returned**. Please note that, during contest season, entries to our World's Best Short Short Story, Poetry, and Creative Nonfiction competitions must still be sent through regular postal mail. "Avoid trendy experimentation for its own sake (present-tense narration, observation that isn't also revelation). Fresh stories, moving, interesting characters and a sensitivity to language are still fiction mainstays. We also publish the winner and runners-up of the World's Best Short Story Contest, Poetry Contest, and Creative Nonfiction Contest."

SOUTHERN CALIFORNIA REVIEW

3501 Trousdale Pkwy., Mark Taper Hall, THH 355J, University of Southern California, Los Angeles CA 90089-0355. **E-mail:** scr@college.usc.edu. **Website:** http://usc.edu/scr. **Contact:** Poetry Editor. *Southern California Review (SCR)*, published semiannually in the fall and spring, "is the literary journal of the Master of Professional Writing program at the University of Southern California. It has been publishing fiction and poetry since 1982 and now also accepts submissions of creative nonfiction, plays, and screenplays." Accepts poetry in experimental and traditional styles. Features new, emerging, and established authors. Has published poetry by Yevgeny Yevtushenko, Philip Appleman, Tomaz Salamun, Joyce Carol Oates, Bei Ling, and Denise Levertov. *Southern California Review* is about 140 pages, digest-sized, perfect-bound, with a semi-glossy color cover with original artwork. Press run is 1,000. Sample: $10.

HOW TO CONTACT Submit up to 3 poems at a time. Considers simultaneous submissions, "but please note this in the cover letter and notify us immediately if your submission is accepted for publication elsewhere." No previously published poems. Reads submissions year round. Guidelines available for SASE or on website. Responds in 3-6 months. Pays 2 contributor's copies. Rights revert to poets upon publication; "author is asked to cite appearance in *Southern California Review* when the work is published elsewhere."

CONTEST/AWARD OFFERINGS The Ann Stanford Poetry Prize (see separate listing in Contests & Awards).

SOUTHERN HUMANITIES REVIEW

Auburn University, 9088 Haley Center, Auburn University AL 36849. (334)844-9088. **E-mail:** shrengl@auburn.edu. **E-mail:** shrsubmissions@auburn.edu. **Website:** www.auburn.edu/english/shr/home.htm. **Contact:** Karen Beckwith. *Southern Humanities Review*, published quarterly, is "interested in poems of any length, subject, genre. Space is limited, and brief poems are more likely to be accepted. Translations welcome, but also send written permission from the copyright holder." Has published poetry by Donald Hall, Andrew Hudgins, Margaret Gibson, Stephen Dunn, Walt McDonald, and R.T. Smith. *Southern Humanities Review* is 100 pages, digest-sized. Press run is 800. Subscription: $10/year for new subscriber, $18/year. Sample: $5. *Southern Humanities Review* publishes fiction, poetry, and critical essays on the arts, literature, philosophy, religion, and history for a well-read, scholarly audience. "We contract for all rights until publication. Then copyright reverts to author." Responds in 1-2 weeks to queries. Sample copy for $5 in U.S.; $7 everywhere else. Guidelines for #10 SASE or at www.auburn.edu/shr

MAGAZINE NEEDS Any kind; short poems preferred.

HOW TO CONTACT Submit 3-5 poems at a time via postal or submissions e-mail. No previously published poems or simultaneous submissions. "Send poems in a business-sized envelope. Include SASE. Avoid sending faint computer printout." Responds in 2 months, "possibly longer in summer." Always sends prepublication galleys. Pays 2 contributor's copies and 2 offprints. Copyright reverts to author upon publication. Reviews books of poetry in approximately 750-1,000 words. Send materials for review consideration.

CONTEST/AWARD OFFERINGS Sponsors the Theodore Christian Hoepfner Award, a $50 prize for the best poem published in a given volume of *Southern Humanities Review.*

TIPS "Send us the ms with SASE. If we like it, we'll take it or we'll recommend changes. If we don't like it, we'll send it back as promptly as possible. Read the journal. Send typewritten, clean copy, carefully proofread. We also award the annual Hoepfner Prize of $100 for the best published essay or short story of the year. Let someone whose opinion you respect read your story and give you an honest appraisal. Rewrite, if necessary, to get the most from your story."

◐ SOUTHERN POETRY REVIEW

Armstrong Atlantic State Univ., 11935 Abercorn St., Savannah GA 31419. (912)344-3196. **E-mail:** tonyraymorris@gmail.com. **Website:** www.southernpoetryreview.org. James Smith, Associate Editor. **Contact:** Tony Morris, managing editor. Member: CLMP. Southern Poetry Review, published twice a year, is one of the oldest poetry journals in America. Wants "poetry eclectically representative of the genre; no restrictions on form, style, or content." Does not want fiction, essays, or reviews. Has published poetry by Cathy Smith Bowers, Carl Dennis, Robert Morgan, Linda Pastan, Margaret Gibson, and R. T. Smith. Southern Poetry Review is 80-88 pages, digest-sized, perfect-bound, with 80 lb. matte cardstock cover with b&w photography, includes ads. Receives about 8,000 poems/year, accepts about 2%. Press run is 1,200. Single copy: $7.00. Considers simultaneous submissions (with notification in cover letter); no previously published poems ("previously published" includes poems published or posted online). No e-mail or disk submissions. Cover letter is preferred. "Include SASE for reply; ms returned only if sufficient postage is included." Reads submissions year round. Poems are circulated to an editorial board ("multiple readers, lively discussion and decision-making"). Sometimes comments on rejected poems. Always sends pre-publication galleys. Pays 2 contributor's copies. Sponsors annual Guy Owen Contest. See website for guidelines. Acquires one-time rights. Publishes ms 6 months after acceptance. Responds in 2 months. Guidelines available in magazine, for SASE, by e-mail, or on website.

Work appearing in *Southern Poetry Review* received a 2005 Pushcart Prize and often has poems selected for VerseDaily.org.

CONTEST/AWARD OFFERINGS Sponsors annual Guy Owen Contest. See website for guidelines.

THE SOUTHERN REVIEW

(225)578-5108. **Fax:** (225)578-5098. **E-mail:** southernreview@lsu.edu. **Website:** www.lsu.edu/tsr. **Contact:** Jeanne Leiby, Editor. Reading period: September1-

June 1. All mss. submitted during summer months will be recycled. Buys first North American serial rights. Pays on publication. Publishes ms an average of 6 months after acceptance. Responds in 2 months. Sample copy for $8. Guidelines available online.

MAGAZINE NEEDS *The Southern Review*, published quarterly, "has been committed to finding the next new voices in literature. In our pages were published the early works of Eudora Welty, John Berryman, Delmore Schwartz, Peter Taylor, Randall Jarrell, Mary McCarthy, and Nelson Algren, to name only a few. More recently, we can claim Robert Pinsky, Michael S. Harper, and David Kirby as being among those whom we helped "discover." Has published poetry by Aimee Baker, Wendy Barker, David Bottoms, Nick Courtright, Robert Dana, Oliver de la Paz, Ed Falco, Piotr Florczyk, Rigoberto Gonzalez, Ava Leavell Haymon, and Philip Schultz. *The Southern Review* is 200 pages, digest-sized, flat-spined, with full color cover. Receives about 10,000 poetry submissions/year. Press run is 3,200 (2,100 subscribers, 70% libraries). Subscription: $40. Sample: $12. 1-4 pages Pays $30/page

HOW TO CONTACT Submit up to 1-5 pages of poetry at a time. No previously published poems. No fax or e-mail submissions. "We do not require a cover letter, but we prefer one giving information about the author and previous publications." Reads submissions September-May. Guidelines available for SASE or on website. Responds in 1-2 months. Pays $25/printed page plus 2 contributor's copies. Acquires first North American serial rights. Staff reviews books of poetry in 3,000 words, multi-book format. Send materials for review consideration.

TIPS "Careful attention to craftsmanship and technique combined with a developed sense of the creation of story will always make us pay attention."

SOUTH POETRY MAGAZINE

P.O. BOX 3744, Cookham Maidenhead SL6 9UY, England. **E-mail:** south@southpoetry.org. **Website:** www.southmagazine.org. *SOUTH Poetry Magazine*, published biannually in Spring and Autumn, is based in "the southern counties of England. Poets from or poems about the South region are particularly welcome, but poets from all over the world are encouraged to submit work on all subjects." Has published poetry by Ian Caws, Stella Davis, Lyn Moir, Elsa Corbluth, Paul Hyland, and Sean Street. *SOUTH* is 68 pages, digest-sized, litho-printed, saddle-stapled, with gloss-laminated duotone cover. Receives about 1,500 poems/year, accepts about 120. Press run is 350 (250 subscribers). Single copy: £5.80; subscription: £10/year, £18/2 years. Make cheques (in sterling) payable to *SOUTH Poetry Magazine*. Deadlines are 31 May for the Autumn issue and 30 November for the Spring issue the following year. You may submit work at any time. Please print and use the submission form on our website which has all the necessary information for submitting to SOUTH.

"SOUTH is run by a management team. The current team is: Anne Clegg, Tim Harris, Peter Keeble, Patrick Osada, Tony Turner, and Chrissie Williams."

MAGAZINE NEEDS No email submissions. Submit up to 3 poems at a time in duplicate. No previously published poems or simultaneous submissions. Accepts disk submissions (if accompanied by hard copy). "Do not put name or address on manuscript. List poem titles on submission form (downloadable from website) or in cover letter with name and address." Selection does not begin prior to the deadline and may take up to eight weeks or more from that date." Time between acceptance and publication is up to 2 months, depending on date of submission. Guidelines available on website.

TIPS "Buy the magazine [and read it. That way you will see the sort of work we publish, and whether your work is likely to fit in. You'll also be contributing to its continued success."

SOUTHWESTERN AMERICAN LITERATURE

Center for the Study of the Southwest, Brazos Hall, Texas State University-San Marcos, San Marcos TX 78666-4616. (512)245-2224. **Fax:** (512)245-7462. **E-mail:** swpublications@txstate.edu. **Website:** http://swrhc.txstate.edu/cssw/. **Contact:** Twister Marquiss, assistant editor; Mark Busby, co-editor; Dick Maurice Heaberlin, co-editor. "We publish fiction, nonfiction, poetry, literary criticism and book reviews. Generally speaking, we want material covering the Greater Southwest or material written by Southwest writers. Ethnic/multicultural, literary, mainstream, regional. "No science fiction or romance." Receives 10-20 unsolicited poems/month. Accepts 5-10 poems/issue; 10-20 poems/year. Publishes 6 months after acceptance. Publishes 1-2 new writers/year. Recently published work by Sherwin Bitsui, Alison Hawthorne Deming,

Keith Ekiss, Sara Marie Ortiz, Karla K. Morton, Jeffrey C. Alfier, Carol Hamilton, and Larry D. Thomas. Length: 100 lines max; average length: 15-25 lines. Also publishes fiction, literary essays, literary criticism. Sometimes comments on rejected mss.

HOW TO CONTACT Include cover letter, estimated word count, 2-5 line bio and list of publications. Accepts email submissions as attachments. Include bio and list of publications in email. Responds in 3-6 months to mss. Sample copy for $10. Writer's guidelines free.

TIPS "We look for crisp language, an interesting approach to material; a regional approach is desired but not required. Read widely, write often, revise carefully. We are looking for stories that probe the relationship between the tradition of Southwestern American literature and the writer's own imagination in creative ways. We seek stories that move beyond stereotype and approach the larger defining elements and also ones that, as William Faulkner noted in his Nobel Prize acceptance speech, treat subjects central to good literature—the old verities of the human heart, such as honor and courage and pity and suffering, fear and humor, love and sorrow."

SOUTHWEST REVIEW

P.O. Box 750374, Dallas TX 75275-0374. (214)768-1037. **Fax:** (214)768-1408. **E-mail:** swr@smu.edu. **Website:** www.smu.edu/southwestreview. **Contact:** Jennifer Cranfill, senior editor. Poetry published in *Southwest Review* has been included in The Best American Poetry and The Pushcart Prize. *Southwest Review*, published quarterly, prints fiction, essays, poetry, and occasional interviews. "We always suggest that potential contributors read several issues of the magazine to see for themselves what we like. We demand very high quality in our poems; we accept both traditional and experimental writing, but avoid unnecessary obscurity and private symbolism. We place no arbitrary limits on length but find shorter poems easier to fit into our format than longer ones. We have no specific limitations as to theme. Poems tend to be lyric and narrative free verse combining a strong voice with powerful topics or situations. Diction is accessible and content often conveys a strong sense of place." Has published poetry by Albert Goldbarth, John Hollander, Mary Jo Salter, James Hoggard, Dorothea Tanning, and Michael Rosen. *Southwest Review* is 144 pages, digest-sized, professionally printed, perfect-bound, with matte text stock cover. Receives about 1,000 poetry submissions/year, accepts about 32. Press run is 1,500. Subscription: $24. Sample: $6.

HOW TO CONTACT No previously published poems or simultaneous submissions. Submit by mail or on website. Please note there is a $2 administrative fee for online submissions. Mailed manuscripts must be typed and should include SASE for a response. Guidelines available for SASE or on website. Responds within 1 month. Always sends prepublication galleys. Pays cash plus contributor's copies.

CONTEST/AWARD OFFERINGS The Elizabeth Matchett Stover Memorial Award presents $250 to the author of the best poem or groups of poems (chosen by editors) published in the preceding year. Also offers The Morton Marr Poetry Prize.

TIPS "Despite the title, we are not a regional magazine. Before you submit your work, it's a good idea to take a look at recent issues to familiarize yourself with the magazine. We strongly advise all writers to include a cover letter. Keep your cover letter professional and concise and don't include extraneous personal information, a story synopsis, or a resume. When authors ask what we look for in a strong story submission the answer is simple regardless of graduate degrees in creative writing, workshops, or whom you know. We look for good writing, period."

SOU'WESTER

Box 1438, Dept. of English, Southern Illinois University, Edwardsville IL 62026-1438. (618)650-3190. **Fax:** (618)650-3509. **E-mail:** sw@siue.edu. **Website:** www.siue.edu/ENGLISH/SW. **Contact:** Adrian Matejka. *Sou'wester* appears biannually in spring and fall. "We lean toward poetry with strong imagery, successful association of images, and skillful use of figurative language." Has published poetry by Robert Wrigley, Beckian Fritz Goldberg, Eric Pankey, Betsy Sholl, and Angie Estes. *Sou'wester* has 30-40 pages of poetry in each digest-sized, 100-page issue. *Sou'wester* is professionally printed, flat-spined, with textured matte card cover, press run is 300 for 500 subscribers of which 50 are libraries. Receives 3,000 poems (from 600 poets) each year, accepts 36-40, has a 6-month backlog. Subscription: $18/2 issues. Returns rights. Responds in 3 months. Sample: $8.

MAGAZINE NEEDS Submit up to 5 poems via online journal manager. Accepts simultaneous submissions. No previously published poems. No e-mail submissions. Reads submissions from September 1 through May 1. Editor comments on rejected poems "usually, in the case of those that we almost accept." Pays 2 contributor's copies and a one-year subscription.

THE SOW'S EAR POETRY REVIEW

217 Brookneill Dr., Winchester VA 22602. **E-mail:** sowsearpoetry@yahoo.com. **Website:** www.sowsear.kitenet.net. **Contact:** Kristin Camitta Zimet. "*The Sow's Ear* prints fine poetry of all styles and lengths, complemented by b&w art. We also welcome reviews, interviews, and essays related to poetry. We are open to group submissions. Our 'Crossover' section features poetry married to any other art form, including prose, music, and visual media." Acquires first publication rights. Publishes ms an average of 1-6 months after acceptance. Responds in 2 weeks to queries. Responds in 3 months to mss. Editorial lead time 1-6 months. Sample copy for $8. Guidelines available for SASE, by e-mail, or on website.

MAGAZINE NEEDS Submit up to 5 poems at a time. Considers simultaneous submissions "if you tell us promptly when work is accepted elsewhere"; no previously published poems, although will consider poems from chapbooks if they were never published in a magazine. Previously published poems may be included in 'Crossover' if rights are cleared. No e-mail submissions, except for poets outside the US; postal submissions only. Include brief bio and SASE. Pays 2 contributor's copies. Inquire about reviews, interviews, and essays. Contest/Award offerings: *The Sow's Ear* Poetry Competition and *The Sow's Ear* Chapbook Contest. Open to any style or length. No limits on line length.

TIPS "We like work that is carefully crafted, keenly felt, and freshly perceived. We respond to poems with voice, a sense of place, delight in language, and a meaning that unfolds. We look for prose that opens new dimensions to appreciating poetry."

SPACE AND TIME

458 Elizabeth Ave., Somerset NJ 08873. **E-mail:** nytebird45@aol.com. **Website:** www.spaceandtimemagazine.com. Established 1966. **Contact:** Linda D. Addison, poetry editor. *Space and Time* was about 100 pages, digest-sized, perfect-bound; however, the magazine will be reformatted to 48 pages, magazine-sized, web press printed on 50 lb. stock and saddle-stapled with glossy card cover and interior b&w illustrations. Receives about 500 poems/year, accepts 5%. Press run is 2,000 (200 subscribers, 10 libraries, 1,200 shelf sales). Single copy: $5; subscription: $10. Sample: $6.50. Magazine. 8×11, 48 pages, matte paper, glossy cover. Contains illustrations. "We love stories that blend elements—horror and science fiction, fantasy with SF elements, etc. We challenge writers to try something new and send us their unclassifiable works—what other publications reject because the work doesn't fit in their 'pigeonholes.'" Quarterly. Receives 250 mss/reading period. Accepts 8 mss/issue; 32 mss/year. Only open during announced reading periods. Check website to see if submissions are open. **Publishes 2-4 new writers/year.** Published PD Cacek, AR Morlan, Jeffrey Ford, Charles De Lint, and Jack Ketchum. Length: 1,000-10,000 words. Average length: 6,500 words. Publishes short shorts. Average length of short shorts: 1,000 words. Also publishes poetry, occasional book reviews. Publication is copyrighted. Acquires first North American serial rights and onetime rights. Pays on publication. Ms published 3-6 months after acceptance. Sample copy available for $6.50. Additional copies $5. Guidelines available only on website.

MAGAZINE NEEDS *Space and Time* is a quarterly magazine that publishes "primarily science fiction/fantasy/horror; some related poetry and articles. We do not want to see anything that doesn't fit science fiction/fantasy/weird genres." Has published poetry by G. O. Clark, Corinne de Winter, Bruce Boston and Ann K. Schwader.

HOW TO CONTACT Submit up to 4 poems at a time. No previously published poems or simultaneous submissions. Time between acceptance and publication is up to 9 months. Often comments on rejected poems. Guidelines available for SASE or on website. Responds in up to 6 weeks, "longer if recommended." Pays 1¢/word ($5 minimum) plus 2 contributor's copies. Acquires first North American serial rights.

SPACEPORTS & SPIDERSILK

Sam's Dot Publishing, P.O. Box 782, Cedar Rapids IA 52406-0782. **Website:** www.samsdotpublishing.com. *Spaceports & Spidersilk*, published quarterly online, prints "fantasy, science fiction, sword and sorcery, alternate history, myths/folktales, spooky short stories, poems, illustrations, puzzles, nonfiction articles, and movie and book reviews, all for a reading audience of 9-18 years old." Wants "fantasy, science fiction, spooky horror, and speculative poetry" appropriate to age group. Does not want "horror with excessive blood and gore." Considers poetry by children and teens. Has published poetry by Bruce Boston, Karen A. Romanko, Guy Belleranti, Aurelio Rico Lopez III, and Kristine Ong Muslim. Receives about 180 poems/year, accepts about 30 (16%). Acquires first, exclusive worldwide electronic rights for 90 days. Publishes ms 1-3 months after acceptance. Responds in 4-6 weeks. Guidelines available online at website.

MAGAZINE NEEDS Submit up to 5 poems at a time. Lines/poem: 25 maximum. Considers previously published poems; no simultaneous submissions. Accepts e-mail submissions only (pasted into body of message). "Submission should include snail mail address and a short (1-2 lines) bio." Reads submissions year round. Often comments on rejected poems. Reviews books/chapbooks of poetry. Send materials for review consideration to Tyree Campbell. Pays $2/original poem, $1/reprint.

SPEEDPOETS ZINE

86 Hawkwood St., Brisbane QL 4122, Australia. (61)(7)3420-6092. **E-mail:** geenunn@yahoo.com.au. **Website:** http://speedpoets.com. **Contact:** Graham Nunn, editor. *SpeedPoets Zine*, published monthly, showcases "the community of poets that perform at the monthly SpeedPoets readings in Brisbane, as well as showcasing poets from all around the world." Wants "shorter, experimental pieces." Does not want long submissions. Has published poetry by Robert Smith, Steve Kilbey, Brentley Frazer, Jayne Fenton Keane, Graham Nunn, and Marie Kazalia. *SpeedPoets Zine* is 28 pages, digest-sized, photocopied, folded and stapled, with color cover. Press run is 100. Single copy: $5 for overseas/interstate contributors. Payable to Graham Nunn via PayPal (in AUD only, or send well-concealed cash). Publishes ms 2 weeks after acceptance. Responds in 2 weeks. Guidelines available by e-mail.

MAGAZINE NEEDS Submit 2 poems at a time. Lines/poem: 25 maximum. Considers previously published poems. Accepts e-mail submissions (pasted into body of message—no attachments); no disk submissions. Cover letter is preferred. Reads submissions year round.

SPIDER

Carus Publishing, 70 E. Lake St., Suite 300, Chicago IL 60601. **Website:** www.cricketmag.com; www.spidermagkids.com. **Contact:** Alice Letvin, editorial director; Margaret Mincks, associate editor. *SPIDER*, published monthly, is a reading and activity magazine for children ages 6-9. "It's specially written and edited for children who have reached that amazing age when they first get excited about reading on their own." Wants "serious and humorous poetry, nonsense rhymes." *SPIDER* is 38 pages, 8x10, staple-bound. Receives more than 1,200 submissions/month, accepts 25-30. Circulation is 70,000. Subscription: $35.97/year (12 issues). Sample: $5; sample pages available on website.

HOW TO CONTACT Submit no more than 5 poems at a time. Lines/poem: no more than 20. Considers previously published poems. Responds in 6 months. Guidelines available for SASE or on website. Pays up to $3/line on publications. Acquires North American publication rights for previously published poems; rights vary for unpublished poems.

TIPS "Before attempting to illustrate for *SPIDER*, be sure to familiarize yourself with this age group, and read several issues of the magazine. Please do not query first."

SPILLWAY

P.O. Box 7887, Huntington Beach CA 92615. (714)968-0905. **E-mail:** mifanwy.kaiser@gmail.com; spillway2@tebotbach.org. **Website:** http://tebotbach.org/spillway.html. **Contact:** Mifanwy Kaiswer, publisher; Susan Terris, editor. Acquires one-time rights. Responds in up to 6 months.

"We recommend ordering a sample copy before you submit, though acceptance does not depend upon purchasing a sample copy."

MAGAZINE NEEDS Submit 3-5 poems at a time (6 pages maximum total). No fiction. Theme for December 2012 issue: 'Nature Red in Tooth and Claw.' Theme for June 2013: 'The Road Not Taken.' For more complete information about upcoming themes and submission periods, check our website. E-mail submissions only to spillway2@tebotbach.org (Microsoft Word attachment); no disk or fax submissions. Cover letter is required. Include brief bio. Responds in up to 6 months. Pays 1 contributor's copy. Acquires one-time rights. Reviews books of poetry in 500-2,500 words. Accepts queries by e-mail. Send materials for review consideration.

SPINNING JENNY

c/o Black Dress Press, P.O. Box 1067, New York NY 10014. **E-mail:** editor@spinning-jenny.com. **Website:** www.spinning-jenny.com. **Contact:** C.E. Harrison, editor. *Spinning Jenny*, published once/year in the fall (usually September), has published poetry by Abraham Smith, Cynthia Cruz, Michael Morse, and Joyelle McSweeney. Authors retain rights. Pays 3 contributor's copies. Responds within 4 months. Single copy: $10; subscription: $20 for 2 issues. Guidelines available on website.

Spinning Jenny is 96 pages, digest-sized, perfect-bound, with heavy card cover. "We accept less than 5% of unsolicited submissions." Press run is 1,000.

MAGAZINE NEEDS Submit up to 6 poems at a time. No previously published poems or simultaneous submissions. Accepts submissions online only (see website for guidelines). Reads submissions September 15-May 15 only. Seldom comments on rejected poems.

SPITBALL: THE LITERARY BASEBALL MAGAZINE

5560 Fox Rd., Cincinnati OH 45239. **Website:** www.spitballmag.com. **Contact:** Mike Shannon, editor-in-chief. *Spitball: The Literary Baseball Magazine*, published semiannually, is "a unique magazine devoted to poetry, fiction, and book reviews exclusively about baseball. Newcomers are very welcome, but remember that you have to know the subject; we do, and our readers do. Perhaps a good place to start for beginners is one's personal reactions to the game, a game, a player, etc., and take it from there." Writers submitting to *Spitball* for the first time must buy a sample copy (waived for subscribers). "This is a one-time-only fee, which we regret, but economic reality dictates that we insist those who wish to be published in *Spitball* help support it, at least at this minimum level." *Spitball* is 96 pages, digest-sized, computer-typeset, perfect-bound. Receives about 1,000 submissions/year, accepts about 40. Press run is 1,000. Subscription: $12. Sample: $6.

MAGAZINE NEEDS Submit a "batch" of poems at a time ("we prefer to use several of same poet in an issue rather than a single poem"). Lines/poem: open. No previously published poems or simultaneous submissions. Cover letter is required. Include brif bio and SASE. "Many times we are able to publish accepted work almost immediately." Pays 2 contributor's copies."All material published in *Spitball* will be automatically considered for inclusion in the next *Best of Spitball* anthology."1) Poems submitted to *Spitball* will be considered automatically for Poem of the Month, to appear on the website. 2) "We sponsor the Casey Award (for best baseball book of the year) and hold the Casey Awards Banquet in late February or early March. Any chapbook of baseball poetry should be sent to us for consideration for the 'Casey' plaque that we award to the winner each year."

TIPS "Take the subject seriously. We do. In other words, get a clue (if you don't already have one) about the subject and about the poetry that has already been done and published about baseball. Learn from it—think about what you can add to the canon that is original and fresh—and don't assume that just anybody with the feeblest of efforts can write a baseball poem worthy of publication. And most importantly, stick with it. Genius seldom happens on the first try."

SPLIZZ

4 St. Marys Rise, Burry Port, Carms SA16 0SH, Wales. **E-mail:** splizzmag@yahoo.co.uk. **Contact:** Amanda Morgan, editor. *Splizz*, published quarterly, features poetry, prose, reviews of contemporary music, and background to poets. Responds in 2 months. Sometimes sends prepublication galleys. Guidelines available in magazine, for SASE (or SAE and IRC), or by e-mail.

Wants "any kind of poetry. We have no restrictions regarding style, length, subjects." Does not want "anything racist or homophobic." Has published Colin Cross (UK), Anders Carson (Canada), Paul Truttman (US), Jan Hansen (Portugal), and Gregory Arena (Italy). *Splizz* is 60-64 pages, A5, saddle-stapled; includes ads. Receives about 200-300 poems/year; accepts about 90%. Press run is 150 (35 subscribers). Single copy: £2.20 (UK); subscription: £8.80 (UK). E-mail for current rates. Payments accepted in cash or PayPal to splizz@tiscali.co.uk. "No checks please."

MAGAZINE NEEDS Submit 5 poems at a time. No previously published poems or simultaneous submissions. Accepts e-mail submissions (as attachment). Cover letter is required. Include short bio. Typed submissions preferred. Name and address must be included on each page of submitted work. Include SAE with IRCs. Time between acceptance and publication is 4 months. Often comments on rejected poems. Charges criticism fee. "Just enclose SAE/IRC for response,and allow 1-2 months for delivery. For those sending IRCs, please ensure that they have been correctly stamped by your post office." Reviews books/chapbooks of poetry or other magazines in 50-300 words. Send materials for review consideration. E-mail for further enquiries.

SPOON

315 Eastern SE, Grand Rapids MI 49503. (616)245-8633; (616)328-4090. **E-mail:** edholman@rocketmail.com. **Contact:** Ed Holman, poetry editor. Publishes ms 2 months after acceptance. Responds in 1 month. Sample copy for $1.50. Guidelines available by e-mail.

"Bimonthly. A creative newsletter by and for homeless and disempowered people in the Heartside area of Grand Rapids. We accept material from everywhere." Considers poetry by children/teens. Has published poetry by Edward Holman, Cathy Bousma Richa, Walter Mathews, Tammy Reindle. Reads submissions year round. No reading fees. Sometimes comments on rejected poems. Never publishes theme issues. Never sends prepublication galleys. Magazine-size with offset printing, no binding; rarely includes ads. Receives 140 poems/year, accepts about 15-20%. Press run is 1,000. Single copy: $3.00; subscription: $15/year. Sample copy for $1.50. Make checks payable to: Cathy Needham, memo: Spoon.

MAGAZINE NEEDS "Does not want vulgar poetry 'for shock value;' however, if a poem has a serious meaning we won't silence it." Pays $5.00 per accepted submission.

ADDITIONAL INFORMATION Considers poetry by children/teens. Senior editor and poetry editor are currentlyconsidering contests in the future.

TIPS "Read, write, and be passionate."

SPOUT MAGAZINE

P.O. Box 581067, Minneapolis MN 55458. **E-mail:** editors@spoutpress.org. **Website:** www.spoutpress.org. **Contact:** Michelle Filkins, poetry editor. As the counterpart to Spout Press, Spout magazine features poetry, art, fiction, and thought pieces with diverse voices and styles.

"We are currently accepting submissions of poetry, short stories, essays, opinion, art, and cartoons — *basically anything creative that can be affixed to an 8 1/2 x 11 page* — **for the upcoming issue of our magazine**. Follow our guidelines online."

MAGAZINE NEEDS Submit up to 5 poems at a time. Considers previously published poems and simultaneous submissions. Cover letter is preferred. Time between acceptance and publication is 2-3 months. "Poems are reviewed by 2 of 3 editors; those selected for final review are read again by all three." Seldom comments on rejected poems. Guidelines available for SASE or on website. Responds in 4 months. Pays 1 contributor's copy.

SRPR (SPOON RIVER POETRY REVIEW)

4241 Department of English, Illinois State University, Normal IL 61790-4241. **E-mail:** krhotel@ilstu.edu. **Website:** www.litline.org/spoon. **Contact:** Kirstin Hotelling Zona, editor. *SRPR (Spoon River Poetry Review)*, published biannually, is "one of the nation's oldest continuously published poetry journals. We seek to publish the best of all poetic genres, experimental as well as mainstream, and are proud of our commitment to regional as well as international poets and readers. *SRPR* includes, alongside poems from emerging and established poets, a chapbook-length selection of poetry by our featured *SRPR* poet, a substantial interview with the featured poet, and a long review-essay on books of recently published poetry written by established poet-critics. The Summer/Fall issue also spotlights the winner and runners-up of our highly competitive editor's prize contest." Acquires first North American serial rights. Pays a year's subscription and 2 contributor's copies. Responds in 3-6 months. Guidelines available in magazine or on website.

SRPR is 128 pages, digest-sized, laser-set, perfect bound. Receives about 3,000 poems/month; accepts 1%. Press run is 1,500. Sponsors the *SRPR* Editor's Prize Contest.

MAGAZINE NEEDS Submit 3-5 poems at a time. Accepts simultaneous submissions "as long as you notify us immediately if a poem has been accepted elsewhere." Include name, e-mail, and address on every poem. Accepts submissions September 15-Feb 15. Comments on rejected poems "many times, if a poet is promising." Reviews books of poetry. Send materials for review consideration. Subscription: $18. Sample: $10 (includes guidelines).

STAND MAGAZINE

School of English, University of Leeds, Leeds LS2 9JT, United Kingdom. (44)(113)343-4794. **E-mail:** stand@leeds.ac.uk. **Website:** www.standmagazine.org. **Contact:** Jon Glover and John Whale, editors. (U.S. Editor: David Latané, Dept. of English, Virginia Commonwealth University, Richmond VA 23284-2005; dlatane@vcu.edu.) "Quarterly literary magazine." Pays on publication. Guidelines available online at website.

"U.S. submissions can be made through the Virginia office (see separate listing)."

MAGAZINE NEEDS *Stand Magazine*, published quarterly, "seeks more subscriptions from U.S. readers and also hopes that the magazine will be seriously treated as an alternative platform to American literary journals." *Library Journal* calls *Stand* "one of England's best, liveliest, and truly imaginative little magazines." Has published poetry by John Ashbery, Mary Jo Bang, Brian Henry, and Michael Mott. *Stand* is about 64 pages, A5 (landscape), professionally printed on smooth stock, flat-spined, with matte color cover, includes ads. Press run is 2,000 (1,000+ subscribers, 600 libraries). Subscription: $49.50. Sample: $13.

HOW TO CONTACT No fax or e-mail submissions. Cover letter is required, "assuring us that work is not also being offered elsewhere." Publishes theme issues. Always sends prepublication galleys. Pays £20 for first poem and £5 for each subsequent poem over 6 lines, and one contributor's copy. Acquires first world serial rights for 3 months after publication. If work appears elsewhere, *Stand* must be credited. Reviews books of poetry in 3,000-4,000 words, multi-book format. Send materials for review consideration.

ST. ANTHONY MESSENGER

(513)241-5615. **Fax:** (513)241-0399. **E-mail:** mageditors@americancatholic.org. **Website:** www.americancatholic.org. **Contact:** Christopher Heffron, poetry editor. *St. Anthony Messenger* is a Catholic family magazine which aims to help its readers lead more fully human and Christian lives. We publish articles which report on a changing church and world, opinion pieces written from the perspective of Christian faith and values, personality profiles, and fiction which entertains and informs. Buys first North American serial rights, buys electronic rights. first worldwide serial rights. Pays on acceptance. Publishes ms an average of 1 year after acceptance. Responds in 3 weeks to queries. Responds in 2 months to mss. Sample copy for 9×12 SAE with 4 first-class stamps. Guidelines available online.

MAGAZINE NEEDS *St. Anthony Messenger*, published monthly, is a mgazine for Catholic families, mostly with children in grade school, high school, or college. Some issues feature a poetry page that uses poems appropriate for their readership. Poetry submissions are always welcome despite limited need. "We seek to publish accessible poetry of high quality. Spiritual/inspirational in nature a plus, but not required." Considers poetry by young writers, ages 14 and older. *St. Anthony Messenger* is 60 pages. Press run 280,000. Our poetry needs are very limited. Up to 20-25 lines; the shorter, the better. Pays $2/line; $20 minimum.

HOW TO CONTACT Submit "a few" poems at a time. Lines/poem: under 25. No previously published poems. Accepts fax and e-mail submissions. "Please include your phone number and a SASE with your submission. Do not send us your entire collection of poetry. Poems must be original." Submit seasonal poems several months in advance. Pays $2/line on acceptance plus 2 contributor's copies.

TIPS "The freelancer should consider why his or her proposed article would be appropriate for us, rather than for *Redbook* or *Saturday Review*. We treat human problems of all kinds, but from a religious perspective. Articles should reflect Catholic theology, spirituality, and employ a Catholic terminology and vocabulary. We need more articles on prayer, scripture, Catholic worship. Get authoritative information (not merely library research); we want interviews with experts. Write in popular style; use lots of examples, stories, and personal quotes. Word length is an important consideration."

STAPLE MAGAZINE

114-116 St. Stephen's Rd., Sneinton, Nottingham NG2 4FJ, England. **Website:** www.staplemagazine.com. **Contact:** Wayne Burrows, editor. *Staple*, published 3 times/year, accepts "poetry, short fiction, and articles about the writing process and general culture in relation to writing, plus some artwork and photography." *Staple* is about 150 pages, perfect-bound. Press run is 500 (350 subscribers). Single copy: £10;

subscription: £25/year, £35/year overseas. Sample: £5.00 (back issue).

MAGAZINE NEEDS Submit 6 poems or 1-2 stories/essays at a time. No previously published poems or simultaneous submissions. Cover letter with author bio note is preferred. Include SAE and 2 IRCs. Issues are themed, contact for details. Reads submissions by the following deadlines: end of March, July, and November. Sometimes comments on rejected poems. Responds in up to 3 months. Pays £10/single poem, £25/group of poems; £25/story or essay.

STAR*LINE

Science Fiction Poetry Association, 1412 NE 35th St., Ocala FL 34479. **E-mail:** SFPASL@aol.com. **Website:** www.sfpoetry.com. **Contact:** Marge Simon, editor. *Star*Line*, published quarterly by the Science Fiction Poetry Association (see separate listing in Organizations), is a newsletter and poetry magazine. "Open to all forms—free verse, traditional forms, light verse—as long as your poetry shows skilled use of the language and makes a good use of science fiction, science, fantasy, horror, or speculative motifs." *Star*Line* is digest-sized, saddle-stapled. Receives about 300-400 submissions/year, accepts about 80. Has 250 subscribers. Subscription: $13 for 6 issues. Sample: $2. Send requests for copies/membership information to Samantha Henderson, SFPA Treasurer, P.O. Box 4846, Covina, CA 91723. Send submissions to *Star*Line* only.

MAGAZINE NEEDS Submit 3-5 poems at a time. Lines/poem: preferably under 50. No simultaneous submissions. Accepts e-mail submissions (preferred; pasted into body of message, no attachments). Cover letter is preferred (brief). Submissions must be typed. Responds in 1 month. Pays $3 for 10 lines or less; $5 for 11-50 lines; 10¢ per line rounded to the next dollar for 51+ lines. Buys first North American serial rights. Reviews books of poetry "within the science fiction/fantasy field" in 50-500 words. Open to unsolicited reviews. Send materials for review consideration.

ALSO OFFERS The Association also publishes *The Rhysling Anthology*, a yearly collection of nominations from the membership "for the best science fiction/fantasy long and short poetry of the preceding year and *Dwarf Stars*, an annual collection of poetry ten lines or fewer."

STEPPING STONES MAGAZINE: A LITERARY MAGAZINE FOR INNOVATIVE ART

First Step Press, P.O. Box 902, Norristown PA 19404-0902. **E-mail:** poetry@fspressonline.org. **Website:** www.fspressonline.org. **Contact:** Trinae A. Ross, publisher. *Stepping Stones Magazine: A Literary Magazine for Innovative Art*, published 4 times/year online, delivered as a PDF document, seeks "poetry as diverse as are the authors themselves. Poems should have something to say other than, 'Hi, I'm a poem please publish me.'" Does not want "poems that promote intolerance for race, religion, gender, or sexual preference." Has published poetry by Clayton Vetter, Michael Hathaway, and Ivan Silverberg. Receives about 300 poems/year, accepts about 10-15%. Reviews chapbooks, Web sites, and other publications of interest to poets. Responds in 2 months.

MAGAZINE NEEDS Submit no more than 5 poems at a time. Considers previously published poems and simultaneous submissions. Prefers e-mail submissions; should include cover letter and formatted with a simple font and saved as .doc, .rtf, or .odf. Attach submissions and cover letter to e-mail and send to poetry@fspressonline.org. Read submissions year round. Guidelines available for SASE, by sending an e-mail to guidelines @fspressonline.org, or on website. Pays one contributor's copy and free advertising space, though will implement a pay schedule when funding permits.

ALSO OFFERS "Free advertising space is available for those wishing to promote their website, book, or other literary venture. The continuing goal of First Step Press is to provide sanctuary for new and established writers, to hone their skills and commune with one another within the comfort of our electronic pages."

THE WALLACE STEVENS JOURNAL

University of Antwerp, Prinsstraat 13, B-200 Antwerp, Belgium. **E-mail:** bart.eeckhout@ua.ac.be. **Website:** www.wallacestevens.com. **Contact:** Bart Eeckhout, editor. *The Wallace Stevens Journal*, published semiannually by the Wallace Stevens Society, uses "poems about or in the spirit of Wallace Stevens or having some relation to his work. No bad parodies of Stevens's anthology pieces." Has published poetry by David Athey, Jacqueline Marcus, Charles Wright, X.J. Kennedy, A.M. Juster, and Robert Creeley. *The*

Wallace Stevens Journal is 96-120 pages, digest-sized, typeset, flat-spined, with glossy cover with art. Receives 200-300 poems/year, accepts 15-20. Press run is 600. Subscription: $30 (includes membership in the Wallace Stevens Society). Sample: $10.

STIRRING: A LITERARY COLLECTION

Stirring: A Literary Collection, c/o Erin Elizabeth Smith, Department of English, 301 McClung Tower, University of Tennessee, Knoxville TN 37996-0430. **E-mail:** eesmith81@gmail.com. **Website:** www.sundresspublications.com/stirring/. **Contact:** Erin Elizabeth Smith, managing and poetry editor. Acquires first North American serial rights. Publishes ms 1-2 weeks after acceptance. Responds in 2-5 months. E-mail for guidelines.

"*Stirring* is one of the oldest continually-published literary journals on the web. *Stirring* is a monthly literary magazine that publishes poetry, short fiction, creative nonfiction, and photography by established and emerging writers."

MAGAZINE NEEDS Wants free verse, formal poetry, etc. Doesn't want religious verse or children's verse. Has published poetry by Dorianne Laux, Sharon Olds, Patricia Smith, Chad Davidson. Receives about 1,500 poems/year, accepts 60.

STONE SOUP

Children's Art Foundation, P.O. Box 83, Santa Cruz CA 95063-0083. (831)426-5557. **Fax:** (831)426-1161. **E-mail:** editor@stonesoup.com. **Website:** www.stonesoup.com. **Contact:** Ms. Gerry Mandel, editor. *Stone Soup* is 48 pages, 7×10, professionally printed in color on heavy stock, saddle-stapled, with coated cover with full-color illustration. Receives 5,000 poetry submissions/year, accepts about 12. Press run is 15,000 (14,000 subscribers, 3,000 shelf sales, 500 other). Subscription: membership in the Children's Art Foundation includes a subscription, $37/year. *Stone Soup*, published 6 times/year, showcases writing and art by children ages 13 and under. "We have a preference for writing and art based on real-life experiences; no formula stories or poems. We only publish writing by children ages 8 to 13. We do not publish writing by adults." Buys all rights. Pays on publication. Publishes ms an average of 4 months after acceptance. Sample copy by phone only. Guidelines available online.

"Stories and poems from past issues are available online."

MAGAZINE NEEDS Wants free verse poetry. Does not want rhyming poetry, haiku, or cinquain. Pays $40/poem, a certificate, and 2 contributor's copies plus discounts.

TIPS "All writing we publish is by young people ages 13 and under. We do not publish any writing by adults. We can't emphasize enough how important it is to read a couple of issues of the magazine. You can read stories and poems from past issues online. We have a strong preference for writing on subjects that mean a lot to the author. If you feel strongly about something that happened to you or something you observed, use that feeling as the basis for your story or poem. Stories should have good descriptions, realistic dialogue, and a point to make. In a poem, each word must be chosen carefully. Your poem should present a view of your subject, and a way of using words that are special and all your own."

STORYSOUTH

5603B W. Friendly Ave., Suite 282, Greensboro NC 27410. **E-mail:** terry@storysouth.com. **Website:** www.storysouth.com. **Contact:** Terry Kennedy, editor. "*storySouth* is interested in fiction, creative nonfiction, and poetry by writers from the New South. The exact definition of New South varies from person to person and we leave it up to the writer to define their own connection to the southern United States." Quarterly. Receives 70 unsolicited mss/month. Accepts 5 mss/issue; 20 mss/year. **Publishes 5-10 new writers/year.** Average length: 4,000 words. Publishes short shorts. Also publishes literary essays, literary criticism, poetry. Often comments on rejected mss. Send complete ms. Accepts online submissions only. Acquires one-time rights. Publishes ms 1 month after acceptance. Responds in 4 months to mss. Writers' guidelines online.

MAGAZINE NEEDS Experimental, literary, regional (south), translations.

TIPS "What really makes a story stand out is a strong voice and a sense of urgency—a need for the reader to keep reading the story and not put it down until it is finished."

THE STORYTELLER

2441 Washington Rd., Maynard AR 72444. (870)647-2137. **E-mail:** storytellermag1@@yahoo.com. **Website:** www.thestorytellermagazine.com. Buys first rights. Publishes ms an average of 1-12 months after acceptance. Responds in 1 week to queries. Responds in 2 weeks to mss. Editorial lead time 6 months. Sample copy for 4 first-class stamps. Guidelines for #10 SASE.

MAGAZINE NEEDS Submit with SASE. Does not want long rambling. Length: 40 lines.

CONTEST/AWARD OFFERINGS Sponsors a quarterly contest. "Readers vote on their favorite poems. Winners receive a copy of the magazine and a certificate. We also nominate for the Pushcart Prize." See website for yearly contest announcements and winners.

TIPS *The Storyteller* is one of the best places you will find to submit your work, especially new writers. Our best advice, be professional. You have one chance to make a good impression. Don't blow it by being unprofessional.

THE STRAY BRANCH

6001 Munger Rd., Dayton OH 45459. **E-mail:** thestraybranchlitmag@yahoo.com. **Website:** www.thestraybranch.org. **Contact:** Debbie Berk, editor/publisher. *The Stray Branch*, published twice per year, is a journal "looking to publish well-crafted material from experienced writers who are serious about their craft. Looking for honest, personal, edgy, raw, real life material that is relatable to the human condition known as existence in all its dark, flawed, secret self.. exposed in the wounds that bleed upon the page and leave a scar within the skull of the reader. Open to subject matter but prefers edgy, raw material written from the gut that reflects the heart and human experience. Wants poetry by real people that can be understood by all readers. *The Stray Branch* prefers works of a darker nature." Acquires one-time rights ("includes material published on the web"). Rights revert to poets upon publication. Responds in 3-4 weeks to submissions. Guidelines available on website.

Does not want "over-schooled, arrogant, self-righteous, religious, political, erotic poetry/fiction, or happy and light, pretty poetry/fiction. Not interested in rants, tantrums, and the use of profanity that is not fitting to the piece. Please, be tactful and respectful of the language." Has published work by Andy Robertson, Keith Estes, Kate Sjostrand, Lena Vanelslander, Michael Grover, and Justin Blackburn. Issue price: $10; $7 for contributors with the use of a contributor discount code.

MAGAZINE NEEDS Submit 6 poems at a time. "Maximum length for poems is no longer than 1 page, shorter poems are preferred and stand a better chance." Considers previously published poems; no simultaneous submissions. (Considers poetry posted on a public website/blog/forum and poetry posted on a private, password-protected forum as published.) Accepts e-mail submissions (pasted into body of message or as attachments); no fax or disk submissions. Cover letter is unnecessary. Reads submissions October-April. Sometimes comments on rejected poems.

STRAYLIGHT

English Department, University of Wisconsin-Parkside, 900 Wood Rd., Kenosha WI 53141. (262)595-2139. **Fax:** (262)595-2271. **E-mail:** straylight@litspot.net. **Website:** www.straylightmag.com. **Contact:** Poetry Editor.

MAGAZINE NEEDS *Straylight*, published biannually, seeks "poetry of almost any style as long as it's inventive." *Straylight* is digest-sized. Single copy: $10; subscription: $19. Make checks payable to *Straylight*.

HOW TO CONTACT Submit 3-6 poems at a time. No previously published poems or simultaneous submissions. Accepts e-mail submissions (preferred, as .rtf or .doc attachment); no fax or disk submissions. Cover letter is required. "Include contact information on all pages of submission." Reads submissions August 15-April 15. Submit seasonal poems 3 months in advance. Time between acceptance and publication is 6 months. Never comments on rejected poems. Sometimes publishes theme issues. Upcoming themes available on website. Guidelines available for SASE or on website. Responds in 2 months. Pays 2 contributor's copies. Additional payment when funding permits. Acquires first North American serial rights. Rights revert to poet upon publication.

TIPS "We tend to publish character-based and inventive fiction with cutting-edge prose. We are unimpressed with works based on strict plot twists or novelties. Read a sample copy to get a feel for what we publish."

STRIDE MAGAZINE

E-mail: editor@stridemagazine.co.uk, submissions@stridemagazine.co.uk. **Website:** www.stridemagazine.co.uk. **Contact:** Rupert Loydell, editor. *Stride Magazine*, published online, is "a gathering of new poetry, short prose, articles, news, reviews, and whatever takes our fancy. *Stride* is regularly updated with new contributions."

MAGAZINE NEEDS Submit 4-5 poems at a time. Accepts e-mail submissions (pasted into body of message; no attachments). "Attachments or snail mail without SAEs will not be considered or replied to."

STRUGGLE: A MAGAZINE OF PROLETARIAN REVOLUTIONARY LITERATURE

P.O. Box 28536, Detroit MI 48228. (313)273-9039. **E-mail:** timhall11@yahoo.com. **Website:** www.strugglemagazine.net. **Contact:** Tim Hall, Editor. Publishes material related to "the struggle of the working class and all progressive people against the rule of the rich—including their war policies, repression, racism, exploitation of the workers, oppression of women and immigrants and general culture, etc." Quarterly. Recently published work by Billie Louise Jones, Tyler Plosia, Margaret Dimacou. Accepts multiple submissions. Magazine: 5×8; 36-72 pages; 20 lb. white bond paper; colored cover; illustrations; occasional photos. No rights acquired. Responds in 3-4 months to queries generally. Sample copies for $3; $5 for double-size issues; subscriptions $10 for 4 issues; make checks payable to Tim Hall, Special Account, not to *Struggle*.

MAGAZINE NEEDS *Struggle: A Magazine of Proletarian Revolutionary Literature*, published quarterly, focuses "on the struggle of the working people and all oppressed against the rich, dealing with such issues as racism, poverty, women's rights, full rights for immigrants, aggressive wars, workers' struggle for jobs and job security, the overall struggle for a non-exploitative society, a genuine socialism." The poetry and songs printed are "generally short, any style; subject matter must criticize or fight—explicitly or implicitly—against the rule of the billionaires. We welcome experimentation devoted to furthering such content. We are open to both subtlety and direct statement." Has published poetry by Christian Weaver, R. Nat Turner, Jose H. Villareal, Ly Doi, Tendai Mwanaka, Teresinka Pereira, Madeleine Michele Egger, Janine Fitzgerald, Nepthali De Leon. *Struggle* is 36 pages, digest-sized, photocopied. Subscription: $10/year (4 issues); $12 for institutions, $15 for foreign, $5 for prisoners. Sample: $5 (for the now-customary double-sized issue of 72 pages). Make checks payable to "Tim Hall—Special Account (not to *Struggle*)."

HOW TO CONTACT Submit up to 8 poems at a time or one story or plan up to 20 pages. Accepts e-mail submissions (pasted into body of message, no attachments), but prefers postal mail. "Writers must include SASE. Name and address must appear on the opening page of each poem."

ADDITIONAL INFORMATION Accepted work usually appears in the next or following issue. Comments on rejected poems "with every submission." Responds in 4 months, if possible, but often becomes backlogged. Pays one contributor's copy. "If you are unwilling to have your poetry published on our website, please inform us."

STUDIO, A JOURNAL OF CHRISTIANS WRITING

727 Peel St., Albury NS 2640, Australia. (61)(2)6021-1135. **Fax:** (61)(2)6021-1135. **E-mail:** studio00@bigpond.net.au. **Website:** http://web.me.com/pdgrover/StudioJournal. **Contact:** Paul Grover, publisher. *Studio, A Journal of Christians Writing*, published quarterly, prints "poetry and prose of literary merit, offering a venue for previously published, new, and aspiring writers, and seeking to create a sense of community among Christians writing." Also publishes occasional articles as well as news and reviews of writing, writers, and events of interest to members. Wants "shorter pieces (of poetry) but with no specification as to form or length (necessarily less than 200 lines), subject matter, style, or purpose. People who send material should be comfortable being published under this banner: *Studio, A Journal of Christians Writing*." Acquires first Australian rights. Pays 1 contributor's copy. Time between acceptance and publication is 6-9 months. Response time is 2 months to poems. Responds in 1 week to queries and to mss. Editorial lead time 3 months. Sample copy for $10 (AUD; airmail to US). Guidelines by e-mail.

Has published poetry by John Foulcher, Les Murray, and other Australian poets. *Studio* is 36 pages, digest-sized, professionally printed on high-quality recycled paper, saddle-stapled, with matte card cover. Press run is 300 (all subscriptions). Subscription: $60 AUD for overseas members. Conducts a biannual poetry and short story contest.

MAGAZINE NEEDS Lines/poem: less than 200. Considers simultaneous submissions. Cover letter is required. Include brief details of previous publishing history, if any. SAE with IRC required. "Submissions must be typed and double-spaced on 1 side of

A4 white paper. Name and address must appear on the reverse side of each page submitted." Reviews books of poetry in 250 words, single-book format. Send materials for review consideration.

CONTEST/AWARD OFFERINGS Conducts a biannual poetry and short story contest.

SUBTROPICS

University of Florida, P.O. Box 112075, 4008 Turlington Hall, Gainesville FL 32611-2075. **E-mail:** dleavitt@ufl.edu; subtropics@english.ufl.edu. **Website:** www.english.ufl.edu/subtropics. **Contact:** David Leavitt. "Magazine published 3 times/year through the University of Florida's English department. *Subtropics* seeks to publish the best literary fiction, essays, and poetry being written today, both by established and emerging authors. We will consider works of fiction of any length, from short shorts to novellas and self-contained novel excerpts. We give the same latitude to essays. We appreciate work in translation and, from time to time, republish important and compelling stories, essays, and poems that have lapsed out of print by writers no longer living." Buys first North American serial rights, buys one-time rights. Pays on acceptance. Publishes ms an average of 6 months after acceptance. Responds in 1 month to queries and mss. Guidelines available online

HOW TO CONTACT Submit in hard copy by mail. Please include cover letter with contact information included both on letter and on submission. Responds by e-mail. period from September 1-May 1. Does not return ms. Reading "We do not accept simultaneous submissions in poetry." Poets are paid $100 per poem.

TIPS "We publish longer works of fiction, including novellas and excerpts from forthcoming novels. Each issue will include a short-short story of about 250 words on the back cover. We are also interested in publishing works in translation for the magazine's English-speaking audience."

THE SUN

107 N. Roberson St., Chapel Hill NC 27516. (919)942-5282. **Fax:** (919)932-3101. **Website:** www.thesunmagazine.org. Sy Safransky, editor. **Contact:** Luc Sanders, assistant editor. "We are open to all kinds of writing, though we favor work of a personal nature." Buys first rights, buys one-time rights. Pays on publication. Publishes ms an average of 6-12 months after acceptance. Responds in 3-6 months to queries. Responds in 3-6 months to mss. Sample copy for $5. Guidelines available online.

MAGAZINE NEEDS Submit up to 6 poems at a time. Considers previously published poems but strongly prefers unpublished work; no simultaneous submissions. "Poems should be typed and accompanied by a cover letter and SASE." Guidelines available with SASE or on website. Responds within 3-6 months. Acquires first serial or one-time rights. Rarely publishes poems that rhyme. Pays $100-500 on publication plus contributor's copies and subscription.

TIPS "Do not send queries except for interviews. We're looking for artful and sensitive photographs that aren't overly sentimental. We're open to unusual work. Read the magazine to get a sense of what we're about. Send the best possible prints of your work. Our submission rate is extremely high. Please be patient after sending us your work. Send return postage and secure return packaging."

O SUNKEN LINES

E-mail: dogger@sunkenlines.com. **Website:** www.sunkenlines.com. **Contact:** Dogger Banks, poetry editor. *Sunken Lines*, published biannually online, is a magazine of poetry, fiction, essays, and artwork "intended as a forum for talented writers looking for more exposure." Wants "poems that evoke a strong response in the reader, whether it be laughter, empathy, the conjuring of a strong image, or admiration of a witty line. Formal or (accessible) free verse." Does not want "poems that are excessively religious, offensive, or miserable." Has published poetry by Larry Rapant, Tony Gruenewald, Suzanne Harvey, Anna Evans, Paul Lench, and Bruce Niedt. Receives about 500 poems/year, accepts about 10%.

MAGAZINE NEEDS Submit up to 5 poems at a time. Lines/poem: 40 maximum. Considers simultaneous submissions; no previously published poems. Accepts e-mail submissions (preferably pasted into body of message, or as attachment in MS Word or RTF format); no disk submissions. Cover letter is required. "Please be prepared to supply a short biography and optional photo upon notification of acceptance." Reads submissions year round. "We cannot consider or acknowledge unsolicited poetry or prose submissions received between July 1 and October 31." Time between acceptance and publication is up to 3 months. Poems are circulated to an editorial board. Sometimes comments on rejected poems. Guidelines available on website. Responds in 3 months. Acquires one-time rights. Rights revert to poet upon publication.

SUNSPINNER

E-mail: sunspinnermagazine@yahoo.com. **Website:** www.sunspinner.org. **Contact:** Ellen Lewis and Lisa Swanstrom, editors. *Sunspinner*, published biannually online, is based in southern California and features "fiction and poetry from writers everywhere. There are no restrictions on style or subject matter, and submissions are always welcome." Has published poetry by Ryan G. Van Cleave, Lyn Lifshin, Linda Mastrangelo, and Gary Lehman.

MAGAZINE NEEDS Submit 3-5 poems at a time. Considers previously published poems ("provided the author retains all rights") and simultaneous submissions. Accepts e-mail (pasted into body of message or as attachment in Microsoft Word) and disk submissions. Cover letter is preferred. "Please include a brief bio with each submission." Reads submissions year round. Time between acceptance and publication is 6 months to a year. Never comments on rejected poems. Guidelines available on website. Responds in 4-6 months. No payment. "Works accepted by *Sunspinner* will be archived for an indefinite period of time and removed at the author's request. Authors retain all rights to work featured in *Sunspinner*."

SUNSTONE

Website: www.sunstonemagazine.com. *Sunstone*, published 6 times/year, prints "scholarly articles of interest to an open, Mormon audience; personal essays; fiction and poetry." Wants "both lyric and narrative poetry that engages the reader with fresh, strong images, skillful use of language, and a strong sense of voice and/or place." Does not want "didactic poetry, sing-song rhymes, or in-process work." Has published poetry by Susan Howe, Anita Tanner, Robert Parham, Ryan G. Van Cleave, Robert Rees, and Virgil Suaárez. *Sunstone* is 64 pages, magazine-sized, professionally printed, saddle-stapled, with semi-glossy paper cover. Receives more than 500 poems/year, accepts 40-50. Press run is 3,000. Subscription: $45 for 6 issues. Sample: $10 postpaid. Acquires first North American serial rights. Publishes ms 2 years after acceptance. Responds in 3 months. Guidelines for SASE.

MAGAZINE NEEDS Submit up to 5 poems at a time. Lines/poem: 40 maximum. No previously published poems or simultaneous submissions. Include name and address on each poem. Seldom comments on rejected poems. Pays 5 contributor's copies.

SWELL

E-mail: swelleditor@yahoo.com. **Website:** www.swellzine.com. **Contact:** Jill Craig, editor. "SWELL aims to reflect a spectrum of perspectives as diverse as the community from which it was born. Ideal publication candidates approach GLBT (gay/lesbian/bisexual/transgender) issues in a fresh way or present universal topics from a unique point of view. Pieces which avoid well-trodden areas of the GLBT canon are of particular interest. Fiction and non-fiction of all styles, as well as poetry and drama, are all acceptable forms for SWELL; aspiring contributors are also encouraged to experiment with the possibilities inherent in internet publication, such as multimedia compositions, creative hyperlinking, and works not easily categorized." Responds in 1-2 months.

MAGAZINE NEEDS Lines/poem: no works over 3,000 words total. Welcomes multiple submissions as long as the total submitted is under the maximum word count. Accepts e-mail submissions only. Rights revert to poet upon publication.

TIPS "SWELL is pleased to sponsor a fiction contest. Prizes Awarded: First Prize: $250; Second Prize: $100; Third Prize: $50. See our website for details."

SYCAMORE REVIEW

Purdue University Dept. of English, 500 Oval Dr., West Lafayette IN 47907. (765) 494-3783. **Fax:** (765) 494-3780. **E-mail:** sycamore@purdue.edu. **Website:** www.sycamorereview.com. *Sycamore Review*, published semiannually in January and June, uses "personal essays, short fiction, short shorts, drama, translations, and quality poetry in any form. We aim to publish many diverse styles of poetry from formalist to prose poems, narrative, and lyric." Has published poetry by Denise Duhamel, Jonah Winter, Amy Gerstler, Mark Halliday, Dean Young, and Ed Hirsch. *Sycamore Review* is about 120 pages, 8×8, professionally printed, flat-spined, with matte color cover. Press run is 1,000 (200 subscribers, 50 libraries). Subscription: $14. Current issue: $7. Back Issue: $5. Make checks payable to Purdue University. "Strives to publish the best writing by new and established writers. Looks for well crafted and engaging work, works that illuminate our lives in the collective human search for meaning. We would like to publish more work that takes a reflective look at our national identity and how we are perceived by the world. We look for diversity of voice, pluralistic worldviews, and political and social context." Buys first North American serial rights.

Sycamore Review is Purdue University's internationally acclaimed literary journal, affiliated with Purdue's College of Liberal Arts and the Dept. of English. Art should present politics in a language that can be felt.

MAGAZINE NEEDS Submissions should be typed, double-spaced,with numbered pages and the author's name and the title easily visible on each page. Does not publish creative work by any student currently attending Purdue University. Former students should wait one year before submitting.

HOW TO CONTACT Submit 3-6 poems at a time. with name and address on each page. Considers simultaneous submissions, if notified immediately of acceptance elsewhere; no previously published poems except translations. No fax or postal submissions. Only accepts submissions via submission manager on website. Cover letter is required. Poem should be typed single-spaced, one poem to a page. Please submit no more than twice per reading period. Reads submissions August 1-March 31 only. Responds in 4-5 months. Pays 2 contributor's copies. Acquires first North American rights. After publication, all rights revert to author. Staff reviews books of poetry. Send materials for review consideration to editor-in-chief.

TIPS "We look for originality, brevity, significance, strong dialogue, and vivid detail. We sponsor the Wabash Prize for Poetry (deadline: mid-October) and Fiction (deadline: March 1). $1,000 award for each. All contest submissions will be considered for regular inclusion in the *Sycamore Review.* No e-mail submissions—no exception. Include SASE.

TAKAHE

P.O. Box 13-335, Christchurch 8001, New Zealand. (03)359-8133. **E-mail:** admin@takahe.org.nz. **Website:** www.takahe.org.nz/index.php. **Contact:** Poetry Editor. The Takahe 2010 Poetry Competition awards 1st Prize: $250 NZD; 2nd Prize: $100 NZD; plus one-year subscriptions to *Takahe* to 2 runners-up. Submit as many poems as you wish, but each much be named separately on the entry form. Submissions must be unpublished and may not be entered in other contests. Poems must be in English and typed on A4 paper, with no identifying information on the ms. Include SASE with entry for results and/or return of entries (or SAE with IRCs for overseas entrants; may also add $2 NZD to entry fee for handling and postage). All entries considered for publication in *Takahe.* Guidelines and entry form available on website. **Entry fee:** $5 NZD/poem. Deadline: September 30, 2010.

MAGAZINE NEEDS No simultaneous submissions. No e-mail submissions. "**Please note:** U.S. stamps should not be used on SAEs. They do not work in New Zealand. Please enclose IRCs or supply e-mail address." Cover letter is required. "

TIPS "We pay a flat rate to each writer/poet appearing in a particular issue regardless of the number/length of items. Editorials and literary commentaries are by invitation only."

TALENT DRIPS EROTIC PUBLISHINGS

(216)799-9775. **E-mail:** talent_drips_eroticpublishing@lycos.com. **Website:** http://ashygirlforgirls.tripod.com/talentdripseroticpublishings. **Contact:** Kimberly Steele, founder. *Talent Drips*, published bimonthly online, focuses solely on showcasing new erotic fiction. Acquires electronic rights only. Rights revert to poets upon publication. Time between acceptance and publication is 2 months. Responds in 3 weeks. Guidelines on website.

MAGAZINE NEEDS Wants erotic poetry and short stories.

HOW TO CONTACT Submit 2-3 poems at a time, maximum 30 lines each by e-mail to talent_drips_eroticpublishing@lycos.com. Considers previously published and simultaneous submissions. Accepts e-mail pasted into body of message. Reads submissions during publication months only. Time between acceptance and publication is 2 months. Guidelines available on website. Responds in 3 weeks. Pays $10 for each accepted poem. Acquires electronic rights only. Work to be archived on the site for a year.

CONTEST/AWARD OFFERINGS Talent Drips Erotic Publishings Poet of the Year Contest is held annually. Prizes: $75, $50, and certificate. Deadline: December 15. Guidelines on website.

TIPS "Does not want sci-fi/fantasy submissions; mythical creatures having pointless sex is not a turn-on; looking for more original plots than 'the beast takes the submissive maiden' stuff."

TALES OF THE TALISMAN

E-mail: hadrosaur@zianet.com. **Website:** www.talesofthetalisman.com. **Contact:** David Lee Summers, editor. "*Tales of the Talisman* is a literary science fiction and fantasy magazine. We publish short stories, poetry, and articles with themes related to science fiction and fantasy. Above all, we are looking for thought-provoking ideas and good writing. Speculative fiction set in the past, present, and future is welcome. Likewise, contemporary or historical fiction is welcome as long as it has a mythic or science fictional element. Our target audience includes adult fans of the science fiction and fantasy genres along with anyone else who enjoys thought-provoking and entertaining writing." Buys one-time rights. Pays on acceptance. Publishes ms an average of 9 months after acceptance. Responds in 1 week to queries. Responds in 1 month to mss. Editorial lead time 9-12 months. Sample copy for $8. Guidelines available online.

Fiction and poetry submissions are limited to reading periods of January 1-February 15 and July 1-August 15.

MAGAZINE NEEDS "Do not send 'mainstream' poetry with no science fictional or fantastic elements. Do not send poems featuring copyrighted characters, unless you're the copyright holder." Length: 3-50 lines.

TIPS "Let your imagination soar to its greatest heights and write down the results. Above all, we are looking for thought-provoking ideas and good writing. Our emphasis is on character-oriented science fiction and fantasy. If we don't believe in the people living the story, we generally won't believe in the story itself."

TALKING RIVER

Division of Literature and Languages, 500 8th Ave., Lewiston ID 83501. (208)792-2189. **Fax:** (208)792-2324. **E-mail:** talkingriver@lcmail.lcsc.edu. **Website:** www.lcsc.edu/talkingriverreview. **Contact:** Kevin Goodan, editorial advisor. Magazine: 6×9; 150-200 pages; 60 lb. paper; coated, color cover; illustrations; photos. "We look for new voices with something to say to a discerning general audience." Semiannual. Circ. 250. Ethnic/multicultural, feminist, humor/satire, literary, regional. "Wants more well-written, character-driven stories that surprise and delight the reader with fresh, arresting yet unselfconscious language, imagery, metaphor, revelation." Nothing sexist, racist, homophobic, erotic for shock value; no genre fiction. Receives 400 unsolicited mss/month. Accepts 5-8 mss/issue; 10-15 mss/year. Reads mss September 1-May 1 only. Publishes ms 1-2 years after acceptance. **Publishes 10-15 new writers/year.** Length: 4,000 words; average length: 3,000 words. Sometimes comments on rejected mss. Responds in 3 months to mss. Does not accept simultaneous submissions. Sample copy for $6. Writer's guidelines for #10 SASE. Acquires one-time rights. Acquires one-time rights. 1-2 years Responds in 3 months to mss. Sample copy for $6. Writer's guidelines for #10 SASE

MAGAZINE NEEDS Pays contributor's copies; additional copies $4

HOW TO CONTACT Send complete manuscript with cover letter. Include estimated word count, 2-sentence bio and list of publications. Send SASE for reply, return of ms or send disposable copy of ms.

TIPS "We look for the strong, the unique; we reject clicheéd images and predictable climaxes."

TAPROOT LITERARY REVIEW

Box 204, Ambridge PA 15003. (724)266-8476. **E-mail:** taproot10@aol.com. **Contact:** Tikvah Feinstein, editor. *Taproot Literary Review*, published annually, is "a very respected anthology with increasing distribution. We publish some of the best poets in the U.S. We enjoy all types and styles of poetry from emerging writers to established writers to those who have become valuable and old friends who share their new works with us." Has published poetry by Shirley Barasch, Holly Day, Alena Horowitz, Chris Waters, Ellaraine Lockie, Craig Sipe, Greg Moglia, Elizabeth Swados, B.Z. Niditch and Robert Penick. *Taproot Literary Review* is about 95 pages, offset-printed on white stock, with one-color glossy cover. Circulation is 500. Single copy: $8.95; subscription: $7.50. Sample: $5.

HOW TO CONTACT Submit up to 5 poems at a time. Lines/poem: 35 maximum. No previously published poems or simultaneous submissions. Accepts submissions by e-mail (pasted into body of message), but "we would rather have a hard copy. Also, we cannot answer without a SASE." Cover letter is required (with general information). Reads submissions September 1-December 31 only. Guidelines available for SASE. Sometimes sends prepublication galleys. Pays 1 contributor's copy; additional copies are $6.50 each. Open to receiving books for review consideration. Send query first.

CONTEST/AWARD OFFERINGS Sponsors the annual Taproot Writer's Workshop Annual Writing Contest. 1st Prize: $25 and publication in *Taproot Literary Review*; 2nd and 3rd Prizes: publication. Submit 5 poems of literary quality, in any form, on any subject except porn, religion, and politics. **Entry fee:** $12/5 poems (no longer than 35 lines each); fee includes copy of *Taproot.* **Deadline:** December 31. Winners announced the following March.

TIPS "*Taproot* is getting more fiction submissions, and every one is read entirely. This takes time, so response can be delayed at busy times of year. Our contest is a good way to start publishing. Send for a sample copy and read it through. Ask for a critique and follow suggestions. Don't be offended by any suggestions—just take them or leave them and keep writing. Looks for a story that speaks in its unique voice, told in a well-crafted and complete, memorable style, a style of signature to the author. Follow writer's guidelines. Research markets. Send cover letter. Don't give up."

TARPAULIN SKY

P.O. Box 189, Grafton VT 05146. **Website:** www.tarpaulinsky.com. **Contact:** Poetry Editors. *Tarpaulin Sky,* published biannually in print and online, features "highest-quality poetry, prose, cross-genre work, art, photography, interviews, and reviews. We are open to all styles and forms, providing the forms appear inevitable and/or inextricable from the poems. We are especially fond of inventive/experimental and cross-/trans-genre work. The best indication of our aesthetic is found in the journal we produce: Please read it before submitting your work. Also, hardcopy submissions may be received by different editors at different times; check guidelines before submitting." Has published poetry by Jenny Boully, Matthea Harvey, Bin Ramke, Eleni Sikelianos, Juliana Spahr, and Joshua Marie Wilkinson. Receives about 3,000 poems/year.

MAGAZINE NEEDS Submit 4-6 poems at a time. Considers simultaneous submissions; no previously published poems. Accepts e-mail submissions ("best received as attachments in .rtf or .pdf formats"); no disk submissions. Cover letter is preferred. Reads submissions year round. Time between acceptance and publication is 2-6 months. "Poems are read by all editors. We aim for consensus." Rarely comments on rejected poems. Guidelines available for SASE, by e-mail, or on website. E-mail: editors@tarpaulinsky.com (inquiries) or submissions@tarpaulinsky.com (submissions). Responds in 1-4 months. Pays in contributor's copies and "by waiving readings fees for Tarpaulin Sky Press Open Reading Periods." Always sends prepublication galleys (electronic). Acquires first rights. Reviews books/chapbooks of poetry.

TAR RIVER POETRY

Mail Stop 139, Erwin Hall, East Fifth St., East Carolina University, Greenville NC 27858. **E-mail:** TarRiverPoetry@gmail.com. **Website:** www.tarriverpoetry.com. **Contact:** Luke Whisnant, Editor. *Tar River Poetry,* published twice/year, is an "'all-poetry' magazine that publishes 40-50 poems per issue, providing the talented beginner and experienced writer with a forum that features all styles and forms of verse." Wants "skillful use of figurative language; poems that appeal to the senses." Does not want "sentimental, flat-statement poetry." Has published poetry by William Stafford, Sharon Olds, Carolyn Kizer, A.R. Ammons, and Claudia Emerson. Has also published "many other well-known poets, as well as numerous new and emerging poets." *Tar River Poetry* is 64 pages, 9×5, professionally printed with color cover. Receives 6,000-8,000 submissions/year, accepts 60-80. Press run is 900 (500 subscribers, 125 libraries). Subscription: $12/year; $20/two years. Sample: $7.00 postpaid.

"We only consider submissions during two six-week reading periods: one in the fall (usually Sept. 15-Nov. 1) and one in the spring (Feb. 1-Mar. 15); check our website for reading periods before submitting. Work submitted at other times will not be considered."

MAGAZINE NEEDS Submit no more than 5 poems at a time. Simultaneous submissions okay. No previously published poems. Accepts e-mail submissions only; no print submissions; print submissions will be returned unread. "Detailed submission instructions appear on the website, along with writer's guidelines." Check website for reading periods: "we do not read manuscripts from May through August—submissions will be returned unread." Rarely comments on rejections "due to volume of submissions." Guidelines available for SASE or on website. Responds in 6 weeks. Acquires first rights and reassigns reprint rights after publication. Reviews books of poetry in 4,000 words maximum, single- or multi-book format. Query for reviews. Pays 2 contributor's copies.

TIPS Familiarize yourself with the type of poetry we publish before submitting. Sample copies are available, or visit our website to read sample poems. "Writers of poetry should first be readers of poetry. Read and study traditional and contemporary poetry."

TATTOO HIGHWAY

E-mail: submissions@tattoohighway.org. **Website:** www.tattoohighway.org. **Contact:** Sara McAulay, editor and graphics; Rochelle Nameroff, poetry editor.

TIPS "Look at past issues online, then bring us your best stuff."

THE TAYLOR TRUST: POETRY AND PROSE

E-mail: lavonne.taylor@sbcglobal.net. **Website:** http://thetaylortrust.wordpress.com. **Contact:** LaVonne Taylor, editor and publisher. The Taylor Trust "considers ourselves egalitarian in that we accept most poetry forms. We also accept flash fiction, short stories, nonfiction." Do not want profanity or sexually explicit material. No age restrictions but child must state age and give a short bio. Prefers uplifting subject matter.

"We have moved away from print publishing to online only."

MAGAZINE NEEDS Humorous poetry also accepted. Considers previously published poems ("as long as the author owns the publication rights") and simultaneous submissions ("with the understanding that it is the author's duty to inform all concerned when a poem is accepted"). "We require a bio of about 150-200 words with publication history and any other information the author cares to provide. We do not accept hard copy submittals; online only, please." Reads submissions year round. Acquires one-time electronic rights. Rights revert to poet upon publication. Reviews poetry books, chapbooks, and other magazines and journals in 500-1,000 words.

THE TEACHER'S VOICE

P.O. Box 150384, Kew Gardens NY 11415. **E-mail:** editor@the-teachers-voice.org. **Website:** www.the-teachers-voice.org. **Contact:** Andres Castro, founding/managing editor. *The Teacher's Voice*, was founded as an experimental hardcopy literary magazine and is now free and online. "We publish poetry, short stories, creative nonfiction, and essays that reflect the many different American teacher experiences." Wants "all styles and forms. We ask to see critical creative writing that takes risks without being overly self-indulgent or inaccessible. We welcome work that ranges from 'art for art's sake' to radically social/political. Writing that illuminates the most pressing/urgent issues in American education and the lives of teachers gets special attention." Has published poetry by Edward Francisco, Sapphire, Hal Sirowitz, and Antler. Receives about 1,000 poems/year, accepts about 10%.

MAGAZINE NEEDS Submit 3-5 poems at a time. Lines/poem: no limits. Considers previously published poems (if rights are held by the author) and simultaneous submissions (contact if submission has been accepted elsewhere). No e-mail or disk submissions. Send prose pieces under 2,000 words. Cover letter is preferred. "Are you a teacher, administrator, parent, student, librarian, custodian, coach, security officer, etc? We do not accept responsibility for submissions or queries not accompanied by a SASE with adequate postage." Reads submissions year round. Time between acceptance and publication is 4 months to 1 year. Poems are circulated to an editorial board. Guidelines available on website. Sometimes sends prepublication galleys "if requested." Acquires first rights and electronic reprint rights. Rights revert to poet "after work is first electronically published and archived on this site; no material on this site may be reproduced in any form without permission from their individual authors." No longer accepts online submissions.

ADDITIONAL INFORMATION "Since we publish open as well as theme issues (that require enough thematic pieces to be compiled) and do rely on readership financial support, our publishing schedule and format may vary from year to year. We publish hardcopy limited press collections when funds allow. Our production goal is to showcase strong cohesive collections that support our mission and satisfy the needs of particular issues. For the moment, our new focus on electronic publishing is a matter of survival that offers many new possibilities and opportunities in keeping with the changing times."

CONTEST/AWARD OFFERINGS Sponsors *The Teacher's Voice* Annual Chapbook Contest and *The Teacher's Voice* Annual Poetry Contest for Unpublished Poets. Final contest judges have included, Sapphire, Jack Hirschman, and Taylor Mali. Guidelines for both contests available for SASE, by e-mail, or on website.

TEARS IN THE FENCE

Website: http://tearsinthefence.com. *Tears in the Fence*, published twice a year, is a "small press magazine of poetry, fiction, interviews, essays, and reviews. We are open to a wide variety of poetic styles. Work that shows social and poetic awareness whilst prompting close and divergent readings. However, we like to publish a variety of work." Sample: $8.

Has published poetry by John Hartley Williams, Sheila E. Murphy, John Kinsella, Donna Hilbert, Anne Blonstein, Anthony Barnett, Glyn Hughes, Carrie Etter, Vahni Capildeo. *Tears in the Fence* is 168 pages, A5, docutech-printed on 110-gms. paper, perfect-bound, with matte card cover. Press run is 800 (522 subscribers). Subscription: $20/3 issues.

MAGAZINE NEEDS Submit 6 poems at a time. Accepts e-mail (pasted into body of message) and disk submissions. Cover letter with brief bio is required. Poems must be typed; include SASE. Time between acceptance and publication is 3 months. Pays 1 contributor's copy. Reviews books of poetry in 2,000-4,000 words, single- or multi-book format. Send materials for review consideration.

ALSO OFFERS The magazine runs a regular series of readings in London, and an annual international literary festival.

TERRAIN.ORG: A JOURNAL OF THE BUILT & NATURAL ENVIROMENTS

Terrain.org, P.O. Box 19161, Tucson AZ 19161. 520-241-7390. **Website:** www.terrain.org. **Contact:** Simmons Buntin, editor-in-chief. Terrain.org is based on and thus welcomes quality submissions from new and experienced authors and artists alike. Our online journal accepts only the finest poetry, essays, fiction, articles, artwork, and other contributions' material that reaches deep into the earth's fiery core, or humanity's incalculable core, and brings forth new insights and wisdom. Sponsors *Terrain.org 2nd Annual Contest in Poetry, Fiction, and Nonfiction!* Submissions due by August 1. How to Submit: Go to Submission Manager Online Tool. "Terrain.org is searching for that interface - the integration among the built and natural environments, that might be called the soul of place. The works contained within Terrain.org ultimately examine the physical realm around us, and how those environments influence us and each other physically, mentally, emotionally and spiritually." Semiannual. All issues are theme-based. List of upcoming themes available on website. Receives 25 mss/month. Accepts 3-5 mss/issue; 6-10 mss/year. Agented fiction 5%. **Publishes 1-3 new writers/year.** Published Al Sim, Jacob MacAurthur Mooney, T.R. Healy, Deborah Fries, Andrew Wingfield, Braden Hepner, Chavawn Kelly, Tamara Kaye Sellman. Sometimes comments on/critiques rejected mss. Sends galleys to author. Publication is copyrighted. Acquires one- time rights. Manuscript published 5 weeks to 18 months after acceptance. Responds to queries in 2 weeks. Responds to mss in 8-12 weeks. Guidelines available online.

HOW TO CONTACT Submit through online submission form.

ADDITIONAL INFORMATION Sponsors *Terrain.org 2nd Annual Contest in Poetry, Fiction, and Nonfiction!* Submissions due by August 1. See guidelines online.

TIPS "We have three primary criteria in reviewing fiction: 1) The story is compelling and well-crafted. 2) The story provides some element of surprise; i.e., whether in content, form or delivery we are unexpectedly delighted in what we've read. 3) The story meets an upcoming theme, even if only peripherally. Read fiction in the current issue and perhaps some archived work, and if you like what you read—and our overall enviromental slant—then send us your best work. Make sure you follow our submission guidelines (including cover note with bio), and that your manuscript is as error-free as possible."

TEXAS POETRY CALENDAR

Dos Gatos Press, 1310 Crestwood Rd., Austin TX 78722. (512)467-0678. **E-mail:** editors@dosgatospress.org. **Website:** www.dosgatospress.org. **Contact:** Scott Wiggerman and Cindy Huyser, co-editors; David Meischen, managing editor. *Texas Poetry* Calendar, published annually in August, features a "week-by-week calendar side-by-side with poems with a Texas connection." Wants "a wide variety of styles, voices, and forms, including rhyme—though a Texas connection is preferred. Humor is welcome! Poetry only!" Does not want "children's poetry, erotic poetry, profanity, obscure poems, previously published work, or poems over 35 lines." Texas Poetry Calendar is about 144 pages, digest-sized, offset-printed, spiral-bound, with full-color cardstock cover. Receives about 600 poems/year, accepts about 70-75. Press run is 1,200; 70 distributed free to contributors. Single copy: $13.95 plus $3 shipping. Make checks payable to Dos Gatos Press.

MAGAZINE NEEDS Submit 3 poems at a time. Lines/poem: 35 maximum, "including spaces and title." No simultaneous submissions; no previously published poems. No fax, e-mail, or disk submissions. Cover letter is required. "Include a short bio (100-200 words) and poem titles in cover letter. Also include e-mail address and phone number. Do not include poet's name on the poems themselves!" Reads submissions Jan-May. Time between acceptance and publication is 3-4 months. Poems are circulated to an editorial board. Never comments on rejected poems. Deadline: February 21 (postmark).

TEXAS REVIEW

Texas Review Press, Department of English, Sam Houston State University, Box 2146, Huntsville TX 77341-2146. (936)294-1992. **Fax:** (936)294-3070. **E-mail:** eng_pdr@shsu.edu; cww006@shsu.edu. **Website:** www.shsu.edu/~www_trp. Established 1976. **Contact:** Robert Phillips, poetry editor. *The Texas Review*, published semiannually, is a "scholarly journal publishing poetry, short fiction, essays and book reviews." Has published poetry by Donald Hall, X.J. Kennedy, and Richard Eberhart. *The Texas Review* is 152 pages, digest-sized, offset printed, perfect-bound, with 4-color cover, includes ads. Press run is 1,000. Single copy: $12; subscription: $24. Sample: $5. Make checks payable to Friends of Texas Review.

HOW TO CONTACT No previously published poems or simultaneous submissions. Include SASE. Reads submissions September 1-April 30 only. Time between acceptance and publication is 6 months. Poems are circulated to an editorial board. Seldom comments on rejected poems. Responds in up to 6 months. Pays one-year subscription and one contributor's copy (may request more). Acquires first North American serial rights. Returns rights "for publication in anthology."

CONTEST/AWARD OFFERINGS Sponsors the X.J. Kennedy Poetry Prize (for best full-length book of poetry) and the Robert Phillips Poetry Chapbook Prize (for best poetry chapbook). Both competitions award $200 and publication for the winning mss. **Entry fee:** $20. Guidelines available for SASE (specifying "for poetry/fiction contest guidelines") or on website.

THEMA

Thema Literary Society, P.O. Box 8747, Metairie LA 70011-8747. **E-mail:** thema@cox.net. **Website:** http://themaliterarysociety.com. **Contact:** Gail Howard, poetry editor.

MAGAZINE NEEDS *THEMA*, published triannually, uses poetry related to specific themes. "Each issue is based on an unusual premise. Please, please send SASE for guidelines before submitting poetry to find out the upcoming themes." Does not want "scatologic language, alternate lifestyle, explicit love poetry." Has published poetry by Edward Beatty, Phil Gruis, Greg Moglia, James Penha, and KH Solomon. *THEMA* is 100 pages, digest-sized professionally printed, with glossy card cover. Receives about 400 poems/year, accepts about 8%. Press run is 400 (230 subscribers, 30 libraries). Subscription: $20 U.S./$30 foreign. Sample $10 U.S./$15 foreign.

HOW TO CONTACT Submit up to 3 poems at a time. Include SASE. "All submissions should be typewritten on standard 8×11 paper. Submissions are accepted all year, but evaluated after specified deadlines." Specify target theme. Editor comments on submissions. Upcoming themes and guidelines available in magazine, for SASE, by e-mail, or on website. Pays $10/poem and 1 contributor's copy. Acquires one-time rights.

THICK WITH CONVICTION

E-mail: twczine@yahoo.com. **Website:** www.twczine.angelfire.com. **Contact:** Acquisitions: Arielle Lancaster-LaBrea, Kayla Middlebrook and Kristina Marie Blanton. *Thick With Conviction*, published biannually online, is "run by three twenty-something women who are looking for fresh and exciting voices in poetry. We don't want to take a nap while we're reading, so grab our attention, make us sit up and catch our breath." Wants all genres of poetry, "poems that make us exhale a deep sigh after reading them. Basically, if we can't feel the words in front of us, we're not going to be happy. We'd like to see new and cutting edge poets who think outside the box, but still know how to keep things from getting too strange and inaccessible." Does not want "teen angst poems, religious poems, or greeting card tripe." Has published poetry by Kendall A. Bell, April Michelle Bratten, KristinaMarie Darling, James H. Duncan, Paul Hostovsky and Kelsey Upward. Receives about 300 poems/year, accepts about 15%. Never comments on rejected poems. Acquires one-time rights. Rights revert to poet upon publication. Publishes ms 3 months after acceptance. Responds in "roughly 2-3 months." Guidelines available on website.

MAGAZINE NEEDS Submit 3-5 poems at a time. Lines/poem: no limit. Considers previously published poems; no simultaneous submissions. Accepts e-mail submissions (pasted into body of message; "any attachments will be deleted"); no disk submissions. Cover letter and bio is required. Reads submissions year-round.

THINK JOURNAL

Reason Publishing LLC, P.O. Box 454, Downingtown PA 19335. **E-mail:** thinkjournal@yahoo.com. **Website:** http://web.me.com/christineyurick/Think_Journal/Home_Page.html. **Contact:** Christine Yurick, editor. "*Think Journal*, published quarterly, "focuses on words that have meaning, that are presented in a clear way, and that exhibit the skills demanded by craft. The journal prints work that achieves a balance between form and content. The most important traits that will be considered are form, structure, clarity, content, imagination, and style. *Think Journal* is 55 pages, digest-sized, desktop-printed, staple-bound with a cardstock cover containing original artwork. Single copy: $7; subscription: $20/year. Sample $6. Make checks payable to Christine Yurick." Buys one-time rights. Publication is payment, along with 1 free contributor's copy. Publishes ms an average of 3-6 months after acceptance. Responds in 2-4 weeks to queries. Responds in 1-2 months to mss. Editorial lead time 3 months.

MAGAZINE NEEDS Submit 3-5 poems at a time, no restrictions in length. Accepts submissions by e-mail, mail. "Always include a SASE with submissions. Cover letter and brief biography preferred. Please include your e-mail address on the cover page for further communications. Include your name and address on each page of your submission." Reads submissions year round. Does not accept previously published or simultaneous submissions.

TIPS "Please visit the website to view samples of previously published work, or purchase a sample issue. Also looking for graphic design artwork for the cover."

THIRD WEDNESDAY: A LITERARY ARTS MAGAZINE

174 Greenside Up, Ypsilanti MI 48197. (734) 434-2409. **E-mail:** submissions@thirdwednesday.org; LaurenceWT@aol.com. **Website:** http://thirdwednesday.org. **Contact:** Laurence Thomas, editor. Acquires first rights. Pays on acceptance. Writers receive $3, 1 contributor's copy. Additional copies $8. Publishes ms 3 months after acceptance. Responds to mss in 6-8 weeks. Sample copy available for $8. Guidelines available for SASE, or via e-mail.

MAGAZINE NEEDS Wants "all styles and forms of poetry, from formal to experimental. Emphasis is placed on the ideas conveyed, craft and language, beauty of expression, and the picture that extends beyond the frame of the poem." Does not want "hate-filled diatribes, pornography (though eroticism is acceptable), prose masquerading as poetry, first drafts of anything." Considers simultaneous submissions. Accepts submissions through e-mail, which is preferred to mail. Include SASE if submitting via postal mail. Reads submissions year round. Submit seasonal poems 3 months in advance. Time between acceptance and publication is 3 months. Poems are circulated to an editorial board. "Submissions are coded by executive editor and sent blind to members of editorial board; said members send up or down votes to executive editor who accepts pieces according to rule of majority." Sometimes comments on rejected poems. Guidelines available in magazine, by e-mail, and on website. Acquires first North American serial rights, electronic rights. "*TW* retains the right to reproduce accepted work as samples on our website." Rights revert to poet upon publication. Has published poetry by Wanda Coleman, Philip Dacey, Richard Luftig, Simon Perchik, Marge Piercy, Charles Harper Webb. Receives 800 poems/year. Press run is 125. Single copy: $8; subscription: $30. Make checks payable to *Third Wednesday.*

TIPS "Of course, originality is important, along with skill in writing, deft handling of language, and meaning, which goes hand in hand with beauty—whatever that is. Short fiction is specialized and difficult, so the writer should read extensively in the field."

TICKLED BY THUNDER

14076-86A Ave., Surrey BC V3W 0V9, Canada. (604)591-6095. **E-mail:** info@tickledbythunder.com. **Website:** www.tickledbythunder.com. **Contact:** Larry Lindner, publisher. *Tickled by Thunder*, published up to 2 times/year, uses poems "about fantasy particularly; writing or whatever. Require original images and thoughts. Welcome humor and creative inspirational verse." Does not want "anything pornographic, childish, unimaginative." Has published poetry by Laleh Dadpour Jackson and Helen Michiko Singh. *Tickled by Thunder* is 24 pages, digest-sized, published on Macintosh. Has 1,000 readers/subscribers. Subscription: $12 CAD/4 issues. Sample: $2.50 CAD.

HOW TO CONTACT Submit 3-5 poems at a time. Lines/poem: up to 40 ("keep them short—not interested in long, long poems"). No e-mail submissions. Cover letter is required. Include "a few facts about yourself and brief list of publishing credits." Comments on rejected poems "80% of the time." Guidelines available for SASE or on website. Responds in up to 6 months. Pays 2¢/line, $2 CAD maximum. Acquires first rights. Reviews books of poetry in up to 300 words. Open to unsolicited reviews. Send materials for review consideration.

ADDITIONAL INFORMATION Publishes **author-subsidized chapbooks.** "We are also interested in student poetry and publish it in our center spread: *Expressions*." Send SASE (or SAE and IRC) for details.

CONTEST/AWARD OFFERINGS Offers a poetry contest 2 times/year. Prize: cash, publication, and subscription. **Entry fee:** $5 CAD for one poem; free for subscribers. **Deadlines:** the 15th of February, 15th of August.

TIPS "Allow your characters to breathe on their own. Use description with action."

TIGER'S EYE

Tiger's Eye Press, P.O. Box 9723, Denver CO 80209. **E-mail:** tigerseyepoet@yahoo.com. **Website:** www.tigerseyejournal.com. **Contact:** Colette Jonopulos and JoAn Osborne, editors. *Tiger's Eye: A Journal of Poetry*, published annually, features both established and undiscovered poets. "Besides publishing the work of several exceptional poets in each issue, we feature two poets in interviews, giving the reader insight into their lives and writing habits." Wants "both free verse and traditional forms; no restrictions on subject or length. We welcome sonnets, haibun, haiku, ghazals, villenelles, etc. We pay special attention to unusual forms and longer poems that may have difficulty being placed elsewhere. Poems with distinct imagery and viewpoint are read and re-read by the editors and considered for publication." Has published poetry by Laura LeHew, Carol Frith, Jose Angel Araguz, Julie Gard. *Tiger's Eye* is 64 pages, saddle-stitched. Receives 1,000 poems/year, accepts 100. Press run is 300. Single copy: $6; subscription: $11 for 2 issues. Make checks payable to Tiger's Eye Press. Acquires one-time rights. Publishes ms 3 months after acceptance. Responds in 6 months. Guidelines available in magazine or on website.

MAGAZINE NEEDS Submit 3-5 poems at a time, no multiple submissions. Considers simultaneous submissions with notification if a poem is accepted elsewhere; no previously published poems. Accepts e-mail submissions in one continuous attachment. Cover letter is required. Include brief bio. SASE for notification only; no submissions are returned. Reads submissions year-round. Journal deadline is January 31. Chapbook contest deadline is August 31. "All poems are read by the editors, then filed as poems we definitely want to publish, those we are still considering, and those we aren't publishing. Our two featured poets are chosen, then letters and e-mails are sent out." Seldom comments on rejected poems. Always sends prepublication galleys. Pays one contributor's copy to each poet, 2 to featured poets. Acquires one-time rights.

ADDITIONAL INFORMATION *Tiger's Eye* nominates for *The Pushcart Prize.*

CONTEST/AWARD OFFERINGS Tiger's Eye Chapbook Contest (see separate listing in Contests & Awards). "Our annual poetry contest awards $500, $100, $50. Send 20-25 poems, cover letter with poet's name and contact information (no identifying information on mss pages) SASE, and $15 entry fee. **Deadline: August 31.**

TIMBER JOURNAL

E-mail: timberjournal@gmail.com. **Website:** www.timberjournal.com. **Contact:** Oren Silverman, managing editor; Caroline Davidson, poetry editor; Gabrielle Fuentes, fiction editor. Timber is a literary journal, run by students in the MFA program at the University of Colorado-Boulder, dedicated to the promotion of innovative literature. "We publish work that explores the boundaries of poetry, fiction, creative nonfiction, and digital literatures. We produce both an online journal in which we explore the potentials of the digital medium, and a semi-annual 'book object,' which is a venue for more traditional print-based work." Reading period September 1-February 15. Include 30-50 word bio with submission. Guidelines available online.

MAGAZINE NEEDS Looking for innovative poetry. Submit 3-5 poems (less than 3 poems will not be reviewed). Pays one contributor copy.

TIPS "We are looking for innovative poetry, fiction, creative nonfiction, and digital lit (screenwriting, digital poetry, multimedia lit, etc.)."

TIME OF SINGING

P.O. Box 149, Conneaut Lake PA 16316. **E-mail:** timesing@zoominternet.net. **Website:** www.timeofsinging.com. **Contact:** Lora Zill, editor. "*Time of Singing* publishes 'Christian' poetry in the widest sense, but prefers 'literary' type. Welcome forms, fresh rhyme, well-crafted free verse. Like writers who take chances, who don't feel the need to tie everything up neatly." Buys first North American serial rights, buys first rights, buys one-time rights, buys second serial (reprint) rights. Publishes ms 1 year after acceptance. Responds in 3 months to mss. Editorial lead time 6 months. Sample copy for $4/each or 2 for $7. Guidelines for SASE or on website.

MAGAZINE NEEDS Wants free verse and well-crafted rhyme; would like to see more forms. Does not want "collections of uneven lines, sermons that rhyme, unstructured 'prayers,' and trite sing-song rhymes." Has published poetry by John Grey, Luci Shaw, Bob Hostetler, Tony Cosier, Barbara Crooker, and Charles Waugaman. It is 44 pages, digest-sized, offset from typescript. Receives more than 800 submissions/year, accepts about 175. Press run is 250 (150 subscribers). Subscription: $17 USD, $21 USD Canada, $30 USD overseas. Sample: $4, or 2 for $7 (postage paid). Accepts e-mail submissions (pasted into body of message or as attachment). Poems should be single-spaced. Comments "with suggestions for improvement if close to publication. TOS has published poets from England, South Africa, Mexico, New Zealand, Scotland, Russia, Australia, and Ireland." Does not want sermons that rhyme or greeting card type poetry. Length: 3-60 lines. All contributors receive one copy of the issue in which their work appears and the opportunity to purchase more at the contributor's rate

ADDITIONAL INFORMATION "*Time of Singing* also welcomes general inspirational and nature poems. I prefer poems that don't preach, and "show" rather than "tell." Sermons and greeting card poetry have valid purposes, but aren't appropriate for this magazine. I suggest you obtain a sample back issue to help you ascertain TOS's style. I welcome fresh rhyme, beg for more forms, appreciate well-crafted free verse, and consider poems up to 60 lines in length. I try to respond within 3 months, and make every effort to publish poems within one year of acceptance."

CONTEST/AWARD OFFERINGS Sponsors theme contests for specific issues. Guidelines available for SASE, by e-mail, or on website.

TIPS "Read widely and study the craft. You need more than feelings and religious jargon to make it into TOS. It's helpful to get honest critiques of your work. Cover letter not necessary. Your poems speak for themselves."

TIN HOUSE

McCormack Communications, P.O. Box 10500, Portland OR 97210. (503)274-4393. **Fax:** (503)222-1154. **E-mail:** info@tinhouse.com. **Website:** www.tinhouse.com. **Contact:** Cheston Knapp, managing editor; Holly Macarthur, founding editor. "We are a general interest literary quarterly. Our watchword is quality. Our audience includes people interested in literature in all its aspects, from the mundane to the exalted." Buys first North American serial rights, buys anthology rights. Pays on publication. Publishes ms an average of 6 months after acceptance. Responds in 6 weeks to queries. Responds in 3 months to mss. Editorial lead time 6 months. Sample copy for $15. Guidelines available online.

MAGAZINE NEEDS "No prose masquerading as poetry." Send complete ms September 1-May 31 via regular mail or online submission form. No fax or e-mail submissions. Pays $50-150.

TIPS "Remember to send an SASE with your submission."

TOAD SUCK REVIEW

E-mail: toadsuckreview@gmail.com. **Website:** http://toadsuckreview.org. **Contact:** Mark Spitzer, Editor. 6×11 magazine, 150 pages. Perfect bound flat spine. Prefers submissions from skilled, experienced poets; will consider work from beginning poets. Born from the legendary *Exquisite Corpse Annual*, the innovative *Toad Suck Review* is a cutting edge mixture of poetry, fiction, creative nonfiction, translations, reviews and artwork with a provocative sense of humor and an interest in diverse cultures and politics. No themes planned for 2012 issues. No previously published work. "Previously published" work includes: poetry posted on a public website/blog/forum, and poetry posted on a private, password-protected forum. Reads mss in the fall. Published Kevin Brockmeie, Teresa Bergen, Daniel Grandbois, William Lychack. Single copy is $15; lifetime subscription is $100. Make checks payable to Univ. of Central Arkansas. Publishes 5 unpublished writers each year. Receives about 777 poems/year; accepts 17. Sometimes comments on rejected poems. Responds to ms in 1 week to 9 months.

Acquires one-time rights; rights revert to poets upon publication. Reviews books of poetry, chapbooks of poetry, and other magazines/journals. Send materials to Book Review Editor. Acquires one-time rights. Pays on publication. 4 months Responds to mss in 1 week to 9 months Sample copy for $15. Guidelines available free for SASE or on website.

MAGAZINE NEEDS All forms and styles are welcome, especially those that take risks and shoot for something new. Does not want rhyming, repetitive, pastoral & religious poetry. Length: 1-111 max. Pays $1-2.

HOW TO CONTACT Submit in e-mail as attached document.

TIPS "See a recent issue or a back issue of the *Exquisite Corpse Annual* for an idea of our aesthetics." "Our guidelines are very open and ambiguous. Don't send us too much and don't make it too long. If you submit in an e-mail, use rtf. We're easy. If it works, we'll be in touch." "It's a brutal world—wear your helmet."

O TOASTED CHEESE

E-mail: editors@toasted-cheese.com. **E-mail:** submit@toasted-cheese.com. **Website:** www.toasted-cheese.com.

MAGAZINE NEEDS E-zine specializing in fiction, creative nonfiction, poetry and flash fiction. "*Toasted Cheese* accepts submissions of previously unpublished fiction, flash fiction, creative nonfiction and poetry. Our focus is on quality of work, not quantity. Some issues will therefore contain fewer/more pieces than previous issues. We don't restrict publication based on subject matter. We encourage submissions from innovative writers in all genres." Quarterly. Adventure, children's/juvenile, ethnic/multicultural, fantasy, feminist, gay, historical, horror, humor/satire, lesbian, literary, mainstream, mystery/suspense, New Age, psychic/supernatural/occult, romance, science fiction, thriller/espionage, western. "No fan fiction. No chapters or excerpts unless they read as a stand-alone story. No first drafts." Receives 150 unsolicited mss/month. Accepts 1-10 mss/issue; 5-30 mss/year. Publishes 15 new writers/year. Publishes short shorts. Also publishes poetry.

HOW TO CONTACT Send complete ms in body of e-mail; no attachments. Accepts submissions by e-mail. Responds in 4 months to mss. No simultaneous submissions. Sample copy online. Follow online submission guidelines. Acquires electronic rights.

CONTEST/AWARD OFFERINGS Sponsors awards/contests.

TIPS "We are looking for clean, professional writing from writers of any level. Accepted stories will be concise and compelling. We are looking for writers who are serious about the craft: tomorrow's literary stars before they're famous. Take your submission seriously, yet remember that levity is appreciated. You are submitting not to traditional 'editors' but to fellow writers who appreciate the efforts of those in the trenches. Follow online submission guidelines."

◐ TORCH: POETRY, PROSE AND SHORT STORIES BY AFRICAN AMERICAN WOMEN

3720 Gattis School Rd., Suite 800, Round Rock TX 78664. **E-mail:** info@torchpoetry.org (inquiries), poetry@torchpoetry.org (submissions). **Website:** www.torchpoetry.org. **Contact:** Amanda Johnston, editor. *TORCH: Poetry, Prose, and Short Stories by African American Women*, published semiannually online, provides "a place to publish contemporary poetry, prose, and short stories by experienced and emerging writers alike. We prefer our contributors to take risks, and offer a diverse body of work that examines and challenges preconceived notions regarding race, ethnicity, gender roles, and identity." Has published poetry by Sharon Bridgforth, Patricia Smith, Crystal Wilkinson, Tayari Jones, and Natasha Trethewey. Receives about 250+ submissions/year, accepts about 20. Number of unique visitors: 600+/month. Submit 3 poems at a time. No previously published poems or simultaneous submissions. Accepts e-mail submissions only (as one MS Word attachment). Send to poetry@torchpoetry.org with "Poetry Submission" in subject line. Cover letter is preferred (in the body of the e-mail). Reads submissions April 15-August 31 only. Sometimes comments on rejected poems. Always sends prepublication galleys. No payment. "Within *TORCH*, we offer a special section called Flame that features an interview, biography, and work sample by an established writer as well as an introduction to their Spark—an emerging writer who inspires them and adds to the boundless voice of creative writing by Black women." A free online newsletter is available; see website. Acquires rights to publish accepted work in online issue and in archives. Rights revert to authors upon publication. Time between acceptance and publication is 2-7 months. Guidelines available on website.

HOW TO CONTACT Submit 3 poems at a time. No previously published poems or simultaneous submissions. Accepts e-mail submissions only (as one MS Word attachment). Send to poetry@torchpoetry.org with "Poetry Submission" in subject line. Cover letter is preferred (in the body of the e-mail). Reads submissions April 15-August 31 only. Always sends prepublication galleys. No payment. Acquires rights to publish accepted work in online issue and in archives. Rights revert to authors upon publication.

ALSO OFFERS "Within *TORCH*, we offer a special section called Flame that features an interview, biography, and work sample by an established writer as well as an introduction to their Spark—an emerging writer who inspires them and adds to the boundless voice of creative writing by Black women." A free online newsletter is available; see website.

TRAVEL NATURALLY

Internaturally, Inc., P.O. Box 317, Newfoundland NJ 07435-0317. (973)697-3552. **Fax:** (973)697-8313. **E-mail:** naturally@internaturally.com. **Website:** www.internaturally.com. *Travel Naturally* looks at why millions of people believe that removing clothes in public is a good idea, and at places specifically created for that purpose—with good humor, but also in earnest. *Travel Naturally* takes you to places where your personal freedom is the only agenda, and to places where textile-free living is a serious commitment. Buys first rights, buys one-time rights. Pays on publication. Editorial lead time 4 months. Sample copy for $9. Guidelines available online.

Travel Naturally is 72 pages, magazine-sized, printed on glossy paper, saddle-stapled.

MAGAZINE NEEDS Wants poetry about the naturalness of the human body and nature, any length. Consideers previously published poems and simultaneous submissions. Accepts e-mail and fax submissions. "Name and address must be submitted with e-mail."

TIPS "*Travel Naturally* invokes the philosophies of naturism and nudism, but also activities and beliefs in the mainstream that express themselves, barely: spiritual awareness, New Age customs, pagan and religious rites, alternative and fringe lifestyle beliefs, artistic expressions, and many individual nude interests. Our higher purpose is simply to help restore our sense of self. Although the term 'nude recreation' may, for some, conjure up visions of sexual frivolities inappropriate for youngsters—because that can also be technically true—these topics are outside the scope of *Travel Naturally*. Here the emphasis is on the many varieties of human beings, of all ages and backgrounds, recreating in their most natural state, at extraordinary places, their reasons for doing so, and the benefits they derive. We incorporate a travel department to advise and book vacations in locations reviewed in travel articles."

TRIBECA POETRY REVIEW

P.O. Box 2061, New York NY 10013. **E-mail:** editor@tribecareview.org. **Website:** www.tribecareview.org. **Contact:** Kenlynne Rini Mulroy, editor. *Tribeca Poetry Review*, published biennially in even-numbered years, is "a publication emerging out of the thick poetic history that is downtown New York. It seeks to expose its readers to the best smattering of poetry we can get our hands on. *TPR* will showcase new pieces by seasoned poets as well as illuminate the work of fresh voices." Acquires first North American serial rights. Reads submissions year round. Time between acceptance and publication is up to 2 years. Sometimes comments on rejected poems. Responds as soon as possible; can be up to 6 months. Guidelines on website.

Tribeca Poetry Review is approximately 100 pages, digest-sized, professionally printed, flat-spine bound, with artwork cover. Press run is 1,000.

MAGAZINE NEEDS Submit no more than 5 poems at a time, up to 10 pages in total. No previously published poems or simultaneous submissions. Cover letter is required. "Please do not use your cover letter as a place to explain your poems. The letter is a place to introduce yourself and your work but not sell or explain either. Your name, address, contact phone, and e-mail should be on each page submitted." Wants "the kind of poetry that squirms in your head for days, hopefully longer, after reading it. Send us your best work. Will publish all forms (including traditional poesy, spoken word, or your experimental pieces) providing they translate well on the page, are intelligent, and well-crafted. New York City poets are always encouraged to submit their work, but this is *not* strictly a regional publication. Does not want "overly self-absorbed poems; pieces so abstract that all meaning and pleasure is lost on anyone but the poet; first drafts, goofy word play, trite nostalgia." Considers poetry by teens. "It's the poem itself that needs to resonate with readers, so the age of the poet means little. Occasionally, poetry by a 14 year old is more profound than the drivel generated by those adults who hang out unnecessarily in coffee shops and believe themselves 'poets.'" Pays 2 contributor's copies.

THE TULE REVIEW

P.O. Box 160406, Sacramento CA 95816. (916)451-5569. **E-mail:** tulereview@sacramentopoetrycenter.org. **Website:** www.sacramentopoetrycenter.org. **Contact:** Theresa McCourt or Linda Collins. *The Tule Review*, published 1-2 times/year, uses "poetry, book reviews, and essays concerning contemporary poetry" Wants "all styles and forms of poetry." Primarily publishes poets living in the greater Sacramento area, but accepts work from anywhere. Has published poetry by Gary Snyder, Diane DiPrima, Jack Hirschman, Julia Connor, Joyce Odam, and Douglas Blazek. *The Tule Review* is 40-60 pages, digest-sized, perfect-bound, with cover artwork. Receives about 500 poems/year, accepts about 10-20%. Press run is 500; 50 distributed free to contributors and for review. Single copy: $10 ppd; subscription: $30/year (includes *Poetry Now*, a monthly publication). Make checks payable to Sacramento Poetry Center. Acquires first North American serial rights. Publishes ms 1-6 months after acceptance. Responds in 3-4 monts. Guidelines and upcoming themes available by e-mail, or on website.

MAGAZINE NEEDS Submit up to 6 poems at a time. Lines/poem: 96 maximum. Considers previously published poems; no simultaneous submissions. Prefers e-mail (include poems in a single attachment). Include name, street, and e-mail address on each page of submission. Provide short, 5 line bio. Reads submissions year round. Submit seasonal poems 6 months in advance. Poems are circulated to an editorial board. Sometimes comments on rejected poems. Sometimes publishes theme issues. See website for other publications and contests. Pays 1 contributor's copy.

TUNDRA: THE JOURNAL OF THE SHORT POEM

22230 NE 28th Place, Sammamish WA 98074-6408. **E-mail:** welchm@aol.com. **Website:** http://sites.google.com/site/tundrashortpoem/. **Contact:** Michael Dylan Welch, editor. *Tundra: The Journal of the Short Poem* showcases all short poetry, including haiku, tanka, and other genres. Wants "short poems of 13 or fewer lines rooted in immediate and objective imagery, including haiku and tanka." Does not want religious, topical, or confessional poetry. Has published poetry by Dana Gioia, X.J. Kennedy, Jane Hirshfield, Peter Pereira, Robert Bly, and Madeleine DeFrees. *Tundra* is 128 pages, digest-sized, offset-printed, perfect-bound, with glossy cover. Receives about 14,000 poems/year, accepts less than 1%. Press run is 1,200 (700 subscribers, 10 libraries, 50 shelf sales); 10 distributed free to such places as poetry centers. Single copy: $9; subscription: $21 for 3 issues. Make checks payable to Michael Dylan Welch. Acquires first rights. Publishes ms 1 year after acceptance. Responds in 3-4 months. Guidelines available for SASE, by e-mail, or on website.

MAGAZINE NEEDS Submit 3-5 poems at a time ("up to 10 is okay if as short as haiku"). No previously published poems or simultaneous submissions. Accepts e-mail submissions (pasted into body of message; no attachments); no disk submissions. "Always include your full postal address with each e-mail submission." Cover letter is optional; "okay the first time you submit, but unnecessary thereafter unless you write something you are sure the editor needs to know. *Tundra* does not publish bios, so there's no need to include them except for the editor's information. Please include a #10 SASE with sufficient postage for return of the manuscript or for a response." Reads submissions year round. Time between acceptance and publication "varies, but is sometimes up to a year. The editor makes the sole decision, and may occasionally offer suggestions on poems whether accepted or returned. The editor will clearly indicate if he wants to see a revision." Recommends reading an issue before submitting, "but no purchase or subscription is required." Sometimes sends prepublication galleys. Acquires first rights. "Rights revert to author after publication, but we may want to include selected poems on website in the future." Reviews books/chapbooks of poetry in 500-2,000 words, single- and multi-book format. Send materials for review consideration to Michael Dylan Welch. Pays 1 contributor's copy.

TIPS "If your work centers on immediate and objective imagery, *Tundra* is interested. All poems must be 13 or fewer lines, with only very rare exceptions (where each line is very short). If you think that a haiku is merely 5-7-5 syllables, then I do not want to see your work (see 'Becoming a Haiku Poet' online at http://sites.google.com/site/graceguts/essays/becoming-a-haiku-poet for reasons why). Due to the excessive volume of inappropriate submissions for *Tundra* in the past, I now encourage only well-established poets to submit."

TURTLE MAGAZINE FOR PRESCHOOL KIDS

Children's Better Health Institute, 1100 Waterway Blvd., Indianapolis IN 46202. **Website:** www.turtlemag.org. *Turtle Magazine for Preschool Kids*, published by Childen's Better Health Institute, is a magazine for children ages 3-5. "Colorful and entertaining.. perfect for reading aloud." Wants light-hearted poetry appropriate for the age group. Reviews submissions for possible use in all Children's Better Health Institute publications. Buys all rights. Pays on publication. Responds in 3 months to queries. Sample copy for $3.99. Guidelines for #10 sase.

Closed to submissions until further notice.

MAGAZINE NEEDS We use short verse on our inside front cover and back cover. Length: 4-12 lines. Pays up to $35.

TIPS We are looking for more short rebus stories, easy science experiments, and simple, nonfiction health articles. We are trying to include more material for our youngest readers. Material must be entertaining and written from a healthy lifestyle perspective.

UP AND UNDER: THE QND REVIEW

P.O. Box 115, Hainesport NJ 08036. **E-mail:** qndpoets@yahoo.com. **Website:** www.quickanddirtypoets.com. **Contact:** Kendall Bell, editor. *Up and Under: The QND Review*, published annually in March, is "a journal with an eclectic mix of poetry: sex, death, politics, IKEA, Mars, food, and jug handles alongside a smorgasbord of other topics covered in such diverse forms as the sonnet, villanelle, haiku, and free verse. We are interested in excellent poetry with no bias between free verse or traditional forms." Does not want "greeting card verse, graphic pornography." Has published poetry by Dan Maguire, Gina Larkin, Leonard Gontarek, Autumn Konopka, John Grey and Taylor Graham. *Up and Under* is 50-60 pages, digest-sized, laser-printed, saddle-stapled, with card cover with photograph, includes ads. Receives about 300 poems/year, accepts about 30 (or 10%). Press run is 100. Single copy: $7. Chapbooks are available online or through U.S. Mail. Make checks payable to Kendall Bell. Acquires one-time rights. Publishes ms 3-6 months after acceptance. Responds in 2-3 months. Guidelines available in magazine, for SASE, or on website.

MAGAZINE NEEDS Pays 1 contributor's copy.

HOW TO CONTACT Submit up to 5 poems at a time. Lines/poem: no limit. Considers simultaneous submissions (with notification); no previously published poems. Accepts e-mail submissions (pasted into body of message). Reads submissions September 1-December 30. Poems are circulated to an editorial board. Sometimes comments on rejected poems.

URTHONA MAGAZINE

Abbey House, Abbey Road, Cambridge CB5 8HQ, England. **E-mail:** urthonamag@gmail.com. **Website:** www.urthona.com. *Urthona*, published biannually, explores the arts and Western culture from a Buddhist perspective. Wants "poetry rousing the imagination." Does not want "undigested autobiography, political, or New Age-y poems." Has published poetry by Peter Abbs, Robert Bly, and Peter Redgrove. *Urthona* is 60 pages, A4, offset-printed, saddle-stapled, with 4-color glossy cover, includes ads. Receives about 300 poems/year, accepts about 40. Press run is 1,200 (200 subscribers, plus shelf sales in Australia and America). "See website for current subscription rates." Sample (including guidelines): $7.99 USD, $8.99 CAD. Publishes ms 8 months after acceptance. Responds in 6 months.

MAGAZINE NEEDS Submit 6 poems at a time. No previously published poems or simultaneous submissions. Accepts e-mail submissions (as attachment). Cover letter is preferred. Poems are circulated to an editorial board and are read and selected by poetry editor. Other editors have right of veto. Acquires one-time rights. Reviews books/chapbooks of poetry and other magazines in 600 words. Send materials for review consideration. Pays 1 contributor's copy.

U.S. 1 WORKSHEETS

U.S. 1 Poets' Cooperative, U.S. 1 Worksheets, P.O. Box 127, Kingston NJ 08528. **E-mail:** info@US1Poets.com. **Website:** www.us1poets.com. "*U.S. 1 Worksheets*, published annually, uses high-quality poetry and, on occasion, short fiction. We prefer complex, well-written work. Has published poetry by Alicia Ostriker, BJ Ward, James Richardson, Lois Marie Harrod, and Baron Wormser. *U.S. 1 Worksheets* is 112 pages, perfect-bound, with b&w cover art. Press run is 500. Subscription: 2 years for $15; sample copy $8. Back issues $5. We are looking for well-crafted poetry with a focused point of view. Representative authors: Baron Wormser, Alicia Ostriker, Richard Jones, Bj

Ward, Lois Harrod." Responds in 3-6 months to mss. Guidelines available online.

MAGAZINE NEEDS Submit up to 5 poems at a time. Considers simultaneous submissions if indicated; no previously published poems. Submit no more than 7 pages.

ALSO OFFERS The U.S. 1 Poets' Cooperative co-sponsors (with the Princeton Public Library) a series of monthly poetry readings (U.S. 1 Poets Invite) at the Princeton Public Library. "There is no formal membership, only the willingness of participants to share their work."

TIPS "Mss are accepted from April 15-June 30 and are read by rotating editors from the cooperative. Send us something unusual, something we haven't seen before, but make sure it's poetry. Proofread carefully."

U.S. CATHOLIC

(312)236-7782. **Fax:** (312)236-8207. **E-mail:** editors@uscatholic.org. **E-mail:** submissions@uscatholic.org. **Website:** www.uscatholic.org. "*U.S. Catholic* is dedicated to the belief that it makes a difference whether you're Catholic. We invite and help our readers explore the wisdom of their faith tradition and apply their faith to the challenges of the 21st century." Buys all rights. Pays on acceptance. Publishes ms an average of 2-3 months after acceptance. Responds in 1 month to queries. Responds in 2 months to mss. Editorial lead time 8 months. Sample copy for large SASE. Guidelines by e-mail or on website.

Please include SASE with written ms.

MAGAZINE NEEDS Submit 3-5 poems at a time. Lines/poem: 50 maximum. Considers simultaneous submissions; no previously published poems. Accepts e-mail submissions (pasted into body of message; no attachments). Cover letter is preferred. "Always include SASE." Time between acceptance and publication is 3 months. Poems are circulated to an editorial board. Seldom comments on rejected poems. Guidelines available for SASE or on website. Responds in 3 months. Pays $75/poem and 5 contributor's copies. Acquires first North American serial rights. No light verse. Length: 50 lines. Pays $75.

VALLUM: NEW INTERNATIONAL POETICS

P.O. Box 598, Victoria Station, Montreal QC H3Z 2Y6, Canada. (514)937-8946. **Fax:** (514)937-8946. **E-mail:** info@vallummag.com. **Website:** www.vallummag.com. **Contact:** Joshua Auerbach and Eleni Zisimatos, editors.

"Poetry/fine arts magazine published twice/year. Publishes exciting interplay of poets and artists. Sample copies available for $10 USD. Submission guidelines available on website. Content for magazine is selected according to themes listed on website. Material is not filed but is returned by SASE. Email response is preferred. Pays $30 honorarium for accepted poems and $65 for accepted reviews or essays on poetry. Buys first North American serial rights. Copyright remains with the author. Seeking exciting, unpublished, traditional or avant-garde poetry that reflects contemporary experience."

MAGAZINE NEEDS *Vallum* is 100 pages, digest sized (7x812), digitally printed, perfect-bound, with color images on coated stock cover. Includes ads. Press run is 1,800. Single copy: $10 CDN; subscription: $17/year CDN; $21 US (shipping included). Make checks payable to *Vallum*. Does not want hate poetry.

ADDITIONAL INFORMATION "The Vallum Chapbook Series publishes 2-3 chapbooks by both well-known and emerging poets. Past editions include *Gospel of X* by George Elliott Clarke, *The Art of Fugue* by Jan Zwicky and *Address* by Franz Wright. *Vallum* does not currently accept unsolicited mss for this project."

CONTEST/AWARD OFFERINGS "Sponsors annual contest. First Prize: $500, Second Prize: $250 and publication in an issue of *Vallum*. Honourable mentions may be selected but are not eligible for cash prizes. Submit 4-5 poems. Entry fee: $20 USD / CAD (includes subscription to *Vallum*). Deadline: June 30. Guidelines available in magazine, by e-mail, and on website. Poems may be submitted in any style or on any subject; max. 4-5 poems, up to 25-40 lines per poem. Entries should be labelled 'Vallum Contest' and submitted by regular mail. Submissions are not returned. In addition to cash prizes, winners will be announced on our website and published in the forthcoming issue."

VALPARAISO POETRY REVIEW

Department of English, Valparaiso University, Valparaiso IN 46383-6493. (219)464-5278. **Fax:** (219)464-5511. **E-mail:** vpr@valpo.edu. **Website:** www.valpo.edu/vpr/. **Contact:** Edward Byrne, editor. *Valparai-*

so Poetry Review: Contemporary Poetry and Poetics, published semiannually online, accepts "submissions of unpublished poetry, book reviews, author interviews, and essays on poetry or poetics that have not yet appeared online and for which the rights belong to the author. Query for anything else." Wants poetry of any length or style, free verse or traditional forms. Has published poetry by Charles Wright, Cornelius Eady, Dorianne Laux, Dave Smith, Claudia Emerson, Billy Collins, Brian Turner, Daisy Fried, Stanley Plumly, and Annie Finch. Receives about 9,000 poems/year, accepts about 1%. Acquires one-time rights. "All rights remain with author." Publishes ms 6-12 months after acceptance. Responds in 6 weeks. Guidelines online.

MAGAZINE NEEDS Submit 3-5 poems at a time (no more than 5). Considers previously published poems ("original publication must be identified to ensure proper credit") and simultaneous submissions. Accepts e-mail submissions (pasted into body of message, no attachments); no fax or disk submissions. **Postal submissions preferred.** Cover letter is preferred. Include SASE. Reads submissions year round. Seldom comments on rejected poems. Reviews books of poetry in single- and multi-book format. Send materials for review consideration.

VEGETARIAN JOURNAL

P.O. Box 1463, Baltimore MD 21203-1463. (410)366-8343. **E-mail:** vrg@vrg.org. **Website:** www.vrg.org. **Contact:** Debra Wasserman, editor. Established 1982. *Vegetarian Journal*, published quarterly, considers poetry by children and teens only. *Vegetarian Journal* is 36 pages, magazine-sized, professionally printed, saddle-stapled, with glossy card cover. Press run is 20,000. Sample: $3. "Please, no submissions of poetry from adults; 18 and under only."The Vegetarian Resource Group offers an annual contest for ages 18 and under: $50 savings bond in 3 age categories for the best contribution on any aspect of vegetarianism. "Most entries are essay, but we would accept poetry with enthusiasm." **Deadline:** May 1 (postmark). Details available at website: http://www.vrg.org/essay.

TIPS Areas most open to freelancers are recipe section and feature articles. "Review magazine first to learn our style. Send query letter with photocopy sample of line drawings of food."

VERANDAH LITERARY & ART JOURNAL

Faculty of Arts, Deakin University, 221 Burwood Hwy., Burwood, Victoria 3125, Australia. (61)(3)9251-7134. **E-mail:** verandah@deakin.edu.au. **Website:** www.deakin.edu.au/verandah. **Contact:** Editorial team. *Verandah*, published annually in September, is "a high-quality literary journal edited by professional writing students. It aims to give voice to new and innovative writers and artists." Acquires first Australian publishing rights. Some prizes awarded. Pays 1 contributor's copy, "with prizes awarded accordingly." Sample: $20 AUD. Guidelines available on website.

"The first edition of *Verandah* was launched in 1985, beneath the shade of the 'wide verandahs' of Victoria College. Established as a student-run publication, from its inception *Verandah* has attracted high quality work by both established and emerging writers and artists for annual publication." Has published work by Christos Tsiolka, Dorothy Porter, Seamus Heaney, Les Murray, Ed Burger, and John Muk Muk Burke. *Verandah* is 120 pages, professionally printed on glossy stock, flat-spined, with full-color glossy card cover.

MAGAZINE NEEDS Length: fewer than 100 lines.

HOW TO CONTACT Submit by mail or e-mail. However, electronic version of work must be available if accepted by *Verandah*. **Do not submit work without the required submission form (available for download on website).** Reads submissions by June 1 deadline (postmark). Guidelines available on website. Some prizes awarded. Pays one contributor's copy, "with prizes awarded accordingly."

CONTEST/AWARD OFFERINGS Prizes awarded in each issue. Prize entry is automatic for Deakin students, no entry fee (student number is required). **Entry fee:** $10 AUD for first entry, $15 AUD for 3. Work submitted by non-Deakin students without an entry fee will not be considered for publication. **Deadline:** June 1. Guidelines available on website.

VERSAL

Postbus 3865, Amsterdam 1054 EJ , The Netherlands. **Website:** www.wordsinhere.com. **Contact:** Shayna Schapp, assistant art editor (artists); Megan Garr, editor (writers and designers). Annual print magazine. "*Versal*, published each May by *worsinhere*, is the only literary magazine of its kind in the Netherlands and publishes new poetry, prose, and art from around the world. *Versal* and the writers behind it are also at the forefront of a growing translocal European literary scene, which includes exciting communities in Amsterdam, Paris and Berlin. *Versal* seeks work that is urgent, involved and unexpected." Pays on publication. Publishes ms an average of 3-4 months after acceptance. Responds in 2 months. Sample copies available for $10. Guidelines available online.

MAGAZINE NEEDS "We publish writers with an instinct for language and line break, content and form that is urgent, involved, and unexpected." Has published poetry by Naomi Shihab Nye, Ben Doller, Marilyn Hacker, Emily Carr, Peter Shippy, William Doresky, Mary Miller, and Sawako Nakayasu. Receives about 1,000+ poems/year, accepts about 4%. Single copy: $15 USD. Ordering information available on website. Submit 3-5 poems at a time. Considers simultaneous submissions; no previously published poems. Pays in copies

HOW TO CONTACT Submit 3-5 poems at a time. Considers simultaneous submissions; no previously published poems. Accepts submissions online only (online submission system can be found on website. Reads submissions September 15–January 15. Time between acceptance and publication is 4-7 months. Poems are circulated to an editorial board. Sometimes comments on rejected poems. Guidelines available on website. Responds in 2 months. Sends prepublication PDF galleys. Pays 1 contributor's copy. Acquires one-time rights. Rights revert to poet upon publication.

TIPS "We ask that all writers interested in submitting work first purchase a copy (available from our website) to get an idea of *Versal*'s personality. All unsolicited submissions must be submitted through our online submission system. The link to this system is live during the submission period, which is September 15–January 15 each year. We like to see that a story is really a story, or, regardless of your definition of story, that the text has a shape. Often, we receive excellent ideas or anecdotes that have no real sense of development, evolution, or involution. Because we have a story limit of 3,000 words, the best stories have carefully considered their shape. A good shape for an 8,000 word story will rarely be successful in a 2,000-3000 word story. We prefer work that has really thought through and utilized detail/imagery which is both vivid and can carry some symbolic/metaphoric weight. While we like stories that test or challenge language and syntax, we do publish plenty of amazing stories that imply traditional syntax. Even in these stories, however, it is clear that the writers pay close attention to sound and language, which allows the stories to best display their power."

⊘ VERSE

English Department, University of Richmond, Richmond VA 23173. **Website:** http://versemag.blogspot.com. Andrew Zawacki, co-editor. **Contact:** Brian Henry. *Verse*, published 3 times/year, is "an international poetry journal which also publishes interviews with poets, essays on poetry, and book reviews." Wants "no specific kind; we look for high-quality, innovative poetry. Our focus is not only on American poetry, but on all poetry written in English, as well as translations." Has published poetry by James Tate, John Ashbery, Barbara Guest, Gustaf Sobin, and Rae Armantrout. *Verse* is 128-416 pages, digest-sized, professionally printed, perfect-bound, with card cover. Receives about 5,000 poems/year, accepts 1%. Press run is 1,000. Single copy: $10; subscription: $18 for individuals, $39 for institutions. Sample: $6. Everyone submitting work to the print magazine will receive a free copy of Verse (cover price $12-15). All contributors to the print magazine will receive at least $200 (possibly more) plus two copies and a one-year subscription.There is no reading fee for submissions to the *Verse* site and no payment for contributors to the *Verse* site. All submissions to the print magazine will also be considered for the VERSE site, so if a portfolio isn't selected for the print magazine, individual pieces still might be accepted for the VERSE site.

TIPS "Read widely and deeply. Avoid inundating a magazine with submissions; constant exposure will not increase your chances of getting accepted."

THE VIEW FROM HERE MAGAZINE

E-mail: editor@viewfromheremagazine.com; rear.view.poetry@gmail.com. **Website:** www.viewfromheremagazine.com. **Contact:** Mike French, senior editor; Kaleem Raja, managing poetry editor; Claire King, managing fiction editor. "We are a print and online literary magazine designed and edited by an international team. We bring an entertaining mix of wit and insight all packaged in beautifully designed pages." Buys first rights. Sample copy online at website or for cost of $6.89.

MAGAZINE NEEDS "The Rear View Poetry realm showcases new, emerging talent as well as the seasoned voice. Our poets are word wizards, prophets, mystics and lyricists who are afraid to demand attention by painting the world with their vision."

TIPS "Due to the amount of submissions, work sent without a brief cover letter or introduction will be dismissed."

THE VILLA

University of Wisconsin-Parkside, English Department, University of Wisconsin-Parkside, 900 Wood Rd., Box 2000, Kenosha WI 53414-2000. (262) 595-2139. **Fax:** (262) 595-2271. **E-mail:** villa@straylightmag.com. **Website:** http://straylightmag.com. Dean Karpowicz, editor. **Contact:** Appropriate genre editor (revolving editors). "*The Villa* is the web counterpart to *Straylight Literary Arts Journal.* We publish some crossover print material, but the *Villa* is centered on publishing work suited to a biannual magazine." Acquires first North American serial rights. Copyrighted. Guidelines available on website. Byline given. Publishes ms an average of 1 month after acceptance. Responds in 2 weeks on queries; 2 months on mss Editorial lead time is one month. Sample copy on website. Guidelines on website.

MAGAZINE NEEDS Needs avant-garde, free verse, haiku, light verse, traditional. Line Length: 3 minimum. No maximum. Pays when funds are available.

HOW TO CONTACT Send 3-6 poems by using submission form on website or by e-mail. Include a cover letter with a brief bio (25 words or so) with your submission.

TIPS "Please submit fiction and poetry through the website or by e-mail, and indicate you are submitting for the web magazine, and provide a short (25 word) bio with your submission. Query for reviews. We have publisher contacts and provide advanced copies."

THE VIRGINIA QUARTERLY REVIEW

P.O. Box 400223, Charlottesville VA 22904-4223. **E-mail:** vqr@vqronline.org. **Website:** www.vqronline.org. *The Virginia Quarterly Review* uses about 45-50 pages of poetry in each issue. No length or subject restrictions. Issues have largely included lyric and narrative free verse, most of which features a strong message or powerful voice. *The Virginia Quarterly Review* is 256 pages, digest-sized, flat-spined. Press run is 7,000. Responds in 1-3 months.

MAGAZINE NEEDS Submit up to 5 poems at a time. No simultaneous submissions. Accepts online submissions only at http://vqronline.org/submission/. Pays $5/line.

CONTEST/AWARD OFFERINGS Sponsors the Emily Clark Balch Prize for Poetry, an annual award of $1,000 given to the best poem or group of poems published in the *Review* during the year.

WATERWAYS: POETRY IN THE MAINSTREAM

Ten Penny Players, Inc., 393 Saint Pauls Ave., Staten Island NY 10304-2127. (718)442-7429. **Website:** www.tenpennyplayers.org. **Contact:** Barbara Fisher and Richard Spiegel, poetry editors. *Waterways: Poetry in the Mainstream*, published 11 times/year, prints work by adult poets. "We publish theme issues and are trying to increase an audience for poetry and the printed and performed word. While we do 'themes,' sometimes an idea for a future magazine is inspired by a submission, so we try to remain open to poets' inspirations. Poets should be guided, however, by the fact that we are children's and animal rights advocates and are a NYC press. We are open to reading material from people we have never published, writing in traditional and experimental poetry forms." Does not want "haiku or rhyming poetry; never use material of an explicit sexual nature." Has published poetry by Ida Fasel, Will Inman, and Richard Kostelanetz. Acquires one-time publication rights. Pays 1 contributor's copy. Responds in less than 1 month. Sample: $5. Guidelines available for SASE or on website.

MAGAZINE NEEDS *Waterways* is 40 pages, 4x7, photocopied from various type styles, saddle-stapled, with matte card cover. Back issues of *Waterways* are published online at www.tenpennyplayers.org and at scribd.com in addition to being available in the limited printing paper edition. Accepts 60% of poems submitted. Press run is 150. Subscription: $45. Sample: $5. Submit less than 10 poems at a time (for first submission). Considers simultaneous submissions. Accepts e-mail submissions (pasted into body of message). "Since we've taken the time to be very specific in our response, writers should take seriously our comments and not waste their emotional energy and our time sending material that isn't within our area of interest. Sending for our theme sheet and a sample issue and then objectively thinking about the writer's own work is practical and wise. Mss that arrive without a return envelope are not sent back." Sometimes comments on rejected poems.

HOW TO CONTACT Guidelines available for SASE or on website. Responds in less than 1 month. Pays 1 contributor's copy. Acquires one-time publication rights.

ADDITIONAL INFORMATION Ten Penny Players publishes chapbooks "by children and young adults only—not by submission—they come through our workshops in the library and schools. Adult poets are published through our Bard Press imprint, **by invitation only**. Books evolve from the relationship we develop with writers we publish in *Waterways* and to whom we would like to give more exposure."

WEBER: THE CONTEMPORARY WEST

Weber State University, 1405 University Circle, Ogden UT 84408-1405. **Website:** www.weber.edu/weberjournal. *Weber: The Contemporary West*, published 3 times/year, is "an interdisciplinary journal interested in relevant works covering a wide range of topics." Wants "three or four poems; we publish multiple poems from a poet." Does not want "poems that are flippant, prurient, sing-song, or preachy." Has published poetry by Naomi Shihab Nye, Carolyn Forche, Stephen Dunn, Billy Collins, William Kloefkorn, David Lee, Gary Gildner, and Robert Dana. *Weber* is 150 pages, offset-printed on acid-free paper, perfect-bound, with color cover. Receives about 250-300 poems/year, accepts 30-40. Press run is 1,000; 90% libraries. Subscription: $20 ($30 for institutions); $40 for outside the US. Sample: $10 (back issue). Acquires all rights. Copyright reverts to author after first printing. Publishes ms 15 months after acceptance. Responds in 6 months. Themes and guidelines available in magazine, for SASE, by e-mail, or on website.

Poetry published in *Weber* has appeared in *The Best American Poetry*.

MAGAZINE NEEDS Submit 3-4 poems at a time, 2 copies of each (one without name). Considers simultaneous submissions; no previously published poems. Cover letter is preferred. Poems are selected by an anonymous (blind) evaluation. Always sends prepublication galleys. Pays 2 contributor's copies, a year's subscription, and a small honorarium ($100-300) depending on fluctuating grant monies.

CONTEST/AWARD OFFERINGS The Dr. Sherwin W. Howard Poetry Award, a $500 cash prize, is awarded annually to the author of the best set of poems published in *Weber* during the previous year. The competition is announced each year in the Spring/Summer issue.

THE WELL TEMPERED SONNET

87 Petoskey St., Suite 120, New Hudson MI 48165. **E-mail:** thewelltemperedsonnet@yahoo.com. **Website:** http://thewelltemperedsonnet.com. **Contact:** James D. Taylor Jr., editor/publisher. *The Well Tempered Sonnet*, published annually, features compositions in sonnet form only and "caters to those who love and appreciate the form Shakespeare made famous." Does not want "erotica, blasphemy, vulgarity, or racism." Considers poetry by children and teens. *The Well Tempered Sonnet* is magazine-sized, desktop-published, spiral-bound, with attractive heavy stock cover. Subscription: $25/year. Make checks payable to James Taylor. "We encourage submissions requesting subscriptions, details included in guidelines."

MAGAZINE NEEDS Submit up to 5 poems at a time. Considers previously published poems; no simultaneous submissions. Accepts submissions by mail or e-mail. Seldom comments on rejected poems. Occasionally publishes theme issues. Guidelines available for SASE or on website. Responds ASAP. Always sends prepublication galleys.

TIPS "We encourage and try to provide the means for interaction between other sonneteers."

WEST BRANCH

Stadler Center for Poetry, Bucknell University, Lewisburg PA 17837-2029. (570)577-1853. **Fax:** (570)577-1885. **E-mail:** westbranch@bucknell.edu. **Website:** www.bucknell.edu/westbranch. *West Branch* publishes poetry, fiction, and nonfiction in both traditional and innovative styles. Buys first North American serial rights. Pays on publication. Sample copy for $3. Guidelines available online.

MAGAZINE NEEDS Pays $20-100 ($10/page).

TIPS "All submissions must be sent via our online submission manager. Please see website for guidelines. We recommend that you acquaint yourself with the magazine before submitting."

WESTERLY

Westerly Centre (M202), The University of Western Australia, 35 Stirling Hwy, Crawley WA 6009, Australia. **E-mail:** westerly@uwa.edu.au. **Website:** http://westerly.uwa.edu.au. *Westerly*, published annually in July and November, prints quality short fiction, poetry, literary critical, socio-historical articles, and book reviews with special attention given to Australia, Asia, and the Indian Ocean region. "We don't dictate to writers on rhyme, style, experimentation, or anything else. We are willing to publish short or long poems. We do assume a reasonably well-read, intelligent audience. Past issues of *Westerly* provide the best guides. Not consciously an academic magazine."

Westerly is about 200 pages, digest-sized, "electronically printed." Press run is 1,200. Subscription information available on website.

MAGAZINE NEEDS Submit up to 3 poems or 1 short story (2 if quite short-suggested maximum length 5,000 words) at a time. No simultaneous submissions. Submit via post or e-mail. Cover letters should be brief and non-confessional. All mss must show the name and address of the sender and should be single spaced in size 12 Times New Roman font. Deadline for July edition is March 31; deadline for November edition is July 31. Time between acceptance and publication may be up to 1 year depending on when work is submitted. "Please wait for a response before forwarding any additional submissions for consideration." Contributors receive payment, plus 1 complimentary copy. Acquires first publication rights; requests acknowledgment on reprints. Reviews books of poetry in multi-book format in an annual review essay. Send materials for review consideration. For further information on contributing, see website.

CONTEST/AWARD OFFERINGS The Patricia Hackett Prize (value approximately $750 AUD) is awarded annually for the best contribution published in the previous year's issue of *Westerly*.

WESTERN HUMANITIES REVIEW

University of Utah, English Department, 255 S. Central Campus Dr., Room 3500, Salt Lake City UT 84112-0494. (801)581-6070. **Fax:** (801)585-5167. **E-mail:** whr@mail.hum.utah.edu. **Website:** www.hum.utah.edu/whr. **Contact:** Dawn Lonsinger, Managing Editor. Buys one-time rights. Pays in contributor copies. Publishes ms an average of 1 year after acceptance. Sample copy for $10. Guidelines available online.

MAGAZINE NEEDS *Western Humanities Review*, published semiannually in April and October, prints poetry, fiction, and a small selection of nonfiction. Wants "quality poetry of any form, including translations." Has published poetry by Charles Simic, Olena Kalytiak Davis, Ravi Shankar, Karen Volkman, Dan Beachy-Quick, Lucie Brock-Broido, Christine Hume, and Dan Chiasson. Innovative prose poems may be submitted as fiction or non-fiction to the appropriate editor. *Western Humanities Review* is 120-160 pages, digest-sized, professionally printed on quality stock, perfect-bound, with coated card cover. Receives about 1,500 submissions/year, accepts less than 5%. Press run is 1,000. Subscription: $16 to individuals in the U.S. Sample: $10.

HOW TO CONTACT Considers simultaneous submissions but no more than 5 poems or 25 pages per reading period. No fax or e-mail submissions. Reads submissions October 1-April 1 only. Time between acceptance and publication is 1-3 issues. Managing editor and assistant editors makes an initial cut, then the poetry editor makes the final selections. Seldom comments on rejected poems. "We do not publish writer's guidelines because we think the magazine itself conveys an accurate picture of our requirements." Responds in up to 6 months. Pays 2 contributor's copies. Acquires first serial rights then rights revert to author.

CONTEST/AWARD OFFERINGS Sponsors an annual contest for Utah writers.

TIPS "Because of changes in our editorial staff, we urge familiarity with recent issues of the magazine. We do not publish writer's guidelines because we think that the magazine itself conveys an accurate picture of our requirements. Please, no e-mail submissions."

WESTVIEW: A JOURNAL OF WESTERN OKLAHOMA

Southwestern Oklahoma State University, 100 Campus Dr., Weatherford OK 73096. **E-mail:** james.silver@swosu.edu; westview@swosu.edu. *Westview: A Journal of Western Oklahoma*, published semiannually, is "particularly interested in writers from the Southwest; however, we are open to quality work by poets from elsewhere. We publish free verse, prose poems, and formal poetry."

Has published poetry by Carolynne Wright, Miller Williams, Walter McDonald, Robert Cooperman, Alicia Ostriker, and James Whitehead. *Westview* is 64 pages, magazine-sized, perfect-bound, with full-color glossy card cover. Receives about 500 poems/year; accepts 7%. Press run is 700 (300 subscribers, about 25 libraries). Subscription: $15/2 years. Sample: $6.

MAGAZINE NEEDS Submit 5 poems at a time. Cover letter is required, including biographical data for contributor's note. Comments on submissions "when close." Mss are circulated to an editorial board. Responds within 4-6 months. Pays 1 contributor's copy.

WESTWARD QUARTERLY: THE MAGAZINE OF FAMILY READING

Laudemont Press, P.O. Box 369, Hamilton IL 62341. (800)440-4043. **E-mail:** editor@wwquarterly.com. **Website:** www.wwquarterly.com. **Contact:** Shirley Anne Leonard, editor. *WestWard Quarterly: The Magazine of Family Reading* prints poetry. Wants "all forms, including rhyme—we welcome inspirational, positive, reflective, humorous material promoting nobility, compassion, and courage." Does not want "experimental or avant-garde forms, offensive language, depressing or negative poetry." Considers poetry by children and teens. Has published poetry by Wynne Alexander, Leland Jamieson, Joyce I. Johnson, Michael Keshigian, Richard Luftig, Arlene Mandell, Dennis Ross, J. Alvin Speers, Jane Stuart, Charles Waugaman. *WestWard Quarterly* is 32 pages, digest-sized, laser-printed, saddle-stapled, with inkjet color cover with scenic photos, includes ads. Receives about 1,500 poems/year, accepts about 12%. Press run is 150 (60 subscribers). Single copy: $4 ($6 foreign); subscription: $15/year ($18 foreign). Contributors to an issue may order extra copies at a discounted price. Make checks payable to Laudemont Press.

MAGAZINE NEEDS Submit up to 5 poems at a time. Lines/poem: 40 maximum. Considers previously published poems and simultaneous submissions. Prefers e-mail submissions (pasted into body of message); no disk submissions. Reads submissions year round. Submit seasonal poems 3 months in advance. Time between acceptance and publication is "months." Often comments on rejected poems. Guidelines available for SASE, by e-mail, or on website. Responds in "weeks." Pays 1 contributor's copy. Acquires one-time rights.

ALSO OFFERS "Every issue includes a 'Featured Writer' and a piece on improving writing skills and a piece on improving writing skills or writing different forms of poetry."

WHISKEY ISLAND MAGAZINE

Rhodes Tower 1636, Cleveland OH 44115. (216)687-2000. **E-mail:** whiskeyisland@csuohio.edu. **Website:** www.csuohio.edu/class/english/whiskeyisland. "This is a nonprofit literary magazine that has been published (in one form or another) by students of Cleveland State University for over 30 years. Also features the Annual Student Creative Writing Contest." Responds in 3 months to mss.

"We accept original poetry, prose, and art submissions from August 15 through May 1 of each year. We accept simultaneous submissions and ask that you identify them as such in your cover letter. No multiple submissions, please, and no previously published work either. Reporting time is about 3 months."

MAGAZINE NEEDS Submit 3-5 poems at one time. Please combine all the poems you wish to submit into one document.

TIPS "See submissions page. Include SASE. Wait at least a year before submitting again."

WHITE PELICAN REVIEW

P.O. Box 7833, Lakeland FL 33813. **Contact:** Nancy Wiegel, editor. *White Pelican Review*, published semiannually in April and October, is dedicated to printing poetry of the highest quality. Wants "writing that goes beyond competency to exceptional acts of imagination and language." Has published poetry by Paul Hostovsky, Michael Hettich, Becky Sakellariou, Lyn Lifshin, and John Grey. *White Pelican Review* is about 48 pages, digest-sized, photocopied from typescript, saddle-stapled, with matte cardstock cover. Receives about 5,000 poems/year, accepts 3%. Circulation is 500. Single copy: $4; subscription: $8/year for individuals, $10/year for institutions. Make checks payable to *White Pelican Review*. Acquires one-time rights. Publishes ms 1-6 months after acceptance. Responds in 6 months. Guidelines for SASE.

MAGAZINE NEEDS Submit 3-5 poems at a time. Lines/poem: "optimal length is 32 lines plus title, although longer poems are given full consideration." No previously published poems or simultaneous submissions. Cover letter is required. SASE is a must. "Please include name, address, telephone number, and (if available) e-mail address on each page. No handwritten poems." Reads submissions year round. Pays 1 contributor's copy.

CONTEST/AWARD OFFERINGS The Hollingsworth Prize of $100 is offered to one distinguished poem published in each issue. No contest or fee is involved.

WHITE WALL REVIEW

Department of English, Ryerson University, 10th Floor, Jorgenson Hall, 350 Victoria St., Toronto ON M5B 2K3, Canada. **E-mail:** wwr@ryerson.ca. **Web-**

site: www.ryerson.ca/wwr/. *White Wall Review*, published annually in August, focuses on printing "clearly expressed, innovative poetry and prose. No style is unacceptable." Has published poetry by Vernon Mooers and David Sidjak. *White Wall Review* is 90-144 pages, digest-sized, professionally printed, perfect-bound, with glossy card cover. Press run is 500. Subscription: $10 plus GST.

MAGAZINE NEEDS Submit up to 5 poems at a time by mail only. Length: 5 pages/piece maximum. Cover letter is required. Include short bio. Guidelines available in magazine, for SASE. Responds "as soon as possible." Pays 1 contributor's copy.

TIPS "Innovative work is especially appreciated."

WICKED ALICE

dancing girl press, 410 S. Michigan #921, Chicago IL 60605. **E-mail:** wickedalicepoetry@yahoo.com. **Website:** www.sundresspublications.com/wickedalice. **Contact:** Kristy Bowen, editor. "*Wicked Alice* is a women-centered poetry journal dedicated to publishing quality work by both sexes, depicting and exploring the female experience." Wants "work that has a strong sense of image and music. Work that is interesting and surprising, with innovative, sometimes unusual, use of language. We love humor when done well, strangenes, wackiness. Hybridity, collage, intertexuality." Does not want greeting card verse. Has published poetry by Daniela Olszewska, Rebecca Loudon, Robyn Art, Simone Muench, Brandi Homan, Karyna McGlynn. Receives about 500 poems/year, accepts about 8%. Acquires one-time rights. Responds in 1-6 months. Guidelines on website.

MAGAZINE NEEDS Wants "work that has a strong sense of image and music. Work that is interesting and surprising, with innovative, sometimes unusual, use of language. We love humor when done well, strangenes, wackiness. Hybridity, collage, intertexuality." Does not want greeting card verse.

WILD GOOSE POETRY REVIEW

Hickory NC 28235-5009. **E-mail:** asowensl@yahoo.com. **Website:** www.wildgoosepoetryreview.com. *Wild Goose Poetry Review*, published quarterly online, is a poetry journal with essays, reviews, and interviews. Wants "good contemporary poetry. No particular biases. Enjoys humor, strong imagery, strong lines, narrative, lyric, etc. Not a fan of abstraction, cliche, form for the sake of form, shock for the sake of shock. As in any good poem, everything should be purposeful."

MAGAZINE NEEDS Wants "poetry that exudes a sense of place, that is well-crafted, with an eye to imagery and an ear to music." Does not want "erotica, abstract stream-of-consciousness, or gratuitous obscenities." Has published poetry by Anthony Abbott. Receives about 1,000 poems/year, accepts about 12%. Has published poetry by Anthony Abbott, Karen Douglass, Lisa Zaran. No previously published poems or simultaneous submissions. Accepts e-mail submissions only, pasted into body of e-mail; no attachments; no disk submissions. Cover letter is preferred; include bio. Reads submissions year round. Usually responds within 1 month. Time between acceptance and publication is up to 3 months. Guidelines available on website. Rights revert to poet upon publication. Reviews books/chapbooks of poetry. Send materials for review consideration to Scott Owens

WILD VIOLET

P.O. Box 39706, Philadelphia PA 19106-9706. **E-mail:** wildvioletmagazine@yahoo.com. **Website:** www.wildviolet.net. **Contact:** Alyce Wilson, editor.

MAGAZINE NEEDS *Wild Violet*, published quarterly online, aims "to make the arts more accessible, to make a place for the arts in modern life." Wants "poetry that is well crafted, that engages thought, that challenges or uplifts the reader. We have published free verse, haiku, blank verse, and other forms. If the form suits the poem, we will consider any form." Does not want "abstract, self-involved poetry; poorly managed form; excessive rhyming; self-referential poems that do not show why the speaker is sad, happy, or in love." Has published poetry by Lyn Lifshin, Andrew H. Oerke, Erik Kestler, Anselm Brocki, Carol Frith, Richard Fammereée, Joanna Weston and Graham Burchell. Accepts about 15% of work submitted.

HOW TO CONTACT Submit 3-5 poems at a time. Considers simultaneous submissions (with notification); no previously published poems. Accepts e-mail submissions (pasted into body of message, or as text or Word attachment); no disk submissions. Cover letter is preferred. Reads submissions year round. Submit seasonal poems 3 months in advance. Time between acceptance and publication is 3 months. "Decisions on acceptance or rejection are made by the editor." Seldom comments on rejected poems, unless requested. Occasionally publishes theme issues. Guidelines available by e-mail or on website. Responds in up to 3 months. Pays by providing a bio and link on contributor's page. Requests electronic rights to publish and archive accepted works. Reviews books/chapbooks of poetry in 250 words, single-book format. Query for review consideration.

CONTEST/AWARD OFFERINGS Sponsors an annual poetry contest, offering 1st Prize: $100 and publication in *Wild Violet*; 2 Honorable Mentions will also be published. Guidelines available by e-mail or on website. **Entry fee:** $5/poem. Judged by independent judges.

TIPS "We look for stories that are well-paced and show character and plot development. Even short shorts should do more than simply paint a picture. Manuscripts stand out when the author's voice is fresh and engaging. Avoid muddying your story with too many characters and don't attempt to shock the reader with an ending you have not earned. Experiment with styles and structures, but don't resort to experimentation for its own sake."

◐ WILLARD & MAPLE

(802)860-2700 ext.2462. **E-mail:** willardandmaple@champlain.edu. 163 S. Willard St., Freeman 302, Box 34, Burlington VT 05401. (802)860-2700 ext. 2462. **E-mail:** willardandmaple@champlain.edu. **Contact:** Poetry Editor. *Willard & Maple*, published annually in spring, is "a student-run literary magazine from Champlain College's Professional Writing Program that publishes a wide array of poems, short stories, creative essays, short plays, pen & ink drawings, photographs, and computer graphics." Wants "creative work of the highest quality." Does not want any submissions over 10 typed pages in length; all submissions must be in English. Considers poetry by children and teens. Has published poetry by Frederick Zydek, Robert Cooperman, Meghan Schardt, Patrick Willwerth, and N.B.Smith. Willard & Maple is 200 pages, digest-sized, digitally printed, perfect-bound. Receives about 500 poems/year, accepts about 20%. Press run is 600 (80 subscribers, 4 libraries); 200 are distributed free to the Champlain College writing community. Single copy: $12. Contact Lulu Press for contributor's copy.

HOW TO CONTACT Submit up to 5 poems at a time. Lines/poem: 100 maximum. Considers simultaneous submissions; no previously published poems. Accepts e-mail and disk submissions. Cover letter is required. "Please provide current contact information including an e-mail address. Single-space submissions, one poem/page." Reads submissions September 1 -March 31. Time between acceptance and publication is less than 1 year. "All editors receive a blind copy to review. They meet weekly throughout the academic year. These meetings consist of the submissions being read aloud, discussed, and voted upon." Seldom comments on rejected poems. Occasionally publishes theme issues. Upcoming themes available by e-mail. Responds in less than 6 months. Pays 2 contributor's copies. Acquires one-time rights. Reviews books/chapbooks of poetry and other magazines/journals in 1,200 words. Send materials for review consideration to the poetry editor.

TIPS "The power of imagination makes us infinite."

O THE WILLOW

The Smithtown Poetry Society, P.O. Box 793, Nesconset NY 11767. (631)656-6690. **Fax:** (631)656-6690. **E-mail:** sherylmint@cs.com; editor@thesmithtownpoetrysociety.com. **Website:** www.thesmithtownpoetrysociety.com. **Contact:** Sheryl Minter, editor. *The Willow*, published quarterly online, features "new and upcoming poets alongside known poets. We also feature art, short stories, and poetry, regardless of length, that inspire intelligent thought and originality." Wants all forms of poetry. Does not want "poetry written without thought or in sing-song rhyme." Considers poetry by children and teens. Has published poetry by Marian Ford and Najwa Brax. Receives about 1,000 poems/year, accepts about 15%. Press run is 600; 300 distributed free to coffee shops. Single copy: $7; subscription: $20. Make checks payable to S. Minter.

MAGAZINE NEEDS Submit up to 3 poems at a time. Lines/poem: 30 maximum (longer poems are considered but may take longer to publish, depending on magazine space; query before submitting). Considers previously published poems; no simultaneous submissions. Accepts disk submissions; no fax or e-mail submissions. Cover letter is preferred. "All submissions must be typed, double-spaced, with submitter's name and address clearly printed. Please include a SASE for all submissions if you would like your original work returned." Reads submissions year round. Submit seasonal poems 6 months in advance. **Charges $1 reading fee.** Time between acceptance and publication is up to one year. Poems are circulated to an editorial board. Sometimes comments on rejected poems. Guidelines available in magazine, for SASE, by e-mail, or on website. Responds in 1 month.

TIPS The Smithtown Poetry Society Yearly Contest is open to all poets and offers 50% of the contest proceeds as first prize; "the other half goes to the distribution of *The Willow*." Submit up to 3 poems, 20 lines maximum each. **Entry fee:** $5. **Deadline:** June 1. Guidelines available in magazine, for SASE, or on website. "All submissions may be edited for grammar and punctuation."

WINDFALL: A JOURNAL OF POETRY OF PLACE

Windfall Press, P.O. Box 19007, Portland OR 97280-0007. **Website:** www.windfalljournal.com. **Contact:** Bill Siverly and Michael McDowell, co-editors. *Windfall: A Journal of Poetry of Place*, published semiannually in March and September, is "looking for poems of place, specifically places in the Pacific Northwest (the broad bioregion extending from the North Slope of Alaska to the San Francisco Bay Area, and from the Rocky Mountains to the Pacific Coast). 'Place' can be named or unnamed; but if unnamed, then location should be clearly implied or suggested by observed detail. The poet does not have to be living in the Pacific Northwest, but the poem does. We favor poetry based on imagery derived from sensory observation. *Windfall* also favors poetry that occurs in lines and stanzas." Does not want "language poetry, metapoetry, surrealism, 'Internet poetry' (constructed from search engine information rather than experience), abstract, or self-centered poetry of any kind." Acquires first North American serial rights. "Poem may appear in sample pages on *Windfall* website." Rights revert to poet upon publication. Pays 2 contributor's copies. Time between acceptance and publication is 2 months. Never comments on rejected poems. Responds in 2 weeks to 6 months ("depends on when poems are submitted in the biannual cycle"). Guidelines available in magazine or on website.

Has published poetry by Judith Barrington, Gloria Bird, Barbara Drake, Clem Starck, Tom Wayman, and Robert Wrigley. *Windfall* is 52 pages, digest-sized, stapled, with art on covers ("all are drawings or prints by Portland artist Sharon Bronzan"). Receives about 160 poems/year, accepts about 60. Press run is 250. Single copy: $7; subscription: $14/year. Make checks payable to Windfall Press.

MAGAZINE NEEDS Submit 5 poems at a time. Lines/poem: up to 50. Considers simultaneous submissions; no previously published poems. Accepts e-mail submissions (as attachment). Cover letter is preferred. "SASE required for submissions by US mail." Reads submissions "after the deadlines for each issue: February 1 for Spring, and August 1 for Fall."

WINDSOR REVIEW

Dept. of English, University of Windsor, Windsor ON N9B 3P4, Canada. (519)253-3000; (519) 253-4232 ext. 2290. **Fax:** (519)971-3676. **E-mail:** uwrevu@uwindsor.ca. **Website:** www.uwindsor.ca. **Contact:** Marty Gervais, art editor. Estab. 1966. Biannual 4-color literary magazine featuring poetry, short fiction and art. Circ. 400. Art guidelines free for #10 SASE with first-class postage. "We try to offer a balance of fiction and poetry distinguished by excellence." Buys one-time rights. Pays on publication. Publishes ms an average of 6 months after acceptance. Responds in 1 month to queries; 6 weeks to mss. Sample copy for $7 (US). Guidelines available online.

TIPS "Good writing, strong characters, and experimental fiction is appreciated."

WISCONSIN REVIEW

University of Wisconsin Oshkosh, 800 Algoma Blvd., Oshkosh WI 54901. (920)424-2267. **E-mail:** wisconsinreview@uwosh.edu. **Website:** www.uwosh.edu/wisconsinreview. *Wisconsin Review*, published annually, is a "contemporary poetry, prose, and art magazine run by students at the University of Wisconsin Oshkosh." Wants all forms and styles of poetry. Does not want "poetry that is racist, sexist, or unnecessarily vulgar." Considers poetry by children and teens. "Minors may submit material by including a written letter of permission from a parent or guardian." *Wisconsin Review* is 250 pages, digest-sized, perfect-bound, with 4-color glossy coverstock. Receives about 400 poetry submissions/year, accepts about 50; Press run is 2,000. Single copy: $10; subscription: $10 plus $3 extra per issue for shipments outside the U.S.

MAGAZINE NEEDS Submit up to 5 poems at a time. Does not consider previously published poems or simultaneous submissions. Accepts e-mail submissions. "Online submissions are accepted only through manuscripthub.com." Type one poem/page, single-spaced, with name and address of writer on each page. Cover letter is required. Include 3-5 sentence bio and SASE if submitting by mail. Reads submissions September through May. Submit seasonal poems 6 months in advance. Time between acceptance and publication is 6-9 months. Sometimes comments on rejected poems. Guidelines available in magazine, for SASE, by e-mail, and on website. Responds in 4-6 months. Pays 2 contributor's copies. Reviews books and chapbooks of poetry, other magazines and journals. Send materials for review consideration to the editors.

HOW TO CONTACT Send complete ms with cover letter and SASE. Sample copy and yearly subscription $10/year. Pays with 2 contributor copies. Acquires first rights. Simultaneous submissions are not accepted.

TIPS "We are open to any poetic form and style, and look for outstanding imagery, new themes, and fresh voices - poetry that induces emotions."

THE WORCESTER REVIEW

1 Ekman St., Worcester MA 01607. (508)797-4770. **E-mail:** rodgerwriter@myfairpoint.net. **Website:** wreview.homestead.com. **Contact:** Rodger Martin, managing editor. *The Worcester Review*, published annually by the Worcester County Poetry Association, encourages "critical work with a New England connection; no geographic limitation on poetry and fiction." Wants "work that is crafted, intuitively honest and empathetic." Has published poetry by Kurt Brown, Cleopatra Mathis, and Theodore Deppe. *The Worcester Review* is 160 pages, digest-sized, professionally printed in dark type on quality stock, perfect-bound, with matte card cover. Press run is 750. Subscription: $30 (includes membership in WCPA). Sample: $8.

HOW TO CONTACT Submit up to 5 poems at a time (recommend 3 or less receive the most favorable readings). Considers previously published poems "if they do not conflict with our readership" and simultaneous submissions "if notified." Cover letter is required. Include brief bio. Poems should be typed on 8×11 paper, with poet's name in upper left corner of each page. Include SASE for return of ms. Sometimes comments on rejected poems. Guidelines available for SASE or on website. Responds in up to 9 months. Pays 2 contributor's copies plus small honorarium. Acquires first rights.

TIPS "Send only one short story—reading editors do not like to read two by the same author at the same time. We will use only one. We generally look for creative work with a blend of craftsmanship, insight and empathy. This does not exclude humor. We won't print work that is shoddy in any of these areas."

THE WRITE PLACE AT THE WRITE TIME

E-mail: submissions@thewriteplaceatthewritetime.org. **Website:** www.thewriteplaceatthewritetime.org. **Contact:** Nicole M. Bouchard, Editor-in-Chief. Acquires electronic rights, archive rights and one-time reprint rights. 2 months Responds to queries in 2-4 weeks. Guidelines available on website or by e-mail: questions@thewriteplaceatthewritetime.org.

"We encourage new and seasoned writers to send in submissions for the next issue, benefit from resources we provide, read the current issue and enjoy themselves. It's a supportive writers' environment dedicated to artistic expression, learning and living the written word. We are a quarterly publication and our writers range from previously unpublished to having written for *The New York Times, Newsweek,* HBO, and *Business Week* and they come from all over the US and Europe." Frequently comments on rejected mss.

TIPS "We sponsor writer's contests—visit the website for details." Our publication is copyrighted. Sends prepublication galleys to author depending on whether the story underwent significant edits. We like to work closely with our writers. If the material is only slightly edited, then we don't.

WRITER'S BLOC

Texas A&M University-Kingsville, Dept. of Language and Literature, MSC 162, Fore Hall 201B, Kingsville TX 78363. (361)593-2640. **E-mail:** octavio.quintanilla@tamuk.edu. **Website:** www.tamuk.edu/langlit/writers-bloc.html. **Contact:** Octavio Quintanilla. *Writer's Bloc*, published annually, prints poetry, fiction, creative nonfiction, and graphic art. "About half of our pages are devoted to the works of Texas A&M University-Kingsville students and half to the works of writers and artists from all over the world." Wants quality poetry; no restrictions on content or form. *Writer's Bloc* is 96 pages, digest-sized. Press run is 300. Subscription: $7. Sample: $7.

MAGAZINE NEEDS Submit no more than 3 pages of poetry at a time ("prose poems okay"). Lines/poem: 50 maximum. No previously published poems or simultaneous submissions. No e-mail submissions; postal submissions only. "Submissions should be typed, double-spaced; SASE required for reply." Reads submissions September-February only. "Manuscripts are published upon recommendation by a staff of students and faculty." Seldom comments on rejected poems. Guidelines available in magazine or for SASE. "Acceptance letters are sent out in October." Pays 1 contributor's copy.

THE WRITER'S CHRONICLE

Association of Writers & Writing Programs (AWP), Carty House MS 1E3, George Mason University, Fairfax VA 22030-4444. (703)993-4301. **Fax:** (703)993-4302. **E-mail:** chronicle@awpwriter.org. **Website:** www.awpwriter.org. "*Writer's Chronicle* strives to: present the best essays on the craft and art of writing poetry, fiction and nonfiction; help overcome the over-specialization of the literary arts by presenting a public forum for the appreciation, debate and analysis of contemporary literature; present the diversity of accomplishments and points of view within contemporary literature; provide serious and committed writers and students of writing the best advice on how to manage their professional lives; provide writers who teach with new pedagogical approaches for their classrooms; provide the members and subscribers with a literary community as a compensation for a devotion to a difficult and lonely art; provide information on publishing opportunities, grants and awards; and promote the good works of AWP, its programs and its individual members." Buys first North American serial rights for print and Web. Pays on publication. Responds in 2 weeks to queries. Editorial lead time 3 months. Sample copy free. Guidelines free and online.

TIPS "In general, the editors look for articles that demonstrate an excellent working knowledge of literary issues and a generosity of spirit that esteems the arguments of other writers on similar topics. When writing essays on craft, do not use your own work as an example. Keep in mind that 18,000 of our readers are students or just-emerging writers. They must become good readers before they can become good writers, so we expect essays on craft to show exemmplary close readings of a variety of contemporary and older works. Essays must embody erudition, generosity, curiosity and discernment rather than self-involvement. Writers may refer to their own travails and successes if they do so modestly, in small proportion to the other examples. We look for a generosity of spirit—a general love and command of literature as well as an expert, writerly viewpoint."

WRITER'S DIGEST

F+W Media, Inc., 10151 Carver Rd., Suite #200, Cincinnati OH 45242. (513)531-2690, ext. 11483. **E-mail:** wdsubmissions@fwmedia.com. **Website:** www.writersdigest.com. "Our readers look to us for specific ideas and tips that will help them succeed, whether success means getting into print, finding personal fulfillment through writing or building and maintaining a thriving writing career and network." Buys first North American print and perpetual world digital rights. Pays 25% print reprint fee. Pays on acceptance. Publishes ms an average of 6-9 months after acceptance. Responds in 2-4 months to queries. Responds in 2-4 months to mss. Guidelines and editorial calendar available online (writersdigest.com/submissionguidelines)

The magazine does not accept or read e-queries with attachments.

TIPS "InkWell is the best place for new writers to break in. We recommend you consult our editorial calendar before pitching feature-length articles. Check our writer's guidelines for more details."

THE WRITING DISORDER

P.O. Box 93613, Los Angeles CA 90093. (323)336-5822. **E-mail:** submit@thewritingdisorder.com. **Website:** www.thewritingdisorder.com. **Contact:** C.E. Lukather, editor; Paul Garson, managing editor. Quarterly literary magazine featuring new and established writers. "*The Writing Disorder* is an online literary magazine devoted to literature, art, and culture. The mission of the magazine is to showcase new and emerging writers—particularly those in writing programs—as well as established ones. The magazine also features original artwork, photography, and comic art. Although it strives to publish original and experimental work, *The Writing Disorder* remains rooted in the classic art of storytelling." Acquires first North American serial rights. Pays on publication Publishes ms an average of 3-6 months after acceptance. Responds in 6-12 weeks to queries; 3-6 months to ms. 3 months Sample copy online. Guidelines available online.

MAGAZINE NEEDS Query. Annual print anthology of best work published online. Pays contributor's a copy of anthology to writer's whose work has been selected for inclusion.

TIPS "We are looking for work from new writers, writers in writing programs, and students and faculty of all ages."

XAVIER REVIEW

Xavier University, 1 Drexel Dr., New Orleans LA 70125-1098. **Website:** www.xula.edu/review. *Xavier Review*, published semiannually, is a journal of poetry, fiction, translations, essays, and reviews (contemporary literature) for professional writers, libraries, colleges, and universities. "Our content includes a focus on African American, Caribbean, and Southern literature, as well as works that touch on issues of religion and spirituality. We do, however, consider quality works on all themes." Has published poetry by Chris Waters, Lisa Sisk, Mark Taksa, Glenn Sheldon, Christine DeSimone, and Holly Pettit. Press run is 300. Subscription: $10/year for individuals, $15/year for institutions. Sample: $5.

MAGAZINE NEEDS Submit 3-5 poems at a time. Include SASE. "Overseas authors only may submit by e-mail attachment." Pays 2 contributor's copies; offers 40% discount on additional copies.

ADDITIONAL INFORMATION *Xavier Review* Press publishes book-length works of poetry and prose. Recent publications include *Turning Up the Volume* by Patrice Melnick and *Vespers at Mount Angel* by Stella Nesanovich. Books are available through website or by e-mailing klaborde@xula.edu. Query via e-mail: klaborde@xula.edu. **"Manuscripts should not be sent without permission of the editor."**

YEMASSEE

(803)777-2085. **Fax:** (803)777-9064. **E-mail:** editor@yemasseejournalonline.org; manager@yemasseejournalonline.org. **E-mail:** See applicable department editor. **Website:** http://yemasseejournalonline.org. Leslie Haynsworth: manager@yemasseejournalonline.org; Robbie Baden, interview editor: interviews@yemasseejournalonline.org. **Contact:** Zack O'Neill and Bhavin Tailor, co-editors. *Yemassee* publishes all genres and forms of writing, including poetry, fiction, drama, nonfiction, reviews, and interviews. Publishes in the fall and spring, printing three to five stories and twelve to fifteen poems per issue. "We tend to solicit reviews, essays, and interviews but welcome unsolicited queries. We do not favor any particular aesthetic or school of writing. Quality of writing is our only concern." "*Yemassee* is the University of South Carolina's literary journal. Our readers are interested in high quality fiction, poetry, drama, and creative nonfiction. We have no editorial slant; quality of work is our only concern." "We publish in the fall and spring, printing three to five stories and 12-15 poems per issue. We tend to solicit reviews, essays, and interviews but welcome unsolicited queries. We do not favor any particular aesthetic or school of writing. Please limit any submission to 7,500 words. Simultaneous submissions are accepted, given that you identify them as such on your cover letter and immediately notify us if the submission is accepted elsewhere. We do not consider any work that has been previously published in any form, print or electronic. We do not accept electronic submissions (exceptions are made for overseas submissions and submissions from incarcerated persons). Address your manuscripts to the appropriate genre editor. Include a cover letter with your contact information (including email address) and a SASE with sufficient postage. NO MANUSCRIPTS WILL BE RETURNED. Response time generally ranges from one to four months. Contributors receive 3 copies of the issue in which their work appears." Buys first North American serial rights, buys electronic rights. Publishes ms an average of 4-6 months after acceptance. Responds in 1-4 months to queries. Responds in 1-4 months to mss. Editorial lead time 3 months. Sample copy for $5. Guidelines available online.

Stories from *Yemassee* have been published in *New Stories From the South.*

MAGAZINE NEEDS "We are open to a variety of subjects and writing styles. We publish primarily fiction and poetry, but we are also interested in one-act plays, brief excerpts of novels, and interviews with literary figures. Our essential consideration for acceptance is the quality of the work." Semiannual. Estab. 1993. Circ. 750. Condensed novels, ethnic/multicultural, experimental, feminist, gay, historical, humor/satire, lesbian, literary, regional. "No romance, religious/inspirational, young adult/teen, children's/juvenile, erotica. Wants more experimental work." Receives 30 unsolicited mss/month. Accepts 1-3 mss/issue; 2-6 mss/year. "We read from August-May and hold ms over to the next year if they arrive in the summer." **Publishes 6 new writers/year.** Recently published work by Robert Coover, Chris Railey, Virgil Suárez, Susan Ludvigson, Kwame Dawes. Publishes short shorts. Also publishes literary essays, poetry. Send complete ms. Include estimated word count, brief bio, list of publications. Send SASE for reply, return of ms, or send disposable copy of ms. Responds in 2 weeks to queries; 4 months to mss. Accepts simultaneous submissions. Does not want workshop poems, unpolished drafts, generic/unoriginal themes, bad Hemingway. Does not want "poems of such a highly personal nature that their primary relevance is to the author; bad Ginsberg." Length: 1-120 lines. Pays in contributor copies.

HOW TO CONTACT Postal or submission manager on website. Response time generally ranges from 1-4 months. Contributors receive 2 copies of the issue in which their work appears.

CONTEST/AWARD OFFERINGS Pocataligo Poetry Contest: $500 award; submission deadline: March 15, annual. See separate listing.

◐ ZEEK: A JEWISH JOURNAL OF THOUGHT AND CULTURE

P.O. Box 1342, New York NY 10116. (212)666-1404. **Fax:** (646)843-4737. **E-mail:** zeek@zeek.net. **Website:** www.zeek.net. *Zeek: A Jewish Journal of Thought and Culture*, published monthly online and in print, seeks poetry that is "poetically daring, with shades of the numinous as it manifests in moments non-poets would ignore." Does not want "clicheéd, 'inspirational,' or ethnocentric writing; something that could serve as a greeting card, political poster, etc.; cynicism." Has published poetry by Hal Sirowitz, Rodger Kamenetz, Linda Zisquit, Yerra Sugarman, Shirley Kaufman, others. *Zeek* (print version) is 96 pages, digest-sized, perfect-bound, includes photography. Receives about 500 poems/year, accepts about 20. Press run (print) is 2,000 (200 subscribers); online version gets 60,000 hits/month. Single copy: $7; subscription: $14/year. Make checks payable to Zeek Media Inc.

MAGAZINE NEEDS Submit 3 poems at a time. Considers simultaneous submissions; no previously published poems. Accepts e-mail submissions only (pasted into body of message). Short cover letter is acceptable. Reads submissions year round. Time between acceptance and publication varies. "Poetry editor has final approval, but editorial board of four can propose or reject." Seldom comments on rejected poems. Occasionally publishes theme issues. Guidelines available on website. Responds anywhere from 1 month to 1 year. Pays 5 contributor's copies (to poets published in print edition). Acquires one-time rights. Reviews books of poetry.

O ZYLOPHONE POETRY JOURNAL

E-mail: faineugenia@yahoo.com. **Website:** poetezines.4mg.com. **Contact:** Eugenia Fain, editor. *Zylophone* is published semiannually in print and online. Wants all common formats. Has published poetry by Edward W. Cousins, Daisy Whitmore, David Barger. *Zylophone* is 16 pages, tabloid-sized, staple-bound with line drawing artwork. Receives about 60 poems/year; accepts about 12. Press run is 20. Sample copy is $6. Publishes ms 6 weeks after acceptance. Guidelines by e-mail.

MAGAZINE NEEDS Submit 3 poems at a time by e-mail. Lines/poem: 4-16 lines. Considers simultaneous submissions; no previously published work. Cover letter is preferred. Reads submissions year round. Pays oe contributor's copy.

BOOK/CHAPBOOK PUBLISHERS

Every poet dreams of publishing a collection of his or her work. However, it's surprising how many poets still envision putting out a thick, hardbound volume containing hundreds of poems. In reality, poetry books are usually slim, often paperback, with varying levels of production quality, depending on the publisher.

More common than full-length poetry books (i.e., 50-150 pages by modern standards) are poetry *chapbooks,* small editions of approximately 24-32 pages. They may be printed on quality paper with beautiful cover art on heavy stock; or they may be photocopied sheets of plain printer paper, folded and stapled or hand-sewn along the spine.

In this section you'll find a variety of presses and publishers of poetry books and chapbooks. However, it's a reflection of how poetry publishing works in the early 21st century that many book/chapbook publishing opportunities appear in the Contest & Awards section instead.

HOW LISTINGS ARE FORMATTED

Content of each listing was provided or verified by a representative of the press or publisher (poetry editor, managing editor, owner, etc.). Here is how that content is arranged in each listing:

CONTACT INFORMATION. Find the information you need to contact the press or publisher, according to what was provided for each listing: name (in bold) of the publisher/press (with areas of specialization noted in parentheses where appropriate); regular mail address; telephone number; fax number; e-mail address; website address; year the publisher/press was established; the name of the person to contact (or an editorial title); and membership in small press/publishing organization(s). (Note: If a publisher or press wants electronic submissions exclusively, no street address may be given.)

NEEDS. This section provides an overview of the publisher/press, including such helpful information as editorial preferences; how manuscripts are considered; the number and kinds of books and/or chapbooks produced; a list of recently published titles; and production information about the titles (number of pages, printing/binding details, type of cover, press run).

HOW TO CONTACT. This section states whether a poet should query with samples or send the complete manuscript; possible reading periods; reading fees, if applicable; response time; payment amount/terms; and how to order sample copies.

ADDITIONAL INFORMATION. Editors/publishers may use this section to explain other types of publishing activities (such as broadsides, postcards or anthologies), elaborate on some aspect of production—anything beyond the basic details of the submission process that readers may find of interest.

CONTEST/AWARD OFFERINGS. This section discusses prizes and competitions associated with the publisher, with either brief guidelines or a cross-reference to a separate listing in the Contests & Awards section.

TIPS. Provides direct quotes from the editor/publisher about everything from pet peeves to tips on writing to views on the state of poetry today.

GETTING STARTED, FINDING A PUBLISHER

If you don't have a publisher in mind, read randomly through the listings, making notes as you go. (Don't hesitate to write in the margins, underline, use highlighters; it also helps to flag markets that interest you with Post-It Notes). Browsing the listings is an effective way to familiarize yourself with the kind of information presented and the publishing opportunities that are available at various skill levels. If you're thinking of a specific publisher by name, however, begin with the General Index. Here all *Poet's Market* listings are alphabetized.

REFINE YOUR SEARCH

To supplement the General Index, we provide a more specific Subject Index to help you refine your marketing plan for your manuscript. Not every listing appears in one of this index, so use it only to reinforce your other research efforts.

AHSAHTA PRESS

MFA Program in Creative Writing, Boise State University, 1910 University Dr., MS 1525, Boise ID 83725. (208)426-4210. **E-mail:** ahsahta@boisestate.edu. **E-mail:** jholmes@boisestate.edu. **Website:** ahsahtapress.boisestate.edu. **Contact:** Janet Holmes, director. Publishes trade paperback originals. Pays 8% royalty on retail price. Publishes ms 2 years after acceptance. Responds in 3 months to mss. Book catalog available online.

NEEDS "We are booked years in advance and are not currently reading manuscripts, with the exception of the Sawtooth Poetry Prize competition, from which we publish 2-3 mss per year."

HOW TO CONTACT Submit complete ms. Considers multiple and simultaneous submissions. Reading period is temporarily suspended due to backlog, but the press publishes runners-up as well as winners of the Sawtooth Poetry Prize. Forthcoming, new, and backlist titles available on website. Most backlist titles: $9.95; most current titles: $17.50.

TIPS "Ahsahta's motto is that poetry is art, so our readers tend to come to us for the unexpected—poetry that makes them think, reflect, and even do something they haven't done before."

AMSTERDAM PRESS

6199 State Hwy 43, Amsterdam OH 43903. (740)543-4333. **E-mail:** editor@amsterdampress.net. **Website:** www.amsterdampress.net. **Contact:** Cindy Kelly, editor. Amsterdam Press publishes chapbooks and broadsides, wants "poetry of place, poetry grounded in sense images, poetry that leaps, and has a clear voice." Does not want "esoteric poetry that focuses on the universal." Manuscripts are selected through open submission. Chapbooks are 36 pages, laser-printed, saddle-stitched, with card cover and black and white art/graphics. Responds in 1-3 months to queries/mss.

HOW TO CONTACT Query first, with a few sample poems and a cover letter with brief bio and publication credits. Chapbook mss may include previously published poems. "Previously published poetry must be recognized on a separate page of mss."

ANAPHORA LITERARY PRESS

104 Banff Dr., Apt. 101, Edinboro PA 16412. (814)273-0004. **E-mail:** pennsylvaniajournal@gmail.com. **Website:** www.anaphoraliterary.wordpress.com. **Contact:** Anna Faktorovich, editor-in-chief (general interest). "We are actively seeking submissions at this time. The genre is not as important as the quality of work. You should have a completed full-length ms ready to be emailed or mailed upon request. In the Winter of 2010, Anaphora began accepting book-length single-author submissions. We are actively seeking single and multiple-author books in fiction (poetry, novels, and short story collections) and nonfiction (academic, legal, business, journals, edited and un-edited dissertations, biographies, and memoirs). E-mail submissions to pennsylvaniajournal@gmail.com. Profits are split 50/50% with single-author writers. There are no costs to have a book produced by Anaphora. We do not offer any free contributor copies." Format publishes in trade paperback originals and reprints; mass market paperback originals and reprints. Pays 10-30% royalty on retail price. "We currently publish journals, which are authored by several people. If we publish a novel or a critical book by a single author, we will share our profits with the author." Responds in 1 month on queries, proposals, and mss. Catalog and guidelines available online at website.

NEEDS Confession, contemporary, experimental, occult, picture books, plays, poetry, poetry in translation

HOW TO CONTACT Contact by mail or e-mail. Looking for single and multiple-author books in poetry. Query. Submit 10 sample poems. Submit complete ms.

TIPS "Our audience is academics, college students and graduates, as well as anybody who loves literature. Regardless of profits, we love publishing great books and we enjoy reading submissions. So, if you are reading this book because you love writing and hope to publish as soon as possible, send a query letter or a submission to us. But, remember—proofread your work (most of our editors are English instructors)."

ANGOOR PRESS LLC

E-mail: submissions@angoorpress.com. **Website:** www.angoorpress.com. **Contact:** Carolina Maine, Founder, Editor. Pays 5%-20% on wholesale price in royalties. 6-12 months Responds 3 months to proposals and manuscripts. No catalog available. Manuscript guidelines are free by request.

HOW TO CONTACT Submit 2-5 number of sample poems and complete manuscript.

TIPS "Christians."

ANHINGA PRESS

P.O. Box 3665, Tallahassee FL 32315. (850)422-1408. **Fax:** (850)442-6323. **E-mail:** info@anhinga.org. **Website:** www.anhinga.org. **Contact:** Rick Campbell, editor. Publishes only full-length collections of poetry (60-80 pages). No individual poems or chapbooks. Publishes hardcover and trade paperback originals. Pays 10% royalty on retail price. Offers Anhinga Prize of $2,000. Responds in 3 months to queries, proposals, and mss. Book catalog and contest for #10 SASE or online. Guidelines available online.

NEEDS Query with SASE and 10-page sample (not full ms) by mail. No e-mail queries.

ARC PUBLICATIONS

Nanholme Mill, Shaw Wood Rd., Todmorden, Lancashire OL14 6DA, England. **E-mail:** info@arcpublications.co.uk. **Website:** www.arcpublications.co.uk. Angele Jarman, director of development. **Contact:** Tony Ward, managing editor.

NEEDS Publishes "contemporary poetry from new and established writers from the UK and abroad, specializing in the work of world poets writing in English, and the work of overseas poets in translation."

HOW TO CONTACT *"At present we are not accepting submissions but keep updated by visiting the website."*

ARCTOS PRESS

P.O. Box 401, Sausalito CA 94966. (415)331-2503. **E-mail:** runes@aol.com. **Website:** www.arctospress.com. **Contact:** CB Follett, editor.

NEEDS "We publish quality, perfect-bound books and anthologies of poetry, usually theme-oriented, in runs of 1,500. as well as individual poetry collections such as *Prism*, poems by David St. John; *Fire Is Favorable to the Dreamer*, poems by Susan Terris; J.D. Whitney, Lowell Jaeger, and others.

HOW TO CONTACT *"We do not accept unsolicited manuscripts."*

ASHLAND POETRY PRESS

401 College Avenue, Ashland OH 44805. (419)289-5957. **Fax:** (419)289-5255. **E-mail:** app@ashland.edu. **Website:** www.ashland.edu/aupoetry. **Contact:** Sarah M. Wells, managing editor. Publishes trade paperback originals. Makes outright purchase of $500-1,000. Publishes book 10 months after acceptance. Responds in 1 month to queries; 6 months to mss. Book catalog available online. Guidelines available online.

NEEDS "We accept unsolicited manuscripts through the Snyder Prize competition each spring-the deadline is April 30. Judges are mindful of dedication to craftsmanship and thematic integrity."

TIPS "We rarely publish a title submitted off the transom outside of our Snyder Prize competition."

AUTUMN HOUSE PRESS

(412)381-261. **E-mail:** info@autumnhouse.org. **Website:** www.autumnhouse.org. Sharon Dilworth, fiction editor. **Contact:** Michael Simms, editor-in-chief (fiction). "We are a non-profit literary press specializing in high-quality poetry and fiction. Our editions are beautifully designed and printed, and they are distributed nationally. Approximately one-third of our sales are to college literature and creative writing classes." **Published 2 new writers last year.** Plans 2 debut novels this year. Averages 6 total titles/year; 2 fiction titles/year. Member CLMP, AWP, Academy of American Poets. "We distribute our own titles. We do extensive national promotion through ads, web-marketing, reading tours, bookfairs and conferences." "We are open to all genres. The quality of writing concerns us, not the genre." You can also learn about our annual Fiction Prize, Poetry Prize and Chapbook Award competitions, as well as our online journal, *Coal Hill Review*. (Please note that Autumn House accepts unsolicited manuscripts *only* through these competitions.) Hardcover, trade paperback, and electronic originals. Format: acid-free paper; offset printing; perfect and casebound (cloth) bound; sometimes contains illustrations. Average print order: 1,500. Debut novel print order: 1,500. Pays 7% royalty on wholesale price Pays $0-2,500 advance. 9 months from acceptance to publication Responds in 1-3 days on queries and proposals; 3 months on mss Catalog free on request Guidelines online at website; free on request; or for #10 SASE

NEEDS All full-length collections of poetry 50-80 pages in length are eligible. Since 2003, the annual Autumn House Poetry Contest has awarded publication of a full-length manuscript and $2,500 to the winner. For the 2011 contest, the preliminary judge is Thom Ward, and the final judge is Denise Duhamel.

HOW TO CONTACT Submit only through our annual contest. See guidelines online.

CONTEST/AWARD OFFERINGS The winners will receive book publication, $1,000 advance against royalties, and a $1,500 travel grant to participate in the 2012 Autumn House Master Authors Series in Pittsburgh.

TIPS "The competition to publish with Autumn House is very tough. Submit only your best work."

THE BACKWATERS PRESS

3502 N. 52nd St., Omaha NE 68104. (402)451-4052. **E-mail:** thebackwaterspress@gmail.com. **Website:** http://www.thebackwaterspress.org. **Contact:** Greg Kosmicki, editor.

NEEDS "The Backwaters Press continues to accept manuscripts for consideration for publication through the Open Submissions category. We're looking for manuscripts between 65 and 80 pages in length. **There is a $25 reading fee.**" The Backwaters Press is not currently seeking submissions in order that we may clear up our backlog. Please watch the website for notice when the press will begin accepting new material.

BEAR STAR PRESS

185 Hollow Oak Dr., Cohasset CA 95973. (530)891-0360. **Website:** www.bearstarpress.com. **Contact:** Beth Spencer, publisher/editor. "Bear Star is committed to publishing the best poetry it can attract. Each year it sponsors the Dorothy Brunsman contest, open to poets from Western and Pacific states. From time to time we add to our list other poets from our target area whose work we admire." Publishes trade paperback originals. Pays $1,000, and 25 copies to winner of annual Dorothy Brunsman contest. Publishes book 9 months after acceptance. Responds in 2 weeks to queries. Guidelines available online.

NEEDS Wants well-crafted poems. No restrictions as to form, subject matter, style, or purpose. "Poets should enter our annual book competition. Other books are occasionally solicited by publisher, sometimes from among contestants who didn't win."

HOW TO CONTACT Query and submit complete ms. Online form.

CONTEST/AWARD OFFERINGS The Dorothy Brunsman Poetry Prize awards $1,000 and publication by Bear Star Press to the best book-length ms by a poet who resides in the Western states (within Mountain or Pacific time zones, plus Alaska and Hawaii) and serves as their primary pool for finding new manuscripts. "You need not enter the contest to submit to us, but our first allegiance is to mss that come with a reading fee since they help to keep the press going."

TIPS "Send your best work, consider its arrangement. A 'wow' poem early keeps me reading."

BIRCH BOOK PRESS

P.O. Box 81, Delhi NY 13753. **Fax:** (607)746-7453. **E-mail:** birchbrook@copper.net. **Website:** www.birchbrookpress.info. **Contact:** Tom Tolnay, editor/publisher; Barbara dela Cuesta, assoc. editor. Member: American Academy of Poets, Small Press Center, Independent Book Publishers Association, American Typefounders Fellowship. Birch Brook Press "is a letterpress book printer/typesetter/designer that uses monies from these activities to publish several titles of its own each year with cultural and literary interest." Specializes in literary work, flyfishing, baseball, outdoors, theme anthologies, occasional translations of classics, and books about books. Has published *Woodstoves & Ravens* by Robert Farmer, *Shadwell Hills*, by Rebecca Lilly, *Seasons of Defiance* by Lance Lee, *And This is What Happens Next*, by Marcus Rome, *Jack's Beans* by Tom Smith, and *Tony's World*, by Barry Wallenstein. Publishes 4 paperbacks and/or hardbacks/year. Specializes "mostly in anthologies with specific themes." Books are "handset letterpress editions printed in our own shop." **Offers occasional co-op contract.** Occasionally publishes trade paperback originals. Pays modest royalty on acceptance. Acceptance to publication is 10-18 months. Responds in 3 to 6 months to mss Book catalog available online.

HOW TO CONTACT Query first with a few sample poems or chapters, or send entire ms. No e-mail submissions; submissions by postal mail only. "Must include SASE with submissions." Occasionally comments on rejected poems. Guidelines available for SASE. Pays from $5-25 for publication in anthology. Royalty on co-op contracts. Order sample books by visiting our online catalog at: www.birchbookpress.info.

TIPS "Write well on subjects of interest to BBP, such as outdoors, flyfishing, baseball, music, literary stories and occasional novellas, books about books."

BLACK LAWRENCE PRESS

115 Center Ave., Aspinwall PA 15215. **E-mail:** editors@blacklawrencepress.com. **E-mail:** submissions@blacklawrencepress.com. **Website:** www.blacklawrencepress.com. **Contact:** Diane Goettel, executive editor. Black Lawrence Press seeks "to publish intriguing books of literature: novels, short story collections, poetry. Will also publish the occasional translation (from the German and French)." Has published poetry by D.C. Berry, James Reidel, and Stefi Weisburd.

Publishes 10-12 books/year, mostly poetry and fiction. Manuscripts are selected through open submission and competition (see below). Books are 48-400 pages, offset-printed or high-quality POD, perfect-bound, with matte 4-color cover.

HOW TO CONTACT "Regular submissions are considered on a year-round basis. Please check the general submissions page on our website for the most up-to-date guidelines information before submitting." Responds in up to 4 months for mss, "sometimes longer depending on backlog." Pays royalties. Sample books available through website.

CONTEST/AWARD OFFERINGS The St. Lawrence Book Award, The Hudson Prize, and The Black River Chapbook Competition.

BLACK MOUNTAIN PRESS

109 Roberts, Asheville NC 28801. (828)273-3332. **E-mail:** jackmoe@theBlackMountainPress.com. **Website:** www.theBlackMountainPress.com. **Contact:** Jack Moe, editor (how-to, poetry); James Robiningski (short story collections, novels). Publishes hardcover, trade paperback, and electronic originals. Pays 5-10% royalty on retail price. Pays $100-500 advance. Publishes ms 5 months after acceptance. Responds in 4-6 months to mss. Book catalog and ms guidelines available online at website.

HOW TO CONTACT Submit complete ms.

TIPS "Don't be afraid of sending your anti-government, anti-religion, anti-art, anti-literature, experimental, avant-garde efforts here. But don't send your work before it's fully cooked, we do, however, enjoy fresh, natural, and sometimes even raw material, just don't send in anything that is "glowing" unless it was savaged from a FoxNews book-burning event."

BLACK OCEAN

Fax: (617)849-5678. **E-mail:** carrie@blackocean.org. **Website:** www.blackocean.org. **Contact:** Carrie Olivia Adams, poetry editor. Responds in 6 months to mss.

NEEDS Wants poetry that is well-considered, risks itself, and by its beauty and/or bravery disturbs a tiny corner of the universe. Manuscripts are selected through open submission. Books are 60+ pages.

HOW TO CONTACT Book/chapbook mss may include previously published poems. We have an open submission period in May of each year; specific guidelines are updated and posted on our website in the months preceding.

BLUE LIGHT PRESS

1563 45th Ave., San Francisco CA 94122. **E-mail:** bluelightpress@aol.com. **Website:** www.bluelightpress.com. **Contact:** Diane Frank, chief editor. "We like poems that are imagistic, emotionally honest, and push the edge—where the writer pushes through the imagery to a deeper level of insight and understanding. No rhymed poetry." Has published poetry by Alice Rogoff, Tom Centolella, Rustin Larson, Tony Krunk, Lisha Adela Garcia, Becky Sakellariou, and Christopher Buckley. "Books are elegantly designed and artistic." Chapbooks are 30 pages, digest-sized, professionally printed, with original cover art.

NEEDS "We have an online poetry workshop with a wonderful group of American and international poets—open to new members 3 times per year. Send an e-mail for info. We work in person with local poets, and will edit/critique poems by mail; $40 for four poems."

HOW TO CONTACT Does not accept e-mail submissions. **Deadlines:** January 30 full-sized ms. and June 15 for chapbooks. "Read our guidelines before sending your ms."

BLUE MOUNTAIN PRESS

Blue Mountain Arts, Inc., P.O. Box 4219, Boulder CO 80306. (800)525-0642. **E-mail:** BMPbooks@sps.com. **Website:** www.sps.com. **Contact:** Patti Wayant, editorial director. Publishes hardcover originals, trade paperback originals, electronic originals. Pays royalty on wholesale price. Publishes ms 6-8 months after acceptance. Responds in 2-4 months to queries, mss, and proposals. Guidelines available by e-mail.

NEEDS "We publish poetry appropriate for gift books, self-help books, and personal growth books. We do not publish chapbooks or literary poetry."

HOW TO CONTACT Query. Submit 10+ sample poems.

BOA EDITIONS, LTD.

250 N. Goodman St., Suite 306, Rochester NY 14607. (585)546-3410. **Fax:** (585)546-3913. **E-mail:** conners@boaeditions.org; hall@boaeditions.org. **Website:** www.boaeditions.org. Melissa Hall, Development Director/Office Manager. **Contact:** Peter Conners, editor. "BOA Editions publishes distinguished collections of poetry, fiction and poetry in translation. Our goal is to publish the finest American contemporary poetry, fiction and poetry in translation." Publishes hardcover and trade paperback originals.

Negotiates royalties. Pays variable advance. Publishes ms 18 months after acceptance. Responds in 1 week to queries; 5 months to mss. Book catalog available online. Guidelines available online.

NEEDS "Readers who, like Whitman, expect of the poet to `indicate more than the beauty and dignity which always attach to dumb real objects. .. They expect him to indicate the path between reality and their souls,' are the audience of BOA's books." BOA Editions, a Pulitzer Prize-winning, not-for-profit publishing house acclaimed for its work, reads poetry mss for the American Poets Continuum Series (new poetry by distinguished poets in mid- and late career), the Lannan Translations Selection Series (publication of 2 new collections of contemporary international poetry annually, supported by The Lannan Foundation of Santa Fe, NM), The A. Poulin, Jr. Poetry Prize (to honor a poet's first book; mss considered through competition), and The America Reader Series (short fiction and prose on poetics). Has published poetry by Naomi Shihab Nye, W.D. Snodgrass, Lucille Clifton, Brigit Pegeen Kelly, and Li-Young Lee.

HOW TO CONTACT Check website for reading periods for the American Poets Continuum Series and The Lannan Translation Selection Series. "Please adhere to the general submission guidelines for each series." Guidelines available for SASE or on website.

⊘ BOTTOM DOG PRESS, INC.

P.O. Box 425, Huron OH 44839. **E-mail:** LsmithDog@smithdocs.net. **Website:** http://smithdocs.net. Allen Frost and Laura Smith, associate editors. **Contact:** Larry Smith, director. Bottom Dog Press, Inc., "is a nonprofit literary and educational organization dedicated to publishing the best writing and art from the Midwest." Has published poetry by Jeff Gundy, Jim Daniels, Maj Ragain, Diane di Prima, and Sue Doro. Publishes the Midwest Series, Working Lives Series, and Harmony Series (105 books to date).

⊕◐ BRICK ROAD POETRY PRESS, INC.

P.O. Box 751, Columbus GA 31902. (706)649-3080. **Fax:** (706)649-3094. **E-mail:** editor@brickroadpoetrypress.com. **Website:** www.brickroadpoetrypress.com. **Contact:** Ron Self and Keith Badkowski, co-editors/founders.

NEEDS Publishes poetry only: books (single author collections), e-zine, and annual anthology. "We prefer poetry that offers a coherent human voice, a sense of humor, attentiveness to words and language, narratives with surprise twists, persona poems, and/or philosophical or spiritual themes explored through the concrete scenes and images." Does not want over-emphasis on rhyme, intentional obscurity or riddling, highfalutin vocabulary, greeting card verse, overt religious statements of faith and/or praise, and/or abstractions. Previous collections include *Dancing on the Rim*, by Clela Reed; *Possible Crocodiles*, by Barry Marks; *Damnatio Memoriae*, by Michael Meyerhofer; *Otherness*, by M. Ayodele Heath; *Etch and Blur*, by Jamie Thomas; and *Chosen*, by Toni Thomas. Publishes 10-12 poetry books/year and 1 anthology/year. Accepted poems meeting our theme requirements are published on our website. Mss accepted through open submission and competition. Books are 110 pages, print-on-demand, perfect-bound, paperback with full color art or photograph covers.

HOW TO CONTACT "We accept .doc, .rtf, or .pdf file formats. We prefer electronic submissions but will reluctantly consider hard copy submissions by mail if USPS Flat Rate Mailing Envelope is used and with the stipulation that, should the author's work be chosen for publication, an electronic version (.doc or .rtf) must be prepared in a timely manner and at the poet's expense." Please include cover letter with poetry publication/recognition highlights and something intriguing about your life story or ongoing pursuits. "We would like to develop a connection with the poet as well as the poetry." Please include the collection title in the cover letter. "We want to publish poets who are engaged in the literary community, including regular submission of work to various publications and participation in poetry readings, workshops, and writers' groups. That said, we would never rule out an emerging poet who demonstrates ability and motivation to move in that direction." Pays royalties and 15 author copies. Initial print run of 150, print-on-demand thereafter. "Submit up to 5 poems per submission via our online submission manager. Poems accepted will be published on our website. Inclusion in a print anthology will be considered as well."

CONTEST/AWARD OFFERINGS Brick Road Poetry Contest is an annual contest with a $1,000 prize. Entry fee: $25. Learn more online.

TIPS "The best way to discover all that poetry can be and to expand the limits of your own poetry is to read expansively. We recommend the following poets: Kim Addonizio, Ken Babstock, Coleman Barks, Billy Collins, Morri Creech, Alice Friman, Beth A. Gylys, Jane

Hirshfield, Jane Kenyon, Ted Kooser, Stanley Kunitz, Thomas Lux, Barry Marks, Michael Meyerhofer, Linda Pastan, Mark Strand, and Natasha D. Trethewey."

BROOKS BOOKS

3720 N. Woodridge Dr., Decatur IL 62526. **E-mail:** brooksbooks@sbcglobal.net. **Website:** www.brooksbookshaiku.com. **Contact:** Randy Brooks, editor (haiku poetry, tanka poetry). "Brooks Books, formerly High/Coo Press, publishes English-language haiku books, chapbooks, magazines, and bibliographies." Publishes hardcover, trade paperback, and electronic originals. Outright purchase based on wholesale value of 10% of a press run. Publishes ms 1 year after acceptance. Responds in 2 months to queries; 3 months to proposals and mss. Book catalog free on request or online at website. Guidelines free on request, for #10 SASE.

NEEDS "We celebrate English language haiku by promoting & publishing in a variety of media. Our goal is to share our joy of the art of reading & writing haiku through our little chapbook-size magazine, *Mayfly*. Also, we celebrate the art of haiga, lifetime contributions of haiku writers, the integration of visual arts (photography or painting) and contemporary English language haiku by leading poets.

HOW TO CONTACT Query.

TIPS "The best haiku capture human perception—moments of being alive conveyed through sensory images. They do not explain nor describe nor provide philosophical or political commentary. Haiku are gifts of the here and now, deliberately incomplete so that the reader can enter into the haiku moment to open the gift and experience the feelings and insights of that moment for his or her self. Our readership includes the haiku community, readers of contemporary poetry, teachers and students of Japanese literature and contemporary Japanese poetics."

⊕ C&R PRESS

812 Westwood Ave., Chattanooga TN 37405. (423)645-5375. **Website:** www.crpress.org. **Contact:** Chad Prevost, editorial director and publisher; Ryan G. Van Cleave, executive director and publisher. Publishes hardcover, trade paperback, mass market paperback, and electronic originals. Publishes ms 1 year after acceptance. Responds in up to 1 month on queries and proposals, 1-2 months on mss. Catalog and guidelines available online at website.

NEEDS "We remain committed to our annual first book of poetry contest, the De Novo Award. However, we also feature 1-2 monthly paid reading periods when we consider any and all poetry projects. Please check the website for updated guidelines."

HOW TO CONTACT Submit complete ms.

⊘ CALAMARI PRESS

Via Titta Scarpetta #28, Rome 00153, Italy. **E-mail:** derek@calamaripress.net. **Website:** www.calamaripress.com. Calamari Press publishes books of literary text and art. Publishes 1-2 books/year. Manuscripts are selected by invitation. Occasionally has open submission period— check website. Helps to be published in *SleepingFish* first." See separate listing in magazines/journals. Order books through the website, Powell's, or SPD. Publishes paperback originals. Pays in author's copies. Manuscript published 2-6 months after acceptance. Responds to mss in 2 weeks. Writer's guidelines on website.

NEEDS Calamari Press publishes books of literary text and art. Publishes 1-2 books/year. Manuscripts are selected by invitation. Occasionally has open submission period— check website.

HOW TO CONTACT Helps to be published in *SleepingFish* first." See separate listing in magazines/journals. Order books through the website, Powell's, or SPD.

CAROLINA WREN PRESS

(919)560-2738. **E-mail:** carolinawrenpress@earthlink.net. **Website:** www.carolinawrenpress.org. **Contact:** Andrea Selch, president. Publishes 1 poetry book/year, "usually through our poetry series. Otherwise we primarily publish women, minorities, and North Carolina authors." Has published *"a half-red sea"* by Evie Shockley, as well as poetry by William Pitt Root, Karen Leona Anderson, Jaki Shelton Green, and Erica Hunt. Guidelines available for SASE, by e-mail, or on website. Carolina Wren Press Poetry Contest for a First of Second Book. Entry Deadline: February 15, 2011. "We publish poetry, fiction, nonfiction, biography, autobiography, literary nonfiction work by, and/or about people of color, women, gay/lesbian issues, health and mental health topics in children's literature." 1 year Responds in 3 months to queries. Responds in 6 months to manuscripts. Guidelines available online.

HOW TO CONTACT Accepts e-mail queries, but send only letter and description of work; no large files. Reads unsolicited poetry submissions during the month of February. "Your best bet is to submit as part of our biennual poetry contest held in autumn of even-numbered years (e.g., 2010)." Query first to see if submissions are open. If so, send 10 pages of sample poems and cover letter with brief bio and publication credits. Include SASE for reply only. Responds to queries in 3 months; to mss in 6 months. Payment varies.

CONTEST/AWARD OFFERINGS The Carolina Wren Press Poetry Series - full-length poetry manuscripts by authors who have not had more than one full-length book published. Submissions are accepted in even-numbered autums, with a final deadline of December 1st, 2010, 2012, 2014, etc. There is a $20 reading fee for this contest. Full guidelines should be followed - check the website in late summer to see the current guidelines.

TIPS Manuscripts are read year-round, but reply time is long unless submitting for a contest.

CITY LIGHTS BOOKS

261 Columbus Ave., San Francisco CA 94133. (415)362-8193. **Fax:** (415)362-4921. **E-mail:** staff@citylights.com. **Website:** www.citylights.com. Established 1953.

NEEDS City Lights Books is the legendary paperback house that achieved prominence with the publication of Allen Ginsberg's *Howl* and other poetry of the "Beat" school. Publishes "poetry, fiction, philosophy, political and social history."

HOW TO CONTACT Does not accept unsolicted mss. No inquiries or submissions by e-mail. "Before sending a book proposal, we urge you to look at our catalog to familiarize yourself with our publication. If you feel certain that your work is appropriate to our list, then please send a query letter that includes your reésumeé (with a list of previous publications and a sample of no more than 10 pages." Include SASE for response. Responds in 3 months. Guidelines available on website.

CLEVELAND STATE UNIVERSITY POETRY CENTER

2121 Euclid Ave., RT 1841, Cleveland OH 44115. (216)687-3986. **Fax:** (216)687-6943. **E-mail:** poetrycenter@csuohio.edu. **Website:** www.csuohio.edu/poetrycenter. **Contact:** Michael Dumanis or Rita Grabowski, managers.

NEEDS The Cleveland State University Poetry Center publishes "full-length collections by established and emerging poets, through competition and solicitation, as well as occasional poetry anthologies, texts on poetics, and novellas. Eclectic in its taste and inclusive in its aesthetic, with particular interest in lyric poetry and innovative approaches to craft. Not interested in light verse, devotional verse, doggerel, or poems by poets who have not read much contemporary poetry." Recent CSU Poetry Center publications include *The Grief Performance*, by Emily Kendal Frey; *The Firestorm*, by Zach Savich; *Rust or Go Missing*, by Lily Brown; *Say So*, by Dora Malech; *Mule*, by Shane McCrae; *You Don't know What you Don't Know*, by John Bradley; *Clamor*, by Elyse Fenton; *Horse Dance Underwater*, by Helena Mesa; *Destruction Myth*, by Mathias Svalina; *Sum of Every Lost Ship*, by Allison Titus; *Trust*, by Liz Waldnere; and *Self-Portrait With Crayon*, by Allison Benis White.

HOW TO CONTACT "Most manuscripts we publish are accepted through the competitions. All manuscripts sent for competitions are considered for publication. Outside of competitions, manuscripts are accepted by solicitation only."

COACH HOUSE BOOKS

(416)979-2217. **Fax:** (416)977-1158. **E-mail:** editor@chbooks.com. **Website:** www.chbooks.com. **Contact:** Alana Wilcox, editor. Publishes trade paperback originals by Canadian authors Pays 10% royalty on retail price. 1 year Responds in 6 months to queries Guidelines available online

NEEDS Consult website for guidelines.

HOW TO CONTACT Query.

TIPS "We are not a general publisher, and publish only Canadian poetry, fiction, artist books and drama. We are interested primarily in innovative or experimental writing."

COFFEE HOUSE PRESS

79 13th NE, Suite 110, Minneapolis MN 55413. (612)338-0125. **Fax:** (612)338-4004. **E-mail:** info@coffeehousepress.org. **Website:** www.coffeehousepress.org. **Contact:** Chris Fischbach, associate publisher. This successful nonprofit small press has received numerous grants from various organizations including the NEA, the McKnight Foundation and Target. Books published by Coffee House Press have won numerous honors and awards. Example: The Book of Medicines by Linda Hogan won the Colorado Book Award for Poetry and the Lannan Foundation Literary Fellowship. Publishes hardcover and

trade paperback originals. Responds in 4-6 weeks to queries; up to 6 months to mss. Book catalog and ms guidelines online.

HOW TO CONTACT As of September 1, 2010, Coffee House Press will only accept submissions during two annual reading periods: September 1-October 31 and March 1-April 30. Submissions postmarked outside of these two reading periods will not be considered or returned. In addition, until further notice, Coffee House Press will not accept unsolicited poetry submissions. Please check our web page periodically for future updates to this policy.

TIPS Look for our books at stores and libraries to get a feel for what we like to publish. No phone calls, e-mails, or faxes."

⊘ COPPER CANYON PRESS

P.O. Box 271, Bldg. 313, Port Townsend WA 98368. (360)385-4925. **Fax:** (360)385-4985. **E-mail:** poetry@coppercanyonpress.org. **Website:** www.coppercanyonpress.org. "Copper Canyon Press is dedicated to publishing poetry in a wide range of styles and from a full range of the world's cultures." Publishes trade paperback originals and occasional cloth-bound editions. Pays royalty. Publishes book 2 years after acceptance. Responds in 4 months to queries. Book catalog & guidelines available online.

NEEDS *No unsolicited mss.*

TIPS "CCP publishes poetry exclusively and is the largest poetry publisher in the U.S. We will not review queries if guidelines are not followed. We will read queries from poets who have published a book. Please read our query guidelines."

COTEAU BOOKS

(306)777-0170. **Fax:** (306)522-5152. **E-mail:** coteau@coteaubooks.com. **Website:** www.coteaubooks.com. **Contact:** Geoffrey Ursell, publisher. "Our mission is to publish the finest in Canadian fiction, nonfiction, poetry, drama, and children's literature, with an emphasis on Saskatchewan and prairie writers. De-emphasizing science fiction, picture books." Publishes trade paperback originals and reprints Pays 10% royalty on retail price. 12 months Responds in 3 months to queries and manuscripts Book catalog available free Guidelines available online

NEEDS Coteau Books is a "small literary press that publishes poetry, fiction, drama, anthologies, criticism, young adult novels—**by Canadian writers only**." Has published *The Crooked Good* by Louise Bernice Halfe, *Wolf Tree* by Alison Calder, and *Love of Mirrors* by Gary Hyland.

HOW TO CONTACT Submit mss (80-100 poems only) typed with at least 12-point font. No simultaneous or non-Canadian submissions. No e-mail or fax submissions. Cover letter is required. Include publishing credits and bio, and SASE for return of ms. Accepts poetry mss from September 1-December 31 only. Responds to queries and mss in 4 months. Always sends prepublication galleys. Author receives 10% royalties and 10 author's copies. Order samples by sending 9x12 SASE for catalog. Submit 20-25 sample poems and complete ms.

ADDITIONAL INFORMATION Website includes title and ordering information, author interviews, awards, news and events, submission guidelines, and links.

TIPS "Look at past publications to get an idea of our editorial program. We do not publish romance, horror, or picture books but are interested in juvenile and teen fiction from Canadian authors. Submissions, even queries, must be made in hard copy only. We do not accept simultaneous/multiple submissions. Check our website for new submission timing guidelines."

⊘ DESCRIBE ADONIS PRESS

297 Blake Blvd. #4, Ottawa ON K1L 6L6, Canada. **Website:** http://vallance22.hpage.com.

NEEDS Describe Adonis Press publishes Japanese form poetry only, "especially haiku, but also senryu, renga, tanka, etc." Does not want any other form or genre of poetry. Publishes one poetry book/year, 5 chapbooks/year on average.

HOW TO CONTACT Contact with up to 12 haikus via e-mail attachment in rtf form only. E-mail is through website form at http://vallance22.hpage.com. Format should be single-spaced with three blank lines between each haiku; subject line should read: "Submission of hiaku (or haikus) by [your name]." Must use Georgia Font 11 points, or, if absolutely unable to use that, in Times New Roman 11 point font. See website for complete guidelines and contact.

DIAL BOOKS FOR YOUNG READERS

Imprint of Penguin Group USA, 345 Hudson St., New York NY 10014. (212)366-2000. **Website:** www.penguin.com/youngreaders. **Contact:** Lauri Hornik, president/publisher; Kathy Dawson, associate publisher; Kate Harrison, senior editor; Liz Waniewski, editor; Alisha Niehaus, editor; Jessica Garrison, editor; Lily Malcom, art director. "Dial Books for Young Readers publishes quality picture books for ages 18 months-6 years; lively, believable novels for middle readers and young adults; and occasional nonfiction for middle readers and young adults." Publishes hardcover originals. Pays royalty. Pays varies advance. Responds in 4-6 months to queries. Book catalog for 9 X12 envelope and 4 first-class stamps.

TIPS "Our readers are anywhere from preschool age to teenage. Picture books must have strong plots, lots of action, unusual premises, or universal themes treated with freshness and originality. Humor works well in these books. A very well-thought-out and intelligently presented book has the best chance of being taken on. Genre isn't as much of a factor as presentation."

DIVERSION PRESS

E-mail: diversionpress@yahoo.com. **Website:** www.diversionpress.com. Publishes hardcover, trade and mass market paperback originals. Pays 10% royalty on wholesale price. Publishes ms 1-2 years after acceptance. Responds in 2 weeks to queries. Responds in 1 month to proposals. Guidelines available online.

NEEDS "Poetry will be considered for anthology series and for our poetry award."

HOW TO CONTACT Submit 5 sample poems.

TIPS "Read our website and blog prior to submitting. We like short, concise queries. Tell us why your book is different, not like other books. Give us a realistic idea of what you will do to market your book—that you will actually do. We will ask for more information if we are interested."

DREAMLAND BOOKS INC.

P.O.Box 1714, Minnetonka MN 55345. (612)281-4704. **E-mail:** dreamlandbooks@inbox.com. **Website:** www.dreamlandbooks.inc.com.

NEEDS "We ARE accpeting poetry and flash story submissions for our poetry journal Cellar Door Poetry. We accept all forms of poetry, but will not publish any work that promotes violence or pornography."

ÉCRITS DES FORGES

992-A, rue Royale, Trois-Rivières QC G9A 4H9, Canada. (819)840-8492. **Website:** www.ecritsdesforges.com. **Contact:** Stéphane Despatie, director. Pays royalties of 10-20%. Responds to queries in 6 months.

NEEDS Écrits des Forges publishes poetry only that is "authentic and original as a signature. We have published poetry from more than 1,000 poets coming from most of the francophone countries: Andreé Romus (Belgium), Amadou Lamine Sall (Seéneégal), Nicole Brossard, Claude Beausoleil, Jean-Marc Desgent, and Jean-Paul Daoust (Québec)." Publishes 45-50 paperback books of poetry/year. Books are usually 80-88 pages, digest-sized, perfect-bound, with 2-color covers with art.

HOW TO CONTACT Query first with a few sample poems and a cover letter with brief bio and publication credits. Order sample books by writing or faxing.

ELOHI GADUGI / THE HABIT OF RAINY NIGHTS PRESS

900 NE 81st Ave., #209, Portland OR 97213. **E-mail:** editors@elohigadugi.org. **Website:** http://rainynightspress.org. **Contact:** Patricia McLean, nonfiction editor (narrative nonfiction); Duane Poncy, fiction editor (general fiction, native American); Ger Killeen, poetry editor. Format publishes in electronic originals Pays 20-25% royalty on retail price (60-70% of wholesale for e-books). Publishes ms 9-12 months after acceptance. Responds in 1-2 months on queries; 2-3 months on mss. Catalog and guidelines available online at website.

NEEDS "All poetry should have a strong narrative quality. Have something to say!" No academic or experimental poetry.

HOW TO CONTACT Submit 5-6 sample poems; submit complete ms.

TIPS "Respect your work. Make sure it is ready for publication. Polish, polish, polish. We cannot consider books that need a lot of basic cleaning up. Have something to say—we are not interested in using up vital resources to publish fluff."

ENITHARMON PRESS

26B Caversham Rd., London NW5 2DU, England. (44)(207)482-5967. **Fax:** (44)(207)284-1787. **E-mail:** info@enithamron.co.uk. **Website:** www.enitharmon.co.uk. **Contact:** Stephen Stuart-Smith, poetry editor. Enitharmon is a publisher of fine editions of poetry and literary criticism in paperback, and some hardback, editions. "We publish about 15 volumes/year, averaging 100 pages each." Has published poetry by John Heath-Stubbs, Ted Hughes, David Gascoyne, Thom Gunn, Ruth Pitter, and Anthony Thwaite.

FABER & FABER INC.

Farrar, Straus & Giroux, 18 W. 18th St., New York NY 10011. (212)741-6900. **Website:** us.macmillan.com/faberandfaber.aspx. Responds in 6-8 weeks.

HOW TO CONTACT "All submissions must be submitted through the mail—we do not accept electronic submissions, or submissions delivered in person. Please include a cover letter describing your submission, along with the first 50 pages of the manuscript. If you are submitting poems, please include 3-4 poems."

FARRAR, STRAUS & GIROUX/ BOOKS FOR YOUNG READERS

Books for Young Readers, 175 Fifth Ave., New York NY 10010. (646)307-5151. **Website:** www.fsgkidsbooks.com. **Contact:** Children's Editorial Department. (Specialized: children) "We publish original and well-written material for all ages." Publishes hardcover originals and trade paperback reprints Pays 2-6% royalty on retail price for paperbacks, 3-10% for hardcovers. Pays $3,000-25,000 advance. 18 months Responds in 2 months to queries. Responds in 3 months to manuscripts For catalog fax request or email to: childrens.publicity@fsgbooks.com Guidelines available online

NEEDS Publishes one book of children's poetry "every once in a while," in trade hardcover only. Open to book-length submissions of children's poetry only. Has published Valerie Worth's *Peacock and Other Poems*, Tony Johnston's *An Old Shell*, and Helen Frost's *Keesha's House* (a novel in poems).

HOW TO CONTACT Query first with sample poems and cover letter with brief bio and publication credits. Considers simultaneous submissions. Seldom comments on rejected poems. Send SASE for reply. Responds to queries in up to 2 months, to mss in up to 4 months. "We pay an advance against royalties; the amount depends on whether or not the poems are illustrated, etc." Also pays 10 author's copies.

TIPS Audience is full age range, preschool to young adult. Specializes in literary fiction.

FENCE BOOKS

(518)591-8162. **E-mail:** fence.fencebooks@gmail.com; robfence@gmail.com. **Website:** www.fenceportal.org. **Contact:** Rob Arnold, Submissions Manager. "*Fence is closed to submissions right now.* We'll have another reading period in the Spring. Fence Books offers 2 book contests (in addition to the National Poetry Series) with 2 sets of guidelines and entry forms on our website." Hardcover originals. Guidelines available online.

NEEDS Enter National Poetry Series Contest. See Open Competition Guidelines online. Also the annual Fence Books Motherwell Prize 2011 ($5,000) for a first or second book of poetry by a woman. Submit 48-60 pages during the month of November; and Fence Modern Poets Series 2011, for a poet writing in English at any stage in his or her career. $25 entry fee.

HOW TO CONTACT Submissions may be sent through regular USPS mail, UPS, Fedex-type couriers, or certified mail.

TIPS "At present Fence Books is a self-selecting publisher; mss come to our attention through our contests and through editors' investigations. We hope to become open to submissions of poetry and fiction mss in the near future."

FIRST EDITION DESIGN PUBLISHING

5202 Old Ashwood Dr., Sarasota FL 34233. (941)921-2607. **Fax:** (617)249-1694. **E-mail:** support@firsteditiondesign.com. **E-mail:** submission@firsteditiondesign.com. **Website:** www.firsteditiondesignpublishing.com. **Contact:** Deborah E. Gordon, executive editor; Tom Gahan, marketing director. Pays royalty 30-70% on retail price. Accept to publish time is one week to two months. Send SAE for catalog. Guidelines available free on request or online at website.

HOW TO CONTACT Submit complete ms electronically.

TIPS "Follow our FAQs listed on our website."

FLARESTACK POETS

P.O. Box 14779, Birmingham, West Midlands B13 3GU, United Kingdom. **E-mail:** meria@btinternet.com; jacquierowe@hotmail.co.uk. **Website:** www.flarestackpoets.co.uk. **Contact:** Meredith Andrea and Jacqui Rowe. Pays 25% royalty and 6 contributor's copies. Responds in 6 weeks.

NEEDS Flarestack Poets wants "poems that dare outside current trends, even against the grain." Does not want "poems that fail to engage with either language or feeling." First chapbooks appearing in Autumn 2009. Publishes 8 chapbooks/year and 1 anthology. Manuscripts are selected through open submission and competition. "Our first chapbooks are winners of the 2009 Flarestack Poets Pamphlet competition. Thereafter we will consider open submissions." Chapbooks are 20-30 pages, professional photocopy, saddle-stitched, card cover.

HOW TO CONTACT Query first with a few sample poems and a cover letter with brief bio and publication credits. Ms may include previously published poems.

FLOATING BRIDGE PRESS

PO Box 18814, Seattle WA 98118. **E-mail:** floatingbridgepress@yahoo.com. **Website:** www.floatingbridgepress.org.

NEEDS Floating Bridge Press publishes chapbooks and anthologies by Washington State poets, selected through an annual competition (see below). Has published *After* by Nancy Pagh, *In the Convent We Become Clouds* by Annette Spaulding-Convy, *Toccata & Fugue* by Timothy Kelly, and *The Former St. Christopher* by Michael Bonacci, among others. The press also publishes *Floating Bridge Review*, an annual anthology featuring the work of Washington State poets. *Floating Bridge Review* is 86-144 pages, digest-sized, offset-printed, perfect-bound, with glossy cardstock cover. For a sample chapbook or anthology, send $13 postpaid.

CONTEST/AWARD OFFERINGS For consideration, **Washington State poets only** should submit a chapbook ms of 20-24 pages of poetry. In addition to publication, the winner receives $500, 15 author's copies, and a reading in the Seattle area. All entrants receive a copy of the winning chapbook and will be considered for inclusion in *Floating Bridge Review*. Poet's name must not appear on the ms. Include a separate page with ms title, poet's name, address, phone number, and acknowledgments of any previous publications. Include SASE for results only; mss will not be returned. **Entry fee:** $12. **Deadline:** usual reading period is November 1-February 15 (postmark). Considers previously published individual poems and simultaneous submissions. Mss are judged anonymously.

FOUR WAY BOOKS

Box 535, Village Station, New York NY 10014. **E-mail:** fourwayeditors@fourwaybooks.com; editors@fourwaybooks.com. **Website:** www.fourwaybooks.com. Established 1993. **Contact:** Martha Rhodes, director.

NEEDS Four Way Books publishes poetry and short fiction. Considers full-length poetry mss only. Does not want individual poems or poetry intended for children/young readers. Has published poetry by D. Nurkse, Noelle Kocot, Susan Wheeler, Nancy Mitchell, Henry Israeli, and Paul Jenkins. Publishes 8-11 books a year. Manuscripts are selected through open submission and through competition. Books are about 70 pages, offset-printed digitally, perfect-bound, with paperback binding, art/graphics on covers.

HOW TO CONTACT See website for complete submission guidelines and open reading period. Book mss may include previously published poems. Responds to submissions in 4 months. Payment varies. Order sample books from Four Way Books online or through bookstores.

FUTURECYCLE PRESS

313 Pan Will Rd., Mineral Bluff GA 30559. (706)622-4454. **E-mail:** submissions@futurecycle.org. **Website:** www.futurecycle.org. **Contact:** Robert S. King, director/editor-in-chief. Pays 10% royalty and 25 author's copies. Responds to mss in 3 months. Guidelines available online at website.

NEEDS Wants "poetry from highly skilled poets, whether well known or emerging. With a few exceptions, we are eclectic in our editorial tastes." Does not want concrete or visual poetry. Has published David Chorlton, John Laue, Temple Cone, Neil Carpathios, Tania Runyan, Timothy Martin, Joanne Lowery. Publishes 4 poetry books/year and 2 chapbooks/year. Ms. selected through open submission and competition. "We read unsolicited mss. but also conduct a yearly poetry book competition." Books are 60-90 pages; offset print, perfect-bound, with glossy, full color cover stock, b&w inside. Chapbooks are 20-40 pages, offset print, saddle-stitched.

HOW TO CONTACT Submit complete ms, no need to query.

GAMBIT PUBLISHING

1725 W. Glenlake Ave., #1W, Chicago IL 60660. **E-mail:** gailglaser@gambitpublishingonline.com. **E-mail:** editor@gambitpublishingonline.com. **Website:** www.gambitpublishingonline.com. **Contact:** Gail Glaser, editor (film, biography, popular culture). Publishes hardcover originals and reprints; trade paperback originals and reprints; mass market paperback originals and reprints; electronic originals and reprints. Pays 10-60% royalty on retail price. No advance. Publishes ms 3 months after acceptance. Responds in 1 month on queries, proposals, and mss. Catalog available online and for #10 SASE. Guidelines free by email at website.

NEEDS "We are open to most poetry."

HOW TO CONTACT Query. Submit 3 sample poems. Submit complete ms.

GERTRUDE PRESS

P.O. Box 83948, Portland OR 97283. (503)515-8252. **E-mail:** edelehoy@fc.edu. **Website:** www.gertrudepress.org. **Contact:** Justus Ballard (all fiction). (Specialized: gay, lesbian, bisexual, transgendered, queer-identified & allied)

NEEDS Gertrude Press, a nonprofit 501(c)(3) organization, showcases and develops "the creative talents of lesbian, gay, bisexual, trans, queer-identified, and allied individuals." Has published *Bone Knowing* by Kate Grant. Gertrude Press publishes 2 chapbooks/year (1 fiction, 1 poetry) as well as *Gertrude*, a semi-annual literary journal (see separate listing in Magazines/Journals). Manuscripts are chosen through competition only (see below). Chapbooks are 20-24 pages, offset-printed, saddle-stapled, with cardstock cover with art. Submit up to 6 poems of any subject matter. There is no line limit; however, poems less than 60 lines are preferable.

HOW TO CONTACT Refer to guidelines for Gertrude Press Poetry Chapbook Contest. Order sample chapbooks for $10.

TIPS Sponsors poetry and fiction chapbook contest. Prize is $50 and 50 contributor's copies. Submission guidelines and fee information on website. "Read the journal and sample published work. We are not impressed by pages of publications; your work should speak for itself."

GHOST PONY PRESS

P.O. Box 260113, Madison WI 53726. **E-mail:** ghostponypress@hotmail.com. **Contact:** Ingrid Swanberg, editor/publisher. Ghost Pony Press has published 3 books of poetry by proóspero saiíz, including *the bird of nothing & other poems* (168 pages, 7x10, with sewn and wrapped binding; paperback available for $20, signed and numbered edition for $35). Also published *zen concrete & etc.* by d.a. levy (268 pages, magazine-sized, perfect-bound, illustrated; paperback available for $27.50).

HOW TO CONTACT Query first, with a few sample poems (5-10) and cover letter with brief bio and publication credits. Include SASE. Considers previously published material for book publication. Accepts submissions by postal mail only; no e-mail submissions. Editor sometimes comments briefly on rejected poems. No promised response time. "We currently have a considerable backlog."

GHOST ROAD PRESS

820 S. Monaco Pkwy, #288, Denver CO 80224. (303)758-7623. **E-mail:** matt.grp@gmail.com. **Website:** ghostroadpress.com.

HOW TO CONTACT *Not currently accepting submissions.* Query via e-mail. "Send an attachment (word or.rtf only) that includes a complete synopsis, a description of your marketing plan and platform and samples. To view a complete list of our titles and changing submission guidelines, please visit website." Responds in 2-3 months. Accepts simultaneous submissions.

GINNINDERRA PRESS

P.O. Box 3461, Port Adelaide 5015, Australia. (61)(2)6258-9060. **Fax:** (61)(2)6258-9069. **E-mail:** stephen@ginninderrapress.com.au. **Website:** www.ginninderrapress.com.au. **Contact:** Stephen Matthews, publisher. Ginninderra Press works "to give publishing opportunities to new writers." Has published poetry by Alan Gould and Geoff Page. Books are usually up to 72 pages, A5, laser-printed, saddle-stapled or thermal-bound, with board covers. Responds to queries within 1 week; mss in 2 months.

HOW TO CONTACT Query first, with a few sample poems and a cover letter with brief bio and publication credits. Considers previously published poems; no simultaneous submissions.

GOOSE LANE EDITIONS

(506)450-4251. **Fax:** (506)459-4991. **Website:** www.gooselane.com/submissions.php. **Contact:** Angela Williams, publishing assistant. "Goose Lane publishes literary fiction and nonfiction from well-read and highly skilled Canadian authors." Publishes hardcover and paperback originals and occasional reprints. Pays 8-10% royalty on retail price. Pays $500-3,000, negotiable advance. Responds in 6 months to queries.

NEEDS Goose Lane is a small literary press publishing Canadian fiction, poetry, and nonfiction. **Considers mss by Canadian poets only.** Receives about 400 mss/year, publishes 15-20 books/year, 4 of which are poetry collections. Has published *Beatitudes* by Herménégilde Chiasson and *I & I* by George Elliott Clarke.

HOW TO CONTACT "Call to inquire whether we are reading submissions." Accepts submissions by postal mail only. Guidelines available on website. Always sends prepublication galleys. Authors may receive royalties of up to 10% of retail price on all copies sold. Copies available to author at 40% discount.

TIPS "Writers should send us outlines and samples of books that show a very well-read author with highly developed literary skills. Our books are almost all by Canadians living in Canada; we seldom consider submissions from outside Canada. If I were a writer trying to market a book today, I would contact the targeted publisher with a query letter and synopsis, and request manuscript guidelines. Purchase a recent book from the publisher in a relevant area, if possible. Always send an SASE with IRCs or suffient return postage in Canadian stamps for reply to your query and for any material you'd like returned should it not suit our needs. Specializes in high quality Canadian literary fiction, poetry, and nonfiction. We consider submissions from outside Canada only when the author is Canadian and the book is of extraordinary interest to Canadian readers. We do not publish books for children or for the young adult market."

GOTHIC CHAPBOOK SERIES

2272 Quail Oak, Baton Rouge LA 70808. **E-mail:** gothicpt12@aol.com. **Website:** www.gwcgothicpress.com. Gothic Press publishes gothic, horror, and dark fantasy poetry in their Gothic Chapbook series. Wants poetry in "any form or style as long as gothic or horror elements are present." Does not want science fiction. Has published Bruce Boston, Joey Froehlich, Scott C. Hocstad. Manuscripts are selected through open submission. Chapbooks are 10-80 pages, offset, saddle-stapled, with cardstock cover or interior illustration by commission. Send samples of art.

HOW TO CONTACT *Gothic Press no longer accepts unsolicited submissions, and seeks chapbooks by invitation only.*

TIPS "Know gothic and horror literature well."

GRAYWOLF PRESS

250 Third Ave. N., Suite 600, Minneapolis MN 55401. **E-mail:** wolves@graywolfpress.org. **Website:** www.graywolfpress.org. **Contact:** Katie Dublinski, editorial manager (nonfiction, fiction). "Graywolf Press is an independent, nonprofit publisher dedicated to the creation and promotion of thoughtful and imaginative contemporary literature essential to a vital and diverse culture." Publishes trade cloth and paperback originals. Pays royalty on retail price. Pays $1,000-25,000 advance. Responds in 3 months to queries. Book catalog available free. Guidelines online.

NEEDS Graywolf Press is considered one of the nation's leading nonprofit literary publishers. "Graywolf introduces and promotes some of the most exciting and creative writers of our times." Considers only mss by poets widely published in magazines and journals of merit; **does not generally consider unsolicited mss but considers queries.** Has published poetry by Elizabeth Alexander, Vijay Seshadri, Tess Gallagher, Tony Hoagland, Matthea Harvey, D.A. Powell, and many more. Publishes around 9 collections of poetry, 1-2 collections of poetry in translation, and 1-2 collections of essays on poetry/year. "We are interested in linguistically challenging work." Query with SASE.

HOW TO CONTACT *No unsolicited mss.* Query first, with 10 pages of poetry (as a sample from the ms) and cover letter with brief bio and publication credits through online submission form. See website for guidelines. SASE required for reply. No e-mail queries. Reads queries in January, May, and September. Responds to queries in 3-6 months. Order sample books through website, or request catalog through online submission form.

⊘✪ GUERNICA EDITIONS

Box 117, Station P, Toronto ON M5S 2S6, Canada. (416)658-9888. **Fax:** (416)657-8885. **E-mail:** antoniodalfonso@sympatico.ca. **Website:** www.guernicaeditions.com. **Contact:** Antonio D'Alfonso, editor/publisher (poetry, nonfiction, novels). "Guernica Editions is an independent press dedicated to the bridging of cultures. We do original and translations of fine works. We are seeking essays on authors and translations with less emphasis on poetry." Publishes trade paperback originals, reprints, and software Pays 8-10% royalty on retail price, or makes outright purchase of $200-5,000. Pays $200-2,000 advance. 15 months Responds in 1 month to queries. Responds in 6 months to proposals. Responds in 1 year to manuscripts. Book catalog available online.

NEEDS "We wish to bring together the different and often divergent voices that exist in Canada and the U.S. We are interested in translations. We are mostly interested in poetry and essays on pluriculturalism." Has published poetry by Pier Paolo Pasolini, Pasquale Verdichio, Carole David, Jean-Marc Desgent, Gilles Cyr, Claudine Bertrand, Paul Beélanger, Denise Desaulets. Feminist, gay/lesbian, literary, multicultural, poetry in translation. We wish to have writers in translation. Any writer who has translated Italian poetry is welcomed. Full books only. No single poems by different authors, unless modern, and used as an anthology. First books will have no place in the next couple of years.

HOW TO CONTACT Query with 1-2 pages of sample poems. Send SASE (Canadian stamps only) or SAE and IRCs for catalog. Query.

HIPPOPOTAMUS PRESS

22 Whitewell Rd., Frome Somerset BA11 4EL, UK. (44)(173)466-6653. **E-mail:** rjhippopress@aol.com. **Contact:** R. John, editor; M. Pargitter (poetry); Anna Martin (translation). "Hippopotamus Press publishes first, full collections of verse by those well represented in the mainstream poetry magazines of the English-speaking world." Publishes hardcover and trade paperback originals. Pays 7 ½-10% royalty on retail price. Pays advance. Publishes book 10 months after acceptance. Responds in 1 month to queries. Book catalog available free.

NEEDS "Read one of our authors—Poets often make the mistake of submitting poetry without knowing the type of verse we publish."

HOW TO CONTACT Query and submit complete ms.

TIPS "We publish books for a literate audience. We have a strong link to the Modernist tradition. Read what we publish."

HOLIDAY HOUSE, INC.

(212)688-0085. **Fax:** (212)421-6134. **E-mail:** info@holidayhouse.com. **Website:** holidayhouse.com. **Contact:** Mary Cash, editor-in-chief. "Holiday House publishes children's and young adult books for the school and library markets. We have a commitment to publishing first-time authors and illustrators. We specialize in quality hardcovers from picture books to young adult, both fiction and nonfiction, primarily for the school and library market." Publishes hardcover originals and paperback reprints. Pays royalty on list price, range varies. Agent's royalty. 1-2 years Responds in 4 months. Guidelines for #10 SASE.

NEEDS A trade children's book house. Has published hardcover books for children by John Updike and Walter Dean Myers. Publishes one poetry book/year, averaging 32 pages.

HOW TO CONTACT "The acceptance of complete book mss of high-quality children's poetry is limited." Please send the entire manuscript, whether submitting a picture book or novel by mail. Does not accept submissions by e-mail or fax.

TIPS "We need manuscripts with strong stories and writing."

HOUSE OF ANANSI PRESS

110 Spadina Ave., Suite 801, Toronto ON M5V 2K4, Canada. (416)363-4343. **Fax:** (416)363-1017. **Website:** www.anansi.ca. Pays 8-10% royalties. Pays $750 advance and 10 author's copies. Responds to queries within 1 year, to mss (if invited) within 4 months.

NEEDS House of Anansi publishes literary fiction and poetry by Canadian and international writers. "We seek to balance the list between well-known and emerging writers, with an interest in writing by Canadians of all backgrounds. We publish Canadian poetry only, and poets must have a substantial publication record—if not in books, then definitely in journals and magazines of repute." Does not want "children's poetry or poetry by previously unpublished poets." Has published *Power Politics* by Margaret Atwood and *Ruin & Beauty* by Patricia Young. Books are generally 96-144 pages, trade paperbacks with French sleeves, with matte covers.

HOW TO CONTACT Canadian poets should query first with 10 sample poems (typed double-spaced) and a cover letter with brief bio and publication credits. Considers simultaneous submissions. Poems are circulated to an editorial board. Often comments on rejected poems.

ILIUM PRESS

2407 S. Sonora Dr., Spokane WA 99037-9011. (509)928-7950. **E-mail:** contact@iliumpress.com; submissions@iliumpress.com. **Website:** www.iliumpress.com. **Contact:** John Lemon, Owner/editor (literature, epic poetry, how-to). Format publishes in trade paperback originals and reprints, electronic originals and reprints. Pays 20%-50% royalties on wholesale price. 6 months Responds in 1 month on queries/proposals and 3 months on manuscripts. Guidelines available on website www.iliumpress.com.

NEEDS "I am primarily interested in epic, narrative book-length poems. See website for details."

HOW TO CONTACT Query. Submit 3 sample chapters.

TIPS "Read submission guidelines on my website."

ITALICA PRESS

595 Main St., Suite 605, New York NY 10044-0047. (212)935-4230. **Fax:** (212)838-7812. **E-mail:** inquiries@italicapress.com. **Website:** www.italicapress.com. **Contact:** Ronald G. Musto and Eileen Gardiner, publishers. "Italica Press publishes English translations of modern Italian fiction and medieval and

Renaissance nonfiction." Publishes trade paperback originals Pays 7-15% royalty on wholesale price; author's copies. 1 year Responds in 1 month to queries. Responds in 4 months to manuscripts. Book catalog and guidelines available online.

NEEDS Italica is a small press publisher of English translations of Italian works in paperbacks, averaging 175 pages. Has published *Contemporary Italian Women Poets*, a dual-language (English/Italian) anthology edited and translated by Anzia Sartini Blum and Lara Trubowitz, and *Women Poets of the Italian Renaissance*, a dual-language anthology, edited by Laura Anna Stortoni, translated by Laura Anna Stortoni and Mary Prentice Lillie. Poetry titles are always translations and generally dual language.

HOW TO CONTACT Query with 10 sample translations of medieval and Renaissance Italian poets. Include cover letter, bio, and list of publications. Accepts simultaneous submissions, but translation should not be "totally" previously published. Accepts e-mail submissions; no fax submissions. Responds to queries in 3 weeks, to mss in 3 months. Always sends prepublication galleys. Pays 7-15% royalties plus 10 author's copies. Acquires English language rights.

TIPS "We are interested in considering a wide variety of medieval and Renaissance topics (not historical fiction), and for modern works we are only interested in translations from Italian fiction by well-known Italian authors." *Only* fiction that has been previously published in Italian. A *brief* call saves a lot of postage. 90% of proposals we receive are completely off base—but we are very interested in things that are right on target. Please send return postage if you want your ms returned.

ALICE JAMES BOOKS

238 Main St., Farmington ME 04938. (207)778-7071. **Fax:** (207)778-7766. **E-mail:** interns@alicejamesbooks.org; Frank@alicejamesbooks.org. **Website:** www.alicejamesbooks.org. **Contact:** Frank Giampietro, managing editor; Carey Salerno, executive director; Meg Willing, editorial assistant. "Alice James Books is a nonprofit cooperative poetry press. The founders' objectives were to give women access to publishing and to involve authors in the publishing process. The cooperative selects mss for publication through both regional and national competitions." Publishes trade paperback originals. Pays through competition awards. Publishes ms 1 year after acceptance. Responds promptly to queries; 4 months to mss. Book catalog for free or on website. Guidelines for #10 SASE or on website.

NEEDS Seeks to publish the best contemporary poetry by both established and beginning poets, with particular emphasis on involving poets in the publishing process. Has published poetry by Jane Kenyon, Jean Valentine, B.H. Fairchild, and Matthea Harvey. Publishes flat-spined paperbacks of high quality, both in production and contents. Does not want children's poetry or light verse. Publishes 6 paperback books/year, 80 pages each, in editions of 1,500.

HOW TO CONTACT Query.

TIPS "Send SASE for contest guidelines or check website. Do not send work without consulting current guidelines."

THE JOHNS HOPKINS UNIVERSITY PRESS

2715 N. Charles St., Baltimore MD 21218. (410)516-6900. **Fax:** (410)516-6968. **E-mail:** jmm@press.jhu.edu. **Website:** www.press.jhu.edu. **Contact:** Jacqueline C. Wehmueller, executive editor (consumer health, psychology and psychiatry, and history of medicine; jcw@press.jhu.edu); Matthew McAdam, editor (mxm@jhu@press.edu); Robert J. Brugger, senior acquisitions editor (American history; rjb@press.jhu.edu); Vincent J. Burke, exec. editor (biology; vjb@press.jhu.edu); Juliana McCarthy, acquisitions editor (humanities, classics, and ancient studies; jmm@press.jhu.edu); Ashleigh McKown, assistant editor (higher education, history of technology, history of science; aem@press.jhu.edu); Suzanne Flinchbaugh, Associate Editor (Political Science, Health Policy, and Co-Publishing Liaison; skf@press.jhu.edu; Greg Nicholl, Assistant Editor (Regional Books, Poetry and Fiction, and Anabaptist and Pietist Studies; gan@press.jhu.edu). Publishes hardcover originals and reprints, and trade paperback reprints. Pays royalty. Publishes ms 1 year after acceptance.

NEEDS "One of the largest American university presses, Johns Hopkins publishes primarily scholarly books and journals. We do, however, publish short fiction and poetry in the series Johns Hopkins: Poetry and Fiction, edited by John Irwin."

ALFRED A. KNOPF

1745 Broadway, 21st Floor, New York NY 10019. **Website:** knopf.knopfdoubleday.com. Publishes hardcover and paperback originals. Royalties vary. Offers advance. Publishes ms 1 year after acceptance. Responds in 2-6 months to queries.

LAPWING PUBLICATIONS

1 Ballysillan Dr., Belfast BT14 8HQ, Northern Ireland. +44 2890 500 796. **Fax:** +44 2890 295 800. **E-mail:** lapwing.poetry@ntlworld.com. **Website:** www.lapwingpoetry.com. **Contact:** Dennis Greig, editor. Pays 20 author's copies, no royalties. Responds to queries in 1 month; mss in 2 months.

NEEDS Lapwing publishes "emerging Irish poets and poets domiciled in Ireland, plus the new work of a suitable size by established Irish writers. Non-Irish poets are also published. Poets based in continental Europe have become a major feature. Emphasis on first collections preferrably not larger than 80 pages. Logistically, publishing beyond the British Isles is always difficult for 'hard copy' editions. PDF copies via e-mail are £3 or 3€ per copy. No fixed upperl limit to number of titles per year. Hard copy prices are £8 to £10 per copy. No e-reader required." Wants poetry of all kinds, but, "no crass political, racist, sexist propaganda, even of a positive or 'pc' tenor." Has published Alastair Thomson, Clifford Ireson, Colette Wittorski, Gilberte de Leger, Aubrey Malone, and Jane Shaw Holiday. Pamphlets up to 32 pages, chapbooks up to 44 pages, books 48-112 pages; New Belfast binding, simulated perfect binding for books, otherwise saddle stitching.

HOW TO CONTACT "Submit 6 poems in the first instance; depending on these, an invitation to submit more may follow." Considers simultaneous submissions. Accepts e-mail submissions in body of message or in DOC format. Cover letter is required. "All submissions receive a first reading. If these poems have minor errors or faults, the writer is advised. If poor quality, the poems are returned. Those 'passing' first reading are retained, and a letter of conditional offer is sent." Often comments on rejected poems. "After initial publication, irrespective of the quantity, the work will be permanently available using 'print-on-demand' production; such publications will not always be printed exactly as the original, although the content will remain the same."

LES FIGUES BOOKS

P.O. Box 7736, Los Angeles CA 90007. **E-mail:** info@lesfigues.com. **Website:** www.lesfigues.com. Co-Directors: Teresa Carmody and Vanessa Place. Les Figues Press creates aesthetic conversations between writers/artists and readers, especially those interested in innovative/experimental/avant-garde work. The Press intends in the most premeditated fashion to champion the trinity of Beauty, Belief, and Bawdry.

LETHE PRESS

118 Heritage Ave., Maple Shade NJ 08052. (609)410-7391. **E-mail:** editor@lethepressbooks.com. **Website:** www.lethepressbooks.com. **Contact:** Steve Berman, publisher. "Lethe Press is a small press seeking gay and lesbian themed poetry collections." Lethe Books are distributed by Ingram Publications and Bookazine, and are available at all major bookstores, as well as the major online retailers.

NEEDS "Lethe Press is an independent publishing house specializing in speculative fiction, books of gay interest, poetry, spirituality, as well as classic works of the occult & supernatural. Named after the Greek river of memory and forgetfulness (and pronounced Lee-Thee), Lethe Press is devoted to ideas that are often neglected or forgotten by mainstream publishers."

HOW TO CONTACT Send query letter. Accepts queries by e-mail. Rarely accepts unsolicited mss.

LOUISIANA STATE UNIVERSITY PRESS

3990 W. Lakeshore Dr., Baton Rouge LA 70808. (225)578-6294. **Fax:** (225)578-6461. **E-mail:** mkc@lsu.edu. **Website:** www.lsu.edu/lsupress. John Easterly, excecutive editor (poetry, fiction, literary studies); Rand Dotson, senior editor (U.S. History & Southern Studies). **Contact:** MK Callaway, director. Publishes in the fall and spring. Publishes hardcover and paperback originals, and reprints. Publishes 8 poetry titles per year and 2 works of original fiction as part of the Yellow Shoe Fiction series. Pays royalty. Publishes ms 1 year after acceptance. Responds in 1 month to queries. Book catalog and ms guidelines free and online.

NEEDS A highly respected publisher of collections by poets such as Claudia Emerson, David Kirby, Brendan Galvin, Fred Chappell, Marilyn Nelson, and Henry Taylor. Publisher of the Southern Messenger Poets series edited by Dave Smith." "No unsolicited poetry mss. for the foreseeable future. We have filled our slots until 2014."

LUNA BISONTE PRODS

E-mail: bennett.23@osu.edu. **Website:** www.johnmbennett.net. **Contact:** John M. Bennett, editor/publisher.

NEEDS "Interested in avant-garde and highly experimental work only." Has published poetry by Jim

Leftwich, Sheila E. Murphy, Al Ackerman, Richard Kostelanetz, Carla Bertola, Olchar Lindsann, and many others.

HOW TO CONTACT Query first, with a few sample poems and cover letter with brief bio and publication credits. "Keep it brief. Chapbook publishing usually depends on grants or other subsidies, and is usually by solicitation. **Will also consider subsidy arrangements on negotiable terms.**" A sampling of various Luna Bisonte Prods products is available for $20.

MAVERICK DUCK PRESS

E-mail: maverickduckpress@yahoo.com. **Website:** www.maverickduckpress.com. **Contact:** Kendall A. Bell, editor. Maverick Duck Press is a "publisher of chapbooks from undiscovered talent. We are looking for fresh and powerful work that shows a sense of innovation or a new take on passion or emotion. Previous publication in print or online journals will increase your chances of us accepting your manuscript." Does not want "unedited work." Pays 20 author's copies (out of a press run of 50).

HOW TO CONTACT Send ms in Microsoft Word format with a cover letter with brief bio and publication credits. Chapbook mss may include previously published poems. "Previous publication is always a plus, as we may be more familiar with your work. Chapbook mss should have at least 20 poems."

MEADOWBROOK PRESS

5451 Smetana Dr., Minnetonka MN 55343. **Fax:** (952)930-1940. **E-mail:** info@meadowbrookpress.com. **Website:** www.meadowbrookpress.com. Publishes trade paperback originals and reprints. Pays 7 1/2% royalty. Pays $50-100/poem plus 1 contributor's copy. Pays small advance. Publishes book 2 years after acceptance. Responds only if interested to queries. Book catalog for #10 SASE. Guidelines available online.

NEEDS Meadowbrook Press is "currently seeking poems to be considered for future funny poetry book anthologies for children." Wants humorous poems aimed at children ages 6-12. "Poems should be fun, punchy, and refreshing. We're looking for new, hilarious, contemporary voices in children's poetry that kids can relate to." Has published poetry by Shel Silverstein, Jack Prelutsky, Jeff Moss, Kenn Nesbitt, and Bruce Lansky. Published anthologies include *Kids Pick the Funniest Poems, A Bad Case of the Giggles,* and *Miles of Smiles.*

HOW TO CONTACT "Please take time to read our guidelines, and send your best work." Submit up to 10 poems at a time; 1 poem to a page with name and address on each; include SASE. Lines/poem: 25 maximum. Considers simultaneous submissions.

TIPS "Always send for guidelines before submitting material. Always submit nonreturnable copies; we do not respond to queries or submissions unless interested."

MELLEN POETRY PRESS

P.O. Box 450, Lewiston NY 14092. (716)754-2266. **Fax:** (716)754-4056. **E-mail:** jrupnow@mellenpress.com. **Website:** www.mellenpress.com. **Contact:** Dr. John Rupnow, acquisitions. "We are a non-subsidy academic publisher of books in the humanities and social sciences. Our sole criterion for publication is that a manuscript makes a contribution to scholarship. We publish monographs, critical editions, collections, translations, revisionist studies, constructive essays, bibliographies, dictionaries, grammars and dissertations. We publish in English, French, German, Spanish, Italian, Portuguese, Welsh and Russian. Our books are well reviewed and acquired by research libraries worldwide. The *Press* also publishes over 100 continuing series, several academic journals, and the research generated by several scholarly institutes."

MERRIAM PRESS

133 Elm St., Suite 3R, Bennington VT 05201. (802)447-0313. **E-mail:** ray@merriam-press.com. **Website:** www.merriam-press.com. "Merriam Press specializes in military history - particularly World War II history." Publishes hardcover and softcover trade paperback originals and reprints Pays 10% royalty on actual selling price. Publishes ms 6 months or less after acceptance. Responds quickly (e-mail preferred) to queries. Book catalog available for $5 or visit website to view all available titles and access writer's guidelines and info.

TIPS "Our military history books are geared for military historians, collectors, model kit builders, wargamers, veterans, general enthusiasts. We now publish some fiction and poetry and will consider well-written books on a variety of historical topics."

MIAMI UNIVERSITY PRESS

356 Bachelor Hall, Miami University, Oxford OH 45056. **E-mail:** tumakw@muohio.edu. **Website:** www.muohio.edu/mupress. **Contact:** Keith Tuma, editor; Dana Leonard, managing editor. Publishes 1-2 books

of poetry/year and one novella, in paperback editions. Recent poetry titles include *Virgil's Cow*, by Frederick Farryl Goodwin; *Between Cup and Lip*, by Peter Manson; and *Talk Poetry*, by Mairéad Byrne. Recent fiction titles include John Cotter, *Under the Small Lights*, Lee Upton, *The Guide to the Flying Island*, and Cary Holladay, *A Fight in the Doctor's Office*.

⊘ MIDMARCH ARTS PRESS

300 Riverside Dr., New York NY 10025. (212)666-6990. **Fax:** (212)865-5509. **E-mail:** info@midmarchartspress.org. **Website:** www.midmarchartspress.org.

HOW TO CONTACT Query by letter or e-mail prior to submitting anything.

◐ MILKWEED EDITIONS

1011 Washington Ave. S., Suite 300, Minneapolis MN 55415. (612)332-3192. **Fax:** (612)215-2550. **E-mail:** submissions@milkweed.org. **Website:** www.milkweed.org. "Milkweed Editions publishes with the intention of making a humane impact on society, in the belief that literature is a transformative art uniquely able to convey the essential experiences of the human heart and spirit. To that end, Milkweed Editions publishes distinctive voices of literary merit in handsomely designed, visually dynamic books, exploring the ethical, cultural, and esthetic issues that free societies need continually to address." Publishes hardcover, trade paperback, and electronic originals; trade paperback and electronic reprints. Pays authors variable royalty based on retail price. Offers advance against royalties. Pays varied advance from $500-10,000. Publishes book in 18 months. Responds in 6 months to queries, proposals, and mss. Book catalog available online at website. Guidelines available online.

NEEDS Milkweed Editions is "looking for poetry manuscripts of high quality that embody humane values and contribute to cultural understanding." Not limited in subject matter. Open to writers with previously published books of poetry or a minimum of 6 poems published in nationally distributed commercial or literary journals. Considers translations and bilingual mss. Has published *Fancy Beasts*, by Alex Lemon, *Reading Novalis in Montana*, by Melissa Kwasny, and *The Book of Props*, by Wayne Miller.

HOW TO CONTACT Submit through website. No fax or e-mail submissions. Do not send originals. Accepts and reads unsolicited mss all year. Guidelines available on website. Responds in up to 6 months. Order sample books through website. Query with SASE; submit completed ms

TIPS "We are looking for excellent writing with the intent of making a humane impact on society. Please read submission guidelines before submitting and acquaint yourself with our books in terms of style and quality before submitting. Many factors influence our selection process, so don't get discouraged. Nonfiction is focused on literary writing about the natural world, including living well in urban environments."

◐◎ MOON TIDE PRESS

P.O. Box 50184, Irvine CA 92619. **E-mail:** publisher@moontidepress.com. **Website:** www.moontidepress.com. **Contact:** Michael Miller, publisher.

HOW TO CONTACT Query first.

TIPS "Keep in mind that when we open and read your ms, it will probably be in the middle of a large stack of other submissions, and many of those will be well-meaning but undistinguished collections about the same few themes. So don't be afraid to take risks. Surprise and entertain us. Give us something that the next ten poets in the stack won't."

⊘ MOVING PARTS PRESS

10699 Empire Grade, Santa Cruz CA 95060. (831)427-2271. **E-mail:** frice@movingpartspress.com. **Website:** www.movingpartspress.com. **Contact:** Felicia Rice, poetry editor. Moving Part Press publishes handsome, innovative books, broadsides, and prints that "explore the relationship of word and image, typography and the visual arts, the fine arts and popular culture." Published *Codex Espangliensis: from Columbus to the Border Patrol* (1998) with performance texts by Guillermo Goómez-Penña and collage imagery by Enrique Chagoya; *Cosmogonie Intime/An Intimate Cosmogony* (2005), a limited edition artists' book with poems by Yves Peyreé, translated by Elizabeth R. Jackson, and drawings by Ray Rice.

HOW TO CONTACT *Does not accept unsolicited mss.*

✪⊘ MULTICULTURAL BOOKS

307 Birchwood Ct., 6311 Gilbert Rd., Richmond BC V7C 3V7, Canada. (60447-0979. **E-mail:** jrmbooks@hotmail.com. **Website:** www.mbooksofbc.com; www.thehypertexts.com. **Contact:** Joe M. Ruggier, publisher. "MBooks of BC is a small press. We publish poetry, prose and poetry leaflets, prose, translations, children's writing, sound recordings, fiction, and literary non-fiction. We also have a publishing services divi-

sion. We belong to an international circle of poets and editors committed to reforming the prevailing order by bringing about a traditionalist revival in writing." Responds to queries and mss 2 months.

HOW TO CONTACT Query first, with a few sample poems and a cover letter with brief bio and publication credits. Book mss may include previously published poems. "The only criteria is quality of work and excellence."

NEW ISSUES POETRY & PROSE

Western Michigan University, 1903 W. Michigan Ave., Kalamazoo MI 49008-5463. (269)387-8185. **Fax:** (269)387-2562. **E-mail:** new-issues@wmich.edu. **Website:** wmich.edu/newissues. **Contact:** Managing Editor. Established 1996. Contests: The Green Rose Prize in Poetry offers $2,000 and publication of a book of poems by an established poet who has published one or more full-length collections of poetry. New Issues may publish as many as 3 additional mss from this competition. Considers simultaneous submissions, but New Issues must be notified of acceptance elsewhere. Submit a ms of at least 48 pages, typed, single-spaced preferred. Clean photocopies acceptable. Do not bind; use manila folder or metal clasp. Include cover page with poet's name, address, phone number, and title of the ms. Also include brief bio, table of contents, and acknowledgments page. No e-mail or fax submissions. Include SASP for notification of receipt of ms and SASE for results only; mss will be recycled. Guidelines available for SASE, by fax, e-mail, or on website. Please visit the AWP website for guidelines to submit to the AWP Award Series in the Novel contest. Guidelines available online, by e-mail, or by SASE.

NEEDS New Issues Poetry & Prose offers two contests annually. The Green Rose Prize is awarded to an author who has previously published at least one full-length book of poems. The New Issues Poetry Prize, an award for a first book of poems, is chosen by a guest judge. Past judges have included Philip Levine, C.K. Williams, C.D. Wright, and Campbell McGrath. New Issues does not read manuscripts outside our contests. Graduate students in the Ph.D. and M.F.A. programs of Western Michigan Univ. often volunteer their time reading manuscripts. Finalists are chosen by the editors. New Issues often publishes up to two additional manuscripts selected from the finalists.

HOW TO CONTACT Query first. All unsolicited mss returned unopened. "The press considers for publication only manuscripts submitted during its competition reading periods and often accepts two or more manuscripts for publication in addition to the winner."

NEW NATIVE PRESS

P.O. Box 661, Cullowhee NC 28723. (828)293-9237. **E-mail:** newnativepress@hotmail.com. **Website:** www.newnativepress.com. **Contact:** Thomas Rain Crowe, publisher. New Native Press has "selectively narrowed its range of contemporary 20th- and 21st-century literature to become an exclusive publisher of writers in marginalized and endangered languages. All books published are bilingual translations from original languages into English." Has published *Kenneth Patchen: Rebel Poet in America* by Larry Smith; Gaelic, Welsh, Breton, Cornish, and Manx poets in an all-Celtic-language anthology of contemporary poets from Scotland, Ireland, Wales, Brittany, Cornwall, and Isle of Man, entitled *Writing The Wind: A Celtic Resurgence* (The New Celtic Poetry); and *Selected Poems* by Kusumagraj (poet from Bombay, India) in the Marathi language. Books are sold by distributors in 4 foreign countries, and in the U.S. by Baker & Taylor, Amazon.com, library vendors, and Small Press Distribution. Books are typically 80 pages, offset-printed on glossy 120 lb. stock, perfect-bound, with professionally designed color cover. Publishes ms 1 year after acceptance. Responds to queries in 2 weeks.

NEEDS Always comments on rejected poems.

HOW TO CONTACT Query first, with 10 sample poems and cover letter with brief bio and publication credits.

NEW RIVERS PRESS

MSU Moorhead, 1104 Seventh Ave. S., Moorhead MN 56563. **E-mail:** kelleysu@mnstate.edu. **Website:** www.newriverspress.com. **Contact:** Suzanne Kelley, managing editor. New Rivers Press publishes collections of poetry, novels or novellas, translations of contemporary literature, and collections of short fiction and nonfiction. "We continue to publish books regularly by new and emerging writers, but we also welcome the opportunity to read work of every character and to publish the best literature available nationwide. Each fall through the MVP competition, we choose 2 books, 1 of them. Poetry and 1 of them Prose."

NEEDS The Many Voices Prize (MVP) awards $1,000, a standard book contract, and publication of a book-length ms by New Rivers Press. All previously published poems must be acknowledged. Considers simultaneous submissions "if noted as such. If your manuscript is accepted elsewhere during the judging, you must notify New Rivers Press immediately. If you do not give such notification and your manuscript is selected, your signature on the entry form gives New Rivers Press permission to go ahead with publication." Submit 50-80 pages of poetry. Entry form (required) and guidelines available on website. **Entry fee:** $20. **Deadline:** submit September 15-November 1 (postmark).

HOW TO CONTACT Book-length mss of poetry, short fiction, novellas, or creative nonfiction are all considered. No fax or e-mail submissions. Guidelines available on website.

⊘ NINETY-SIX PRESS

Furman University, 3300 Poinsett Hwy., Greenville SC 29613. (864)294-3152. **Fax:** (864)294-2224. **E-mail:** gil.allen@furman.edu. **Contact:** Gilbert Allen, editor.

HOW TO CONTACT **"We currently accept submissions by invitation only."** For a sample, send $10.

OOLIGAN PRESS

P.O. Box 751, Portland OR 97207. (503)725-9410. **E-mail:** ooligan@ooliganpress.pdx.edu. **Website:** www.ooliganpress.pdx.edu. Publishes trade paperback, and electronic originals and reprints. Pays negotiable royalty on retail price. Book catalog available online. Guidelines available online.

NEEDS Ooligan is a general trade press that "specializes in publishing authors from the Pacific Northwest and/or works that have specific value to that community. We are limited in the number of poetry titles that we publish as poetry represents only a small percentage of our overall acquisitions. We are open to all forms of style and verse; however, we give special preference to translated poetry, prose poetry, and traditional verse. Although spoken word, slam, and rap poetry are of interest to the press, we will not consider such work if it does not translate well to the written page. Ooligan does not publish chapbooks." Has published *Deer Drink the Moon*, edited by Liz Nakazawa and *American Scream* and *Palindrome Apocalypse* by the Croatian poet Durbravaka Oraic-Tolid, translated by Julienne Eden Busic.

HOW TO CONTACT Query, submit 20 sample poems, submit complete ms.

TIPS "For children's books, our audience will be middle grades and young adult, with marketing to general trade, libraries, and schools. Good marketing ideas increase the chances of a manuscript succeeding."

⊘ ORCHISES PRESS

P.O. Box 320533, Alexandria VA 22320. (703)683-1243. **E-mail:** lathbury@gmu.edu. **Website:** mason.gmu.edu/~lathbury. **Contact:** Roger Lathbury, editor-in-chief. Orchises Press is a general literary publisher specializing in poetry with selected reprints and textbooks. No new fiction or children's books. Publishes hardcover and trade paperback originals and reprints. Pays 36% of receipts after Orchises has recouped its costs. Publishes book 1 year after acceptance. Responds in 3 months to queries. Guidelines available online.

NEEDS Poetry must have been published in respected literary journals. Orchises Press is a general literary publisher specializing in poetry with selected reprints and textbooks. *Orchises Press no longer reads unsolicited mss.* Poetry must have been published in respected literary journals. Publishes free verse, but has strong formalist preferences.

HOW TO CONTACT Query and submit 5 sample poems.

PALETTES & QUILLS

330 Knickerbocker Ave., Rochester NY 14615. (585)456-0217. **E-mail:** palettesnquills@gmail.com. **Website:** www.palettesnquills.com. **Contact:** Donna M. Marbach, publisher/owner.

NEEDS Palettes & Quills "is at this point, a poetry press only, and produces only a handful of publications each year, specializing in anthologies, individual chapbooks, and broadsides." Wants "work that should appeal to a wide audience." Does not want "poems that are sold blocks of text, long-lined and without stanza breaks. Wildly elaborate free-verse would be difficult and in all likelihood fight with art background, amateurish rhyming poem, overly sentimental poems, poems that use excessive profanity, or which denigrate other people, or political and religious diatribes."

HOW TO CONTACT Query first with 3-5 poems and a cover letter with brief bio and publication credits for individual unsolicited chapbooks. May include previously published poems. Chapbook poets would get 20 copies of a run; broadside poets and artists get 5-10 copies and occasionally paid $10 for reproduction rights. Anthology poets get 1 copy of the anthology. All poets and artists get a discount on purchases that include their work.

CONTEST/AWARD OFFERINGS Palettes & Quills Biennial Chapbook Contest, held biennually. Prize: $200 plus 50 copies of chapbook and discount on purchase of others. Guidelines available for SASE or on website. Entry fee: $20. Past judges: Ellen Bass and Dorianne Laux.

PATH PRESS, INC.

1229 Emerson St., Evanston IL 60201. (847)492-0177. **Fax:** (773)651-0210. **E-mail:** pathpressinc@aol.com. **Contact:** Bennett J. Johnson, president. Path Press is a small publisher of books and poetry primarily "by, for, and about African American and Third World people." Open to all types of poetic forms; emphasis is on high quality. Books are "hardback and quality paperbacks."

HOW TO CONTACT Query first, with a few sample poems and cover letter with brief bio and publication credits. Submissions should be typewritten in ms format. Accepts submissions by e-mail (as attachment).

PECAN GROVE PRESS

Box AL, 1 Camino Santa Maria, San Antonio TX 78228. (210)436-3442. **Fax:** (210)436-3782. **E-mail:** phall@stmarytx.edu. **Website:** http://library.stmarytx.edu/pgpress. **Contact:** H. Palmer Hall, editor/director. Member, CLMP. Pecan Grove Press is a poetry-only press and conducts one national chapbook competition each year. Aside from that, the press publishes approximately 7-8 books and chapbooks each year outside of the competition. Manuscripts are selected through open submission. Books are 52-100 pages, off-set or laser print, perfect-bound with color index stock cover and full color art. Chapbooks are 32-45 pages, laser printed, perfect-bound, index stock cover with color in-house graphics. Pays poet 50% of proceeds after printing/binding costs are covered.

HOW TO CONTACT Submit complete ms via submission manager on website only.

PELICAN PUBLISHING COMPANY

1000 Burmaster St., Gretna LA 70053. (504)368-1175. **Fax:** (504)368-1195. **E-mail:** editorial@pelicanpub.com. **Website:** www.pelicanpub.com. **Contact:** Nina Kooij, editor-in-chief. "We believe ideas have consequences. One of the consequences is that they lead to a best-selling book. We publish books to improve and uplift the reader. Currently emphasizing business and history titles." Publishes 20 young readers/year; 3 middle readers/year. "Our children's books (illustrated and otherwise) include history, biography, holiday, and regional. Pelican's mission is to publish books of quality and permanence that enrich the lives of those who read them." Publishes hardcover, trade paperback and mass market paperback originals and reprints. Pays authors in royalties; buys ms outright "rarely." Illustrators paid by "various arrangements." Advance considered. Publishes a book 9-18 months after acceptance. Responds in 1 month to queries; 3 months to mss. Book catalog and ms guidelines online.

NEEDS Pelican Publishing Company is a medium-sized publisher of popular histories, cookbooks, regional books, children's books, and inspirational/motivational books. Considers poetry for "hardcover children's books only (1,100 words maximum), preferably with a regional focus. However, our needs for this are very limited; we publish 20 juvenile titles per year, and most of these are prose, not poetry." Has published *Alaskan Night Before Christmas* by Tricia Brown and *Hawaiian Night Before Christmas* by Carolyn Macy. Two of Pelican's popular series are prose books about Gaston the Green-Nosed Alligator by James Rice, and Clovis Crawfish by Mary Alice Fontenot. Books are 32 pages, magazine-sized, include illustrations.

TIPS "We do extremely well with cookbooks, popular histories, and business. We will continue to build in these areas. The writer must have a clear sense of the market and knowledge of the competition. A query letter should describe the project briefly, give the author's writing and professional credentials, and promotional ideas."

PERUGIA PRESS

P.O. Box 60364, Florence MA 01062. **E-mail:** info@perugiapress.com. **Website:** www.perugiapress.com. **Contact:** Susan Kan, director.

PLAN B PRESS

P.O. Box 4067, Alexandria VA 22303. (215)732-2663. **E-mail:** planbpress@gmail.com. **Website:** www.planbpress.com. **Contact:** Steven Allen May, president. Plan B Press is a "small publishing company with an international feel. Our intention is to have Plan B Press be part of the conversation about the direction and depth of literary movements and genres. Plan B Press's new direction is to seek out authors rarely-to-never published, sharing new voices that might not otherwise be heard. Plan B Press is determined to merge text with image, writing with art." Publishes poetry and short fiction. Wants "experimental poetry, concrete/visual work." Has published poetry by Lamont B. Steptoe, Michele Belluomini, Jim Mancinelli, Lyn Lifshin, Robert Miltner, and Steven Allen May. Publishes 1 poetry book/year and 5-10 chapbooks/year. Manuscripts are selected through open submission and through competition (see below). Books/chapbooks are 24-48 pages, with covers with art/graphics. Pays author's copies. Responds to queries in 1 month; mss in 3 months.

NEEDS Wants to see: experimental, concrete, visual poetry Does not want "sonnets, political or religious poems, work in the style of Ogden Nash."

HOW TO CONTACT Query first, with a few sample poems and a cover letter with brief bio and publication credits. Book/chapbook mss may include previously published poems.

POETRY SALZBURG

University of Salzburg, Department of English, Akademiestrasse 24, Salzburg A-5020, Austria. (43) (662)8044-4422. **Fax:** (43)(662)8044-167. **E-mail:** editor@poetrysalzburg.com. **Website:** www.poetrysalzburg.com. **Contact:** Dr. Wolfgang Goertschacher, Andreas Schachermayr. Poetry Salzburg publishes "collections of at least 100 pages by mainly poets not taken up by big publishers." Publishes 6-8 paperbacks/year. Books are usually 100-350 pages, A5, professionally printed, perfect-bound, with card covers. Payment varies. Responds to queries in 1 month; mss in 3 months.

HOW TO CONTACT Query first, with a cover letter with brief bio and publication credits. Suggests authors publish in *Poetry Salzburg Review* first.

PRESA :S: PRESS

P.O. Box 792, 8590 Belding Rd. NE, Rockford MI 49341. **E-mail:** presapress@aol.com. **Website:** www.presapress.com. **Contact:** Roseanne Ritzema, editor. Presa :S: Press publishes "perfect-bound paperbacks and saddle-stitched chapbooks of poetry. Wants "imagistic poetry where form is an extension of content, surreal, experimental, and personal poetry." Does not want "overtly political or didactic material." Pays 10-25 author\quotes copies. Time between acceptance and publication is 8-12 weeks. Responds to queries in 2-4 weeks; to mss in 8-12 weeks Guidelines available in magazine, for SASE, and by e-mail.

NEEDS Needs poems, reviews, essays, photos, criticism, and prose. Dedicates 6-8 pages of each issue to a featured poet. Considers previously published poems. (Considers poetry posted on a public website/ blog/forum and poetry posted on a private, password-protected forum as published.) Acquires first North American serial rights and the right to reprint in anthologies. Rights revert to poets upon publication. Accepts postal submissions only. Cover letter is preferred. Reads submissions year round. Poems are circulated to an editorial board. Never comments on rejected poems. Never publishes theme issues. Reviews books and chapbooks of poetry. Send materials for review consideration to Roseanne Ritzema.

HOW TO CONTACT Query first, with a few sample poems and a cover letter with brief bio and publication credits. Book/chapbook mss may include previously published poems.

PRINCETON UNIVERSITY PRESS

41 William St., Princeton NJ 08540. (609)258-4900. **Fax:** (609)258-6305. **Website:** www.pupress.princeton.edu. **Contact:** Hanne Winarsky, editor. "The Lockert Library of Poetry in Translation embraces a wide geographic and temporal range, from Scandinavia to Latin America to the subcontinent of India, from the Tang Dynasty to Europe of the modern day. It especially emphasizes poets who are established in their native lands and who are being introduced to an English-speaking audience. The series, many of whose titles are bilingual editions, calls attention to some of the most widely-praised poetry available today. In the Lockert Library series, each book is given individual design treatment rather than stamped into a series mold. We have published a wide range of poets from other cultures, including well-known writers such as Hoölderlin and Cavafy, and those who have not yet had their due in English translation, such as Goöran Sonnevi. Manuscripts are judged with several criteria in mind: the ability of the translation to stand on its own as poetry in English; fidelity to the tone and spirit of the original, rather than literal accuracy; and the importance of the translated poet to the literature of his or her time and country."

NEEDS Submit hard copy of proposal with sample poems or full ms. Cover letter is required. Reads submissions year round. Mss will not be returned. Comments on finalists only. Responds in 3-4 months.

PUCKERBRUSH PRESS

413 Neville Hall, Orono ME 04469. (207)581-3832. **Website:** http://puckerbrushreview.com. **Contact:** Sanford Phippen, editor. Publishes trade paperback originals and reprints of literary fiction and poetry. Pays 10-15% royalty on wholesale price. Responds in 1 month to queries; 2 months to proposals; 3 months to mss. Guidelines for SASE.

NEEDS Submit highest literary quality.

HOW TO CONTACT Submit complete ms. Please submit your poetry, short stories, literary essays and reviews through the link on website. Hard-copy submissions will no longer be accepted.

TIPS "Be true to your vision, not to fashion. For sophisticated readers who retain love of literature. Maine writers continue to be featured."

THE PUDDIN'HEAD PRESS

P.O. Box 477889, Chicago IL 60647. (708)656-4900. **E-mail:** phbooks@att.net. **Website:** www.puddinheadpress.com. "In the last several years we have been increasingly active across the country. There are numerous readings and events that we sponsor. We do our own distribution, primarily in the Midwest, and also do distribution for other small presses. Please send a SASE for a list of our current publications and publication/distribution guidelines. We sell poetry books, not just print them. Submitted poetry is evaluated for its marketability and quality." Responds to queries in 2 months.

NEEDS The Puddin'head Press is interested in "well-rounded poets who can support their work with readings and appearances." Wants "quality poetry by active poets who read and lead interesting lives. We occasionally publish chapbook-style anthologies and let poets on our mailing lists know what type of work we're interested in for a particular project." Does not want experimental, overly political poetry, or poetry with overt sexual content; no shock or novelty poems. Has published poetry by Jared Smith, Carol Anderson, Larry Janowski, Sandy Goldsmith, and Norman Porter. Puddin'head Press publishes 2-3 books and 2-3 chapbooks per year. Books/chapbooks are 30-100 pages, perfect-bound or side-stapled ("we use various formats").

HOW TO CONTACT "Please visit our website for submission guidelines." Poets must include SASE with submission.

QED PRESS/CYPRESS HOUSE

Cypress House, 155 Cypress St., Fort Bragg CA 95437. (800)773-7782. **Fax:** (707)964-7531. **E-mail:** joeshaw@cypresshouse.com. **Website:** www.cypresshouse.com. **Contact:** Joe Shaw, editor. Pays royalties of 7-12% and 25 author's copies. Publishes book 1 year after acceptance. Responds to queries and mss in 1 month. Order sample books through website.

NEEDS QED Press publishes "clear, clean, intelligent, and moving work." Wants "concrete, personal, and spare writing. No florid rhymed verse." Has published poetry by Victoria Greenleaf, Luke Breit, Paula Tennant (Adams), Cynthia Frank, et al. Publishes no more than 1 poetry book/year. Books are usually about 96 pages (75-80 poems), digest-sized, offset-printed, perfect-bound, with full-color cover. Also offers book packaging, and promotion and marketing services to start-up publishers.

HOW TO CONTACT We prefer to see 6 representative poems." Considers simultaneous submissions. Cover letter and SASE for return of materials are required.

RAGGED SKY PRESS

P.O. Box 312, Annandale NJ 08801. **E-mail:** info@raggedsky.com. **Website:** www.raggedsky.com. Publisher: Ellen Foos. Managing Editor: Vasiliki Katsarou. Editor: Arlene Weiner. Produces books of poetry and inspired prose. Ragged Sky is a small, highly selective cooperative press. "We work with our authors closely." Learn more online.

RATTAPALLAX PRESS

217 Thompson St., Suite 353, New York NY 10012. **E-mail:** info@rattapallax.com. **Website:** www.rattapallax.com. **Contact:** Ram Devineni, editor and publisher; Flavia Rocha; Idra Novey. Rattapallax Press publishes "contemporary poets and writers with unique, powerful voices." Publishes 5 paperbacks and 3 chapbooks/year. Books are usually 64 pages, digest-sized, offset-printed, perfect-bound, with 12-pt. CS1 covers.

HOW TO CONTACT Query first, with a few sample poems and cover letter with brief bio and publication credits. Include SASE. Requires authors to first be published in *Rattapallax*. Responds to queries in 1 month; to mss in 2 months. Pays royalties of 10-25%. Order sample books from website.

RED DRAGON PRESS

P.O. Box 320301, Alexandria VA 22320. **Website:** www.reddragonpress.com. Red Dragon Press is a proponent "of works that represent the nature of man as androgynous, as in the fusing of male and female symbolism, and we support works that deal with psychological and parapsychological topics." Wants "innovative and experimental poetry and prose using literary symbolism and aspiring to the creation of meaningful new ideas, forms, and methods." Publishes ms 8 months after acceptance. Responds to queries in 10 weeks; mss in 1 year.

NEEDS "Poems are selected for consideration by the publisher, then circulated to senior editor and/or poets previously published for comment. Poems are returned to the publisher for further action, i.e., rejection or acceptance for publication in an anthology or book by a single author. Frequently, submission of additional works is required before final offer is made, especially in the process for a book by a single author." Often comments on rejected poems.

HOW TO CONTACT Submit up to 5 poems at a time with SASE. Cover letter with brief bio is preferred. **Reading fee: $5 for poetry and short fiction, $10 for novels.**

RED HEN PRESS

P.O. Box 3537, Granada Hills CA 91394. (818)831-0649. **Fax:** (818)831-6659. **E-mail:** redhenpressbooks.com. **Website:** www.redhen.org. **Contact:** Mark E. Cull, publisher/editor (fiction). "*Red Hen Press is not currently accepting unsolicited material.* At this time, the best opportunity to be published by Red Hen is by entering one of our contests. Please find more information in our award submission guidelines." Publishes trade paperback originals. Publishes ms 1 year after acceptance. Responds in 1 month to queries; 2 months to proposals; months to mss. Book catalog available free. Guidelines available online.

CONTEST/AWARD OFFERINGS The Benjamin Saltman Award is awarded annually for the best poetry book collection. Submit 48 to 96 pages of poetry. Postmark deadline is August 31. $25 entry fee. SASE for notification only. Please include name, address, title, email address, and telephone number on cover sheet only. Award: $3,000 and publication of collection.

TIPS "Audience reads poetry, literary fiction, intelligent nonfiction. If you have an agent, we may be too small since we don't pay advances. Write well. Send queries first. Be willing to help promote your own book."

RED MOON PRESS

P.O. Box 2461, Winchester VA 22604. (540)722-2156. **E-mail:** jim.kacian@redmoonpress.com. **Website:** www.redmoonpress.com. **Contact:** Jim Kacian, editor/publisher. Red Moon Press "is the largest and most prestigious publisher of English-language haiku and related work in the world." Publishes 6-8 volumes/year, usually 3-5 anthologies and individual collections of English-language haiku, as well as 1-3 books of essays, translations, or criticism of haiku. Under other imprints, the press also publishes chapbooks of various sizes and formats.

HOW TO CONTACT Query with book theme and information, and 30-40 poems or draft of first chapter. Responds to queries in 2 weeks, to mss (if invited) in 3 months. "Each contract separately negotiated."

RONSDALE PRESS

3350 W. 21st Ave., Vancouver BC V6S 1G7, Canada. (604)738-4688. **Fax:** (604)731-4548. **E-mail:** ronsdale@shaw.ca. **Website:** http://ronsdalepress.com. **Contact:** Ronald B. Hatch, director (fiction, poetry, social commentary); Veronica Hatch, managing director (children's literature). "Ronsdale Press is a Canadian literary publishing house that publishes 12 books each year, three of which are children's titles. Of particular interest are books involving children exploring and discovering new aspects of Canadian history." Publishes trade paperback originals. Pays 10% royalty on retail price. Publishes book 1 year after acceptance. Responds to queries in 2 weeks; mss in 2 months. Book catalog for #10 SASE. Guidelines available online.

NEEDS Poets should have published some poems in magazines/journals and should be well-read in contemporary masters.

HOW TO CONTACT Submit complete ms.

TIPS "Ronsdale Press is a literary publishing house, based in Vancouver, and dedicated to publishing books from across Canada, books that give Canadians new insights into themselves and their country. We aim to publish the best Canadian writers."

ROSE ALLEY PRESS

4203 Brooklyn Ave. NE, #103A, Seattle WA 98105. (206)633-2725. **E-mail:** rosealleypress@juno.com. **Website:** www.rosealleypress.com. **Contact:** David Horowitz. Rose Alley Press was founded by David D. Horowitz in November 1995. It was named for the London street where, on December 18th, 1679, poet and playwright John Dryden was brutally beaten by three thugs. Evidence suggests that an aristocrat who mistakenly attributed a satire's authorship to Dryden hired the assailants. Undaunted, Dryden continued writing, even more boldly than before the assault. Inspired by such perseverance, David established Rose Alley Press, which publishes rhymed and metered poetry, cultural commentary, and an annually updated booklet about writing and publication.

SAKURA PUBLISHING & TECHNOLOGIES

P.O. Box 1681, Hermitage PA 16148. (330)360-5131. **E-mail:** skpublishing124@gmail.com. **Website:** www.sakura-publishing.com. **Contact:** Derek Vasconi, talent finder and CEO. Publishes hardcover, trade paperback, mass market paperback and electronic originals and reprints. Pays royalty of 20-60% on wholesale price or retail price. Publishes ms 6 months after acceptance. Responds in 1 month to queries, mss, proposals. Book catalog available for #10 SASE. Guidelines available online at website or by e-mail.

SALMON POETRY

Knockeven, Cliffs of Moher, County Clare, Ireland. 353(0)65 708 1941. **Fax:** 353(0)65 708 1941. **E-mail:** info@salmonpoetry.com. **E-mail:** jessie@salmonpoetry.com. **Website:** www.salmonpoetry.com. **Contact:** Jessie Lendennie, editor. Publishes mass market paperback originals.

NEEDS "Salmon Press has become one of the most important publications in the Irish literary world, specialising in the promotion of new poets, particularly women poets. Established as an alternative voice. Walks tightrope between innovation and convention. Was a flagship for writers in the west of Ireland. Salmon has developed a cross-cultural, internatonal literary dialog, broadening Irish Literature and urging new perspectives on established traditions."

TIPS "If we are broad minded and willing to nurture the individual voice inherent in the work, the artist will emerge."

SAM'S DOT PUBLISHING

P.O. Box 782, Cedar Rapids IA 52406. **E-mail:** samsdot@samsdotpublishing.com. **Website:** www.samsdotpublishing.com. **Contact:** Tyree Campbell, managing editor. Pays royalties of 12.5% minimum and 1-2 author's copies (out of a press run of 50-100). Responds to queries in 2 weeks; mss in 4-6 weeks.

NEEDS Sam's Dot Publishing prints collections of scifaiku, horror-ku, and minimalist poetry. Publishes 2-3 chapbooks/year and one anthology/year. Mss are selected through open submission. Chapbooks are 32 pages, offset-printed, saddle-stapled, with cardstock covers.

HOW TO CONTACT Query first, with a few sample poems and a cover letter with brief bio and publication credits, up to 500 words. Chapbook mss may include previously published poems.

SATURNALIA BOOKS

105 Woodside Rd., Ardmore PA 19003. (267) 278-9541. **E-mail:** info@saturnaliabooks.com. **Website:** www.saturnaliabooks.org. **Contact:** Henry Israeli, publisher. "We do not accept unsolicited submissions. We hold a contest, the Saturnalia Books Poetry Prize, annually in which 1 anonymously submitted title is chosen by a poet with a national reputation for publication. Submissions are accepted during the month of March. The submission fee is $30, and the prize is $2,000 and 20 copies of the book. See website for details." Publishes trade paperback originals Pays authors 4-6% royalty on retail price. Pays $400-2,000 advance. Responds in 4 months on mss Catalog on website Guidelines available on website

HOW TO CONTACT "Saturnalia Books has no bias against any school of poetry, but we do tend to publish writers who take chances and push against convention in some way, whether it's in form, language, content, or musicality." Submit complete ms to contest only.

TIPS "Our audience tend to be young avid readers of contemporary poetry. Read a few sample books first."

SEAWEED SIDESHOW CIRCUS

P.O. Box 234, Jackson WI 53037. **E-mail:** sscircus@aol.com. **Website:** www.facebook.com/sscircus. **Contact:** Andrew Wright Milam, editor. eaweed Sideshow Circus is "a place for young or new poets to publish a chapbook." Has published *Main Street* by Steven Paul Lansky and *The Moon Incident* by Amy McDonald. Publishes one chapbook/year. Chapbooks are usually

30 pages, digest-sized, photocopied, saddle-stapled, with cardstock covers. Pays 10 author's copies (out of a press run of 100). Responds to queries in 6-9 weeks; to mss in 6-9 months.

HOW TO CONTACT Query first, with 5-10 sample poems and cover letter with brief bio and publications credits.

SECOND AEON PUBLICATIONS

19 Southminster Rd., Roath, Cardiff CF23 5AT, Wales. +44(29)2049-3093. **Fax:** +44(29)2049-3093. **E-mail:** peter@peterfinch.co.uk. **Website:** www.peterfinch.co.uk. **Contact:** Peter Finch, poetry editor.

HOW TO CONTACT *Does not accept unsolicited mss.*

SPOUT PRESS

P.O. Box 581067, Minneapolis MN 55458. (612) 782-9629. **E-mail:** spoutpress@hotmail.com; editors@spoutpress.org. **Website:** www.spoutpress.org. **Contact:** Carrie Eidem, fiction editor. Publishes book 12-15 months after acceptance. Responds in 1 month to queries; 3-5 months to mss. Ms guidelines for SASE or on website.

HOW TO CONTACT Submit via mail with cover letter and SASE.

TIPS "We tend to publish writers after we know their work via publication in our journal, *Spout Magazine*."

SPS STUDIOS, INC.

P.O. Box 1007, Dept. PM, Boulder CO 80306-1007. **E-mail:** editorial@spsstudios.com. **Website:** www.sps.com. **Contact:** Editorial Staff. Submissions must be typewritten, one poem/page or sent by e-mail (no attachments). Include SASE. Simultaneous submissions "discouraged but okay with notification." Accepts fax and e-mail (pasted into body of message) submissions. Submit seasonal material at least 4 months in advance. Pays $300/poem, all rights for each of the first 2 submissions chosen for publication (after which payment scale escalates), for the worldwide, exclusive right, $50/poem for one-time use in an anthology. Responds in up to 6 months. Guidelines available for SASE or by e-mail.

NEEDS SPS Studios publishes greeting cards, books, calendars, prints, and other gift items. Looking for poems, prose, and lyrics ("usually non-rhyming") appropriate for publication on greeting cards and in poetry anthologies. Also actively seeking "book-length manuscripts that would be appropriate for book and gift stores. We are also very interested in receiving book and card ideas that would be appropriate for college stores, as well as younger buyers. Poems should reflect a message, feeling, or sentiment that one person would want to share with another. We'd like to receive creative, original submissions about love relationships, family members, friendships, philosophies, and any other aspect of life. Poems and writings for specific holidays (Christmas, Valentine's Day, etc.) and special occasions, such as graduation, anniversary, and get well are also considered. Only a small portion of the material we receive is selected each year and the review process can be lengthy, but be assured every manuscript is given serious consideration."

CONTEST/AWARD OFFERINGS SPS Studios sponsors Biannual Poetry Card Contest.

STEEL TOE BOOKS

Department of English, Western Kentucky University, 1906 College Heights Blvd. #11086, Bowling Green KY 42101. (270)745-5769. **E-mail:** tom.hunley@wku.edu. **Website:** www.steeltoebooks.com. **Contact:** Dr. Tom C. Hunley, director. Steel Toe Books publishes "full-length, single-author poetry collections. Our books are professionally designed and printed. We look for workmanship (economical use of language, high-energy verbs, precise literal descriptions, original figurative language, poems carefully arranged as a book); a unique style and/or a distinctive voice; clarity; emotional impact; humor (word plays, hyperbole, comic timing); performability (a Steel Toe poet is at home on the stage as well as on the page)." Does not want "dry verse, purposely obscure language, poetry by people who are so wary of being called 'sentimental' they steer away from any recognizable human emotions, poetry that takes itself so seriously that it's unintentionally funny." Has published poetry by Allison Joseph, Susan Browne, James Doyle, Martha Silano, Mary Biddinger, John Guzlowski, Jeannine Hall Gailey, and others. Publishes 1-3 poetry books/year. Manuscripts are normally selected through open submission.

HOW TO CONTACT "Check the website for news about our next open reading period." Book mss may include previously published poems. Responds to mss in 3 months. Pays $500 advance on 10% royalties and 10 author's copies. Order sample books by sending $12 to Steel Toe Books. *Must purchase a manuscript in order to submit.* See website for submission guidelines.

SWAN SCYTHE PRESS

515 P Street, #804, Sacramento CA 95814. **E-mail:** jimzbookz@yahoo.com. **Website:** www.swanscythe.com. **Contact:** James DenBoer, editor.

NEEDS "After publishing 25 chapbooks, a few full-sized poetry collections,and 1 anthology, then taking a short break from publishing, Swan Scythe Press is now re-launching its efforts with some new books, under a new editorship, in 2010. We have also begun a new series of books, called Poetas/Puentes, from emerging poets writing in Spanish, translated into English. We will also consider manuscripts in indigenous languages from North, Central and South America, translated into English. Has published poetry by Emmy Perez, Maria Melendez, John Olivares Espinoza, Karen An-hwei Lee, Pos Moua, and Walter Pavlich. Order books/chapbooks by using paypal at the Swan Scythe Press or order through website.

HOW TO CONTACT Query first before submitting a ms via email or through website.

SYNERGEBOOKS

205 S. Dixie Dr., Haines City FL 33844. (863)956-3015. **Fax:** (863)588-2198. **E-mail:** synergebooks@aol.com. **Website:** www.synergebooks.com. **Contact:** Debra Staples, publisher/acquisitions editor. "SynergEbooks is first and foremost a digital publisher, so most of our marketing budget goes to those formats. Authors are required to direct-sell a minimum of 100 digital copies of a title before it's accepted for print." Publishes trade paperback and electronic originals. Pays 15-40% royalty; makes outright purchase. Book catalog and guidelines online.

NEEDS Anthologies must be a unique topic or theme.

HOW TO CONTACT Query and submit 1-5 sample poems.

TIPS "At SynergEbooks, we work with the author to promote their work."

◐ TARPAULIN SKY PRESS

P.O. Box 189, Grafton VT 05146. **E-mail:** editors@tarpaulinsky.com. **Website:** www.tarpaulinsky.com. **Contact:** Colie Collen, editor-in-chief. Tarpaulin Sky Press publishes cross- and trans-genre works as well as innovative poetry and prose. Produces full-length books and chapbooks, hand-bound books and trade paperbacks, and offers both hand-bound and perfect-bound paperback editions of full-length books. "We're a small, author-centered press endeavoring to create books that, as objects, please our authors as much their texts please us." Has published books and chapbooks by Jenny Boully, Danielle Dutton, Joyelle McSweeney, Chad Sweeney, Andrew Michael Roberts, and Max Winter, as well as a collaborative book by Noah Eli Gordon as Joshua Marie Wilkinson.

HOW TO CONTACT Writers whose work has appeared in or been accepted for publication in *Tarpaulin Sky* (see separate listing in Magazines/Journals) may submit chapbook or full-length manuscripts at any time, with no reading fee. Tarpaulin Sky Press also considers chapbook and full-length manuscripts from writers whose work has not appeared in the journal, but **asks for a $20 reading fee**. Make checks/money orders to Tarpaulin Sky Press. Cover letter is preferred. Reads periods may be found on the website.

⊘ TEBOT BACH

P.O. Box 7887, Huntington Beach CA 92615. (714)968-0905. **E-mail:** info@tebotbach.org. **Website:** www.tebotbach.org. **Contact:** Mifanwy Kaiser, editor/publisher. 2 years Responds to queries and mss, if invited, in 3 months.

HOW TO CONTACT Query first via e-mail, with a few sample poems and cover letter with brief bio.

ADDITIONAL INFORMATION Offers an anthology of California poets. Must be current or former resident of California in order to submit, but no focus or theme required for poetry. Submit up to 6 poems with "California Anthology" written on lower left corner of envelope. Accepts submissions by e-mail (pasted into body of message or as attachment in Word). Deadline for submission is in August of the year call for submissions is announced. Please check the website for calls for submissions. Also publishes *Spillway: A Literary Journal.*

⊘ TEXAS TECH UNIVERSITY PRESS

P.O. Box 41037, Lubbock TX 79409. (806)742-2982. **Fax:** (806)742-2979. **E-mail:** judith.keeling@ttu.edu. **Website:** www.ttupress.org. **Contact:** Judith Keeling, editor-in-chief; Robert Mandel, director. Texas Tech University Press, the book publishing office of the university since 1971 and an AAUP member since 1986, publishes nonfiction titles in the areas of natural history and the natural sciences; eighteenth-century and Joseph Conrad studies; studies of modern Southeast Asia, particularly the Vietnam War; costume and textile history; Latin American literature and culture; and all aspects of the Great Plains and the American West, especially history, biography, memoir, sports history, and travel. In addition, the Press publishes several scholarly journals, acclaimed series for young readers, an annual invited poetry collection, and literary fiction of Texas and the West.

TIGHTROPE BOOKS

602 Markham St., Toronto ON M6G 2L8, Canada. (647)348-4460. **E-mail:** shirarose@tightropebooks.com. **Website:** www.tightropebooks.com. **Contact:** Shirarose Wilensky, editor. Publishes hardcover and trade paperback originals. Pays 5-15% royalty on retail price. Pays advance of $200-300. Publishes book 1 year after acceptance. Responds if interested. Catalog and guidelines free on request and online.

HOW TO CONTACT Query. Submit 10 sample poems. Submit complete ms.

TIPS "Audience is young, urban, literary, educated, unconventional."

TIMBERLINE PRESS

5710 S. Kimbark #3, Chicago IL 60637. **E-mail:** steven_schroeder@earthlink.net. **Website:** http://vacpoetry.org/timberline/.

NEEDS "We publish limited letterpress editions with the goal of blending strong poetry with well-crafted and designed printing. We lean toward natural history or strongly imagistic nature poetry but will look at any good work. Also, good humorous poetry." Has published *Stark Beauty* by Larry D. Thomas, *Menagerie* by William Heyen, *Crossing Crocker Township* by Robert Tremmel, and *The Body of Water* by Walter Bargen. Sample copies may be obtained by sending $7.50, requesting sample copy, and noting you saw the listing in *Poet's Market*. Responds in less than one month. Pays "50-50 split with author after Timberline Press has recovered its expenses."

HOW TO CONTACT Query before submitting full ms.

TOKYO ROSE RECORDS/CHAPULTEPEC PRESS

4222 Chambers, Cincinnati OH 45223. **E-mail:** ChapultepecPress@hotmail.com. **Website:** www.tokyoroserecords.com. **Contact:** David Garza. Publishes trade paperback originals. Pays 50% of profits and author's copies. Publishes book 6 months after acceptance. Book catalog available online.

NEEDS Chapultepec Press publishes books of poetry/literature, essays, social/political issues, art, music, film, history, popular science; library/archive issues, and bilingual works. Wants "poetry that works as a unit, that is caustic, fun, open-ended, worldly, mature, relevant, stirring, evocative. Bilingual. Looking for authors who have a publishing history. No poetry collections without a purpose, that are mere collections. Also looking for broadsides/posters/illuminations." Publishes 1-2 books/year. Books are usually 1-100 pages.

HOW TO CONTACT Query first. Submit 5-15 sample poems.

TIPS Tokyo Rose Records/Chapultepec Press specializes in shorter-length publications (100 pages or less). Order sample books by sending $5 payable to David Garza.

TUPELO PRESS

P.O. Box 1767, North Adams MA 01247. (413)664-9611. **E-mail:** publisher@tupelopress.org. **E-mail:** www.tupelopress.org/submissions. **Website:** www.tupelopress.org. **Contact:** Jeffrey Levine, publish/editor-in-chief; Elyse Newhouse, associate publisher; Jim Schley, managing editor. "We're an independent nonprofit literary press. Also sponsor these upcoming competitions: Dorset Prize: $10,000. Entries must be postmarked between September 1 and December 31, 2011. Guidelines are online; Snowbound Series chapbook Award: $1,000 and 50 copies of chapbook. See website for submission period and guidelines. Every July we have Open Submissions. We accept book-length poetry, poetry collections (48 + pages), short story collections, novellas, literary nonfiction/memoirs and up to 80 pages of a novel." Guidelines available online.

NEEDS "Our mission is to publish thrilling, visually and emotionally and intellectually stimulating books of the highest quality, inside and out. We want contemporary poetry, etc. by the most diverse list of emerging and established writers in the U.S."

HOW TO CONTACT Submit complete ms.

THE UNIVERSITY OF AKRON PRESS

120 E. Mill St., Suite 415, Akron OH 44325. (330)972-5342. **Fax:** (330)972-8364. **E-mail:** uapress@uakron.edu. **Website:** www.uakron.edu/uapress. **Contact:** Thomas Bacher, director and acquisitions. "The University of Akron Press is the publishing arm of The University of Akron and is dedicated to the dissemination of scholarly, professional, and regional books and other content." Publishes hardcover and paperback originals and reissues. Pays 7-15% royalty. Publishes book 9-12 months after acceptance. Responds in

2 weeks to queries/proposals; 3-4 months to solicited mss. Query prior to submitting Book catalog available free. Guidelines available online.

NEEDS Follow the guidelines and submit mss only for the contest: www.uakron.edu/uapress/poetry.html. "We publish two books of poetry annually, one of which is the winner of The Akron Poetry prize. We also are interested in literary collections based around one theme, especially collections of translated works."

HOW TO CONTACT If you are interested in publishing with The University of Akron Press, please fill out form online.

THE UNIVERSITY OF CHICAGO PRESS

1427 E. 60th St., Chicago IL 60637. Voicemail: (773)702-7700. **Fax:** (773)702-2705 or (773)702-9756. **Website:** www.press.uchicago.edu. **Contact:** Randolph Petilos, poetry editor. "The University of Chicago Press has been publishing scholarly books and journals since 1891. Annually, we publish an average of four books in our Phoenix Poets series and four books of poetry in translation. Occasionally, we may publish a book of poetry outside Phoenix Poets, or as a paperback reprint from another publisher." Has published poetry by Peter Balakian, Don Bogen, Peter Campion, Gendun Chopel, David Gewanter, Reginald Gibbons, Fulke Greville, Randall Mann, Lucrezia Marinella, Greg Miller, Gabriela Mistral, Marguerite de Navarre, Robert Polito, Francisco de Quevedo, Atsuro Riley, Pedro Salinas, Gaspara Stampa, Sarra Copia Sulam, Garcilaso de la Vega, and Tom Yuill.

UNIVERSITY OF IOWA PRESS

100 Kuhl House, 119 W. Park Rd., Iowa City IA 52242. (319)335-2000. **Fax:** (319)335-2055. **E-mail:** uipress@uiowa.edu. **Website:** www.uiowapress.org. **Contact:** Holly Carver, director; Joseph Parsons, acquisitions editor. "We publish authoritative, original nonfiction that we market mostly by direct mail to groups with special interests in our titles, and by advertising in trade and scholarly publications." Publishes hardcover and paperback originals. Pays 7-10% royalty on net receipts. Publishes book 1 year after acceptance. Book catalog available free. Guidelines available online.

NEEDS Currently publishes winners of the Iowa Poetry Prize Competition, Kuhl House Poets, poetry anthologies. Competition guidelines available on website.

UNIVERSITY OF NEW MEXICO PRESS

(505)277-3324 or (800)249-7737. **Fax:** (505)277-3343. **E-mail:** clark@unm.edu. **E-mail:** wcwhiteh@unm.edu. **Website:** www.unmpress.com. **Contact:** W. Clark Whitehorn, editor-in-chief. "The Press is well known as a publisher in the fields of anthropology, archeology, Latin American studies, art and photography, architecture and the history and culture of the American West, fiction, some poetry, Chicano/a studies and works by and about American Indians. We focus on American West, Southwest and Latin American regions." Publishes hardcover originals and trade paperback originals and reprints. Pays variable royalty. Pays advance. Book catalog available for free. Please read and follow the submission query guidelines on the Author Information page online. Do not send your entire ms or additional materials until requested. If your book is accepted for publication, you will be notified.

VANHOOK HOUSE

925 Orchard St., Charleston WV 25302. **E-mail:** editor@vanhookhouse.com. **E-mail:** acquisitions@vanhookhouse.com. **Website:** www.vanhookhouse.com. **Contact:** Jim Whyte, acquisitions, all fiction/true crime/military/war. "VanHook House is a small press focused on the talents of new, unpublished authors. We are looking for works of fiction and non-fiction to add to our catalog. No erotica or sci-fi, please. Query via email. Queries accepted ONLY during submissions periods." hardcover and trade paperback originals; trade paperback reprints. Pays authors 8-10% royalty on wholesale price. Advance negotiable. Publishes ms 6 months after acceptance. Responds in 1 month on queries; 2 months on proposals; 3 months on mss. Book catalog and guidelines free on request and available online at website.

VÉHICULE PRESS

Box 125, Place du Parc Station, Montreal QC H2X 4A3, Canada. (514)844-6073. **Fax:** (514)844-7543. **E-mail:** vp@vehiculepress.com. **Website:** www.vehiculepress.com. **Contact:** Simon Dardick, president/publisher. "Montreal's Véhicule Press has published the best of Canadian and Quebec literature-fiction, poetry, essays, translations, and social history." Publishes trade paperback originals by Canadian authors mostly. Pays 10-15% royalty on retail price. Pays $200-500 advance. Publishes ms 1 year after acceptance. Responds in 4 months to queries. Book catalog for 9 x 12 SAE with IRCs.

NEEDS Contact Carmine Starnino with SASE. Vehicule Press is a "literary press with a poetry series, Signal Editions, publishing the work of Canadian poets only." Publishes flat-spined paperbacks. Has published *The Empire's Missing Links* by Walid Bitar, *36 Cornelian Avenue* by Christopher Wiseman, and *Morning Gothic* by George Ellenbogen. Publishes Canadian poetry that is "first-rate, original, content-conscious."

TIPS "Quality in almost any style is acceptable. We believe in the editing process."

WAKE FOREST UNIVERSITY PRESS

P.O. Box 7333, Winston-Salem NC 27109. (336)758-5448. **Fax:** (336)758-5636. **E-mail:** wfupress@wfu.edu. **Website:** www.wfu.edu/wfupress. **Contact:** Jefferson Holdridge, director/poetry editor; Dillon Johnston, advisory editor. "We publish only poetry from Ireland. I am able to consider only poetry written by native Irish poets. I must return, unread, poetry from American poets." Query with 4-5 samples and cover letter. Sometimes sends prepublication galleys. Buys North American or U.S. rights. Pays on 10% royalty contract, plus 6-8 author's copies. Negotiable advance. Responds to queries in 1-2 weeks; to submissions (*if invited*) in 2-3 months.

NEEDS Has published *Collected Poems* by John Montague; *Ghost Orchid* by Michael Longley; *Selected Poems* by Medbh McGuckian; and *The Wake Forest Book of Irish Women's Poetry.*

WASHINGTON WRITERS' PUBLISHING HOUSE

C/O Bravo Household, 3541 S. St., NW, Washington DC 20007. **E-mail:** wwphpress@gmail.com. **Website:** www.washingtonwriters.org. **Contact:** Patrick Pepper, president. Washington Writers' Publishing House considers book-length mss for publication by poets living within 60 driving miles of the U.S. Capitol (Baltimore area included) through competition only (see below).

NEEDS Washington Writers' Publishing House publishes books by Washington, D.C.- and Baltimore-area poets through its annual book competition. "No specific criteria, except literary excellence." Has published books by Holly Karapetkova, Jehanne Dubrow, Brandel France de Bravo, Carly Sachs, Bruce MacKinnon, Piotr Gwiazda, Patric Pepper, Mary Ann Larkin, Moira Egan, Bernard jankowski, Kim Roberts, Sid Gold, Jane Satterfield, Ned Balbo, Jean Nordhaus, Grace Cavalieri, E.ethelbert Miller, and Gray Jacobik. Publishes 1-2 poetry books/year.

CONTEST/AWARD OFFERINGS Offers $500 and 50 copies of published book plus additional copies for publicity use. Manuscripts may include previously published poems. Submit 2 copies of a poetry ms of 50-60 pages, single-spaced (poet's name should not appear on ms pages). Include separate page of publication acknowledgments plus 2 cover sheets: one with ms title, poet's name, address, telephone number, and e-mail address, the other with ms title only. Include SASE for results only; mss will not be returned (will be recycled). Guidelines available for SASE or on website. "Author should indicate where they heard about WWPH." **Entry fee:** $20. **Deadline:** July 1-November 1 (postmark). Order sample books on website or by sending $12 plus $3 s&h to Washington Writers' Publishing House, P.O. Box 15271, Washington DC 20003.

WAVE BOOKS

1938 Fairview Ave. E., Suite 201, Seattle WA 98102. (206)676-5337. **E-mail:** info@wavepoetry.com. **Website:** www.wavepoetry.com. **Contact:** Charlie Wright, publisher; Joshua Beckman and Matthew Zapruder, editors; Heidi Broadhead, managing editor. "Wave Books is an independent poetry press based in Seattle, Washington. Dedicated to publishing the best in contemporary American poetry and poetry in translation, Wave Books was founded in 2005, joining forces with already-established publisher Verse Press. Wave Books seeks to build on and expand the mission of Verse Press by publishing strong innovative work and encouraging our authors to expand and interact with their readership through nationwide readings and events, affirming our belief that the audience for poetry is larger and more diverse than commonly thought." Hardcover and trade paperback originals. Catalog online.

NEEDS "We are dedicated to publishing the best in American poetry by new & established authors. We seek to build on & expand by publishing strong innovative work & encouraging our authors to expand & interact with their readership through nationwide readings & events, affirming our belief that the audience for poetry is larger & more diverse than commonly thought." No children's, fiction, or nonfiction for Wave library. No magazine contributions right now.

HOW TO CONTACT Submit with cover letter. Galleys & advance reader's copies are acceptable.

⊘ WHITE EAGLE COFFEE STORE PRESS

P.O. Box 383, Fox River Grove IL 60021. **E-mail:** WECSPress@aol.com. **Website:** whiteeaglecoffeestorepress.com. **Contact:** Frank Edmund Smith, publisher. White Eagle is a small press publishing 2-3 chapbooks/year. "Alternate chapbooks are published by invitation and by competition. Author published by invitation becomes judge for next competition." Wants "any kind of poetry. No censorship at this press. Literary values are the only standard." Does not want "sentimental or didactic writing." Has published poetry by Timothy Russell, Connie Donovan, Scott Lumbard, Linda Lee Harper, Scott Beal, Katie Kingston, and Brian Brodeur. Sample: $6.95. *Regular submissions by invitation only.*

NEEDS Winner receives $500 and 25 author's copies. All entrants will receive a copy of the winning chapbook. Considers previously published poems and simultaneous submissions, with notice. Submit complete chapbook ms (20-24 pages), paginated, with table of contents. Poet's name should not appear on ms pages. Include 2 cover sheets: 1 with ms title, poet's name, address, phone number, and brief biography; second with ms title and 125-word statement about poet's work to be included in chapbook (poet's name should not appear on second cover sheet). Include list of credits for previously published poems. **Entry fee:** $15. **Deadline:** October 31 (postmark). "Each competition is judged by either the author of the most recent chapbook published by invitation or by previous competition winners." Responds 3 months after deadline.

HOW TO CONTACT No e-mail submissions. Include SASE for results only; mss will not be returned. Guidelines available for SASE or on website.

TIPS "Poetry is about a passion for language. That's what we're about. We'd like to provide an opportunity for poets of any age who are fairly early in their careers to publish something substantial. We're excited by the enthusiasm shown for this press and by the extraordinary quality of the writing we've received."

WISDOM PUBLICATIONS

199 Elm St., Somerville MA 02144. (617)776-7416, ext. 28. **Fax:** (617)776-7841. **E-mail:** editors@wisdompubs.org. **Website:** www.wisdompubs.org. **Contact:** David Kittlestrom, senior editor. "Wisdom Publications is dedicated to making available authentic Buddhist works for the benefit of all. We publish translations, commentaries, and teachings of past and contemporary Buddhist masters and original works by leading Buddhist scholars. Currently emphasizing popular applied Buddhism, scholarly titles." Publishes hardcover originals and trade paperback originals and reprints. Pays 4-8% royalty on wholesale price. Pays advance. Publishes ms within 2 years of acceptance. Book catalog and ms guidelines online.

TIPS "We are basically a publisher of Buddhist books-all schools and traditions of Buddhism. Please see our catalog or our website before you send anything to us to get a sense of what we publish."

WOODLEY MEMORIAL PRESS

English Dept., Washburn University, Topeka KS 66621. **E-mail:** karen.barron@washburn.edu. **Website:** www.washburn.edu/reference/woodley-press. **Contact:** Kevin Rabas, acquisitions editor. "Woodley Memorial Press is a small, nonprofit press which publishes novels and fiction collections by Kansas writers only; by 'Kansas writers' we mean writers who reside in Kansas or have a Kansas connection." Publishes paperback originals. Publishes ms 1 year after acceptance. Responds in 2 weeks to queries; 6 months to mss. Guidelines available on website.

TIPS "We only publish one to three works of fiction a year, on average, and those will definitely have a Kansas connection. We seek authors who are dedicated to promoting their works."

WORDSONG

815 Church St., Honesdale PA 18431. **Fax:** (570)253-0179. **E-mail:** submissions@boydsmillspress.com; eagarrow@boydsmillspress.com. **Website:** www.wordsongpoetry.com. "We publish fresh voices in contemporary poetry." Pays authors royalty or work purchased outright. Responds to mss in 3 months.

NEEDS Submit complete ms or submit through agent. Label package "Manuscript Submission" and include SASE. "Please send a book-length collection of your own poems. Do not send an initial query."

TIPS "Collections of original poetry, not anthologies, are our biggest need at this time. Keep in mind that the strongest collections demonstrate a facility with multiple poetic forms and offer fresh images and insights. Check to see what's already on the market and on our website before submitting."

CONTESTS & AWARDS

This section contains a wide array of poetry competitions and literary awards. These range from state poetry society contests (with a number of modest monetary prizes) to prestigious honors bestowed by private foundations, elite publishers and renowned university programs. Because these listings reflect such a variety of skill levels and degrees of competitiveness, it's important to read each carefully and note its unique requirements. *Never* enter a contest without consulting the guidelines and following directions to the letter (including manuscript formatting, number of lines or pages of poetry accepted, amount of entry fee, entry forms needed and other details).

IMPORTANT NOTE: As we gathered information for this edition of *Poet's Market*, we found that some competitions hadn't yet established their 2013 fees and deadlines. In such cases, we list the most recent information available as a general guide. Always consult current guidelines for updates before entering any competition.

WHAT ABOUT ENTRY FEES?

Most contests charge entry fees, and these are usually quite legitimate. The funds are used to cover expenses such as paying the judges, putting up prize monies, printing prize editions of magazines and journals, and promoting the contest through mailings and ads. If you're concerned about a poetry contest or other publishing opportunity, see "Is It a 'Con'?" for advice on some of the more questionable practices in the poetry world.

10 MINUTE PLAY CONTEST & FESTIVAL

Weathervane Playhouse, 1301 Weathervane Lane, Akron OH 44313. (330)836-2626. **E-mail:** 10minuteplay@weathervaneplayhouse.com. **Website:** www.weathervaneplayhouse.com. Annual 8x10 TheatreFest. Must be US citizen 18 years or older. All rights remain with writers. "The mission of the Weathervane Playhouse 8x10 TheatreFest is to promote the art of play writing, present new works, and introduce area audiences to the short play form. The competition will provide Weathervane with recognition for quality and innovative theatre." Deadline for submissions is mid-May. Eight finalists receive full productions of their plays during TheatreFest, held in mid-July. Winners will be announced after the final performance. Cash prizes include 1st Place: $350; 2nd Place: $250; Audience Favorite: $150; 5 runners-up: $50. First round judges include individuals with experience in every area of stagecraft, including tech designers, actors, directors, stage managers, and playwrights.

TIPS "Please see visit www.weathervaneplayhouse.com/special-events for this year's specific dates, guidelines, etc."

THE 49TH PARALLEL POETRY AWARD

Western Washington University, Mail Stop 9053, Bellingham WA 98225. **E-mail:** bhreview@wwu.edu. **Website:** www.wwu.edu/~bhreview. The annual 49th Parallel Poetry Award offers 1st Prize of $1,000, plus publication in and a year's subscription to Bellingham Review. Runners-up and finalists may be considered for publication. Submissions must be unpublished and not accepted for publication elsewhere. Considers simultaneous submissions, but work must be withdrawn from the competition if accepted for publication elsewhere. Submit up to 3 poems. "Poems within a series will each be treated as a separate entry." For each entry, include a 3x5 index card stating the title of the work, the category (poetry), the poet's name, phone number, address, and e-mail. "Make sure writing is legible on this card. Author's name must not appear anywhere on the manuscript." Include SASE for results only; mss will not be returned. Guidelines available for SASE or on website. **Entry fee:** $18 for first entry (up to 3 poems); $10 each additional poem. Make checks payable to Bellingham Review. "Everyone entering the competition will receive a complimentary two-issue subscription to Bellingham Review ." **Deadline:** April 1.

ACORN-PLANTOS AWARD FOR PEOPLES POETRY

Acorn-Plantos Award Committee, 36 Sunset Ave., Hamilton ON L8R 1V6, Canada. **E-mail:** jeffseff@allstream.net. **Contact:** Jeff Seffinga. "Annual contest for work that appeared in print in the previous calender year. This award is given to the Canadian poet who best (through the publication of a book of poems) exemplifies populist or peoples poetry in the tradition of Milton Acorn, Ted Plantos, et al. Work may be entered by the poet or the publisher; the award goes to the poet. Entrants must submit 5 copies of each title. Poet must be a citizen of Canada or a landed immigrant. Publisher need not be Canadian." Deadline: June 30 $500 (CDN) and a medal. Judged by a panel of poets in the tradition who are not entered in the current year.

AKRON POETRY PRIZE

The University of Akron Press, 120 E. Mill St., Suite 415, Akron OH 44308. (330)972-5342. **Fax:** (330)972-8364. **E-mail:** uapress@uakron.edu; marybid@uakron.edu. **Website:** www3.uakron.edu/uapress/poetryprize.html. **Contact:** Mary Biddinger, editor/award director. Offers annual award of $1,500 plus publication of a book-length ms. Submissions must be unpublished. Considers simultaneous submissions (with notification of acceptance elsewhere). Submit 48 or more pages, typed, single-spaced; optional self-addressed postcard for confirmation. Mss will not be returned. Do not send mss bound or enclosed in covers. See website for complete guidelines. **Entry fee:** $25. **Deadline:** Entries accepted May 1-June 15 only. Competition receives 500+ entries. 2011 winner was Emily Rosko for *Prop Rockery*. 2012 judge: Dara Wier. Winner posted on website by September 30. "Intimate friends, relatives, current and former students of the final judge (students in an academic, degree-conferring program or its equivalent) are not eligible to enter the 2013 Akron Poetry Prize competition."

AGHA SHAHID ALI PRIZE IN POETRY

University of Utah Press, J. Willard Marriott Lib., Ste 5400, 295 S. 1500 East, Salt Lake City UT 84112. (801)581-6771. **Fax:** (801)581-3365. **Website:** www.uofupress.com/ali-poetry-prize.php. The University of Utah Press and the University of Utah Department of English offer an annual award of $1,000, publication of a book-length poetry ms, and a reading in the

Guest Writers Series. Poems must be unpublished as a collection, but individual poems may have been previously published elsewhere. Considers simultaneous submissions; "however, entrants must notify the Press immediately if the collection submitted is accepted for publication elsewhere during the competition." Submit 48-64 typed pages of poetry, with no names or other identifying information appearing on title page or within ms. Include cover sheet with complete contact information (name, address, telephone, e-mail address). Submissions must be in English. Mss will not be returned. Guidelines available on website. **Entry fee:** $25/book submission. **Deadline:** 2012: February 1-March 31. Competition receives over 300 mss/year. Winner announced on press website in November; series editor contacts winning poet. Copies of winning books are available for $14.95 from University of Utah Press ((800)621-2736 for order fulfillment) or through website.

AMERICAN LITERARY REVIEW SHORT FICTION AWARD

P.O. Box 311307, University of North Texas, Denton TX 76203-1307. (940)565-2755. **E-mail:** americanliteraryreview@gmail.com. **Website:** www.engl.unt.edu/alr. "To award excellence in short fiction." Three prizes of $1,000 each and publication in the *American Literary Review* will be given for a poem, a short story, and an essay. 2010 **Poetry Judge: Claire Bateman; Fiction Judge: Donald Hays; Creative Nonfiction Judge: Debra Monroe**. Judged by rotating outside writer. Entry fee: $15. For guidelines, send SASE or visit website. Accepts inquiries by email and phone. Deadline: November 1. Entries must be unpublished. Contest open to anyone not affiliated with the University of North Texas. "Only solidly crafted, character-driven stories will have the best chance for success." Winners announced and notified by mail and phone in February. List of winners available for SASE.

O THE AMY AWARD FOR POETRY

Poets & Writers, 90 Broad St., Suite 2100, New York NY 10004. **E-mail:** admin@pw.org. **Website:** www.pw.org/about-us/amy_award. **Contact:** Elliot Figman, executive director. The Amy Award, sponsored by Poets & Writers, Inc., offers honorarium, books, plus a reading in NYC. **Entrants must be women 30 years of age or under who reside on Long Island or in the New York metropolitan region.** Submit 3 lyric poems of no more than 50 lines each, online or with SASE, and application. Guidelines available on website. **Entry fee:** none. **Deadline:** June 1, 2012. Past winners include Genevieve Burger-Weiser, Lisabeth Burton, K.D. Henley, and Alexandra Wilder. "The Amy Award was established by Edward Butscher and Paula Trachtman of East Hampton in memory of Mrs. Trachtman's daughter, Amy Rothholz, an actor and poet who died at age 25."

◐ ANABIOSIS PRESS CHAPBOOK CONTEST

2 South New St., Bradford MA 01835. (978)469-7085. **E-mail:** rsmyth@anabiosispress.org. **Website:** www.anabiosispress.org. **Contact:** Acquisitions: Richard Smyth, editor. The Anabiosis Press Chapbook Contest offers $100, plus publication of the winning chapbook, and 75 copies of the first run. Submit 16-20 pages of poetry on any subject. Include separate pages with a biography, table of contents, and acknowledgments for any previous publications. Include SASE with correct postage for return of ms. **Entry fee:** $12 (all entrants receive a copy of the winning chapbook). Make checks payable to The Anabiosis Press. **Deadline:** June 30 (postmark). Winners announced by September 30. The 2011 winner was Jessie Brown's *Lucky.* Deadline: June 30 (postmark) $100, plus publication of the winning chapbook, and 75 copies of the first run.

ANDERBO POETRY PRIZE

Anderbo Poetry Prize, 270 Lafayette St., Suite 1412, New York NY 10012. **E-mail:** editors@anderbo.com. **Website:** www.anderbo.com. **Contact:** Rick Rofihe. Judge: Linda Bierds; Contest Assistant: Charity Burns. Reading Fee: $10; make check payable to Rick Rofihe. "Poet must not have have been previously published on anderbo.com. Limit 6 poems per poet. Poems should be typed on 8½ x 11 paper with the poet's name and contact info on the upper right corner of each poem. Mail submissions. Enclose SASE to receive names of winner and honorable mentions. See guidelines online. Prize: $500, publication on anderbo.com.

ANNUAL BOOK COMPETITION

E-mail: wwphpress@gmail.com. **Website:** www.washingtonwriters.org. Poets living within 60 driving miles of the Capitol (Baltimore area included) are invited to submit TWO copies of a POETRY manuscript (50-70 pages, single or 1-1/2 spaced), each copy with an acknowledgments page for poems previously published in journals or anthologies, a reading fee of $20.00, and a stamped, self-addressed reply envelope. Manuscripts will not be returned; rather they will be recycled. **General Info:** Author's name should not appear on the manuscript. The title page of each copy should contain the title only. Provide name, address, telephone number, e-mail address, and title on a separate cover sheet accompanying the submission. A separate page for acknowledgments may be included for stories or excerpts previously published in journals and anthologies. The winner will receive $500 and 50 copies of the book.

ANNUAL GIVAL PRESS OSCAR WILDE AWARD

Gival Press, LLC, P.O. Box 3812, Arlington VA 22203. (703)351-0079. **E-mail:** givalpress@yahoo.com. **Website:** www.givalpress.com. **Contact:** Robert L. Giron. "Award given to the best previously unpublished original poem—written in English of any length, in any style, typed, double-spaced on 1 side only—which best relates gay/lesbian/bisexual/transgendered life, by a poet who is 18 years or older. Entrants are asked to submit their poems without any kind of identification (with the exception of titles) and with a separate cover page with the following information: name, address (street, city, and state with zip code), telephone number, e-mail address (if available), and a list of poems by title. Checks drawn on American banks should be made out to Gival Press, LLC." Deadline: June 27 (postmarked). Prize: $100 and the poem, along with information about the poet, will be published on the Gival Press website.

ANNUAL VENTURA COUNTY WRITERS CLUB POETRY CONTEST WITH TWO DIVISIONS FOR YOUNG POETS

Ventura County Writers Club Poetry Contest, P.O. Box 3373, Thousand Oaks CA 91362. (805)524-6970. **E-mail:** kathleen@kathleenkaiser.com. **E-mail:** venturacountywriters@yahoo.com. **Website:** www.venturacountywriters.com. **Contact:** Katherine Kaiser. Contest includes two youth categories for poets under 18. Division A is open to entrants ages 13 to 18. Division B is open to poets ages 12 and under. Poets 18 and older are invited to enter in the Adult category. The contest is open to poets throughout the country and does accept international entries. "This contest enriches the culture of our community and supports our poets," states Melissa Grossman, contest chair. "Poetry is alive in Ventura County! We must do all we can to nurture new poets and promote established writers." All winning poems will be published in the club's newsletter, *The Write Stuff*, and the winning poets will be invited to recite their works at the April club meeting. All winners and families will be honored at a reception following the readings. The winning poems will appear in the next volume of the club's anthology, to be published in 2012. There will be additional publicity for the winners to help promote their winning works. "Last year we divided the youth category into two parts and received an outstanding response from many area schools," commented club president Lee Wade. "Inspiring a new generation to embrace poetry and other forms of written communication goes to the core of VCWC's mission, to encourage the craft." Full details and rules are available for download from the club's website http://www.venturacountywriters.com Categories and Fees: Adult Category: $4.00 per poem for VCWC members, $5.00 per poem for others. Youth Categories - $3.00 per poem. Entry fees cannot be accepted online at this time. For both print and electronic entries, checks should be made payable to Ventura County Writers Club or VCWC and mail to: Ventura County Writers Club Poetry Contest, P. O. Box 3373 Thousand Oaks, CA 91362. Enter as many poems as you like. No poems that have been previously published in any form (including digital) are to be entered. Include a separate cover sheet with name, address, phone number, title(s) of submitted poem(s), with the category and division in which they are entered. Do not place your name or any other identification on the poem pages. This is to ensure authors are not identified during the judging process. Include a separate cover sheet with name, address, phone number, titles of submitted poems, with the category and division in which they are entered. For print submissions, submit one poem per page using Times New Roman 12 point type on white 8 1/2 X 11 inch paper. Send two copies of each poem. For electronic submissions, email VenturaCountyWriters@yahoo.com with 'Poetry Contest' in the subject line. Send one poem per attachment. Send cover sheet in separate attachment with information as shown above. Include a cover sheet copy with your entry fee(s). Deadline: February 28 (postmark-mail, email by 12:00 midnight)

ANNUAL WORLD HAIKU COMPETITION & ANNUAL WORLD TANKA CONTEST

P.O. Box 17331, Arlington VA 22216. **E-mail:** lpezinesubmissions@gmail.com. **Website:** http://lyricalpassionpoetry.yolasite.com. **Contact:** Raquel D. Bailey. Contest is open to all writers. "Promotes Japanese short form poetry." Deadline: November 30, 2012. (Dates are subject to change each year. See website for details.) Monetary compensation and publication. Judged by experienced editors and award-winning writers from the contemporary writing community.

TIPS "E-mail and snail mail entries accepted."

ARIZONA LITERARY CONTEST & BOOK AWARDS

6145 W. Echo Lane, Glendale AZ 85302. (623)847-9343. **E-mail:** info@azauthors.com. **Website:** www.azauthors.com. Arizona Authors Association sponsors annual literary contest in poetry, short story, essay, unpublished novels, and published books (fiction, nonfiction, and children's literature). Awards publication in *Arizona Literary Magazine*, prizes by Five Star Publications, Inc., and $100 1st Prize, $50 2nd Prize, and $25 3rd Prize in each category. Poetry submissions must be unpublished. Considers simultaneous submissions. Submit any number of poems on any subject up to 50 lines. Entry form and guidelines available on website or for SASE. **Entry fee:** $15/poem. **Deadline:** Reads submissions January 1-July 1. Competition receives 1,000 entries/year. Recent poetry winners include Dennis Schwesinger and Kelly Nelson. Judges: Arizona authors, editors, and reviewers. Winners announced at an award banquet by November 8. Arizona Authors Association sponsors annual literary contest in poetry, short story, essay, unpublished novels, and published books (fiction, nonfiction, and children's literature). Judges: Arizona authors, editors, and reviewers. Winners announced at an award banquet by November 8.

O ARIZONA STATE POETRY SOCIETY ANNUAL CONTEST

37427 N. Ootam Rd., #104, Cave Creek AZ 85331. (480)575-1222. **Website:** www.azpoetry.org. Offers a variety of cash prizes in several categories ranging from $10-125; 1st, 2nd, and 3rd Prize winners are published in Sandcutters, ASPS's quarterly publication, which also lists names of Honorable Mention winners. See guidelines for detailed submission information (available for SASE or on website). **Entry fee:** varies according to category; see guidelines. **Deadline:** approximately September 15 (postmark). Competition receives over 1,000 entries/year. "ASPS sponsors a variety of monthly contests for members. Membership is available to anyone anywhere."

ARROWHEAD REGIONAL ARTS COUNCIL INDIVIDUAL ARTIST SUPPORT GRANT

Arrowhead Regional Arts Council, 1301 Rice Lake Rd., Suite 120, Duluth MN 55811. (218)722-0952 or (800)569-8134. **E-mail:** info@aracouncil.org. **Website:** www.aracouncil.org. Award is to provide financial support to regional artists wishing to take advantage of impending, concrete opportunities that will advance their work or careers. Deadline: August, November, March. Prize: up to $2,500. Judged by the ARAC Board.

ART AFFAIR ANNUAL WRITING CONTEST

Art Affair, P.O. Box 54302, Oklahoma City OK 73154. **E-mail:** artaffair@aol.com. **Website:** www.shadetreecreations.com. **Contact:** Barbara Shepherd. Purpose of contest is to encourage new and established writers and to publicly recognize them for their efforts. Open to any writer or poet. Deadline: October 1 (every year). "Fiction and poems must be unpublished. Multiple entries accepted and may be mailed in the same packet. For (general) Short Story, double-space in 12-point font (put page and word count in upper right-hand corner of first page—5,000 word limit. Include cover page with writer's name, address, phone number, and title of story. For Western Short Story, follow same directions but type 'Western' on cover page. For Poetry, submit original poems on any subject, in any style, no more than 60 lines (put line count in the upper right-hand corner of first page). Include cover page with poet's name, address, phone number, and title. Do not include SASE; mss will not be returned." $3/each poem. Make check payable to Art Affair. Poetry: 1st Prize: $40; 2nd Prize: $25; 3rd Prize: $15. (All winners also receive certificates. Additional certificates for Honorable Mentions will be awarded at discretion of the judges). "Winners' list will be published on our website in December. Highly-qualified and professional judges—different each year (blind judging)."

TIPS "Guidelines and entry forms available for SASE and on website."

THE ART OF MUSIC ANNUAL WRITING CONTEST

P.O. Box 85, Del Mar CA 92014-0085. (619)884-1401. **Fax:** (858)755-1104. **E-mail:** info@theartofmusicinc.org. **E-mail:** eaxford@aol.com. **Website:**

www.theartofmusicinc.org; www.pianopress.com. **Contact:** Elizabeth C. Axford. Offered biannually. Categories are: Essay, short story, poetry, song lyrics, and illustrations for cover art. Acquires one-time rights. All entries must be accompanied by an entry form indicating category and age; parent signature is required of all writers under age 18. Poems may be of any length and in any style; essays and short stories should not exceed 5 double-spaced, typewritten pages. All entries shall be previously unpublished (except poems and song lyrics) and the original work of the author. Inquiries accepted by e-mail, phone. Short stories should be no longer than 5 pages typed and double spaced. Open to any writer. "Make sure all work is fresh and original. Music-related topics only." Results announced October 31. Winners notified by mail. For contest results, send SASE or visit website. "The purpose of the contest is to promote the art of music through writing." Deadline: June 30. Prize: Cash, medal, certificate, publication in the anthology *The Art of Music: A Collection of Writings*, and copies of the book. Judged by a panel of published poets, authors and songwriters.

ATLANTIC WRITING COMPETITION FOR UNPUBLISHED MANUSCRIPTS

Writers' Federation of Nova Scotia, 1113 Marginal Rd., Halifax NS B3H 4P7. (902)423-8116. **Fax:** (902)422-0881. **E-mail:** director@writers.ns.ca; talk@writers.ns.ca. **Website:** www.writers.ns.ca. **Contact:** Nate Crawford, program coordinator. "Annual contest for beginners to try their hand in a number of categories: novel, short story, poetry, writing for younger children, writing for juvenile/young adult. Only 1 entry/category is allowed. Established writers are also eligible, but must work in an area that's new to them. Because our aim is to help Atlantic Canadian writers grow, judges return written comments when the competition is concluded. Anyone residing in the Atlantic Provinces for at least 6 months prior to the contest deadline is eligible to enter." Deadline: First Friday in December. **Novel**—1st Place: $200; 2nd Place: $150; 3rd Place: $75. **Writing for Younger Children and Juvenile/Young Adult**—1st Place: $150; 2nd Place: $75; 3rd Place: $50. **Poetry and Short Story**—1st Place: $150; 2nd Place: $75; 3rd Place: $50. a team of 2-3 professional writers, editors, booksellers, librarians, or teachers.

AUTUMN HOUSE POETRY, FICTION, AND NONFICTION PRIZES

P.O. Box 60100, Pittsburgh PA 15211. (412)381-4261. **E-mail:** msimms@autumnhouse.org. **Website:** http://autumnhouse.org. **Contact:** Michael Simms, editor. Offers annual prize of $2,500 and publication of book-length ms with national promotion. Submission must be unpublished as a collection, but individual poems, stories, and essays may have been previously published elsewhere. Considers simultaneous submissions. Submit 50-80 pages of poetry or 200-300 pages of prose ("blind judging—2 cover sheets requested"). Guidelines available for SASE, by e-mail, or on website. **Entry fee:** $30/ms. **Deadline:** June 30 annually. Competition receives 1,500 entries/year. 2012 judges were Stephen Dunn, Stewart O'Nan, and Phillip Lopate. Winners announced through mailings, website, and ads in *Poets & Writers*, *American Poetry Review*, and *Writer's Chronicle* (extensive publicity for winner). Copies of winning books available from Amazon.com, Barnes & Noble, and other retailers. "Autumn House is a nonprofit corporation with the mission of publishing and promoting poetry and other fine literature. We have published books by Gerald Stern, Ruth L. Schwartz, Ed Ochester, Andrea Hollander Budy, George Bilgere, Jo McDougall, and others."

TIPS "Include only your best work."

BARROW STREET PRESS BOOK CONTEST

P.O. Box 1558, Kingston RI 02881. **Website:** www.barrowstreet.org. Barrow Street Press publishes one poetry book/year through the annual Barrow Street Press Book Contest. Winner receives $1,000 and publication. Submit a 50- to 70-page ms of original, previously unpublished poetry in English. Manuscript should be typed, single-spaced on white 812x11 paper. Clear photocopies acceptable. Include 2 title pages and an acknowledgments page listing any poems previously published in journals or anthologies. Author's name, address, and daytime phone number should appear on first title page only, and nowhere else in ms. Include SASE for results only; no mss will be returned. Guidelines available on website. **Entry fee:** $25; include mailer with $2.13 postage for copy of winning book. Make checks payable to Barrow Street. **Deadline:** June 30. 2012 Judge is Lynn Emanuel.

THE BASKERVILLE PUBLISHERS POETRY AWARD & THE BETSY COLQUITT POETRY AWARD

(817)257-6537. **Fax:** (817)257-6239. **E-mail:** descant@tcu.edu. **Website:** www.descant.tcu.edu. **Contact:** Dan Williams and Alex Lemon. "Annual award for an outstanding poem published in an issue of *descant.*" Deadline: September - April. $250 for Baskerville Award; $500 for Betsy Colquitt Award. Publication retains copyright, but will transfer it to the author upon request.

● THE PATRICIA BIBBY FIRST BOOK AWARD

Tebot Bach, P.O. Box 7887, Huntington Beach CA 92615-7887. **E-mail:** mifanwy@tebotbach.org. **Website:** www.tebotbach.org. **Contact:** Mifanwy Kaiser. Deadline: October 31 (postmark), annually Judges are selected annually. Winner announced each year in April.

● BINGHAMTON UNIVERSITY MILT KESSLER POETRY BOOK AWARD

Binghamton University Creative Writing Program, P.O. Box 6000, Binghamton NY 13902. (607)777-2713. **Fax:** (607)777-2408. **E-mail:** cwpro@binghamton.edu. **Website:** english.binghamton.edu/cwpro/bookawards/kesslerguidelines.htm. **Contact:** Maria Mazziotti Gillan, creative writing program director. Offers annual award of $1,000 for a book of poetry judged best of those published during the previous year. Submit books published that year; do not submit manuscripts." Entry form and guidelines available for SASE, by e-mail, or on website. **Entry fee:** none; "just submit 3 copies of book." **Deadline:** March 1. Competition receives 500 books/year.

BLUE MOUNTAIN ARTS/SPS STUDIOS POETRY CARD CONTEST

P.O. Box 1007, Boulder CO 80306. (303)449-0536. **Fax:** (303)447-0939. **E-mail:** poetrycontest@sps.com. **Website:** www.sps.com. "We're looking for original poetry that is rhyming or non-rhyming, although we find that non-rhyming poetry reads better. Poems may also be considered for possible publication on greeting cards or in book anthologies. Contest is offered biannually. Guidelines available online." Deadline: December 31 and June 30 1st Place: $300; 2nd Place: $150; 3rd Place: $50. Blue Mountain Arts editorial staff.

●● THE BOARDMAN TASKER AWARD FOR MOUNTAIN LITERATURE

The Boardman Tasker Charitable Trust, 8 Bank View Rd., Darley Abbey Derby DE22 1EJ, UK. Phone/fax: UK 01332342246. **E-mail:** steve@people-matter.co.uk. **Website:** www.boardmantasker.com. **Contact:** Steve Dean. Offered annually to reward a work of nonfiction or fiction, in English or in translation, which has made an outstanding contribution to mountain literature, in English or in translation, which has made an outstanding contribution to mountain literature. May be fiction, nonfiction, poetry or drama. Not an anthology. Subject must be concerned with a mountain environment. Previous winners have been books on expeditions, climbing experiences, a biography of a mountaineer, novels." Guidelines available in January by e-mail or on website. Entries must be previously published. Open to any writer. Results announced in November. Winners notified by phone or e-mail. For contest results, e-mail or visit website. "The winning book needs to be well written to reflect a knowledge of and a respect and appreciation for the mountain environment." "The award is to honor Peter Boardman and Joe Tasker, who disappeared on Everest in 1982." Deadline: Midnight of August 17. Prize: £3,000 Judged by a panel of 3 judges elected by trustees.

THE FREDERICK BOCK PRIZE

(312)787-7070. **E-mail:** poetry@poetrymagazine.org. **Website:** www.poetrymagazine.org. Offered annually for poems published in *Poetry* during the preceding year (October through September). Upon acceptance, *Poetry* licenses exclusive worldwide first serial rights, including electronic rights, for publication, as well as non-exclusive rights to reprint, reuse, and archive the work, in any format, in perpetuity. Copyright reverts to author upon first publication. Any writer may submit poems to *Poetry.* Prize: $500

BOSTON GLOBE-HORN BOOK AWARDS

The Boston Globe, Horn Book, Inc., 56 Roland St., Suite 200, Boston MA 02129. (617)628-0225. **Fax:** (617)628-0882. **E-mail:** info@hbook.com; khedeen@hbook.com. **Website:** hbook.com/bghb/. **Contact:** Katrina Hedeen. Offered annually for excellence in literature for children and young adults (published June 1-May 31). Categories: picture book, fiction and poetry, nonfiction. Judges may also name several honor books in each category. Books must be published in the US, but may be written or illustrated by citizens of any country. The Horn Book Magazine publishes speeches given at awards ceremonies. Guidelines for SASE or online. Deadline for entries: May 15. Winners receive $500 and an engraved silver bowl; honor book recipients receive an engraved silver plate. Judged by a panel of 3 judges selected each year.

BARBARA BRADLEY PRIZE

New England Poetry Club, 654 Green St., No. 2, Cambridge MA 02139. **E-mail:** contests@nepoetryclub.org. **Website:** www.nepoetryclub.org. **Contact:** NEPC contest coordinator. For a lyric poem under 21 lines, written by a woman. Deadline: May 31. Prize: $200. Judges are well-known poets and sometimes winners of previous NEPC contests.

THE BRIAR CLIFF REVIEW FICTION, POETRY, AND CREATIVE NONFICTION COMPETITION

The Briar Cliff Review, Briar Cliff University, 3303 Rebecca St., Sioux City IA 51104-0100. **E-mail:** tricia.currans-sheehan@briarcliff.edu (editor); jeanne.emmons@briarcliff.edu (poetry). **Website:** www.briarcliff.edu/bcreview. **Contact:** Tricia Currans-Sheehan, editor. *The Briar Cliff Review* sponsors an annual contest offering $1,000 and publication to each 1st Prize winner in fiction, poetry, and creative nonfiction. Previous year's winner and former students of editors ineligible. Winning pieces accepted for publication on the basis of first-time Rights. Considers simultaneous submissions, "but notify us immediately upon acceptance elsewhere." Submit 3 poems, single-spaced on 8 1/2x11 paper; no more than 1 poem per page. Include separate cover sheet with author's name, address, e-mail, and poem title(s); no name on ms. Include SASE for results only; mss will not be returned. Guidelines available on website. **Entry fee:** $20 for 3 poems. "All entrants receive a copy of the magazine (a $15 value) containing the winning entries." **Deadline:** November 1. Judge: The editors of *The Briar Cliff Review*. Offered annually for unpublished poetry, fiction and essay. "Send us your best work. We want stories with a plot." Award to reward good writers and showcase quality writing.

BRICK ROAD POETRY BOOK CONTEST

Brick Road Poetry Press, Inc., P.O. Box 751, Columbus GA 31902. (706)649-3080. **Fax:** (706)649-3094. **E-mail:** editor@brickroadpoetrypress.com. **Website:** www.brickroadpoetrypress.com. **Contact:** Ron Self and Keith Badowski, co-editors/founders. Offers annual award. The 1st Prize winner will receive a publication contract with Brick Road Poetry Press, $1,000, and 25 copies of the printed book. The winning book will be published in both print and e-book formats. "We may also offer publication contracts to the top finalists." Submissions must be unpublished as a collection, but individual poems may have been previously published elsewhere. Submit 70-100 pages of poetry. Guidelines available by e-mail or online. **Entry fee:** $25. **Deadline:** November 1. Competition receives 150 entries/year. Judged by Ron Self and Keith Badowski. Winners notified February 15. Copies of winning books available for $15.95. "The mission of Brick Road Poetry Press is to publish and promote poetry that entertains, amuses, edifies and surprises a wide audience of appreciative readers. We are not qualified to judge who deserves to be published, so we concentrate on publishing what we enjoy. Our preference is for poetry geared toward dramatizing the human experience in a language rich with sensory image and metaphor, recognizing that poetry can be, at one and the same time, both familiar as the perspiration of daily labor and outrageous as a carnival sideshow."

TIPS "The best way to discover all that poetry can be and to expand the limits of your own poetry is to read expansively."

THE BRIDPORT PRIZE

P.O. Box 6910, Dorset DT6 9QB, United Kingdom. +44 (0)1308 428 333. **E-mail:** frances@bridportprize.org.uk. **Website:** www.bridportprize.org.uk. **Contact:** Frances Everitt, administrator. Award to "promote literary excellence, discover new talent." Categories: Short stories, poetry, flash fiction. 2010 introduced a new category for flash fiction: £1,000 sterling 1st Prize for the best short, short story of under 250 words. Deadline: May 31. Prize: £5,000 sterling; £1,000 sterling; £500 sterling; various runners-up prizes and publication of approximately 13 best stories and 13 best poems in anthology; plus 6 best flash fiction stories. Judged by 1 judge for fiction (in 2012, Patrick Gale) and 1 judge for poetry (in 2012, Gwyneth Lewis).

BRIGHT HILL PRESS POETRY CHAPBOOK AWARD

Bright Press Hill & Literary Center, P.O. Box 193, 94 Church St., Treadwell NY 13846. (607)829-5055. **E-mail:** brighthillpress@stny.rr.com. **Website:** www.

brighthillpress.org. The annual Bright Hill Press Chapbook Award offers $300, publication of a chapbook-length ms, and 25 author's copies. Guidelines available for SASE, by e-mail, or on website. Deadline: July 31 (postmark).

TIPS "Publish your poems in literary magazines before trying to get a whole ms published. Publishing individual poems is the best way to hone your complete ms."

BRITTINGHAM PRIZE IN POETRY

University of Wisconsin Press, Department of English, 600 N. Park St., Madison WI 53706. **E-mail:** rwallace@wisc.edu. **Website:** www.wisc.edu/wisconsinpress/index.html. **Contact:** Ronald Wallace, poetry editor. The annual Brittingham Prize in Poetry is 1 of 2 prizes awarded by The University of Wisconsin Press (see separate listing for the Felix Pollak Prize in Poetry in this section). Offers $1,000, plus publication, with an additional $1,500 honorarium to cover expenses of a reading in Madison. Submissions must be unpublished as a collection, but individual poems may have been published elsewhere (publication must be acknowledged). Considers simultaneous submissions if notified of selection elsewhere. Submit 50-80 unbound ms pages, typed single-spaced (with double spaces between stanzas). Clean photocopies are acceptable. Include 1 title page with poet's name, address, and telephone number and 1 with title only. No translations. SASE required. Will return results only; mss will not be returned. Guidelines available for SASE or on website. **Entry fee:** $25. **NOTE:** $25 fee applies to consideration of same entry for the Felix Pollak Prize in Poetry—1 fee for 2 contest entries. Make checks/money orders payable to University of Wisconsin Press. **Deadline:** Submit September 1-27 (postmark). 2012 Brittingham Prize winner was Jazzy Danziger, *Darkroom*. Qualified readers will screen all mss. Judge by "a distinguished poet who will remain anonymous until the winners are announced in mid-February."

BURNSIDE REVIEW CHAPBOOK COMPETITION

P.O. Box 1782, Portland OR 97207. **E-mail:** sid@burnsidereview.org. **Website:** www.burnsidereview.org. **Contact:** Sid Miller, editor. The annual Burnside Review Chapbook Competition awards $200, publication, and 10 author's copies to winning poet. Guidelines available for SASE or electronic submission on website. **Entry fee:** $15. **Deadline:** March 15-June 30. 2011 winner was Amalia Gladhart (*Detours*). 2012 Judge is Emily Kendal Frey. (See separate listing for Burnside Review in Magazines/Journals.)

GERALD CABLE BOOK AWARD

Silverfish Review Press, P.O. Box 3541, Eugene OR 97403. (541)344-5060. **E-mail:** sfrpress@earthlink.net. **Website:** www.silverfishreviewpress.com. **Contact:** Rodger Moody, Editor. Offers annual award of $1,000, publication by Silverfish Review Press, and 25 author copies to a book-length ms of original poetry by an author who has not yet published a full-length collection. No restrictions on the kind of poetry or subject matter; no translations. Individual poems may have been previously published elsewhere, but must be acknowledged. Considers simultaneous submissions (notify immediately of acceptance elsewhere). Submit at least 48 pages of poetry, no names or identification on ms pages. Include separate title sheet with poet's name, address, and phone number. Include SASP for notification of receipt and SASE for results; no mss will be returned. Accepts e-mail submissions in Word, plain text, or rich text; send entry fee and SASE by regular mail. Guidelines available for SASE, by e-mail, or on website. **Entry fee:** $25. Make checks payable to Silverfish Review Press. **Deadline:** October 15 (postmark). Winner announced in March. Copies of winning books available through website. "All entrants who enclose a booksize envelope and $2.23 in postage will receive a free copy of a recent winner of the book award."

TIPS "Now accepting email submissions (save money on postage and photocopying); use Paypal for reading fee payment, see website for instructions."

CAKETRAIN CHAPBOOK COMPETITION

P.O. Box 82588, Pittsburgh PA 15218. **E-mail:** caketrainjournal@hotmail.com. **Website:** www.caketrain.org/competitions. Annual chapbook contest sponsored by *Caketrain* literary journal. Can submit by mail with SASE or by e-mail. See website for guidelines. Winner receives a $250 cash prize and 25 copies of their chapbook. **Entry fee:** $15 for reading fee only or $20 for entry fee and copy of winning chapbook. **Deadline:** October 1. Recent winners include Claire Hero's *afterpastures* (2008); Tina May Hall's *All the Day's Sad Stories* (2009); Ben Mirov's *Ghost Machine* (2010); Sarah Rose Etter's *Tongue Party* (2011); and Meredith Stricker's *Mistake* (2012).

◐ CAROLINA WREN PRESS POETRY CONTEST FOR A FIRST OR SECOND BOOK

120 Morris St., Durham NC 27701. (919)560-2738. **Fax:** (919)560-2759. **E-mail:** carolinawrenpress@earthlink.net. **Website:** www.carolinawrenpress.org. **Contact:** Contest Director. The biennial Carolina Wren Press Poetry Contest for a First or Second Book offers $1,000 and publication by Carolina Wren Press (see separate listing in Book/Chapbook Publishers). Open only to poets who have published no more than 1 full-length collection (48 pages or more). Submissions must be unpublished as a collection, but individual poems may have been previously published elsewhere. Manuscripts that have been previously self-published or that are available online in their entirety are not eligible. Considers simultaneous submissions (notify immediately of acceptance elsewhere). Submit 2 copies of a poetry ms of 48-72 pages. Page count should include title page, table of contents, and optional dedication page. See guidelines for complete formatting and submission details. Include SASE for results only; mss will not be returned. Guidelines available for SASE, by e-mail, or on website (in September). **Entry fee:** $20. **Deadline:** Entry Deadline: March 15, 2011. (postmark). 2011 judge: Lee Ann Brown. Past judges: William Pitt Root, Evie Shockley, Minnie Bruce Pratt. Copies of winning books available through website, Amazon, or local bookstore.

JAMIE CAT CALLAN HUMOR PRIZE

Category in the Soul Making Keats Literary Competition, The Webhallow House, 1544 Sweetwood Dr., Broadmoor Village CA 94015-2029. **E-mail:** pennobhill@aol.com. **Website:** www.soulmakingcontest.us. **Contact:** Eileen Malone. "Any form, 2,500 words or less, 1 piece per entry. Previously published material is accepted. Indicate category on cover page. Identify only with 3x5 card. Open annually to any writer." Deadline: November 30. 1st Place: $100; 2nd Place: $50; 3rd Place: $25.

◐◎ THE CENTER FOR BOOK ARTS POETRY CHAPBOOK COMPETITION

The Center for Book Arts, 28 W. 27th St., 3rd Floor, New York NY 10001. (212)481-0295. **Fax:** (866)708-8994. **E-mail:** info@centerforbookarts.org. **Website:** www.centerforbookarts.org. Contest needs poetry chapbooks. Offered annually for unpublished collections of poetry. Individual poems may have been previously published. Collection must not exceed 500 lines or 24 pages (does not include cover page, title pages, table of contents, or acknowledgements pages). Copies of winning chapbooks available through website. "Center for Book Arts is a nonprofit organization dedicated to the traditional crafts of bookmaking and contemporary interpretations of the book as an art object. Through the Center's Education, Exhibition, and Workspace Programs, we ensure that the ancient craft of the book remains a viable and vital part of our civilization." Deadline: December 1 (postmarked). $500 award, $500 honorarium for a reading, publication, and 10 copies of chapbook. 2012 judges were Phillis Levin and Sharon Dolin.

◐ CIDER PRESS REVIEW BOOK AWARD

P.O. Box 33384, San Diego CA 92163. **E-mail:** editor@ciderpressreview.com. **Website:** http://ciderpressreview.com/bookaward. **Contact:** Contest director. Annual award from *Cider Press Review*. Deadline: submit September 1 - November 30 (postmark). Prize: $1,500, publication, and 25 author's copies of a book length collection of poetry. Author receives a standard publishing contract. Initial print run is not less than 1,000 copies. CPR acquires first publication rights. 2012 judge was Gray Jacobik. The 2011 winner was Joseph Fasano.

◐ CLEVELAND STATE UNIVERSITY POETRY CENTER FIRST BOOK

Dept. of English, 2121 Euclid Ave., Cleveland OH 44115-2214. **E-mail:** poetrycenter@csuohio.edu. **Website:** www.csuohio.edu/poetrycenter/contest1.html. **Contact:** Poetry Center Manager. Offers $1,000, publication in the CSU Poetry Series, and a paid reading at Cleveland State for the best full-length volume of original poetry by a poet who has not published or committed to publish a collection of poetry in a book of 48 or more pages with a press run of at least 500 copies. "The CSU Poetry Center reserves the right to consider all finalists for publication." Considers simultaneous submissions; "please inform us if the manuscript is accepted elsewhere." "Eclectic in taste and inclusive in its aesthetic, with particular interest in lyric poetry and innovative approaches to craft. Not interested in light verse, devotional verse, doggerel, or poems by poets who have not read my contemporary poetry." Submit a minimum of 48 pages of poetry, numbered. Include table of contents and acknowledgements page. Include 2 cover pages: one with ms title, poet's name, address, phone number, and e-mail; one with ms title only. No identifying information on ms pages; no cover letter or biographical information. Clearly mark outside of mailing envelope and each cover page "First Book." Accepts multiple submissions with separate entry fee for each; send in the same envelope marked " Multiple." Include SASP for notification of receipt of ms (optional) and SASE for notification of results; mss are not returned. Guidelines available on website. **Entry fee:** $25. Make checks payable to Cleveland State University. **Deadline:** submit November 1-February 15 (postmark). Entrants notified by mail in summer. 2012 judge: Nick Flynn (intimate friends, relatives, current and former students of the First Book judge, students in an academic degree-conferring program or its equivalent are not eligible to enter)."

◐ CLEVELAND STATE UNIVERSITY POETRY CENTER OPEN COMPETITION

Dept. of English, 2121 Euclid Ave., Clevleand OH 44115-2214. **E-mail:** poetrycenter@csuohio.edu. **Website:** www.csuohio.edu/poetrycenter/contest1.html. **Contact:** Center Manager. Offers $1,000 and publication in the CSU Poetry Series for the best full-length volume of original poetry by a poet who has published at least one full-length collection of poetry in a book of 48 pages or more with a press run of 500. The CSU Poetry Center reserves the right to consider all finalists for publication. No submissions previously published in their entirety (including self-published) or translations. Considers simultaneous submissions; "please inform us if the manuscript is accepted elsewhere. Eclectic in its taste and inclusive in its aesthetic, with particular interest in lyric poetry and innovative approaches to craft. Not interested in light verse, devotional versr, doggerel, or poems by poets who have not read much contemporary poetry." Submit a minimum of 48 pages of poetry, numbered. Include table of contents and acknowledgements page. Include 2 cover pages: one with ms title, poet's name, address, phone number, and e-mail; one with ms title only. No identifying information on ms pages; no cover letter or biographical information. Clearly mark outside of mailing envelope and each cover page "Open Competition." Include SASP for notification of receipt of ms (optional) and SASE for notification of results; mss are not returned. Guidelines available on website. **Entry fee:** $25. Make checks payable to Cleveland State University. **Deadline:** submit November 1-February 15 (postmark). Entrants notified by mail in summer.

CLOCKWISE CHAPBOOK AWARD

Tebot Bach, 20592 Minerva Lane, Huntington Beach CA 92646. (714)968-0905. **Fax:** (714)968-4677. **E-mail:** mifanwy@tebotbach.org. **Website:** www.tebotbach.org. **Contact:** Gail Wrongsky. Purpose of award is to honor the winning entry. Deadline: April 30. Prize: $500 award, chapbook publication. Judged by Gail Wronsky.

◐ THE COLORADO PRIZE FOR POETRY

(970)491-5449. **E-mail:** creview@colostate.edu. **Website:** http://coloradoprize.colostate.edu. **Contact:** Stephanie G'Schwind, editor. The annual Colorado Prize for Poetry awards an honorarium of $2,000 and publication of a book-length ms. Submission must be unpublished as a collection, but individual poems may have been published elsewhere. Submit mss of 48-100 pages of poetry (no set minimum or maximum) on any subject, in any form, double- or single-spaced. Include 2 titles pages: 1 with ms title only, the other with ms title and poet's name, address, and phone number. Enclosed SASP for notification of receipt and SASE for results; mss will not be returned. Guidelines available for SASE or by e-mail. **Entry fee:** $25; includes 1-year subscription to *Colorado Review*. **Deadline:** January 14. Winner was Eric Baus. 2011 judge was Cole Swensen. "Offered annually to an unpublished collection of poetry. Guidelines available for SASE or online at website. Poets can also submit online via our online submission manager through our website." To connect writers and readers by publishing exceptional writing. Deadline: January 14 Prize: $2,000 and publication of book. Cole Swenson

COMMONWEALTH CLUB OF CALIFORNIA BOOK AWARDS

595 Market St., San Francisco CA 94105. (415)597-6724. **Fax:** (415)597-6729. **E-mail:** bookawards@commonwealthclub.org. **Website:** www.commonwealthclub.org/bookawards. "Offered annually for published submissions appearing in print January 1-December 31 of the previous year. Purpose of award is the encouragement and production of literature in California. Can be nominated by publisher as well. Open to California residents (or residents at time of publication)." Annual awards "consisting of not more than two gold and eight silver medals" plus $2,000 cash prize to gold medal winners and $300 to

silver medal winners. For books of "exceptional literary merit" in poetry, fiction, and nonfiction (including work related to California and work for children), plus 2 "outstanding" categories. Submissions must be previously published. Submit at least 3 copies of each book entered with an official entry form. (Books may be submitted by author or publisher.) Open to books, published during the year prior to the contest, whose author "must have been a legal resident of California at the time the manuscript was submitted for publication." Entry form and guidelines available for SASE or on website. Competition receives approximately 50 poetry entries/year. Most recent award winners were Czeslaw Milosz and Carolyn Kizer. Deadline: December 31. Medals and cash prizes to be awarded at publicized event. Judged by jury.

TIPS "Guidelines available on website."

○ CONCRETE WOLF POETRY CHAPBOOK CONTEST

P.O. Box 1808, Kingston WA 98346. **E-mail:** concretewolf@yahoo.com. **Website:** http://concretewolf.com. **Contact:** Contest Coordinator. Member: CLMP. The Concrete Wolf Poetry Chapbook award offers publication and 100 author copies of a perfectly bound chapbook. Considers simultaneous submissions if notified of acceptance elsewhere. "We prefer chapbooks that have a theme, either obvious (i.e., chapbook about a divorce) or understated (i.e., all the poems mention the color blue). We like a collection that feels more like a whole than a sampling of work. We have no preference as to formal or free verse. We probably slightly favor lyric and narrative poetry to language and concrete, but excellent examples of any style get our attention." Submit up to 26 pages of poetry, paginated. Include table of contents and acknowledgments page. Include 2 cover sheets: 1 with ms title, poet's name, address, phone number, and e-mail; 1 without poet's identification. Include SASE for results; mss will not be returned. Guidelines available on website. **Entry fee:** $20; include 10x12 envelope stamped with $2.20 postage for a copy of the winning chapbook. Make checks payable to Concrete Wolf. **Deadline:** November 3 each year. Competition receives about 20 entries. Winner announced in February. Judge: Editors and a final guest judge. Copies of winning chapbooks available through website and Amazon.com.

THE CONNECTICUT RIVER REVIEW POETRY CONTEST

P.O. Box 270554, West Hartford CT 06127. **E-mail:** connpoetry@comcast.net. **Website:** ct-poetry-society.org. Prizes of $400, $100, and $50 will be awarded and winning poems will be published in *Connecticut River Review.* Send up to 3 unpublished poems, any form, 80 line limit. Include two copies of each poem: one with complete contact information in the upper right hand corner and one with NO contact information.Include SASE for results only (no poems will be returned). Winning poems must be submitted electronically following notification. Submit: April 1-May 31 (postmark). Entry fee: $15 for up to 3 poems. Simultaneous submissions acceptable if we are notifited immediately when a poem is accepted elsewhere. Please make out check to Connecticut Poetry Society. See separate entries in Magazines and Organizations sections of this book.

⊕◐ CPR EDITOR'S PRIZE BOOK AWARD

P.O. Box 33384, San Diego CA 92163. **E-mail:** editor@ciderpressreview.com. **Website:** http://ciderpressreview.com/bookaward. **Contact:** Contest director. Annual award from *Cider Press Review.* Deadline: submit April 1 - June 30 (postmark). Prize: $1,000, publication, and 25 author's copies of a book length collection of poetry. Author receives a standard publishing contract. Initial print run is not less than 1,000 copies. CPR acquires first publication rights. Judged by *Cider Press Review* editors.

◐ CRAB ORCHARD SERIES IN POETRY FIRST BOOK AWARD

Department of English, Mail Code 4503, Faner Hall 2380, Southern Illinois University of Carbondale, Carbondale IL 62901. **E-mail:** jtribble@siu.edu. **Website:** www.craborchardreview.siu.edu. **Contact:** Jon Tribble, series editor. Annual award. 2011 winner was Tyler Mills (*Tongue Lyre).* Deadline: See guidelines or check website. Prize: Offers $2,500 ($1,000 prize plus $1,500 honorarium for a reading at Southern Illinois University Carbondale) and publication.

● CRAB ORCHARD SERIES IN POETRY OPEN COMPETITION AWARDS

Department of English, Mail Code 4503, Faner Hall 2380, Southern Illinois University at Carbondale, Carbondale IL 62901. **E-mail:** jtribble@siu.edu. **Website:** www.craborchardreview.siu.edu. **Contact:** Jon Tribble, series editor. Annual competition. 2011 winners were Jacob Shores-Arguello ("In the Absence of Clocks") and Wally Swist ("Huang Po and the Dimensions of Love"). Deadline: See guidelines or check website Prize: Offers 2 winners $3,500 and publication of a book-length ms. Cash prize totals reflect a $1,500 honorarium for each winner for a reading at Southern Illinois University Carbondale. Publication contract is with Southern Illinois University Press.

◐ LOIS CRANSTON MEMORIAL POETRY PRIZE

CALYX, Inc., P.O. Box B, Corvallis OR 97339. **E-mail:** calyx@proaxis.com. **Website:** www.calyxpress.org. CALYX offers the annual Lois Cranston Memorial Poetry Prize of $300, publication in CALYX, and a one-volume subscription. Finalists will be published on the CALYX website and receive a one-volume subscription. No previously published poems or simultaneous submissions. Submit up to 3 poems/entry (6 pages total maximum). Include separate cover letter with poet's name, address, phone number, e-mail address, and title(s) of poem(s). No names on poems. No mss will be returned. Guidelines available for SASE, by e-mail, or on website. **Entry fee:** $15 for up to 3 poems. Make checks payable to CALYX. **Deadline:** submit March 1-May 31 (inclusive postmark dates). Winners notified by October 30 and announced on Calyx' s website.

CWW ANNUAL WISCONSIN WRITERS AWARDS COMPETITION

Council for Wisconsin Writers, **Website:** www.wisconsinwriters.org. **Contact:** Geoff Gilpin; Karla Huston, awards co-chairs; and Carolyn Washburne, Christopher Latham Sholes Award and Major Achievement Award co-chair. Offered annually for work published by Wisconsin writers the previous calendar year. Nine awards: Major/life achievement alternate years; short fiction; short nonfiction; nonfiction book; poetry book; fiction book; children's literature; Lorine Niedecker Poetry Award; Sholes Award for Outstanding Service to Wisconsin Writers Alternate Years; Essay Award for Young Writers. Open to Wisconsin residents. Guidelines, rules, and entry form on website. Deadline: January 31 (postmark) Prizes: $500 and a week-long residency at Shake Rag Alley in Mineral Point. Essay Contest: $150. "This year only the Essay Award for Young Writers prize will be $250."

● THE ROBERT DANA ANHINGA PRIZE FOR POETRY

Anhinga Press, P.O. Box 3665, Tallahassee FL 32315. (850)442-1408. **Fax:** (850)442-6323. **E-mail:** info@anhinga.org. **Website:** www.anhinga.org. **Contact:** Rick Campbell, poetry editor. Offered annually for a book-length collection of poetry by an author who has not published more than 1 book of poetry. Guidelines for SASE or on website. Open to any writer writing in English. Deadline: February 15-May 1. $2,000, and publication Past judges include Donald Hall, Joy Harjo, Robert Dana, Mark Jarman, and Tony Hoagland. Past winners include Frank X. Gaspar, Earl S. Braggs, Julia Levine, Keith Ratzlaff, and Lynn Aarti Chandhok, and Rhett Iseman Trull.

◐ DANA AWARD IN POETRY

200 Fosseway Dr., Greensboro NC 27455. (336)644-8028 (for emergency questions only). **E-mail:** danaawards@pipeline.com. **Website:** www.danaawards.com. **Contact:** Mary Elizabeth Parker, award chair. Offers annual award of $1,000 for the best group of 5 poems. Submissions must be unpublished and not under promise of publication when submitted. Considers simultaneous submissions. Submit 5 poems on any subject, in any form; no light verse. Include separate cover sheet with name, address, phone, e-mail address, and titles of poems. Entries by regular mail only. Include SASE for winners list only; no mss will be returned. Guidelines available for SASE, by e-mail, or on website. **Entry fee:** $15 for 5 poems. **Deadline:** October 31 (postmark). Winner will be announced in early spring by phone, letter, and e-mail.

○ DANCING POETRY CONTEST

704 Brigham Ave., Santa Rosa CA 95404-5245. (707)528-0912. **E-mail:** jhcheung@comcast.net. **Website:** www.dancingpoetry.com. **Contact:** Judy Cheung, contest chair. Annual contest offers three Grand Prizes of $100 each, six 1st Prizes of $50, twelve 2nd Prizes of $25, and thirty 3rd Prizes of $10. The 3 Grand Prize-winning poems will be choreographed, costumed, danced, and videotaped at the annual Dancing Poetry Festival at Palace of the Legion of Honor, San Francisco; Natica Angilly's Poetic Dance Theater Company will perform the 3 Grand Prize-winning poems. In addition, all prizes include an invitation to read your prize poem at the festival, and a certificate suitable for framing. Submissions must be unpublished or poet must own rights. Submit 2 copies of any number of

poems, 40 lines maximum (each), with name, address, phone number on 1 copy only. Foreign language poems must include English translations. No entries by fax or e-mail. Entry form available for SASE. Entry fee: $5/poem or $10 for 3 poems. Deadline: May 15 annually. Competition receives about 500-800 entries. Winners will be announced by August 1; Ticket to festival will be given to all prize winners. Artist Embassy International has been a nonprofit educational arts organization since 1951, "Furthering intercultural understanding and peace through the universal language of the arts."

DELAWARE DIVISION OF THE ARTS

820 N. French St., Wilmington DE 19801. (302)577-8278. **Fax:** (302)577-6561. **E-mail:** kristin.pleasanton@state.de.us. **Website:** www.artsdel.org. **Contact:** Kristin Pleasanton, coordinator. Award "to help further careers of emerging and established professional artists." For Delaware residents only. Prize: $10,000 for masters; $6,000 for established professionals; $3,000 for emerging professionals. Judged by out-of-state, nationally recognized professionals in each artistic discipline. No entry fee. Guidelines available after May 1 on website. Accepts inquiries by e-mail, phone. Expects to receive 25 fiction entries. Deadline: August 1. Open to any Delaware writer. Results announced in December. Winners notified by mail. Results available on website.

TIPS "Follow all instructions and choose your best work sample."

DER-HOVANESSIAN PRIZE

New England Poetry Club, 654 Green St., No. 2, Cambridge MA 02139. **E-mail:** contests@nepoetryclub.org. **Website:** www.nepoetryclub.org. **Contact:** NEPC contest coordinator. For a translation from any language into English. Send a copy of the original. Funded by John Mahtesian. Deadline: May 31 Prize: $250. Judges are well-known poets and sometimes winners of previous NEPC contests.

◐ DIAGRAM/NEW MICHIGAN PRESS CHAPBOOK CONTEST

Department of English, P.O. Box 210067, University of Arizona, Tucson AZ 85721. **E-mail:** nmp@thediagram.com. **Website:** www.newmichiganpress.com/nmp. **Contact:** Ander Monson, editor. The annual DIAGRAM /New Michigan Press Chapbook Contest offers $1,000, plus publication and author's copies, with discount on additional copies. Also publishes 2-4 finalist chapbooks each year. Submit 18-44 pages of poetry, fiction, mixed-genre, or genre-bending work ("images OK if b&w and you have permissions"). Include SASE. Guidelines available on website. **Entry fee:** $16. **Deadline:** March 30.

DOBIE PAISANO PROJECT

The Graduate School, The University of Texas at Austin, #1 University Ave., Mail Stop G0400, Austin TX 78712. (512)471-8528. **Fax:** (512)471-7620. **E-mail:** adameve@mail.utexas.edu. **Website:** www.utexas.edu/ogs/Paisano. **Contact:** Dr. Michael Adams. "The annual Dobie-Paisano Fellowships provide solitude, isolation, and an extended period of time to live and work at J. Frank Dobie's 250-acre ranch outside of Austin, Texas. At the time of the application, the applicant must: be a native Texan; have lived in Texas at some time for at least 3 years; or have published writing that has a Texas subject. Criteria for making the awards include quality of work, character of proposed project, and suitability of the applicant for ranch life at Paisano, the late J. Frank Dobie's ranch near Austin, TX. Applicants must submit examples of their work in triplicate. Guidelines for SASE or online." Deadline is January 15, 2013 for fellowships in 2013-2014. Winners are announced in early May. "The Ralph A. Johnston memorial Fellowship is for a period of 4 months with a stipend of $5,000 per month. It is aimed at writers who have already demonstrated some publishing and critical success. The Jesse H. Jones Writing Fellowship is for a period of approximately 6 months with a stipend of $3,000 per month. It is aimed at, but not limited to, writers who are early in their careers."

TIPS "Guidelines and application forms are on the website or may be requested by sending a SASE (2-ounce postage) to the above address and attention of 'Dobie Paisano Fellowship Project.'"

T.S. ELIOT PRIZE

Dutch Houses, 307-308 High Holborn, London WCIV 7LL, United Kingdom. **Website:** www.poetrybooks.co.uk. Offers annual award for the best poetry collection published in the UK/Republic of Ireland each year. Prize: $29,500 to winner and $1,960 to shortlisted poets (donated by Mrs. Valerie Eliot). Submissions must be previously published and may be entered in other contests. Book/manuscipt must be submitted by publisher and have been published (or scheduled to be published) the year of the contest. Entry form and guidelines available for SASE or by fax or e-mail. Deadline: early August. Competition receives 100 entries/year.

T.S. ELIOT PRIZE FOR POETRY

Truman State University Press, 100 E. Normal Ave., Kirksville MO 63501-4221. (660)785-7336. **Fax:** (660)785-4480. **E-mail:** tsup@truman.edu. **Website:** tsup.truman.edu. **Contact:** Nancy Rediger. Offers annual award of $2,000 and publication. "The manuscript may include individual poems previously published in journals or anthologies, but may not include a significant number of poems from a published chapbook or self-published book." Submit 60-100 pages. Include 2 title pages: 1 with poet's name, address, phone number, and ms title; the other with ms title only. Include SASE for acknowledgment of ms receipt only; mss will not be returned. Guidelines available for SASE or on website. Competition receives about 500 entries/year. 2012 winner was David Livewell (*Shackamaxon*). Deadline: October 31. 2012 judge: Sandra McPherson.

◐ EMERGING VOICES

P.O. Box 6037, Beverly Hills CA 90212. (424)258-1180. **Fax:** (424)258-1184. **E-mail:** ev@penusa.org; pen@penusa.org. **Website:** www.penusa.org. Annual program offering $1,000 stipend and 8-month fellowship to writers in the early stages of their literary careers. Program includes one-on-one sessions with mentors, seminars on topics such as editing or working with agents, courses in the Writers' Program at UCLA Extension, and literary readings. Participants selected according to potential and lack of access to traditional publishing and/or educational opportunities. Must be over the age of 18. Graduates of Creative Writing B.A., M.F.A., and Ph.D. programs or students currently enrolled in B.A., M.A., or M.F.A. programs are not eligible. Participants need not be published, but "the program is directed toward poets and writers of fiction and creative nonfiction with clear ideas of what they hope to accomplish through their writing. Mentors are chosen from PEN's comprehensive membership of professional writers and beyond. Participants are paired with established writers sharing similar writing interests and often with those of the same ethnic and cultural backgrounds." Program gets underway in January. See website for brochure and complete guidelines. Application Fee: $10. Deadline: September 5. "Materials must arrive in the PEN offices by the submission deadline—no exceptions."

◐ ERSKINE J. POETRY PRIZE

P.O. Box 22161, Baltimore MD 21203. **E-mail:** sreichert@smartishpace.com. **Website:** www.smartishpace.com. **Contact:** Stephen Reichert, editor. The annual Erskine J. Poetry Prize offers 1st Prize: $200 and publication of the winning poem in Smartish Pace; 2nd and 3rd Prizes: winning poems will be published in Smartish Pace. Winners also receive additional Internet and advertising exposure. Honorable mention (usually 5 to 12) also published in Smartish Pace. All entries will be considered for publication in Smartish Pace. Submit 3 poems, with poet's name, address, e-mail, telephone number (preferred), and "Erskine J." at the top of each page of poetry submitted. Include bio. Entries may be submitted online or by e-mail (as attachment) or regular mail. Include SASE with postal entries. Guidelines available on website. **Entry fee:** $5/3 poems; additional poems may be submitted for $1/poem (limit of 12 poems). Make checks/money orders payable to Smartish Pace. **Deadline:** September 1.

⊕◐ FALL POETRY CHAPBOOK CONTEST

White Eagle Coffee Store Press, P.O. Box 383, Fox River Grove IL 60021-0383. (847)639-9200. **E-mail:** wecspress@aol.com. **Website:** whiteeaglecoffeestorepress.com. **Contact:** Frank Edmund Smith, publisher. "This contest is designed to promote and reward the writing of a small collection of poetry—20-22 pages. Typically, poets wish to publish chapbooks early in their careers, as a way of marking an achievement and having inexpensive books to sell at poetry readings. Many poets continue to publish chapbooks throughout their careers. This press especially welcomes writers of any age who have just begun to publish, but it is open to more successful writers, too." Deadline: October 31. Publication, $500, and 25 copies of the published chapbook; 10 copies for press kits. All contest entrants receive a copy of the book. "The final judge is always announced and is someone who has already published with the press, usually a previous contest winner. Thus, the press is always open to new styles and new writers. Author maintains copyright. White Eagle Coffee Store Press acquires first publishing rights and the exclusive right to print and reprint the chapbook."

FAR HORIZONS AWARD FOR POETRY

The Malahat Review, University of Victoria, P.O. Box 1700, Stn CSC, Victoria BC V8W 2Y2, Canada. (250)721-8524. **Fax:** (250)472-5051. **E-mail:** malahat@uvic.ca. **Website:** www.malahatreview.ca. **Contact:** John Barton, editor. The biennial Far Horizons Award for Poetry offers $1,000 CAD and publication in The Malahat Review. Open to "emerging poets from Canada, the United States, and elsewhere" who have not yet published a full-length book (48 pages or more). Submissions must be unpublished. No simultaneous submissions. Submit up to 3 poems per entry, each poem not to exceed 60 lines; no restrictions on subject matter or aesthetic approach. Include separate page with poet's name, address, e-mail, and poem title(s); no identifying information on mss pages. No e-mail submissions. Do not include SASE for results; mss will not be returned. Guidelines available on website. **Entry fee:** $25 CAD for Canadian entries, $30 USD for US entries ($35 USD for entries from Mexico and outside North America); includes a one-year subscription to *The Malahat Review.* **Deadline:** May 1 (postmark) of alternate years (2010, 2012, etc.). 2010 winner: Darren Bifford. Winner and finalists contacted by e-mail. Winner published in fall in *The Malahat Review* and announced on website, Facebook page, and in quarterly e-newsletter, *Malahat lite.*

JANICE FARRELL POETRY PRIZE

E-mail: pennobhill@aol.com. **Website:** www.soulmakingcontest.us. **Contact:** Eileen Malone. "Poetry may be double- or single-spaced. One-page poems only, and only 1 poem/page. All poems must be titled. Three poems/entry. Indicate category on each poem. Identify with 3x5 card only. Open to all writers." $5/entry (make checks payable to NLAPW). **Deadline:** November 30 (annually). **Prizes:** 1st Place: $100; 2nd Place: $50; 3rd Place: $25. Judged by a local San Francisco successfully published poet.

FIELD POETRY PRIZE

Oberlin College Press/FIELD, 50 N. Professor St., Oberlin OH 44074. (440)775-8408. **Fax:** (440)775-8124. **E-mail:** oc.press@oberlin.edu. **Website:** www.oberlin.edu/ocpress/prize.htm. **Contact:** Drew Krewer, managing editor. The annual FIELD Poetry Prize for a book-length collection of poems offers $1,000 and publication in the FIELD Poetry Series. Mss of 50-80 pages must be submitted during May through our online submissions manager. See our website for details. Entry Fee: $28; includes one-year subscription to FIELD: Contemporary Poetry and Poetics. **Deadline:** submit during May only. 2011 winner was Mark Neely (Beasts of the Hill). "Offered annually for unpublished work. Contest seeks to encourage the finest in contemporary poetry writing. Open to any writer." Deadline: Submit in May only $1,000 and the book is published in Oberlin College Press's FIELD Poetry Series.

THE FINCH PRIZE FOR POETRY

The National Poetry Review, P.O. Box 2080, Aptos CA 95001-2080. **E-mail:** editor@nationalpoetry review.com. **Website:** www.nationalpoetryreview.com. **Contact:** C.J. Sage, editor. The Finch Prize for Poetry offers $500 plus publication in *The National Poetry Review.* All entries will be considered by the editor for publication. Deadline: June 30 (postmark).

FIRMAN HOUGHTON PRIZE

New England Poetry Club, 654 Green St., No. 2, Cambridge MA 02139. **E-mail:** contests@nepoetryclug.org. **Website:** www.nepoetryclub.org. **Contact:** NEPC contest coordinator. For a lyric poem in honor of the former president of NEPC. Deadline: May 31 Prize: $250. Judges are well-known poets and sometimes winners of previous NEPC contests.

FIRST BOOK AWARD

Saskatchewan Book Awards, Inc., 100-2400 College Ave., Regina SK S4P 0K1, Canada. (306)569-1585. **Fax:** (306)569-4187. **E-mail:** director@bookawards.sk.ca. **Website:** www.bookawards.sk.ca. **Contact:** Executive director, book submissions. Offered annually. "This award is presented to a Saskatchewan author for the best first book, judged on the quality of writing." Books from the following categories will be considered: Children's; drama; fiction (short fiction by a single author, novellas, novels); nonfiction (all categories of nonfiction writing except cookbooks, directories, how-to books, or bibliographies of minimal critical content); and poetry. Deadline: November 1. Prize: $2,000 (CAD).

FLORIDA FIRST COAST WRITERS' FESTIVAL NOVEL, SHORT FICTION, PLAYWRITING & POETRY AWARDS

FCCJ North Campus, 4501 Capper Rd., Jacksonville FL 32218-4499. (904)766-6760. **Fax:** (904)766-6654. **Website:** opencampus.fccj.org/WF/. Conference and contest "to create a healthy writing environment, honor writers of merit and find a novel manuscript to recommend to New York publishers for 'serious consideration.'" Judged by university faculty and freelance and professional writers. Entry fee: $7 for poetry or $18 for 3 poems. **Deadline: December 1 for poetry.** Entries must be unpublished. Word length: 30 lines for poetry. Open to any writer. Guidelines available on the website or in the fall for SASE. Accepts inquiries by fax and e-mail. "For stories and novels, make the opening pages sparkle. For plays, make them at least two acts and captivating. For poems, blow us over with imagery and insight and avoid clichés and wordiness." Results announced on the website and at FCCJ's Florida First Coast Writers' Festival held in the spring.

FOLEY POETRY CONTEST

America, 106 W. 56th St., New York NY 10019. (212)581-4640. **Fax:** (212)399-3596. **Website:** www.americamagazine.org. *America*, the national Catholic weekly by the Jesuits of North America, sponsors the annual Foley Poetry Contest. Offers $1,000 and 2 contributor's copies for the winning poem. Winner will be announced in the mid-June issue of America and on the website. Runners-up will have their poems printed in subsequent issues of *America*. Submissions must be unpublished and may not be entered in other contests. "Submit 1 poem per person, not to exceed 30 lines of verse, in any form. Name, address, telephone number, and e-mail address (if applicable) should be appended to the bottom of the page. Poems will not be returned, and e-mailed submissions are not accepted." Guidelines available in magazine, for SASE, or on website. **Deadline:** January 1-April 18 (postmark). Competition receives more than 1,000 entries/year. 2011 winner was Mara Faulkner (for "Things I Didn't Know I Loved". Judge: James Torrens, S.J.

FREEFALL SHORT PROSE AND POETRY CONTEST

Freefall Literary Society of Calgary, 922 9th Ave. SE, Calgary AB T2G 0S4, Canada. **E-mail:** freefallmagazine@yahoo.ca. **Website:** www.freefallmagazine.ca. **Contact:** Lynn C. Fraser, managing editor. Offered annually for unpublished work in the categories of poetry (5 poems/entry) and prose (3,000 words or less). The purpose of the award in both categories is to recognize writers and offer publication credits in a literary magazine format. Contest rules and entry form online. Acquires first Canadian serial rights; ownership reverts to author after one-time publication. Deadline: December 31. 1st Place: $300 (CAD); 2nd Place: $150 (CAD); 3rd Place: $75; Honourable Mention: $25. All prizes include publication in the spring edition of *FreeFall Magazine*. Winners will also be invited to read at the launch of that issue if such a launch takes place. Honorable mentions in each category will be published and may be asked to read. Travel expenses not included. Judged by current guest editor for issue (who are also published authors in Canada).

THE ROBERT FROST FOUNDATION ANNUAL POETRY AWARD

The Robert Frost Foundation, Lawrence Library, 51 Lawrence St., Lawrence MA 01841. (978)725-8828. **E-mail:** frostfoundation@comcast.net. **Website:** www.frostfoundation.org. Established 1997. Offers annual award of $1,000. Submissions may be entered in other contests. Submit up to 3 poems of not more than 3 pages each (2 copies of each poem, 1 with name, address, and phone number), written in the spirit of Robert Frost. Guidelines available for SASE and on website. **Entry fee:** $10/poem. **Deadline:** September 15. Competition receives over 600 entries/year.

THE KINERETH GENSLER AWARDS

Alice James Books, University of Maine at Farmington, 238 Main St., Farmington ME 04938. (207)778-7071. **Fax:** (207)778-7766. **E-mail:** ajb@alicejamesbooks.org. **Website:** www.alicejamesbooks.org. **Contact:** Meg Willing, managing editor. "For complete contest guidelines, visit our website or send a SASE. Entry fee: $25 for hardcopy submissions; $28 for online submissions." "Offered annually for unpublished full-length poetry collection." Deadline: October 1. Winner receives $2,000, publication, and servers a three-year term on the Alice James Books Cooperative Board.

GEORGETOWN REVIEW

Georgetown Review, 400 East College St., Box 227, Georgetown KY 40324. (502) 863-8308. **Fax:** (502) 863-8888. **E-mail:** gtownreview@georgetowncollege.edu. **Website:** http://georgetownreview.georgetowncollege.edu. **Contact:** Steve Carter, editor. "Annual. Publishes short stories, poetry, and creative nonfiction. Reading period September 1-December 31. Also sponsors yearly writing contest for short stories, poetry, and creative nonfiction." Receives about 300 entries for each category. Entries are judged by the editors. Guidelines available in July. Accepts inquiries by e-mail. Contest open to anyone except family and friends of the editors. "Sometimes our contests are themed, so check the website for details." Results announced Februry or March. Winners notified by e-mail. Results made available to entrants with SASE. Cover letter and ms should include name, address, phone, e-mail, novel/story title. Writers may submit own work. Purpose is to publish quality work. Deadline: October 15 $1,000 and publication; runners-up receive publication.

GERTRUDE PRESS POETRY CHAPBOOK CONTEST

P.O. Box 83948, Portland OR 97283. **E-mail:** editor@gertrudepress.org. **Website:** www.gertrudepress.org. Gertrude Press sponsors an annual chapbook competition. Deadline: April 15. Offers $100, publication, and 50 author copies (out of a press run of 200) to the winning poet.

ALLEN GINSBERG POETRY AWARDS

(973)684-6555. **Fax:** (973)523-6085. **E-mail:** mgillan@pccc.edu. **Website:** www.pccc.edu/poetry. **Contact:** Maria Mazziotti Gillan, executive director. The Allen Ginsberg Poetry Awards offer annual prizes of 1st Prize: $1,000; 2nd Prize: $200; and 3rd Prize: $100. All winning poems, honorable mentions, and editor's choice poems will be published in *Paterson Literary Review*. Winners will be asked to participate in a reading that will be held in the Paterson Historic District. Submissions must be unpublished. Submit up to 5 poems (no poem more than 2 pages long). Send 4 copies of each poem entered. Include cover sheet with poet's name, address, phone number, e-mail address and poem titles. Poet's name should not appear on poems. Include SASE for results only; poems will not be returned. Guidelines available for SASE or on website. **Entry fee:** $18 (includes subscription to *Paterson Literary Review*). Write "poetry contest" in memo section of check and make payable to PCCC. **Deadline:** April 1 (postmark). Winners will be announced the following summer by mail and in newspaper announcements.

GIVAL PRESS POETRY AWARD

Gival Press, LLC, P.O. Box 3812, Arlington VA 22203. (703)351-0079. **E-mail:** givalpress@yahoo.com. **Website:** www.givalpress.com. **Contact:** Robert L. Giron, editor. "Offered annually for a previously unpublished poetry collection as a complete ms, which may include previously published poems; previously published poems must be acknowledged, and poet must hold rights. The competition seeks to award well-written, original poetry in English on any topic, in any style. Guidelines for SASE, by e-mail, or online. Entrants are asked to submit their poems without any kind of identification (with the exception of the titles) and with a separate cover page with the following information: Name, address (street, city, state, and zip code), telephone number, e-mail address (if available), short bio, and a list of the poems by title. Checks drawn on American banks should be made out to Gival Press, LLC." Deadline: December 15 (postmarked). $1,000, publication, and 20 author's copies. The editor narrows entries to the top 10; previous winner selects top 5 and chooses the winner—all done anonymously. **TIPS** "Open to any writer, as long as the work is original, not a translation, and is written in English. The copyright remains in the author's name; certain rights fall to the publisher per the contract."

GOLDEN ROSE AWARD

New England Poetry Club, 654 Green St., No. 2, Cambridge MA 02139. **Website:** www.nepoetryclub.org. **Contact:** NEPC contest coordinator. "Given annually to the poet who has done the most for the art in the previous year or in a lifetime. Chosen by board." May 31 Judges are well-known poets and sometimes winners of previous NEPC contests.

GOVERNOR GENERAL'S LITERARY AWARD FOR POETRY

Canada Council for the Arts, 350 Albert St., P.O. Box 1047, Ottawa ON K1P 5V8, Canada. (613)566-4414, ext. 5573. **Fax:** (613)566-4410. **Website:** www.canadacouncil.ca/prizes/ggla. Offered for the best English-language and the best French-language work of poetry by a Canadian. Publishers submit titles for consideration. Deadline depends on the book's publication date. Books in English: March 15, June 1, or August 7. Books in French: March 15 or July 15. Each laureate receives $25,000; non-winning finalists receive $1,000.

GRANTS FOR ARTIST'S PROJECTS

Artist Trust, 1835 12th Ave., Seattle WA 98122. (206) 467-8734, ext. 11. **Fax:** (206) 467-9633. **E-mail:** miguel@artisttrust.org. **Website:** www.artisttrust.org. **Contact:** Monica Miller, director of programs. "The GAP Program provides support for artist-generated projects, which can include (but are not limited to) the development, completion or presentation of new work." Annual. Prize: maximum of $1,500 for projects. Accepted are poetry, fiction, graphic novels, experimental works, creative non-fiction, screen plays, film scripts and teleplays. Entries are judged by work sample as specified in the guidelines. Winners are selected by a discipline-specific panel of artists and artist professionals. No entry fee. Guidelines available in March. Accepts inquiries by mail, phone. Submission period is March-May. **Deadline: May 2013**; check website for specific date. Entries can be unpublished or previously published. Washington state residents only. Length: 8 pages max for poetry, fiction, graphic novels, experimental work and creative nonfiction; up to 12 pages for screen plays, film scripts and teleplays. All mss must be typed with a 12-point font size or larger and cannot be single-spaced (except for poetry). Include application with project proposal and budget, as well as resume with name, address, phone, e-mail, and novel/story title. "GAP awards are highly competitive. Please follow guidelines with care." Results announced in the fall. Winners notified by email. Results made available to entrants by e-mail and on website. "The GAP grant is awarded annually to 60 artists of all disciplines including writers. The award is meant to help finance a specific project, which can be in very early stages or near completion. Full-time students are not eligible. Open to Washington state residents only. Up to $1,500 for artist-generated projects."

◐ GREAT LAKES COLLEGES ASSOCIATION NEW WRITERS AWARD

535 W. William, Suite 301, Ann Arbor MI 48103. (734)661-2350. **Fax:** (734)661-2349. **E-mail:** wegner@glca.org. **Website:** www.glca.org. **Contact:** Gregory R. Wegner. Offers annual award to the best first book of poetry, fiction, and creative nonfiction among those submitted by publishers. The winning authors tour several of the 13 GLCA-member colleges (as invited) reading, lecturing, visiting classes, doing workshops, and publicizing their books. Each writer receives an honorarium of at least $500 from each college visited, as well as travel expenses, hotel accommodations, and hospitality. Tours are scheduled during the academic year. Submissions must be previously published. Publishers should submit 4 copies of galleys or the printed book plus a statement of the author's agreement to commit to the college tour. Galleys of Books to be published within the judging period may also be submitted. Guidelines available for SASE, by e-mail, or on the GLCA website. **Deadline:** July 25. Additional details as well as a listing of winning writers are also available on the GLCA website. The New Writers Award is given for an author's first published volume, 1 in each category of fiction, creative nonfiction, and poetry.

◐ THE GREEN ROSE PRIZE IN POETRY

New Issues Poetry & Prose, Deptartment of English, Western Michigan University, 1903 W. Michigan Ave., Kalamazoo MI 49008-5331. (269)387-8185. **Fax:** (269)387-2562. **Website:** www.wmich.edu/newissues. The Green Rose Prize in Poetry offers $2,000 and publication of a book of poems by an established poet who has published 1 or more full-length collections of poetry. *New Issues* may publish as many as 3 additional mss from this competition. Considers simultaneous submissions, but *New Issues* must be notified of acceptance elsewhere. Submit a ms of at least 48 pages, typed; single-spaced preferred. Clean photocopies acceptable. Do not bind; use manila folder or metal clasp. Include cover page with poet's name, address, phone number, and title of the ms. Also include brief bio, table of contents, and acknowledgments page. Submissions are also welcome through the online submission manager www.submishmash.com. "For hardcopy manuscripts only, you may include SASP for notification of receipt of ms and SASE for results only; mss will be recycled." Guidelines available for SASE, by fax, e-mail, or on website. **Entry fee**: $25. Make checks payable to New Issues Poetry & Prose. **Deadline:** Submit May 1-September 30 (postmark). Winner is announced in January or February on website. 2012 winner was Jaswinder Bolina (*Phantom Camera*). Judge: *New Issues* editors. The winning manuscript will be published in spring 2014. Offered annually for unpublished poetry. The university will publish a book of poems by a poet writing in English who has published 1 or more full-length collections of poetry. *New Issues* may publish as many as 3 additional mss from this competition. Guidelines for SASE or online. *New Issues Poetry & Prose* obtains rights for first publication. Book is copyrighted in the author's name.

● GUGGENHEIM FELLOWSHIPS

90 Park Ave., New York NY 10016. (212)687-4470. **E-mail:** fellowships@gf.org. **Website:** www.gf.org. Guggenheim Fellowships are awarded each year to poets, as well as fiction and creative nonfiction writ-

ers, "on the basis of unusually distinguished achievement in the past and exceptional promise for future accomplishment." 2009 Fellowships were awarded to 34 writers; amounts averaged $36,672 each. Submit career summary, statement of intent, and no more than 3 published books. Guidelines, application form (required), and additional information available for SASE, by e-mail, or on website. **Deadline:** September 15.

HACKNEY LITERARY AWARDS

(205)226-4921. **E-mail:** info@hackneyliteraryawards.org. **Website:** www.hackneyliteraryawards.org. **Contact:** Myra Crawford, PhD, executive director. Offered annually for unpublished novels, short stories (maximum 5,000 words) and poetry (50 line limit). Guidelines on website. Deadline: September 30 (novels), November 30 (short stories and poetry) Prize: $5,000 in annual prizes for poetry and short fiction ($2,500 national and $2,500 state level). 1st Place: $600; 2nd Place: $400; 3rd Place: $250); plus $5,000 for an unpublished novel. Competition winners will be announced on the website each March.

KATHRYN HANDLEY PROSE POEM PRIZE

E-mail: pennobhill@aol.com. **Website:** www.soulmakingcontest.us. **Contact:** Eileen Malone. Open annually to all writers. Poetry may be double- or single-spaced. 1-page poems only, and only 1 prose poem/page. Three poems/entry. Indicate category on each poem. Identify only with 3x5 card. **Entry fee:** $5/entry (make checks payable to NLAPW). **Deadline:** November 30. Prizes: 1st Place: $100; 2nd Place: $50; 3rd Place: $25.

THE BEATRICE HAWLEY AWARD

Alice James Books, University of Maine at Farmington, 238 Main St., Farmington ME 04938. (207)778-7071. **Fax:** (207)778-7766. **E-mail:** ajb@alicejamesbooks.org. **Website:** www.alicejamesbooks.org. **Contact:** Meg Willing, managing editor. "For complete contest guidelines, visit our website or send a SASE. Entry fee: $25 for hardcopy submissions; $28 for online submissions." "Offered annually for unpublished full-length poetry collections." Deadline: December 1. Winner receives $2,000 and publication.

THE HODDER FELLOWSHIP

Lewis Center for the Arts, Princeton University, 6 New South, Princeton NJ 08544. (609)258-4096. **E-mail:** jbraude@princeton.edu. **Website:** www.princeton.edu/arts/lewis_center/society_of_fellows. **Contact:** Janine Braude, program assistant-Creative Writing. "The Hodder Fellowship will be given to writers of exceptional promise to pursue independent projects at Princeton University during the 2011-2012 academic year. Typically the fellows are poets, playwrights, novelists, creative nonfiction writers and translators who have published one highly acclaimed work and are undertaking a significant new project that might not be possible without the "studious leisure" afforded by the fellowship. Preference is given to applicants outside academia. Candidates for the Ph.D. are not eligible. Submit a resumè, sample of previous work (10 pages maximum, not returnable), and a project proposal of 2-3 pages. Guidelines available on website. Princeton University is an equal opportunity employer and complies with applicable EEO and affirmative action regulations. Apply online at http://jobs.princeton.edu or for general application information and how to self-identify, see http://www.princeton.edu/dof/ApplicantsInfo.htm. We strongly recommend, however, that all interested candidates use the online application process. Stipend: $63,900." Deadline: November 1, 2010 (postmarked).

ERIC HOFFER AWARD

Fax: (609)964-1718. **E-mail:** info@hopepubs.com. **Website:** www.hofferaward.com. **Contact:** Christopher Klim, chair. "Annual contest for previously published books. Recognizes excellence in independent publishing in many unique categories: Art (titles capture the experience, execution, or demonstration of the arts); Poetry (all styles); General Fiction (non-genre-specific fiction); Commercial Fiction (genre-specific fiction); Children (titles for young children); Young Adult (titles aimed at the juvenile and teen markets); Culture (titles demonstrating the human or world experience); Memoir (titles relating to personal experience); Business (titles with application to today's business environment and emerging trends); Reference (titles from traditional and emerging reference areas); Home (titles with practical applications to home or home-related issues, including family); Health (titles promoting physical, mental, and emotional well-being); Self-help (titles involving new and emerging topics in self-help); Spiritual (titles involving the mind and spirit, including relgion); Legacy (titles over 2 years of age that hold particular relevance to any subject matter or form). Open to any writer of published work within the last 2 years, including categores for older books." "This contest recognizes excellence in independent publishing in many unique categories: Art, Poetry, General Fiction, Commercial Fiction, Children, Young Adult, Culture, Memoir, Business, Reference, Home, Health, Self-help, Spiritual, and Legacy (fiction and nonfiction)."

THE BESS HOKIN PRIZE

Poetry, 61 W. Superior St., Chicago IL 60654. (312)787-7070. **E-mail:** poetry@poetrymagazine.org. **Website:** www.poetrymagazine.org. Offered annually for poems published in *Poetry* during the preceding year (October-September). Upon acceptance, *Poetry* licenses exclusive worldwide first serial rights, including electronic rights, for publication, as well as non-exclusive rights to reprint, reuse, and archive the work, in any format, in perpetuity. Copyright reverts to author upon first publication. $1,000.

◐ TOM HOWARD/JOHN H. REID POETRY CONTEST

Tom Howard Books, c/o Winning Writers, 351 Pleasant St., PMB 222, Northampton MA 01060-3961. (866)946-9748. **Fax:** (413)280-0539. **E-mail:** johnreid@mail.qango.com. **Website:** www.winningwriters.com. **Contact:** John Reid, award director. Offers annual award of 1st Prize: $3,000; 2nd Prize: $1,000; 3rd Prize: $400; 4th Prize: $250; 6 Most Highly Commended Awards of $150 each; plus a new $250 bonus prize for humorous verse. The top 10 entries will be published on the Winning Writers website. Submissions may be published or unpublished and may have won prizes elsewhere. Considers simultaneous submissions. Submit poems in any form, style, or genre. "There is no limit on the number of lines or poems you may submit." No name on ms pages; type or computer-print on letter-size white paper, single-sided. Submit online or by regular mail. Guidelines available for SASE or on website. **Entry fee:** $7 USD for every 25 lines (exclude poem titles and any blank lines from line count). **Deadline:** December 15-September 30. Competition receives about 1,000 entries/year. 2012 judges: John H. Reid and Dee C. Konrad. Winners announced in February at WinningWriters.com. Entrants who provide valid e-mail addresses will also receive notification. Offers annual awards.

THE JULIA WARD HOWE/BOSTON AUTHORS AWARD

(617)783-1357. **E-mail:** bostonauthors@aol.com; lawson@bc.edu. **Website:** www.bostonauthorsclub.org. **Contact:** Alan Lawson. This annual award honors Julia Ward Howe and her literary friends who founded the Boston Authors Club in 1900. It also honors the membership over 110 years, consisting of novelists, biographers, historians, governors, senators, philosophers, poets, playwrights, and other luminaries. There are 2 categories: trade books and books for young readers (beginning with chapter books through young adult books). Works of fiction, nonfiction, memoir, poetry, and biography published in 2010 are eligible. Authors must live or have lived (college counts) within a 100-mile radius of Boston within the last 5 years. Subsidized books, cook books and picture books are not eligible. Fee is $25 per title.

◐ HENRY HOYNS & POE/FAULKNER FELLOWSHIPS

Creative Writing Program, 219 Bryan Hall, P.O. Box 400121, University of Virginia, Charlottesville VA 22904-4121. (434)924-6675. **Fax:** (434)924-1478. **E-mail:** creativewriting@virginia.edu. **Website:** www.creativewriting.virginia.edu. **Contact:** Jeb Livingood, associate director. Two-year MFA program in poetry and fiction; all students receive first-year fellowships of $16,000. Sample poems/prose required with application. **Deadline:** December 15.

◐ THE LYNDA HULL MEMORIAL POETRY PRIZE

Crazyhorse, Dept. of English, College of Charleston, 66 George St., Charleston SC 29424. (843)953-7740. **E-mail:** crazyhorse@cofc.edu. **Website:** www.crazyhorsejournal.org. **Contact:** Prize Director. The annual Lynda Hull Memorial Poetry Prize offers $2,000 and publication in Crazyhorse. All entries will be considered for publication. Submissions must be unpublished. Submit online or by mail up to 3 original poems (no more than 10 pages). Include cover page (placed on top of ms) with poet's name, address, e-mail, and telephone number; no identifying information on mss (blind judging). Accepts multiple submissions with separate fee for each. Include SASP for notification of receipt of ms and SASE for results only; mss will not be returned. Guidelines available for SASE or on website. **Entry fee:** $16/ms for new entrants. Fee includes a one-year/2 issue subscription to Crazyhorse;

for each poetry ms entered and fee paid, subscription is extended by 1 year. Make checks payable to Crazyhorse; credit card payments also accepted (see website for details). **Deadline:** January 15.

THE HUNGER MOUNTAIN CREATIVE NONFICTION PRIZE

Vermont College, 36 College St., Montpelier VT 05602. (802)828-8517. **E-mail:** hungermtn@vcfa.edu. **Website:** www.hungermtn.org. **Contact:** Miciah Bay Gault, editor. The annual Hunger Mountain Creative Nonfiction Prize offers $1,000 and publication in *Hunger Mountain* online; 2 runners-up receive $100 and are considered for publication. Submit essay under 10,000 words. Guidelines available on website. Deadline: September 10.

INDIANA REVIEW K (SHORT-SHORT/PROSE-POEM) CONTEST

Indiana Review, Ballantine Hall 465, 1020 E. Kirkwood Ave., Indiana University, Bloomington IN 47405-7103. (812)855-3439. **Fax:** (812)855-9535. **E-mail:** inreview@indiana.edu. **Website:** http://indianareview.org. **Contact:** Alessandra Simmons, editor. Offered annually for unpublished work. Maximum story/poem length is 500 words. Guidelines available in March for SASE, by phone, e-mail, on website, or in publication. Deadline: June. Prize: $1,000, plus publication, contributor's copies, and a year's subscription to *Indiana Review*.

INDIANA REVIEW POETRY PRIZE

Indiana Review, Ballantine Hall 465, Indiana University, Bloomington IN 47405-7103. (812)855-3439. **Fax:** (812)855-9535. **E-mail:** inreview@indiana.edu. **Website:** www.indianareview.org. **Contact:** Alessandra Simmons, Editor. Offered annually for unpublished work. Judged by guest judges; 2012 prize will be judged by Dean Young. Open to any writer. Send no more than 3 poems per entry. Guidelines on website and with SASE request. This year's deadline: March 31, 2012. Prize: $1,000 and publication in *Indiana Review*. Costs: $20 fee (includes a 1-year subscription).

INKWELL ANNUAL POETRY CONTEST

Manhattanville College, 2900 Purchase St., Purchase NY 10577. (914)323-5239. **Fax:** (914)323-3122. **E-mail:** inkwell@mville.edu. **Website:** www.inkwelljournal.org. **Contact:** Competition Poetry Editor. The Inkwell Annual Poetry Competition awards $1,000 grand prize and publication in *Inkwell* for best poem. Submissions must be unpublished. Submit up to 5 poems at a time, no more than 40 lines/poem, typed in 12 pt. font. Include cover sheet with poet's name, address, phone number, e-mail, and poems titles and line counts. No name or address should appear on mss. Also include Submission Checklist (download from website). Indicate "Poetry Competition" on envelope. Include SASE for results only; mss will not be returned. Guidelines available on website. **Entry fee:** $10 for first poem, $5 for each additional poem (USD only). Make checks payable to Manhattanville—Inkwell. **Deadline:** August 1-October 30 (postmark)..

THE INTRO PRIZE IN POETRY

Four Way Books, P.O. Box 535, Village Station, New York NY 10014. (212)334-5430. **E-mail:** editors@fourwaybooks.com. **Website:** www.fourwaybooks.com. The Intro Prize in Poetry, offered biennially in even-numbered years, awards publication by Four Way Books, honorarium ($1,000), and a reading at one or more participating series. Open to U.S. poets who have not yet published a book-length collection. "Submit one manuscript, 48-100 pages suggested. You may submit via e-mail or regular mail by the deadline. For complete information, you must refer to our guidelines on our website." **Entry fee:** $28. **Deadline:** March 31 (postmark). Winner announced by mail and on website. Copies of winning books available through Four Way Books online and at bookstores (to the trade through University Press of New England).

THE IOWA REVIEW AWARD IN POETRY, FICTION, AND NONFICTION

308 EPB, University of Iowa, Iowa City IA 52242. **E-mail:** iowa-review@uiowa.edu. **Website:** www.iowareview.org. **Contact:** Contest Coordinator. *The Iowa Review* Award in Poetry, Fiction, and Nonfiction presents $1,500 to each winner in each genre, $750 to runners-up. Winners and runners-up published in *The Iowa Review*. Deadline: Submit January 1-31 (postmark). 2012 Judges: Timothy Donnelly, Ron Currie, Jr., and Meghan Daum.

JOSEPH HENRY JACKSON AWARD

225 Bush Street, Suite 500, San Francisco CA 94104. (415)733.8500. **Fax:** (415)477.2783. **E-mail:** info@sff.org. **Website:** www.sff.org. The Joseph Henry Jackson Award offers $2,000 to the author of an unpublished work-in-progress of fiction (novel or short stories), nonfictional prose, or poetry. Applicants must be residents of northern California or Nevada for 3

consecutive years immediately prior to the March 31 deadline and must be between the ages of 20 and 35 as of the deadline. There are no applications for this award. Only applicant names submitted by a nominating jury will be considered. **Entry fee:** none. **Deadline:** March 31. Competition receives 150-180 entries.

● JUNIPER PRIZE FOR POETRY

University of Massachusetts Press, Amherst MA 01003. (413)545-2217. **Fax:** (413)545-1226. **E-mail:** info@umpress.umass.edu. **Website:** www.umass.edu/umpress. **Contact:** Carla J. Potts. The University of Massachusetts Press offers the annual Juniper Prize for Poetry, awarded in alternate years for the first and subsequent books. Deadline: August 1 - September 29 (postmark). Winners announced online in April on the press website. Prize: includes publication and $1,500 in addition to royalties. In even-numbered years (2012, etc.), only "subsequent" books will be considered—mss whose authors have had at least 1 full-length book or chapbook (of at least 30 pages) of poetry published or accepted for publication. Self-published work is not considered to lie within this "books and chapbooks" category. In odd-numbered years (2013, etc.), only "first books' will be considered—mss by writers whose poems may have appeared in literary journals and/or anthologies but have not been published or accepted for publication in book form.

● HAROLD MORTON LANDON TRANSLATION AWARD

The Academy of American Poets, 75 Maiden Lane, Suite 901, New York NY 10038. (212)274-0343 ext. 15. **E-mail:** awards@poets.org. **Website:** www.poets.org. **Contact:** Alex Dimitrov, awards coordinator. Offers one $1,000 award each year to recognize a published translation of poetry from any language into English. Guidelines available for SASE or on website. **Deadline:** January 31, 2012 for a book published in 2010.

● THE LAUREATE PRIZE FOR POETRY

The National Poetry Review, P.O. Box 2080, Aptos CA 95001-2080. **E-mail:** editor@nationalpoetryreview.com. **Website:** www.nationalpoetryreview.com. **Contact:** C.J. Sage, editor. Honors "1 new poem that *The National Poetry Review* believes has the greatest chance, of those entered, of standing the test of time and becoming part of the literary canon." Deadline: September 30. Prize: $500, plus publication in *The National Poetry Review.*

TIPS "Simultaneous submission acceptable, but if the work is selected by *TNPR* for the prize or for publication, it must be withdrawn from elsewhere unless you have withdrawn it from us 2 weeks before our acceptance. Multiple submissions are acceptable with a reading fee for each group of 3 poems; 10-page limit per group."

O THE LEAGUE OF MINNESOTA POETS CONTEST

57310 166th Lane, Good Thunder MN 56037. **Website:** www.mnpoets.org. **Contact:** Susan Stevens Chambers. Annual contest offers 18 different categories, with 3 prizes in each category, ranging from $10-125. See guidelines for poem lengths, forms, and subjects. Guidelines available for #10 SASE, by e-mail, or on website. Additional information regarding LOMP membership available on website. Deadline: July 31. Judged by nationally known, non-Minnesota judges. Winners will be announced at the October LOMP Conference and by mail.

LEAGUE OF UTAH WRITERS CONTEST

420 W. 750 N., Logan UT 84321. (435)755-7609. **E-mail:** luwriters@gmail.com. **Website:** www.luwriters.org. **Contact:** Dianne Hardy, membership chair. Open to any writer, the LUW Contest provides authors an opportunity to get their work read and critiqued. Contest submission period opens March 1 and closes June 1. Multiple categories are offered; see webpage for details. Entries must be the original and unpublished work of the author. Winners are announced at the Annual Writers Round-Up in September. Those not present will be notified by e-mail. Cash prizes are awarded. Deadline: June 1 Entries are judged by professional authors and editors from outside the League.

⊕ LES FIGUES PRESS NOS BOOK CONTEST

P.O. Box 7736, Los Angeles CA 90007. **E-mail:** info@lesfigues.com. **Website:** www.lesfigues.com. Les Figues Press creates aesthetic conversations between Writers/Artists and readers, especially those interested in innovative/experimental/avant-garde work. The Press intends in the the most premeditated fashion to champion the trinity of Beauty, Belief, and Bawdry. Prize given for best ms of poetry or prose. See website for contest guidelines. Deadline: September 9. $1,000, plus publication by Les Figues Press.

LET'S WRITE LITERARY CONTEST

E-mail: writerpllevin@gmail.com. **Website:** www.gcwriters.org. **Contact:** Philip Levin. "The Gulf Coast Writers Association sponsors this nationally recognized contest, which accepts unpublished poems and short stories from authors all around the US. This is an annual event which has been held for over 20 years." Deadline: April 15 1st Prize: $80; 2nd Prize: $50; 3rd Prize: $20.

TIPS "See guidelines online."

THE LEVINSON PRIZE

Poetry, 61 W. Superior St., Chicago IL 60654. (312)787-7070. **Fax:** (312)787-6650. **E-mail:** poetry@poetrymagazine.org. **Website:** www.poetrymagazine.org. Offered annually for poems published in *Poetry* during the preceding year (October-September). Upon acceptance, *Poetry* licenses exclusive worldwide first serial rights, including electronic rights, for publication, as well as non-exclusive rights to reprint, reuse, and archive the work, in any format, in perpetuity. Copyright reverts to author upon first publication. Prize: $500.

LEVIS READING PRIZE

(804)828-1329. **Fax:** (804)828-8684. **E-mail:** tndidato@vcu.edu. **Website:** www.has.vcu.edu/eng/resources/levis_prize/levis_prize.htm. **Contact:** Thom Didato. "Offered annually for books of poetry published in the previous year to encourage poets early in their careers. The entry must be the writer's first or second published book of poetry. Previously published books in other genres, or previously published chapbooks or self-published material, do not count as books for this purpose." Deadline: January 15 $1,500 honorarium and an expense-paid trip to Richmond to present a public reading.

THE RUTH LILLY POETRY PRIZE

E-mail: poetry@poetrymagazine.org. **Website:** www.poetrymagazine.org. Offered annually to a poet whose accomplishments in the field of poetry warrant extraordinary recognition. No applicants or nominations are accepted. Deadline: Varies. Prize: $100,000.

◐ LITERAL LATTE FOOD VERSE AWARDS

200 East 10th St., Suite 240, New York NY 10003. **Website:** www.literal-latte.com. **Contact:** Lisa Erdman. The annual Literary Latté Food for Verse Awards offers 1st Prize: $500 for best poem with food as an ingredient. All styles and subjects welcome. All entries considered for publication in Literal Latte. Submissions must be unpublished. Include cover page with poet's name, address, phone number, e-mail, and poem titles/first lines; no identifying information on mss pages. Guidelines available by e-mail, or on website. **Entry fee:** $10 for up to 6 poems, $15 for 12 poems. Make checks/money orders payable to Literal Latté. **Deadline:** January 15 (postmark).

LITERAL LATTÉ POETRY AWARD

Literal Latté, 200 E. 10th St., Suite 240, New York NY 10003. (212)260-5532. **E-mail:** LitLatte@aol.com. **Website:** www.literal-latte.com. **Contact:** Jenine Gordon Bockman, editor. "Offered annually to any writer for unpublished poetry (maximum 2,000 words per poem). All styles welcome. Winners published in *Literal Lattè*." Deadline: Postmark by July 15. 1st Place: $1,000; 2nd Place: $300; 3rd Place: $200.

THE MACGUFFIN NATIONAL POET HUNT CONTEST

The MacGuffin, 18600 Haggerty Rd., Livonia MI 48152. (734)462-4400, ext. 5327. **Fax:** (734)462-4679. **E-mail:** macguffin@schoolcraft.edu. **Website:** www.macguffin.org. **Contact:** Gordon Krupsky, managing editor. Work is judged blindly by a renowned, published poet. Offered annually for unpublished work. Guidelines available by mail, e-mail, or on the website. Acquires first rights (if published). Once published, all rights revert to the author. Open to any writer. All non-winning poems will also be considered by staff for publication in an upcoming issue of *The MacGuffin*. Also accepting unpublished stories up to 5,000 words and poetry up to 400 lines for normal publication. Please direct all correspondence to Gordon Krupsky. **Costs:** $15 for a 5-poem entry. Check or MO payable to Schoolcraft College. **Deadline:** April 2-June 4 (postmarked). Prize: 1st Place: $500; 2 Honorable Mentions will be published. 2012 Judge: Dorianne Laux. Past judges include Terry Blackhawk, Jim Daniels, Thomas Lynch, and Vivian Shipley.

NAOMI LONG MADGETT POETRY AWARD

Lotus Press, Inc., P.O. Box 21607, Detroit MI 48221. **E-mail:** lotuspress@comcast.net. **Website:** www.lotuspress.org. **Contact:** Constance Withers. Offered annually to recognize an unpublished poetry ms by an African American. Guidelines for SASE, by e-mail, or online. **Deadline:** January 2-March 1. Prize: $500 and publication by Lotus Press. Offered annually to recognize an unpublished poetry ms by an African

American. Guidelines for SASE, by e-mail, or online. Deadline: January 2-March 1 $500 and publication by Lotus Press.

MAIN STREET RAG'S ANNUAL CHAPBOOK CONTEST

P.O. Box 690100, Charlotte NC 28227-7001. (704)573-2516. **E-mail:** editor@mainstreetrag.com. **Website:** www.MainStreetRag.com. **Contact:** M. Scott Douglass, editor/publisher. Annual chapbook contest by *Main Street Rag* offers a 1st Prize of $500 and 50 copies of chapbook. "Runners-up are offered publication, and every ms entered is also considered for publication." All entrants receive a copy of the winning chapbook. Submit 24-32 pages of poetry; no more than 1 poem/page. Guidelines available for SASE, by e-mail, or on website. **Entry fee:** $17. **Deadline:** May 31.

MAIN STREET RAG'S ANNUAL POETRY BOOK AWARD

P.O. Box 690100, Charlotte NC 28227-7001. (704)573-2516. **E-mail:** editor@mainstreetrag.com. **Website:** www.MainStreetRag.com. **Contact:** M. Scott Douglass, editor/publisher. Main Street Rag' s Annual Poetry Book Award offers a 1st Prize of $1,000 and 50 copies of book; runners-up may also be offered publication. Submit 48-84 pages of poetry, no more than 1 poem/page (individual poems may be longer than 1 page). Guidelines available on website. **Entry fee:** $22 (or $27 to include a copy of the winning book). **Deadline:** January 31. Deadline: January 31 Offers a 1st Prize of $1,000 and 50 copies of book; runners-up may also be offered publication.

THE MALAHAT REVIEW LONG POEM PRIZE

E-mail: malahat@uvic.ca (queries only). **Website:** www.malahatreview.ca. **Contact:** John Barton, editor. The biennial Long Poem Prize offers 2 awards of $1,000 CAD each for a long poem or cycle (10-20 printed pages). Includes publication in The Malahat Review. Open to "entries from Canadian, American, and overseas authors." Submissions must be unpublished. No simultaneous submissions. Submit a single poem or cycle of poems, 10-20 published pages (a published page equals 32 lines or less, including breaks between stanzas); no restrictions on subject matter or aesthetic approach. Include separate page with poet's name, address, e-mail, and title; no identifying information on mss pages. No e-mail submissions. Do not include SASE for results; mss will not be returned. Guidelines available on website. **Entry fee:** $35 CAD for Canadian entries, $40 USD for US entries ($45 USD for entries from Mexico and outside North America); includes 1-year subscription to *The Malahat Review*. **Deadline:** February 1 (postmark) of alternate years (2011, 2013, etc.). Winners published in the summer issue of *The Malahat Review*, announced in summer on website, Facebook page, and in quarterly e-newsletter *Malahat lite*. "Long Poem Prize offered in alternate years with the Novella Contest. Open to unpublished long poems. Preliminary reading by editorial board; final judging by 3 recognized poets. Obtains first world rights. After—publication rights revert to the author. Open to any writer."

THE MORTON MARR POETRY PRIZE

Southern Methodist University, P.O. Box 750374, Dallas TX 75275-0374. (214)768-1037. **Fax:** (214)768-1408. **E-mail:** swr@mail.smu.edu. **Website:** www.smu.edu/southwestreview. **Contact:** Prize coordinator. The annual Morton Marr Poetry Prize awards 1st Prize: $1,000 and 2nd Prize: $500 to a poet who has not yet published a first book of poetry. Winners will be published in Southwest Review. Submit 6 poems in a "traditional" form (e.g., sonnet, sestina, villanelle, rhymed stanzas, blank verse, et al). Include cover letter with poet's name, address, and other relevant information; no identifying information on entry pages. Manuscripts will not be returned. Guidelines available on website. **Entry fee:** $5/poem. **Deadline:** September 30 (postmark).

MARSH HAWK PRESS POETRY PRIZE

P.O. Box 206, East Rockaway NY 11518-0206. **E-mail:** marshhawkpress1@aol.com. **Website:** www.MarshHawkPress.org. **Contact:** Prize director. The Marsh Hawk Press Poetry Prize offers $1,000, plus publication of a book-length ms. Submissions must be unpublished as a collection, but individual poems may have been previously published elsewhere. Submit 48-70 pages of original poetry in any style in English, typed single-spaced, and paginated. (Longer manuscripts will be considered if the press is queried before submission.) Contest mss may be submitted by electronic upload. See website for more information. If submitting via Post Office mail, the ms must be bound with a spring clip. Include 2 title pages: 1 with ms title, poet's name, and contact information only; 1 with ms title only (poet's name must not appear anywhere in the ms). Also include table of contents and acknowledgments page. Include SASE for results only; ms will not be returned. Guidelines available on website. **Entry fee:** $20; make check/money order payable to Marsh Hawk Press. **Deadline:** April 30.

KATHLEEN MCCLUNG SONNET PRIZE CATEGORY

Category in the Soul Making Keats Literary Competition, National League of American Pen Women, The Webhallow House, 1544 Sweetwood Dr., Broadmoor Village CA 94015-2029. **E-mail:** pennobhill@aol.com. **Website:** www.soulmakingcontest.us. **Contact:** Eileen Malone. "Call for Shakespearean and Petrarchan sonnets on the theme of the 'beloved.'" Deadline: November 30 (annually) 1st Place: $100; 2nd Place: $50; 3rd Place: $25.

MELBOURNE POETS UNION NATIONAL POETRY COMPETITION

Melbourne Poets Union, P.O. Box 266, Flinders Lane VI 8009, Australia. **Website:** http://home.vicnet.net.au/~mpuinc. **Contact:** Leon Shann. Offers annual prizes of $1,500 AUD, plus book vouchers and book prizes. Submissions must be unpublished. Submit unlimited number of poems on any subject, in any form, up to 50 lines. "Open to Australian residents living in Australia or overseas." Entry form and guidelines available for SASE (or SAE and IRC). **Entry fee:** $8 AUD; MPU members $7 AUD/poem; $14 AUD/2 poems; $18 AUD/3 poems. Under 18s (3) Aus 50¢ postage stamps or equivalent. **Deadline:** October 31. Competition receives over 500 entries/year. Winners announced on the last Friday of November by newsletter, mail, phone, and on website. "The $1,500 prize money comes directly from entry money; the rest going to paying the judge and costs of running the competition."

MIDLAND AUTHORS AWARD

Society of Midland Authors, P.O. Box 10419, Chicago IL 60610-0419. **E-mail:** writercc@aol.com. **Website:** www.midlandauthors.com. **Contact:** Carol Jean Carlson. "Established in 1915, the Society of Midland Authors Award (SMA) is presented to one title in each of six categories 'to stimulate creative effort,' one of SMA's goals, to be honored at the group's annual awards banquet in May." Annual. Competition/award for novels, story collections (by single author). Prize: cash prize of at least $300 and a plaque that is awarded at the SMA banquet. Categories: children's nonfiction and fiction, adult nonfiction and fiction, adult biography, and poetry. Judging is done by a panel of three judges for each category that includes a mix of experienced authors, reviewers, book sellers, university faculty and librarians. No entry fee. Guidelines available in September-November with SASE, on website, in publication. Accepts inquiries by e-mail, phone. **Deadline: Feb. 1.** "The contest is open to any title with a recognized publisher that has been published within the year prior to the contest year." Open to authors or poets who reside in, were born in, or have strong ties to a Midland state, which includes Illinois, Indiana, Iowa, Kansas, Michigan, Minnesota, Missouri, Nebraska, North Dakota, South Dakota, Ohio and Wisconsin. SMA only accepts published work accompanied by a completed award form. Writers may submit own work. Entries can also be submitted by the publisher's rep. "Write a great story and be sure to follow contest rules by sending a copy of the book to each of the three judges for the given category who are listed on SMA's website." Results announced at the SMA Awards Banquet each May. Other announcements follow in the media. Winners notified by mail, by phone. Results made available to entrants on website, in our monthly membership newsletter. Results will also go to local media in the form of press releases.

MILFORD FINE ARTS COUNCIL NATIONAL POETRY CONTEST

40 Railroad Ave., South, Milford CT 06460. **E-mail:** milfordfac@optonline.net. **Website:** www.milford-arts.org. **Contact:** Tom Bouton, Writer's Group Chairperson. Offers annual award of 1st Prize: $100; 2nd Prize: $50; 3rd Prize: $25; plus winners will be published in Milford Fine Arts Council's annual publication, *High Tide*. Submissions must be unpublished. No simultaneous submissions. Poems entered may not have won any other prizes or honorable mentions. Poets must be 18 years and older. "Poems must be typed single-spaced on white standard paper, 10-30 lines (including title), no more than 48 characters/line, on any subject, in any style, rhymed or unrhymed. Use standard font, clear and legible, 1 poem/page, no script or fax. NO foul language. No bio or date, only the words 'Unpublished Original' typed above the poem." Include poet's name, address, ZIP code, and phone number or e-mail address in the middle back of the submitted poem, no identifying information on the front of the page. Poems will be judged on form, clarity, originality, and universal appeal. "En-

tries may be considered for publication in *High Tide*. If you do not want your poems considered for publication, then you must print on the back of the poem (below your name, address, and ZIP code) 'For National Poetry Contest Only.'" Include SASE for results only, with NOTIFICATION printed on bottom left corner of envelope; no poems will be returned. Guidelines available for SASE or on website. **Entry fee:** $3 for one poem, $6 for 3 poems, $2 for each additional poem after 3. Contestants may enter an unlimited number of poems (will be judged individually, not as a group). Check or money order accepted, no cash. **Deadline:** March 31.

VASSAR MILLER PRIZE IN POETRY

University of North Texas Press, 1155 Union circle, #311336, Denton TX 76203-5017. (940)565-2142. **Fax:** (940)565-4590. **Website:** http://untpress.unt.edu/. **Contact:** John Poch. "Annual prize awarded to a collection of poetry." Deadline: November 15 Winner will receive $1000 and publication by University of North Texas Press. Judged by a "different eminent writer selected each year. Some prefer to remain anonymous until the end of the contest."

TIPS "No limitations to entrants. In years when the judge is announced, we ask that students of the judge not enter to avoid a perceived conflict. All entries should contain identifying material only on the one cover sheet. Entries are read anonymously."

MISSISSIPPI REVIEW PRIZE

Mississippi Review, 118 College Dr., #5144, Hattiesburg MS 39406-0001. (601)266-4321. **Fax:** (601)266-5757. **E-mail:** editors@mississippireview.com; rief@mississippireview.com. **Website:** www.mississippireview.com. "Our annual contest awards prizes of $1,000 in fiction and in poetry. Winners and finalists will make up next winter's print issue of the national literary magazine *Mississippi Review*. Contest is open to all writers in English except current or former students or employees of The University of Southern Mississippi. Fiction entries should be 1000-5000 words, poetry entries should be three poems totaling 10 pages or less. There is no limit on the number of entries you may submit. Entry fee is $15 per entry, payable to the *Mississippi Review*. Each entrant will receive a copy of the prize issue. No manuscripts will be returned. Previously published work is ineligible. Contest opens April 2. Deadline is October 1. Winners will be announced in late January and publication is scheduled for May next year. Entries should have "MR Prize," author name, address, phone, e-mail and title of work on page one."

TIPS No mss returned.

JENNY MCKEAN MOORE VISITING WRITER

English Deptartment, George Washington University, Rome Hall, 801 22nd St. NW, Suite 760, Washington DC 20052. (202)994-6180. **Fax:** (202)994-7915. **E-mail:** tvmallon@gwu.edu. **Website:** http://columbian.gwu.edu/departmentsprograms/english/creativewriting/activitiesevents. **Contact:** Thomas Mallon, director of Creative Writing. "The position is filled annually, bringing a visiting writer to The George Washington University. During each semester the Writer teaches 1 creative-writing course at the university as well as a community workshop. Each year we seek someone specializing in a different genre—fiction, poetry, creative nonfiction. For the 2012-13 academic year we will be looking for a poet. Guidelines for application will be announced in *The Writer's Chronicle*. Annual stipend between $50,000 and $60,000, plus reduced-rent townhouse on campus (not guaranteed)." Application Deadline: November 1 Annual stipend varies, depending on endowment performance; most recently, stipend was $58,000, plus reduced-rent townhouse (not guaranteed).

THE KATHRYN A. MORTON PRIZE IN POETRY

Sarabande Books, Inc., P.O. Box 4456, Louisville KY 40204. (502)458-4028. **E-mail:** info@sarabandebooks.org. **Website:** www.SarabandeBooks.org. **Contact:** Sarah Gorham, editor-in-chief. Member: CLMP. The Kathryn A. Morton Prize in Poetry is awarded annually to a book-length ms (at least 48 pages). All finalists are considered for publication. Competition receives approximately 1,400 entries. *Easy Math*. 2012 judge was Cole Swensen. "To avoid conflict of interest, students in a degree-granting program or close friends of a judge are ineligible to enter the contest in the genre for which their friend or teacher is serving as judge. Sarabande, as a member of CLMP, complies with its Contest Code of Ethics." Deadline: Submit January 1-February 15 (postmark) only. $2,000, publication, and a standard royalty contract.

THE HOWARD FRANK MOSHER SHORT FICTION PRIZE

Vermont College, 36 College St., Montpelier VT 05602. (802)828-8517. **E-mail:** hungermtn@vcfa.edu. **Website:** www.hungermtn.org. **Contact:** Miciah Bay Gault, editor. The annual Howard Frank Mosher Short Fiction Prize offers $1,000 and publication in *Hunger Mountain*; 2 runners-up receive $100 and are considered for publication. Submit story under 10,000 words. Guidelines available on website. Deadline: June 30.

SHEILA MARGARET MOTTON PRIZE

New England Poetry Club, 2 Farrar St., Cambridge MA 02138. **E-mail:** contests@nepoetryclub.org. **Website:** www.nepoetryclub.org. **Contact:** NEPC contest coordinator. Checks for all contests should be made to New England Poetry Club. All entries should be sent in duplicate with name, address, phone, and email of writer on only one copy. (Judges receive copies without names). Deadline: May 31. Prize: $500. Judges are well-known poets and sometimes winners of previous NEPC contests.

ERIKA MUMFORD PRIZE

New England Poetry Club, 654 Green St., No. 2, Cambridge MA 02139. **E-mail:** contests@nepoetryclub.org. **Website:** www.nepoetryclub.org/contests.htm. **Contact:** NEPC contest coordinator. Offered annually for a poem in any form about foreign culture or travel. Funded by Erika Mumford's family and friends. Deadline: May 31. Prize: $250. Judges are well-known poets and sometimes winners of previous NEPC contests.

NATIONAL BOOK AWARDS

The National Book Foundation, 90 Broad St., Suite 609, New York NY 10004. (212)685-0261. **E-mail:** nationalbook@nationalbook.org. **Website:** www.nationalbook.org. Presents $10,000 in each of 4 categories (fiction, nonfiction, poetry, and young people's literature), plus 16 short-list prizes of $1,000 each to finalists. Submissions must be previously published and **must be entered by the publisher**. General guidelines available on website; interested publishers should phone or e-mail the Foundation. **Entry fee:** $125/title. **Deadline:** See website for current year's deadline. Presents $10,000 in each of 4 categories (fiction, nonfiction, poetry, and young people's literature), plus 16 short-list prizes of $1,000 each to finalists. Submissions must be previously published and **must be entered by the publisher**. General guidelines available on website; interested publishers should phone or e-mail the Foundation. Deadline: See website for current year's deadline.

NATIONAL POETRY COMPETITION

Poetry Society, 22 Betterton St., London WC2H 9BX, United Kingdom. **E-mail:** info@poetrysociety.org.uk. **Website:** www.poetrysociety.org.uk. **Contact:** Competition organiser. The National Poetry Competition offers 1st Prize: £5,000; 2nd Prize: £2,000; 3rd Prize: £1,000; plus 7 commendations of £100 each. Winners will be published in *Poetry Review*, and on the Poetry Society website; the top 3 winners will receive a year's free membership in the Poetry Society (see separate listing in Organizations). Open to anyone aged 17 or over. Entries "received from all around the world. All entries are judged anonymously and past winners include both published and previously unknown poets." Submissions must be unpublished (poems posted on websites are considered published). Submit original poems in English, on any subject, no more than 40 lines/poem, typed on 1 side only of A4 paper, double- or single-spaced. Each poem must be titled. No identifying information on poems. Do not staple pages. Accepts online submissions; full details available on the National Poetry Competition pages on the Poetry Society website. Entry form (required) available for A5 SAE (1 entry form covers multiple entries, may be photocopied). Include stamped SAE for notification of receipt of postal entries (confirmation of online entries will be e-mailed at time of submission); poems will not be returned. Guidelines available on website. **Entry fee:** £6 for first poem, £3 for each subsequent entry (Poetry Society members can enter a second poem free of charge). Make cheques, in sterling only, payable to the Poetry Society. **Deadline:** October 31.

THE NATIONAL POETRY REVIEW BOOK PRIZE

The National Poetry Review, P.O. Box 2080, Aptos CA 95001-2080. **E-mail:** editor@nationalpoetryreview.com. **Website:** www.nationalpoetryreview.com. **Contact:** C.J. Sage, editor. *The National Poetry Review* Book Prize offers $1,000, publication of a book-length ms, and 15 author copies. All entries will be considered for publication. Deadline: June 30 (postmark).

NATIONAL WRITERS ASSOCIATION POETRY CONTEST

The National Writers Association, 10940 S. Parker Rd. #508, Parker CO 80134. (303)841-0246. **E-mail:** natlwritersassn@hotmail.com. **Website:** www.nationalwriters.com. **Contact:** Sandy Whelchel, director. "Annual contest to encourage the writing of poetry, an important form of individual expression but with a limited commercial market." Deadline: October 1. 1st Place: $100; 2nd Place: $50; 3rd Place: $25.

HOWARD NEMEROV SONNET AWARD

E-mail: mona.3773@yahoo.com. **Website:** http://theformalist.evansville.edu/Home.htm. **Contact:** Mona Baer, contest coordinator. *The Formalist* sponsors the annual Howard Nemerov Sonnet Award. 2011 winner was Robert W. Crawford. 2011 judge was A. M. Juster. Deadline: November 15, 2012 (postmark). Offers $1,000 prize for a single sonnet. Winner and 11 finalists will be published in *Measure: A Review of Formal Poetry.*

● THE PABLO NERUDA PRIZE FOR POETRY

(918)631-3080. **Fax:** (918)631-3033. **E-mail:** nimrod@utulsa.edu. **Website:** www.utulsa.edu/nimrod. **Contact:** Francine Ringold. The annual Nimrod Literary Awards include The Pablo Neruda Prize for Poetry, which offers: 1st Prize—$2,000 and publication in *Nimrod: International Journal of Prose and Poetry*; and 2nd Prize—$1,000 and publication. *Nimrod* retains the right to publish any submission. Submissions must be unpublished. Work must be in English or translated by original author. Submit 3-10 pages of poetry (1 long poem or several short poems). Poet's name must not appear on ms. Include cover sheet with poem title(s), poet's name, address, phone and fax numbers, and e-mail address (poet must have a US address by October of contest year to enter). Mark "Contest Entry" on submission envelope and cover sheet. Include SASE for results only; mss will not be returned. Guidelines available for #10 SASE or on website. **Entry fee:** $20; includes 1-year subscription (2 issues) to *Nimrod.* Make checks payable to *Nimrod.* 2011 winners were Hayden Saunider ("Sideways Glances in the Rear-View Mirror") and Suzanne Cleary ("Amazing" and other poems). Winners will be announced on *Nimrod*'s website. Annual award to discover new writers of vigor and talent. Open to US residents only. 2011 winners were Hayden Saunider ("Sideways Glances in the Rear-View Mirror") and Suzanne Cleary ("Amazing" and other poems). Winners will be announced on *Nimrod*'s website. Deadline: April 30.

◐ THE NEW CRITERION POETRY PRIZE

Website: www.newcriterion.com. 900 Broadway, Suite 602, New York NY 10003. **Website:** www.newcriterion.com. **Contact:** Contest Coordinator. The annual New Criterion Poetry Prize offers $3,000 and publication by Ivan R. Dee, Chicago for a book-length poetry ms that pay close attention to form. All entrants will receive a copy of the winning submission upon publication. Submit a ms of no more than 60 pages. Manuscripts will not be returned. Guidelines available on website. **Entry fee:** $25. No personal checks; money order or certified check must accompany each entry. **Deadline:** September 30 (postmark). Winner announced in February.

◐ THE NEW ISSUES POETRY PRIZE

New Issues Poetry & Prose, New Issues Poetry & Prose, Department of English, Western Michigan University, 1903 W. Michigan Ave., Kalamazoo MI 49008-5331. (269)387-8185. **Fax:** (269)387-2562. **E-mail:** new-issues@wmich.edu. **Website:** www.wmich.edu/newissues. The New Issues Poetry Prize offers $2,000, plus publication of a book-length ms. Open to "poets writing in English who have not previously published a full-length collection of poems. Additional mss will be considered from those submitted to the competition for publication. Considers simultaneous submissions, but *New Issues* must be notified of acceptance elsewhere. Submit ms of at least 48 pages, typed, single-spaced preferred. Clean photocopies acceptable. Do not bind; use manila folder or metal clasp. Include cover page with poet's name, address, phone number, and title of the ms. Also include brief bio and acknowledgments page. Submissions are also welcome through the online submission manager www.submishmash.com. For hardcopy submissions only, you may include SASP for notification of receipt of ms and SASE for results only; no mss will be returned. **Entry fee:** $20. Make checks payable to New Issues Poetry & Prose. **Deadline:** November 30 (postmark). "Winning manuscript will be named in May and published in the next spring. A national judge selects the prize winner and recommends other manuscripts. The editors decide on the other books considering the judge's recommendation, but are not bound by it." 2012 judge: Jean Valentine; 2013 judge: TBD. Offered annually for publication of a first book of poems by a poet writing in English who has not previously published a full-length collection of poems in an edition of 500 or more copies. *New Issues Poetry & Prose* obtains rights for first publication. Book is copyrighted in author's name. Guidelines for SASE or online. Deadline: November 30 (postmark).

NEW LETTERS PRIZE FOR POETRY

New Letters Awards for Writers, UMKC, University House, 5101 Rockhill Rd., Kansas City MO 64110-2499. **Website:** www.newletters.org. The annual New Letters Poetry Prize awards $1,500 and publication in *New Letters* to the best group of 3-6 poems. All entries will be considered for publication in *New Letters*. Submissions must be unpublished. Considers simultaneous submissions with notification upon acceptance elsewhere. Accepts multiple entries with separate fee for each. Submit up to 6 poems (need not be related). Include 2 cover sheets: 1 with poet's name, address, e-mail, phone number, prize category (poetry), and poem title(s); the second with category and poem title(s) only. No identifying information on ms pages. Accepts electronic submissions. Include SASE for notification of receipt of ms and entry number, and SASE for results only (send only 1 envelope if submitting multiple entries); mss will not be returned. Guidelines available by SASE or on website. **Entry fee:** $15 for first entry, $10 for each subsequent entry; includes cost of a 1-year subscription, renewal, or gift subscription to *New Letters* (shipped to any address within the US). Make checks payable to New Letters. **Deadline:** May 18 (postmark). Current students and employees of the University of Missouri-Kansas City, and current volunteer members of the *New Letters* and BkMk Press staffs, are not eligible.

NEW MILLENNIUM AWARDS FOR FICTION, POETRY, AND NONFICTION

P.O. Box 2463, Room M2, Knoxville TN 37901. (423)428-0389. **Website:** www.newmillenniumwritings.com/awards; www.writingawards.com. "No restrictions as to style, content or number of submissions. Previously published pieces OK if online or under 5,000 print circulation. Send any time between now and midnight, June 17, for the Summer Awards program, January 31 for the Winter Awards. Simultaneous and multiple submissions welcome. Each fiction or nonfiction piece is a separate entry and should total no more than 6,000 words, except for the Short-Short Fiction Award, which should total no more than 1,000 words. (Nonfiction includes essays, profiles, memoirs, interviews, creative nonfiction, travel, humor, etc.) Each poetry entry may include up to 3 poems, not to exceed 5 pages total. All 20 poetry finalists will be published. Include name, phone, address, e-mail, and category on cover page only." Entries should be postmarked on or before June 17 or January 31. Prize: $1,000 for Best Poem; $1,000 for Best Fiction; $1,000 for Best Nonfiction; $1,000 for Best Short-Short Fiction.

NEW SOUTH WRITING CONTEST

E-mail: newsouth@gsu.edu. **Website:** www.review.gsu.edu. **Contact:** Editor. Offered annually to publish the most promising work of up-and-coming writers of poetry (up to 3 poems) and fiction (9,000 word limit). Rights revert to writer upon publication. Guidelines online. Deadline: March 5 1st Place: $1,000 in each category; 2nd Place: $250; and publication to winners. **TIPS** "We look for engagement with language and characters we care about."

NEW WOMEN'S VOICES CHAPBOOK COMPETITION

Finishing Line Press, P.O. Box 1626, Georgetown KY 40324. (859)514-8966. **E-mail:** FinishingBooks@aol.com. **Website:** www.finishinglinepress.com. **Contact:** Leah Maines, poetry editor. The New Women's Voices Chapbook Competition offers $1,000 and publication by Finishing Line Press for a chapbook-length ms by a woman poet who has not yet published a full-length collection (previous chapbook publication is okay). All entries will be considered for publication; up to 10 entries will be selected for the New Women's Voices series. Submit up to 26 pages of poetry. Include bio, acknowledgments, and SASE. Guidelines available on website. **Entry fee:** $15. **Deadline:** February 15 (postmark). Judge: Varies.

JESSE BRYCE NILES MEMORIAL CHAPBOOK AWARD

4956 St. John Dr., Syracuse NY 13215. (315)488-8077. **E-mail:** poetry@comstockreview.org. **Website:** www.comstockreview.org. The Jesse Bryce Niles Memorial Chapbook Award runs every other year, next in 2013, and offers $1,000 plus publication and 50 author's copies; each entrant also receives a copy. Submissions must be unpublished as a collection, but individual poems may have been previously published in journals. Considers simultaneous submissions "as long as the poet notifies us immediately upon acceptance elsewhere." Submit 25-34 pages of poetry, single-spaced (1 page=38 lines maximum, including spacing between lines; poems may run longer than 1 page). **Manuscripts either too short or too long will be disqualified.** "Do not count title page, acknowledgments, dedication, or bio in the page length. Do not send illustrations, photos, or any other graphics attached to the poems. You may submit a table of contents, which may list the manuscript name only, not the poet's name (not counted in page total for manuscript)." Manuscripts should be paginated and secured with a binder clip; no staples or plastic covers. Include 2 cover pages: 1 with ms title, poet's name, address, phone number, and e-mail address; second with ms title only. List acknowledgments on a separate, removable page with same identifying information. Poet's name should not appear on poems. Include SASE for results only; mss will not be returned. Guidelines available for SASE or on website. **Entry fee:** $25/chapbook. **Deadline:** submit August 1-September 30 (postmark). **Offered every other year.**

THE JOHN FREDERICK NIMS MEMORIAL PRIZE

Poetry, 61 W. Superior St., Chicago IL 60654. (312)787-7070. **E-mail:** poetry@poetrymagazine.org. **Website:** www.poetrymagazine.org. Offered annually for poems published in *Poetry* during the preceding year (October-September). Upon acceptance, *Poetry* licenses exclusive worldwide first serial rights, including electronic rights, for publication, as well as nonexclusive rights to reprint, reuse, and archive the work, in any format, in perpetuity. Copyright reverts to author upon first publication. Copyrights are returned to the authors on request. Prize: $500.

NORTH CAROLINA WRITERS' FELLOWSHIPS

North Carolina Arts Council, Dept. of Cultural Resources, Raleigh NC 27699-4632. (919)807-6500. **Fax:** (919)807-6532. **E-mail:** davidpotorti@ncdcr.gov. **Website:** www.ncarts.org. **Contact:** David Potorti, literature director. Offered every even year to support writers of fiction, poetry, literary nonfiction, literary translation, and spoken word. See website for guidelines and other eligibility requirements. Writers must be current residents of North Carolina for at least 1 year, must remain in residence in North Carolina during the grant year, and may not pursue academic or professional degrees while receiving grant. Fellowships offered to support writers in the development and creation of their work. See website for details. Prize: $10,000 grant. Reviewed by a panel of literature professionals (writers and editors).

NORTHERN CALIFORNIA BOOK AWARDS

Northern California Book Reviewers Association, c/o Poetry Flash, 1450 Fourth St. #4, Berkeley CA 94710. (510)525-5476. **E-mail:** editor@poetryflash.org. **Website:** www.poetryflash.org. **Contact:** Joyce Jenkins, executive director. Annual Northern California Book Award for outstanding book in literature, open to books published in the current calendar year by Northern California authors. Annual award. NCBR presents annual awards to Bay Area (northern California) authors annually in fiction, nonfiction, poetry and children's literature. Purpose is to encourage writers and stimulate interest in books and reading." Previously published books only. Must be published the calendar year prior to spring awards ceremony. Submissions nominated by publishers; author or agent could also nominate published work. Deadline for entries: December. No entry forms. Send 3 copies of the book to attention: NCBR. No entry fee. Awards $100 honorarium and award certificate. Judging by voting members of the Northern California Book Reviewers. Books that reach the "finals" (usually 3-5 per category) displayed at annual award ceremonies (spring). Nominated books are displayed and sold at the Northern California Book Awards in the spring of each year; the winner is asked to read at the San Francisco Public Library's Main Branch.

NSW PREMIER'S LITERARY AWARD THE KENNETH SLESSOR PRIZE

Website: www.arts.nsw.gov.au. (Specialized: Australian citizens only) Offers annual award of $30,000 for a book of poetry (collection or long poem) published in the previous year. **Open to Australian citizens only.** Books may be nominated by poets or by their agents or publishers. Write for entry form and guidelines or check website. **Deadline:** November (check guidelines). Winners will be announced in May. "Obtain copy of guidelines before entering."

OHIOANA POETRY AWARD

Ohioana Library Association, 274 E. First Ave., Suite 300, Columbus OH 43201. (614)466-3831. **Fax:** (614)728-6974. **E-mail:** ohioana@ohioana.org. **Web-**

site: www.ohioana.org. (Helen and Laura Krout Memorial) (Specialized: native & resident OH authors) "Offers annual Ohioana Book Awards. Up to 6 awards may be given for books (including books of poetry) by authors born in Ohio or who have lived in Ohio for at least 5 years." The Ohioana Poetry Award of $1,000 (with the same residence requirements), made possible by a bequest of Helen Krout, is given yearly "to an individual whose body of published work has made, and continues to make, a significant contribution to poetry, and through whose work as a writer, teacher, administrator, or in community service, interest in poetry has been developed." **Deadline:** nominations to be received by December 31. Competition receives several hundred entries. 2009 Ohioana Poetry Award winner was William Greenway (*Everywhere at Once*). Ohioana Quarterly regularly reviews books by Ohio authors and is available through membership in Ohioana Library Association ($25/year).

OPEN SEASON AWARDS

The Malahat Review, University of Victoria, P.O. Box 1700, Stn CSC, Victoria BC V8V 2Y2, Canada. **Fax:** (250)472-5051. **E-mail:** malahat@uvic.ca. **Website:** www.malahatreview.ca. **Contact:** John Barton, editor. The annual Open Season Awards offers $1,000 CAD and publication in *The Malahat Review*. The Open Season Awards accepts entries of poetry, fiction, and creative nonfiction. Submissions must be unpublished. No simultaneous submissions. Submit up to 3 poems per entry, each poem not to exceed 100 lines; one piece of fiction (2500 words max.), or one piece of creative nonfiction (2500 words max.), no restrictions on subject matter or aesthetic approach. Include separate page with writer's name, address, e-mail, and title(s); no identifying information on mss pages. No e-mail submissions. Do not include SASE for results; mss will not be returned. Guidelines available on website. Entry fee: $35 CAD for Canadian entries, $40 USD for U.S. entries, ($45 USD for entries from Mexico and outside North America); includes a one-year subscription to *The Malahat Review*. Deadline: November 1 (postmark) every year. 2011 winner in Poetry category: Cynthia Woodman Kerkham. Winner and finalists contacted by e-mail. Winners published in spring issue of *Malahat Review* announced in winter on website, facebook page, and in quarterly e-newsletter, *Malahat lite*. Offers $1,000 CAD and publication in *The Malahat Review* in each category.

OREGON BOOK AWARDS

224 NW 13th Ave., Suite 306, #219, Portland OR 97209. (503)227-2583. **E-mail:** susan@literary-arts.org. **Website:** www.literary-arts.org. **Contact:** Susan Denning. The annual Oregon Book Awards celebrate Oregon authors in the areas of poetry, fiction, nonfiction, drama and young readers' literature published between August 1, 2010 and July 31, 2011. Prize: Finalists are invited on a statewide reading tour and are promoted in bookstores and libraries across the state. Judged by writers who are selected from outside Oregon for their expertise in a genre. Past judges include Mark Doty, Colson Whitehead and Kim Barnes. Entry fee determined by initial print run; see website for details. Deadline: last Friday in August. Entries must be previously published. Oregon residents only. Accepts inquiries by phone and e-mail. Finalists announced in January. Winners announced at an awards ceremony in November. List of winners available in April.

GUY OWEN AWARD

Southern Poetry Review, Department of Languages, Literature, and Philosophy, Armstrong Atlantic State University, 11935 Abercorn St., Savannah GA 31419-1997. (912)344-3196. **E-mail:** tonyryamorris@gmail.com. **Website:** www.southernpoetryreview.org. **Contact:** Tony Morris, managing editor. The annual Guy Owen Prize offers $1,000 and publication in *Southern Poetry Review* to the winning poem selected by a distinguished poet. All entries will be considered for publication. 2011 winner was Catherine Staples. Deadline: March 1-June 15 (postmarked).

THE PATERSON POETRY PRIZE

(973)684-6555. **Fax:** (973)523-6085. **E-mail:** mgillan@pccc.edu. **Website:** www.pccc.edu/poetry. **Contact:** Maria Mazziotti Gillan, executive director. The Paterson Poetry Prize offers an annual award of $1,000 for the strongest book of poems (48 or more pages) published in the previous year. The winner will be asked to participate in an awards ceremony and to give a reading at The Poetry Center. Minimum press run: 500 copies. Publishers may submit more than 1 title for prize consideration; 3 copies of each book must be submitted. Include SASE for results; books will not be returned (all entries will be donated to The Poetry Center Library). Guidelines and application form (required) available for SASE or on website. **Entry fee:** None. **Deadline:** February 1 (postmark). Winners will be announced in *Poets & Writers* magazine and on website. 2011 winner was Elizabeth Alexander for the book *Crave Radiance: New and Selected Poems 1990-2010*. "Offered annually for a book of poetry 48 pages or more, with a print run of 500 or more, published in the previous year."

THE KATHERINE PATERSON PRIZE FOR YOUNG ADULT AND CHILDREN'S WRITING

Vermont College, 36 College St., Montpelier VT 05602. (802)828-8517. **E-mail:** hungermtn@vcfa.edu. **Website:** www.hungermtn.org. **Contact:** Miciah Bay Gault, editor. The annual Katherine Paterson Prize for Young Adult and Children's Writing offers $1,000 and publication in *Hunger Mountain*; 3 runners-up receive $100 and are also published. Submit young adult or middle grade mss, and writing for younger children, short stories, picture books, or novel excerpts, under 10,000 words. Guidelines available on website. Deadline: June 30.

◐ PAVEMENT SAW PRESS CHAPBOOK AWARD

321 Empire St., Montpelier OH 43543-1301. **E-mail:** info@pavementsaw.org. **Website:** www.pavementsaw.org. **Contact:** David Baratier, editor. "Pavement Saw Press has been publishing steadily since the fall of 1993. Each year since 1999, we have published at least 4 full-length paperback poetry collections, with some printed in library edition hard covers, 1 chapbook and a yearly literary journal anthology. We specialize in finding authors who have been widely published in literary journals but have not published a chapbook or full-length book." 2012 winner was Amy Wright. Deadline: December 31 (postmark) Chapbook Award offers $500, publication, and 50 author copies.

◐ PEARL POETRY PRIZE

Pearl Editions, 3030 E. Second St., Long Beach CA 90803. (562)434-4523. **Fax:** (562)434-4523. **E-mail:** pearlmag@aol.com. **Website:** www.pearlmag.com. **Contact:** Marilyn Johnson, editor/publisher. The annual Pearl Poetry Prize awards $1,000, publication, and 25 author's copies for a book-length ms. Guidelines available for SASE or on website. **Entry fee:** $20. **Deadline:** Submit May 1-June 30 only. 2010 winner was Jerry Neren (*Once Upon a Time in Vietnam*). 2012 judge: Andrea Carter Brown. "Offered annually to provide poets with further opportunity to publish their poetry in book-form and find a larger audience for their work. Mss must be original works written in English. Guidelines for SASE or online. Open to all writers." Deadline: Submit May 1-June 30 only $1,000 and publication by Pearl Editions

○ JUDITH SIEGEL PEARSON AWARD

Wayne State University/Family of Judith Siegel Pearson, Attn: Writing Awards Committee, 5057 Woodward Ave., Suite 9408, Detroit MI 48202. (313)577-2450. **Fax:** (313)577-8618. **E-mail:** ad2073@wayne.edu. **Contact:** Royanne Smith, contest coordinator. Offers an annual award of up to $500 for the best creative or scholarly work on a subject concerning women. The type of work accepted rotates each year: Drama in 2012; poetry in 2013 (poetry, 20 pages maximum); essays in 2014; fiction in 2015. Open to all interested writers and scholars. Submissions must be unpublished. Guidelines available by e-mail. No late or electronic submissions accepted. Deadline: Mid-late February. Offers an annual award of up to $500 for the best creative or scholarly work on a subject concerning women. The type of work accepted rotates each year: Drama in 2012; poetry in 2013 (poetry, 20 pages maximum); essays in 2014; fiction in 2015. Open to all interested writers and scholars. Submissions must be unpublished. Guidelines available by e-mail. Deadline: Mid-late February.

● JEAN PEDRICK PRIZE

New England Poetry Club, 2 Farrar St., Cambridge MA 02138. **E-mail:** contests@nepoetryclub.org. **Website:** www.nepoetryclub.org. **Contact:** NEPC contest coordinator. Deadline: May 31. Prize: $100. Judges are well-known poets and sometimes winners of previous NEPC contests.

PEN AWARD FOR POETRY IN TRANSLATION

(212)334-1660, ext. 108. **E-mail:** awards@pen.org. **Website:** www.pen.org. **Contact:** Literary awards manager. This award recognizes book-length translations of poetry from any language into English, published during the current calendar year. All books must have been published in the US. Translators may be of any nationality. US residency/citizenship not required. Deadline: February 1. $3,000. Judged by a single translator of poetry appointed by the PEN Translation Committee.

PEN/JOYCE OSTERWEIL AWARD FOR POETRY

(212)334-1660, ext. 126. **E-mail:** awards@pen.org. **Website:** www.pen.org. **Contact:** Jasmine Davey, literary awards coordinator. *Candidates may only be nominated by members of PEN.* This award recognizes the high literary character of the published work to date of a new and emerging American poet of any age, and the promise of further literary achievement. Nominated writer may not have published more than 1 book of poetry. Offered in odd-numbered years and alternates with the PEN/Voelcker Award for Poetry. Deadline: February 1, 2013. $5,000. Judged by a panel of 3 judges selected by the PEN Awards Committee.

PEN/VOELCKER AWARD FOR POETRY

(212)334-1600, ext. 108. **E-mail:** awards@pen.org. **Website:** www.pen.org. **Contact:** Jasmine Davey, literary awards coordinator. Deadline: See website. $5,000 stipend. Judged by a panel of 3 poets or other writers.

◐ PERUGIA PRESS PRIZE

Perugia Press, P.O. Box 60364, Florence MA 01062. **E-mail:** info@perugiapress.com. **Website:** www.perugiapress.com. **Contact:** Susan Kan. The Perugia Press Prize for a first or second poetry book by a woman offers $1,000 and publication. Poet must have no more than 1 previously published book of poems (chapbooks don't count). Submissions must be unpublished as a collection, but individual poems may have been previously published in journals, chapbooks, and anthologies. Considers simultaneous submissions if notified of acceptance elsewhere. "Follow online guidelines carefully. Electronic submissions available through our website." No translations or self-published books. Multiple submissions accepted if accompanied by separate entry fee for each. **Entry fee:** $25. Make checks payable to Perugia Press. **Deadline:** Submit August 1-November 15 (postmark). "Use USPS or electronic submission, not FedEx or UPS." Winner announced by April 1 by e-mail or SASE (if included with entry). Judges: Panel of Perugia authors, booksellers, scholars, etc.

◐ THE RICHARD PETERSON POETRY PRIZE

Crab Orchard Review, Department of English, Mail Code 4503, Faner Hall 2380, Southern Illinois University at Carbondale, Carbondale IL 62901. **Website:** www.craborchardreview.siu.edu. **Contact:** Jon Tribble, managing editor. The Richard Peterson Poetry Prize offers $2,000 plus publication in the Winter/Spring issue of *Crab Orchard Review.* Deadline: March 1-May 4.

THE PINCH LITERARY AWARD IN FICTION AND POETRY

(901)678-4591. **E-mail:** editor@thepinchjournal.com. **Website:** www.thepinchjournal.com. Offered annually for unpublished short stories of 5,000 words maximum or up to three poems. Guidelines on website. Cost: $20, which is put toward one issue of *The Pinch.* Deadline: March 15. Prize: 1st place Fiction: $1,500 and publication; 1st place Poetry: $1,000 and publication. Offered annually for unpublished short stories of 5,000 words maximum or up to three poems. Guidelines on website. Deadline: March 15 1st place Fiction: $1,500 and publication; 1st place Poetry: $1,000 and publication.

◐ PLAN B PRESS POETRY CHAPBOOK CONTEST

P.O. Box 4067, Alexandria VA 22303. (215)732-2663. **E-mail:** planbpress@gmail.com. **Website:** www.planbpress.com. **Contact:** Contest Coordinator. The annual Plan B Press Poetry Chapbook Contest offers $235, publication by Plan B Press (see separate listing in Book/Chapbook Publishers), and 50 author's copies. Poems may be previously published individually. Accepts multiple submissions with separate fee for each. Submit up to 24 poems (48 pages total maximum) in English. Include table of contents and list of acknowledgments. Include e-mail address or SASE for notification of winner; mss will not be returned. Author retains copyright of poems, but Plan B reserves rights to layout and/or cover art and design. Guidelines available on website. **Entry fee:** $15. **Deadline:** March 1.

PNWA LITERARY CONTEST

Pacific Northwest Writers Association, PMB 2717-1420 NW Gilman Blvd, Suite 2, Issaquah WA 98027. (425)673-2665. **Fax:** (206)824-4559. **E-mail:** staff@pnwa.org. **Website:** www.pnwa.org. **Contact:** Kelli Liddane. **Open to students.** Annual contest. Purpose of contest: "Valuable tool for writers as contest submissions are critiqued (2 critiques)." Unpublished submissions only. Submissions made by author. Deadline for entries: February 18, 2011. Entry fee is $35/entry for members, $50/entry for nonmembers. Awards $700-1st; $300-2nd. Awards in all 12 categories.

THE POCATALIGO POETRY CONTEST

Yemassee, Department of English, Pocataligo Poetry Contest, University of South Carolina, Columbia SC 29208. (803)777-2085. **E-mail:** editor@yemasseejournalonline.org. **Website:** http://yemasseejournalonline.org. **Contact:** Contest coordinator. The annual Pocataligo Poetry Contest offers a $500 prize and publication in *Yemassee*. Submissions must be unpublished. Considers simultaneous submissions with notice of acceptance elsewhere. Accepts multiple entries with separate $10 fee and SASE for each. Submit 3-5 poems (15 pages total), typed. Include cover letter with poet's name, contact information, and poem title(s); no identifying information on ms pages except poem title (which should appear on every page). Include SASE for results only; mss will not be returned. Electronic submissions (with secure online payment system) preferred at www.yemassee.submishmash.com. Guidelines available on website. **Entry fee:** $10. Make checks payable to Educational Foundation/English Literary Magazine Fund. **Deadline:** March 31 (postmark). The annual Pocataligo Poetry Contest offers a $500 prize and publication in *Yemassee*. Deadline: March 31 (postmark).

POETRY 2012 INTERNATIONAL POETRY COMPETITION

Atlanta Review, P.O. Box 8248, Atlanta GA 31106. **E-mail:** atlrev@yahoo.com. **Website:** www.atlantareview.com. **Contact:** Dan Veach, Editor/Publisher. *Atlanta Review* sponsors an annual international poetry competition, offering $1,000 Grand Prize, 20 International Publication Awards (winners will be published in *Atlanta Review*), and 30 International Merit Awards (includes certificate, Honorable Mention in *Atlanta Review*, and free issue). Poems must not have been published in a nationally distributed print publication. Online entry available at journal website. For mail entry: put your name and address on each page (e-mail and phone optional). Include SASE for results only; no entries will be returned. Guidelines available on website. **Entry fee:** $5 for the first poem, $3 for each additional poem. Make checks payable to *Atlanta Review*. International entrants must use online entry. **Deadline:** March 1, 2013. Winners will be announced in the summer; Contest Issue published in October. Contest Issue available for $4, or free with $10 subscription to *Atlanta Review*.

THE POETRY SOCIETY OF VIRGINIA ADULT AND STUDENT CONTESTS

P.O. Box 341, Montpelier VA 23192-0341. **E-mail:** musicsavy45@yahoo.com. **Website:** www.PoetrySocietyOfVirginia.org. **Contact:** Judith K. Bragg. Adult contest offers many categories for original, unpublished poems—both specified and unspecified forms and topics. Student contest is school grade-specific. Offers numerous cash prizes (varies by year). One poem per category may be submitted. Submit 2 copies of each poem. Both copies must have the category name and number on top left of page. One copy must contain poet's name, address, e-mail, and phone number on top right of page, as well as membership status. Guidelines available for SASE or on website (guidelines must be followed). **Entry fee:** $4/poem for adults; no fee for students and PSV members. ("Membership fee of $25 covers entries in all categories and can be sent with entry and membership form, available on website or for SASE.") Designate entries as "adult" or "student" and send to Contest Chair at the above address. **Deadline:** January 19 (postmark) annually (Edgar Allan Poe's birthday). Winning entries may be published in a booklet or on the PSV website unless author indicates otherwise on each poem entered. "Follow guidelines to ensure inclusion of poem in contest. Always include SASE for any return information."

POETS & PATRONS ANNUAL CHICAGOLAND POETRY CONTEST

Sponsored by Poets & Patrons of Chicago, 416 Gierz St., Downers Grove IL 60515-3838. **E-mail:** eatonb1016@aol.com. **Website:** www.poetsandpatrons.org. **Contact:** Barbara Eaton, director. Annual contest for unpublished poetry. Guidelines available for self-addressed, stamped envelope. The purpose of the contest is to encourage the crafting of poetry. Deadline: September 1. Prize is $45, $20, $10 cash. Poet retains rights. Judged by out-of -state professionals.

FELIX POLLAK PRIZE IN POETRY

University of Wisconsin Press, Department of English, 600 N. Park St., Madison WI 53706. **E-mail:** rwallace@wisc.edu. **Website:** www.wisc.edu/wisconsinpress/index.html. **Contact:** Ronald Wallace, Poetry Series editor. The annual Felix Pollak Prize in Poetry is 1 of 2 prizes awarded by the University of Wisconsin Press (see separate listing for the Brittingham Prize in Poetry). Offers $1,000, plus publication, with an additional $1,500 honorarium to cover expenses of a reading in Madison. Submissions must be unpublished as a collection, but individual poems may have been published elsewhere (publication must be acknowledged). Considers simultaneous submissions if notified of selection elsewhere. Submit 50-80 unbound ms pages, typed single-spaced (with double spaces between stanzas). Clean photocopies are acceptable. Include 1 title page with poet's name, address, and telephone number; 1 title page with title only. No translations. Include SASE for results only; mss will not be returned. Guidelines available for SASE or on website. **Entry fee:** $25. **NOTE:** $25 fee applies to consideration of same entry for the Brittingham Prize in Poetry—1 fee for 2 contest awards. Make checks/money orders payable to University of Wisconsin Press. **Deadline:** Submit September 1-27 (postmark). 2011 Pollak Prize winner was Mark Wagenaar, *Voodoo Inverso*. Qualified readers will screen all mss. Judge by "a distinguished poet who will remain anonymous until the winners are announced in mid-February."

A. POULIN, JR. POETRY PRIZE

BOA Editions, Ltd., 250 N. Goodman St., Suite 306, Rochester NY 14607. **E-mail:** conners@boaeditions.org. **Website:** www.boaeditions.org. BOA Editions, Ltd. sponsors the annual A. Poulin, Jr. Poetry Prize for a poet's first book. Deadline: Submit between August 1-Nov. 30 (annually). Awards $1,500 honorarium and book publication in the A. Poulin, Jr. New Poets of America Series.

PRAIRIE SCHOONER BOOK PRIZE

Prairie Schooner and the University of Nebraska Press, 123 Andrews Hall, University of Nebraska, Lincoln NE 68588-0334. (402)472-0911. **E-mail:** jengelhardt2@unlnotes.unl.edu; jengelhardt2@unl.edu. **Website:** prairieschooner.unl.edu. **Contact:** Kwame Dawes, editor. Annual. Competition/award for story collections. Prize: $3,000 and publication through the University of Nebraska Press for one book of short fiction and one book of poetry. Entry fee: $25. Make checks payable to Prairie Schooner. Deadline: Submissions are accepted between January 15 and March 15; check website for updates. Entries should be unpublished. Send full manuscript (the author's name should not appear anywhere on the ms). Send two cover pages: one listing only the title of the ms, and the other listing the title, author's name, address, telephone number, and e-mail address. Send SASE for notification of results. All mss will be recycled. You may also send an optional SAS postcard for confirmation of receipt of ms. Winners notified by phone, by e-mail. Results made available to entrants on website, in publication. $3,000 and publication through the University of Nebraska Press (1 award in fiction and 1 award in poetry). Kwame Dawes, editor of *Prairie Schooner*, and members of the Book Series Literary Board.

THE PSA NEW YORK CHAPBOOK FELLOWSHIPS

Poetry Society of America, 15 Gramercy Park, New York NY 10003. (212)254-9628. **Fax:** (212)673-2352. **Website:** www.poetrysociety.org. **Contact:** Contest Coordinator. The PSA New York Chapbook Fellowships offer 2 prizes of $1,000 and publication of each of winning chapbook mss, with distribution by the Poetry Society of America. Open to any New York City resident (in the 5 boroughs) who is 30 or under and has not published a full-length poetry collection. **(Poets who apply to this contest may not apply to The PSA National Chapbook Fellowships.)** Does not accept entries by fax or e-mail. Guidelines available for SASE or on website. **Entry fee:** $12 for both PSA members and nonmembers. Make checks/money orders payble to Poetry Society of America. **Deadline:** submit October 1-December 22 (postmarked).

PUSHCART PRIZE

Pushcart Press, P.O. Box 380, Wainscott NY 11975. (631)324-9300. **Website:** www.pushcartprize.com. **Contact:** Bill Henderson. "Little magazine and small book press editors (print or online) may make up to six nominations from their year's publications by our December 1, (postmark) deadline. The nominations may be any combination of poetry, short fiction, essays or literary whatnot. Editors may nominate self-contained portions of books — for instance, a chapter from a novel. We welcome translations, reprints and both traditional and experimental writing. One copy of each selection should be sent. No nominations can be returned. There is no entry fee and no forms to fill out. We also accept nominations from our staff of distinguished Contributing Editors." Deadline: December 1.

RATTLE POETRY PRIZE

RATTLE, 12411 Ventura Blvd., Studio City CA 91604. (818) 505-6777. **E-mail:** tim@rattle.com. **Website:** www.rattle.com. **Contact:** Timothy Green, Editor. The RATTLE Poetry Prize awards 1st Prize of

$5,000, plus ten $100 Finalists. One $1,000 Reader's Choice Award will then be chosen from among the finalists by subscriber and entrant vote. Additional entries may be offered publication as well. Open to writers worldwide (see website for special international guidelines). Poems must be written in English (no translations). No previously published poems or works accepted for publication elsewhere. No simultaneous submissions. Submit no more than 4 poems/entry. Multiple entries by a single poet accepted; however, each 4-poem group must be treated as a separate entry with its own cover sheet and entry fee. Include cover sheet with poet's name, address, e-mail address, phone number, and poem titles. No contact information should appear on poems. Include SASE for results only; no poems will be returned. **Note:** Poems also may be entered through online submission on website. Guidelines available by e-mail or on website. **Entry fee:** $18; includes one-year subscription to RATTLE. Make checks/money orders payable to RATTLE (for credit card entries, see website). **Deadline:** August 1 (postmark). Judge: Finalists selected by editors of RATTLE in blind review; winner voted on by subscribers/entrants after publication. Finalists announced in September; winner announced the following February.

THE RBC BRONWEN WALLACE AWARD FOR EMERGING WRITERS

(416)504-8222. **Fax:** (416)504-9090. **E-mail:** info@writerstrust.com. **Website:** www.writerstrust.com. **Contact:** Amanda Hopkins. Presented annually to "a Canadian writer under the age of 35 who is not yet published in book form. The award, which alternates each year between poetry and short fiction, was established in memory of poet Bronwen Wallace." Prize: $5,000 and $1,000 to 2 finalists.

REGINA BOOK AWARD

Saskatchewan Book Awards, Inc., 100-2400 College Ave., Regina SK S4P 0K1, Canada. (306)569-1585. **Fax:** (306)569-4187. **E-mail:** director@bookawards.sk.ca. **Website:** www.bookawards.sk.ca. **Contact:** Executive director, book submissions. Offered annually. "In recognition of the vitality of the literary community in Regina, this award is presented to a Regina author for the best book, judged on the quality of writing." Books from the following categories will be considered: Children's; drama; fiction (short fiction by a single author, novellas, novels); nonfiction (all categories of nonfiction writing except cookbooks, directories, how-to books, or bibliographies of minimal critical content); poetry. Deadline: November 1. Prize: $2,000 (CAD).

MARGARET REID POETRY CONTEST FOR TRADITIONAL VERSE

c/o Winning Writers, 351 Pleasant St., PMB 222, Northampton MA 01060-3961. **E-mail:** johnreid@mail.qango.com. **Website:** www.winningwriters.com. **Contact:** John Reid. Offers annual award of 1st Prize: $3,000; 2nd Prize: $1,000; 3rd Prize: $400; 4th Prize: $250; and 6 Most Highly Commended Awards of $150 each. The top 10 entries will be published on the Winning Writers website. Submissions may be published or unpublished, may have won prizes elsewhere, and may be entered in other contests. Submit poems in traditional verse forms; see website for guidelines. No limit on number of lines or number of poems submitted. No name on ms pages; type or computer-print on letter-size white paper, single-sided. Guidelines available for SASE or on website. Submit online or by mail. **Entry fee:** $8 USD for every 25 lines (exclude poem title and any blank lines from count). **Deadline:** November 15-June 30. 2011 winner was Jacie Ragan ("In the Shadow of the Condor"). 2011 judges: John H. Reid and Dee C. Konrad. Winners announced in December at WinningWriters.com; entrants who provide valid e-mail addresses also receive notification. "Seeks poems in traditional verse forms, such as sonnets." Both unpublished and published work accepted.

RHINO FOUNDERS' PRIZE

RHINO, The Poetry Forum, P.O. Box 591, Evanston IL 60204. **E-mail:** editors@rhinopoetry.org. **Website:** www.rhinopoetry.org. **Contact:** Ralph Hamilton. Accepting poetry, including translations, and flash fiction of 1,000 words or less from April 1, 2012, to October 1, 2012. "We look forward to reading your work! Send up to 5 unpublished poems—please no more than 5 pages total. *RHINO* looks for originality. It is helpful to review our poetry samples online and review past issues. Submit on our website or by mail. Submissions must include a cover letter listing your name, address, e-mail, and/or telephone number as well as titles of the poems. No identifying information should appear on the poems. Mss will not be returned. Include an SASE for notification of results and mail to address above."

RHODE ISLAND ARTIST FELLOWSHIPS AND INDIVIDUAL PROJECT GRANTS

(401)222-3880. **Fax:** (401)222-3018. **E-mail:** Cristina.DiChiera@arts.ri.gov. **Website:** www.arts.ri.gov. **Contact:** Cristina DiChiera, director of individual artist programs. Annual fellowship competition is based upon panel review of mss for poetry, fiction, and playwriting/screenwriting. Project grants provide funds for community-based arts projects. Rhode Island artists may apply without a nonprofit sponsor. Applicants for all RSCA grant and award programs must be at least 18 years old and not currently enrolled in an arts-related degree program. Online application and guidelines can be found at www.arts.ri.gov/grants/guidelines/. Deadline: April 1 and October 1. Fellowship awards: $5,000 and $1,000. Grants range from $500-10,000, with an average of around $3,000.

ROANOKE-CHOWAN POETRY AWARD

The North Carolina Literary & Historical Assoc., 4610 Mail Service Center, Raleigh NC 27699-4610. (919)807-7290. **Fax:** (919)733-8807. **E-mail:** michael.hill@ncdcr.gov. **Website:** www.history.ncdcr.gov/affiliates/lit-hist/awards/awards.htm. **Contact:** Michael Hill, awards coordinator. Offers annual award for "an original volume of poetry published during the 12 months ending June 30 of the year for which the award is given." Open to "authors who have maintained legal or physical residence, or a combination of both, in North Carolina for the 3 years preceding the close of the contest period." Submit 3 copies of each entry. Guidelines available for SASE or by fax or e-mail. **Deadline:** July 15. Competition receives about 15 entries. 2010 winner was Joseph R. Bathanti, professor in Appalachian State University's Department of English and co-director of the creative writing program there for Bathantiâ's poetry collection *Restoring Sacred Art,* in which Bathanti shares rich ethnic associations, religious themes and vivid memories. The collectionwas published by Star Cloud Press.

◐ BEULLAH ROSE POETRY PRIZE

P.O. Box 22161, Baltimore MD 21203. **E-mail:** cbanks@smartishpace.com. **Website:** www.smartishpace.com. **Contact:** Clare Banks, associate editor. The annual Beullah Rose Poetry Prize for exceptional poetry by women offers 1st Prize: $200 and publication of the winning poem in *Smartish Pace*; 2nd and 3rd Prizes: winning poems will be published in Smartish Pace. Winners also receive additional Internet and advertising exposure. Submit 3 poems, with poet's name, address, e-mail, telephone number (preferred), and "Beulah Rose Poetry Prize" at the top of each page of poetry submitted. Include bio. Entries may be submitted online or by e-mail (as attachment) or regular mail. Include SASE with postal entries. Guidelines available on website. **Entry fee:** $5 for 3 poems; additional poems may be submitted for $1/poem (12 poem maximum). Make checks/money orders payable to *Smartish Pace*. **Deadline:** October 1. Judges: Clare Banks and Traci O'Dea, associate editors.

● THE SACRAMENTIO POETRY CENTER BOOK PRIZE

PO Box 160406, Sacramento CA 95816. (916)451-5569. **E-mail:** buchanan@csus.edu. **Website:** www.sacramentopoetrycenter.org. **Contact:** Brad Buchanan. (Formerly the Cathy Washington Prize) The Sacramento Poetry Center Book Prize offers an annual prize of book publication, $500, and 12 free copies of the winning book. Winning mss will be sold via Amazon.com and SPC website. Submissions must be unpublished as a collection, but individual poems may have been previously published elsewhere. Considers simultaneous submissions, with notification. Submit 48-70 pages of poetry. Include 2 title pages: name and contact information (including email address, if possible) should appear on first title page only. Staff, volunteers, or board members of the Sacramento Poetry Center, or their relations, may not submit manuscripts for consideration in this contest. Guidelines available for SASE, on website, or by e-mail. **Entry fee**: $20. Check should be made out to The Sacramento Poetry Center. **Deadline**: April 30, 2011. Winner announced in June by email. Copies of winning books available for $12 from The Sacramento Poetry Center. "The Sacramento Poetry Center is a non-profit organization dedicated to furthering the cause of poetry in the Sacramento area and nationwide. We welcome work from anyone, anywhere."

● ERNEST SANDEEN PRIZE IN POETRY

Dept. of English, University of Notre Dame, Notre Dame IN 46556-5639. (574)631-7526. **Fax:** (574)631-4795. **E-mail:** creativewriting@nd.edu. **Website:** http://english.nd.edu/creative-writing/publications/sandeen-sullivan-prizes. **Contact:** Director of Creative Writing. The Sandeen Prize in Poetry offers $1,000 (a $500 award and a $500 advance against royalties from the Notre Dame Press) and publication of a book-length ms. Open to poets who have published at least 1 volume of poetry. "Please include a photocopy of the copyright and the title page of your previous volume. Vanity press publications do not fulfill this requirement. We will pay special attention to second volumes. Please include a vita and/or a biographical statement that includes your publishing history. We will be glad to see a selection of reviews of the earlier collection." Submit 2 copies of ms (inform if ms is available on computer disk). Include SASE for acknowledgment of receipt of ms and SASE for return of ms. **Entry fee:** $15; includes one-year subscription to Notre Dame Review. Make checks payable to University of Notre Dame. **Deadline:** Submit May 1- September 1. 2011 winner was Janet Kaplan (*Dreamlife of a Philanthropist*). Winners announced by the end of January.

MAY SARTON AWARD

New England Poetry Club, 654 Green St., No. 2, Cambridge MA 02139. **Website:** www.nepoetryclub.org. **Contact:** NEPC contest coordinator. "Given intermittently to a poet whose work is an inspiration to other poets. Recipients are chosen by the board." Deadline: May 31. Prize: $250. Judges are well-known poets and sometimes winners of previous NEPC contests.

SASKATCHEWAN POETRY AWARD

Saskatchewan Book Awards, Inc., 100-2400 College Ave., Regina SK S4P 0K1, Canada. (306)569-1585. **Fax:** (306)569-4187. **E-mail:** director@bookawards.sk.ca. **Website:** www.bookawards.sk.ca. **Contact:** Executive director, book submissions. Offered annually. "This award is presented to a Saskatchewan author for the best book of poetry, judged on the quality of writing." Deadline: November 1. Prize: $2,000 (CAD).

SASKATOON BOOK AWARD

Saskatchewan Book Awards, Inc., 100-2400 College Ave., Regina SK S4P 0K1, Canada. (306)569-1585. **Fax:** (306)569-4187. **E-mail:** director@bookawards.sk.ca. **Website:** www.bookawards.sk.ca. **Contact:** Executive director, book submissions. Offered annually. "This award is presented to a Saskatoon author (or pair of authors) for the best book, judged on the quality of writing." Books from the following categories will be considered: Children's; drama; fiction (short fiction by a single author, novellas, novels); nonfiction (all categories of nonfiction writing except cookbooks, directories, how-to books, or bibliographies of minimal critical content); poetry. Deadline: November 1. Prize: $2,000 (CAD).

THE SCARS EDITOR'S CHOICE AWARDS

829 Brian Court, Gurnee IL 60031-3155. **E-mail:** editor@scars.tv. **Website:** http://scars.tv. **Contact:** Janet Kuypers, editor/publisher (whom all reading fee checks need to be made out to). Award "to showcase good writing in an annual book." Categories: short stories, poetry. Entry fee: $19/short story, and $15/poem. Deadline: Revolves for appearing in different upcoming books as winners. Prize: Publication of story/essay and 1 copy of the book. Entries may be unpublished or previously published, "as long as you retain the rights to your work." Open to any writer. For guidelines, visit website. Accepts inquiries by e-mail. "E-mail is always preferred for inquiries and submissions. (If you have access to e-mail, we will request that you e-mail your contest submission, and we will hold it until we receive the reading fee payment for the submission.)" Length: "We appreciate shorter works. Shorter stories, more vivid and more real storylines in writing have a good chance." Results announced at book publication, online. Winners notified by mail when book is printed. For contest results, send SASE or e-mail or look at the contest page at website. "

THE SCENT OF AN ENDING™

White Eagle Coffee Store Press, P.O. Box 383, Fox River Grove IL 60021-0383. (847)639-9200. **E-mail:** scentofanending@aol.com. **Website:** www.thescentofanending.com, or www.whiteeaglecoffeestorepress.com. **Contact:** Frank Edmund Smith, publisher. "Contest is offered annually for unpublished submissions. We're searching for the best bad ending to an imaginary novel—an ending that's a real stinker. We're looking for a memorably bad ending to a novel that has not been written. Submit the invented title of the novel and the final 25-125 words. The entry must be completely your own invention and cannot be taken from or closely based on anything actually published." Initial publication on website, then in chapbook format. Deadline: September 30 annually. Prize: 1st place: $89.25; 2nd place: $67.32; 3rd place: $31.18, "plus dubious fame and publication for winner and all finalists. Initial publication on website, then publication in chapbook format. Winners and finalists receive copies of the published chapbook." Rights to any winning and published materials revert to author upon publication. WECSPress holds the rights to first publication in print and on the Internet and to permanent reprint rights. Please see website for complete contest information and sample endings and current finalists. Judged by editors of White Eagle Coffee Store Press.

THE MONA SCHREIBER PRIZE FOR HUMOROUS FICTION & NONFICTION

E-mail: brad.schreiber@att.net. **Website:** www.brashcyber.com. **Contact:** Brad Schreiber. "The purpose of the contest is to award the most creative humor writing, in any form less than 750 words, in either fiction or nonfiction, including but not limited to stories, articles, essays, speeches, shopping lists, diary entries, and anything else writers dream up." Deadline: December 1. 1st Place: $500; 2nd Place: $250; 3rd Place: $100. Brad Schreiber, author, journalist, consultant, and instructor at MediaBistro.com. Complete rules and previous winning entries on website.

TIPS "No SASE's, Please."

SHORT GRAIN CONTEST

Box 67, Saskatoon SK S7K 3K1, Canada. (306)244-2828. **Fax:** (306)244-0255. **E-mail:** grainmag@sasktel.net. **Website:** www.grainmagazine.ca. **Contact:** Mike Thompson, business administrator (inquiries only). The annual Short Grain Contest includes a category for poetry of any style up to 100 lines, offering 3 prizes with a 1st Prize of $1,000, plus publication in *Grain Magazine*. "Each entry must be original, unpublished, not submitted elsewhere for publication or broadcast, nor accepted elsewhere for publication or broadcast, nor entered simultaneously in any other contest or competition for which it is also eligible to win a prize. Entries must be typed on 8- ½x 11 paper. It must be legible. Faxed and/or electronic entries not accepted. No simultaneous submissions. A separate covering page must be attached to the text of your entry, and must provide the following information: Poet's name, complete mailing address, telephone number, e-mail address, entry title, category name, and line count. An absolutely accurate word or line count is required. No identifying information on the text pages. Entries will not be returned. Names of the winners and titles of the winning entries will be posted on the *Grain Magazine* website in August; only the winners will be notified. Entry fee: $35 CAD; $40 for US and international entrants, in US funds; includes 1 year subscription to *Grain Magazine*. Deadline: April 1."

SKIPPING STONES HONOR (BOOK) AWARDS

P.O. Box 3939, Eugene OR 97403-0939. Phone/fax: (541)342-4956. **E-mail:** editor@skippingstones.org. **Website:** www.skippingstones.org. **Contact:** Arun N. Toké. Annual awards since 1994 to "promote multicultural and/or nature awareness through creative writings for children and teens and their educators." Prize: Honor certificates; gold seals; reviews; press release/publicity. Categories: Short stories, novels, story collections, poetry, nonfiction, and teaching resources, including DVDs. Judged by "a multicultural committee of teachers, librarians, parents, students and editors." Entry fee: $50. **Deadline: February 1** post mark/ship date each year. Entries must be previously published. Open to published books and teaching resources that appeared in print during a two year period prior to the deadline date. Guidelines for SASE or e-mail and on website. Accepts inquiries by e-mail, fax, phone. "We seek authentic, exceptional, child/youth friendly books that promote intercultural, international, intergenerational harmony, and understanding through creative ways. Writings that come out of your own experiences and cultural understanding seem to have an edge." Results announced in May each year. Winners notified through personal notifications, press release and by publishing reviews of winning titles in the summer issue and on website. Reviews are often reprinted in several other educational publications and reported in others. Attractive gold honor seals available for winners. For contest results, send SASE, e-mail, or visit website. Annual awards to "promote multicultural and/or nature awareness through creative writings for children and teens and their educators." Categories: Short stories, novels, story collections, poetry, nonfiction, and teaching resources, including DVDs. "We seek authentic, exceptional, child/youth friendly books that promote intercultural, international, intergenerational harmony, and understanding through creative ways. Writings that come out of your own experiences and cultural understanding seem to have an edge." Results announced in May each year. Winners notified through personal notifications, press release and by publishing reviews of winning titles in the summer issue and on website. Reviews are often reprinted in several other educational publications and reported in others. Attractive gold honor seals available for winners. For contest results, send SASE, e-mail, or visit website. Deadline: February 1 post mark/ship date each year. Honor certificates; gold seals; reviews; press release/publicity. Judged by "a multicultural committee of teachers, librarians, parents, students and editors."

SKIPPING STONES YOUTH AWARDS

P.O. Box 3939, Eugene OR 97403-0939. Phone/fax: (541)342-4956. **E-mail:** editor@skippingstones.org. **Website:** www.skippingstones.org. **Contact:** Arun N. Toké. Annual awards to "promote creativity as well as multicultural and nature awareness in youth." Prize: Publication in the autumn issue of *Skipping Stones*, honor certificate, subscription to magazine, plus 5 multicultural and/or nature books. Categories: Short stories, nonfiction, and poetry. **Entry fee:** $3/entry; make checks payable to Skipping Stones. Cover letter should include name, address, phone, and e-mail. **Deadline:** June 20. Entries must be unpublished. Length: 1,000 words maximum. Open to any writer between 7 and 17 years old. Guidelines available by SASE, e-mail, or on website. Accepts inquiries by e-mail or phone. "Be creative. Do not use stereotypes or excessive violent language or plots. Be sensitive to cultural diversity." Results announced in the September-October issue of *Skipping Stones*. Winners notified by mail. For contest results, visit website. Everyone who enters receives the issue which features the award winners.

SLIPSTREAM ANNUAL POETRY CHAPBOOK COMPETITION

E-mail: editors@slipstreampress.org. **Website:** www.slipstreampress.org. **Contact:** Dan Sicoli, co-editor. The annual Slipstream Poetry Chapbook Contest awards $1,000, publication of a chapbook ms, and 50 author's copies. All entrants receive copy of winning chapbook and an issue of *Slipstream*. Considers simultaneous submissions if informed of status. Accepts previously published work with acknowledgments. Submit up to 40 pages of poetry, any style, format, or theme. Manuscripts will not be returned. Guidelines available for SASE or on website. **Entry fee:** $20. **Deadline:** December 1. Latest winner is Moriah Erickson for *Three Crows Laughing*. "Offered annually to help promote a poet whose work is often overlooked or ignored. Open to any writer." Winner is featured prominently on the *Slipstream* website for 1 year, as well as in all *Slipstream* catalogs, press releases, and promotional material. Winning chapbooks are submitted by Slipstream for review by various national and international poetry/writing pubications and may also be featured in the Grants & Awards section of *Poets & Writers* magazine.

TIPS "Winner announced in late spring/early summer."

◐ SLOPE EDITIONS BOOK PRIZE

847 Bernardston Road, Greenfield MA 01301. **E-mail:** ethan@slope.org. **Website:** www.SlopeEditions.org. **Contact:** Christopher Janke, senior editor and Ethan Paquin, editor-in-chief. The Slope Editions Book Prize offers an annual award of $1,000 and publication of a book-length ms; author copies offered in lieu of royalties. Submissions must be unpublished as a collection. Submit 40-90 typed pages, bound only by a clip. Include 2 title pages: one with ms title, poet's name, address, phone number, and e-mail; and one with ms title only. Also include table of contents and acknowledgments page. Guidelines available by e-mail or on website. Do not include SASE or postcards for notification; they will not be returned. **Entry fee:** $20; entitles entrant to one Slope Editions book (see guidelines for details). Make checks/money orders payable to Slope Publishing Inc. **Deadline:** March 15. 2012 judge is Matthea Harvey.

THE BERNICE SLOTE AWARD

Prairie Schooner, 123 Andrews Hall, PO Box 880334, Lincoln NE 68588-0334. (402)472-0911. **Fax:** (402)472-9771. **E-mail:** jengelhardt2@unl.edu. **Website:** www.prairieschooner.unl.edu. **Contact:** Kwame Dawes. Offered annually for the best work by a beginning writer published in Prairie Schooner in the previous year. Categories: short stories, essays and poetry. Judged by editorial staff of Prairie Schooner. No entry fee. For guidelines, send SASE or visit website. "Only work published in the journal during the previous year will be considered." Work is nominated by the editorial staff. Results announced in the Spring issue. Winners notified by mail in February or March. Prize is $500.

HELEN C. SMITH MEMORIAL AWARD FOR POETRY

E-mail: tilsecretary@yahoo.com. **Website:** http://texasinstituteofletters.org/. Offered annually for the best book of poems published January 1-December 31 of previous year. Poet must have been born in Texas, have lived in the state at some time for at least 2 consecutive years, or the subject matter must be associated with the state. See website for guidelines. Deadline: Early January. Prize: $1,200.

KAY SNOW WRITERS' CONTEST

9045 SW Barbur Blvd. #5A, Portland OR 97219-4027. (503)452-1592. **Fax:** (503)452-0372. **E-mail:** wilwrite@teleport.com. **Website:** www.willamettewriters.com. **Contact:** Lizzy Shannon, contest director. Annual contest. **Open to students.** Purpose of contest: "to encourage beginning and established writers to continue the craft." Unpublished, original submissions only. Submissions made by the author. Deadline for entries: April 23rd. SASE for contest rules and entry forms. Entry fee is $10, Williamette Writers' members; $15, nonmembers; free for student writers grades 1-12. Awards cash prize of $300 per category (fiction, nonfiction, juvenile, poetry, script writing), $50 for students in three divisions: 1-5, 6-8, 9-12. Judges are anonymous.

SOUL MAKING KEATS LITERARY COMPETITION

The Webhallow House, 1544 Sweetwood Dr., Broadmoor Vlg CA 94015-2029. **E-mail:** PenNobHill@aol.com. **Website:** www.soulmakingcontest.us. **Contact:** Eileen Malone, Award Director. Annual open contest offers cash prizes in each of 13 literary categories, including poetry and prose poem. 1st Prize: $100; 2nd Prize: $50; 3rd Prize: $25. Submissions in some categories may be previously published. No names or other identifying information on mss; include 3x5 card with poet's name, address, phone, fax, e-mail, title(s) of work, and category entered. Include SASE for results only; mss will not be returned. Guidelines available on website. **Entry fee:** $5/entry. **Deadline:** November 30. Competition receives 600 entries/year. Names of winners and judges are posted on website. Winners announced in January by SASE and on website. Winners are invited to read at the Koret Auditorium, San Francisco. Event is televised.

THE SOW'S EAR CHAPBOOK COMPETITION

The Sow's Ear Review, P.O. Box 127, Millwood VA 22646. (540)955-3955. **E-mail:** rglesman@gmail.com. **Website:** www.sows-ear.kitenet.net. **Contact:** Robert G. Lesman, managing editor. *The Sow's Ear Poetry Review* sponsors an annual chapbook competition. Open to adults. Deadline: May 1 (postmark). Prize: Offers $1,000, publication as the spring issue of the magazine, and 25 author's copies.

THE SOW'S EAR POETRY COMPETITION

The Sow's Ear Review, P.O. Box 127, Millwood VA 22646. **E-mail:** rglesman@gmail.com. **Website:** www.sows-ear.kitenet.net. **Contact:** Robert G. Lesman, managing editor. *The Sow's Ear Poetry Review* sponsors an annual contest for unpublished poems. Offers $1,000 and publication in *The Sow's Ear Poetry Review*. Submit up to 5 unpublished poems. Include separate sheet with poem titles, poet's name, address, phone number, and e-mail address (if available). "We will check with finalists regarding publication status of poems before sending to final judge." Poet's name should not appear on poems. Include SASE for results only; entries will not be returned. Guidelines available for SASE, by e-mail, or on website. **Entry fee:** $27 for up to 5 poems. Contestants receive a year's subscription. Make checks payable to The Sow's Ear Poetry Review. Submit in September or October. **Deadline:** November 1 (postmark). Past judges include Gregory Orr and Marge Piercy. "Four criteria help us judge the quality of submissions: 1) Does the poem make the strange familiar or the familiar strange, or both? 2) Is the form of the poem vital to its meaning? 3) Do the sounds of the poem make sense in relation to the theme? 4) Does the little story of the poem open a window on the Big Story of the human situation?"

SRPR EDITORS' PRIZE CONTEST

Spoon River Poetry Review, 4241 Department of English, Publications Unit, Illinois State University, Normal IL 61790-4241. (309)438-3025. **Website:** www.litline.org/spoon. Offered annually for unpublished poetry to identify and reward excellence. Guidelines available online. Open to all writers. Deadline: April 15 1st Place: $1,000 and publication; Runners-Up (2): $100 each and publication.

STAGE OF LIFE ESSAY WRITING CONTESTS

StageofLife.com, P.O. Box 580950, Minneapolis MN 55458-0950. **Fax:** (717)650-3855. **E-mail:** contact@stageoflife.com. **Website:** www.stageoflife.com. "Monthly writing contests for teens, college students, brides, grooms, married couples, homeowners, parents, and grandparents using a non-fiction, memoir, blogging, essay-style format. Submitted essays must be 500 words or less. Style, grammar, point of view, and authentic voice are all important aspects in the submissions. Press for the StageofLife.com writing contest has appeared on Time.com, ABC TV'S "Mary Talks Money", *The Wall Street Journal*'s MarketWatch, Socialtimes.com, and other media outlets." Deadline: 12am PST the last day of the month. Offers $25-50 cash prize or equivalent gift card from current contest sponsor, swag consisting of a "what's Your Story" t-shirt and writing pen, "Featured Writer" status on StageofLife.com and mention in the site's monthly press release. Editorial staff headed by Eric Thiegs, CEO; Rebecca Thiegs, senior editor; Megan Colyer, PR coordinator; Michelle Pease, essay editor; and a panel of 12 freelance editors judge monthly contests. **TIPS** "Writer must be in the life stage for the contest they are entering."

WALLACE E. STEGNER FELLOWSHIPS

Creative Writing Program, Stanford University, Stanford CA 94305-2087. (650)723-0011. **Fax:** (650)723-3679. **E-mail:** krystalg@stanford.edu. **Website:** www.stanford.edu/group/creativewriting/stegner. **Contact:** Admissions coordinator: Krystal Griffiths, program assistant. Offers 5 fellowships in poetry and 5 in fiction of $26,000 plus tuition of over $7,000/year for promising writers who can benefit from 2 years of instruction and participation in the program. "We do not require a degree for admission. No school of writing is favored over any other. Chronological age is not a consideration." Accepts applications between September 1 and December 1 (postmark). Applicants may apply online. Competition receives about 1,700 entries/year. Offers 5 fellowships in poetry and 5 in fiction of $26,000 plus tuition of over $7,000/year for promising writers who can benefit from 2 years of instruction and participation in the program. "We do not require a degree for admission. No school of writing is favored over any other. Chronological age is not a consideration." Accepts applications between September 1 and December 1 (postmark). Applicants may apply online. Competition receives about 1,700 entries/year.

STEVENS POETRY MANUSCRIPT CONTEST

832 Tacoma Dr., Auburn AL 22614. **E-mail:** downejm@auburn.edu. **Website:** www.nfsps.org. **Contact:** Jeremy Downes, contest chair. National Federation of State Poetry Societies (NFSPS) offers annual award of $1,000, publication of ms, and 50 author's copies. Individual poems may have been previously published in magazines, anthologies, or chapbooks, but not the entire ms as a collection. Simultaneous submissions allowed. Submit 48-70 pages of poetry by a single author, typewritten, or computer printed, beginning each poem on a new page. Pages numbered, with table of contents, but no author identification anywhere in ms. Include 2 title pages; 1 with no author identification, the other with name of poet, address, phone number, e-mail address and state poetry society member affiliation, if applicable. No staples or binders; plain manila folder and/or manuscript clip permitted. No illustrations. No disk submissions; no certified or registered mail. Optional: Include SASE for results only; mss will not be returned. Guidelines available for SASE or on website. **Entry fee:** $20 for NFSPS members; $25 for nonmembers. Make checks/money orders payable to NFSPS. **Deadline:** October 15 (postmark). Winners announced in January following deadline; entrants who include an e-mail address or SASE will be notified of winner. Book will be published by June and sold at annual NFSPS convention and winning poet (if present) will read from it. Copies of books available through NFSPS website.

THE RUTH STONE PRIZE IN POETRY

Vermont College, 36 College St., Montpelier VT 05602. (802)828-8517. **E-mail:** hungermtn@vcfa.edu. **Website:** www.hungermtn.org. **Contact:** Miciah Bay Gault, editor. The annual Ruth Stone Prize in Poetry offers $1,000 and publication in *Hunger Mountain: The VCFA Journal of the Arts*; 2 runners-up receive $100 and are also published. Submit up to 3 poems, not to exceed 6 pages. **Entry fee:** $20. **Deadline:** December 10. Guidelines available on website. "Include SASE and index card with poem titles and address; do not put name on poems."

THE ELIZABETH MATCHETT STOVER MEMORIAL AWARD

(214)768-1037. **Fax:** (214)768-1408. **E-mail:** swr@mail.smu.edu. **Website:** www.smu.edu/southwestreview. **Contact:** Jennifer Cranfill, senior editor, and Willard Spiegelman, editor-in-chief. "Offered annually to the best works of poetry that have appeared in the magazine in the previous year. Please note that mss are submitted for publication, not for the prizes themselves. Guidelines for SASE and online." $300 Judged by Jennifer Cranfill and Willard Spiegelman.

STROKESTOWN INTERNATIONAL POETRY COMPETITION

Strokestown International Poetry Festival, Strokestown Poetry Festival Office, Strokestown, County Roscommon, Ireland. (+353) 71 9633759. **E-mail:** office@strokestownpoetry.org. **Website:** www.strokestownpoetry.org. **Contact:** Director. This annual competition was established to promote excellence in poetry and participation in the reading and writing of it. Acquires first publication rights. Deadline: January 1st Prize: 4,000 euros (approximately $3,900) for a poem in English of up to 70 lines, plus others totalling about $3,000. Up to 10 shortlisted poets will be invited to read at the Strokestown International Poetry Festival and paid a reading fee.

MAY SWENSON POETRY AWARD

Utah State University Press, 7800 Old Main Hill, Logan UT 84322-7800. (435)797-1362. **Fax:** (435)797-0313. **E-mail:** michael.spooner@usu.edu. **Website:** www.usupress.org. **Contact:** Michael Spooner, director. The annual Swenson Award Competition offers a $1,000 prize plus publication for a full-length poetry collection. Must be original poetry in English, 50 to 100 pages. No restrictions on form or subject. $25 reading fee (includes copy of winning book). Postmark deadline September 30. Previous winners include Idris Anderson, Jason Whitmarsh, Elisabeth Murawski. Previous judges include Harold Bloom, Grace Schulman, Billy Collins, and Edward Field. See website for guidelines and the full series of Swenson volumes.

TEXAS INSTITUTE OF LETTERS BOB BUSH MEMORIAL AWARD FOR FIRST BOOK OF POETRY

Website: http://texasinstituteofletters.org. Offered annually for best first book of poetry published in previous year. Writer must have been born in Texas, have lived in the state at least 2 consecutive years at some time, or the subject matter should be associated with the state. Deadline: See website for exact date. Prize: $1,000.

THE TEXAS INSTITUTE OF LETTERS POETRY AWARD

E-mail: Betwx@aol.com. **Website:** www.texasinstituteofletters.org. The Texas Institute of Letters gives annual awards for books by Texas authors, including the Helen C. Smith Memorial Award for Best Book of Poetry. Books must have been first published in the year in question, and entries may be made by authors or by their publishers. Complete guidelines and award information available on website.

THE BITTER OLEANDER PRESS LIBRARY OF POETRY BOOK AWARD

The Bitter Oleander Press, 4983 Tall Oaks Dr., Fayetteville NY 13066-9776. (315)637-3047. **Fax:** (315)637-5056. **E-mail:** info@bitteroleander.com. **Website:** www.bitteroleander.com. **Contact:** Paul B. Roth. "The Bitter Oleander Press Library of Poetry Book Award replaces the 15-year long run of the Frances Locke Memorial Poetry Award. We suggest reading the complete guidelines available on our website." Deadline: May 1 - June 15 (postmarked). Early or late entries will be disqualified. Prize: $1,000, plus book publication of the winning ms.

TIGER'S EYE POETRY CHAPBOOK CONTEST

Tiger's Eye Press, P.O. Box 9723, Denver CO 80209. **E-mail:** tigerseyepoet@yahoo.com. **Website:** www.tigerseyejournal.com. The Tiger's Eye Poetry Chapbook Contest awards $100 and publication of the winning chapbook. Considers simultaneous submissions. Submit 20-25 pages of poetry; include a short bio, SASE, and cover page with poet's name and contact information. No identifying information on mss pages. No restrictions on form, subject, or length. Guidelines available on website. Deadline: August 31 (postmark).

LENA-MILES WEVER TODD POETRY SERIES BOOK COMPETITION

Pleiades Press, Dept of English, Martin 336, University of Central Missouri, Warrensburg MO 64093. (660)543-8106. **E-mail:** pleiades@ucmo.edu. **Website:** www.ucmo.edu/pleiades/. **Contact:** Wayne Miller, editor. The annual Lena-Miles Wever Todd Poetry Series Book Competition offers $2,000 and publication of a book-length ms. Open to all American writers, regardless of previous publication. Submission must be unpublished as a collection, but individual poems may have been previously published elsewhere. Submit at least 48 pages of poetry (one copy). Include 2 cover sheets: one with ms title, poet's name, address, and phone number; the second with ms title only. Also include acknowledgments page for previously published poems. Include SASE for results; for an additional large SASE with $1.28 postage affixed, entrant will receive a copy of the winning book. Guidelines available for SASE or on website. **Entry fee:** $25. Make checks/money orders payable to Pleiades Press. **Deadline:** November 1st (postmark). 2012 winner was Katy Didden for *Avalanche*. The judge for 2012-13 will be Dana Levin.

TRANSCONTINENTAL POETRY AWARD

Pavement Saw Press, 321 Empire St., Montpelier OH 43543. (419)485-0524. **E-mail:** info@pavementsaw.org. **Website:** pavementsaw.org. **Contact:** David Baratier, editor. The Transcontinental Poetry Award offers $1,000, publication, and a percentage of the print run for a first or second book. "Each year, Pavement Saw Press will seek to publish at least 1 book of poetry and/or prose poems from manuscripts received during this competition, which is open to anyone who has not previously published a volume of poetry or prose. Poets who have not published a book, who have published 1 collection, or who have published a second collection of fewer than 40 pages, or who have published a second full-length collection with a print run of no more than 500 copies are eligible. More than 1prize may be awarded." Submit 48-70 pages of poetry (1 poem/page), paginated and bound with a single clip. Include 2 cover sheets: 1 with ms title, poet's name, address, phone number, and e-mail; if available, the second with ms title only (this sheet should be clipped to ms). Also include 1-page cover letter (a brief biography, ms title, poet's name, address, and telephone number, e-mail, and poet's signature) and acknowledgments page (journal, anthology, chapbook, etc., and poem published). Include SASP for acknowledgment of receipt; SASE unnecessary as result will be sent with free book and no mss will be returned. Guidelines available for SASE or on website. **Entry fee:** $20; electronic submissions $27. "All US entrants will receive books, chapbooks, and journals equal to, or more than, the entry fee. Add $3 (USD) for other countries to cover the extra postal charge if sending by mail." Make checks payable to Pavement Saw Press. **Deadline:** Reads submissions in June, July, and until August 15 (must have August 15 or earlier postmark). "Offered annually for a first or second book of poetry. Judged by the editor and a guest judge. Guidelines available online."

TUFTS POETRY AWARDS

Claremont Graduate University, 160 E. 10th St., Harper East B7, Claremont CA 91711-6165. (909)621-8612. **Website:** www.cgu.edu/tufts. **Contact:** Wendy Martin, program director. The annual Kingsley Tufts Poetry Award offers $100,000 for a work by an emerging poet, "one who is past the very beginning but has not yet reached the acknowledged pinnacle of his/her career." 2012 winner is Timothy Donnelly (*The Cloud Corporation*). The Kate Tufts Discovery Award ($10,000) is for a first book. 2012 winner is Katherine Larson (*Radial Symmetry*). To be considered for the 2013 awards, books must have been published between September 1, 2011 and August 31, 2012. Entry form and guidelines available for SASE or on website. Check website for updated deadlines and award information.

UTMOST CHRISTIAN POETRY CONTEST

Utmost Christian Writers Foundation, 121 Morin Maze, Edmonton AB T6K 1V1, Canada. **E-mail:** nnharms@telusplanet.net. **Website:** www.utmostchristianwriters.com. **Contact:** Nathan Harms, executive director. The Utmost Christian Poetry Contest opens annually for entries on September 1 "for Christian poets only!" $3,000 in cash prizes. The purpose of this contest is "to promote excellence in poetry by poets of Christian faith. All entries are eligible for most of the cash awards, but there is a special category for rhyming poetry with prizes of $300 and $100. All entries must be unpublished." See rules and entry form online at website. Deadline: February 28 annually. 1st Place: $1,000; 2nd Place: $600; 10 prizes of $100 are offered for honorable mention. Rights are acquired to post winning entries on the organization's website. Judged by a committee of the Directors of Utmost Christian Writers Foundation (who work under the direction of Barbara Mitchell, chief judge).

TIPS "Besides providing numerous resources for Christian writers and poets, Utmost also provides a marketplace where Christian writers and poets can sell their work. Please follow our guidelines. We receive numerous unsuitable submissions from writers. We encourage writers to submit suitable material. The best way to do this is to read the guidelines specific to your project—poetry, book reviews, articles—and then take time to look at the material we have already published in that area. The final step is to evaluate your proposed submission in comparison to the material we have used previously. If you complete these steps and strongly feel that your material is appropriate for us, we encourage you to submit it. Please use the submission link on the appropriate Web page. For example, if you are submitting a poem, please click the 'Poetry Gallery' link and use the submission link 'Poetry Guidelines'. If you fail to follow these instructions, it's possible your submission will be lost."

⊙ DANIEL VAROUJAN AWARD

New England Poetry Club, 654 Green St., No. 2, Cambridge MA 02139. **E-mail:** contests@nepoetryclub.org. **Website:** www.nepoetryclub.org. **Contact:** NEPC contest coordinator. "For an unpublished poem (not a translation)worthy of Daniel Varoujan, a poet killed by the Turks in the genocide that destroyed three-fourths of the Armenian population. Previous winners may not enter again." Deadline: May 31. Prize: $1,000. Judges are well-known poets and sometimes winners of previous NEPC contests.

O MARICA AND JAN VILCEK PRIZE FOR POETRY

Bellevue Literary Review, New York University School of Medicine, OBV-A612, 550 First Ave., New York NY 10016. (212)263-3973. **E-mail:** info@BLReview.org. **Website:** www.BLReview.org. **Contact:** Stacy Bodziak. The annual Marica and Jan Vilcek Prize for Poetry recognizes outstanding writing related to themes of health, healing, illness, the mind, and the body. Offers $1,000 for best poem and publication in Bellevue Literary Review. All entries will be considered for publication. No previously published poems (including Internet publication). Submit up to 3 poems (5 pages maximum). Electronic (online) submissions only; combine all poems into 1 document and use first poem as document title. See guidelines for additional submission details. Guidelines available for SASE or on website. **Entry fee:** $15/submission; limit of 2 submissions per person (1-year subscription available for additional $5). **Deadline:** July 1. Winner announced in December. 2013 judge: Mark Doty. Previous judges include Cornelius Eady, Naomi Shihab Nye, and Tony Hoagland.

THE WASHINGTON PRIZE

Dearlove Hall, Adirondack Community College, 640 Bay Rd., Queensbury NY 12804. **E-mail:** editor@wordworksdc.com. **Website:** www.wordworksdc.com. **Contact:** Nancy White, Washington Prize administrator. Word Works is "a nonprofit literary organization publishing contemporary poetry in single-author editions." Levels of membership/dues: $35 (basic), $50 (sustaining). Membership benefits at the basic level include choice of 2 books from The Word Works book list, newsletter, and 20% discount on additional book orders; in addition to these benefits, sustaining members are eligible for online critique of several poems via e-mail. Sponsors an ongoing poetry reading series, educational programs, and the Hilary Tham Capital Collection (2012 judge will be Cornelius Eady). Sponsors The Washington Prize, one of the older manuscript publishing prizes, and The Jacklyn Potter Young Poets Competition. Additional information available on website. Winners announced in August. Book publication planned for January 2013. Deadline: Submit January 15-March 15 (postmark). Offers $1,500 and publication of a book-length ms of original poetry in English by a living American poet (US or Canadian citizen or resident).

WERGLE FLOMP HUMOR POETRY CONTEST

Winning Writers, 351 Pleasant St., PMB 222, Northampton MA 01060-3961. (866)946-9748. **Fax:** (413)280-0539. **E-mail:** adam@winningwriters.com. **Website:** www.winningwriters.com. **Contact:** Adam Cohen. Offers annual award of 1st Prize: $1,500; 2nd Prize: $800; 3rd Prize: $400; plus 12 Honorable Mentions of $75 each. Both published and unpublished poems are welcome. Final judge: Jendi Reiter. See the complete guidelines and past winners. All prizewinners receive online publication at WinningWriters.com. Submissions may be previously published. Considers simultaneous submissions. Submit 1 humorous poem of any length, in any form. See website for examples." Entries accepted only through website; no entries by regular mail. Guidelines available on website. **Entry fee:** None. **Deadline:** April 1. Competition receives about 2,000 entries/year. Winners announced at WinningWriters.com and in free e-mail newsletter. "Please read the past winning entries and the judge's comments published at WinningWriters.com." See separate listing for the Sports Poetry & Prose Contest in this section. "This annual contest seeks today's best humor poems. One poem of any length should be submitted. The poem should be in English. Inspired gibberish is also accepted. See website for guidelines, examples, and to submit your poem. Nonexclusive right to publish submissions on WinningWriters.com, in e-mail newsletter, and in press releases."

TIPS "Submissions may be previously published and may be entered in other contests. Competition receives about 2,000 entries/year. Winners are announced on August 15 at WinningWriters.com. Entrants who provide a valid e-mail address will also receive notification."

WESTERN AUSTRALIAN PREMIER'S BOOK AWARDS

State Library of Western Australia, Alexander Library Bldg., Perth Cultural Centre, Perth WA 6000, Australia. **Website:** www.slwa.wa.gov.au/pba.html. Offers annual poetry prize of $10,000 AUD for a published book of poetry. Winner also eligible for Premier's Prize of $25,000 AUD. Submissions must be published. Open to residents of Australia or Australian citizens. Entry form and guidelines available for SASE or on website. Online entry form and guidelines on website. **Entry fee:** None. **Deadline:** January 31 each year. Competition receives about 30-40 entries in poetry category per year. 2010 poetry winner was Mark Tredinnick for *Fire Diary.* Winners announced in September each year at a presentation given by the Premier of Western Australia. "The contest is organized by the State Library of Western Australia, with money provided by the Western Australian State Government to support literature."

STAN AND TOM WICK POETRY PRIZE

301 Satterfield Hall, Kent State University, P.O. Box 5190, Kent OH 44242-0001. (330)672-2067. **E-mail:** www.kent.edu/wick. **Website:** www.dept.kent.edu/wick. **Contact:** David Hassler, director. Offers annual award of $2,500 and publication by Kent State University Press. Open to poets writing in English who have not yet published a full-length collection. Submissions must be unpublished as a collection, but individual poems may have been previously published elsewhere. Considers simultaneous submissions as long as the Wick Poetry Center receives notice upon acceptance elsewhere. Submit 50-70 pages of poetry. Include cover sheet with poet's name, address, telephone number, e-mail address, and title of ms. Guidelines available for SASE or on website. **Reading fee:** $25. **Deadline:** Submit February 1-May 1. Competition receives700-800 entries. Open to anyone writing in English who has not previously published a full-length book of poems (a volume of 50 pages or more published in an edition of 500 or more copies). Send SASE or visit the website for guidelines. Competition receives 700-800 entries.

WILLA LITERARY AWARD

E-mail: slyon.www@gmail.com. **Website:** www.womenwritingthewest.org. **Contact:** Alice D. Trego, contest director; Suzanne Lyon, WILLA chair. The WILLA Literary Award honors the best in literature featuring women's or girls' stories set in the West published each year. Women Writing the West (WWW), a nonprofit association of writers and other professionals writing and promoting the Women's West, underwrites and presents the nationally recognized award annually (for work published between January 1 and December 31). The award is named in honor of Pulitzer Prize winner Willa Cather, one of the country's foremost novelists. The award is given in 7 categories: Historical fiction, contemporary fiction, original softcover fiction, creative nonfiction, scholarly nonfiction, poetry, and children's/young adult fiction/nonfiction. Deadline: February 1 Winner receives $100 and a trophy. Finalist receives a plaque. Award announcement is in early August, and awards are presented to the winners and finalists at the annual WWW Fall Conference. Judged by professional librarians not affiliated with WWW.

WISCONSIN INSTITUTE FOR CREATIVE WRITING FELLOWSHIP

6195B H.C. White Hall, 600 N. Park St., Madison WI 53706. **E-mail:** rfkuka@wisc.edu. **Website:** www.wisc.edu/english/cw. **Contact:** Ron Kuka, program coordinator. Fellowship provides time, space and an intellectual community for writers working on first books. Receives approximately 300 applicants a year for each genre. Judged by English Department faculty and current fellows. "Candidates must not yet have published, or had accepted for publication, a book by application deadline." Open to any writer with either an M.F.A. or Ph.D. in creative writing. Please enclose a SASE for notification of results. Results announced by May 1. "Send your best work. Stories seem to have a small advantage over novel excerpts." Applicants should submit up to 10 pages of poetry or one story of up to 30 pages and a résumé or vita directly to the program during the month of February. An applicant's name must not appear on the writing sample (which must be in ms form) but rather on a separate sheet along with address, social security number, phone number, e-mail address and title(s) of submission(s). Candidates should also supply the names and phone numbers of two references. Accepts inquiries by e-mail and phone. Deadline: February. Prize: $27,000 for a 9-month appointment.

THE J. HOWARD AND BARBARA M.J. WOOD PRIZE

Poetry, 61 W. Superior St., Chicago IL 60654. (312)787-7070. **E-mail:** poetry@poetrymagazine.org. **Website:** www.poetrymagazine.org. Offered annually for poems published in *Poetry* during the preceding year (October-September). Upon acceptance, *Poetry* licenses exclusive worldwide first serial rights, including electronic rights, for publication, as well as non-exclusive rights to reprint, reuse, and archive the work, in any format, in perpetuity. Copyright reverts to author upon first publication. $5,000.

◐ WORKING PEOPLE'S POETRY COMPETITION

Blue Collar Review, P.O. Box 11417, Norfolk VA 23517. **E-mail:** red-ink@earthlink.net. **Website:** www.partisanpress.org. The Working People's Poetry Competition offers $100 and a 1-year subscription to *Blue Collar Review* and "1 year posting of winning poem on our website. Poetry should be typed as you would like to see it published, with your name and address on each page. Include cover letter with entry." Guidelines available on website. Deadline: May 15. Previous winner was Gregg Shotwell.

WORLD'S BEST SHORT-SHORT STORY FICTION CONTEST, NARRATIVE NONFICTION CONTEST & SOUTHEAST REVIEW POETRY CONTEST

E-mail: southeastreview@gmail.com. **Website:** www.southeastreview.org. **Contact:** Katie Cortese, acquisitions editor. Annual award for unpublished short-short stories (500 words or less), poetry, and narrative nonfiction (6,000 words or less). Deadline: March 15. $500 per category. Winners and finalists will be published in *The Southeast Review*.

WRITER'S DIGEST ANNUAL WRITING COMPETITION

F+W Media, Inc., 10151 Carver Rd., Blue Ash OH. (513)531-2690, ext. 1328. **E-mail:** writing-competition@fwmedia.com; nicole.florence@fwmedia.com. **Website:** www.writersdigest.com. **Contact:** Nicki Florence. Writing contest with 10 categories: Inspirational Writing (spiritual/religious, maximum 2,500 words); Memoir/Personal Essay (maximum 2,000 words); Magazine Feature Article (maximum 2,000 words); Short Story (genre, maximum 4,000 words); Short Story (mainstream/literary, maximum 4,000 words); Rhyming Poetry (maximum 32 lines); Non-rhyming Poetry (maximum 32 lines); Stage Play (first 15 pages and 1-page synopsis); TV/Movie Script (first 15 pages and 1-page synopsis). Entries must be original, in English, unpublished*/unproduced (except for Magazine Feature Articles), and not accepted by another publisher/producer at the time of submission. *Writer's Digest* retains one-time publication rights to the winning entries in each category. Deadline: May. Grand Prize: $3,000 and a trip to New York City to meet with editors and agents; *Writer's Digest* will fly you and a guest to The Big Apple for the conference.

WRITER'S DIGEST INTERNATIONAL SELF-PUBLISHED BOOK AWARDS

F+W Media, Inc., Iola WI. (715)445-4612, ext. 13430. **E-mail:** writing-competition@fwmedia.com. **Website:** www.writersdigest.com. **Contact:** Nicole Florence. Contest open to all English-language self-published books for which the authors have paid the full cost of publication, or the cost of printing has been paid for by a grant or as part of a prize. Categories include: Mainstream/Literary Fiction, Nonfiction, Inspirational (spiritual/new age), Life Stories (biographies/autobiographies/family histories/memoirs), Children's Books, Reference Books (directories/encyclopedias/guide books), Poetry, Middle-Grade/Young Adult Books. Deadline: April 20 Grand Prize: $3,000, promotion in *Writer's Digest* and *Publisher's Weekly*, and 10 copies of the book will be sent to major review houses with a guaranteed review in *Midwest Book Review*; 1st Place (9 winners): $1,000, promotion in *Writer's Digest*.

WRITERS-EDITORS NETWORK ANNUAL INTERNATIONAL WRITING COMPETITION

E-mail: contest@writers-editors.com. **Website:** www.writers-editors.com. **Contact:** Dana K. Cassell, executive director. "Annual award to recognize publishable talent. Categories: Nonfiction (previously published article/essay/column/nonfiction book chapter; unpublished or self-published article/essay/column/nonfiction book chapter); fiction (unpublished or self-published short story or novel chapter); children's literature (unpublished or self-published short story/nonfiction article/book chapter/poem); poetry (unpublished or self-published free verse/traditional)." Guidelines available online. Deadline: March 15 1st

Place: $100; 2nd Place: $75; 3rd Place: $50. All winners and Honorable Mentions will receive certificates as warranted. Judged by editors, librarians, and writers.

WRITERS' FELLOWSHIP

Department of Cultural Resources, Raleigh NC 27699-4632. **Website:** www.ncarts.org. Fellowships are awarded to support the creative development of NC writers and to stimulate the creation of new work. Prize: $10,000. Categories: short stories, novels, literary nonfiction, literary translation, spoken word. Work for children also invited. Judged by a panel of literary professionals appointed by the NC Arts Council, a state agency. No entry fee. Mss must not be in published form. We receive approximately 300 applications. Word length: 20 double-spaced pages (max). The work must have been written within the past 5 years. Only writers who have been full-time residents of NC for at least 1 year as of the application deadline and who plan to remain in the state during the grant year may apply. Guidelines available in late August on website. Accepts inquiries by fax, e-mail, phone. Results announced in late summer. All applicants notified by mail.

WRITERS GUILD OF ALBERTA AWARDS

Writers Guild of Alberta, Percy Page Centre, 11759 Groat Rd., Edmonton AB T5M 3K6, Canada. (780)422-8174. **Fax:** (780)422-2663. **E-mail:** mail@writersguild.ab.ca. **Website:** www.writersguild.ab.ca. **Contact:** Executive Director. Offers the following awards: Wilfrid Eggleston Award for Nonfiction; Georges Bugnet Award for Fiction; Howard O'Hagan Award for Short Story; Stephan G. Stephansson Award for Poetry; R. Ross Annett Award for Children's Literature; Gwen Pharis Ringwood Award for Drama; Jon Whyte Memorial Essay Prize; James H. Gray Award for Short Nonfiction; Amber Bowerman Memorial Travel Writing Award. Eligible entries will have been published anywhere in the world between January 1 and December 31 of the current year; the authors must have been residents of Alberta for at least 12 of the 18 months prior to December 31. Unpublished mss, except in the drama, essay, and short nonfiction categories, are not eligible. Anthologies are not eligible. Works may be submitted by authors, publishers, or any interested parties. Deadline: December 31. Winning authors receive $1,500; essay prize winners receive $700.

GRANTS:

State & Provincial

Arts councils in the United States and Canada provide assistance to artists (including poets) in the form of fellowships or grants. These grants can be substantial and confer prestige upon recipients; however, only state or province residents are eligible. Because deadlines and available support vary annually, query first (with a SASE) or check websites for guidelines.

UNITED STATES ARTS AGENCIES

ALABAMA STATE COUNCIL ON THE ARTS, 201 Monroe St., Montgomery AL 36130-1800. (334)242-4076. E-mail: staff@arts.alabama.gov. Website: www.arts.state.al.us.

ALASKA STATE COUNCIL ON THE ARTS, 411 W. Fourth Ave., Suite 1-E, Anchorage AK 99501-2343. (907)269-6610 or (888)278-7424. E-mail: aksca_info@eed.state.ak.us. Website: www.eed.state.ak.us/aksca.

ARIZONA COMMISSION ON THE ARTS, 417 W. Roosevelt St., Phoenix AZ 85003-1326. (602)771-6501. E-mail: info@azarts.gov. Website: www.azarts.gov.

ARKANSAS ARTS COUNCIL, 1500 Tower Bldg., 323 Center St., Little Rock AR 72201. (501)324-9766. E-mail: info@arkansasarts.com. Website: www.arkansasarts.com.

CALIFORNIA ARTS COUNCIL, 1300 I St., Suite 930, Sacramento CA 95814. (916)322-6555. E-mail: info@caartscouncil.com. Website: www.cac.ca.gov.

COLORADO COUNCIL ON THE ARTS, 1625 Broadway, Suite 2700, Denver CO 80202. (303)892-3802. E-mail: online form. Website: www.coloarts.state.co.us.

COMMONWEALTH COUNCIL FOR ARTS AND CULTURE (Northern Mariana Islands), P.O. Box 5553, CHRB, Saipan MP 96950. (670)322-9982 or (670)322-9983. E-mail: galaidi@vzpacifica.net. Website: www.geocities.com/ccacarts/ccacwebsite.html.

CONNECTICUT COMMISSION ON CULTURE & TOURISM, Arts Division, One Financial Plaza, 755 Main St., Hartford CT 06103. (860)256-2800. Website: www.cultureandtourism.org.

DELAWARE DIVISION OF THE ARTS, Carvel State Office Bldg., 4th Floor, 820 N. French St., Wilmington DE 19801. (302)577-8278 (New Castle Co.) or (302)739-5304 (Kent or Sussex Counties). E-mail: delarts@state.de.us. Website: www.artsdel.org.

DISTRICT OF COLUMBIA COMMISSION ON THE ARTS & HUMANITIES, 410 Eighth St. NW, 5th Floor, Washington DC 20004. (202)724-5613. E-mail: cah@dc.gov. Website: http://dcarts.dc.gov.

FLORIDA ARTS COUNCIL, Division of Cultural Affairs, R.A. Gray Building, Third Floor, 500 S. Bronough St., Tallahassee FL 32399-0250. (850)245-6470. E-mail: info@florida-arts.org. Website: http://dcarts.dc.gov.

GEORGIA COUNCIL FOR THE ARTS, 260 14th St., Suite 401, Atlanta GA 30318. (404)685-2787. E-mail: gaarts@gaarts.org. Website: www.gaarts.org.

GUAM COUNCIL ON THE ARTS & HUMANITIES AGENCY, P.O. Box 2950, Hagatna GU 96932. (671)646-2781. Website: www.guam.net.

HAWAII STATE FOUNDATION ON CULTURE & THE ARTS, 2500 S. Hotel St., 2nd Floor, Honolulu HI 96813. (808)586-0300. E-mail: ken.hamilton@hawaii.gov. Website: http.state.hi.us/sfca.

IDAHO COMMISSION ON THE ARTS, 2410 N. Old Penitentiary Rd., Boise ID 83712. (208)334-2119 or (800)278-3863. E-mail: info@arts.idaho.gov. Website: www.arts.idaho.gov.

ILLINOIS ARTS COUNCIL, James R. Thompson Center, 100 W. Randolph, Suite 10-500, Chicago IL 60601. (312)814-6750. E-mail: iac.info@illinois.gov. Website: www.state.il.us/agency/iac.

INDIANA ARTS COMMISSION, 150 W. Market St., Suite 618, Indianapolis IN 46204. (317)232-1268. E-mail: IndianaArtsCommission@iac.in.gov. Website: www.in.gov/arts.

INSTITUTE OF PUERTO RICAN CULTURE, P.O. Box 9024184, San Juan PR 00902-4184. (787)724-0700. E-mail: www@icp.gobierno.pr. Website: www.icp.gobierno.pr.

IOWA ARTS COUNCIL, 600 E. Locust, Des Moines IA 50319-0290. (515)281-6412. Website: www.iowaartscouncil.org.

KANSAS ARTS COMMISSION, 700 SW Jackson, Suite 1004, Topeka KS 66603-3761. (785)296-3335. E-mail: KAC@arts.state.ks.us. Website: http://arts.state.ks.us.

KENTUCKY ARTS COUNCIL, 21st Floor, Capital Plaza Tower, 500 Mero St., Frankfort KY 40601-1987. (502)564-3757 or (888)833-2787. E-mail: kyarts@ky.gov. Website: http://artscouncil.ky.gov.

LOUISIANA DIVISION OF THE ARTS, Capitol Annex Bldg., 1051 N. 3rd St., 4th Floor, Room #420, Baton Rouge LA 70804. (225)342-8180. Website: www.crt.state.la.us/arts.

MAINE ARTS COMMISSION, 193 State St., 25 State House Station, Augusta ME 04333-0025. (207)287-2724. E-mail: MaineArts.info@maine.gov. Website: www.mainearts.com.

MARYLAND STATE ARTS COUNCIL, 175 W. Ostend St., Suite E, Baltimore MD 21230. (410)767-6555. E-mail: msac@msac.org. Website: www.msac.org.

MASSACHUSETTS CULTURAL COUNCIL, 10 St. James Ave., 3rd Floor, Boston MA 02116-3803. (617)727-3668. E-mail: mcc@art.state.ma.us. Website: www.massculturalcouncil.org.

MICHIGAN COUNCIL OF HISTORY, ARTS, AND LIBRARIES, 702 W. Kalamazoo St., P.O. Box 30705, Lansing MI 48909-8205. (517)241-4011. E-mail: artsinfo@michigan.gov. Website: www.michigan.gov/hal/0,1607,7-160-17445_19272---,00.html.

MINNESOTA STATE ARTS BOARD, Park Square Court, 400 Sibley St., Suite 200, St. Paul MN 55101-1928. (651)215-1600 or (800)866-2787. E-mail: msab@arts.state.mn.us. Website: www.arts.state.mn.us.

MISSISSIPPI ARTS COMMISSION, 501 N. West St., Suite 701B, Woolfolk Bldg., Jackson MS 39201. (601)359-6030. Website: www.arts.state.ms.us.

MISSOURI ARTS COUNCIL, 815 Olive St., Suite 16, St. Louis MO 63101-1503. (314)340-6845 or (866)407-4752. E-mail: moarts@ded.mo.gov. Website: www.missouriartscouncil.org.

MONTANA ARTS COUNCIL, 316 N. Park Ave., Suite 252, Helena MT 59620-2201. (406)444-6430. E-mail: mac@mt.gov. Website: www.art.state.mt.us.

NATIONAL ASSEMBLY OF STATE ARTS AGENCIES, 1029 Vermont Ave. NW, 2nd Floor, Washington DC 20005. (202)347-6352. E-mail: nasaa@nasaa-arts.org. Website: www.nasaa-arts.org.

NEBRASKA ARTS COUNCIL, 1004 Farnam St., Plaza Level, Omaha NE 68102. (402)595-2122 or (800)341-4067. Website: www.nebraskaartscouncil.org.

NEVADA ARTS COUNCIL, 716 N. Carson St., Suite A, Carson City NV 89701. (775)687-6680. E-mail: online form. Website: http://dmla.clan.lib.nv.us/docs/arts.

NEW HAMPSHIRE STATE COUNCIL ON THE ARTS, 21/2 Beacon St., 2nd Floor, Concord NH 03301-4974. (603)271-2789. Website: www.nh.gov/nharts.

NEW JERSEY STATE COUNCIL ON THE ARTS, 225 W. State St., P.O. Box 306, Trenton NJ 08625. (609)292-6130. Website: www.njartscouncil.org.

NEW MEXICO ARTS, DEPT. OF CULTURAL AFFAIRS, P.O. Box 1450, Santa Fe NM 87504-1450. (505)827-6490 or (800)879-4278. Website: www.nmarts.org.

NEW YORK STATE COUNCIL ON THE ARTS, 175 Varick St., New York NY 10014. (212)627-4455. Website: www.nysca.org.

NORTH CAROLINA ARTS COUNCIL, 109 East Jones St., Cultural Resources Building, Raleigh NC 27601. (919)807-6500. E-mail: ncarts@ncmail.net. Website: www.ncarts.org.

NORTH DAKOTA COUNCIL ON THE ARTS, 1600 E. Century Ave., Suite 6, Bismarck ND 58503. (701)328-7590. E-mail: comserv@state.nd.us. Website: www.state.nd.us/arts.

OHIO ARTS COUNCIL, 727 E. Main St., Columbus OH 43205-1796. (614)466-2613. Website: www.oac.state.oh.us.

OKLAHOMA ARTS COUNCIL, Jim Thorpe Building, 2101 N. Lincoln Blvd., Suite 640, Oklahoma City OK 73105. (405)521-2931. E-mail: okarts@arts.ok.gov. Website: www.arts.state.ok.us.

OREGON ARTS COMMISSION, 775 Summer St. NE, Suite 200, Salem OR 97301-1280. (503)986-0082. E-mail: oregon.artscomm@state.or.us. Website: www.oregonartscommission.org.

PENNSYLVANIA COUNCIL ON THE ARTS, 216 Finance Bldg., Harrisburg PA 17120. (717)787-6883. Website: www.pacouncilonthearts.org.

RHODE ISLAND STATE COUNCIL ON THE ARTS, One Capitol Hill, Third Floor, Providence RI 02908. (401)222-3880. E-mail: info@arts.ri.gov. Website: www.arts.ri.gov.

SOUTH CAROLINA ARTS COMMISSION, 1800 Gervais St., Columbia SC 29201. (803)734-8696. E-mail: info@arts.state.sc.us. Website: www.southcarolinaarts.com.

SOUTH DAKOTA ARTS COUNCIL, 711 E. Wells Ave., Pierre SD 57501-3369. (605)773-3301. E-mail: sdac@state.sd.us. Website: www.artscouncil.sd.gov.

TENNESSEE ARTS COMMISSION, 401 Charlotte Ave., Nashville TN 37243-0780. (615)741-1701. Website: www.arts.state.tn.us.

TEXAS COMMISSION ON THE ARTS, E.O. Thompson Office Building, 920 Colorado, Suite 501, Austin TX 78701. (512)463-5535. E-mail: front.desk@arts.state.tx.us. Website: www.arts.state.tx.us.

UTAH ARTS COUNCIL, 617 E. South Temple, Salt Lake City UT 84102-1177. (801)236-7555. Website: http://arts.utah.gov.

VERMONT ARTS COUNCIL, 136 State St., Drawer 33, Montpelier VT 05633-6001. (802)828-3291. E-mail: online form. Website: www.vermontartscouncil.org.

VIRGIN ISLANDS COUNCIL ON THE ARTS, 5070 Norre Gade, St. Thomas VI 00802-6872. (340)774-5984. Website: http://vicouncilonarts.org.

VIRGINIA COMMISSION FOR THE ARTS, Lewis House, 223 Governor St., 2nd Floor, Richmond VA 23219. (804)225-3132. E-mail: arts@arts.virginia.gov. Website: www.arts.state.va.us.

WASHINGTON STATE ARTS COMMISSION, 711 Capitol Way S., Suite 600, P.O. Box 42675, Olympia WA 98504-2675. (360)753-3860. E-mail: info@arts.wa.gov. Website: www.arts.wa.gov.

WEST VIRGINIA COMMISSION ON THE ARTS, The Cultural Center, Capitol Complex, 1900 Kanawha Blvd. E., Charleston WV 25305-0300. (304)558-0220. Website: www.wvculture.org/arts.

WISCONSIN ARTS BOARD, 101 E. Wilson St., 1st Floor, Madison WI 53702. (608)266-0190. E-mail: artsboard@arts.state.wi.us. Website: www.arts.state.wi.us.

WYOMING ARTS COUNCIL, 2320 Capitol Ave., Cheyenne WY 82002. (307)777-7742. E-mail: ebratt@state.wy.us. Website: http://wyoarts.state.wy.us.

CANADIAN PROVINCES ARTS AGENCIES

ALBERTA FOUNDATION FOR THE ARTS, 10708-105 Ave., Edmonton AB T5H 0A1. (780)427-9968. Website: www.affta.ab.ca/index.shtml.

BRITISH COLUMBIA ARTS COUNCIL, P.O. Box 9819, Stn. Prov. Govt., Victoria BC V8W 9W3. (250)356-1718. E-mail: BCArtsCouncil@gov.bc.ca. Website: www.bcartscouncil.ca.

THE CANADA COUNCIL FOR THE ARTS, 350 Albert St., P.O. Box 1047, Ottawa ON K1P 5V8. (613)566-4414 or (800)263-5588 (within Canada). Website: www.canadacouncil.ca.

MANITOBA ARTS COUNCIL, 525-93 Lombard Ave., Winnipeg MB R3B 3B1. (204)945-2237 or (866)994-2787 (in Manitoba). E-mail: info@artscouncil.mb.ca. Website: www.artscouncil.mb.ca.

NEW BRUNSWICK ARTS BOARD (NBAB), 634 Queen St., Suite 300, Fredericton NB E3B 1C2. (506)444-4444 or (866)460-2787. Website: www.artsnb.ca.

NEWFOUNDLAND & LABRADOR ARTS COUNCIL, P.O. Box 98, St. John's NL A1C 5H5. (709)726-2212 or (866)726-2212. E-mail: nlacmail@nfld.net. Website: www.nlac.nf.ca.

NOVA SCOTIA DEPARTMENT OF TOURISM, CULTURE, AND HERITAGE, Culture Division, 1800 Argyle St., Suite 601, P.O. Box 456, Halifax NS B3J 2R5. (902)424-4510. E-mail: cultaffs@gov.ns.ca. Website: www.gov.ns.ca/dtc/culture.

ONTARIO ARTS COUNCIL, 151 Bloor St. W., 5th Floor, Toronto ON M5S 1T6. (416)961-1660 or (800)387-0058 (in Ontario). E-mail: info@arts.on.ca. Website: www.arts.on.ca.

PRINCE EDWARD ISLAND COUNCIL OF THE ARTS, 115 Richmond St., Charlottetown PE C1A 1H7. (902)368-4410 or (888)734-2784. E-mail: info@peiartscouncil.com. Website: www.peiartscouncil.com.

QUÉBEC COUNCIL FOR ARTS & LITERATURE, 79 boul. René-Lévesque Est, 3e étage, Quebec QC G1R 5N5. (418)643-1707 or (800)897-1707. E-mail: info@calq.gouv.qc.ca. Website: www.calq.gouv.qc.ca.

THE SASKATCHEWAN ARTS BOARD, 2135 Broad St., Regina SK S4P 1Y6. (306)787-4056 or (800)667-7526 (Saskatchewan only). E-mail: sab@artsboard.sk.ca. Website: www.artsboard.sk.ca.

YUKON ARTS FUNDING PROGRAM, Cultural Services Branch, Dept. of Tourism & Culture, Government of Yukon, Box 2703 (L-3), Whitehorse YT Y1A 2C6. (867)667-8589 or (800)661-0408 (in Yukon). E-mail: arts@gov.yk.ca. Website: www.tc.gov.yk.ca/216.html.

CONFERENCES, WORKSHOPS & FESTIVALS

There are times when we want to immerse ourselves in learning. Or perhaps we crave a change of scenery, the creative stimulation of being around other artists, or the uninterrupted productivity of time alone to work.

That's what this section of *Poet's Market* is all about, providing a selection of writing conferences and workshops, artist colonies and retreats, poetry festivals, and even a few opportunities to go traveling with your muse. These listings give the basics: contact information, a brief description of the event, lists of past presenters, and offerings of special interest to poets. Contact an event that interests you for additional information, including up-to-date costs and housing details. **(Please note that most directors had not finalized their 2013 plans when we contacted them for this edition of *Poet's Market*. However, where possible, they provided us with their 2012 dates, costs, faculty names or themes to give you a better idea of what each event has to offer.)**

Before you seriously consider a conference, workshop or other event, determine what you hope to get out of the experience. Would a general conference with one or two poetry workshops among many other types of sessions be acceptable? Or are you looking for something exclusively focused on poetry? Do you want to hear poets speak about poetry writing, or are you looking for a more participatory experience, such as a one-on-one critiquing session or a group workshop? Do you mind being one of hundreds of attendees, or do you prefer a more intimate setting? Are you willing to invest in the expense of traveling to a conference, or would something local better suit your budget? Keep these questions and others in mind as you read these listings, view websites and study conference brochures.

ABROAD WRITERS CONFERENCES

17363 Sutter Creek Rd., Sutter Creek CA 95685. (209)296-4050. **E-mail:** abroadwriters@yahoo.com. **Website:** www.abroad-crwf.com/index.html. "Abroad Writers Conferences are devoted to introducing our participants to world views here in the United States and Abroad. Throughout the world we invite several authors to come join us to give readings and to participate on a panel. Our discussion groups touch upon a wide range of topics from important issues of our times to publishing abroad and in the United States. Our objective is to broaden our cultural and scientific perspectives of the world through discourse and writing." Conferences are held throughout the year in various places worldwide. See website for scheduling details. Conference duration: 7-10 days. "Instead of being lost in a crowd at a large conference, Abroad Writers' Conference prides itself on holding small group meetings where participants have personal contact with everyone. Stimulating talks, interviews, readings, Q&A's, writing workshops, film screenings, private consultations and social gatherings all take place within a week to ten days. Abroad Writers' Conference promises you true networking opportunities and full detailed feedback on your writing."

COSTS/ACCOMMODATIONS Prices start at $2,750. Discounts and upgrades may apply. Particpants must apply to program no later than 3 months before departure. To secure a place you must send in a deposit of $700. Balance must be paid in full twelve weeks before departure. See website for pricing details.

ADDITIONAL INFORMATION Agents participate in conference. Application is online at website.

AEC CONFERENCE ON SOUTHERN LITERATURE

Arts & Education Council (AEC), 3069 S. Broad St., Suite 2, Chattanooga TN 37408-3056. (423)267-1218 or (800)267-4232. **Fax:** (423)267-1018. **E-mail:** srobinson@artsedcouncil.org. **Website:** http://artsedcouncil.org; http://southernlitconference.org. **Contact:** Susan Robinson. "The AEC Conference stands out because of its unique collaboration with the Fellowship of Southern Writers, an organization founded by towering literary figures like Eudora Welty, Cleanth Brooks, Walker Percy and Robert Penn Warren to recognize and encourage literature in the South. The 2012 Conference marked 23 YEARS since the Fellowship selected Chattanooga for its headquarters and chose to collaborate with the Conference on Southern Literature. Up to 50 members of the Fellowship will participate in this year's event, discussing hot topics and reading from their latest works. The Fellowship will also award nine literary prizes and induct eight new members, making this event the place to discover up-and-coming voices in Southern literature. The AEC Conference attracts over 1,000 readers and writers from all over the United States. It strives to maintain an informal atmosphere where conversations will thrive, inspired by a common passion for the written word. This conference started as one of 12 pilot agencies founded by a Ford Foundation grant. In 1983, the AEC organization changed its name to the Arts & Education Council to more accurately reflect its outreach in Chattanooga. The AEC is the only organization of the 12 still in existence. The AEC produces innovative events and programs that enrich the Chattanooga community, including the Conference on Southern Literature and its school literacy outreach, the Chattanooga Festival of Writers, Culture Fest, TheatreExpress, the Back Row Film Series, Independent Film Series, and current affairs television programs "Point of View" and "First View." In 2009, they reached 70,000 through these outreach initiatives.

AMERICAN CHRISTIAN WRITERS CONFERENCES

P.O. Box 110390, Nashville TN 37222-0390. (800)219-7483. **Fax:** (615)834-7736. **E-mail:** acwriters@aol.com. **Website:** www.acwriters.com. **Contact:** Reg Forder, director. Conference duration: 2 days. Average attendance: 60. Annual conferences promoting all forms of Christian writing (fiction, nonfiction, scriptwriting). Conferences are held throughout the year in 36 US cities. ACW hosts dozens of annual one-, two-, and three-day writers conferences across America taught by editors and professional freelance writers. These conferences provide excellent instruction, networking opportunities, and valuable one-on-one time with editors. For schedule, click on city name for an online brochure.

COSTS/ACCOMMODATIONS Special rates are available at the host hotel (usually a major chain like Holiday Inn). $150 for one day, $250 for two days, plus meals and accommodations.

ADDITIONAL INFORMATION Send a SASE for conference brochures/guidelines.

ANNUAL SPRING POETRY FESTIVAL

City College, 160 Convent Ave., New York NY 10031. (212)650-6356. **Website:** wwwl.ccny.cuny.edu/prospective/humanities/poetry. Writer workshops geared to all levels. **Open to students.** Annual poetry festival. Festival held May 17, 2011. Registration limited to 325. Cost of workshops and festival: free. Write for more information. Site: Theater B of Aaron Davis Hall.

ART WORKSHOPS IN GUATEMALA

4758 Lyndale Ave. S, Minneapolis MN 55419-5304. (612)825-0747. **E-mail:** info@artguat.org. **Website:** www.artguat.org. **Contact:** Liza Fourre, director. Annual. Workshops held year-round. Maximim class size: 10 students per class.

COSTS/ACCOMMODATIONS All transportation and accommodations included in price of conference. See website. ncludes tuition, lodging, breakfast, ground transportation.

ADDITIONAL INFORMATION Conference information available now. For brochure/guidelines visit website, e-mail, fax or call. Accepts inquiries by e-mail, phone.

ASPEN SUMMER WORDS LITERARY FESTIVAL & WRITING RETREAT

Aspen Writers' Foundation, 110 E. Hallam St., #116, Aspen CO 81611. (970)925-3122. **Fax:** (970)925-5700. **E-mail:** info@aspenwriters.org. **Website:** www.aspenwriters.org. **Contact:** Natalie Lacy, programs coordinator. Annual conference held the fourth week of June. Conference duration: 5 days. Average attendance: 150 at writing retreat; 300+ at literary festival. Retreat for fiction, creative nonfiction, poetry, magazine writing, food writing, and literature. Festival includes author readings, craft talks, panel discussions with publishing industry insiders, professional consultations with editors and agents, and social gatherings.

COSTS/ACCOMMODATIONS Discount lodging at the conference site will be available. 2011 rates to be announced. Free shuttle around town. Check website each year for updates.

ADDITIONAL INFORMATION Workshops admission deadline is April 15. Manuscripts for juried workshops must be submitted by April 15 for review and selection. 10 page limit for workshop application manuscript. A limited number of partial-tuition scholarships are available. Deadline for agent/editor meeting registration is May 27th. Brochures available for SASE, by e-mail and phone request, and on website.

ATLANTIC CENTER FOR THE ARTS

1414 Art Center Ave., New Smyrna Beach FL 32618. (386)427-6975. **E-mail:** program@atlanticcenterforthearts.org. **Website:** http://atlanticcenterforthearts.org.

COSTS/ACCOMMODATIONS $850; $25 non-refundable application fee. Financial aid is available. Participants responsible for all meals. Accommodations available on site. See website for application schedule and materials.

AUSTIN INTERNATIONAL POETRY FESTIVAL

(512)777-1888. **E-mail:** aipfdirector@gmail.com. **Website:** www.aipf.org. **Contact:** Ashley S. Kim, festival director.

COSTS/ACCOMMODATIONS Includes anthology submission fee, program bio, scheduled reading at one of AIPF's 15 venues, participation in all events, 1 catered meal, workshop participation, and more.

ADDITIONAL INFORMATION Offers multiple poetry contests as part of festival. Guidelines available on website. Registration form available on website. "Largest non-juried poetry festival in the U.S.!"

BREAD LOAF WRITERS' CONFERENCE

(802)443-5286. **Fax:** (802)443-2087. **E-mail:** ncargill@middlebury.edu. **Website:** www.middlebury.edu/blwc. Annual conference held in late August. Conference duration: 11 days. Offers workshops for fiction, nonfiction, and poetry. Agents, editors, publicists, and grant specialists will be in attendance.

COSTS/ACCOMMODATIONS Bread Loaf Campus in Ripton, Vermont. $2,345 (includes tuition, housing).

ADDITIONAL INFORMATION 2011 Conference Dates: August 10-20. Location: mountain campus of Middlebury College. Average attendance: 230.

FINE ARTS WORK CENTER

24 Pearl St., Provincetown MA 02657. (508)487-9960 ext. 103. **Fax:** (508)487-8873. **E-mail:** workshops@fawc.org. **Website:** www.fawc.org. **Contact:** Dorothy Antczak, summer program director. Weeklong workshops in creative writing and the visual arts. Location: The Fine Arts Work Center in Provincetown.

COSTS/ACCOMMODATIONS 2012 cost: Summer Workshop Program fees range $600-725. Accommodations available at the Work Center for $675 for 6 nights. Additional accommodations available locally. Cost: $600-725/week, $675/week (housing).

ADDITIONAL INFORMATION See website for details and an application form.

FISHTRAP, INC.

400 Grant Street, P.O. Box 38, Enterprise OR 97828-0038. (541)426-3623. **E-mail:** director@fishtrap.org. **Website:** www.fishtrap.org. **Contact:** Barbara Dills, interim director. In 21 years, Fishtrap has hosted over 200 published poets, novelists, journalists, song writers, and non-fiction writers as teachers and presenters. Although workshops are kept small, thousands of writers, teachers, students and booklovers from around the west have participated in Fishtrap events on a first come first served basis. Writer workshops geared toward beginner, intermediate, advanced and professional levels. Open to students, scholarships available. A series of writing workshops and a writers' gathering is held each July. During the school year Fishtrap brings writers into local schools and offers workshops for teachers and writers of children's and young adult books. Other programs include writing and K-12 teaching residencies, writers' retreats, and lectures. College credit available for many workshops. See website for full program descriptions and to get on the e-mail and mail lists.

GREAT LAKES WRITERS FESTIVAL

Lakeland College, P.O. Box 359, Sheboygan WI 53082-0359. **E-mail:** elderk@lakeland.edu. **Website:** www.greatlakeswritersfestival.org. Annual. Last conference held November 3-4, 2011. Conference duration: 2 days. "Festival celebrates the writing of poetry, fiction, and creative nonfiction." Site: "Lakeland College is a small, 4-year liberal arts college of 235 acres, a beautiful campus in a rural setting, founded in 1862." No themes or panels; just readings and workshops. 2011 faculty: Joyce Dyer and Hailey Leithauser.

COSTS/ACCOMMODATIONS Does not offer overnight accommodations. Provides list of area hotels or lodging options. Free and open to the public. Participants may purchase meals and must arrange for their own lodging.

ADDITIONAL INFORMATION All participants who would like to have their writing considered as an object for discussion during the festival workshops should submit it to Karl Elder electronically by October 15. Participants may submit material for workshops in 1 genre only (poetry, fiction, or creative nonfiction). Sponsors contest. Contest entries must contain the writer's name and address on a separate title page, typed, and be submitted as clear, hard copy on Friday at the festival registration table. Entries may be in each of 3 genres per participant, yet only 1 poem, 1 story, and/or 1nonfiction piece may be entered. There are 2 categories—high school students on 1 hand, all others on the other—of cash awards for first place in each of the 3 genres. The judges reserve the right to decline to award a prize in 1 or more of the genres. Judges will be the editorial staff of *Seems* (a.k.a. Word of Mouth Books), excluding the festival coordinator, Karl Elder. Information available in September. For brochure, visit website.

HAIKU NORTH AMERICA CONFERENCE

1275 Fourth St. PMB #365, Santa Rosa CA 95404. **E-mail:** welchm@aol.com. **Website:** www.haikunorthamerica.com. **Contact:** Michael Dylan Welch. Five days, held every two years at varying locations throughout North America. Dates: August 3-7, 2011 (Eleventh) biennial conference. 2013 dates to be determined. Site: Seattle Center, Seattle, Washington.

COSTS/ACCOMMODATIONS Typically around $200, including a banquet and some additional meals. Accommodations at discounted hotels nearby are an additional cost. Information available on website as details are finalized closer to the conference date.

ADDITIONAL INFORMATION Past conferences have been held in San Francisco (twice), Toronto, Portland (Oregon), Chicago, Boston, New York City, Port Townsend (Washington), Winston-Salem (North Carolina), and Ottawa (Ontario). In the words of Jim Kacian, founder of the Haiku Foundation, "Haiku North America. .. is intellectually diverse, socially expansive, emotionally gratifying, and provides more than any other single experience the sense that haiku is a literary force to be reckoned with and capable of work that matters in the rest of the world."

HIGHLAND SUMMER CONFERENCE

Box 7014, Radford University, Radford VA 24142-7014. (540)831-5366. **Fax:** (540)831-5951. **E-mail:** tburriss@radford.edu; rbderrick@radford.edu. **Website:** www.radford.edu/~arsc. **Contact:** Dr. Theresa Burriss, Ruth Derrick. The Highland Summer Writers' Conference is a two-week lecture-seminar workshop combination conducted by well-known guest writers. It offers the opportunity to study and practice creative and expository writing within the context of regional culture. The course is graded on Pass/Fail basis for undergraduates and letter grades for graduate students. It may be taken twice for credit. The class runs Monday through Friday afternoons, 1:30-4:30, with readings and receptions by visiting authors on Tuesday and Thursday evening in McConnell Library from 7:30-9:30. The evening readings are free and open to the public.

COSTS/ACCOMMODATIONS We do not have special rate arrangements with local hotels. We do offer accommodations on the Radford University campus in a recently refurbished residence hall.

ADDITIONAL INFORMATION Conference leaders typically critique work done during the 2-week conference, but do not ask to have any writing submitted prior to the conference. Conference brochures/guidelines are available in March for a SASE.

HOFSTRA UNIVERSITY SUMMER WRITING WORKSHOPS

University College for Continuing Education, 250 Hofstra University, Hempstead NY 11549-2500. (516)463-7600. **Fax:** (516)463-4833. **E-mail:** ce@hofstra.edu. **Website:** ce.hofstra.edu/summerwriters. **Contact:** Richard Pioreck, co-director. Hofstra University's 2-week Summer Writers Program, a cooperative endeavor of the Creative Writing Program, the English Department, and Hofstra University Continuing Education (Hofstra CE), offers 8 classes which may be taken on a noncredit or credit basis, for both graduate and undergraduate students. Led by master writers, the Summer Writing Program operates on the principle that true writing talent can be developed, nurtured and encouraged by writer-in-residence mentors. Through instruction, discussion, criticism and free exchange among the program members, writers begin to find their voice and their style. The program provides group and individual sessions for each writer. The Summer Writing Program includes a banquet, guest speakers, and exposure to authors such as Oscar Hijuelos, Robert Olen Butler (both Pulitzer Prize winners), Maurice Sendak, Cynthia Ozick, Nora Sayre, and Denise Levertov. Often agents, editors, and publishers make presentations during the conference, and authors and students read from published work and works in progress. These presentations and the conference banquet offer additional opportunities to meet informally with participants, master writers and guest speakers. Average attendance: 65. Conference offers workshops in short fiction, nonfiction, poetry, and occasionally other genres such as screenplay writing or writing for children. Site is the university campus on Long Island, 25 miles from New York City.

COSTS/ACCOMMODATIONS Free bus operates between Hempstead Train Station and campus for those commuting from New York City on the Long Island Rail Road. Dormitory rooms are available. Check website for current fees. Credit is available for undergraduate and graduate students. Choose one of 9 writing genres and spend two intensive weeks studying and writing in that genre.

ADDITIONAL INFORMATION Students entering grades 9-12 can now be part of the Summer Writers Program with a special section for high school students. Through exercises and readings, students will learn how to use their creative impulses to improve their fiction, poetry and plays and learn how to create cleaner and clearer essays. During this intensive 2-week course, students will experiment with memoir, poetry, oral history, dramatic form and the short story, and study how to use character, plot, point of view and language.

IOWA SUMMER WRITING FESTIVAL

C215 Seashore Hall, University of Iowa, Iowa City IA 52242. (319)335-4160. **Fax:** (319)335-4743. **E-mail:** iswfestival@uiowa.edu. **Website:** www.uiowa.edu/~iswfest. Annual festival held in June and July. Conference duration: Workshops are 1 week or a weekend. Average attendance: Limited to 12 people/class, with over 1,500 participants throughout the summer. "We offer courses across the genres: novel, short story, poetry, essay, memoir, humor, travel, playwriting, screenwriting, writing for children, and women's writing. Held at the University of Iowa campus." Speakers have included Marvin Bell, Lan Samantha Chang, John Dalton, Hope Edelman, Katie Ford, Patricia Foster, Bret Anthony Johnston, Barbara Robinette Moss, among others.

COSTS/ACCOMMODATIONS Accommodations available at area hotels. Information on overnight accommodations available by phone or on website. $560 for full week; $280 for weekend workshop. Housing and meals are separate.

ADDITIONAL INFORMATION Brochures are available in February. Inquire via e-mail or on website.

IWWG ANNUAL SUMMER CONFERENCE

International Women's Writing Guild "Remember the Magic" Annual Summer Conference, International Women's Writing Guild, P.O. Box 810, Gracie Station, New York NY 10028. (212)737-7536. **Fax:** (212)737-9469. **E-mail:** iwwg@iwwg.org. **Website:** www.iwwg.org. **Contact:** Hannelore Hahn, executive director. Writer and illustrator workshops geared toward all levels. Offers over 50 different workshops—some are for children's book writers and illustrators. Also sponsors other events throughout the U.S. Annual workshops. Workshops held every summer for a week. Length of each session: 90 minutes; sessions take place for an entire week. Registration limited to 500. Write for more information.

JACKSON HOLE WRITERS CONFERENCE

PO Box 1974, Jackson WY 83001. (307)413-3332. **E-mail:** nicole@jacksonholewritersconference.com. **Website:** www.jacksonholewritersconference.com. Annual conference held in June. Conference duration: 4 days. Average attendance: 110. Covers fiction, creative nonfiction, and young adult and offers ms critiques from authors, agents, and editors. Agents in attendance will take pitches from writers. Paid manuscript critique programs are available.

COSTS/ACCOMMODATIONS $355-385, includes all workshops, speaking events, cocktail party, BBQ, and goodie bag with dining coupons. $75 spouse/guest registration; $50 ms evaluation; $75 extended ms evaluation. "You must register for conference to be eligible for ms evaluation."

ADDITIONAL INFORMATION Held at the Center for the Arts in Jackson, Wyoming and online.

KENTUCKY WOMEN WRITERS CONFERENCE

232 E. Maxwell St., Lexington KY 40506. (859)257-2874. **E-mail:** kentuckywomenwriters@gmail.com. **Website:** www.uky.edu/wwc/. **Contact:** Julie Wrinn, director. Conference held in second or third weekend of September. Conference duration: 2 days. Average attendance: 150-200. Conference covers all genres: poetry, fiction, creative nonfiction, playwriting. Writing workshops, panels, and readings featuring contemporary women writers. Site: Held at the University of Kentucky and several historic downtown Lexington locations, including the Carnegie Center for Literacy and Learning.

COSTS/ACCOMMODATIONS $150 for 2 days, $80 for 1 day, $30 for students. Some snacks included. Meals and accommodations are not included.

ADDITIONAL INFORMATION Sponsors prizes in poetry ($200), fiction ($200), nonfiction ($200), playwriting ($500), and spoken word ($500). Winners also invited to read during the conference. Pre-registration opens May 1.

KENYON REVIEW WRITERS WORKSHOP

Kenyon College, Gambier OH 43022. (740)427-5207. **Fax:** (740)427-5417. **E-mail:** kenyonreview@kenyon.edu; writers@kenyonreview.org. **Website:** www.kenyonreview.org. **Contact:** Anna Duke Reach, director. Annual 8-day workshop held in June. Participants apply in poetry, fiction, or creative nonfiction, and then participate in intensive daily workshops which focus on the generation and revision of significant new work. Held on the campus of Kenyon College in the rural village of Gambier, Ohio. Workshop leaders have included David Baker, Ron Carlson, Rebecca McClanahan, Meghan O'Rourke, Linda Gregorson, Dinty Moore, Tara Ison, Jane Hamilton, Lee K. Abbott, and Nancy Zafris.

COSTS/ACCOMMODATIONS The workshop operates a shuttle to and from Gambier and the airport in Columbus, Ohio. Offers overnight accommodations. Participants are housed in Kenyon College student housing. The cost is covered in the tuition. $1,995 includes tuition, room and board.

ADDITIONAL INFORMATION Application includes a writing sample. Admission decisions are made on a rolling basis. Workshop information is available online at www.kenyonreview.org/workshops in November. For brochure send e-mail, visit website, call, fax. Accepts inquiries by SASE, e-mail, phone, fax.

KUNDIMAN POETRY RETREAT

P.O. Box 4248, Sunnyside NY 11104. **E-mail:** info@kundiman.org. **Website:** www.kundiman.org. **Contact:** Sarah Gambito, executive director. "Opento Asian American poets. Renowned faculty will conduct workshops and provide one-on-one mentorship sessions with fellows. Readings and informal social gatherings will also be scheduled. Fellows selected based on sample of 6-8 poems and short essay answer. Applications should be received between December 15-February 1."

ADDITIONAL INFORMATION Additional information, guidelines, and online application available on website.

MENDOCINO COAST WRITERS CONFERENCE

(707)937-9983. **E-mail:** info@mcwc.org. **Website:** www.mcwc.org. Annual conference held in July. Average attendance: 80. Provides workshops for fiction, nonfiction, and poetry. Held at a small community college campus on the northern Pacific Coast. Workshop leaders have included Kim Addonizio, Lynne Barrett, John Dufresne, John Lescroart, Ben Percy, Luis Rodriguez, and Ellen Sussman. Agents and will be speaking and available for meetings with attendees.

COSTS/ACCOMMODATIONS Information on overnight accommodations is made available. $525+ (includes panels, meals, 2 socials with guest readers, 4 public events, 3 morning intensive workshops in 1 of 6 subjects, and a variety of afternoon panels and lectures).

ADDITIONAL INFORMATION Emphasis is on writers who are also good teachers. Brochures are online after in mid-February. Send inquiries via e-mail.

MONTEVALLO LITERARY FESTIVAL

Sta. 6420, University of Montevallo, Montevallo AL 35115. (205)665-6420. **Fax:** (205)665-6422. **E-mail:** murphyj@montevallo.edu. **Website:** www.montevallo.edu/english. **Contact:** Dr. Jim Murphy, director.

COSTS/ACCOMMODATIONS Offers overnight accommodations at Ramsay Conference Center on campus. Call (205)665-6280 for reservations. Free on-campus parking. Additional information available at www.montevallo.edu/cont_ed/ramsay.shtm.

ADDITIONAL INFORMATION To enroll in a fiction workshop, contact Bryn Chancellor (bchancellor@montevallo.edu). Information for upcoming festival available in February For brochure, visit website. Accepts inquiries by mail (with SASE), e-mail, phone, and fax. Editors participate in conference. "This is a friendly, relaxed festival dedicated to bringing literary writers and readers together on a personal scale." Poetry workshop participants submit up to 5 pages of poetry; e-mail as Word doc to Jim Murphy (murphyj@montevallo.edu) at least 2 weeks prior to festival.

JENNY MCKEAN MOORE COMMUNITY WORKSHOPS

English Department, George Washingtion University, 801 22nd St. NW, Rome Hall, Suite 760, Washington DC 20052. (202) 994-6180. **Fax:** (202) 994-7915. **E-mail:** tvmallon@gwu.edu. **Website:** www.gwu.edu/~english/creative_jennymckeanmoore.html. **Contact:** Thomas Mallon, director of creative writing. Workshop held each semester at the university. Average attendance: 15. Concentration varies depending on professor—usually fiction or poetry. The Creative Writing department brings an established poet or novelist to campus each year to teach a writing workshop for GW students and a free community workshop for adults in the larger Washington community.

ADDITIONAL INFORMATION Admission is competitive and by ms.

MOUNT HERMON CHRISTIAN WRITERS CONFERENCE

37 Conference Drive, Mount Hermon CA 95041. **E-mail:** info@mounthermon.org. **Website:** www.mounthermon.org/writers. Annual professional conference (always held over the Palm Sunday weekend, Friday noon through Tuesday noon). Average attendance: 450. Sponsored by and held at the 440-acre Mount Hermon Christian Conference Center near San Jose, California in the heart of the coastal redwoods, we are a broad-ranging conference for all areas of Christian writing, including fiction, nonfiction, fantasy, children's, teen, young adult, poetry, magazines, inspirational and devotional writing. This is a working, how-to conference, with Major Morning tracks in all genres (including a track especially for teen writers), and as many as 20 optional workshops each afternoon. Faculty-to-student ratio is about 1 to 6. The bulk of our more than 70 faculty members are editors and publisher representatives from major Christian publishing houses nationwide. Speakers have included T. Davis Bunn, Debbie Macomber, Jerry Jenkins, Bill Butterworth, Dick Foth and others.

COSTS/ACCOMMODATIONS Registrants stay in hotel-style accommodations. Meals are buffet style, with faculty joining registrants. See website Nov. 1 for cost updates. Registration fees include tuition, all major morning sessions, keynote sessions, and refreshment breaks. Room and board varies depending on choice of housing options. See website for current costs.

ADDITIONAL INFORMATION "The residential nature of our conference makes this a unique setting for one-on-one interaction with faculty/staff. There is also a decided inspirational flavor to the conference, and general sessions with well-known speakers are a highlight. Registrants may submit 2 works for critique in advance of the conference, then have personal interviews with critiquers during the conference. All conference information is online by December 1 of each year. Send inquiries via e-mail. Tapes of past conferences are also available online."

NAPA VALLEY WRITERS' CONFERENCE

Napa Valley College, 1088 College Ave., St. Helena CA 94574. (707)967-2900. **Website:** www.napawritersconf.org. **Contact:** John Leggett and Anne Evans, program directors. Established 1981. Annual week-long event. Location: Upper Valley Campus in the historic town of St. Helena, 25 miles north of Napa in the heart of the valley's wine growing community. Excellent cuisine provided by Napa Valley Cooking School. Average attendance: 48 in poetry and 48 in fiction. "Serious writers of all backgrounds and experience are welcome to apply." Offers poets workshops, lectures, faculty readings, ms critiques, and meetings with editors. "Poetry session provides the opportunity to work both on generating new poems and on revising previously written ones."

ADDITIONAL INFORMATION The conference is held at the Upper Valley Campus of Napa Valley College, located in the heart of California's Wine Country.The campus is in the historic town of St. Helena, about 25 miles north of the city of Napa, and about two hours' drive north of the San Francisco or Oakland airports.During the conference week, attendees' meals are provided by the Napa Valley Cooking School, which offers high quality, intensive training for aspiring chefs. The goal of the program is to provide each student with hands-on, quality, culinary and pastry skills required for a career in a fine-dining establishment. The disciplined and professional learning environment, availability of global externships, low student teacher ratio and focus on sustainability make the Napa Valley Cooking School unique.

PHILADELPHIA WRITERS' CONFERENCE

(215) 619-7422. **E-mail:** dresente@mc3.edu. **Website:** www.pwcwriters.org. **Contact:** Dana Resente. Annual. Conference held June 8-10 for 2012. Average attendance: 160-200. Conference covers many forms of writing: novel, short story, genre fiction, nonfiction book, magazine writing, blogging,juvenile, poetry.

COSTS/ACCOMMODATIONS Holiday Inn, Independence Mall, Fourth and Arch Streets, Philadelphia, PA 19106-2170. "Hotel offers discount for early registration." Advance registration postmarked by April 15 is $205; after April 8 and walk-in registration is $225. The banquet and buffet are $40 each. Master classes are $50.

ADDITIONAL INFORMATION Sponsors contest. "Length is generally 2,500 words for fiction or nonfiction. 1st Prize, in addition to cash and certificate, gets free tuition for following year." Also offers ms critique. Accepts inquiries by e-mail and SASE. Agents and editors attend conference. Visit us on the web for further agent and speaker details."

PIMA WRITERS' WORKSHOP

Pima College, 2202 W. Anklam Rd., Tucson AZ 85709. (520)206-6084. **Fax:** (520)206-6020. **E-mail:** mfiles@pima.edu. **Contact:** Meg Files, director. Writer conference geared toward beginner, intermediate and advanced levels. **Open to students.** The conference features presentations and writing exercises on writing and publishing stories for children and young adults, among other genres. Annual conference. Workshop held in May. 2011 dates: May 27-29. Cost: $100 (can include ms critique). Participants may attend for college credit. Meals and accommodations not included. Features a dozen authors, editors, and agents talking about writing and publishing fiction, nonfiction, poetry, and stories for children. Write for more information.

SAN DIEGO STATE UNIVERSITY WRITERS' CONFERENCE

(619)594-2517. **Fax:** (619)594-8566. **E-mail:** sdsuwritersconference@mail.sdsu.edu. **Website:** www.ces.sdsu.edu/writers. Annual conference held in January/February. Conference duration: 2 days. Average attendance: 375. Covers fiction, nonfiction, scriptwriting and e-books. Held at the Doubletree Hotel in Mission Valley. Each year the conference offers a variety of workshops for the beginner and advanced writers. This conference allows the individual writer to choose which workshop best suits his/her needs. In addition to the workshops, editor reading appointments and agent/editor consultation appointments are provided so attendees may meet with editors and agents one-on-one to discuss specific questions. A reception is offered Saturday immediately following the workshops, offering attendees the opportunity to socialize with the faculty in a relaxed atmosphere. Last year, approximately 60 faculty members attended.

COSTS/ACCOMMODATIONS Attendees must make their own travel arrangements. Approximately $365-485

SANTA BARBARA WRITERS CONFERENCE

27 W. Anapamu St., Suite 305, Santa Barbara CA 93101. (805)568-1516. **E-mail:** info@sbwriters.com. **Website:** www.sbwriters.com. Annual conference held in June. Check website for specific dates. Average attendance: 200. Coversfiction, nonfiction, journalism, memoir, poetry, playwriting, screenwriting, travel writing, young adult, children's literature, humor, and marketing.

COSTS/ACCOMMODATIONS Hyatt Santa Barbara.

ADDITIONAL INFORMATION Register online or contact for brochure and registration forms.

SASKATCHEWAN FESTIVAL OF WORDS

217 Main St. N., Moose Jaw SK S6J 0W1, Canada. **Website:** www.festivalofwords.com. Annual 4-day event, third week of July (2012 dates: July 19-22). Location: Moose Jaw Library/Art Museum complex in Crescent Park. Average attendance: about 4,000 admissions. "Canadian authors up close and personal for readers and writers of all ages in mystery, poetry, memoir, fantasy, graphic novels, history, and novel. Each summer festival includes 60 events within 2 blocks of historic Main Street. Audience favourite activities include workshops for writers, audience readings, drama, performance poetry, concerts, panels, and music.

COSTS/ACCOMMODATIONS Available at www.templegardens.sk.ca, campgrounds, and bed and breakfast establishments. Complete information about festival presenters, events, costs, and schedule available on website.

SCHOOL OF THE ARTS AT RHINELANDER UW-MADISON CONTINUING STUDIES

21 N Park St., 7th Floor, Madison WI 53715-1218. (608)263-6322. **E-mail:** soa@dcs.wisc.edu; ltarnoff@dcs.wisc.edu. **Website:** www.soawisconsin.org. "Each summer for nearly 50 years, more than 250 people have gathered in northern Wisconsin for a week of study, performance, exhibits, and other creative activities. More than 50 workshops in writing, body/mind/spirit; food and fitness; art and folk art; music; and digital media are offered. Participants can choose from any and all 1-, 2-, and 5-day classes to craft their own mix for creative exploration and renewal." 2012 dates: July 22-27. Location: James Williams Middle School, Rhinelander, WI. Average attendance: 250.

COSTS/ACCOMMODATIONS Informational available from Rhinelander Chamber of Commerce. 2012 cost: Registration costs range from $50-300. Online registration preferred.

ADDITIONAL INFORMATION Online catalog at www.soawisconsin.org. Additional information available by phone, e-mail, website.

SEWANEE WRITERS' CONFERENCE

735 University Ave., 123 Gailor Hall, Stamlor Center, Sewanee TN 37383-1000. (931) 598-1141. **Website:** www.sewaneewriters.org. **Contact:** Caki Wilkinson. Annual conference held in the second half of July. Conference duration: 12 days. Average attendance: 144. "We offer genre-based workshops in fiction, poetry, and playwriting. The conference uses the facilities of Sewanee: The University of the South. The university is a collection of ivy-covered Gothic-style buildings located on the Cumberland Plateau in mid-Tennessee. Editors, publishers, and agents structure their own presentations, but there is always opportunity for questions from the audience." A score of writing professionals will visit. The Conference will offer its customary Walter E. Dakin Fellowships and Tennessee Williams Scholarships as well as awards in memory of Stanley Elkin, Donald Justice, Howard Nemerov, Father William Ralston, Peter Taylor, Mona Van Duyn, and John N. Wall. Additional scholarships have been made possible by Georges and Anne Borchardt and Gail Hochman. Each participant—whether contributor, scholar, or fellow—receives financial support.

COSTS/ACCOMMODATIONS Participants are housed in single rooms in university dormitories. Bathrooms are shared by small groups. Motel or B&B housing is available, but not abundantly so.

STEAMBOAT SPRINGS WRITERS CONFERENCE

Steamboat Springs Arts Council, Eleanor Bliss Center for the Arts at the Depot, 1001 13th St., Steamboat Springs CO 80487. (970)879-9008. **Fax:** (970)879-8138. **E-mail:** info@steamboatwriters.com. **Website:** www.steamboatwriters.com. **Contact:** Susan de Wardt. Annual conference held in mid-July. Conference duration: 1 day. Average attendance: approximately 35. Attendance is limited. Featured areas of instruction change each year. Held at the restored train Depot. Speakers have included Carl Brandt, Jim Fergus, Avi, Robert Greer, Renate Wood, Connie Willis, Margaret Coel, and Kent Nelson.

ADDITIONAL INFORMATION Brochures are available in April for a SASE. Send inquiries via e-mail.

TAOS SUMMER WRITERS' CONFERENCE

Department of English Language and Literature, MSC 03 2170, University of New Mexico, Albuquerque NM 87131-0001. (505)277-5572. **Fax:** (505)277-2950. **E-mail:** taosconf@unm.edu. **Website:** www.unm.edu/~taosconf. **Contact:** Sharon Oard Warner. Annual conference held in July. Conference duration: 7 days. Offers workshops in novel writing, short story writing, screenwriting, poetry, creative nonfiction, travel writing, historical fiction, memoir, and revision. Participants may also schedule a consultation with a visiting agent/editor.

MARK TWAIN CREATIVE WRITERS WORKSHOPS

5101 Rockhill Rd., Kansas City MO 64110-2499. (816)235-1168. **Fax:** (816)235-2611. **E-mail:** BeasleyM@umkc.edu. **Website:** www.newletters.org/writingConferences.asp. **Contact:** Betsy Beasley, administrative associate.

COSTS/ACCOMMODATIONS Offers list of area hotels or lodging options. Fees for regular and noncredit courses.

ADDITIONAL INFORMATION Submit for workshop 6 poems/one short story prior to arrival. Conference information is available in March by SASE, e-mail or on website. Editors participate in conference.

WESLEYAN WRITERS CONFERENCE

Wesleyan University, 294 High St., Room 207, Middletown CT 06459. (860)685-3604. **Fax:** (860)685-2441. **E-mail:** agreene@wesleyan.edu. **Website:** www.wesleyan.edu/writers. Annual conference held the third week of June. Average attendance: 100. Focuses on the novel, fiction techniques, short stories, poetry, screenwriting, nonfiction, literary journalism, memoir, mixed media work and publishing. The conference is held on the campus of Wesleyan University, in the hills overlooking the Connecticut River. Features a faculty of award-winning writers, seminars and readings of new fiction, poetry, nonfiction and mixed media forms - as well as guest lectures on a range of topics including publishing. Both new and experienced writers are welcome. Participants may attend seminars in all genres. Speakers have included Esmond Harmsworth (Zachary Schuster Agency), Daniel Mandel (Sanford J. Greenburger Associaties), Dorian Karchmar, Amy Williams (ICM and Collins McCormick), Mary Sue Rucci (Simon & Schuster), Denise Roy (Simon & Schuster), John Kulka (Harvard University Press), Julie Barer (Barer Literary) and many others. Agents will be speaking and available for meetings with attendees. Participants are often successful in finding agents and publishers for their mss. Wesleyan participants are also frequently featured in the anthology *Best New American Voices*.

COSTS/ACCOMMODATIONS Meals are provided on campus. Lodging is available on campus or in town.

ADDITIONAL INFORMATION Ms critiques are available, but not required. Scholarships and teaching fellowships are available, including the Joan Jakobson Awards for fiction writers and poets; and the Jon Davidoff Scholarships for nonfiction writers and journalists. Inquire via e-mail, fax, or phone.

WESTERN RESERVE WRITERS & FREELANCE CONFERENCE

7700 Clocktower Dr., Kirtland OH 44094. (440) 525-7812. **E-mail:** deencr@aol.com. **Website:** www.deannaadams.com. **Contact:** Deanna Adams, director/conference coordinator. Biannual. Last conference held March 31, 2012. Conference duration: 1 day or half-day. Average attendance: 120. "The Western Reserve Writers Conferences are designed for all writers, aspiring and professional, and offer presentations in all genres—nonfiction, fiction, poetry, essays, creative nonfiction, and the business of writing, including Web writing and successful freelance writing." Site: "Located in the main building of Lakeland Community College, the conference is easy to find and just off the I-90 freeway. The Fall 2011 conference featured top-notch presenters from newspapers and magazines, along with published authors, and freelance writers. Presentations included developing issues in today's publishing (*Do you need an agent?*), as well as workshops on creating credible characters, the elements of mystery, romance writing and, tips on e-books and storytelling for both fiction and nonfiction writers. Included throughout the day are one-on-one editing consults, Q&A panel, and book sale/author signings."

COSTS/ACCOMMODATIONS Fall all-day conference includes lunch: $95. Spring half-day conference, no lunch: $69.

ADDITIONAL INFORMATION Brochures for the conferences are available by January (for spring conference) and July (for fall). Also accepts inquiries by e-mail and phone, or see website. Editors and agents often attend the conferences.

WINTER POETRY & PROSE GETAWAY IN CAPE MAY

(888)887-2105. **E-mail:** info@wintergetaway.com. **Website:** www.wintergetaway.com. **Contact:** Peter Murphy. Annual conference. This is not your typical writers' conference. Energize your writing with challenging and supportive workshos thpfocus on at starting new material. Advance your craft with feedback from our award-winning faculty including Pulitzer Prize & National Book Award winners. Thousands of people have enjoyed the getaway over the past 17 years, developing their craft as writers and making lifelong friends. The focus isn't on our award-winning faculty, it's on helping you improve and advance your skills."

COSTS/ACCOMMODATIONS Please see website or call for current fee information.

ADDITIONAL INFORMATION Previous faculty has included Julianna Baggott, Christian Bauman, Laure-Anne Bosselaar, Kurt Brown, Mark Doty (National Book Award Winner), Stephen Dunn (Pulitzer Prize Winner), Carol Plum-Ucci, James Richardson, Mimi Schwartz, Terese Svoboda, and more.

WRITE IT OUT

P.O. Box 704, Sarasota FL 34230-0704. (941)359-3824. **E-mail:** rmillerwio@aol.com. **Website:** www.writeitout.com. **Contact:** Ronni Miller, director. Workshops held 2-3 times/year in March, June, July and August. Conference duration: 5-10 days. Average attendance: 4-10. Workshops retreats on "expressive writing and painting, fiction, poetry, memoirs. We also offer intimate, motivational, in-depth free private conferences with instructors." Past facilitators included Arturo Vivante, novelist. Acquisitions:

COSTS/ACCOMMODATIONS 2012 fees: Italy, $1,450; Cape Cod, $675. Price includes tution, private conferences and salons. Room, board, and airfare not included.

ADDITIONAL INFORMATION "Critiques on work are given at the workshops." Conference information available year round. For brochures/guidelines e-mail, call, or visit website. Accepts inquiries by phone, e-mail. Workshops have "small groups, option to spend time writing and not attend classes, with personal appointments with instructors."

WRITERS OMI AT LEDIG HOUSE

55 Fifth Ave., 15th Floor, New York NY 10003. (212)206-6114. **E-mail:** writers@artomi.org. **Website:** www.artomi.org. Residency duration: 2 weeks to 2 months. Average attendance and site: "Up to 20 writers per session—10 at a given time—live and write on the stunning 300 acre grounds and sculpture park that overlooks the Catskill Mountains." Deadline: October 20.

COSTS/ACCOMMODATIONS Residents provide their own transportation. Offers overnight accommodations.

ADDITIONAL INFORMATION "Agents and editors from the New York publishing community are invited for dinner and discussion. Bicycles, a swimming pool, and nearby tennis court are available for use."

WRITING WORKSHOP AT CASTLE HILL

1 Depot Rd., P.O. Box 756, Truro MA 02666-0756. **E-mail:** cherie@castlehill.org. **Website:** www.castlehill.org. Poetry, Fiction, Memoir workshops geared toward intermediate and advanced levels. **Open to students.** Workshops by Keith Althaus: Poetry; Anne Bernays: Elements of Fiction; Elizabeth Bradfield: Poetry in Plein Air & Broadsides and Beyond: Poetry as Public Art; Melanie Braverman: In Pursuit of Exactitude: Poetry; Josephine Del Deo: Preoccupation in Poetry; Martin Espada: Barbaric Yamp: A Poetry Workshop; Judy Huge: Finding the Me in Memoir; Justin Kaplan: Autobiography. See website under Summer 2011 Writers for dates and more information.

THE HELENE WURLITZER FOUNDATION

P.O. Box 1891, Taos NM 87571. (575)758-2413. **Fax:** (575)758-2559. **E-mail:** hwf@taosnet.com. **Website:** www.wurlitzerfoundation.org. **Contact:** Michael A. Knight, executive director. Three-month residencies. "The Foundation's purpose is to provide a quiet haven where artists may pursue their creative endeavors without pressure to produce while they are in residence." The Foundation's purpose is to provide a quiet haven where artists may pursue their creative endeavors without pressure to produce while they are in residence.

COSTS/ACCOMMODATIONS "Provides individual housing in fully furnished studio/houses (casitas), rent and utility free. Artists are responsible for transportation to and from Taos, their meals, and the materials for their work. Bicycles are provided upon request."

ORGANIZATIONS

There are many organizations of value to poets. These groups may sponsor workshops and contests, stage readings, publish anthologies and chapbooks or spread the word about publishing opportunities. A few provide economic assistance or legal advice. The best thing organizations offer, though, is a support system to which poets can turn for a pep talk, a hard-nosed (but sympathetic) critique of a manuscript or simply the comfort of talking and sharing with others who understand the challenges, and joys, of writing poetry.

Whether national, regional or as local as your library or community center, each organization has something special to offer. The listings in this section reflect the membership opportunities available to poets with a variety of organizations. Some groups provide certain services to both members and nonmembers.

To find out more about groups in your area (including those that may not be listed in *Poet's Market*), contact your YMCA, community center, local colleges and universities, public library and bookstores (and don't forget newspapers and the Internet). If you can't find a group that suits your needs, consider starting one yourself. You might be surprised to discover there are others in your locality who would welcome the encouragement, feedback and moral support of a writer's group.

THE ACADEMY OF AMERICAN POETS

75 Maiden Lane, Suite 901, New York NY 10038. (212)274-0343. **Fax:** (212)274-9427. **E-mail:** academy@poets.org. **Website:** www.poets.org. Executive Director: Tree Swenson. Established 1934. The Academy of American Poets was founded to support the nation's poets at all stages of their careers and to foster the appreciation of contemporary poetry. Levels of membership/dues: begin at $35/year (contributing member). Administers The Walt Whitman Award; The James Laughlin Award; The Harold Morton Landon Translation Award; The Lenore Marshall Poetry Prize; The Raiziss/de Palchi Translation Award; and The Wallace Stevens Award. Also awards The Fellowship of the Academy of American Poets ($25,000 to honor distinguished poetic achievement, no applications accepted) and The University & College Poetry Prizes. Publishes American Poet, an informative semiannual journal sent to all Academy members. The Academy's other programs include National Poetry Month (April), the largest literary celebration in the world; the Poetry Audio Archive, a 700-volume audio library capturing the voices of contemporary American poets for generations to come; an annual series of poetry readings and special events; and Poets.org, which includes thousands of poems, hundreds of essays and interviews, lesson plans for teachers, a National Poetry Almanac, a national Calendar of Events, and the National Poetry Map.

ARIZONA AUTHORS ASSOCIATION

6145 West Echo Lane, Glendale AZ 85302. (623)847-9343. **E-mail:** info@azauthors.com. **Website:** www.azauthors.com. **Contact:** Toby Heathcotte, president. Purpose of organization: to offer professional, educational and social opportunities to writers and authors, and serve as a network. Members must be authors, writers working toward publication, agents, publishers, publicists, printers, illustrators, etc. Membership cost: $45/year writers; $30/year students; $60/year other professionals in publishing industry. Holds regular workshops and meetings. Publishes bimonthly newsletter and *Arizona Literary Magazine*. Sponsors Annual Literary Contest in poetry, essays, short stories, novels, and published books with cash prizes and awards bestowed at a public banquet. Winning entries are also published or advertised in the *Arizona Literary Magazine*. First and second place winners in poetry, essay and short story categories are entered in the Pushcart Prize. Winners in published categories receive free listings by www.fivestarpublications.com. Send SASE or view website for guidelines.

THE ASSOCIATION OF WRITERS & WRITING PROGRAMS (AWP)

Mail Stop 1E3, George Mason University, Fairfax VA 22030-4444. (703)993-4301. **E-mail:** services@awpwriter.org (membership contact). **Website:** www.awpwriter.org. Established 1967. Offers a variety of services for writers, teachers, and writing programs, including networking and resources, job placement assistance (helps writers find jobs in teaching, editing, and other related fields), writing contests, literary arts advocacy, and forums. Levels of membership/dues: annual individual membership is $65/year; $110 for 2 years; students who provide photocopy of valid student ID pay $40/year (all prices apply to U.S. residents only). Membership includes 6 issues of The Writer's Chronicle (containing information about grants and awards, publishing opportunities, fellowships, and writing programs); access to the online AWP Job List (employment opportunity listings for writers); access to AWP eLink, a members-only website; a 50% discount on AWP Award Series entry fees; discount on registration for annual conference; and more. The Writer's Chronicle is available by subscription only for $20/year (6 issues). The AWP Award Series for novel, poetry, fiction, and creative nonfiction includes the Donald Hall Prize for Poetry (see separate listing in Contests & Awards). Additional information available on website.

THE AUTHORS GUILD, INC.

31 E. 32nd St., 7th Floor, New York NY 10016. (212)564-5904. **Fax:** (212)564-5363. **E-mail:** staff@authorsguild.org. **Website:** www.authorsguild.org. **Contact:** Paul Aiken, executive director. Purpose of organization: to offer services and materials intended to help authors with the business and legal aspects of their work, including contract problems, copyright matters, freedom of expression and taxation. Guild has 8,000 members. Qualifications for membership: Must be book author published by an established American publisher within 7 years or any author who has had 3 works (fiction or nonfiction) published by a magazine or magazines of general circulation in the last 18 months. Associate membership also available. Annual dues: $90. Different levels of membership include: associate membership with

all rights except voting available to an author who has a firm contract offer or is currently negotiating a royalty contract from an established American publisher. "The Guild offers free contract reviews to its members. The Guild conducts several symposia each year at which experts provide information, offer advice and answer questions on subjects of interest and concern to authors. Typical subjects have been the rights of privacy and publicity, libel, wills and estates, taxation, copyright, editors and editing, the art of interviewing, standards of criticism and book reviewing. Transcripts of these symposia are published and circulated to members. The *Authors Guild Bulletin*, a quarterly journal, contains articles on matters of interest to writers, reports of Guild activities, contract surveys, advice on problem clauses in contracts, transcripts of Guild and League symposia and information on a variety of professional topics. Subscription included in the cost of the annual dues."

BOWERY POETRY CLUB

308 Bowery Street, New York NY 10012. (212)614-0505. **Fax:** (212)614-8539. **E-mail:** mail@bowerypoetry.com. **Website:** www.bowerypoetry.com. Established 2002. **Contact:** Gary Glazner. The Bowery Poetry Club and Cafe hosts regional open mic and poetry events. "Hosting between 20 and 30 shows a week, the Bowery Poetry Club (BPC) is proud of our place in the lineage of populist art: The Yiddish theater, burlesque, vaudeville, beat poetry, jazz, and punk that gave the Bowery its name." Offers workshops for adults and young poets. "Each Tuesday night at 6:30 pm touring Slam poets give a craft talk as part of our WordShop series." Nationally known writers give readings that are open to the public. Sponsors open mic readings for the public each Tuesday night at 7 pm as part of the Urbana Poetry Slam; format: open mic, featured poet, poetry slam. See website for more information and schedule.

BRIGHT HILL LITERARY CENTER

P.O. Box 193, 94 Church St., Treadwell NY 13846-0193. (607)829-5055. **Fax:** (607)829-5054. **E-mail:** wordthur@stny.rr.com. **Website:** www.brighthillpress.org. Bright Hill Literary Center serves residents in the Catskill Mountain region, greater New York, and throughout the U.S. Includes the Bright Hill Library & Internet Center, with "thousands of volumes of literary journals, literary prose and poetry, literary criticism and biography, theater, reference, art, and children's books available for reading and research (noncirculating, for the time being). Wireless Internet access is available." Sponsors workshops for children and adults. Sponsors contests/awards (Bright Hill Press book and chapbook competitions; see separate listings in Contests & Awards). Publishes 5-7 books of poetry each year.

CALIFORNIA STATE POETRY SOCIETY

CSPS/CQ, P.O. Box 7126, Orange CA 92863. **E-mail:** pearlk@covad.net. **Website:** www.californiaquarterly.blogspot.com. **Contact:** The Membership Chair. The California State Poetry Society "is dedicated to the adventure of poetry and its dissemination. Although located in California, its members are from all over the U.S. and abroad." Levels of membership/dues: $30/year. Benefits include membership in the National Federation of State Poetry Societies (NFSPS); 4 issues of California Quarterly (see separate listing in Magazines/Journals), *Newsbriefs*, and *The Poetry Letter*. Sponsors monthly and annual contests. Additional information available for SASE.

CANADIAN POETRY ASSOCIATION

331 Elmwood Dr., Suite 4-212, Moncton NB E1A 1X6, Canada. (506)204-1732. **Fax:** (506)380-1222. **E-mail:** poemata@live.ca; poemata@live.com. **Website:** www.canadianpoetryassoc.com. "We promote all aspects of the reading, writing, publishing, purchasing, and preservation of poetry in Canada. The CPA promotes the creation of local chapters to organize readings, workshops, publishing projects, and other poetry-related events in their area." Membership is open to anyone with an interest in poetry, including publishers, schools, libraries, booksellers, and other literary organizations. Levels of membership/dues: $35 CAD/year; seniors, students, and fixed income, $25 CAD; International, $45 USD. Publishes a magazine, Poemata, featuring news articles, chapter reports, poetry by new members, book reviews, markets information, announcements, and more. Membership form available for SASE or on website. Also sponsors The CPA Annual Poetry Contest, with 3 cash prizes plus up to 10 Honorable Mentions. **Open to the public.** Winning poems published in Poemata and on CPA website. **Deadline:** June 30, 2010. Guidelines available for SASE or on website. "Send in your best verse!"

CONNECTICUT POETRY SOCIETY

P.O. Box 702, Manchester CT 06040. **E-mail:** connpoetry@comcast.net. **Website:** www.ct-poetry-society.org/. Established 1978. **Contact:** Christine Beck, president. The Connecticut Poetry Society is a nonprofit organization dedicated to the promotion and enjoyment of poetry through chapter meetings, contests, and poetry-related events. Statewide organization open to non-Connecticut residents. Currently has about 175 members. Levels of membership/dues: full, $25/year; student, $10/year. Membership benefits include automatic membership in The National Federation of State Poetry Societies (NFSPS); a free copy of The Connecticut River Review, a national poetry journal published by CPS (see separate listing in Magazines/Journals); opportunity to publish in Long River Run II, a members-only poetry journal; quarterly CPS and NFSPS newsletters; annual April poetry celebration; and membership in any of 10 state chapters. Sponsors conferences and workshops. Sponsors The Connecticut River Review Annual Poetry Contest, The Brodinsky-Brodine Contest, The Winchell Contest, and The Lynn Decaro High School Competition. Members and nationally known writers give readings that are open to the public. Members meet monthly. Additional information available by SASE or on website.

COUNCIL OF LITERARY MAGAZINES AND PRESSES (CLMP)

154 Christopher St., Suite 3C, New York NY 10014. (212)741-9110. **E-mail:** info@clmp.org. **Website:** www.clmp.org. Established 1967. "Dedicated to supporting and actively promoting the field of independent literary publishing." Open to publishers who are primarily literary in nature, have published at least one issue/title prior to applying for membership, publish at least one issue/title annually on an ongoing basis, have a minimum print run of 500 per issue or title, do not charge authors a fee, are not primarily self-publishing, and do not primarily publish children's/students' work. Currently has over 500 members. Levels of membership/dues: based on publishing organization's annual budget. See website for complete member application process. Benefits include free and discounted monographs, subscription to email listserves and online databases, annual copy of The Literary Press and Magazine Directory. Additional information available by e-mail or on website.

GEORGIA POETRY SOCIETY

P.O. Box 2184, Columbia GA 31902. **E-mail:** gps@georgiapoetrysociety.org. **Website:** www.georgiapoetrysociety.org. Statewide organization open to any person who is in accord with the objectives to secure fuller public recognition of the art of poetry, stimulate an appreciation of poetry, and enhance the writing and reading of poetry. Currently has 200 members. Levels of membership/dues: Active, $30 ($40 family), fully eligible for all aspects of membership; Student, $15, does not vote or hold office, and must be full-time enrolled student through college level; Lifetime, same as Active but pays a one-time membership fee of $500, receives free anthologies each year, and pays no contest entry fees. Membership includes affiliation with NFSPS. Holds at least one workshop annually. Contests are sponsored throughout the year, some for members only. "Our contests have specific general rules, which should be followed to avoid the disappointment of disqualification. See the website for details." Publishes Georgia Poetry Society Newsletter, a quarterly, and The Reach of Song, an annual anthology devoted to contest-winning poems and member works. Each quarterly meeting (open to the public) features at least one poet of regional prominence. Also sponsors a monthly open mic at the Columbus Library (Macon Rd) in Columbus, GA (open to the public). Sponsors Poetry in the Schools project. Additional information available on website. Statewide organization open to any person who is in accord with the objectives to secure fuller public recognition of the art of poetry, stimulate an appreciation of poetry, and enhance the writing and reading of poetry. Currently has 200 members. Levels of membership/dues: Active, $30 ($40 family), fully eligible for all aspects of membership; Student, $15, does not vote or hold office, and must be full-time enrolled student through college level; Lifetime, same as Active but pays a one-time membership fee of $500, receives free anthologies each year, and pays no contest entry fees. Membership includes affiliation with NFSPS. Holds at least one workshop annually. Contests are sponsored throughout the year, some for members only. "Our contests have specific general rules, which should be followed to avoid the disappointment of disqualification. See the website for details." Publishes Georgia Poetry Society Newsletter, a quarterly, and The Reach of Song, an annual anthology devoted to contest-winning poems and member works. Each quarterly meeting (open to the public) features at least one poet of regional prominence. Also sponsors a monthly open mic at the Columbus Library (Macon Rd) in Columbus, GA (open to the public). Sponsors Poetry in the Schools project. Additional information available on website.

HAIKU SOCIETY OF AMERICA

P.O. Box 31, Nassau NY 12123. **E-mail:** hsa-9AT@comcast.net. **Website:** www.hsa-haiku.org. The Haiku Society of America is composed of haiku poets, editors, critics, publishers, and enthusiasts dedicated to "promoting the creation and appreciation of haiku and related forms (haibun, haiga, renku, senryu, sequences, and tanka) among its members and the public." Currently has over 800 members. Levels of membership/dues: $33 U.S.; $30 seniors or full-time students (in North America); $35 USD in Canada and Mexico; $45 USD for all other areas. Membership benefits include a year's subscription (3 issues in 2011) to the Society's journal, Frogpond (see separate listing in Magazines/Journals), and to the quarterly HSA Newsletter Ripples; the annual information sheet; an annual address/e-mail list of HSA members; and eligibility to submit work to the members' anthology. Administers the following annual awards: The Harold G. Henderson Awards for haiku, The Gerald Brady Awards for senryu, The Bernard Lionel Einbond Awards for renku, The Merit Book Awards, and The Nicholas Virgilio Haiku Awards for youth. For 2011, A Haibun contest is being offered as well.Guidelines available in the newsletter or on website. Meets quarterly at various locations throughout the U.S. Additional information available for SASE or on website.

THE HUDSON VALLEY WRITERS' CENTER

300 Riverside Dr., Sleepy Hollow NY 10591. (914)332-5953. **Fax:** (914)332-4825. **E-mail:** info@writerscenter.org. **Website:** www.writerscenter.org. Established 1988. **Contact:** Jerri Lynn Fields, executive director. "The Hudson Valley Writers' Center is a nonprofit organization devoted to furthering the literary arts in our region. Its mission is to promote the appreciation of literary excellence, to stimulate and nurture the creation of literary works in all sectors of the population, and to bring the diverse works of gifted poets and prose artists to the attention of the public." Open to all. Currently has 350 members. Levels of membership/dues: individual ($35/year), family ($50/year), senior/student ($25/year), and friend ($100/year and up). Offerings include public readings by established and emerging poets/writers, workshops and classes, monthly open mic nights, paid and volunteer outreach opportunities, and an annual chapbook competition with Slapering Hol Press (see separate listing in Contests & Awards). Additional information available for SASE, by fax, e-mail, or on website.

INTERNATIONAL WOMEN'S WRITING GUILD

International Women's Writing Guild, P.O. Box 810, Gracie Station, New York NY 10028. (212)737-7536. **Fax:** (212)737-9469. **E-mail:** iwwg@iwwg.org; dirhahn@iwwg.org. **Website:** www.iwwg.org. **Contact:** Hannelore Hahn, founder/executive editor. IWWG is "a network for the personal and professional empowerment of women through writing." Qualifications: Open to any woman connected to the written word regardless of professional portfolio. Membership cost: $55/65 annually. "IWWG sponsors several annual conferences a year in all areas of the U.S. The major conference is held in June of each year at Yale University in New Haven, Connecticut. It is a week-long conference attracting 350 women internationally." Also publishes a 32-page newsletter, *Network*, 4 times/year; offers dental and vision insurance at group rates, referrals to literary agents.

IOWA POETRY ASSOCIATION

2325 61st St., Des Moines IA 50322. (515)279-1106. **Website:** www.iowapoetry.com. Established 1945. **Contact:** Lucille Morgan Wilson, editor. Statewide organization open to "anyone interested in poetry, with a residence or valid address in the state of Iowa." Currently has about 425 members. Levels of membership/dues: Regular ($8/year) and Patron ($15 or more/year; "same services, but patron members contribute to cost of running the association"). Offerings include "semiannual workshops to which a poem may be sent in advance for critique; annual contest--also open to nonmembers--with no entry fee; IPA Newsletter, published 5 or 6 times/year, including a quarterly national publication listing of contest opportunities; and an annual poetry anthology, Lyrical Iowa, containing prize-winning and high-ranking poems from contest entries, available for $10 postpaid. No requirement for purchase to ensure publication." Semiannual workshops "are the only 'meetings' of the association." Additional information available for SASE or on website.

THE KENTUCKY STATE POETRY SOCIETY

E-mail: www.tcscott@cebridge.com. **Website:** www.kystatepoetrysociety.org. Established 1966. **Contact:** A. Carol Scott, president. Regional organization open to all. Member of The National Federation of State Poetry Societies (NFSPS). Currently has about 230 members. Levels of membership/dues: students ($5); adults ($20); senior adults ($15); other categories: Life; Patron; Benefactor. Offerings include association with other poets; information on contests and poetry happenings across the state and nation; annual state and national contests; national and state annual conventions with workshops, selected speakers, and open poetry readings. Sponsors workshops, contests, awards. Membership includes the quarterly KSPS Newsletter. Also includes a quarterly newsletter, Strophes, of the NFSPS; and the KSPS journal, Pegasus, published 3 times/year: a Spring/ Summer and Fall/Winter issue which solicits good poetry for publication (need not be a member to submit), and a Prize Poems issue of 1st Place contest winners in over 30 categories. Members or nationally known writers give readings that are open to the public. Members meet annually. Membership information available by e-mail or on website.

THE LOFT LITERARY CENTER

Suite 200, Open Book, 1011 Washington Ave. S, Minneapolis MN 55414. (612)215-2575. **E-mail:** loft@loft.org. **Website:** www.loft.org. "The Loft is the largest and most comprehensive literary center in the country, serving both writers and readers with a variety of readings, Spoken Word performances, educational programs, contests and grants, and writing facilities." Supporting members (starting at $60/year - $25 for students/low income) receive benefits including discounted tuition, admission charges, and contest fees; check-out privileges at The Loft's Rachel Anne Gaschott Resource Library; rental access to the Book Club Meeting Room and writers' studios and more. Information on additional benefit levels, classes/workshops, contests and grants, and readings by local and national writers available at the website.

MASSACHUSETTS STATE POETRY SOCIETY

64 Harrison Ave., Lynn MA 01905. **E-mail:** msps.jcmaes@comcast.net. **Website:** http://mastatepoetrysociety.tripod.com/. Dedicated to the writing and appreciation of poetry and promoting the art form. Statewide organization open to anyone with an interest in poetry. Currently has 200 members. Levels of membership/dues: $15/year. Member benefits include subscription to Bay State Echo, published 5 times/year with members' news and announcements; members-only contests; round-robin critique groups; members-only annual anthology; workshops at society meetings; and automatic membership in National Federation of State Poetry Societies (NFSPS). Sponsors contests open to all poets. Guidelines available for SASE or on website. Members or nationally known writers give readings that are open to the public. Sponsors open mic readings for members and the public for National Poetry Day. Members meet 5 times/year. Additional information available for SASE or on website.

MISSISSIPPI POETRY SOCIETY, INC.

608 N. Pearl St., Luka MS 38852-2223. **E-mail:** poet@vol.com. **Website:** www.mississippipoetrysociety.org. Established 1932. **Contact:** Dr. Emory D. Jones, state president. ("This changes annually when new officers are installed.") Purpose is "to foster interest in the writing of poetry through a study of poetry and poetic form; to provide an opportunity for, and give recognition to, individual creative efforts relating to poetry; and to create an audience for poetry; and suggest or otherwise make known markets and contests for poetry to its members." Statewide organization, affiliated with the National Federation of State Poetry Societies (NFSPS), consisting of 3 branches open to "anyone who writes poetry or is interested in fostering the interests of poetry." Currently has 100 members. Levels of membership/dues: Regular (in-state members, $25; 2 members in same household, $45); At-Large (out-of-state members, $15); Student (elementary school through college undergraduate, $10). Offerings include monthly meetings, annual contests, an annual awards banquet, and opportunities to have poems critiqued in sessions at state and branch meetings. State also holds a one-day Mini-Festival in the fall and an annual 2-day Spring Festival; includes noted speakers and contests. Publishes bimonthly newsletter Magnolia Muse (members who win places in contests are published in The Mississippi Poetry Journal ; student winners are published in Fledglings). Branches publish newsletters and/or journals periodically. "The state organization publishes journals of all winning poems each year, and often of other special contests." Members give readings that are open to the public. Members meet at various times (North, South, and Central Branches may meet monthly, bimonthly, or quarterly; state organization meets in the fall and spring). Additional information available for SASE, by e-mail, or on website.

NATIONAL FEDERATION OF STATE POETRY SOCIETIES (NFSPS)

Website: www.nfsps.org. Established 1959. "NFSPS is a nonprofit organization exclusively educational and literary. Its purpose is to recognize the importance of poetry with respect to national cultural heritage. It is dedicated solely to the furtherance of poetry on the national level and serves to unite poets in the bonds of fellowship and understanding." Currently has 7,000 members. Any poetry group located in a state not already affiliated, but interested in affiliating, with NFSPS may contact the membership chairman (see website). In a state where no valid group exists, help may also be obtained by individuals interested in organizing a poetry group for affiliation. Most reputable state poetry societies are members of the National Federation and advertise their various poetry contests through the NFSPS quarterly newsletter Strophes (sample copy available for SASE and $1), edited by Caroline Walton, 6176 W. Pinedale Circle, Crystal River, FL 34429 (e-mail: carowalton@tampabay.rr.com). **Beware of organizations calling themselves state poetry societies (however named) that are not members of NFSPS, as such labels are sometimes used by vanity schemes trying to sound respectable.** NFSPS holds an annual 3-day convention in a different state each year with workshops, an awards banquet, and addresses by nationally known poets. Sponsors an annual 50-category national contest. Additional information available by e-mail or on website.

NATIONAL WRITERS ASSOCIATION

10904 S. Parker Rd., #508, Parker CO 80138. (303)841-0246. **Fax:** (303)841-2607. **E-mail:** natlwritersassn@hotmail.com. **Website:** www.nationalwriters.com. Purpose of organization: association for freelance writers. Qualifications for membership: associate membership--must be serious about writing; professional membership--must be published and paid writer (cite credentials). Membership cost: $65 associate; $85 professional; $35 student. Sponsors workshops/conferences: TV/screenwriting workshops, NWAF Annual Conferences, Literary Clearinghouse, editing and critiquing services, local chapters, National Writer's School. Open to non-members. Publishes industry news of interest to freelance writers; how-to articles; market information; member news and networking opportunities. Nonmember subscription: $20. Sponsors poetry contest; short story contest; article contest; novel contest. Awards cash for top 3 winners; books and/or certificates for other winners; honorable mention certificate places 5-10. Contests open to nonmembers.

NATIONAL WRITERS UNION

256 W. 38th St., Suite 703, New York NY 10018. (212)254-0279. **Fax:** (212)-254-0673. **E-mail:** nwu@nwu.org. **Website:** www.nwu.org. Purpose of organization: Advocacy for freelance writers. Qualifications for membership: "Membership in the NWU is open to all qualified writers, and no one shall be barred or in any manner prejudiced within the Union on account of race, age, sex, sexual orientation, disability, national origin, religion or ideology. You are eligible for membership if you have published a book, a play, three articles, five poems, one short story or an equivalent amount of newsletter, publicity, technical, commercial, government or institutional copy. You are also eligible for membership if you have written an equal amount of unpublished material and you are actively writing and attempting to publish your work" Membership cost: annual writing income less than $5,000-$120/year; $5,001-15,000-$195; $15,001-30,000-$265/year; $30,001-$45,000-$315 a year; $45,001- and up -$340/year. Holds workshops throughout the country. Members only section on website offers rich resources for freelance writers. Skilled contract advice and grievance help for members.

NEVADA POETRY SOCIETY

P.O. Box 7014, Reno NV 89510. (775)322-3619. Established 1976. **Contact:** Sam Wood, president. Statewide organization. Currently has 30 members. Levels of membership/dues: Active and Emeritus ($10). Offerings include membership in the National Federation of State Poetry Societies (NFSPS), which includes a subscription to their publication, Strophes ; monthly challenges followed by critiquing of all new poems; lessons on types of poetry. Members of the society are occasionally called upon to read to organizations or in public meetings. Members meet monthly. Additional information available for SASE. "We advise poets to enter their poems in contests before thinking about publication."

NEW HAMPSHIRE WRITERS' PROJECT

2500 North River Rd., Manchester NH 03106. (603)314-7980. **Fax:** (603)314-7981. **E-mail:** info@nhwritersproject.org. **Website:** www.nhwritersproject.org. **Contact:** Kathy Wurtz, Exec. Director. Statewide organization open to writers at all levels in all genres. Currently has 600+ members. Levels of membership/dues: $55/year; $25/year for seniors and students. Offerings include workshops, seminars, an annual conference, and a literary calendar. Sponsors daylong workshops and 4- to 6-week intensive courses. Also sponsors the biennial New Hampshire Literary Awards for outstanding literary achievement (including The Jane Kenyon Award for Outstanding Book of Poetry). Publishes *NH Writer*, a quarterly newsletter for and about New Hampshire writers. Members and nationally known writers give readings that are open to the public. Additional information available by fax, e-mail, or on website.

NEW YORK CENTER FOR INDEPENDENT PUBLISHING

The General Society of Mechanics & Tradesmen, 20 W. 44th, New York NY 10036. (212)764-7021. **Fax:** (212)840-2046. **E-mail:** info@smallpress.org. **Website:** http://nycip.org. Established 1984. "The Small Press Center is a nonprofit educational program and resource center for independent publishing, as well as a membership organization of independent and small press publishers and their enthusiasts." National organization open to "any person, company, or organization that supports the small press." Levels of membership/dues: Friends Membership ($50 Individual, $75 Dual/Family, $100 Contributing Friends, $250 Literary Benefactors, $300 Corporate Sponsors, $500 Patrons); Publisher Membership ($75 for one year; $100 for 2 years). Membership benefits include the quarterly Small Press Center Newsletter ; discounts on workshops, lectures, and audiotapes; invitations to readings and special events; and discount on Books on Writing & Publishing: A Bibliography in Progress, with 1,700 listings (additional or unique benefits available according to membership type and level). Sponsors the Small Press Book Fair in March and the New York Round Table Writers' Conference (www.writersconferencenyc.org) in April. Offers "a place in which the public may examine and order the books of independent publishers, free from commercial pressures. The Center is open five days a week." Additional information available for SASE, by fax, e-mail, or on website.

THE NORTH CAROLINA POETRY SOCIETY

NCPS, 3814 Hulon Dr., Durham NC 27705. **E-mail:** caren@windstream.net. **Website:** www.ncpoetrysociety.org. The North Carolina Poetry Society holds poetry-related contests and gives away several awards each year, for both Adults and Students (which includes 3rd Graders all the way to University Undergraduates). Contact through website: www.ncpoetrysociety.org or mail to: NCPS, 3814 Hulon Drive, Durham, NC 27705. Include SASE for reply. Established 1932. Statewide organization open to non-NC residents. Purpose: to encourage the reading, writing, study, and publication of poetry. NCPS brings poets together in meetings that feature workshops, presentations by noted poets and publishers, book and contest awards, and an annual anthology of award-winning poems. Currently has 350 members from NC and beyond. Levels of membership: Adult ($25/year) and Student ($10/year). NCPS conducts 6 general meetings and numerous statewide workshops/events each year. Sponsors annual Poetry Contest with categories for adults and students. Contests are open to anyone, with small fee for nonmembers. **Deadline** in January (verify date via Website or mail.) Winning poems are published in *Pinesong*, NCPS's annual anthology. A free copy is given to all winners, who are also invited to read at Awards Day. NCPS also sponsors the annual Brockman-Campbell Book Award for a book of poetry over 20 pages by a North Carolina poet (native-born or current resident for 3 years. Prize: $200 and a reading. Entry fee: none for members, $10 for nonmembers. Deadline: May 1.) NCPS also cosponsors the Gilbert-Chappell Distinguished Poet Series with The North Carolina Center for the Book, for the purpose of mentoring young poets across the state. Please visit NCPS's Website for more information or to see additional benefits offered to members. The North Carolina Poetry Society holds poetry-related contests and gives away several awards each year, for both Adults and Students (which includes 3rd Graders all the way to University Undergraduates).

NORTH CAROLINA WRITERS' NETWORK

P.O. Box 21591, Winston-Salem NC 27120. (336)293-8844. **E-mail:** mail@ncwriters.org. **Website:** www.ncwriters.org. Supports the work of writers, writers' organizations, independent bookstores, little magazines and small presses, and literary programming statewide. Currently has 1,000 members. Levels of membership/dues: $75/year; seniors/students, $55/year. Membership benefits include The Writers' Network News, a 24-page quarterly newsletter containing organizational news, trend in writing and publishing, and other literary material of interest to writers; and access to the NCWN online resources, other writers, workshops, writer's residencies, conferences, readings and competitions, and NCWN's critiquing and editing service. Annual fall conference features nationally known writers, publishers, and editors, held in a different North Carolina location each November. Sponsors competitions in short fiction, nonfiction, and poetry for North Carolina residents and NCWN members. Guidelines available for SASE or on website.

OHIO POETRY ASSOCIATION

5580 Beverly Hills Dr., Apt B, Columbus OH 43213. (740)694-5013. **E-mail:** david@ohiopoetryassn.org. **Website:** www.ohiopoetryassn.com. Established in 1929 as Verse Writers' Guild of Ohio. **Contact:** Bob Casey, president. Promotes the art of poetry, and furthers the support of poets and others who support poetry. Statewide membership with additional members in several other states, Japan, and England. Affiliated with the National Federation of State Poetry Societies (NFSPS). Open to poets and writers of all ages and ability, as well as to non-writing lovers of poetry. Currently has about 215 members. Levels of membership/dues: Regular ($18); Student (including college undergrads, $8); Associate ($8); Senior ($15); Life; and Honorary. Member benefits include regular contests; meeting/workshop participation; assistance with writing projects; networking; twice-yearly magazine, Common Threads (see separate listing in Magazines/Journals), publishing only poems by members; quarterly Ohio Poetry Association Newsletter ; quarterly NFSPS newsletters (Strophes); automatic NFSPS membership; and contest information and lower entry fees for NFSPS contests. Members are automatically on the mailing list for Ohio Poetry Day contest guidelines (OPA financially supports Ohio Poetry Day; see separate listing in Contests & Awards). Individual chapters regularly host workshops and seminars. Members and nationally known writers give readings that are open to the public (at quarterly meetings; public is invited). Sponsors open mic readings for members and the public. Past readers have included Lisa Martinovic, David Shevin, Michael Bugeja, David Citino, and Danika Dinsmore. Members meet quarterly (September, December, March, May). Additional information available by e-mail or on website. "In short, OPA provides poets with opportunities to share info, critique, publish, sponsor contests, and just socialize."

PEN AMERICAN CENTER

588 Broadway, Suite 303, New York NY 10012. (212)334-1660. **Fax:** (212)334-2181. **E-mail:** pen@pen.org. **Website:** www.pen.org. Purpose of organization: "An association of writers working to advance literature, to defend free expression, and to foster international literary fellowship." Qualifications for membership: "The standard qualification for a writer to become a member of PEN is publication of two or more books of a literary character, or one book generally acclaimed to be of exceptional distinction. Also eligible for membership: editors who have demonstrated commitment to excellence in their profession (usually construed as five years' service in book editing); translators who have published at least two book-length literary translations; playwrights whose works have been produced professionally; and literary essayists whose publications are extensive even if they have not yet been issued as a book. Candidates for membership may be nominated by a PEN member or they may nominate themselves with the support of two references from the literary community or from a current PEN member. Membership dues are $100 per year and many PEN members contribute their time by serving on committees, conducting campaigns and writing letters in connection with freedom-of-expression cases, contributing to the PEN journal, participating in PEN public events, helping to bring literature into underserved communities, and judging PEN literary awards. PEN members receive a subscription to the PEN journal, the PEN Annual Report, and have access to medical insurance at group rates. Members living in the New York metropolitan and tri-state area, or near the Branches, are invited to PEN events throughout the year. Membership in PEN American Center includes reciprocal privileges in PEN American Center branches and in foreign PEN Centers for those traveling abroad. Application forms are available on the Web at www.pen.org. Associate Membership is open to everyone who supports PEN's mission, and your annual dues ($40; $20 for students) provides crucial support to PEN's programs. When you join as an Associate Member, not only will you receive a subscription to the *PEN Journal* http://pen.org/page.php/prmID/150 and notices of all PEN events but you are also invited to participate in the work of PEN. PEN

American Center is the largest of the 141 centers of PEN International, the world's oldest human rights organization and the oldest international literary organization. PEN International was founded in 1921 to dispel national, ethnic, and racial hatreds and to promote understanding among all countries. PEN American Center, founded a year later, works to advance literature, to defend free expression, and to foster international literary fellowship. The Center has a membership of 3,400 distinguished writers, editors, and translators. In addition to defending writers in prison or in danger of imprisonment for their work, PEN American Center sponsors public literary programs and forums on current issues, sends prominent authors to inner-city schools to encourage reading and writing, administers literary prizes, promotes international literature that might otherwise go unread in the United States, and offers grants and loans to writers facing financial or medical emergencies. In carrying out this work, PEN American Center builds upon the achievements of such dedicated past members as W.H. Auden, James Baldwin, Willa Cather, Robert Frost, Langston Hughes, Thomas Mann, Arthur Miller, Marianne Moore, Susan Sontag, and John Steinbeck. The Children's Book Authors' Committee sponsors annual public events focusing on the art of writing for children and young adults and on the diversity of literature for juvenile readers. The PEN/Phyllis Naylor Working Writer Fellowship was established in 2001 to assist a North American author of fiction for children or young adults (**E-mail:** awards@pen.org). Visit www.pen.org for complete information. Sponsors several competitions per year. Monetary awards range from $2,000-35,000.

THE POETRY FOUNDATION

444 N. Michigan Ave., Suite 1850, Chicago IL 60611-4034. (312)787-7070. **Fax:** (312)787-6650. **E-mail:** mail@poetryfoundation.org. **Website:** http://poetryfoundation.org. "The Poetry Foundation is an independent literary organization committed to a vigorous presence for poetry in our culture. It exists to discover and celebrate the best poetry and to place it before the largest possible audience. Initiatives include publishing Poetry magazine (see separate listing in Magazines/Journals); distributing Ted Kooser's *American Life in Poetry* newspaper project; funding and promotion of Poetry Out Loud: National Recitation Contest (in partnership with the National Endowment for the Arts and state arts associations); *Poetry Everywhere*, a series of short poetry films airing on public television and on transportation systems across the country; *The Essential American Poets* podcast series featuring seminal recordings of major American Poets reading from their work, as selected by former Poet Laureate Donald Hall; and www.poetryfoundation.org, an award-winning comprehensive online resource for poetry featuring an archive of more than 6,500 poems by more than 600 classic and contemporary poets. The site also includes the poetry blog "Harriet," poetry-related articles, a bestseller list, video programming, a series of poetry podcasts, and reading guides about poets and poetry. The Poetry Foundation annually awards the Ruth Lilly Poetry Prize, of $100,000, and the Ruth Lilly Poetry Fellowships, 5 annual awards of $15,000 to young poets to support their further studies in poetry. In 2004 the Foundation established a family of prizes called the Pegasus Awards to honor under-recognized poets and types of poetry (The Neglected Masters Award, The Emily Dickinson First Book Award, The Mark Twain Poetry Award, The Randall Jarrell Award in Criticism, The Children's Poet Laureate, and The Verse Drama Award). Additional information available on website. "

POETRY LIBRARY

The Saison Poetry Library, Royal Festival Hall, London SE1 8XX, England. (44)(207)921-0943/0664. **Fax:** (44)(207)921-0607. **E-mail:** info@poetrylibrary.org.uk. **Website:** www.poetrylibrary.org.uk. **Contact:** Chris McCabe and Miriam Valencia, assistant librarians. A "free public library of modern poetry. It contains a comprehensive collection of all British poetry published since 1912 and an international collection of poetry from all over the world, either written in or translated into English. As the United Kingdom's national library for poetry, it offers loan and information services and a large collection of poetry magazines, cassettes, compact discs, videos, records, poem posters, and cards; also press cuttings and photographs of poets."

POETRY SOCIETY OF AMERICA

15 Gramercy Park, New York NY 10003. (212)254-9628. **Website:** www.poetrysociety.org. Established 1910. Executive Director: Alice Quinn. The Poetry Society of America is a national nonprofit organization for poets and lovers of poetry. Levels of membership/dues: Student ($25); Member ($45); Supporter ($65);

Sustainer ($100); Patron ($250); Benefactor ($500); and Angel ($1,000). All paid members receive Crossroads: The Journal of the Poetry Society of America ; additional benefits available as membership levels increase. Sponsors readings and lectures as well as the Poetry in Motion program. Provides free-to-join PSA electronic mailing list for news of upcoming events. PSA also sponsors a number of competitions for members and nonmembers.

POETRY SOCIETY OF NEW HAMPSHIRE

31 Reservoir, Farmington NH 03835. (603)332-0732. **E-mail:** poetrysocietyofnh@gmail.com. **Website:** www.poetrysocietyofnewhampshire.org. A statewide organization for anyone interested in poetry. Currently has 200 members. Levels of membership/dues: Junior ($10); Regular ($20). Offerings include annual subscription to quarterly magazine, The Poet's Touchstone ; critiques, contests, and workshops; public readings; and quarterly meetings with featured poets. The Poet's Touchstone is available to nonmembers for $6 (single issue). Members and nationally known writers give readings that are open to the public. Sponsors open mic readings for members and the public. Additional information available for SASE or by e-mail. "We do sponsor a national contest four times a year with $100, $50, and $25 prizes paid out in each one. People from all over the country enter and win."

THE POETRY SOCIETY OF SOUTH CAROLINA

P.O. Box 1090, Charleston SC 29402. **E-mail:** flatbluesky@hotmail.com. **Website:** www.poetrysocietysc.org. The Poetry Society of South Carolina supports "the reading, writing, study, and enjoyment of poetry." Statewide organization open to anyone interested in poetry. Offers programs in Charleston that are free and open to the public September-May (except for members-only holiday party in December). Currently has 150 members. Levels of membership/dues: $15 student, $25 individual, $35 family, $50 patron, and $100 business or sponsor. Membership year runs July 1-June 30. Membership benefits include discounts to PSSC-sponsored seminars and workshops held in various SC locations; a copy of the annual Yearbook of contest-winning poems; eligibility to read at the open mic and to enter contests without a fee; and an invitation to the annual holiday party. Sponsors a monthly Writers' Group, a January open mic reading featuring PSSC members, a Charleston Poetry Walk during Piccolo Spoleto in June, and a May Forum leading to an audience-selected poetry prize. Sponsors two yearly contests, totaling 20-25 contest categories, some with themes; some are open to all poets, others open only to SC residents or PSSC members. Guidelines available on website. **Deadline:** November 15 (Fall round) and February 15 (Spring round). Also offers the Skylark Prize, a competition for SC high school students. Sometimes offers a chapbook competition. Members and nationally known writers give readings that are open to the public. Poets have included Billy Collins, Henry Taylor, Cathy Smith Bowers, and Richard Garcia, as well as emerging poets from the region. Additional information available by e-mail or on website.

POETRY SOCIETY OF TENNESSEE

18 S. Rembert, Memphis TN 38104. **E-mail:** RSTRpoet@cs.com. **Website:** www.tpstn.org. **Contact:** Russell H. Strauss. Purpose is "to promote writing, reading, and appreciation of poetry among members of the society and the community; to improve poetry writing skills of members and local students. State poetry society, with some out-of-state members. Affiliate of National Federation of State Poetry Societies (NFSPS). Current membership about 70. Dues $20 a year for adults, $25 to include the yearbook (Tennessee Voices); $8 for students, including yearbook. Yearbook contains names, addresses, e-mail addresses of officers and members; winning poems by members and student members; and more. Society activities include programs with speakers; poetry contests, readings, and workshops; one meeting a year dedicated to students; plus Mid-South Poetry Festival first Saturday in October with workshop and prizes. Poetry readings about four times a year in local restaurants and bookstores. Regular meetings at 2 p.m. on first Saturday of each month (September-May) in basement of Evergreen Presbyterian Church across from Rhodes College (Parkway at College St.). No meetings in summer months. Newsletter Tennessee Voices Bulletin) every 2 months to members or for SASE.

THE POETRY SOCIETY OF TEXAS

610 Circle View Dr., Dallas TX 75248. (817)477-1754. **E-mail:** jlstrother@sbcglobal.net. **Website:** www.poetrysocietyoftexas.org. "The purpose of the society shall be to secure fuller public recognition of the art of poetry, to encourage the writing of poetry by Texans,

and to kindle a finer and more intelligent appreciation of poetry, especially the work of living poets who interpret the spirit and heritage of Texas." Poetry Society of Texas is a member of the National Federation of State Poetry Societies (NFSPS). Has 25 chapters in cities throughout the state. Currently has 300 members. Levels of membership/dues: Active ($25) for native Texans, Citizens of Texas, or former Citizens of Texas who were active members; Associate ($25) for all who desire to affiliate; also Student ($12.50); Sustaining; Benefactors; and Patrons of the Poets. Offerings include annual contests with prizes in excess of $5,000 as well as monthly contests (general and humorous); 8 monthly meetings; annual awards banquet; annual summer conference in a different location each year; round-robin critiquing opportunities sponsored at the state level; and Poetry in Schools with contests at state and local chapter levels. "Our monthly state meetings are held at the Preston Royal Branch of the Dallas Public Library. Our annual awards banquet is held at the Crown Plaza Suites in Dallas. Our summer conference is held at a site chosen by the hosting chapter. Chapters determine their meeting sites." PST publishes A Book of the Year, which presents annual and monthly award-winning poems, coming contest descriptions, minutes of meetings, by-laws of the society, history, and information. Also publishes the Poetry Society of Texas Bulletin, a monthly newsletter that features statewide news documenting contest winners, state meeting information, chapter and individual infor! mation, news from the NFSPS, and announcements of coming activities and offerings for poets. "A Book of the Year is available to nonmembers for $8." Members and nationally known writers give readings. "All of our meetings are open to the public." Additional information available for SASE, by e-mail, or on website.

POETS & WRITERS, INC.

90 Broad St., Suite 2100, New York NY 10004. (212)226-3586. **Website:** www.pw.org. Established 1970. Poets & Writers' mission is "to foster the professional development of poets and writers, to promote communication throughout the U.S. literary community, and to help create an environment in which literature can be appreciated by the widest possible public." The largest nonprofit literary organization in the nation, P&W offers information, support, resources, and exposure to poets, fiction writers, and nonfiction writers at all stages in their careers. Sponsors the Readings/Workshops Program, through which P&W sponsors more than 1,700 literary events in New York, California, and other cities in the U.S. Publishes the online Directory of American Poets and Writers with a searchable database of over 7,000 writers; Poets & Writers Magazine (print); and Poets & Writers Online, which offers topical information, the Speakeasy Message Forum (a central meeting place for writers), and links to over 1,500 websites of interest to writers. Sponsors the Writers Exchange Contest (emerging poets and fiction writers are introduced to literary communities outside their home states); the Jacobson Poetry Prize ($50,000 award for an early to mid-career poet; no nominations accepted); the Barnes & Noble Writers for Writers Award; and the Amy Award (see separate listing in Contests & Awards).

POETS HOUSE

10 River Terrace, New York NY 10282. (212)431-7920. **Fax:** (212)431-8131. **E-mail:** info@poetshouse.org. **Website:** www.poetshouse.org. Poets House, a national poetry library and literary center, is a "home for all who read and write poetry." Levels of membership/dues: begin at $50/year; along with other graduated benefits, each new or renewing member receives free admission to all regularly scheduled programs. Resources include the 50,000-volume poetry collection, conference room, exhibition space, a programming hall, and a Children's Room. Over 200 annual public programs include panel discussions and lectures, readings, seminars and workshops, and children's events. In addition, Poets House continues its collaboration with public library systems, Poetry in The Branches, a multi-faceted program model to help libraries nationwide create a complete environment for poetry locally (see website for information). Finally, each year Poets House hosts the Poets House Showcase, a comprehensive exhibit of the year's new poetry releases from commercial, university, and independent presses across the country. (**Note: Poets House is not a publisher.**) Copies of new titles become part of the library collection, and comprehensive listings for each of the books are added to Directory of American Poetry Books, a free, searchable online database featuring over 50,000 poetry titles published 1996-2007. "Poets House depends, in part, on tax-deductible contributions of its nationwide members." Additional information available by fax, e-mail, or on website.

SCIENCE FICTION POETRY ASSOCIATION

PO Box 4846, Covina CA 91723. **E-mail:** SFPATreasurer@gmail.com. **Website:** www.sfpoetry.com. **Contact:** Samantha Henderson, treasurer. The Science Fiction Poetry Association was founded "to bring together poets and readers interested in science fiction poetry (poetry with some element of speculation, usually science fiction, fantasy, or horror)." Levels of membership/dues: $21 USD (U.S., Canada, Mexico) for one-year memberships/renewals; $25 USD for overseas. Membership benefits include 6 issues/year of Star*Line (see separate listing in Magazines/Journals), a journal filled with poetry, reviews, articles, and more; one issue of the annual Rhysling Anthology of the best science fiction poetry of the previous year; opportunity to nominate one short poem and one long poem to be printed in the anthology, and to vote for which poems should receive that year's Rhysling award; half-priced advertising on the SFPA website, with greater subject matter leeway than nonmembers; eligibility to vote for SFPA officers (or run for officer); mailings with the latest news. Additional information available on website.

UNIVERSITY OF ARIZONA POETRY CENTER

1508 E. Helen St., P.O. Box 210129, Tucson AZ 85721. (520)626-3765. **E-mail:** poetry@email.arizona.edu. **Website:** www.poetrycenter.arizona.edu. **Contact:** Gail Browne, Exec. Director. 1508 E. Helen St., P.O. Box 210150, Tucson AZ 85721. (520)626-3765. **Fax:** (520)621-5566. **E-mail:** poetry@u.arizona.edu. **Website:** www.poetrycenter.arizona.edu. **Contact:** Gail Browne, executive director. Established 1960. "Open to the public, the University of Arizona Poetry Center is a contemporary poetry archive and a nationally acclaimed poetry collection that includes over 70,000 items. Programs and services include a library with a noncirculating poetry collection and space for small classes; online lesson plan library; High School Bilingual Corrido Contest; K-16 field trip program; summer camps; poetry-related meetings and activities; facilities, research support, and referral information about poetry and poets for local and national communities; Reading Series; community creative writing classes and workshops; a summer residency offered each year to two writers (one prose, one poetry) selected by jury; and poetry awards, readings, and special events for high school, undergraduate, and graduate students. Additional information available by phone, e-mail, or website. Become a 'Friend of the Poetry Center' by making an annual contribution."

WASHINGTON POETS ASSOCIATION

Website: www.washingtonpoets.org. Established 1971. **Contact:** president. The Washington Poets Association seeks to "serve and inspire individuals and communities across the state by supporting the creation, presentation, and appreciation of poetry through events, publications, recognition, and education." Regional organization open to poets and fans of poetry. Currently has 380 members. Levels of membership/dues: $20/year. Membership benefits include e-newsletter; discounted admission to events; ability to submit to Cascade Journal (plus one free copy and discounts on the purchase of additional copies); and advance notification of contests, events, readings, and publishing opportunities. Sponsors conferences/workshops and poetry festivals. Also sponsors On the Road poetry workshops for underserved areas in Washington state. Sponsors the Washington Poets Association Annual Poetry Contest (see separate listing in Contests & Awards). Publishes quarterly newsletter, Word! ; available to nonmembers free on website. Members and nationally known writers give readings that are open to the public. Sponsors open mic readings for the public "scheduled weekly, monthly, and quarterly at venues across the state." Additional information available on website.

WISCONSIN FELLOWSHIP OF POETS

2105 E. Lake Bluff Blvd., Shorewood WI 53211. **E-mail:** nevers@wisc.edu. **Website:** www.wfop.org. President: Lester Smith. Statewide organization open to residents and former residents of Wisconsin who are interested in the aims and endeavors of the organization. Currently has 485 members. Levels of membership/dues: Active ($25); Student ($12.50). Sponsors biannual conferences, workshops, contests and awards. Publishes Wisconsin Poets' Calendar, poems of Wisconsin (resident) poets. Also publishes Museletter, a quarterly newsletter. Members or nationally known writers give readings that are open to the public. Sponsors open mic readings. Additional information available for SASE to WFOP membership chair at the above address, by e-mail, or on website.

THE WRITER'S CENTER

4508 Walsh St., Bethesda MD 20815. (301)654-8664. **Fax:** (801)730-6233. **E-mail:** postmaster@writer.org. **Website:** www.writer.org. Established 1976. **Contact:** Gregory Robison, executive director. Voluntary, membership organization open to all skill levels. "The Writer's Center is a nonprofit community of writers supporting each other in the creation and marketing of literary texts." Levels of membership/dues: $40/year individual; $25/year full-time student; $50/year family. Annually conducts hundreds of workshops; hosts literary events, readings, and conferences; publishes Writer's Carousel, a quarterly magazine of articles and writing news for members. Also publishes Poet Lore, America's oldest poetry journal (see separate listing in Magazines/Journals). Additional information available by e-mail or on website.

WRITERS' FEDERATION OF NOVA SCOTIA

1113 Marginal Rd., Halifax NS B3H 4P7, Canada. (902)423-8116. **Fax:** (902)422-0881. **E-mail:** talk@writers.ns.ca. **Website:** www.writers.ns.ca. Purpose of organization: "to foster creative writing and the profession of writing in Nova Scotia; to provide advice and assistance to writers at all stages of their careers; and to encourage greater public recognition of Nova Scotian writers and their achievements." Regional organization open to anybody who writes. Currently has 800+ members. Levels of membership/dues: $45 CAD annually ($20 CAD students). Offerings include resource library with over 2,500 titles, promotional services, workshop series, annual festivals, mentorship program. Publishes *Eastword*, a bimonthly newsletter containing "a plethora of information on who's doing what; markets and contests; and current writing events and issues." Members and nationally known writers give readings that are open to the public. Additional information available on website.

WRITERS GUILD OF ALBERTA

11759 Groat Rd., Edmonton AB T5M 3K6, Canada. (780)422-8174. **Fax:** (780)422-2663. **E-mail:** mail@writersguild.ab.ca. **Website:** www.writersguild.ab.ca. Purpose of organization: to support, encourage and promote writers and writing, to safeguard the freedom to write and to read, and to advocate for the well-being of writers in Alberta. Currently has over 1,000 members. Offerings include retreats/conferences; monthly events; bimonthly magazine that includes articles on writing and a market section; weekly electronic bulletin with markets and event listings; and the Stephan G. Stephansson Award for Poetry (Alberta residents only). Membership cost: $60/year; $30 for seniors/students. Holds workshops/conferences. Publishes a newsletter focusing on markets, competitions, contemporary issues related to the literary arts (writing, publishing, censorship, royalties etc.). Sponsors annual Literary Awards in five categories (novel, nonfiction, children's literature, poetry, drama). Awards include $1,500, leather-bound book, promotion and publicity. Open to nonmembers.

POETS IN EDUCATION

Whether known as PITS (Poets in the Schools), WITS (Writers in the Schools), or similar names, programs exist nationwide that coordinate residencies, classroom visits and other opportunities for experienced poets to share their craft with students. Many state arts agencies include such "arts in education" programs in their activities (see Grants on page 424 for contact information). Another good source is the National Assembly of State Arts Agencies (see below), which offers an online directory of contact names and addresses for arts education programs state-by-state. The following list is a mere sampling of programs and organizations that link poets with schools. Contact them for information about their requirements (some may insist poets have a strong publication history, others may prefer classroom experience) or check their websites where available.

THE ACADEMY OF AMERICAN POETS, 584 Broadway, Suite 604, New York NY 10012-5243. (212)274-0343. E-mail: academy@poets.org. website: www.poets.org (includes links to state arts in education programs).

ARKANSAS WRITERS IN THE SCHOOLS, WITS Director, 333 Kimpel Hall, University of Arkansas, Fayetteville AR 72701. (479)575-5991. E-mail: wits@cavern.uark.edu. website: www.uark.edu/~wits.

CALIFORNIA POETS IN THE SCHOOLS, 1333 Balboa St. #3, San Francisco CA 94118. (415)221-4201. E-mail: info@cpits.org. website: www.cpits.org.

E-POETS.NETWORK, a collective online cultural center that promotes education through videoconferencing (i.e., "distance learning"); also includes the *Voces y Lugares* project. website: http://learning.e-poets.net (includes online contact form).

IDAHO WRITERS IN THE SCHOOLS, Log Cabin Literary Center, 801 S. Capitol Blvd., Boise ID 83702. (208)331-8000. E-mail: info@thecabinidaho.org. website: www.thecabinidaho.org.

INDIANA WRITERS IN THE SCHOOLS, University of Evansville, Dept. of English, 1800 Lincoln Ave., Evansville IN 47722. (812)488-2962. E-mail: rg37@evansville.edu. website: http://english.evansville.edu/WritersintheSchools.htm.

MICHIGAN CREATIVE WRITERS IN THE SCHOOLS, ArtServe Michigan, 17515 W. Nine Mile Rd., Suite 1025, Southfield MI 48075. (248)557-8288 **OR** 1310 Turner St., Suite B, Lansing MI 48906. (517)371-1720 (toll free at (800)203-9633). E-mail: online form. website: www.artservemichigan.org.

NATIONAL ASSEMBLY OF STATE ARTS AGENCIES, 1029 Vermont Ave. NW, 2nd Floor, Washington DC 20005. (202)347-6352. E-mail: nasaa@nasaa-arts.org. website: www.nasaa-arts.org.

NATIONAL ASSOCIATION OF WRITERS IN EDUCATION (NAWE), P.O. Box 1, Sheriff Hutton, York YO60 7YU England. (44)(1653)618429. website: www.nawe.co.uk.

OREGON WRITERS IN THE SCHOOLS, Literary Arts, 224 NW 13th Ave., Suite 306, Portland OR 97209. (503)227-2583. E-mail: john@literary-arts.org. website: www.literary-arts.org/wits.

PEN IN THE CLASSROOM (PITC), Pen Center USA, Þco Antioch University, 400 Corporate Pointe, Culver City CA 90230. (310)862-1555. E-mail: pitc@penusa.org. website: www.penusa.org/go/classroom.

"PICK-A-POET," The Humanities Project, Arlington Public Schools, 1439 N. Quincy St., Arlington VA 22207. (703)228-6299. E-mail: online form. website: www.humanitiesproject.org.

POTATO HILL POETRY, 6 Pleasant St., Suite 2, South Natick MA 01760. (888)5-POETRY. E-mail: info@potatohill.com. website: www.potatohill.com (includes online contact form).

SEATTLE WRITERS IN THE SCHOOLS (WITS), Seattle Arts & Lectures, 105 S. Main St., Suite 201, Seattle WA 98104. (206)621-2230. website: www.lectures.org/wits.html.

TEACHERS & WRITERS COLLABORATIVE, 520 Eighth Ave., Suite 2020, New York NY 10018. (212)691-6590 or (888)BOOKS-TW (book orders). E-mail: info@twc.org. website: www.twc.org. "A catalog of T&W books is available online, or call toll-free to request a print copy.

TEXAS WRITERS IN THE SCHOOLS, 1523 W. Main, Houston TX 77006. (713)523-3877. E-mail: mail@witshouston.org. website: www.writersintheschools.org.

WRITERS & ARTISTS IN THE SCHOOLS (WAITS), COMPAS, Landmark Center, Suite 304, 75 Fifth St. West, St. Paul MN 55102-1496. (651)292-3254. E-mail: daniel@compas.org. website: www.compas.org.

YOUTH VOICES IN INK, Badgerdog Literary Publishing, Inc., P.O. Box 301209, Austin TX 78703-0021. (512)538-1305. E-mail: info@badgerdog.org. website: www.badgerdog.org.

GLOSSARY OF LISTING TERMS

A3, A4, A5. Metric equivalents of 11¾×16½, 8¼×11¾, and 5⅞×8¼ respectively.

ACKNOWLEDGMENTS PAGE. A page in a poetry book or chapbook that lists the publications where the poems in the collection were originally published; may be presented as part of the copyright page or as a separate page on its own.

ANTHOLOGY. A collection of selected writings by various authors.

ATTACHMENT. A computer file electronically "attached" to an e-mail message.

AUD. Abbreviation for Australian Dollar.

B&W. Black & white (photo or illustration).

BIO. A short biographical statement often requested with a submission.

CAD. Abbreviation for Canadian Dollar.

CAMERA-READY. Poems ready for copy camera platemaking; camera-ready poems usually appear in print exactly as submitted.

CHAPBOOK. A small book of about 24-50 pages.Circulation. The number of subscribers to a magazine/journal.

CLMP. Council of Literary Magazines and Presses; service organization for independent publishers of fiction, poetry, and prose.

CONTRIBUTOR'S COPY. Copy of book or magazine containing a poet's work, sometimes given as payment.

COVER LETTER. Brief introductory letter accompanying a poetry submission.

COVERSTOCK. Heavier paper used as the cover for a publication.

DIGEST-SIZED. About 5½×8½, the size of a folded sheet of conventional printer paper.

DOWNLOAD. To "copy" a file, such as a registration form, from a website.

ELECTRONIC MAGAZINE. See *online magazine*.E-mail. Mail sent electronically using computer and modem or similar means.

EURO. Currency unit for the 27 member countries of the European Union; designated by EUR or the INSERT EURO symbol.

FAQ. Frequently Asked Questions.

FONT. The style/design of type used in a publication; typeface.

GALLEYS. First typeset version of a poem, magazine, or book/chapbook.

GLBT. Gay/lesbian/bisexual/transgender (as in "GLBT themes").

HONORARIUM. A token payment for published work.Internet. A worldwide network of computers offering access to a variety of electronic resources.

IRC. International Reply Coupon; a publisher can exchange IRCs for postage to return a manuscript to another country.

JPEG. Short for *Joint Photographic Experts Group*; an image compression format that allows digital images to be stored in relatively small files for electronic mailing and viewing on the Internet.

MAGAZINE-SIZED. About 8½×11, the size of an unfolded sheet of conventional printer paper.

MS. Manuscript.

MSS. Manuscripts.

MULTI-BOOK REVIEW. Several books by the same author or by several authors reviewed in one piece.

OFFSET-PRINTED. Printing method in which ink is transferred from an image-bearing plate to a "blanket" and then from blanket to paper.

ONLINE MAGAZINE. Publication circulated through the Internet or e-mail.

P&H. Postage & handling.

P&P. Postage & packing.

"PAYS IN COPIES." See *contributor's copy.*

PDF. Short for *Portable Document Format*, developed by Adobe Systems, that captures all elements of a printed document as an electronic image, allowing it to be sent by e-mail, viewed online, and printed in its original format.

PERFECT-BOUND. Publication with glued, flat spine; also called "flat-spined."

POD. See *print-on-demand.*

PRESS RUN. The total number of copies of a publication printed at one time.

PREVIOUSLY PUBLISHED. Work that has appeared before in print, in any form, for public consumption.

PRINT-ON-DEMAND. Publishing method that allows copies of books to be published as they're requested, rather than all at once in a single press run.

PUBLISHING CREDITS. A poet's magazine publications and book/chapbook titles.

QUERY LETTER. Letter written to an editor to raise interest in a proposed project.

READING FEE. A monetary amount charged by an editor or publisher to consider a poetry submission without any obligation to accept the work.

RICH TEXT FORMAT. Carries the .rtf filename extension. A file format that allows an exchange of text files between different word processor operating systems with most of the formatting preserved.

RIGHTS. A poet's legal property interest in his/her literary work; an editor or publisher may acquire certain rights from the poet to reproduce that work.

ROW. "Rest of world."

ROYALTIES. A percentage of the retail price paid to the author for each copy of a book sold.

SADDLE-STAPLED. A publication folded, then stapled along that fold; also called "saddle-stitched."

SAE. Self-addressed envelope.

SASE. Self-addressed, stamped envelope.

SASP. Self-addressed, stamped postcard.Simultaneous submission. Submission of the same manuscript to more than one publisher at the same time.

SUBSIDY PRESS. Publisher who requires the poet to pay all costs, including typesetting, production, and printing; sometimes called a "vanity publisher."

TABLOID-SIZED. 11×15 or larger, the size of an ordinary newspaper folded and turned sideways.

TEXT FILE. A file containing only textual characters (i.e., no graphics or special formats).

UNSOLICITED MANUSCRIPT. A manuscript an editor did not ask specifically to receive.

URL. Stands for "Uniform Resource Locator," the address of an Internet resource (i.e., file).

USD. Abbreviation for United States Dollar.website. A specific address on the Internet that provides access to a set of documents (or "pages").

GLOSSARY OF POETRY TERMS

This glossary is provided as a quick-reference only, briefly covering poetic styles and terms that may turn up in articles and listings in *Poet's Market*. For a full understanding of the terms, forms, and styles listed here, as well as common literary terms not included, consult a solid textbook or handbook, such as John Drury's *The Poetry Dictionary* (Writer's Digest Books). (Ask your librarian or bookseller for recommendations).

ABSTRACT POEM: conveys emotion through sound, textures, and rhythm and rhyme rather than through the meanings of words.

ACROSTIC: initial letters of each line, read downward, form a word, phrase, or sentence.

ALLITERATION: close repetition of consonant sounds, especially initial consonant sounds. (Also known as *consonance*.)

ALPHABET POEM: arranges lines alphabetically according to initial letter.

AMERICAN CINQUAIN: derived from Japanese haiku and tanka by Adelaide Crapsey; counted syllabic poem of 5 lines of 2-4-6-8-2 syllables, frequently in iambic feet.

ANAPEST: foot consisting of 2 unstressed syllables followed by a stress (- - ‘).

ASSONANCE: close repetition of vowel sounds.Avant-garde: work at the forefront--cutting edge, unconventional, risk-taking.

BALLAD: narrative poem often in ballad stanza (4-line stanza with 4 stresses in lines 1 and 3, 3 stresses in lines 2 and 4, which also rhyme).

BALLADE: 3 stanzas rhymed *ababbcbC* (*C* indicates a refrain) with envoi rhymed *bcbC*.

BEAT POETRY: anti-academic school of poetry born in '50s San Francisco; fast-paced free verse resembling jazz.

BLANK VERSE: unrhymed iambic pentameter.

CAESURA: a deliberate rhetorical, grammatical, or rhythmic pause, break, cut, turn, division, or pivot in poetry.

CHANT: poem in which one or more lines are repeated over and over.

CINQUAIN: any 5-line poem or stanza; also called "quintain" or "quintet." (See also *American cinquain.*)

CONCRETE POETRY: see *emblematic poem.*

CONFESSIONAL POETRY: work that uses personal and private details from the poet's own life.

CONSONANCE: see *alliteration.*

COUPLET: stanza of 2 lines; pair of rhymed lines.

DACTYL: foot consisting of a stress followed by 2 unstressed syllables (' - -).

DIDACTIC POETRY: poetry written with the intention to instruct.

ECLECTIC: open to a variety of poetic styles (as in "eclectic taste").

EKPHRASTIC POEM: verbally presents something originally represented in visual art, though more than mere description.

ELEGY: lament in verse for someone who has died, or a reflection on the tragic nature of life.

EMBLEMATIC POEM: words or letters arranged to imitate a shape, often the subject of the poem.

ENJAMBMENT: continuation of sense and rhythmic movement from one line to the next; also called a "run-on" line.

ENVOI: a brief ending (usually to a ballade or sestina) no more than 4 lines long; summary.

EPIC POETRY: long narrative poem telling a story central to a society, culture, or nation.

EPIGRAM: short, witty, satirical poem or saying written to be remembered easily, like a punchline.

EPIGRAPH: a short verse, note, or quotation that appears at the beginning of a poem or section; usually presents an idea or theme on which the poem elaborates, or contributes background information not reflected in the poem itself.

EPITAPH: brief verse commemorating a person/group of people who died.

EXPERIMENTAL POETRY: work that challenges conventional ideas of poetry by exploring new techniques, form, language, and visual presentation.

FIBS: short form based on the mathematical progression known as the Fibonacci sequence; syllable counts for each line are 1/1/2/3/5/8/13 (count for each line is derived by adding the counts for the previous two lines).

FLARF: a malleable term that may refer to 1) poetic and creative text pieces by the Flarflist Collective; any poetry created from search engine (such as Google) results; any intentionally bad, zany, or trivial poetry.

FOOT: unit of measure in a metrical line of poetry.Found poem: text lifted from a non-poetic source such as an ad and presented as a poem.

FREE VERSE: unmetrical verse (lines not counted for accents, syllables, etc.).

GHAZAL: Persian poetic form of 5-15 unconnected, independent couplets; associative jumps may be made from couplet to couplet.

GREETING CARD POETRY: resembles verses in greeting cards; sing-song meter and rhyme.

HAIBUN: originally, a Japanese form in which elliptical, often autobiographical prose is interspersed with haiku.

HAIKAI NO RENGA: see *renku*.

HAY(NA)KY: a 3-line form, with 1 word in line 1, 2 words in line 2, and 3 words in line 3.

HAIKU: originally, a Japanese form of a single vertical line with 17 sound symbols in a 5-7-5 pattern. In English, typically a 3-line poem with fewer than 17 syllables in no set pattern, but exhibiting a 2-part juxtapositional structure, seasonal reference, imagistic immediacy, and a moment of keen perception of nature or human nature. The term is both singular and plural.

HOKKU: the starting verse of a renga or renku, in 5, 7, and then 5 sound symbols in Japanese; or in three lines, usually totaling fewer than 17 syllables, in English; the precursor for what is now called haiku. (See also *haiku*).

IAMB: foot consisting of an unstressed syllable followed by a stress (- ‘).Iambic pentameter: consists of 5 iambic feet per line.

IMAGIST POETRY: short, free verse lines that present images without comment or explanation; strongly influenced by haiku and other Oriental forms.

KYRIELLE: French form; 4-line stanza with 8-syllable lines, the final line a refrain.

LANGUAGE POETRY: attempts to detach words from traditional meanings to produce something new and unprecedented.Limerick: 5-line stanza rhyming *aabba*; pattern of stresses/line is traditionally 3-3-2-2-3; often bawdy or scatalogical.

LINE: basic compositional unit of a poem; measured in feet if metrical.

LINKED POETRY: written through the collaboration of 2 or more poets creating a single poetic work.Long poem: exceeds length and scope of short lyric or narrative poem; defined arbitrarily, often as more than 2 pages or 100 lines.

LYRIC POETRY: expresses personal emotion; music predominates over narrative or drama.

METAPHOR: 2 different things are likened by identifying one as the other (A=B).Meter: the rhythmic measure of a line.

MINUTE: a 12-line poem consisting of 60 syllables, with a syllabic line count of 8,4,4,4,8,4,4,4, 8,4,4,4; often consists of rhyming couplets.

MODERNIST POETRY: work of the early 20th century literary movement that sought to break with the past, rejecting outmoded literary traditions, diction, and form while encouraging innovation and reinvention.

NARRATIVE POETRY: poem that tells a story.

NEW FORMALISM: contemporary literary movement to revive formal verse.

NONSENSE VERSE: playful, with language and/or logic that defies ordinary understanding.

OCTAVE: stanza of 8 lines.

ODE: a songlike, or lyric, poem; can be passionate, rhapsodic, and mystical, or a formal address to a person on a public or state occasion.

PANTOUM: Malayan poetic form of any length; consists of 4-line stanzas, with lines 2 and 4 of one quatrain repeated as lines 1 and 3 of the next; final stanza reverses lines 1 and 3 of the previous quatrain and uses them as lines 2 and 4; traditionally each stanza rhymes *abab*.

PETRARCHAN SONNET: octave rhymes *abbaabba*; sestet may rhyme *cdcdcd, cdedce, ccdccd, cddcdd, edecde*, or *cddcee*.

PROSE POEM: brief prose work with intensity, condensed language, poetic devices, and other poetic elements.

QUATRAIN: stanza of 4 lines.

REFRAIN: a repeated line within a poem, similar to the chorus of a song.

REGIONAL POETRY: work set in a particular locale, imbued with the look, feel, and culture of that place.

RENGA: originally, a Japanese collaborative form in which 2 or more poets alternate writing 3 lines, then 2 lines for a set number of verses (such as 12, 18, 36, 100, and 1,000). There are specific rules for seasonal progression, placement of moon and flower verses, and other requirements. (See also *linked poetry.*)

RENGAY: an American collaborative 6-verse, thematic linked poetry form, with 3-line and 2-line verses in the following set pattern for 2 or 3 writers (letters represent poets, numbers indicate the lines in each verse): A3-B2-A3-B3-A2-B3 or A3-B2-C3-A2-B3-C2. All verses, unlike renga or renku, must develop at least one common theme.

RENKU: the modern term for renga, and a more popular version of the traditionally more aristocratic renga. (See also *linked poetry.*)

RHYME: words that sound alike, especially words that end in the same sound.

RHYTHM: the beat and movement of language (rise and fall, repetition and variation, change of pitch, mix of syllables, melody of words).

RONDEAU: French form of usually 15 lines in 3 parts, rhyming *aabba aabR aabbaR* (*R* indicates a refrain repeating the first word or phrase of the opening line).

SENRYU: originally, a Japanese form, like haiku in form, but chiefly humorous, satirical, or ironic, and typically aimed at human foibles. (See also *haiku* and *zappai.*)

SEQUENCE: a group or progression of poems, often numbered as a series.

SESTET: stanza of 6 lines.

SESTINA: fixed form of 39 lines (6 unrhymed stanzas of 6 lines each, then an ending 3-line stanza), each stanza repeating the same 6 non-rhyming end-words in a different order; all 6 end-words appear in the final 3-line stanza.

SHAKESPEAREAN SONNET: rhymes *abab cdcd efef gg.*Sijo: originally a Korean narrative or thematic lyric form. The first line introduces a situation or problem that is countered or developed in line 2, and concluded with a twist in line 3. Lines average 14-16 syllables in length.

SIMILE: comparison that uses a linking word (*like, as, such as, how*) to clarify the similarities.

SONNET: 14-line poem (traditionally an octave and sestet) rhymed in iambic pentameter; often presents an argument but may also present a description, story, or meditation.Spondee: foot consisting of 2 stressed syllables (' ').

STANZA: group of lines making up a single unit; like a paragraph in prose.

STROPHE: often used to mean "stanza"; also a stanza of irregular line lengths.

SURREALISTIC POETRY: of the artistic movement stressing the importance of dreams and the subconscious, nonrational thought, free associations, and startling imagery/juxtapositions.

TANKA: originally, a Japanese form in one or 2 vertical lines with 31 sound symbols in a 5-7-5-7-7 pattern. In English, typically a 5-line lyrical poem with fewer than 31 syllables in no set syllable pattern, but exhibiting a caesura, turn, or pivot, and often more emotional and conversational than haiku.

TERCET: stanza or poem of 3 lines.

TERZA RIMA: series of 3-line stanzas with interwoven rhyme scheme (*aba, bcb, cdc* . . .).

TROCHEE: foot consisting of a stress followed by an unstressed syllable (' -).

VILLANELLE: French form of 19 lines (5 tercets and a quatrain); line 1 serves as one refrain (repeated in lines 6, 12, 18), line 3 as a second refrain (repeated in lines 9, 15, 19); traditionally, refrains rhyme with each other and with the opening line of each stanza.

VISUAL POEM: see *emblematic poem.*

WAKA: literally, "Japanese poem," the precursor for what is now called tanka. (See also *tanka.*)

WAR POETRY: poems written about warfare and military life; often written by past and current soldiers; may glorify war, recount exploits, or demonstrate the horrors of war.

ZAPPAI: originally Japanese; an unliterary, often superficial witticism masquerading as haiku or senryu; formal term for joke haiku or other pseudo-haiko.

ZEUGMA: a figure of speech in which a single word (or, occasionally, a phrase) is related in one way to words that precede it, and in another way to words that follow it.

SUBJECT INDEX

AFRICAN AMERICAN

ANIMALS/PETS

ANTHOLOGY/ANIMAL/BEST OF

BILINGUAL/FOREIGN LANGUAGE

BUDDHISM

CHRISTIAN

COWBOY POETRY/AMERICAN WEST

CULTURES/COMMUNITIES VARIOUS

EROTICA

FANTASY

FORM/STYLE

FORM/STYLE ASIAN

GAY/LESBIAN/BISEXUAL/TRANSGENDERED

GOTHIC/HORROR/DARK POETRY

HISPANIC/LATINO

HUMOR/SATIRE

JEWISH

LOVE/ROMANCE

MEDICAL/HEALTH ISSUES

MEMBERSHIP/SUBSCRIPTION

MINORITIES

MYSTERY/SUSPENSE

NATURE ECOLOGY, SEASONS, OUTDOORS

ONLINE MARKETS

POETRY BY CHILDREN

POETRY BY TEENS

POETRY FOR CHILDREN

SPORTS/RECREATION

STUDENTS

THEMES

TRANSLATIONS

WOMEN VARIOUS

WORKING CLASS ISSUES

WRITING

GENERAL INDEX

C

D

E

F

Q

R

S